8/18

Thailand

Chiang Mai Province
p307

Northern Thailand
p201

Northeastern Thailand
p366

Central Thailand
p163

Bangkok & Around
p65

Ko Chang & the Eastern Seaboard
p448

Hua Hin & the Upper Gulf
p490

Phuket & the Andaman Coast
p593

Ko Samui & the Lower Gulf
p523

Anita Isalska, Austin Bush, Tim Bewer, Celeste Brash,
David Eimer, Damian Harper, Andy Symington

Contents

STIR-FRIED CURRY NOODLES P44

MARK WENS / LONELY PLANET ©

PHAYRE'S LANGUR, KAENG KRACHAN NATIONAL PARK P496

PRASIT CHANSAREEKORN / GETTY IMAGES ©

SURIYA99 / SHUTTERSTOCK ©

Contents

YI PENG, UBON RATCHATHANI
PROVINCE P425

ON THE ROAD

TÚK-TÚK, BANGKOK P65

DAVID BUFFINGTON / BLEND IMAGES / GETTY IMAGES ©

RMNUNES / GETTY IMAGES ©

TALING CHAN FLOATING
MARKET, BANGKOK P148

KAREN MASSIER / GETTY IMAGES ©

WAT RONG KHUN P209,
CHIANG RAI

Contents

Welcome to Thailand

Friendly and fun-loving, cultured and historic, Thailand radiates a golden hue, from its glittering temples and tropical beaches through to the ever-comforting Thai smile.

Sand Between Your Toes

With a long coastline (actually, two coastlines) and jungle-topped islands anchored in azure waters, Thailand is a tropical getaway for the hedonist and the hermit, the prince and the pauper. This paradise offers a varied menu: playing in the gentle surf of Ko Lipe, diving with whale sharks off Ko Tao, scaling the sea cliffs of Krabi, kiteboarding in Hua Hin, partying on Ko Phi-Phi, recuperating at a health resort on Ko Samui and feasting on the beach wherever sand meets sea.

A Bountiful Table

Adored around the world, Thai cuisine expresses fundamental aspects of Thai culture: it is generous, warm, refreshing and relaxed. Thai dishes rely on fresh, local ingredients – pungent lemongrass, searing chillies and plump seafood. A varied national menu is built around the four fundamental flavours: spicy, sweet, salty and sour. Roving appetites go on eating tours of Bangkok noodle shacks, seafood pavilions in Phuket, and Burmese market stalls in Mae Sot. Cooking classes reveal the simplicity behind the seemingly complicated dishes, and mastering the market is an important survival skill.

Sacred Spaces

The celestial world is a close confidant in this Buddhist nation, and religious devotion is colourful and ubiquitous. Gleaming temples and golden Buddhas frame both the rural and the modern landscape. Ancient banyan trees are ceremoniously wrapped in sacred cloth to honour the resident spirits, fortune-bringing shrines decorate humble homes as well as monumental malls, while garland-festooned dashboards ward off traffic accidents. Visitors can join the conversation through meditation retreats in Chiang Mai, religious festivals in northeastern Thailand, underground cave shrines in Kanchanaburi and Phetchaburi and hilltop temples in northern Thailand.

Fields & Forests

In between the cluttered cities and towns is the rural heartland, which is a mix of rice paddies, tropical forests and squat villages tied to the agricultural clock. In the north, the forests and fields bump up against toothy blue mountains decorated with silvery waterfalls. In the south, scraggy limestone cliffs poke out of the cultivated landscape like prehistoric skyscrapers. The usually arid northeast emits an emerald hue during the rainy season when tender green rice shoots carpet the landscape.

Why I Love Thailand

By Austin Bush, Writer

I'm tempted to say that the thing I love most about Thailand is the food. But then I'm reminded of that feeling of freedom when on a motorcycle trip upcountry. And of the sensory overload of a busy morning market or a wild night out in Bangkok. And of encounters with history and culture, the new and the old, at just about every turn. Did I mention the white-sand beaches, jungles, ancient ruins and Buddhist temples? Indeed, the food satisfies, but on second thought Thailand offers so much more.

For more about our writers, see p800

Above: Stupas at Doi Inthanon National Park (p363)

Thailand

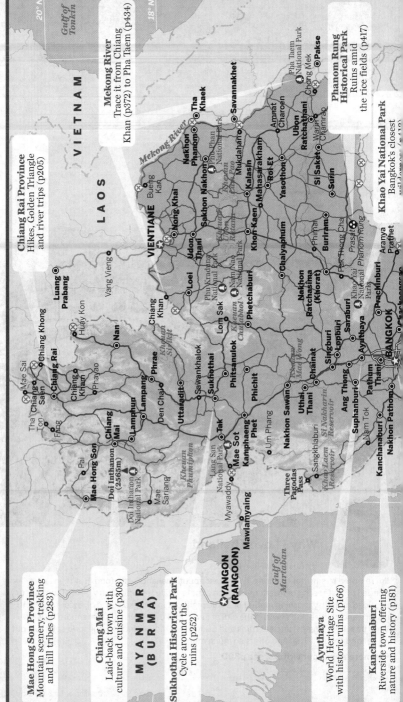

Mae Hong Son Province
Mountain scenery, trekking and hill tribes (p283)

Chiang Mai
Laid-back town with culture and cuisine (p308)

Sukhothai Historical Park
Cycle around the ruins (p252)

Ayuthaya
World Heritage Site with historic ruins (p166)

Kanchanaburi
Riverside town offering nature and history (p181)

Chiang Rai Province
Hikes, Golden Triangle and river trips (p205)

Mekong River
Trace it from Chiang Khan (p372) to Pha Taem (p434)

Phanom Rung Historical Park
Ruins amid the rice fields (p417)

Khao Yai National Park
Bangkok's closest wilderness (p419)

200 km
100 miles

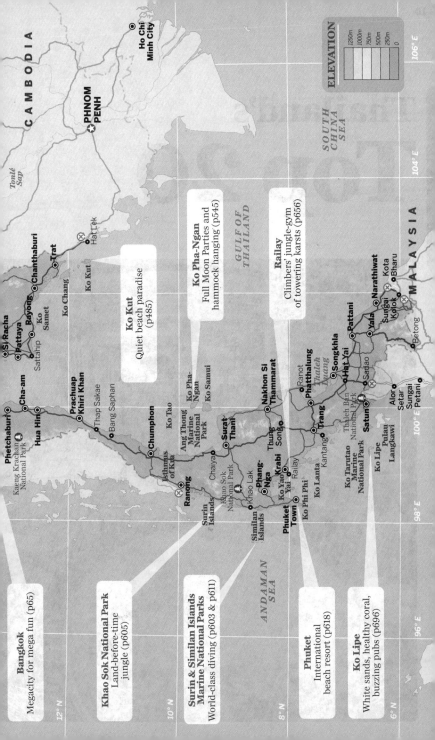

Thailand's
Top 20

Bangkok

1 Glittering temples, towering skyscrapers, a dynamic nightlife and, oh – the food! What's not to love about Bangkok (p65)? Traffic jams, humidity and political instability aside, the Thai capital is now tidier and easier to navigate than ever. Zip between golden shrines, colourful markets, glitzy mega-malls and fascinating museums, stopping to refuel at sizzling streetside food stands and some of Asia's best restaurants. Head up to one of the city's famous rooftop bars on your first night to get your bearings in this heaving, twinkling metropolis, and prepare to dive straight in. Khao San Road (p111)

Chiang Mai

2 The cultural capital of the north, Chiang Mai (p308) is beloved by culture geeks, temple-spotters and families. The old city is jam-packed with temples born during the time of the once independent Lanna kingdom. These and the area's winding side roads are best explored on bicycle. Cooking schools teach visitors the art of Thai food, while the scenic countryside boasts jungle treks, elephant encounters and minority villages. The city enjoys fantastic dining thanks to imports such as Japanese sushi and Burmese curries, plus home-grown northern specialities and vegetarian fare. The surrounding areas are rich with traditional handicraft outlets. Royal Park Rajapruek (p322)

Railay

3 At the tip of the Krabi peninsula are some of Thailand's most famous natural features: the soaring limestone karsts of Railay (p656), anchored in the ocean. The beaches are sugar-white and the forested interior is traversed by foot traffic, not cars. No traffic jams, no transport hassles. Visitors come and go by long-tail boats. Come to lounge, swim, dive or rock-climb. Beginners can learn basic skills, and some stay so long they get good enough to do a free solo on a pinnacle then fall harmlessly into a cobalt sea.

Chiang Rai Province

4 The days of the Golden Triangle opium trade are over, but Chiang Rai (p205) still packs intrigue in the form of fresh-air fun such as hiking and self-guided exploration. It is also a great destination for unique cultural experiences, ranging from a visit to an Akha village to a stay at the Yunnanese hamlet of Doi Mae Salong. From the Mekong River to the mountains, Chiang Rai is arguably Thailand's most beautiful province, and if you've set your sights further, it's a convenient gateway to Myanmar and Laos. Tea plantation, Doi Mae Salong (p215)

Ayuthaya

5 A once vibrant, glittering capital packed with hundreds of temples, the Ayuthaya (p166) of today retains ample hints of its erstwhile glory. Cycle around the brick-and-stucco ruins, which form part of a Unesco World Heritage Site, and try to imagine how the city must have looked in its prime, when it greeted merchants from around the globe. On the outskirts of the city sit several more attractions, including an enormous handicraft centre and the most eclectic royal palace you will ever see. Wat Chai Wattanaram (p169)

Kanchanaburi

6 Once you've explored this western province's wartime past – the infamous Bridge Over the River Kwai is here – get ready to walk on the wild side in Kanchanaburi (p181), where dragon-scaled limestone mountains gaze down upon dense jungle. Activities from kayaking to rock-climbing are all on offer at this popular adventure-traveller hub. Trek past silvery waterfalls, clamber into caves, then spend the night in lavish riverside resorts, tree-top bungalows or traditional village homestays.

Similan Islands Marine National Park

7 The world-renowned dive sites off the Similan Islands (p611) have anchored Thailand as a global diving destination. Live-aboard trips set out from Khao Lak, allowing for more time hanging out with aquatic residents, including manta rays and whale sharks, as well as soft corals. Above the water line, the islands are an attraction in their own right, with jungle-filled interiors and smooth white beaches surrounded by coral reefs, and national park accommodation on Ko Miang (also known as Island 4).

6

Pai

8 Combine a beautiful mountain valley, a party scene reminiscent of a Thai island, an old-school hippie vibe and laid-back northern Thai roots and you have Pai (p283), still northern Thailand's coolest destination. Its popularity means it can get crowded, especially at the peak of Thailand's 'winter' in December and January. But a huge spread of accommodation that caters to every budget, and a host of outdoor and laid-back activities mean that your visit won't be quite like anybody else's. Hot springs, Mae Hong Son (p294)

Sukhothai Historical Park

9 Step back some 800 years in time at one of Thailand's most impressive historical parks (p253). Exploring the ruins of this former capital by bicycle is a leisurely way to wind through the crumbling temples, graceful Buddha statues and fish-filled ponds. Worthwhile museums and some of the country's best-value accommodation round out the package. Sukhothai rarely feels crowded, but for something off the beaten track head to nearby Si Satchanalai-Chaliang Historical Park, where you might be the only person scaling an ancient stairway.

Mekong River

10 From the historic timber shophouses of Chiang Khan to the waterfalls of Pha Taem National Park (p434), northeast Thailand's glorious arc of the Mekong River offers a smorgasbord of culture and beauty. Chase the meandering river aboard a rickety bus, long-tail boat or even a bicycle. View the cross-pollination of Thai-Lao culture in local fishing villages, Nong Khai's bizarre sculpture park (above; p380), and prehistoric rock paintings in Ubon Ratchathani. Those who follow this little-visited trail are rewarded with true travellers' tales to tell.

Ko Pha-Ngan

11 Famous for its techno-fuelled Full Moon Parties, Ko Pha-Ngan (p545) has long since graduated from a sleepy bohemian island to an Asian Ibiza. Comfort-seekers have an alternative to Ko Samui thanks to a bevy of boutique bungalows. On the northern and eastern coasts, ascetic hammock-hangers can still find castaway bliss. Just offshore is Sail Rock, one of the Gulf of Thailand's best dive sites, while much of the island's interior is spectacular, unspoiled forest.

Phetchaburi

12 A delightful mix of culture and nature combine in this provincial capital (p492), which some call a living Ayuthaya. Explore an antique hilltop palace, sacred cave shrines and bustling temples. Wander the old shophouse neighbourhood filled with DIY businesses run by Thai aunties and grannies. Then head off to the wilds of Kaeng Krachan National Park to spot wild gibbons and exotic birds. Phetchaburi is also a clever layover for travellers returning from the south. Tham Khao Luang (p492)

Ko Lipe

13 Where creature comforts meet laid-back island escape, Ko Lipe (p696) takes work to reach but the ever-growing band of devotees agree that it's worth it. The days of solitude are over, especially in the high season when the island is overrun, but it is still a wonderful blend of white-sand beaches, authentic Thai kitchens, groovy guesthouses, boutique resorts and nature adventures in the national park. The diving and living are best here during the early wet season (mid-April to June). But keep that hush-hush.

Khao Sok National Park

14 A deep, dark jungle hugs the mid-section of southern Thailand. This ancient rainforest (p605) is filled with long, sweaty hiking routes up dramatic limestone formations that pay off with postcard-perfect views. Birds and bats call this forest home, as does the rare *Rafflesia kerrii*, one of the largest and stinkiest flowers on the planet. After trying out tubing, kayaking and rafting, you can reward your outdoor work with riverside camping or sleep on the floating lake-top huts at Chiaw Lan.

13

Khao Yai National Park

15 This park is home to elephants, monkeys, gibbons, hornbills, pythons, bears, a million bats and even a few wily tigers. Wildlife sightings are mostly at the mercy of chance, but your odds are excellent at this vast Unesco-listed reserve (p413), just a few hours out of Bangkok. And even if you don't meet many big animals, the orchids, birds, waterfalls and sense of adventure that inevitably arises when hiking in the jungle guarantee a good day out. Khao Yai's mix of scenery and accessibility is hard to beat. Pig-tailed macaques

Ko Kut

16 Still looking for that paradise island where the crowds are thin, the water aquamarine and clear, and the beaches wide and long? Try Ko Kut (p485). There is Hat Khlong Chao, one of the most beautiful stretches of sand anywhere in Thailand, fine snorkelling and hidden waterfalls to hike to. Best of all, Ko Kut retains a supremely unhurried pace of life that visitors soon find themselves imitating. There is nothing in the way of nightlife, apart from listening to the ocean. But that's why you're here.

PHENTI PRASOMPHETHIRAN / SHUTTERSTOCK ©

Mae Hong Son Province

17 Tucked away in the country's northwest corner, this province (p283) has a lot more in common with Myanmar than anywhere else in Thailand. With its remote location, soaring mountains and unique culture and cuisine, Mae Hong Son can seem like an entirely different country. Exploration is the reason to make the journey here, and can involve tramping through one of the province's many caves, taking a hairpin turn on your motorcycle or doing a self-guided trek from Mae La-Na to Soppong.

Phanom Rung Historical Park

18 Perched high atop an extinct volcano, Thailand's most impressive Khmer ruin (p417) is something special. As you amble along the promenade, up the stairs and over the *naga*-flanked bridges, the sense of anticipation builds. And when you enter the temple, completely restored and still rich with Hindu sculpture, you experience a moment of timelessness. While Phanom Rung is not as awe-inspiring as Cambodia's Angkor Wat, the experience here is unique enough that you should definitely consider visiting both.

Phuket

19 An international beach resort, Phuket (p618) is an easy destination for all ages. You can fly in from Bangkok (or even Dubai), and then retreat into a five-star resort or arty boutique hotel for a trouble-free tropical vacation. There are slinky stretches of sand, hedonistic party pits and world-class spas. Culture capital Phuket Town is now an attraction in its own right, plus there are day trips to mangrove forests, an elephant rescue sanctuary and a ton of water sports to take part in, from diving to surfing. Hat Patong (p634)

Ko Lanta

20 A beach bum's best friend, Ko Lanta (p671) sports a mellow island vibe and a parade of peachy sand. Social butterflies alight on the northern beaches for the party scene. Solitude-seekers migrate southwards to low-key beach huts and a sleepy village ambience. Activities abound, from hiking through limestone caves to diving off Hin Muang and Hin Daeng, with the chance to glimpse rays and even whale sharks. Sprinkle in some culture by visiting the east coast's charismatic Old Town, home to a Muslim community and charming seafront coffee shops.

JUSTANOTHERWORLDTRIP / GETTY IMAGES ©

Need to Know

For more information, see Survival Guide (p751)

Currency
Thai baht (B)

Language
Thai

Visas
For visitors from most countries, visas are generally not required for stays of up to 30 days.

Money
Most places in Thailand deal only with cash. Some foreign credit cards are accepted in high-end establishments.

Mobile Phones
Buying a pre-paid SIM card is the simplest option for travellers – they are widely available and sold at 7-Eleven stores. They usually include both talk and data packages.

Time
GMT plus seven hours

When to Go

Mae Hong Son
GO Nov–Mar

Chiang Mai
GO Nov–Feb

BANGKOK
GO Nov–Feb

Ko Samui
GO Dec–Aug

Phuket
GO Oct–Apr

Tropical climate, rain year-round

Tropical climate, wet & dry seasons

High Season
(Nov–Mar)

➡ A cool and dry season follows the monsoons, meaning the landscape is lush and temperatures are comfortable.

➡ Western Christmas and New Year's holidays bring crowds and inflated rates.

Shoulder Season
(Apr–Jun, Sep & Oct)

➡ April to June is generally very hot and dry, with an average Bangkok temperature of 30°C. Sea breezes make coastal areas more bearable.

➡ September and October are ideal for the north and the gulf coast.

Low Season
(Jul–Oct)

➡ Monsoon season ranges from afternoon showers to major flooding. Rain is usually in short, intense bursts.

➡ Some islands shut down; boat service is limited during stormy weather. Be flexible with travel plans.

Useful Websites

Thaivisa (www.thaivisa.com) Expat site for news and discussions.

Lonely Planet (www.lonelyplanet.com/thailand) Destination information, hotel bookings, traveller forum and more.

Richard Barrow (www.richardbarrow.com) Prolific blogger and tweeter focusing on Thai travel.

Tourism Authority of Thailand (TAT; www.tourismthailand.org) National tourism department covering info and special events.

Thai Language (www.thailanguage.com) Online dictionary and Thai tutorials.

Important Numbers

Thailand's country code	☑66
Emergency	☑191
International access codes	☑001, 007, 008, 009 (& other promotional codes)
Operator-assisted international calls	☑100
Tourist police	☑1155

Exchange Rates

Australia	A$1	26B
Canada	C$1	25B
China	Y10	50B
Euro	€1	37B
Japan	¥100	32B
New Zealand	NZ$1	24B
South Korea	1000W	30B
UK	£1	44B
US	US$1	34B

For current exchange rates see www.xe.com.

Daily Costs

**Budget:
Less than 1000B**

➡ Basic guesthouse room: 600–1000B

➡ Market/street stall meal: 40–100B

➡ Small bottle of beer: 100B

➡ Public transport around town: 20–50B

**Midrange:
1000–4000B**

➡ Flashpacker guesthouse or midrange hotel room: 1000–4000B

➡ Western lunches and seafood dinner: 150–350B

➡ Organised tour or activity: 1000–1500B

➡ Motorbike hire: 150–250B

**Top end:
More than 4000B**

➡ Boutique hotel room: 4000B

➡ Meal at fine-dining restaurant: 350–1000B

➡ Private tours: 2000B

➡ Car hire: from 800B per day

Opening Hours

Banks and government offices close for national holidays. Some bars and clubs close during elections and certain holidays when alcohol sales are banned. Shopping centres have banks that open late.

Banks 8.30am–4.30pm; 24hr ATMs

Bars 6pm–midnight or 1am

Clubs 8pm–2am

Government Offices 8.30am–4.30pm Mon–Fri; some close for lunch

Restaurants 8am–10pm

Shops 10am–7pm

Arriving in Thailand

Suvarnabhumi International Airport (Bangkok; p767) The Airport Rail Link runs from Phaya Thai station to Suvarnabhumi, a new bus line runs from Suvarnabhumi to Th Khao San, and meter taxis run 24 hours.

Don Mueang International Airport (Bangkok; p767) There are four bus lines from Bangkok's de facto budget airport, meter taxis run 24 hours, and a free shuttle bus runs to Suvarnabhumi.

Chiang Mai International Airport (p767) Taxis to the city centre charge a flat fare.

Phuket International Airport (p767) Metered taxis run to the beaches and Phuket Town for a flat fare, buses connect with Phuket Town, and minivans run to Phuket Town and the beaches.

Getting Around

Air Cheap and frequent domestic connections on budget airlines.

Bus Extensive and affordable for travel between towns.

Car & motorcycle Easy to hire for local touring.

Local transport Shared and chartered taxis and motorcycles are widely available.

Train Slow but scenic between Bangkok, the north, the north-east and the south.

For much more on **getting around**, see p769

PLAN YOUR TRIP NEED TO KNOW

First Time Thailand

For more information, see Survival Guide (p751)

Checklist

➡ Ensure your passport is valid for at least six months.

➡ Apply for a tourist visa from a Thai consulate for visits longer than 30 days.

➡ Organise travel insurance, diver's insurance and international driving permit.

➡ Visit your doctor for a check-up and medical clearance if intending to dive.

➡ Inform your bank and credit-card company of your travel plans.

What to Pack

➡ Driving licence and international driving permit (IDP)

➡ Thai phrasebook

➡ GSM mobile phone and charger

➡ Hat and sunglasses

➡ Sandals

➡ Earplugs

➡ Rain-gear and dry bag if travelling in the rainy season

Top Tips for Your Trip

➡ Eat at markets or street stalls for true Thai flavour.

➡ Hop aboard local transport – it's cheap and sociable.

➡ Learn a few Thai phrases and always smile.

➡ Hire a bicycle to tour towns and neighbourhoods.

➡ Avoid the first-timer scams (p154): one-day gem sales in Bangkok, insanely low (or high) transport prices, dodgy tailors etc.

➡ Learn how to bargain (p763) without being a jerk.

➡ Don't touch the Thais on the head and don't point with your feet.

➡ Dress conservatively (don't expose shoulders or too much leg) and remove your shoes when visiting Buddhist temples.

➡ Don't make any disparaging remarks about any member of Thailand's royal family; it's illegal.

What to Wear

In general, light, loose-fitting clothes will prove the most comfortable in the tropical heat. It's worth bringing one jacket that can double as a raincoat and keep you warm in higher elevations and on air-conditioned buses (or in movie theatres). When you visit temples, wear clothes that cover to your elbows and knees. Bring a smart outfit if you plan on fine-dining or clubbing in Bangkok or Phuket.

Sleeping

For peace of mind, book a room for your arrival night. After that, you can wing it – except during certain holidays and peak travel periods when vacancies are scarce.

Guesthouses Family-run options are the best. Rooms run from basic (bed and fan) to plush (private bathroom and air-con).

Hotels Comfortable, mostly modern rooms, with extra services like breakfast included in the rate.

Hostels As the cost and standard of Thailand's guesthouses have increased, dorms have become better value.

Money

Most places in Thailand deal only with cash. Some foreign credit cards are accepted in high-end establishments.

For more information, see p760.

Bargaining

Thais respect a good haggler. Always let the vendor make the first offer, then ask 'Can you lower the price?'. This usually results in a discount. Now it's your turn to make a counter-offer. Always start low, but don't bargain unless you're serious about buying. If you're buying several of an item, you have much more leverage to request and receive a lower price. It helps immeasurably to keep the negotiations relaxed and friendly.

Tipping

Tipping is not generally expected in Thailand, though it is appreciated. The exception is loose change from a large restaurant bill – if a meal costs 488B and you pay with a 500B note, some Thais will leave the change. It's a way of saying 'I'm not so money-grubbing as to grab every last baht'. At many hotel restaurants and upmarket eateries, a 10% service charge will be added to your bill.

AUSTIN BUSH / LONELY PLANET ©

Bangkok market

Etiquette

Thais are generally very understanding and hospitable, but there are some important taboos and social conventions.

Monarchy It is a criminal offence to disrespect the royal family; treat objects depicting the king (like money) with respect.

Temples Wear clothing that covers to your knees and elbows. Remove all footwear before entering. Sit with your feet tucked behind you, so they are not facing the Buddha image. Women should never touch a monk or a monk's belongings; step out of the way on footpaths and don't sit next to them on public transport.

Modesty At the beach, avoid public nudity or topless sunbathing.

Body language Avoid touching anyone on the head and be careful where you point your feet.

Saving face The best way to win over the Thais is to smile (p730) – visible anger or arguing is embarrassing.

LANGUAGE

Tourist towns have plenty of English speakers, though bus drivers, market vendors and taxi drivers are less fluent so it helps to know how to order food and count in Thai. Learn more in the language chapter (p780).

Thailand has its own script. Street signs are transliterated into English, but there is no standard system so spellings vary widely. Not all letters are pronounced as they appear ('Ph' is an aspirated 'p' not an 'f').

What's New

Chang Chui

This tough-to-pin-down venue, which spans everything from bars to performance spaces to an abandoned airplane, is one of the most eclectic openings Bangkok has seen in years. (p97)

Hua Hin to Pattaya Ferry

This new link across the sometimes-choppy waters of the Gulf of Thailand links the beaches and islands of Thailand's south and east, saving a long haul through Bangkok. (p506)

Craft Beer

Thailand seems to be in the midst of a beer renaissance, and good ol' Singha and Chang are being crowded out by craft beers, both imported and domestic. Bangkok heads the way, with fun bars such as Hair of the Dog, but Chiang Mai and Ko Samui also have their own craft beer scenes. (p141)

E-Thong

Great coffee shops, numerous welcoming homestays and a relaxing vibe are increasingly luring Thai city dwellers for weekends in this forest-fringed border outpost in Kanchanaburi Province. Now, if only they'd fix that road... (p196)

New Trains

The State Railway of Thailand has upgraded some of its rolling stock, introducing shiny new train cars on routes linking Bangkok with Chiang Mai and destinations in the northeast. (p772)

Homestays

Want to delve deeper into Thai culture than a typical hotel stay might allow? Consider a stint in one of the growing number of homestay programs in just about every corner of the country; the operation in charming Muang Pon, in Mae Hong Son Province, is one of our favourites. (p755)

Chanthaburi

There's little new about this town in eastern Thailand, but its charming waterfront district is becoming trendy, with hipster coffee bars and handcraft boutiques making an interesting contrast with the historic ambience. (p467)

Bangkok Nightlife

A host of new speakeasy-influenced drinkeries such as Ku Bar, offering progressive cocktails and craft beers, are quickly shifting the perception of Bangkok's drinking scene from sketchy to sophisticated. (p138)

Hip Hostels

Hostels continue to be the one of the fastest-growing sectors of accommodation in Thailand, and fresh design and fun amenities at places like Fin Hostel, in Phuket, mean that sharing a bathroom is no longer a compromise. (p641)

For more recommendations and reviews, see lonelyplanet.com/thailand

If You Like...

Fabulous Food

Curries Thai curry is pungent, fiery and colourful. Bangkok, southern Thailand and northern Thailand all whip up their own variations. (p44)

Isan cuisine The northeast's triumvirate dishes – *gài yâhng* (grilled chicken), *sôm·đam* (spicy green papaya salad) and *kôw něe·o* (sticky rice) – have converts across the country. (p414)

Seafood Grilled prawns, spicy squid stir-fries, crab curries, fried mussels – get thee to the coast and dine on the fruits of the sea.

Fruit Luscious, dessert-like tropical fruits are piled into pyramid displays at day markets or arranged like precious jewels in vendors' glass cases. (p45)

Cooking courses Learn how to replicate the tricks of the trade at cooking schools in Bangkok, Chiang Mai, Ko Chang or Ko Samui. (p47)

Temples & Ruins

Bangkok The city's most exalted Buddha figure resides comfortably in Wat Phra Kaew, the seat of Thai Buddhism. (p68)

Ayuthaya The ruins of this fabled city stand testament to Thailand's formative years. (p166)

Sukhothai This ancient city is the capital of one of Thailand's first home-grown kingdoms. (p252)

Chiang Mai Chiang Mai's old walled city is filled with antique teak temples. (p308)

Phanom Rung This Khmer outpost built in the Angkor style has surveyed the rural landscape for centuries. (p417)

Lopburi Leaders from the Khmer and Dvaravati empires used to rule here; today hundreds of monkeys scamper around the ruins. (p176)

Beaches

Railay Adrenaline junkies scale the limestone crags while sun-seekers bask on the powder-soft sands. (p656)

Ko Phi-Phi The laid-back vibe on visually stunning Phi-Phi is hard to resist. (p663)

Ko Lanta The jumping-off spot for some stellar dive sites, and more character than most due to a strong Muslim community. (p671)

Ko Tarutao So far south it's almost in Malaysia, Tarutao has wide, open beaches and almost no facilities – precisely the appeal. (p695)

Ko Chang Top-notch resorts and spas, several escape-from-it-all guesthouses where the only facility is a hammock, and jaw-droppingly good sunsets. (p474)

Ko Samet Favoured by flashpackers, some of Samet's beaches are lively affairs, while those further south are far more tranquil. (p461)

Wildlife Encounters

Khao Yai National Park Spot elephants, monkeys, snakes and creepy-crawlies in Thailand's oldest national park. (p413)

Kaeng Krachan National Park Wake up to dense morning mists, then go trekking to spot elephants and gibbons in this little-visited park, south of Bangkok. (p496)

Ao Khanom A lovely and un-touristy bay south of Surat Thani that hosts pink dolphins, a rare albino breed. (p581)

Kui Buri National Park Take a Thai safari for virtually guaranteed wild elephant encounters. (p508)

Nam Nao National Park One of the best spots for ornithologists, this park is also home to elephants, leopards and tigers. (p443)

Thong Pha Phum National Park
The elephants, tigers and bears may be elusive, but overnight park visitors will likely see serow, barking deer and a plethora of bird life. (p195)

Festivals

Songkran Thailand's biggest festival is about using water to show respect. Once that's done, water fights erupt in every town.

Music festivals With a jazz festival in **Hua Hin** and international DJs in Bangkok and Ko Samui, music fans are well catered for. (p503)

Loi Krathong Every November, Thais pray for their sins to be forgiven by creating lanterns and setting them afloat in waterways. (p32)

Fruit festivals Rural towns honour their agricultural produce with a range of festivals. In Chiang Rai the lychee is revered, while Chanthaburi takes time to honour the world's stinkiest fruit, the durian. (p31)

Escaping the Crowds

Ko Tarutao A wild jungle interior and vast empty beaches mean you can really get away from it all here. (p695)

Phu Wua Wildlife Sanctuary A wild outpost in Thailand's northeast. (p397)

Ko Ngai One of the quieter southern islands, Ko Ngai has superb snorkelling and top beaches. (p686)

Si Satchanalai-Chaliang Historical Park The ruins nobody seems to know about. (p260)

Top: Loi Krathong (p333), Chiang Mai Province.

Bottom: Green pork curry

Diving & Snorkelling

Surin & Similan Islands National Marine Parks These Andaman islands have dramatic rocky gorges, hard and soft coral reefs and myriad marine life. (p603), (p611)

Ko Lanta A smorgasbord of dive sites surrounds this Andaman island; look out for manta rays, whale sharks and other large pelagic fish. (p671)

Ko Tao Cheap dive schools, shallow waters and year-round conditions, Ko Tao remains the country's dive-training headquarters. (p563)

Ko Lipe Dive sites with healthy coral, a deep pinnacle and good visibility in the early rainy season. (p696)

World-Class Pampering

Ko Samui Get lean, aligned and beautified on this wellness retreat island. (p526)

Bangkok Massages in the City of Angels are an everyday treat, not unlike picking up dry cleaning or going to the post office. (p65)

Phuket Five-star spas make pampering an all-day affair on this resort island. (p618)

Chiang Mai This low-key city does massages for the masses without the painful 'spa' price tag. (p308)

Ko Chang As if lounging on the beach isn't enough, Ko Chang boasts top-class spas for that extra level of de-stressing. (p474)

Shopping & Markets

Bangkok Pick from the capital's mega-malls packed with designer gear, sprawling markets like Chatuchak or chic independent shops. (p147)

Chiang Mai The bustling Night Bazaar is filled with souvenirs and antiques. Outside the city, handicraft centres offer silk garments and colourful umbrellas. (p348)

Phuket Town Check out the boutiques, galleries and weekend market in Phuket's hipster heart. (p629)

Mae Sot Myanmar or Thailand? It's hard to tell in what is one of the country's most exotic fresh markets. (p277)

Khon Kaen Gleefully deplete your baht at one of this northeastern city's many night markets. (p439)

Hill-Tribe Culture

Chiang Mai The Karen, Lahu, Hmong and several other hill tribes live around Chiang Mai. (p308)

Chiang Rai The Akha, who live in the mountains surrounding Chiang Rai, have distinct traditions, including a giant swing festival. (p205)

Sangkhlaburi Volunteer at one of several charities in this border town that look after displaced hill tribes from Myanmar. (p197)

Mae Sot A fascinatingly diverse city, where Hmong, Karen and Burmese folk stroll the streets. (p274)

Nightlife

Bangkok International DJs regularly hold court in the capital's clubs, while a more chilled clientele sip mojitos from the city's sky bars. Th Khao San remains the backpackers' favourite haunt. (p138)

Phuket Clubs, live-music bars and cabaret shows ensure there's plenty of post-beach action to be had. (p593)

Pattaya Mega-clubs aimed largely at foreign visitors have arrived, and an increasing number of five-star venues have their own fancy bars with live music. (p455)

Ko Pha-Ngan Home of the Full Moon Party, buckets of whisky and almighty hangovers. (p545)

Outdoor Adventure

Kanchanaburi Waterfall spotting, rafting and ziplining are just a short journey from Bangkok. (p181)

Mae Hong Son Hike into the mountainous frontier between Thailand and Myanmar to visit hill-tribe villages. (p294)

Ko Chang When you tire of the sea, plunge into the jungle-covered hills with local guides. (p474)

Khao Sok National Park Canoe and hike through Thailand's ancient rainforest studded with limestone mountains. (p605)

Railay Claw your way up the limestone cliffs in Krabi Province for a breathtaking and breathless ocean view. (p656)

Chiang Mai Every known activity – mountain biking, kayaking, abseiling, trekking, ziplining etc – has a following in this nature-loving city. (p308)

Month by Month

January

The weather is cool and dry, ushering in the peak tourist season.

Chinese New Year

Thais with Chinese ancestry celebrate the Chinese lunar new year (*drùd jeen*) with a week of house-cleaning and fireworks.

February

Still in the high season, Thailand is sun and fun for anyone snowed out.

Makha Bucha

One of three holy days marking significant moments of Buddha's life, Makha Bucha (*mah·ká boo·chah*) commemorates the day when 1250 *arhant* (Buddhists who had achieved enlightenment) assembled to visit Buddha and received the principles of Buddhism; the festival falls on the full moon of the third lunar month. It is a public holiday.

Flower Festival

Chiang Mai displays its floral beauty during a three-day period. The festival highlight is the flower-decorated floats that parade through town.

March

The hot and dry season approaches and the beaches start to empty out.

Pattaya International Music Festival

Pattaya showcases pop and rock bands from across Asia at this free music event, attracting bus-loads of Bangkok uni students.

Kite-Flying Festivals

During the windy season, colourful kites battle it out over the skies of Sanam Luang in Bangkok and elsewhere in the country.

Mango Season

Luscious ripe mangoes come into season from March to June and are sliced before your eyes, packed in a container with sticky rice and accompanied with a coconut-milk-based dressing.

April

Hot, dry weather sweeps across the land. Though the main tourist season is winding down, make reservations well in advance – the whole country is on the move for Songkran.

Songkran

Thailand's traditional new year (13–15 April) starts out as a respectful affair then degenerates into a water war. Morning visits to the temple involve colourful processions and water-sprinkling ceremonies of sacred Buddha images. Afterwards, Thais load up their water guns and head out to the streets for combat. Chiang Mai and Bangkok are the epicentres.

Poy Sang Long

This Buddhist novice ordination festival held in late March/early April in Mae Hong Son and Chiang Mai sees young Shan (Tai Yai) boys between the ages of seven and 14 parading

in festive costumes, head-dresses and make up.

May

Leading up to the rainy season, festivals encourage plentiful rains and bountiful harvests. Prices are low and tourists are few but it is still remorselessly hot.

🎆 Rocket Festival

In the northeast, where rain can be scarce, villagers craft painted bamboo rockets *(bâng fai)* that are fired into the sky to encourage precipitation. This festival is celebrated in Yasothon, Ubon Ratchathani and Nong Khai.

🎆 Visakha Bucha

The holy day of Visakha Bucha *(wí·săh·kà boo·chah)* falls on the 15th day of the waxing moon in the sixth lunar month and commemorates the date of the Buddha's birth, enlightenment and *parinibbana* (passing away).

June

In some parts of the country, the rainy season is merely an afternoon shower, leaving the rest of the day for music and merriment. This month is a shoulder season.

🍴 Chanthaburi Fruit Festival

Held at the end of May or the start of June, this festival in Chanthaburi is an opportunity to enjoy an abundance of fruit: mangosteen, rambutan, longkong,

Top: Flower Festival (p333), Chiang Mai.

Bottom: Lopburi Monkey Festival (p178)

longan, salak and the pungent durian.

Phi Ta Khon

The Buddhist holy day of Bun Phra Wet is given a carnival makeover in Dan Sai village in northeast Thailand. Revellers disguise themselves in garish 'spirit' costumes and parade through the streets wielding wooden phalluses and downing rice whisky. Dates vary between June and July.

July

The start of the rainy season ushers in Buddhist Lent, a period of reflection and meditation. Summer holidays bring tourists.

Asahna Bucha

The full moon of the eighth lunar month commemorates Buddha's first sermon, in which he described the religion's four noble truths. It is considered one of Buddhism's holiest days.

Khao Phansaa

The day after Asahna Bucha marks the beginning of Buddhist Lent (the first day of the waning moon in the eighth lunar month), the traditional time for men to enter the monastery. In Ubon Ratchathani, traditional candle offerings have grown into a festival of elaborately carved wax sculptures.

HM the King's Birthday

The king's birthday is a public holiday on 28 July.

August

Overcast skies and daily showers mark the middle of the rainy season.

HM the Queen's Birthday

The Queen Mother's birthday (12 August) is a public holiday and national Mother's Day.

September

September is the wettest month in and around Bangkok, and tourist numbers are correspondingly low.

October

Religious preparations for the end of the rainy season and the end of Buddhist Lent begin. The monsoons are reaching the finish line (in most of the country).

Vegetarian Festival

A holiday from meat is taken for nine days in adherence with Chinese beliefs of mind and body purification. In Phuket the festival gets extreme, with entranced marchers turning themselves into human shish kebabs. Generally held late September/early October.

King Chulalongkorn Day

Rama V is honoured on the anniversary of his death at the Royal Plaza in Bangkok's Dusit neighbourhood. Held on 23 October.

November

The cool, dry season has arrived, and if you get here early enough, you'll beat the tourist crowds.

Loi Krathong

One of Thailand's most beloved festivals, Loi Krathong is celebrated on the first full moon of the 12th lunar month. Small origami-like boats (called *kràthong* or *grà·tong*) festooned with flowers and candles are sent adrift in the waterways.

Lopburi Monkey Festival

During the last week of November, the town's troublesome macaques get pampered with their very own banquet, while merit-makers watch on.

December

The peak of the tourist season has returned with fair skies, busy beach resorts and a holiday mood.

Chiang Mai Red Cross & Winter Fair

A 10-day festival that displays Chiang Mai's cultural heritage with a country-fair atmosphere; expect food (lots of it) and traditional performances.

Rama IX's Birthday

Honouring the late king's birthday on 5 December, this public holiday hosts parades and merit-making events, and is combined with Father's Day.

Itineraries

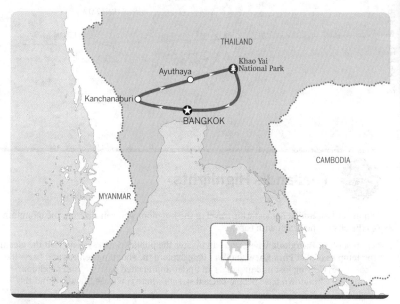

 Bangkok & Around

If time is not on your side, you can still explore jungles, temples and Thai culture – all of which are within easy reach of Bangkok.

After a quick look around the major temples and markets in the **capital**, and hitting its top restaurants, embark on the wonderfully scenic train ride to **Kanchanaburi**. Here, enjoy a dip in the seven-tiered Erawan waterfall before visiting the Hellfire Pass Memorial, a poignant tribute to the thousands of prisoners of war who died making the Death Railway during WWII. The nearby forests are ideal for adventure activities or outdoor excursions, such as ziplining over the forest canopies or cruising along the River Kwai.

Next, jump in a minivan bound for **Ayuthaya** and cycle around the impressive ruins of this erstwhile capital. Finally, head over to **Khao Yai National Park**, transiting through Pak Chong. Spend a day hiking through the jungle in search of elephants and tigers, and a night camping under the stars before winding your way back to Bangkok.

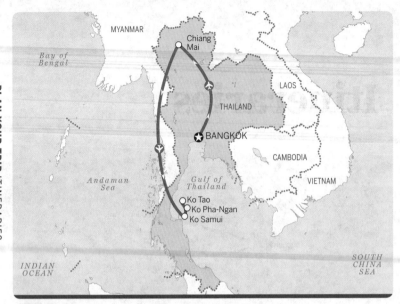

Thailand's Highlights

Thanks to expanded domestic air travel in the kingdom, you can zip from the mountains to the city to the beach with ease.

Start off in **Bangkok**, where you can master the public transit system, visit the gleaming temples of Wat Phra Kaew and Wat Pho, explore the shopping centres and party like a rock star. Getting lost in Bangkok is an under-appreciated pastime, and neighbourhoods like Chinatown have people-packed streets where you'll see the weird and the wonderful.

Fly (or take the scenic train) to **Chiang Mai**, which can keep you busy for several days with its Thai cooking classes, temples, monk chats, markets and fabulous food. Take a road trip to the surrounding countryside, where you can hike to hill-tribe villages and zipline through the forest. Don't forget to visit the cool highlands of Doi Suthep or Doi Inthanon, two famous northern mountains.

Ready for the beach? Take a direct flight from Chiang Mai south to the tropical island of **Ko Samui**, where you can choose to live it up in a five-star resort or villa, or relax in a low-key beach bungalow in one of the island's quieter corners (yes, some still exist).

Make a day trip to uninhabited Ang Thong Marine National Marine Park before a stop at **Ko Pha-Ngan**, an easy boat trip from Ko Samui. Head to one of its famous Full Moon Parties, or time your visit to miss the crowds and enjoy laid-back hammock hanging instead. Virtually next door is tiny **Ko Tao**, Thailand's diving-certification headquarters; there are plenty of shallow reefs near the shore for snorkellers, too.

Head back to Samui to fly on to your next destination, or make your way back to Bangkok for some last-minute shopping.

Top: Chinatown (p81), Bangkok

Bottom: Ang Thong National Marine Park (p577)

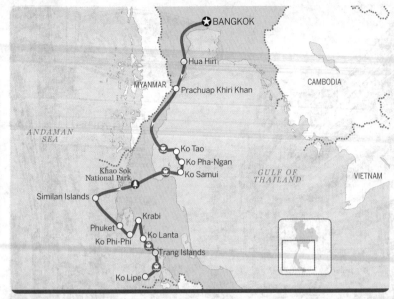

Southern Islands & Beaches

3 WEEKS

Hitting all of Thailand's top beaches in one trip isn't easy, but some serious island-hopping means you can do it and still have bags of hammock time. This trip takes you there by land and sea, but if you need to hurry up, hop on a flight along the way.

From **Bangkok**, dip south into **Hua Hin**, an upmarket resort town where all the top hotel chains have a spot on the beach. Then on to **Prachuap Khiri Khan**, where you can hire a bike and check out the undulating coast, bays and laid-back beach scene.

Now for some island time, first stop **Ko Tao** (via Chumphon). Sign up for a dive course or enjoy a few days of snorkelling before island-hopping to **Ko Pha-Ngan** for Full Moon Party fun or an other-side-of-the-island escape. Retire to the resort island of **Ko Samui** for some pampering (or, if you have the energy, more partying), from where it's a short ferry ride to transport hub Surat Thani. Buses leave hourly for **Khao Sok National Park**, where you can enjoy some jungle time in one of the world's oldest rainforests before making the short transfer to Khao Lak, a sleepy beach resort that serves as the perfect base for dive trips to the world-famous **Similan Islands** and, to the north, the Surin Islands. Consider spending a few days on a live-aboard to linger in the underwater world full of rays, sharks and seahorses. Once you surface, go south to **Phuket** – Thailand's largest island – and gulp down the numerous attractions and activities on offer here (don't miss a day trip to Ao Phang-Nga).

From Phuket, jump on a boat bound for **Ko Phi-Phi**, a party island that stays up all night and still looks fantastic in the morning. From here you can head back to the mainland and explore the gorgeous coastline of **Krabi** (be sure to take a long-boat to Railay beach, regarded as one of the finest in Thailand) or ferry straight to **Ko Lanta** to collapse in a hammock and drink in the bucolic island life. Continue south by ferry past the beautiful **Trang Islands** to increasingly popular but still relatively undeveloped **Ko Lipe**, and catch a speedboat back to the mainland when you're ready to begin your journey home.

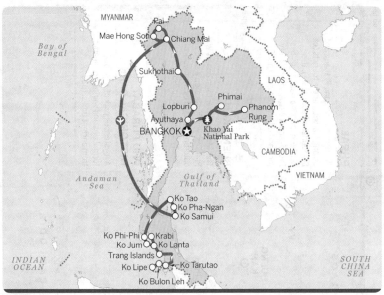

 The Grand Tour

4 WEEKS

A fully rounded trip to Thailand meanders through almost every corner of the kingdom. If you need to save time, hop on a flight – planes go everywhere these days.

Start off in **Bangkok**, and then take a train north to the ancient capital of **Ayuthaya**. Make a detour to the monkey town of **Lopburi**. From here, follow the culture trail north to **Sukhothai**, where you can cycle through the historic and crumbling ruins of another ancient capital. Hightail it to **Chiang Mai**, the 'rose of the north', and cycle around the old temples. Then switch back into the mountains to the party scene of **Pai**. Climb deeper into the hills to the Myanmar-influenced town of **Mae Hong Son**. Loop back to Chiang Mai.

By now the beach should be calling. Fly to the Gulf of Thailand and stop by **Ko Samui** for its resort-island trappings, **Ko Pha-Ngan** for beach bumming and partying, and **Ko Tao** for diving and snorkelling.

Next, get over to the Andaman Coast and its limestone mountains jutting out of the sea. **Ko Phi-Phi** is the prettiest, priciest and most party-fuelled of them all. Little **Ko Jum** holds tight to a fast-disappearing beach-shack, hippie vibe. the dive scene is the real attraction at gentrified **Ko Lanta**. Rock-climbers opt for mainland Krabi, particularly **Railay**.

If you've got the itch for more sand then continue down the peninsula to the **Trang Islands**, another collection of limestone sea mountains lapped by clear waters. Or opt for the idyllic islands offshore from Satun. There's also emerging and midrange **Ko Bulon Leh**, rustic **Ko Tarutao** and laid-back **Ko Lipe**.

Or, you could skip the beaches south of Krabi and instead take a cultural antidote to the northeast, Thailand's agricultural heartland. Transit through Bangkok and then crawl through the jungles of **Khao Yai National Park**. From here, head to Nakhon Ratchasima (Khorat), a transit point for trips to the Angkor ruins at **Phimai**. Follow the Khmer trail east to **Phanom Rung**, the most important and visually impressive of the Angkor temples in Thailand. Surrounding Phanom Rung are a handful of smaller, more remote and forgotten temples with regal ambience.

Off the Beaten Track: Thailand

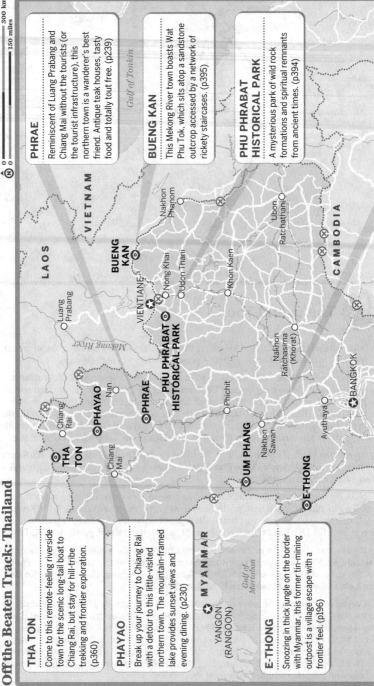

THA TON

Come to this remote-feeling riverside town for the scenic long-tail boat to Chiang Rai, but stay for hill-tribe trekking and frontier exploration. (p360)

PHAYAO

Break up your journey to Chiang Rai with a detour to this little-visited northern town. The mountain-framed lake provides sunset views and evening dining. (p230)

E-THONG

Snoozing in thick jungle on the border with Myanmar, this former tin-mining outpost is a village escape with a frontier feel. (p196)

PHRAE

Reminiscent of Luang Prabang and Chiang Mai without the tourists (or the tourist infrastructure), this northern town is a wanderer's best friend. Antique teak houses, tasty food and totally tout free. (p239)

BUENG KAN

This Mekong River town boasts Wat Phu Tok, which sits atop a sandstone outcrop accessed by a network of rickety staircases. (p395)

PHU PHRABAT HISTORICAL PARK

A mysterious park of wild rock formations and spiritual remnants from ancient times. (p394)

KUIBURI NATIONAL PARK

Take a Thai safari for virtually guaranteed wild elephant encounters. (p508)

KO PHAYAM

A beach retreat for the resort-averse, Ko Phayam has fine sand, a range of accommodation and motorbike-friendly paths. Sand and sea without the distractions. (p600)

KO TARUTAO

Tarutao, part of a marine park, is so far south it is practically in Malaysia. But it is a top castaway contender with secluded alabaster beaches. (p695)

UM PHANG

In Thailand's western frontier, this mostly Karen village is surrounded by unspoilt wilderness, perfect for rafting, trekking and waterfall-spotting. (p279)

AO KHANOM

A pretty Gulf of Thailand bay with long beaches and regular visits from pink albino dolphins. It is a dreamy natural setting without much development. (p581)

KO SUKORN

Ko Sukorn is a cultural paradise filled with tawny beaches and rubber plantations. It's the perfect place to experience village life. (p690)

Phetchaburi · Kuiburi National Park · Prachuap Khiri Khan · Chumphon · Ranong · Ko Phayam · Surin Islands · Similan Islands · Surat Thani · Ko Tao · Ko Pha-Ngan · Ko Samui · Ao Khanom · Phuket Town · Ko Sukorn · Satun · Pulau Langkawi · Ko Tarutao · Pattani · Kota Bharu

Chanthaburi · GULF OF THAILAND · PHNOM PENH · Ho Chi Minh City · VIETNAM · MALAYSIA

Plan Your Trip
Activities

With oceans and islands to explore, jungles and mountains to discover and a rich and varied culture to embrace, Thailand overflows with activities. For adventure-seekers, there are canopy-skimming ziplines, hard-kicking *moo·ay tai* (Thai boxing) lessons and world-class dive sites. Alternatively, chill out on spiritual retreats and massage courses.

When to Go

January to March

What is laughingly known locally as the cold season is a great time to focus on outdoor pursuits, as the temperatures are warm but bearable. Trekking in the northern provinces is particularly good around this time.

November to April

The Andaman displays its best features, when diving visibility can be incredible. Between May and October resorts tend to grind to a halt or close due to the rainy season.

January to September

Dive capital Ko Tao is primed for diving nearly all year round, but many resorts here and on nearby islands close between October and December when the rains come.

Diving & Snorkelling

The waters off Thailand are filled with myriad marine life. Nearly all the signature dive sites are in the south, though the eastern seaboard has some good coral and wreck dives. Always go with a responsible (p753) operator that enforces sustainable practices.

Where to Go

Surin & Similan Islands Both the Surin (p603) and Similan (p611) islands are stunning national parks. Their dive sites are regularly named as being among the finest in the world due to the visiting pelagics, superb visibility (up to 35m) and the array of canyons. Dive trips and live-aboards, for all levels, can be arranged from Phuket or Hat Khao Lak.

Hin Daeng & Hin Muang Accessible from Ko Lanta, sightings below these two remote rocks often include manta rays and barracuda. With depths of up to 40m and strong currents, divers should have some experience.

Ko Tao New to diving? Check out Ko Tao (p563), the cheapest and best place to get your open-water certification. For non-divers, there are plenty of simple snorkelling coves.

Hiking & Trekking

Northern Thailand has excellent hiking routes filled with cascading waterfalls, dense jungle and soaring mountain ranges.

Top: Snorkelling off Ao
Phang-Nga (p614)

Bottom: Hiking in Doi
Chiang Dao Wildlife
Sanctuary (p357)

HORIZONMAN / SHUTTERSTOCK

Stay overnight with hill tribes or pitch a tent with nature as your only neighbour. Along with treks, guides can arrange cycling, kayaking and rafting excursions. Choose environmentally responsible operators (p754).

Where to Go

Chiang Mai (p326) is the main jumping-off point for treks, such as day trips to Doi Inthanon (p363), Thailand's highest mountain. Hard-core trekkers head to more remote spots such as Um Phang Wildlife Sanctuary (p280), home to the kingdom's largest waterfall, or learn survival skills from guides who grew up near the jungles.

Loei (p367) has some spectacular trekking options. Among them is Phu Kradueng National Park (p378), where you can take the 5.5km trail to the plateau, or experience the relatively cooler climes of the pine forests and savannah.

Meditation & Spiritual Retreats

Thais often go on spiritual retreats to rejuvenate themselves. You can join them at temples or meditation centres.

Where to Go

Bangkok Some of the city's temples offer day courses (p100) in meditation for English-speaking beginners.

Chiang Mai The monk chats (p330) offered at several temples can function as informal introductions to Buddhism. Several temples also offer meditation lessons.

Ubon Ratchathani The northeast is the heartland of Thailand's forest meditation temples (p432). For those with a bit more experience, consider Wat Pa Nanachat (p432).

Moo·ay Tai (Thai Boxing)

Ever dreamed of becoming a Thai boxing champ? *Moo·ay tai* (also spelt muay thai) training camp packages include general fitness and ring work.

Where to Go

Bangkok Thailand's capital is home to a number of schools spanning every level. Beginners are particularly well catered for at gyms such as Jaroenthong Muay Thai Gym (p101) and Eight Limbs (p101).

Pattaya Fairtex Sports Club (☎038 253888; www.fairtexpattaya.com; 179/185-212 Mu 5, Th Pattaya Neua; sessions 800B) has excellent facilities aimed at training foreign visitors with any level of fitness or fighting experience. National champions and MMA (mixed martial arts) fighters also drop in to spar.

Chiang Mai The northern capital has several top *moo·ay tai* gyms, including Lanna Muay Thai Boxing Camp (p330) and Chai Yai Muay Thai (p330), where everyone – from national champions to total beginners – comes to train.

Climbing

Thailand has a range of climbing options, ranging in skill from total beginner to those who rival Spiderman. Most climbs are in the south, but the north has several challenging peaks.

Where to Go

Railay Scaling these limestone crags while surrounded by azure seas and a fabulous beach makes Railay (p656) the number-one climbing site in Thailand. More than 700 bolted routes can be assaulted on your own or with the help of guides.

Lopburi Khao Chin Lae (p181) is a 240m-high limestone peak surrounded by sunflower fields. Guides in Lopburi (p176) can arrange transport and explain the routes.

Surfing & Kiteboarding

The monsoon's mid-year swell creates surfable barrels off Phuket, while almost year-round gusty winds lure kiteboarders to the east coast.

Where to Go

Phuket The best waves arrive between June and September, when annual surfing competitions are held on Hat Kata Yai, the most popular surf spot on Phuket (p621), and Hat Kalim, just north of Patong.

Hua Hin Thailand's kiteboarding, or kitesurfing, capital Hua Hin (p500) is blessed with strong, gusty winds, shallow water and a long beach off which to practise your moves.

Damnoen Saduak Floating Market (p148), Bangkok

Eat & Drink Like a Local

Incendiary curries, oodles of noodles, fresh seafood and the tropical fruit you've been dreaming about – Thailand has it all. To experience the true flavours of Thailand, you need to familiarise yourself with the dishes of Thailand's various regions and ethnic groups.

The Year in Food

Summer (March to June)

Thailand's hot season is the best time of year for fruit. Durian, mangoes, mangosteen and lychees are all at their juicy peak during these months.

Rainy Season (July to October)

One event to look out for during the rainy season is Thailand's annual Vegetarian Festival, typically held in late September or early October. The festival is celebrated particularly in places with large Chinese populations, such as Bangkok, Phuket Town and Trang.

Winter (November to January)

During Thailand's brief cool season, open-air beer halls, many serving spicy Thai drinking snacks, spring up in the larger cities.

The Four Flavours

Simply put, sweet, sour, salty and spicy are the parameters that define Thai food, and although many associate the cuisine with fiery heat, virtually every dish is an exercise in balancing these four tastes. This balance might be obtained by a squeeze of lime juice, a spoonful of sugar and a glug of fish sauce, or a tablespoon of fermented soybeans and a strategic splash of vinegar. Bitter also factors into many Thai dishes, and often comes from the addition of a vegetable or herb. Regardless of the source, the goal is the same: a favourable balance of four clear, vibrant flavours.

Thai Staples

Curries & Soups

In Thai, *gaang* (it sounds somewhat similar to the English 'gang') is often translated as 'curry', but it actually describes any dish with a lot of liquid and can thus refer to soups (such as *gaang jèut*) as well as classic chilli-paste-based curries. The prepara-

tion of the latter begins with a *krêu·ang gaang,* created by mashing, pounding and grinding an array of fresh ingredients with a stone mortar and pestle to form an aromatic paste. Typical ingredients include chilli, galangal, lemongrass, kaffir lime zest, shallots, garlic, shrimp paste and salt.

Another food celebrity is *dôm yam,* the famous Thai spicy-and-sour soup. Fuelling the fire beneath *dôm yam's* often velvety surface are fresh *prík kêe nǒo* (tiny chillies) or, alternatively, half a teaspoonful of *nám prík pǒw* (roasted chilli paste).

Spicy Salads

Standing right alongside curries in terms of Thai-ness is the ubiquitous *yam,* a hot and tangy 'salad' typically based around seafood, meat or vegetables. Lime juice provides the tang, while the abundant use of chilli generates the heat. Most *yam* are served at room temperature, or just slightly warmed by any cooked ingredients. The dish functions equally well as part of a meal or on its own as *gàp glâam,* snack food to accompany a night of boozing.

Rice & Noodles

Rice is so central to Thai food culture that the most common term for 'eat' is *gin kôw* (literally, 'consume rice') and one of the most common greetings is *Gin kôw rěu yang?* (Have you consumed rice yet?). The grain is customarily served alongside main dishes such as curries, stir-fries or soups.

Thai noodle dishes are often served slightly under-seasoned. The idea is to season your own bowl, typically using some or all of four condiments: *prík nám sôm* (sliced mild chillies in vinegar), *nám plah* (fish sauce), *prík pòn* (dried red chilli, flaked or ground to a near powder) and *nám·dahn* (plain white sugar). You'll find four main kinds of noodle in Thailand:

Bà·mèe Made from wheat flour and egg, this noodle is yellowish in colour and sold only in fresh bundles.

Kà·nǒm jeen This noodle is produced by pushing a rice-based dough through a sieve into boiling water, much the way some types of Italian pasta are made.

Sên gǒo·ay děe·o The most common type of noodle in Thailand is made from rice flour mixed with water to form a paste, which is steamed to form wide, flat sheets, then sliced into various widths.

Wún·sên An almost clear noodle made from mung-bean starch and water, it features occasionally in soups, but is usually the central ingredient in *yam wún sên*, a hot and tangy salad.

Nám Prík

Although more home than restaurant food, *nám prík* is a spicy chilli-based dip. Typically eaten with rice and vegetables and herbs, they're also among the most regional of Thai dishes – you could probably pinpoint the province you're in by simply looking at the *nám prík* on offer.

Stir-Fries & Deep Fries

Pàt (stir-fries) were introduced to Thailand by the Chinese, and many dishes cling to their roots, such as the ubiquitous *pàt pàk bûng fai daang* (morning glory flash-fried with garlic and chilli). Others are Thai-Chinese hybrids, such as *pàt pèt* (literally 'spicy stir-fry').

Tôrt (deep-frying in oil) is mainly reserved for snacks such as *glôo·ay tôrt* (deep-fried bananas) or *pò·pée·a* (egg rolls). An exception is *plah tôrt* (deep-fried fish), which is a common way to prepare fish.

Mangosteen

Fruits

Being a tropical country, Thailand excels in the fruit department. *Má·môo·ang* (mangoes) alone come in a dozen varieties that are eaten at different stages of ripeness. Other common fruit include *sàp·pà·rót* (pineapple), *má·lá·gor* (papaya) and *daang moh* (watermelon), all of which are sold from ubiquitous vendor carts and accompanied by a dipping mix of salt, sugar and ground chilli. A highlight of visiting Thailand is sampling the huge variety of indigenous fruits of which you've probably never heard. Many are available year-round nowadays, but April and May is peak season for several of the most beloved varieties, including durian, mangoes and mangosteen.

Here is a list of other lesser-known tropical fruits:

Custard apple Known in Thai as *nóy nàh*, the knobbly green skin of this fruit conceals hard black seeds and sweet, gloopy flesh with a granular texture.

Durian Known in Thai as *tú·ree·an*, the king of fruit is also Thailand's most infamous, due to its intense flavour and odour, which can suggest everything from custard to onions.

Guava A native of South America, *fa·ràng* – the same as the word for Westerner – is a green, apple-like ball containing pink or white flesh that's sweet and crispy.

Jackfruit The gigantic green pod of *kà·nŭn* – it's considered the world's largest fruit – conceals dozens of waxy yellow sections that taste like a blend of pineapple and bananas (it reminds us of Juicy Fruit chewing gum).

Langsat Strip away the yellowish peel of this fruit, known in Thai as *long·gong*, to find a segmented, perfumed pearlescent flesh with a lychee-like flavour.

Longan *Lam yai* takes the form of a tiny hard ball; it's like a mini lychee with sweet, perfumed flesh. Peel it, eat the flesh and spit out the hard seed.

Lychee The pink skin of *lín·jèe* conceals an addictive translucent flesh similar in flavour to a grape. It's generally only available between April and June.

Mangosteen The hard purple shell of *mang·kút*, the queen of Thai fruit, conceals delightfully fragrant white segments, some containing a hard seed.

Pomelo Like a grapefruit on steroids, *sôm oh* takes the form of a thick pithy green skin hiding sweet, tangy segments. Cut into the skin, peel off

NAIT029 / SHUTTERSTOCK ©

Kà·nŏm (bite-sized sweet snack)

the pith and then break open the segments and munch on the flesh inside.

Rambutan People have different theories about what *ngó* look like, not all repeatable in polite company. Regardless, the hairy shell contains sweet translucent flesh that you scrape off the seed with your teeth.

Rose apple Known in Thai as *chom·pôo*, rose apple is an elongated pink or red fruit with a smooth, shiny skin and pale, watery flesh. It's a good thirst-quencher on a hot day.

Salak Also known as snake fruit because of its scaly skin. The exterior of *sàlà* looks like a mutant strawberry and the soft flesh tastes like unripe bananas.

Starfruit The star-shaped cross-section of *má·feu·ang* is the giveaway. The yellow flesh is sweet and tangy and believed by many to lower blood pressure.

Sweets

Thai-style sweets are generally consumed as breakfast or as a sweet snack, not directly following a meal. *Kŏrng wăhn*, which translates as 'sweet things', are small, rich sweets that often have a slightly salty flavour. Prime ingredients for *kŏrng wăhn* include grated coconut, coconut milk, rice flour (from white rice or sticky rice), cooked sticky rice, tapioca, mung-bean starch, boiled taro and various fruits.

Closer to the European concept of pastries are *kà·nŏm*. Probably the most popular type are bite-sized items wrapped in banana leaves, especially *kôw đôm gà·tí* and *kôw đôm mát*. Both consist of sticky rice grains steamed with *gà·tí* (coconut milk) inside a banana-leaf wrapper.

Coffee

Thais are big coffee drinkers, and good-quality arabica and robusta are cultivated in the hilly areas of northern and southern Thailand. The traditional filtering system is nothing more than a narrow cloth bag attached to a steel handle. This type of coffee is served in a glass, mixed with sugar and sweetened with condensed milk – if you don't want either, be sure to specify *gah·faa dam* (black coffee) followed with *mâi sài nám·đahn* (without sugar).

Chah tai (Thai-style tea)

Black tea, both local and imported, is available at the same places that serve real coffee. *Chah tai* (Thai-style tea) derives its characteristic orange-red colour from ground tamarind seed added after curing.

Fruit drinks appear all over Thailand and are an excellent way to rehydrate. Most *nám pŏn·lá·mái* (fruit juices) are served with a touch of sugar and salt and a whole lot of ice. Many foreigners object to the salt, but it serves a metabolic role in helping the body to cope with tropical temperatures.

Food Experiences

Top Restaurants

Krua Apsorn (p127) This award-winning Bangkok restaurant has a thick menu of decadent fare influenced by Bangkok and central Thailand.

One Chun (p627) Southern-style curries and seafood served in a Phuket Town Sino-Portuguese shophouse that looks like it hasn't been touched since the 1950s.

Gai Yang Rabeab (p438) Some of the best *gài yâhng* (grilled chicken) you'll get in Isan, in breezy, busy Khon Kaen surrounds.

Chanthorn (p470) Just up from the waterfront in Chanthaburi, this is a fine spot to try traditional flavours like pork with chamung leaves.

Larp Khom Huay Poo (p289) Simple but profoundly delicious northern-style *lâhp* (a type of minced meat 'salad') is the highlight at this Pai restaurant.

Khao Soi Lam Duan Fah Ham (p341) Chiang Mai's top bowl of *kôw soy* – northern Thailand's famous curry noodles – served to enthusiastic lunchtime crowds.

Koti (p505) You know a restaurant in Thailand is good when the queue for a table stretches around the corner; in Hua Hin.

Blue Rice (p188) Pomelo salad and the signature massaman curry are best served with the namesake pea-flower-coloured rice at this Kanchanaburi restaurant.

In Town Seafood (p514) Fantastic seafood and views of Prachuap Khiri Khan's awesome bay at this locals' favourite.

Krua Thara (p663) One of Thailand's very best seafood kitchens attracts domestic tourists from around the country to Krabi.

Cooking Courses

A standard one-day course usually features a shopping trip to a local market to choose ingredients, followed by preparation of curry pastes, soups, curries, salads and desserts.

Amita Thai Cooking Class (p101), **Bangkok** Learn to make Thai dishes at this canalside family compound.

Small House Chiang Mai Thai Cooking School (p331), **Chiang Mai** Northern Thai–style dishes are taught at this home-bound school.

Apple & Noi Thai Cooking (p186), **Kanchanaburi** Cooking lessons in a rural setting.

Borderline Shop cookery course (p277), **Mae Sot** Dip into the dishes of Thailand's neighbour, Myanmar.

Samui Institute of Thai Culinary Arts (p530), **Ko Samui** Courses in fruit-carving are also available here.

Phuket Thai Cookery School (p631), **Ko Sireh** A menu of dishes that changes on a daily basis is taught here.

Top: Pork-leg stew

Bottom: Thai-style boiled chicken

Regional Specialities

Unlike the way it is often touted abroad, Thai food is anything but a single entity. It is made up of a vast repertoire of ingredients, cooking techniques and dishes that can often pinpoint a particular province, or even a town.

Bangkok & Central Thai Cuisine

When foreigners think of Thai food, they're often thinking of the dishes of Bangkok (p126) and the central plains (p163). A wealth of agriculture, access to the sea and foreign influences have come together in a cuisine that is both sophisticated and diverse.

Northern Thai Cuisine

You may have heard of *kôw soy* (curry noodle soup), but most people, including many Thais, would be hard-pressed to name more than a few northern Thai dishes. In addition to being the country's least-known regional cuisine, northern Thai food is probably also the mildest and most seasonal, largely due to the north's elevation and climate.

Northeastern Thai Cuisine

Northeastern Thai food (p414) is undoubtedly the country's most rustic regional cooking style, and is most likely indicative of what the ethnic Tai people have been eating for hundreds, if not thousands, of years. Spicy, tart flavours and simple cooking methods, such as grilling and soups, dominate the northeastern kitchen, in which the predominant carb is sticky rice.

Southern Thai Cuisine

Although you might not notice it in the guesthouse food you're served, the dishes of Thailand's southern provinces are arguably the country's spiciest. Eat outside the tourist track and you'll find an entire inventory of incendiary soups, piquant curries and full-flavoured stir-fries.

Fusion Specialities

In addition to geography, the country's predominant minorities – Muslims and the Chinese – have had different but profound influences on the local cuisine.

Thai-Chinese Cuisine

It was Chinese labourers and vendors who most likely introduced the wok and several varieties of noodle dishes to Thailand. Look out for the following dishes:

Bà·mèe Chinese-style wheat-and-egg noodles are typically served with slices of barbecued pork, a handful of greens and/or wontons.

Gŏo·ay dĕe·o kôo·a gài Wide rice noodles fried with little more than egg, chicken, squid and garlic oil. A popular dish in Bangkok's Chinatown.

Kôw kăh mŏo Braised pork leg served over rice, often with a side of greens and a hard-boiled egg, is the epitome of the Chinese-style one-dish meal.

FOOD HABITS & CUSTOMS

➡ To achieve the right mix of flavours and textures, traditionally a party orders a curry, a steamed or fried fish, a stir-fried vegetable dish and a soup, taking care to balance cool and hot, sour and sweet, salty and plain.

➡ Whether at home or in a restaurant, Thai meals are always served 'family-style' – that is, from common serving platters. Put no more than one spoonful onto your plate at a time. Heaping your plate will look greedy to Thais.

➡ To dine the Thai way, use a serving spoon, or your own, to take a single mouthful of food from a central dish and ladle it over your rice. A fork is then used to push the now-food-soaked portion of rice back onto the spoon before entering the mouth.

➡ Chopsticks are reserved for eating Chinese-style food from bowls, or for eating in all-Chinese restaurants (you will be supplied with chopsticks without having to ask).

Má·đà·bà (stuffed pancake)

Kôw man gài Chicken rice, originally from the Chinese island of Hainan, is now found in just about every corner of Thailand.

Sah·lah·bow Steamed buns are a favourite at old-school Chinese-style coffee shops across Thailand.

Thai-Muslim Cuisine

When Muslims first visited Thailand during the late 14th century, they brought with them a halal (religiously permissible) cuisine based on meat and dried spice from their homelands in India and the Middle East. Nearly 700 years later, the impact of this culinary commerce can still be felt. Common dishes influenced by the Islamic world include:

Gaang mát·sà·màn 'Muslim curry' is a rich coconut-milk-based dish, which, unlike most Thai curries, gets much of its flavour from dried spices.

Kôw mòk Biryani, found across the Islamic world, also has a foothold in Thailand. Here it's typically made with chicken and served with dipping sauce and chicken broth.

Má·đà·bà Known as *murtabak* in Malaysia and Indonesia, these are pancakes that have been stuffed with a savoury or sometimes sweet filling and fried until crispy.

Sà·đé (satay) The savoury, peanut-based dipping sauce served with these grilled skewers of meat is often mistakenly associated with Thai cooking.

Sà·làt kàak Literally 'Muslim salad' (*kàak* is a somewhat derogatory word used to describe people or things of South Asian and/or Muslim origin), this dish combines lettuce, tofu, cucumber, egg, tomato and peanut sauce.

Best Cheap Eats

MBK Food Island (p132), **Bangkok** A cheap, clean and tasty introduction to Thai and Thai-Chinese staples.

Paa Suk (p210), **Chiang Rai** Some of the north's best noodles – at a pocket-change price tag.

Abdul's Roti Shop (p626), **Phuket Town** A local legend, friendly Abdul has been cooking delicious *roh·dee* (a fried 'pancake') at the front of his shop for years, served either sweet with sticky banana or savoury with spicy fish or meat curries.

Satay sticks

FOOD GLOSSARY

a·ròy – the Thai word for delicious

bà·mèe – wheat-and-egg noodles

đôm yam – Thailand's famous sour and spicy soup

gaang – curry

gŏo·ay đĕe·o – the generic term for noodle soup

gài – chicken

kà·nŏm – Thai-style sweet snacks

kôw – rice

kôw nĕe·o – sticky rice

lâhp – a 'salad' of minced meat

mŏo – pork

nám dèum – drinking water

nám prík – chilli-based dips

nám þlah – fish sauce

pàk – vegetables

pàt – fried

pàt see·éw – wide rice noodles fried with pork and greens

pàt tai – thin rice noodles fried with egg and seasonings

pèt – spicy

pŏn·lá·mái – fruit

prík – chili

ráhn ah·hăhn – restaurant

tôrt – deep-fried

yam – a Thai-style salad

Bang Ian Night Market (p172), **Ayuthaya** Feast on mouthwatering barbecued fish or colourful *roh·đee săi măi* (candyfloss in a crêpe) at this lively local market.

Talat Pratu Chang Pheuak (p342), **Chiang Mai** Come hungry to this bustling food market to dine on an array of local fare including the famous and sublime *kôw kăh mŏo* (braised pork leg with rice) prepared by the hard-to-miss 'Cowboy Hat Lady'.

Jek Pia (p504), **Hua Hin** Some of the city's best cooks work together at this culinary gem.

Krua Talay (p584), **Nakhon Si Thammarat** Simply superb Thai seafood in an alluring garden setting.

Sai Ngam (p411), **Phimai** Where eating *pàt mèe pímai* (local-style fried noodles) from one of the restaurants is almost obligatory.

Blues Blues Restaurant (p483), **Ko Chang** This arty oasis does brilliant stir-fries and makes a great break from the brasher face of the island.

Vegetarians & Vegans

Vegetarianism isn't widespread, but many tourist-oriented restaurants cater to vegetarians, and there are also a handful of *ráhn ah·hăhn mang·sà·wí·rát* (vegetarian restaurants) where inexpensive food is served buffet-style. Dishes are almost always 100% vegan (ie no meat, poultry, fish or fish sauce, dairy or egg products).

The phrase 'I'm vegetarian' in Thai is *pŏm gin jair* (for men) or *dì·chăn gin jair* (for women). Loosely translated this means 'I eat only vegetarian food', which includes no eggs and no dairy products – in other words, total vegan.

The downloadable Vegetarian Thai Food Guide (www.eatingthaifood.com/vegetarian-thai-food-guide) is a handy resource for vegetarians visiting Thailand.

Food Spotter's Guide

Spanning four distinct regions, influences from China to the Middle East, a multitude of ingredients and a reputation for spice, Thai food can be more than a bit overwhelming. So to point you in the direction of the good stuff, we've put together a shortlist of the country's must-eat dishes.

1. Đôm yam
The 'sour Thai soup' moniker featured on many menus is a feeble description of this mouthpuckeringly tart and intensely spicy herbal broth.

2. Pàt tai
Thin rice noodles fried with egg, tofu and shrimp, and seasoned with fish sauce, tamarind and dried chilli, have emerged as the poster child for Thai food.

3. Gaang kěe·o wǎhn
Known outside of Thailand as green curry, this intersection of a piquant, herbal spice paste and rich coconut milk is single-handedly emblematic of Thai cuisine's unique flavours and ingredients.

4. Yam
This family of Thai 'salads' combines meat or seafood with a tart and spicy dressing and fresh herbs.

5. Lâhp
Minced meat seasoned with roasted rice powder, lime, fish sauce and fresh herbs is a one-dish crash course in the rustic flavours of Thailand's northeast.

6. Bà·mèe
Although Chinese in origin, these wheat-and-egg noodles, typically served with roast pork and/or crab, have become a Thai hawker-stall staple.

7. Kôw mòk
The Thai version of biryani couples golden rice and tender chicken with a sweet and sour dip and a savoury broth.

8. Sôm·đam
'Papaya salad' hardly does justice to this tearinducingly spicy dish of strips of crunchy unripe papaya pounded in a mortar and pestle with tomato, long beans, chilli, lime and fish sauce.

9. Kôw soy
Even outside of its home in Thailand's north, there's a cult following for this soup that combines flat egg-and-wheat noodles in a rich, spice-laden, coconut-milk-based broth.

10. Pàt pàk bûng fai daang
Crunchy green vegetables, flash-fried with heaps of chilli and garlic, is Thai comfort food.

Plan Your Trip
Choose Your Beach

It's a terrible dilemma: Thailand has too many beaches to choose from. Choices can be daunting even for those visiting a second time, and development is so rapid that where you went five years ago may now be completely different. Here, we break it down for you so you can find your dream beach.

Best Beaches For...

Relaxation and Activities

Ko Mak Beach bar scene, explorably flat and vast expanses of sand.

Ko Phayam Bike back roads to empty beaches or to parties.

Hat Mae Nam Quiet Ko Samui beach close to lots of action.

Ko Bulon Leh Chilled-out vibe but lots to do.

Local Culture

Ko Yao Noi Thai-Muslim fishing island with beautiful karst scenery.

Ko Sukorn Agricultural and fishing gem filled with mangroves and water buffalo.

Ko Phra Thong Look for rare orchids with a *chow lair* (a Moken 'sea gypsy') guide.

Hua Hin Mingle with middle-class Thais in this urban beach getaway.

The Price of Paradise

The personality of a Thai resort town depends a lot on the prices. In places where midrange options dominate, you'll usually find package tourists, rows of beach loungers and umbrellas along the beach, and plenty of big boats full of snorkelling tours.

At upscale places things settle down. The ritzier beaches of Phuket like Surin and Ao Bang Thao are among the quieter on the island yet still have some dining and cocktail options. Ko Kut off the eastern seaboard has lovely resorts on some of the country's most unspoiled beaches, while the more secluded beaches of northeastern Ko Samui have some of the most luxurious resorts in Thailand. Once you go very high-end, privacy and seclusion become a bigger part of the picture.

There are a few remaining beach huts that are mostly found on some of the country's most secluded beaches.

Easy Access from Bangkok

Nowadays the closest beaches to Bangkok aren't necessarily the quickest and easiest to get to. There are international flights direct to Phuket and Ko Samui that allow you to skip the big city altogether, and flights from Bangkok (and some other Southeast Asian countries) can shuttle you to several southern towns with ease.

If you don't want to fly but are still short on time, the nearest beach island to Bangkok is Ko Samet (count on around four hours' total travel time), while the closest beach resorts are Bang Saen (one hour by bus) and Pattaya (1½ hours). The next-closest stops by land are the beach towns of Cha-am (2½ hours) and Hua Hin (three hours). It takes around six hours to get to Ko Chang, which beats the minimum of 10 hours to reach the Lower Gulf islands. If you're in a hurry and want to take the bus, the Andaman Coast is not your best choice.

Activities

What you can do besides lounging on the beach is the deciding factor for many visitors when choosing a beach.

Diving & Snorkelling

Thailand is a diving and snorkelling paradise. The Andaman Coast and Ko Tao in the Lower Gulf have the best undersea views in the country. Islands like Ko Samui and Ko Lanta don't have great snorkelling from the beach, but snorkelling tours can take you to nearby sites where you'll see some corals and fish, and a turtle or shark if you're lucky.

Culture

For a taste of authentic Thai culture, head out of the main tourist zones to coastal towns like Trang, Surat Thani or Nakhon Si Thammarat, to lesser known islands like Ko Si Chang or Ko Sukorn, or to the less visited parts of islands like the south coast of Ko Samui or the east coast of Ko Lanta. But even tourist-central Patong or Ko Phi-Phi can give you a taste of what's beyond resort land, just by eating at food stalls and talking to the owners, smiling a lot and being open to interactions with locals.

Climbing

Railay is the best-known place to climb in southern Thailand; it's ideal for both beginners and experienced climbers, and a fun scene. Ko Phi-Phi has some great climbing options alongside its lively party scene – although the climbing operators are on Railay – as well as an abundance of water and land activities. There are less busy and more off-the-beaten-path climbing options around the appealing mainland town of Krabi. The Ko Yao islands are slowly getting bolted and offer horizons to more seasoned climbers. Ko Tao also attracts rock-climbers.

Hiking

The mainland national parks like Khao Sok have the most jungle-trekking opportunities, but more forested islands such as Ko Chang, Ko Pha-Ngan and even Phuket have great hiking, often to waterfalls or vistas looking across the blue sea.

WHEN TO GO

REGION	JAN-MAR	APR-JUN	JUL-SEP	OCT-DEC
Bangkok	hotter towards Mar	hot & humid	rainy season	cooler towards Dec
Eastern Seaboard	peak season; thins towards Mar	rainy season begins in May	smaller islands close for the monsoon	cooler weather; low hotel rates
Southern Gulf	hot & dry	hot & dry	occasional rains & strong winds	occasional rains & strong winds
Lower Gulf	clear & sunny	hot & dry	clear & sunny, increasing wind & rain on Ko Tao	monsoon & rough waters
Northern Andaman	high season; high prices	fringe season with variable weather	rainy season & surf season	high season picks up again
Southern Andaman	high season	monsoons usually begin in May	some resorts close for rainy season	crowds return with the sun

OVERVIEW OF THAILAND'S ISLANDS & BEACHES

BEACHES	PACKAGE, TOURISTS	BACK-PACKERS	FAMILIES	PARTIES	DIVE/ SNORKEL	PERSONALITY
Ko Chang & Eastern Seaboard						
Ko Samet	✓	✓	✓	✓		pretty beaches, easy getaway from Bangkok
Ko Chang	✓	✓	✓	✓	✓	international resort, mediocre beaches, jungle
Ko Wai		✓	✓		✓	primitive; day-trippers, deserted in the evening
Ko Mak	✓	✓				mediocre beaches, great island vibe
Ko Kut	✓	✓				lovely semi-developed island, great for solitude
Hua Hin & the Upper Gulf						
Hua Hin	✓	✓	✓			international resort, easy access to Bangkok
Pranburi area	✓		✓			quiet & close to Bangkok
Ban Krut		✓	✓			low-key, popular with Thais
Bang Saphan Yai		✓	✓			cheap mainland beach
Ko Samui & the Lower Gulf						
Ko Samui	✓	✓	✓	✓		international resort for social beach-goers
Ko Pha-Ngan	✓	✓	✓	✓	✓	popular beaches, some secluded; boozy Hat Rin
Ko Tao	✓	✓	✓	✓	✓	dive schools galore
Ang Thong		✓	✓			karst scenery, rustic
Ao Khanom		✓	✓			quiet, little-known
Phuket & the Andaman Coast						
Ko Chang (Ranong)		✓	✓		✓	rustic and secluded
Ko Phayam		✓	✓		✓	quiet, getting more popular
Surin & Similan Islands		✓			✓	dive sites accessed by live-aboards
Ko Yao	✓	✓	✓			poor beaches but nice vibe, great scenery
Phuket	✓	✓	✓	✓	✓	international resort for social beach-goers
Ao Nang	✓	✓	✓		✓	touristy, close to Railay
Railay	✓	✓	✓			rock-climbing centre with some superb beaches
Ko Phi-Phi	✓	✓		✓	✓	pretty party island
Ko Jum	✓	✓	✓			mediocre beach, nice vibe
Ko Lanta	✓	✓	✓		✓	reasonable beaches
Trang Islands	✓	✓	✓		✓	Ko Ngai is good for kids
Ko Bulon Leh		✓	✓		✓	pretty, little-known
Ko Tarutao		✓	✓			developing national park
Ko Lipe	✓	✓	✓	✓	✓	hotspot, good beaches, handy for visa runs
Ko Adang		✓			✓	popular with day-trippers

Top: Phra Nang Beach, Railay (p656)

Bottom: Ko Tao (p563)

MATT MUNRO / LONELY PLANET ©

Staying Safe

Drownings are common. Pay attention to red- and yellow-flag warnings and be aware that many beaches do not have life guards. Also beware of rip tides, which can carry you out to sea. If caught in a rip tide in deep water, do not fight against it as you may rapidly, and dangerously, tire. It is more advisable to try to call for help, but go with the flow and conserve energy; the rip tide will take you further out to sea, but you should be able to swim back. Rip-tide channels are quite narrow, so another technique is to gradually swim parallel to the shore when caught in a rip tide and you should escape it.

Signs on some beaches warn of box jellyfish, so check before swimming. Stings from box jellyfish can be fatal, and although there are few deaths, there were three fatalities in Ko Pha-Ngan and Ko Samui waters in a 12-month period between 2014 and 2015.

Watch out for jet skis and long-tail boats coming in to the shore when swimming. Do not expect them to see you.

If renting a scooter or motorbike, you may not be insured. Insurance is not included in most rentals and your own insurance may not cover the cost of any accident. It is likely that you will be liable for medical expenses and repair or replacement costs for any damaged vehicle. If you don't have a Thai driving licence or an international driving licence, you will also be driving illegally (many rental outfits don't check). If you do rent, watch out for sand or grit on the road (especially if braking), drive slowly (under 40km/h), particularly after rain, and avoid alcohol. Above all, wear a helmet.

NIGHTLIFE IN PARADISE

To Party or Not to Party

A big percentage of travellers to southern Thailand aim to party, and the local tourism industry happily accommodates them, with an array of thumping beach bars lining many of the main beaches. Luckily, it's just as easy to escape the revelry as it is to join in. The main party zones are well known to be just that. Anywhere you go that's not a major tourist enclave will have peace and quiet on offer.

The Girly-Bar Issue

Bangkok, Pattaya and Patong in Phuket are the capitals of push-up bras and short skirts, while Hat Lamai on Ko Samui is the centre of this small universe in the lower Gulf Islands. Islands like Ko Chang and mid-sized towns such as Hat Yai and Ao Nang have small enclaves of questionable massage parlours and bars, but it won't be in your face. Smaller islands will be clear of this sort of thing, as will most mainland towns.

Your Party Level

Level One: Dead Calm Surin and Similan Islands, Laem Son National Park, Hat Pak Meng and Hat Chang Lang

Level Two: A Flicker of Light Ko Tarutao, Ko Libong, Prachuap Khiri Khan

Level Three: There's a Bar Ko Yao Islands, Ao Khanom, Ko Kut

Level Four: Maybe a Few Bars Hat Khao Lak, Ko Muk, Ao Thong Nai Pan (Ko Pha-Ngan)

Level Five: Easy to Find a Drink Hua Hin, Bo Phut (Ko Samui), Ao Nang

Level Six: There's a Beach-Bar Scene Ko Mak, Ko Phayam, Railay

Level Seven: Magic Shake Anyone? Ko Lanta, Ko Chang, Ban Tai (Ko Pha-Ngan)

Level Eight: I Forget What Eight Was For Hat Lamai (Ko Samui), Ko Lipe, Ko Samet

Level Nine: What Happened Last Night? Hat Chaweng (Ko Samui), Pattaya, Ko Tao

Level Ten: Don't Tell Me What Happened Last Night Patong (Phuket), Ko Phi-Phi, Hat Rin (Ko Pha-Ngan)

Plan Your Trip
Travel With Children

Looking for an exotic destination that the kids can handle? Thailand has it: beaches, mountains, elephants, sparkling temples and bustling markets; there's something for each age range. Plus Thais are serious 'cute' connoisseurs, and exotic-looking foreign children trump stuffed animals and fluffy dogs.

Kingdom for Kids

Small foreign children are instant celebrities in Thailand and attract paparazzi-like attention. Babies do surprisingly well with their new-found stardom, soaking up adoration from gruff taxi drivers who transform into loving uncles wanting to play a game of peekaboo (called *'já ăir'*). If you've got a babe in arms, food vendors will often hold the child while you eat, or take the child for a brief stroll to visit the neighbours.

If your children are shy, stick to tourist centres instead of trotting off to far-flung places where foreigners, especially children, will attract attention. A polite way to deflect spectators is to say the child is 'shy' (*'kîi ai'*). Older children should be safe from Thai attention.

Planning & Practicalities

Amenities specially geared towards young children – such as child-safety seats for cars, high chairs in restaurants or nappy-changing facilities in public restrooms – are spotty in Thailand. Therefore parents will have to be resourceful in seeking out substitutes or just do without.

Baby formula and nappies (diapers) are available at mini-markets and 7-Elevens in

Best Regions for Kids

Eastern Seaboard & Ko Chang
Shallow seas are kind to young swimmers and the low evening tides make for good beach-combing. Older children will like the interior jungle, elephant interactions and mangrove kayaking.

Upper Gulf
Hua Hin has a long sandy coastline for pint-sized marathons, and hillside temples for monkey-spotting. Phetchaburi's cave temples are home to bats.

Ko Samui & Lower Gulf
Ko Samui, especially its northern beaches, is a hit with pram-pushers and toddlers, while Hat Chaweng is social, commercial and ideal for teens. Older children can snorkel at Ko Tao.

Phuket & Andaman Coast
Phuket has amusements galore (including great surf schools), though steer clear of the Patong party scene. There are at least a dozen islands along this coast where families can frolic in the sea.

Chiang Mai
Families come in droves during European summer holidays to expose their kids to culture, zipline among the gibbons and cycle about town.

PARENTS' MEDICAL KIT

A medical kit designed specifically for children may include paracetamol or Tylenol syrup for fevers, an antihistamine, itch cream, first-aid supplies, nappy-rash treatment, sunscreen and insect repellent. It is a good idea to carry a general antibiotic (best used under medical supervision) – Azithromycin is an ideal paediatric formula used to treat bacterial diarrhoea, as well as ear, chest and throat infections.

the larger towns and cities, but sizes are usually small, smaller and smallish. If your kid wears size 3 or larger, head to Tesco Lotus, Big C or Tops Market stores.

Hauling around little ones can be a challenge. Thailand's footpaths are often too crowded to push a pram, especially full-size SUV versions. Instead opt for a compact umbrella stroller that can squeeze past the fire hydrants and mango carts and can be folded up and thrown in a túk-túk. A baby pack (sling) is also useful, but make sure the child's head doesn't sit higher than yours: there are lots of hanging obstacles poised at forehead level.

For all-round information and advice, check out *Lonely Planet's Travel with Children*.

Eating with Kids

In Thailand, the vagaries of children's food preferences are further complicated by a cuisine known for its spiciness. Luckily, even Thai children are shielded from chillies and there are a handful of child-friendly dishes that every server can recommend. Because of the heat, remember to keep your little ones well hydrated, either with water or a variety of fruit juices, including fresh young coconuts or lime juice (a surprising hit).

kài jee-o (omelette) A safe, non-spicy restaurant or street-stall option.

gài yâhng/tôrt (grilled/fried chicken) Common market and street-stall meal.

kôw něe-o (sticky rice) Straight-up carbs but picky eaters won't resist; sold in markets alongside grilled or fried chicken.

gài pàt mét má·môo·ang (chicken stir-fried with cashew nuts) Mild stir-fry, popular at restaurants.

kôw man gài (Hainanese chicken rice) A popular morning and afternoon meal.

City Hassles

Some kids might get nervous about the natural chaos of Thai cities and the confusion that arises from being in a new place and having to negotiate transport. Consider giving your children a role in travel planning: reading the map, setting up an itinerary or carrying the water bottles. You're moulding future travellers.

Thai cities can also be claustrophobic and the heat can make it hard to wear out energetic children. Staying at a hotel or resort with a pool will give the kids enough exercise not to bounce off the proverbial walls.

Health & Safety

For the most part, parents needn't worry too much about health concerns.

➡ Regular hand-washing should be enforced.

➡ Thai children are bathed at least twice a day and powdered afterwards to reduce skin irritation from the humid climate; foreigners should aim for at least daily showers.

➡ Children should be warned not to play with animals as rabies is relatively common, and some pets (not to mention wild monkeys) may be aggressive.

➡ Dengue is an increasing concern in Thailand and has reached record highs in recent years. Parents should take care to prevent mosquito bites (a difficult task) in children. Repellent creams containing 12% DEET are widely available from 7-Elevens and other convenience stores, but pack some from home before you travel. If your child is bitten, there are a variety of locally produced balms that can reduce swelling and itching. All the usual health precautions apply.

➡ Thai cities are very loud and can be a sensory overload for young children. Be sure that your child understands street safety guidelines as it will be difficult to focus on your instructions amid all the street noise outside.

Children's Highlights

Beaches

➡ **Swimming, Trang Islands & Ko Samui** The shallow, gentle bays of the Trang Islands (p684) and the northern beaches of Ko Samui (p526) are perfect for beginner or younger swimmers.

➡ **Snorkelling, Ko Lipe & Ko Wai** Older kids can strap on a mask and snorkel close to the beach on Ko Lipe (p696) and Ko Wai (p488).

➡ **Surfing** (p640), **Hat Kata Yai** The gentle breaks at Hat Kata Yai on Phuket are ideal for beginners. Sign the older ones up for a day's surf school.

➡ **Diving** (p563), **Ko Tao** Children are eligible to take an open-water course from the age of 10. With many reputable dive schools and shallow diving, Ko Tao is the ideal place to learn.

➡ **Kayaking** (p615), **Ao Phang-Nga Marine National Park** Take a kayaking tour in this spectacular preserve.

➡ **Resorts, Phuket, Ko Chang & Ko Samui** Many of the big resorts on Phuket (p618), Ko Samui (p526) and Ko Chang (p474) offer organised water sports ideal for children aged six years and older.

Animal Amusements

➡ **Queen Saovabha Memorial Institute** (p86), **Bangkok** This 'snake farm' is a hit with kids.

➡ **Animal rescue, Ko Lanta & Ko Chang** There are a few animal rescue organisations, including Lanta Animal Welfare (p755) and the Koh Chang Animal Project (p755), where you can see the animals and volunteer to walk the dogs or play with the kittens.

➡ **Phuket Aquarium** (p630) Tons of colourful fish, and sharks and electric eels too at this impressive aquarium.

➡ **Phuket Elephant Sanctuary** (p755) Children love to feed the retired elephants and watch them bathe and hang out.

➡ **Phuket Gibbon Rehabilitation Project** (p651) Children can't get too close to the gibbons but they still like looking at them.

➡ **Monkeys, Ko Phi-Phi, Railay & Phetchaburi** On the beach at Ko Phi-Phi (p663), dangling from limestone cliffs in Railay (p656) and hanging out at the temples of Phetchaburi (p492).

Outdoor Activities

➡ **Ancient City** (p161), **Bangkok Region** Open-air museum outside Bangkok that displays the country's most famous monuments.

➡ **River Kwai Canoe Travel Services** (p186), **Kanchanaburi** Entry-level kayaking experiences in central Thailand.

➡ **Lumphini Park** (p86), **Bangkok** Central Bangkok's largest park has paddle boats, play areas and giant monitor lizards.

➡ **Amusement parks, Phuket** Plentiful on Phuket. Try Splash Jungle (p622) or Phuket Wake Park (p622).

➡ **Cycling, Hua Hin & Phuket** Hua Hin Bike Tours (p502) and Amazing Bike Tours (p625) on Phuket offer great cycling tours.

➡ **Khao Sok National Park** (p605).Trek through the rainforest and search for hidden waterfalls and caves.

➡ **Rock-climbing, Railay** The region's best climbing, along with good instructors and many beginner routes suitable for children, can be found on stunning Railay (p656).

➡ **Ziplining, Ko Chang & Phuket** Kids over the age of seven can whizz through the air on ziplines above the jungly interiors of Ko Chang (p474) and Phuket (p618).

Indoor Activities

➡ **Children's Discovery Museum** (p87), **Bangkok** Learning disguised as fun.

➡ **KidZania** (p87), **Bangkok** Hyper-sophisticated play park in the city's centre.

➡ **Museum of Siam** (p69), **Bangkok** An introduction to Thai culture with a kid-forward feel.

➡ **Malls, Hua Hin & Phuket** Great air-con, shops, restaurants and cinemas in the malls at Hua Hin (p500), Phuket (p623) and the bigger towns. They make good rain shelters in the monsoon season.

Boats & Trains

➡ **BTS** Bangkok's above-ground train system is a hit with young kids.

➡ **Chao Phraya Express Boat** (p156), **Bangkok** River taxis are the most fun way to get around the city.

➡ **State Railways of Thailand** Loads of kids like overnight train journeys, where they can be assigned lower sleeping berths with views of the stations.

Regions at a Glance

Central Thailand

History
Nature
Getaways

Monumental Ruins

The ruins of Ayuthaya, Thailand's greatest empire, are a Unesco World Heritage Site. Lopburi and its ancient ruins are ruled by troops of monkeys. Kanchanaburi has poignant memorials to the POWs who worked on the Death Railway during WWII.

Rugged National Parks

Kanchanaburi is the gateway to the misty mountains of western Thailand. Rivers and waterfalls carve the contours, and a collection of national parks makes this one of Thailand's wildest corners.

Spellbinding Escapes

Sangkhlaburi and Thong Pha Phum are intoxicating getaways that are easy to reach, but hard to leave.

p163

Northern Thailand

Culture
Mountains
Food

Ancient Kingdoms

The remains of ancient city-states, with their fortressed walls and sandstone Buddhist monuments, are dotted throughout northern Thailand. Sukhothai is the most impressive.

Spectacular Scenery

The hills and mountains here form some of the country's most dramatic scenery. The high-altitude villages of ethnic minorities, are the highlights of provinces such as Chiang Rai and Mae Hong Son.

Distinctive Cuisine

The north's cooler climate has shaped a menu of dishes characterised by sour and bitter notes, many influenced by Thai, Shan, Burmese and Yunnanese cuisine.

p201

Bangkok & Around

Food
Culture
Nightlife

Global Cuisine

The residents of this multi-wát city love to eat. Food can be found in every nook and cranny, from noodle pushcarts and grease-stained wok shops to fine dining and fashion-minded cafes. All of Bangkok's expat communities have their culinary outposts, providing exotic flavours to all.

Gleaming Temples

The great temples along Mae Nam Chao Phraya (Chao Phraya River) are national pilgrimage sites cradling revered religious symbols and the country's greatest displays of classical art and architecture.

Beer & Cocktails

The quintessential night out in Bangkok is still a plastic table filled with sweating Chang beers, but rooftop bars, with cool breezes and fizzy cocktails, Instagram better. University students are always out on the town, filling indie clubs or pop discos.

p65

Chiang Mai Province

Culture
Food
Outdoor Adventures

Chiang Mai showcases northern Thailand's history and culture in its antique-fortified city. Culture geeks come for sightseeing or courses in cooking, language and massage. While just beyond the city limits a mountainous landscape waits to be explored.

p307

Northeastern Thailand

History
Festivals
Outdoors

The Lower Isan region is the site of the Ancient Khmer Hwy. Remnants of the Khmer empire can still be seen in Phanom Rung and Phimai. Not to be missed are the Rocket Festivals and Phi Ta Khon festival, which are wild and spectacular affairs.

p366

Ko Chang & Eastern Seaboard

Beaches
Diving & Snorkelling
Small Towns

Jungle-covered Ko Chang is loved for its tropical ambience and thriving party scene, while offshore it's surrounded by a national marine park. Quiet Ko Kut excels in seaside seclusion, Ko Mak boasts a laid-back island vibe, and little Ko Wai has the prettiest views you have ever seen.

p448

Hua Hin & the Upper Gulf

Beaches
History
Food

Beach-lovers will delight in Prachuap Khiri Khan, a mellow town with karst-studded bays, and Hua Hin, a resort ideal for families and honeymooners, while history-lovers will enjoy Phetchaburi and its historic hilltop palace and cave shrines.

p490

Ko Samui & the Lower Gulf

Beaches
Diving & Snorkelling
Nightlife

The three sister islands of the Lower Gulf have been pursued by island-hoppers for decades. Professional Ko Samui has stunning sugar-white beaches, Ko Pha-Ngan is more bohemian, while the warm gentle seas and wallet-friendly prices keep Ko Tao beloved for dive training.

p523

Phuket & the Andaman Coast

Scenery
Beaches
Diving & Snorkelling

Limestone mountains jut out of cerulean waters. A variety of activities, based out of Krabi, Trang and Ko Yao, turn the pinnacles into an outdoor playground. Andaman beaches come in every shape and flavour, while Phuket excels in comfort for the masses and top-end luxury.

p593

On the Road

Chiang Mai
Province
p307

Northern
Thailand
p201

Northeastern
Thailand
p366

Central
Thailand
p163

Bangkok &
Around
p65

Ko Chang & the
Eastern Seaboard
p448

Hua Hin & the
Upper Gulf
p490

Phuket & the
Andaman Coast
p593

Ko Samui & the
Lower Gulf
p523

Bangkok & Around

Best Places to Eat

➡ nahm (p131)

➡ Eat Me (p132)

➡ Krua Apsorn (p127)

➡ Jay Fai (p129)

➡ MBK Food Island (p132)

Best Places to Stay

➡ AriyasomVilla (p123)

➡ Phra-Nakorn Norn-Len (p125)

➡ Siam Heritage (p121)

➡ Loy La Long (p116)

➡ Lamphu Treehouse (p113)

Why Go?

Same same, but different. This Thailish T-shirt philosophy sums up Bangkok (กรุงเทพฯ), a city where the familiar and the exotic collide like the flavours on a plate of *pàt tai*.

Climate-controlled megamalls sit side by side with 200-year-old village homes; gold-spired temples share space with neon-lit strips of sleaze; slow-moving traffic is bypassed by long-tail boats plying the royal river. For adventurous foodies who don't need white tablecloths, there's probably no better dining destination. And with immigration bringing every regional Thai and international cuisine to the capital, it's a truly diverse experience.

With so much daily life conducted on the street, exploring Bangkok is handsomely rewarded. Cap off a boat trip with a visit to a hidden market. Get lost in Chinatown's lanes and stumble upon a Chinese opera performance. Or after dark, let the Skytrain escort you to Sukhumvit, where the nightlife reveals a cosmopolitan and dynamic city.

When to Go

➡ Bangkok is one of the world's hottest cities, maintaining an average high temperature between 32°C and 34°C.

➡ Bangkok's high season (November to March) is arguably the best time of the year to visit as the weather is relatively cool and dry, although it also means crowds and inflated rates.

➡ The rainy season runs from May to October; in this period the city can receive more than 200mm of rain monthly.

➡ Virtually the only break from the relentless heat and humidity comes in winter, a couple of weeks of relative coolness in December/January.

History

Since the late 18th century, the history of Bangkok has essentially been the history of Thailand. Many of the country's defining events have unfolded here, and today the language and culture of the city have come to represent those of the entire country. This situation may once have seemed impossible, given the city's origins as little more than an obscure Chinese trading port, but, today boasting a population of almost 10 million, Bangkok will continue to shape Thailand's history.

Moving the Capital

Before it became the capital of Siam – as Thailand was then known – in 1782, the tiny settlement known as Bang Makok was merely a backwater village opposite the larger Thonburi Si Mahasamut on the banks of Mae Nam Chao Phraya, not far from the Gulf of Siam.

Thonburi had been founded by a group of wealthy Siamese during the reign of King Chakkraphat (r 1548–68) as an important relay point for sea- and river-borne trade between the Gulf of Siam and Ayuthaya, 86km upriver. Ayuthaya served as the royal capital of Siam from 1350 to 1767. When the Burmese sacked Ayuthaya in 1767, the remaining Siamese regrouped under Phraya Taksin, a half-Chinese, half-Thai general who decided to move the capital further south along Mae Nam Chao Phraya, closer to the Gulf of Siam. Thonburi was a logical choice for the new capital.

---

① BANGKOK: STOP OVER OR STICK AROUND?

Bangkok is a major stopover point for long-haul flights (and connecting flights to the islands), with many visitors spending a couple of days here before moving on. If you're keen to see more than the top temples and the insides of Bangkok's shopping malls, spend at least four days here. This way, you'll also be able to eat at some of the best restaurants, check out a few rooftop bars, spend a morning at Chatuchak Weekend Market and squeeze in a cooking class, with time to spare for a famous Thai massage (or two).

Taksin was deposed by another important military general, Chao Phraya Chakri, in 1782. Fearing Thonburi to be vulnerable to Burmese attack from the west, Chakri moved the Siamese capital across the river to Bang Makok. The succession of his son in 1809 established the present-day royal dynasty, and Chao Phraya Chakri was posthumously dubbed Rama I.

Building Bangkok

The first task set before the planners of the new city was to create hallowed ground for royal palaces and Buddhist monasteries. Rama I augmented Bangkok's natural canal and river system with hundreds of artificial waterways feeding into Thailand's hydraulic lifeline, the broad Mae Nam Chao Phraya. Rama I also ordered the construction of 10km of city walls and *klorng rôrp grung* (canals around the city) to create a royal 'island' – Ko Ratanakosin – between Mae Nam Chao Phraya and the canal loop. The city soon became a regional centre for Chinese trading ships, slowly surpassing in importance even the British port at Singapore.

European Influences

European aesthetics and technologies filtered east in the late 19th century. In 1855 Rama IV (King Mongkut; r 1851–68) signed the Bowring Treaty with Britain, marking Siam's break from exclusive economic involvement with China. The signing of this document, and the subsequent ascension of Rama V (King Chulalongkorn; r 1868–1910), led to the largest period of European influence on Siam. Rama V gave Bangkok 120 new roads during his reign, inspired by street plans from Batavia (the Dutch colonial centre now known as Jakarta), Calcutta, Penang and Singapore. Germans were hired to design and build railways emanating from the capital, while the Dutch contributed the design of Bangkok's Hualamphong train station, today considered a minor masterpiece of civic art deco.

In 1893, Bangkok opened its first railway line, extending 22km from Bangkok to Pak Nam. A 20km electric tramway opened the following year. Americans established Siam's first printing press along with the kingdom's first newspaper in 1864. The first Siamese-language newspaper came along in 1874 and by 1900 Bangkok boasted three daily English-language newspapers.

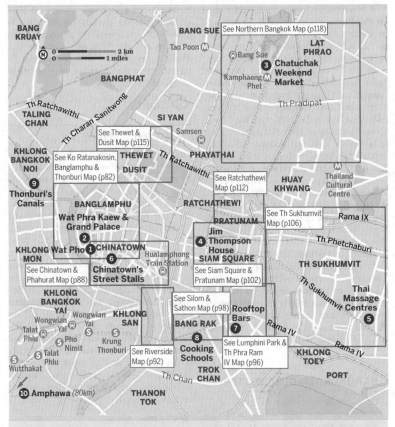

Bangkok & Around Highlights

1 Wat Pho (p69) Trying to stop your jaw from dropping to the floor upon encountering the enormous reclining Buddha.

2 Wat Phra Kaew & Grand Palace (p68) Basking in the glow of the Emerald Buddha.

3 Chatuchak Weekend Market (p151) Burning baht on colourful souvenirs, vintage gear and food galore.

4 Jim Thompson House (p90) Admiring the best of Thai architecture and artwork.

5 Thai Massage (p98) Being blissfully pounded into submission at a terrific-value massage centre.

6 Chinatown (p128) Eating yourself into a stupor at Chinatown's street stalls.

7 Rooftop Bars (p136) Toasting the stars and the

twinkling skyscraper lights from a lofty bar.

8 Cooking Schools (p101) Mastering spices and learning authentic recipes in a Thai cookery class.

9 Thonburi's Canals (p80) Gliding between sightseeing spots on a leisurely cruise.

10 Amphawa (p159) Exploring quaint wooden buildings in this canalside town outside Bangkok.

The Last Century

As Bangkok prospered, many wealthy merchant families sent their children to study in Europe. In 1924 a handful of Siamese students in Paris formed the Promoters of Political Change, a group that met to discuss ideas for a future Siamese government modelled on Western democracy.

A bloodless revolution in 1932, initiated by the Promoters of Political Change and a willing Rama VII (King Prajadhipok; r 1925–35), transformed Siam from an absolute monarchy into a constitutional one.

In the 1950s the US military developed bases in Thailand during the war in Vietnam in exchange for economic incentives. During this time Bangkok gained notoriety as a 'rest and recreation' spot for foreign troops stationed in Southeast Asia.

It wasn't until the boom years of the 1980s and 1990s that Bangkok exploded into a fully fledged metropolis crowded with hulking skyscrapers and an endless spill of concrete that gobbled up rice paddies and green space. The city's extravagant tastes were soon tamed by the 1997 economic meltdown, when the Thai currency fell into a deflationary tailspin and the national economy screeched to a virtual halt.

In recent years the military junta has embarked on several policies and projects that have had a huge impact on Bangkok. A ban on street vendors in certain neighbourhoods has already altered the city's sidewalks. Bangkok is furiously expanding its public transportation network. A plan to build a 14km promenade along Mae Nam Chao Praya has already resulted in the demolition of nearly 300 riverside structures, many of which were decades old. These forces, coupled with commercial interests, mean that Bangkok is changing at an astonishing rate.

◉ Sights

◉ Ko Ratanakosin

The birthplace of Bangkok, the artificial island of Ko Ratanakosin is where it all started more than 200 years ago. The remnants of this history – today Bangkok's biggest sights – draw just about every visitor to the city. The big-hitters, Wat Phra Kaew and Grand Palace and Wat Pho, are a short walk from the Chao Phraya Express Boat piers at Chang Pier, Maharaj Pier and Tien Pier, and are within walking distance of each other, although the hot sun may make doing this a more demanding task than it appears. Alternatively, túk-túks (pronounced *dúk dúk;* a type of motorised rickshaw) are a dime a dozen around here. If you're planning on visiting several sights, it's a good idea to arrive early in the morning for the cooler weather and to avoid the crowds. Evening is best for photography, particularly if you're hoping for the classic sunset shot of Wat Arun.

★**Wat Phra Kaew & Grand Palace** BUDDHIST TEMPLE
(วัดพระแก้ว, พระบรมมหาราชวัง; Map p82; Th Na Phra Lan; 500B; ⊙8.30am-3.30pm; ⊠Chang Pier, Maharaj Pier, Phra Chan Tai Pier) Also known as the Temple of the Emerald Buddha, Wat Phra Kaew is the colloquial name of the vast, fairy-tale compound that also includes the former residence of the Thai monarch, the Grand Palace.

This ground was consecrated in 1782, the first year of Bangkok rule, and is today Bangkok's biggest tourist attraction and a pilgrimage destination for devout Buddhists and nationalists. The 94.5-hectare grounds encompass more than 100 buildings that represent 200 years of royal history and architectural experimentation.

Housed in a fantastically decorated *bòht* (ordination hall), the Emerald Buddha is the temple's primary attraction.

Except for an anteroom here and there, the buildings of the Grand Palace are now

---

BANGKOK TONGUE-TWISTER

Upon completion of the royal district of Ko Ratanakosin in 1785, the capital of Siam was given a new name: 'Krungthep mahanakhon amonratanakosin mahintara ayuthaya mahadilok popnopparat ratchathani burirom udomratchaniwet mahasathan amonpiman avatansathit sakkathattiya witsanukamprasit'. This lexical gymnastic feat translates roughly as: 'Great City of Angels, the Repository of Divine Gems, the Great Land Unconquerable, the Grand and Prominent Realm, the Royal and Delightful Capital City full of Nine Noble Gems, the Highest Royal Dwelling and Grand Palace, the Divine Shelter and Living Place of Reincarnated Spirits'.

Understandably, foreign traders continued to call the capital Bang Makok, which eventually truncated itself to 'Bangkok'. These days all Thais understand 'Bangkok' but use a shortened version of the official name, Krung Thep (City of Angels).

put to use by the king only for certain ceremonial occasions, such as Coronation Day, and are largely off limits to visitors. Formerly, Thai kings housed their huge harems in the inner palace area, which was guarded by combat-trained female sentries. Outer palace buildings that visitors can view include **Borombhiman Hall**, a French-inspired structure that served as a residence for Rama VI (King Vajiravudh; r 1910–25). The building to the west is **Amarindra Hall** (open from Monday to Friday), originally a hall of justice, more recently used for coronation ceremonies, and the only palace building that tourists are generally allowed to enter. The largest of the palace buildings is the **Chakri Mahaprasat**, the Grand Palace Hall. Last is the Ratanakosin-style **Dusit Hall**, which initially served as a venue for royal audiences and later as a royal funerary hall.

Guides can be hired at the ticket kiosk; ignore offers from anyone outside. An audio guide can be rented for 200B for two hours.

Admission for the complex includes entrance to Dusit Palace Park (p95), which includes Vimanmek Teak Mansion and Abhisek Dusit Throne Hall.

★ **Wat Pho** BUDDHIST TEMPLE
(วัดโพธิ์/วัดพระเชตุพน, Wat Phra Chetuphon; Map p82; Th Sanam Chai; 100B; ⊙8.30am-6.30pm; ⛴Tien Pier) You'll find (slightly) fewer tourists here than at Wat Phra Kaew, but Wat Pho is our fave among Bangkok's biggest sights. In fact, the compound incorporates a host of superlatives: the city's largest reclining Buddha, the largest collection of Buddha images in Thailand and the country's earliest centre for public education.

Almost too big for its shelter is Wat Pho's highlight, the genuinely impressive **Reclining Buddha**.

The rambling grounds of Wat Pho cover 8 hectares, with the major tourist sites occupying the northern side of Th Chetuphon and the monastic facilities found on the southern side. The temple compound is also the national headquarters for the teaching and preservation of traditional Thai medicine, including Thai massage, a mandate legislated by Rama III when the tradition was in danger of extinction. The famous massage school has two massage pavilions (p99) located within the temple area and additional rooms within the training facility (p105) outside the temple.

Museum of Siam MUSEUM
(สถาบันพิพิธภัณฑ์การเรียนรู้แห่งชาติ; Map p82; www.museumsiam.org; Th Maha Rat; 300B; ⊙10am-6pm Tue-Sun; 👶; ⛴Tien Pier) Although temporarily closed for renovation when we stopped by, this fun museum's collection employs a variety of media to explore the origins of the Thai people and their culture. Housed in a European-style 19th-century building that was once the Ministry of Commerce, the exhibits are presented in a contemporary, engaging and interactive fashion not typically found in Thailand's museums. They are also refreshingly balanced and entertaining, with galleries dealing with a range of questions about the origins of the nation and its people.

Amulet Market MARKET
(ตลาดพระเครื่องวัดมหาธาตุ; Map p82; Th Maha Rat; ⊙7am-5pm; ⛴Chang Pier, Maharaj Pier, Phra Chan Tai Pier) This arcane and fascinating market claims both the footpaths along Th Maha Rat and Th Phra Chan, as well as a dense network of covered market stalls that runs south from Phra Chan Pier; the easiest entry point is clearly marked 'Trok Maha That'. The trade is based around small talismans carefully prized by collectors, monks, taxi drivers and people in dangerous professions.

Potential buyers, often already sporting many amulets, can be seen bargaining and flipping through magazines dedicated to the amulets, some of which command astronomical prices. It's a great place to just wander and watch men (because it's rarely

ⓘ **WAT PHRA KAEW: DRESS CODE & TICKET TIPS**

➡ Enter Wat Phra Kaew and the Grand Palace complex through the clearly marked third gate from the river pier. Tickets are purchased inside the complex; anyone telling you it's closed is a gem tout or a con artist.

➡ At Wat Phra Kaew and the Grand Palace grounds, dress rules are strictly enforced. If you're flashing a bit too much skin, expect to be shown into a dressing room and issued with a shirt or sarong (rental is free, but you must provide a refundable 200B deposit).

➡ Admission to the complex includes entrance to Dusit Palace Park.

Wat Phra Kaew & Grand Palace

EXPLORE BANGKOK'S PREMIER MONUMENTS TO RELIGION & REGENCY

The first area tourists enter is the Buddhist temple compound generally referred to as Wat Phra Kaew. A covered walkway surrounds the area, the inner walls of which are decorated with the **❶ ❷ murals of the Ramakian**. Originally painted during the reign of Rama I (r 1782–1809), the murals, which depict the Hindu epic the *Ramayana*, span 178 panels

that describe the struggles of Rama to rescue his kidnapped wife, Sita.

After taking in the story, pass through one of the gateways guarded by **❸ yaksha** to the inner compound. The most important structure here is the **❹ bòht, or ordination hall**, which houses the **❺ Emerald Buddha**.

Kinaree
These graceful half-swan, half-women creatures from Hindu-Buddhist mythology stand outside Prasat Phra Thep Bidon.

Amarindra Hall

Borombhiman Hall

Prasat Phra Thep Bidon

Phra Si Ratana

The Murals of the Ramakian
These wall paintings, which begin at the eastern side of Wat Phra Kaew, often depict scenes more reminiscent of 19th-century Thailand than of ancient India.

Hanuman
Rows of these mischievous monkey deities from Hindu mythology appear to support the lower levels of two small *chedi* near Prasat Phra Thep Bidon.

Head east to the so-called Upper Terrace, an elevated area home to the **6 spires of the three primary chedi**. The middle structure, Phra Mondop, is used to house Buddhist manuscripts. This area is also home to several of Wat Phra Kaew's noteworthy mythical beings, including beckoning **7 kinaree** and several grimacing **8 Hanuman**.

Proceed through the western gate to the compound known as the Grand Palace. Few of the buildings here are open to the public. The most noteworthy structure is **9 Chakri Mahaprasat**. Built in 1882, the exterior of the hall is a unique blend of Western and traditional Thai architecture.

The Three Spires
The elaborate seven-tiered roof of Phra Mondop, the Khmer-style peak of Prasat Phra Thep Bidon, and the gilded Phra Si Ratana *chedi* are the tallest structures in the compound.

LEPNEVA IRINA / SHUTTERSTOCK ©

Emerald Buddha
Despite the name, this diminutive statue (it's only 66cm tall) is actually carved from nephrite, a type of jade.

ALEXEY STOP / GETTY IMAGES ©

The Death of Thotsakan
The panels progress clockwise, culminating at the western edge of the compound with the death of Thotsakan, Sita's kidnapper, and his elaborate funeral procession.

Chakri Mahaprasat
This structure is sometimes referred to as *fa·ràng sài chá·dah* (Westerner in a Thai crown) because each wing is topped by a *mon·dòp*: a spire representing a Thai adaptation of a Hindu shrine.

DESIGN PICS / BLAKE KENT / GETTY IMAGES ©

Dusit Hall

Yaksha
Each entrance to the Wat Phra Kaew compound is watched over by a pair of vigilant and enormous *yaksha*, ogres or giants from Hindu mythology.

ZZVET / GETTY IMAGES ©

Bòht (Ordination Hall)
This structure is an early example of the Ratanakosin school of architecture, which combines traditional stylistic holdovers from Ayuthaya along with more modern touches from China and the West.

Wat Pho

A WALK THROUGH THE BIG BUDDHAS OF WAT PHO

The logical starting place is the main *wi·hăhn* (sanctuary), home to Wat Pho's centre piece, the immense ❶ **Reclining Buddha**. In addition to its enormous size, note the ❷ **mother-of-pearl inlay** on the soles of the statue's feet. The interior walls of the *wi·hăhn* are covered with murals that depict previous lives of the Buddha, and along the south side of the structure there are 108 bronze monk bowls; for 20B you can buy 108 coins, each of which is dropped in a bowl for good luck.

Exit the *wi·hăhn* and head east via the two ❸ **stone giants** who guard the gateway to the rest of the compound. Directly south of these are the four towering ❹ **royal chedi**.

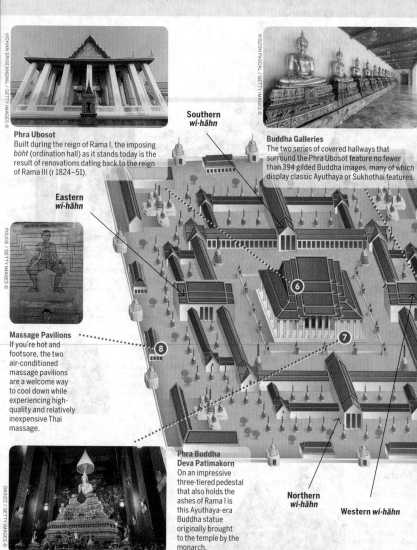

Southern *wi·hăhn*

Phra Ubosot
Built during the reign of Rama I, the imposing *bòht* (ordination hall) as it stands today is the result of renovations dating back to the reign of Rama III (r 1824–51).

Buddha Galleries
The two series of covered hallways that surround the Phra Ubosot feature no fewer than 394 gilded Buddha images, many of which display classic Ayuthaya or Sukhothai features.

Eastern *wi·hăhn*

Massage Pavilions
If you're hot and footsore, the two air-conditioned massage pavilions are a welcome way to cool down while experiencing high-quality and relatively inexpensive Thai massage.

Phra Buddha Deva Patimakorn
On an impressive three-tiered pedestal that also holds the ashes of Rama I is this Ayuthaya-era Buddha statue originally brought to the temple by the monarch.

Northern *wi·hăhn*

Western *wi·hăhn*

VICHAN SRISENGNIL / GETTY IMAGES ©

KISZON PASCAL / GETTY IMAGES ©

PIDJOE / GETTY IMAGES ©

QASIZZ / GETTY IMAGES ©

Continue east, passing through two consecutive **5** galleries of Buddha statues linking four *wí·hǎhn*, two of which contain notable Sukhothai-era Buddha statues; these comprise the exterior of **6** **Phra Ubosot**, the immense ordination hall that is Wat Pho's second-most noteworthy structure. The base of the building is surrounded by bas-relief inscriptions, and inside is the notable Buddha statue, **7** **Phra Buddha Deva Patimakorn**.

Wat Pho is often referred to as Thailand's first university, a tradition that continues today in an associated traditional Thai medicine school and, at the compound's eastern extent, two **8** **massage pavilions**.

Interspersed throughout the eastern half of the compound are several additional minor *chedi* and rock gardens.

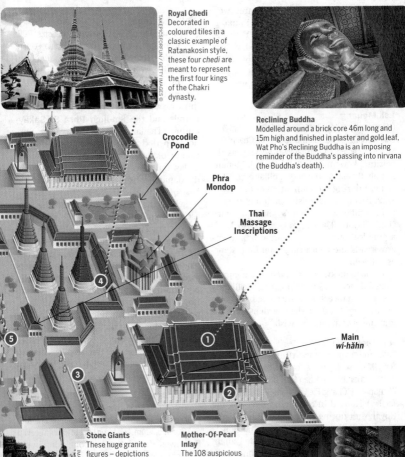

Royal Chedi
Decorated in coloured tiles in a classic example of Ratanakosin style, these four *chedi* are meant to represent the first four kings of the Chakri dynasty.

Reclining Buddha
Modelled around a brick core 46m long and 15m high and finished in plaster and gold leaf, Wat Pho's Reclining Buddha is an imposing reminder of the Buddha's passing into nirvana (the Buddha's death).

Crocodile Pond

Phra Mondop

Thai Massage Inscriptions

Main *wí·hǎhn*

Stone Giants
These huge granite figures – depictions range from Chinese opera characters to Marco Polo – originally arrived in Thailand in the 19th century as ballast aboard Chinese junks.

Mother-Of-Pearl Inlay
The 108 auspicious *lák·sà·nà*, physical characteristics of the Buddha, are depicted on the soles of the feet of the Reclining Buddha.

women) looking through magnifying glasses at the tiny amulets, seeking hidden meaning and, if they're lucky, hidden value.

National Museum   MUSEUM
(พิพิธภัณฑสถานแห่งชาติ; Map p82; 4 Th Na Phra That; 200B; ⊙9am-4pm Wed-Sun; ⛴Chang Pier, Maharaj Pier, Phra Chan Tai Pier) Often touted as Southeast Asia's biggest museum, Thailand's National Museum is home to an impressive, albeit occasionally dusty, collection of items, best appreciated on one of the museum's free twice-weekly guided **tours** (⊙9.30am Wed & Thu).

Most of the museum's structures were built in 1782 as the palace of Rama I's viceroy, Prince Wang Na. Rama V turned it into a museum in 1874, and today there are three permanent exhibitions spread out over several buildings. When we stopped by, several of the exhibition halls were being renovated.

Lak Meuang   MONUMENT
(ศาลหลักเมือง; Map p82; cnr Th Sanam Chai & Th Lak Meuang; ⊙6.30am-6.30pm; ⛴Chang Pier, Maharaj Pier, Phra Chan Tai Pier) Serving as the spiritual keystone of Bangkok, Lak Meuang is a phallus-shaped wooden pillar erected by Rama I during the foundation of the city in 1782. Part of an animistic tradition, the city pillar embodies the city's guardian spirit (Phra Sayam Thewathirat) and also lends a practical purpose as a marker of a town's crossroads and measuring point for distances between towns.

If you're lucky, *lá·kon gâa bon* (a commissioned dance) may be in progress. Brilliantly costumed dancers measure out subtle movements as gratitude to the guardian spirit for granting a worshipper's wish.

National Gallery   GALLERY
(พิพิธภัณฑ์สถานแห่งชาติหอศิลป์/หอศิลป์เจ้า ฟ้า; Map p82; www.facebook.com/thenational gallerythailand; 4 Th Chao Fa; 200B; ⊙9am-4pm Wed-Sun; ⛴Chang Pier, Maharaj Pier, Phra Chan Tai Pier) Housed in a building that was the Royal Mint during the reign of Rama V, the National Gallery's permanent exhibition is admittedly a rather dusty and dated affair. Secular art is a relatively new concept in Thailand and most of the country's best examples of fine art reside in the temples for which they were created – much as historic Western art is often found in European cathedrals. As such, most of the permanent

collection here documents Thailand's homage to modern styles.

◉ Banglamphu

Next to Ko Ratanakosin, leafy lanes, antique shophouses, buzzing wet markets and golden temples convene in Banglamphu – easily the city's most quintessentially 'Bangkok' neighbourhood. It's a quaint postcard picture of the city that used to be, that is until you stumble upon Th Khao San (p111), arguably the world's most famous backpacker enclave.

★ Wat Suthat   BUDDHIST TEMPLE
(วัดสุทัศน์; Map p82; Th Bamrung Meuang; 20B; ⊙8.30am-9pm; ⛴klorng boat to Phanfa Leelard Pier) Other than being just plain huge and impressive, Wat Suthat also holds the highest royal temple grade. Inside the *wí·hăhn* (sanctuary for a Buddha sculpture) are intricate *Jataka* (stories of the Buddha) murals and the 8m-high **Phra Si Sakayamuni**, Thailand's largest surviving Sukhothai-period bronze, cast in the former capital of Sukhothai in the 14th century. Today, the ashes of Rama VIII (King Ananda Mahidol; r 1935–46) are contained in the base of the image.

Behind the *wí·hăhn*, the *bòht* is the largest of its kind in the country. To add to its list of 'largests', Wat Suthat holds the rank of Rachavoramahavihan, the highest royal temple grade. It also maintains a special place in the national religion because of its association with the Brahman priests who perform important ceremonies, such as the Royal Ploughing Ceremony in May. These priests also perform religious rites at two Hindu shrines near the *wát* – **Dhevasathan** (เทวสถาน/โบสถ์พราหมณ์; ⊙daylight hours) FREE on Th Din So, and the smaller **Vishnu Shrine** (ศาลเทวาลัยพระวิษณุนารายณ์; ⊙daylight hours) FREE on Th Unakan.

Golden Mount   BUDDHIST TEMPLE
(ภูเขาทอง, Phu Khao Thong; Map p82; off Th Boriphat; admission to summit of Golden Mount 10B; ⊙7.30am-5.30pm; ⛴klorng boat to Phanfa Leelard Pier) Even if you're *wát*-ed out, you should tackle the brisk ascent to the Golden Mount. Serpentine steps wind through an artificial hill shaded by gnarled trees, some of which are signed in English, and past graves and pictures of wealthy benefactors. At the peak,

City Walk
Ko Ratanakosin Stroll

START CHANG PIER
END WAT ARUN
LENGTH 4KM; THREE TO FIVE HOURS

The bulk of Bangkok's 'must-see' destinations are in the former royal district, Ko Ratanakosin. Start early to beat the heat and get in before the hordes have descended.

Start at Chang Pier and follow Th Na Phra Lan east, with a quick diversion to **1 Silpakorn University**, Thailand's premier fine-arts university. If you haven't already been, continue east to the main gate into **2 Wat Phra Kaew & Grand Palace** (p68), two of Bangkok's most famous attractions.

Return to Th Maha Rat and proceed north, through an enclave of herbal apothecaries and footpath amulet sellers. Immediately after passing the cat-laden newsstand (you'll know it when you smell it), turn left into **3 Trok Tha Wang**, a narrow alleyway holding a hidden classic Bangkok neighbourhood. Returning to Th Maha Rat, continue moving north; on your right is **4 Wat Mahathat**, one of Thailand's most respected Buddhist universities.

Across the street, turn left into narrow Trok Maha That to discover the cramped **5 Amulet Market** (p69). As you continue north alongside the river, amulets soon turn to food vendors. The emergence of white-and-black uniforms is a clue that you are approaching **6 Thammasat University**, known for its law and political science departments.

Exiting at Phra Chan Pier, cross Th Maha Rat and continue east until you reach **7 Sanam Luang**, the 'Royal Field'. Cross the field and continue south along Th Ratchadamnoen Nai until you reach the home of Bangkok's city spirit, **8 Lak Meuang** (p74). After paying your respects, head south along Th Sanam Chai and turn right onto Th Thai Wang, which will lead you to the entrance of **9 Wat Pho** (p69), home of the giant Reclining Buddha.

If you've still got the energy, head to adjacent Tien Pier to catch the cross-river ferry to **10 Wat Arun** (p80).

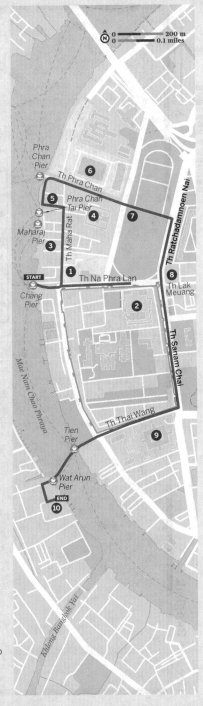

BANGKOK & AROUND

Greater Bangkok

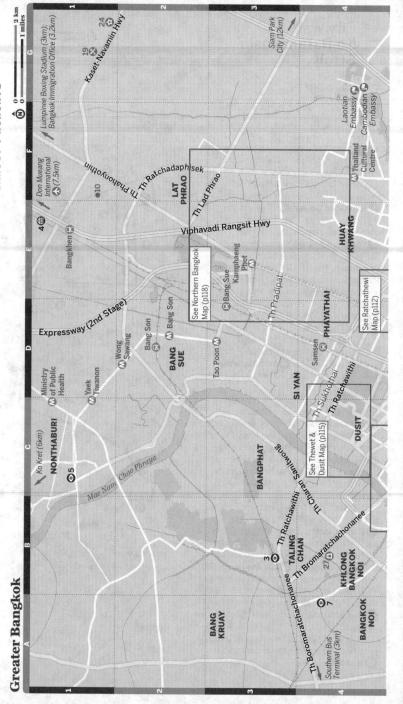

N 0 — 2 km
0 — 1 miles

Lumpinee Boxing Stadium (3km);
Bangkok Immigration Office (3.2km)

Kaset-Navamin Hwy

Siam Park City (12km)

Laotian Embassy
Cambodian Embassy

Don Mueang International (7.5km)

Th Ratchadaphisek

Th Phahonyothin

LAT PHRAO

Th Lad Phrao

Thailand Cultural Centre

Viphavadi Rangsit Hwy

HUAY KHWANG

Bangkhen

See Northern Bangkok Map (p118)

Bang Sue Kamphaeng Phet

PHAYATHAI

See Ratchathewi Map (p112)

Expressway (2nd Stage)

Th Pradipat

Th Pradiphat

Bang Son

Wong Sawang

Bang Son

BANG SUE

Tao Poon

Samsen

Ministry of Public Health

Yaek Tiwanon

NONTHABURI

Th Sukhothai

SI YAN

Th Ratchawithi

Ko Kret (6km)

Mae Nam Chao Phraya

BANGPHAT

See Thewet & Dusit Map (p115)

DUSIT

Th Charan Sanitwong

BANG KRUAY

Th Ratchawithi

TALING CHAN

Th Bromaratchachonanee

KHLONG BANGKOK NOI

Th Boromaratchachonanee

BANGKOK NOI

Southern Bus Terminal (3km)

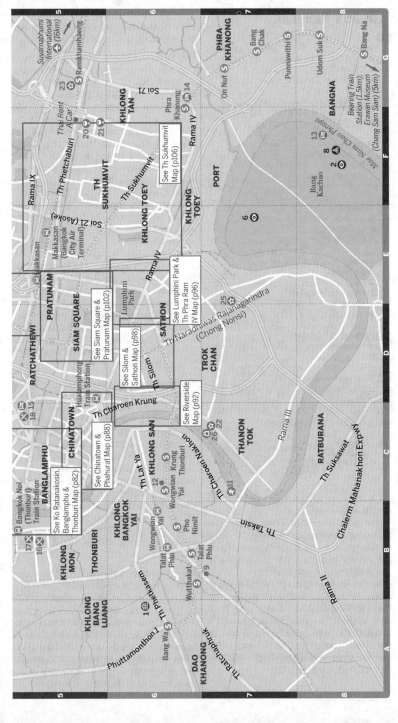

Suvarnabhumi International (16km)

Ramkhamhaeng Ⓢ

23

PHRA KHANONG

Bang Chak Ⓢ

Ⓢ On Nut

Bang Na Ⓢ

Punnawithi Ⓢ

Udom Suk Ⓢ

Ⓖ

Thai Rent A Car

20 21

Soi 71

KHLONG TAN

Phra Khanong Ⓢ

14

Rama IV

BANGNA

Bearing Train Station (1.5km); Erawan Museum (5km) (Chang Sam Sian)

Rama IX

Th Phetchaburi

TH SUKHUMVIT

Th Sukhumvit

See Th Sukhumvit Map (p106)

13

8

2

Ⓕ

Mae Nam Chao Phraya

Makkasan

Soi 21 (Asoke)

KHLONG TOEY

PORT

Bang Kachao

Makkasan (Bangkok City Air Terminal)

KHLONG TOEY

6

Ⓔ

RATCHATHEWI

PRATUNAM

SIAM SQUARE

See Siam Square & Pratunam Map (p102)

Rama IV

Lumphini Park

SATHON

See Lumphini Park & Th Phra Ram IV Map (p96)

25

Th Naradhiwas Rajanagarindra (Chong Nonsi)

Ⓓ

Hualamphong Train Station

See Silom & Sathon Map (p98)

Th Silom

SILOM

TROK CHAN

CHINATOWN

18 15

See Chinatown & Phahurat Map (p88)

Th Charoen Krung

See Riverside Map (p92)

26 22

THANON TOK

Rama III

Ⓒ

Bangkok Noi (Thonburi) Train Station

17 16

BANGLAMPHU

See Ko Ratanakosin, Banglamphu & Thonburi Map (p82)

Th Lat Ya

Ⓢ KHLONG SAN

12 Ⓢ

Wongwian Krung Yai Thonburi

Th Charoen Nakhon

11

RATBURANA

Th Suksawat

Chalerm Mahanakhon Expwy

Ⓑ

KHLONG MON

THONBURI

KHLONG BANGKOK YAI

Ⓢ Wongwian Yai

Pho Nimit

Th Taksin

Rama II

Talat Phlu Ⓢ

Talat Phlu

Wutthakat Ⓢ

9

KHLONG BANG LUANG

1

Th Phetkasem

Phuttamonthon I Ⓢ

Bang Wa Ⓢ

DAO KHANONG

Th Ratchadaphisek

Greater Bangkok

you'll find a breezy 360-degree view of Bangkok's most photogenic side.

The hill was created when a large stupa, under construction by Rama III (King Phranangklao; r 1824–51), collapsed because the soft soil beneath would not support it. The resulting mud-and-brick hill was left to sprout weeds until Rama IV (King Mongkut; r 1851–68) built a small stupa on its crest. Rama V (King Chulalongkorn; r 1868–1910) later added to the structure and housed a Buddha relic from India (given to him by the British government) in the stupa. The concrete walls were added during WWII to prevent the hill from eroding.

In November there's a festival in the grounds that includes an enchanting candlelight procession up the Golden Mount.

Wat Bowonniwet   BUDDHIST TEMPLE
(วัดบวรนิเวศวิหาร; Map p82; www.watbowon.org; Th Phra Sumen; ⊙8.30am-5pm; ⊜Phra Athit/Banglamphu Pier) FREE Founded in 1826, Wat Bowonniwet (known colloquially as Wat Bowon) is the national headquarters for the Thammayut monastic sect, a reformed version of Thai Buddhism. The rest of us should visit the temple for the noteworthy murals in its *bòht*, which include Thai depictions of Western life (possibly copied from magazine illustrations) during the early 19th century.

Because of its royal status, visitors should be particularly careful to dress properly for admittance; shorts and sleeveless clothing are not allowed.

Rama IV (King Mongkut; r 1851–68), who set out to be a scholar, not a king, founded the Thammayut sect and began the royal tradition of ordination at this temple. In fact, Mongkut was the abbot of Wat Bowon for several years. Rama IX (King Bhumibol Adulyadej; r 1946–2016) and Rama X (King Maha Vajiralongkorn; r 2016–), as well as several other males in the royal family, have been ordained as monks here.

Thanon Bamrung Meuang Religious Shops   AREA
(ถนนบำรุงเมือง; Map p82; Th Bamrung Meuang; ⊙9am-6pm; ⊜klorng boat to Phanfa Leelard Pier) The stretch of Th Bamrung Meuang (one of Bangkok's oldest streets and originally an elephant path leading to the Grand Palace) from Th Mahachai to Th Tanao is lined with shops selling all manner of Buddhist religious paraphernalia. You probably don't need a car-sized Buddha statue or an eerily lifelike effigy of a famous monk, but browsing is fun, and who knows when you might need to do a great deal of Thai-style merit making?

King Prajadhipok Museum   MUSEUM
(พิพิธภัณฑ์พระบาทสมเด็จพระปกเกล้าเจ้าอยู่หัว; Map p82; www.kingprajadhipokmuseum.org; 2 Th Lan Luang; ⊙9am-4pm Tue-Sun; ⊜klorng boat to Phanfa Leelard Pier) FREE This museum assembles old photos and memorabilia to illustrate the rather dramatic life of Rama VII (King Prajadhipok; r 1925–35), Thailand's last absolute monarch. It occupies a grand neocolonial-style building constructed on

LOCAL KNOWLEDGE

BANGKOK LIKE A LOCAL

Don't want to feel like a sheltered package holidaymaker? Rest assured that it's a cinch to get local in Bangkok, a city where hectic tourist attractions often rub shoulders with classic local neighbourhoods. Often it takes little more than a tiny detour from the big-hitter sights.

The Banglamphu (p138) neighbourhood is home to heaps of bars frequented mostly by young locals, the dance clubs of Royal City Avenue (p141) pull the majority of local partiers and Silom (p140) is the magnet for the local LGBT crowd.

Come dinnertime, it doesn't get more local than the street stalls of Bangkok's Chinatown (p129). Alternatively, head to the hoods north of Bangkok, such as the area surrounding the Victory Monument, for unpretentious street food. At some point during your stay, be sure to hit a food court, like MBK Food Island (p132), to see how the locals dine.

BK (www.bk.asia-city.com) is probably the best English-language guide to cover what the locals are up to.

the orders of Rama V for his favourite firm of Bond St merchants – the only foreign business allowed on the royal road linking Bangkok's two palace districts.

Ban Baat
AREA

(บ้านบาตร, Monk's Bowl Village; Map p82; off Soi Ban Bat; ⏱9am-5pm; 🚤klorng boat to Phanfa Leelard Pier) The residents of Ban Baat inhabit the only remaining village of three established in Bangkok by Rama I (King Phraphutthayotfa Chulalok; r 1782–1809) to produce *bàht*, the distinctive bowls used by monks to receive morning food donations. Tourists – not temples – are among the customers these days, and a bowl purchase is usually rewarded with a bowl-making demonstration.

As cheaper factory-made bowls are now the norm, the artisanal tradition has shrunk to one extended family. You can observe the process of hammering the bowls together from eight separate pieces of steel, said to represent Buddhism's eightfold path. The joints are then fused with melted copper wire, and the bowl is beaten, polished and coated with several layers of black lacquer.

To find the village – today just a single alleyway – from Th Bamrung Meuang, turn down Soi Ban Bat, then take the first right.

Sao Ching-Cha
MONUMENT

(เสาชิงช้า, Giant Swing; Map p82; Th Bamrung Meuang; 🚤klorng boat to Phanfa Leelard Pier) This spindly red arch – a symbol of Bangkok – formerly hosted a Brahman festival in honour of Shiva, in which participants

would swing in ever higher arcs in an effort to reach a bag of gold suspended from a 15m-high bamboo pole. Whoever grabbed the gold could keep it, but that was no mean feat, and deaths were as common as successes. A black-and-white photo illustrating the risky rite can be seen at the ticket counter at adjacent Wat Suthat (p74).

Wat Ratchanatdaram
BUDDHIST TEMPLE

(วัดราชนัดดาราม; Map p82; Th Mahachai; ⏱8am-5pm; 🚤klorng boat to Phanfa Leelard Pier) FREE This temple was built for Rama III (King Phranangklao; r 1824-51) in the 1840s, and its design is said to derive from metal temples built in India and Sri Lanka more than 2000 years ago.

Phra Sumen Fort &
Santi Chai Prakan Park
NOTABLE BUILDING, PARK

(ป้อมพระสุเมรุ, สวนสันติชัยปราการ; Map p82; Th Phra Athit; ⏱5am-9pm; 🚤Phra Athit/Banglamphu Pier) FREE Formerly the site of a sugar factory, today Santi Chai Prakan Park is a tiny patch of greenery with a great river view and lots of evening action, including comical communal aerobics classes. The riverside pathway heading southwards makes for a serene promenade.

The park's most prominent landmark is the blindingly white Phra Sumen Fort, which was built in 1783 to defend the city against a river invasion.

Named for the mythical Phra Sumen (Mt Meru) of Hindu-Buddhist cosmology, the octagonal brick-and-stucco bunker was one of 14 city watchtowers that formerly punctuated the old city wall alongside Khlong Rop

WORTH A TRIP

THONBURI: CRUISING THE 'VENICE OF THE EAST'

Bangkok was formerly known as the Venice of the East, as the city used to be criss-crossed by an advanced network of *klorng* (also spelt *khlong*), artificial canals that inhabitants used both for transport and to ship goods. Today, cars and motorcycles have superseded boats, and the majority of Bangkok's canals have been filled in and covered by roads, or are fetid and drying up. Yet a peek into the watery Bangkok of yesteryear can still be had west of Mae Nam Chao Phraya, in Thonburi.

Thonburi's network of canals and river tributaries still carries a motley fleet of water-craft, from paddle canoes to rice barges. Homes, trading houses and temples are built on stilts with front doors opening out to the water. According to residents, these waterways protect them from the seasonal flooding that plagues the capital. **Khlong Bangkok Noi** is lined with greenery and historic temples; smaller **Khlong Mon** is largely residen-tial. **Khlong Bangkok Yai** was in fact the original course of the river until a canal was built to expedite transits. Today, long-tail boats that ply these and other Thonburi canals are available for charter at Chang Pier and Tien Pier, both on Ko Ratanakosin. Prices at these piers are slightly higher than elsewhere and allow little room for negotiation, but you stand the least chance of being conned or hit up for tips and other unexpected fees.

Trips generally traverse Khlong Bangkok Noi and Khlong Mon, taking in the Royal Barges National Museum, Wat Arun and a riverside temple with fish feeding. Longer trips diverge into Khlong Bangkok Yai, and can include a visit to an orchid farm. On weekends, you have the option of visiting the **Taling Chan Floating Market** (p148). However, it's worth pointing out that to actually disembark and explore any of these sights, the most common tour of one hour (1000B, up to six people) is simply not enough time; you'll most likely need 1½ or two hours (1300B or 1500B respectively). Most operators have set tour routes, but if you have a specific destination in mind, you can request it. Tours are generally conducted from 8am to 5pm.

If you'd prefer something longer or more personalised, **Pandan Tour** (p109) con-ducts a variety of mostly full-day tours. And a budget alternative is to take the one-way-only **commuter long-tail boat** (Map p82; Chang Pier, off Th Maha Rat; 25B; ⊙4.30am-7.30pm) from Chang Pier to Bang Yai, at the distant northern end of Khlong Bangkok Noi, although foreigners are sometimes discouraged from doing so.

Krung (now Khlong Banglamphu but still called Khlong Rop Krung on most signs). Apart from **Mahakan Fort** (ป้อมมหากาฬ; Map p82; Th Ratchadamnoen Klang; ⊙24hr; 🚢klorng boat to Phanfa Leelard Pier) **FREE**, this is the only one still standing.

◎ Thonburi

Thonburi, located across Mae Nam Chao Phraya from Banglamphu, is a seemingly forgotten yet visit-worthy zone of sleepy residential districts connected by *klorng* (canals; also spelt *khlong*). The area is ac-cessible via the 3B river-crossing ferries at Chang Pier and Tien Pier.

★ Wat Arun
BUDDHIST TEMPLE

(วัดอรุณฯ; Map p82; www.watarun.net; off Th Arun Amarin; 50B; ⊙8am-6pm; 🚢cross-river ferry from Tien Pier) After the fall of Ayuthaya, King Tak-sin ceremoniously clinched control here on the site of a local shrine and established a

royal palace and a temple to house the Em-erald Buddha. The temple was renamed af-ter the Indian god of dawn (Aruna) and in honour of the literal and symbolic founding of a new Ayuthaya. Today the temple is one of Bangkok's most iconic structures – not to mention one of the few Buddhist temples one is encouraged to climb on.

It wasn't until the capital and the Em-erald Buddha were moved to Bangkok that Wat Arun received its most promi-nent characteristic: the 82m-high *prahng* (Khmer-style tower). The tower's construc-tion was started during the first half of the 19th century by Rama II (King Phraphut-thaloetla Naphalai; r 1809–24) and later completed by Rama III (King Phranang-klao; r 1824–51). Steep stairs lead to the top, from where there's amazing views of Mae Nam Chao Phraya. Not apparent from a distance are the ornate floral **mosaics** made from broken, multihued Chinese porcelain, a common temple ornamentation in the early Ratanakosin period, when Chinese ships calling at the port of Bangkok discarded tonnes of old porcelain as ballast.

Also worth an inspection is the interior of the *bòht*. The main Buddha image is said to have been designed by Rama II himself. The **murals** date from the reign of Rama V (King Chulalongkorn; r 1868–1910); particularly impressive is one that depicts Prince Siddhartha encountering examples of birth, old age, sickness and death outside his palace walls, an experience that led him to abandon the worldly life. The ashes of Rama II are interred in the base of the presiding Buddha image.

Royal Barges
National Museum   MUSEUM
(พิพิธภัณฑสถานแห่งชาติ เรือพระราชพิธี/เรือพระที่นั่ง; Map p82; Khlong Bangkok Noi or 80/1 Th Arun Amarin; admission 100B, camera 100B; ⊙9am-5pm; 📷 Phra Pin Klao Bridge Pier) The royal barges are slender, fantastically ornamented vessels used in ceremonial processions. The tradition dates back to the Ayuthaya era, when travel (for commoners and royals) was by boat. When not in use, the barges are on display at this Thonburi museum.

The most convenient way to get here is by motorcycle taxi from Phra Pin Klao Bridge Pier (ask the driver to go to *rew·a prá têe nâng*). The museum is also an optional stop on long-tail boat trips through Thonburi's canals.

Suphannahong, the king's personal barge, is the most important of the six boats on display here. Made from a single piece of timber, it's said to be the largest dugout in the world. The name means Golden Swan, and a huge swan head has been carved into the bow. Lesser barges feature bows that are carved into other Hindu-Buddhist mythological shapes such as the *naga* (mythical sea serpent) and *garuda* (Vishnu's bird mount).

Historic photos help envision the grand processions in which the largest of the barges would require a rowing crew of 50 men, plus seven umbrella bearers, two helmsmen and two navigators, as well as a flagsman, rhythm keeper and chanter. Today, the royal barge procession is an infrequent occurrence, most recently performed in 2012 in honour of the late King Bhumibol Adulyadej's 85th birthday.

Siriraj Medical Museum   MUSEUM
(พิพิธภัณฑ์นิติเวชศาสตร์สงกรานต์นิยมเสน; Map p82; 2nd fl, Adulyadejvikrom Bldg, Siriraj Hospital; 200B; ⊙10am-4pm Wed-Mon; 📷 Wang Lang/Siriraj Pier, Thonburi Railway Station Pier) Various appendages, murder weapons and crime-scene evidence, including a bloodied T-shirt from a victim stabbed to death with a dildo, are on display at these linked museums – collectively dubbed the Museum of Death – dedicated to anatomy, pathology and forensic science.

The easiest way to reach the Siriraj museum is by taking the river-crossing ferry from Chang Pier to Wang Lang/Siriraj Pier in Thonburi. At the exit to the pier, turn right (north) to enter Siriraj Hospital and follow the green Museum signs.

◉ Chinatown & Phahurat

Chinatown embodies everything that's hectic, noisy and polluted about Bangkok, but that's what makes it such a fascinating area to explore. The area's big sights – namely Wat Traimit (Golden Buddha) and the street markets – are worth hitting, but be sure to set aside enough time to do some map-free wandering among the neon-lit gold shops, hidden temples, crumbling shopfronts and pencil-thin alleys, especially the tiny winding lanes that extend from Soi Wanit 1 (aka Sampeng Lane).

For ages, Chinatown was home to Bangkok's most infamous traffic jams, but the arrival of the MRT (Metro) in 2005 finally made the area a sane place to visit. Still, the station is about a kilometre from many sights, so you'll have to take a longish walk or a short taxi ride. An alternative is to take the Chao Phraya Express Boat to the stop at Ratchawong Pier, from where it's a brief walk to most restaurants and a bit further to most sights.

At the western edge of Chinatown is a small but thriving Little India, Phahurat.

★ Wat Traimit
(Golden Buddha)   BUDDHIST TEMPLE
(วัดไตรมิตร, Temple of the Golden Buddha; Map p88; Th Mittaphap Thai-China; 100B; ⊙8am-5pm; 📷 Ratchawong Pier, Ⓜ Hua Lamphong exit 1) The attraction at Wat Traimit is undoubtedly the impressive 3m-tall, 5.5-tonne, **solid-gold**

Ko Ratanakosin, Banglamphu & Thonburi

Somdej Prapinklao Soi 2 🏨 51

Santi Chai Prakan Park

Phra Athit/ Banglamphu Pier 🚢 74

Th Phra Athit 67

Phra Pin Klao Bridge Pier 🚢

Saphan Phra Pin Klao

52
79
65
30 84
81
Soi Rami Buttri

Th Chao Fa

Th Rongmai

Bangkok Information Center ℹ️

16 🏛
Khlong Bangkok Noi

Bangkok Noi (Thonburi) Train Station 🚉

THONBURI

Thonburi Railway Station Pier 🚢

Siriraj Hospital 20 🏛

Th Phrannok

Wang Lang/ Siriraj Pier 🚢

Phra Chan Pier 🚢

Soi Tambon Wanglang 1

Phra Chan Tai Pier 🚢

Maharaj Pier 🚢

Th Phra Chan

5
27

Th Maha Rat

94
13 🏛
87

14 🏛

21

Sanam Luang

17

Th Na Phra That

Th Ratchadamnoen Nai

Wat Rakhang Pier 🚢

BANGKOK NOI

Chang Pier 🚢 19

Commuter Long-tail Boat 🚢

Silpakorn University

Th Na Phra Lan

10 ℹ️ Th Lak Meuang

Th Sanam Chai

Mae Nam Chao Phraya

Wat Phra Kaew & Grand Palace 3 🛕

KO RATANAKOSIN

Saranrom Royal Garden

Enlargement

0 ————— 200 m
0 ————— 0.1 miles

2 🛕
31

Wat Pho

Th Maha Rat

Soi Tha Tian 33

Th Chetuphon

86 78
72
43 34

Soi Pratu Nokyung

Soi Phen Phat 53
28
64
39

12 🏛

Th Maha Rat

Tien Pier 🚢

Wat Arun Pier 🚢

Th Maha Rat

Th Thai Wang

Th Chetuphon

Wat Arun
🛕 1

See Enlargement

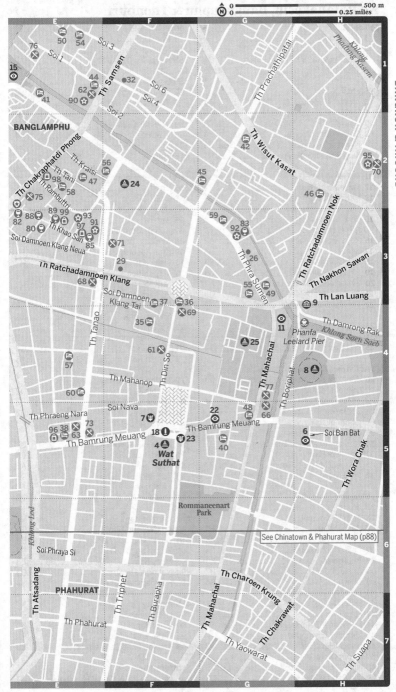

0 500 m
0 0.25 miles

BANGLAMPHU

Th Samsen

Soi 3
Soi 1
Soi 6
Soi 4
Soi 2

Th Prachathipatai
Khlong Phadung Kasem

Th Wisut Kasat

Th Chakraphatdi Phong
Th Kraisi
Th Tani
Th Rambuttri
Th Khao San
Soi Damnoen Klang Neua

Th Ratchadamnoen Klang
Soi Damnoen Klang Tai

Th Tanao

Th Ratchadamnoen Nok

Th Nakhon Sawan

Th Lan Luang

Th Damrong Rak
Khlong Saen Saeb
Phanfa
Leelard Pier

Th Mahachai

Th Boriphat

Th Mahanop
Th Din So

Soi Nava

Th Phraeng Nara

Th Bamrung Meuang

Th Bamrung Meuang

Wat Suthat

Soi Ban Bat

Th Wora Chak

Rommaneenart Park

See Chinatown & Phahurat Map (p88)

Khlong Lod

Soi Phraya Si

PHAHURAT

Th Atsadang

Th Phahurat

Th Triphet

Th Burapha

Th Mahachai

Th Charoen Krung

Th Chakrawat

Th Yaowarat

Th Suapa

Ko Ratanakosin, Banglamphu & Thonburi

Buddha image, which gleams like, well, gold. Sculpted in the graceful Sukhothai style, the image was 'discovered' some 60 years ago beneath a stucco/plaster exterior, when it fell from a crane while being moved to a new building within the temple compound.

It has been theorised that the covering was added to protect it from marauding hordes, either during the late Sukhothai period or later in the Ayuthaya period when the city was under siege by the Burmese. The temple itself is said to date from the early 13th century.

Donations and a constant flow of tourists have proven profitable, and the statue is now housed in an imposing four-storey marble structure. The 2nd floor of the building is home to the **Phra Buddha Maha Suwanna Patimakorn Exhibition** (นิทรรศการพระพุทธมหาสุวรรณปฏิมากร; 40B; ⊙8am-5pm Tue-Sun), which has exhibits on how the statue was made, discovered and came to arrive at its current home, while the 3rd floor is home to the **Yaowarat Chinatown Heritage Center** (ศูนย์ประวัติศาสตร์เยาวราช; 40B; ⊙8am-5pm Tue-Su), a small but engaging museum with multimedia exhibits on the history of Bangkok's Chinatown and its residents.

Talat Mai MARKET
(ตลาดใหม่; Map p88; Soi Yaowarat 6/Charoen Krung 16; ⊙6am-6pm; ⛴Ratchawong Pier, Ⓜ Hua Lamphong exit 1 & taxi) With nearly two centuries of commerce under its belt, New Market is no longer an entirely accurate name for this strip of commerce. Regardless, this is Bangkok's, if not Thailand's, most Chinese market, and the dried goods, seasonings, spices and sauces will be familiar to anyone who's ever spent time in China. Even if you're not interested in food, the hectic atmosphere (be on guard for motorcycles squeezing between shoppers) and exotic sights and smells create something of a surreal sensory experience.

While much of the market centres on cooking ingredients, the section north of Th Charoen Krung (equivalent to Soi 21, Th Charoen Krung) is known for selling incense, paper effigies and ceremonial sweets – the essential elements of a traditional Chinese funeral.

Wat Mangkon Kamalawat BUDDHIST TEMPLE
(วัดมังกรกมลาวาส; Map p88; cnr Th Charoen Krung & Th Mangkon; ⊙6am-6pm; ⛴Ratchawong Pier, Ⓜ Hua Lamphong exit 1 & taxi) FREE Clouds of incense and the sounds of chanting form the backdrop at this Chinese-style Mahayana Buddhist temple. Surrounding the temple are vendors selling food for the gods – steamed lotus-shaped dumplings and oranges – which are donated to the temple in exchange for merit. Dating back to 1871, it's the largest and most important religious structure in the area, and during the annual Vegetarian Festival (p110), religious and culinary activities are particularly active here.

Talat Noi AREA
(ตลาดน้อย; Map p92; off Th Charoen Krung; ⊙7am-7pm; ⛴Marine Department Pier) This microcosm of soi life is named after a small (nóy) market (dà·làht) that sets up between Soi 22 and Soi 20, off Th Charoen Krung. Wandering here you'll find streamlike soi turning in on themselves, weaving through noodle shops, grease-stained machine shops and people's living rooms.

Phahurat AREA
(พาหุรัด; Map p88; Th Chakkaraphet; ⊙9am-5pm; ⛴Saphan Phut/Memorial Bridge Pier, Pak Klong Taladd Pier) Heaps of South Asian traders set up shop in Bangkok's small but bustling Little India, where everything from Bollywood movies to bindis is sold by enthusiastic, small-time traders. It's a great area to just wander through, stopping for masala chai and a Punjabi sweet as you go.

The bulk of the action unfolds along unmarked Soi ATM, which runs alongside the large **India Emporium** (⊙10am-10pm) shopping centre.

Church of Santa Cruz CHURCH
(โบสถ์ซางตาครู้ส; Map p88; Soi Kuti Jiin; ⊙7am-noon Sat & Sun; ⛴river-crossing ferry from Atsadang Pier) Centuries before Sukhumvit became Bangkok's international district, the Portuguese claimed fa·ràng (Western) supremacy on a riverside plot of land given to them by King Taksin in appreciation for their support after the fall of Ayuthaya. Located on this concession, the Church of Santa Cruz dates to 1913.

◉ Riverside

The Riverside area is great for an aimless wander among old buildings. This stretch of Mae Nam Chao Phraya was formerly Bangkok's international zone, and today retains a particularly Chinese and Muslim feel. Most of the sights in this area can be seen in a morning; the BTS stop at Saphan Taksin is a good starting point.

★ Bangkokian Museum   MUSEUM

(พิพิธภัณฑ์ชาวบางกอก; Map p92; 273 Soi 43, Th Charoen Krung; admission by donation; ⊙10am-4pm Wed-Sun; ⑤Si Phraya/River City Pier) A collection of three antique structures built during the early 20th century, the Bangkokian Museum illustrates an often-overlooked period of the city's history, and functions as a peek into a Bangkok that, these days, is disappearing at a rapid pace.

The main building was built in 1937 as a home for the Surawadee family and, as the signs inform us, was finished by Chinese carpenters on time and for less than the budgeted 2400B (which would barely buy a door handle today). This building and the large wooden one to the right, which was added as a boarding house to help cover costs, are filled with the detritus of postwar family life and offer a fascinating window into the period. The third building, at the back of the block, was built in 1929 as a surgery for a British doctor, though he died soon after arriving in Thailand.

Number 1 Gallery   GALLERY

(Map p92; www.number1gallery.com; 19 Soi 21, Th Silom; ⊙10am-7pm Mon-Sat; ⑤Surasak exit 3) FREE This gallery has established itself by featuring the often attention-grabbing contemporary work of Thai artists such as Vasan Sitthiket, Sutee Kunavichayanont and Thaweesak Srithongdee.

Old Customs House   HISTORIC BUILDING

(กรมศุลกากร; Map p92; Soi 36, Th Charoen Krung; ⑤Oriental Pier) The country's former Customs House was once the gateway to Thailand, levying taxes on traders moving in and out of the kingdom. It was designed by an Italian architect and built in the 1890s; the front door opened onto its source of income (the river) and the grand facade was ceremoniously decorated in columns and transom windows.

Sathorn Unique Tower   NOTABLE BUILDING

(Map p92; Soi 51, Th Charoen Krung; ⑤Sathorn/Central Pier, ⑤Saphan Taksin) Construction began on Sathorn Unique, known colloquially as the Ghost Tower because locals believe the plot of land it occupies to be a former cemetery in 1990. In 1997, with an estimated 75% of the tower completed, the Asian crisis reached its peak, funds disappeared, and construction on the tower was simply halted, leaving it in its partially finished state ever since.

◎ Lumphini Park & Rama IV

At 58 hectares, Lumphini is central Bangkok's largest and most popular park. The easiest ways to reach the area are via the BTS stop at Sala Daeng or the MRT stops at Si Lom and Lumphini.

★ Lumphini Park   PARK

(สวนลุมพินี; Map p96; bounded by Th Sarasin, Rama IV, Th Witthayu/Wireless Rd & Th Ratchadamri; ⊙4.30am-9pm; ▣; Ⓜ Lumphini exit 3, Si Lom exit 1, ⑤Sala Daeng exit 3, Ratchadamri exit 2) Named after the Buddha's place of birth in Nepal, Lumphini Park is the best way to escape Bangkok without actually leaving town. Shady paths, a large artificial lake and swept lawns temporarily blot out the roaring traffic and hulking concrete towers.

There are paddleboats for lovers, playgrounds for the kids and enormous monitor lizards for the whole family. One of the best times to visit the park is before 7am, when the air is fresh (well, relatively so for Bangkok) and legions of Thai-Chinese are practising t'ai chi. The park reawakens with the evening's cooler temperatures – aerobics classes collectively sweat to a techno soundtrack. Late at night the borders of the park are frequented by streetwalking prostitutes, both male and female.

◎ Silom & Sathon

Th Silom, with its towering hotel and office buildings, is Bangkok's de facto financial district, while adjacent Th Sathon is home to many of the city's embassies. Incongruously, lower Th Silom functions as Bangkok's gaybourhood.

The BTS stop at Sala Daeng and the MRT stop at Si Lom put you at lower Th Silom, perfect jumping-off points for either Lumphini Park or the area's restaurants and sights.

Queen Saovabha Memorial Institute   ZOO

(สถานเสาวภา, Snake Farm; Map p98; cnr Rama IV & Th Henri Dunant; adult/child 200/50B; ⊙9.30am-3.30pm Mon-Fri, to 1pm Sat & Sun; ▣; Ⓜ Si Lom exit 1, ⑤Sala Daeng exit 3) Thailand's snake farms tend to gravitate towards carnivalesque rather than humanitarian, except

BANGKOK FOR KIDS

Kids are welcome almost anywhere and you'll rarely experience the sort of eye-rolling annoyance sometimes seen in the West.

Kid-Friendly Museums

The **Children's Discovery Museum** (พิพิธภัณฑ์เด็ก; Map p118; Th Kamphaengphet 4, Queen Sirikit Park; ⏲9am-5pm Tue-Fri, 10am-6pm Sat & Sun; 👪; Ⓜ Chatuchak Park exit 1, Ⓢ Mo Chit exit 1) FREE has interactive displays ranging in topic from construction to culture. Although not specifically targeted towards children, the **Museum of Siam** (p69) has lots of interactive exhibits that will appeal to kids. Siam Discovery has a branch of the famous **Madame Tussauds** (Map p102; www.madametussauds.com; 4th fl, Siam Discovery, cnr Rama I & Th Phayathai; adult/child 990/790B; ⏲10am-9pm; Ⓢ Siam exit 1) wax museum.

Outside of town, the open-air **Ancient City** (p161) re-creates Thailand's most famous monuments. They're linked by bicycle paths and were practically built for being climbed on.

Parks, Playgrounds & Zoos

Lumphini Park is a trusty ally in the cool hours of the morning and afternoon for kite flying, swan-boat rentals and fish feeding. Nearby, kids can view lethal snakes becoming reluctant altruists at the antivenin-producing **Queen Saovabha Memorial Institute**.

Dusit Zoo (สวนสัตว์ดุสิต/เขาดิน; Map p115; www.dusitzoo.org; Th Ratchawithi; adult/child 150/70B; ⏲8am-6pm; ⛴ Thewet Pier, Ⓢ Phaya Thai exit 3 & taxi) has shady grounds, plus a lake with paddle boats for hire and a children's playground.

For kid-specific play centres, consider **Fun-arium** (Map p106; ☎02 665 6555; www.funarium.co.th; 111/1 Soi 26, Th Sukhumvit; 110-330B; ⏲9am-6pm Mon-Thu, to 7pm Fri-Sun; 👪; Ⓢ Phrom Phong exit 1 & taxi), central Bangkok's largest, or the impressive **KidZania** (Map p102; ☎02 683 1888; www.bangkok.kidzania.com; 5th fl, Siam Paragon, 991/1 Rama I; adult 425-500B, child 425-1000B; ⏲10am-5pm Mon-Fri, 10.30am-8pm Sat & Sun; Ⓢ Siam exits 3 & 5). Alternatively, **Siam Park City** (Map p158; ☎02 919 7200; www.siamparkcity.com; 203 Th Suansiam; adult/child US$30/25; ⏲10am-6pm; Ⓜ Chatuchak Park exit 2 & taxi, Ⓢ Mo Chit exit 1 & taxi) and **Dream World** (Map p158; ☎02 577 8666; www.dreamworld.co.th; 62 Mu 1, Th Rangsit-Nakornnayok, Pathum Thani; from 1200B; ⏲10am-5pm Mon-Fri, to 7pm Sat & Sun; Ⓜ Chatuchak Park exit 2 & taxi, Ⓢ Mo Chit exit 1 & taxi) are vast amusement parks found north of the city.

Rainy-Day Fun

If you're visiting during the rainy season (approximately from June to October), you'll need a few indoor options in your back pocket.

MBK Center (p151) and **Siam Paragon** (Map p102; www.siamparagon.co.th; 991/1 Rama I; ⏲10am-10pm; Ⓢ Siam exits 3 & 5) both have bowling alleys to keep the older ones occupied. The latter also has an IMAX theatre and **Sea Life Ocean World** (Map p102; www.sealifebangkok.com; basement, Siam Paragon, 991/1 Rama I; adult/child from 490/350B; ⏲10am-9pm; Ⓢ Siam exits 3 & 5). For very hot days, **CentralWorld** (Map p102; www.centralworld.co.th; Th Ratchadamri; ⏲10am-10pm; Ⓢ Chit Lom exit 9 to Sky Walk, Siam exit 6 to Sky Walk) has an ice rink. Most malls have amusement centres with video games, small rides and playgrounds. **Gateway Ekamai** (Map p106; www.gatewayekamai.com; 982/22 Th Sukhumvit; ⏲10am-10pm; ❄; Ⓢ Ekkamai exit 4) has an arcade and a branch of **Stanley MiniVenture** (Map p106; www.stanleyminiventure.com; 2nd fl, Gateway Ekamai, 982/22 Th Sukhumvit; adult/child 500/400B; ⏲10am-8pm), a model-train-like miniature town.

Web Resources

Bambi (www.bambiweb.org) A useful resource for parents in Bangkok.

Bangkok.com (www.bangkok.com/kids) Lists a dizzying array of things to do with kids.

Thorn Tree Kids To Go forum (www.lonelyplanet.com/thorntree/forums/kids-to-go) Questions and answers from other travellers with children on Lonely Planet's community forum.

BANGKOK & AROUND

Chinatown & Phahurat

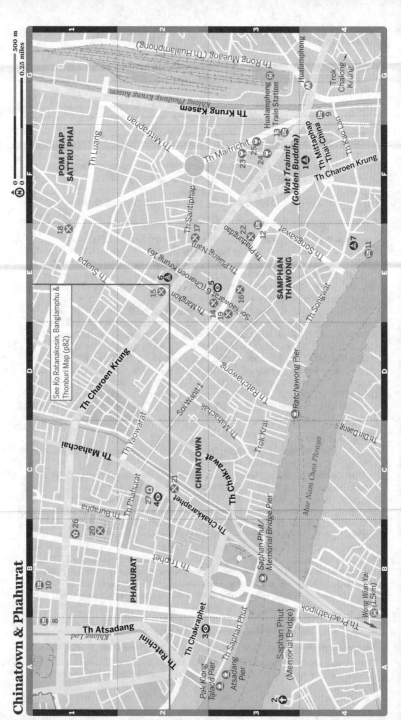

at the Queen Saovabha Memorial Institute. Founded in 1923, the snake farm gathers antivenom by milking the snakes' venom, injecting it into horses, and harvesting and purifying the antivenom they produce. The antivenoms are then used to treat human victims of snake bites. Regular milkings (11am Monday to Friday) and snake-handling performances (2.30pm Monday to Friday and 11am Saturday and Sunday) are held at the outdoor amphitheatre.

MR Kukrit Pramoj House HISTORIC BUILDING
(บ้านหม่อมราชวงศ์คึกฤทธิ์ปราโมช; Map p98; ☑ 02 286 8185; Soi 7, Th Naradhiwas Rajanagarindra/ Chong Nonsi; adult/child 50/20B; ⊙ 10am-4pm; ⑤ Chong Nonsi exit 2) Author and statesman Mom Ratchawong Kukrit Pramoj (1911–95) once resided in this charming complex now open to the public. Surrounded by a manicured garden, the five teak buildings introduce visitors to traditional Thai architecture, arts and the former resident, who served as prime minister of Thailand in 1974 and '75, wrote more than 150 books and spent 20 years decorating the house.

Sri Mariamman Temple HINDU TEMPLE
(วัดพระศรีมหาอุมาเทวี/วัดแขก, Wat Phra Si Maha Umathewi; Map p98; cnr Th Silom & Th Pan; ⊙ 6am-8pm Mon-Thu, to 9pm Fri, to 8.30pm Sat & Sun; ⑤ Surasak exit 3) ᖴᖇᗴᗴ Arrestingly flamboyant, the Sri Mariamman Hindu temple is a wild collision of colours, shapes and deities. It was built in the 1860s by Tamil immigrants and features a 6m facade of intertwined, full-colour Hindu deities. While most of the people working in the temple hail from the Indian subcontinent, you will likely see plenty of Thai and Chinese devotees praying here as well. This is because the Hindu gods figure just as prominently in their individualistic approach to religion.

The official Thai name of the temple is Wat Phra Si Maha Umathewi, but it's often referred to as Wat Khaek – *kàak* being a common expression for people of Indian descent. The literal translation is 'guest', an obvious euphemism for any group of people not particularly wanted as permanent residents; hence most Indian Thais aren't fond of the term.

◎ **Siam Square & Pratunam**

Multistorey malls, outdoor shopping precincts and never-ending markets leave no

doubt that this is Bangkok's commercial district. If you're serious about shopping, set aside the better part of a day to burn your baht here. Try to arrive around 11am, when the crowds are minimal. Likewise, try to avoid Sundays when half of Bangkok seems to flock to the area's air-conditioned malls.

Siam Sq is most easily accessed via the BTS (Skytrain).

TROUBLE & TRAGEDY AT THE ERAWAN SHRINE

One of the more clichéd tourist images of Bangkok is that of elaborately dressed classical Thai dancers performing at the Hindu shrine in front of the Grand Hyatt Erawan hotel. Although not a fabrication, as with many things in Thailand, there is great deal hidden behind the serene facade.

After 50 years of largely benign existence, the Erawan Shrine became a point of focus when just after midnight on 21 March 2006, 27-year-old Thanakorn Pakdeepol, a man with a history of mental illness and depression, destroyed the highly revered, gilded plaster image of Brahma with a hammer. Thanakorn was almost immediately attacked and beaten to death by two Thai rubbish collectors who were in the vicinity. Although the government ordered a swift restoration of the statue, the incident became a galvanising omen for the protest movement opposing then Prime Minister Thaksin Shinawatra, which was in full swing at the time. At a rally the following day, protest leader Sondhi Limthongkul suggested that the prime minister had masterminded the image's destruction in order to replace the deity with a 'dark force'. Rumours spreading through the capital claimed that Thaksin had hired Cambodian shamans to put spells on Thanakorn so that he would perform the unspeakable deed. Thaksin, when asked to comment on Sondhi's accusations, simply replied, 'That's insane'. A new statue, which incorporated pieces of the previous one, was installed a month later. Thaksin was ousted in a military coup in 2006 and has remained in exile since 2008.

In 2010, the Ratchaprasong Intersection, where the shrine is located, became the main gathering point for anti-government Red Shirt protesters, who occupied the area for several months. Images of the predominantly lower-class rural protesters camped out in front of the Ratchaprasong's luxury storefronts became a media staple. When the Red Shirts were forcibly cleared out by the military on 19 May, five people were killed and fleeing protesters set fire to the nearby CentralWorld mall.

CentralWorld was renovated in 2012, but a year later Ratchaprasong Intersection yet again became a major protest site, this time occupied by opponents of Thaksin's sister, then Prime Minister Yingluck Shinawatra. The protests were known colloquially as Shutdown Bangkok (complete with protest merchandise featuring the computer shutdown button icon), and this time media images of the largely middle- and upper-class urban protesters in front of chic malls drew comparisons rather than contrasts. On 20 May 2014, the Thai Army declared martial law and took over the government in a coup d'état, leading the protesters to disperse.

Yet undoubtedly the most significant event in the shrine's history came on the evening of 17 August 2015, when a bomb planted in the Erawan Shrine compound exploded, killing 20 and injuring more than 120 people, an apparent act of terrorism that Prime Minister Prayut Chan-o-cha described as the 'worst incident that has ever happened' in Thailand. More than two years on, two suspects have been arrested and are undergoing trial, although their motives remain unclear and a verdict has yet to be reached.

Why so much turmoil associated with a shrine that most believe to have positive powers? Some feel that the Erawan Shrine sits on land that carries long-standing and potentially conflicting supernatural powers. Others feel that the area is currently spiritually overcrowded, as other nearby structures also have their own, potentially competing, Hindu shrines. What's certain is that in Thailand, politics, faith, fortune and tragedy are often linked.

★ **Jim Thompson House** HISTORIC BUILDING
(เรือนไทยจิมทอมป์สัน; Map p102; www.jimthompsonhouse.com; 6 Soi Kasem San 2; adult/student 150/100B; ⊙9am-6pm, compulsory tours every 20min; 🚤klorng boat to Sapan Hua Chang Pier, Ⓢ National Stadium exit 1) This jungly compound is the former home of the eponymous American silk entrepreneur and art collector. Born in Delaware in 1906, Thompson briefly served in the Office of Strategic Services (the forerunner of the CIA) in Thailand during WWII. He settled in Bangkok after the war, when his neighbours' handmade silk caught his eye and piqued his business sense; he sent samples to fashion houses in

Milan, London and Paris, gradually building a steady worldwide clientele.

In addition to textiles, Thompson also collected parts of various derelict Thai homes and had them reassembled in their current location in 1959. Some of the homes were brought from the old royal capital of Ayuthaya; others were pulled down and floated across the *klorng* (canal; also spelt *khlong*) from Baan Khrua, including the first building you enter on the tour. One striking departure from tradition is the way each wall has its exterior side facing the house's interior, thus exposing the wall's bracing system. His small but splendid Asian art collection and his personal belongings are also on display in the main house.

Thompson's story doesn't end with his informal reign as Bangkok's best-adapted foreigner, however. While out for an afternoon walk in the Cameron Highlands of western Malaysia in 1967, Thompson mysteriously disappeared. That same year his sister was murdered in the USA, fuelling various conspiracy theories. Was it communist spies? Business rivals? Or a man-eating tiger? Although the mystery has never been solved, evidence revealed by American journalist Joshua Kurlantzick in his profile of Thompson, *The Ideal Man,* suggests that the vocal anti-American stance Thompson took later in his life may have made him a potential target of suppression by the CIA.

Beware well-dressed touts in soi near the Thompson house who will tell you it is closed and try to haul you off on a dodgy buying spree.

Erawan Shrine   MONUMENT
(ศาลพระพรหม; Map p102; cnr Th Ratchadamri & Th Phloen Chit; ⊙6am-11pm; ⑤Chit Lom exit 8) FREE The Erawan Shrine was originally built in 1956 as something of a last-ditch effort to end a string of misfortunes that occurred during the construction of a hotel, at that time known as the Erawan Hotel.

After several incidents ranging from injured construction workers to the sinking of a ship carrying marble for the hotel, a Brahman priest was consulted. Since the hotel was to be named after the elephant escort of Indra in Hindu mythology, the priest determined that Erawan required a passenger, and suggested it be Lord Brahma. A statue was built and, lo and behold, the misfortunes miraculously ended.

THE SINKING CITY

With much of the city around 1.5m above sea level, low-lying Bangkok has been sinking at a rate of 2cm per year. Some scientists estimate that the city may face submersion within approximately 15 years due to rising sea levels.

Although the original Erawan Hotel was demolished in 1987, the shrine still exists, and today remains an important place of pilgrimage for Thais, particularly those in need of some material assistance. Those making a wish at the statue should ideally come between 7am and 8am, or 7pm and 8pm, and should offer a specific list of items that includes candles, incense, sugar cane or bananas, all of which are almost exclusively given in multiples of seven. Particularly popular are teak elephants, with money from the sale of these items donated to a charity run by the current hotel, the Grand Hyatt Erawan. And as the tourist brochures depict, it is also possible to charter a classical Thai dance, often done as a way of giving thanks if a wish is granted.

A bomb exploded near the shrine in August 2015, killing 20 and slightly damaging the shrine. It was repaired and reopened just two days later.

Lingam Shrine   MONUMENT
(ศาลเจ้าแม่ทับทิม; Map p102; Swissôtel Nai Lert Park, Th Witthayu/Wireless Rd; ⊙24hr; ⑤klorng boat to Wireless Pier, ⑤Phloen Chit exit 1) FREE Every village-neighbourhood has a local shrine, either a sacred banyan tree tied up with coloured scarves or a spirit house. But it isn't every day you see a phallus garden like this lingam shrine, tucked back behind the staff quarters of the Swissôtel Nai Lert Park.

When facing the entrance of the hotel, follow the small concrete pathway to the right, which winds down into the building beside the car park. The shrine is at the end of the building next to the *klorng.*

Clusters of carved stone and wooden shafts surround a spirit house and shrine built by millionaire businessman Nai Loet to honour Jao Mae Thap Thim, a female deity thought to reside in the old banyan tree on the site. Someone who made an offering shortly after the shrine was built had a baby,

Riverside

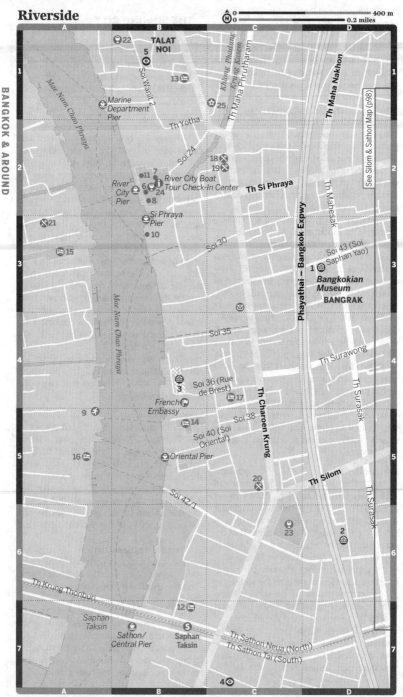

Riverside

and the shrine has received a steady stream of worshippers – mostly young women seeking fertility – ever since.

⊙ Sukhumvit

Japanese enclaves, burger restaurants, Middle Eastern nightlife zones, tacky 'sexpat' haunts: it's all here along Th Sukhumvit, Bangkok's unofficial international district. Where temples and suburban rice fields used to be, today you'll also find shopping centres, nightlife and a host of other amenities that cater to middle-class Thais and resident foreigners.

The BTS (Skytrain) runs along the length of Th Sukhumvit, making it a snap to reach just about anywhere around here.

★Siam Society & Kamthieng House   MUSEUM
(สยามสมาคม & บ้านคำเที่ยง; Map p106; www.siam-society.org; 131 Soi 21/Asoke, Th Sukhumvit; adult/child 100B/free; ⊙9am-5pm Tue-Sat; Ⓜ Sukhumvit exit 1, Ⓢ Asok exit 3 or 6) Kamthieng House transports visitors to a northern Thai village complete with informative displays of daily rituals, folk beliefs and everyday household chores, all within the setting of a traditional wooden house. This museum is operated by and shares space with the Siam Society, publisher of the renowned *Journal*

of the Siam Society and a valiant preserver of traditional Thai culture.

Khlong Toey Market   MARKET
(ตลาดคลองเตย; Map p106; cnr Th Ratchadaphisek & Rama IV; ⊙5-10am; Ⓜ Khlong Toei exit 1) This wholesale market, one of the city's largest, is the origin of many of the meals you'll eat during your stay in Bangkok. Get there early, and bring a camera; although some corners of the market can't exactly be described as photogenic, the cheery fishmongers and stacks of durians make great happy snaps. By 10am, most vendors have already packed up and left.

⊙ Ratchathewi

Ratchathewi has a lot less to offer than neighbouring districts – unless you want to check out Bangkok's suburban/workaday side. The attractions in this area can be covered in a couple of hours, and most are within walking distance of the BTS stop at Victory Monument.

★Suan Pakkad Palace Museum   MUSEUM
(วังสวนผักกาด; Map p112; Th Si Ayuthaya; 100B; ⊙9am-4pm; Ⓢ Phaya Thai exit 4) An overlooked treasure, Suan Pakkad is a collection of eight traditional wooden Thai houses that was once the residence of Princess Chumbon of Nakhon Sawan and before that a

WORTH A TRIP

SILK-WEAVING IN BAAN KHRUA

The canalside neighbourhood of **Baan Khrua** (บ้านครัว; Map p102; ⚓klorng boat to Sapan Hua Chang Pier, ⑤Ratchathewi exit 1, National Stadium exit 1) dates back to the turbulent years at the end of the 18th century, when Cham Muslims from Cambodia and Vietnam fought on the side of the new Thai king and were rewarded with this plot of land east of the new capital. The immigrants brought their silk-weaving traditions with them, and the community grew when the residents built Khlong Saen Saeb to better connect them to the river.

The 1950s and '60s were boom years for Baan Khrua after Jim Thompson hired the weavers and began exporting their silks across the globe. The last 50 years, however, haven't been so great. Silk production was moved elsewhere following Thompson's disappearance, and the community spent 15 years successfully fighting to stop a freeway being built right through it. Through all this, many Muslims moved out of the area; today it is estimated that only about 30% of the population is Muslim, the rest primarily immigrants from northeast Thailand.

Today's Baan Khrua consists of old, tightly packed homes threaded by tiny paths barely wide enough for two people to pass. There's a mosque, and two family-run outfits, **Phamai Baan Krua** (ผ้าไหมบ้านครัว; Map p102; www.phamaibaankrua.com; Soi 9, Soi Phaya Nak; ⏰8.30am-5pm) and **Aood Bankrua Thai Silk** (อูช็อดบ้านครัวไหมไทย; Map p102; ☎02 215 9864; Soi 9, Soi Phaya Nak; ⏰9am-8pm), continue to be involved in every step of silk cloth production, from the dyeing of threads to weaving the cloth by hand on old wood looms. Of the two, Phamai Baan Krua claims to be the original. Run by English- and German-speaking Niphon Manuthas, the company continues to produce the type of high-quality handwoven silk that originally attracted Jim Thompson, at much cheaper prices than a certain more famous store across the klorng.

Baan Khrua is an easy stop after visiting Jim Thompson House (p90); simply cross the bridge over the canal at the end of Soi Kasem San 3. Alternatively, from the BTS stop at Ratchathewi, enter Soi Phaya Nak, take the third left, the street that leads to **Da-Ru-Fa-Lah Mosque** (มัสยิดดารุลฟะละฮ์; Map p102; ⏰daylight hours; ⑤Ratchathewi exit 1), following it to the canal; turn right and look for the signs.

lettuce farm (in Thai, Suan Pakkad means Lettuce Farm). Within the stilt buildings are displays of art, antiques and furnishings, and the landscaped grounds are a peaceful oasis complete with ducks, swans and a semi-enclosed garden.

The diminutive **Lacquer Pavilion**, at the back of the complex, dates from the Ayuthaya period and features gold-leaf *Jataka* and *Ramayana* murals, as well as scenes from daily Ayuthaya life. The building originally sat in a monastery compound on Mae Nam Chao Phraya, just south of Ayuthaya. Larger residential structures at the front of the complex contain displays of Khmerstyle Hindu and Buddhist art, Ban Chiang ceramics and a very interesting collection of historic **Buddhas**, including a beautiful late U Thong–style image.

Baiyoke Tower II   NOTABLE BUILDING
(ตึกใบหยก ๒; Map p112; 22 Th Ratchaprarop; 300B; ⏰9am-11pm; ⚓klorng boat to Pratunam Pier) Cheesiness and altitude run in equal

parts at Baiyoke Tower II, Bangkok's tallest building (to be usurped by a 'super tower' slated to be finished in 2021). Ascend through a corridor decked with aliens and planets (and the *Star Wars* theme song) to emerge at the 84th-floor, open-air revolving platform that looks over a city whose concrete sprawl can appear never-ending.

👁 Thewet & Dusit

Thewet, particularly the area near Th Samsen, has the hectic, buzzy feel often associated with Bangkok. The adjacent river is the only respite from the action, and it also functions as a good point from which to approach the area, as most sights and restaurants are a short walk from the river ferry pier.

Dusit, on the other hand, is possibly Bangkok's most orderly district, home to the kind of tree-lined avenues and regal monuments you'd expect to find in Paris. Dusit's sights are relatively far apart and are best approached by taxi or túk-túk.

★**Dusit Palace Park**   MUSEUM, HISTORIC SITE
(วังสวนดุสิต; Map p115; bounded by Th Ratchawithi, Th U Thong Nai & Th Nakhon Ratchasima; admission for all Dusit Palace Park sights adult/child 100/20B, with Grand Palace ticket free; ⊙ 9.30am-4pm Tue-Sun; ⛴ Thewet Pier, ⑤ Phaya Thai exit 2 & taxi) Following his first European tour in 1897, Rama V (King Chulalongkorn; r 1868–1910) returned with visions of European castles and set about transforming these styles into a uniquely Thai expression, today's Dusit Palace Park. These days, the current king has yet another home and this complex now holds a house museum and other cultural collections.

When we stopped by, Dusit Palace Park was temporarily closed for renovation and is expected to be open again in 2018; enquire at the ticket office of the Grand Palace (p68).

Originally constructed on Ko Si Chang in 1868 and moved to the present site in 1910, **Vimanmek Teak Mansion** (พระที่นั่ง วิมานเมฆ) contains 81 rooms, halls and anterooms, and is said to be the world's largest golden-teak building, allegedly built without the use of a single nail. The mansion was the first permanent building on the Dusit Palace grounds, and served as Rama V's residence in the early 20th century. The interior of the mansion contains various personal effects of the king and a treasure trove of early Ratanakosin-era art objects and antiques. Compulsory tours (in English) leave every 30 minutes between 9.45am and 3.15pm, and last about an hour.

The nearby **Ancient Cloth Museum** (พิพิธภัณฑ์ผ้าไทยโบราณ) presents a beautiful collection of traditional silks and cottons that make up the royal cloth collection.

Originally built as a throne hall for Rama V in 1904, the smaller **Abhisek Dusit Throne Hall** (พระที่นั่งอภิเศกดุสิต) is typical of the finer architecture of the era. Victorian-influenced gingerbread architecture and Moorish porticoes blend to create a striking and distinctly Thai exterior. The hall houses an excellent display of regional handiwork crafted by members of the Promotion of

---

GALLERY-HOPPING IN BANGKOK

Although Bangkok often seems to cater to the inner philistine in all of us, the city is home to a diverse but low-key art scene. Our picks of the city's better galleries:

Bangkok CityCity Gallery (Map p96; ☑ 083 087 2725; www.bangkokcitycity.com; 13/3 Soi 1, Th Sathon Tai/South; ⊙ 1-7pm Wed-Sun; Ⓜ Lumphini exit 2) FREE New attention-grabbing art space.

100 Tonson Gallery (Map p102; www.100tonsongallery.com; 100 Th Ton Son; ⊙ 11am-7pm Thu-Sun; ⑤ Chit Lom exit 4) FREE Low-key hub for contemporary art.

Kathmandu Photo Gallery (Map p98; www.kathmanduphotobkk.com; 87 Th Pan; ⊙ 11am-7pm Tue-Sun; ⑤ Surasak exit 3) FREE The city's only dedicated photography gallery.

Subhashok the Arts Centre (SAC; Map p106; www.sac.gallery; 160/3 Soi 33, Th Sukhumvit; ⊙ 10am-5.30pm Sat, noon-6pm Sun; ⑤ Phrom Phong exit 6 & taxi) One of the city's most ambitious galleries.

H Gallery (Map p98; www.hgallerybkk.com; 201 Soi 12, Th Sathon Neua/North; ⊙ 10am-6pm Wed-Sat, by appointment Tue; ⑤ Chong Nonsi exit 1) FREE Classy gallery/jumping-off point for domestic artists.

Jim Thompson Art Center (Map p102; www.jimthompsonhouse.com; Jim Thompson House, Soi Kasem San 2, Rama I; ⊙ 9am-8pm; ⛴ klorng boat to Sapan Hua Chang Pier, ⑤ National Stadium exit 1) FREE Revolving, predominantly Southeast Asia–themed, art exhibitions.

Museum of Contemporary Art (MOCA; Map p76; www.mocabangkok.com; 3 Th Viphawadee Rangsit; 250B; ⊙ 10am-5pm Tue-Fri, 11am-6pm Sat & Sun; Ⓜ Chatuchak Park exit 2 and taxi, ⑤ Mo Chit exit 1 & taxi) Don't expect New York City's MOMA, but this is the best place in Thailand to familiarise oneself with the genre.

Numthong Gallery (Map p118; www.gallerynumthong.com; 72/3 Soi Ari 5; ⊙ 11am-6pm Mon-Sat; ⑤ Ari exit 3) This long-standing gallery has a new home in the hip Ari hood, with changing exhibitions devoted to Thai artists.

Lumphini Park & Th Phra Ram IV

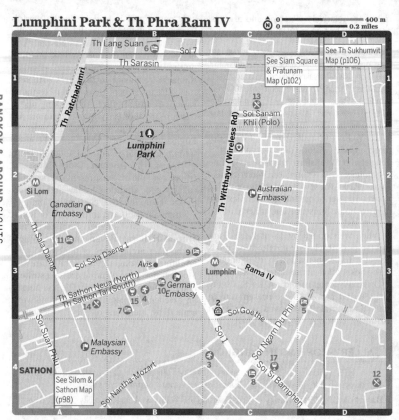

Supplementary Occupations & Related Techniques (Support) foundation, a charity organisation sponsored by Queen Sirikit.

Near the Th U Thong Nai entrance, two large stables that once housed three white elephants – animals whose auspicious albinism automatically make them crown property – now form the **Royal Thai Elephant Museum** (พิพิธภัณฑ์ช้างต้น). One of the structures contains artefacts and photos outlining the importance of elephants in Thai history and explaining their various rankings according to physical characteristics. The second stable holds a life-sized model of the previous king's first royal white elephant. Draped in royal vestments, the statue is more or less treated as a shrine by the visiting Thai public.

Because this is royal property, visitors should wear shirts with sleeves and long pants (no capri pants) or long skirts.

Wat Benchamabophit   BUDDHIST TEMPLE

(วัดเบญจมบพิตร/วัดเบญจฯ; Map p115; cnr Th Si Ayuthaya & Rama V; 20B; ⊙8am-6pm; 🚤Thewet Pier, 🚇Phaya Thai exit 3 & taxi) You might recognise this temple from the back of the 5B coin. Made of white marble imported from Italy, the distinctive *bòht* of Wat Ben, as it's colloquially known, was built in the late 19th century under Rama V. The base of the central Buddha image, a copy of the revered Phra Phuttha Chinnarat in Phitsanulok, northern Thailand, contains his ashes.

The structure is a unique example of modern Thai temple architecture, as is the interior design, which melds Thai features with European influences: the red carpets, the gold-on-white motifs painted repetitively on the walls, the walls painted like stained-glass windows and the royal blue wall behind the central Buddha image are strongly reminiscent of a European palace. It's not all that surprising when you consider

Lumphini Park & Th Phra Ram IV

how enamoured Rama V was with Europe – just walk across the street to Dusit Palace Park for further evidence.

The courtyard behind the *bòht* has 53 Buddha images (33 originals and 20 copies) representing every *mudra* (gesture) and style from Thai history, making this the ideal place to compare Buddhist iconography. If religious imagery isn't your thing, this temple still offers a pleasant stroll beside landscaped canals filled with blooming lotus and Chinese-style footbridges.

◉ Northern Bangkok

There are several reasons to visit greater Bangkok, but most people come for markets like Chatuchak Weekend Market (p151). For the day markets you'll want to arrive as early as possible.

Most of the markets are located within easy access of the northern extents of the BTS (Skytrain) and/or MRT (Metro). Reaching other destinations in Bangkok's burbs often involves a taxi ride from BTS or MRT terminal stations and a bit of luck. A smartphone with a mapping function is an invaluable tool for helping you arrive at the right place and on time.

Chang Chui   MARKET
(ช่างชุ่ย; Map p76; www.en.changchuibangkok.com; 460/8 Th Sirindhorn; 20-40B; ⊙11am-11pm Tue-Sun) An abandoned aeroplane, craft-beer bars, a hipster barber shop, performance spaces, a skull-shaped florist, an insect-themed restaurant... This tough-to-pin-down marketplace is one of the most eclectic and exciting openings Bangkok has seen in years. Spanning 18 different structures (all

of which are made from discarded objects), a handful of the outlets are open during the day, but the best time to go is during weekend evenings, when the place has the vibe of an artsy, more sophisticated Chatuchak Weekend Market.

Nonthaburi Market   MARKET
(ตลาดนนทบุรี; Map p76; Tha Nam Nonthaburi, Nonthaburi; ⊙5-9am; 🚢Nonthaburi Pier) Exotic fruits, towers of dried chillies, smoky grills and the city's few remaining rickshaws form a very un-Bangkok backdrop at this, one of the most expansive and atmospheric produce markets in the area. Come early though, as most vendors are gone by 9am.

To get to the market, take the Chao Phraya Express Boat to Nonthaburi Pier, the northernmost stop for most lines. The market is a two-minute walk east along the main road from the pier.

🏃 Activities

Massage & Spas

According to the teachings of traditional Thai healing, the use of herbs and massage should be part of a regular health-and-beauty regimen, not just an excuse for pampering. In other words, you need no excuse to get a massage in Bangkok.

The most common variety is traditional Thai massage (*nôo·at păan boh·rahn*). Although it sounds relaxing, at times it can seem more closely related to Thai boxing than to shiatsu. Techniques involve pulling, stretching, bending and manipulating pressure points. If done well, a traditional massage will leave you sore but revitalised. Full-body massages usually include cam-

Silom & Sathon

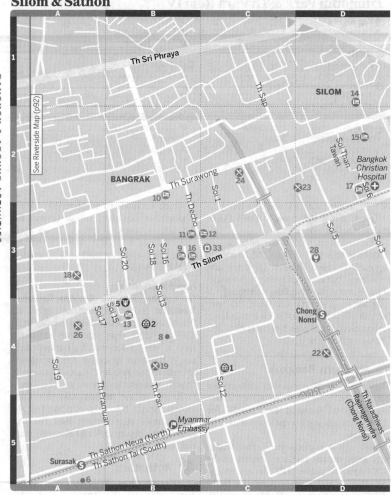

phor-scented balms or herbal compresses. Note that 'oil massage' is sometimes taken as code for 'sexy massage'.

Within the enormous spa category there are many options: there's plenty of pampering going around, but some spas now focus more on the medical than the sensory, while plush resort-style spas offer a menu of appealing beauty treatments.

Oriental Spa
SPA
(Map p92; ☎ 02 659 9000; www.mandarinorien tal.com; Mandarin Oriental, 48 Soi 40/Oriental, Th Charoen Krung; massage & spa packages from

2900B; ☺ 9am-10pm; ☐ Oriental Pier or hotel shuttle boat from Sathon/Central Pier) Regarded as among the premier spas in the world, the Oriental Spa sets the standard for Asian-style spa treatment. Depending on where you flew in from, the jet-lag massage might be a good option, but all treatments require advance booking.

Health Land
MASSAGE
(Map p106; ☎ 02 261 1110; www.healthlandspa.com; 55/5 Soi 21/Asoke, Th Sukhumvit; Thai massage 2hr 550B; ☺ 9am-11pm; Ⓜ Sukhumvit exit 1, Ⓢ Asok exit 5) A winning formula of affordable pric-

temple sightseeing it's hard to think of a better way to cool down and chill out.

Yunomori Onsen & Spa ONSEN

(Map p106; www.yunomorionsen.com; 120/5 Soi 26, Th Sukhumvit; onsen 450B, massage 1hr 350B; ⏱10.30am-11pm; ⑤Phrom Phong exit 3 & taxi) Bangkok as a whole can often seem like a sauna, but for a more refined approach to sweating, consider this *onsen* (Japanese-style hot-spring bath). The thermal water is trucked up from southern Thailand and employed in the gender-divided, open pools. In addition to sauna, steam bath and soak pools, massage and other spa treatments are also available.

Spa 1930 SPA

(Map p102; ☎02 254 8606; www.spa1930.com; 42 Th Ton Son; Thai massage from 1000B, spa packages from 3500B; ⏱9.30am-9.30pm; ⑤Chit Lom exit 4) Discreet and sophisticated, Spa 1930 rescues relaxers from the contrived spa ambience of New Age music and ingredients you'd rather see at a dinner party. The menu is simple (face, body care and body massage) and the scrubs and massage oils are logical players.

Babylon SPA

(Map p96; www.babylonbangkok.com; 34 Soi Nantha-Mozart; sauna 230-350B; ⏱10.30am-10.30pm; Ⓜ Lumphini exit 2) Bangkok's most famous gay sauna remains extremely popular with visitors, many from neighbouring Singapore and Hong Kong. B&B-style accommodation is also available.

Asia Herb Association MASSAGE

(Map p106; ☎02 392 3631; www.asiaherbassociation.com; 58/19-25 Soi 55/Thong Lor, Th Sukhumvit; Thai massage 1hr 500B, with herbal compress 1½hr 1100B; ⏱9am-midnight; ⑤Thong Lo exit 3) With multiple branches along Th Sukhumvit, this Japanese-owned chain specialises in massage using *prà·kóp* (traditional Thai herbal compresses) filled with 18 different herbs.

es, expert treatments and pleasant facilities has created a small empire of Health Land centres across Bangkok.

Massage Pavilions MASSAGE

(Map p82; Wat Pho, Th Sanam Chai; Thai massage per hour 420B; ⏱9am-4pm; 🚢Tien Pier) These two air-conditioned *săh·lah* (pavilions; often spelt *Sala*) near the eastern entrance to the temple grounds are run by the school (p105) affiliated with Wat Pho, which is the country's primary training centre for Thai traditional massage. The menu is short but the quality is guaranteed, and after a day of

Ruen-Nuad Massage Studio MASSAGE

(Map p98; ☎02 632 2662; 42 Th Convent; massage per hour 350B; ⏱10am-9pm; Ⓜ Si Lom exit 2, ⑤Sala Daeng exit 2) Set in a refurbished wooden house, this charming place successfully avoids both the tackiness and New Agedness that characterise most Bangkok Thai-massage joints. Prices are relatable, too.

Silom & Sathon

Baan Dalah MASSAGE
(Map p106; ☑ 02 653 3358; www.baandalahmind bodyspa.com; 2 Soi 8, Th Sukhumvit; Thai massage per hour 350B; ⊙10am-midnight; ⓈNana exit 4) A small, conveniently located spa with services ranging from foot massage to full-body Thai massage.

Coran MASSAGE
(Map p106; ☑ 02 726 9978; www.coranbangkok. com; 94-96/1 Soi Ekamai 10, Soi 63/Ekamai, Th Sukhumvit; Thai massage per hour from 600B; ⊙11am-10pm; ⓈEkkamai exit 4 & taxi) A classy, low-key spa housed in a Thai villa. Aroma and Thai-style massage are also available.

Thann Sanctuary SPA
(Map p102; ☑ 02 658 6557; www.thannsanctuary spa.info; 2nd fl, CentralWorld, Th Ratchadamri; Thai massage from 2000B, spa treatments from 2800B; ⊙10am-9pm; ⓈChit Lom exit 9 to Sky Walk, Siam exit 6 to Sky Walk) This local brand of herbal-based cosmetics also has a series of mall-based spas – perfect for post-shopping therapy.

Banyan Tree Spa SPA
(Map p96; ☑ 02 679 1052; www.banyantreespa. com; 21st fl, Banyan Tree Hotel, 21/100 Th Sathon Tai/South; massage/spa packages from 2800/6000B; ⊙9am-10pm; ⓂLumphini exit 2) A combination of highly trained staff and

high-tech facilities have provided this hotel spa with a glowing reputation. Come for pampering regimens based on Thai tradtions, or unique signature treatments.

Meditation & Yoga
Although most of the time Bangkok seems like the most un-Buddhist place on earth, there are a few places where foreigners can practise Theravada Buddhist meditation. Some, like Center Meditation Wat Mahadhatu allow drop-ins on a daily basis, while others, such as House of Dhamma, require advance notice.

Meanwhile, yoga studios – and enormous accompanying billboards of smiling gurus – have popped up faster than mushrooms at a Full Moon Party. Expect to pay about 500B for a one-off class.

Center Meditation Wat Mahadhatu MEDITATION
(Map p82; ☑ 02 222 6011, 02 223 3813; Section 5, Wat Mahathat, Th Maha Rat; donations accepted; ⊙classes 7am, 1pm & 6pm; 🚢Chang Pier, Maharaj Pier, Phra Chan Tai Pier) Located within Wat Mahathat, this small centre offers informal daily meditation classes. Taught by English-speaking Prasuputh Chainikom (Kosalo), classes last three hours. Longer periods of study, which include accommodation and

food, can be arranged, but students are expected to follow a strict regimen of conduct.

Yoga Elements Studio YOGA

(Map p106; ☑02 255 9552; www.yogaelements. com; 7th fl, 185 Dhammalert Bldg, Th Sukhumvit; classes from 600B; ⓢChit Lom exit 5) Run by American Adrian Cox, who trained at Om in New York and who teaches primarily vinyasa and ashtanga, this is the most respected yoga studio in town. The high-rise location helps you rise above it all, too.

House of Dhamma MEDITATION

(Map p118; ☑02 511 0439; www.houseofdhamma. com; 26/9 Soi 15, Th Lat Phrao; fee by donation; ⓜLat Phrao exit 3) Helen Jandamit has opened her suburban Bangkok home to meditation retreats and two-day classes in *vipassana* (insight meditation). Check the website to see what workshops are on offer and be sure to reserve a spot at least a week in advance.

Absolute Yoga YOGA

(Map p102; ☑02 252 4400; www.absoluteyoga bangkok.com; 4th fl, Amarin Plaza, Th Phloen Chit; classes from 750B; ⓢChit Lom exit 6) This is the largest of Bangkok's yoga studios, teaching Bikram hot yoga plus a host of other styles.

Pilates Studio HEALTH & FITNESS

(Map p102; ☑02 650 7797; www.pilates.co.th; 888/58-59 Mahatun Plaza, Th Phloen Chit; classes from 550B; ⊙8am-7pm; ⓢPhloen Chit exit 2) The first choice for those in Bangkok looking for Pilates instruction and training.

Thai Boxing (Moo·ay tai)

Training in *moo·ay tai* (Thai boxing; also spelt *muay Thai*) for foreigners has increased in popularity in the last decade and many camps all over the country are tailoring their programs for English-speaking fighters of both sexes. Food and accommodation can often be provided for an extra charge. The website Muay Thai Camps (www.muaythaicampsthailand.com) contains detailed information on Thailand's various training centres.

Jaroenthong Muay Thai Gym MARTIAL ARTS

(Map p82; ☑02 629 2313; www.jaroenthongmuay thaikhaosan.com; Th Phra Athit; lessons from 600B; ⊙drop-in hours 10-11.30am & 2-9pm; 🚤Phra Athit/Banglamphu Pier) With branches around the country, this lauded gym has opened up an outlet a short walk from Th Khao San. Beginners can drop in and train in

air-conditioned comfort, or the more experienced can opt for longer training regimens.

MuayThai Institute MARTIAL ARTS

(Map p158; ☑082 985 1115; www.muaythai-insti tute.net; Rangsit Stadium, 336/932 Th Prachatipat, Pathum Thani; weeklong course from 6900B; ⓜChatuchak Park exit 2 & taxi, ⓢMo Chit exit 3 & taxi) Associated with the respected World Muay Thai Council, the institute offers a fundamental course in Thai boxing (consisting of three levels of expertise), as well as courses for instructors, referees and judges.

Eight Limbs MARTIAL ARTS

(Map p106; ☑090 987 9590; www.facebook. com/8limbsluaythaigym; Soi 24, Th Sukhumvit; lessons from 580B; ⊙10am-8.30pm Tue-Sun; ⓢPhrom Phong exit 2) This small gym in downtown Bangkok offers 1½-hour walk-in lessons in *moo·ay tai* for all skill levels. See the Facebook page for times.

Fairtex Muay Thai MARTIAL ARTS

(Map p158; ☑086 776 0488; www.fairtexbangplee. com; 99/5 Mu 3, Soi Buthamanuson, Th Thaeparak, Samut Prakan; tuition & accommodation per day from 1450B; ⓢChong Nonsi exit 2 & taxi) A popular, long-running Thai boxing camp south of Bangkok.

🍽 Courses

Cooking

Having consumed everything Bangkok has to offer is one thing, but imagine the points you'll rack up if you can make the same dishes for your friends back at home. A visit to a Thai cooking school has become a must-do on many Bangkok itineraries and for some visitors it's a highlight of their trip.

Courses range in price and value, but a typical half-day course should include at least a basic introduction to Thai ingredients and flavours and a hands-on chance to both prepare and cook several dishes. Nearly all lessons include a set of printed recipes and end with a communal lunch consisting of your handiwork.

★ Amita Thai Cooking Class COOKING

(Map p76; ☑02 466 8966; www.amitathaicooking. com; 162/17 Soi 14, Th Wutthakat, Thonburi; classes 3000B; ⊙9.30am-1pm Thu-Tue; 🚤klorng boat from Maharaj Pier) One of Bangkok's most charming cooking schools is held in this canalside house in Thonburi. Taught by the delightfully enthusiastic Piyawadi 'Tam' Jantrupon, a course here includes a romp

Siam Square & Pratunam

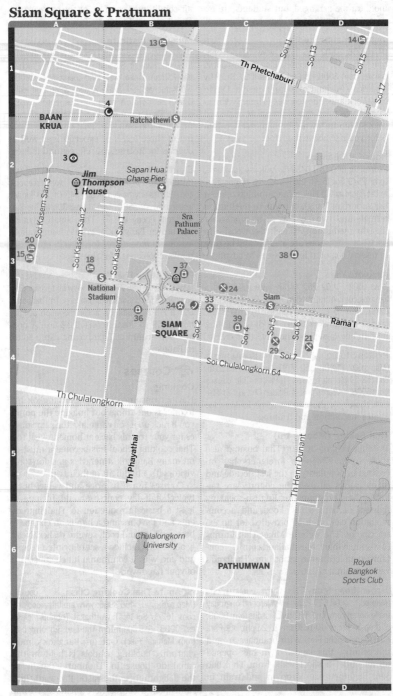

BAAN KRUA

Ratchathewi

Th Phetchaburi

Soi 11
Soi 13
Soi 15
Soi 17

13

14

4

3

Jim Thompson House 1

Sapan Hua Chang Pier

Soi Kasem San 3
Soi Kasem San 2
Soi Kasem San 1

Sra Pathum Palace

20
15

18

38

National Stadium

7 37

24

Siam

Rama I

36

34 33

SIAM SQUARE

Soi 2

39

Soi 4
Soi 5
Soi 6

21

29 Soi 7

Soi Chulalongkorn 64

Th Chulalongkorn

Th Phayathai

Th Henri Dunant

Chulalongkorn University

PATHUMWAN

Royal Bangkok Sports Club

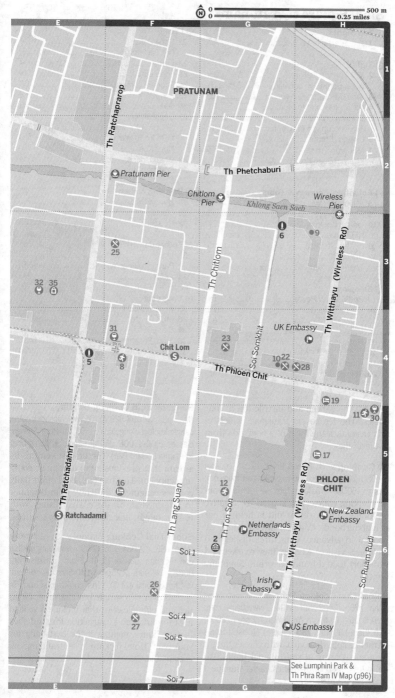

N 0
0
500 m
0.25 miles

PRATUNAM

Th Ratchaprarop

Pratunam Pier

Chitlom Pier

Th Phetchaburi

Wireless Pier

Khlong Saen Saeb

6

9

25

32 35

Th Chitlom

Th Witthayu (Wireless Rd)

31

Chit Lom

5 8

23

Soi Somkhit

UK Embassy

10 22
28

Th Phloen Chit

19

11 30

17

Th Ratchadamri

16

Th Lang Suan

12

Th Ton Son

PHLOEN CHIT

Ratchadamri

Netherlands
Embassy

New Zealand
Embassy

2

Soi 1

Irish
Embassy

Soi Ruam Rudi

26

Soi 4

27

Soi 5

US Embassy

Soi 7

See Lumphini Park &
Th Phra Ram IV Map (p96)

Siam Square & Pratunam

through the garden and instruction in four dishes. The fee covers transport, which in this case takes the form of a boat ride from Maharaj Pier.

★ **Cooking with Poo & Friends**   COOKING
(☑080 434 8686; www.cookingwithpoo.com; classes 1500B; ☺8.30am-1pm; ⊕) This popular cooking course was started by a native of Khlong Toey's slums and is held in her neighbourhood. Courses, which must be booked in advance, span three dishes and include a visit to Khlong Toey Market and transport to and from Emporium Shopping Centre.

Baipai Thai Cooking School   COOKING
(Map p76; ☑02 561 1404; www.baipai.com; 8/91 Soi 54, Th Ngam Wong Wan; classes 2200B; ☺9.30am-1.30pm & 1.30-5.30pm) Housed in an attractive suburban villa, with classes taught by a small army of staff, Baipai offers two daily lessons of four dishes each. Transport there is provided.

Bangkok Bold Cooking Studio   COOKING
(Map p82; ☑098 829 4310; www.facebook.com/bangkokboldcookingstudio; 503 Th Phra Sumen; classes 2500-4500B; ☺11am-2pm; ⊛klorng boat to Phanfa Leelard Pier) The newest venture by a team that previously ran a popular cooking school on Th Khao San, Bold offers daily courses ranging in difficulty from beginner to intermediate in three Thai dishes, with lessons taught in a chic shophouse setting.

Silom Thai Cooking School   COOKING
(Map p98; ☑084 726 5669; www.bangkokthaicooking.com; 68 Soi 13, Th Silom; classes from 900B; ☺9am-12.20pm, 1.40-5pm & 6-9pm; ⑤Chong Nonsi exit 3) This cooking school is spread over two simple but charming facilities and offers lessons that include a visit to a local market and instruction for six dishes in four hours, making it the best bang for your baht. Hotel pick-up in central Bangkok is available.

Issaya Cooking Studio COOKING

(Map p102; ☑ 02 160 5636; www.issayastudio.
com; Eatthai, level LG, Central Embassy, 1031 Th
Phloen Chit; classes 2000-3000B; ☺ 11am-2pm,
3-6pm & 6-8pm; ⓢ Phloen Chit exit 5) Started
up by home-grown celebrity chef Pongta-
wat 'Ian' Chalermkittichai, morning lessons here include instruction in four dishes
from his linked restaurant, Issaya Siamese
Club (p131), while afternoon and evening
lessons focus on desserts and mixology;
check the calendar to see what's coming up.
Specialised and private lessons can also be
arranged.

Blue Elephant Thai
Cooking School COOKING

(Map p98; ☑ 02 673 9353; www.blueelephantcook
ingschool.com; 233 Th Sathon Tai/South; classes
from 3295B; ☺ 8.45am-1pm & 1.30-4.30pm Mon-
Sat; ⓢ Surasak exit 2) Bangkok's most chichi
Thai cooking school offers two lessons daily. The morning class squeezes in a visit to
a local market, while the afternoon session
includes a detailed introduction to Thai
ingredients.

Oriental Hotel Thai
Cooking School COOKING

(Map p92; ☑ 02 659 9000; www.mandarinorien
tal.com; Mandarin Oriental, 48 Soi 40/Oriental, Th
Charoen Krung; classes from 3735B; ☺ 9am-1pm
Wed-Mon, to 2pm Sat & Sun; ⓢ Oriental Pier or
hotel shuttle boat from Sathon/Central Pier) Located across the river in an antique wooden
house, the Oriental's cooking classes span
a daily revolving menu of four Thai dishes, and in some cases, excursions to a local
market. It's worth noting that the courses
here are less 'hands on' compared to others
in Bangkok.

Thai Massage

Chetawan Traditional
Massage School HEALTH & WELLBEING

(Map p82; ☑ 02 622 3551; www.watpomassage.
com; 392/32-33 Soi Phen Phat; lessons from
2500B; Thai massage per hour 420B; ☺ lessons
9am-4pm, massage 9am-8pm; ⓢ Tien Pier) Associated with the nearby temple (p69) of the
same name, this institute offers basic and
advanced courses in traditional massage;
basic courses offer 30 hours spread over five
days and cover either general massage or
foot massage. Thai massage is also available
for non-students.

CANALSIDE CULTURE

Sort of a gallery, kind of a coffeeshop,
more a cultural centre... It's tough to
catagorise the **Artist's House** (บ้าน
ศิลปิน; Map p76; www.facebook.com/
baansilapin; Khlong Bang Luang; ☺ 9am-
6pm; ⓢ Wongwian Yai exit 2), an old
wooden house on Khlong Bang Luang
in Thonburi. There's food available on
weekends, as well as a free traditional
Thai puppet show scheduled for 2pm,
but the best excuse to come is simply to
soak up the old-world canalside vibe.

Artist's House is most easily accessible via Soi 3, Th Charansanitwong; cross
the canal at the bridge by the 7-Eleven,
turn left and it's about 100m down.

The school is outside the temple compound in a restored Bangkok shophouse in
Soi Phen Phat.

The school's advanced level course spans
165 hours, requires the basic course as a
prerequisite, and covers therapeutic and
healing massage. Other advanced courses
include oil massage and aromatherapy, and
infant and child massage.

Phussapa Thai
Massage School HEALTH & WELLBEING

(Map p106; ☑ 02 204 2922; www.facebook.com/
phussapa; 25/8 Soi 26, Th Sukhumvit; tuition from
6000B, Thai massage per hour 250B; ☺ lessons
9am-4pm, massage 11am-11pm; ⓢ Phrom Phong
exit 4) Run by a long-time Japanese resident
of Bangkok, the basic course in Thai massage here spans 30 hours over five days;
there are shorter courses in foot massage
and self massage.

☞ Tours

Bangkok is a big, intimidating place and
some visitors might appreciate a bit of
hand-holding in the form of a guided tour.
But even if you already know your way
around, themed tours led by a private guide
or bicycle tours are great ways to see another side of the city.

Walking & Themed Tours

Although the pollution and heat are significant obstacles, Bangkok is a fascinating
city to explore on foot – particularly in the

Th Sukhumvit

N

0   0.5 miles
0   1 km

Th Watthana Tham

Rama IX

Th Phetchaburi

Phra Ram 9 M

Soi 21 (Asoke)

Makkasan (Bangkok City Air Terminal)

Tourism Authority of Thailand

Chinese Visa Application Service Center

Phetchaburi M

Asoke M

Soi 21 (Asoke)

Nana Chard Pier

Asoke-Phetchaburi Pier

Nana Nua Pier

Bumrungrad International Hospital

SUKHUMVIT

Soi 1

Soi 3 (Nana)

Soi 5

Soi 4

Soi 2

Phloen Chit S

Nana S

Soi 6

Soi 7

Soi 11/1

Soi 11

Soi 13

Soi 15

Soi 19

Soi 23

Siam Society & Kamthieng House

Sukhumvit M

Soi 31 S

Soi 39 S

Soi Phrom Si 2

Soi Ekamai 21

Italthai Pier

Wat Mai Chonglom Pier

Klong Saen Saeb

Baan Don Mosque Pier

Soi Thong Lor Pier

Kamphaeng Phet 7

Th Phetchaburi

RCA (Royal City Ave)

Budget

Th Phetchaburi

Th Sukhumvit

15

26

47
49

53
54

4

41

46

29

11

48

25

31
44

60

13

43

32

1

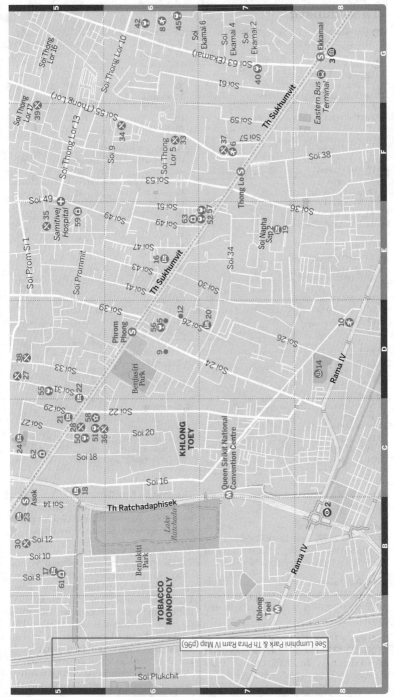

See Lumphini Park & Th Phra Ram IV Map (p96)

Th Sukhumvit

company of an expert guide on a themed walking tour.

Bangkok Food Tours   WALKING
(☏ 095 943 9222; www.bangkokfoodtours.com; tours from 1150B) Half-day culinary tours of Bangkok's older neighbourhoods.

Tour With Tong   TOURS
(☏ 081 835 0240; tours from 1000B) Established outfit whose guides conduct tours in and around Bangkok.

Chili Paste Tours   TOURS
(☏ 085 143 6779, 094 552 2361; www.foodtours bangkok.com; tours from 2000B) Culinary tours of Bangkok's older neighbourhoods.

Thai Private Tour Guide   TOURS
(☏ 082 799 1099; www.thaitourguide.com; tours from 2000B) Tours of Bangkok led by guides who garner heaps of positive feedback.

River & Canal Cruises

The cheapest and most obvious way to commute between riverside attractions is on the commuter boats run by Chao Phraya Express Boat (p156). The terminus for most northbound boats is Nonthaburi Pier, while for most southbound boats it's Sathon Pier (also called Central Pier), near the Saphan Taksin BTS station (although some boats run as far south as Wat Ratchasingkhon).

For a more personal view, you might consider chartering a long-tail boat along the city's canals (p80). Another option is one of the dinner cruises (p134) that ply Mae Nam Chao Phraya at night.

A little faster than the days of sailing ships, river cruises from Bangkok north to the ruins of the former royal capital of Ayuthaya take in all the romance of the river. Normally only one leg of the journey between Bangkok and Ayuthaya is aboard a boat, while the return or departing trip is by bus.

Asian Oasis BOATING

(Map p102; ☑088 809 7047, 081 496 4516; www. asian-oasis.com; 7th fl, Nai Lert Tower, 2/4 Th Witthayu/Wireless Rd; 2-day trip 7850-16,100B; ☉9am-5pm Mon-Fri; ⑤ Phloen Chit exit 1) Cruise Mae Nam Chao Phraya aboard a fleet of restored rice barges with old-world charm and modern conveniences. Trips include either an upstream or downstream journey to/from Ayuthaya with bus transfer in the opposite direction. Costs vary according to season and direction.

Pandan Tour BOATING

(☑02 689 1232, 087 109 8873; www.thaicanaltour. com; tours from 2395B) This outfit conducts a variety of mostly full-day boat tours of Thonburi's canals.

Thanatharee BOATING

(Map p76; ☑02 440 1979; www.thanatharee.com; 21/8 Th Krung Thonburi; 2-day trip 11,900-16,200B; ⑤ Wongwian Yai exit 1) Overnight boat tours to Ayuthaya on a restored wooden barge with six cabins.

Bicycle Tours

You might be wondering who would want to get on a bike in the notorious traffic jams and sauna-like conditions of Bangkok's streets. But these trips allow discovery of a whole side of the city that's virtually off limits to four-wheeled transport. Routes include unusual circuits around Chinatown and Ko Ratanakosin, but the pick are journeys across the river to Thonburi and, in particular, to the Phrapradaeng Peninsula (p123), an exquisite expanse of mangrove, banana and coconut plantations just a stone's throw from the frantic city centre.

Several companies run regular, well-received tours starting at about 1000B for a half-day.

Grasshopper Adventures CYCLING

(Map p82; ☑02 280 0832; www.grasshopper adventures.com; 57 Th Ratchadamnoen Klang; half-/full-day tours from 1350/2400B; ☉8.30am-6.30pm; ☒ klorng boat to Phanfa Leelard Pier) This lauded outfit runs a variety of unique bicycle tours in and around Bangkok, including a night tour and a tour of the city's historic zone.

ABC Amazing Bangkok Cyclists CYCLING

(Map p106; ☑081 812 9641; www.realasia.net; 10/5-7 Soi Aree, Soi 26, Th Sukhumvit; tours from 1300B; ☉daily tours at 8am, 10am, 1pm & 6pm; ⚑; ⑤ Phrom Phong exit 4) A long-running operation offering morning, afternoon and all-day bike tours of Bangkok and its suburbs.

Co van Kessel Bangkok Tours CYCLING

(Map p92; ☑02 639 7351; www.covankessel.com; ground fl, River City, 23 Th Yotha; tours from 950B; ☉6am-7pm; ☒ River City Pier) This originally Dutch-run outfit offers a variety of tours in Chinatown, Thonburi and Bangkok's green zones, many of which also involve boat rides. Tours depart from the company's office in the River City shopping centre.

Bangkok Bike Rides CYCLING

(☑02 381 7490; www.bangkokbikerides.com; tours from 1250B; ⚑) A division of tour company Spice Roads, this outfit offers a variety of cycling tours, both urban and rural, including a night tour of Bangkok. Pick-up is available.

Velo Thailand CYCLING

(Map p82; ☑02 628 8628, 089 201 7782; www. velothailand.com; 29 Soi 4, Th Samsen; tours from 1000B; ☉10am-7pm; ☒ Phra Athit/Banglamphu Pier) Velo is a small and personal bike-tour outfit based out of Banglamphu. Day and night tours to Thonburi and further afield are on offer.

★★ Festivals & Events

Many Thai festivals follow the lunar calendar (a complex system based on astrology) and therefore change annually relative to the Gregorian calendar. Contact local tourist offices for exact festival dates.

January to March

Chinese New Year CULTURAL

(☉Jan or Feb) Thai-Chinese celebrate the Lunar New Year with a week of house-cleaning, lion dances and fireworks. Most festivities centre on Chinatown. Dates vary.

Kite-Flying Season CULTURAL

(☺Mar) During the windy season, colourful kites battle it out over the skies of Sanam Luang and Lumphini Park.

April & May

Songkran CULTURAL

(☺mid-Apr) The celebration of the Thai New Year has morphed into a water war with high-powered water guns and water balloons being launched at suspecting and unsuspecting participants. The most intense water battles take place on Th Silom and Th Khao San.

Royal Ploughing Ceremony CULTURAL

(☺May) His Majesty the King commences rice-planting season with a ceremony at Sanam Luang. Dates vary.

August

Queen Sirikit's Birthday/Mother's Day CULTURAL

(☺12 Aug) The former queen's birthday is recognised as Mother's Day throughout the country. In Bangkok, festivities centre on Th Ratchadamnoen Klang and the Grand Palace.

September & October

Vegetarian Festival FOOD & DRINK

(☺Sep or Oct) This 10-day Chinese-Buddhist festival wheels out yellow-bannered streetside vendors serving meatless meals. The greatest concentration of vendors is found in Chinatown (p130). Dates vary.

King Chulalongkorn Day CULTURAL

(☺23 Oct) Rama V is honoured on the anniversary of his death at the Royal Plaza in Dusit. Crowds of devotees come to make merit with incense and flower garlands.

November & December

Loi Krathong CULTURAL

(☺early Nov) A beautiful festival where, on the night of the full moon, small lotus-shaped boats made of banana leaf and containing a lit candle are set adrift on Mae Nam Chao Phraya.

Wat Saket Fair FAIR

(☺Nov) The grandest of Bangkok's temple fairs *(ngahn wát)* is held at Wat Saket and the Golden Mount around Loi Krathong. The temple grounds turn into a colourful, noisy fair selling flowers, incense, bells, saffron cloth and tonnes of Thai food.

King Bhumibol's Birthday/Father's Day CULTURAL

(☺5 Dec) Locals celebrate the previous monarch's birthday with lots of parades and fireworks.

🛏 Sleeping

If your idea of the typical Bangkok hotel was influenced by *The Hangover Part II*, you'll be relieved to learn that the city is home to a variety of modern hostels, guesthouses and hotels. To further improve matters, much of Bangkok's accommodation offers excellent value and competition is so intense that fat discounts are almost always available. And the city is home to so many hotels that, apart from some of the smaller, boutique places, booking ahead isn't generally required.

🛏 Ko Ratanakosin & Thonburi

If you've opted to rest your head in Ko Ratanakosin or Thonburi, you've got the bulk of Bangkok's most famous sights at your door. Riverside views and a glut of charming midrange places along Th Maha Rat are even more reasons to stay here; a relative lack of drinking and dining, and the schlep to the newer parts of Bangkok aren't.

Arom D HOSTEL $$

(Map p82; ☎02 622 1055; www.aromdhostel.com; 336 Th Maha Rat; r incl breakfast 1200-1600B; ❄@🛜; 🚢Tien Pier) The rooms here are united by a cutesy design theme and a host of inviting communal areas including a rooftop deck, computers and a ground-floor cafe. They don't have much space and could use a bit of TLC, but they do have style.

Royal Tha Tien Village HOTEL $$

(Map p82; ☎095 151 5545; www.facebook.com/theroyalthatienvillage; 392/29 Soi Phen Phat; r 1200B; ❄@🛜; 🚢Tien Pier) These 12 rooms spread over two converted shophouses are relatively unassuming, but TV, fridge, aircon, lots of space and shiny wood floors, not to mention a cosy homestay atmosphere, edge this place into the recommendable category. It's popular, so be sure to book ahead.

★ Inn a Day HOTEL $$$

(Map p82; ☎02 221 0577; www.innaday.com; 57-61 Th Maha Rat; incl breakfast r 3500-4200B, ste 7500-9000B; ❄@🛜; 🚢Tien Pier) Inn a Day wows with its hyper-cool retro/industrial theme (the hotel is in a former sugar factory) and its location (it towers over the

UNDERSTANDING KHAO SAN ROAD

Th Khao San, better known as Khao San Rd, is genuinely unlike anywhere else on earth. It's an international clearing house of people either entering the liberated state of travelling in Southeast Asia or returning to the coddling bonds of 'real' life, all coming together in a neon-lit melting pot in Banglamphu. Its uniqueness is probably best illustrated by a question: apart from airports, where else could you share space with the citizens of dozens of countries at the same time, people ranging from first-time backpackers scoffing banana pancakes to 75-year-old grandparents ordering G&Ts, and everyone in between, including hippies, hipsters, nerds, glamazons, package tourists, global nomads, people on a week's holiday and those taking a gap year, people of every colour and creed looking at you looking at them looking at everyone else?

Th Khao San (*kâw sǎhn*, meaning 'uncooked rice') is perhaps the most high-profile bastard child of the age of independent travel. Of course, it hasn't always been this way. For its first two centuries or so it was just another unremarkable road in old Bangkok. To see what it was like back in the day, you can stop into the **Khaosan Museum** (ข้าวสาร มิวเซียม; Map p82; 1st fl, 201 Th Khao San; ⊙9am-9pm; 🚤 Phra Athit/Banglamphu Pier) **FREE**. The first guesthouses appeared in 1982, and as more backpackers arrived through the '80s the old wooden homes were converted one by one into low-rent dosshouses. By the time Alex Garland's novel *The Beach* was published in 1997, with its opening scenes set in the seedier side of Khao San, staying here had become a rite of passage for backpackers coming to Southeast Asia.

The publicity from Garland's book and the movie that followed pushed Khao San into the mainstream, romanticising the seedy, and stereotyping the backpackers it attracted as unwashed and counterculturalist. It also brought the long-simmering debate about the relative merits of Th Khao San to the top of backpacker conversations across the region. Was it cool to stay on KSR? Was it uncool? Was this 'real travel' or just an international anywhere surviving on the few baht Western backpackers spent before they headed home to start their high-earning careers? Was it really Thailand at all?

Perhaps one of Garland's characters summed it up most memorably when he said: 'You know, Richard, one of these days I'm going to find one of those Lonely Planet writers and I'm going to ask him, what's so fucking lonely about the Khao San Road?'

Today more than ever the answer would have to be: not that much. With the help of all that publicity, Khao San continued to evolve, with bedbug-infested guesthouses replaced by boutique hotels, and downmarket TV bars showing pirated movies transformed into hip design bars peopled by flashpackers in designer threads. But the most interesting change has been in the way Thais see Khao San.

Once written off as home to cheap, dirty *fa·ràng kêe ngók* (stingy foreigners), Banglamphu has become just about the coolest district in Bangkok. Attracted in part by the long-derided independent traveller and their modern ideas, the city's own counterculture kids have moved in and brought with them a tasty selection of small bars, organic cafes and shops. Indeed, Bangkok's indie crowd has proved to be the Thai spice this melting pot always lacked.

Not that Khao San has moved completely away from its backpacker roots. The strip still anticipates every traveller need: meals to soothe homesickness, cafes and bars for swapping travel tales about getting to the Cambodian border, tailors, travel agents, teeth whitening, secondhand books, hair braiding and, of course, the perennial Akha women trying to harass everyone they see into buying wooden frogs. No, it's not very lonely at all…

river and Wat Arun). The 11 rooms aren't huge, but they include unique touches such as clear neon shower stalls, while the top-floor suites have two levels and huge clawfoot tubs.

⭐**Arun Residence** HOTEL **$$$**
(Map p82; ☎02 221 9158; www.arunresidence. com; 36-38 Soi Pratu Nokyung; incl breakfast r 3500-4200B, ste/villas 5800/12,000B; ❀@🛜; 🚤Tien Pier) Although strategically located on the river directly across from Wat Arun,

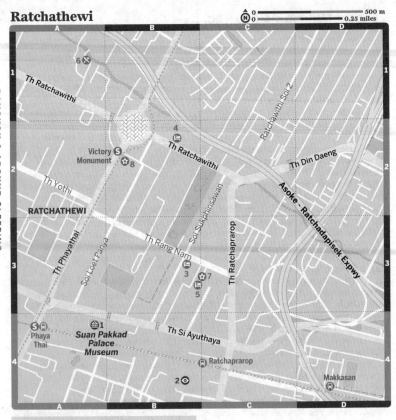

this multilevel wooden house boasts much more than just great views. The seven rooms here manage to feel both homey and stylish (the best are the top-floor, balcony-equipped suites). There are also inviting communal areas, including a library, rooftop bar and restaurant. Reservations essential.

Chakrabongse Villas HOTEL $$$
(Map p82; ☎ 02 622 1900; www.chakrabongse villas.com; 396/1 Th Maha Rat; incl breakfast r 5000B, ste 10,000-25,000B; ❋@🛜🏊; 🚤Tien Pier) This almost fairy-tale-like compound incorporates three sumptuous but cramped rooms and four larger suites and villas, some with great river views, all surrounding a still-functioning royal palace dating back to 1908. There's a pool, jungle-like gardens and an elevated deck for romantic riverside dining. No walk-ins.

🛏 Banglamphu & Around

Banglamphu still holds the bulk of Bangkok's budget places, although nowadays it's also home to nearly the entire spectrum of accommodation in Bangkok. Lots of eating, drinking and shopping options are other clever reasons to stay in Banglamphu, although it can feel somewhat isolated from the rest of Bangkok.

Suneta Hostel Khaosan
HOSTEL $

(Map p82; 02 629 0150; www.sunetahostel.com; 209-211 Th Kraisi; incl breakfast dm 470-570B, r 1180B; ❄@🖥; ☗Phra Athit/Banglamphu Pier) A pleasant, low-key atmosphere, a unique, retro-themed design (some of the dorm rooms resemble sleeping-car carriages), a location just off the main drag and friendly service are what make Suneta stand out.

Vivit Hostel
HOSTEL $

(Map p82; 02 224 5888; www.vivithostel.com; 510 Th Tanao; dm/r incl breakfast 475/965B; ❄🖥; ☗klorng boat to Phanfa Leelard Pier) Flower-patterned curtains, framed portraits of flowers and grandfather clocks provide this hostel with an overwhelmingly mature feel, despite it having opened in 2017. Nonetheless, the dorms represent excellent – if slightly bland – value.

Fortville Guesthouse
HOTEL $

(Map p82; 02 282 3932; www.fortvilleguesthouse.com; 9 Th Phra Sumen; r 820-1190B; ❄@🖥; ☗Phra Athit/Banglamphu Pier) With an exterior that combines elements of a modern church and/or castle, and an interior that relies on mirrors and industrial themes, the design concept of this hotel is tough to pin down. The rooms themselves are stylishly minimalist, and the more expensive ones include perks such as a fridge and balcony.

Khaosan Immjai
HOSTEL $

(Map p82; 02 629 3088; www.khaosanimmjai.com; 240 Soi 1, Th Samsen; dm incl breakfast 300-350B; ❄@🖥; ☗Phra Athit/Banglamphu Pier) There's nothing flashy or particularly exceptional about this hostel. But a homely feel and positive feedback edge it into the recommendable column. Dorms, which range from four to 14 beds, are clean, done out in pastel tones and have ample natural light. There's access to lots of convenient amenities (washing machines, computers etc), although none of these are free.

★Lamphu Treehouse
HOTEL $$

(Map p82; 02 282 0991; www.lamphutreehotel.com; 155 Wanchat Bridge, off Th Prachathipatai; incl breakfast r 1650-2500B, ste 3500-4500B; ❄@🖥❄; ☗klorng boat to Phanfa Leelard Pier) Despite the name, this attractive midranger has its feet firmly on land, and as such represents brilliant value. The wood-panelled rooms are attractive, inviting and well maintained, and the rooftop sun lounge, pool, internet cafe, restaurant and quiet canalside location ensure that you may never feel the need to leave. An annexe a few blocks away increases the odds of snagging an elusive reservation.

Baan Dinso
HOSTEL $$

(Map p82; 02 621 2808; www.baandinso.com; 113 Trok Sin; r incl breakfast 900-2500B; ❄@🖥; ☗klorng boat to Phanfa Leelard Pier) This antique wooden villa may not represent the best value in Bangkok, but for accommodation with a nostalgic feel and palpable sense of place, it's almost impossible to beat. Of the 10 small yet spotless rooms, only five have en suite bathrooms, while all have access to functional and inviting communal areas.

Baan Noppawong
HOTEL $$

(Map p82; 02 224 1047; www.facebook.com/baannoppawong; 112-114 Soi Damnoen Klang Tai; incl breakfast r 2500-3400B, ste 4400-5100B; ❄🖥; ☗klorng boat to Phanfa Leelard Pier) If your nana ran a hotel in Bangkok, it might resemble the seven rooms in this fastidiously tidy antique house. Rooms don't have much space, but are light-filled, comfortable and homely, and attractively decorated with antique furnishings. A secluded location augments the homestay vibe.

Sourire
HOTEL $$

(Map p82; 02 280 2180; www.sourirebangkok.com; Soi Chao Phraya Si Phiphat; r incl breakfast 1500-3500B; ❄@🖥; ☗klorng boat to Phanfa Leelard Pier) More home than hotel, the 38 rooms here exude a calming, matronly vibe. Soft lighting, comfortable and sturdy wood furniture, and the friendly, aged owners complete the package. To reach the hotel, follow Soi Chao Phraya Si Phiphat to the end and knock on the tall brown wooden door immediately on your left.

Nanda Heritage
HOTEL $$

(Map p82; 02 282 2900; www.nandaheritage.com; 632 Th Wisut Kasat; incl breakfast r 2500-4000B, ste 6000B; ❄🖥; ☗klorng boat to Phanfa Leelard Pier) Taking cues from the teak home that used to reside here and the wooden buildings that still surround it, is this new,

WHERE TO STAY IN BANGKOK

NEIGHBOURHOOD	FOR	AGAINST
Ko Ratanakosin & Thonburi	Bangkok's most famous sights at your door; river views; (relatively) fresh air; old-school Bangkok feel.	Difficult to reach; few budget options; touts.
Banglamphu	Close to main sights; proximity to classic Bangkok hood; numerous good-value budget beds; melting-pot feel; virtually interminable dining options; one of the city's best nightlife areas.	Getting to and from the area can be troublesome; Th Khao San can be noisy; budget places can have low standards; relentless touts.
Chinatown & Phaturat	Some interesting budget and midrange options; off the beaten track; easy access to worthwhile sights and some of the city's best food; close to Bangkok's main train station.	Noisy; polluted; hectic.
Riverside, Lumphini, Silom & Sathan	Some of the city's best upscale accommodation; river boats and river views; superconvenient access to BTS and MRT (Metro); lots of dining and nightlife options; gay-friendly.	Can be noisy and polluted; budget options can be pretty dire; hyperurban feel away from the river.
Siam Square, Pratunam & Ratchathewi	Wide spread of accommodation alternatives; megaconvenient access to shopping; steps away from BTS (Skytrain).	Touts; unpristine environment; relative lack of dining and entertainment options in immediate area; lacks character.
Sukhumvit	Some of the city's most sophisticated hotels; lots of midrange options; easy access to BTS and MRT; international dining; easy access to some of the city's best bars; home to several reputable spas and massage parlours.	Annoying street vendors and sexpat vibe; noisy; hypertouristy.
Thewet & Dusit	Good budget options; riverside village feel; fresh air; close to a handful of visit-worthy sights.	Few midrange and upscale options; not very convenient access to rest of Bangkok; relatively few dining and drinking options; comatose at night.
Northern Bangkok	Less hectic setting; good value; convenient airport access.	Transport can be inconvenient; lack of drinking and entertainment options.

design-forward hotel. Rooms are well-equipped, and come decked out in subtle, earthy colours, with spacious en suite bathrooms. A clever choice for the sophisticated but still-want-to-be-near-Th-Khao-San crowd.

The Warehouse　　　　　HOTEL $$
(Map p82; ☏ 02 622 2935; www.thewarehouse bangkok.com; 120 Th Bunsiri; r incl breakfast 2280-2580B; ❄ @ ❋; ❂ klorng boat to Phanfa Leelard

Pier) Wooden pallets as furniture, yellow-and-black wall art, and exposed fittings and other industrial elements contribute to the factory theme here. Against all odds, the Warehouse pulls it off, and what you get are 36 rooms that are fun, functional and relatively spacious, if not stupendous value.

Hotel Dé Moc　　　　　HOTEL $$
(Map p82; ☏ 02 282 2831; www.hoteldemoc.com; 78 Th Prachathipatai; r incl breakfast 2000-4000B;

Thewet & Dusit

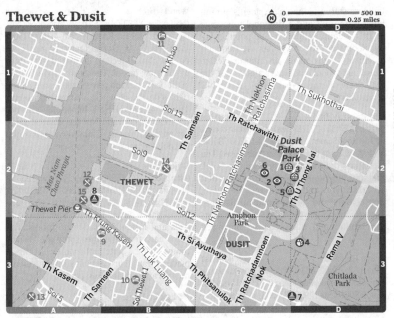

Thewet & Dusit

[✱] @ ⌾ ≋ ; ⬙ klorng boat to Phanfa Leelard Pier) With high ceilings and generous windows, the rooms at this 1960s-era hotel feel spacious, although the furnishings, like the exterior, are still stuck in the previous century. The grounds include an inviting and retro-feeling pool and cafe; complimentary

transport to Th Khao San and free use of bikes are thoughtful perks.

Baan Dinso @ Ratchadamnoen   HOTEL $$

(Map p82; ☑ 086 815 3300; www.baandinso.com; 78/3 Th Ratchadamnoen Klang; r incl breakfast 650-2520B; [✱] ⌾ ; ⬙ klorng boat to Phanfa Leelard Pier) Overlooking what is arguably the most famous intersection in Bangkok, the 27 rooms here run the spectrum from modern but tiny singles with shared bathrooms to the more spacious Grand rooms, most of which offer fleeting views of the Democracy Monument.

Villa Phra Sumen   HOTEL $$

(Map p82; ☑ 080 085 0085; www.villaphrasumen. com; 457 Th Phra Sumen; r incl breakfast 2500-3700B; [✱] @ ⌾ ; ⬙ klorng boat to Phanfa Leelard Pier) Surrounding a garden and edging the canal, Villa Phra Sumen boasts a secluded, secret feel. Gain access to the compound and inside you'll find 24 somewhat tight (and likewise overpriced) rooms, all of which come equipped with balconies and contemporary amenities, and are looked after by service-minded staff.

Villa Cha-Cha   HOTEL $$

(Map p82; ☑ 02 280 1025; www.villachacha.com; 36 Th Tani; r 2000-5500B; [✱] ⌾ ≋ ; ⬙ Phra Athit/ Banglamphu Pier) Wind your way between

Balinese statues, lounging residents, a rambling restaurant and a tiny pool to emerge at this seemingly hidden but popular hotel. Rooms are capable – bar the frequently clumsy stabs made at interior design (think art-school nude portraits) – but the real draw is the hyper-social, resort-like atmosphere.

Old Capital Bike Inn
HOTEL $$$

(Map p82; ☑ 02 629 1787; www.oldcapitalbkk.com; 609 Th Phra Sumen; r incl breakfast 3200-7800B; ❄@🛜; 🚤klorng boat to Phanfa Leelard Pier) The dictionary definition of a honeymoon hotel, this antique shophouse has 10 rooms that are decadent and sumptuous, blending rich colours and heavy wood furnishings. True to its name, the bicycle theme runs throughout, and bikes can be borrowed free.

Praya Palazzo
HOTEL $$$

(Map p82; ☑ 02 883 2998; www.prayapalazzo.com; 757/1 Somdej Prapinklao Soi 2; incl breakfast r 6900-8900B; ste 11,900-18,900B; ❄🛜🏊; 🚤hotel shuttle boat from Phra Athit/Banglamphu Pier) After lying dormant for nearly 30 years, this elegant 19th-century mansion has been reborn as an attractive riverside boutique hotel. The 17 rooms can seem rather tight, and river views can be elusive, but the meticulous renovation, handsome antique furnishings and bucolic atmosphere convene in a boutique hotel with authentic old-world charm.

Riva Surya
HOTEL $$$

(Map p82; ☑ 02 633 5000; www.rivasuryabangkok.com; 23 Th Phra Athit; r incl breakfast 3500-5500B; ❄@🏊; 🚤Phra Athit/Banglamphu Pier) A former condo has been transformed into one of the more design-conscious hotels in this part of town. The 68 rooms are decked out in greys and blacks, with contemporary furnishings, and in the case of the Deluxe and Riva rooms, great river views, although not always tonnes of space.

🏨 Chinatown & Phahurat

Chinatown is home to some good-value budget and midrange accommodation options. Downsides include noise, pollution and the neighbourhood's relative distance from both public transport and 'new' Bangkok.

Wanderlust
HOSTEL $

(Map p88; ☑ 083 046 8647; www.facebook.com/onederlust; 149-151 Rama IV; dm 450B, r 1300-1800B; ❄🛜; 🚇, Ⓜ Hua Lamphong exit 1) An almost clinical-feeling industrial vibe rules at this new hostel. The dorms span four to eight beds, and the private rooms are on the tight side, the cheapest sharing bathrooms. These are united by a hyper-chic ground-floor cafe-restaurant. Not the greatest value accommodation in Chinatown, but quite possibly the most image-conscious.

Chic Hostel
HOSTEL $

(Map p88; ☑ 02 237 9989; www.chicth.com; 23/48-51 Th Traimit; incl breakfast dm 390B, r 800-1100B; ❄@🛜🏊; Ⓜ Hua Lamphong exit 1) This new hostel packs dorms ranging from two to 14 beds and a handful of private rooms. The latter have few amenities (only the 'deluxe' rooms have en suite bathrooms), but this is made up for all-around via a bright, colourful vibe and a swimming pool.

★ Loy La Long
HOTEL $$

(Map p88; ☑ 02 639 1390; www.loylalong.com; 1620/2 Th Songwat; r incl breakfast 2700-4900B; ❄@🛜; 🚤Ratchawong Pier, Ⓜ Hua Lamphong exit 1 & taxi) Rustic, retro, charming: the six rooms in this 100-year-old wooden house can lay claim to more than their fair share of personality. United by a unique location elevated over Mae Nam Chao Phraya, it's also privy to a hidden, almost secret, feel.

The only hitch is in finding it; to get here proceed to Th Songwat and cut through Wat Patumkongka Rachaworawiharn (วัดปทุมคงคาราชวรวิหาร) FREE to the river.

Feung Nakorn Balcony
HOTEL $$

(Map p88; ☑ 02 622 1100; www.feungnakorn.com; 125 Th Fuang Nakhon; incl breakfast r 2200-4400B, ste 4300-4800B; ❄@🛜; 🚤Saphan Phut/Memorial Bridge Pier, Pak Klong Taladd Pier) Located in a former school, the 42 rooms here surround an inviting garden courtyard and are generally large, bright and cheery. Amenities such as a free minibar, safe and flat-screen TV are standard, and the hotel has a quiet and secluded location away from the strip, with capable staff. A charming and inviting (if not exceedingly great-value) place to stay.

Shanghai Mansion
HOTEL $$$

(Map p88; ☑ 02 221 2121; www.shanghaimansion.com; 479-481 Th Yaowarat; incl breakfast r 2500-4500B, ste 4500B; ❄@🛜; 🚤Ratchawong Pier, Ⓜ Hua Lamphong exit 1 & taxi) Easily the

AIRPORT HOTELS

The vast majority of visitors to Bangkok need not consider the airport hotel rigmarole as taxis are cheap and plentiful, and early morning traffic means the trip shouldn't take too long. That said, those worried about a super-early departure or late arrival may consider a stay at one of the following:

Novotel Suvarnabhumi Airport Hotel (Map p158; ☑ 02 131 1111; www.novotelairportbkk. com; incl breakfast r 4500-7300B; ste 9500-10,400B; ✳ @ 🕿; 🛐 Phra Khanong exit 3 & taxi, 🚇 Suvarnabhumi Airport & hotel shuttle bus) Has 600-plus luxurious rooms; located within the Suvarnabhumi International Airport compound.

The Cottage (Map p158; ☑ 02 727 5858; www.thecottagebangkokairport.com; 888/8 Th Lad Krabang; r incl breakfast 880-1379B; ✳ @ 🕿 🗷; 🛐 Phra Khanong exit 3 & taxi, 🚇 Suvarnabhumi Airport & hotel shuttle bus) This solid midranger is near the Suvarnabhumi International Airport compound and within walking distance of food and shopping; has an airport shuttle.

Sleep Box (Map p158; ☑ 02 535 7555; Terminal 2; r 1800B; ✳ 🕿) Finally, an alternative to snoozing on the chairs at Don Mueang International Airport. Rooms may induce claustrophobia, but include en suite bathrooms, water, wi-fi and even food coupons. Short stays (1000B for three hours) and showers (300B) are also available.

Amari Airport Hotel (Map p158; ☑ 02 566 1020; www.amari.com/donmuang; 333 Th Choet Wutthakat; r 1845-2205B; ste 2205-3105B; ✳ @ 🕿 🗷; Ⓜ Chatuchak Park exit 2 & taxi, 🛐 Mo Chit exit 3 & taxi) International-standard hotel located directly opposite Don Mueang International Airport.

---

most consciously stylish place to stay in Chinatown, if not in all of Bangkok, this award-winning boutique hotel screams Shanghai c1935 with stained glass, an abundance of lamps, bold colours and cheeky Chinatown kitsch. If you're willing to splurge, ask for one of the bigger streetside rooms with tall windows that allow more natural light.

Asadang   HOTEL **$$$**
(Map p88; ☑ 085 180 7100; 94-94/1 Th Atsadang; r incl breakfast 3900-6000B; ✳ @ 🕿; 🛳 Saphan Phut/Memorial Bridge Pier, Pak Klong Taladd Pier) Travel a century back in time by booking one of the nine rooms in this beautiful antique shophouse located in a classic Bangkok neighbourhood. They're not particularly huge, but are big on atmosphere and come equipped with both antique furnishings and modern amenities. The sister hotel, **Bhuthorn** (Map p82; ☑ 02 622 2270; www.thebhu thorn.com; 96-98 Th Phraeng Phuthon; r incl breakfast 5000-6300B; ✳ @ 🕿), a couple of blocks away, offers a similar package.

🛏 Riverside

Budget and luxury accommodation, with relatively little between.

Glur Bangkok   HOSTEL **$**
(Map p92; ☑ 02 630 5595; www.glurbangkok.com; 45 Soi 50, Th Charoen Krung; incl breakfast dm 285-720B, r 1300-1600B; ✳ 🕿; 🛳 Sathon/Central Pier, 🛐 Saphan Taksin exit 1) A narrow shophouse with three attractive and comfy eight-bed dorms. Space is limited, but Glur makes the most of it with fun and functional communal areas, including a ground-floor cafe.

Swan Hotel   HOTEL **$$**
(Map p92; ☑ 02 235 9271; www.swanhotelbkk. com; 31 Soi 36/Rue de Brest, Th Charoen Krung; r incl breakfast 1200-2000B; ✳ @ 🕿 🗷; 🛳 Oriental Pier) The 1960s-era furnishings date this classic Bangkok hotel, despite renovations. But the rooms are airy and virtually spotless, and the antiquated vibe provides the Swan, particularly its pool area, with a fun, groovy vibe.

Mandarin Oriental   HOTEL **$$$**
(Map p92; ☑ 02 659 9000; www.mandarinoriental. com; 48 Soi 40/Oriental, Th Charoen Krung; incl breakfast r 14,000-30,000B; ste 26,700-160,000B; ✳ @ 🕿 🗷; 🛳 Oriental Pier, or hotel shuttle boat from Sathon/Central Pier) For the true Bangkok experience, a stay at this grand old riverside hotel is a must. The majority of rooms are in the modern and recently refurbished New Wing, but we prefer the old-world ambience

Northern Bangkok

of the Garden and Authors' Wings. The hotel is also home to one of the region's most acclaimed spas, a legendary fine-dining restaurant and a cooking school.

Peninsula Hotel HOTEL $$$
(Map p92; ☎02 861 2888; www.peninsula.com; 333 Th Charoen Nakhon; incl breakfast r 7500-8100B; ste 10,600-130,000B; ❄@☎☎; ☎hotel shuttle boat from Sathon/Central Pier) At the age of 20, the Pen still seems to have it all: the location (towering over the river), the rep (it's consistently one of the top-ranking luxury hotels in the world) and one of the highest levels of service in town. If money is no obstacle, stay on one of the upper floors where you literally have all of Bangkok at your feet.

Millennium Hilton HOTEL $$$
(Map p92; ☎02 442 2000; www.bangkok.hilton.com; 123 Th Charoen Nakhon; incl breakfast r 4000-5900B; ste 6500-7000B; ❄@☎☎; ☎ho-tel shuttle boat from Sathon/Central Pier) As soon as you enter the dramatic lobby, it's obvious that this is among Bangkok's youngest, most modern riverside hotels. Rooms, all of which boast widescreen river views, carry on the theme and are decked out with funky furniture and Thai-themed photos. A glass elevator and an artificial beach are just some of the fun touches.

🛏 Lumphini Park & Rama IV

ETZzz Hostel HOSTEL $
(Map p96; ☎02 286 9424; www.etzhostel.com; 5/3 Soi Ngam Du Phli; dm 180-350B; r 750-900B; ❄@☎; Ⓜ Lumphini exit 1) This narrow shophouse includes dorms ranging in size from four to 12 beds, and two private rooms (the latter equipped with en suite bathroom), all of which are united by a neat, primary colour theme and a convenient location near the MRT.

Northern Bangkok

Urban House　　　　　　　HOTEL $$
(Map p96; ☎081 492 7778; www.urbanh.com; 35/13 Soi Yommarat; incl breakfast r 800-2300B, ste 1580B; ❈🖥; Ⓜ Si Lom exit 2, Ⓢ Sala Daeng exit 4) There's nothing showy about this shophouse with six rooms, but that's exactly what we like about it. Rooms are subtle, comfortable and relatively spacious, and the place boasts a peaceful, homely atmosphere, largely due to the kind host and the quiet residential street it's located on.

LUXX XL　　　　　　　HOTEL $$
(Map p96; ☎02 684 1111; www.staywithluxx.com; 82/8 Th Lang Suan; incl breakfast r 1500-2400B, ste 3700-7700B; ❈@🖥⛱; Ⓢ Ratchadamri exit 2) LUXX oozes with a contemporary, minimalist hipness that wouldn't be out of place in London or New York. Floor-to-ceiling windows allow heaps of natural light, suites have an added kitchenette, and all rooms are decked out with appropriately stylish furnishings. There's another slightly cheaper (and smaller) **Th Decho branch** (Map p98; ☎02 635 8844; 6/11 Th Decho; r 1060-1445B, ste 1570B; ❈@🖥; Ⓢ Chong Nongsi exit 3), off Th Silom.

Sukhothai Hotel　　　　　　HOTEL $$$
(Map p96; ☎02 344 8888; www.sukhothai.com; 13/3 Th Sathon Tai/South; incl breakfast r 4000-5200B, ste 6000-80,000B; ❈@🖥⛱; Ⓜ Lumphini exit 2) This is one of Bangkok's classiest luxury options, and, as the name suggests, the Sukhothai employs brick stupas, courtyards and antique sculptures to create a peaceful, almost temple-like atmosphere. The rooms contrast this with high-tech TVs, phones and in some cases, high-tech toilets.

Sofitel So　　　　　　　HOTEL $$$
(Map p96; ☎02 624 0000; www.sofitel.com; 2 Th Sathon Neua/North; incl breakfast r 8100-9100B, ste 13,000-48,000B; ❈@🖥⛱; Ⓜ Lumphini exit 2) Taking inspiration from (and featuring amazing views of) adjacent Lumphini Park, this is one of a handful of large-yet-hip brand-name hotels to open in Bangkok over the last few years. The four-elements-inspired design theme has no two rooms looking quite the same, but all are spacious and stylish, contemporary and young.

🛏 Silom & Sathon

Silom, Bangkok's de facto financial district, is frenetic and modern, while Th Sathon is a more subdued embassy zone.

Mile Map Hostel　　　　　　HOSTEL $
(Map p98; ☎02 635 1212; 36/4 Th Pan; dm 250-285B, r 600-900B; ❈@🖥; Ⓢ Chong Nonsi exit 3) Despite the quasi-industrial theme, this hostel feels inviting, warm and fun. The 10-bed dorms are one of the best deals in town, and the private rooms have a funky, minimalist feel, although not much natural light.

Mad Cow Hostel　　　　　　HOSTEL $
(Map p98; ☎087 972 0955; 18 Th Decho; dm 150-180B, r shared bathroom 440B; ❈🖥; Ⓢ Chong Nonsi exit 3) The fan-cooled dorms here just might be the cheapest beds in town. As such, you'd be foolish to expect anything beyond the basics, but they're clean and service is friendly. The closet-sized private rooms share bathroom facilities.

★ Smile Society　　　　　　HOTEL $$
(Map p98; ☎081 442 5800, 081 444 1596; www.smilesocietyhostel.com; 30/3-4 Soi 6, Th Silom; incl breakfast dm 450-600B, r 1100-2200B; ❈@🖥; Ⓜ Si Lom exit 2, Ⓢ Sala Daeng exit 1) Part boutique hotel, part hostel, this four-storey shophouse combines small but comfortable and well-equipped rooms, and dorms with

BANGKOK'S BEST HOSTELS

If you're on a shoestring budget, Bangkok has heaps of options for you, ranging from high-tech, pod-like dorm beds in a brand-new hostel to cosy bunk beds in a refurbished Chinatown shophouse. (And if you decide that you need a bit more privacy, nearly all of Bangkok's hostels also offer private rooms.)

Lub*d (Map p102; ☑ 02 612 4999; www.siamsquare.lubd.com; Rama I; dm 550B, r 1900-2500B; ❄ @ 🛜; Ⓢ National Stadium exit 1) The title is a play on the Thai *làp dee*, meaning 'sleep well', but the fun atmosphere at this modern-feeling hostel might make you want to stay up all night. Diversions include an inviting communal area stocked with games and a bar, and thoughtful facilities range from washing machines to a theatre room.

Chern (Map p82; ☑ 02 621 1133; www.chernbangkok.com; 17 Soi Ratchasak; dm 400B, r 1400-1900B; ❄ @ 🛜; 🚤 klorng boat to Phanfa Leelard Pier) The vast, open spaces and white, over-exposed tones of this hostel converge in an almost afterlife-like feel.

Niras Bangkoc (Map p82; ☑ 02 221 4442; www.nirasbankoc.com; 204-206 Th Mahachai; dm 450-500B, r 1300-1500B; ❄ 🛜; 🚤 klorng boat to Phanfa Leelard Pier) Niras takes advantage of its location in an antique shophouse to arrive at a charmingly old-school feel. Both the four- and six-bed dorms here feature dark woods and vintage furniture, with access to friendly staff, a cosy ground-floor cafe and a location in an atmospheric corner of the city.

Silom Art Hostel (Map p98; ☑ 02 635 8070; www.silomarthostel.com; 198/19-22 Soi 14, Th Silom; dm 300-350B, r 1300-1500B; ❄ @ 🛜; Ⓢ Chong Nonsi exit 3) Quirky, artsy, bright and fun, Silom Art Hostel combines recycled materials, unconventional furnishings and colourful wall paintings to culminate in a hostel that's quite unlike anywhere else in town. It's not all about style though: beds are functional and comfortable, with lots of appealing communal areas.

Loftel 22 (Map p92; www.loftel22bangkok.com; 952 Soi 22, Th Charoen Krung; dm 250-300B, r with shared bathroom 850-1300B; ❄ @ 🛜; 🚤 Marine Department Pier, Ⓜ Hua Lamphong exit 1) Stylish, inviting dorms have been coaxed out of these two adjoining shophouses. Friendly service and a location in one of Chinatown's most atmospheric corners round out the package.

NapPark Hostel (Map p82; ☑ 02 282 2324; www.nappark.com; 5 Th Tani; dm 440-600B; ❄ @ 🛜; 🚤 Phra Athit/Banglamphu Pier) This popular hostel features dorm rooms of various sizes, the smallest and most expensive of which boasts six pod-like beds outfitted with power points, mini-TV, reading lamp and wi-fi.

Chao Hostel (Map p102; ☑ 02 217 3083; www.chaohostel.com; 8th fl, 865 Rama I; incl breakfast dm 550B, r 1600-1800B; ❄ @ 🛜; Ⓢ National Stadium exit 1) Blending modern minimalist and Thai design elements, not to mention tonnes of open space, the new Chao is one of the most sophisticated hostels we've encountered in Bangkok.

Pause Hostel (Map p106; ☑ 02 108 8855; www.onedaybkk.com; Oneday, 51 Soi 26, Th Sukhumvit; incl breakfast dm 450-600B, r 1300-1500B; ❄ @ 🛜; Ⓢ Phrom Phong exit 4) Attached to a cafe/coworking space is this modern, open-feeling hostel. Dorms span four to eight beds and are united by a handsome industrial-design theme and inviting, sun-soaked communal areas.

S1 Hostel (Map p96; ☑ 02 679 7777; www.facebook.com/s1hostelbangkok; 35/1-4 Soi Ngam Du Phli; dm 330-380B, r 700-1300B; ❄ @ 🛜; Ⓜ Lumphini exit 1) A huge new hostel with dorm beds decked out in a simple yet attractive primary-colour scheme. A host of facilities (laundry, kitchen, rooftop garden) and a convenient location within walking distance of the MRT make it great value.

Bed Station Hostel (Map p102; ☑ 02 019 5477; www.bedstationhostel.com; 486/149-150 Soi 16, Th Phetchaburi; incl breakfast dm 500-650B, r 1350-1550B; ❄ @ 🛜; Ⓢ Ratchathewi exit 3) A handsome industrial-chic theme unites the dorms at this modern-feeling hostel. They range from four to eight beds and include access to tidy toilet facilities and a laundry room.

spotless shared bathrooms. A central location, overwhelmingly positive guest feedback, and helpful, English-speaking staff are other perks. And a virtually identical annexe next door helps with spillover as Smile Society gains more fans.

★**kokotel** HOTEL $$
(Map p98; ☑02 235 7555; www.kokotel.com; 181/1-5 Th Surawong; r 1400-3400B; ❄@🛜; ⑤Chong Nonsi exit 3) Quite possibly the city's family-friendliest accommodation, kokotel unites big, sun-filled rooms with puffy beds, an expansive children's play area and a downstairs cafe (with, appropriately, a slide). Friendly rates also make it great value.

Amber HOTEL $$
(Map p98; ☑02 635 7272; www.amberboutique silom.com; 200 Soi 14, Th Silom; r incl breakfast 1900-2400B; ❄@🛜; ⑤Chong Nonsi exit 3) Spanning design themes such as Moroccan, Sino-Portuguese and Modern, it's easy to assume that Amber might emphasise style over comfort. But nothing here is flashy or overwrought, and what you'll get are 19 excellent-value, spacious rooms with lots of amenities and natural light in a quiet location. Frequent promotions bring the rates down even lower than this, making it terrific value.

Rose Hotel HOTEL $$
(Map p98; ☑02 266 8268; www.rosehotelbkk.com; 118 Th Surawong; incl breakfast r 1900-2300B; ste 3300-3800B; ❄@🛜🏊; Ⓜ Si Lom exit 2, ⑤ Sala Daeng exit 3) Don't let the unremarkable exterior fool you: the convenient location, modern rooms, pool, gym and sauna make this Vietnam War–era vet a pretty solid deal.

★**Siam Heritage** HOTEL $$$
(Map p98; ☑02 353 6101; www.thesiamheritage. com; 115/1 Th Surawong; incl breakfast r 3500-3800B, ste 5000-6500B; ❄@🛜🏊; Ⓜ Si Lom exit 2, ⑤ Sala Daeng exit 1) Tucked off busy Th Surawong, this hotel overflows with homey Thai charm – probably because the owners also live in the same building. The 73 rooms are decked out in silk and dark woods with classy design touches and thoughtful amenities. There's an inviting rooftop garden/pool/spa, and it's all cared for by a team of professional, accommodating staff. Highly recommended.

★**Metropolitan by COMO** HOTEL $$$
(Map p96; ☑02 625 3333; www.comohotels.com; 27 Th Sathon Tai/South; incl breakfast r 3500-

ROOMS WITH VIEWS

Arun Residence (p111) Handsome rooms directly across from Wat Arun.

Millennium Hilton (p118) Tall riversider featuring some of Bangkok's best watery views.

Bangkok Tree House (p123) Take in the greenery and river from these elevated bungalows in Bangkok's 'green lung'.

Sofitel So (p119) Rooms peering over the urban oasis that is Lumphini Park.

5300B, ste 6200-27,000B; ❄@🛜🏊; Ⓜ Lumphini exit 2) The exterior of Bangkok's former YMCA has changed relatively little, but a peek inside reveals one of the city's sleekest, sexiest hotels. The 171 rooms come in striking tones of black, white and yellow, yet it's worth noting that the City rooms tend to feel a bit tight, while in contrast the two-storey penthouse suites are like small homes.

🛏 Siam Square & Pratunam

A good selection of budget and midrange accommodation in a central location.

Boxpackers Hostel HOSTEL $
(Map p102; ☑02 656 2828; www.boxpackershostel. com; 39/3 Soi 15, Th Phetchaburi; incl breakfast dm 390-570B, r 1360-2000B; ❄🛜; ⑤Ratchathewi exit 1 & taxi) A contemporary, sparse hostel with dorms ranging in size from four to 12 double-decker pods – some of which are double beds. Communal areas are inviting, and include a ground-floor cafe and a lounge with pool table. A linked hotel also offers 14 small but similarly attractive private rooms.

★**Siam@Siam** HOTEL $$$
(Map p102; ☑02 217 3000; www.siamatsiam. com; 865 Rama I; r incl breakfast 4500-7800B; ❄@🛜🏊; ⑤National Stadium exit 1) A seemingly random mishmash of colours and industrial/recycled materials in the lobby here result in a style one could only describe as 'junkyard chic' – but in a good way, of course. The rooms, which largely continue the theme, are found between the 14th and 24th floors, and offer terrific city views. There's a rooftop restaurant and an 11th-floor pool, and a recent renovation has it looking better than ever.

Hansar
HOTEL $$$

(Map p102; ☑ 02 209 1234; www.hansarbangkok.com; 3 Soi Mahadlekluang 2; ste incl breakfast 5800-24,000B; ❋ @ 🛜 ☒; ⑤ Ratchadamri exit 4) The Hansar can claim that elusive intersection of style and value. All 94 rooms here are handsome and feature huge bathrooms and giant desks, but the smallest (and cheapest) studios are probably the best deal, as they have a kitchenette, washing machine, stand-alone tub, free wi-fi and in most, a balcony.

Hotel Indigo
HOTEL $$$

(Map p102; ☑ 02 207 4999; www.ihg.com; 81 Th Witthayu/Wireless Rd; incl breakfast r 3300-4200B, ste 13,600B; ❋ @ 🛜 ☒; ⑤ Phloen Chit exit 5) An international chain with local flavour, the Indigo has borrowed from the history and culture of this corner of Bangkok to arrive at a hotel that is retro, modern, Thai and artsy all at the same time. Many of the 192 rooms overlook some of the greener areas of Bangkok's embassy district, and all are decked out with colourful furnishings and functional amenities.

Okura Prestige
HOTEL $$$

(Map p102; ☑ 02 687 9000; www.okurabangkok.com; 57 Th Witthayu/Wireless Rd; incl breakfast r 6300-8500B, ste 29,000-110,000B; ℗ ❋ @ 🛜 ☒; ⑤ Phloen Chit exit 5) The Bangkok venture of this Japanese chain – the first branch outside of its homeland – is, unlike other recent, big-name openings in Bangkok, distinctly unflashy. But we like the minimalist, almost contemplative feel of the lobby and the 240 rooms, and the subtle but thoughtful, often distinctly Japanese touches. Significant online discounts are available.

🛏 Sukhumvit

Th Sukhumvit is home to a significant slice of Bangkok's accommodation, and as such there's a bit of everything, although the area probably excels in the top-end chain type hotel.

FU House Hostel
HOSTEL $

(Map p106; ☑ 098 654 5505; www.facebook.com/fuhouseghostel; 77 Soi 8, Th Sukhumvit; dm/r incl breakfast 500/1650B; ❋ 🛜; ⑤ Nana exit 4) Great for a quiet, low-key stay is this two-storey wooden villa on a residential street. Choose between attractive bunk beds in one of two spacious, private-feeling dorms, or rooms with en suite bathrooms.

★ Tints of Blue
HOTEL $$

(Map p106; ☑ 099 289 7744; www.tintsofblue.com; 47 Soi 27, Th Sukhumvit; r incl breakfast 1800-2000B; ❋ 🛜 ☒; Ⓜ Sukhumvit exit 2, ⑤ Asok exit 6) The location in a leafy, quiet street is reflected in the rooms here, which manage to feel secluded, homey and warm. Equipped with kitchenettes, lots of space and natural light, and balconies, they're also a steal at this price.

S31
HOTEL $$

(Map p106; ☑ 02 260 1111; www.s31hotel.com; 545 Soi 31, Th Sukhumvit; incl breakfast r 3700B, ste 4200-25,000B; ❋ 🛜 ☒; ⑤ Phrom Phong exit 5) The bold patterns and graphics of its interior and exterior make the S31 a fun, youthful choice. Thoughtful touches like kitchenettes with large fridge, super-huge beds and courses (Thai boxing and yoga) prove that the style also has substance. Significant discounts can be found online, and additional branches are located on Soi 15 and Soi 33.

Beat Hotel
HOTEL $$

(Map p76; ☑ 02 178 0077; www.beathotelbangkok.com; 69/1 Th Sukhumvit; r incl breakfast 2000-2500B; ❋ @ 🛜 ☒; ⑤ Phra Khanong exit 3) This art-themed hotel has a vibrant, youthful vibe that kicks off in the lobby. The 54 rooms continue this feeling, ranging in design from those with colourful floor-to-ceiling wall art to others painted in a monochromatic bold hue. It's worth shelling out for the super-huge Deluxe rooms.

S-Box
HOTEL $$

(Map p106; ☑ 02 262 0991; www.sboxhotel.com; 4 Soi 31, Th Sukhumvit; r incl breakfast 1100-2200B; ❋ @ 🛜; ⑤ Phrom Phong exit 5) The name says it all: the rooms here are little more than boxes – albeit attractive, modern boxes with stylish furniture and practical amenities. The cheapest are pod-like and lack natural light, while the more expensive have floor-to-ceiling windows.

RetrOasis
HOTEL $$

(Map p106; ☑ 02 665 2922; www.retroasishotel.com; 503 Th Sukhumvit; r incl breakfast 1400-2300B; ❋ 🛜 ☒; Ⓜ Sukhumvit exit 2, ⑤ Asok exit 6) This former tryst hotel dating back to the '60s has been converted to a fun mid-ranger. Bright paint and an inviting central pool give the hotel a young, fresh vibe, while vintage furniture and architecture serve as reminders of its real age.

WORTH A TRIP

PHRAPRADAENG PENINSULA: BANGKOK'S GREEN LUNG

If you've been to any of Bangkok's rooftop bars, you may have noticed the rural-looking zone just southeast of the city centre. Known in English as the Phrapradaeng Peninsula, the conspicuously green finger of land is surrounded on three sides by Mae Nam Chao Phraya, a feature that seems to have shielded it from development.

The Phrapradaeng Peninsula encompasses rural homes, orchards, canals and lots of wet, unruly jungle. Most people visit the peninsula for the **Bang Nam Pheung Market** (ตลาดบางน้ำผึ้ง; Map p76; Bang Kachao; ⊙8am-3pm Sat & Sun), a fun, weekends-only market with an emphasis on food. While there, you can check out the wonderfully dilapidated, 250-year-old **Wat Bang Nam Pheung Nok** (วัดบางน้ำผึ้งนอก; Map p76; Bang Kachao; ⊙daylight hours), a Buddhist temple.

For something more active, the area is on the itinerary of many Bangkok bike tours, which take advantage of the peninsula's elevated walkways. Alternatively, there's **Si Nakhon Kheun Khan Park** (สวนศรีนครเขื่อนขันธ์; Map p76; Bang Kachao; ⊙6am-7pm) **FREE**, a vast botanical park with a large lake and birdwatching tower.

If you're really enjoying the Phrapradaeng Peninsula, you can extend your stay by overnighting at **Bangkok Tree House** (Map p76; ☑082 995 1150; www.bangkoktreehouse.com/cozy-nests.html; bungalow incl breakfast 6000-10,000B; ❄@🌐), near Wat Bang Na Nork.

To get to Phrapradaeng, take the BTS to Bang Na and jump in a taxi for the short ride to the pier at Wat Bang Na Nork via Th Sanphawut. From there, take the river-crossing ferry (4B) followed by a short motorcycle taxi (10B) ride if you're going to Bang Nam Pheung Market.

Napa Place HOTEL $$
(Map p106; ☑02 661 5525; www.napaplace.com; 11/3 Soi Napha Sap 2; incl breakfast r 2200-2600B, ste 3400-4600B; ❄@🌐; ⑤Thong Lo exit 2) Hidden in the confines of a typical Bangkok urban compound is what must be the city's homeliest accommodation. The 12 expansive rooms have been decorated with dark woods from the family's former lumber business and light-brown cloths from the hands of Thai weavers, while the cosy communal areas might not be much different from the suburban living room you grew up in.

U Sukhumvit HOTEL $$
(Map p106; ☑02 651 3355; 81 Soi 15, Th Sukhumvit; r incl breakfast 2600-3200B; ❄🌐; Ⓜ️Sukhumvit exit 3, ⑤Asok exit 5) A modern hotel featuring the Thai regions as a design theme. Rooms are colourful, with lively rustic touches, not to mention spacious and well-equipped. A midrange keeper.

★ **AriyasomVilla** HOTEL $$$
(Map p106; ☑02 254 8880; www.ariyasom.com; 65 Soi 1, Th Sukhumvit; r incl breakfast 6900-10,500B; ❄@🌐; ⑤Phloen Chit exit 3) Located at the end of Soi 1 behind a wall of tropical greenery, this beautifully renovated 1940s-era villa is one of the worst-kept accommodation secrets in Bangkok. The 24 rooms are spacious and meticulously outfitted with thoughtful Thai design touches and sumptuous, beautiful antique furniture. There's also a spa and an inviting tropical pool. Book well in advance.

Breakfast is vegetarian and served in the villa's stunning glass-encased dining room.

Cabochon Hotel BOUTIQUE HOTEL $$$
(Map p106; ☑02 259 2871/3; www.cabochonhotel.com; 14/29 Soi 45, Th Sukhumvit; incl breakfast r 4900-6500B, ste 7200-13,000B; 🅿️♿❄🌐; ⑤Phrom Phong exit 3) The Cabochon, which means polished gem, is indeed a diamond in rowdy Bangkok. Rooms are light-filled and unfussy, and packed with thoughtful curiosities like antique telephones, typewriters, tortoise shells, model aeroplanes and vintage tea sets. Venture to the rooftop pool or nosh street-food style on mouthwatering Thai and Laotian dishes at the cosy Thai Lao Yeh Restaurant.

Sheraton Grande Sukhumvit HOTEL $$$
(Map p106; ☑02 649 8888; www.sheratongrandesukhumvit.com; 250 Th Sukhumvit; incl breakfast r 11,000-13,800B, ste 19,000-56,000B; ❄🌐; Ⓜ️Sukhumvit exit 3, ⑤Asok exit 2) This conveniently located, business-oriented hotel offers some of the biggest rooms in town and fills them with a generous spread of amenities. Guest feedback is overwhelmingly positive, and by the time you read this, ongoing

THE FLAVOURS OF BANGKOK

You can't say you've tried Bangkok-style Thai food unless you've tasted at least a couple of the following:

Pàt tai Thin rice noodles stir-fried with dried and/or fresh shrimp, bean sprouts, tofu, egg and seasonings, traditionally served with lime halves and a few stalks of Chinese chives and a sliced banana flower. **Thip Samai** (p127), in Banglamphu, is probably Bangkok's most lauded destination for the dish.

Yam blah dùk foo Fried shredded catfish, chilli and peanuts served with a sweet/tart mango dressing. Try it at **Kimleng** (Map p82; 158-160 Th Tanao; mains 60-150B; ⏰10am-10pm Mon-Sat; ❄; ⛴klorng boat to Phanfa Leelard Pier), in Bangkok's Banglamphu district.

Đôm yam Lemon grass, kaffir lime leaf and lime juice give this soup its characteristic tang; fresh chillies or an oily chilli paste provide it with its legendary sting. Available just about everywhere, but it's hard to beat the version at **Krua Apsorn** (p127).

Yen đah foh Combining a slightly sweet crimson-coloured broth with a variety of meatballs, cubes of blood and crispy greens, yen đah foh is probably both the most intimidating and popular noodle dish in Bangkok. Available at **Soi 10 Food Centres** (p131) and many street stalls.

Gaang sôm Central Thailand's famous 'sour soup' often includes freshwater fish, vegetables and/or herbs, and a thick, tart broth. Available at **Poj Spa Kar** (Map p82; 443 Th Tanao; mains 65-200B; ⏰12.30-8.30pm; ❄; ⛴klorng boat to Phanfa Leelard Pier).

Gŏo•ay đĕe•o reu•a Known as boat noodles because they were previously served from small boats along the canals of central Thailand, these intense pork- or beef-based bowls are among the most full-flavoured of Thai noodle dishes. Try a bowl at **Bharani** (Sansab Boat Noodle; Map p106; 96/14 Soi 23, Th Sukhumvit; mains 60-250B; ⏰11am-10pm; ❄; Ⓜ Sukhumvit exit 2, Ⓢ Asok exit 3).

renovations will be making what was already a very good hotel an excellent one.

Ma Du Zi HOTEL $$$
(Map p106; ☎02 615 6400; www.maduzihotel.com; cnr Th Ratchadaphisek & Soi 16, Th Sukhumvit; incl breakfast r 5100-5500B, ste 7700-11,700B; ❄@☎; Ⓜ Sukhumvit exit 3, Ⓢ Asok exit 6) The name is Thai for 'come take a look', somewhat of a misnomer for this reservations-only, no-walk-ins hotel. If you've gained access, behind the gate you'll find a modern, sophisticated midsized hotel steeped in dark, chic tones and designs. We particularly like the immense bathrooms, equipped with a walk-in tub and minimalist shower.

🍽 Ratchathewi

HI Mid Bangkok HOSTEL $$
(Map p112; ☎02 644 5744; www.midbangkok.com; 481/3 Th Ratchawithi; dm 390B, r 1000-2400B; ❄@☎; Ⓢ Victory Monument exit 4) Contemporary elements (industrial influences, smooth concrete) and old-school Bangkok touches (faux-antique tiles, wood furniture) mingle at this inviting hostel. Dorm rooms are cosy and share clean bathrooms, while private rooms are spacious, if somewhat bare (only the larger deluxe rooms have TV), with lots of natural light.

Bizotel HOTEL $$
(Map p112; ☎02 245 2424; www.bizotelbkk.com; 104/40 Th Rang Nam; r incl breakfast 1900-2100B; ❄@☎; Ⓢ Victory Monument exit 4) Attractive, bright and stuffed with useful amenities: you could be fooled into believing that the rooms at this hotel cost twice this much. A location in a relatively quiet part of town is another bonus, and helpful, friendly staff seal the deal.

K Maison BOUTIQUE HOTEL $$
(Map p112; ☎02 245 1953; www.kmaisonboutique. com; Soi Ruam Chit; incl breakfast r 2200-3500B, ste 6500B; ❄☎; Ⓢ Victory Monument exit 4) The lobby, with its virginal white, swirling marble and streaks of blue, sets the tone of this boutique hotel. The 21 rooms follow suit, and are handsome in a delicate and attractively sparse way. Lest you think it's all about image, fear not: K Maison is also functional and comfortable.

🛏 Thewet & Dusit

Good budget options, a riverside village feel and proximity to visit-worthy sights are the benefits of staying in Thewet and Dusit.

Penpark Place   HOTEL $
(Map p82; ☑02 628 8896; www.penparkplace. com; 22 Soi 3, Th Samsen; r 300-1700B, ste 2200B; ❄@⏶; ⛴Thewet Pier) This former factory has been turned into a good-value budget hotel. A room in the original building is little more than a bed and a fan, but an adjacent add-on sees a handful of well-equipped apartment-like rooms and suites.

★Sam Sen Sam Place   GUESTHOUSE $$
(Map p82; ☑02 628 7067; https://samsensam. com; 48 Soi 3, Th Samsen; r incl breakfast 600-2400B; ❄@⏶; ⛴Thewet Pier) One of the homeliest places in this area, if not Bangkok, this colourful, refurbished antique villa gets glowing reports about its friendly service and quiet location. Of the 18 rooms here, all are extremely tidy, and the cheapest are fan-cooled and share a bathroom.

★Phra-Nakorn Norn-Len   HOTEL $$
(Map p115; ☑02 628 8188; www.phranakorn-norn-len.com; 46 Soi Thewet 1; r incl breakfast 2200-4200B; ❄@⏶; ⛴Thewet Pier) Set in an enclosed garden compound decorated like a Bangkok neighbourhood of yesteryear, this bright and cheery hotel is a fun and atmospheric, if not necessarily stupendous-value, place to stay. Although the 31 rooms are attractively furnished with antiques and paintings, it's worth noting that they don't include TV, a fact made up for by daily activities, massage and endless opportunities for peaceful relaxing.

Baan Manusarn   GUESTHOUSE $$
(Map p115; ☑02 281 2976; www.facebook.com/ baanmanusarn; Th Krung Kasem; r incl breakfast 1400B; ❄@⏶; ⛴Thewet Pier) Steps from Thewet Pier is this inviting vintage shophouse with four rooms. All feature beautiful wood floors and lots of space – with the two family rooms being the most generous – and half boast balconies and en suite bathrooms.

Loog Choob Homestay   GUESTHOUSE $$
(Map p76; ☑085 328 2475; www.loogchoob.com; 463/5-8 Th Luk Luang; incl breakfast r 2100B, ste 3800-4400B; ❄@⏶; ⛴Thewet Pier, Ⓢ Phaya Thai exit 3 & taxi) Five rooms in a former gem factory outside the tourist zone might sound iffy, but the rooms here are stylish and inviting, and come supplemented with a huge array of thoughtful amenities and friendly, heartfelt service.

The Siam   HOTEL $$$
(Map p115; ☑02 206 6999; www.thesiamhotel. com; 3/2 Th Khao; incl breakfast r 16,100-22,400B, villa 26,300-37,000B; ❄@⏶⏳; ⛴Thewet Pier, or hotel shuttle boat from Sathon/Central Pier) Zoom back to the 1930s in this contemporary riverside hotel, where art deco influences, copious marble and beautiful antiques define the look. Rooms are spacious and well-appointed, while villas up the ante with rooftop balcony and plunge pool. Yet it's not just about self-indulging, with activities ranging from Thai boxing lessons to a private theatre to keep you busy.

🛏 Northern Bangkok

Staying outside of Bangkok's centre can offer great value, especially when it comes to budget and midrange accommodation. And improved public transport means that it doesn't have to feel like a compromise.

The Yard   HOSTEL $
(Map p118; ☑089 677 4050; www.theyardhostel. com; 51 Soi 5, Th Phahonyothin; incl breakfast dm 550-650B, r 1200-1900B; ❄⏶; ⓈAri exit 1) This fun hostel is comprised of 10 converted shipping containers. Predictably, neither the dorm nor private rooms are huge (nor great value), but are attractive and cosy, and have access to inviting communal areas ranging from the eponymous lawn (which also functions as a bar) to a kitchen.

Siamaze   HOSTEL $
(Map p118; ☑02 693 6336; www.siamaze.com; Soi 17, Th Ratchadaphisek; incl breakfast dm 390-490B, r 1200-2000B; ❄@⏶; ⓂSutthisan exit 4) Siamaze is an unflashy, casual budget hotel with spacious private rooms and tech-outfitted bunk-bed dorms. The latter share big, clean bathrooms and access to thoughtful, convenient facilities. If you're OK with staying away from the main tourist drag, it's an excellent deal.

ℹ **HUNGRY MONDAYS**

Most of Bangkok's street-food vendors close up shop on Monday, so don't plan on eating in Chinatown on this day.

Mystic Place
HOTEL $$

(Map p118; ☎02 270 3344; www.mysticplacebkk.com; 224/5-9 Th Pradiphat; r incl breakfast 2200-2650B; ❄@☎; ⓢSaphan Khwai exit 2 & taxi) This hotel unites 36 rooms, each of which is individually and playfully designed. One we checked out combined a chair upholstered with stuffed animals and walls covered with graffiti, while another was swathed in eye-contorting op art. Heaps of fun and perpetually popular, so be sure to book ahead.

Be My Guest Bed & Breakfast
GUESTHOUSE $$

(Map p118; ☎02 692 4037; 212/4 Soi 1, Soi 7, Th Ratchadaphisek; r incl breakfast 900-1400B; ❄@☎; ⓜThailand Cultural Centre exit 4 & taxi) With only four rooms and the owner living upstairs, you really are the eponymous guest at this friendly, tidy guesthouse. Rooms are neat but simple, and supplemented by user-friendly communal areas, personal service and a genuinely homey vibe. Contact in advance, both to ensure vacancy and to ask for detailed instructions on locating the place.

Eating

Nowhere else is the Thai reverence for food more evident than in Bangkok. To the outsider, the life of a Bangkokian appears to be a string of meals and snacks punctuated by the odd stab at work, not the other way

---

around. If you can adjust your mental clock to this schedule, your visit will be a delicious one indeed.

The people of central Thailand are fond of sweet, savoury, herbal flavours, and many dishes include freshwater fish, pork, coconut milk and palm sugar – common ingredients in the central Thai plains. Because of the region's proximity to the Gulf of Thailand, central Thai eateries, particularly those in Bangkok, also serve a wide variety of seafood.

Ko Ratanakosin

In stark contrast to the rest of Bangkok, there aren't many restaurants or stalls in Ko Ratanakosin, and those that are here predominantly serve Thai cuisine. For something more international, consider heading to Banglamphu, a short taxi ride away.

Pa Aew
THAI $

(Map p82; Th Maha Rat; mains 20-60B; ⏱10am-5pm Tue-Sat; 🚢Tien Pier) Pull up a plastic stool for some rich, seafood-heavy, Bangkok-style fare. It's a bare-bones, open-air curry stall, but for taste, Pa Aew is one of our favourite places to eat in this part of town.

There's no English-language sign; look for the exposed trays of food directly in front of the Krung Thai Bank near the corner with Soi Pratu Nokyung.

★ Tonkin-Annam
VIETNAMESE $$

(Map p82; ☎093 469 2969; www.facebook.com/tonkinannam; 69 Soi Tha Tien; mains 140-300B; ⏱10am-10pm Wed-Mon; ❄; 🚢Tien Pier) The retro/minimalist interior here might be red flags for hipster ethnic cuisine, but Tonkin-Annam serves some of the best Vietnamese food in Bangkok. Come for the deliciously tart and peppery banana blossom salad, or dishes you won't find elsewhere, such as *bánh bèo* (steamed cups of rice flour topped with pork), a speciality of Hue.

Err
THAI $$

(Map p82; www.errbkk.com; off Th Maha Rat; mains 65-360B; ⏱11am-late Tue-Sun; ❄; 🚢Tien Pier) Think of all those different smoky, spicy, crispy, meaty bites you've encountered on the street. Now imagine them assembled in one funky, retro-themed locale, and coupled with tasty Thai-themed cocktails and domestic microbrews. If Err (a Thai colloquialism for agreement) seems too good to be true, we empathise, but insist that it's true.

BEST VEGETARIAN EATS

Bonita Cafe & Social Club (Map p98; www.bonitacafesocialclub.wordpress.com; 100 Soi 26, Th Silom; mains 100-300B; ⏱9.30am-9.30pm Wed-Mon; ❄☎✐; ⓢSurasak exit 3) Foreign-influenced vegan dining.

Anotai (Map p106; www.facebook.com/anotaigo; 976/17 Soi Rama 9 Hospital, Rama IX; mains 150-300B; ⏱10am-9.30pm Thu-Tue; ❄✐; ⓜPhra Ram 9 exit 3 & taxi) Sophisticated meat-free meals.

Saras (p133) Fast-food-feeling southern Indian.

Arawy Vegetarian Food (Map p82; 152 Th Din So; mains from 30B; ⏱7am-8pm; ✐; 🚢klorng boat to Phanfa Leelard Pier) Long-standing Thai vegetarian.

Chennai Kitchen (p131) Homecooked southern Indian.

✕ Banglamphu

Banglamphu is famous for its old-school central Thai food – the predominant cuisine in this part of town. For something more international, head to Th Khao San, where you'll find a few international fast-food franchises as well as foreign and vegetarian restaurants.

Somsong Phochana   THAI $

(Map p82; off Th Lamphu; mains from 30B; ⊙ 9.30am-4pm; ⚑ Phra Athit/Banglamphu Pier) This is one of the few places in Bangkok that serves *gŏo·ay dĕe·o sù·kŏh·tai*, Sukhothai-style noodles: barbecued pork and thin rice noodles in a clear broth seasoned with a little sugar, supplemented with sliced green beans, and garnished with ground peanuts.

There's no English-language sign. To find Somsong, enter Th Lamphu, then take the first left, opposite Watsungwej School; the restaurant is on the right.

Karim Roti-Mataba   THAI $

(Map p82; 136 Th Phra Athit; mains 40-130B; ⊙ 9am-10pm Tue-Sun; ⚑ ⚑; ⚑ Phra Athit/Banglamphu Pier) This classic Bangkok eatery may have grown a bit too big for its britches in recent years, but it still serves tasty Thai-Muslim dishes such as roti, *gaang mát·sà·màn* ('Muslim curry'), tart fish curry and *má·đà·bà* (something of a stuffed pancake). An upstairs air-con dining area and a couple of outdoor tables provide barely enough seating for loyal fans and curious tourists alike.

Nuttaporn   THAI $

(Map p82; 94 Th Phraeng Phuthon; mains from 20B; ⊙ 9am-4pm Mon-Sat; ⚑; ⚑ Phra Athit/Banglamphu Pier) A crumbling shophouse that for the last 70 years has been churning out some of Bangkok's most famous coconut ice cream – in our opinion, the ideal palate cleanser after a bowl of spicy noodles. Other uniquely domestic flavours include mango, Thai tea, and for the daring, durian.

Thip Samai   THAI $

(Map p82; 313 Th Mahachai; mains 50-250B; ⊙ 5pm-2am; ⚑ klorng boat to Phanfa Leelard Pier) Brace yourself: you should be aware that the fried noodles sold from carts along Th Khao San have little to do with the dish known as *pàt tai*. Luckily, less than a five-minute túk-

SOUTHERN THAI FEAST

The area around Thonburi's Siriraj Hospital is one of the best places in Bangkok for southern-Thai food, the theory being that the cuisine took root here because of the nearby train station that served southern destinations. In particular, between Soi 8 and Soi 13 of Th Wang Lang there is a knot of authentic, southern Thai-style curry shops: **Dao Tai** (Map p76; 508/26 Th Wang Lang, no roman-script sign; mains from 30B; ⊙ 7am-8.30pm; ⚑ Wang Lang/Siriraj Pier), **Ruam Tai** (Map p76; 376/4 Th Wang Lang, no roman-script sign; mains from 30B; ⊙ 7am-9pm; ⚑ Wang Lang/Siriraj Pier) and **Chawang** (Map p76; 375/5-6 Th Wang Lang; mains from 30B; ⊙ 7am-7pm; ⚑ Wang Lang/Siriraj Pier). A menu isn't necessary as all feature bowls and trays of prepared curries, soups, stir-fries and relishes; simply point to whatever looks tastiest. And when eating, don't feel ashamed if you're feeling the heat; even Bangkok Thais tend to find southern Thai cuisine spicy.

túk ride away lies Thip Samai, home to some of the most legendary fried noodles in town.

Note that Thip Samai is closed on alternate Wednesdays.

Chote Chitr   THAI $

(Map p82; 146 Th Phraeng Phuthon; mains 60-200B; ⊙ 11am-10pm; ⚑ klorng boat to Phanfa Leelard Pier) This third-generation shophouse restaurant boasting just six tables is a Bangkok foodie landmark. The kitchen can be inconsistent and the service is consistently grumpy, but when they're on, dishes like *mèe gròrp* (crispy fried noodles) and *yam tòo·a ploo* (wing-bean salad) are in a class of their own.

May Kaidee's   THAI $

(Map p82; www.maykaidee.com; 59 Th Tanao; mains 80-120B; ⊙ 9am-10pm; ⚑ ⚑; ⚑ Phra Athit/Banglamphu Pier) A long-standing restaurant that serves up meat-free Thai dishes, and that also houses a vegie Thai cooking school.

★ Krua Apsorn   THAI $$

(Map p82; www.kruaapsorn.com; Th Din So; mains 100-450B; ⊙ 10.30am-8pm Mon-Sat; ⚑; ⚑ klorng boat to Phanfa Leelard Pier) This cafeteria-like

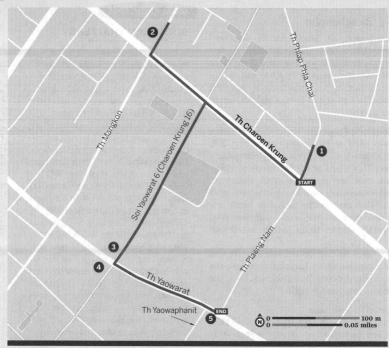

City Walk
Chinatown Eating Tour

START CNR TH PLAENG NAM & TH CHAROEN KRUNG
END CNR TH YAOWAPHANIT & TH YAOWARAT
LENGTH 1KM; TWO TO THREE HOURS

Street food rules in Chinatown, making the area ideal for a culinary adventure. Although many vendors stay open late, the more popular stalls tend to sell out quickly, so the best time to feast in this area is from 7pm to 9pm. Don't try this walk on a Monday, when most of the city's street vendors stay at home. Bringing a friend (or three) and sharing is a good way to ensure that you can try as many dishes as possible.

Start your walk at the intersection of Th Plaeng Nam and Th Charoen Krung. Head north along Th Phlap Phla Chai, staying on the right-hand side for about 50m, until you reach **❶ Nai Mong Hoi Tho**, a shophouse restaurant renowned for its delicious *or hŏy tôrt* (oysters fried with egg and a sticky batter).

Backtrack to Th Charoen Krung and turn right. Upon reaching Th Mangkon make a right; on your left-hand side you'll see **❷ Jék Pûi**, a table-less stall famous for its Chinese-style Thai curries.

Cross Th Charoen Krung again, turn left, and continue east until you reach Soi Yaowarat 6/Charoen Krung 16, also known as Talat Mai, the area's most famous strip of commerce. At the end of the alley you'll see a gentleman making **❸ gŏo·ay đĕe·o kôo·a gài**, rice noodles fried with chicken, egg and garlic oil.

Upon emerging at Th Yaowarat, cross over to the busy market area directly across the street. The first vendor on the right, **❹ Nay Lék Ûa**, sells *gŏo·ay jáp nám sǎi*, an intensely peppery broth containing noodles and pork offal.

Returning back to Th Yaowarat, turn right and continue until the next intersection. On the corner of Th Yaowaphanit and Th Yaowarat you'll see **❺ Mangkorn Khǎ**, a stall selling *bà·mèe* (Chinese-style wheat noodles) and barbecued pork, and wontons.

dining room is a favourite of members of the Thai royal family and restaurant critics alike. Just about all of the central and southern Thai dishes are tasty, but regulars never miss the chance to order the decadent stir-fried crab with yellow pepper chili or the *tortilla Española*–like fluffy crab omelette.

There's another branch (p136) on Th Samsen in Thewet and Dusit.

Shoshana ISRAELI $$
(Map p82; 88 Th Chakraphatdi Phong; mains 80-320B; ⊗10am-midnight; ✤🖋; 🚢Phra Athit/Banglamphu Pier) One of Khao San's longest-running Israeli restaurants, Shoshana resembles your grandparents' living room right down to the tacky wall art and plastic placemats. Feel safe in ordering anything deep-fried – staff do an excellent job of it – and don't miss the deliciously garlicky eggplant dip.

Hemlock THAI $$
(Map p82; 56 Th Phra Athit; mains 75-280B; ⊗4pm-midnight Mon-Sat; ✤🖋; 🚢Phra Athit/Banglamphu Pier) Taking full advantage of its cosy shophouse location, this perennial favourite has enough style to feel like a special night out, but doesn't skimp on flavour or preparation. The eclectic menu reads like an ancient literary work, reviving old dishes from aristocratic kitchens across the country, not to mention several meat-free items.

Bangkok Poutine INTERNATIONAL $$
(Map p82; www.facebook.com/bangkokpoutine; Th Samsen; mains 70-200B; ⊗noon-midnight Tue-Sun; ✤🖋; 🚢Phra Athit/Banglamphu Pier) You've conquered the deep-fried scorpion, now wrangle with poutine: French fries topped with cheese curds and gravy. Run by guys from Québec, this is the place to go for Francophone pop and the latest hockey game, as well as dishes ranging in cuisine from Thai to Lebanese, including lots of meat-free items.

★ Jay Fai THAI $$$
(Map p82; 327 Th Mahachai; mains 180-1000B; ⊗3pm-2am Mon-Sat; 🚢klorng boat to Phanfa Leelard Pier) With its bare-bones dining room, it's hard to believe Jay Fai is renowned for serving Bangkok's most expensive *pàt kêe mow* ('drunkard's noodles': wide rice noodles fried with seafood and Thai herbs). The price, however, is justified by the copious fresh seafood, plus a distinct frying style resulting in an almost oil-free finished dish.

It's in a virtually unmarked shophouse, opposite a 7-Eleven.

🍴 Chinatown & Phahurat

When you mention Chinatown, most Bangkokians immediately dream of street food, the bulk of which is found just off Th Yaowarat.

On the western side of the neighbourhood is Phahurat, Bangkok's Little India, filled with small Indian and Nepali restaurants tucked into the tiny soi off Th Chakkaraphet.

Nay Hong STREET FOOD $
(Map p88; off Th Yukol 2, no Roman-script sign; mains 35-50B; ⊗4-10pm; 🚢Ratchawong Pier, Ⓜ Hua Lamphong exit 1 & taxi) The reward for locating this hole-in-the-wall is one of Bangkok's best fried noodle dishes – *gŏo·ay đĕe·o kôo·a gài* (flat rice noodles fried with garlic oil, chicken and egg). No English-language menu.

To find Nay Hong, proceed north from the corner of Th Suapa and Th Luang, then turn right into the first side street; it's at the end of the narrow alleyway.

Old Siam Plaza SWEETS $
(Map p88; cnr Th Phahurat & Th Triphet; mains 30-90B; ⊗10am-7pm; ✤; 🚢Saphan Phut/Memorial Bridge Pier, Pak Klong Taladd Pier) Sugar junkies, be sure to include this stop on your Bangkok eating itinerary. The ground floor of this shopping centre is a candyland of traditional Thai sweets and snacks, most made right before your eyes.

80/20 INTERNATIONAL $$
(Map p92; 📞02 639 1135; www.facebook.com/8020bkk; 1052-1054 Th Charoen Krung; mains from 240B; ⊗6pm-midnight Wed-Mon; ✤; 🚢Ratchawong Pier, Ⓜ Hua Lamphong exit 1) Don't call it fusion; rather, 80/20 excels at taking and blending Thai and Western ingredients and dishes, arriving at something altogether unique. The often savoury-leaning desserts, overseen by a Japanese pastry chef, are especially worth the trip. A progressive breath of air in otherwise conservative Chinatown.

Little Market AMERICAN $$
(Map p92; www.facebook.com/littlemarketbkk; 1056/7 Soi 28, Th Charoen Krung; mains 100-180B; ⊗10am-10pm Tue-Sun; 🚢Ratchawong Pier, Ⓢ Hua Lamphong exit 1) They may not look like much, but the sliders here are some of the best burgers in town. Throw into the mix

LOCAL KNOWLEDGE

CHINATOWN'S VEGETARIAN FESTIVAL

During the annual Vegetarian Festival in September/October, Bangkok's Chinatown becomes a virtual orgy of non-meat cuisine. The festivities centre on Chinatown's main street, Th Yaowarat, and the Talat Noi (p85) area, but food shops and stalls all over the city post yellow flags to announce their meat-free status.

Celebrating alongside the ethnic Chinese are Thais who look forward to the special dishes that appear during the festival period. Most restaurants put their normal menus on hold and instead prepare soy-based substitutes for standard Thai dishes like *đôm yam* (Thai-style spicy/sour soup) and *gaang kĕe·o wǎhn* (green curry). Even Thai regional cuisines are sold (without the meat, of course). Yellow Hokkien-style noodles often make an appearance in the special festival dishes, usually in stir-fries along with meaty mushrooms and big hunks of vegetables.

Along with abstinence from meat, the 10-day festival is celebrated with special visits to the temple, often requiring worshippers to dress in white.

the crispy tater tots, American-style breakfasts and a fun retro vibe with a classic rock soundtrack, and Little Market just might be the most authentically American eatery in Bangkok.

Thanon Phadungdao
Seafood Stalls   STREET FOOD $$
(Map p88; cnr Th Phadungdao & Th Yaowarat; mains 100-600B; ⊙4pm-midnight Tue-Sun; ⍟Ratchawong Pier, Ⓜ Hua Lamphong exit 1 & taxi) After sunset, these two opposing open-air restaurants – each of which claims to be the original – become a culinary train wreck of outdoor barbecues, screaming staff, iced seafood trays and messy pavement seating. True, the vast majority of diners are foreign tourists, but this has little impact on the cheerful setting, the fun experience and the cheap bill.

Royal India   INDIAN $$
(Map p88; 392/1 Th Chakkaraphet; mains 135-220B; ⊙10am-10pm; ⍟✎; ⍟Saphan Phut/Memorial Bridge Pier, Pak Klong Taladd Pier) Yes, we're aware that this hole-in-the-wall has been in every edition of our guide since the beginning, but after all these years it's still the most reliable place to eat in Bangkok's Little India. Try any of the delicious breads or rich curries, and don't forget to finish with a homemade Punjabi sweet.

✖ Riverside

Le Normandie   FRENCH $$$
(Map p92; ✆02 659 9000; www.mandarinoriental.com; Mandarin Oriental, 48 Soi 40/Oriental, Th Charoen Krung; mains 2100-3300B; ⊙noon-2.30pm & 7-11pm Mon-Sat, 7-11pm Sun; ⍟; ⍟Oriental Pier

or hotel shuttle boat from Sathon/Central Pier) Although today's Bangkok boasts a plethora of upmarket choices, Le Normandie has maintained its niche and is still the only place to go for a genuinely old-world 'Continental' dining experience. A revolving cast of Michelin-starred guest chefs and some of the world's most decadent ingredients keep up the standard, and appropriately formal attire (including jacket) is required. Book ahead.

Never Ending Summer   THAI $$$
(Map p92; ✆02 861 0953; www.facebook.com/theneverendingsummer; 41/5 Th Charoen Nakhon; mains 200-1000B; ⊙11am-11pm; ⍟; ⍟river-crossing ferry from River City Pier) The cheesy name doesn't do justice to this surprisingly sophisticated Thai restaurant located in a former warehouse by the river. Join Bangkok's beautiful crowd for antiquated Thai dishes such as cubes of watermelon served with a dry 'dressing' of fish, sugar and deep-fried shallots, or fragrant green curry with pork and fresh bird's-eye chilli.

✖ Lumphini Park & Rama IV

Kai Thort Jay Kee   THAI $$
(Polo Fried Chicken; Map p96; 137/1-3 Soi Sanam Khli/Polo; mains 50-350B; ⊙11am-9pm; ⍟; Ⓜ Lumphini exit 3) Although the *sôm·đam* (spicy green papaya salad), sticky rice and *lâhp* (a spicy salad of minced meat) of this former street stall give the impression of a northeastern-Thai-style eatery, the restaurant's namesake deep-fried bird is more southern in origin. Regardless, smothered in a thick

layer of crispy deep-fried garlic, it is none other than a truly Bangkok experience.

★ nahm
THAI $$$

(Map p96; ☑ 02 625 3388; www.comohotels.com; ground fl, Metropolitan Hotel, 27 Th Sathon Tai/South; set lunch 600-1600B, set dinner 2500B, mains 310-800B; ⊙ noon-2pm Mon-Fri, 7-10.30pm daily; ❉; Ⓜ Lumphini exit 2) Australian chef-author David Thompson is the man behind one of Bangkok's – and if you believe the critics, the world's – best Thai restaurants. Using ancient cookbooks as his inspiration, Thompson has given new life to previously extinct dishes with exotic descriptions such as 'smoked fish curry with prawns, chicken livers, cockles, chillies and black pepper'.

Issaya Siamese Club
THAI $$$

(Map p96; ☑ 02 672 9040; www.issaya.com; 4 Soi Sri Aksorn; mains 150-600B; ⊙ 11.30am-2.30pm & 6-10.30pm; ❉✐; Ⓜ Khlong Toei exit 1 & taxi) Housed in a charming 1920s-era villa, Issaya is Thai celebrity-chef Ian Kittichai's first effort at a domestic outpost serving the food of his homeland. Dishes alternate between somewhat saucy, meaty items and lighter dishes using produce from the restaurant's organic garden.

The restaurant can be a bit tricky to find, and is best approached in a taxi via Soi Ngam Du Phli.

🍴 Silom & Sathon

Th Silom has a bit of everything, from old-school Thai to some of the city's best upmarket international dining.

Jay So
THAI $

(Map p98; 146/1 Soi Phiphat 2; mains 45-80B; ⊙ 10am-4pm Mon-Sat; Ⓜ Si Lom exit 2, Ⓢ Sala Daeng exit 2) Jay So has no menu, but a mortar and pestle and a huge grill are the telltale signs of ballistically spicy *sôm·dam* (green papaya salad), sublime herb-stuffed, grilled catfish and other northeastern Thai specialities.

There's no English signage (nor an English-language menu), so look for the ramshackle, white and green, Coke-decorated shack about halfway down Soi Phiphat 2.

Muslim Restaurant
THAI $

(Map p92; 1354-6 Th Charoen Krung; mains 40-140B; ⊙ 6.30am-5.30pm; 🚢 Oriental Pier, Ⓢ Saphan Taksin exit 1) Plant yourself in any random wooden booth of this ancient eatery for a glimpse into what restaurants in Bangkok used to be like. The menu, much like the interior design, doesn't appear to have changed much in the restaurant's 70-year history, and the biryanis, curries and samosas remain more Indian-influenced than Thai.

Chennai Kitchen
INDIAN $

(Map p98; 107/4 Th Pan; mains 70-150B; ⊙ 10am-3pm & 6-9.30pm; ❉✐; Ⓢ Surasak exit 3) This thimble-sized mum-and-dad restaurant puts out some of the best southern Indian vegetarian food in town. The metre-long *dosai* (a crispy southern Indian bread) is always a good choice, but if you're feeling indecisive (or exceptionally famished) go for the banana-leaf thali (set meal) that seems to incorporate just about everything in the kitchen.

Soi 10 Food Centres
THAI $

(Map p98; Soi 10, Th Silom; mains 20-60B; ⊙ 8am-3pm Mon-Fri; Ⓜ Si Lom exit 2, Ⓢ Sala Daeng exit 1) These two adjacent hangar-like buildings tucked behind Soi 10 are the main lunchtime fuelling stations for the area's office staff. Choices range from southern-style *kôw gaang* (point-and-choose curries ladled over rice) to just about every incarnation of Thai noodle.

Sushi Tsukiji
JAPANESE $$

(Map p98; 62/19-20 Th Thaniya; sushi per item 60-700B; ⊙ 11.30am-2.30pm & 5.30-10.30pm; ❉; Ⓜ Si Lom exit 2, Ⓢ Sala Daeng exit 1) Our pick of the numerous Japanese joints along Th Thaniya is Tsukiji, named after Tokyo's famous seafood market. Dinner at this sleek sushi joint will leave a significant dent in the wallet, so instead come for lunch on a weekday, when Tsukiji does generous set meals for a paltry 300B.

Taling Pling
THAI $$

(Map p98; Baan Silom, Soi 19, Th Silom; mains 110-275B; ⊙ 11am-10pm; ❉✐; Ⓢ Surasak exit 3) Don't be fooled by the flashy interior; long-standing Taling Pling continues to serve a thick menu of homey, full-flavoured Thai dishes. It's a good starting point for rich, southern and central Thai fare such as *gaang kôo·a* (crabmeat curry with wild betel leaves), with tasty pies and cakes and refreshing drinks rounding out the choices.

DON'T MISS

BANGKOK'S BEST FOOD COURTS

The Siam Square area has more than its share of mall-based food courts. They're generally cheap, clean, air-conditioned and have English-language menus. At most, paying is done by exchanging cash for vouchers or a temporary credit card at one of several counters; your change is refunded at the same desk.

MBK Food Island (Map p102; 6th fl, MBK Center, cnr Rama I & Th Phayathai; mains 35-150B; ⊙10am-9pm; ※✐; ⑤National Stadium exit 4) Dozens of vendors selling Thai-Chinese, regional Thai and international dishes.

Food Republic (Map p102; 4th fl, Siam Center, cnr Rama I & Th Phayathai; mains 30-200B; ⊙10am-10pm; ※✐; ⑤Siam exit 1) A good mix of Thai and international (mostly Asian) outlets in an open, modern-feeling locale.

Eathai (Map p102; www.facebook.com/eathaibycentral; basement, Central Embassy, 1031 Th Phloen Chit; mains 60-360B; ⊙10am-10pm; ※✐; ⑤Phloen Chit exit 5) This expansive food court spans Thai dishes from just about every corner of the country.

Gourmet Paradise (Map p102; ground fl, Siam Paragon, 991/1 Rama I; mains 35-500B; ⊙10am-10pm; ※✐; ⑤Siam exits 3 & 5) Unites international fast-food chains, domestic restaurants and food-court-style stalls, with an emphasis on the sweet stuff.

Food Loft (Map p102; www.centralfoodloft.com; 6th fl, Central Chidlom, 1027 Th Phloen Chit; mains 65-950B; ⊙10am-10pm; ※✐; ⑤Chit Lom exit 5) Pioneered the concept of the upscale food court.

FoodPark (Map p102; 4th fl, Big C, 97/11 Th Ratchadamri; mains 30-90B; ⊙9am-9pm; ※; ⑤Chit Lom exit 9 to Sky Walk) Selections here may not inspire you, but they are representative of the kind of 'fast food' Thais enjoy eating.

★ **Eat Me**　　　　　INTERNATIONAL **$$$**
(Map p98; ☑02 238 0931; www.eatmerestaurant. com; Soi Phiphat 2; mains 300-1400B; ⊙3pm-1am; ※✐; ⓜSi Lom exit 2, ⑤Sala Daeng exit 2) With descriptions like 'charred witlof and mozzarella salad with preserved lemon and dry-aged Cecina beef', the dishes may sound all over the map or perhaps somewhat pretentious, but they're actually just plain tasty. A casual yet sophisticated atmosphere, excellent cocktails, a handsome wine list, and some of the city's best desserts also make this one of our favourite places in Bangkok to dine.

L'Atelier de
Joël Robuchon　　　INTERNATIONAL **$$$**
(Map p98; ☑02 001 0698; www.robuchon-bang kok.com; 5th fl, Mahanakorn Cube, 96 Th Naradhiwas Rajanagarindra/Chong Nonsi; set lunch 950-1950B, set dinner 7500-11,500B, mains 1350-3200B; ⊛11.30am-2pm & 6.30-10pm; ※✐; ⑤Chong Nonsi exit 3) We'd like to think that you came to Bangkok to eat Thai, but we'd be remiss not to mention this place. Helmed by the chef who holds more Michelin stars than anyone else, it's one of the biggest openings in the city's recent past. Expect modern, French-inspired dishes, some with local touches, served in a sexy, sultry atmosphere where counter-top 'atelier' seating is encouraged.

Somboon Seafood　　　　CHINESE **$$$**
(Map p98; ☑02 233 3104; www.somboonseafood. com; cnr Th Surawong & Th Naradhiwas Rajanagarindra/Chong Nonsi; mains 120-900B; ⊙4-11pm; ※; ⑤Chong Nonsi exit 3) Somboon, a hectic seafood hall with a reputation far and wide, is known for doing the best curry-powder crab in town. Soy-steamed sea bass (*plah grà·pong nêung see·éw*) is also a speciality and, like all good Thai seafood, should be enjoyed with an immense platter of *kôw pàt boo* (fried rice with crab) and as many friends as you can gather together.

✕ **Siam Square, Pratunam & Around**

If you find yourself hungry in this part of central Bangkok, you're largely at the mercy of shopping-mall food courts and chain restaurants. However, this is still Thailand, and if you can ignore the prefabricated atmosphere, the food can often be quite good.

Open House CAFE

(Map p102; ☏02 119 7777; www.centralembassy.
com/anchor/open-house; 6th fl, Central Embassy, 1031 Th Phloen Chit; ◷10am-10pm; ❄🛜♿;
Ⓢ Phloen Chit) Housed in posh Central Embassy mall, Open House is a chic, light-filled
multi-use space from the same team who
designed YouTube and Google's Tokyo headquarters. The open floor plan incorporates
restaurants, galleries, a bookstore, a breezy
balcony for lounging and 180-degree views
of buzzy Th Sukhumvit. Pop in to recharge
with an iced latte and connect to the fast
wi-fi.

Nuer Koo CHINESE $

(Map p102; 4th fl, Siam Paragon, 991/1 Rama I;
mains 85-970B; ◷11.30am-9.15pm; ❄; Ⓢ Siam
exits 3 & 5) Is this the future of the noodle
stall? Mall-bound Nuer Koo does a luxe version of the formerly humble bowl of beef
noodles. Choose your cut of beef (including
Kobe beef from Japan), enjoy the rich broth
and cool air-con, and quickly forget about
the good old days.

Somtam Nua THAI $

(Map p102; 392/14 Soi 5, Siam Sq; mains 75-120B;
◷10.45am-9.30pm; ❄; Ⓢ Siam exit 4) It can't
compete with the street stalls for flavour
and authenticity, but if you need to be seen,
particularly while in air-con and trendy surroundings, this is a good place to sample
northeastern Thai specialities. Expect a line
at dinner.

Gaa INTERNATIONAL $$$

(Map p102; ☏091 419 2424; www.gaabkk.com;
68/4 Soi Langsuan; set menu 1800-2400B; ◷6-
9.30pm; ❄; Ⓢ Ratchadamri) A bright yellow
and pink shophouse opposite Gaggan (☏02
652 1700; www.eatatgaggan.com; 68/1 Th Langsu-
an; set menu 5000B; ◷6-11pm; ❄🖊) has been
taken over by Gaggan's former sous chef,
Garima Arora, who also honed her craft at
Copenhagen's famed Noma. Classic Indian
and Thai dishes are the specialities here,
upgraded with modern cooking techniques
and presented in artful 8-12-course tasting
menus. Reservations are strongly recom-
mended.

Din Tai Fung CHINESE $$

(Map p102; 7th fl, CentralWorld, Th Ratchadamri; mains 65-350B; ◷11am-10pm; ❄🖊; Ⓢ Chit
Lom exit 9 to Sky Walk, Siam exit 6 to Sky Walk)
Most come to this lauded Taiwanese chain
for the *xiao long bao* (broth-filled 'soup'

dumplings). And so should you. But the other northern-Chinese-style dishes are just as
good, and justify exploring the more remote
regions of the menu.

Coca Suki CHINESE, THAI $$

(Map p102; 416/3-8 Th Henri Dunant; mains 100-
800B; ◷11am-11pm; ❄🖊; Ⓢ Siam exit 6) Im-
mensely popular with Thai families, *sù·gêe*
takes the form of a bubbling hotpot of broth
and the raw ingredients to dip therein. Coca
is one of the oldest purveyors of the dish,
and this branch reflects the brand's efforts
to appear more modern. Insider tip for fans
of spice: be sure to request the tangy *tom
yam* broth.

🍴 Sukhumvit

With the city's largest selection of interna-
tional restaurants, this seemingly endless
ribbon of a road is where to go if, for the
duration of a meal, you wish to forget that
you're in Thailand.

Gokfayuen CHINESE $

(Map p106; www.facebook.com/wuntunmeen;
161/7 Soi Thong Lor 9; mains 70-140B; ◷11am-
11.30pm; ❄; Ⓢ Thong Lo exit 3 & taxi) Gokfayuen
has gone to great lengths to re-create classic
Hong Kong dishes in Bangkok. Couple your
house-made wheat-and-egg noodles with
roasted pork, steamed vegetables with oys-
ter sauce, or the Hong Kong–style milk tea.

Saras INDIAN $

(Map p106; www.saras.co.th; Soi 20, Th Sukhum-
vit; mains 90-200B; ◷9am-10.30pm; ❄🖊;
Ⓜ Sukhumvit exit 2, Ⓢ Asok exit 4) Describing
your restaurant as a 'fast-food feast' may not
be the cleverest PR strategy we've encoun-
tered, but it's a pretty spot-on description of
this Indian restaurant. Order at the counter
to be rewarded with *dosai* (crispy southern
Indian bread), meat-free regional set meals
or rich curries (dishes are brought to your
table). We wish all fast food could be this
satisfying.

Klang Soi Restaurant THAI $

(Map p106; Soi 49/9, Th Sukhumvit; mains 80-
250B; ◷11am-2.30pm & 5-10pm Tue-Sun; ❄;
Ⓢ Phrom Phong exit 3 & taxi) If you had a Thai
grandma who lived in the Sukhumvit area,
this is where she'd eat. The mimeographed
menu spans old-school specialties from cen-
tral and southern Thailand, as well as a few
Western dishes.

DINNER CRUISES

A dinner cruise along Mae Nam Chao Phraya is touted as an iconic Bangkok experience, and several companies cater to this. Yet it's worth mentioning that, in general, the vibe can be somewhat cheesy, with loud live entertainment and mammoth boats so brightly lit inside you hardly know you're on the water. The food, typically served as a buffet, usually ranges from mediocre to forgettable. But the atmosphere of the river at night, bordered by illuminated temples and skyscrapers, and the cool breeze chasing the heat away, is usually enough to trump all of this.

A good one-stop centre for all your dinner cruise needs is the **River City Boat Tour Check-In Center** (Map p92; www.rivercity.co.th; ground fl, River City, 23 Th Yotha; ⊙10am-10pm; ⊠Si Phraya/River City Pier, or shuttle boat from Sathon/Central Pier), where tickets can be purchased for **Grand Pearl** (Map p92; ☑02 861 0255; www.grandpearlcruise.com; cruises 2000B; ⊙cruise 7.30-9.30pm), **Chaophraya Cruise** (Map p92; ☑02 541 5599; www.chao phrayacruise.com; cruises 1700B; ⊙cruise 7-9pm), **Wan Fah** (Map p92; ☑02 622 7657; www.wan fah.in.th; cruises 1500B; ⊙cruise 7-9pm), **Chao Phraya Princess** (Map p92; ☑02 860 3700; www.thaicruise.com; cruises 1500B; ⊙cruise 7-9.30pm) and **White Orchid** (Map p92; ☑02 438 8228; www.whiteorchidrivercruise.com; cruises 1400B; ⊙cruise 7.20-9.45pm). All cruises depart from River City Pier; take a look at the websites to see exactly what's on offer.

For something slightly more upscale, consider **Manohra Cruises** (Map p76; ☑02 476 0022; www.manohracruises.com; cruises 2300B; ⊠hotel shuttle boat from Sathon/Central Pier) or **Supanniga Cruise** (Map p92; ☑02 714 7608; www.supannigacruise.com; cruises 1250-3250B; ⊙cruises 4.45-5.45pm & 6.15-8.30pm; ⊠Si Phraya/River City Pier), more intimate experiences that also get positive feedback for their food.

Located at the end of Soi 49/9, in the Racquet Club complex.

★ **Sri Trat**   THAI **$$**
(Map p106; www.facebook.com/sritrat; 90 Soi 33, Th Sukhumvit; mains 180-450B; ⊙noon-11pm Wed-Mon; ❄; ⑤Phrom Phong exit 5) This new restaurant specialises in the unique fare of Thailand's eastern provinces, Trat and Chanthaburi. What this means is lots of rich, slightly sweet, herbal flavours, fresh seafood and dishes you won't find anywhere else in town. Highly recommended.

★ **Soul Food Mahanakorn**   THAI **$$**
(Map p106; ☑02 714 7708; www.soulfood mahanakorn.com; 56/10 Soi 55/Thong Lor, Th Sukhumvit; mains 140-290B; ⊙5.30pm-midnight; ❄☙; ⑤Thong Lo exit 3) This contemporary staple gets its interminable buzz from its dual nature as both an inviting restaurant – the menu spans tasty interpretations of rustic Thai dishes – and a bar serving deliciously boozy, Thai-influenced cocktails. Reservations recommended.

★ **Jidori Cuisine Ken**   JAPANESE **$$**
(Map p106; ☑02 661 3457; www.facebook.com/jidoriken; off Soi 26, Th Sukhumvit; mains 60-350B; ⊙5pm-midnight Mon-Sat, to 10pm Sun; ❄; ⑤Phrom Phong exit 4) This cosy Japanese restaurant does tasty tofu dishes, delicious salads and even excellent desserts; basically everything here is above average, but the highlight is the smoky, perfectly seasoned chicken skewers. Reservations recommended.

Daniel Thaiger   AMERICAN **$$**
(Map p106; ☑084 549 0995; www.facebook.com/danielthaiger; Soi 11, Th Sukhumvit; mains from 140B; ⊙11am-late; ⑤Nana exit 3) Bangkok's best burgers are served from this American-run stall that, at the time of research, had a long-standing location on Soi 11. Check the Facebook page to see where the food truck will be when you're in town.

Game Over   AMERICAN **$$**
(Map p106; www.gameover.co.th; Liberty Plaza, 1000/39 Soi 55/Thong Lor, Th Sukhumvit; mains 160-340B; ⊙5.30pm-2am Tue-Fri, 11.30am-2am Sat & Sun; ❄; ⊠Soi Thong Lor Pier, ⑤Thong Lo exit 3 & taxi) Indulge your inner teen by playing *Call of Duty* while downing burgers and truffle fries at this video-game centre/restaurant. For the old at heart, there's Scrabble and an impressive selection of imported microbrews.

Cabbages & Condoms
THAI $$

(Map p106; www.pda.or.th; Soi 12, Th Sukhumvit; mains 120-470B; ⏰11am-11pm; ✳🌶; Ⓜ Sukhumvit exit 3, Ⓢ Asok exit 2) ✈ This long-standing garden restaurant is a safe place to gauge the Thai staples. It also stands for a safe cause: instead of after-meal mints, diners receive packaged condoms, and all proceeds go towards the Population and Community Development Association (PDA), a sex education/AIDS prevention organisation.

★ Appia
ITALIAN $$$

(Map p106; ✆02 261 2056; www.appia-bangkok.com; 20/4 Soi 31, Th Sukhumvit; mains 400-1000B; ⏰6.30-11pm Tue-Sat, 11.30am-2.30pm & 6.30-11pm Sun; ✳🌶; Ⓢ Phrom Phong exit 5) Handmade pastas, slow-roasted meats and a carefully curated and relatively affordable wine list are the selling points of this restaurant serving Roman-style cuisine – for our baht, one of the best places in town for non-Thai dinner. Reservations recommended.

★ Ginzado
JAPANESE $$$

(Map p106; ✆02 392 3247; Panjit Tower, 117 Soi 55/Thong Lor, Th Sukhumvit; mains 120-900B; ⏰5-11pm; ✳; Ⓢ Thong Lo exit 3) Make a reservation or queue for some really excellent *yakitori* (DIY grilled beef) not to mention a mean *bibimbap* (rice and toppings served in a sizzling stone bowl). Ginzado is located between Soi Thong Lor 3 and Soi Thong Lor 5, through the large white archway.

The Commons
MARKET $$$

(Map p106; www.thecommonsbkk.com; 335 Soi 17, Soi 55/Thong Lor, Th Sukhumvit; mains 500-2000B; ⏰8am-midnight; ✳🌶; Ⓢ Thong Lo exit 3 & taxi) Trendy Thong Lor gets even cooler with this marketplace-style eatery that is packed with reliable names such as Soul Food 555, Peppina and Meat & Bones, along with a coffee roaster, a craft beer bar and wine vendor. It's an ideal place to idle away an evening listening to Jack Johnson wannabes strum acoustic sets.

Bei Otto
GERMAN $$$

(Map p106; ✆02 260 0869; www.beiotto.com; 1 Soi 20, Th Sukhumvit; mains 200-1000B; ⏰11am-midnight; ✳🌶; Ⓜ Sukhumvit exit 2, Ⓢ Asok exit 4) Claiming a Bangkok residence for more than 30 years, Bei Otto's culinary bragging point is its pork knuckles, reputedly the best in town. A good selection of German beers and an attached delicatessen with brilliant breads and super sausages make it even more attractive to go Deutsch.

⚔ Ratchathewi

Toy
THAI $

(Map p112; Soi 18, Th Ratchawithi, no roman-script sign; mains from 15B; ⏰8am-5pm; Ⓢ Victory Monument exit 3) The area surrounding the Victory Monument is home to heaps of simple restaurants selling spicy, rich 'boat noodles' – so-called because they used to be sold directly from boats that plied central Thailand's rivers and canals. Our pick of the lot is Toy, located at the edge of the canal at the

---

LGBT BANGKOK

Bangkok has a notoriously pink vibe to it. From kinky male-underwear shops mushrooming at street corners to lesbian-only get-togethers, as a LGBT person you could eat, shop and play here for days without ever leaving the comfort of gay-friendly venues. Unlike elsewhere in Southeast Asia, homosexuality is not criminalised in Thailand and the general attitude remains extremely laissez-faire.

Bangkok Lesbian (www.bangkoklesbian.com) is the city's premier website for ladies who love ladies, while **BK** (www.bk.asia-city.com) and **Siam2nite** (www.siam2nite.com) are good sources for LGBT events in Bangkok. Noted pop parodists **Trasher** (www.facebook.com/trasherbangkok) organise gay-friendly parties – check the website to see if one's on when you're in town.

Don't miss **DJ Station** (p141), one of the most iconic gay nightclubs in Asia. Other highlights are **Telephone Pub** (Map p98; www.telephonepub.com; 114/11-13 Soi 4, Th Silom; ⏰6pm-1am; 🛜; Ⓜ Si Lom exit 2, Ⓢ Sala Daeng exit 1), a long-standing bar right in the middle of Bangkok's pinkest zone, and the city's premier drag show, **Playhouse Magical Cabaret** (Map p118; ✆02 024 5522; www.playhousethailand.com; 5 Th Ratchadapisek, Chompol Sub-District, Chatuchak; 960B; ⏰show times 8pm & 9.30pm; Ⓢ Lat Phrao exit 1).

DON'T MISS

ROOFTOP BARS

In Bangkok, nobody seems to mind if you slap the odd bar on top of a skyscraper. Indeed, the city has become associated with open-air rooftop bars, and the area around Th Sathon and Th Silom is home to some of its best, with locales boasting views that range from riverside to hyper-urban.

Note that nearly all of Bangkok's hotel-based rooftop bars have strictly enforced dress codes barring access to those wearing shorts and/or sandals.

Moon Bar (Map p96; www.banyantree.com; 61st fl, Banyan Tree Hotel, 21/100 Th Sathon Tai/South; ⊙5pm-1am; Ⓜ Lumphini exit 2) An alarmingly low barrier at this rooftop bar is all that separates patrons from the street, 61 floors down. Located on top of the Banyan Tree Hotel, Moon Bar claims to be among the highest alfresco bars in the world. It's also a great place from which to see the Phrapradaeng Peninsula, the vast green area that's colloquially known as Bangkok's green lung.

Park Society (Map p96; 29th fl, Sofitel So, 2 Th Sathon Neua/North; ⊙5pm-2am; Ⓜ Lumphini exit 2) Gazing down at the green expanse of Lumphini Park, abruptly bordered by tall buildings on most sides, you can be excused for thinking that Bangkok almost, kinda, sorta feels like Manhattan. The drink prices at Park Society, 29 floors above the ground, may also remind you of New York City, although there are monthly promotions.

Sky Bar (Map p92; www.lebua.com; 63rd fl, State Tower, 1055 Th Silom; ⊙6pm-1am; Ⓔ Sathon/Central Pier, Ⓢ Saphan Taksin exit 3) Descend the Hollywood-like staircase to emerge at this bar that juts out over the city's skyline and Mae Nam Chao Phraya. This is the classic Bangkok rooftop bar – scenes from *The Hangover Part II* were filmed here – and the views are breathtaking, although the excessive drink prices and photo-snapping crowds have made it an increasingly hectic destination.

northern end of Soi 18, Th Ratchawithi. No English-language menu.

✕ Thewet & Dusit

While Thewet may lack in culinary diversity, it excels in riverfront views. There's little in the way of dining in Dusit.

Nang Loeng Market THAI $
(Map p76; btwn Soi 8-10, Th Nakhon Sawan; mains 30-80B; ⊙10am-2pm Mon-Fri; Ⓔ Thewet Pier, Ⓢ Phaya Thai exit 3 & taxi) Dating back to 1899, this atmospheric fresh market offers a charming glimpse of old Bangkok – not to mention a great place to grab a bite. Nang Loeng is renowned for its Thai sweets, and at lunchtime it's also an excellent place to fill up on central-Thai-style curries or Chinese-influenced noodles.

Kaloang Home Kitchen THAI $
(Map p115; Th Si Ayuthaya; mains 80-300B; ⊙10am-10pm; Ⓔ Thewet Pier) Don't be alarmed by the peeling paint and dilapidated deck – the return customers at Kaloang Home Kitchen certainly aren't. The laid-back atmosphere and seafood-heavy menu will quickly dispel any concerns about sinking into Mae Nam

Chao Phraya, and a beer and the breeze will temporarily erase any scarring memories of Bangkok traffic.

To reach the restaurant, follow the final windy stretch of Th Si Ayuthaya all the way to the river.

★ Likhit Kai Yang THAI $$
(Map p82; off Th Ratchadamnoen Nok, no Roman-script sign; mains 50-300B; ⊙9am-9pm; ❋; Ⓔ Thewet Pier, Ⓢ Phaya Thai exit 3 & taxi) Located just behind Rajadamnern Stadium (avoid the grotty branch directly adjacent to the stadium), this decades-old restaurant is where locals come for a northeastern-Thai-style meal before a Thai boxing match. The friendly English-speaking owner will steer you through the ordering process, but don't miss the deliciously herbal, eponymous 'charcoal roasted chicken'. There's no English-language sign; look for the huge yellow banner.

★ Krua Apsorn THAI $$
(Map p115; www.kruaapsorn.com; 503-505 Th Samsen; mains 100-450B; ⊙10.30am-7.30pm Mon-Fri, to 6pm Sat; ❋; Ⓔ Thewet Pier) This is the original branch of this homey, award-winning and royally patronised restaurant. Expect

a clientele of fussy families and big-haired, middle-aged ladies, and a cuisine revolving around full-flavoured, largely seafood- and vegetable-heavy central and southern Thai dishes. If you have dinner in mind, be sure to note the early closing times.

Khinlom Chom Sa-Phan
THAI $$

(Map p115; ☑ 02 628 8382; www.khinlomchom saphan.com; 11/6 Soi 3, Th Samsen; mains 100-2500B; ⊙ 11.30am-midnight; ☑ Thewet Pier) Locals come to this open-air restaurant for the combination of riverfront views and tasty, seafood-based eats; it also doubles quite neatly as a pub. It's popular, so be sure to call ahead to book a riverfront table.

Steve Café & Cuisine
THAI $$

(Map p115; www.stevecafeandcuisine.com; 68 Soi 21, Th Si Ayuthaya; mains 180-1900B; ⊙ 11.30am-2.30pm Mon-Fri, to 11pm Sat & Sun; ☑ Thewet Pier) The cheesy name is seemingly a cover for this sophisticated, house-bound, riverside Thai restaurant. The menu spans a good selection of Thai dishes, and service is friendly and efficient, even when the place is mobbed.

To get here, enter Th Si Ayuthaya and walk through **Wat Thewaratkunchorn** (วัด เทวราชกุญชร) until you reach the river; locals will help point the way.

🍴 Northern Bangkok

Although a bit of a trek, an excursion to Bangkok's suburbs can be a profoundly tasty experience, with heaps of restaurants that don't tone down their flavours for foreigners. The city's outskirts are also a great place to sample regional Thai cuisine.

Yusup
THAI $

(Map p76; 531/12 Kaset-Navamin Hwy; mains 50-120B; ⊙ 8.30am-3pm; ☑ Mo Chit exit 3 & taxi) The Thai-language sign in front of this restaurant boldly says *rah·chah kôw mòk* (King of Biryani) and Yusup indeed backs it up with flawless biryani, not to mention sour oxtail soup and decadent *gaang mát·sà·màn* ('Muslim curry'). For dessert try *roh·dee wăhn,* a paratha-like crispy pancake with sweetened condensed milk and sugar – a dish that will send most carb-fearing Westerners running away screaming.

To get here, take a taxi heading north from BTS Mo Chit and tell the driver to take you to the Kaset intersection and turn right

> ℹ Smoking is banned indoors at bars and restaurants.

on Th Kaset-Navamin. Yusup is on the left-hand side, about 1km past the first stoplight.

Kaobahn
THAI $$

(Map p118; www.facebook.com/kaobahn; Aran Bicicletta, 128/10 Soi, Th Phahonyothin; mains 50-120B; ⊙ 11am-9pm Fri-Wed; ☑ Ari exit 2) Kaobahn means, roughly, home cooking, which is an accurate description of the no-frills-yet-full-flavoured central Thai dishes here. There's no English-language menu, but there's an iPad with images of the dishes, which range from a rich, spicy red curry with pork and pumpkin to a dip of grilled mackerel. Nor will you find an English-language sign, but the restaurant is located behind Aran Bicicletta cafe.

Baan Pueng Chom
THAI $$

(Map p118; Soi Chua Chit, off Soi 7/Ari, Th Phahonyothin; mains 90-250B; ⊙ 11am-2pm & 4-10pm Mon-Sat; ❄; ☑ Ari exit 1) These days, it takes venturing to the burbs to find an old-school Thai restaurant like this. Ensconced in a watery jungle of a garden, Baan Pueng Chom has a fat, illustrated menu of typically full-flavoured, fragrant Thai dishes you're unlikely to find elsewhere. Call ahead if you wish to sit indoors.

Puritan
DESSERTS $$

(Map p118; 46/1 Soi Ari 5, Th Phahonyothin; cakes & pastries from 120B; ⊙ 1-10pm Tue-Fri, 11am-10pm Sat & Sun; ❄; ☑ Ari exit 1) In an attempt to describe the vibe of this uniquely bizarre dessert cafe, our source uttered the words 'a knight wearing a tiara'. Oddly enough this is a pretty accurate summary of Puritan, although the 16-plus chandeliers, taxidermied animals, cherubs and other antiquated, Europhile touches need to be seen in person. Most importantly, however, there are excellent and authentic cakes and pies.

Fatbird
INTERNATIONAL $$

(Map p118; ☑ 02 619 6609; www.facebook.com/fatbird; Soi 7/Ari, Th Phahonyothin; mains 160-300B; ⊙ 5.30pm-midnight Tue-Sun; ❄; ☑ Ari exit 3) The dishes here, which range from tater tots to 'tom-yum-kung fried rice', don't quite cut it for dinner. But approach them as bar snacks, especially when combined with Fatbird's great drinks, eclectic shophouse atmosphere and fun soundtrack, and you have yourself a winner.

 Drinking & Nightlife

Shame on you if you think Bangkok's only nightlife options include the word 'go-go'. As in any big international city, the drinking and partying scene in Bangkok ranges from trashy to classy and touches on just about everything in between.

Way back in 2001, the Thaksin administration started enforcing closing times and curtailing other excesses that had previously made the city's nightlife famous. Since his 2006 ousting, the laws have been increasingly circumvented or inconsistently enforced. Post the 2014 coup, there are indications that Bangkok is seeing something of a return to the 2001-era strictly enforced operating hours and zoning laws.

Ko Ratanakosin, Thonburi & Banglamphu

Rowdy Th Khao San is one of the city's best areas for a night out. If the main drag is too intense, consider the (sightly) quieter places along Soi Ram Buttri and Th Samsen.

Bars are a rare sight in Ko Ratanakosin, although there is a growing number of hotel-based bars along the riverfront.

Hippie de Bar   BAR
(Map p82; www.facebook.com/hippie.debar; 46 Th Khao San; ☺3pm-2am; 🚢Phra Athit/Banglamphu Pier) Hippie boasts a funky retro vibe and indoor and outdoor seating, all set to the type of indie/pop soundtrack that you're unlikely to hear elsewhere in town. Despite being located on Th Khao San, there are surprisingly few foreign faces, and it's a great place to make some new Thai friends.

The Club   CLUB
(Map p82; www.facebook.com/theclubkhaosanbkk; 123 Th Khao San; admission Fri & Sat 120B; ☺9pm-2am; 🚢Phra Athit/Banglamphu Pier) Located right in the middle of Th Khao San, this cavern-like dancehall hosts a good mix of locals and backpackers; check the Facebook page for upcoming events and guest DJs.

Madame Musur   BAR
(Map p82; www.facebook.com/madamemusur; 41 Soi Ram Buttri; ☺8am-midnight; 🚢Phra Athit/Banglamphu Pier) Saving you the trip north to Pai, Madame Musur pulls off that elusive

combination of northern Thailand meets *The Beach* meets Th Khao San. It's a fun place to chat, drink and people-watch, and it's also not a bad place to eat, with a short menu of northern Thai dishes priced from 100B to 200B.

Ku Bar   BAR
(Map p82; www.facebook.com/ku.bangkok; 3rd fl, 469 Th Phra Sumen; ☺7pm-midnight Thu-Sun) Tired of buckets and cocktails that revolve around Red Bull? Head to Ku Bar, in almost every way the polar opposite of the Khao San party scene. Climb three floors of stairs (look for the tiny sign) to emerge at an almost comically minimalist interior where sophisticated fruit- and food-heavy cocktails (sample names: Lychee, Tomato, Pineapple/Red Pepper) and obscure music augment the underground vibe.

Roof   BAR
(Map p82; www.salaresorts.com/rattanakosin; 5th fl, Sala Rattanakosin, 39 Th Maha Rat; ☺5pm-midnight Mon-Thu, to 1am Fri-Sun; 🚢Tien Pier) The open-air bar on top of the Sala Rattanakosin hotel has upped the stakes for sunset views of Wat Arun – if you can see the temple at all through the wall of selfie-snapping tourists. Be sure to get there early for a good seat.

The Bank   BAR
(Map p82; 3rd fl, 44 Th Chakraphatdi Phong; ☺6pm-late; 🚢Phra Athit/Banglamphu Pier) This vaguely Middle Eastern–themed bar represents the posh alter ego of Th Khao San. There's live music, lounges for puffing on *shisha* (waterpipes), and a dark club. And the bar's elevated setting appears to lend it some leniency with the city's strict closing times.

Chinatown & Phahurat

A handful of new, artsy bars on Soi Nana and along Th Charoen Krung have finally made Chinatown an interesting nightlife destination.

★ Tep Bar   BAR
(Map p88; www.facebook.com/tepbar; 69-71 Soi Nana; ☺5pm-midnight Tue-Sun; Ⓜ Hua Lamphong exit 1) We never expected to find a bar this sophisticated – yet this fun – in Chinatown. Tep does it with a Thai-tinged, contemporary interior, tasty signature cocktails, Thai drinking snacks, and raucous live Thai music performances from Thursday to Sunday.

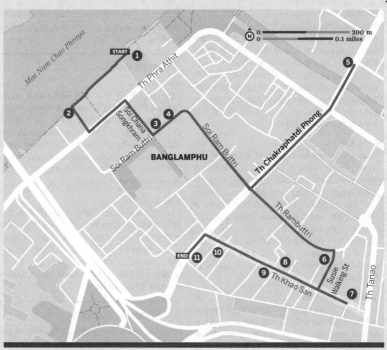

⚡ City Walk
Banglamphu Pub Crawl

START SHEEPSHANK
END THE BANK
LENGTH 1.5KM; THREE TO SIX HOURS

You don't need to go too far to find a bar in Banglamphu, but why limit yourself to one? With this in mind, we've assembled a pub crawl that spans river views, people-watching, live music and late-night shenanigans.

Begin your crawl in sophisticated, air-conditioned comfort at ❶ **Sheepshank**, a gastropub with an intriguing menu of bar snacks and classic cocktails. If you still have space for tapas, head west along the riverfront promenade until you reach ❷ **Babble & Rum**, the Riva Surya hotel's open-air restaurant-bar.

From Th Phra Athit, enter Soi Chana Songkhram and take a left on Soi Ram Buttri, where you begin phase two of your crawl: people-watching. ❸ **Gecko Bar** is a fun and frugal place to gawk at other patrons and passers-by, while a few doors down, ❹ **Madame Musur** offers the same perks,

but with a bit more sophistication and tasty northern-style eats.

It's time to add some music to the mix, so for phase three, head north on Th Chakraphatdi Phong to the long-standing blues bar ❺ **Ad Here the 13th** (p146) or to one of the open-air live music bars along Th Rambuttri, such as ❻ **Molly Bar**.

At this point, you should be lubricated enough for the main event, so, crossing via Susie Walking St, proceed to Th Khao San. If you need a bathroom or a blast of air-con, make a pit stop at ❼ **Mulligans**, an Irish-themed bar in the Buddy Lodge. Otherwise, get a bird's-eye view of the human parade from elevated ❽ **The Roof Bar**, or ringside at the noisy and buzzy ❾ **Center Khao Sarn**.

End the night on a good note by planting yourself at ❿ **Hippie de Bar**, one of Banglamphu's best bars. Or if 2am is too early to call it a night, crawl over to ⓫ **The Bank**, a rooftop lounge and nightclub that stays open until late.

Ba Hao
BAR

(Map p88; www.ba-hao.com; 8 Soi Nana; ⏱6pm-midnight Tue-Sun; 🚢Ratchawong Pier, Ⓜ️Hua Lamphong exit 1) At this point, there's little original about this retro Chinese-themed refurbished shophouse on Soi Nana, but potable craft beer, inventive cocktails and really excellent Chinese-style bar snacks (don't miss the Chinese pancake with braised pork belly, herbs and fried egg) make Ba Hao stand out.

Pijiu Bar
BAR

(Map p88; www.facebook.com/pijiubar; 16 Soi Nana; ⏱5pm-midnight Tue-Sun; 🚢Ratchawong Pier, Ⓜ️Hua Lamphong exit 1) Old West meets old Shanghai at this new yet classic-feeling bar. The emphasis here is on beer ('pijiu' is Chinese for beer), with four revolving craft brews on tap, but perhaps even more enticing are the charcuterie platters (300B) that unite a variety of smoked and preserved meats from some of the best vendors in Chinatown.

Teens of Thailand
BAR

(Map p88; 76 Soi Nana; ⏱7pm-midnight Tue-Sun; Ⓜ️Hua Lamphong exit 1) Probably the edgiest of the new bars in Chinatown's Soi Nana. Squeeze through the tiny wooden door of this refurbished shophouse to emerge at an artsy warehouse-like interior, with hipster barkeeps serving creative gin-based drinks, and an upright piano we're guessing doesn't get too much play time.

El Chiringuito
BAR

(Map p88; ☎086 340 4791; www.facebook.com/elchiringuitobangkok; 221 Soi Nana; ⏱6pm-midnight Thu-Sun; Ⓜ️Hua Lamphong exit 1) Come to this retro-feeling bar for sangria, Spanish gin and bar snacks, or the revolving art ex-hibitions. Opening hours can be sporadic, so call or check the Facebook page before heading out.

Riverside

River Vibe
BAR

(Map p92; 8th fl, River View Guesthouse, off Soi Charoen Phanit; ⏱7.30-11pm; 🚢Marine Department Pier, Ⓜ️Hua Lamphong exit 1) Can't afford the overpriced cocktails at Bangkok's up-scale rooftop bars? The excellent river views from the top of this guesthouse will hardly feel like a compromise. We suggest getting dinner elsewhere, though.

Viva & Aviv
BAR

(Map p92; www.vivaaviv.com; ground fl, River City, 23 Th Yotha; ⏱11am-midnight; 🚢Si Phraya/River City Pier) An enviable riverside location, casual open-air seating and a funky atmosphere make this restaurant-ish bar a contender for one of Bangkok's better sunset cocktail destinations.

Silom & Sathon

Lower Silom is Bangkok's gaybourhood, but the area as a whole has several fun bars and dance clubs for all comers.

★Smalls
BAR

(Map p96; www.facebook.com/smallsbkk; 186/3 Soi Suan Phlu; ⏱8.30pm-late; Ⓜ️Lumphini exit 2 & taxi) Even though it only opened its doors in 2014, Smalls is the kind of bar that feels like it's been here forever. Fixtures include a cheekily decadent interior, an inviting rooftop, food-themed nights (check the Facebook page) and live jazz on Wednesdays. The eclectic house cocktails are strong, if

---

BEST AFTER-HOURS NIGHTLIFE

Wong's Place (Map p96; 27/3 Soi Si Bamphen; ⏱9pm-late Tue-Sun; Ⓜ️Lumphini exit 1) Open from midnight until the last punter crawls out.

The Bank (p138) Puff on *shisha* or dance into the wee hours on Th Khao San.

Narz (Map p106; www.narzclubbangkok.net; 112 Soi 23, Th Sukhumvit; from 400B; ⏱9pm-2am; Ⓜ️Sukhumvit exit 2, Ⓢ️Asok exit 3) With three vast zones to keep clubbers raving till dawn.

Levels (Map p106; www.levelsclub.com; 6th fl, Aloft, 35 Soi 11, Th Sukhumvit; 500B; ⏱9pm-late; Ⓢ️Nana exit 3) When most Soi 11 bars begin to close, this club heats up.

Mixx (Map p102; www.mixx-discotheque.com; basement, InterContinental Hotel, 973 Th Phloen Chit; 300B; ⏱10pm-2am; Ⓢ️Chit Lom exit 7) Basement-level late-night disco.

Scratch Dog (Map p106; basement, Windsor Suites Hotel, 8-10 Soi 20, Th Sukhumvit; 400B; ⏱midnight-late; Ⓜ️Sukhumvit exit 2, Ⓢ️Asok exit 4) For when closing times trump quality music.

WORTH A TRIP

LIVIN' IT UP ALONG ROYAL CITY AVENUE

By day a bland-looking strip of offices, come Friday and Saturday nights, Royal City Ave – known by everybody as RCA – transforms into one of Bangkok's most popular nightlife zones. Although some of the bigger clubs can draw thousands, keep in mind that they often require an ID check and also maintain a dress code (no shorts or sandals).

The easiest way to approach RCA is via taxi from the MRT stop at Phra Ram 9; taxis generally can't enter RCA itself, so you'll have to U-turn or cross busy Th Phet Uthai on foot. Approaching the strip from Th Phet Uthai, you'll find the following venues:

Onyx (Map p106; www.facebook.com/onyxbkk; RCA/Royal City Ave; 500B; ⊙8pm-2am) Probably the most sophisticated club along RCA – evidenced by the hefty entry fee and the coiffed and coddled clientele. Check the Facebook page for upcoming DJ events.

Route 66 (Map p106; www.route66club.com; 29/33-48 RCA/Royal City Ave; 300B; ⊙8pm-2am) This vast club has been around just about as long as RCA has, but frequent facelifts and expansions have kept it relevant. Top 40 hip hop rules the main space here, although there are several different themed 'levels', featuring anything from Thai pop to live music.

Vesbar (Map p106; www.facebook.com/govesbar; 29/68 RCA/Royal City Ave; ⊙11am-midnight Mon-Sat) This Vespa-themed bar-restaurant serves up international dishes, import beers and jazzy live music (Wednesday, Friday and Saturday).

Taksura (Map p106; 9 RCA/Royal City Avenue; ⊙6pm-2am) Existing somewhere between restaurant and pub is retro-themed Taksura. If you're fuelling up for the clubs, the spicy *gàp glâam* (Thai drinking snacks) won't disappoint.

sweet, and bar snacks range from rillettes to quesadillas.

DJ Station
CLUB

(Map p98; www.dj-station.com; 8/6-8 Soi 2, Th Silom; from 150B; ⊙10pm-2am; M Si Lom exit 2, S Sala Daeng exit 1) One of Bangkok's and indeed Asia's most legendary gay dance clubs, here the crowd is a mix of Thai guppies (gay professionals), money boys and a few Westerners. There are several similar clubs in Soi 2.

Vesper
BAR

(Map p98; www.vesperbar.co; 10/15 Th Convent; ⊙noon-2.30pm & 6pm-1am Mon-Fri, 6pm-midnight Sat, noon-2.30pm Sun; M Si Lom exit 2, S Sala Daeng exit 2) One of the freshest faces on Bangkok's drinking scene is this deceptively classic-feeling bar-restaurant. As the name suggests, the emphasis here is on cocktails, including several revived classics and mixed drinks mellowed by ageing for six weeks in white-oak barrels.

Namsaah Bottling Trust
BAR

(Map p98; www.namsaah.com; 401 Soi 7, Th Silom; ⊙5pm-2am; M Si Lom exit 2, S Sala Daeng exit 2) Namsaah is all about twists. From its home (a former mansion incongruously painted hot pink), to the cocktails (classics with a

tweak or two) and the bar snacks and dishes (think *pàt tai* with foie gras), everything's a little bit off in just the right way.

The Stranger
BAR

(Map p98; www.facebook.com/thestrangerbar; Soi 4, Th Silom; ⊙5.45pm-2am; M Si Lom exit 2, S Sala Daeng exit 1) Probably the most low-key, sophisticated venue on Soi 4 – except during the drag shows on Monday, Friday and Saturday nights.

🍸 Siam Square, Pratunam & Around

Bangkok's most central zone is home to a scant handful of bars.

Hair of the Dog
BAR

(Map p102; www.hairofthedogbkk.com; 1st fl, Mahathun Plaza, 888/26 Th Phloen Chit; ⊙5pm-midnight; S Phloen Chit exit 2) The craft-beer craze that has swept Bangkok over the last few years is epitomised at this semi-concealed bar. With a morgue theme, dozens of bottles and 13 rotating taps, it's a great place for a weird, hoppy night.

Red Sky
BAR

(Map p102; www.centarahotelsresorts.com; 55th fl, Centara Grand, CentralWorld, Th Ratchadamri;

PATPONG: TOURISTS IN THE GO-GO BAR ZONE

The neon signs leave little doubt about the dominant industry in Patpong, arguably the world's most infamous strip of go-go bars and clubs running 'exotic' shows.

For years opinion on **Patpong** (Map p98; Th Phat Phong & Soi Phat Phong 2; ⊘ 4pm-2am; M Si Lom exit 2, S Sala Daeng exit 1) has been polarised between people who see it as an exploitative, immoral place and the very definition of sleaze, and others for whom a trip to Bangkok is about immersing themselves in planet Patpong. But Patpong has become such a caricature of itself that in recent times a third group has emerged: the curious tourist.

Prostitution is technically illegal in Thailand but there are as many as two million sex workers, the vast majority of whom – women and men – cater to Thai men. Many come from poorer regional areas, such as Isan in the northeast, while others might be students helping themselves through university. Sociologists suggest Thais often view sex through a less moralistic or romantic filter than Westerners. That doesn't mean Thai wives like their husbands using prostitutes, but it's only recently that the gradual empowerment of women through education and employment has led to a more vigorous questioning of this very widespread practice.

The unintended consequence of prostitution prohibition is the lawless working environment it creates for people who enter the industry. Sex workers are not afforded the rights of other workers and bars can set their own punitive rules that fine a worker if they don't smile enough, arrive late or don't meet the drink quota.

Patpong actually occupies two soi that run between Th Silom and Th Surawong in Bangkok's financial district. The two streets are privately owned by – and named for – the Thai-Chinese Patpongpanich family, who bought the land in the 1940s and initially built Th Phat Phong and its shophouses; Soi Phat Phong 2 was laid later. During the Vietnam War the first bars and clubs opened to cater to American soldiers on 'R&R'. The scene and its international reputation grew through the '70s and peaked in the '80s, when official Thai tourism campaigns made the sort of 'sights' available in Patpong a pillar of their marketing.

These days Patpong has mellowed considerably, if not matured. Thanks in part to the popular night market that fills the street after 5pm, it draws so many tourists that it has become a sort of sex theme park. There are still plenty of the stereotypical middle-aged men ogling pole dancers and paying 'bar fines' to take girls to hotels that charge by the hour. But you'll also be among other tourists and families who come to see what all the fuss is about.

Most tourists go no further than stolen glances into the ground-floor go-go bars, where women in bikinis drape themselves around stainless-steel poles. Others will be lured to the dimly lit upstairs clubs by men promising sex shows. But it should be said that the so-called 'ping pong' shows usually feature bored-looking women performing acts that feel demeaning to everyone involved. Several of these clubs are also infamous for their scams, usually involving the nonperforming (ie clothed, if just barely) staff descending on wide-eyed tourists like vultures. Before you know it you've bought a dozen drinks, racked up a bill for thousands of baht, followed up with a loud, aggressive argument flanked by menacing-looking bouncers.

⊘ 6pm-1am; S Chit Lom exit 9 to Sky Walk, Siam exit 6 to Sky Walk) Perched on the 55th floor of a skyscraper smack-dab in the modern centre of Bangkok, Red Sky provides one of Bangkok's most stunning rooftop views. The dramatic arch and all that glass provide the bar with a more upscale feel than Bangkok's other rooftoppers.

Hyde & Seek BAR

(Map p106; www.hydeandseek.com; ground fl, Athenee Residence, 65/1 Soi Ruam Rudi; ⊘ 4.30pm-1am; S Phloen Chit exit 4) The tasty and comforting English-inspired bar snacks and meals here have earned Hyde & Seek the right to call itself a 'gastro bar'. But we reckon the real reasons to come are one of Bangkok's best-stocked liquor cabinets and some of the city's tastiest and most sophisticated cocktails.

 ## Sukhumvit

This long street is home to Bangkok's most sophisticated bars and clubs.

★ WTF
BAR
(Map p106; www.wtfbangkok.com; 7 Soi 51, Th Sukhumvit; ⊘6pm-1am Tue-Sun; 🛜; Ⓢ Thong Lo exit 3) Wonderful Thai Friendship (what did you think it stood for?) is a funky and friendly neighbourhood bar that also packs in a gallery space. Arty locals and resident foreigners come for the old-school cocktails, live music and DJ events, poetry readings, art exhibitions and tasty bar snacks. And we, like them, give WTF our vote for Bangkok's best bar.

★ Q&A Bar
BAR
(Map p106; www.qnabar.com; 235/13 Soi 21/Asoke, Th Sukhumvit; ⊘7pm-2am Mon-Sat) Imagine a mid-century modern dining car or airport lounge, and you're close to picturing the interior of Q&A. The short list of featured cocktails can appear to be a divergence from the classic vibe, but an old-world dress code and manners are encouraged.

★ Studio Lam
BAR, CLUB
(Map p106; www.facebook.com/studiolambangkok; 3/1 Soi 51, Th Sukhumvit; ⊘6pm-1am Tue-Sun; Ⓢ Thong Lo exit 3) Studio Lam is an extension of uberhip record label ZudRangMa, and boasts a Jamaican-style sound system custom-built for world and retro-Thai DJ sets and the occasional live show. For a night of dancing in Bangkok that doesn't revolve around Top 40 cheese, this is the place.

★ Tuba
BAR
(Map p76; www.facebook.com/tubabkk; 34 Room 11-12 A, Soi Thong Lor 20/Soi Ekamai 21; ⊘11am-2am; Ⓢ Ekamai exit 1 & taxi) Part storage room for over-the-top vintage furniture, part restaurant, part friendly local boozer; this quirky bar certainly doesn't lack in diversity – nor fun. Indulge in a whole bottle (they'll hold onto it for your next visit if you don't finish it) and don't miss the moreish chicken wings or the delicious deep-fried *lâhp* (a tart/spicy salad of minced meat).

Waon
KARAOKE
(Map p106; 10/11 Soi 26, Th Sukhumvit; ⊘8pm-1am Mon-Sat) Is the canned soundtrack the only thing that's preventing you from obtaining karaoke superstardom? At Waon, muzak is replaced by a real live piano player. The music and clientele are predominately Japanese, but the friendly owner is happy to play Western standards. And even if you can't sing, you can pitch in via maracas, bongos or acoustic guitar.

Sky on 20
ROOFTOP BAR
(Map p106; 📞02 009 4999; www.novotelbangkoksukhumvit20.com; 26th fl, Novotel, 19/9 Soi Sukhumvit 20; ⊘5pm-2am; 🛜; Ⓢ Phrom Phong) With drinks averaging 250B, Sky on 20 has a reputation as a laid-back place for bargain sundowners. Electro house beats fill the open-air bar that has circular couches and lounge chairs overlooking Sirikit Lake and Benjasiri Park. Drinks made with local fruit juices rule the menu, and there is a retractable roof to keep the rainy season downpours at bay.

Mikkeller
BAR
(Map p106; www.mikkellerbangkok.com; 26 Yaek 2, Soi Ekamai 10; ⊘5pm-midnight; Ⓢ Ekamai exit 1 & taxi) These buzz-generating Danish 'gypsy' brewers have set up shop in Bangkok, granting us more than 30 beers on tap. Expect brews ranging from the local (Sukhumvit Brown Ale) to the insane (Beer Geek, a 13% alcohol oatmeal stout), as well as an inviting atmosphere and good bar snacks.

Dim Dim
BAR
(Map p106; 📞02 085 2788; www.facebook.com/dimdimbarbkk; 27/1 Soi 33, Th Sukhumvit; ⊘6.30pm-1.30am Mon-Sat; Ⓢ Phrom Phong exit 5) Bangkok's love of Chinese-themed bars reaches its zenith at Dim Dim, a candlelit cocktail bar in Phrom Phong. China's lucky colour of red dominates the decor, and a row of gold waving cats beckons you to try the house specialty chrysanthemum vodka, or sip an Oolong Tea and Orange Sour, an Asian take on the whiskey sour, made with oolong tea and orange-peel-infused bourbon.

A R Sutton & Co Engineers Siam
BAR
(Map p106; Parklane, Soi 63/Ekamai, Th Sukhumvit; ⊘6pm-midnight; Ⓢ Ekamai exit 2) Skeins of copper tubing, haphazardly placed one-of-a-kind antiques, zinc ceiling panels, and rows of glass vials and baubles culminate in one of the most unique and beautifully fantastical bars in Bangkok – if not anywhere. An adjacent distillery provides fuel for the bar's largely gin-based cocktails.

BANGKOK'S SILVER SCREENS

Each Bangkok mall has its own cinema, but few can rival **Paragon Cineplex** (Map p102; ☑ 02 129 4635; www.paragon cineplex.com; 5th fl, Siam Paragon, 991/1 Rama I; ⑤ Siam exits 3 & 5). In addition to 16 screens, more than 3000 seats and Thailand's largest IMAX screen, the options here include the Blue Ribbon Screen, a cinema with a maximum of 72 seats, where you're plied with pillows, blankets, complimentary snacks and drinks, and of course, a 15-minute massage; and Enigma, where in addition to a sofa-like love seat designed for couples, you'll be served cocktails and food (as well as blankets and a massage).

If you're looking for something with less glitz and a bit more character, consider the old-school stand-alone theatres just across the street, such as **Scala** (Map p102; ☑ 02 251 2861; Soi 1, Siam Sq; ⑤ Siam exit 2) and **Lido** (Map p102; ☑ 02 252 6498; www.apex siam-square.com; btwn Soi 2 & Soi 3, Siam Sq; ⑤ Siam exit 2).

For film showtimes at theatres across Bangkok, check in with moveedoo (www.moveedoo.com).

Sugar Ray
BAR
(Map p76; www.facebook.com/sugarraybkk; off Soi Ekamai 21; ⊙ 8pm-2am Wed, Fri & Sat; ⑤ Ekkamai exit 1 & taxi) Run by a team of fun and funky Thai dudes who make flavoured syrups, Sugar Ray is a fun, funky hidden bar serving fun, funky cocktails; think an Old Fashioned made with aged rum, orange and cardamom syrup, and garnished with a piece of caramelised bacon.

Golden Coins Taproom
MICROBREWERY
(Map p106; ☑ 082 675 9673; www.facebook.com/ goldencoinstaproom; Ekamai Mall, Ekkamai Soi 10; ⊙ 5pm-midnight; ⑤ Ekkamai) Thailand's craft beer laws forced Golden Coins microbrewery to shut down their Chinatown outpost (RIP Let the Boy Die) and partner with local breweries in Vietnam to produce the ales that are on tap at their Ekkamai location. Six are on offer, including a dessert-style stout and a not-too-hoppy IPA that pairs perfectly with the American-style BBQ menu.

Walden
BAR
(Map p106; 7/1 Soi 31, Th Sukhumvit; ⊙ 6.30pm-1am Mon-Sat; ⑤ Phrom Phong exit 5) Get past the hyper-minimalist/*Kinfolk* vibe, and the thoughtful Japanese touches of this bar make it one of the more welcoming places in town. The brief menu of drinks spans Japanese-style 'highballs', craft beers from the US, and simple, delicious bar snacks.

🍷 Northern Bangkok

The epicentre of entertainment is the strip known as Royal City Ave (p141). The area broadly known as Ari is also home to an increasingly sophisticated spread of restaurants that function equally well as bars.

Fake Club The Next Gen
CLUB, GAY
(Map p118; www.facebook.com/fakeclubthe nextgen; 222/32 Th Ratchadaphisek; ⊙ 9pm-3am; Ⓜ Sutthisan exit 3) In new digs is this long-standing, popular gay staple. Expect live music, cheesy choreography and lots of lasers.

Aree
BAR
(Map p118; cnr Soi Ari 4/Nua & Soi 7/Ari, Th Phahonyothin; ⊙ 6pm-1am; ⑤ Ari exit 3) Exposed brick, chunky carpets and warm lighting give Aree a cosier feel than your average Bangkok bar. It also offers live music (from 8pm Tuesday to Sunday), contemporary Thai drinking snacks, and a relatively sophisticated drinks list.

O'glee
BAR
(Map p118; www.facebook.com/ogleeari1; Soi Ari 1, Soi 7/Ari, Th Phahonyothin; ⊙ 5.30pm-midnight; ⑤ Ari exit 3) The name and decor of this bar vaguely call to mind an Irish pub. But rather than shamrocks and clichés, you get an astonishing selection of imported microbrews – both in bottles and draught – served by a charming Thai family.

Viva's
BAR
(Map p150; Section 26, Stall 161, Chatuchak Weekend Market, Th Phahonyothin; ⊙ 10am-10pm Sat & Sun; Ⓜ Chatuchak Park exit 1, Kamphaeng Phet exits 1 & 2, ⑤ Mo Chit exit 1) This café-bar in Bangkok's Chatuchak Weekend Market features live music and stays open late.

☆ Entertainment

Shame on you if you find yourself bored in Bangkok. With traditional cultural performances, dance, art, live music and, yes, the infamous go-go bars, you have a city whose entertainment scene spans from – in local parlance – lo-so (low society) to hi-so (high society).

Gà·teu·i Cabaret

Over the last decade, watching *gà·teu·i* (also spelt *kàthoey*) – Thai cross-dressers or transgender people – perform choreographed stage shows featuring Broadway high kicks and lip-synched pop tunes has become a 'must-do' fixture on the Bangkok tourist circuit. Playhouse Magical Cabaret (p135) caters to the trend, as does **Calypso Bangkok** (Map p76; ☑ 02 688 1415; www.calypsocabaret. com; Asiatique, Soi 72-76, Th Charoen Krung; adult/child 900/600B; ⊙ show times 8.15pm & 9.45pm; ⛴ shuttle ferry from Sathon/Central Pier), located in Asiatique night market.

Thai Boxing (Moo·ay tai)

Quintessentially Thai, almost anything goes in *moo·ay tai* (also spelt *muay Thai*), the martial art more commonly known elsewhere as Thai boxing or kickboxing. If you don't mind the violence, a Thai-boxing match is well worth attending for the pure spectacle: the wild musical accompaniment, the ceremonial beginning of each match and the frenzied betting.

The best of the best fight at Bangkok's two boxing stadiums. Built on royal land at the end of WWII, the art-deco-style **Rajadamnern Stadium** (สนามมวย ราชดำเนิน; Map p82; www.rajadamnern.com; off Th Ratchadamnoen Nok; tickets 3rd class/2nd class/ringside 1000/1500/2500B; ⊙Matches Mon-Thur from 6.30-11pm, Sun 3pm & 6.30pm; ⛴Thewet Pier, ⑤Phaya Thai exit 3 & taxi) is the original and has a relatively formal atmosphere. The other main stage, **Lumpinee Boxing Stadium** (สนามมวยลุมพิ นี; Map p158; ☑02 282 3141; www.muaythai lumpinee.net; 6 Th Ramintra; tickets 3rd class/2nd class/ringside 1000/1500/2500B; ⊙Matches Tue & Fri 6.30-11pm, Sat 2-8.30pm; Ⓜ Chatuchak Park exit 2 & taxi, ⑤Mo Chit exit 3 & taxi), has moved from its eponymous hood to a modern home north of Bangkok.

Admission fees vary according to seating. Ringside seats (from 2500B) are the most expensive and will be filled with subdued VIPs; tourists usually opt for the 2nd-class seats (from 1500B); diehard *moo·ay tai* fans bet and cheer from 3rd class (1000B). If you're thinking these prices sound a bit steep for your average fight fan (taxi drivers are big fans and they make about 600B a day), then you're right – foreigners pay several times what the Thais do.

We recommend the 2nd- or 3rd-class seats. The 2nd-class area is filled with numbers-runners who take bets from fans in rowdy 3rd class, which is fenced off from the rest of the stadium. Akin to a stock-exchange pit, hand signals communicate bets and odds fly between the areas. Most fans in 3rd class follow the match (or their bets) too closely to sit down, and we've seen stress levels rise to near-boiling point. It's all very entertaining.

Most programs have eight to 10 fights of five rounds each. English-speaking 'staff' outside the stadium, who practically tackle you upon arrival, will hand you a fight roster and steer you to the foreigners' ticket windows; they can also be helpful in telling you which fights are the best match-ups (some say that welterweights, between 61.2kg and 66.7kg, are the best). To avoid supporting scalpers, purchase your tickets from the ticket window or online, not from a person outside the stadium.

Live Music

As Thailand's media capital, Bangkok is the centre of the Thai music industry, packaging and selling pop, crooners, *lôok tûng* (Thaistyle country music) and the recent phenomenon of indie bands.

Music is a part of almost every Thai social gathering; the matriarchs and patriarchs like dinner with an easy-listening soundtrack – typically a Filipino band and a synthesiser. Patrons pass their request (on a napkin) up to the stage.

Bars and clubs with live music are allowed to stay open until 1am, but this is subject to police discretion. The drinking age is 20 years old.

★ Parking Toys   LIVE MUSIC

(Map p76; ☑ 02 907 2228; 17/22 Soi Mayalap, off Kaset-Navamin Hwy; ⊙ 4pm-2am; Ⓜ Chatuchak

---

ⓘ CHILD ABUSE

In 1996, Thailand passed a reform law to address the issue of child prostitution. Help stop child-sex tourism by reporting suspicious behaviour on a dedicated hotline (☑1300) or by reporting perpetrators directly to the embassy of their home country.

Park exit 2 & taxi, ⑤ Mo Chit exit 3 & taxi) One of Bangkok's best venues for live music, Parking Toys hosts an eclectic revolving cast of fun bands ranging in genre from rockabilly to electro-funk jam acts.

To get here, take a taxi heading north from BTS Mo Chit (or the MRT Chatuchak Park) and tell the driver to take you to the Kaset intersection and turn right on Th Kaset-Navamin; Parking Toys is just past the second stoplight on this road.

★ Brick Bar
LIVE MUSIC

(Map p82; www.brickbarkhaosan.com; basement, Buddy Lodge, 265 Th Khao San; admission Sat & Sun 150B; ⊙ 7pm-1.30am; 🛳 Phra Athit/ Banglamphu Pier) This basement pub, one of our favourite destinations in Bangkok for live music, hosts a nightly revolving cast of bands for an almost exclusively Thai crowd – many of whom will end the night dancing on the tables. Brick Bar can get infamously packed, so be sure to get there early.

★ The Living Room
LIVE MUSIC

(Map p106; 🖂 02 649 8888; www.thelivingroomat bangkok.com; level 1, Sheraton Grande Sukhumvit, 250 Th Sukhumvit; ⊙ 6pm-midnight; Ⓜ Sukhumvit exit 3, ⑤ Asok exit 2) Don't let looks deceive you: every night this bland hotel lounge transforms into the city's best venue for live jazz. True to the name, there's comfy, sofa-based seating, all of it within earshot of the music. Enquire ahead of time to see which sax master or hide-hitter is in town. An entry fee of 300B is charged after 8.30pm.

ⓘ GEM SCAMS

Countless tourists are sucked into the prolific and well-rehearsed gem scam in which they are taken to a store by a helpful stranger and tricked into buying bulk gems that can supposedly be resold in their home country for 100% profit. The expert con artists (part of a well-organised cartel) seem trustworthy and convince tourists that they need a citizen of the country to circumvent tricky customs regulations. Unsurprisingly, the gem world doesn't work like that and what most tourists end up with are worthless pieces of glass. By the time you sort all this out, the store has closed and changed names and the police can do little to help.

Lam Sing
LIVE MUSIC

(Map p76; www.facebook.com/isanlamsing; 57/5 Th Phet Phra Ram; ⊙ 9.30pm-4am; ⑤ Ekkamai exit 1 & taxi) Even Ziggy Stardust–era David Bowie has nothing on this dark, decadent, rhinestone-encrusted den, one of Bangkok's best venues for *mŏr lam* and *lôok tûng*, music with roots in Thailand's rural northeast. Come for raucous live-music performances accompanied by tightly choreographed, flagrantly costumed backup dancers.

There's no English-language sign here, but most taxi drivers are familiar with the place.

Saxophone Pub & Restaurant
LIVE MUSIC

(Map p112; www.saxophonepub.com; 3/8 Th Phayathai; ⊙ 7.30pm-1.30am; ⑤ Victory Monument exit 2) After 30 years, Saxophone remains Bangkok's premier live-music venue – a dark, intimate space where you can pull up a chair just a few metres away from the band and see their every bead of sweat. If you prefer some mystique in your musicians, watch the blues, jazz, reggae or rock from the balcony.

Tawandang German Brewery
LIVE MUSIC

(Map p76; www.tawandang.co.th; cnr Rama III & Th Narathiwat Ratchanakharin/Chong Nonsi; ⊙ 5pm-1am; ⑤ Chong Nonsi exit 2 & taxi) It's Oktoberfest all year round at this hangar-sized music hall. The Thai-German food is tasty, the house-made brews are entirely potable, and the nightly stage shows make singing along a necessity. Music starts at 8.30pm.

Bamboo Bar
LIVE MUSIC

(Map p92; 🖂 02 236 0400; www.mandarinoriental. com; ground fl, Mandarin Oriental, 48 Soi 40/Oriental, Th Charoen Krung; ⊙ 5pm-1am Sun-Thu, to 2am Fri & Sat; 🛳 Oriental Pier or hotel shuttle boat from Sathon/Central Pier) After more than 60 years of service, the Mandarin Oriental's Bamboo Bar remains one of the city's premier locales for live jazz. Guest vocalists are flown in from across the globe – check the website to see who's in town – and the music starts at 9pm nightly.

Ad Here the 13th
LIVE MUSIC

(Map p82; www.facebook.com/adhere13thblues bar; 13 Th Samsen; ⊙ 6pm-midnight; 🛳 Phra Athit/Banglamphu Pier) This closet-sized blues bar is everything a neighbourhood joint should be: lots of regulars, cold beer and heart-warming tunes delivered by a masterful house band (starting at 10pm).

Everyone knows each other, so don't be shy about mingling.

Brown Sugar LIVE MUSIC

(Map p82; www.brownsugarbangkok.com; 469 Th Phra Sumen; ⊙5pm-1am Tue-Thu & Sun, to 2am Fri & Sat; ⊕klorng boat to Phanfa Leelard Pier, Phra Athit/Banglamphu Pier) Located in a cavernous shophouse is this long-standing live-music staple. The music, which spans from funk to jazz, starts at 8pm most nights, and on weekends in particular, draws heaps of locals.

Raintree LIVE MUSIC

(Map p112; Soi Ruam Chit; ⊙6pm-1am Mon-Sat; ⑤Victory Monument exit 2) This rustic pub is one of the few remaining places in town to hear 'songs for life', Thai folk music with roots in the political movements of the 1960s and '70s. Tasty bar snacks also make it a clever place to have a bite to eat.

SoulBar LIVE MUSIC

(Map p92; www.facebook.com/livesoulbarbangkok; 945 Th Charoen Krung; ⊙7pm-midnight Tue-Sun; ⊕Marine Department Pier, ⓂHua Lamphong exit 1) An unlikely venue – and neighbourhood – for live music, this converted shophouse nonetheless plays host to live blues, jazz and soul from 9pm just about every night.

Titanium LIVE MUSIC

(Map p106; www.titaniumbangkok.com; 2/30 Soi 22, Th Sukhumvit; ⊙8pm-1am; ⑤Phrom Phong exit 6) Many come to this cheesy 'ice bar' for the chill, the skimpily dressed working girls and the flavoured vodka, but we come for Unicorn, the all-female house band, who rock the house from Monday to Saturday.

Go-Go Bars

Although technically illegal, prostitution is fully 'out' in Bangkok, and the influence of organised crime and lucrative kickbacks mean that it will be a long while before the existing laws are ever enforced. Yet despite the image presented by much of the Western media, the underlying atmosphere of Bangkok's red-light districts is not one of illicitness and exploitation (although these do inevitably exist), but rather an aura of tackiness and boredom. Patpong (p142) earned notoriety during the 1980s for its wild sex shows.

BEST MARKET-BROWSING

Pak Khlong Talat (ปากคลองตลาด, Flower Market; Map p88; Th Chakkaraphet; ⊙24hr; ⊕Pak Klong Taladd Pier, Saphan Phut/Memorial Bridge Pier) The capital's famous flower market; come late at night and don't forget your camera.

Talat Mai (p85) This frenetic fresh market is a slice of China in Bangkok.

Nonthaburi Market (p97) An authentic upcountry market only minutes from Bangkok.

Khlong Toey Market (p93) The city's largest fresh market.

Theatre

Sala Chalermkrung THEATRE

(Map p88; ☑02 224 4499; www.salachalermkrung.com; 66 Th Charoen Krung; tickets 800-1200B; ⊙shows 7.30pm Thu & Fri; ⊕Saphan Phut/Memorial Bridge Pier, ⓂHua Lamphong exit 1 & taxi) This art deco Bangkok landmark, a former cinema dating to 1933, is one of the few remaining places *kŏhn* (masked dance-drama based on stories from the *Ramakian*, the Thai version of the Indian epic *Ramayana*) can be witnessed. The traditional dance-drama is enhanced here by laser graphics, high-tech audio and English subtitles. Concerts and other events are also held; check the website for details.

National Theatre THEATRE

(Map p82; ☑02 224 1342; 2 Th Ratchini; tickets 60-100B; ⊕Chang Pier, Maharaj Pier, Phra Chan Tai Pier) The National Theatre holds performances of *kŏhn* at 2pm on the first and second Sundays of the month from January to September, and *lá·kon* (classical dance-dramas) at 2pm on the first and second Sundays of the month from October to December. Tickets go on sale an hour before performances begin.

🔒 Shopping

Prime your credit card and shine your baht – shopping is serious business in Bangkok. Hardly a street corner in this city is free from a vendor, hawker or impromptu stall, and it doesn't stop there: Bangkok is also home to one of the world's largest outdoor markets, not to mention some of Southeast Asia's largest malls.

WORTH A TRIP

FLOATING MARKETS

Pictures of đà·làht nám (floating markets) jammed full of wooden canoes pregnant with colourful exotic fruits have defined the official tourist profile of Thailand for decades. The idyllic scenes are as iconic as the Grand Palace or the Reclining Buddha, but they are also almost completely contrived for, and dependent upon, foreign and domestic tourists – roads and motorcycles moved Thais' daily errands onto dry ground long ago. That said, if you can see them for what they are, a few of Thailand's floating markets are worth a visit.

Tha Kha Floating Market (ตลาดน้ำท่าคา; Map p158; Tha Kha, Samut Songkhram; ☺7am-noon, 2nd, 7th & 12th day of waxing & waning moons plus Sat & Sun) The most real-feeling floating market is also the most difficult to reach. A handful of vendors coalesce along an open rural klorng (canal; also spelt Khlang) lined with coconut palms and old wooden houses. Boat rides (20B per person, 45 minutes) can be arranged along the canal and there are lots of tasty snacks and fruits for sale. Contact Amphawa's **tourist office** (☏034 752 847; 71 Th Prachasret; ☺8.30am-4.30pm) to see when the next one is. To get here, take one of the morning sŏrng·tăa·ou (passenger pick-up trucks; 20B, 45 minutes) from Samut Songkhram's market area.

Amphawa Floating Market (ตลาดน้ำอัมพวา; Amphawa; dishes 20-40B; ☺4-9pm Fri-Sun) The Amphawa Floating Market, located in Samut Songkhram Province, convenes near Wat Amphawa. The emphasis is on edibles and tourist knick-knacks; because the market is only there on weekends and is popular with tourists from Bangkok, things can get pretty hectic.

Taling Chan Floating Market (ตลาดน้ำตลิ่งชัน; Map p76; Khlong Bangkok Noi, Thonburi; ☺7am-4pm Sat & Sun; Ⓢ Wongwian Yai exit 3 & taxi) Located just outside Bangkok on the access road to Khlong Bangkok Noi, Taling Chan looks like any other fresh-food market busy with produce vendors from nearby farms. But the twist emerges at the canal where several floating docks serve as informal dining rooms and the kitchens are canoes tethered to the docks. Taling Chan is in Thonburi and can be reached via taxi from Wongwian Yai BTS station or via air-con bus 79 (16B, 25 minutes), which makes stops on Th Ratchadamnoen Klang. Long-tail boats from any large Bangkok pier can also be hired for a trip to Taling Chan and the nearby Khlong Chak Phra.

Damnoen Saduak Floating Market (ตลาดน้ำดำเนินสะดวก; Map p158; Damnoen Saduak, Ratchaburi; ☺7am-noon) This 100-year-old floating market – the country's most famous – is now essentially a floating souvenir stand filled with package tourists. This in itself can be a fascinating insight into Thai culture, as the vast majority of tourists here are Thais and watching the approach to this cultural 'theme park' is instructive. But beyond the market, the residential canals are quite peaceful and can be explored by hiring a boat (100B per person) for a longer duration. Trips stop at small family businesses, including a Thai candy maker, a pomelo farm and a knife crafter. Minivans from the Southern Bus Terminal in Thonburi can link you with Damnoen Saduak (80B, two hours, frequent from 6am to 9pm).

Don Wai Market (ตลาดดอนหวาย; Map p158; Don Wai, Nakhon Pathom; ☺6am-6pm) Not technically a swimmer, this market claims a riverbank location in Nakhon Pathom Province, having originally started out in the early 20th century as a floating market for pomelo and jackfruit growers and traders. As with many tourist attractions geared towards Thais, the main draw is food, including fruit, traditional sweets and pèt pah·lôh (five-spice stewed duck), which can be consumed aboard large boats that cruise Mae Nam Nakhorn Chaisi (60B, one hour). The easiest way to reach Don Wai Market is to take a minibus (45B, 35 minutes) from beside **Central Pinklao** (Map p76; Th Somdet Phra Pin Klao; ☺10am-10pm; Ⓢ Talat Phlu exit 3 & taxi or Victory Monument exit 3 & taxi) in Thonburi.

🔒 Banglamphu & Chinatown

Shopping in Banglamphu means street markets and traditional items, and Chinatown might be the city's most commerce-heavy hood, but the bulk of wares are utilitarian and will hold little interest for travellers.

★ **Thanon Khao**
San Market   GIFTS & SOUVENIRS
(Map p82; Th Khao San; ☺10am-midnight; 🚤Phra
Athit/Banglamphu Pier) The main guesthouse
strip in Banglamphu is a day-and-night
shopping bazaar peddling all the backpacker 'essentials': profane T-shirts, bootleg
MP3s, hemp clothing, fake student ID cards,
knock-off designer wear, selfie sticks, orange
juice and, of course, those croaking wooden
frogs.

Heritage Craft   ARTS & CRAFTS
(Map p82; 35 Th Bamrung Meuang; ☺11am-6pm
Mon-Fri; 🚤klorng boat to Phanfa Leelard Pier)
Handicrafts with a conscience: this new
boutique is an atmospheric showcase for the
quality domestic wares of **ThaiCraft** (Map
p106; www.thaicraft.org; L fl, Jasmine City Bldg, cnr
Soi 23 & Th Sukhumvit; Ⓜ Sukhumvit exit 2, Ⓢ A-
sok exit 3), some of which are produced via
fair-trade practices. Items include silks from
Thailand's northeast, baskets from the south
and jewellery from the north, and there's
also an inviting on-site cafe.

Lofty Bamboo   ARTS & CRAFTS
(Map p82; ground fl, Buddy Lodge, 265 Th Khao San;
☺10.30am-8pm; 🚤Phra Athit/Banglamphu Pier)
No time to make it to northern Thailand?
No problem. At this shop you can get the
type of colourful, hill-tribe-inspired clothes,
cloth items and other handicrafts you'd find
at the markets in Chiang Mai and Chiang
Rai. And best of all, a purchase supports economic self-sufficiency in upcountry villages.

Nittaya Thai Curry   FOOD & DRINKS
(Map p82; 136-40 Th Chakraphatdi Phong;
☺9am-7pm Mon-Sat; 🚤Phra Athit/Banglamphu
Pier) Follow your nose: Nittaya is famous
throughout Thailand for her pungent,
high-quality curry pastes. Pick up a couple of takeaway canisters for prospective
dinner parties or peruse the snack and gift
sections, where visitors to Bangkok load up
on local specialities for friends and family
back in the provinces.

🏠 Riverside, Silom & Sathon

Asiatique   MARKET
(Map p76; Soi 72-76, Th Charoen Krung; ☺4-11pm;
🚤shuttle boat from Sathon/Central Pier) One
of Bangkok's more popular night markets,
Asiatique takes the form of warehouses of
commerce next to Mae Nam Chao Phraya.
Expect clothing, handicrafts, souvenirs and
quite a few dining and drinking venues.

Frequent, free shuttle boats depart from
Sathon/Central Pier from 4pm to 11.30pm.

House of Chao   ANTIQUES
(Map p98; 9/1 Th Decho; ☺9.30am-7pm; Ⓢ Chong
Nonsi exit 3) This three-storey antique shop,
appropriately located in an antique shophouse, has everything necessary to deck
out your fantasy colonial-era mansion.
Particularly interesting are the various
weather-worn doors, doorways, gateways
and trellises that can be found in the covered area behind the showroom.

ⓘ ONE NIGHT IN BANGKOK...ISN'T ENOUGH TO TAILOR A SUIT

Many tourists arrive in Bangkok with the notion of getting clothes custom-tailored at a
bargain price. The golden rule is that you get what you pay for. Although an offer may
seem great on the surface, the price may fluctuate significantly depending on the fabric
you choose. Have a good idea of what you want before walking into a shop.

Set aside a week to get clothes tailored. Shirts and trousers can often be turned
around in 48 hours or less with only one fitting, but no matter what a tailor may tell you,
it takes more than one and often more than two fittings to create a good suit.

July (Map p98; 📞02 233 0171; www.julytailor.com; 30/6 Th Sala Daeng; ☺9am-6pm Mon-Sat;
Ⓜ Si Lom exit 2, Ⓢ Sala Daeng exit 4) Suits at this tailor to Thailand's royalty and elite don't
come cheap and the cuts can be somewhat conservative, but the quality is unsurpassed.

Rajawongse (Map p106; 📞02 255 3714; www.dress-for-success.com; 130 Th Sukhumvit;
☺10.30am-8pm Mon-Sat; Ⓢ Nana exit 2) A legendary and long-standing Bangkok tailor;
Jesse and Victor's creations are particularly renowned among American visitors and
residents.

Duly (Map p106; 📞02 662 6647; www.laladuly.co.th; Soi 49, Th Sukhumvit; ☺10am-7pm;
Ⓢ Phrom Phong exit 1) High-quality Italian fabrics and experienced tailors make Duly one
of the best places in Bangkok to commission a sharp shirt.

Chatuchak Market

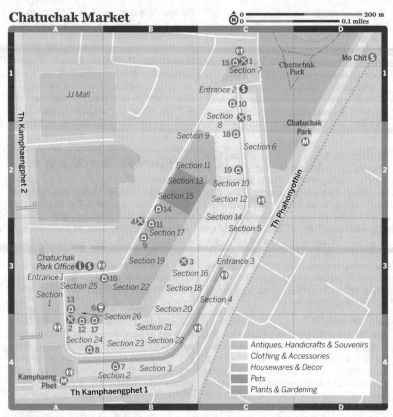

Chatuchak Market

⊗ Eating

1 Café Ice	C1
2 Foontalop	A4
3 Saman Islam	B3
4 Toh-Plue	B3
5 Viva 8	C1

⊖ Drinking & Nightlife

6 Viva's	A3

⊕ Shopping

7 AnyaDharu Scent Library	B4

8 Baan Sin Thai	A4
9 D-narn	B3
10 Kitcharoen Dountri	C1
11 Marché	B3
12 Meng	A4
13 Orange Karen Silver	A3
14 Papachu	B2
15 Pariwat A-nantachina	C1
16 PL Bronze	B3
17 Spice Boom	A4
18 Ton-Tan	C2
19 Tuptim Shop	C2

Tamnan Mingmuang   ARTS & CRAFTS
(Map p98; 2nd fl, Thaniya Plaza, Th Thaniya;
⊙10am-7pm; M Si Lom exit 2, S Sala Daeng exit 1)
As soon as you step through the doors of this
museum-like shop, the earthy smell of dried
grass and stained wood rushes to meet you.
Rattan, *yahn lí·pow* (a fern-like vine) and
water hyacinth woven into patterns, and co-

conut shells carved into delicate bowls are
among the exquisite pieces that will outlast
flashier souvenirs available on the streets.

⌂ Siam Square, Pratunam & Around

The area around Siam Sq is home to the
city's greatest concentration of malls; if

name brands are your thing, this is your place. Cheap stuff, namely clothes, is found just north, in the Pratunam area.

★ Siam Discovery SHOPPING CENTRE

(Map p102; www.siamdiscovery.co.th; cnr Rama I & Th Phayathai; ☺10am-10pm; ⑤ Siam exit 1) With an open, almost-market-like feel and an impressive variety of unique goods ranging from housewares to clothing (including lots of items by Thai designers), the recently renovated Siam Discovery is hands down the most design-conscious mall in town.

★ MBK Center SHOPPING CENTRE

(Map p102; www.mbk-center.com; cnr Rama I & Th Phayathai; ☺10am-10pm; ⑤ National Stadium exit 4) This eight-storey market in a mall has emerged as one of Bangkok's top attractions. On any given weekend half of Bangkok's residents (and most of its tourists) can be found here combing through a seemingly inexhaustible range of small stalls, shops and merchandise.

★ Siam Square SHOPPING CENTRE

(Map p102; Rama I; ☺11am-9pm; ⑤ Siam exits 2, 4 & 6) This open-air shopping zone is ground zero for teenage culture in Bangkok. Pop music blares out of tinny speakers, and gangs of hipsters in various costumes ricochet between fast-food restaurants and closet-sized boutiques. It's a great place to pick up labels and designs you're guaranteed not to find anywhere else, though most outfits require a barely there waistline.

🄰 Sukhumvit

Tailor on Ten CLOTHING

(Map p106; 📱 084 877 1543; www.tailoronten.com; 93 Soi 8, Th Sukhumvit; ☺9.30am-7pm Mon-Sat) It's not the cheapest in town, but set prices, foreign management and, most importantly, good tailoring, have earned this outfit heaps of praise and repeat customers.

ZudRangMa Records MUSIC

(Map p106; www.zudrangmarecords.com; 7/1 Soi 51, Th Sukhumvit; ☺2-9pm Tue-Sun; ⑤ Thong Lo exit 1) The headquarters of this retro/world label is a chance to finally combine the university-era pastimes of record-browsing and drinking. Come to snicker at corny old Thai vinyl covers or invest in some of the label's highly regarded compilations of classic *mŏr lam* and *lôok tûng*.

🄰 Northern Bangkok

★ Chatuchak Weekend Market MARKET

(ตลาดนัดจตุจักร, Talat Nat Jatujak; Map p118; www.chatuchakmarket.org; 587/10 Th Phahonyothin; ☺7am-6pm Wed & Thu plants only, 6pm-midnight Fri wholesale only, 9am-6pm Sat & Sun; Ⓜ Chatuchak Park exit 1, Kamphaeng Phet exits 1 & 2, ⑤ Mo Chit exit 1) Among the largest markets in the world, Chatuchak seems to unite everything buyable, from used vintage sneakers to baby squirrels. Plan to spend a full day here, as there's plenty to see, do and buy. But come early, ideally around 10am, to beat the crowds and the heat.

There is an information centre and a bank with ATMs and foreign-exchange booths at the **Chatuchak Park Office** (Map p150; ☺9am-6pm Sat & Sun), near the northern end of the market's Soi 1, Soi 2 and Soi 3. Schematic maps and toilets are located throughout the market.

Friday nights from around 8pm to midnight, several vendors, largely those selling clothing, accessories and food, open up shop in Chatuchak. There are a few vendors on weekday mornings, and a daily vegetable, plant and flower market opposite the market's southern side. One section of the latter, known as the **Or Tor Kor Market** (องค์กร ตลาดเพื่อเกษตรกร; Map p118; Th Kamphaengphet 1; ☺8am-6pm; Ⓜ Kamphaeng Phet exit 3), sells fantastically gargantuan fruit and seafood, and has a decent food court as well.

Once you're deep in the bowels of Chatuchak, it will seem like there is no order and no escape, but the market is arranged into relatively coherent sections. Use the clock tower as a handy landmark.

➡ *Antiques, Handicrafts & Souvenirs*

Section 1 is the place to go for Buddha statues, old LPs and other random antiques. More secular arts and crafts, such as musical instruments and hill-tribe items, can be found in Sections 25 and 26. **Baan Sin Thai** (Map p150; Section 24, Stall 130, Soi 1; ☺9am-6pm Sat & Sun) sells a mixture of *kŏhn* masks and old-school Thai toys, all of which make fun souvenirs, and **Kitcharoen Dountri** (Map p150; Section 8, Stall 464; ☺9am-6pm Sat & Sun) specialises in Thai musical instruments, including flutes, whistles, drums and CDs of classical Thai music. Other quirky gifts include the lifelike plastic Thai fruit and vegetables at **Marché** (Map p150; Section 17, Stall 254, Soi 1; ☺9am-6pm Sat & Sun), or their

❶ NOT-SO-FANTASTIC PLASTIC

Buy a can of beer at any store in Bangkok, and it will be presented to you in a tiny plastic bag. Do your shopping at any supermarket, and you'll find that your groceries have been thematically divided into a comical and inconvenient-to-carry number of plastic bags.

In Thailand, a huge producer of plastic products, bags are ubiquitous and very cheap. A survey conducted by the country's Department of Environmental Quality Promotion (DEQP) estimated that the average Thai uses eight plastic bags per day and that plastic bags form 20% of the country's rubbish.

Over the last decade, retailers, such as 7-Eleven and Tesco Lotus, and municipal and government authorities have kick-started numerous informal initiatives to reduce the distribution of plastic bags. Indeed, a 2015 campaign initiated by the Thai Ministry of Natural Resources and Environment pleaded with Thais to part with their precious plastic bags – for one day a month.

Tell your checkout person *mâi sài tǔng* ('no bag, please'), but the response may be a blank stare, followed by the person putting your purchase in a plastic bag.

scaled-down miniature counterparts nearby at **Papachu** (Map p150; Section 17, Stall 23; ◷9am-6pm Sat & Sun).

➧ *Clothing & Accessories*

Clothing dominates most of Chatuchak, starting in Section 8 and continuing through the even-numbered sections to 24. Sections 5 and 6 deal in used clothing for every Thai youth subculture, from punks to cowboys, while Soi 7, where it transects Sections 12 and 14, is heavy on the more underground hip-hop and skate fashions. Somewhat more sophisticated independent labels can be found in Sections 2 and 3, while tourist-sized clothes and textiles are in Sections 8 and 10.

For accessories, several shops in Sections 24 and 26, such as **Orange Karen Silver** (Map p150; Section 26, Stall 229, Soi 34/8; ◷9am-6pm Sat & Sun), specialise in chunky silver jewellery and semiprecious uncut stones.

➧ *Eating & Drinking*

Lots of Thai-style eating and snacking will stave off Chatuchak rage (cranky behaviour brought on by dehydration or hunger), and numerous food stalls set up shop between Sections 6 and 8. Long-standing standouts include **Foontalop** (Map p150; Section 26, Stall 319, no roman-script sign; mains 20-70B; ◷10am-6pm Sat & Sun), an incredibly popular Isan restaurant; **Café Ice** (Map p150; Section 7, Stall 267; mains 250-490B; ◷10am-6pm Sat & Sun), a Western-Thai fusion joint that does good, if overpriced, *pàt tai* and tasty fruit shakes; **Toh-Plue** (Map p150; opposite Section 17; mains 150-400B; ◷noon-8pm Sat & Sun), which does all the Thai standards; and **Saman Islam** (Map p150; Section 16, Stall 34, Soi 24; mains 40-100B; ◷10am-6pm Sat & Sun), a Thai-Muslim

restaurant that serves a tasty chicken biryani. **Viva 8** (Map p150; www.facebook.com/viva8JJ; Section 8, Stall 371; mains 150-300B; ◷9am-10pm Sat & Sun) features a DJ and, when we stopped by, a chef making huge platters of paella. And as evening draws near, down a beer at Viva's (p144), a cafe-bar that features live music.

➧ *Housewares & Decor*

The western edge of the market, particularly Sections 8 to 26, specialises in all manner of housewares, from cheap plastic buckets to expensive brass woks. This area is a particularly good place to stock up on inexpensive Thai ceramics, ranging from celadon to the traditional rooster-themed bowls from Lampang.

PL Bronze (Map p150; Section 25, Stall 185, Soi 4; ◷9am-6pm Sat & Sun) has a huge variety of stainless-steel flatware, and **Ton-Tan** (Map p150; Section 8, Stall 460, Soi 15/1; ◷9am-6pm Sat & Sun) deals in coconut- and sugar-palm-derived plates, bowls and other utensils.

Those looking to spice up the house should stop by **Spice Boom** (Map p150; Section 26, Stall 246, Soi 8; ◷9am-6pm Sat & Sun), were you can find dried herbs and spices for both consumption and decoration. Other notable olfactory indulgences include the handmade soaps, lotions, salts and scrubs at **D-narn** (Map p150; Section 19, Stall 203, Soi 1; ◷9am-6pm Sat & Sun), and the fragrant perfumes and essential oils at **AnyaDharu Scent Library** (Map p150; Section 3, Stall 3, Soi 43/2; ◷9am-6pm Sat & Sun).

For less utilitarian goods, Section 7 is a virtual open-air gallery – we particularly liked **Pariwat A-nantachina** (Map p150; Section 7, Stall 117, Soi 63/3; ⏱9am-6pm Sat & Sun) for Bangkok-themed murals. Several shops in Section 10, including **Tuptim Shop** (Map p150; Section 10, Stall 261, Soi 19; ⏱9am-6pm Sat & Su), sell new and antique Burmese lacquerware. **Meng** (Map p150; Section 26, Stall 195, Soi 8; ⏱9am-6pm Sat & Sun) features a dusty mishmash of quirky antiques from both Thailand and Myanmar.

➡ *Pets*

Possibly the most fun you'll ever have window-shopping will be petting puppies and cuddling kittens in Sections 13 and 15. Soi 9 of the former features several shops that deal solely in clothing for pets. It's also worth noting that this section has, in the past, been associated with the sale of illegal wildlife, although much of this trade has been driven underground.

➡ *Plants & Gardening*

The interior perimeter of Sections 2 to 4 feature a huge variety of potted plants, flowers, herbs, fruits, and the accessories needed to maintain them. Many of these shops are also open on weekday afternoons.

ℹ Information

DANGERS & ANNOYANCES

Bangkok is generally a safe city, but there are a few things to be aware of:

➡ In recent years, Bangkok has been the site of political protests that have occasionally turned violent; check your embassy's advisory travel warnings before leaving.

➡ Criticising the Thai monarchy in any way is a very serious social faux pas that carries potentially incriminating repercussions; don't do it.

➡ Avoid the common scams: one-day gem sales, suspiciously low transport prices, dodgy tailors.

➡ Bangkok's streets are extremely dangerous and its drivers rarely yield to pedestrians. Look in both directions before crossing any street (or footpath) and yield to anything with more metal than you.

➡ Bangkok's rainy season is from May to October, when daily downpours – and occasional flooding – are the norm.

Thais are generally so friendly and laid-back that some visitors are lulled into a false sense of security. While your personal safety is rarely at risk in Thailand, you may be unwittingly charmed out of the contents of your wallet or fall prey to a scam (p154).

EMERGENCY

The police contact number functions as the de facto universal emergency number in Thailand and can also be used to call an ambulance or report a fire.

Bangkok area code	☎02
Country code	☎66
Directory assistance (free)	☎1133
International access code	☎001, 007
Operator-assisted international calls	☎100
Police	☎191
Tourist Police	☎1155

INTERNET & TELEPHONE

Wi-fi is standard in guesthouses and cafes. Signal strength deteriorates in the upper floors of multistorey buildings; you can always request a room near a router. Cellular data networks continue to expand and increase in capability.

The easiest phone option in Thailand is to acquire a mobile (cell) phone equipped with a local SIM card. Buying a prepaid SIM is as simple as finding a 7-Eleven. SIM cards include talk and data packages and you can add more funds with a prepaid reload card.

A convenient place to take care of your communication needs in the centre of Bangkok is **TrueMove** (Map p102; www.truemove.com; Soi 2, Siam Sq; ⏱7am-10pm; Ⓢ Siam exit 4), which has high-speed internet computers equipped with Skype, sells phones and mobile subscriptions, and can also provide information on citywide wi-fi access for computers and phones.

MEDIA

➡ Bangkok's predominant English-language newspapers are the *Bangkok Post* (www.bangkokpost.com) and the business-heavy *Nation* (www.nationmultimedia.com).

➡ *Bangkok 101* (www.bangkok101.com) is a tourist-friendly listings magazine; *BK* (www.bk.asia-city.com) is a slightly more in-depth listings mag; and *Coconuts Bangkok* (https://bangkok.coconuts.co) is where to go for listings and offbeat local 'news'.

➡ On Twitter, Richard Barrow (@RichardBarrow) is a great source of tourist information.

MEDICAL SERVICES

Bangkok is considered a centre of medical excellence in Southeast Asia. Private hospitals are more expensive than other medical facilities, but offer a superior standard of care and English-speaking staff. The cost of health care is relatively cheap in Thailand compared to most Western countries.

The following hospitals have English-speaking doctors:

Bangkok Christian Hospital (Map p98; ☎ 02 625 9000; www.bch.in.th; 124 Th Silom; Ⓜ Si Lom exit 2, Ⓢ Sala Daeng exit 1) Modern hospital in central Bangkok.

BNH (Map p98; ☎ 02 686 2700; www.bnhhospital.com; 9 Th Convent; Ⓜ Si Lom exit 2, Ⓢ Sala Daeng exit 2) Modern, centrally located hospital.

Bumrungrad International Hospital (Map p106; ☎ 02 667 1000; www.bumrungrad.com; 33 Soi 3, Th Sukhumvit; ⊙24hr; Ⓢ Phloen Chit exit 3) An internationally accredited hospital.

Samitivej Hospital (Map p106; ☎ 02 022 2222; www.samitivejhospitals.com; 133 Soi 49, Th Sukhumvit; Ⓢ Phrom Phong exit 3 & taxi) Modern hospital.

Pharmacies are plentiful, and in central areas most pharmacists will speak English. If you don't find what you need in a Boots, Watsons or a local pharmacy, try one of the hospitals.

MONEY

Banks generally open between 8.30am and 3.30pm, although branches in busy areas and shopping malls may open later. ATMs function around the clock and are common throughout Bangkok. The downside is that Thai ATMs charge a 200B foreign-transaction fee on top of whatever currency conversion and out-of-network fees your home bank charges.

Some foreign credit cards are accepted in high-end establishments but most places deal only with cash. Go to 7-Eleven shops or other reputable places to break 1000B bills; don't expect a vendor or taxi to be able to change a bill 500B or larger.

POST

Main Post Office (Map p92; ☎ 02 233 1050; Th Charoen Krung; ⊙8am-8pm Mon-Fri, to 1pm Sat & Sun; 🚤Oriental Pier)

TOILETS

Increasingly, the Asian-style squat toilet is less of the norm in Thailand and the Western-style toilet appears wherever foreign tourists are found. Even in places where sit-down toilets are installed, the septic system may not be designed to take toilet paper. In such cases there will be a waste basket where you're supposed to place used toilet paper and feminine hygiene products. For public toilets in Bangkok, your best bet is to head for a shopping centre or fast-food restaurant.

TOURIST INFORMATION

Bangkok Information Center (Map p82; ☎ 02 225 7612-4; www.bangkoktourist.com; 17/1 Th Phra Athit; ⊙8am-7pm Mon-Fri, 9am-5pm Sat & Sun; 🚤Phra Athit/Banglamphu Pier) Handles city-specific tourism information.

Tourism Authority of Thailand (TAT; Map p106; ☎ 02 250 5500, nationwide 1672; www.tourismthailand.org; 1600 Th Phetchaburi; ⊙8.30am-4.30pm; Ⓜ Phetchaburi exit 2) Government-operated tourist information and promotion service founded in 1960. Produces excellent pamphlets on sightseeing; check the website for contact information.

ⓘ Getting There & Away

AIR

Located 30km east of central Bangkok is **Suvarnabhumi International Airport** (☎ 02 132 1888; www.suvarnabhumiairport.com), pronounced sù·wan·ná·poom. The airport website has real-time details of arrivals and departures.

Bangkok's other airport, **Don Mueang International Airport** (☎ 02 535 2111; www.don

---

ⓘ COMMON BANGKOK SCAMS

Commit these classic rip-offs to memory and join us in our ongoing crusade to outsmart Bangkok's crafty scam artists.

Gem scam We're begging you – if you aren't a gem trader, then don't buy unset stones in Thailand. Period.

Closed today Ignore any 'friendly' local who tells you that an attraction is closed for a Buddhist holiday or for cleaning.

Túk-túk rides for 20B These alleged 'tours' bypass the sights and instead cruise to all the fly-by-night gem and tailor shops that pay commissions.

Flat-fare taxi ride Flatly refuse any driver who quotes a flat fare, which will usually be three times more expensive than the reasonable meter rate.

Friendly strangers Be wary of smartly dressed men who approach you asking where you're from and where you're going.

mueangairportthai.com), 25km north of central Bangkok, is the city's de facto budget hub. Terminal 1 handles international flights, while Terminal 2 is for domestic destinations.

BUS

Bangkok is the centre for bus services that fan out all over the kingdom. Buses using government bus stations are far more reliable and less prone to incidents of theft than those departing from Th Khao San or other tourist centres.

Allow an hour to reach all bus terminals from most parts of Bangkok.

Eastern Bus Terminal (Map p106; ☑ 02 391 2504; Soi 40, Th Sukhumvit; ⑤ Ekkamai exit 2) The departure point for buses to Pattaya, Rayong, Chanthaburi and other points east, except for the border crossing at Aranya Prathet. Most people call it *sà·tăh·nee èk·gà·mai* (Ekamai station). It's near the Ekkamai BTS station.

Northern & Northeastern Bus Terminal (Mo Chit; Map p118; ☑ northeastern routes 02 936 2852, ext 602/605, northern routes 02 936 2841, ext 325/614; Th Kamphaengphet; Ⓜ Kamphaeng Phet exit 1 & taxi, ⑤ Mo Chit exit 3 & taxi) Located just north of Chatuchak Park. This hectic bus station is also commonly called *kŏn sòng mŏr chít* (Mo Chit station) – not to be confused with Mo Chit BTS station. Buses depart from here for all northern and northeastern destinations, as well as international destinations including Pakse (Laos; 900B, 12 hours, 8.30pm), Phnom Penh (Cambodia; 750B, 11 hours, 1.30am), Siem Reap (Cambodia; 750B, seven hours, 9am) and Vientiane (Laos; 900B, 10 hours, 8pm). To reach the bus station, take BTS to Mo Chit or MRT to Kamphaeng Phet and transfer onto city bus 3, 77 or 509, or hop on a taxi or motorcycle taxi.

Southern Bus Terminal (Sai Tai Mai; Map p158; ☑ 02 422 4444, call centre 1490; Th Boromaratchachonanee) Commonly called *săi dâi mài*, lies a long way west of the centre of Bangkok. Besides serving as the departure point for all buses south of Bangkok, transport to Kanchanaburi and western Thailand also departs from here. The easiest way to reach the station is by taxi, or you can take bus 79, 159, 201 or 516 from Th Ratchadamnoen Klang.

Suvarnabhumi Public Transport Centre (Map p158; ☑ 02 132 1888; Suvarnabhumi Airport) Located 3km from Suvarnabhumi International Airport, this terminal has relatively frequent departures to points east and northeast including Aranya Prathet (for the Cambodian border), Chanthaburi, Ko Chang, Nong Khai (for the Lao border), Pattaya, Rayong, Trat and Udon Thani. It can be reached from the airport by a free shuttle bus.

TRAIN

The city's main train terminus is known as **Hualamphong** (☑ 02 220 4334, call centre 1690; www.railway.co.th; off Rama IV; Ⓜ Hua Lamphong exit 2). It's advisable to ignore all touts here and avoid the travel agencies. To check timetables and prices for destinations visit the website of the State Railway of Thailand (www.railway.co.th/main/index_en.html).

Also known as Thonburi, **Bangkok Noi** (☑ 02 418 4310, call centre 1690; www.railway.co.th; off Th Itsaraphap; 🛳 Thonburi Railway Station, Wang Lang/Siriraj Pier, ⑤ Wongwian Yai exit 4 & taxi) is a minuscule train station with (overpriced) departures for Kanchanaburi.

Wong Wian Yai (☑ 02 465 2017, call centre 1690; www.railway.co.th; off Th Phra Jao Taksin; ⑤ Wongwian Yai exit 4 & taxi) is a tiny hidden station, the jumping-off point for the commuter line to Samut Sakhon (also known as Mahachai).

ⓘ Getting Around

Bangkok may seem chaotic and impenetrable at first, but its transport system is gradually improving, and although you'll almost certainly find yourself stuck in traffic at some point, the traffic jams aren't as legendary as they used to be.

BTS The elevated Skytrain runs from 6am to midnight. Tickets 16B to 44B.

MRT The Metro runs from 6am to midnight. Tickets 16B to 42B.

Taxi Outside of rush hours, Bangkok taxis are a great bargain. Flagfall 35B.

Chao Phraya Express Boat Runs 6am to 8pm, charging 10B to 40B.

Klorng boat Bangkok's canal boats run from 5.30am to 8pm most days. Tickets 9B to 19B.

Bus Cheap but a slow and confusing way to get around Bangkok. Tickets 5B to 30B.

TO/FROM THE AIRPORTS

Train

➡ From **Suvarnabhumi International Airport** the **Airport Rail Link** (☑ call centre 1690; www.srtet.co.th) connects Suvarnabhumi with the BTS stop at Phaya Thai (45B, 30 minutes, from 6am to midnight) and the MRT stop at Phetchaburi (45B, 25 minutes, from 6am to midnight).

➡ From **Don Mueang International Airport** the walkway that crosses from the airport to the Amari Airport Hotel also provides access to Don Muang Train Station, which has trains to Hualamphong Train Station every one to 1½ hours from 4am to 11.30am and then roughly every hour from 2pm to 9.30pm (from 5B to 10B).

Bus & Minivan

➡ From **Suvarnabhumi International Airport** there is a public transport centre 3km from the airport that includes a bus terminal with buses to a handful of provinces and inner-city-bound buses and minivans. A free airport shuttle connects the transport centre with the passenger terminals. Bus lines that city-bound tourists are likely to use include line 551 to BTS Victory Monument station (40B, frequent from 5am to 10pm) and 552 to BTS On Nut (20B, frequent from 5am to 10pm). From these points, you can continue by public transport or taxi to your hotel.

➡ Outside the **Don Mueang International Airport** arrivals hall there are four bus lines: bus A1 makes stops at BTS Mo Chit (50B, frequent from 7.30am to 11.30pm); A2 makes stops at BTS Mo Chit and BTS Victory Monument (50B, every 30 minutes from 7.30am to 11.30pm); A3 makes stops at Pratunam and Lumphini Park (50B, every 30 minutes from 7.30am to 11.30pm); and A4 at Th Khao San and Sanam Luang (50B, every 30 minutes from 7.30am to 11.30pm). Public buses stop on the highway in front of the airport. Useful lines include 29, with a stop at Victory Monument BTS station, before terminating at Hualamphong Train Station (24 hours); line 59, with a stop near Th Khao San (24 hours); and line 538, stopping at Victory Monument BTS station (4am to 10pm); fares are approximately 20B.

Taxi

➡ From **Suvarnabhumi International Airport**-Metered taxis are available kerbside at Floor 1 – ignore the 'official airport taxi' touts who approach you inside the terminal. Typical metered fares from Suvarnabhumi include 200B to 250B to Th Sukhumvit; 250B to 300B to Th Khao San; and 400B to Mo Chit. Toll charges (paid by passengers) vary between 25B and 70B. Note that there's a 50B surcharge added to all fares departing from the airport, payable directly to the driver.

➡ From **Don Mueang International Airport** public taxis leave from outside both arrival halls and there is a 50B airport charge added to the meter fare.

BICYCLE

Over the past few years, cycling has exploded in popularity in Bangkok. Bike sales are booming, the 23km bicycle track that circles Suvarnabhumi International Airport was being upgraded at the time of writing and a Bangkok cycling event in mid-2015 drew nearly 40,000 participants. There's even a bike-share initiative, although it appeared to be on its last legs at the time of writing. Yet despite all this, dangerous roads, traffic, heat, pollution and lack of bike lanes mean that Bangkok is still far from a safe or convenient place to use a bicycle as a means of transportation.

BOAT

A fleet of boats, both those that run along Mae Nam Chao Phraya and along the city's canals, serve Bangkok's commuters.

Canal Routes

Canal taxi boats run along Khlong Saen Saep (Banglamphu to Ramkhamhaeng) and are an easy way to get between Banglamphu and Jim Thompson House, the Siam Sq shopping centres (get off at Sapan Hua Chang Pier for both) and other points further east along Th Sukhumvit – after a mandatory change of boat at Pratunam Pier.

These boats are mostly used by daily commuters and pull into the piers for just a few seconds – jump straight on or you'll be left behind.

Fares range from 9B to 19B and boats run from 5.30am to 7.15pm from Monday to Friday, from 6am to 6.30pm on Saturday and from 6am to 6pm on Sunday.

River Routes

The **Chao Phraya Express Boat** (☑ 02 623 6001; www.chaophrayaexpressboat.com) operates the main ferry service along Mae Nam Chao Phraya. The central pier is known as Tha Sathon, Saphan Taksin or sometimes Sathon/Central Pier, and connects to the BTS at Saphan Taksin station.

➡ Boats run from 6am to 8pm. You can buy tickets (10B to 40B) at the pier or on board; hold on to your ticket as proof of purchase (an occasional formality).

➡ The most common boats are the orange-flagged express boats. These run between Wat Rajsingkorn, south of Bangkok, to Nonthaburi, north, stopping at most major piers (15B, frequent from 6am to 7pm).

➡ A blue-flagged tourist boat (40B, every 30 minutes from 9.30am to 5pm) runs from Sathon/Central Pier to Phra Athit/Banglamphu Pier, with stops at eight major sightseeing piers and barely comprehensible English-language commentary. Vendors at Sathon/Central Pier tout a 150B all-day pass, but unless you plan on doing a lot of boat travel, it's not great value.

➡ There are also dozens of cross-river ferries, which charge 3B and run every few minutes until late at night.

➡ Private long-tail boats can be hired for sightseeing trips at Phra Athit/Banglamphu Pier, Chang Pier, Tien Pier and Oriental Pier.

BTS & MRT

The elevated **BTS** (☑ 02 617 6000, tourist information 02 617 7341; www.bts.co.th), also known as the Skytrain (rót fai fáa), whisks you through 'new' Bangkok (Silom, Sukhumvit and Siam Sq). The interchange between the two lines is at Siam station and trains run frequently from 6am to midnight. Fares range from 16B to 44B or 140B for a one-day pass. Most ticket machines only accept coins, but change is available at the information booths.

Bangkok's Metro, the **MRT** (☎ 02 354 2000; www.bangkokmetro.co.th) is most helpful for people staying in the Sukhumvit or Silom area to reach the train station at Hualamphong. Fares cost from 16B to 42B or 120B for a one-day pass. The trains run frequently from 6am to midnight.

BUS

Bangkok's public buses are run by the **Bangkok Mass Transit Authority** (☎ 02 246 0973, call centre ☎ 1348; www.bmta.co.th).

➜ As the routes are not always clear, and with Bangkok taxis being such a good deal, you'd really have to be pinching pennies to rely on buses as a way to get around Bangkok.

➜ Air-con bus fares range from 10B to 23B and fares for fan-cooled buses start at 6.50B.

➜ Most of the bus lines run between 5am and 10pm or 11pm, except for the 'all-night' buses, which run from 3am or 4am to midmorning.

➜ You'll most likely require the help of thinknet's *Bangkok Bus Guide*.

CAR

For short-term visitors, you will find parking and driving a car in Bangkok more trouble than it is worth. If you need private transport, consider hiring a car and driver through your hotel or hire a taxi driver that you find trustworthy. One reputable operator is **Julie Taxi** (☎ 082 664 4789, 081 846 2014; www.facebook.com/tourwith julietaxi), which offers a variety of vehicles and excellent service.

But if you still want to give it a go, all the big car-hire companies have offices in Bangkok,

as well as counters at Suvarnabhumi and Don Mueang International Airports. Rates start at around 1000B per day for a small car. A passport plus a valid licence from your home country (with English translation if necessary) or an International Driving Permit are required for all rentals.

MOTORCYCLE TAXI

Motorcycle taxis (known as *motorsai*) serve two purposes in Bangkok.

Most commonly and popularly they form an integral part of the public transport network, running from the corner of a main thoroughfare, such as Th Sukhumvit, to the far ends of sois that run off that thoroughfare. Riders wear coloured, numbered vests and gather at either end of their soi, usually charging 10B to 20B for the trip (without a helmet unless you ask).

Their other purpose is as a means of beating the traffic. You tell your rider where you want to go, negotiate a price (from 20B for a short trip up to about 150B going across town), strap on the helmet (they will insist for longer trips) and say a prayer to whichever god you're into.

RIDE-SHARE APPS

App-based alternatives to the traditional taxis that operate in Bangkok:

All Thai Taxi (www.allthaitaxi.com)

GrabTaxi (www.grab.com/th)

Uber (www.uber.com/cities/bangkok)

TAXI

➜ Although many first-time visitors are hesitant to use them, in general, Bangkok's taxis are new and comfortable and the drivers are courteous and helpful, making them an excellent way to get around.

➜ All taxis are required to use their meters, which start at 35B, and fares to most places within central Bangkok cost 60B to 90B. Free-

---

ℹ **BANGKOK TAXI TIPS**

➜ Never agree to take a taxi that won't use the meter; usually these drivers park outside hotels and in tourist areas. Simply get one that's passing by instead.

➜ Bangkok taxi drivers will generally not try to 'take you for a ride' as happens in some other countries; they make more money from passenger turnover.

➜ It's worth keeping in mind that many Bangkok taxi drivers are in fact seasonal labourers fresh from the countryside and may not know their way around.

➜ If a driver refuses to take you somewhere, it's probably because he needs to return his hired cab before a certain time, not because he doesn't like how you look.

➜ Very few Bangkok taxi drivers speak much English, so an address written in Thai can help immensely.

➜ Older cabs may be less comfortable but typically have more experienced drivers because they are driver-owned, as opposed to the new cabs, which are usually hired.

Around Bangkok

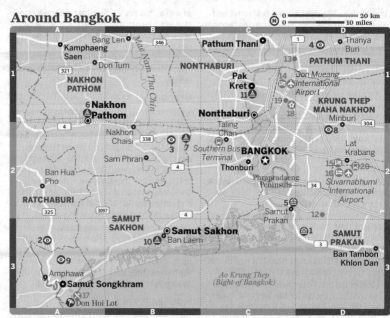

way tolls – 25B to 70B depending on where you start – must be paid by the passenger.

➡ **Taxi Radio** (1681; www.taxiradio.co.th) and other 24-hour 'phone-a-cab' services are available for 20B above the metered fare.

➡ If you leave something in a taxi your best chance of getting it back (still pretty slim) is to call 1644.

TÚK-TÚK

➡ Bangkok's iconic túk-túk (pronounced *đúk đúk;* a type of motorised rickshaw) are used by Thais for short hops not worth paying the taxi flagfall for. For foreigners, however, these emphysema-inducing machines are part of the Bangkok experience, so despite the fact that they overcharge outrageously and you can't see anything due to the low roof, pretty much everyone takes a túk-túk at least once.

➡ Túk-túk are notorious for taking little 'detours' to commission-paying gem and silk shops and massage parlours. En route to 'special' temples, you'll meet 'helpful' locals who will steer you to even more rip-off opportunities. Ignore anyone offering too-good-to-be-true 20B trips.

➡ The vast majority of túk-túk drivers ask too much from tourists (expat *fa·ràng* never use them). Expect to be quoted a 100B fare, if not more, for even the shortest trip. Try bargaining them down to about 60B for a short trip, preferably at night when the pollution (hopefully) won't be quite so bad. Once you've done

it, you'll find taxis are cheaper, cleaner, cooler and quieter.

WALKING

You'll notice very few Thais walking around in Bangkok, and it doesn't take long to see why: hot weather, pollution, uneven or nonexistent footpaths, footpaths clogged with vendors and motorcycles and the sheer expanse of the city make walking one of the least convenient ways to get around.

AROUND BANGKOK

If you're itching to get out of the capital, but don't have a lot of time, consider a day trip to one of the neighbouring towns and provinces. On Bangkok's doorstep are all of Thailand's provincial charms – you don't have to go far to find ancient religious monuments, floating markets, architectural treasures and laid-back fishing villages.

The provinces adjacent to Bangkok are most easily reached via bus and train. The former depart from the Southern Bus Terminal, in Thonburi, while trains can be boarded at Wong Wian Yai train station, also in Thonburi.

Around Bangkok

Ko Kret   เกาะเกร็ด

An easy rural getaway from Bangkok, Ko Kret is an artificial island, the result of a canal having been dug nearly 300 years ago to shorten an oxbow bend in Mae Nam Chao Phraya. The area is one of Thailand's oldest settlements of Mon people, who were a dominant people of central Thailand between the 6th and 10th centuries AD. Today, Ko Kret is a popular weekend getaway, known for its hand-thrown terracotta pots and its busy weekend market.

◉ Sights

There are a couple of temples worth peeking into at Ko Kret, such as the leaning stupa at **Wat Poramai Yikawat** (วัดปรมัยยิกาวาส; Map p158; ⊙9am-5pm), but the real highlight is taking in the bucolic riverside atmosphere.

A 6km paved path circles the island and can be easily completed on foot or by bicycle, the latter available for rent from the pier (40B per day). Alternatively, it's possible to charter a boat for up to 10 people for 500B; the typical **island tour** stops at a batik workshop, a sweets factory and, on weekends, a floating market.

Ko Kret is known for its **hand-thrown terracotta pots**, sold at markets throughout Bangkok; order an iced coffee from just about any vendor on the island and you'll get a small pot as a souvenir. From Wat Poramai Yikawat, go in either direction to find both abandoned kilns and working pottery centres on the east and north coasts.

If you come to Ko Kret on a weekday you'll likely be the only visitor. On weekends things change drastically as Ko Kret is an extremely popular destination for urban Thais. There's heaps more food, drink and things for sale, but with this come the crowds.

✖ Eating

On weekends, droves of Thais flock to Ko Kret to eat deep-fried snacks and Thai-style sweets. One snack to look for is *khâw châa,* an unusual but delicious Mon dish of savoury titbits served with chilled fragrant rice.

Pa Ka Lung   THAI **$**
(Restaurant River Side; Map p158; mains 30-60B; ⊙8am-4pm Mon-Fri, to 6pm Sat & Sun) An open-air food court with an English-language menu. This is a good place for *khâw châa* and other local dishes. It's found on the northern edge of the island, not far from Wat Poramai Yikawat.

◉ Getting There & Away

Ko Kret is in Nonthaburi, about 15km north of central Bangkok. To get there, take bus 166 from the Victory Monument or a taxi to Pak Kret before boarding the cross-river ferry (2B, 5am to 9pm) that leaves from Wat Sanam Neua.

Amphawa   อัมพวา

☑ 034 / POP 5000

The canalside village of Amphawa has become a popular destination for city folk who seek out its quintessentially 'Thai' setting. This urban influx has sparked some gentrification, but the canals, old wooden buildings,

THE LONG WAY TO AMPHAWA

Amphawa is only 80km from Bangkok, but you can reach the town via a long journey involving trains, boats, a motorcycle ride and a short jaunt in the back of a truck. Why? Because sometimes the journey is just as interesting as the destination.

The adventure begins at Thonburi's Wong Wian Yai (p155) train station. Just past the Wong Wian Yai traffic circle is a fairly ordinary food market that camouflages the unspectacular terminus of this commuter line. Hop on one of the hourly trains (10B, one hour, 5.30am to 8.10pm) to Samut Sakhon.

After 15 minutes on the rattling train, the city density yields to squat villages. From the window you can peek into homes, temples and shops built a carefully considered arm's length from the passing trains.

The backwater farms evaporate quickly as you enter **Samut Sakhon**, a bustling port town and the end of the first rail segment. Before the 17th century it was called Tha Jiin (Chinese Pier) because of the large number of Chinese junks that called here.

After working your way through one of the most hectic fresh markets in the country, you'll come to a vast harbour clogged with water hyacinths and wooden fishing boats. Take the ferry across to Baan Laem (3B to 5B). If the infrequent 5B ferry hasn't already deposited you there, take a motorcycle taxi (10B) for the 2km ride to **Wat Chawng Lom** (วัดช่องลม; Map p158; ☺ daylight hours) **FREE**, home to the **Jao Mae Kuan Im Shrine**, a 9m-high fountain in the shape of the Mahayana Buddhist Goddess of Mercy. Beside the shrine is Tha Chalong, a train stop with three daily departures for Samut Songkhram at 8.10am, 12.05pm and 4.40pm (10B, one hour). The train rambles out of the city on tracks that the surrounding forest threatens to engulf.

The jungle doesn't last long, and any illusion that you've entered a parallel universe free of concrete is shattered as you enter **Samut Songkhram**. Between train arrivals and departures hectic market stalls are set up directly on the tracks and must be hurriedly cleared away when the train arrives – it's quite an amazing scene.

Commonly known as Mae Klong, Samut Songkhram is a tidier version of Samut Sakhon and offers a great deal more as a destination. Owing to flat topography and abundant water sources, the area surrounding the provincial capital is well suited to the steady irrigation needed to grow guava, lychee and grapes. From Mae Klong Market pier (*tâh dà·làht mâa glorng*), you can charter a boat (1000B) or hop in a *sŏrng·tăa·ou* (passenger pick-up truck; 8B) near the market for the 10-minute ride to Amphawa.

atmospheric cafes and quaint waterborne traffic still retain heaps of charm. From Friday to Sunday, Amphawa puts on an extremely popular floating market (p148). Alternatively, visit on a weekday and you'll probably be the only tourist.

◉ Sights & Activities

Steps from Amphawa's central footbridge is **Wat Amphawan Chetiyaram** (วัดอัมพวัน เจติยาราม; ☺ daylight hours), a graceful temple believed to be located at the place of the family home of Rama II, and which features accomplished murals. A short walk from the temple is **King Buddhalertla (Phuttha Loet La) Naphalai Memorial Park** (อุทยาน พระบรมราชานุสรณ์พระบาทสมเด็จพระพุทธเลิศ หล้านภาลัย/อุทยาน ร. ๒; 20B; ☺ 8.30am-5pm), a museum housed in a collection of traditional central Thai houses set on 1.5 landscaped

hectares. Dedicated to Rama II, the museum contains a library of antiques from early 19th-century Siam.

At night **long-tail boats** (☺ dusk) zip through Amphawa's sleeping waters to watch the Christmas light–like dance of the *hìng hôy* (fireflies), most populous during the wet season. From Friday to Sunday, operators from several piers lead tours, charging 60B for a seat. Outside of these days, it costs 500B for a two-hour charter.

The Amphawa area's second-most-famous tourist attraction is **Don Hoi Lot** (ดอนหอย หลอด), a bank of fossilised shells at the mouth of Mae Nam Mae Klong, not far from Samut Songkhram. These shells come from *hŏy lòrt* (clams with a tube-like shell). While nearby seafood restaurants are popular with city folk year-round, the shell bank is best seen during April and May when the river surface has receded to its lowest level.

🛏 Sleeping & Eating

Amphawa is exceedingly popular with Bangkok's weekend warriors and it seems like virtually every other house has opened its doors to tourists as a homestay. These can range from little more than a mattress on the floor and a mosquito net to upscale guesthouse-style accommodation. Rooms with fan start at about 250B, while rooms with air-con (many share bathrooms) begin at about 1000B. Prices are half this on weekdays.

In addition to many canalside restaurants and the weekends-only floating market (p148), Amphawa has a simple night market open each evening. There are some excellent **seafood restaurants** (Map p158; mains 70-200B; ⊙10am-10pm) at Don Hoi Lot, about 20km east.

ChababaanCham Resort   HOTEL $$$
(☑081 984 1000; www.chababaancham.com; Th Rim Khlong; r incl breakfast 1900-2400B; ❉ 🔊) Located just off the canal, this place has attractive, modern and spacious duplex-style rooms, the more expensive of which come equipped with a rooftop lounge area.

Baan Ku Pu   HOTEL $$$
(☑081 941 1249; Th Rim Khlong; bungalows incl breakfast 1600-2000B; ❉ 🔊) A Thai-style 'resort' featuring wooden bungalows in a relatively peaceful, canalside enclave.

Ploen Amphawa Resort   HOTEL $$$
(☑081 458 9411; www.facebook.com/ploenamphawa; Th Rim Khlong; r incl breakfast 1400-3000B; ❉ 🔊) Not a resort at all, but rather a handful of rooms in a refurbished wooden home in the thick of the canal area.

ℹ Getting There & Away

From Bangkok's **Southern Bus Terminal** (p155) in Thonburi, board any bus bound for Damnoen Saduak and ask to get off at Amphawa (80B, two hours, frequent 6am to 9pm). Alternatively, there are also frequent minivans to Samut Songkhram (also known as Mae Klong; 70B, 1½ hours, frequent from 6am to 9pm). From there, you can hop in a *sŏrng·tăa·ou* (passenger pick-up truck; 8B) near the market for the 10-minute ride to Amphawa.

WORTH A TRIP

ANCIENT CITY

Don't have the time to see Thailand's most famous historic monuments? Then consider visiting scaled-down versions of them at **Ancient City** (เมืองโบราณ, Muang Boran; Map p158; www.ancient citygroup.net/ancientsiam; 296/1 Th Sukhumvit, Samut Prakan; adult/child 600/350B; ⊙9am-7pm; [S]Bearing exit 1), which claims to be the largest open-air museum in the world. It's an excellent place to explore by bicycle (daily hire 50B) as it's usually quiet and rarely crowded.

On the way to Ancient City and created by the same visionary, the **Erawan Museum** (พิพิธภัณฑ์ช้างเอราวัณ/ช้างสามเศียร; Map p158; www.ancientcitygroup.net/erawan; Soi 119, Th Sukhumvit; adult/child 300/200B; ⊙9am-8pm; [S]Bearing exit 1) is a five-storey sculpture of Indra's three-headed elephant mount from Hindu mythology. The interior is filled with antique sculptures but is most impressive for the stained-glass ceiling.

Ancient City lies east of Bangkok outside Samut Prakan, which is most conveniently accessed via the park's shuttle bus from BTS Bearing station (see website for departure times).

Nakhon Pathom   นครปฐม

☑034 / POP 120,000

Nakhon Pathom is a typical central Thai city, with Phra Pathom Chedi as a visible link to its claim to the country's oldest settlement. The town's name, which derives from the Pali 'Nagara Pathama' meaning 'First City', appears to lend some legitimacy to this boast.

The modern town is quite sleepy, but it is an easy destination in which to see everyday Thai ways and practice your newly acquired language skills on a community genuinely appreciative of such efforts.

⊙ Sights

Phra Pathom Chedi   BUDDHIST TEMPLE
(พระปฐมเจดีย์; Map p158; by donation; ⊙temple daylight hours, museum 9am-4pm Wed-Sun) This stupa, located in the centre of Nakhon

Pathom and rising to 127m, is one of the tallest Buddhist monuments in the world.

The original structure was erected in the early 6th century by the Theravada Buddhists of Dvaravati. But, in the early 11th century the Khmer king, Suriyavarman I of Angkor, conquered the city and built a Brahman *prang* (Hindi/Khmer-style stupa) over the sanctuary. The Burmese of Bagan, under King Anawrahta, sacked the city in 1057 and the *prang* lay in ruins until Rama IV (King Mongkut) had it restored in 1860.

On the eastern side of the monument, in the *bòht*, is a **Dvaravati-style Buddha** seated in a European pose similar to the one in Wat Phra Meru in Ayuthaya. It may, in fact, have come from there.

Also of interest are the many examples of Chinese sculpture carved from a greenish stone that came to Thailand as ballast in the bottom of 19th-century Chinese junks. Opposite the *bòht* is a **museum**, with some interesting Dvaravati sculpture and lots of old junk. Within the *chedi* complex is **Lablae Cave**, an artificial tunnel containing the shrine of several Buddha figures.

The **wát** surrounding the stupa enjoys the kingdom's highest temple rank, Rachavoramahavihan; it's one of only six temples so honoured in Thailand. King Rama VI's ashes are interred in the base of the Sukhothai-era Phra Ruang Rochanarit, a large standing Buddha image in the wát's northern *wí-hǎhn* (sanctuary).

The stupa is located just south of Nakhon Pathom's railway station.

Phutthamonthon
BUDDHIST TEMPLE

(พุทธมณฑล; Map p158; ⊙ daylight hours) Southeast of the city stands this Sukhothai-style standing Buddha designed by Corrado Feroci. At 15.8m it is reportedly the world's tallest, and it's surrounded by a 400-hectare landscaped park that contains sculptures representing the major stages in the Buddha's life.

All Bangkok–Nakhon Pathom buses pass by the access road to the park at Phra Phutthamonthon Sai 4; from there you can walk, hitch or flag down a *sǒrng·tǎa·o* into the park itself. From Nakhon Pathom you can also take a white-and-purple Salaya bus; the stop is on Th Tesa across from the post office.

✖ Eating

Nakhon Pathom has an excellent market (p148) along the road between the train station and Phra Pathom Chedi. There are many good, inexpensive food vendors and restaurants in this area.

❶ Getting There & Away

Nakhon Pathom is 64km west of Bangkok. The city doesn't have a central bus station, but most transport arrives and departs from near the market and train station.

The most convenient and fastest way to get to Nakhon Pathom from Bangkok is via a minivan, which depart from the Southern Bus Terminal (60B, one hour, frequent 6am to 6pm).

There are also more frequent trains from Bangkok's Hualamphong station throughout the day (14B to 60B, one hour).

Central Thailand

Best Places to Eat

➡ Blue Rice (p188)

➡ Keeree Tara (p188)

➡ Sainam Pomphet (p172)

➡ On's Thai-Issan (p188)

➡ Toy's (p199)

Best Places to Stay

➡ Oriental Kwai Resort (p187)

➡ River Kwai Resotel (p194)

➡ P Guesthouse (p199)

➡ Good Times Resort (p187)

➡ Ayothaya Riverside House (p171)

➡ Phu Chom Mork Resort (p199)

Why Go?

History lives and breathes in central Thailand's misty valleys and jungle-fringed rivers. The region's crowning glory is Ayuthaya, Siam's former royal capital. The town is practically an open-air museum, with dozens of breathtaking temple ruins peopled by stone Buddhas. Khmer-style temples are also a draw in Lopburi, 50km north, though the atmosphere is far less serene in Thailand's 'Monkey City'.

Heading west, Kanchanaburi's museums chronicle the dark history of the Thailand–Burma Railway (aka the Death Railway) and WWII memorials pay tribute to thousands of lost lives. Scenery gets wetter and wilder following Mae Nam Khwae Yai northwest. The river's tributaries are hugged by sedate villages (and the occasional riverside resort) and skirt national parks such as the waterfall-kissed Erawan and Sai Yok.

Life dawdles at an even slower pace in Sangkhlaburi in the multi-ethnic northwest, where villages and national parks bordering Myanmar have a beguiling, frontier feel.

When to Go

➡ Central Thailand experiences the country's three seasons in equal measure. It's hot from February to June, rainy from June to October, and cool (relatively speaking) from October to January. The one constant is the humidity.

➡ Because of altitude, it is wetter and cooler (and sometimes even a little chilly) in Sangkhlaburi and its surrounding national parks than elsewhere, making this region a comparatively refreshing break from low-lying towns...just be sure to bring an umbrella.

➡ Ayuthaya and Lopburi sit in a wide open plain that receives similar amounts of rain and heat as Bangkok.

Central Thailand Highlights

1 Ayuthaya (p166) Cycling between enigmatic ruins and colossal Buddhas, and watching the sunset paint them gold.

2 Kanchanaburi (p181) Being rendered speechless by the harrowing history of the Death Railway.

3 Erawan National Park (p190) Clambering up seven levels of waterfall to splash in aquamarine pools.

4 Prang Sam Yot (p176) Admiring Lopburi's most famous 13th-century temple while dodging myriad monkeys.

5 River Resorts (p194) Escaping to the wilderness at Nam Tok's resorts, which float on water or hide in forest.

6 Saphan Mon (p197) Striding across Thailand's longest wooden bridge for views of Sangkhlaburi's glassy lake.

7 E-Thong (p196) Being jolted along a potholed road en route to this picturesque border village.

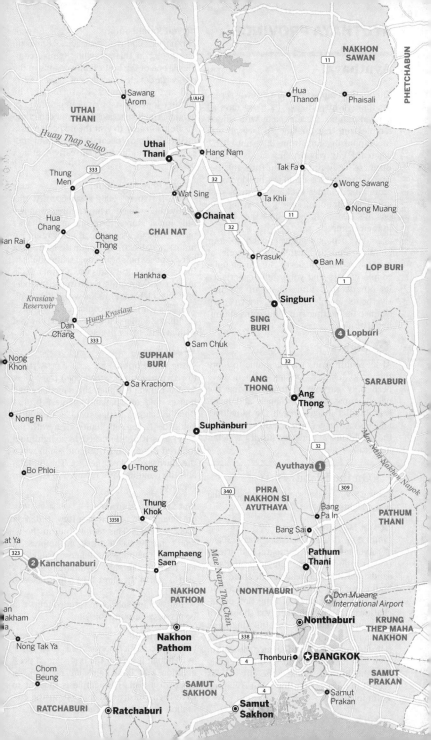

AYUTHAYA PROVINCE

Ayuthaya   อยุธยา

📞 035 / POP 18,600

Enigmatic temple ruins are strewn across Ayuthaya, whispering of its glory days as a royal capital. Once replete with gilded temples and treasure-laden palaces, it was the capital of Siam from 1350 until 1767, when the city was brutally sacked by the Burmese. Only ruins remain from this period of thriving trade and art, but dozens of crumbling temples evoke Ayuthaya's past grandeur. Standing among towering stupas, it's easy to imagine how they looked in their prime.

A day trip is usually enough to tour temple ruins and catch the flavour of Ayuthaya's faded majesty. But linger for a couple of days and you'll fully experience its otherworldly atmosphere of sloshing riverboats, temple silhouettes drawn sharp against the setting sun, and ruins illuminated at night.

👁 Sights

At its zenith, Ayuthaya was home to more than 400 temples. Dozens of them have been only partially restored, leaving the naked stupas, roofless chapels and headless Buddha images to tell the kingdom's tale. It's easy to get between sites by bicycle, though hiring a guide for historical detail is useful.

👁 On the Island

Central Ayuthaya's 'island' has most of the major sights.

⭐ Wat Mahathat   RUINS

(วัดมหาธาตุ; Th Chee Kun; 50B; ⊙ 8am-6.30pm; 🅿) Ayuthaya's most photographed attraction is found in these temple grounds: a sandstone Buddha head tangled within a bodhi tree's entwined roots. Founded in 1374, during the reign of King Borom Rachathirat I, Wat Mahathat was the seat of the supreme patriarch and the kingdom's most important temple. The central *prang* (Hindi/Khmer-style stupa) once stood 43m high and it collapsed on its own long before the Burmese sacked the city. It was rebuilt in more recent times, but collapsed again in 1911.

⭐ Wat Ratchaburana   RUINS

(วัดราชบูรณะ; off Th Naresuan; 50B; ⊙ 8am-6pm) The *prang* in this sprawling temple complex is one of the best extant versions in the city, with detailed carvings of lotus flowers and mythical creatures; it's surrounded by another four stupas. If you aren't afraid of heights, small spaces or bats, you can climb inside the *prang* to visit the crypt (the largest in Thailand), decorated with faint murals of the Buddha from the early Ayuthaya period.

⭐ Wat Phra Si Sanphet   RUINS

(วัดพระศรีสรรเพชญ์; 50B; ⊙ 8am-6pm) At this captivating ruined temple, three wonderfully intact stupas form one of Ayuthaya's most iconic views; unlike at many other ruins, it's possible to clamber up the stairs for a lofty vantage point (and epic selfie). Built in the late 15th century, this was a royal temple inside palace grounds; these were the model for Bangkok's Wat Phra Kaew and Royal Palace. This temple once contained a 16m-high standing Buddha (Phra Si Sanphet) covered with at least 143kg of gold.

⭐ Wihan Phra Mongkhon Bophit   BUDDHIST TEMPLE

(วิหารพระมงคลบพิตร; ⊙ 8am-5pm) FREE Next to Wat Phra Si Sanphet, this sanctuary hall houses one of Thailand's largest bronze Buddha images, dating to 1538. Coated in gold, the 12.5m-high figure (17m with the base) was badly damaged by a lightning-induced fire around 1700, and again when the Burmese sacked the city. The Buddha and the building were repaired in the 20th century.

Wat Lokayasutharam   RUINS, STATUE

(วัดโลกยสุธาราม; off Th Khlong Thaw; ⊙ daylight hours; 🅿) FREE This temple ruin in the island's northwest features an impressive 42m-long reclining Buddha, ostensibly dating back to the early Ayuthaya period. A visit is worth the short bike trip it takes to reach it.

Touts selling snacks and guided tours can be persistent around this site.

Wat Phra Ram   RUINS

(วัดพระราม; off Th Naresuan; 50B; ⊙ 8am-6pm; 🅿) Though it isn't in the best state of preservation, Wat Phra Ram's tall main *prang* is worth a visit. The temple is thought to have been constructed in 1369 on the cremation site of King U Thong (the Ayuthaya kingdom's first sovereign), though details of its history are unclear. It's a 500m walk east of Wihan Phra Mongkhon Bophit.

Unlike some of the other temple ruins in Ayuthaya, the site attracts only a trickle of tourists.

Chao Sam Phraya National Museum
MUSEUM

(พิพิธภัณฑสถานแห่งชาติเจ้าสามพระยา; ☏035 244570; cnr Th Rotchana & Th Si Sanphet; adult/child 150B/free; ⊙9am-4pm Wed-Sun; Ⓟ) The most impressive treasure of Ayuthaya's largest museum is the haul of royal gold (jewellery, utensils, gourds, spittoons) unearthed from the crypts of Wat Mahathat and Wat Ratchaburana. Beautifully carved teak friezes, some flecked with gold leaf, and numerous Buddha statues (some sculpted in the 7th century) are also on display.

Million Toy Museum
MUSEUM

(พิพิธภัณฑ์ล้านของเล่นเกริกยุ้นพันธ์; ☏081 890 5782; www.milliontoymuseum.com; Th U Thong; adult/child 50/20B; ⊙9am-4pm Tue-Sun; Ⓟ) Thousands of toys from across the decades are amassed in this private museum. Much of the exhibition is unlabelled, so it remains a mystery why rare porcelain elephants and retro racing cars are filed alongside mass-produced Shrek and Pikachu figurines. Still, the collection is in a pleasantly cool atrium, a refreshing change from sweating it out at Ayuthaya's temple ruins.

Ayutthaya Tourist Center
MUSEUM

(ศูนย์ท่องเที่ยวอยุธยา; ☏035 246076; off Th Si Sanphet; ⊙8.30am-4.30pm) FREE Two floors of historical exhibitions contextualise Ayuthaya's history from ancient to present-day within this impressive building crowned with militaristic statues. Downstairs is the tourist information centre (p174).

Wat Maheyong
RUINS

(วัดมเหยงค์; Han Tra; 50B; ⊙8am-4.30pm) Despite requiring an admission fee, Wat Maheyong is not an especially interesting structure, although the walled corridor leading to a large *ubosot* (chapel) is an unusual feature.

Thai Boat Museum
MUSEUM

(พิพิธภัณฑ์เรือไทย; ☏035 241195; www.thaiboat museum.com; Th Ho Rattanachai; by donation; ⊙9am-noon & 1-5pm) Think you can tell a round-bottomed tug from a triple-planked fishing boat? This interesting little private museum is full of wooden boats, both real and artistic miniatures. Many such vessels can still be seen plying Ayuthaya's rivers today.

Wat Suwandararam
BUDDHIST TEMPLE

(วัดสุวรรณดาราราม; ⊙daylight hours) FREE Although there was a temple here in the Ayuthaya era, the present buildings are from the current reign, with the *bòht* (ordination hall) built by King Rama I and the adjacent *wí·hǎhn* (sanctuary) by King Rama IV. Both have fascinating murals inside that show, among other things, scenes of daily life and stories from the life of King Naresuan. It's in the southwest part of town, north of Th U Thong.

Chantharakasem National Museum
MUSEUM

(พิพิธภัณฑสถานแห่งชาติจันทรเกษม; ☏035 251586; Th U Thong; 100B; ⊙9am-4pm Wed-Sun) This museum is within the grounds of Wang Chan Kasem (Chan Kasem Palace), built for King Rama IV at the site of a palace used by King Naresuan and seven subsequent Ayuthaya kings. The museum is large, but the collection (Buddhist art, pottery, ancient weapons, lacquered cabinets and original furnishings) isn't – the highly decorated buildings themselves are the main attraction.

Wat Thammikarat
RUINS, TEMPLE

(วัดธรรมิกราช; off Th U Thong; 20B; ⊙8am-7pm; Ⓟ) To the west of Wat Ratchaburana, this is both an active temple and a pleasant place to sit among the ruins. The most prominent feature is a central *chedi* (stupa) surrounded by 13 *singha* (guardian lion) sculptures.

Ayuthaya

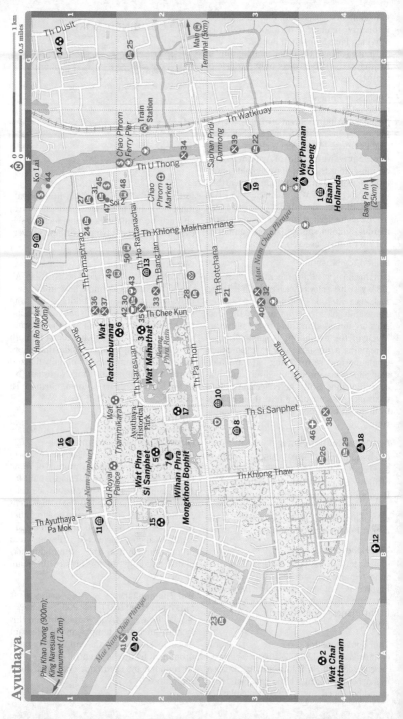

Ayuthaya

⊙ Off the Island

On the opposite side of the water that envelops central Ayuthaya are several famous temples. You can reach some sites by bicycle, but others require a motorbike, car or túk-túk ride. Evening boat tours around the island are another way to see the highlights.

★ Wat Chai Wattanaram   RUINS
(วัดไชยวัฒนาราม; Ban Pom; 50B; ⊙8am-6pm; P) Glorious at sunset, this temple is Ayuthaya's most impressive off-island site thanks to its 35m-high Khmer-style central *prang* and fine state of preservation. Relief panels are heavily eroded, but you can make out carved scenes from the Buddha's life.

★ Wat Phanan Choeng   BUDDHIST TEMPLE
(วัดพนัญเชิง; Khlong Suan Plu; 20B; ⊙daylight hours) This lively temple, believed to date to 1324, is a fascinating place to observe merit-making ceremonies, which unfold beneath the gaze of the 19m-high Phra Phanan Choeng Buddha. This enormous statue, a guardian for seafarers, is the focus of most visits. He sits within a soaring *wí·hăhn* (open 8am to 5pm) surrounded by 84,000 small Buddha images lining the walls.

★ Wat Yai Chai Mongkhon   RUINS
(วัดใหญ่ชัยมงคล; 20B; ⊙6am-6pm) Visitors to this photogenic ruin can climb stairs up the bell-shaped *chedi* for a view of sculpted gardens and dozens of stone Buddhas. There's a 7m-long reclining Buddha near the entrance

ⓘ ELEPHANT WARNING

Guided elephant rides are frequently offered to tourists as a way to tour Ayuthaya's temples but we strongly advise against partaking in this cruel activity.

and the local belief is that if you can get a coin to stick to the Buddha's feet, good luck will come your way.

It's 2km east of the island's southeast corner.

Wat Na Phra Men
BUDDHIST TEMPLE

(วัดหน้าพระเมรุ; Lum Phli; 20B; ⊙ daylight hours; Ⓟ) Housing a gorgeous 6m-high Buddha flanked by maroon columns, this temple was one of the few to escape the wrath of Burma's invading army in 1767; it survived by serving as the army's main base and weapons storehouse. The *bòht* is massive, larger than most modern ones, and the Buddha image wears 'royal attire', which was very common in the late Ayuthaya era. Despite what the English sign inside says, it's made of bronze, not gold.

Wat Tha Ka Rong
BUDDHIST TEMPLE

(วัดท่าการ้อง; ⊙ daylight hours; Ⓟ) FREE With animatronic skeletons, super-sized crow sculptures and armless statues, Wat Tha Ka Rong is eerie and playful in equal measure. The temple, northwest of the island, is peopled by Buddhist, Hindu, animist and just-for-fun statues. Beware the skeletons doing the *wâi* (palms-together Thai greeting); they have motion sensors.

There's a weekend **floating market** (dishes from 20B; ⊙ 8am-5pm Sat & Sun) nearby.

Wat Phutthai Sawan
BUDDHIST TEMPLE

(วัดพุทไธศวรรย์; Samphao Lom; ⊙ 8am-5.30pm) FREE Atmospheric ruins and lively temple worship can both be experienced at Wat Phutthai Sawan. King Ramathibodi I founded this temple in 1353, the first built off Ayuthaya island. It's one of the few places

---

DON'T MISS

AYUTHAYA'S FOREIGN QUARTER

One reason Ayuthaya's rulers thrived was their adroit diplomacy and tolerance towards other cultures and religions. At its peak, more than 40 ethnic groups resided here. People from nearby places, such as the Mon, Lao and Khmer, as well as the Chinese, lived more or less freely among the locals. Those from further away, such as Indians, Persians, Javanese and Malay, were given land, mostly to the south of the island, by the king to create their own settlements.

The Portuguese, who arrived in 1511, were the first Europeans to reach Siam and they were granted land to settle here in the 1540s. They were followed in the next century by the Dutch, English, Spanish and French. The Europeans brought arms and other luxuries, and returned mostly with spices, tin, deerskins, porcelain, sappan wood and rice.

In 1767 these settlements met the same fate as the rest of the city when it was sacked by the Burmese. Three nations have memorialised their ancient Thai ties here.

Baan Hollanda (บ้านฮอลันดา; ☑ 035 245683; www.baanhollanda.org; Soi Khan Rua, Mu 4; 50B; ⊙ 9am-5pm Wed-Sun; Ⓟ) The bright and beautifully curated 'Dutch House' features an excellent exhibition of Thai-Dutch history alongside the excavated foundations of centuries-old Dutch buildings. The Dutch East India Company (VOC) arrived in Ayuthaya in 1604 and set up a trading post here, hoping to use Thailand (then Siam) as a gateway to China. Adjoining the museum is a charming clog-adorned cafe offering *stroopwafels* and other Dutch-themed snacks alongside Western and Thai-style coffees and tea.

Japanese Village (หมู่บ้านญี่ปุ่น; ☑ 035 259867; 25/3 Mu 7, Tambon Kohrian; adult/child 50/20B; ⊙ 8am-5pm; Ⓟ) Set within manicured, hibiscus-fringed gardens, this small museum complex details the lives of the estimated 1500 Japanese who came to settle in Ayuthaya in the early 17th century. Some came to trade, but most were Christians fleeing persecution in their homeland. Both exhibition halls feature a video presentation.

Portuguese Village (หมู่บ้านโปรตุเกส; Samphao Lom; ⊙ 9am-4pm) FREE Arriving in the 16th century, the Portuguese were the first European settlers in Ayuthaya. Several of their skeletal remains are on view at this burial site excavation. More than 200 Portuguese and Christian converts were interred here. Behind the burial ground is the foundation of the 1540 San Petro Church, the first church built in Thailand.

spared by Burmese invaders and its bone-white Khmer-style *prang* still rises high above the temple complex; you can go inside.

St Joseph Church
CHURCH

(วัดนักบุญยอแซฟ; Samphao Lom; ⊙8.30am-noon & 1-4.30pm Mon-Sat, 10.30-11.30am Sun; P) FREE In 1673, King Narai gave the French the land next to the Christian Vietnamese settlement and donated money towards building the first St Joseph Church. This attractive, mustard-coloured church is the modern rebuild of the original wooden sanctuary on this spot. The brick church dates to 1695, though it's been modified since then with decorative turrets and columns.

Wat Kudi Dao
RUINS

(วัดกุฎีดาว; Phai Ling) FREE Though it's not yet near *Indiana Jones* levels, forest is slowly reclaiming this attractive ruin. Knowledge is hazy about its construction date and history, but its huge bell-shaped stupa and imposing walls are worth exploring nonetheless.

👉 Tours

Most guesthouses are happy to arrange tours, though you may get more options and flexibility by talking to a travel agency such as **Tour With Thai** (☑086 982 6265, 035 958226; http://tour-with-thai.business.site; Soi 2, Th Naresuan; ⊙8am-7pm).

One of the most common itineraries is a two-hour boat tour (around 250B) taking in Wat Phanan Choeng (p169), Wat Phutthai Sawan and Wat Chai Wattanaram (p169); it's worthwhile if you don't have private transport. **Ayutthaya Boat & Travel** (☑081 733 5687; www.ayutthaya-boat.com; cnr Th Chee Kun & Th Rotchana; ⊙9am-5pm Mon-Sat) offers dinner cruises on a teak rice barge, as well as longer cycling and paddling tours with homestay accommodation.

⚔ Festivals & Events

Wai Kru Muay Thai Ceremony
CULTURAL

(⊙mid-Mar) Thai boxing fighters and their fans flock to Ayuthaya for this one-day event. Attendees can watch *moo·ay tai* matches, take lessons, observe sword making and the ancient, sacred practice of *yant* tattooing, and witness the sacred Wai Kru Muay Thai Ceremony, in which boxers pay respect to their masters and calm their minds before fighting.

Ayutthaya World Heritage Fair
LIGHT SHOW

(⊙Dec or Jan) The sound and light shows (500B) at Wat Mahathat (p166) are the highlight of this event, held in December or January. Check dates with the Tourism Authority of Thailand (p174).

🛏 Sleeping

Most backpackers head for Soi 2, Th Naresuan (known as 'foreigner street'); the area in front of the train station also has plenty of low-priced rooms. Staying riverside on the island's west is pleasant, but less convenient. Most lodgings only accept cash.

★ Ayothaya Riverside House
GUESTHOUSE $

(☑081 644 5328; www.facebook.com/ayothaya riversidehouse; 17/2 Mu 7, Tambon Banpom; d without bathroom 400B, d on boat 1500B; ❄🖙) Across Mae Nam Chao Phraya on the west side of Ayutthaya, this wonderful guesthouse offers a choice between pleasant rooms with fans and mosquito nets or satin-and-wood-decorated rooms on a boat (with air-con).

11:11 Hostel
HOSTEL $

(☑035 950138; www.facebook.com/11.11hostel; Th U Thong; dm incl breakfast 200B; ❄🖙) If you prefer modern dorm rooms to teak houses, you'll sigh with delight upon entering the cheerful and efficient 11:11 Hostel. Monochrome dorms have iron-frame bunks, each with its own light and plug socket, plus there's a dining area and a small terrace where you can look out over the river.

Chantana House
GUESTHOUSE $

(☑035 323200; chantanahouse@yahoo.com; 12/22 Soi 2, Th Naresuan; d with fan/air-con incl breakfast from 400/500B; P❄🖙) Rooms are plain, but modern Chantana House arguably offers the best value on the backpacker strip. Staff are friendly, though English is limited.

Baan Lotus Guest House
GUESTHOUSE $

(☑035 251988; Th Pamaphrao; s 250B, d & tw 350-600B; P❄🖙) Near, but completely separate from, the backpacker strip, this converted teak schoolhouse with a large deck out back has a soothing air, inset from the main road with a shambling yard filled with lilies and chirruping crickets. Wood-shuttered rooms are clean and comfortable, and it's so chill that almost nothing happens after 6pm, including check-in.

★**Promtong Mansion** GUESTHOUSE $$
(☑089 165 6297; www.promtong.com; off 23 Th Pa Thon; d 1100B; ❄ 🤶) Extending the warmest welcome in Ayuthaya, Promtong Mansion is filled with fabulous wood-carved sculptures. Large, comfortable rooms are decked with elephant-shaped bedside lamps and other local trimmings. The owner is a fount of local knowledge, complimentary fruit platters are offered throughout guests' stays, and the location is quiet but convenient.

Baifern GUESTHOUSE $$
(☑035 242051; www.baifernhomestay.com; Th Khlong Thaw; d incl breakfast 1200-1750B; ❄ 🤶) One of the classiest guesthouses in Ayuthaya, Baifern's rooms are priced by size (sleeping up to four people) and attired with traditional fabrics and antique-effect furniture. There's an inviting lounge, a garden stalked by cats (and, unfortunately, plenty of mosquitoes) and an on-site restaurant (mains around 120B) serving tasty Thai food.

Tamarind Guesthouse GUESTHOUSE $$
(☑089 010 0196, 081 655 7937; tamarind thai2012@gmail.com; off Th Chee Kun; d & tw incl breakfast 650-1200B; ❄ 🤶) Service couldn't be friendlier at this guesthouse within an attractively modified wooden building. Hidden in a back street across from Wat Mahathat (p166), Tamarind feels like a retreat despite being close to major attractions. As in many wooden guesthouses, creaky floors and thin walls aren't ideal for light sleepers; we think the traditional decor (stained glass, colourfully painted wood) amply compensates.

Tony's Place GUESTHOUSE $$
(☑035 252578; Soi 2, 8 Th Naresuan; d 850-1200B, f 1500B; ❄ 🤶 ☀) Tony's remains a prime destination for flashpackers thanks to its large outdoor **restaurant** (mains 70-300B; ☺8am-10pm; 🤶 🖉) area (ideal for mingling), mini-pool and spacious, characterful rooms. Lodgings on the upper floor are the most attractive.

★**Sala Ayutthaya** BOUTIQUE HOTEL $$$
(☑035 242588; www.salaayutthaya.com; 9/2 Mu 4, Th U Thong; d incl breakfast 4700-9400B; P❄🤶☀) Stepping inside Sala Ayutthaya is reminiscent of entering a wát, thanks to maze-like brick alcoves that lead to pure white and wood-accented rooms and an equally minimalist pool and spa zone. The excellent (though pricey) restaurant, and some rooms, enjoy views across the river to Wat Phutthai Sawan (p170), especially magical when illuminated at night.

★**Baan Thai House** RESORT $$$
(☑080 437 4555; www.baanthaihouse.com; Pai Ling; villas 1900-2800B, d/f all incl breakfast 2500/3800B; P❄🤶☀) Stone walkways threading through lush grounds, complete with lagoon and fountain, set the tone for this tranquil resort. Thai-style villas are awash in golden yellow and have fridges and TVs. Spacious double and family rooms are wood-lined, snug and similarly well-equipped.

✖ Eating

Centuries of mingling with foreign traders have resulted in a wealth of food options. The defining dishes are river prawns, Thai-Muslim snacks and boat noodles (noodles in a meaty, soy-rich broth, originally served by boat vendors and allegedly created in Ayuthaya).

★**Sainam Pomphet** THAI $
(Th U Thong; mains 100-150B; ☺10am-10pm; 🤶) Spider crab – either steamed or whipped into fried rice – is the house speciality at this excellent riverside restaurant. Fish 'steamboat' dishes (in a simmering tureen) are immensely popular too. Those who aren't fans of seafood can tuck into a range of other Thai fare (try the pineapple spare ribs).

★**Malakor** THAI $
(www.facebook.com/malakorrestaurant; Th Chee Kun; mains 40-200B; ☺restaurant noon-10pm, coffee shop 8am-4pm; ❄🤶) Touristy but satisfying, Malakor has a big menu, a great cook whipping up catfish curry and *pàd gàprow gài* (chicken with basil), and a relaxing wooden hut to enjoy it in. You will need to be patient with the service.

The attached coffee shop serves quality lattes and ice-blended drinks, best enjoyed with its green-tea gateau or strawberry cheesecake.

Bang Ian Night Market MARKET $
(Th Bang Ian; snacks from 10B, mains 30-100B; ☺5-8.30pm) This big, busy night market on its namesake street is a great destination for noshing on barbecued river fish, glass noodles, curry and rice dishes, rainbow-coloured

kà·nŏm chan (layered coconut jellies) and much more besides.

Lung Lek
NOODLES $
(Th Chee Kun; mains 30-50B; ⏱8.30am-4pm) This locally adored noodle emporium serves some of the most notable *gŏo·ay dĕe·o mŏo đun* (stewed pork noodles, aka boat noodles) in town.

Roti Săi Măi Stalls
DESSERTS $
(Th U Thong; desserts from 35B; ⏱8am-8pm) The dessert *roti săi măi* (silk thread *roti*) was invented in Ayuthaya and is sold all over town, though these stalls fronting the hospital are the most famous.

Buy a bag then make your own by rolling together thin strands of melted palm sugar and wrapping them inside the sweet flatbread.

Ban U Thong
THAI $
(Th U Thong; mains 50-120B; ⏱noon-9.30pm) Overhanging the water, Ban U Thong has a satisfying menu featuring dishes such as chicken with sour melon, catfish salad, and lip-smackingly sour *đôm yam gûng* (prawn soup).

★ Coffee Old City
CAFE, THAI $$
(Th Chee Kun; mains 100-200B; ⏱8am-5.30pm Mon-Sat; ❄🛜) Energise for a day of temple-hopping with shrimp rice soup and a caffeine hit at this friendly cafe. Wicker chairs, greenery, bare-brick feature walls and traditional Thai decorations establish a calming ambience. It serves an excellent *pàt tai*.

Bann Kun Pra
THAI $$
(📞035 241978; www.bannkunpra.com; Th U Thong; mains 70-350B; ⏱11am-9.30pm) More intimate than most of Ayuthaya's riverside restaurants, this century-old teak house is a great place to sit and watch river life pass by. Service quality varies, but the menu is loaded with seafood – including multiple preparations of local river prawns and fresh, tasty shrimp omelettes – and features other dishes such as chicken with cashew nuts.

Sai-Thong
THAI $$
(Th U Thong; mains 60-350B; ⏱10.30am-9.30pm; 🅿✏) One of many restaurants with riverside decks along this stretch of Mae Nam Chao Phraya, Sai-Thong has perhaps the merriest ambience, thanks

DESSERT DOYENNE

A half-Japanese, half-Portuguese chef from Ayuthaya is fondly remembered for her contribution to tooth-tingling Thai desserts. Madame Maria Guyomar de Pinha (aka Thao Thong Kip Ma) rose to local fame as a chef in King Narai's court thanks to her Portuguese-inspired sweets recipes, which she disseminated among ladies of the court. Guyomar is credited with creating numerous classic desserts, so spare a thought for this 17th-century chef when you nibble on *thong yot* (syrupy golden droplets of flour and egg) and *foi thong* (sweet threads made from duck egg yolk).

CENTRAL THAILAND AYUTHAYA

to occasional live music and jokey serving staff. The menu is broader than most, featuring local favourites such as river prawns plus a number of tasty northeastern Thai delicacies, as well as all shades of vegetarian Thai curry.

🍷 Drinking & Nightlife

Most travellers head to the pack of streetside bars on Soi 2, Th Naresuan.

Busaba
CAFE
(Th Chee Kun; ⏱9am-6pm; 🛜) Iced mango smoothies and coffees come garnished with edible flowers and Ayuthaya's favourite sweet treat, *săi mài* (palm sugar floss) at this photogenic, brick-walled cafe.

Coffee House
BAR
(Th Naresuan; ⏱11am-midnight) This oddly named bar has a stage and plenty of outdoor tables, with live rock and pop music starting at 8pm most nights.

🛍 Shopping

Chao Phrom Market
MARKET
(Th Naresuan; ⏱hours vary) Ayuthaya is famous for its sweet Muslim snacks, curries and *nám prík* (spicy dip), and the bustling undercover Chao Phrom Market is the place to find them, plus assorted Thai-Chinese and other Muslim dishes. Operating hours of this daytime market depend on individual vendors but it's at its peak during the early afternoon.

ℹ Information

DANGERS & ANNOYANCES

When cycling, wear your bags around your body; don't put them in baskets where they could be snatched. At night many packs of dogs roam the streets – be sure to keep your distance.

EMERGENCY

Tourist Police (☏ 035 241446, 1155; Th Si Sanphet)

IMMIGRATION

Immigration Office (☏ 035 328411; Th U Thong; ☉ 8.30am-noon & 1pm-4.30pm Mon-Fri) For Thailand visa extensions.

MEDICAL SERVICES

Phra Nakorn Si Ayuthaya Hospital (☏ 035 211888; www.ayhosp.go.th/ayh; Th U Thong) Has an emergency centre and English-speaking doctors.

Rajthanee Hospital (☏ 035 335555; www.rajthanee.com; off Hwy 309) Private hospital with some English-speaking doctors, 5km east of the island.

MONEY

All the major banks have offices (and ATMs) on Th Naresuan, including a number of foreign exchanges; **Krungthai Bank** (KTB; ☏ 035 251663; ground flr, Amporn Department Store, Th Naresuan; ☉ 10am-1pm & 2-5.30pm) opens at the weekends.

Bangkok Bank (Th U Thong)

Krungsri Bank (☏ 035 245718; cnr Th Ho Ratthanchai & Th U Thong; ☉ 8.30am-3.30pm Mon-Fri)

POST

Main Post Office (Th U Thong; ☉ 8.30am-4.30pm Mon-Fri, 9am-noon Sat)

ℹ TOURING BY TÚK-TÚK

Túk-túks are readily available. The drivers' initial offer is certain to be high, but for most one-way trips on the island the rate should be 50B to 100B. Going rates per hour are 200B to 300B, but multi-hour trips get discounts. For a túk-túk from the bus terminal to the old city, expect to pay upwards from 150B. If rates sound cheap, check that they aren't giving you the rate per person, rather than the total price.

Túk-túks in Ayuthaya are different from the classic Thai design thanks to their dome-shaped fronts, resembling Darth Vader's iconic mask.

Post Office (Th Pa Thon; ☉ 8am-6pm Mon-Fri, to noon Sat)

TOURIST INFORMATION

Tourism Authority of Thailand (TAT; ☏ 035 246076; tatyutya@tat.or.th; Th Si Sanphet; ☉ 8.30am-4.30pm) Has an information counter with maps and good advice at the Ayutthaya Tourist Center (p167).

ℹ Getting There & Away

BOAT

There are no public boats between Bangkok and Ayuthaya. Be aware that 'cruises' from Bangkok are usually bus tours featuring a short boat ride through Bangkok at the start or end (or they bus you there and boat you part of the way back). Scrutinise itineraries carefully.

BUS

Ayuthaya's minivan **bus stop** (Th Naresuan) is just south of the backpacker strip (ask for the *đà-làht tâh rót jôw prom*). Minivans to Suphanburi (transfer here for Kanchanaburi), Saraburi (transfer here for Pak Chong and Khorat) and various places in Bangkok leave from here. There's a second Bangkok **departure point** (Th Naresuan) one block west.

For destinations further afield, you'll need to go out to the **main bus terminal** (off Hwy 32), 3km east of the island, though you can buy tickets for Chiang Mai and Sukhothai from a town-centre **bus ticket office** (Th Naresuan; ☉ 6.30am-5pm) for a fee (from 20B). For a túk-túk between the terminal and the island, try for 100B but expect to pay around 150B (or roughly half that for a motorcycle taxi). Or you can ride the purple *sŏrng·tăa·ou* (7B; passenger pick-up truck).

Many people pay premium prices to book tickets at their hotel. The markup includes transport to the station and sometimes a shower before departure. Many guesthouses also sell seats in private minivans to Kanchanaburi (350B to 400B, 2½ to 3½ hours), Bangkok's Th Khao San (200B to 300B, 1½ hours), Hua Hin (750B, six hours) and Chiang Mai (540B to 990B, 10 hours); prices usually include hotel pick-up.

TRAIN

Ayuthaya's train station is just across the river from the town's main island. Trains are usually slower than buses and minibuses, except for those to Khao Yai National Park (Pak Chong station). For Bangkok (20B to 65B, 1½ to 2½ hours, frequent), most trains stop at Bang Sue station before arriving at Hua Lamphong. There are five daily departures from Ayuthaya to Chiang Mai (396B to 1848B, 10 to 14 hours).

TRANSPORT TO/FROM AYUTHAYA

Buses

DESTINATION	FARE (B)	DURATION (HR)	FREQUENCY
Bangkok (Rangsit)	40	¾	frequent (minivan)
Bangkok Northern (Mo Chit) bus terminal	55-70	1-1½	frequent (minivan)
Chiang Mai	419-837	8½-10	at least eight daily
Lopburi	80	1½-1¾	every 30min (minivan)
Saraburi	45	1½	frequent
Sukhothai	266-342	7	at least 10 daily
Suphanburi	50-80	1½	more than hourly (minivan)

Trains

DESTINATION	FARE (B)	DURATION (HR)	FREQUENCY
Bang Pa In	3-12	¼	16 daily
Bangkok Hualamphong station	20-65	1½-2½	frequent
Chiang Mai	396-1848	10-14	5 daily
Nong Khai	202-1750	9-11	3 daily
Pak Chong	53-465	2-3	12 daily

If you are visiting Ayuthaya as a day trip before boarding an overnight train, there is luggage storage at the train station; most guesthouses offer showers for about 30B.

ℹ️ Getting Around

Cycling is the ideal way to see the city. Many guesthouses hire bicycles (40B to 50B per day) and motorcycles (250B to 300B) and there are several rental stands opposite Wat Mahathat (p166) and Wat Ratchaburana (p166). You can also rent bikes from Tour with Thai (p171). A deposit of ID will be required.

River ferries cost 5B per person plus 5B for a bike. The **ferry** (⊘5am-7.30pm) nearest the train station operates 5am to 7.30pm, and the westernmost can carry motorcycles.

Around Ayuthaya

⭐ Bang Pa In Palace   PALACE

(พระราชวังบางปะอิน; 100B; ⊘8am-4pm, last entrance 3.15pm; [P]) Ornate buildings are sprinkled across Bang Pa In Palace's 19-hectare gardens. First established in the 17th century, the palace was revived in the 19th century by kings Rama IV and V, the latter adding most of its European styling. Today an eclectic assortment of architectural styles is arranged around manicured lawns, including the intricate Chinese-style **Wehart Chamrun**, the orange-and-red-striped observatory **Ho Withun Thasana** (1881) and a Thai **pavilion** that appears to float on the water. Dress modestly.

The palace grounds are ideal for strolling but renting an electric buggy (400B for one hour, 100B per hour thereafter) is a handy way to stay in the shade.

Certain buildings require women to don traditional sarongs before entering. Sarongs are available for use free of charge.

To reach the palace, take the train from Ayuthaya (3B to 12B, 15 minutes, 16 daily) and then jump on a motorcycle taxi (around 20B) or túk-túk (from 60B) to the palace, which is 1.7km away. If you're driving, there's a large car park nearby (30B per vehicle).

Private taxi transfers from Ayuthaya cost around 1300B one way.

Wat Niwet Thamaprawat   BUDDHIST TEMPLE

(วัดนิเวศธรรมประวัติราชวรวิหาร; Bang Pa In; by donation; ⊘daylight hours) On an island next to Bang Pa In Palace, this unique *ubosot* (chapel) was designed to resemble a European Gothic cathedral, complete with a spire topping the showy, buttercup-yellow

BANG PA IN'S TRAGIC QUEEN

Queen Sunanda Kumariratana drowned when her royal barge overturned on the way to Bang Pa In Palace (p175) in 1880. There were heavy taboos on physical contact between royals and non-royals – the penalty was death – so distraught onlookers watched helplessly as she drowned. The tragic queen and her children are memorialised with a marble obelisk in the palace grounds.

building. Inside you can admire cathedral-style windows, stained glass and gilded filigree that wouldn't look out of place in a European church.

Take a free, monk-operated **cable car** across the river from the palace parking lot (leave a donation in the boxes).

Bang Sai Arts & Crafts Centre
CULTURAL CENTRE

(ศูนย์ศิลปาชีพบางไทร; adult/child 100/50B; ⊙ 9am-5pm Tue-Sun) Observe basket weaving, ceramic painting and myriad traditional Thai crafts at this cultural complex, 30km south of Ayuthaya. Whether you're in the market for delicate silk purses or carved wooden furniture, it's an excellent place to browse handmade souvenirs. You'll need private transport to visit the centre from Ayuthaya.

LOPBURI PROVINCE

Lopburi
ลพบุรี

✔ 036 / POP 161,000

In Thailand's 'Monkey City', imposing Khmer-style temples are assailed by an army of furry menaces. These adorable mischief-makers have the run of the town and are impossible to avoid – and for many, monkeys are the headline attraction of Lopburi.

One of Thailand's oldest cities, Lopburi developed during the Dvaravati period (6th to 10th centuries), when it was known as Lavo. King Narai (r 1657–88) made Lopburi a second capital, hosting many foreign dignitaries in the town. An array of palaces and

temples from the Khmer and Ayuthaya empires still stand, though in various states of decay.

It only takes 24 hours to see Lopburi's main sights, but it's worth staying a second day to explore the countryside. Sunflowers carpet the fields east of town from November to January, needle-like limestone peaks beckon to climbers, and temples such as Wat Khao Chin Lae (p181) overlook jaw-dropping vistas.

◉ Sights

All of Lopburi's main sites reside in a conveniently compact area and can be visited in a leisurely day. If you're staying overnight, take a stroll through the city after dark to see the ruins and shrine (p178) lit up, each to very different effect.

★ Prang Sam Yot
RUINS

(ปรางค์สามยอด; cnr Th Wichayen & Th Prang Sam Yot; 50B; ⊙ 8.30am-6pm) As well known for its resident monkeys as its looming towers, this is Lopburi's most famous attraction. The three linked towers were built from laterite and sandstone by the Khmer in the 13th century as a Buddhist temple. It was later converted to Shiva worship but was returned to Buddhism by King Narai in the 17th century. There are two ruined headless Buddha images inside; a third, more complete Buddha sits photogenically in front of the main *prang* (Hindi/Khmer-style stupa).

Visitors can enter but a heavy metal door keeps the monkeys out – keep your distance unless you want macaques swinging from your rucksack and making off with your sunglasses.

★ Phra Narai Ratchaniwet
MUSEUM

(วังนารายณ์ราชนิเวศน์, Somdet Phra Narai National Museum; ✔ 036 414372; entrance Th Sorasak; 150B; ⊙ 8.30am-4.30pm Wed-Sun) An excellent museum is enclosed within these ruins of a 17th-century palace. Built from 1665 with help from French and Italian engineers, the palace was originally used to welcome foreign dignitaries. A trim promenade leads between King Narai's elephant stables, banquet rooms, wells and dozens of storage buildings to the Somdet Phra Narai National Museum. Allow a couple of hours to explore this 7-hectare historical site inside and out.

Lopburi

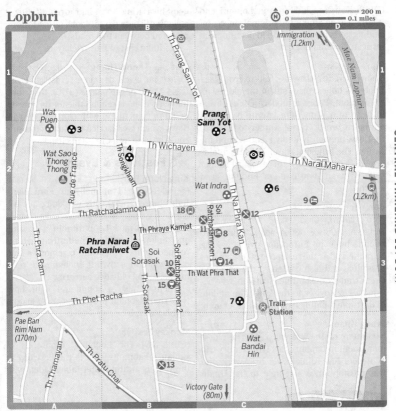

Lopburi

◉ Top Sights
1 Phra Narai Ratchaniwet	B3
2 Prang Sam Yot	C2

◉ Sights
3 Ban Wichayen	A2
4 Prang Khaek	B2
5 San Phra Kan	C2
6 Wat Nakhon Kosa	C2
7 Wat Phra Si Ratana Mahathat	C3

🛏 Sleeping
8 Noom Guesthouse	C3
9 Pee Homestay	D2

✴ Eating
10 Baan Sahai	B3
11 Matini	C3
12 Night Market	C2
Noom Restaurant	(see 8)
13 Vietnamese Restaurant	B4

🍸 Drinking & Nightlife
14 Come On Bar	C3
15 Sahai Phanta	B3

ℹ Transport
16 Minivans to Bangkok	C2
17 Minivans to Bangkok	C3
18 Sŏrng·tăa·ou to Bus Station	B2

Wat Phra Si Ratana Mahathat   RUINS
(วัดพระศรีรัตนมหาธาตุ; Th Na Phra Kan; 50B;
⊙8.30am-4pm) For a peaceful, monkey-free
experience of a Khmer wát, stroll around
this beautiful site opposite the train station.
Built in the 12th century and heavily modified over the centuries, this now-ruined
temple has the tallest central *prang*

(Hindi/Khmer-style stupa) in Lopburi and retains a good amount of original stucco, including gorgeous lotus-shaped detailing and intricate Buddha images.

San Phra Kan SHRINE

(ศาลพระกาฬ; Th Wichayen; ⊙ 5.30am-6pm) **FREE** Lopburi's holiest place sits in the old town's roundabout. It has a modern (1951) shrine in front of a Khmer-era laterite base from a toppled *prang* (Hindi/Khmer-style stupa) that was previously known as the 'supreme shrine'. The principal statue inside is a four-armed Vishnu body in Lopburi-Khmer style with an Ayuthaya-era Buddha head attached.

Ban Wichayen RUINS

(บ้านวิชาเยนทร์, Chao Phraya Wichayen; Th Wichayen; 50B; ⊙ 8.30am-4pm) This compound, built in European style by King Narai, served as the residence of foreign ambassadors and also contained the palace of Greek trader Constantine Phaulkon, who became a key adviser to the king. The middle of the three buildings was a Catholic church.

Prang Khaek RUINS

(ปรางค์แขก; off Th Wichayen) **FREE** The oldest monument in Lopburi, this 11th-century trio of towers has Khmer-style brickwork and was possibly once a temple to the Hindu god Shiva. King Narai had it rebuilt after it collapsed. These days it looks rather forlorn, pincered between two roads.

It's 100m east of Ban Wichayen.

Wat Sao Thong Thong BUDDHIST TEMPLE

(วัดเสาธงทอง; Rue de France; ⊙ daylight hours) **FREE** North of the palace (p176), this working temple site is remarkable for its unusual *wí·hǎhn* (sanctuary) with Gothic-style windows, which were added by King Narai so it could be used as a Christian chapel.

🎎 Festivals & Events

King Narai Fair CULTURAL

(⊙ mid-Feb) Held annually at Phra Narai Ratchaniwet (p176), this weeklong fair celebrates Ayuthaya's most revered monarch, who transformed Lopburi into a cultural and diplomatic centre. The festival features re-enactments of period ceremonies and other cultural activities, including a 'retro market' using old-style currency.

There is also a sound-and-light-show. Note that elephant processions may feature in this festival.

Monkey Festival CULTURAL

(⊙ late Nov) For Lopburi's thousands of simian inhabitants, this is the best day of the year. Beautiful buffet tables laden with

---

LOCAL KNOWLEDGE

MONKEY MAYHEM

Grown men arm their catapults, old women grab 2m-long poles and tourists alternately shriek and pose for photos. Welcome to Lopburi, a town that fights a losing battle to keep its iconic monkeys at bay. Hundreds of rhesus and crab-eating macaques (and crossbreeds of the two species) roam a wide swathe of the old city via its rooftops and power cables. They climb on cars, slide down sunshades and squabble over scraps, putting on a non-stop show that has put 'Monkey City' on the travel map.

Many locals loathe their simian neighbours, but the monkeys are never harmed due to the belief that they are disciples of the Hindu god Hanuman (in the Thai version of the Ramayana, Rama gave this land to Hanuman, who founded the city), and so to injure one would be seriously bad karma. However, it will only take a few minutes in Lopburi for you to understand why many residents support plans to round some monkeys up and ship them to a forest outside town.

Monkeys may be cute, but they are wild animals. Don't carry food (or anything that could be mistaken for food) within the monkey zone; otherwise, expect a dash-and-grab robbery. If you do suffer a mugging (they're common at Prang Sam Yot (p176) and the nearby railway crossing), don't resist – monkeys bite, and if this happens you'll need medical attention. It's also prudent to avoid walking below them (unless you're carrying an umbrella).

Most of the monkeys live at Prang Sam Yot and San Phra Kan. Stand still long enough and monkeys may sneak up to steal your hat or jump on your back; avoid eye contact and keep moving slowly around the site if you want to escape their attentions.

fruits and sweets are set out four times during the day for the monkeys to devour. There's also a street fair and dance shows around town.

🛏 Sleeping

Budget rooms are the only choice in the old town, and the new town surprises with its lack of genuinely good choices. If you have your own wheels, there are some better midrange resort options 5km east of town.

★ Noom Guesthouse GUESTHOUSE $
(📞036 427693; www.noomguesthouse.com; Th Phraya Kamjat; s/d/tr with shared bathroom & fan 250/350/450B, d with air-con 500B; ✸🏠) Weary backpackers sigh with relief upon arrival at family-run Noom, easily the most fa·ràng-friendly spot in town. Even if you aren't staying in one of their clean, simple rooms (or the comfy garden bungalows out back), it's worth swinging by to rent a motorbike (from 250B), book a climbing tour or swap travel stories with the backpackers at the bar.

You can buy breakfast from the great on-site **restaurant** (📞036 427693; www.noomguesthouse.com; Th Phraya Kamjat; mains 50-150B; ⏱8am-9.30pm; 🏠🍴).

Pee Homestay HOMESTAY $
(📞086 164 2184; www.lopburimassage.com; Soi Promachan; d with fan 280B, d with air-con 340-500B; ✸🏠) On the wrong side of the tracks (in a good way), this homestay behind the train station is run by the super-friendly Kanaree, a beautician and massage therapist. It's a laid-back local experience. Spic-and-span rooms are priced by size.

Lopburi Inn Resort HOTEL $$
(📞036 420777; www.lopburiinnresort.com; off Th Phrakiat; d/ste incl breakfast 1000/1400B; 🅿✸🏠🏊) Want to sleep in the shade of gigantic monkey statues? Of course you do. Lopburi Inn Resort embraces the town's monkey theme, arranging comical chimps around its grounds. Decorated in vanilla and beige, rooms are simple but have fridges and good-quality beds.

It's 7km east of the old town.

Windsor Resort HOTEL $$
(📞036 411689; off Hwy 3196; d incl breakfast from 650B; 🅿✸🏠) With a windmill at its entrance and bright chalets, Windsor Resort is a cheery little enclave. Lodgings don't quite match the buildings' merry exteriors (the peach-coloured rooms in the main hotel building

BUDDHA'S FOOTPRINT

An imprint of the Buddha's foot, protected by a bone-white shrine, is the focus of merit-making rituals at lofty **Wat Phra Puttachai** (วัดพระพุทธบาท; Saraburi; ⏱daylight hours; 🅿) **FREE**. In front of the imprint, devotees daub petals of gold leaf on to a symbolic outline of the foot. Outside the shrine is a rocky outline representing Thailand's borders. The temple is 10km south of Saraburi town, accessed by a meandering, monkey-ridden road. From the car park, climb the stairs and turn left to reach the shrine.

With private transport, you can visit on a half-day excursion from Lopburi (60km northwest) or Ayuthaya (50km west). If you're staying in Lopburi, Noom Guesthouse offers afternoon tours that include a stop at this temple (800B to 1250B for groups of one to five people).

are especially bland) though it's a great-value, functional place with helpful service.

It's 750m south of the train station (p181).

Benjatara Boutique Place Resort RESORT $$
(📞089 904 2121, 036 422608; off Th Phahonyothin; d incl breakfast 750B; 🅿✸🏠) The description as 'boutique' is pushing it, given Benjatara inhabits a dreary block. Still, rooms are modern and clean (if a little worn), and the resort is well-run.

It's located 5.5km east of the old town and so best suited to travellers with private transport.

🍴 Eating & Drinking

Lopburi isn't renowned for nightlife, but it does have a handful of places for a beer-steeped evening. Traveller havens Noom and Matini (p180) both attract foreigners keen to shoot the breeze over pool and cocktails, while locals head to **Come On** (Th Wat Phra That; ⏱hours vary) for beers and **Sahai Phanta** (Soi Sorasak; ⏱7pm-midnight) for whisky and live music.

Night Market MARKET, THAI $
(Th Na Phra Kan; ⏱4-11pm) The best bet for a cheap dinner in the old town is these stalls running parallel to the railway track.

Tip: eating at stalls further south along the strip increases your distance from monkey ground zero, reducing the risk of losing your fried chicken or corn on the cob to a ravenous macaque.

Vietnamese Restaurant VIETNAMESE $

(☑ 036 411220; 43 Th Sorasak; mains 60-120B; ☺ 11am-7.30pm) Its proprietors may not have worked too hard on the name, but this casual restaurant is otherwise excellent. Searingly spicy pork with lemongrass and chilli, Vietnamese-style omelettes and fresh, mint-stuffed spring rolls are among the dishes served by the smiling staff.

Baan Sahai THAI $

(Soi Sorasak; mains 40-250B; ☺ 11am-10pm; ☜) With a touch of European flair, this little spot styles itself as a bistro, serving Thai main courses and a range of loosely French-inspired desserts. It's as good for a full-blown meal as for a fresh, ice-blended pineapple shake.

Matini INTERNATIONAL, THAI $$

(18 Th Phraya Kamjat; mains 50-350B; ☺ 9am-late; ☜ ☝) Free pool, a Blues Brothers motif on the wall and good food (both Thai and Western) plant Matini firmly in the sights of backpackers. With indoor and outdoor areas, this is a great spot to tuck into sizeable portions of richly spiced curries (including veggie options), sip on smoothies or kick back late with a few beers.

Bua Luang CHINESE, THAI $$

(☑ 036 413009; off Th Phahonyothin; mains 80-200B; ☺ 10am-11pm; ⓟ) This crowd-pleasing out-of-town restaurant has a leafy outdoor dining area and efficient service. It serves a medley of Chinese and Thai dishes, including local favourite *plaa salid tôrd* (deep-fried salted fish) and basil-fried squid.

The main drawback is the location, 7km east of the old town.

About Coffee Garden COFFEE

(☑ 063 597 9291; Th Phrakiat; ☺ 7am-5pm) This coffee stand, 7km east of the old town, is a welcome surprise with its award-winning brews and charmingly ramshackle garden shed ambience.

ⓘ Information

There are several banks in the northern half of old Lopburi, along Th Songkhram and Th Ratchadamnoen, though none are open evenings or weekends. **Siam Commercial Bank** (Th Songkhram; ☺ 8.30am-3.30pm Mon-Fri) has a 24-hour ATM.

Post Office (Th Prang Sam Yot; ☺ 8.30am-7pm Mon-Fri, 9am-noon Sat & Sun)

DANGERS & ANNOYANCES

Being bitten by a monkey is a real possibility in macaque-packed Lopburi, and you're more of a target if you walk while carrying food or wear jewellery or accessories that catch the light. Stray dogs are also a problem, and they're especially bold at night. You'll need medical care if you're bitten by either, even if the injury

TRANSPORT TO/FROM LOPBURI

Buses & Minivans

DESTINATION	FARE (B)	DURATION (HR)	FREQUENCY
Ayuthaya	80	1½	every 30min (minivan)
Bangkok	110-120	2	frequent (minivan)
Chiang Mai	502-582	9-12	four daily
Nakhon Ratchasima (Khorat)	130-164	3½	every 30min (minivan & bus)
Pak Chong	70	2	every 30min (minivan)

Trains

DESTINATION	FARE (B)	DURATION (HR)	FREQUENCY
Ayuthaya	13-58	½-1½	18 daily
Bangkok Hualamphong	28-123	2-3½	16 daily
Chiang Mai	236-1800	9-12	5 daily
Phitsanulok	49-1046	3-5	11 daily

KHAO CHIN LAE

Khao Chin Lae, the rugged mountain visible in the distance from Lopburi, makes for a worthwhile day trip for outdoor enthusiasts and temple-hoppers.

For a serene excursion to the mountain, head to **Wat Khao Chin Lae** (วัดเวฬุวัน, Peacock Temple; Khao Chin Lae; ☉ daylight hours; P) FREE perched on the eastern edge of the mountain (15km from Lopburi by road). Climb 436 steps to the large Buddha to admire forest-clad mountains and **sunflower fields** (between November and January); the flowers are Lopburi's second claim to fame (after its monkeys). Just 5km east of the mountain by road is **Ang Sap Lek** (อ่างเก็บน้ำซับเหล็ก), a reservoir lined by restaurants with bamboo piers for eating lunch and dinner out over the water.

Want something more adrenalin drenched? Book a rock climbing excursion with Noom Guesthouse (p179). The main point for rock climbing is a 240m sheer peak visible as you approach **Wat Pa Suwannahong** (northeast of Wat Khao Chin Lae). Another thrill is **Kao Ta Kla**, home to a large **bat cave**, where hundreds of thousands of bats emerge for their nocturnal hunt just before sunset. Noom offers afternoon tours (800B to 1250B for groups of one to five people) which include all these sites plus Wat Phra Puttachai (p179) the famous Buddha footprint temple in nearby Saraburi Province.

If you just want to see the sunflowers, take the bus heading to Wang Muang (15B, 30 minutes); fields of sunflowers unfurl around the turn-off north to Wat Khao Chin Lae.

is slight. There's a first-aid point at San Phra Kan (p178); if it's closed, call the emergency number 1669, or get to **hospital** (☑ 036 785444; www.kingnaraihospital.go.th; Th Phahonyothin).

❶ Getting There & Away

BUS & MINIVAN

Lopburi lies well off the main north–south highway, which means direct bus routes are limited. For Kanchanaburi, you'll need to change buses in Ayuthaya or Suphanburi (50B, two hours). Lopburi's **bus station** (Sa Kaew Circle) is 2km east of the old town. Buy Chiang Mai tickets ahead of time through Noom Guesthouse (p179).

Minivans to Bangkok depart from two spots on Th Na Phra Kan; one (Th Na Phra Kan) is near the train station and another (cnr Th Wichayen & Th Na Phra Kan) is slightly north). Minivans to Ayuthaya depart from the bus station. As with minivans everywhere in Thailand, big bags require their own tickets.

TRAIN

The **train station** (Th Na Phra Kan) is in the old town. Depending on size, luggage storage costs 10B to 15B per bag per day and is available 24 hours.

❶ Getting Around

Sŏrng·tăa·ou run from **Th Ratchadamnoen** (Th Ratchadamnoen) to the bus station (8B per journey). Săhm·lór (pedicabs, also spelt săamláw) and motorcycle taxis will go anywhere in the old town for around 20B.

KANCHANABURI PROVINCE

Given the jaw-dropping natural beauty of Kanchanaburi Province, it seems paradoxical that the region is best known for the horrors of WWII's Death Railway. The provincial capital's war memorials are a mandatory stop before heading deeper into the parks and preserves that comprise the Western Forest Complex, one of Asia's largest protected areas.

Kanchanaburi กาญจนบุรี

☑ 034 / POP 94,600

Beyond its hectic modern centre and river views, Kanchanaburi has a dark history, paid tribute to at excellent memorials and museums.

During WWII, Japanese forces used Allied prisoners of war (POWs) and conscripted Asian labourers to build a rail route between Thailand and Burma (Myanmar). The harrowing story became famous after the publication of Pierre Boulle's book *The Bridge Over the River Kwai,* based loosely on real events, and the 1957 movie that followed. War cemeteries, museums and the chance to ride a section of the so-called 'Death Railway' draw numerous visitors to Kanchanaburi. Interest in the railway has been reignited by Richard Flanagan's Man Booker

Kanchanaburi

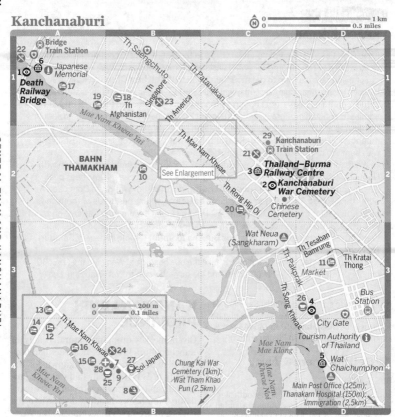

Prize-winning novel *The Narrow Road to the Deep North* (2013), inspired by the experiences of Flanagan's father as a POW.

Kanchanaburi is also an ideal gateway to national parks in Thailand's wild west, and home to an array of lush riverside resorts.

⊙ Sights

⊙ In Town

★ Death Railway Bridge   HISTORIC SITE

(สะพานข้ามแม่น้ำแคว, Bridge Over the River Kwai; ⊘24hr) **FREE** This 300m-long bridge is heavy with the history of the Thailand–Burma Railway, the construction of which cost thousands of imprisoned labourers their lives. Its centre was destroyed by Allied bombs in 1945; only the outer curved spans are original. You're free to roam over the bridge; stand in a safety point if a train

appears. Food and souvenir hawkers surround the bridge, so the site can have a jarring, funfair-like atmosphere; come early or late to avoid the scrum.

The three old trains in the park near the station were used during WWII. Across the river, pop in to the Chinese temple on the right and view the bridge from its tranquil garden. Nothing remains of a second (wooden) bridge the Japanese built 100m downstream.

During the last weekend of November and first weekend of December, an informative **sound and light show** (⊘late Nov/early Dec) tells the history of the Death Railway.

★ Thailand–Burma
Railway Centre   MUSEUM

(ศูนย์รถไฟไทย-พม่า; ☏ 034 512721; www.tbrconline.com; 73 Th Jaokannun; adult/child 140/60B; ⊘9am-5pm) This excellent museum strikes

Kanchanaburi

CENTRAL THAILAND KANCHANABURI

a balance of statistics and historical context with personal accounts of the conditions endured by POWs and other imprisoned labourers forced to build the Thailand–Burma Railway. Kanchanaburi's role in WWII is thoroughly explained, but most of the museum traces the journey of railway workers from transport in cramped boxcars to disease-ridden labour camps in the jungle, as well as survivors' fates after the war. Allow time for the poignant video with testimony from both POWs and Japanese soldiers.

★**Kanchanaburi War Cemetery**   CEMETERY
(สุสานทหารพันธมิตรดอนรัก, Allied War Cemetery; Th Saengchuto; ⊘24hr) Immaculately maintained by the Commonwealth War Graves Commission, this, the largest of Kanchanaburi's two war cemeteries, is right in town. Of the 6982 soldiers buried here, nearly half were British; the rest came mainly from Australia and the Netherlands. As you stand at the cemetery entrance, the entire right-hand side contains British victims, the front-left area contains Australian graves, the rear left honours Dutch and unknown soldiers, and those who were cremated lie at the furthest spot to the left.

All remains of American POWs were returned to the USA. If you're looking for the resting place of a loved one, a register is kept at the entrance.

JEATH War Museum   MUSEUM
(พิพิธภัณฑ์สงคราม; cnr Th Wisuttharangsi & Th Pak Phraek; 50B; ⊘8.30am-4.30pm) This small, open-air museum displays correspondence and artwork from former POWs involved in the building of the Death Railway. Their harsh living conditions are evident in the many photos on display alongside personal effects and war relics, including an unexploded Allied bomb dropped to destroy the bridge. One of the three galleries is built from bamboo in the style of the shelters (called *attap*) the POWs lived in; another has a 10-minute video presentation.

Heritage Walking Street   AREA
(ถนนปากแพรก; Th Pakprak) A stroll along this enchanting street offers a glimpse of a bygone Kanchanaburi. Many buildings date to the interwar period. Though worn by the passage of time, their Sino-Portuguese, Thai, Vietnamese and Chinese styles have been preserved; yellow signs reveal their history, architecture and current owners. The walk begins at the restored City Gate.

BUILDING THE 'DEATH RAILWAY'

The so-called 'Death Railway' was an astonishing feat of engineering constructed at immense human cost. Built by hard labour rather than modern machines, Japan's Allied prisoners of war and conscripted workers were armed only with basic tools and dynamite as they toiled. Well over 12,000 POWs and as many as 90,000 recruited and forced labourers (many of them Malay, Chinese and Indian) died due to disease, poor hygiene, lack of medical equipment and brutal treatment by camp guards. Many Thais risked their lives to aid the POWs, most of whom were Australian, American, British and Dutch, but they could offer only limited help.

The 415km railway was built during the WWII Japanese occupation of Thailand (1941–45). Its objective was to secure an overland supply route to Burma (Myanmar) for the Japanese conquest of other west Asian countries.

Construction began in October 1942 at existing stations at Thanbyuzayat in Myanmar and Nong Pladuk (Ban Pong) in Thailand. On 16 October 1943, the rails were joined 18km south of Three Pagodas Pass.

Most workers arrived at their labour camps already weakened by imprisonment, four-day-long journeys in cramped, overheated boxcars, and forced marches to reach their camps. Working conditions were initially survivable, but food supplies were already meagre. Cholera, malaria and dysentery were rife and medical care was mostly improvised. Japanese and Korean guards employed barbaric punishments for anyone who stepped out of line. As the Japanese demand for faster construction grew, conditions worsened. The most deadly section of railway construction was dubbed 'Hellfire Pass', because of immense rock cutting undertaken in perilous terrain; a memorial (p191) has since been built there.

Because of the mountainous landscape, 688 bridges were built along the route. Most of them were wooden trestle bridges, such as those at the oft-visited Tham Krasae. The bridge that spans the 'River Kwai' near Kanchanaburi city – which is now referred to as the Death Railway Bridge (p182) – was the only steel bridge built in Thailand; Burma had seven. It was bombed several times by the Allies, but the POWs were sent to rebuild it. When the war's tide turned, the railway became an escape path for the Japanese troops.

On the Thai side, the State Railway of Thailand (SRT) assumed control and continues to operate trains on 130km of the original route between Nong Pladuk, southeast of Kanchanaburi, and Nam Tok.

Highlights include the elegant parapets of **Sirichumsang Shophouse** (1932), the gold-flecked former jewellery shop **Chansiri House** (1927) and the Chinese-style **Kanchanaburi Hotel** (1937), which retains its original coloured glass.

WWII Museum　　　　　　　MUSEUM
(พิพิธภัณฑ์สงครามโลกครั้งที่สอง; Th Mae Nam Khwae; 40B; ☉8am-6pm) Though it's close to the Death Railway Bridge, this eclectic museum shouldn't be your first stop for understanding Kanchanaburi's wartime history. It's well-intentioned, but the museum's dispersed (and usually context-free) displays have limited educational value. Still, you'll see trains, Japanese motorcycles, anchors and old helmets, plus the museum has a great view of the bridge (the

tower in the northwest corner has the best viewpoint).

◉ Outside Town

★ **Wat Tham Seua**　　　BUDDHIST TEMPLE
(วัดถ้ำเสือ; Muang Chum; ☉daylight hours; P)
FREE The centrepiece of this hilltop temple is a striking 18m-high Buddha covered in golden mosaics. One of the merit-making ceremonies for devotees is to place coins in small trays on a conveyor belt that drops donations into a central bowl with a resounding clang. It's fun to ride the steep cable car (20B per person) to the top of the temple, but you can also climb the stairs.

Surrounding the main Buddha image are several styles of stupa. The biggest, nine stories (69m) high, is full of murals – mostly war related – of Kanchanaburi's history, and Buddha images, including many in seldom-seen postures. The namesake **Tiger Cave**, flanked by brightly painted tiger statues, is at the base of the hill, to the right of the cable car. The Chinese-style temple next door is **Wat Tham Khao Noi**, which is more interesting outside than in.

Wat Tham Seua is 12km southeast of central Kanchanaburi. After crossing the city's southernmost bridge, make the first left and follow the river. There's no public transport.

⭐ **Wat Tham Khao Pun**   BUDDHIST TEMPLE
(วัดถ้ำเขาปูน; Nong Ya; 30B; ◷6am-6pm) The nearest cave temple to Kanchanaburi town is a spellbinding labyrinth of stone passageways. The marked trail can be slippery (and a bit of a squeeze) in places, but ducking beneath limestone protrusions to discover these subterranean shrines is an otherworldly experience; it's pin-drop silent (aside from fluttering bats) down here. The temple is 4km southwest of the town centre, beyond Chung Kai War Cemetery.

Wat Ban Tham   BUDDHIST TEMPLE
(วัดบ้านถ้ำ; ◷temple daylight hours, stairway 8am-5pm; P) FREE In the countryside around Kanchanaburi, cave temples are almost as common as convenience stores are inside the city, but this is one of the most interesting. Walk up the steps and into the dragon's mouth to reach the large main cave.

You'll need a car or bike in order to reach the temple; it's 10km east of town on the south bank of the river, 4km before Wat Tham Seua.

Chung Kai War Cemetery   CEMETERY
(สุสานทหารพันธมิตรช่องไก่; Nong Ya; ◷7am-6pm) FREE Smaller and less visited than the war cemetery (p183) in town (but just as well maintained), Chung Kai Cemetery honours 1400 Commonwealth and 300 Dutch soldiers. This was the site of one of the biggest Allied POW camps. Prisoners built their own hospital and church close by and the majority of those buried here died at the hospital.

The cemetery is near the river, 2.5km southwest of the Wat Neua bridge. It's easily reached by bicycle.

🏃 **Activities**

Tours & Trekking

Tours are a convenient way to see the main sights outside the city, though if you have a small group it may be cheaper to hire a driver and plan your movements independently. Day trips generally cost 800B to 1100B per person, usually including admission fees and lunch. Kanchanaburi is rich in natural wonders, and many standard tours include bamboo rafting and short jungle treks.

Many companies offer similar itineraries. One of the most popular programs is a day to Erawan Falls (p190), Hellfire Pass Memorial (p191) and the Death Railway's 'wooden bridge' at Tham Krasae. But more adventurous options – such as cycling tours and overnight jungle trekking, usually staying in a Karen village – are available if enough people are interested. As a rule of thumb, the further north you go, the wilder things get. Posted prices are often negotiable. Trips can be cancelled if not enough people sign up, so check where things stand before booking.

ETHICAL ELEPHANT EXPERIENCES

Regrettably, a number of elephant-riding outfits exist around Kanchanaburi and numerous guesthouses and travel agencies are quick to recommend them. For animal welfare reasons, we strongly advise against rides; it's worth researching whether a place described to you as an 'elephant sanctuary' is just a glorified riding operation.

But you can get close to these endearing pachyderms without harming them: **Elephant Haven** (☑ 053 272855; www.elephantnaturepark.org; Sai Yok; half-day/full-day 1500/2500B; ◷by arrangement) 🌿 (an easy day trip from either Kanchanaburi town or Nam Tok) allows visitors to prepare and hand-feed balls of rice to elephants, observe them in their natural forest stamping ground, and join them for a dip in the river. Staff treat these intelligent creatures – most of them rescued or retired from elephant-riding outfits – with affection and care. Day-long programs include lunch, refreshments and transport to and from Kanchanaburi.

DON'T BE A BUFFALO

The movie *The Bridge on the River Kwai* (1957) made the waterway globally famous, but also left a generation pronouncing it incorrectly. You should talk about the River Khwae (sounds like 'square' without the 's' and 'r'), not Kwai (sounds like 'why'). Pronounce it like the film and you'll be referring to river buffalo, which Thais find amusing.

During the war, the bridge didn't cross the River Khwae either. Though the railway ran next to the river for much of its length, the bridge, in fact, crossed Mae Khlong – Pierre Boulle had it wrong when he wrote his book.

After the movie (filmed in Sri Lanka, so its bridge bears no resemblance to the real thing), tourists began visiting Kanchanaburi to see the bridge. To avoid confusion and disappointment, Mae Khlong officially became Khwae Yai ('yai' means 'big') in 1960.

AS Mixed Travel (☑ 034 512017; www.applenoikanchanaburi.com/a-s-mixed-travel; Apple's Retreat; per person from 950B), **Good Times Travel** (☑ 034 624441, 081 913 7758; www.good-times-travel.com; Th Mae Nam Khwae; day tour per person from 800B; ☺ hours vary) and **Toi's Tours** (☑ 081 856 5523, 034 514209; Th Mae Nam Khwae; day tour per person from 890B; ☺ hours vary) are reputable agencies for excursions in and around Kanchanaburi, though many others advertise their services (particularly along Th Mae Nam Khwae). Be aware that elephant rides, which we urge you to avoid, sometimes feature in cultural or outdoor tour programmes – scrutinise your itinerary and make it clear you don't wish to partake in this unpleasant practice.

For in-depth wartime and railway history, the Thailand–Burma Railway Centre (p182) can organise half-day to weeklong tours in and around Kanchanaburi; enquire via its website (under 'Railway Pilgrimages').

Kayaking

River Kwai Canoe
Travel Services   KAYAKING
(☑ 087 001 9137, 086 168 5995; riverkwaicanoe@yahoo.com; 11 Th Mae Nam Khwae; ☺ hours vary) Takes you out of town and lets you paddle back. The three-hour, 15km trip (500B per person) is the most popular option, but longer and shorter trips are available.

Also offers elephant ride excursions, which we strongly advise you to avoid for animal welfare reasons.

🎓 Courses

Apple & Noi Thai Cooking (☑ 034 512017; www.applenoikanchanaburi.com/apple-noi-cooking; Apple's Retreat; per person 1990B; ☺ by arrangment) Book ahead for a day course at this friendly riverside **guesthouse** (☑ 062 324 5879, 034 512017; www.applenoikanchanaburi.com; 153/4 Mu 4, Ban Tamakham; d/tw incl breakfast 990B; P ✳ 🛜) and restaurant.

On's Thai-Issan (p188) is a vegetarian restaurant offering informal two-hour cooking classes for 600B.

🛏 Sleeping

Travellers flock to the plentiful accommodation along Th Mae Nam Khwae. Budget and midrange digs sit alongside (or literally on) the river. The best high-end resorts are in the surrounding countryside (where it's a good idea to have a car).

🛏 In Town

Blue Star Guest House   GUESTHOUSE $
(☑ 034 512161, 064 984 4329; www.bluestar-guesthouse.com; 241 Th Mae Nam Khwae; d with fan/aircon 350/450B, bungalow 550-750B; P ✳ 🛜) Nature wraps itself around Blue Star's waterside lodgings, which range from simple rooms and thatch-roofed huts to more solid, bungalow-style accommodation. With a jungly vibe and helpful staff, this family-run guesthouse is one of the best budget choices in town.

Sugar Cane 2 Guesthouse   GUESTHOUSE $
(☑ 034 514988; Th Cambodia; d with fan/air-con 300/550B; P ✳ 🛜) Though it feels way out in the countryside, Sugar Cane 2 is just a 10-minute walk from the restaurants and bars of Th Mae Nam Khwae. A spot of renovation wouldn't hurt, but both land-side rooms and the bamboo-made raft rooms are a fair price.

★ Sabai@Kan   RESORT $$
(☑ 034 521559; www.sabaiatkan.com; 317/4 Th Mae Nam Khwae; d incl breakfast 1400-1700B, tr 2100B; P ✳ 🛜 ▨) Hospitable and impeccably managed, this boutique resort has modern cream-and-mahogany rooms arranged

around a swimming pool. Rooms have huge windows overlooking the pretty poolside garden, and it has the feel of a haven despite being close to Kanchanaburi's main tourist drag.

Pong Phen   GUESTHOUSE $$

(☑ 034 512981; www.pongphen.com; Soi Bangladesh, Th Mae Nam Khwae; d incl breakfast 650-1300B, tr1300B; P ✳ ☎ ☎) With river views, a warm welcome and staff who can arrange anything from motorbike rental (200B) to guided tours, Pong Phen is a great all-rounder. Cheaper rooms are spotless, if a little beige; at the pricier end, they overlook the river and are tastefully decorated with gleaming wood or tiled floors.

Ploy Guesthouse   GUESTHOUSE $$

(☑ 090 964 2653; www.ployresorts.com; 79/2 Th Mae Nam Khwae; d 680-1400B, f 1850-2200B, incl breakfast; P ✳ @ ☎ ☎) This stylish guesthouse-resort has rooms in a classic style, all cream walls and dark-wood furnishings. The best accommodation is cottage-style, featuring bamboo four-poster beds. Its back porch area is one of the prettiest places in town to relax along the river.

Tara Raft   GUESTHOUSE $$

(☑ 092 829 9419; www.tararoom.com; Th Rong Hip Oi; d & tw 600-900B; ✳ ☎) Though it's just 300m from the bustle of Th Mae Nam Khwae, there's an entirely different atmosphere along Rong Hip Oi road; it's peaceful and very local. The overall character of Tara could be better, but it has the best raft rooms in town (from 700B) – they're bright, nicely decorated and even have mini-fridges and in-room safes.

Baan Ma Feung   GUESTHOUSE $$

(☑ 034 511090; www.facebook.com/baanmafeung; Th Saengchuto; d from 650B; ✳ ☎) In a secluded location with a little garden, Baan Ma Feung's cosy and clean rooms are a pleasant surprise. It's 500m from the bus station, though a little far from the river and main backpacker drag on Th Mae Nam Khwae.

★ Good Times Resort   HOTEL $$$

(☑ 090 143 4925; www.good-times-resort.com; 265/5 Th Mae Nam Khwae; d incl breakfast 1250-2700B; P ✳ ☎ ☎) At this palm-lined riverside oasis, ample rooms are flooded with natural light and attractively flecked with colour. Beaming staff keep rooms spotless

and happily offer tips, while perks such as laundry service and lockers add peace of mind. An excellent choice.

River Kwai Bridge Resort   RESORT $$$

(☑ 034 514522; www.riverkwaibridgeresort.com; 8 Th Vietnam; d incl breakfast 1500-1950B; P ✳ ☎ ☎) This garden resort is within walking distance of the Death Railway Bridge (p182) (you can see half of it from the **restaurant**). It feels a little worn around the edges, but rooms and bungalows are tidy and comfortable, and you'll be lulled to sleep by a chorus of frogs.

Bridge Residence   HOTEL $$$

(☑ 034 515001; www.thebridgeresidence.com; 263/6 Th Mae Nam Khwae; d incl breakfast from 2600B; P ✳ ☎ ☎) At the Bridge Residence, monochrome feature walls, tasteful furnishings and high-end amenities (safes, minibars and fridges) keep well-heeled guests in the style to which they're accustomed. Service and breakfast varied in quality on our stay, but rooms are very elegant with deliciously comfy beds.

Outside Town

★ Ban Sabai Sabai   GUESTHOUSE $$

(☑ 089 040 5268; www.bansabaisabai.com; 102/3 Mu 4, Nong Bua; d 400-800B, f from 1650B; P ✳ ☎) Out in the countryside, 7km or so west of town along Hwy 323, this friendly place lives up to its name: 'Relaxation House'. Tile-floored rooms arranged around the florid garden are simple but very well maintained, and hosts can arrange anything from cooking classes to onward transport.

You can ask ahead for a free pick-up from town, but it's best to have your own wheels if staying here for a few days.

★ Oriental Kwai Resort   RESORT $$$

(☑ 616 730670; www.orientalkwai.com; 194/5 Mu 1, Tambon Lat Ya; cottages incl breakfast 2800-4900B; ✳ ☎ ☎) This Thai-Dutch-run spot has an exclusive feel. Set in a semi-wild garden, all four cottages are sumptuously decorated with Thai sculpture and fabrics and brooding oxblood walls. Amenities include fridges and flat-screen TVs. Two are designed for families and sleep up to six people. It's located 13km northwest of town, almost 2km off the road to Erawan National Park (p190).

X2 River Kwai
RESORT $$$

(☏ 034 552124; www.X2resorts.com; 138 Mu 4, Nong Ya; ste incl breakfast 3500-12,400B; P ❄ 🛜 🛝) Mannerly staff and water features immediately establish the tone of this sleek riverside resort, 10km southwest of the city. X2 has gorgeously designed rooms – think slate feature walls and tasteful modern art – facing an idyllic stretch of the river. We loved the cabins, each with floor-to-ceiling windows and a private roof sunbed (pricier 'luxe' cabins have their own kayak).

 ## Eating

Don't leave Kanchanaburi without dining at one of its charming riverside restaurants. Offerings along Th Mae Nam Khwae are variable in quality, with one tourist trap for every high-quality Thai restaurant. For better or worse, you'll also find a glut of Western food including English breakfasts, Aussie pies and pizza. A more authentic option is **JJ Market** (Th Saengchuto; snacks from 15B; ⊙ 5.30-10pm).

★ Blue Rice
THAI $

(www.applenoikanchanaburi.com; 153/4 Mu 4, Ban Tamakahm; mains from 135B; ⊙ noon-2pm & 6-10pm; P 🛜 🍴) Masterful spice blends, a creative menu and peaceful river views make this one of the most irresistible restaurants in Kanchanaburi. The signature massaman curry is perfectly balanced, and the menu is packed with reinvented Thai classics such as *yam sôm oh* (pomelo salad) and chicken-coconut soup with banana plant. The eponymous rice is stained with pea-flower petals, if you're wondering.

★ On's Thai-Issan
VEGETARIAN $

(☏ 087 364 2264; www.onsthaiissan.com; Th Mae Nam Khwae; mains from 70B; ⊙ noon-10pm; ❄ 🍴) At this casual restaurant, vegetarian and vegan recipes borrow Isan flavours and reinvent classic Thai dishes from entirely plant-based ingredients, with other healthy flourishes such as brown rice. Banana flower salad, ginger tofu and 'morning glory' (pan-seared greens) are cooked before your eyes on fryers outside and served in generous portions.

★ Keeree Tara
THAI $$

(☏ 034 513855; www.facebook.com/keereeTara; 431/1 Th Mae Nam Khwae; mains 150-400B; ⊙ 11am-11pm) This refined riverside eatery is ever so slightly upriver from the melee around the bridge. It serves upmarket Thai dishes from duck stuffed with lily to succulent catfish heaped with red curry. Still hungry? Choose from Thai desserts including *da·go peu·ak* (taro pearls in coconut milk) and French-inspired gateaux and white chocolate mousse.

Library Cafe
DESSERTS $$

(☏ 034 514300; Soi Singapore, Th Mae Nam Khwae; sweets from 170B; ⊙ 9am-10.30pm; ❄ 🛜) It's eye-wateringly expensive if you compare it to Kanchanaburi's markets, but a platter of *bingsu* (a Korean-style shaved ice dessert) served in Library Cafe's sultry surrounds is a guilty pleasure. The *bingsu* arrives big, adorned with mango, chocolate brownies, red beans and all manner of treats.

🍷 Drinking & Nightlife

Tourists and expats spend their evenings along bar-lined Th Mae Nam Khwae. Many venues have pool tables and screen sports matches (particularly the numerous Australian and British-themed bars). For the brave, streetside bars here offer shots for 10B.

Th Song Khwae, along the river in the centre of town, has a variety of bars; most don't get started until late.

★ 10 O'Clock
CAFE

(off Th Mae Nam Khwae; ⊙ 10am-10pm; 🛜) Flanked by a fountain that wouldn't look out of place in a Viennese palace, 10 O'Clock (guess the opening hours) has outdoor tables under shady trees. Within the clock-bedecked cafe, passionfruit frappés and good coffee are served to the clickety-clack of patrons using the free wi-fi.

★ Sitthisang
CAFE

(Th Pakprak; ⊙ 8am-6pm; 🛜) Hunker down with a bit of history – plus great coffee and dainty baked goods – in this primrose-yellow building on the Heritage Walking Street (p183). This house (built in 1920) has been owned by the same family for generations; it's one of the best-preserved buildings along this storied street.

Sugar Member
BAR

(Th Mae Nam Khwae; ⊙ 6pm-late) 'Drink! Drunk! Dance!' urges the sign above Sugar Member, and punters happily comply. This is a classic Kanchanaburi backpacker bar, with a vague reggae theme and friendly staff who will sip whisky buckets with you all night.

ℹ Information

EMERGENCY

Police Station (☏ 034 621040; cnr Th Saeng-chuto & Th Lak Meuang)

Tourist Police (☏ 034 512795; Th Saengchuto)

Tourist Police Booth (◷ 9am-4pm) Near Death Railway Bridge (p182).

IMMIGRATION

Immigration (☏ 034 564279; www.kan-immigration.com; Hwy 3429; ◷ 8.30am-noon & 1-4.30pm Mon-Fri) For visa extensions.

MEDICAL SERVICES

Pharmacy (Th Mae Nam Khwae; ◷ 9am-10pm) Sells over-the-counter medication. Yes, they have mossie repellent.

Thanakarn Hospital (☏ 034 622366; off Th Saengchuto) The best-equipped hospital to deal with foreign visitors.

MONEY

Most major Thai banks can be found on Th Saengchuto near the bus terminal. Three exchange booths in front of the WWII Museum (p184) open daily during normal business hours.

POST

Main Post Office (Th Saengchuto; ◷ 8.30am-4.30pm Mon-Fri, 9am-noon Sat & Sun)

TOURIST INFORMATION

Tourism Authority of Thailand (TAT; ☏ 034 511200; www.tourismthailand.org/Kanchanaburi; Th Saengchuto; ◷ 8.30am-4.30pm) Provides free maps of the town and province, along with bus timetables.

ℹ Getting There & Away

BUS

Kanchanaburi's **bus station** (☏ 034 515907; Th Lak Meuang) is in the centre of town just off Th Saengchuto, and minivans outnumber buses. (Remember, with a minivan, you need to buy an extra seat for large bags.) For Ayuthaya, you'll need to go to Suphanburi first. If heading south, it's quickest to transfer at Ratchaburi rather than Bangkok, but only old buses without air-con go there. Minivans to Bangkok depart until around 10pm.

There are also minivans to Bangkok catering to tourists; these pick up passengers along Th Mae Nam Khwae. Tickets, sold from dozens of shops, cost anywhere from 20B to 60B more per person. Unlike vehicles departing the bus station, these tourist minivans offer direct routes to Suvarnabhumi Airport (500B, three hours) and Ayuthaya (400B, 3½ hours).

TRAIN

Kanchanaburi is on the Bangkok Noi–Nam Tok rail line (trains don't use Hualamphong station). The SRT promotes this as a historic route, and so charges foreigners 100B for any one-way journey along the line, regardless of the distance. The trains are 3rd class, meaning wooden benches and no air-con, and you should not expect them to run on time. If you are planning a day trip to Kanchanaburi and time is tight, take a bus.

The most interesting part of the journey begins after Kanchanaburi as the train crosses the Death Railway Bridge (p182) and terminates at Nam Tok station, which is near Hellfire Pass (p191). It takes two hours, leaving

BUSES TO/FROM KANCHANABURI

DESTINATION	FARE (B)	DURATION (HR)	FREQUENCY
Bangkok Khao San Rd	120	2½	frequent (minivan)
Bangkok Northern (Mo Chit) bus terminal	100-150	2½	frequent (minivan)
Bangkok Southern (Sai Tai Mai) bus terminal	100	2½	every 20min (minivan)
Chiang Mai	594	10-11	three daily (8.30am, 6pm, 7pm)
Hua Hin	220	3½	every two hours (5am-6pm)
Nong Khai	495-829	11	one daily (7pm)
Ratchaburi	50	2½	every 20min
Sangkhlaburi (via Thong Pha Phum)	145-175	3½-5	every 30min (7am-5pm
Suphanburi	48-65	2½	every 30min

ⓘ GETTING TO MYANMAR: PHU NAM RON TO HTEE KHEE

This crossing is still something of an adventure. Myanmar visas are not available at the border.

Getting to the border There are around six daily buses (70B to 80B, two hours) and minivans (100B, 1½ hours) from Kanchanaburi's bus station (p189) right to the border starting at 9am. If you leave early you can make it to Dawei in a day, though there are guesthouses in Phu Nam Ron if you need them.

At the border After getting stamped out of Thailand, wait for the shuttle (50B) or take a motorcycle taxi to Myanmar immigration. Formalities are hassle-free, though a bit slow, on both sides.

Moving on Not far from immigration, you'll be introduced to minivan drivers who will take you to Dawei for 800B per person, though this is sometimes negotiable. It's five hours through the beautiful mountains to Dawei on what is still a mostly dirt – and sometimes rough – road, though improvements are under way.

Kanchanaburi's **main station** (☏ 034 511285) at 6.07am, 10.35am and 4.26pm. Most people headed from Kanchanaburi to Nam Tok board the train at the little station next to the Death Railway Bridge, so to be sure you get a seat (the left side of the train has the best views) board at the main station in town instead. Another option is a 'special car': tour companies near the bridge sell 300B tickets that include a cushion, a snack and a guaranteed seat.

Trains to Bangkok Noi (three hours) depart at 7.19am and 2.48pm.

ⓘ Getting Around

BICYCLE & MOTORCYCLE

Motorcycles can be rented at guesthouses and shops along Th Mae Nam Khwae for around 200B per day. Bicycle rentals cost from 50B per day.

BOAT

Long-tail boats can be hired near the Death Railway Bridge (p182) and the JEATH War Museum (p183). The standard program is a 1½-hour trip to Chung Kai War Cemetery (p185), Wat Tham Khao Pun (p185) and – depending on where you begin – either the bridge or the museum. The set price for up to six people is 800B, but this is sometimes negotiable.

PUBLIC TRANSPORT

Motorcycle taxis, many with sidecars that can carry several people and large luggage, are much more common than túk-túks (motorised transport, pronounced đúk đúk). A trip from the bus station to the guesthouse area will probably cost you 50B.

Yellow and blue *sŏrng·tǎa·ou* (passenger pick-up trucks) run up and down Th Saengchuto (get off at the cemetery if you want the guesthouse area) for 10B per passenger. You can board them on the west edge of the bus station (p189). Orange *sŏrng·tǎa·ou* do more work as taxis than they do running regular routes.

Around Kanchanaburi

It's possible to squeeze the major attractions around Kanchanaburi into a rushed day trip, but it takes a couple of days to do them justice. All but Muang Sing are easily reached by public transport. If you plan to spend a night at a national park on a weekend, book in advance.

Erawan National Park
อุทยานแห่งชาติเอราวัณ

 Erawan National Park   NATIONAL PARK
(☏ 034 574222; adult/child 300/200B, car/motorbike 30/20B; ◷ 8am-4.30pm; ℗) Splashing in cerulean pools under **Erawan Falls** is the highlight of this 550-sq-km park. Seven tiers of waterfall tumble through the forest, and bathing beneath these crystalline cascades is equally popular with locals and visitors. Reaching the first three tiers is easy; beyond here, walking shoes and some endurance are needed to complete the steep 2km hike (it's worth it to avoid the crowds in the first two pools).

Bring a swimming costume (and cover-up T-shirt) but be aware you're sharing the bathing area with large, nibbling fish; monkeys have been known to snatch swimmers' belongings. Level four has a natural rock slide and level six usually has the fewest swimmers. Buggies (adult/child 30/15B) can transport people with limited mobility to the first level. Picnickers, be aware that you can't take food and drink to level three or beyond. Bottles of water are permitted but to prevent littering, visitors are asked to register bottles and leave a 20B deposit (which is returned when you show the bottle on your way back down).

Elsewhere in the park, **Tham Phra That** (ถ้ำพระธาตุ; ⊘ 8am-4pm; P) is a cave with a variety of shimmering limestone formations. Geologists find the caves of interest due to a clearly visible fault line. Contact the **visitor centre** (☑ 034 574222; http://portal.dnp. go.th/; ⊘ 8am-4pm) before driving the 12km out there and a guide will meet you with paraffin lamps. There are several other fantastic caves in the park, but they're currently closed to the public.

The park was named for Erawan, the three-headed elephant of Hindu mythology, whom the top tier is thought to resemble. Mixed deciduous forest covers over 80 per cent of the park, but there's also dry evergreen and dry dipterocarp forest and big swathes of bamboo. Tigers, elephants, sambar deer, gibbons, red giant flying squirrels, king cobras and hornbills call the park home, but they don't frequent the waterfall area and you're unlikely to see them along the park's limited trails.

From the visitor centre, **Mong Lay Dry Trail** only takes an hour; for something more taxing, embark on the 5km **Khao Hin Lan Pee Trail**, a three-hour walk that takes you to the falls' fifth tier.

Park **bungalows** (☑ 02 562 0760; www.dnp. go.th; bungalows 800-4000B) sleep between two to eight people. Tent hire is 150B to 300B; if you bring your own tent, there's a 30B fee.

From Kanchanaburi, buses (50B, 1½ hours) run hourly from 8am to 5pm and go right to the visitor centre. The last bus back to town is at 4pm, and on weekends it will be packed. Touts at the bus station will try to talk you into hiring a private driver instead of taking the bus, but this isn't necessary.

Hellfire Pass Memorial ช่องเขาขาด

★ **Hellfire Pass Memorial**   MUSEUM
(☑ 034 919605; Hwy 323; ⊘ museum 9am-4pm, grounds 7.30am-6pm; P) **FREE** A poignant museum and memorial trail pay tribute to those who died building the Thailand–Burma Railway in WWII. Begin at the museum and ask for the free audio guide, which provides historical detail and fascinating first-person accounts from survivors.

CENTRAL THAILAND AROUND KANCHANABURI

KANCHANABURI REGION IN...

Two Days

Start in Kanchanaburi town, delving into wartime history at the **Thailand–Burma Railway Centre** (p182) and nearby **Kanchanaburi War Cemetery** (p183). Stroll along the charming **Heritage Walking Street** (p183) and head to the river for lunch; chic **Keeree Tara** (p188) is next to the **Death Railway Bridge** (p182).

On day two, catch a bus to **Erawan National Park**. Its seven-tiered waterfall feeds swimmable turquoise pools, and the higher you climb, the less crowded they get. Back in Kanchanaburi, bar-hop along Th Mae Nam Khwae.

Four Days

On day three, set out early for remote **Sangkhlaburi** (p197). Time it right and you can pause at **Hellfire Pass Memorial**; buses to Sangkhlaburi pass nearby. In town, admire the sunset from iconic **Saphan Mon** (p197).

On day four, enjoy a misty morning **boat ride** (p197) and head to **Baan Unrak Bakery** (p199) for vegan nibbles and local handicrafts.

One Week

On day five, bus your way to charming **E-Thong village** (p196) via **Thong Pha Phum** (p195) and crash at a welcoming homestay.

On day six, en route back to Thong Pha Phum town, stop in the less explored **Thong Pha Phum National Park** (p195) to snooze in a **treetop hut** (p195).

On your last day, book into a riverside resort (p194) near Nam Tok (p194) for peak relaxation before returning to busy Kanchanaburi.

Kanchanaburi Province

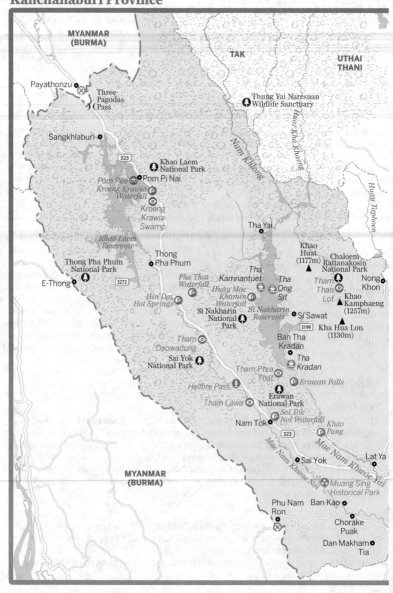

Then descend behind the museum to a trail following the original rail bed. The infamous cutting known as Hellfire Pass was the largest along the railway's length and the most deadly for the labourers forced to construct it.

Locally referred to as Konyu Cutting, this 600m stretch earned its 'hellfire' nickname following the final 'Speedo' construction period where shifts of 500 prisoners worked 16 to 18 hours a day, and even the 'light sick' were marched back to work. The glow from

face, the audio guide does an excellent job of conjuring up the conditions endured by prisoners.

The full walking route is 4km and ends at Compressor Cutting (allow three hours). If arranged in advance, pickup services are available from near Hin Tok Station (1.5km before Compressor Cutting).

The museum is 80km northwest of Kanchanaburi on Hwy 323 and can be reached by Sangkhlaburi and Thong Pha Phum buses (45B to 65B, two hours, every 30 minutes). The last bus back to Kanchanaburi passes here around 5pm.

Muang Sing Historical Park
อุทยานประวัติศาสตร์เมืองสิงห์

The restored ruins of 'Lion City', **Muang Sing Historical Park** (☏034 591122; 100B, car 50B; ⊙8am-4.30pm) is a 13th-century Khmer outpost, are girded by 880m of laterite walls at this expansive archaeological site. Set amid limestone hills 40km west of Kanchanaburi town, Muang Sing is thought to have been a relay point for trade along Mae Nam Khwae Noi. The ruins (Mahayana Buddhist sanctuaries, stocky city gates) show evidence of Bayon form, a decorative 12th- and 13th-century Khmer sculptural style.

Around the wall are additional layers of ramparts and moats, which are visible outside the main entrance. The ponds inside the wall were probably used for religious purposes.

There are two large main monuments at the site, and the remnants of two others. The principal shrine, **Prasat Muang Sing**, is in the centre and faces east (the cardinal direction of most Angkor temples). Found inside are replica statues of the eight-armed Bodhisattva Avalokitesavara and the goddess Prajnaparamita; the latter was probably installed in the other large shrine.

Outside the wall, right next to the river, is a burial site that shows two skeletons, pottery and jewellery thought to date back 2000 years.

Muang Sing is located 40km west of Kanchanaburi. Tha Kilen train station (100B) is just a 1.5km walk away, but it's wisest to come with your own transport since trains are infrequent and the grounds are large.

burning torches cast eerie shadows of the Japanese guards and of the gaunt prisoners' faces, so that the scene was said to resemble Dante's *Inferno*. As you walk past imposing walls of rock, catching sight of occasional nails protruding from the chiselled sur-

DON'T MISS

RIVERSIDE LUXURY

Central Thailand has countless raft resorts and waterside hotels, but Nam Tok does riverbank chic especially well. Guests glide on a long-boat to reach **River Kwai Resotel** (☎ booking line 02 642 5497, hotel 081 734 5238; www.riverkwai resotel.net; 55 Mu 5, Tambol Wangkrajae; d incl breakfast 1815-3300B; 🅿❄@≋) with its thatched-roof chalets set amid lush gardens; chalet interiors are beautifully modern with stone-effect bathrooms. Over at sister resort **FloatHouse** (☎ 02 642 5497; www.thefloathouseriverkwai.com; Wang Krachae; d incl breakfast 5250-7300B; 🅿❄📶), luxurious bamboo rooms shift with the movement of the river.

Both are accessed by long-boat (included in the room rate) from private **Phutakien Pier**, 2km west of Hwy 323, where you can park your car. All that remains is to decide whether you want to be lulled to sleep by a forest soundtrack of twittering birds and cicadas, or the gentle bobbing of a raft room.

Nam Tok

น้ำตก

For travellers riding the heritage Death Railway route from Kanchanaburi, Nam Tok is the final destination. But it can also be a starting point for tramping into caves, placid river rowing and luxuriating in water's-edge resorts.

Nam Tok train station serves the eponymous (and not overly exciting) town. A few kilometres north of here, resorts snooze along the riverbanks. For many visitors, a day or two relaxing by the river is reason enough to pass through Nam Tok. Otherwise, explore the southern part of Sai Yok National Park, which includes **Tham Lawa** (ถ้ำละว้า, Lawa Cave; Sai Yok National Park, Wang Krachae; ⏲ 8am-4.30pm), or join the locals picnicking at **Sai Yok Noi Waterfall** (น้ำตกไทรโยคน้อย, Nam Tok Sai Yok Noi; ⏲ daylight hours; 🅿) FREE.

🛏 Sleeping & Eating

Chokchai Hotel HOTEL $

(☎ 089 550 4361; www.facebook.com/chokchai hotel; Hwy 323; d 300-500B, f 1000B; 🅿❄📶) Basic, pastel-hued rooms equipped with fridges, on the highway between Sai Yok Noi Falls and Nam Tok village.

Yuk Coffee COFFEE

(☎ 081 016 4253; Hwy 323; ⏲ 9am-6pm) Excellent coffee and desserts are available from this enormously friendly roadside cafe, 15km southeast of Nam Tok train station.

ℹ Getting There & Away

Trains to Kanchanaburi (100B, two hours) depart **Nam Tok station** (Tha Sao) at 5.20am, 12.55pm and 3.30pm, while buses between Kanchanaburi (45B to 55B, 1¼ hours) and Thong Pha Phum (70B, one hour) pass through at least every 30 minutes. Six buses (leaving from near the train station) go all the way to Sangkhlaburi (80B to 90B, four hours), the last leaving at about 2.30pm.

Sai Yok National Park

อุทยานแห่งชาติไทรโยค

In **Sai Yok National Park** (☎ 034 686024; www.dnp.go.th; adult/child 300/200B; ⏲ daylight hours), mountains reach as high as 1125m and limestone caves burrow beneath the ground. Hemmed by Mae Nam Khwae Noi, this 958-sq-km preserve doesn't have waterfalls as impressive as those in Erawan National Park (p190), but it receives a fraction of the visitors. Home to rare wildlife, it's a bucolic place of walking trails amid mixed forests of bamboo, evergreen and deciduous greenery. For total immersion in nature, there are simple riverside bungalows where you can listen to a chorus of birdlife as the sun sets.

It's easy to explore Sai Yok independently, thanks to several sights (including waterfalls) reached along well-marked and maintained trails leading directly from the visitor centre. Many trails are open to bikes. The park's elevated location means temperatures are fresher than in surrounding towns, adding to the enjoyment of hiking or biking.

👁 Sights & Activities

The best-known attractions are **Sai Yok Yai Waterfall** (Nam Tok Sai Yok Yai, น้ำตกไทรโยคใหญ่) and – on the other side of the suspension bridge – **Sai Yok Lek Waterfall**. Both are small, but they're beautiful because of how they flow out of the forest. It's also worth visiting **Tham Daowadung** (ถ้ำดาวดึงส์), a cave rich with rock formations and bats, crickets and snakes throughout its eight chambers. There are lights but not stairs; the entrance can be treacherous when wet. A ranger will accompany you in (though it's not required, a tip is deserved). It's 6km northwest of the park entrance by road, or go by boat (1000B return); either way it's a steep 1.5km walk to the cave.

Long-tail boat hire (around 400B per 30 minutes) is available close to the suspension bridge, near the waterfalls.

🛏 Sleeping & Eating

For all accommodation within the park, you'll need to pay the park entrance fee on top of lodging costs. Most river resorts here are basic, with no air-conditioning or wi-fi, though they do have electricity (note that some only switch power on in the evenings). You'll also find floating restaurants by the river; they're near the suspension bridge, soon after you enter the park and start on the short trail to Sai Yok Yai Waterfall.

Krit Raft House (☑ 081 942 8107; d 800-1000B incl breakfast) offers spartan, fan-cooled bungalows overhanging the river. They're light on luxury but ideal if you want to swim, plus there are hammocks to bounce in. Service is friendly (though English isn't spoken). The national park accommodation consists of simple stilt houses and **bungalows** (☑ 02 562 0760; www.dnp.go.th; bungalows 800-2100B; P). They're slightly inset from the main road leading into the park. There's a booking booth by the main car park, though little English is spoken.

ℹ Information

The **Visitor Centre** is 1.5km along the road from the park admission fee booth. Little to no English is spoken, but pamphlets are available.

ℹ Getting There & Away

Sai Yok National Park is halfway between Sangkhlaburi and Kanchanaburi. Buses (60B, 1½ hours, every 30 minutes) between these destinations pass the park turn-off, and stop by request. The visitor centre is 3km off the highway. Motorcycle taxis (around 20B) wait near, but not right at, the junction; ask the visitor centre to call them when you're leaving the park. The last bus to Kanchanaburi passes at around 4.30pm.

Thong Pha Phum National Park

อุทยานแห่งชาติทองผาภูมิ

This less explored **park** (☑ 034 532114; adult/child 200/100B, car/motorbike 30/20B) sprawls across a serrated mountain range along the Myanmar border, a challenging 62km drive west from Thong Pha Phum town. Billed as a land of fog and freezing rainforest, mornings at the park have a brooding beauty, particularly when cold season mist fills the valleys. It's best known for **treetop accommodation** (☑ national parks service 02 562 0760; Thong Pha Phum National Park; d 800-2000B; P), comprising basic 6m- to 10m-high 'Tarzan' rooms.

The park teems with wildlife, including elephants, tigers, bears, marbled cats and palm civets, though most animals are shy.

CENTRAL THAILAND THONG PHA PHUM NATIONAL PARK

THONG PHA PHUM STOPOVER

The mountain-backed town of Thong Pha Phum (ทองผาภูมิ) – located between Kanchanaburi and Sangkhlaburi's wild northwest – is a gateway to its namesake national park and picturesque E-Thong village. The town itself doesn't have A-list attractions but it's worth stopping at **Hin Dat Hot Springs** (adult/child 60/40B; ☉ 9am-6pm), 20km south of Thong Pha Phum, to soak in three soothing geothermal pools or brave the adjacent fast-running stream. The springs are accessible via the Sangkhlaburi–Kanchanaburi bus on Hwy 323 (Km 105 marker).

If you're crashing overnight, **ThongPhaphum Place** (☑ 034 599544; Th Thetsaban 14; r 600-1200B; P ❄ 🛜) has perfectly clean rooms with fast wi-fi; it's near the main **market** (snacks from 10B; ☉ 6am-6pm), where you can grab a crab curry or some pastries. South of here, get info from the **tourist service** (Th Thetsaban; ☉ hours vary).

Buses depart from the market north to Sangkhlaburi (70B to 80B, two hours, three daily) or west to E-Thong (70B, 2½ hours, usually 10.30am and 11.30pm but ask ahead). Buses south to Kanchanaburi (80B to 110B, three hours) leave every 30 minutes, 200m northwest of the main market.

That said, serow (Asian mountain goats) and Fea's muntjac (barking deer) often wander through the visitor centre and lodging area. With a 4WD you can drive within 300m of **Jokkadin Waterfall**, which falls 30m with force. It's 2km southwest of the **visitor centre** then 3km down a steep side road.

Thais know the park for its ranger-led overnight treks (16km round-trip). The hikes go through to grassland much of the way to Chang Pheuk mountain, offering 360-degree views over Myanmar. Treks are possible from October to January and cost 1200B for up to 10 people; porters are available. People rarely trek elsewhere, but rangers can lead you through the forest to various waterfalls and viewpoints.

The latter half of the drive from Thong Pha Phum is along one of Thailand's most remote and winding roads. It is paved, but is heavily potholed in many places. It's best avoided in bad weather conditions and a 4WD is ideal. Yellow *sŏrng·tăa·ou* (passenger pick-up trucks) to E-Thong pass the visitor centre.

E-Thong

อีต่อง

☑ 034 / POP 300

Guarded on all sides by jungle and mist, E-Thong has a fairy-tale setting and charming small-town ambience. A frontier village in Pilok district, near Thailand's border with Myanmar, E-Thong once thrived as a multicultural outpost for tin and tungsten mining. It gained the name *mĕuang pĕe·lôrk* (Ghost Mine) as a result of many mining-related deaths; the industry began to close in the 1980s.

Traces of the town's mining heyday remain, but the village is now reinventing itself as a tourism curiosity: thanks to the beginnings of cafe culture and homestays in town, E-Thong is becoming popular with Bangkokians seeking a far-flung weekend away.

◉ Sights

A trip to E-Thong is more for enjoying nature than sightseeing. Follow the uphill road from the village's car park (and bus stop area) to reach a decorative set of stairs leading up to the hilltop scarlet-and-gold **temple** (วัดอีต่อง; ⊘ daylight hours). A large seated Buddha is visible from the village below.

Walking uphill and left from the car park, you can see relics of E-Thong's mining days in the form of retired **mining equipment**.

The Myanmar border is closed, even to locals, but you can walk up to the Thai flag on the ridge.

🛌 Sleeping & Eating

Hill House   HOMESTAY **$$**

(☑ 080 781 5702; www.pilokhillhouse.com; Sun-Fri s/d from 700/900B, Sat s/d from 1000/1200B; ☎) This welcoming guesthouse, tucked into a leafy corner on the village's east fringe, is one of the best homestay-style lodgings in E-Thong. Tile-floored rooms are airy; the best have balconies overlooking a flower-filled garden.

Walk to the eastern end of the village's main street and follow signs for the guesthouse down the steps.

Che Ni Bistro   THAI **$**

(mains 60-120B; ⊘ noon-7.30pm) This easy-going restaurant, halfway along the village's main pedestrian-only street, serves an array of Thai dishes. Best is the seafood hauled across from Myanmar; some dishes are served steamboat-style (in a bubbling tureen). Thai staples such as *pàd gàprow* pork (basil and chilli-flecked mince with fried egg) are hot and tasty.

❶ Getting There & Away

BUS

Minibuses (70B, 2½ hours, usually 10.30am and 11.30pm) run from Thong Pha Phum. The return trips leave at 6.30am and 7am. Buses only run when there's demand, so ask ahead in Thong Pha Phum.

CAR & MOTORCYCLE

If driving from Thong Pha Phum, think twice about setting out in bad weather unless you have a 4WD; the road zigzags and is heavily potholed in places. The drive takes around 1¾ hours each way; follow signs to Pilok (the district) and you'll find E-Thong village 8km after the entrance to Thong Pha Phum National Park (p195).

Non-resident vehicles aren't allowed inside the village's tiny nucleus, so park as soon as you see the pondside parking spaces.

Sangkhlaburi สังขละบุรี

♬ 034 / POP 8000

Remote Sangkhlaburi is eye-opening in more ways than one. Girded by forest and with the Khao Laem Reservoir wrapped almost entirely around the town, Sangkhlaburi has natural and manufactured beauty. Thailand's longest wooden bridge, a marvel of engineering, reaches across from the shambling town centre to a Mon village. Short-term visitors usually spend their days canoeing, trekking or shopping for handicrafts. Sangkhlaburi also has an international spark, with a small but prominent community of NGO volunteers.

Few places in Thailand are as multicultural as this low-slung town, where Thai, Karen and Mon locals mingle with Lao and Burmese. Most were born here, but others crossed the Myanmar border looking for a safer, more stable life. For travellers, Sangkhlaburi is often the end of the line; but for so many residents it represents the start of a new journey.

◉ Sights

★ Saphan Mon   BRIDGE

(สะพานมอญ) Sangkhlaburi's iconic, 440m-long wooden bridge, the largest in Thailand, was dubbed the 'bridge of faith' after being built largely through manual labour. Saphan Mon connects the main town, home mostly to Thai and Karen, with the Mon settlement. This village is a striking place to explore, peopled by cheroot-smoking women, sarong-wearing men and faces covered in *thanaka* (a yellow paste made from tree bark, used both as sunblock and decoration). Parts of the bridge are uneven, so watch your step.

A 70m section of the bridge collapsed during torrential rain in July 2013 and was hurriedly restored a year later. During Buddhist festivals, the bridge is a popular site for offering alms to monks.

At the Mon end of the bridge is a typical Thai souvenir market selling Karen shirts and dresses among other souvenirs. If you follow the street uphill from the bridge and turn left on the main road to visit the Mon market, which sells traditional food, weaving and other souvenirs.

★ Khao Laem Reservoir   LAKE

(เขื่อนเขาแหลม; ⊙6am-6pm) FREE Backed by fuzzy green hills, this gigantic lake – formerly known Vajiralongkorn Dam – wrapped almost entirely around Sangkhlaburi was formed in the 1980s. Two of the villages submerged under the new lake were moved up to their present location; Saphan Mon was built to connect them. About all that remains now are ruined buildings from three temples. A boat ride (Saphan Mon; per person 500B) allows you to see them up close, as well as feel the pace of life on the lake.

The nearest temple, just visible from the bridge, is Wat Wang Wiwekaram Gao (*gao* means old); this was the site of the Mon village. When the lake rises to its highest point, only the very top of the *ubosot* (chapel) and bell tower stay dry. Nearby, Wat Si Suwannaram Gao was the temple in the Thai-Karen village. It emerges when the lake is very low, while Wat Somdet Gao sits in the forest high on a hill and stays dry year-round. The new Wat Somdet (วัดสมเด็จ; Hwy 323) FREE is along the road into town.

Chedi Phuttakhaya   BUDDHIST TEMPLE

(เจดีย์พุทธคยา; ⊙daylight hours; ℗) FREE This striking stupa rises 59m high; it's 600m southeast of Wat Wang Wiwekaram (p198). Constructed in the style of the Mahabodhi *chedi* (Buddhist stupa) in Bodhgaya, India, its gold-painted, art deco-like surface is full of niches holding little Buddha images. Two relics of the Buddha's thumb are enshrined within.

Sangkhlaburi Cultural Center   CULTURAL CENTRE

(ศูนย์วัฒนธรรมอำเภอสังขละบุรี; ☏086 178 4096; Th Sangkhlaburi; ⊙8am-4pm Mon-Fri, to noon Sat & Sun) FREE This little cultural centre mostly works to promote appreciation of Karen, Mon and Thai culture to local children, but visitors are welcomed inside to admire the privately owned collection of drums, *rá·nâht èhk* (bamboo-keyed xylophones), baskets and old-style farmers' hats.

To find it, walk to the east side of town and head south past the school; it's opposite Toy's (p199) restaurant.

There's no English spoken or displayed on the walls, but the friendly owner sometimes mimes the different objects' uses (and even models the hats).

OFF THE BEATEN TRACK

KHAO LAEM NATIONAL PARK

With the Khao Laem Reservoir at its heart and limestone mountains all around, dramatic landscapes define the 1497-sq-km **Khao Laem National Park** (อุทยานแห่งชาติเขาแหลม; ☑ 034 510431; adult/child 200/100B). But despite the park's size and potential, **Kroeng Krawia Waterfall**, a wide, 5m-high cascade flowing through a small patch of forest, is pretty much all anybody ever visits; it's 34km north of Thong Pha Phum along Hwy 323, and unlike the rest of the park, access is free.

A park visitor centre (usually open 8am to 4pm) is across the road from Kroeng Krawia Waterfall; it's essential to contact park rangers before setting out for anywhere other than that waterfall. **Kra Teng Cheng Waterfall** is accessed by an occasionally challenging 4km trail (allow three hours, trailhead 4km from visitor centre) while **Kroeng Krawia Swamp** can be productive for birdwatchers in the cool season (roughly two hours; trailhead 5km south of visitor centre).

There's lodging and camping available near Kroeng Krawia Swamp, but accommodation is more attractive at **Pom Pee** (☑ national parks service 02 562 0760; www.dnp. go.th; bungalows 900B; ℗), which has sunset views over the lake; it's 9km north of Kroeng Krawia Waterfall.

From Thong Pha Phum, *sŏrng·tăa·ou* reach Kroeng Krawia waterfall (35B, one hour, every 30 minutes).

Wat Wang Wiwekaram BUDDHIST TEMPLE
(วัดวังก์วิเวการาม; ⊙ daylight hours; ℗) FREE
Poking out of the forest on the south side of Saphan Mon (p197), this temple is the spiritual centre of Thailand's Mon people. The temple was established by Luang Phaw Uttama (1910–2006); the *wí·hăhn* (sanctuary) with three richly decorated green-and-yellow towers is a shrine to this highly respected monk, whose body is inside.

🏃 Activities & Tours

⭐ **Villa Scenns Cookery** COOKING
(☑ 080 602 3184; www.scenns.com; Th Si Suwankhiri; per person 800-2950B; ⊙ by arrangement) Charming Scenn runs expert Thai cookery classes, catering with ease to vegetarians and those with other dietary requirements. A classically trained dancer as well as a chef, Scenn imparts the secrets of seasonal food and soy milk preparation, and offers a choice of menus from Burmese to northern Thai for guests to prepare.

Uniquely decorated rooms are available at the small, family-run guesthouse, too.

Baan Unrak VOLUNTEERING
(บ้านอุ่นรัก; www.baanunrak.org) 🖉 With a neohumanist philosophy of vegetarianism, universal love and meditation, Baan Unrak runs this home caring for around 150 orphaned or abandoned children, including young Mon and Karen people. Accommodation and food are provided for volunteers staying six months or longer; helpers who stay for shorter periods are asked to donate US$150 per week (to a maximum US$900) for expenses.

Many of the children at Baan Unrak have fled persecution in neighbouring Myanmar, while others were born in border areas and lack identity papers. As well as running the children's home, Baan Unrak helps single mothers, works with HIV/AIDS patients and runs a bakery and souvenir shop to provide an income for local women.

Sangkhlaburi Jungle Trekking TREKKING
(☑ 085 425 4434; jarunsaksri1@gmail.com) The forest around Sangkhlaburi is wilder and less visited than most trekking destinations in northern Thailand. 'Jack', who has years of experience as a guide, can tailor trips for different fitness levels and for family groups, but the most adventurous option is a week hiking the Myanmar border from Sangkhlaburi to Um Phang (p279), staying in Karen villages along the way.

Prices depend on group size and trip length, but expect 1500B per person per day for three people or more.

🛌 Sleeping

⭐ P Guesthouse
GUESTHOUSE $

(📱 081 450 2783, 034 595061; www.p-guesthouse. com; off Th Si Suwankhiri; d with fan 300B, d/tr with air-con 400/600B; 🅿 ❄ 🛜) You don't-often get views like this on a budget. Stone and log-built rooms gaze upon tranquil waters at this family-run spot. Fan rooms share cold-water bathrooms, while air-conditioned rooms have en suites and the best views. The restaurant is a fantastic place to lounge. You can rent a canoe almost from your door.

The owners can arrange good day trips into the surrounding forest.

J Family Homestay
HOMESTAY $

(📱 034 595511; d with shared bathroom 150B; 🛜) Rooms are just mattresses on the floor with a shared bathroom, but this welcoming homestay offers a pleasant local experience. It's signed one road east over from the temple on Th Si Suwankhiri. Bicycles and motorbikes are available to rent (from 70/200B per day).

Villa Scenns
GUESTHOUSE $$

(📱 080 602 3184; www.scenns.com; Th Si Suwankhiri; r incl breakfast 1000-2000B; 🛜) Facing views of mist-draped forest, the high-ceilinged rooms at this family-run guesthouse boast wooden antiques and comfy beds, and you have access to a shared kitchen and common room. Rooms are fan-only (but stay naturally cool) and they're priced by size.

Ban Thor Phan
HOTEL $$

(📱 081 824 3369; Hwy 323; d incl breakfast from 1000B; 🅿 ❄ 🛜) Just north of the road bridge, this colourful, labyrinthine place feels more like a fantasy village than a hotel. Rooms are comfortable and well-appointed, while common areas are decorated with a delightful tangle of greenery, floral cushions and swinging wicker lamps.

⭐ Phu Chom Mork Resort
RESORT $$$

(📱 064 964 7767; www.phuchommorkresort.com; 32/6 Mu 3, Nong Lu; d incl breakfast 1500-2000B; 🅿 ❄ 🛜) Delightful service and a verdant setting set Phu Chom Mork apart as Sangkhlaburi's fanciest place to stay. Spacious rooms with sumptuous stone-effect bathrooms are spread across banan-tree-hemmed parkland, where your only soundtrack is crickets and the pounding rain.

🍴 Eating & Drinking

A sizeable range of resorts, restaurants and food stands operates in Sangkhlaburi; eateries are mostly no-frills and great value. Look out for *kà·nŏm jeen* (rice noodles with fish sauce), barbecued lake fish, *yam Mon* (salad of noodles, cucumber and cabbage) and variations on *sôm·đam* (tongue-stingingly spicy green papaya salad).

By day, hide from the heat with cream-topped chocolate frappes or fruity iced tea at **Cath Coffee** (Th Si Suwankhiri; drinks 40B, mains 80-280B; ⏱ 8am-6pm; 🛜). After sundown, grab a beer and get travel tips at grungy, casual **Blue Rock** (Th Si Suwankhiri; ⏱ 4pm-late).

⭐ Baan Unrak Bakery
VEGETARIAN, BAKERY $

(📱 034 595 006; www.baanunrak.org; Th Si Suwankhiri; snacks 25-90B, mains 80-150B; ⏱ 8am-7.30pm Mon-Sat; 🛜 🍴) 🍃 This mostly vegan cafe, part of the nonprofit Baan Unrak organisation, is a crowd-pleaser for its meat-free *pad thai*, green curry and freshly baked pizzas, not to mention the homemade baked goods, from banana sponge cake to chocolate doughnuts.

⭐ Toy's
THAI $

(Th Sangkhlaburi; mains 50-150B; ⏱ 9am-8pm Sat-Thu) Superb Isan-style dishes are served with a smile at Toy's. Offerings vary according to what's in season, but you can expect *gài tôrt* (crispy-coated fried chicken) and *lâhp kôo·a* (spicy, herb-speckled mincemeat salad) as well as thick, flavourful massaman curry.

Barbecue Stall
BARBECUE, THAI $

(Th Si Suwankhiri; mains 50-100B; ⏱ approx 11am-5pm) A nameless food stand near the post office (p200) serves sensational *sôm·đam* (spicy green papaya salad) and barbecued lake fish.

It's not far from the corner with Th Sam Prasob.

Night Market
MARKET $

(Soi Thetsaban 1 & 2; ⏱ 4.30-9.30pm) There is as much Burmese food as Thai at the night market, where a medley of dishes are cooked up at open-air stalls in the centre of town. Keep an eye out for regional salad *yam Mon*, with noodles, cucumber and cabbage, and the noodle soup with a banana-tree bark base.

CENTRAL THAILAND SANGKHLABURI

Walking Street Market

MARKET $

(Th Sangkhlaburi; ⊙approx 6-10pm Sat) Food stalls spring up around sundown, one block east of the night market (p199; opposite the hospital). Closed during the rainy season.

Shopping

Delicate Karen weaving is on sale at the **Baan Unrak Shop** (www.baanunrak.org; Th Si Suwankhiri; ⊙8am-7.30pm Mon-Sat) ✎, hand-crafted by a local women's cooperative.

① Information

Sangkhlaburi Hospital (☎034 595058; Th Sangkhlaburi; ⊙24hr) Best to bring a local to translate.

The tiny town centre has a few ATMs and banks including **SCB** (Soi Thetsaban 2; ⊙8.30am-3.30pm Mon-Fri), which has a currency exchange.

Post Office (Th Si Suwankhiri; ⊙8.30am-4.30pm Mon-Fri, to noon Sat)

① Getting There & Away

From a **parking lot** (off west end of Thetsaban 1) on the west side of the town centre, old red buses depart for Kanchanaburi (130B, four hours, 6.30am, 8am, 9.30am and 1pm) and air-conditioned buses go to Bangkok's Mo Chit terminal (281B, seven hours, 8.30am). Mini-vans to Kanchanaburi (175B, 3½ hours, almost hourly) depart near **Blend Cafe** (Soi Thetsaban 1; ⊙8am-8pm; 🛜), where you can buy bus tickets and check schedules at a kiosk window.

The minivans' only regular stop between Sangkhlaburi and Kanchanaburi is Thong Pha Phum, so if you want to stop anywhere else, such as Sai Yok National Park (p194), you need to pay the full Kanchanaburi fare.

① Getting Around

J Family Homestay (p199) and **P Guesthouse** (p199) offer rental bikes (70B to 100B per day) and motorcycles (200B). The latter also has canoes.

A motorbike taxi between guesthouses and the town centre or the bridge costs around 20B.

Northern Thailand

Best Places to Eat

➜ Larp Khom Huay Poo (p289)

➜ Muu Thup (p305)

➜ Khao Soi Pa Orn (p228

Best Places to Stay

➜ Boklua View (p239)

➜ Bamboo Nest de Chiang Rai (p214)

➜ Rai Saeng Arun (p230)

Why Go?

What can't you do in northern Thailand?

The region's premier draw is its nature, and its rugged geography is a playground for outdoor pursuits ranging from a rafting excursion in Um Phang to a hike among wild orchids in Mae Hong Son.

For those drawn to the human side of things, there's also northern Thailand's buffet of cultural attractions. The region is regarded as the birthplace of much of Thai culture and is a great place to take part in activities, from exploring a Buddhist temple in Phrae to crashing at a homestay in rural Sukhothai.

In the north, even niche players are catered for: intrepid explorers can join a hill-tribe trek in Mae Sariang or a road trip to Phayao; history buffs can travel back in time at Sukhothai Historical Park; and even the most devout beach bum could be converted by the inland party scene in Pai.

When to Go

➜ Winter (which stretches from approximately November to January) is the time to head to Northern Thailand, when daytime temperatures at the higher elevations are a relatively comfortable 20°C to 23°C. Nighttime temperatures can, in some places, dip perilously close to freezing.

➜ From March to May, the hottest time of year in northern Thailand, daytime temperatures can exceed 40°C and smoke from slash-and-burn agriculture can fill the skies.

➜ The rainy season (from approximately June to October) should generally be avoided if you plan to do any hiking; otherwise showers are strong but brief, and it can be a pleasant time to visit northern Thailand.

Northern Thailand Highlights

1 Phu Hin Rong Kla National Park (p269) Exploring one of Thailand's lesser-known protected areas.

2 Nam Tok Thilawsu (p279) Hiking and rafting to the country's most beautiful waterfall.

3 Doi Mae Salong (p215) Investigating the unique culture of northern Thailand's remote Chinese outposts.

4 Nan (p232) Kicking back and becoming a local in one of the region's little-visited cities.

5 Sukhothai Historical Park (p253) Time-travelling back to Thailand's golden age.

6 Lampang
(p246) Exploring cool cafes, designer hotels and the north's best market in the Brooklyn of northern Thailand.

7 Chiang Khong to Phayao (p229) Hiring a vehicle and driving one of the country's most stunning routes.

8 Ban Na Ton Chan (p258) Diving headfirst into northern Thai life at a community-based homestay.

9 Pai (p283) Enjoying live music, fun bars and fresh-air activities that have made this formerly tiny village a serious backpacker destination.

ⓘ TRANSPORT IN NORTHERN THAILAND

Public Transport

Just about everywhere in the region is accessible by bus and increasingly minivan, except among the communities along the Myanmar border, where the *sŏrng·tǎa·ou* (passenger pick-up truck, also spelt *songthaew*) is the transport of choice.

Going by train is the most comfortable way to get up north, although there's only one main northern line and it is comparatively slow.

Car & Motorcycle

Despite the obvious risks of driving in Thailand, hiring a vehicle is the best way to explore the countryside at your own pace. Car and motorcycle hire are available at most urban centres.

For motorcycle hire, unless you're intending to go off-road or plan on crossing unpaved roads during the wet season, it's highly unlikely you'll need one of the large dirt bikes you'll see for rent in Chiang Mai. The automatic transmission 110cc to 150cc scooter-like motorcycles found across Thailand are fast and powerful enough for most roads.

The best source of information on motorcycle touring in the north is **Golden Triangle Rider** (GT Rider; www.gt-rider.com). Publishers of a series of terrific motorcycle touring-based maps, their website includes heaps of information on hiring bikes (including recommended hire shops in Chiang Mai and Chiang Rai) and bike insurance, plus a variety of suggested tours with maps and an interactive forum.

Air

For those in a hurry, northern Thailand's air links are surprisingly good. At research time, **Nok Air** (☎ nationwide 1318; www.nokair.com), a subsidiary of THAI, had the most expansive network, with flights connecting several provincial capitals in the region with Bangkok or Chiang Mai. Other domestic airlines that cover the north include:

Air Asia (☎ nationwide 02 515 9999; www.airasia.com) Within northern Thailand, Air Asia flies between Bangkok's Don Mueang International Airport and Chiang Rai, Nan and Phitsanulok.

Bangkok Airways (☎ nationwide 1771; www.bangkokair.com) Destinations in northern Thailand include Chiang Rai, Lampang, Mae Hong Son and Sukhothai.

Thai Lion Air (☎ 02 529 9999; www.lionairthai.com) Destinations in northern Thailand include Chiang Rai and Phitsanulok.

Thai Smile (☎ nationwide 02 118 8888; www.thaismileair.com) Flights to/from Chiang Rai.

History

One of the most significant early cultural influences in the north was the Mon kingdom of Hariphunchai (based in contemporary Lamphun), which held sway from the late 8th century until the 13th century.

The Thais, who are thought to have migrated south from China around the 7th century, united various principalities in the 13th century – this resulted in the creation of Sukhothai and the taking of Hariphunchai from the Mon. In 1238 Sukhothai declared itself an independent kingdom under King Si Intharathit and quickly expanded its sphere of influence. Because of this, and the significant influence the kingdom had on Thai art and culture, Sukhothai is considered by Thais to be the first true Thai kingdom.

In 1296 King Mengrai established Chiang Mai after conquering Hariphunchai. Later, in the 14th and 15th centuries, Chiang Mai, in an alliance with Sukhothai, became a part of the larger kingdom of Lan Na Thai (Million Thai Rice Fields), popularly referred to as Lanna. This empire extended as far south as Kamphaeng Phet and as far north as Luang Prabang in Laos. The golden age of Lanna was in the 15th century and, for a short time during this period, the Sukhothai capital was moved to Phitsanulok, and Chiang Mai increased in influence as a religious and cultural centre. However, during the 16th century, many of Lan Na Thai's important alliances weakened or fell apart, ultimately leading to the Burmese capturing Chiang Mai in 1556. Burmese control of Lanna lasted for the next two centuries. The northern Thais regrouped after the Burmese took Ayuthaya in 1767 and, under King Kawila, Chiang Mai was recaptured in 1774 and the Burmese were pushed north.

In the late 19th century, Rama V of Bangkok made efforts to integrate the northern region with the centre to ward off the colonial threat. The completion of the northern railway to Chiang Mai in 1921 strengthened those links until the northern provinces finally became part of the kingdom of Siam in the early part of the 20th century.

Language

Thailand's regional dialects vary greatly and can even be unintelligible to native speakers of Thai not familiar with the vernacular being spoken. *Gǎm méuang,* the northern Thai dialect, is no exception and, in addition to an entirely different set of tones to master, it possesses a wealth of vocabulary specific to the north. The northern dialect also has a slower rhythm than Thailand's three other main dialects, an attribute reflected in the relaxed, easygoing manner of the people who speak it.

CHIANG RAI PROVINCE

จังหวัดเชียงราย

Chiang Rai Province, Thailand's northernmost province, has a bit of everything: the mountains in the far east are among the most dramatic in the country, the lowland Mekong River floodplains to the northeast are not unlike those one would find much further south in Isan, and the province shares borders with Myanmar and Laos. In terms of people, it's also among Thailand's most ethnically diverse provinces and is home to a significant minority of hill tribes, Shan and other Tai groups, and more recent Chinese immigrants.

Chiang Rai
เชียงราย

📞 053 / POP 70,000

Chiang Rai Province has such a diversity of attractions that its capital is often overlooked. This small, delightful city is worth getting to know, however, with its relaxed atmosphere, good-value accommodation and great local food. It's also the logical base from which to plan excursions to the more remote corners of the province or abroad.

Founded by Phaya Mengrai in 1262 as part of the Lao–Thai Lanna kingdom, Chiang Rai (เชียงราย) didn't become a Siamese territory until 1786 and a province until 1910.

👁 Sights

⭐ Mae Fah Luang Art & Culture Park
MUSEUM

(ไร่แม่ฟ้าหลวง; www.maefahluang.org/rmfl; 313 Mu 7, Ban Pa Ngiw; adult/child 200B/free; ⊗8.30am-4.30pm Tue-Sun) In addition to a museum that houses one of Thailand's biggest collections of Lanna artefacts, this vast, meticulously landscaped compound includes antique and contemporary art, Buddhist temples and other structures.

It's located about 4km west of the centre of Chiang Rai; a túk-túk or taxi here will run to around 100B.

⭐ Hilltribe Museum & Education Center
MUSEUM

(พิพิธภัณฑ์และศูนย์การศึกษาชาวเขา; www.pdacr.org; 3rd fl, 620/25 Th Thanalai; 50B; ⊗8.30am-6pm Mon-Fri, 10am-6pm Sat & Sun) This museum and cultural centre is a good place to visit before undertaking any hill-tribe trek. Run by the nonprofit Population & Community Development Association (PDA), the venue has displays that are underwhelming in their visual presentation but contain a wealth of information on Thailand's various tribes and the issues that surround them.

Oub Kham Museum
MUSEUM

(พิพิธภัณฑ์อูบคำ; www.oubkhammuseum.com; Th Nakhai; adult/child incl tour 300/200B; ⊗8am-5pm) This slightly zany private museum houses an impressive collection of paraphernalia from virtually every corner of the former Lanna kingdom. The items, some of which truly are one of a kind, range from a monkey-bone food taster used by Lanna royalty to an impressive carved throne from Chiang Tung, Myanmar.

It's located 2km west of the town centre and can be a bit tricky to find; túk-túk will go here for about 60B.

Wat Phra Kaew
BUDDHIST TEMPLE

(วัดพระแก้ว; Th Trairat; donations appreciated; ⊗temple 7am-7pm, museum 9am-5pm) Originally called Wat Pa Yia (Bamboo Forest Monastery) in the local dialect, this is the city's most revered Buddhist temple. The main prayer hall is a medium-sized, well-preserved wooden structure. The octagonal

Chiang Rai

Chiang Rai

chedi (stupa) behind it dates from the late 14th century and is in typical Lanna style. The adjacent two-storey wooden building is a museum housing various Lanna artifacts.

Wat Phra Singh
BUDDHIST TEMPLE

(วัดพระสิงห์; Th Singhaclai; donations appreciated; ☉daylight hours) This temple dates back to the late 14th century, and its oldest surviving original buildings are typical northern Thai-style wooden structures with low, sweeping roofs. The main *wí·hǎhn* (sanctuary) houses impressive wooden doors thought to have been carved by local artists, as well as a copy of Chiang Mai's sacred Phra Singh Buddha.

Tham Tu Pu & Buddha Cave
BUDDHIST TEMPLE

(ถ้ำตู้ปู/ถ้ำพระ; Th Ka Salong; ☉daylight hours) FREE Cross the Mae Fah Luang Bridge (located just northwest of the city centre) to the northern side of Mae Nam Kok and you'll come to a turn-off for both Tham Tu Pu and the Buddha Cave. Neither attraction is particularly amazing on its own, but the surrounding country is beautiful and would make an ideal destination for a lazy bike or motorcycle ride.

Follow the road for 1km, then turn off onto a dirt path for 200m to the base of a limestone cliff, where there is a steep set of stairs leading to a main chamber holding a dusty Buddha statue; this is **Tham Tu Pu**.

Continue along the same road for 3km more (the sign says 'Buddha Images Cave') and you'll reach **Buddha Cave**, a cavern by Mae Nam Kok containing a tiny but active Buddhist temple, a lone monk and numerous cats. The temple was one of several destinations on a visit to the region by King Rama V in the early 20th century.

🏃 Activities

Nearly every guesthouse and hotel in Chiang Rai offers hiking excursions in hill-tribe country, some of which have grassroots, sustainable or nonprofit emphases.

In general, trek pricing depends on the type of activities and the number of days and participants. Rates, per person, for two people, for a two-night trek range from 2300B to 6000B. Generally, everything from accommodation to transport and food is included in this price.

★ Rai Pian Karuna
TREKKING

(☎062 246 1897; www.facebook.com/raipiankaruna) This community-based social enterprise conducts one-day and multiday treks and homestays at Akha, Lahu and Lua villages in Mae Chan, north of Chiang Rai. Other activities, from week-long volunteering stints to cooking courses, are also on offer.

Mirror Foundation
TREKKING

(☎053 737616; www.thailandecotour.org) Although its rates are higher, trekking with this nonprofit NGO helps support the training of its local guides. Treks range from one to three days and traverse the Akha, Karen and Lahu villages of Mae Yao District, north of Chiang Rai.

Chiang Rai Bicycle Tours
CYCLING

(☎053 774506, 085 662 4347; www.chiangraibicycletour.com; tours from 1450B) Offers a variety of two-wheeled-based excursions in the areas surrounding Chiang Rai.

Thailand Hilltribe Holidays
TREKKING

(☎085 548 0884; www.thailandhilltribeholidays.com) This outfit offers sustainably minded guided tours and homestays in and around Chiang Rai.

NORTHERN THAILAND CHIANG RAI

ℹ MOTORCYCLE TOURING

A good introduction to motorcycle touring in northern Thailand is the 100km Samoeng loop, which can be tackled in half a day. The route extends north from Chiang Mai and follows Routes 107, 1096 and 1269, passing through excellent scenery and with plenty of curves and providing a taste of what a longer ride up north will be like. The 470km Chiang Rai loop, which passes through scenic Fang and Tha Ton along Routes 107, 1089 and 118, is another popular ride that can be broken up with a stay in Chiang Rai.

The classic northern route is the Mae Hong Son loop, a 600km ride that begins in Chiang Mai and takes in Rtes 1095's 1864 curves with possible stays in Pai, Mae Hong Son and Mae Sariang, before looping back to Chiang Mai via Rte 108. A lesser known but equally fun ride is to follow Rtes 1155 and 1093 from Chiang Khong in Chiang Rai Province to the little-visited city of Phayao, a day trip that passes through some of the most dramatic mountain scenery in the country.

PDA Tours & Travel
TREKKING

(☑ 053 740088; Hilltribe Museum & Education Center, 3rd fl, 620/25 Th Thanalai; ⊙ 8.30am-6pm Mon-Fri, 10am-6pm Sat & Sun) One- to three-day treks are available through this NGO. Profits go back into community projects that include HIV/AIDS education, mobile health clinics, education scholarships and the establishment of village-owned banks.

🐉 Courses

Suwannee
COOKING

(☑ 084 740 7119; www.suwanneethaicookingclass chiangrai.blogspot.com; lessons 1250B; ⊙ courses 9.30am-2pm) Suwannee's cooking courses involve a visit to a local market and instruction in cooking four dishes. Her house is about 3km outside the city centre, but she can pick you up at most centrally located hotels and guesthouses.

Cook Thai Yourself
COOKING

(☑ 081 844 9913; www.cookthaiyourself.wix.com/home; lessons from 1000B; ⊙ lessons 9am-3pm) This outfit offers full-day 'food adventures', including Thai cookery lessons, in a semi-rural location, 20 minutes from Chiang Rai. Transportation is included in the fee.

🛏 Sleeping

Most budget places are in the centre, clustered around Th Jetyod; the majority of midrange places are a brief walk from 'downtown'; and Chiang Rai's upscale accommodation is generally located outside the town centre.

🏨 Town Centre

Baan Warabordee
HOTEL $

(☑ 053 754488; baanwarabordee@hotmail.com; 59/1 Th Sanpanard; r 500-600B; ❄ 🛜) A handsome, good-value hotel has been made from this three-storey Thai villa. Rooms are decked out in dark woods and light fabrics, and are equipped with air-con, fridge and hot water.

FUN-D Hostel
HOSTEL $

(☑ 053 712123; www.facebook.com/fundhostel chiangrai; 753 Th Phahonyothin; incl breakfast dm 200-300B, r 600B; ❄ @ 🛜) A lively hostel located, appropriately, above a restaurant-bar-cafe. Dorms are spacious and bright and range from six to eight beds, the more expensive of which have semi-private, en suite bathroom facilities.

Moon & Sun Hotel
HOTEL $

(☑ 053 719279; 632 Th Singhaclai; r 399-499B, ste 699B; ❄ 🛜) Bright and sparkling clean, this little hotel offers large, modern, terrific-value rooms. Some feature four-poster beds, while all come with desk, cable TV and refrigerator. Suites have a separate, spacious sitting area.

Orchids Guest House
GUESTHOUSE $

(☑ 053 718361; www.orchidsguesthouse.net; 1012/3 Th Jetyod; r 400-500B; ❄ 🛜) This collection of spotless rooms in a residential compound is a good budget catch. In addition to accommodation, various services are available, including internet, laundry, taxi transfer and trekking.

Chok Dee Friend House
GUESTHOUSE $

(☑ 094 672 7921; cnr Th Jetyod & Th Thaiviwat; dm 100B, r 150-250B; 🛜) The rooms are basic and the ground-floor tattoo parlour and bar can be noisy, but for those who fancy a social backpacker scene, this is your place.

Golden Triangle Palace
HOTEL $$

(☑ 053 711 339; 590 Th Phahonyothin; r incl breakfast 13000-1500B; ❄ ❄ 🛜) A recent renovation has left the lobby here looking rather gaudy, but the 32 rooms remain subtle and comfortable, with tile or wood floors, wooden furniture and twin beds.

Na-Rak-O Resort
HOTEL $$

(☑ 081 951 7801; www.facebook.com/narako resort; off Th Sanpanard; r incl breakfast 700-1100B; P ❄ 🛜) Nâh·rák is Thai for 'cute', a spot-on description of this small hotel. Rooms are bright and airy, with big bathrooms and a colourful design theme that calls to mind a day-care centre.

Baan Rub Aroon
GUESTHOUSE $$

(☑ 053 711827; www.baanrubaroon.net; 893 Th Ngummuang; r incl breakfast 650-2000B; ❄ @ 🛜) The rooms in this handsome villa, located just west of the city centre, aren't quite as charming as the exterior suggests, and most share bathrooms, but it's a good choice if you're looking for a quiet, homey stay.

Wiang Inn
HOTEL $$$

(☑ 053 711533; www.wianginn.com; 893 Th Phahonyothin; incl breakfast r 2400-3200B, ste 6000-10,000B; ❄ @ 🛜 ⊠) The funky, 1970s-era exterior is an accurate indicator of this centrally located, business-class hotel's age, but a recent renovation means the rooms are

DON'T MISS

HEAVEN & HELL: TEMPLES OUTSIDE CHIANG RAI

Lying just outside Chiang Rai are Wat Rong Khun and Baandam, two of the province's most touted, bizarre and worthwhile destinations.

Whereas most of Thailand's Buddhist temples have centuries of history, **Wat Rong Khun's** (White Temple, วัดร่องขุ่น; off Rte 1/AH2; ⊙8am-5pm Mon-Fri, to 5.30pm Sat & Sun) FREE construction began in 1997 by noted Thai painter-turned-architect Chalermchai Kositpipat. To enter, you must walk over a bridge and a pool of reaching arms (symbolising desire), where inside, instead of the traditional Buddha life scenarios, the artist has painted contemporary scenes representing *samsara* (the realm of rebirth and delusion). Images such as a plane smashing into the Twin Towers and, oddly enough, Keanu Reeves as Neo from *The Matrix,* dominate the one finished wall of this work in progress. The temple suffered minor damage in an earthquake in 2014.

The temple is located about 13km south of Chiang Rai. To get here, hop on one of the regular buses that run from Chiang Rai to Wiang Pa Pao (20B, hourly from 6.15am to 6.10pm).

The bizarre brainchild of Thai National Artist Thawan Duchanee, and a rather sinister counterpoint to Wat Rong Khun, **Baandam** (บ้านดำ, Black House; off Rte 1/AH2; adult/child 80B/free; ⊙9am-5pm) unites several structures, most of which are stained black and ominously decked out with animal pelts and bones.

The centrepiece is a black, cavernous, temple-like building holding a long wooden dining table and chairs made from deer antlers – a virtual Satan's dining room. Other buildings include white, breast-shaped bedrooms, dark phallus-decked bathrooms and a bone- and fur-lined 'chapel'.

The site is located 13km north of Chiang Rai in Nang Lae; any Mae Sai–bound bus will drop you off here for around 20B.

well maintained and include a few decorative Thai touches.

Hi Chiangrai
HOTEL $$$
(☑053 716699; www.hichiangrai.com; 902/3 Th Phahonyothin; r incl breakfast 1400-3400B; ❄❂☯) The pastel colours, cheesy murals and interior design touches in the exterior and lobby of this new hotel serve as a front for rooms that, by contrast, are rather plain. There's a tiny pool, and the place gets positive feedback from guests.

🛏 Outside Town

Ben Guesthouse
GUESTHOUSE $$
(☑053 716775; www.benguesthousechiangrai.com; 351/10 Soi 4, Th Sankhongnoi; r 500-700B, ste 1000-1500B; ❄@❂☯) One of the best budget-to-midrange places in the north. The spotless compound has a bit of everything, from fan-cooled cheapies to immense suites, not to mention a pool.

It's 1.2km from the town centre, at the end of Soi 4 on Th Sankhongnoi (the street is called Th Sathanpayabarn where it intersects with Th Phahonyothin).

A túk-túk costs 60B.

De Hug
HOTEL $$
(☑053 711789; www.dehughotel.com; Rte 1211; r incl breakfast 1200-1400B; ❄@❂) A four-storey hotel complex with vast rooms, all outfitted with modern amenities and furniture. Despite its relatively large scale, De Hug manages to feel homey.

The hotel is located 2km west of the town centre, across from the Oub Kham Museum; túk-túk will go here for about 60B.

Chezmoi
GUESTHOUSE $$
(☑089 747 5683, 089 148 5257; www.chezmoimyhome.com; 34/2 Th Sankhongnoi; r incl breakfast 500-700B; ❄❂) The seven rooms in this home/studio are fashionably sparse, with clean shared bathrooms, and are looked after by a friendly, welcoming family.

Chezmoi is about 1.5km from the centre of town at the western end of Th Sankhongnoi (the street is called Th Sathanpayabarn where it intersects with Th Phahonyothin) – a 60B túk-túk ride from the centre of Chiang Rai.

Legend of Chiang Rai
HOTEL $$$
(☑053 910400; www.thelegend-chiangrai.com; 124/15 Th Kohloy; incl breakfast r 3000-10,000B, bungalows 7000-12,000B; ❄@❂☯) Boasting

DON'T MISS

CAFE CULTURE, CHIANG RAI STYLE

The relatively small town of Chiang Rai has an enviable spread of high-quality, Western-style cafes. This is largely due to the fact that many of Thailand's best coffee beans are grown in the more remote corners of the province.

BaanChivitMai Bakery (www.bcmthai.com/home; Th Prasopsook; ⊙ 8am-7pm Mon-Fri, to 6pm Sat & Sun; 🛜) In addition to a proper cup of joe made from local beans, you can snack on surprisingly authentic Swedish-style sweets and Western-style meals and sandwiches at this popular bakery. Profits go to BaanChivitMai, an organisation that runs homes and education projects for vulnerable, orphaned or AIDS-affected children.

Prompt Cafe (www.facebook.com/promptcafedripcoffee; 417/4 Th Phahonyothin; ⊙ 7.30am-5.30pm) This closet-sized cafe – probably the city's most sophisticated – serves single-origin drip coffees (with locally sourced beans as an option) and espresso drinks.

Doi Chaang (Th Thanalai; ⊙ 8am-8pm; 🛜) Doi Chaang is the leading brand among Chiang Rai coffees, and its beans are now sold as far abroad as Canada and Europe.

Pangkhon Coffee (Th Sookathit; ⊙ 7am-10pm; 🛜) Combine coffee brewed from local beans with views of Chiang Rai's gilded clock tower.

Roast (Th Sankhongluang; ⊙ 7.30am-5pm) This 'drip bar' treats local beans with the utmost respect. Th Sankhongluang is a block south of Chiang Rai Technical College, about 1.2km from the centre of town.

a riverside location, this upscale resort feels like a traditional Lanna village. Rooms are romantic and luxuriously understated, with furniture in calming creams and rattan. The riverside infinity pool and spa are the icing on the comfort-filled cake. Significant online discounts are available.

Le Meridien Chiang Rai Resort HOTEL $$$
(✆ 053 603333; www.lemeridien.com; 221/2 Th Kwaewai; incl breakfast r 5000-7500B, ste 18,000-20,000B; 🅿🌐🛜🌊) Chiang Rai's grandest upscale resort is about 2km outside of the city centre on a beautiful stretch of Mae Nam Kok. Rooms are immense and decked out in greys, whites and blacks, and the compound includes two restaurants and an infinity pool, in addition to the usual amenities of a hotel of this price range.

🍴 Eating

Come mealtime, you'll inevitably be pointed in the direction of Chiang Rai's night bazaar, but the food there is generally pretty dire – you've been warned. Instead, if you're in town on a weekend, hit the vendors at Chiang Rai's open-air markets, Thanon Khon Muan and the Walking Street, which feature a good selection of local dishes.

★ Lung Eed NORTHERN THAI $
(Th Watpranorn; mains 40-100B; ⊙ 11.30am-9pm Mon-Sat, 3-7pm Sun) One of Chiang Rai's most delicious dishes is available at this simple shophouse restaurant. There's an English-language menu on the wall, but don't miss the sublime *lâhp gài* (minced chicken fried with local spices and topped with crispy deep-fried chicken skin, shallots and garlic).

The restaurant is about 150m east of Rte 1/AH2.

★ Paa Suk NORTHERN THAI $
(Th Sankhongnoi; mains 10-25B; ⊙ 8.30am-3pm) Paa Suk does big, rich bowls of *kà·nŏm jeen nám ngée·o* (a broth of pork or beef and tomatoes served over fresh rice noodles).

The restaurant is between Soi 4 and Soi 5 of Th Sankhongnoi (the street is called Th Sathanpayabarn where it intersects with the southern end Th Phahonyothin). There's no Roman-script sign; look for the yellow sign.

Khao Soi Phor Jai NORTHERN THAI $
(Th Jetyod; mains 40-50B; ⊙ 7am-4pm) Phor Jai serves mild but tasty bowls of the eponymous curry noodle dish, as well as a few other northern Thai staples. There's no Roman-script sign, but look for the open-air shophouse with the white-and-blue interior.

Namnigew Pa Nuan VIETNAMESE, THAI $
(Th Sanpanard; mains 10-120B; ⊙ 9am-5pm) This semi-concealed place (there's no Roman-script sign) serves a unique mix of

NORTHERN THAI CUISINE

The cuisine of Thailand's northern provinces is indicative of the region's seasonal and relatively cool climate, not to mention a love for pork, vegies and all things deep fried. Northern Thai cuisine is probably the most seasonal and least spicy of Thailand's regional schools of cooking, often relying on bitter or other dried spice flavours.

Paradoxically (and unfortunately), it can be difficult to find authentic local food in northern Thailand. Outside of Chiang Mai and the other large cities in northern Thailand, there are relatively few restaurants serving northern-style dishes, and the vast majority of authentic local food is sold from stalls in 'to go' bags. Some must-try dishes include:

Đam sôm oh The region's version of *sôm·đam* substitutes pomelo for green papaya.

Đôm yam The northern Thai version of this Thai soup staple is flavoured with some of the same dried spices that feature in *lâhp kôo·a*.

Gaang hang·lair Burmese in origin (*hang* is a corruption of the Burmese *hin*, meaning curry), this rich pork curry is often seen at festivals and ceremonies. Try a bowl at **Phu Lae**, in Chiang Rai.

Kà·nŏm jeen nám ngée·o Fresh rice noodles served with a meaty and tart pork- and tomato-based broth. An excellent bowl can be slurped at **Paa Suk**, in Chiang Rai.

Kâap mŏo Deep-fried pork crackling is a common, delicious side dish in northern Thailand.

Kôw gân jîn Banana leaf packets of rice mixed with blood, steamed and served with garlic oil. Available at **Paa Suk**, in Chiang Rai.

Kôw soy This popular curry-based noodle dish is possibly Burmese in origin and was probably introduced to northern Thailand by travelling Chinese merchants. A mild but tasty version is available at **Khao Soi Phor Jai**, in Chiang Rai.

Lâhp kôo·a Literally 'fried *lâhp*', this dish takes the famous Thai minced-meat 'salad' and fries it with a mixture of unique dried spices. Try the version at **Pu Som Restaurant** (p237), in Nan.

Lôo Raw blood mixed with curry paste and served over deep-fried intestines and crispy noodles – the most hardcore northern dish and one often associated with Phrae Province.

Năam Fermented raw pork, a sour delicacy that tastes much better than it sounds.

Nám prík nùm Green chillies, shallots and garlic that are grilled then mashed into a stringy and spicy paste served with sticky rice, parboiled vegies and deep-fried pork crackling. Available at just about every evening market in northern Thailand.

Nám prík òrng A chilli dip of Shan origin made from tomatoes and minced pork – a northern Thai bolognese of sorts.

Sâi òo·a A grilled pork sausage seasoned with copious fresh herbs. Available at **Muu Thup** (p305), in Mae Sariang.

Vietnamese and northern Thai dishes. Tasty food, friendly service and a fun, barn-like atmosphere make us wish it was open for dinner as well.

Muang Thong　　　　CHINESE, THAI $
(cnr Th Sanpanard & Th Phahonyothin; mains 30-100B; ⊘24hr) Comfort food for Thais and travellers alike: this long-standing open-air place serves the usual repertoire of satisfyingly salty and spicy Chinese-Thai dishes.

Phu Lae　　　　THAI $
(673/1 Th Thanalai; mains 80-320B; ⊘11.30am-3pm & 5.30-11pm; ▣) This air-conditioned restaurant is popular with Thai tourists for its tasty but somewhat gentrified northern Thai fare. Recommended local dishes include the *gaang hang·lair* (pork belly in a rich Burmese-style curry) served with cloves of pickled garlic, and *sâi òo·a* (herb-packed pork sausages).

BUSES TO/FROM CHIANG RAI

DESTINATION	FARE (B)	DURATION (HR)	FREQUENCY
Bangkok	423-958	11-12	frequent 7am-7pm (new bus station)
Bokeo (Laos)	240	3	4pm (new bus station)
Chiang Khong	65	2	frequent 6.30am-4.30pm (interprovincial bus station)
Chiang Mai	129-258	3-7	frequent 6am-7pm (interprovincial bus station)
Chiang Saen	37	1½	frequent 5.30am-7pm (interprovincial bus station)
Lampang	98-137	4-5	5 departures 12.45-4.30pm (new bus station)
Lampang	137	5	hourly 7am-3.15pm (interprovincial bus station)
Luang Prabang (Laos)	950	16	1pm (new bus station)
Mae Chan (for Mae Salong/Santikhiri)	25	45min	frequent 5am-7.30pm (interprovincial bus station)
Mae Sai	39	1½	frequent 6am-6.30pm (interprovincial bus station)
Mae Sot	416	12	8.15am & 8.45am (new bus station)
Nakhon Ratchasima (Khorat)	569-664	12-13	6 departures 6.30am-7.20pm (new bus station)
Phayao	43	1½-2	hourly 10am-3.30pm (new bus station)
Phayao	66	2	frequent 7.30am-3.30pm (interprovincial bus station)
Phitsanulok	260-335	6-7	hourly 6.15am-7.20pm (new bus station)
Phrae	144	4	half-hourly 6am-6pm (new bus station)
Sukhothai	231	8	hourly 7.30am-noon (new bus station)
Ubon Ratchathani	884	12	4pm (new bus station)

Drinking & Nightlife

Th Jetyod is Chiang Rai's rather tacky drinking strip, on which there are a couple of standouts.

Chiang Rai Ramluek BAR

(Th Phahonyothin; ⏰ 4pm-midnight) For a Thai-style night out on the town, consider this popular place. There's no English-language sign, but follow the live music and look for the knot of outdoor tables. Food is also available.

Cat Bar   BAR
(1013/1 Th Jetyod; ☺5pm-1am) Long-standing Cat Bar has a pool table and, on some nights, live music from 10.30pm.

🛍 Shopping

Thanon Khon Muan   MARKET
(Th Sankhongnoi; ☺6-9pm Sun) Come Sunday evening, the stretch of Th Sankhongnoi from Soi 2 heading west is closed to traffic and in its place are vendors selling clothes, handicrafts and local food. Th Sankhong-noi is called Th Sathanpayabarn where it intersects with the southern end of Th Phahonyothin.

Walking Street   MARKET
(Th Thanalai; ☺4-10pm Sat) If you're in town on a Saturday evening, be sure not to miss the open-air Walking Street, an expansive street market focusing on all things Chiang Rai, from handicrafts to local dishes. The market spans Th Thanalai from the Hilltribe Museum to the morning market.

Night Bazaar   MARKET
(off Th Phahonyothin; ☺6-11pm) Adjacent to the bus station off Th Phahonyothin is Chiang Rai's night market. On a much smaller scale than the one in Chiang Mai, it is nevertheless an OK place to find an assortment of handicrafts and touristy souvenirs.

ℹ Information

There are several banks with foreign exchange and ATMs on both Th Phahonyothin and Th Thanalai.

ℹ Getting There & Away

AIR
Chiang Rai International Airport (Mae Fah Luang International Airport; ☎053 798 000; http://chiangraiairportthai.com) is approximately 8km north of the city. The terminal has airline offices, restaurants, a money exchange, a post office and several car-rental booths. Taxis run into town from the airport for 200B. From town, a metered trip with Chiang Rai Taxi (p214) will cost around 120B.

There are 13 daily flights to Bangkok's Don Mueang International Airport (from 690B, one hour and 20 minutes) and six to Bangkok's Su-varnabhumi International Airport (from 1290B, one hour and 20 minutes), as well as flights to Hat Yai. At the time of writing the only international flight was to Kunming (China).

BOAT
Passenger boats ply Mae Nam Kok between Chiang Rai and Tha Ton (in Chiang Mai), stopping at Ban Ruam Mit along the way. Boats depart from the **CR Pier** (☎053 750009; ☺7am-4pm), 2km northwest of town; a túk-túk to the pier should cost about 80B.

Passenger boats depart from CR Pier at 10.30am daily; the trip to Tha Ton takes about three hours (400B), to Ruam Mit around an hour (100B). Alternatively, you can charter a boat for 800B for around three hours.

MINIVANS TO/FROM CHIANG RAI

DESTINATION	FARE (B)	DURATION (HR)	FREQUENCY
Chiang Saen	45	1½	hourly 6.20am-4.20pm (interprovincial bus station)
Mae Sai	46	1½	frequent 6.30am-6pm (interprovincial bus station)
Phayao	63	1	half-hourly 5am-6pm (interprovincial bus station)
Phrae	165	3½	half-hourly 5am-6pm (new bus station)
Sop Ruak (Golden Triangle)	50	2	hourly 6.20am-4.20pm (interprovincial bus station)

BUS & MINIVAN

Buses bound for destinations within Chiang Rai Province, as well as a couple of minivans and mostly slow, fan-cooled buses bound for a handful of destinations in northern Thailand, depart from the **interprovincial bus station** (☑ 053 715952; Th Prasopsook) in the centre of town (the station was being renovated when we were in town and buses were temporarily shifted a couple blocks east). If you're heading beyond Chiang Rai (or are in a hurry), you'll have to go to the **new bus station** (☑ 053 773989; Rte 1/AH2), 5km south of town; frequent *sŏrng·tăa·ou* (passenger pick-up trucks) linking the new bus station and the interprovincial station run from 6am to 5.30pm (15B, 15 minutes).

Internationally, there's a direct bus from Chiang Rai to Luang Prabang (Laos). There's also a daily bus to Bokeo (Laos), from where it's possible to connect to buses to Luang Nam tha (Laos), Kunming (China) and Vang Vieng (Laos).

ℹ Getting Around

Central Chiang Rai is easy enough to tackle on foot. Otherwise, a túk-túk charges approximately 20B per person for destinations in town.
Chiang Rai Taxi (☑ 053 773477) operates inexpensive metered taxis in and around town.

A number of car-rental companies have offices at the airport.
Avis Rent-A-Car (☑ 053 793827, nationwide 02 251 1131; www.avisthailand.com; Chiang Rai International Airport; ⊙ 7.30am-9pm)
Hertz (☑ 083 540 6157, nationwide 02 266 4666; www.hertzthailand.com; Chiang Rai International Airport; ⊙ 8am-8pm)
Thai Rent A Car (☑ 053 793 393, nationwide 1647; www.thairentacar.com; Chiang Rai International Airport; ⊙ 8am-8pm)

Ban Ruam Mit & Around   บ้านร่วมมิตร

☑ 053 / POP 3000

Ruam Mit means 'mixed', an accurate description of this riverside village, a convenient jumping-off point for the surrounding hilly area that's home to ethnic groups including Thai, Karen, Lisu and Akha. And only 20km from Chiang Rai via a recently paved road, Ban Ruam Mit's ethnic diversity and natural beauty are more accessible than ever.

◉ Sights & Activities

Most visitors come to Ban Ruam Mit to ride elephants (which we don't recommend as it's been proven to be harmful to the animals).

But better, not to mention more sustainable, reasons for hiking among the surrounding area's numerous villages and to visit the hot springs and national park.

Pha Soet Hot Spring   HOT SPRINGS
(บ่อน้ำพุร้อนผาเสริฐ; Ban Pha Soet; adult/child 30/10B; ⊙ 8am-6pm) The hot water from this natural spring has been redirected into a communal pool; for a more private experience, rooms are also available (50B to 100B).

Ban Pha Soet is located about 3km west of Ban Ruam Mit.

Lamnamkok National Park   NATURE RESERVE
(อุทยานแห่งชาติลำน้ำกก; Ban Ruam Mit; ⊙ 8am-4.30pm) Dating back to 2002, this is one of Thailand's youngest national parks. The area is home to waterfalls and, most notably, a hot spring. The latter is a short walk from the headquarters, while longer excursions require a guide.

The park headquarters are about 3km west of Ban Ruam Mit.

🛏 Sleeping & Eating

There are a few basic eateries in Ban Ruam Mit, and each of the hotels has its own restaurant.

Akha Hill House   HOTEL $
(☑ 089 997 5505; www.akhahill.com; r 300-500B, bungalows 600-2000B; ✸ 🛜) On a steep hillside approaching an Akha village is this beautifully situated yet generally underwhelming hotel. Accommodation ranges from fan-cooled, shared-bathroom rooms to spacious, air-con bungalows. Most people stay as part of trekking packages, which get mixed reviews. It's located about 5km south of Ban Pha Soet.

★ **Bamboo Nest de Chiang Rai**   GUESTHOUSE $$
(☑ 095 686 4755, 089 953 2330; www.bamboonest-chiangrai.com; bungalows incl breakfast 800-1600B) The Lahu village that's home to this unique accommodation is only 23km from Chiang Rai but feels a world away. Bamboo Nest takes the form of simple but spacious bamboo huts perched on a hill overlooking tiered rice fields.

The only electricity is provided by solar panels, so leave your laptops in town and instead take part in activities that range from birdwatching to hiking.

Bamboo Nest is located about 2km from the headquarters of Lamnamkok National

Park; free transport to/from Chiang Rai is available for those staying two nights or more.

ⓘ Getting There & Away

From Chiang Rai, the easiest way to get to Ban Ruam Mit is via boat. A daily passenger boat departs from CR Pier, 2km northwest of Chiang Rai, at 10.30am (100B, about one hour); a charter will run to about 800B. In the opposite direction, boats stop in Ban Ruam Mit around 2pm.

Doi Mae Salong (Santikhiri) ดอยแม่สลอง

For a taste of China without crossing any international borders, head to this atmospheric village perched on the back hills of Chiang Rai.

Doi Mae Salong was originally settled by Chinese soldiers who fled communist rule in 1949. Generations later, the descendants and culture of this unique community persists, and the Yunnanese dialect of Chinese still remains the predominant language; residents tend to watch Chinese, rather than Thai, TV; and you'll find more Chinese than Thai food. And although Doi Mae Salong is now thoroughly on the beaten track, the distinctly Chinese vibe, hilltop setting and abundance of hill tribes and tea plantations converge in a destination quite unlike anywhere else in Thailand. It's a great place to kick back for a couple of days, and the surrounding area is exceptional for self-guided exploration.

◎ Sights & Activities

Shin Sane Guest House and Little Home Guesthouse have free maps showing approximate trekking routes to Akha, Lisu, Mien, Lahu and Shan villages in the area. Nearby Akha and Lisu villages are less than half a day's walk away.

The best hikes are north of Mae Salong between Ban Thoet Thai and the Myanmar border. Ask first about political conditions before heading off in this direction; Shan and Wa armies competing for control over this section of the Thailand–Myanmar border do occasionally clash in the area. A steady trade in methamphetamines and, to a lesser extent, heroin flows across the border via several conduit villages.

Shin Sane Guest House leads **horseback treks** to four nearby villages for 500B for about three or four hours.

YUNNANESE NOSH

Many Thai tourists come to Doi Mae Salong simply to eat Yunnanese dishes such as *màn·tŏh* (steamed Chinese buns) served with braised pork belly and pickled vegetables, or black chicken braised with Chinese-style herbs. The very Chinese breakfast of *pah·tôrng·gŏh* (deep-fried dough sticks) and hot soybean milk at the morning market is a great way to start the day. Homemade wheat-and-egg noodles are another speciality of Doi Mae Salong, and are served with a local broth that combines pork and a spicy chilli paste.

Morning Market   MARKET
(ตลาดเช้าดอยแม่สลอง; ◎6-8am) A tiny but busy and vibrant morning market convenes at the T-intersection near Shin Sane Guest House. The market attracts town residents and tribespeople from the surrounding districts and is worth waking up early for.

Wat Santikhiri   VIEWPOINT
(วัดสันติคีรี) To soak up the great views from Wat Santikhiri, go past the market and ascend 718 steps (or drive if you have a car). The wát is of the Mahayana tradition and Chinese in style.

**Chinese Martyr's
Memorial Museum**   MUSEUM
(พิพิธภัณฑ์วีรชนอดีตทหารจีนคณะชาติภาคเหนือ; 20B; ◎8am-6pm) South of the turn-off to the KMT general's tomb is the Chinese Martyr's Memorial Museum, an elaborate Chinese-style building that houses displays on the KMT experience (p216) – battles, migration, culture – in Thailand.

🛏 Sleeping

Don't fret if your first pick is full: there are many, many budget and midrange places to choose from in Doi Mae Salong. The competition means that prices are often negotiable, except during the high season (November to January). And the cool weather means that few places have air-con.

🛏 In Town

Shin Sane Guest House   GUESTHOUSE **$**
(☏ 053 765026; www.maesalong-shinsane.blog spot.com; r 200-400B, bungalows 400-500B;

LOCAL KNOWLEDGE

MAE SALONG, PAST AND PRESENT

Mae Salong was originally settled by the 93rd Regiment of the Kuomintang (KMT), who had fled to Myanmar from China after the 1949 Chinese revolution. The renegades were forced to leave Myanmar in 1961 when the Yangon government decided it wouldn't allow the KMT to remain legally in northern Myanmar. Crossing into northern Thailand with their pony caravans, the ex-soldiers and their families settled into mountain villages and re-created a society like the one they'd left behind in Yunnan.

After the Thai government granted the KMT refugee status in the 1960s, efforts were made to incorporate the Yunnanese KMT and their families into the Thai nation. Until the late 1980s they didn't have much success. Many ex-KMT persisted in involving themselves in the Golden Triangle (p225) opium trade in a three-way partnership with opium warlord Khun Sa and the Shan United Army (SUA). Because of the rough, mountainous terrain and lack of sealed roads, the outside world was rather cut off from the goings-on in Doi Mae Salong, so the Yunnanese were able to ignore attempts by the Thai authorities to suppress opium activity and tame the region.

Infamous Khun Sa made his home in nearby Ban Hin Taek (now Ban Thoet Thai) until the early 1980s, when he was routed by the Thai military. Khun Sa's retreat to Myanmar seemed to signal a change in local attitudes, and the Thai government finally began making progress in its pacification of Doi Mae Salong and the surrounding area. In an attempt to quash opium activity, and the more recent threat of *yah bâh* (methamphetamine) trafficking, the Thai government has created crop-substitution programs to encourage hill tribes to cultivate tea, coffee, corn and fruit trees.

In a further effort to separate the area from its old image as an opium fiefdom, the Thai government officially changed the name of the village from Doi Mae Salong to Santikhiri (Hill of Peace), although few people use this name. Until the 1980s packhorses were used to move goods up the mountain to Doi Mae Salong, but today the 36km road from Ban Pasang is paved and well travelled. But despite the advances in infrastructure, the town is unlike any other in Thailand and retains a strong Chinese cultural presence.

@ 🛜) The rooms in the original building of Mae Salong's oldest hotel are bare but spacious with shared bathrooms, while those in the new annexe and the bungalows are much more comfortable, with en suite bathrooms and TV. Located near the morning market intersection.

Sabaidee Maesalong
HOTEL $

(📞 085 705 5570; Rte 1130; r 500-700B; 🛜) Upscale mountain views at a budget price; the rooms here are spacious, modern and come in a jaunty shade of mint green. Little, if any, English is spoken.

★ Little Home Guesthouse
GUESTHOUSE $$

(📞 053 765389; www.maesalonglittlehome.com; Rte 1130; r & bungalows 500-800B; @🛜) Located near the market intersection is this recently renovated, large yellow building backed by a handful of attractive, great-value bungalows. Rooms are spacious, tidy and sunny, and the owners are extremely friendly and helpful.

Baan Hom Muen Li
HOTEL $$$

(Osmanthus; 📞 053 765271; osmanhouse@hotmail.com; Rte 1130; r incl breakfast 1200-2000B; 🛜) Across from Sweet Maesalong cafe, in the middle of town, this stylish place consists of 22 rooms artfully decked out in modern and classic Chinese themes. Go for the upstairs rooms in the new structure that have huge balconies with views over the surrounding tea plantations. There's no Roman-script sign.

🛏 Outside Town

Khumnaiphol Resort
HOTEL $$

(📞 081 493 5242; https://th-th.facebook.com/khumnaiphol.chiangrai; Rte 1130; incl breakfast r 600-800B, bungalows 1500B; ❄🛜) This resort has comfortable but somewhat tackily decorated bungalows perched on a hillside. The covered porches give great views of the tea plantations below. Cheaper rooms in the main structure are also available.

It's located 1km south of town near the afternoon market intersection. There's no Roman-script sign.

Maesalong Flower Hills Resort
RESORT $$

(☑ 053 765496; www.maesalongflowerhills.com; Rte 1130; incl breakfast r 1000-7000B, bungalows 1300-5900B; ❋☏☤) Located 2km east of Mae Salong's town centre, you can't miss this monument to flower-based landscaping. There's a variety of tidy if rather characterless rooms and bungalows, and the huge pool and larger bungalows make this the logical choice for families.

★ Phu Chaisai Resort & Spa
RESORT $$$

(☑ 053 910500; www.phu-chaisai.com; off Rte 1130; bungalows incl breakfast 3900-20,000B; ❋☏☤) Approximately 7km from Ban Pasang (the turn-off for Mae Salong) on a remote bamboo-covered hilltop, this resort is the most unique place to stay in the area. The decidedly rustic adobe/bamboo bungalows are fittingly without TV, but have amazing views of the surrounding mountains.

Maesalong Mountain Home
HOTEL $$$

(☑ 084 611 9508; www.maesalongmountainhome.com; off Rte 1130; r & bungalows 1000-3300B; @☏) Down a dirt road 1km east of Mae Salong's town centre (look for the orange sign), this boutique place is a great choice if you've got your own wheels or don't mind walking. The 14 bungalows are in the middle of a working farm and are generally bright and airy, with wide balconies and huge bathrooms.

✗ Eating

The culinary offerings in Doi Mae Salong are not unlike those of a village in Yunnan (in southern China). It's a great place to dig into exotic noodles and other dishes not found elsewhere in Thailand.

Countless tea houses sell locally grown teas (mostly oolong and jasmine) and offer complimentary tastings.

★ Salima Restaurant
CHINESE $

(Rte 1130; mains 60-220B; ☉ 7am-8pm) One of the friendliest restaurants in town also happens to be the one serving the most delicious food. Salima does tasty Muslim-Chinese dishes, including a rich Yunnan-style beef curry and a deliciously tart, spicy tuna and tea-leaf salad. The noodle dishes are equally worthwhile and include a beef *kôw soy* (wheat-and-egg noodles in a curry broth).

Sweet Maesalong
CAFE $

(Rte 1130; mains 45-155B; ☉ 8.30am-5pm; ☏) If you require more caffeine than the local tea leaves can provide, stop by this modern cafe with an extensive menu of coffee drinks using local beans. Surprisingly sophisticated baked goods and one-plate dishes are also available. Located more or less in the middle of town.

Sue Hai
CHINESE $$

(Rte 1130; mains 80-300B; ☉ 7am-9pm; ✐) Just east of the town centre, this simple, family-run tea shop and Chinese restaurant has an English-language menu of regional specialities, including local mushrooms fried with soy sauce and delicious air-dried pork fried with fresh chilli.

❶ Information

There is an ATM at the Thai Military Bank opposite Khumnaiphol Resort, at the southern end of town.

An **internet cafe** (Rte 1130; per hour 20B; ☉ 9am-11pm) can be found at the southern end of town, near the bank.

❶ Getting There & Around

If you don't have your own wheels, probably the easiest way to get to Doi Mae Salong from Chiang Rai is to take a bus to Mae Chan, from where there are frequent green *sŏrng·tăa·ou* to Doi Mae Salong (60B, one hour, four departures daily). Alternatively, it's also possible to take a Mae Sai–bound bus to Ban Pasang, from where blue *sŏrng·tăa·ou* can be chartered for around 400B. In the reverse direction, you can flag down *sŏrng·tăa·ou* near Doi Mae Salong's 7-Eleven.

You can also reach Doi Mae Salong by road from Tha Ton, in Chiang Mai. Yellow *sŏrng·tăa·ou* bound for Tha Ton stop near Little Home Guesthouse four times daily (60B, one hour).

Much of Doi Mae Salong is approachable on foot. If you want to go further (or are struggling with the hills), motorcycles can be hired at most guesthouses for around 200B for 24 hours.

Mae Sai
แม่สาย

☑ 053 / POP 22,000

At first glance, Thailand's northernmost town can appear to be little more than a large open-air market. But Mae Sai serves as a convenient base for exploring the Golden Triangle and Doi Mae Salong, and its

BAN THOET THAI: VILLAGE OF THE OPIUM KING

Located in a narrow river valley about 20km north of Mae Salong, Ban Thoet Thai (บ้าน เทอดไทย) is a multiethnic village with a remote, border-town vibe and an interesting back story.

The village is probably most famous for having formerly served as the base of Khun Sa, the Shan narco-warlord known as the Opium King. Until the early 1980s, proximity to the Golden Triangle, the rough, mountainous terrain and lack of sealed roads meant that the outside world was essentially cut off from Ban Thoet Thai (then known as Ban Hin Taek – Broken Stone Village), allowing Khun Sa to establish a virtual monopoly on the world opium trade. Find displays on the Opium King, as well as Shan culture and history, at the **Khunsa Museum** (พิพิธภัณฑ์ขุนส่า; ☉ 8am-5pm) **FREE**, located in his former headquarters (about 500m north of the market area). Don't miss the VIP Living Room that boasts a creepy life-sized model of Khun Sa.

The best place to stay in Ban Thoet Thai is **Rim Taan Guest House** (☎ 053 730209; 15 Mu 1, Thoet Thai; r & bungalows 350-2000B; ❄ ☎), located roughly in the middle of town, with basic fan bungalows and air-con rooms in an attractive stream-side garden. Next door, **Restaurant Ting Ting** (mains 40-150B; ☉ 7am-9pm), practically the only eatery open at night in Ban Thoet Thai, has a thick English-language menu of tasty Chinese dishes. There's an **internet cafe** (per hr 20B; ☉ 9am-11pm) located near the town's 7-Eleven.

To Ban Thoet Thai, blue *sŏrng·tăa·ou* make stops in front of Mae Salong's 7-Eleven between 7am and 5pm (60B, 40 minutes); in the opposite direction, trucks depart from Ban Thoet Thai's market area from 6am to 5pm (60B).

position across from Myanmar also makes it a jumping-off point for those wishing to explore some of the more remote parts of Shan State.

Because occasional fighting within Myanmar or disputes between the Thai and Myanmar governments can lead to the border being closed temporarily, it's always a good idea to check the current situation before travelling to Mae Sai.

◉ Sights

Wat Phra That Doi Wao BUDDHIST TEMPLE
(วัดพระธาตุดอยเวา; Soi 1, Th Phahonyothin; ☉ daylight hours) **FREE** Take the steps up the hill near the border to Wat Phra That Doi Wao for superb views over Mae Sai and Myanmar. This *wát* was reportedly constructed in memory of a couple of thousand Burmese soldiers who died fighting the KMT here in 1965 (you'll hear differing stories around town, including a version wherein the KMT are the heroes).

🛏 Sleeping

Maesai Momhome GUESTHOUSE $
(☎ 053 731537; haritchayahana@gmail.com; off Th Sailomjoy; r 300-500B; ❄ ☎) A shiny new three-storey building holding nine rooms equipped with TV, refrigerator and hot water showers; the price depends on whether you go with fan or air-con. Call in at the signed office at the three-way junction on Th Sailomjoy.

Maesai Guest House HOTEL $
(☎ 053 732021; 688 Th Wiengpangkam; bungalows 300-600B; ☎) This long-standing collection of fan-cooled, A-frame bungalows ranges from simple rooms with shared cold-water showers to bungalows on the river with terraces and private bathrooms.

Khanthongkham Hotel HOTEL $$
(☎ 053 734222; 7 Th Phahonyothin; incl breakfast r 850B, ste 1200-1800B; ❄ ☎) This hotel, located steps from the border, features huge rooms that have been tastefully decorated in light woods and brown cloths. Suites are exceptionally vast, and all rooms have flat-screen TVs and spacious and inviting bathrooms. A downside is that many rooms don't have windows.

Afterglow HOTEL $$
(☎ 053 734188; www.afterglowhostel.com; 139/5 Th Phahonyothin; r 600-800B, bungalows 500B; ❄ ☎) Boasting a ground-floor cafe and rooms with a minimalist feel, Afterglow is probably the hippest place to

Mae Sai

Mae Sai

◎ Sights
1 Wat Phra That Doi Wao B2

⬛ Sleeping
2 Khanthongkham Hotel C1
3 Maesai Guest House A1
4 Maesai Momhome A1
5 Piyaporn Place Hotel C3

✕ Eating
6 Bismillah Halal Food C2
7 Night Market C1
8 Sukhothai Cuisine B1

🛍 Shopping
9 Gem Market C2

ⓘ Information
10 Overbrook Clinic C3
11 Thai Immigration Office C1

ⓘ Transport
12 Motorcycle Taxis to Bus Station C2
13 Siam First C3
14 Sŏrng·tăa·ou to Bus Station C1
15 Sŏrng·tăa·ou to Sop Ruak &
        Chiang Saen C2

stay in Mae Sai. An addition sees a few equally stylish bungalows out back. The downside: it's located about 4km from the border.

Piyaporn Place Hotel HOTEL **$$**
(☎053 734511; 77/1 Th Phahonyothin; incl breakfast r 800B; ste 1800B; ❄@🛜) On the main road by Soi 7, this seven-storey business hotel is good value. The large, contemporary-styled rooms have wooden floors, a small sofa and the usual business-class amenities like bathroom, cable TV and minibar.

Maekhong Delta Boutique Hotel HOTEL **$$**
(☎053 642517; 230/5-6 Th Phahonyothin; incl breakfast r 900-1200B, ste 1200-3600B; ❄@🛜) It's an odd name, considering that the Mekong Delta is way down in Vietnam. Odder still that, with their light wood panelling, the rooms here are somehow reminiscent of a ski lodge. Regardless, they're modern and attractive, albeit nearly 4km from the border.

✕ Eating

An expansive **night market** (Th Phahonyothin; mains 30-60B; ☉5-11pm) unfolds every

❶ GETTING TO MYANMAR: MAE SAI TO TACHILEIK

The Mae Sai–Tachileik border is a popular visa run destination, but there are a few caveats about crossing here for those who want to go further abroad. Border-crossing information is liable to change, so be sure to check the situation locally before you travel.

Getting to the border The border and Thai immigration office are a short walk from most accommodation in Mae Sai.

At the border After taking care of the usual formalities at the **Thai immigration office**, cross the bridge and head to the Myanmar immigration office. If you've already procured a Myanmar visa, you'll be allowed to proceed by land to Kyaingtong (also known as Kengtung) or via air to other points in Myanmar.

If you haven't already obtained a Myanmar visa, it's straightforward to cross to Tachileik for the day and slightly more complicated to get a two-week border pass to visit Kyaingtong.

Day-trippers must pay a fee of 500B for a temporary ID card; your passport will be kept at the border. There is little to do in Tachileik apart from sample Burmese food and shop – the prices are about the same as on the Thai side and everyone accepts baht. There's an interesting morning market and it can be fun to hang about in the teashops.

If you'd like to visit Kyaingtong but haven't already received a Myanmar visa, proceed directly to the Myanmar Travels & Tours (MTT) office. There you'll need to inform the authorities exactly where you're headed and you'll need three photos and US$10 or 500B to process a border pass valid for 14 days; your passport will be kept at the border ensuring that you return the way you came. It's also obligatory to hire a guide for the duration of your stay. Guides cost 1000B per day (plus a 400B 'guiding tax'), and if you haven't already arranged for a Kyaingtong-based guide to meet you at the border, you'll be assigned one by MTT and will also have to pay for your guide's food and accommodation during your stay. Recommended Kyaingtong-based guides include **Leng** (☏ +95 9490 31470; sairoctor.htunleng@gmail.com) and **Freddie** (Sai Yot; ☏ +95 9490 31934; yotkham@gmail.com).

Moving on Buses bound for Kyaingtong (K10,000, five hours, 8am to 8.30am and 11.30am to 12.30pm) depart from Tachileik's bus station, 2km and a 20B *sŏrng·tăa·ou* ride (passenger pick-up truck) or a 50B motorcycle taxi ride from the border. Alternatively, you can charter a taxi from the same station from K100,000 or, if you're willing to wait until it's full, a seat in a share taxi for K12,000 or K15,000.

evening along Th Phahonyothin. During the day, several snack and drink vendors can be found in front of the police station on Th Phahonyothin.

Sukhothai Cuisine THAI $
(399/9 Th Sailomjoy; mains 35-40B; ⊙ 7am-5pm) This open-air restaurant serves the namesake noodles from Sukhothai, as well as satay and a few other basic dishes. There's no English-language sign here, but it's the busy place right on the corner.

Bismillah Halal Food THAI $
(Soi 4, Th Phahonyothin; mains 30-100B; ⊙ 5am-5pm) This tiny restaurant does an excellent biryani, not to mention virtually everything else Muslim, from roti to samosas.

Shopping

Commerce is ubiquitous in Mae Sai, although most of the offerings are of little interest to Western travellers. One particularly common commodity is gems, and a walk down Soi 4 will reveal several open-air **gem dealers** (Soi 4, Th Phahonyothin) diligently counting hundreds of tiny semi-precious stones on the side of the street.

❶ Information

There are several banks with ATMs near the border.

Immigration Main Office (☏ 053 731008; Th Phahonyothin; ⊙ 8.30am-4.30pm Mon-Fri) Located about 3km from the border, near Soi 17.

Internet Cafe (Th Phahonyothin; per hr 10B; ⊙ 8am-11pm) Behind the Wang Thong Hotel, by the car park.

Overbrook Clinic (☎ 053 734422; 20/7 Th Phahonyothin; ⊗ 8am-5pm) Connected to the modern hospital in Chiang Rai.

Police Station (Th Phahonyothin) Mae Sai's main police station.

Thai Immigration Office (☎ 053 733261; Th Phahonyothin; ⊗ 6am-9pm) Located at the entrance to the border bridge.

Tourist Police (☎ 115; Th Phahonyothin; ⊗ 8.30am-6pm) With a booth in front of the border crossing before immigration.

❶ Getting There & Around

Mae Sai's **bus station** (☎ 053 646403; Th Phahonyothin) is 4km from the border; **shared sŏrng·tăa·ou** (Th Phayhonyothin) ply the route between the bus station and a stop on Soi 2, Th Phahonyothin (15B, five minutes, 6am to 6pm). Alternatively, it's a 40B **motorcycle taxi** (Th Phahonyothin) ride to/from the stand at the corner of Th Phahonyothin and Soi 4.

If you're headed to Bangkok, you can avoid going all the way to the bus station by buying your tickets at **Siam First** (☎ 053 731504; near cnr Soi 9 & Th Phahonyothin; ⊗ 8am-5.30pm) – it's on the corner of Soi 9, Th Phahonyothin, next door to the motorcycle dealership.

On Th Phahonyothin, by Soi 8, is a sign saying 'bus stop'; this is where you'll find the **stop** (Th Phahonyothin) for sŏrng·tăa·ou bound for Sop Ruak and Chiang Saen.

Sŏrng·tăa·ou around town cost 15B. Motorcycle taxis cost 20B to 40B.

Chiang Saen เชียงแสน
☎ 053 / POP 11,000

The dictionary definition of a sleepy river town, Chiang Saen is the site of a former Thai kingdom thought to date back to as early as the 7th century. Scattered throughout the modern town are the ruins of this empire – surviving architecture includes several *chedi* (stupa), Buddha images, *wí·hăhn* (sanctuary) pillars and earthen city ramparts. Chiang Saen later became loosely affiliated with various northern Thai kingdoms, as well as 18th-century Myanmar, but didn't become a Siamese possession until the 1880s.

Today huge river barges from China moor at Chiang Saen, carrying fruit, engine parts and all manner of other imports, keeping

NORTHERN THAILAND CHIANG SAEN

TRANSPORT TO/FROM MAE SAI

Buses

DESTINATION	FARE (B)	DURATION (HR)	FREQUENCY
Bangkok	581-904	12-13	7am & frequent 4.20-5.40pm
Chiang Mai	160-319	5	9 departures 6.15am-10.40pm
Chiang Rai	39	1½	frequent 5.45am-6pm
Mae Sot	416	12	6.45am
Phayao	95-122	3	3 departures 7-10.30am
Phitsanulok	344	8	7am & 10.30am
Phrae	225	5	7am & 10.30am

Minivans & Sŏrng·tăa·ou

DESTINATION	FARE (B)	DURATION (HR)	FREQUENCY
Chiang Rai	46	1	frequent minivans 6am-6pm
Chiang Saen	50	1	frequent sŏrng·tăa·ou 8am-noon
Fang	120	3	minivan 8am & 2pm
Sop Ruak (Golden Triangle)	40	45min	frequent sŏrng·tăa·ou 8am-1pm
Tha Ton	120	2	8am & 2pm

Chiang Saen

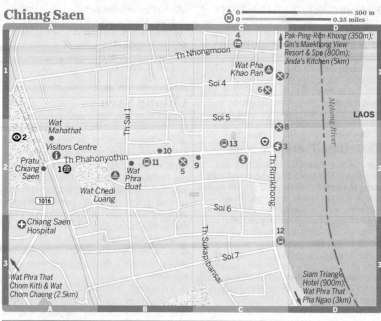

the old China–Siam trade route open. Despite this trade, the town hasn't changed too much over the last decade, and because of this it's a more pleasant base than the comparatively hectic, touristy Sop Ruak, the so-called 'Golden Triangle', 9km east.

◎ Sights & Activities

Wat Pa Sak
HISTORIC SITE

(วัดป่าสัก; off Rte 1290; historical park admission 50B; ⊘8.30am-4.30pm Wed-Sun) FREE
About 200m from the Pratu Chiang Saen (the historic main gateway to the town's western flank) are the remains of Wat Pa

Sak, where the ruins of seven monuments are visible in a historical park. The main mid-14th-century *chedi* combines elements of the Hariphunchai and Sukhothai styles with a possible Bagan influence, and still holds a great deal of attractive stucco relief work.

Chiang Saen National Museum
MUSEUM

(พิพิธภัณฑสถานแห่งชาติเชียงแสน; 702 Th Phahonyothin; 100B; ⊘8.30am-4.30pm Wed-Sun) This museum is a great source of local information considering its relatively small size.

Wat Phra That Pha Ngao
BUDDHIST TEMPLE

(วัดพระธาตุผาเงา; off Rte 1129; ⊘ daylight hours) **FREE** Located 3km south of town in the village of Sop Kham, this Buddhist temple complex contains a large prayer hall built to cover a partially excavated Chiang Saen–era Buddha statue. There is a beautiful golden teak *hŏr đrai* (manuscript depository) and a steep road leads to a hilltop pagoda and temple with views over the area and the Mekong River.

Wat Phra That Chom
Kitti & Wat Chom Chaeng
HISTORIC SITE

(วัดพระธาตุจอมกิตติ/วัดจอมแจ้ง; off Rte 1290; ⊘ daylight hrs) **FREE** The remains of Wat Phra That Chom Kitti and Wat Chom Chaeng can be found about 2.5km northwest of town on a hilltop. The round *chedi* of Wat Phra That Chom Kitti is thought to have been constructed before the founding of the kingdom.

Mekong River Trips
BOATING

(📞 085 392 4701; Th Rimkhong; ⊘ 8am-5pm) Five-passenger speedboats leave from the waterfront jetty to Sop Ruak (per boat one-way/return 600/700B, one hour), or all the way to Chiang Khong (per boat one-way/return 2500/3000B, 1½ hours).

🛏 Sleeping

Jay Nay
GUESTHOUSE $

(📞 081 960 7551; Th Nhongmoon; r 400-1000B; ❄ 🖤 📶) Jay Nay consists of 13 nearly identical rooms in a two-storey complex. They're plain but new, clean and comfy. Look for the 'Rooms For Rent' sign. A great budget catch.

Gin's Maekhong
View Resort & Spa
HOTEL $$

(📞 084 485 1376; www.facebook.com/ginsmaekhongview; Th Rimkhong; incl breakfast r 1000-1500B, bungalows 1500B; ❄ 📶 🏊) Here you can choose between rather tight riverside bungalows or spacious and attractive rooms in a two-storey structure. There's a pool, vast sunflower field, spa and cafe.

Gin's is located about 1km north of the centre of Chiang Saen, near the reconstructed city walls.

Pak-Ping-Rim-Khong
GUESTHOUSE $$

(📞 053 650151; www.facebook.com/pakpingrimkhong; 484 Th Rimkhong; r incl breakfast 1200-1800B; ❄ 📶) A new and tidy villa compound just north of town. Rooms are spacious and come equipped with air-con, TV and fridge.

If you don't need river views, this is one of the best all-around places to stay in town.

Viang Yonok
GUESTHOUSE $$$

(📞 053 650444; www.viangyonok.com; off Rte 1016; bungalows incl breakfast 2100-2450B; ❄ @ 📶 🏊) The emphasis at this well-manicured compound of seven comfortable, modern bungalows is activities, and if a swimming pool, sauna, weights room, bicycles, kayaks and birdwatching aren't enough, well, you're a pretty tough customer.

It's located approximately 5km west of Chiang Saen in Ban Khu Tao, off the road that leads to Mae Chan; follow the yellow signs that appear after the Esso station.

Siam Triangle Hotel
HOTEL $$$

(📞 053 651115; www.siamtriangle.com; 267 Th Rimkhong; incl breakfast r 2000-2500B, ste 4500B; ❄ @ 📶 🏊) Chiang Saen's biggest hotel generally lacks charm, but the gigantic suites with river-view jacuzzi tubs are pretty impressive. There's a new wing with slightly cheaper rooms across the street.

The hotel is just outside Chiang Saen, about 400m south of the former city wall.

✗ Eating & Drinking

Cheap noodle and rice dishes are available at food stalls (mains 30B to 60B) near the covered bus shelter on Th Phahonyothin. Come nightfall, **evening food vendors** (Th Phahonyothin; mains 30-60B; ⊙4-10pm) set up just west of here. Every Saturday evening, a section of Th Rimkhong is closed to vehicle traffic for the busy **Walking Street** (mains 20-60B; ⊙4-9pm Sat), which has lots of food.

Chiang Saen's drinking scene largely revolves around the **riverside food vendors** (Th Rimkhong; mains 30-60B; ⊙4-11pm) who set up shop every evening.

Kiaw Siang Hai   CHINESE **$**
(44 Th Rimkhong; mains 50-200B; ⊙8am-8pm) Serving the workers of Chinese boats that dock at Chiang Saen, this authentic Chinese restaurant prepares a huge menu of dishes in addition to the namesake dumplings. Try the spicy Sichuan-style fried tofu or one of the Chinese herbal soups.

There's no English-language sign, but the restaurant can be identified by the giant ceramic jars out front.

Jinda's Kitchen   THAI **$**
(Rte 1290; mains 25-100B; ⊙8am-9pm; 🛜) This roadside restaurant has been serving up local dishes for more than 50 years and does a mean *kà·nŏm jeen nám ngée·o* (fresh rice noodles served with a meaty and tart pork- and tomato-based broth).

It's roughly halfway between Chiang Saen and Sop Ruak.

2 be 1   BAR
(Th Rimkhong; ⊙5.30pm-midnight) By the river is this tiny bar with indoor and outdoor seating and a pool table – pretty much the extent of Chiang Saen's nightlife scene.

ℹ Information

Chiang Saen Hospital (☑053 777017; Rte 1016; ⊙24hr) Government hospital just south of Wat Pa Sak.

Immigration Office (☑053 777118; cnr Th Phahonyothin & Th Sukapibansai; ⊙8.30am-4.30pm Mon-Fri) Chiang Saen's main immigration office.

Police (Th Phahonyothin; ⊙24hr) Chiang Saen's main police station.

Siam Commercial Bank (Th Phahonyothin; ⊙8.30am-4.30pm Mon-Fri) Bank with foreign exchange and ATM.

Visitors Centre (☑053 777084; Th Phahonyothin; ⊙8.30am-4.30pm Mon-Sat) Has a good relief display showing the major ruin sites as well as photos of various *chedi* before, during and after restoration.

ℹ Getting There & Away

Blue sŏrng·tăa·ou (Th Phahonyothin) bound for Sop Ruak (20B) and Mae Sai (50B) wait at a stall at the eastern end of Th Phahonyothin from 7.20am to 3pm. If you're bound for Chiang Khong, you'll need to board one of the **green sŏrng·tăa·ou** (Th Rimkhong) bound for Hat Bai (50B, one hour, 9am to 2pm) at a stall on Th Rimkhong, south of the riverside immigration office; at Hat Bai you'll need to transfer to yet another *sŏrng·tăa·ou*.

Chiang Saen has no proper bus terminal, rather there is a covered bus shelter at the eastern end of Th Phahonyothin where buses pick up and drop off passengers. From this stop there are frequent buses to Chiang Rai (37B, 1½ hours, 5.30am to 5.30pm) and a daily bus to Chiang Mai (222B, five hours, 9am).

Sombat Tour (☑053 650 788; Th Phahonyothin; ⊙8.20am-5.20pm) operates two daily VIP buses to Bangkok (1058B, 12 hours, 5pm and 5.30pm), departing from a small office on Th Phahonyothin.

ℹ Getting Around

Motorbike taxis will do short trips in town for 20B. They congregate near and across from the bus stop.

A good way to see the Chiang Saen area is on two wheels. Mountain bikes and motorcycles can be rented at the **motorcycle hire shop** (☑089 429 5798; 247/1 Th Phahonyothin; per 24hr bike/motorcycle 80/200B; ⊙8am-7pm) linked with a barber shop.

Sop Ruak   สบรวก
☑053

The borders of Myanmar, Thailand and Laos meet at Sop Ruak, the so-called centre of the Golden Triangle, at the confluence of Nam Ruak and the Mekong River. The town's two opium-related museums, the **House of Opium** (บ้านฝิ่น; Rte 1290; 50B; ⊙7am-7pm) and **Hall of Opium** (หอฝิ่น; Rte 1290; adult/child 200B/free; ⊙8.30am-4pm Tue-Sun), are both worth a visit, and a boat trip is an enjoyable way to pass an hour. But the only reason to overnight here is if you've already booked a room in one of the area's outstanding luxury hotels.

NORTHERN THAILAND SOP RUAK

THE GOLDEN TRIANGLE, PAST & PRESENT

In historical terms, the Golden Triangle refers to an area, stretching thousands of square kilometres into Myanmar, Laos and Thailand, within which the opium trade was once prevalent. From the early 20th century to the 1980s, this region was the world's biggest grower of *Papaver somniferum*, the poppy that produces opium. Poverty and lack of infrastructure and governance in the largely rebel-controlled areas meant that growing poppies and transporting opium proceeded virtually unchecked, eventually making its way around the world as refined heroin.

Undoubtedly the single most significant player in the Golden Triangle drug trade was Khun Sa, a Shan-Chinese warlord dubbed the Opium King by the press. Starting in the mid-1970s from his headquarters in Chiang Rai Province, Khun Sa, his Shan United Army (SUA), ex-KMT fighters in Doi Mae Salong and other cohorts in the region formed a partnership that would eventually claim a virtual monopoly of the world's opium trade.

In 1988, after having been the victim of two unsuccessful assassination attempts, Khun Sa offered to sell his entire crop of opium to the Australian government for A$50 million a year, claiming that this would essentially end the world's entire illegal trade in heroin. He made a similar offer to the US, but he was dismissed by both. With a US DEA bounty of US$2 million on his head, in 1996 Khun Sa surrendered to Burmese officials. They refused to extradite him to the US and Khun Sa eventually died in Yangon in 2007.

Khun Sa's surrender seemed to be the last nail in the coffin for the Golden Triangle opium trade – land dedicated to poppy cultivation in the region hit an all-time low in 1998 – and since the early 21st century, Afghanistan's Golden Crescent has replaced the region as the world's pre-eminent producer of opium. But a recent report by the UN Office of Drugs & Crime claims that trade in the Golden Triangle has yet again spiked – most likely due to increased demand from China – and in 2012 Myanmar alone was thought to have produced 25% of the world's opium.

However, most agree that the contemporary Golden Triangle drug trade has shifted from opium to methamphetamines. Manufactured in Myanmar in factories with alleged links to the United Wa State Army, the drug, known in Thai as *yah bâh* (crazy drug), has become the scourge of the region – footage of tweaked-out users holding hostages was a Thai news staple in the early 2000s. Although recent efforts to eradicate methamphetamines by the Thai authorities have led to higher prices, trafficking and use are thought to have increased.

Thailand's opium-growing days are long gone, but hoteliers and tour operators in Chiang Rai have been quick to cash in on the name by rebranding the tiny village of Sop Ruak as the 'Golden Triangle'. The name is undoubtedly meant to conjure up images of illicit adventure, exotic border areas and contraband caravans, but these days the only caravans you're likely to see is the endless parade of buses carrying package tourists. Sop Ruak's opium has been fully relegated to museums, and even the once beautiful natural setting has largely been obscured by ATMs, stalls selling tourist tat and the seemingly never-ending loud announcements from the various temples. Yet perhaps most tellingly, Khun Sa's formerly impenetrable headquarters in Ban Thoet Thai are today a low-key tourist attraction.

🏃 Activities

Long-tail boat trips on the Mekong River can be arranged at one of various piers throughout the day. One-hour cruises for a maximum of five people per boat cost 500B; upon arrival in Laos, a 30B tax is collected from each visitor.

🛏 Sleeping & Eating

The only reason to stay in or around Sop Ruak is to take advantage of some of northern Thailand's best upscale lodgings; those on a budget are better off in Chiang Saen. Elephant rides and other pachyderm-related 'experiences' are on offer at resorts – activities of this kind have been shown to be harmful to animals, so think twice before joining in.

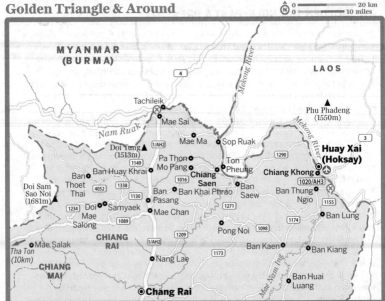

Several tourist-oriented restaurants overlook the Mekong River.

Four Seasons Tented Camp HOTEL $$$
(053 910200; www.fourseasons.com; 2 nights all-inclusive 104,000-116,000B; ✳@🖵🏊) If you can fit it into your schedule (and budget), this safari-inspired resort is among the most unusual accommodation experiences in Thailand. The 'tents' are appropriately luxurious and are decked out in colonial-era safari paraphernalia. A minimum stay of at least two nights is required, and guests take part in daily activities ranging from longboat river excursions to spa treatments.

Anantara Golden Triangle Resort & Spa HOTEL $$$
(053 784084; www.anantara.com; Rte 1290; r & ste per night all inclusive 36,500-44,000B; ✳@🖵🏊) This award-winning resort takes up a large patch of beautifully landscaped ground directly opposite the Hall of Opium. The rooms combine Thai and international themes, and all have balconies looking over the Mekong River. Jacuzzi, squash and tennis courts, gym, sauna and spa round out the luxury amenities, and activities such as cooking courses are included in most packages.

❶ Getting There & Away

There are frequent *sŏrng·tăa·ou* to Chiang Saen (20B, 15 minutes, 7am to noon) and Mae Sai (45B, 30 minutes, every 40 minutes from 8am to 1pm), both of which can be flagged down along the main strip. Minivans to Chiang Rai (50B, one hour, hourly from 5.50am to 4pm) wait in the car park west of Phra Chiang Saen Si Phaendin. It's an easy 9km bicycle ride from Chiang Saen to Sop Ruak.

Chiang Khong เชียงของ
053 / POP 12,000

Chiang Khong was historically an important market town for local hill tribes and for trade with northern Laos. In 2013, a bridge over Mae Nam Khong was completed and today the riverside town is a sleepy travellers' gateway. From Huay Xai, on the opposite side of the Mekong, it's a two-day slowboat or a 13-hour bus trip to Luang Prabang. And for those who have set their sights even further, Huay Xai is only an eight-hour bus ride from Boten, a border crossing to and from China.

🛏 Sleeping

The vast majority of accommodation in Chiang Khong is geared towards the budget market.

LOCAL KNOWLEDGE

COLOSSAL CATFISH

The Mekong River stretch that passes Chiang Khong is a traditional habitat for the *plah bèuk* (giant Mekong catfish, *Pangasianodon gigas* to ichthyologists), the largest freshwater fish in the world. A *plah bèuk* takes at least six and possibly 12 years (no one's really sure) to reach full size, when it will measure 2m to 3m in length and can weigh up to 300kg.

In Thailand and Laos the mild-tasting flesh has long been revered as a delicacy. Fishermen held a special annual ceremony to propitiate Chao Mae Pla Beuk, a female deity believed to preside over the giant catfish.

Today, the *plah bèuk* is on the Convention on International Trade in Endangered Species (CITES) list of endangered species, and the fishing of it has been banned since 2006. Because of the danger of extinction, in 1983 Thailand's Inland Fisheries Department developed a program to breed the fish in captivity. The program was largely unsuccessful until 2001, when 70,000 hatchlings survived. Because of this, *plah bèuk* is again being seen on menus around the country.

★**Namkhong Resort** HOTEL $
(☑053 791055; www.namkhongriverside.com/boutique-resort; 94/2 Th Sai Klang; r 200-800B; ❄️🛜🏊) Just off the main drag is this semi-secluded compound of tropical plants and handsome wooden structures. Even the fan-cooled, shared-bathroom cheapies are charming, and the swimming pool is a bonus.

Baan-Fai Guest House GUESTHOUSE $
(☑053 791394; 108 Th Sai Klang; r 200-700B; ❄️🛜) A renovation has this inviting wooden house looking better than ever. The six rooms in the main structure have air-con and en suite bathrooms, while the newer rooms are fan-cooled and share bathroom facilities; all are linked to an attached cafe.

Ban Tammila HOTEL $
(☑053 791234; 113 Th Sai Klang; r & bungalows 450-700B; ❄️🛜) Although the exterior looks a bit ragged, the rooms and bungalows here are neat, clean and decorated in warm colours. Some rooms boast wide balconies and hammocks; room 12 in particular has breezy views over to Laos.

Baan Pak Pon GUESTHOUSE $
(☑081 791 6735, 053 655092; baanpakpon@hotmail.co.th; off Th Sai Klang; r 400-600B; ❄️🛜) This rambling wooden house off Th Sai Klang features large rooms with wood panelling, and a couple of rooms in a relatively new adjacent cement add-on.

Funky Box HOSTEL $
(☑082 7651839; Soi 2, Th Sai Klang; dm 100B, s/d 250/300; ❄️🛜) Pretty much what the label says: a box-like structure holding 16, fan-cooled dorm beds. Five shared-bathroom rooms have been added to the main building and all are united by a fun bar/restaurant.

Day Waterfront Hotel HOTEL $$
(☑053 791789; www.hoteldaywaterfront.com; 789 Th Sai Klang; r incl breakfast 700-900B; ❄️🛜) The rooms here are tidy and well equipped (the more expensive boast more space, a fridge and teapot) but relatively plain; the real highlight is the friendly service and the great views over to Laos.

River House HOTEL $$
(☑053 792022; theriverhouse_chiangkhong@hotmail.com; 419 Th Sai Klang; dm 150B, r 300-1000B; ❄️@🛜) This homey white house overlooking the Mekong River is a great choice. The cheaper rooms are small, fan cooled and share bathrooms, while the more expensive rooms are spacious and come with air-con, fridge, TV and balcony.

Namkhong Riverside Hotel HOTEL $$
(☑053 791796; www.namkhongriverside.com; 174-176 Th Sai Klang; r incl breakfast 1300-1500B; ❄️@🛜) This modern and popular three-storey hotel holds heaps of clean, neat rooms, most with private balconies overlooking the river. It's a great midrange catch, the only downside being the noise from nightly karaoke parties.

Ibis Styles HOTEL $$$
(☑053 792008; www.ibis.com; 666 Th Sai Klang; r incl breakfast 1500-2300B; ❄️@🛜🏊) Chiang Khong has made it into the modern world with this imposing, big-chain hotel. Choose

Chiang Khong

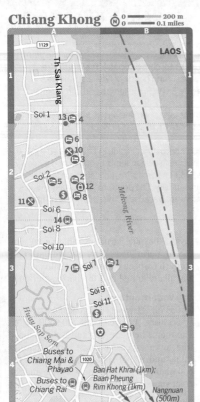

from rooms in the six-storey main structure or the garden- or riverside duplex bungalows.

🍴 Eating & Drinking

On Wednesday and Saturday during the tourist season (from around November to May), Chiang Khong's main drag hosts a **Walking Street market** (Th Sai Klang; ⊙6-10pm Wed & Sat Nov-May), which has a decent selection of local eats.

Guesthouse-based bars form Chiang Khong's nightlife scene.

★ Khao Soi Pa Orn   THAI $
(Soi 6, Th Sai Klang; mains 30-40B; ⊙8am-4pm) You may think you know *kôw soy*, the famous northern curry noodle soup, but the version served in Chiang Khong forgoes the curry broth and replaces it with clear soup topped with a rich, spicy minced-pork

mixture. A few non-noodle dishes are also available.

There's no Roman-script sign, but it's located next to the giant highway-distance marker.

Nangnuan   THAI $
(Ban Hat Khrai; mains 60-200B; ⊙8am-9pm) Freshwater fish from the Mekong is the emphasis here, and it's prepared in a variety of ways, as the extensive English-language menu describes.

It is located at the end of the road that leads to Ban Hat Khrai, about 1km south of town.

Bamboo Mexican House   INTERNATIONAL $$
(Th Sai Klang; mains 70-250B; ⊙7.30am-8.30pm; 🛜🍴) Run by the manager of a now-defunct guesthouse who learned to make Mexican dishes from her American and Mexican guests. To be honest, though, we never got past the coffee and tasty homemade breads and cakes. Opens early and also does boxed lunches for the boat ride to Luang Prabang.

Hub   BAR
(Soi 2, Th Sai Klang; ⊙noon-midnight) After having cycled around the world in record time, Brit Alan Bate decided to plant roots

ROAD TRIP: CHIANG KHONG TO PHAYAO

If you're in Chiang Khong and happen to have your own wheels, we have an excellent suggestion for a drive. Routes 1155 and 1093 are among Thailand's most dramatic roads, hugging steep mountainsides along the Thai–Lao border and passing waterfalls, incredible vistas and national parks. If you need a destination, you can continue all the way to Phayao (p230), a little-visited town with ample accommodation and good food.

From Chiang Khong, the trip is as straightforward as heading south on Rte 1020 and following the signs to **Phu Chi Fa**, a national park near the Lao border. For Thailand, the signs are unusually clear, but a good companion is the Golden Triangle Rider's *Golden Triangle* map.

At the mountaintop village of Doi Pha Tang, consider a quick detour to **Pratu Siam** (1653m), one of Thailand's most impressive viewpoints. There is basic lodging and food here.

Rte 1093 narrows and the roadside becomes markedly less populated as you approach **Phu Chi Fa**, a mountaintop that offers high-altitude views into Laos. There are a few different ways to approach the peak, the most popular being via Ban Rom Fah Thai. There is a variety of accommodation and some basic restaurants on either side of Phu Chi Fa.

Upon passing Phu Chi Fa, stay on Rte 1093 and follow the signs to **Ban Huak**. This is a picturesque village in Phayao Province, 2km from the Lao border. There's a border market on the 10th and 30th of every month, homestay-style accommodation in the town, and nearby **Nam Tok Phu Sang** is a unique waterfall of thermally heated water.

From Ban Huak, follow signs to Chiang Kham, then take Rte 1021 to Chun, from where it's a straight shot to Phayao (via Dok Kham Tai).

If you do the drive in one go, allow at least six hours, including stops for taking photos, coffee and a meal.

in Chiang Khong and opened this tiny, fun cycling-themed bar.

ℹ Information

A handful of banks along Th Sai Klang have ATMs and foreign-exchange services.
Easy Trip (☎ 089 635 5999, 053 655174; www.discoverylaos.com; 183 Th Sai Klang; ⊙ 9am-7pm) This professional travel agency can help you arrange boat or bus transport in Laos.
Government Savings Bank (Th Sai Klang) Bank with ATM.
Police Station (Th Sai Klang) Chiang Khong's main police station.
Siam Commercial Bank (Th Sai Klang) Bank with foreign exchange and ATM.

ℹ Getting There & Around

Chiang Khong has a shiny new **bus station** (☎ 053 792000; Rte 1020) located 3km south of town, which is where you'll need to go if you're bound for a destination in Laos. Otherwise, buses pick up and drop off passengers at various points near the market, south of the centre of town. If you're bound for Chiang Saen, you'll first need to take a **sŏrng·tăa·ou to Hat Bai** (Th Sai Klang) from a stall on Th Sai Klang (50B, one hour, around 8am), where you'll need to transfer to another Chiang Saen-bound *sŏrng·tăa·ou*.

Bus services from Chiang Khong include the following:

Destination	Price (B)	Duration (hr)	Departures
Bangkok	592-921	13	7am, 7.25am & frequent departures 3-4pm
Chiang Mai	254-395	6-7	7.15am, 9.45am & 10.30am
Chiang Rai	65-126	2½	hourly 5am-4pm
Luang Namtha (Laos)	280	4	2.30pm (Mon, Wed, Fri & Sat)
Luang Prabang (Laos)	730	13	2.30pm (Mon, Wed, Fri & Sat)
Phayao	151	3	10.30am
Udomxai (Laos)	460	10	2.30pm (Mon, Wed, Fri & Sat)

RIVERSIDE RETREAT

Located 22km from Chiang Khong on Rte 4007, leading to Chiang Saen, **Rai Saeng Arun** (☑ 081 802 7062; www.raisaengarun.com; Rte 4007; bungalows incl breakfast 4500-5500B; ✳ 🛜) brings together 14 bungalows in a breathtaking plot of land adjacent to the Mekong River. They aren't huge, but they are stylish and comfortable, feature balconies and open-air showers, and are connected by bridged walkways over rice fields. Considerable discounts are available during the low season.

A săhm lór between the bus station and Friendship Bridge, the border crossing to Laos, costs 120B.

PHAYAO PROVINCE

Phayao   พะเยา

☑ 054 / POP 20,000

Few people, including many Thais, are aware of this quiet but attractive northern city. In an overzealous effort to remedy this, a tourist brochure we came across described Phayao as the 'Vienna of South East Asia'. Although this is just *slightly* stretching the truth, Phayao is certainly one of the more pleasant towns in northern Thailand. Its setting on Kwan Phayao, a vast wetland, gives the town a back-to-nature feel that's utterly lacking in most Thai cities, and the tree-lined streets, temples and old wooden houses of 'downtown' Phayao provide a pleasing old-school Thai touch.

The little-visited town is the perfect place to break up your journey to/from Chiang Rai, and can also serve as a bookend to a drive from Chiang Khong (p229).

👁 Sights & Activities

⭐ **Kwan Phayao**   LANDMARK

(กว๊านพะเยา; Th Chaykawan) This vast body of water is the largest swamp in northern Thailand and a symbol of Phayao. Although naturally occurring, the water level is artificially controlled - otherwise the wetlands would go dry outside of the wet season. Framed by mountains, the swamp is in fact more scenic than the name suggests and is the setting for what must be among the most beautiful sunsets in Thailand.

Rowing crews can be seen practising in the evenings, and there's a pier at the southern end of Th Chaykawan where there are **boat rides** (per person 20B; ⊙ 8am-6pm) to what remains of **Wat Tiloke Aram**, a submerged 500-year-old temple. There are ambitious plans to rebuild the temple, one of many submerged religious structures in Kwan Phayao.

In addition to lost Buddhist artefacts, there are at least 50 types of fish native to these waters, and there's a **small fish breeding area** where for 5B you can feed the fish.

Wat Sri Khom Kham   BUDDHIST TEMPLE

(วัดศรีโคมคำ; Th Chaykawan; ⊙ daylight hours) Phayao's most important temple is thought to date back to 1491, but its present structure was finished in 1923. The immense prayer hall holds the Phra Jao Ton Luang, the largest Chiang Saen–era Buddha statue in the country. Standing 18m high, legend has it that the construction of the statue took more than 30 years. It's not the most beautiful or well-proportioned Buddha image in Thailand, but it certainly is impressive.

Phayao Cultural Exhibition Hall   MUSEUM

(หอวัฒนธรรมนิทัศน์; Th Chaykawan; 40B; ⊙ 8.30am-4.30pm) This two-storey museum is packed with artefacts and a good amount of information on local history and culture (in English). Standout items include a unique 'black' Buddha statue and a fossil of two embracing crabs labelled 'Wonder Lover'. It's next door to Wat Sri Khom Kham, about 2km from the northern end of Th Chaykawan.

🛌 Sleeping

Phayao is home to heaps of budget and midrange hotels, many of which are found along Th Chayakwan, the town's lakeside road, and offer great views.

Huanpak Jumjai   GUESTHOUSE $$

(☑ 054 482659; 37/5-6 Th Prasat; r 600B; ✳ 🛜) Rooms here are spacious, clean and decked out in handsome wood, although they don't offer lake views. It's located just off Th

Chaykawan, a short walk from the waterfront.

Gateway Hotel
HOTEL **$$**

(☎054 411333; 7/36 Soi 2, Th Pratu Khlong; incl breakfast r 900-1100B, ste 2000-2500B; ❄ 🛜 🛗) Ostensibly Phayao's grandest hotel, the rooms here boast a slightly aged midrange/business feel and include all the amenities you'd expect from such a place. It's next door to the bus station.

✖ Eating & Drinking

For such a small town, Phayao has an abundance of food. There are literally dozens of lakefront restaurants at the edge of Kwan Phayao, beginning at Th Thakawan and extending all the way to the public park.

There's not much of a nightlife scene in Phayao per se, but the lakefront restaurants function equally well as bars.

Kaat Boran
THAI, MARKET **$**

(Th Chaykawan; mains 30-60B; ⊙6-10pm) This largely food-based night market sets up every evening near the King Ngam Muang monument.

Night Market
THAI **$**

(Th Rob Wiang; mains 30-60B; ⊙6-10pm) An extensive night market convenes along the north side of Th Rob Wiang every evening.

Chue Chan
THAI **$$**

(Th Chaykawan; mains 80-240B; ⊙10am-10.30pm; ❄) Of all the waterfront restaurants, this place has received the most acclaim from the various Thai food authorities. The lengthy menu, which has both pictures and English, spans tasty dishes you won't find elsewhere, such as stuffed pig leg or sour fish fried with egg.

ⓘ GETTING TO LAOS: CHIANG KHONG TO HUAY XAI

Late 2013 saw the completion of the Fourth Thai–Lao Friendship Bridge over the Mekong River. Since then, foreigners are no longer allowed to cross to Huay Xai by boat, which (paradoxically) has made getting to Laos both less convenient and more expensive for most tourists.

Getting to the border The jumping-off point is the Friendship Bridge, around 10km south of Chiang Khong, via a 120B chartered sǎhm·lór (three-wheeled pedicab) ride or a 60B white passenger truck ride running the route from downtown or the bus-stop market area.

At the border After completing border formalities at the Thai immigration office, you'll board a shuttle bus (from 20B, 8am to 6pm) across the 630m span. On the Lao side, foreigners can purchase a 30-day visa for Laos upon arrival in Huay Xai for US$30 to US$42, depending on nationality. On your return to Thailand, unless you've already received a Thai visa, immigration will grant you permission to stay in the country for 15 days.

Moving on From the Lao side of the bridge, it's an exorbitant 100B/25,000K per person sǎhm·lór ride to the boat pier or Huay Xai's new bus terminal. Bus destinations from Huay Xai include Luang Nam Tha (60,000K to 85,000K, 4½ hours, 8.30am and 10am), Luang Prabang (145,000K to 170,000K, 12 hours, 8.30am, 10am and 6pm), Udomxai (90,000K to 100,000K, nine hours, 9.30am), Vang Vieng (215,000K, 24 hours, 10am) and Vientiane (250,000K, 24 hours, 10am).

If time is on your side, the daily **slowboat** (1350B or 220,000K, around 10.30am) to Luang Prabang takes two days, including a night in the village of Pak Beng. Avoid the noisy **fast boats** (360,000K, six to seven hours, frequent from 9am to 11am) as there have been reports of bad accidents. Booking tickets through a Chiang Khong-based agent such as Easy Trip (p229) costs slightly more, but they arrange tickets for you and provide transport and a boxed lunch for the boat ride.

If you already hold a Chinese visa, it's also possible to go directly to China from Chiang Khong. After obtaining a 30-day Lao visa on arrival in Huay Xai, simply board one of the buses bound for Mengla (120,000K, eight hours, 8.30am) or Kunming (430,000K, 18 hours, 10.30am), which are both in China's Yunnan Province.

ℹ️ Information

There are several banks along Th Donsanam, near the town's morning market, many with ATM and exchange services.

ℹ️ Getting There & Away

Phayao's **bus station** (☏ 054 431 488; Th Pratu Khlong), at the northern end of Th Chaykawan, is quite busy, primarily because the city lies on the main north–south highway. Because of this, if you're bound for Bangkok, it's possible to hop on one of the 40 or so buses that pass through the station from points further north.

BUS & MINIVAN

In addition to buses, there are also minivans to Chiang Rai (63B, one hour, half-hourly 7.15am to 7pm) and Phrae (102B, two hours, half-hourly 7.15am to 7pm).

Destination	Price (B)	Duration (hr)	Departures
Bangkok	484-795	11	frequent 8.30am-9pm
Chiang Khong	169	3½	12.40pm & 4.30pm
Chiang Mai	171-221	5	5 departures 9am-5.45pm
Chiang Rai	60-77	3	frequent 9am-3pm
Lampang	176	3	7pm
Mae Sai	122	3	2.15pm
Mae Sot	315	5	10.10am
Nan	119	4	8am & 1.30pm
Sukhothai	183	6	3 departures 9am-noon

NAN PROVINCE

Tucked into Thailand's northeastern corner, Nan is a remote province to be explored for its natural beauty. Nan's ethnic groups are another highlight and differ significantly from those in other northern provinces. Outside the Mae Nam Nan Valley, the predominant hill tribes are Mien, with smaller numbers of Hmong, while dispersed throughout Nan are four lesser-known groups seldom seen outside this province: the Thai Lü, Mabri, Htin and Khamu.

Nan   น่าน
☏ 054 / POP 20,000

Due to its remote location, Nan is not the kind of destination most travellers are going to stumble upon. But if you've taken the time to get here, you'll be rewarded by a city rich in both culture and history.

Many of Nan's residents are Thai Lü, the ancestors of immigrants from Xishuangbanna, in southwestern China. This cultural legacy is seen in the city's art and architecture, particularly in its exquisite temples. A Lanna influence on the town can also be seen in the remains of the old city wall and several early wát.

History

For centuries Nan was an isolated, independent kingdom with few ties to the outside world. Ample evidence of prehistoric habitation exists, but it wasn't until several small *meuang* (city states) consolidated to form Nanthaburi in the mid-14th century that the city became a power to contend with. Towards the end of the 14th century, Nan became one of the nine northern Thai–Lao principalities that comprised Lan Na Thai. The city state flourished throughout the 15th century under the name Chiang Klang (Middle City), a reference to its position approximately midway between Chiang Mai (New City) and Chiang Thong (Golden City, today's Luang Prabang). The Burmese took control of the kingdom in 1558 and transferred many of the inhabitants to Burma as slaves; the city was all but abandoned until western Thailand was wrested from the Burmese in 1786. The local dynasty then regained regional sovereignty and it remained semi-autonomous until 1931, when Nan finally (and reluctantly) accepted full Bangkok sponsorship.

◉ Sights

★ **Wat Phumin**   BUDDHIST TEMPLE
(วัดภูมินทร์; cnr Th Suriyaphong & Th Pha Kong; donations appreciated; ⊙ daylight hours) Nan's most famous Buddhist temple is celebrated for its exquisite murals (p237) that were executed during the late 19th century by a Thai Lü artist named Thit Buaphan. The exterior of the temple takes the form of

Nan

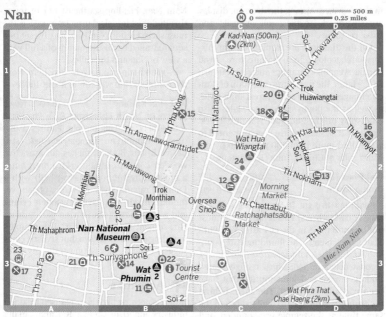

NORTHERN THAILAND NAN

a cruciform *bòht* that was constructed in 1596 and restored during the reign of Chao Anantavorapitthidet (1867–74). The ornate altar in the centre of the *bòht* has four sides, with four Sukhothai-style sitting Buddhas facing in each direction.

★ **Nan National Museum**　MUSEUM
(พิพิธภัณฑสถานแห่งชาติน่าน; Th Pha Kong; 100B; ◷9am-4pm Wed-Sun) Housed in the 1903 vin-tage palace of Nan's last two feudal lords, this museum first opened its doors in 1973. In terms of collection and content, it's one of the country's better provincial museums and has English labels for most items. It was closed for renovations at the time of writing, but is expected to reopen in 2019 with much the same focus.

The ground floor has ethnological exhib-its covering the various ethnic groups found in the province. Among the items on display are silverwork, textiles, folk utensils and tribal costumes.

On the 2nd floor are exhibits on Nan history, archaeology, local architecture, royal regalia, weapons, ceramics and religious art. Of the latter, the museum's collection of Buddha images includes some rare Lanna styles as well as the floppy-eared local styles. Also on display on the 2nd floor is a rare 'black' elephant tusk said to have been presented to a Nan lord more than 300 years ago by the Khün ruler of Chiang Tung (Kyaingtong).

Wat Phra That Chang Kham
BUDDHIST TEMPLE

(วัดพระธาตุช้างค้ำ; cnr Th Suriyaphong & Th Pha Kong; ⊙ daylight hours) This is the second-most important temple in the city after Wat Phra That Chae Haeng. The founding date is unknown, but the main *wí·hǎhn* (sanctuary), reconstructed in 1458, has a huge seated Buddha image and faint murals that have been partially recovered. The *chedi* behind the *wí·hǎhn* is thought to date to around the same time as the temple was founded, and features elephant supports similar to those seen in Sukhothai and Si Satchanalai.

Next to the *chedi* is a small, undistinguished *bòht* (ordination hall) from the same era. Wat Phra That Chang Kham's current abbot tells an interesting story involving the *bòht* and a Buddha image that was once kept inside. According to the abbot, in 1955 art historian AB Griswold offered to purchase the 145cm-tall Buddha inside the small *bòht*. The image appeared to be a crude Sukhothai-style walking Buddha moulded of plaster. After agreeing to pay the abbot 25,000B for the image, Griswold began removing the image – but as he did it fell and the plaster around the statue broke away to reveal an original Sukhothai Buddha of pure gold underneath. Needless to say, the abbot made Griswold give it back, much to the latter's chagrin. Did Griswold suspect what lay beneath the plaster? The abbot refuses to say.

The image is now kept behind a glass partition in the *hǒr đrai* (manuscript library) adjacent to the *wí·hǎhn,* the largest of its type in Thailand.

Wat Phra That Chae Haeng
BUDDHIST TEMPLE

(วัดพระธาตุแช่แห้ง; off Rte 1168; ⊙ daylight hours) Located 2km past the bridge that spans Mae Nam Nan, heading southeast out of town, this Buddhist temple dating from 1355 is the most sacred wát in Nan Province. It's set in a square walled enclosure on top of a hill with a view of Nan and the valley.

A round-trip motorcycle taxi here from the centre of Nan will run to about 100B.

Wat Hua Khuang
BUDDHIST TEMPLE

(วัดหัวข่วง; cnr Th Mahaphrom & Th Pha Kong; ⊙ daylight hours) This temple features a distinctive Lanna/Lan Xang-style *chedi* (stupa) with four Buddha niches, an attractive wooden *hǒr đrai* (manuscript library) and a noteworthy *bòht* (ordination hall) with a Luang Prabang–style carved wooden verandah. Inside is a carved wooden ceiling and a huge *naga* (semi-divine part-human, part-serpent creatures) altar. The temple's founding date is unknown, but stylistic clues suggest that this may be one of the city's oldest wát.

🏃 Activities

Nan has nothing like the organised trekking industry found in Chiang Rai and Chiang Mai, and many visitors, particularly Thais, opt to float rather than walk. White-water rafting along Mae Nam Wa, in northern Nan, is only possible when the water level is high (September to December), and is said to be best during the early part of the rainy season. The rapids span from classes I to IV and pass through intact jungle and remote villages.

Nan Touring
RAFTING

(☑ 081 961 7711; www.nantouring.com; 11/12 Th Suriyaphong; 3 days & 2 nights per person 5900B; ⊙ 9am-5pm) This outfit offers a variety of rafting trips for groups of at least five people.

Fhu Travel
TREKKING

(☑ 054 710636, 081 287 7209; www.facebook.com/fhutravel; 453/4 Th Sumon Thevarat; trekking per person 1700B; ⊙ 9am-6pm) This established outfit currently offers one-day treks around Nan.

🛏 Sleeping

Fah Place
HOTEL $

(☑ 054 710222; 237/8 Th Sumon Thevarat; r 400-450B; ❀ 🛜) The rooms here are vast and have been outfitted with attractive teak furniture, including flat-screen TVs and the kinds of puffy, inviting beds you'd expect at

WAT PHUMIN'S MAGNIFICENT MURALS

Wat Phumin is northern Thailand's Sistine Chapel, and the images on its walls are now found on everything from knick-knacks at Chiang Mai's night bazaar to postcards sold in Bangkok. Yet despite the seemingly happy scenes depicted, the murals were executed during a period that saw the end of Nan as a semi-independent kingdom. This resulted in several examples of political and social commentary manifesting themselves in the murals, a rarity in Thai religious art.

The murals commissioned by Jao Suliyaphong, the last king of Nan, include the *Khad-dhana Jataka,* a relatively obscure story of one of the Buddha's lives that, according to Thai historian David K Wyatt in his excellent book, *Reading Thai Murals,* has never been illustrated elsewhere in the Buddhist world. The story, which is on the left side of the temple's northern wall, depicts an orphan in search of his parents. Wyatt argues that this particular tale was chosen as a metaphor for the kingdom of Nan, which also had been abandoned by a succession of 'parents': the Thai kingdoms of Sukhothai, Chiang Mai and Ayuthaya. At roughly the same time as the murals were painted, Nan was fully incorporated into Siam by King Rama V, and much of its territory was allotted to France. Apparent discontent with this decision can be seen in a scene on the western wall that shows two male monkeys attempting to copulate against a background that, not coincidentally, according to Wyatt, resembles the French flag.

The murals are also valuable purely for their artistic beauty, something that is even more remarkable if you step back and consider the limited palette of colours that the artist, Thit Buaphan, had to work with. The paintings are also fascinating for their fly-on-the-wall depictions of local life in Nan during the end of the 19th century. A portrayal of three members of a hill tribe on the western wall includes such details as a man's immense goitre and a barking dog, suggesting this group's place as outsiders. Multiple depictions of a man wearing a feminine shawl, often seen performing traditionally female-only duties, are among the earliest depictions of *gà·teu·i* (transsexuals). And in what must be one of the art world's most superfluous cameos, the artist painted himself on the western wall, flirting with a woman. Considering that the murals took Thit Buaphan more than 20 years to complete, we'll grant him this indulgence.

places that charge several times this much; a terrific bargain.

Kaampuju
GUESTHOUSE $

(☏081 647 5758; www.facebook.com/kaampuju. nan; 14 Soi 2, Th Pha Kong; r incl breakfast 450-1200B; ✳️🛜) For a warm, homestay-like experience in Nan, consider Kaampuju. Rooms in the old wooden house are simple but spacious and welcoming. Be, your host, bakes her own bread, makes her own jams and knows all the best places in town to eat.

Banban Nannan Library
GUESTHOUSE $

(☏089 859 5898; www.facebook.com/banban nannan; 14/1 Th Monthian; r 350-1000B; 🛜) Although the four rooms in this wooden house are simple (all are fan-cooled and only one has an en suite bathroom), the setting – which spans an inviting garden – the eponymous library and a homely atmosphere more than make up for this.

Nan Guest House
HOTEL $

(☏054 771849, 081 288 8484; www.nanguest house.net; 57/15 Soi 2, Th Mahaphrom; r 300-450B; ✳️@🛜) In a quiet residential area a short walk from Nan's most famous temples, this long-standing and well-maintained place has 10 spotless, spacious rooms, half of which have private hot-water bathrooms, air-con, TV and fridge.

Nan Lanna Hotel
HOTEL $$

(☏054 772720; Trok Monthian; r 690-890B; ✳️🛜) Cool rooms with little natural light, but lots of space, big bathrooms and attractive retro-themed design touches. The location – it's near Nan's most famous temples – is another bonus.

Srinual Lodge
HOTEL $$

(☏054 710174; www.facebook.com/srinuallodge fanpage; 40/5 Th Nokham; r 880-1400B; ✳️🛜) This two-storey brick structure holds a couple dozen rooms decked out in a *faux rustique* style with logs, bamboo and local textiles. Despite the earthy design theme, the rooms look comfortable and are about as close as you'll get to sleeping near Mae Nam Nan.

★Pukha Nanfa Hotel HOTEL **$$$**
(☎054 771111; www.pukhananfahotel.co.th; 369 Th Sumon Thevarat; r incl breakfast 2600-4700B; ❄@📶) The former and forgettable Nan Fah Hotel has been painstakingly transformed into this charming boutique lodging. The 14 rooms are cosy and classy, with aged wood accentuated by touches such as local cloth, handicrafts and art. Antique adverts and pictures add to the old-world feel and, to top it off, the place is conveniently located and has highly capable staff.

Nan Nakara Boutique Hotel HOTEL **$$$**
(☎093 284 2707; www.nannakara.com; 16/1 Soi 1, Th Pha Kong; r incl breakfast 1600-2200B; ❄📶) This new, boutique place has white, almost dreamy rooms that consist of a separate sitting room with a wide-screen TV, and bedrooms (with yet another wide-screen) with spacious bathrooms with glass-fronted showers. A downside is the lack of natural light.

Eating

Despite its other charms, Nan has one of the least inspiring restaurant scenes in northern Thailand.

The town's **night market** (Th Pha Kong; mains 30-60B; ⏲5-11pm) provides a few decent food-stall offerings. Better yet is Nan's Saturday Walking Street, where dishes and tables are provided for takeaway northern Thai-style food.

Wan Da THAI **$**
(Th Kha Luang; mains 30-50B; ⏲8am-5pm) This local legend serves just about everything from curries ladled over rice to satay, but those in the know come for *kà·nŏm jeen* (fresh rice noodles served with various toppings).

Rak Khun THAI **$**
(Th Mano; mains 60-210B; ⏲11am-10pm Mon-Sat) In new digs by the bus station (there's no Roman-script sign), this place is a long-standing hit among locals. Don't miss *gài tôrt má·kwàan* (chicken fried with local spices) or *yam pàk gòot* (a salad of ferns).

Hot Bread INTERNATIONAL, THAI **$**
(38/1-2 Th Suriyaphong; mains 25-140B; ⏲7am-4pm; 🖉) This charming, retro-themed cafe and restaurant has a generous menu of Western-style breakfast dishes – including the eponymous and delicious homemade bread – and other Western and Thai items. Come for *kôw soy* (northern-style curry noodle soup) in the mornings.

NORTHERN THAILAND NAN

BUSES TO/FROM NAN

In addition to buses, there are also minivans to Ban Huay Kon (on the border with Laos; 95B, three hours, five departures from 5am to noon) and Phrae (83B, two hours, half-hourly 5.30am to 6pm).

DESTINATION	FARE (B)	DURATION (HR)	FREQUENCY
Bangkok	396-725	10-11	frequent 8-10am & 6.15-7.45pm
Chiang Mai	213-395	6	frequent 7.30am-5pm & 10.30pm
Chiang Rai	181	6	9am
Lampang	146-291	4	frequent 7.30am-10.30pm
Luang Prabang (Laos)	660	10	8am
Phayao	197	4	1.30pm
Phitsanulok	178	4	5 departures 7.45am-5.15pm
Phrae	78	2½	frequent 7.30am-10.30pm
Pua (for Doi Phu Kha National Park)	50	2	hourly 7am-5pm

Pu Som Restaurant
NORTHERN THAI $

(203/1 Th Khamyot; mains 35-90B; ⊙10am-10pm)
The emphasis here is on meat, served in the
local style as *lâhp* (a type of minced-meat 'salad') or *néu·a·nêung* (beef steamed over herbs
and served with a delicious galangal-based
dip). There's no English-language sign; look
for the illuminated 'est cola' ad.

Som Tam Thawt
THAI $

(Th Sumon Thevarat; mains 35-60B; ⊙10am-9pm
Tue-Sun) This tiny restaurant is known for its
sôm·đam tôrt (deep-fried papaya salad), an
equal parts crunchy and refreshing snack.
It also does fruit smoothies and other basic
dishes.

There's no Roman-script sign; it's located
roughly across from Fah Place hotel.

Shopping

Nan is one of the best places in northern
Thailand to pick up souvenirs. Good buys
include local textiles, especially the Thai
Lü weaving styles, which typically feature
red-and-black thread on white cotton in
floral, geometric and animal designs. Local
Hmong appliqué and Mien embroidery are
of excellent quality. Htin grass-and-bamboo
baskets and mats are worth a look, too.

Walking Street
MARKET

(Th Pha Kong; ⊙5-10pm Fri-Sun) Every Friday,
Saturday and Sunday afternoon, the stretch
of Th Pha Kong in front of Wat Phumin is
closed and vendors selling food, textiles,
clothing and local handicrafts set up shop.

> **WORTH A TRIP**
>
> ## NONG BUA
>
> The neat and tidy Thai Lü village of
> Nong Bua is famous for the Lü-style
> **Wat Nong Bua** (วัดหนองบัว; ⊙daylight
> hours). Featuring a typical two-tiered
> roof and carved wooden portico, the
> *wí·hǎhn* (sanctuary) design is simple
> yet striking – note the carved naga (ser-
> pent) heads at the roof corners. There
> is a model Thai Lü house directly behind
> the wát where weaving is done and you
> can buy attractive local textiles.
>
> Nong Bua is about 30km north of
> Nan, near the town of Tha Wang Pha.
> To get there, take a northbound bus or
> *sǒrng·tǎa·ou* (35B) to Tha Wang Pha.
> Get off at Samyaek Longbom, walk west
> to a bridge over Mae Nam Nan and turn
> left. Continue until you reach another
> small bridge, after which Wat Nong Bua
> will be on your right. It's a long 3km
> from the highway to the wát.

Nan Silver
ARTS & CRAFTS

(430/1 Th Sumon Thevarat; ⊙7.30am-6.30pm)
This small but classy shop sells a huge variety of locally designed and produced silver
items.

Amnouy Porn
ARTS & CRAFTS

(Th Sumon Thevarat; ⊙8am-7pm) This shop
sells a variety of local goods with an emphasis on textiles and clothing. There are a couple other similar shops nearby.

> ### ⓘ GETTING TO LAOS: BAN HUAY KON TO MUANG NGEUN
>
> Located 140km north of Nan, Ban Huay Kon is a sleepy village in the mountains near the
> Lao border. There's a border market on Saturday morning, but most will come here be-
> cause of the town's status as an international border crossing to Laos.
>
> **Getting to the border** To Ban Huay Kon, there are five daily minivans originating in
> Phrae and stopping in Nan between 5am and noon (95B, three hours). In the opposite
> direction, minivans bound for Nan (95B, three hours), Phrae (172B, five hours) and Den
> Chai (for the train; 200B) leave Ban Huay Kon at 9.15am, 10am, 11am, noon and 3pm.
>
> **At the border** After passing the Thai immigration booth, foreigners can purchase a 30-
> day visa for Laos for US$30 to US$42, depending on nationality. There is an extra US$1
> or 50B charge after 4pm and on weekends.
>
> **Moving on** You can then proceed 2.5km to the Lao village of Muang Ngeun, where
> you could stay at the Phouxay Guesthouse or, if you're heading onward, go to the tiny
> Passenger Car Station beside the market, from where *sǒrng·tǎa·ou* leave for Hongsa
> (40,000K, 1½ hours) between 2pm and 4pm.

GHOST-LAND

The name **Phae Meuang Phi**
(แพะเมืองผี; off Rte 101; ⊙6am-6pm)
FREE means Ghost-Land, a reference to
bizarre pillars of soil and rock that look
like giant fungi, most likely the result of
erosion rather than the paranormal. The
area has been made a provincial park;
a few walking trails and viewpoints are
recent additions. There are picnic pavilions in the park and food vendors selling
gài yâhng (grilled chicken), *sôm·đam*
(papaya salad) and sticky rice near the
entrance.

The park is located approximately
18km northeast of Phrae off Rte 101;
getting there by public transport
is not an option. You can charter a
sŏrng·tăa·ou for about 600B.

Peera
ARTS & CRAFTS

(26 Th Suriyaphong; ⊙8am-7pm) A short
walk from Wat Phumin, this place offers
high-quality local textiles, mostly comprising women's skirts and blouses.

Kad-Nan
MARKET

(43 Th Mahayot; ⊙10am-10pm) This open-air
mall is Nan's answer to Bangkok's Chatuchak
Weekend Market. Here you'll find shops selling local knick-knacks, art and clothing, restaurants, coffee shops and bars. The market
is technically open from 10am, but evening,
when most shops and restaurants are open
and live music gives the place a fair-like atmosphere, is the best time to visit.

ⓘ Information

Bangkok Bank (Th Sumon Thewarat;
⊙8.30am-4.30pm Mon-Sat) Operates foreign-exchange services and has ATMs. It is near
the Nan Fah and Dhevaraj hotels.

Police Station (☑24hr emergency 191; cnr Th
Suriyaphong & Th Sumon Thewarat; ⊙24hr)
Nan's main police station.

Siam Commercial Bank (Th Anantaworarit-
tidet; ⊙8.30am-4.30pm Mon-Sat) ATM and
foreign exchange.

Tourist Centre (☑054 751 169; Th Pha Kong;
⊙8.30am-noon & 1-4.30pm) Opposite Wat
Phumin, this helpful information centre is
hidden behind vendors and coffee shops.

Tourist Police (☑nationwide 1155; Th Suriyaphong; ⊙24hr)

ⓘ Getting There & Away

Nan's recently renovated Nan Nakhon Airport
is located about 3km north of town. **Air Asia**
(☑Nan Nakhon Airport 054 772635, nationwide
02 515 9999; www.airasia.com; Nan Nakhon
Airport; ⊙7am-4.30pm) and **Nok Air** (☑Nan
Nakhon Airport 091 119 9834, nationwide
1318; www.nokair.com; Nan Nakhon Airport;
⊙8am-7pm) have flights to/from Bangkok's
Don Mueang International Airport (from 935B,
1½ hours, five to six daily). **Klay Airport Taxi**
(☑086 188 0079; Nan Nakhon Airport) offers
airport transfers for about 100B per person.

From Nan, all buses, minivans and *sŏrng·tăa·o*
(passenger pick-up trucks) leave from the **bus
station** (☑054 711 662; Th Jao Fa) at the southwestern edge of town. A motorcycle taxi between
the station and the centre of town costs 30B.

If you're connecting to the train station at Den
Chai in Phrae, you can hop on any bus bound for
Chiang Mai or Bangkok.

ⓘ Getting Around

Avis (☑Nan Nakhon Airport 061 386 9646,
nationwide 02 251 1131; www.avisthailand.
com; Nan Nakhon Airport; ⊙8am-7pm) and
Thai Rent a Car (☑Nan Nakhon Airport 054
059649, nationwide 1647; www.thairentacar.
com; Nan Nakhon Airport; ⊙8am-6pm) have
booths at Nan Airport.

Săhm·lór (pedicabs) around town cost 30B to
40B. **Nan Taxi** (☑054 773555, 084 610 7777)
has metered taxis.

Oversea Shop (☑054 710258; 488 Th Sumon
Thevarat; ⊙8.30am-5.30pm) and **Thana Sin
Motors** (TS; ☑089 953 0896; 1-7 Th Sumon
Thevarat; ⊙8am-5pm Mon-Sat) , as well as
several guesthouses, hire out motorcycles
(from 200B).

Around Nan

Ban Bo Luang
บ้านบ่อหลวง

☑054 / POP 1000

Ban Bo Luang (also known as Ban Bo Kleua
or Salt Well Village) is a picturesque Htin
village southeast of Doi Phu Kha National
Park where the long-standing occupation
has been the extraction of salt from local salt
wells. It's easy to find the main community
salt wells, which are more or less in the centre of the village.

If you have your own transport, the village is a good base for exploring the nearby
national parks, Doi Phu Kha and **Khun Nan
National Park** (อุทยานแห่งชาติขุนน่าน; ☑054
778140; adult/child 100/50B; ⊙8am-4.30pm).

The latter is located a few kilometres north of Ban Bo Luang and has a 2km walk from the visitor centre that ends in a viewpoint looking over local villages and nearby Laos.

🛏 Sleeping & Eating

There is a handful of places to stay in Ban Bo Luang, including a few simple midrange 'resorts' and homestay-style accommodation. Alternatively, there is accommodation at Khun Nan National Park and farther afield, at Doi Phu Kha National Park.

★**Boklua View**   RESORT **$$$**
(📞081 809 6392; www.bokluaview.com; r & bungalows incl breakfast 1850B; ❄️ 🛜) By far the best place to stay in Ban Bo Luang is Boklua View, an attractive and well-run hillside resort overlooking the village and Nam Mang which runs through it. The resort has its own garden and serves good food (be sure to try Chef Toun's chicken deep-fried with northern Thai spices).

Hua Saphan   THAI **$**
(mains 70-120B; ⊗9am-9pm) This is probably the best of the few small restaurants serving basic dishes in Ban Bo Luang; there's no Roman-script sign, but it's located at the foot of the bridge.

ℹ Information

At the time of research, Bo Luang's only ATM did not accept foreign cards, so be sure to bring cash.

ℹ Getting There & Away

To reach Ban Bo Luang from Nan, take a bus to Pua (50B, two hours, hourly from 6am to 6pm). Get off at the 7-Eleven and cross the highway to take the *sŏrng·tăa·ou* that terminates in the village (80B, one hour, departing 7.30am, 9.30am and 11.30am). To Pua, *sŏrng·tăa·ou* leave from near Bo Luang's T-intersection at 9am, 10.30am and 12.30pm.

Doi Phu Kha National Park   อุทยานแห่งชาติดอยภูคา

This **national park** (📞082 194 1349, accommodation 02 562 0760; www.dnp.go.th; 200B) is centred on 2000m-high Doi Phu Kha, the province's highest peak, in Amphoe Pua and Amphoe Bo Kleua, about 75km northeast of Nan. There are several Htin, Mien, Hmong and Thai Lü villages in the park and vicinity, as well as a couple of caves and waterfalls,

and endless opportunities for forest walks. The park is often cold in the cool season and especially wet in the wet season.

Park HQ has a basic map, and staff can arrange a local guide for walks or more extended excursions around the area, plus rafting on Nam Wa.

The park offers a variety of bungalows (two to seven people 300B to 2000B), and there is a nearby restaurant and basic shop.

To reach the national park by public transport you must first take a bus or *sŏrng·tăa·ou* to Pua (50B, two hours, hourly 7am to 5pm). Get off at the 7-Eleven then cross the highway to board one of the three daily *sŏrng·tăa·ou* (50B, 30 minutes) that depart at 7.30am, 9.30am and 11.30am.

PHRAE PROVINCE

Phrae (จังหวัดแพร่) is a rural, mountainous province most often associated with teak. Despite a nationwide ban on logging, there's not a whole lot of the hardwood left, and the little that does exist is under threat.

Phrae   แพร่
📞054 / POP 18,000

Walking around the older parts of Phrae, one is struck by similarities with the historic Lao city of Luang Prabang: ample greenery, traditional wood buildings and scenic temples dominate the scenery, and monks form a significant part of the traffic. The city's residents must be among the friendliest folks in Thailand, and Phrae's location on the banks of Mae Nam Yom and its ancient wall also invite comparisons with Chiang Mai. Yet despite all this, Phrae is a little-visited city and a great destination for those who require little more than a few low-key attractions, good local food and cheery company.

⊙ Sights

⊙ In Town

Wat Luang   BUDDHIST TEMPLE
(วัดหลวง; Soi 1, Th Kham Leu; ⊗daylight hours) This is the oldest *wát* in Phrae, probably dating from the founding of the city in the 12th or 13th century.

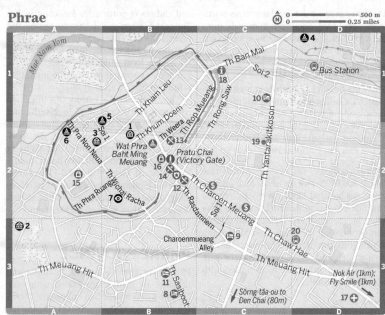

Phrae

Phrae

The verandah of the main *wí·hăhn* (sanctuary) is in the classic Luang Prabang–Lan Xang style but has unfortunately been bricked in with laterite. Opposite the front of the *wí·hăhn* is Pratu Khong, part of the city's original entrance gate. No longer used as a gate, it now contains a statue of Chao Pu, an early Lanna ruler.

Phra That Luang Chang Kham, the large octagonal Lanna-style *chedi*, sits on a square base with elephants supporting it on all four sides. As is sometimes seen in Phrae and Nan, the *chedi* is occasionally swathed in Thai Lü fabric.

Also on the temple grounds is a **museum** displaying temple antiques, ceramics and religious art dating from the Lanna, Nan, Bago and Mon periods. The 16th-century, Phrae-made sitting Buddha on the 2nd floor is particularly exquisite. There are also some 19th-century photos with English labels on display, including some gruesome shots of a beheading. The museum is usually open weekends only, but the monks will sometimes open it on weekdays on request.

Wat Phra Non
BUDDHIST TEMPLE

(วัดพระนอน; Th Phra Non Neua; ⊙daylight hours) Located west of Wat Luang is a 300-year-old wát named after its highly revered reclining Buddha image. The *bòht* (ordination hall) was built around 200 years ago and has an impressive roof with a separate, two-tiered portico and gilded, carved, wooden facade with Ramayana scenes. The adjacent *wí·hăhn* contains the Buddha image, swathed in Thai Lü cloth with bead and foil decoration.

Wat Jom Sawan
BUDDHIST TEMPLE

(วัดจอมสวรรค์; Th Ban Mai; ⊙daylight hours) Outside the old city, this temple was built by local Shan in the late 19th and early 20th centuries, and shows Shan and Burmese influences throughout. An adjacent copper-crowned *chedi* has lost most of its stucco to reveal the artful brickwork beneath. Since a recent renovation, Wat Jom Sawan is more of a museum piece than a functioning temple.

◉ Outside of Town

Wat Phra That Cho Hae
BUDDHIST TEMPLE

(วัดพระธาตุช่อแฮ; off Rte 1022; ⊙daylight hrs) **FREE** Named for the cloth that worshippers wrap around it, this hilltop wát is famous for its 33m-high gilded *chedi* (stupa). Like Chiang Mai's Wat Doi Suthep, it is an important pilgrimage site for Thais living in the north.

Tiered *naga* stairs lead to the temple compound. The interior of the *bòht* (chapel) is rather tackily decorated with a gilded wooden ceiling, rococo pillars and walls with lotus-bud mosaics. The Phra Jao Than Jai Buddha image here, which resembles the Phra Chinnarat in Phitsanulok, is reputed to impart fertility to women who make offerings to it.

The temple is 9km southeast of town off Rte 1022. Sŏrng·tăa·ou between Phrae and Phra That Cho Hae (20B) depart from a stop near Talat Phrae Preeda, on Th Chaw Hae, from 6am to 4.30pm; outside these hours *sŏrng·tăa·ou* can be chartered for 400B.

🛏 Sleeping

Paradorn Hotel
HOTEL $

(☎054 511177; kanthatham@hotmail.com; 177 Th Yantarakitkoson; incl breakfast r 330-590B, ste 900-1200B; ❄️ 🛜) A decent budget choice a short walk from the bus terminal. Rooms here feel authentically vintage, have private balconies and are fan- or air-con-cooled.

Phoomthai Garden
HOTEL $$

(☎054 627359; www.phoomthaigarden.com; 31 Th Sasiboot; r incl breakfast 1200-2000B; ❄️ @ 🛜 ♨️) Although it's a bit of a hike from the old town, this boutique hotel is the best all-around choice in Phrae. The rooms are attractive, modern and comfortable, and all have balconies overlooking the hotel's garden. A new swimming pool seals the deal.

It's about 300m south of the former town wall on Th Sasiboot.

Mee Bed & Breakfast
HOTEL $$

(☎054 061073; www.facebook.com/meebedandbreakfast; 16/5 Th Rasdamnern; ⊙r incl breakfast 690B; ❄️ 🛜) An industrial-chic-themed cube holding 12 rooms. There's little natural light, but lots of space, wall paintings and free use of bikes make up for this. A great midrange catch.

Huern na na
HOTEL $$$

(☎054 524800; 7/9 Th Sasiboot; incl breakfast r 1800, ste 3200-3600B; ❄️ 🛜 ♨️) Rooms at Phrae's most sophisticated hotel are spacious and come decked out in both contemporary and northern Thai-style themes, as well as thoughtful amenities: suites throw in a jacuzzi or kitchenette.

You'll find it off Th Sasiboot, about 250m south of Th Meuang Hit.

🍴 Eating & Drinking

Phrae's entertainment zone is the road leading to the bus station; there you'll fine several loud bars and karaoke joints.

Saeng Fah Laep
THAI $

(Th Charoen Meuang; mains 10-40B; ⊙9am-7pm) This friendly, family-run establishment sells Thai sweets, including a tasty *kôw něe·o má·môo·ang* (mango sticky rice). There's no English sign, but it's the old shophouse just west of the police station.

Night Market
THAI $

(Th Rop Mueang; mains 30-60B; ⊙6-10pm) A small but fun night market convenes around

PHRAE'S TEAK MANSIONS

The lucrative teak trade led to Phrae being home to more than its fair share of beautiful antique mansions, some of which are open for visitors to peek inside.

Vongburi House (บ้านวงศ์บุรี; 50 Th Kham Leu; 30B; ⊙9am-5pm) The two-storey teak house of the last prince of Phrae has been converted into a private museum. It was constructed between 1897 and 1907 for Luang Phongphibun and his wife Chao Sunantha, who once held a profitable teak concession in the city. Inside, many of the house's 20 rooms display late 19th-century teak antiques, documents (including early 20th-century slave concessions), photos and other artefacts from the bygone teak-dynasty era.

Khum Jao Luang (คุ้มเจ้าหลวง; Th Khum Doem; ⊙8.30am-5pm) FREE Built in 1892, this imposing building, sporting a mixture of Thai and European architectural styles, was the home of the final Lord, or Chao Luang, of Phrae. The structure subsequently served as a governor's residence, and is today a museum on local history (no English signage). Ask to see the basement, which was used to punish and house slaves and prisoners.

Wichairacha House (คุ้มวิไชยราชา; 8 Th Wichai Racha; ⊙daylight hours) FREE This beautiful teak mansion is thought to have been built in 1898 by Cantonese artisans. Efforts are being made to turn the house into a museum, though at the time of research the work was far from complete.

Pratubjai House (บ้านประทับใจ; 100B; ⊙8am-5pm) Known in Thai as Baan Pratubjai (Impressive House), this is a large northern Thai-style teak house that was built using more than 130 teak logs, each over 300 years old. It's rather tackily decorated, so don't take the moniker 'impressive' too seriously. It's somewhat difficult to find; your best bet is to exit at the west gate of the former city wall and follow the signs, turning right after the school. A săhm·lór (three-wheel pedicab) here should cost about 60B.

the Pratu Chai (Victory Gate) intersection every evening.

Pan Jai
NORTHERN THAI $

(2 Th Weera; mains 20-40B; ⊙7am-10pm) During the day, the emphasis here is on *kà·nŏm jeen* (fresh rice noodles served with various curries and herbs). At night, locals come for *mŏo gà·tá* (DIY barbecue). There's no Roman-script marking, so look for the yellow sign.

Gingerbread House Café & Gallery
THAI $

(Th Charoen Meuang; mains 50-120B; ⊙8.30am-6pm Mon-Fri, to 7pm Sat & Sun; ❄ 🔊) This modern cafe offers air-con and an English-language menu of quick, light, fried-rice-type dishes. There's a small handicrafts shop here.

🛍 Shopping

Phrae is known for the distinctive *sêua môr hôrm,* the indigo-dyed cotton farmer's shirt seen all over northern Thailand. The cloth is made in Ban Thung Hong, just outside the city, but you can pick it up in town at **Maw Hawm Anian** (36 Th Charoen Meuang; ⊙7am-8.30pm).

Kat Korng Kow
MARKET

(Th Kham Leu; ⊙2-8pm Sat) Every Saturday afternoon Phrae hosts Kat Korng Kow, an open-air market held at the western end of Th Kham Leu. It's mostly food, but there's also a few souvenirs and handicrafts.

ℹ Information

Bangkok Bank (Th Charoen Meuang; ⊙8.30am-4.30pm Mon-Fri) A bank with ATM in Phrae.

Krung Thai Bank (Th Charoen Meuang; ⊙8.30am-4.30pm Mon-Fri) Bank with ATM in Phrae.

Phrae Hospital (☑054 522444; Th Chaw Hae) Phrae's main hospital is located southeast of town.

Police Station (Th Charoen Meuang; ⊙24hr) Phrae's main police station.

Tourism Authority of Thailand (TAT; ☑054 521127, nationwide 1627; tatphrae@tat.or.th; Th Ban Mai; ⊙8.30am-4.30pm) Brand-new office just east of the centre of town. English-speaking staff and volunteers are keen to lend a hand.

ℹ Getting There & Away

At research time, the only airline operating out of Phrae's tiny airport was **Nok Air** (☑054

522189, nationwide 1318; www.nokair.com; Phrae Airport; ⊗ 8am-5pm), with two daily flights (1810B, one hour) to/from Bangkok's Don Mueang International Airport. From the airport, 2.5km east of the city centre, **Fly Smile** (☑ 094 629 5151; Phrae Airport; ⊗ 8am-5pm Mon-Sat) can provide transport to your hotel (100B).

Unlike most cities in Thailand, Phrae's **bus and minivan terminal** (☑ 054 511800; off Th Yantarakitkoson) is located within walking distance of a few accommodation options.

Phrae's closest rail link, **Den Chai station** (☑ 054 613260, nationwide 1690; www.railway.co.th; Den Chai), is 23km south of town. There are frequent **blue sŏrng·tăa·ou** (Th Yantakarakitkoson) to Den Chai (40B, 40 minutes, 6.30am to 5.30pm), departing from a stop in front of Phrae Vocational College, or you can charter one for 400B.

Getting Around

A săhm·lór within the old town costs around 40B. Motorcycle taxis are available at the bus

TRANSPORT TO/FROM PHRAE
Buses

DESTINATION	FARE (B)	DURATION (HR)	FREQUENCY
Bangkok	385-599	8	hourly 9.15am-9pm
Chiang Khong	238-298	4½	5 departures 2am-4pm
Chiang Mai	171-266	4	frequent 12.10am-5.45pm
Chiang Rai	185-216	4	frequent 5am-6pm
Chiang Saen	261	5	2.30pm
Lampang	99-154	2	frequent 12.10am-5.45pm
Mae Sai	225-263	5	hourly 1.30am-11.40pm
Nan	101-157	2	6 departures 10.30am-8.45pm
Phayao	121-141	2	frequent 5am-6pm
Phitsanulok	133-160	3	5 departures 10am-2.20pm
Sukhothai	105-127	3	5 departures 10am-2.20pm

Minivans

DESTINATION	FARE (B)	DURATION (HR)	FREQUENCY
Ban Huay Kon (border with Laos)	180	5	5 departures 3am-7.10pm
Chiang Rai	165	4½	hourly 5am-6pm
Lampang	80	2	hourly 6am-5.20pm
Nan	83	2	frequent 3am-6.50pm
Phayao	102	2	hourly 5am-6pm

Trains

DESTINATION	FARE (B)	DURATION (HR)	FREQUENCY
Bangkok	155-1291	9-11	8 daily
Chiang Mai	72-549	4-6	7 daily
Lampang	50-968	2	4 daily
Phitsanulok	30-348	3½	8 daily

terminal; a trip from here to Pratu Chai (Victory Gate) should cost around 40B. **Sangfa Motor** (☑ 054 521598; 163/8 Th Yantarakitkoson; per 24hr 200B; ◷ 8am-4.30pm) is a motorcycle dealership that also hires out bikes.

LAMPHUN PROVINCE

This tiny province southeast of Chiang Mai consists of little more than a small city surrounded by farms, villages and an easily accessible national park.

Lamphun   ลำพูน

☑ 053 / POP 14,000

A convenient culture stop for Chiang Mai sightseers, this provincial capital sits quietly along the banks of Mae Kuang, a tributary of Mae Ping.

There's not much fanfare regarding Lamphun's status as one of Thailand's oldest cities. The old fortress wall and ancient temples are surviving examples of the city's former life as the northernmost outpost of the ancient Mon Dvaravati kingdom, then known as Hariphunchai (AD 750–1281). During part of this period, the area was ruled by Chama Thewi, a Mon queen who has earned legendary status among Thailand's constellation of historic rulers.

The 26km voyage along a former highway between Chiang Mai and Lamphun is one of the city's primary attractions. It's a beautiful country road, stretches of which are canopied by tall dipterocarp trees.

◉ Sights

Wat Phra That Hariphunchai   BUDDHIST TEMPLE
(วัดพระธาตุหริภุญชัย; Th Inthayongyot; 20B; ◷ 6am-9pm) This temple, Lamphun's most famous, spans back to the Mon period, having originally been built on the site of Queen Chama Thewi's palace in 1044 (or 1108 or 1157 according to some datings). The temple boasts some interesting architecture, a couple of fine Buddha images and two old *chedi* (stupas) in the original Hariphunchai style. The compound lay derelict until Khru Ba Sriwichai, a famous northern Thai monk, ordered renovations in the 1930s.

Hariphunchai National Museum   MUSEUM
(พิพิธภัณฑสถานแห่งชาติหริภุญไชย; Th Inthayongyot; 100B; ◷ 9am-4pm Wed-Sun) Across the street from Wat Phra That Hariphunchai is the informative Hariphunchai National Museum. Inside is a collection of Mon and Lanna artefacts and Buddhas from the Dvaravati kingdom, as well as a stone inscription gallery with Mon and Thai Lanna scripts. There is a small bookshop with some English titles.

Wat Chama Thewi   BUDDHIST TEMPLE
(วัดจามเทวี; Th Chamadevi; ◷ daylight hours) An unusual Hariphunchai *chedi* (stupa) can be seen at Wat Chama Thewi. The structure dates to around the 13th century, but has been restored many times since then and is now a mixture of several schools of architecture. Each side of the *chedi* has five rows of three Buddha figures, diminishing in size on each higher level. The standing Buddhas, although recently sculpted, are in Dvaravati style.

It's located about 1.5km from Wat Phra That Hariphunchai; you can take a motorcycle taxi (20B) from in front of the national museum.

USE YOUR MELON

Diminutive Wat Suchadaram, at **Wat Phra Kaew Don Tao** (p246), is said to be located on the former melon patch (*dorn dôw*) of Mae (Mother) Suchada, a pious local woman. It is said that during a time of famine, a monk appeared and was given an unusually shaped melon by Mae Suchada. Upon opening the melon, the monk found a large green gem inside, and with the help of Mae Suchada, as well as the divine intervention of Indra, the gem was shaped into a Buddha image.

Villagers suspected the collaboration between the monk and Mae Suchada of being a bit too friendly, and in a fit of rage, beheaded Suchada. Upon later realising their mistake (the beheading led to yet another famine), a temple was built in the woman's honour. Today the emerald Buddha image is held at **Wat Phra That Lampang Luang** (p251).

SPEAKING NORTHERN THAI

Northerners used to take offence when outsiders tried speaking *găm méuang* (the colloquial name for the northern dialect) to them, an attitude that dates back to a time when central Thais considered northerners to be very backward and made fun of their dialect. Nowadays, most northerners are proud of their native language, and speaking a few words of the local lingo will go a long way in getting them to open up. The following are words and phrases that will help you talk to, flirt with, or perhaps just win some smiles from the locals.

Ôo găm méuang bòr jâhng I can't speak northern Thai.

A yăng gór? What did you say?

An née tôw dai? How much is this?

Mee kôw nêung bòr? Do you have sticky rice?

Lám đáa đáa Delicious

Mâan lâ Yes/That's right.

Yin dee nôe Thank you

Bòr mâan No

Gàht Market

Jôw (A polite word used by women; equivalent to the central Thai *ka*.)

⭐ Festivals & Events

Songkran　　　　　　　　　　CULTURAL
(⊘mid-Apr) Should Chiang Mai's water fight be too wet and wild for your taste, Lamphun hosts a milder, more traditional affair in mid-April.

Lam Yai Festival　　　　　FOOD & DRINK
(⊘mid-Aug) During the second week of August, Lamphun hosts the annual festival spotlighting its primary agricultural product. It features floats made of fruit and, of course, a Miss Lam Yai contest.

🛏 Sleeping & Eating

You're unlikely to stay overnight as Lamphun is so close to Chiang Mai.

There is a string of decent **noodle shops** (Th Inthayongyot; mains 30-90B) on Lamphun's main street, just south of Wat Phra That Hariphunchai.

Dao Kanong　　　　　　　　　THAI $
(340 Th Charoen Rat (Th Chiang Mai-Lamphun); mains 30-90B; ⊘9.30am-8pm) Long-standing Dao Kanong has a huge selection of northern Thai dishes. It's 1.5km east of Wat Phra That Hariphunchai.

🛍 Shopping

Kad Khua Moong Tha Sing　　MARKET
(Th Rop Mueang Nai; ⊘9am-6pm) Located just east of Wat Phra That Hariphunchai, Kad Khua Moong Tha Sing is a souvenir market selling local items such as dried *lam yai* (longan fruit) and silk.

ℹ Getting There & Away

Frequent blue *sŏrng·tǎa·ou* and purple buses bound for Lamphun leave from Chiang Mai's Chang Pheuak terminal, a stop on Th Praisani in front of Talat Warorot, and from another stop on the eastern side of the river on Th Chiang Mai-Lamphun, just south of the Tourist Authority of Thailand (TAT) office, during daylight hours (25B, 30 minutes). Both can drop you off on Th Inthayongyot at the stop in front of the national museum and Wat Phra That Hariphunchai.

Minibuses and *sŏrng·tǎa·ou* (25B, 30 minutes, 6am to 5.30pm) return to Chiang Mai from the stop in front of the national museum or from the city's bus terminal on Th Sanam.

Doi Khun Tan National Park

This 225-sq-km **national park** (อุทยานแห่งชาติดอยขุนตาล; ☏053 546335, accommodation 02 562 0760; www.dnp.go.th; 200B; ⊘8am-5pm) straddles the mountains between Lamphun and Lampang Provinces. It ranges in elevation from 350m at the bamboo forest lowlands to 1363m at the pine-studded summit of Doi Khun Tan. Wildflowers, including orchids, ginger and lilies, are abundant. At the park headquarters there are maps of well-marked trails that range from short walks around the headquarter's vicinity to hikes covering the mountain's four peaks; there's also a trail to **Nam Tok Tat Moei** (7km roundtrip).

The park is very popular on cool-season weekends.

Intersecting the mountain slopes is Thailand's longest train tunnel (1352m), which opened in 1921 after six years of manual labour by thousands of Lao workers (several of whom are said to have been killed by tigers).

Bungalows (500B to 2700B) sleeping between two and nine people are available near the park headquarters, where there's also a restaurant.

The main access to the park is from the Khun Tan train station. To check timetables and prices from various destinations, call the **State Railway of Thailand** (☏ 053 245363, nationwide 1690; Th Charoen Muang) or check its website. Once at the Khun Tan station, cross the tracks and follow a steep, marked path 1.3km to the park headquarters. By car, take the Chiang Mai–Lampang highway to the Mae Tha turn-off then follow the signs along a steep unpaved road for 18km.

LAMPANG PROVINCE

Formerly associated with the logging trade, today Lampang Province (จังหวัดลำปาง) is more closely linked to industries such as mining and ceramics. It's a vast, mountainous province known for its natural beauty, a pleasant provincial capital and for some of northern Thailand's most emblematic Buddhist temples.

Lampang ลำปาง

☏ 054 / POP 59,000

Are you the type of traveller who wants to say that you were there first, before it became *too* cool? Well you just might have your chance in Lampang. Drawn to the city's riverside charm, locals and outsiders have

opened a small but growing spread of hip cafes, tasty restaurants and image-conscious hotels in recent years – in addition to the city's gorgeous antique buildings and two of the best markets in the north. Yet despite all this, Lampang sees relatively few visitors, giving it more of an undiscovered feel than some of the more touristy destinations in the north.

History

Although Lampang Province was inhabited as far back as the 7th century in the Dvaravati period, legend has it that Lampang city was founded by the son of Hariphunchai's (modern-day Lamphun's) Queen Chama Thewi and that the city played an important part in the history of the Hariphunchai Kingdom.

Like Chiang Mai, Phrae and other older northern cities, modern Lampang was built as a walled rectangle alongside a river (in this case, Mae Wang). At the end of the 19th and beginning of the 20th century, Lampang, along with nearby Phrae, became an important centre for the domestic and international teak trade. A large British-owned timber company brought in Burmese supervisors familiar with the teak industry in Burma to train Burmese and Thai loggers in the area. These well-paid supervisors, along with independent Burmese teak merchants who plied their trade in Lampang, sponsored the construction of more than a dozen temples in the city, a legacy that lives on in several of Lampang's most impressive wát and the beautiful antique homes along Th Talad Gao.

◎ Sights & Activities

Wat Phra Kaew Don Tao   BUDDHIST TEMPLE
(วัดพระแก้วดอนเต้า; off Th Phra Kaew; 20B; ⊙daylight hours) The main *chedi* shows Hariphunchai influence, while the adjacent *mon·dòp* (the small square-sided building with a spire) was built in 1909. The *mon·dòp* is decorated with glass mosaic in typical Burmese style and contains a Mandalay-style Buddha image. From 1436 to 1468, Wat Phra Kaew Don Tao was among four wát in northern Thailand to have housed the Emerald Buddha (now in Bangkok's Wat Phra Kaew).

A display of Lanna artefacts can be viewed in the wát's **Lanna Museum** (พิพิธภัณฑ์ล้านนา; Wat Phra Kaew Don Tao; admission by donation; ⊙7am-6pm).

Adjacent to the temple complex, **Wat Suchadaram** (วัดสุชาดาราม; off Th Phra Kaew; ☉daylight hours) dates back to 1809 and is named after Mae Suchada, the central figure in a local legend.

Th Talad Gao
AREA

(ถนนตลาดเก่า; Th Talad Gao) Lampang's multicultural history can be seen along this riverside street, which is lined with old homes, temples and shophouses showcasing Thai, English, Chinese and Burmese architectural styles. It's also where the town's weekly Walking Street (p251) market is held.

Dhanabadee Ceramic Museum
MUSEUM

(พิพิธภัณฑ์เซรามิคธนบดี; www.dhanabadeeceramicmuseum.com; off Soi 1, Th Phrabat; incl guided tour 100B; ☉9am-5pm) Dhanabadee claims to be the first producer of the emblematic 'chicken bowls' used across Thailand. In 2013 the company opened its doors to visitors and began running guided tours (English-language tours are given every hour on the hour from 9am to 4pm) that span a history of the chicken bowl in Thailand and the various steps involved in making them.

The museum is located about 500m south of Th Phahonyothin/AH2.

Baan Sao Nak
MUSEUM

(บ้านเสานัก; 85 Th Radwattana; 50B; ☉10am-5pm) A huge Lanna-style house built in 1895 and supported by 116 square teak pillars, Baan Sao Nak was once owned by a local *kun-yǐng* (a title equivalent to 'Lady' in England); it now serves as a local museum. The entire house is furnished with mildly interesting Burmese and Thai antiques, but the structure itself and its manicured garden are the highlights.

Wat Pongsanuk Tai
BUDDHIST TEMPLE

(วัดปงสนุกใต้; Th Pongsnook; ☉daylight hours) Despite having lost much of its character in a renovation, the *mon-dòp* at Wat Pongsanuk Tai is still one of the few remaining local examples of original Lanna-style temple architecture, which emphasised open-sided wooden buildings. To get an idea of what it was like previously, look at the carved wooden gateway at the entrance to the north stairway.

A couple of informal museums on the temple grounds display local artefacts, but they include little English explanation.

Wat Si Rong Meuang
BUDDHIST TEMPLE

(วัดศรีรองเมือง; Th Thakhrao Noi; ☉daylight hours) Wat Si Rong Meuang was built in the late 19th century by Burmese artisans. The temple building was constructed in the Burmese 'layered' style, with tin roofs gabled by intricate woodcarvings.

Phum Lakhon Museum
MUSEUM

(พิพิธภัณฑ์เมืองของชาวลำปาง; cnr Th Chatchai & Th Thakhrao Noi; ☉8.30am-4.30pm Mon-Fri) **FREE** A brief but engaging museum that employs multimedia displays to tell the story of the history, people and culture of Lampang.

Horse Carts

Lampang is the only town in Thailand where horse carts are still found. Now fully relegated to tourists, you can't miss the brightly coloured carts that drip with plastic flowers and are handled by stetson-wearing drivers. A 30-minute tour (300B) goes along Mae Wang, while a one-hour tour (400B) stops at Wat Phra Kaew Don Tao and Wat Si Rong Meuang.

Horse carts can be found waiting on Th Suandawg, across from Pin Hotel, and at another stall on Th Boonyawat, just east of the market, from around 5am to 9pm.

🛏 Sleeping

Chita Coffee & Guesthouse
GUESTHOUSE $

(☎054 323370; www.facebook.com/chitacoffeeguesthouse; 143 Th Talad Gao; r 350-750B; ❊🛜) Located smack dab in the middle of historic Th Talad Gao, Chita offers relatively stylish budget rooms above a cafe. The cheapest are closet-sized, fan-cooled and share a bathroom.

Akhamsiri Home
HOTEL $

(☎054 228791; 54/1 Th Pamaikhet; r 590B; ❊@🛜) The tagline here ought to be 'Mid-range amenities at a budget price'. The large cool rooms are located in a tidy residential compound and all have TV, fridge and a garden/balcony. Communicating in English may be problematic.

TT&T Guest House
GUESTHOUSE $

(☎054 221303; 82 Th Pa Mai; r 250-650B; ❊🛜) This long-standing place has an appropriately old-school backpacker vibe. Rooms are bare (only two have air-con) and most bathrooms are shared, but the pleasant riverfront location and expansive chill-out areas downstairs make up for this.

Lampang

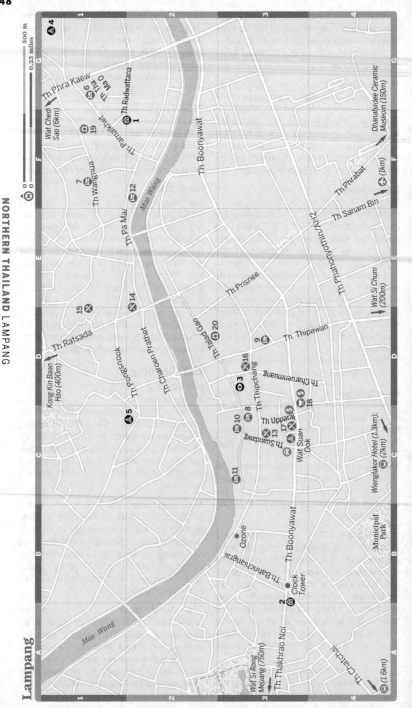

0   500 m
0   0.25 miles

Wat Chedi
Sao (6km)

Th Phra Kaew

Th Tha O

Th Radwattana

Th Pamakkhet

1

19

Th Boonyawat

7

Th Wangnua

12

Mae Wang

Th Pa Mai

Dhanabadee Ceramic
Museum (150m)

Th Phrabat

Th Sanam Bin

Th Phahonyothin/AH2

Wat Si Chum
(200m)

Th Prisnee

15

14

Th Ratsada

Th Pongsnook

Th Charoen Prathet

Th Talap Gao

20

Th Thipawan

9

Th Thipchang

16

3

Th Charuenmuang

Kong Kin Baan
Hao (400m)

5

10

8

13

17

Th Upparaj

Th Suandaw

Wat Suan
Dok

18

Wienglakor Hotel (1.3km);
(2km)

11

Mae Wang

Ozone

Th Bahnchiangrai

Municipal
Park

Th Boonyawat

2

Clock
Tower

Th Thakhrao Noi

Wat Si Rong
Meuang (750m)

Th Chatchai

(1.6km)

Lampang

Prink   HOTEL **$**

(☑ 083 589 6921; 262-264 Th Talad Gao; dm 200, r 300-800B; 🅿🛜) One of Th Talad Gao's noblest historic buildings has been turned into a cutesy boutique hotel. The six rooms, located above a cafe and ice-cream shop, share a fun retro design theme – and bathrooms – although some lack windows and feel somewhat claustrophobic. Avoid this by requesting one of the more expensive balcony rooms.

★**Auangkham Resort**   GUESTHOUSE **$$**

(☑ 054 221305; www.auangkhamlampang.com; 49-51 Th Wangnua; r incl breakfast 1000B; 🅿🛜) Not a resort at all, but rather an exceptionally well-run, boutique-style guesthouse. The 14 rooms feel bright and airy, and all have balconies overlooking an attractive garden. The homey service complements the peaceful vibe, and there are bonus perks such as the free use of bicycles and a location steps from Friday's Cultural Street (p251) market.

★**Hug Lampang**   HOTEL **$$**

(☑ 054 224999; www.huglampangboutiquehotel. com; 59-61 Th Thipawan; r 590-790; 🅿🛜) This former bank has been converted into a stylish, spacious boutique. Opt for the slightly more expensive rooms, which boast huge windows that let in heaps of warm light, a sofa and a vast balcony.

★**Riverside Guest House**   GUESTHOUSE **$$**

(☑ 054 227005; www.theriverside-lampang.com; 286 Th Talad Gao; r 400-900B; ste 1800-2000B; 🅿🛜) Although still mostly within budget range, this leafy compound of refurbished wooden houses is one of the more pleasant places to stay in Lampang, if not all of northern Thailand. It couldn't be any nearer the river, shaded tables for chatting or eating abound, and motorcycle rental and other tourist amenities are available.

Try to score one of the two upstairs rooms in the main structure that feature vast balconies overlooking Mae Wang, or the huge two-room suite.

Karpenter   HOTEL **$$**

(☑ 089 042 9059; www.karpenterlampang. com; Th Nah Guam; r incl breakfast 1500B) 'Post-modern barn' is the self-professed theme at this design-conscious hotel. Indeed, the eight rooms are lofty, decked out in exposed wood, concrete and steel, and minimally rustic, if a bit of a hike from 'downtown' Lampang.

Wienglakor Hotel   HOTEL **$$$**

(☑ 054 316430-5; www.lampangwienglakor.com; 138/35 Th Phahonyothin; incl breakfast r 1200-1600B, ste 3500B; 🅿@🛜) If you're going upscale, this is Lampang's best choice. The entry is tastefully decorated in a teak and northern-Thai-temple theme, a design that continues into the rooms. Deluxe rooms feature an added sitting area and walk-in closet, and the hotel's attractive outdoor dining area with carp pond is a classy, natural touch.

It's about 1.5km west of the centre of Lampang, at the junction of Th Phahonyothin/ AH2 and Th Duangrat.

🍴 Eating & Drinking

Lampang's nightlife scene consists of a few riverside restaurants.

★ **Khun Manee** THAI $

(35 Th Ratsada; mains from 25B; ⊙7am-7pm) Lampang is known for its addictive *kôw dǎan* (deep-fried rice cakes seasoned with watermelon juice and drizzled with palm sugar). You can pick up a few bags and watch the sweets being made at this homey factory just off Th Ratsada – there's no Roman-script sign; look for the white, illuminated sign with green letters.

Phat Thai Yay Fong THAI $

(Th Boonyawat; mains 35-60B; ⊙5-10pm) How do northern Thais take their *pàt tai*? With minced pork and pork rinds, of course. This popular stall is located just east of Wat Suan Dok. There's no Roman-script sign.

Long Jim AMERICAN $

(Th Charuenmuang; pizzas 115-130B; ⊙5-9pm Tue-Fri, to 10pm Sat & Sun; 🔊 🖋) New York-style pizza – available by the slice on Saturday and Sunday – as well as pasta dishes, soups and salads, all overseen by an authentic American.

Evening Market MARKET $

(Th Ratsada; mains 40-150B; ⊙4-8pm) Self-caterers or those interested in local eats will want to check out Lampang's evening market, where steaming baskets of sticky rice and dozens of sides to dip it in are on daily display.

Aroy One Baht THAI $

(cnr Th Suandawg & Th Thipchang; mains 30-100B; ⊙4-11pm) Some nights it can seem like everybody in Lampang is here, and understandably so: the food is tasty and embarrassingly cheap, and the setting in a wooden house is heaps of fun.

Kong Kin Baan Hao THAI $$

(72 Th Jama Thewi; mains 50-250B; ⊙10am-midnight) This local favourite is most popular after dark when a bottle of whisky is regarded as a typical side dish. Flip through the English-language menu's Local Cuisine pages for northern Thai staples such as *gaang kaa gòp* (a herb-laden soup with frog) or *lâhp kôo·a* (*lâhp* that has been stir-fried with local spices).

TRANSPORT TO/FROM LAMPANG

Buses

DESTINATION	FARE (B)	DURATION (HR)	FREQUENCY
Bangkok	328-655	9	frequent 7.50am-10.30pm
Chiang Mai	66-132	2	frequent 2am-11pm
Chiang Rai	137-176	4	frequent 6.30am-3pm
Mae Sai	218	6	10.10am & 2.50pm
Mae Sot	223	4	3 departures 10am-2.50pm
Nan	146-291	4	6 departures 9am-5.15pm
Phayao	87-112	3	9.15am, 11.30am & 3pm
Phitsanulok	154-189	4½	hourly 6.30am-8.45pm
Phrae	77-154	2	6 departures 9am-5.15pm
Sukhothai	155	3½	hourly 6.30am-7pm

Trains

DESTINATION	FARE (B)	DURATION (HR)	FREQUENCY (DAILY)
Bangkok	256-1872	12	6
Chiang Mai	23-413	3	6
Phitsanulok	48-1542	5	6

It's located about 1km outside of town. To get there, head north on Th Ratsada, crossing the river, and turn left at the stoplight. Do a U-turn at the next stoplight; the restaurant is on the left – there's no Roman-script sign; look for the trees.

MAHAMITr   CAFE

(147 Th Boonyawat; ☺8.30am-5pm) The first sign of gentrification? Perhaps, but we're still happy to enjoy this sophisticated cafe. Stop in for excellent espresso drinks, a refreshing nitro coffee or simply to pet the shop's fat cat.

🛍 Shopping

Walking Street   MARKET

(Th Talad Gao; ☺4-10pm Sat & Sun) Lampang has its own Walking Street market along charming Th Talad Gao. On Saturday and Sunday evenings, the usual traffic is replaced by souvenir, handicraft and food stalls.

Cultural Street   MARKET

(Th Wangnua; ☺5-8pm Fri) A Cultural Street market, similar to the Walking Street, is held across the river on Th Wang Nuea every Friday evening.

❶ Information

Several banks with ATMs can be found along Th Boonyawat.

❶ Getting There & Away

Lampang's shiny new **airport** (☎054 821 505; off Th Phahonyothin/AH2) is about 1.5km south of the centre of town, at the eastern end of Th Phahonyothin/AH2. At research time, **Bangkok Airways** (☎054 821522, nationwide 1771; www.bangkokair.com; Lampang Airport; ☺6.30am-6.30pm), with three daily flights to/from Bangkok's Suvarnabhumi International Airport (1540B, 1½ hours), and **Nok Air** (☎094 494 3440, Nationwide 1318; www.nokair.com; Lampang Airport; ☺8am-6.30pm), with three daily flights to/from Bangkok's Don Muang International Airport (1500B, 1½ hours), were the only airlines operating out of Lampang. Taxis from the airport to downtown cost 50B per person, or 100B to book the whole car.

Lampang's **bus and minivan terminal** (☎054 218219; cnr Th Phahonyothin/AH2 & Th Chantarasurin) is nearly 2km south of the centre of town; frequent *sŏrng·tăa·ou* (20B, 15 minutes, 3am to 9pm) run between the station and town. Minibuses head to Chiang Mai (73B, 1½ hours, frequent from 6am to 4pm) and Phrae (70B, two hours, half-hourly from 6.40am to 5pm).

WAT LAI HIN

If you're visiting Wat Phra That Lampang Luang and you've got your own transport, consider a visit to beautiful **Wat Lai Hin** (วัดไหล่หิน; off Rte 1034; ☺daylight hours), also near Ko Kha. Built by artists from Kengtung (also known as Kyaingtong and Chiang Tung), Myanmar, the tiny temple is one of the most characteristically Lanna temples around. It was a significant influence on the design of the Dhara Dhevi hotel in Chiang Mai, not to mention a set for the 2001 Thai historical blockbuster, *Suriyothai*.

There's an interesting folk museum on the grounds that the monks can unlock for you.

If coming from Ko Kha, the temple is located about 6km down a road that turns off 1km before reaching Wat Phra That Lampang Luang.

Lampang's historic **train station** (☎054 217024, nationwide 1690; www.railway.co.th; Th Phahonyothin), dating back to 1916, is about 2.5km from the centre of town, a fair hike from most accommodation. A túk-túk (pronounced *đúk đúk*) between here and the centre of town should run to around 80B.

❶ Getting Around

Getting around central Lampang is possible on foot. The Tourism Authority of Thailand office has free bicycle hire from 10am to 4pm; bring your passport. For destinations outside of town, there is a **taxi stall** (☎054 217233; Th Suandawg; ☺6.30am-5pm) near the Pin Hotel.

Both bicycles and motorcycles are available for hire at **Ozone** (395 Th Thipchang; bicycle per day 60B, motorcycle per day 200-250B; ☺8am-8pm).

Cars can be hired (from 800B per day) via **Thai Rent A Car** (☎054 821699, nationwide 1647; www.thairentacar.com; Lampang Airport; ☺8am-7pm) and **Eddy Rent A Car** (☎095 641 7080; www.eddy-rentacar.com; Lampang Airport; ☺7am-7pm), at Lampang Airport.

Around Lampang

⭐**Wat Phra That Lampang Luang**   BUDDHIST TEMPLE

(วัดพระธาตุลำปางหลวง; off Rte 1034; ☺daylight hrs) This ancient Buddhist temple compound houses several interesting religious structures, including what is arguably the most beautiful wooden Lanna temple in northern Thailand, the open-sided **Wihan Luang**. Dating back to 1476 and thought to be the oldest-standing wooden structure in the country, the impressive *wí·hǎhn* (sanctuary) features a triple-tiered wooden roof supported by immense teak pillars and early 19th-century *Jataka* murals (showing stories of the Buddha's previous lives) painted on wooden panels around the inside upper perimeter.

A huge, gilded *mon·dòp* (the small square-sided building with a spire) in the back of the wí·hǎhn contains a Buddha image cast in 1563.

The small and simple **Wihan Ton Kaew**, to the north of the main *wí·hǎhn,* was built in 1476, while the tall Lanna-style *chedi* (stupa) behind the main *wí·hǎhn,* raised in 1449 and restored in 1496, is 45m high.

Wihan Nam Taem, to the north of the *chedi,* was built in the early 16th century and, amazingly, still contains traces of the original murals, making them among the oldest in the country.

South of the main *chedi,* **Wihan Phra Phut** dates back to the 13th century and is the oldest structure in the compound.

Unfortunately, only men are allowed to see a camera obscura image of the *wí·hǎhn* and *chedi* in the **Haw Phra Phutthabaht**, a small white building behind the *chedi*. The image is projected (upside down) onto a white cloth and clearly depicts the colours of the structures outside.

The lintel over the entrance to the compound features an impressive dragon relief, once common in northern Thai temples but rarely seen today. This gate allegedly dates to the 15th century.

In the arboretum outside the southern gate of the wát, there are now three museums. One displays mostly festival paraphernalia and some Buddha figures. Another, called House of the Emerald Buddha, contains a miscellany of coins, banknotes, Buddha figures, silver betel-nut cases, lacquerware and other ethnographic artefacts, along with three small, heavily gold-leafed Buddhas placed on an altar behind an enormous repoussé silver bowl. The third, a small museum, features shelves of Buddha figures, lacquered boxes, manuscripts and ceramics, all well labelled in Thai and English.

ℹ Getting There & Away

Wat Phra That Lampang Luang is 18km southwest of Lampang in Ko Kha. To get there by public transport from Lampang, flag a blue eastbound *sŏrng·tǎa·ou* (20B) on Th Boonyawat. From the Ko Kha *sŏrng·tǎa·ou* stop, it's a 3km chartered motorcycle taxi ride to the temple (60B). Alternatively, you can charter a *sŏrng·tǎa·ou* from Lampang's bus station for 400B, or taxis will take you there and back for around the same price.

If you're driving or cycling from Lampang, head south on Th Phahonyothin/AH2 and take the Ko Kha exit, then follow the road over a bridge and bear right. Follow the signs and continue for 3km over another bridge until you see the temple on the left.

SUKHOTHAI PROVINCE

The lure of ancient history draws most people to Sukhothai Province (จังหวัดสุโขทัย), as it's home to one of Thailand's most visited and impressive destinations, the ruins of the eponymous former kingdom.

Also worth visiting are the province's other ruins, those of the former Si Satchanalai-Chaliang kingdoms.

Sukhothai   สุโขทัย

☑ 055 / POP 37,000

The Sukhothai (Rising of Happiness) Kingdom flourished from the mid-13th century to the late 14th century. This period is often viewed as the golden age of Thai civilisation. The remains of the kingdom, known as *meuang gòw* (old city), feature around 45 sq km of partially rebuilt ruins, making up one of the most visited ancient sites in Thailand.

Located 12km east of the historical park on Mae Nam Yom, the market town of Sukhothai is not particularly interesting. Yet its friendly and relaxed atmosphere, good transport links and excellent-value accommodation make it a pleasant base from which to explore the old city ruins.

Set among peaceful hills, the 13th- to 15th-century ruins of the old cities of Si Satchanalai and Chaliang lie 50km north of Sukhothai. Chaliang, 1km southeast, is an older city site (dating to the 11th century), though its two temples date to the 14th century.

History

Sukhothai is typically regarded as the first capital of Siam, although this is not entirely accurate. The area was previously the site of a Khmer empire until 1238, when two Thai rulers, Pho Khun Pha Muang and Pho Khun Bang Klang Hao, decided to unite and form a new Thai kingdom.

Sukhothai's dynasty lasted 200 years and spanned nine kings. The most famous was King Ramkhamhaeng, who reigned from 1275 to 1317 and is credited with developing the Thai script – his inscriptions are also considered the first Thai literature. Ramkhamhaeng eventually expanded his kingdom to include an area even larger than that of present-day Thailand. But a few kings later, in 1438, Sukhothai was absorbed by Ayuthaya.

◉ Sights

The **Sukhothai Historical Park ruins** (อุทยานประวัติศาสตร์สุโขทัย; ☎055 697 527; Central Zone 100B, plus per bicycle/motorcycle/car 10/20/50B; Northern Zone 100B, plus per bicycle/motorcycle/car 10/20/50B; Western Zone 100B, plus per bicycle/motorcycle/car 10/20/50B; ⏰Central Zone 6.30am-6pm Sun-Fri, to 9pm Sat; Northern Zone 7.30am-5.30pm; Western Zone 8am-4.30pm) are one of Thailand's most impressive World Heritage Sites. The park includes the remains of 21 historical sites and four large ponds within the old walls, with an additional 70 sites within a 5km radius. The ruins are divided into five zones; the central, northern and western zones each have a separate 100B admission fee.

◉ Central Zone

The historical park's main zone is home to some of its most impressive ruins. On Saturday night much of the central zone is illuminated and remains open until 9pm.

Wat Mahathat   HISTORIC SITE
(วัดมหาธาตุ; Central Zone, Sukhothai Historical Park; Central Zone 100B, plus per bicycle/motorcycle/car 10/20/50B; ⏰6.30am-6pm Sun-Fri, to 9pm Sat) Completed in the 13th century, the largest wát in Sukhothai is surrounded by brick walls (206m long and 200m wide) and a moat that is believed to represent the outer wall of the universe and the cosmic ocean.

The *chedi* spires feature the famous lotus-bud motif, and some of the original stately Buddha figures still sit among the ruined columns of the old *wí·hǎhn* (sanctuary). There are 198 *chedi* within the monastery walls – a lot to explore in what is believed to be the former spiritual and administrative centre of the old capital.

Ramkhamhaeng
National Museum   MUSEUM
(พิพิธภัณฑสถานแห่งชาติรามคำแหง; Sukhothai Historical Park; 150B; ⏰9am-4pm) Near the entrance of the Central Zone, this museum is a decent starting point for exploring the historical park ruins. A replica of the famous Ramkhamhaeng inscription, said to be the earliest example of Thai writing, is kept here among an impressive collection of Sukhothai artefacts. Admission to the museum is not included in the ticket to the central zone.

Wat Si Sawai   HISTORIC SITE
(วัดศรีสวาย; Central Zone, Sukhothai Historical Park; park entry 100B, plus per bicycle/motorcycle/car 10/20/50B; ⏰6.30am-6pm Sun-Fri, to 9pm Sat) Just south of Wat Mahathat, this Buddhist shrine (dating from the 12th and 13th centuries) features three Khmer-style towers and a picturesque moat. It was originally built by the Khmers as a Hindu temple.

Wat Sa Si   HISTORIC SITE
(วัดสระศรี, Sacred Pond Monastery; Central Zone, Sukhothai Historical Park; Central Zone 100B, plus per bicycle/motorcycle/car 10/20/50B; ⏰6.30am-6pm Sun-Fri, to 9pm Sat) Wat Sa Si sits on an island west of the bronze monument of King Ramkhamhaeng (the third Sukhothai king). It's a simple, classic Sukhothai-style wát containing a large Buddha, one *chedi* and the columns of the ruined *wí·hǎhn*.

Wat Trapang Thong   BUDDHIST TEMPLE
(วัดตระพังทอง; off Rte 12; ⏰daylight hours) Next to the Ramkhamhaeng National Museum, this small, still-inhabited wát with fine stucco reliefs is reached by a footbridge across the large lotus-filled pond that surrounds it. This reservoir, allegedly the original site of Thailand's Loi Krathong festival, supplies the Sukhothai community with most of its water.

◉ Northern Zone

The **northern zone**, 500m north of the old city walls, is easily reached by bicycle.

Sukhothai Historical Park

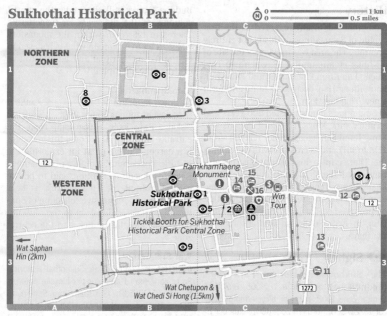

Sukhothai Historical Park

Wat Si Chum   HISTORIC SITE
(วัดศรีชุม; Northern Zone, Sukhothai Historical Park; Northern Zone 100B, plus per bicycle/
motorcycle/car 10/20/50B; ⊙7.30am-5.30pm)
This wát is northwest of the old city and
contains an impressive *mon·dòp* with a
15m brick-and-stucco seated Buddha. This
Buddha's elegant, tapered fingers are much
photographed. Archaeologists theorise that
this image is the 'Phra Atchana' mentioned
in the famous Ramkhamhaeng inscription.
A passage in the *mon·dòp* wall that leads
to the top has been blocked so that it's no
longer possible to view the *Jataka* inscriptions that line the tunnel ceiling.

Wat Phra Phai Luang   HISTORIC SITE
(วัดพระพายหลวง; Sukhothai Historical Park;
park entry 100B, plus per bicycle/motorcycle/car
10/20/50B; ⊙7.30am-5.30pm) This somewhat
isolated wát features three 12th-century
Khmer-style towers, bigger than those at
Wat Si Sawai in the Central Zone. This may
have been the centre of Sukhothai when it
was ruled by the Khmers of Angkor prior to
the 13th century.

◎ Western Zone

The **western zone**, at its furthest extent
2km west of the old city walls, is the most

expansive. In addition to Wat Saphan Hin, several mostly featureless ruins can be found. A bicycle or motorcycle is necessary to explore this zone.

Wat Saphan Hin
HISTORIC SITE

(วัดสะพานหิน; Western Zone, Sukthothai Historical Park; Western Zone 100B, plus per bicycle/motorcycle/car 10/20/50B; ⏰8am-4.30pm) Located on the crest of a hill that rises about 200m above the plain, the name of the wát, which means 'stone bridge', is a reference to the slate path and staircase that lead up to the temple, which are still in place.

All that remains of the original temple are a few *chedi* and the ruined *wí·hǎhn*, consisting of two rows of laterite columns flanking a 12.5m-high standing Buddha image on a brick terrace. The site is 3km west of the former city wall and gives a good view of the Sukhothai ruins to the southeast and the mountains to the north and south.

◉ Outside The Centre

A few worthwhile destinations lie outside the more popular paid zones.

Sangkhalok Museum
MUSEUM

(พิพิธภัณฑ์สังคโลก; Rte 1293; adult/child 100/50B; ⏰8am-5pm) This small but comprehensive museum is an excellent introduction to ancient Sukhothai's most famous product and export, its ceramics.

The ground floor displays an impressive collection of original Thai pottery found in the area, plus some pieces traded from Vietnam, Burma and China. The 2nd floor features examples of non-utilitarian pottery made as art, including some beautiful and rare ceramic Buddha statues.

The museum is about 2.5km east of the centre of New Sukhothai; a túk-túk here is about 100B.

Wat Chetupon
HISTORIC SITE

(วัดเชตุพน; ⏰24hr) **FREE** Located 1.4km south of the old city walls, this temple once held a four-sided *mon·dòp* (a *chedi*-like spire) featuring the four classic poses of the Buddha (sitting, reclining, standing and walking). The graceful lines of the walking Buddha can still be made out today.

Wat Chedi Si Hong
HISTORIC SITE

(วัดเจดีย์สี่ห้อง; ⏰24hr) **FREE** Directly across from Wat Chetupon, the main *chedi* here has retained much of its original stucco relief work, which shows still vivid depictions of elephants, lions and humans.

Wat Chang Lom
HISTORIC SITE

(วัดช้างล้อม; ⏰24hr) **FREE** Off Rte 12 in the eastern zone, Wat Chang Lom (Elephant Circled Monastery) is about 1km east of the main park entrance. A large bell-shaped *chedi* is supported by 36 elephants sculpted into its base.

🏃 Activities & Tours

Cycling Sukhothai
CYCLING

(☑085 083 1864, 055 612519; www.cycling-sukhothai.com; off Th Jarodvithithong; half/full day 800/990B, sunset tour 450B) A resident of Sukhothai for nearly 20 years, Belgian cycling enthusiast Ronny Hanquart offers themed bike tours, such as the Historical Park Tour, which also includes stops at lesser-seen wát and villages.

The office is about 1.2km west of Mae Nam Yom, off Th Jarodvithithong in New Sukhothai; free transport can be arranged.

Sukhothai Bicycle Tour
CYCLING

(☑086 931 6242; www.sukhothaibicycletour.com; 34/1 Th Jarodvithithong; half day 750B, full day 1050-1150B) A bicycle-based tour outfit that gets overwhelmingly positive feedback.

✨ Festivals & Events

Loi Krathong
CULTURAL

(⏰Nov) Spanning five days in November, Sukhothai Historical Park is one of the most popular destinations to celebrate this holiday. In addition to the magical floating

ELEPHANT RETIREMENT HOME

Located 8km from the village of Baan Tuek in Sukhothai Province, the brilliant **Boon Lott's Elephant Sanctuary** (www.blesele.org; per person per night incl meals & transfers 5000B) allows guests to observe rescued and retired working pachyderms in their natural environment. It welcomes overnight and multi-day visitors, with guests involved in all aspects of sanctuary life, from walking elephants to grazing grounds, to planting vegetation.

Three teak guesthouses each sleep two people; book ahead.

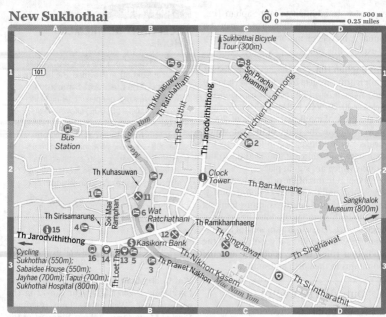

New Sukhothai

🛏 Sleeping
1 4T Guesthouse......................................A2
2 At Home Sukhothai..............................C2
3 Ban Thai...B3
4 Blue House..A3
5 Foresto..B3
6 J&J Guest House B2
7 Lotus Village...B2
8 Ruean Thai Hotel C1
9 Sila Resort..B1

🍴 Eating
10 Dream Café..C3
11 Fueang Fah B2

12 Night Market.......................................B3

🍸 Drinking & Nightlife
13 Chopper Bar..B3
14 Poo Restaurant.....................................B3

ℹ Information
15 Tourism Authority of Thailand A3

ℹ Transport
16 Sŏrng·tăa·ou to Sukhothai
Historical Park A3

lights, there are fireworks, folk-dance performances and a light-and-sound production.

🛏 Sleeping

New Sukhothai has some of the best-value budget accommodation in northern Thailand. Clean, cheerful hotels and guesthouses abound, with many places offering attractive bungalows, free pick-up from the bus station and free use of bicycles.

There's an increasing number of options near the park, many of them upscale. Prices tend to go up during the Loi Krathong festival (p255).

🛏 New Sukhothai

Sila Resort
HOTEL **$**

(📞 055 620344; www.silaresort-sukhothai.com; 3/49 Th Kuhasuwan; incl breakfast r 230-500B, bungalows 750-1200B; ❄@🛜) We couldn't help but think of Disneyland when we first encountered this compound of flowering trees, a gingerbread Thai villa, wood bungalows, statues, resort-like A-frames and a restaurant. And like Disneyland, it comes together in a cheerful, colourful package

FARMER FOR A DAY

Sukhothai's **Organic Agriculture Project** (☑ 055 647290; off Rte 1195; half-day incl lunch 900B; ☺ 8am-5pm Thu-Tue) allows visitors to take part in traditional Thai farm activities.

The compound is also home to a restaurant serving dishes made from the farm's organic produce (mains 50B to 120B, open 8am to 5pm Thursday to Tuesday).

Taking place at Sukhothai Airport's organic farm, the half-day begins by donning the outfit of a Thai rice farmer and riding an *ee đàan* (a traditional utility vehicle) to gather duck eggs. This is followed by riding a buffalo, checking into an orchid farm, witnessing the stages of rice production and, ultimately, planting or gathering rice. The session ends with an informal cooking lesson and meal using organic produce from the farm. Book in advance for an English-speaking guide.

The project is located on the same road as Sukhothai's airport, 27km from New Sukhothai off Rte 1195, and is not accessible by public transport. If you don't have your own wheels, you can arrange a ride with the Sukhothai Airport's minivan service (p259).

looked after by smiling people. The only downside is that it's a fair hike from the centre of New Sukhothai.

Ban Thai　　　　GUESTHOUSE $
(☑ 055 610163; banthai_guesthouse@yahoo.com; 38 Th Prawet Nakhon; r & bungalows 250-800B; ✳☎) The rooms here range from plain to stylish, but the convergence of a friendly atmosphere, an attractive garden setting and low prices makes for a winner.

4T Guesthouse　　　　HOTEL $
(☑ 055 614679; fourthouse@yahoo.com; 122 Soi Mae Ramphan; r 300-1000B; ✳☎⊠) An expansive budget 'resort'. There's a smorgasbord of spacious yet plain rooms to consider, and the swimming pool makes the decision even easier.

Foresto　　　　HOTEL $$
(☑ 083 213 4112; www.forestosukhothai.com; 16/1-3 Th Prawet Nakhon; r 1200-1600B; ✳@☎) Wind past the somewhat messy reception area and through a semi-secluded garden to this union of 15 stylish rooms. Choose from the vast linked rooms in the main structure or the newer rooms that resemble glass cubes.

Sabaidee House　　　　HOTEL $$
(☑ 055 616303; www.sabaideehouse.com; 81/7 Th Jarodvithithong; r 300-1000B; ✳☎⊠) This cheery guesthouse in a semi-rural setting has seven attractive bungalows and four rooms in the main structure – and a brand-new pool.

It's off Th Jarodvithithong, about 200m before the intersection with Rte 101; look for the sign.

At Home Sukhothai　　　　GUESTHOUSE $$
(☑ 055 610172; 184/1 Th Vichien Chamnong; incl breakfast r 450-850B, bungalows 900-1100B; ✳@☎) Located in the 50-year-old childhood home of the proprietor, the simple but comfortable rooms here – both the fan-cooled ones in the original structure and the newer air-con ones – really do feel like home. A new addition has provided four bungalows overlooking a pond. The only downside is the relative distance from 'downtown' Sukhothai.

Blue House　　　　HOTEL $$
(☑ 055 614863; www.sukhothaibluehouse. wordpress.com; off Th Sirisamarung; dm 140B, r 600-850B; ✳@☎) A big azure villa with 18 rooms, all equipped with en suite bathrooms, air-con TV, refrigerator and hot showers. If you don't need such creature comforts, consider the adjacent Green House, where shared-bathroom, fan-cooled beds in a dorm run to 140B.

Lotus Village　　　　HOTEL $$
(☑ 055 621 484; www.lotus-village.com; 170 Th Ratchathani; incl breakfast r 950-1500B, bungalows 1300-2600B; ✳@☎) Village is an apt label for this peaceful compound of wooden bungalows elevated over lotus ponds. Smaller, if overpriced, fan-cooled rooms in a wooden building are also available, and an attractive Burmese-Indian design theme runs through the entire place. Both the breakfast and the staff get great reports, and an on-site spa offers a variety of services.

J&J Guest House　　　　GUESTHOUSE $$
(☑ 055 620095; 12 Th Kuhasuwan; bungalows 600-700B; ✳☎) Located in a manicured garden

VILLAGE HOMESTAY

The residents of Ban Na Ton Chan, a picturesque village in rural Sukhothai, have formed a worthwhile and award-winning **Homestay Program** (☑ 089 885 1639; http://homestaynatonchan.blogspot.com; per person incl breakfast & lunch 700B). Approximately 20 households are involved, and the fee includes breakfast and dinner (for lunch you can try *kôw bóep*, a local noodle dish), and involvement in daily activities such as cooking, furniture-making and weaving.

The locals are keen to open their homes and share their knowledge, but it must be noted that most speak little English.

The village is 15km east of Rte 101, down a signed turn-off north of Ban Hat Siaw. A motorcycle taxi from Ban Hat Siaw will take people here for 150B.

by the river, the eight bungalows here are attractive, cool and relatively spacious. They're identical and price depends on whether you go with fan or air-con.

★ Ruean Thai Hotel
HOTEL $$$

(☑ 055 612444; www.rueanthaihotel.com; 181/20 Soi Pracha Ruammit; r incl breakfast 1480-4200B; ❋ 🛜 ☀) At first glance, you may mistake this eye-catching complex for a Buddhist temple or a traditional Thai house. The upper-level rooms follow a distinct Thai theme, while the poolside rooms are slightly more modern; there's a concrete building with simple air-con rooms out the back. Service is both friendly and flawless, and the whole place boasts a resort-like feel.

Call for free pick-up from the bus station.

🛏 Sukhothai Historical Park

Vitoon Guesthouse
GUESTHOUSE $

(☑ 055 697045; 49 Rte 12; r 300-900B; ❋ 🛜) Within walking distance of the old city, the fan rooms here are starkly bare, but the air-con rooms, in a newer building, are spotless and represent a good deal.

★ Orchid Hibiscus
Guest House
HOTEL $$

(☑ 055 633284; www.orchidhibiscus-guesthouse. com; 407/2 Rte 1272; r/bungalows 900/1400B; ❋ 🛜 ☀) This collection of rooms and bungalows is set in relaxing, manicured grounds with a swimming pool as a centrepiece and the self-professed 'amazing breakfast' (100B) as a highlight. Rooms are spotless and fun, featuring colourful design details and accents.

It's on Rte 1272, about 500m off Rte 12; the turn-off is between the Km 48 and Km 49 markers.

Wake Up @ Muang Kao
GUESTHOUSE $$

(☑ 055 697153; www.facebook.com/wakeupat muangkaoboutiquehotel; 1/1 Rte 12; r incl breakfast 1000B; ❋ @ 🛜) If there's a homestay equivalent to a flashpacker, Wake Up has nailed it. The five rooms here are spacious and tasteful, come decked out with local touches and are looked after by a friendly local couple. A breath of fresh air in Old Sukhothai.

Legendha
HOTEL $$$

(☑ 055 697215; www.legendhasukhothai.com; Rte 12; incl breakfast r 3900-4400B; villa 900B; ❋ @ 🛜 ☀) Water, greenery and traditional structures come together at this lauded resort, culminating in the feel of a northern Thai village. Service-minded staff, a pool, an ongoing renovation that's leaving the rooms looking better than ever and a location relatively close to the historical park are other perks.

Le Charme Sukhothai
HOTEL $$$

(☑ 055 633333; www.lecharmesukhothai.com; 9/9 Rte 1272; r & bungalows 1500-4500; ❋ 🛜 ☀) It may not look like much from a distance, but a closer peek reveals an inviting cluster of bright bungalows linked by an elevated wooden walkway, lush gardens and lotus ponds. Rooms, which are in the process of being renovated, are large and simple but tastefully decorated, with inviting balconies looking out over all that water.

🍴 Eating

Sukhothai's signature dish is *gŏo·ay dĕe·o sù·kŏh·tai* (Sukhothai-style noodles), which features a slightly sweet broth with different preparations of pork, ground peanuts and thinly sliced green beans. Most places to eat are in New Sukhothai, but along the road that leads to the historical park is a string of food stalls and simple tourist-oriented restaurants, the best of which is **Coffee Cup** (Rte 12; dishes 30-150B; ⏱ 8am-10pm; 🛜).

Jayhae
THAI $

(Th Jarodvithithong; dishes 30-120B; ⊙8am-4pm) You haven't been to Sukhothai if you haven't tried the noodles at Jayhae, an extremely popular restaurant that serves Sukhothai-style noodles, *pàt tai* and tasty coffee drinks. Located about 1.3km west of Mae Nam Yom, off Th Jarodvithithong.

Night Market
MARKET $

(Th Ramkhamhaeng; mains 30-60B; ⊙6-11pm) A wise choice for cheap eats in New Sukhothai's tiny night market. Most vendors here are accustomed to accommodating foreigners and even provide bilingual menus.

Tapui
THAI $

(off Th Jarodvithithong; dishes 30-50B; ⊙7am-3pm) Consisting of little more than a brick floor with a tin roof over it, Tapui claims to be the first shop in Sukhothai to have sold the city's namesake dish, *gŏo·ay đěe·o sù·kŏh·tai* (Sukhothai-style noodles). Located about 1.3km west of Mae Nam Yom, off Th Jarodvithithong; there's no Roman-script sign.

Dream Café
THAI $$

(86/1 Th Singhawat; mains 120-350B; ⊙5-11pm; ▣🦌) A meal at Dream Café is like dining in an antique shop. Eclectic but tasteful furnishings and knick-knackery abound, staff members are competent and friendly and, most importantly of all, the food is good. Try one of the well-executed *yam* (Thai-style 'salads').

Fueang Fah
THAI $$

(107/2 Th Khuhasuwan; dishes 50-350B; ⊙10am-10pm) Pretend you're a local in-the-know and take a meal at this long-standing riverside restaurant. The speciality is freshwater fish dishes, such as the tasty 'fried fish', the first item on the barely comprehensible English-language menu. There's no Roman-script sign; it's just after the bridge on Th Khuhasuwan.

🍷 Drinking & Nightlife

Chopper Bar
BAR

(Th Prawet Nakhon; ⊙10am-12.30am; 🛜) Travellers and locals congregate at this restaurant-bar from morning till hangover for food (mains 30B to 150B), drinks and live music. Take advantage of Sukhothai's cool evenings on the rooftop terrace.

Poo Restaurant
BAR

(24/3 Th Jarodvithithong; ⊙11am-midnight; 🛜) Unfortunately named and deceptively simple, Poo has a small selection of Belgian beers. Meals are available too (mains 30B to 150B).

ℹ Information

There are banks with ATMs scattered all around the central part of New Sukhothai, particularly in the area west of Mae Nam Yom, and several in the old city as well.

Kasikorn Bank (Th Jarodvithithong; ⊙8.30am-4.30pm Mon-Sat)

Police Station (📞055 611010, 24hr emergency 191; Th Singhawat; ⊙24 hr) In New Sukhothai.

Siam Commercial Bank (Rte 12; ⊙8.30am-4.30pm Mon-Fri)

Sukhothai Hospital (📞055 610280; Th Jarodvithithong) Located just west of New Sukhothai.

Tourism Authority of Thailand (TAT; 📞055 6162 28, nationwide 1672; Th Jarodvithithong; ⊙8.30am-4.30pm) In new digs since 2016 and about 750m west of the bridge in New Sukhothai, this office has a pretty good selection of maps and brochures.

Tourist Police (📞24hr 1155; Rte 12; ⊙24hr)

ℹ Getting There & Away

Sukhothai's airport is located a whopping 27km north of town off Rte 1195. **Bangkok Airways** (📞055 647224, nationwide 1771; www.bangkokair.com; Sukhothai Airport; ⊙7am-6pm) is the only airline operating here, with three daily flights to/from Bangkok's Suvarnabhumi International Airport (from 1890B, one hour and 15 minutes). There is a **minivan service** (📞055 647220; Sukhothai Airport; ⊙7am-7pm) between the airport and New Sukhothai or Sukhothai Historical Park. Alternatively, **Air Asia** (📞Phitsanulok 094 7193645, nationwide 02 515 9999; www.airasia.com; Phitsanulok Airport; ⊙7am-6.30pm) and **Nok Air** (📞055 301051, nationwide 1318; www.nokair.co.th; Phitsanulok Airport; ⊙6am-7pm) offer minivan transfers to/from both old and new Sukhothai via the airport in Phitsanulok, less than an hour away.

Sukhothai's minivan and **bus station** (📞055 614529; Rte 101) is almost 1km northwest of the centre of New Sukhothai; a motorcycle taxi between here and central New Sukhothai should cost around 50B, or you can hop on any *sŏrng·tǎa·ou* bound for Sukhothai Historical Park – they stop at the bus station on their way out of town (20B, 10 minutes, frequent 6am to 5.30pm).

Alternatively, if you're staying near the historical park, **Win Tour** (☏ 099 135 5645; Rte 12; ⊘ 6am-9.40pm) has an office where you can board buses to Bangkok (310B, six hours, 8am, noon and 9.50pm) and Chiang Mai (210B, five hours, six departures from 6am to 2pm).

🛈 Getting Around

A *săhm·lór* (three-wheeled pedicab) ride within New Sukhothai should cost no more than 40B.

Relatively frequent **sŏrng·tăa·ou** (Th Jarodvithithong; 30B; ⊘ 6am-5.30pm) run between New Sukhothai and Sukhothai Historical Park (30B, 30 minutes, 6am to 5.30pm), leaving from a stop on Th Jarodvithithong. Motorcycle taxis go between the town or bus station and the historical park for 120B.

The best way to get around the historical park is by bicycle; bikes can be hired at shops outside the park entrance for 30B per day (6am to 6pm).

Motorbikes (from 250B for 24 hours) can be hired at nearly every guesthouse in New Sukhothai.

Si Satchanalai-Chaliang Historical Park

อุทยานประวัติศาสตร์ศรีสัชนาลัย-เชลียง

Set among peaceful hills, the 13th- to 15th-century ruins of the old cities of Si Satchanalai and Chaliang lie 50km north of Sukhothai. The park off Rte 101; 100B; ⊘8.30am-4.30pm) covers roughly 720 hectares and is surrounded by a 12m-wide

TRANSPORT TO/FROM SUKHOTHAI

Buses

DESTINATION	FARE (B)	DURATION (HR)	FREQUENCY
Bangkok	241-310	6-7	half-hourly 7.50am-10.40pm
Chiang Mai	195-374	5-6	frequent 6.20am-2am
Chiang Rai	231	9	4 departures 6.40-11.30am
Kamphaeng Phet	53-68	1½	half-hourly 7.50am-10.40pm
Khon Kaen	221-334	7	frequent 10.30am-12.40am
Lampang	155-205	3	frequent 6.20am-2am
Mae Sot	130-176	3	3 departures 9.15am-2.30am
Mukdahan	476	10	7.50pm & 9.40pm
Nan	176	4	3pm
Phitsanulok	39-50	1	half-hourly 7.50am-10.40pm
Sawankhalok	27	1	hourly 6.40am-5pm
Si Satchanalai	45	1½	hourly 6.40am-5pm

Minivans

DESTINATION	FARE (B)	DURATION (HR)	FREQUENCY
Kamphaeng Phet	53	2	frequent *sŏrng·tăa·ou* 9am-4pm
Mae Sot	130	3	4 minivan departures 9.15am-4.15pm
Phitsanulok	39	1	hourly 7.30am-5pm
Sukhothai Historical Park	30	30min	frequent *sŏrng·tăa·ou* 6am-5.30pm

moat. Chaliang, 1km southeast, is an older city site (dating to the 11th century), though its two temples date to the 14th century.

The nearby towns of Ban Hat Siaw and Sawankhalok are the main centres for the area.

Sights & Activities

An admission fee of 250B allows entry to Si Satchanalai, Wat Chao Chan (at Chaliang) and the Si Satchanalai Centre for Study & Preservation of Sangkalok Kilns.

Si Satchanalai

Wat Chang Lom HISTORIC SITE
(วัดช้างล้อม; Si Satchanalai-Chaliang Historical Park; 100B; ⊙8.30am-4.30pm) This fine temple, marking the centre of the old city of Si Satchanalai, has elephants surrounding a bell-shaped *chedi* (stupa) that is somewhat better preserved than its counterpart in Sukhothai. An inscription states that the temple was built by King Ramkhamhaeng between 1285 and 1291.

Wat Khao Phanom Phloeng HISTORIC SITE
(วัดเขาพนมเพลิง; Si Satchanalai-Chaliang Historical Park; 100B; ⊙8.30am-4.30pm) On the hill overlooking Wat Chang Lom are the remains of Wat Khao Phanom Phloeng, including a *chedi,* a large seated Buddha and stone columns that once supported the roof of the *wí·hăhn.* From here you can make out the general design of the once-great city.

The slightly higher hill west of Phanom Phloeng is capped by a large Sukhothai-style *chedi* – all that remains of **Wat Khao Suwan Khiri**.

Wat Chedi Jet Thaew HISTORIC SITE
(วัดเจดีย์เจ็ดแถว; Si Satchanalai-Chaliang Historical Park; 100B; ⊙8.30am-4.30pm) Next to Wat Chang Lom, these ruins contain seven rows of *chedi,* the largest of which is a copy of one at Wat Mahathat in Sukhothai. An interesting brick-and-plaster *wí·hăhn* features barred windows designed to look like lathed wood (an ancient Indian technique used all over Southeast Asia).

Wat Nang Phaya HISTORIC SITE
(วัดนางพญา; Si Satchanalai-Chaliang Historical Park; 100B; ⊙8.30am-4.30pm) South of Wat Chedi Jet Thaew, this *chedi* is Sinhalese in style and was built in the 15th or 16th century, a bit later than the other monuments at Si Satchanalai. Stucco reliefs on the large laterite *wí·hăhn* in front of the *chedi* – now sheltered by a tin roof – date from the Ayuthaya period when Si Satchanalai was known as Sawankhalok. Goldsmiths in the district still craft a design known as *nahng pá·yah,* modelled after these reliefs.

Chaliang

Wat Phra Si Ratana Mahathat HISTORIC SITE
(วัดพระศรีรัตนมหาธาตุ; Si Satchanalai-Chaliang Historical Park; 20B; ⊙8am-4.30pm) These ruins consist of a large laterite *chedi* (dating back to 1448–88) between two *wí·hăhn.* One of the *wí·hăhn* holds a large seated Sukhothai Buddha image, a smaller standing image and a bas-relief of the famous walking Buddha, exemplary of the flowing, boneless Sukhothai style. The other *wí·hăhn* contains some less distinguished images.

Wat Chao Chan HISTORIC SITE
(วัดเจ้าจันทร์; Si Satchanalai-Chaliang Historical Park; 100B, combined entry with Si Satchanalai & Si Satchanalai Centre for Study & Preservation of Sangkalok Kilns 250B; ⊙8am-5pm) The central attraction here is a large Khmer-style tower similar to later towers built in Lopburi and probably constructed during the reign of Khmer King Jayavarman VII (1181–1217). The tower has been restored and is in fairly good shape. The roofless *wí·hăhn* (sanctuary) on the right contains the laterite outlines of a large standing Buddha that has all but melted away from exposure and weathering. Admission isn't always collected here.

Sawankhalok Kilns

At one time, more than 200 huge pottery kilns lined the banks of Mae Nam Yom in the area around Si Satchanalai. In China – the biggest importer of Thai pottery during the Sukhothai and Ayuthaya periods – the pieces produced here came to be called Sangkalok, a mispronunciation of Sawankhalok. Ceramics are still made in the area, and a local ceramic artist even continues to fire his pieces in an underground wood-burning oven.

Si Satchanalai Centre for Study & Preservation of Sangkalok Kilns MUSEUM
(ศูนย์ศึกษาและอนุรักษ์เตาสังคโลก; 100B, combined ticket with Si Satchanalai & Wat Chao Chan 250B;

Si Satchanalai-Chaliang Historical Park

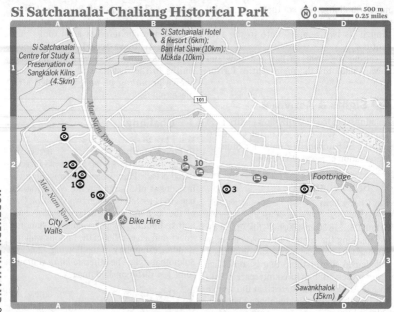

Si Satchanalai-Chaliang Historical Park

⊙8am-4.30pm) Located 5km northwest of the Si Satchanalai ruins, this centre has large excavated kilns and many intact pottery samples. The exhibits are interesting despite the lack of English labels.

⊙ Sawankhalok

**Sawanworanayok National
Museum**   MUSEUM
(พิพิธภัณฑสถานแห่งชาติสวรรควรนายก;   69
Th Phracharat; 50B; ⊙9am-4pm Wed-Sun) In Sawankhalok town, near Wat Sawankhalam on the western river bank, this state-sponsored museum houses an impressive collection of 12th- to 15th-century artefacts. The ground floor focuses on the area's ceramic legacy, while the 2nd floor features several beautiful bronze and stone Sukhothai-era Buddha statues.

🛏 Sleeping & Eating

Accommodation near any of the historical sites is mostly limited to basic homestays and hotels. Alternatives include Sawankhalok, 15km to the south, or Ban Hat Siaw, about 9km north of the park.

There are some basic stalls and restaurants near the park.

Swankaburi Boutique Hotel   HOTEL $
(📞087 312 6767; 15/31 Th Si Satchanalai, Sawankhalok; incl breakfast r 450-900B; ste 1600B; ❄️🛜) This charming boutique means that staying in Sawankhalok will no longer feel like a compromise. The 33 rooms are decked out in woods, tile and attractive local touches; suites are huge while the cheapest rooms are rather tight and share a bathroom.

Located at the northern end of Sawankhalok.

Mukda Resort HOTEL $

(☑ 055 671024; Rte 101, Ban Hat Siaw; r incl breakfast 400-950B; ❄ ⑤) Tidy, comfortable rooms relatively close to the historical park, the cheapest of which are fan-cooled.

It's at the northern end of Ban Hat Siaw, at the turn-off to Uttaradit.

Papong Homestay GUESTHOUSE $

(☑ 087 313 4782, 055 631557; off Rte 1201, Chaliang; r incl breakfast 500B; ❄ ⑤) A locally run outfit near the historical park, the five rooms here include private bathrooms and feel new, tidy and comfortable.

Sisatchanalai Heritage HOTEL $$

(☑ 055 615423; www.sisatchanalaiheritage.com; Chaliang; incl breakfast r 1200-1500B, bung 800-1000B) When we visited in 2017, this expansive riverside compound – complete with restaurant and coffee shop – had only three new-feeling, spacious rooms. But an additional 10 bungalows were being built, which when finished will comprise the only proper hotel close to the park.

Homestay GUESTHOUSE $$

(☑ 084 048 8595, 055 631063; www.baansilalang.com; off Rte 1201, Chaliang; r 600B; ❄ ⑤) A local artist has opened her family's home/studio to guests. A single room, separate from the house, is equipped with private bath and air-con.

Look for the 'Homestay' sign directly across from Wat Khok Singkharam, near the entrance to Si Satchanalai.

Sukhothai Heritage Resort RESORT $$$

(☑ 055 647564; www.sukhothaiheritage.com; 999 Mu 2, Sukhothai Airport; incl breakfast r 2500-3500B, ste 7900B; ❄ @ ⑤ ☒) Approximately 32km from Si Satchanalai Historical Park near Sukhothai Airport is this upscale yet rural, isolated resort. Seemingly a continuation of the historical park, the low-lying brick and peak-roofed structures are interspersed by green fields and calming lotus-filled ponds, culminating in a temple-like environment. The rooms take you back to the contemporary world with large flat-screen TVs and modern furniture.

❶ Information

Information Centre (Si Satchanalai-Chaliang Historical Park; 100B; ⊙ 8am-4.30pm) An information centre at the park distributes free maps and has a small exhibit outlining the history and attractions.

❶ Getting There & Around

You can **hire bicycles** (Si Satchanalai-Chaliang Historical Park; per day 30B; ⊙ 7am-7pm) from near the food stalls at the entrance to the historical park.

BUS

Si Satchanalai-Chaliang Historical Park is off Rte 101 between Sawankhalok and Ban Hat Siaw. From New Sukhothai, take a Si Satchanalai bus (45B, 1½ hours, hourly 6.40am to 5pm) or one of four buses to Chiang Rai between 6.40am and 11.30am (46B) and ask to get off at meuang gòw (old city).

To get to the park from Sawankhalok, you can hop on just about any northbound line from the town's government **bus station** (☑ 055 642037), south of the train station on Rte 1180 (around 20B, 30 minutes, frequent 7am to 5pm).

TRAIN

Sawankhalok's original **train station** is one of the local sights. King Rama VI built a 60km railway spur from Ban Dara (a small town on the main northern trunk) to Sawankhalok just so that he could visit the ruins. Amazingly, there's a daily special express from Bangkok to Sawankhalok (482B, seven hours, 10.50am). The train heads back to Bangkok at 7.40pm, arriving in the city at 3.30am. You can also take this train to Phitsanulok (328B, 3½ hours, 5.55pm). It's a 'Sprinter' – 2nd class air-con and no sleepers. The fare includes dinner and breakfast.

PHITSANULOK PROVINCE

Although most visitors regard Phitsanulok Province (จังหวัดพิษณุโลก) as more a base for visiting the historical ruins in neighbouring provinces than a destination. It's home to visit-worthy natural attractions and a pleasant provincial capital.

Phitsanulok พิษณุโลก

☑ 05584,000 / POP 84,000

Phitsanulok sees relatively few independent travellers but a fair amount of package tourists, probably because the city is a convenient base from which to explore the attractions of historical Sukhothai, Si Satchanalai and Kamphaeng Phet. The frenetic and extremely friendly city also boasts some interesting sites and museums, chief of which is Wat Phra Si Ratana Mahathat (p264), which contains one of the country's most revered Buddha images.

Those willing to forge their own path can also use the city as a base to visit the nearby national parks and wildlife sanctuaries of Thung Salaeng Luang (p267) and Phu Hin Rong Kla (p269), the former the strategic headquarters of the Communist Party of Thailand.

◉ Sights

★ Sergeant Major
Thawee Folk Museum   MUSEUM
(พิพิธภัณฑ์พื้นบ้านจ่าทวี; Th Wisut Kasat; adult/child 50/25B; ⊗8.30am-4.30pm) This fascinating museum displays a remarkable collection of tools, textiles and photographs from Phitsanulok Province. It's spread throughout five traditional-style Thai buildings with well-groomed gardens, and the displays are all accompanied by informative and legible English descriptions. Those interested in cooking will find much of interest in the display of a traditional Thai kitchen and the various traps used to catch game.

★ Wat Phra Si
Ratana Mahathat   BUDDHIST TEMPLE
(วัดพระศรีรัตนมหาธาตุ; Th Phutta Bucha; ⊗temple 6am-9pm, museum 9am-5.30pm Wed-Sun) FREE The main *wí·hǎhn* (sanctuary) at this temple, known by locals as Wat Yai, appears small from the outside, but houses the **Phra Phuttha Chinnarat**, one of Thailand's most revered and copied Buddha images. This famous bronze statue is probably second in importance only to the Emerald Buddha in Bangkok's Wat Phra Kaew.

The story goes that construction of this wát was commissioned under the reign of King Li Thai in 1357. When it was completed, King Li Thai wanted it to contain three high-quality bronze images, so he sent for well-known sculptors from Si Satchanalai, Chiang Saen and Hariphunchai (Lamphun), as well as five Brahman priests. The first two castings worked well, but the third required three attempts before it was decreed the best of all. Legend has it that a white-robed sage appeared from nowhere to assist in the final casting, then disappeared. This last image was named the Chinnarat (Victorious King) Buddha and it became the centrepiece in the *wí·hǎhn*. The other two images, Phra Chinnasi and

Phra Si Satsada, were later moved to the royal temple of Wat Bowonniwet in Bangkok.

The image was cast in the late Sukhothai style, but what makes it strikingly unique is the flame-like halo around the head and torso that turns up at the bottom to become dragon-serpent heads on either side of the image. The head of this Buddha is a little wider than standard Sukhothai, giving the statue a very solid feel.

Another sanctuary to one side has been converted into a free **museum**, displaying antique Buddha images, ceramics and other historic artefacts.

Despite the holiness of the temple, endless loud broadcasts asking for donations, Thai musicians, a strip of vendors hawking everything from herbs to lottery tickets, several ATM machines and hundreds of visitors all contribute to a relentlessly hectic atmosphere. Come early (ideally before 7am) if you're looking for quiet contemplation or simply wish to take photos, and regardless of the time be sure to dress appropriately – no shorts or sleeveless tops.

Wat Ratburana   BUDDHIST TEMPLE
(วัดราชบูรณะ; Th Phutta Bucha; ⊗daylight hours) FREE Across the street from Wat Phra Si Ratana Mahathat, Wat Ratburana draws fewer visitors but in some ways is more interesting than its famous neighbour. In addition to a *wí·hǎhn* with a 700-year-old gold Buddha, there's a *bòht* (chapel), with beautiful murals thought to date back to the mid-19th century, and two wooden *hǒr đrai* (manuscript libraries).

The temple is also home to a few quirky attractions that offer a fascinating insight into the practices of Thai Buddhism. The most apparent of these is a large wooden boat decked with garlands that originally served to transport King Rama V on an official visit to Phitsanulok. Today the boat is believed to grant wishes to those who make an offering and crawl under its entire length three or nine times. Next to the *wí·hǎhn* is a sacred tree with ladders on either side that visitors climb up, leave an offering, then ring a bell and descend, again repeating the action a total of three or nine times. And directly adjacent to the tree is an immense gong that, when rubbed the right way, creates a unique ringing sound.

Near each of these attractions you'll find somebody stationed who, in addition to sell-

Phitsanulok

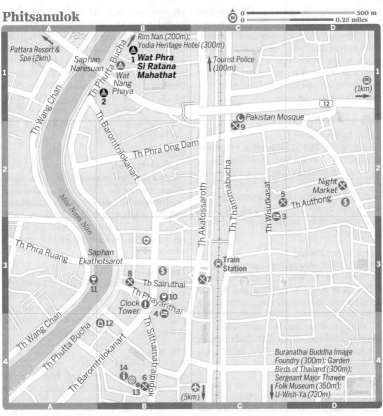

Phitsanulok

ing the coins, incense and flowers used in offerings, will instruct visitors in exactly how to conduct each particular ritual, including how many times to pass, what to offer and what prayer to say.

Buranathai Buddha Image Foundry

WORKSHOP

(โรงหล่อพระบูรณะไทย; 26/43 Th Wisut Kasat; ⊙8am-5pm) FREE Across the street from Sergeant Major Thawee Folk Museum and also belonging to Sergeant Major Thawee is the Buranathai Buddha Image Foundry, where bronze Buddha images of all sizes are cast. Visitors are welcome to watch the process, and there are photo exhibits demonstrating the lost-wax method of metal casting. Some of the larger images take a year or more to complete. There is a small gift shop at the foundry where you can purchase bronze images of various sizes.

🛏 Sleeping

Lithai Guest House
HOTEL $

(☑055 219626; 73/1-5 Th Phayarithai; r incl breakfast 300-580B; ❄️📶) The light-filled 60 or so rooms here don't have much character but they are clean. Air-con rooms include perks such as large private bathrooms with hot water, cable TV, fridge and breakfast, while the cheapies are fan-cooled and share bathrooms.

Ayara Grand Palace
HOTEL $$

(☑055 909993; www.ayaragrandpalacehotel.com; Th Authong; incl breakfast r 1200-1500B, ste 1800-3500B; ❄️@📶🏊) The '90s-era pastels, fake fireplaces and relentless flower theme of this hotel give it an undeniably cheesy feel. But it's all in good fun, and the vast suites – the most expensive of which is decked out with an electric massage chair – are pretty good value.

⭐ Pattara Resort & Spa
HOTEL $$$

(☑055 282966; www.pattararesort.com; 349/40 Th Chaiyanupap; incl breakfast r 3800-4500B, villa 7500-9000B; ❄️@📶🏊) This natural-feeling resort about 2km east from the city centre is Phitsanulok's classiest place to stay. Rooms feel vast and all have huge bathrooms with tubs and wide balconies looking out over lotus ponds and a pool. Better yet, go for one of the two pool villas with private pool, or the two floating villas built over the lotus pond.

Yodia Heritage Hotel
BOUTIQUE HOTEL $$$

(☑055 214677; www.yodiaheritage.com; 89/1 Th Phutta Bucha; incl breakfast r 3300-4500B, ste 8900B; ❄️📶🏊) Located along a quiet stretch of Mae Nam Nan is this retro-themed boutique, which boasts huge suites with similarly large tubs, and a semi-private swimming pool.

🍴 Eating

Phitsanulok takes its cuisine seriously. The city is particularly obsessive about night markets, and there are no fewer than three dotted in various locations around town.

Phitsanulok's **night bazaar** (Th Phutta Bucha; ⊘7pm-midnight) is also good for eats, and the southernmost restaurant along the strip specialises in *pàk bûng loy fáh* (literally 'floating-in-the-sky morning glory vine'), in which the cook fires up a batch of the eponymous vegetable in a wok and then flings it through the air to a waiting server who catches it on a plate.

Yasmeen Halal Food Restaurant
THAI $

(Th Phra Ong Dam; mains 10-50B; ⊘5am-8pm) There are several Thai-Muslim cafes near the Pakistan Mosque on Th Phra Ong Dam, and this is probably the best of them. Thick *roh·đee* (crispy dough 'pancakes') are served up with rich curries, and are best coupled with a cup of sweet tea.

Paknang
CHINESE, THAI $

(Th Sairuthai; mains 40-280B; ⊘10am-10pm) This corner of old Phitsanulok has a distinctly old-world Chinese feel, an excellent pairing with the tasty Chinese-style dishes at this long-standing restaurant.

Rim Nan
THAI $

(5/4 Th Phutta Bucha; mains 20-35B; ⊘9am-4pm) Just north of Wat Phra Si Ratana Mahathat, Rim Nan is one of a few similar restaurants along Th Phutta Bucha that offer *gŏoay·đĕe·o hôy kăh*, literally 'legs-hanging' noodles, named for the benches that make eating a bowl an even more informal endeavour.

Jaroen Rat
THAI $

(Th Sithamatraipidok; mains 15-40B; ⊘8am-3pm; 🍴) This simple place serves a choice of vegetarian dishes paired with husky brown rice. There are at least three other meat-free places along the same strip – there's no Romanscript sign so look for the yellow banners.

Night Market
THAI $

(off Th Akatossaroth; mains 30-60B; ⊘4-8pm) Located just south of the train station, this market features mostly takeaway items including *kôw nĕe·o hòr* (tiny banana-leaf parcels of sticky rice with various toppings). There are two vendors opposite each other near the Th Akatossaroth entrance to the market.

WATERFALLS & RIVER RAPIDS: DRIVING THE GREEN ROUTE

Route 12, which runs along the scenic, rapid-studded Lam Nam Khek between Phitsanulok and Lom Sak, is known as the Green Route. Off this road are waterfalls, resorts and the Phu Hin Rong Kla and Thung Salaeng Luang National Parks.

The Phitsanulok TAT office distributes a good map of the attractions found along this 130km stretch of road. You may want to bypass the first two waterfalls, **Nam Tok Sakhunothayan** (at the Km 33 marker) and **Kaeng Song** (at the Km 45 marker), which on weekends can be overwhelmed with visitors. The third, **Kaeng Sopha** (at the Km 72 marker), is a larger area of small falls and rapids where you can walk from rock formation to rock formation – there are more or fewer rocks depending on rainfall. When there's enough water (typically from September to November) any of the resorts along this section can organise **white-water rafting** trips on the Lam Nam Khek.

Further east along the road is the 1262-sq-km **Thung Salaeng Luang National Park** (อุทยานแห่งชาติทุ่งแสลงหลวง; ☑ 055 268019, accommodation 02 562 0760; www.dnp. go.th; Rte 12; 300-500B; ☺8am-5pm), one of Thailand's largest and most important wildlife sanctuaries. The entrance is at the Km 80 marker, where the park headquarters has information on walks and accommodation.

If you have your own wheels, you can turn south at the Km 100 marker onto Rte 2196 and head for **Khao Kho** (Khow Khor), another mountain lair used by the Communist Party of Thailand during the 1970s.

If you've made the side trip to Khao Kho you can choose either to return to the Phitsanulok–Lom Sak highway, or take Rte 2258, off Rte 2196, until it terminates at Rte 203. On Rte 203 you can continue north to Lom Sak or south to Phetchabun.

Resort-style accommodation can be found along most of the Green Route, with budget accommodation clumping near Kaeng Song, around Km 45, and at the various national parks. Several restaurants are located on the banks of Nam Khek, most taking full advantage of the views and breezes.

Buses between Phitsanulok and Lom Sak cost 85B, and run from 6.15am to 6.15pm. For more freedom it's best to do this route with your own wheels; cars can be hired via several companies at Phitsanulok's airport (p268).

★ **Ban Mai** THAI **$$**
(93/30 Th Authong; mains 100-290B; ☺11am-10pm; ❄) Dinner at this local favourite is like a meal at your grandparents' place: opinionated conversation resounds, frumpy furniture abounds and an overfed cat appears to rule the dining room. The likewise homey dishes include *gaang pèt bèt yâhng* (grilled duck curry) and *yam dà krái* (herbal lemongrass salad). There's no Roman-script sign; look for the yellow compound across from Ayara Grand Palace Hotel.

🍷 Drinking & Nightlife

U-Wish-Ya BAR
(www.facebook.com/Uwishya; 36/110 Th Chan Wetchakit; ☺5pm-midnight) A biker bar as perceived through the Thai lens – which means it's a heck of a lot friendlier. There's live music most nights and a menu of Thai-style bar bites.

In Town BAR
(Th Phayarithai; ☺5.30pm-midnight) With eight beers on tap and about 50 different bottles in the refrigerator, this is the place to come if you want to forget about Chang or Singha for a night.

Shew Shew BAR
(off Th Wang Chan; ☺6pm-midnight) As the only remaining floating pub in Mae Nam Nan, Shew Shew is a dying breed. Snacks and more substantial Thai dishes are available.

ℹ️ Information

Several banks in town offer foreign-exchange services and ATMs. There are also several ATMs inside the Wat Phra Si Ratana Mahathat compound.

@net (off Th Baromtrilokanart; per hr 8B; ☺24hr) Twenty-four-hour internet access.
Golden House Tour (☑ 055 259973; 55/37-38 Th Baromtrilokanart; ☺7am-7pm Mon-Sat) This experienced travel agency can book airline

tickets and arrange ground transport in and around Phitsanulok.

Krung Thai Bank (Th Naresuan; ⊙8.30am-4.30pm Mon-Fri) Bank with ATM in Phitsanulok.

Police Station (☑24hr emergency 191; Th Baromtrilokanart)

Thai Military Bank (Th Authong; ⊙8.30am-4.30pm Mon-Fri) Bank with ATM.

Tourism Authority of Thailand (TAT; ☑055 252742, nationwide 1672; tatphlok@tat.or.th; 209/7-8 Th Baromtrilokanart; ⊙8.30am-4.30pm) Off Th Baromtrilokanart, with helpful staff who hand out free maps of the town and a walking-tour sheet. This office also oversees the provinces of Sukhothai, Phichit and Phetchabun.

Tourist Police (☑nationwide 1155; Th Akatossaroth)

ⓘ Getting There & Away

Phitsanulok's **airport** (☑055 301002) is about 5km south of town; a taxi counter can arrange trips to/from town for 150B. Air Asia (p259), Nok Air (p259) and **Thai Lion Air** (☑call centre 02 529 9999; www.lionairthai.com; Phitsanulok Airport; ⊙7am-7pm) conduct flights to/from Bangkok's Don Mueang International Airport (from 640B, 55 minutes, seven daily).

The city's **bus station** (☑055 212090; Rte 12) is 2km east of town on Hwy 12; túk-túk and motorcycle taxis to/from town cost 60B. Transport options out of Phitsanulok are good as it's a junction for several bus and minivan routes.

Phitsanulok's **train station** (☑055 258005, nationwide 1690; www.railway.co.th; Th Akatossaroth) is within walking distance of accommodation and offers a left-luggage service. The station is a significant train terminal and virtually every northbound and southbound train stops here.

TRANSPORT TO/FROM PHITSANULOK

Buses & Minivans

In addition to these bus routes, there are also minivans to Mae Sot (172B, four hours, five departures 8am to 3pm) and Sukhothai Historical Park (70B, 1½ hours, frequent 5.20am to 6pm).

DESTINATION	FARE (B)	DURATION (HR)	FREQUENCY
Bangkok	263-361	5-6	hourly 8.45am-11pm
Chiang Khong	273	10	9am
Chiang Mai	202-304	6	frequent 5.40am-12.40pm
Chiang Rai	237-304	7-8	6 departures 5.30am-1pm
Lom Sak (for Green Route)	85	1-2	hourly 6.15am-6.15pm
Lampang	238	4	4 departures 11am-10pm
Mae Sai	267-344	7	6 departures 5.30am-1pm
Nakhon Thai (for Phu Hin Rong Kla National Park)	45-64	2	hourly 5am-6pm
Nan	178	6	hourly 6am-5.30pm
Phrae	112	4	hourly 6.30am-5.30pm
Sukhothai	39	1	hourly 7am-6.10pm

Trains

DESTINATION	FARE (B)	DURATION (HR)	FREQUENCY
Bangkok	69-1664	5-7	10 daily
Chiang Mai	65-1645	7-9	6 daily
Lampang	158-1042	5	5 daily

ⓘ Getting Around

Rides on the town's Darth Vader-like sǎhm·lór (three-wheel pedicabs) start at about 60B. Outside the train station there's a sign indicating prices for different destinations around town. Phitsanulok now also has a small fleet of **taxis** (☑ 055 338888).

Car hire out of Phitsanulok's airport costs from around 900B per day.

Phu Hin Rong Kla National Park

อุทยานแห่งชาติภูหินร่องกล้า

Today a national park, Phu Hin Rong Kla was formerly an important base for the CPT, the Communist Party of Thailand. As such, it offers a good mix of man-made and natural attractions that should appeal to most visitors.

History

Between 1967 and 1982, the mountain that is known as Phu Hin Rong Kla served as the strategic headquarters for the CPT and its tactical arm, the People's Liberation Army of Thailand (PLAT). The remote, easily defended summit was perfect for an insurgent army. China's Yunnan Province is only 300km away and it was here that CPT cadres received their training in revolutionary tactics. (This was until the 1979 split between the Chinese and Vietnamese communists, when the CPT sided with Vietnam.)

For nearly 20 years the area around Phu Hin Rong Kla served as a battlefield for Thai troops and the communists. In 1972 the Thai government launched an unsuccessful major offensive against the PLAT. The CPT camp at Phu Hin Rong Kla became especially active after the Thai military killed hundreds of students in Bangkok during the October 1976 student-worker uprising. Many students subsequently fled here to join the CPT, setting up a hospital and a school of political and military tactics. By 1978 the PLAT ranks here had swelled to 4000. In 1980 and 1981 the Thai armed forces tried again and were able to recapture some parts of CPT territory. But the decisive blow to the CPT came in 1982, when the government declared an amnesty for all the students who had joined the communists after 1976. The departure of most of the students broke the spine of the movement, which had become dependent

on their membership. A final military push in late 1982 resulted in the surrender of the PLAT, and Phu Hin Rong Kla was declared a national park in 1984.

◉ Sights & Activities

Phu Hin Rong Kla National Park   NATURE RESERVE
(อุทยานแห่งชาติภูหินร่องกล้า; ☑ 055 233527; www. dnp.go.th; 500B; ⊙ 8.30am-5pm) The park covers about 307 sq km of rugged mountains and forest, much of it covered by rocks and wildflowers. The elevation at park headquarters is about 1000m, so the area is refreshingly cool even in the hot season. The main attractions don't tend to stray too far from the main road through the park and include the remains of the CPT stronghold – a rustic meeting hall, the school of political and military tactics – and the CPT administration building.

There are also waterfalls, hiking trails and scenic views, as well as some interesting rock formations – jutting boulders called Lan Hin Pum and an area of deep rocky crevices where PLAT troops would hide during air raids, called Lan Hin Taek. Ask at the visitor centre for maps.

Phu Hin Rong Kla can become quite crowded on weekends and holidays; for a more peaceful visit schedule for midweek.

Pha Chu Thong   HISTORIC SITE
(ผาชูธง; Flag Raising Cliff; Phu Hin Rong Kla National Park) A 1km trail leads to Pha Chu Thong (sometimes called Red Flag Cliff), where the communists would raise the red flag to announce a military victory. Also in this area is an air-raid shelter, a lookout and the remains of the main CPT headquarters – the most inaccessible point in the territory before a road was constructed by the Thai government.

The buildings in the park are made out of wood and bamboo and have no plumbing or electricity – a testament to how primitive the living conditions were.

There is a small **museum** at the park headquarters that displays relics from CPT days, although there's not a whole lot of English explanation. At the end of the road into the park is a small White Hmong village.

🛏 Sleeping & Eating

Accommodation in the park is limited to that run by **Thailand's Royal Forest**

Department (☑ 02 562 0760; www.dnp.go.th; 2-8 person tent 150-600B, bungalows 800-2400B), and must be booked online or via phone. Golden House Tour (p267), near the TAT office in Phitsanulok, can help book accommodation at the national park.

Inside the park, the only food available is in the canteen near the visitor centre, which can be closed during the rainy season (from approximately June to October).

ℹ️ Getting There & Away

The park headquarters is about 125km from Phitsanulok. To get here, first take an early bus to Nakhon Thai (45B to 64B, two hours, hourly from 5am to 6pm). From there, near the market, you can charter a *sŏrng·tăa·ou* to the park (700B). As a day trip from Phitsanulok, Golden House Tour (p267) charges 2500B for car and driver; petrol is extra. This is a delightful trip if you're on a motorcycle since there's not much traffic along the way, but a strong engine is necessary to conquer the hills to Phu Hin Rong Kla.

KAMPHAENG PHET PROVINCE

Kamphaeng Phet กำแพงเพชร

☑ 055 / POP 30,000

Located halfway between Bangkok and Chiang Mai, Kamphaeng Phet translates as 'Diamond Wall', a reference to the apparent strength of this formerly walled city's protective barrier. This level of security was necessary, as the city helped to protect the Sukhothai and, later, Ayuthaya kingdoms against attacks from Burma or Lanna. Parts of the wall can still be seen today, as well as impressive ruins of several religious structures. The modern city stretches along a shallow section of Mae Nam Ping and is one of Thailand's more pleasant provincial capitals.

◉ Sights

A Unesco World Heritage Site, the **Kamphaeng Phet Historical Park** (อุทยาน ประวัติศาสตร์กำแพงเพชร; 100B, with walled city 150B; ⊘8am-6.30pm) features the ruins of structures dating back to the 14th century, roughly the same time as the better-known kingdom of Sukhothai. Kamphaeng Phet's Buddhist monuments continued to be built up until the Ayuthaya period, nearly 200

years later, and thus possess elements of both Sukhothai and Ayuthaya styles, resulting in a school of Buddhist art quite unlike anywhere else in Thailand. The park consists of two distinct sections.

◉ Walled City

Just north of modern Kamphaeng Phet, this **walled zone** is the origin of the city's name, and was formerly inhabited by *gamavasi* (living in the community) monks. It's a long walk or an approximately 40B motorcycle taxi ride from the centre of town.

Wat Phra Kaew   HISTORIC SITE
(วัดพระแก้ว; Kamphaeng Phet Historical Park; 100B; ⊘8am-6.30pm) This former temple, adjacent to what is believed to have been the royal palace (now in ruins), dominates the walled city. There's an immense reclining Buddha and several smaller, weather-corroded Buddha statues that have assumed slender, porous forms, reminding some visitors of the sculptures of Alberto Giacometti.

Wat Phra That   HISTORIC SITE
(วัดพระธาตุ; Kamphaeng Phet Historical Park; 100B; ⊘8am-6.30pm) The ruins of this temple are distinguished by a large round-based brick and laterite Kamphaeng Phet–style *chedi* surrounded by columns.

◉ Outside Town

The majority of Kamphaeng Phet's ruins are found in this expansive zone (admission 100B), located about 1.5km north of the city walls. The area was previously home to *aranyavasi* (living in forests) monks and (in addition to Wat Phra Si Iriyabot and Wat Chang Rob) contains more than 40 other former compounds, including an additional six currently being excavated, although most are not much more than flat-brick foundations with the occasional weather-worn Buddha image.

There is an excellent visitor centre (p273) at the entrance where bicycle hire (per day 30B) can be arranged.

A motorcycle taxi from central Kamphaeng Phet to the entrance will run to about 80B.

Wat Phra Si Iriyabot   HISTORIC SITE
(วัดพระสี่อิริยาบถ; Kamphaeng Phet Historical Park; 100B; ⊘8am-6.30pm) The highlight here is a towering *mon·dòp* (the small square build-

Kamphaeng Phet

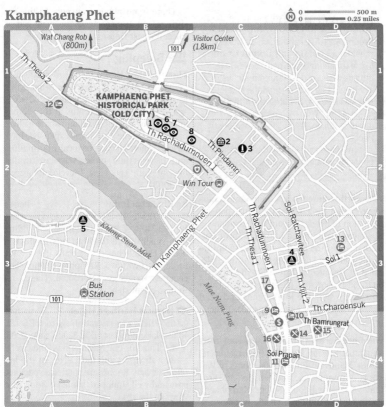

Kamphaeng Phet

⊙ Sights
1 Kamphaeng Phet Historical Park B2
2 Kamphaeng Phet National Museum C2
3 Shiva Shrine C2
4 Wat Khu Yang D3
5 Wat Phra Borommathat A3
6 Wat Phra Kaew B2
7 Wat Phra Si Iriyabot B2
8 Wat Phra That B2

🛏 Sleeping
9 Chakungrao Riverview C3
10 Ko Chokchai Hotel D4

11 Navarat Heritage Hotel C4
12 Scenic Riverside Resort A1
13 Three J Guest House D3

🍴 Eating
14 Bamee Chakangrao D4
15 Kitti D4
16 Night Market C4

🍸 Drinking & Nightlife
17 Rong Tiam C3

ing with a spire in a wát) that contains the shattered remains of standing, sitting, walking and reclining Buddha images, all sculpted in the classic Sukhothai style.

Wat Chang Rob   HISTORIC SITE
(วัดช้างรอบ; Kamphaeng Phet Historical Park; 100B; ⊙ 8am-6.30pm) Meaning 'Elephant-Encircled

Temple', this ruin is just that – a temple buttressed with 68 stucco-covered elephants.

Other Sights

**Kamphaeng Phet
National Museum**   MUSEUM
(พิพิธภัณฑสถานแห่งชาติกำแพงเพชร; Th Pindamri; 100B; ⊙ 9am-4pm Wed-Sun) Kamphaeng Phet's

BOXING CONTEST

Around April, Thai and Burmese boxers meet for a **Thai Boxing Competition** in the traditional style, held somewhere outside Mae Sot. Five-round matches are fought in a circular ring; the first four rounds last three minutes, the fifth has no time limit. With their hands bound in hemp, boxers fight till first blood or knockout.

You'll have to ask around to find the changing venue for this annual slugfest.

visit-worthy museum has undergone an extensive renovation. It's home to an expansive collection of artefacts from the Kamphaeng Phet area, including an immense Shiva statue that is the largest bronze Hindu sculpture in the country. The image was formerly located at the nearby **Shiva Shrine** (ศาลพระ อิศวร; off Th Pindamri) FREE until a German missionary stole the idol's hands and head in 1886 (they were later returned). Today a replica stands in its place.

Wat Phra Borommathat BUDDHIST TEMPLE
(วัดพระบรมธาตุ; off Rte 1078; ⏲ daylight hours) Across Mae Nam Ping are the ruins of Wat Phra Borommathat, located in an area that was settled long before Kamphaeng Phet's heyday, although visible remains are post-classical Sukhothai. The compound has a few small *chedi* (stupas) and one larger *chedi* of the late Sukhothai period, which is now crowned with a Burmese-style umbrella added early in the 20th century.

Wat Khu Yang BUDDHIST TEMPLE
(วัดคูยาง; Soi 1, Soi Ratchavithee; ⏲ daylight hours) Located just north of central Kamphaeng Phet, this Buddhist temple contains a handsome wooden *hŏr đrai* (manuscript library) dating back to the 19th century.

Phra Ruang Hot Springs HOT SPRINGS
(บ่อน้ำพร้อนพระร่วง; Ban Lan Hin; 30B; ⏲ 8.30am-6pm) Along the road to Sukhothai, 20km from Kamphaeng Phet, this complex of hot springs is the Thai version of a rural health retreat. The reputedly therapeutic hot waters have been channelled into seven private bathing rooms (50B) and there are also several places offering traditional Thai massage.

There is no public transport to the hot springs, but transport can be arranged at Three J Guest House.

🛏 Sleeping

Three J Guest House GUESTHOUSE **$**
(📞 081 887 4189, 055 713129; www.threejguesthouse.com; 79 Soi 1, Soi Ratchavitee; r 300-900B; ❄@🅦) The cheapest rooms at this homey guesthouse are fan-cooled and share a clean bathroom, while the more expensive have air-con. There's heaps of local information, and bicycles and motorcycles are available for hire (per day bicycle/motorcycle 50/200B).

Ko Chokchai Hotel HOTEL **$**
(📞 055 711531; 19-43 Soi 8, Th Rachadaumnoen 1; r 260-340B; ❄🅦) This imposing building with smallish and tired but tidy rooms is a decent budget choice, especially if you want to be in 'downtown' Kamphaeng Phet. The cheapest rooms are fan-cooled. There's no Roman-script sign.

★ **Navarat Heritage Hotel** HOTEL **$$**
(📞 055 711211; www.navaratheritage.com; 2 Soi 21, Th Tesa 1; incl breakfast r 1100-3200B, ste 15,000B; ❄🅦) The '70s-era Navarat has undergone a renovation, erasing most signs of the hotel's true age. Rooms are modern, spacious, cosy and well equipped, some boasting nice views of the river.

Chakungrao Riverview HOTEL **$$**
(📞 055 714900; www.chanukungraoriverview.com; 149 Th Thesa 1; incl breakfast r 800-1100B, ste 3000B; ❄@🅦) At Kamphaeng Phet's grandest digs, rooms are tastefully decked out in dark woods and forest green, and feature balconies with river or city views. Suites are huge and are generally available at a considerable discount.

Scenic Riverside Resort HOTEL **$$$**
(📞 055 722009; www.scenicriversideresort.com; 325/16 Th Thesa 2; incl breakfast 1500-3700B; ❄🅦🏊) Picture a Greek fishing village in which the interior design has been overseen by a pre-teen Thai girl and you start to get an idea of this wacky but fun resort. The eight dome-shaped, whitewashed villas here are decked out with stuffed dolls and other kitsch, but are spacious and share a pool and a pleasant riverside location.

✖ Eating & Drinking

★ Bamee Chakangrao THAI $

(cnr Soi 9 & Th Rachadumnoen 1; mains 30-35B;
⊙8.30am-3pm) Thin wheat-and-egg noodles
(bà·mèe) are a speciality of Kamphaeng
Phet, and this famous restaurant is one of
the best places to try them. The noodles are
made fresh every day behind the restaurant,
and pork satay is also available. There's no
Roman-script sign; look for the green ban-
ners on the corner.

Night Market THAI $

(Th Thesa 1; mains 30-60B; ⊙4-10pm) For cheap
Thai eats, a busy night market sets up every
evening near the river just north of the
Navarat Hotel.

Kitti CHINESE, THAI $$

(cnr Th Vijit 2 & Th Bamrungrat; mains 50-1200B;
⊙10am-2pm & 4-10pm; ✲) Long-standing Kitti
excels at seafood-forward, Chinese-style din-
ing. Try the unusual but delicious fried chick-
en with cashew nuts, which also includes
pickled garlic and slices of sweet pork.
  There's no Roman-script sign.

Rong Tiam BAR

(Soi 9, Th Thesa 1; ⊙6pm-1am) Live music (from
8.30pm), snacks and beer are available at
this friendly pub located in a converted an-
tique shophouse.

❶ Information

Most of the major banks also have branches with
ATMs along the main streets near the river and
on Th Charoensuk.

Bangkok Bank (Th Charoensuk; ⊙8.30am-
4.30pm Mon-Sat)

Police Station (☑24hr emergency 191; Rte
101; ⊙24hr)

Visitor Centre (Kamphaeng Phet Historical
Park; 100B; ⊙8am-6.30pm) There is an excel-
lent visitor centre at the entrance where bicycle
hire (per day 30B) can be arranged.

❶ Getting There & Away

Kamphaeng Phet's **bus station** (☑055 799103;
Rte 101) is about 1km west of the Mae Nam Ping.
Motorcycles (50B) and sŏrng·tǎa·ou (20B, fre-
quent 7.30am to 3pm) run between the station
and town. If coming from Sukhothai or Phitsanu-
lok, get off in the old city or at the roundabout on
Th Thesa 1 to save yourself the trouble of having
to get a sŏrng·tǎa·ou back into town.
  Alternatively, if you're bound for Bangkok
(295B, five hours, frequent from 9am to 11pm)
you can circumvent the bus station altogether by
buying tickets and boarding a bus at **Win Tour**
(☑055 713971; Th Kamphaeng Phet), near the
roundabout.

❶ Getting Around

There are very few motorcycle taxis or túk-túk in
Kamphaeng Phet. As such, it's wise to consider
hiring a bicycle or motorbike – **Three J Guest
House** has both (per day bicycle/motorcycle
50/200B).

NORTHERN THAILAND KAMPHAENG PHET

BUSES TO/FROM KAMPHAENG PHET

In addition to the buses listed here, there are minivans to Mae Sot (140B, three hours, hourly from
8am to 6pm) and Sukhothai (65B, one hour, 3pm) and sŏrng·tǎa·ou to Sukhothai (60B, two hours,
three departures from 8am to noon).

DESTINATION	PRICE (B)	DURATION (HR)	FREQUENCY
Bangkok	200-400	5	frequent 9am-10pm
Chiang Mai	256-298	5	hourly 9.30am-11pm
Chiang Rai	265-397	7	5 departures noon-10.30pm
Lampang	147-225	4	5 departures noon-10.30pm
Mae Hong Son	466-544	11	10pm & 10.30pm
Mae Sot	164	3	2am & 4am
Phayao	212-326	6	5 departures noon-10.30pm
Phitsanulok	73	2½	hourly 5am-6pm
Sukhothai	57-74	1	hourly noon-4am

TAK PROVINCE

Tak (จังหวัดตาก) is a vast, mountainous province whose proximity to Myanmar (Burma) has resulted in a complex history and unique cultural mix.

Perhaps due its relative isolation, much of Tak still remains quite wild. The linked Um Phang Wildlife Sanctuary, Thung Yai Naresuan National Park, Huay Kha Kaeng Wildlife Sanctuary and Khlong Lan and Mae Wong National Parks together form one Thailand's largest wildlife corridors and one of the largest intact natural forests in Southeast Asia.

Yet with the opening of Myanmar's first land border at Mae Sot–Myawaddy in 2013, Tak finds itself less isolated, and it remains to be seen how its new role as an increasingly important international crossroads will change the province.

Mae Sot   แม่สอด

☎ 055 / POP 52,000

Despite its remote location and relatively small size, Mae Sot is among the most culturally diverse cities in Thailand. Walking down the town's streets you'll see a fascinating ethnic mixture of Burmese men in their *longyi* (sarongs), Hmong and Karen women in traditional hill-tribe dress, bearded Muslims, Thai army rangers and foreign NGO workers. Burmese and Karen are spoken as much as Thai, shop signs along the streets are in Thai, Burmese and Chinese, and much of the temple architecture is Burmese. Mae Sot has also become the most important jade and gem centre along the border with much of the trade controlled by Chinese and Muslim immigrants from Myanmar.

Although there aren't many formal sights in Mae Sot, many visitors end up staying

Around Tak & Mae Sot

longer than expected. The multicultural vibe, not to mention a vibrant market, fun activities and good food have become attractions in their own right.

◉ Sights & Activities

Border Market
MARKET

(ตลาดริมน้ำเมย; Rte 12/AH1; ⊙7am-7pm) Alongside Mae Nam Moei on the Thai side is an expansive market that sells a mixture of workaday Burmese goods, black-market clothes, cheap Chinese electronics and food, among other things.

It's located 5km west of town; *sŏrng·tǎa·ou* depart from a spot on Th Chid Lom between approximately 6am and 6pm (20B).

Herbal Sauna
BATHHOUSE

(Wat Mani, Th Intharakhiri; 20B; ⊙3-7pm) Wat Mani has separate herbal sauna facilities for men and women. The sauna is towards the back of the monastery grounds, past the monks' *gù·đì* (living quarters).

Cookery Course
COOKING

(☑055 546584; borderlineshop@yahoo.com; 674/14 Th Intharakhiri; lessons 1000B; ⊙lessons 9am-noon & 3-6pm Tue-Sun) The courses here include instruction in four Shan, Burmese and Karen dishes, a trip to the market, a cookbook and the chance to share the results in the adjoining cafe. The cost decreases with bigger groups. Held at Borderline Shop (p277).

Yoga For Life
YOGA

(☑083 092 2772; Irawadee Resort, 758/1 Th Intharakhiri; ⊙classes 9.30-10.30am, 4.50-5.30pm & 6-7pm Mon-Sat, 7.15-8.15pm Tue & Thu) Daily yoga instruction, held at Irawadee Resort (p276).

Highland Farm Gibbon Sanctuary
VOLUNTEERING

(☑081 727 1364; www.gibbonsathighlandfarm. org; Mae Sot) Gives a permanent home to orphaned, abandoned and mistreated gibbons; volunteers are asked for a one-month commitment and to help with daily farm chores. Contact ahead of time via phone or the website to arrange a volunteer stint.

🛏 Sleeping

Many places in Mae Sot are in the budget range and cater to NGO workers who tend to stay for the long-term.

Sleep Nest Hostel
HOSTEL $

(☑081 845 5579; www.facebook.com/sleepnesthostel; Th Intharakhiri; dm 300-450B; ❋❂�)) Pod-like dorm beds in a roomy, young, artsy hostel. The more expensive pods are at ground level and offer much more leg room. The shared facilities have a bar-like feel, and bathrooms are clean and convenient.

Phan Nu House
GUESTHOUSE $

(☑081 972 4467; 563/3 Th Intharakhiri; r 300-500B; ❋�]) This place consists of 29 large rooms in a residential strip just off the street. Most rooms are equipped with air-con, TV, fridge and hot water, making them a good deal.

Bai Fern Guesthouse
HOTEL $

(☑055 531349; 660 Th Intharakhiri; r 150-350B; ❋☞) Set just off the road in a large house, the shared-bathroom budget rooms here are tidy but plain. Service is friendly and a stay includes use of a kitchen, fridge and wireless internet in the communal area.

★Picturebook Guesthouse
HOTEL $$

(☑090 459 6990; www.picturebookthailand.org; 125/4-6 Soi 19, Th Intharakhiri; r incl breakfast 600-800B; ❋☞) Located in an attractive garden, the 10 rooms here, with their smooth concrete, artsy details and custom wood furniture, call to mind trendy dorms. Staff are friendly and keen to help, and are part of a not-for-profit training program.

You'll find the hotel in unmarked Soi 19, directly behind the J2 hotel, about 1km east of Mae Sot.

★Ban Thai Guest House
HOTEL $$

(☑055 531590; banthai_mth@hotmail.com; 740 Th Intharakhiri; r 288-1000B; ❋@☞) This tiny neighbourhood of converted Thai houses includes spacious, stylish, suite-like air-con rooms with Thai-style furniture, axe lounging pillows and Thai textiles, and a couple of fan-cooled, shared-bathroom rooms in the main structure. The whole package is neat, homey and comfortable, not to mention popular with long-stay NGO workers, so booking ahead is a good idea.

J2
HOTEL $$

(☑055 546999; www.facebook.com/j2hotel; 149/8 Th Intharakhiri; r incl breakfast 900-2200B; ❋@☞) The imposing J2 has 47 spacious rooms decked out in an intriguing minimalist-retro theme – think repro '60s- and '70s-era furniture. The tariff isn't a steal, but you're paying for style, and the J2 is probably the

Mae Sot

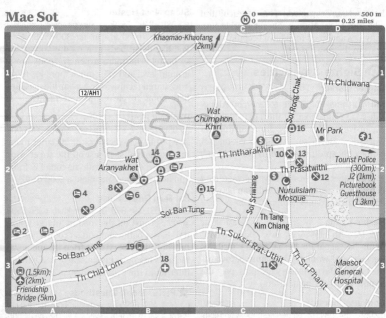

Mae Sot

most image-conscious hotel in town. Located about 1km east of the centre of Mae Sot.

Baan Rabiangmai   HOTEL $$
(☎ 055 532144; 3/3 Th Don Kaew; r incl breakfast 850-2000B; ❉ ☎) Baan Rabiangmai is the type of clean, homey, no-fuss hotel every town should have. The 19 rooms come thoughtfully equipped with kitchenette, big fridge, sitting area, flat-screen TV and a small balcony.

Irawadee Resort   HOTEL $$
(☎ 055 535430; www.irawadee.com; 758/1 Th Intharakhiri; incl breakfast r/ste 1200/2100B; ❉ ☎) The Irawadee has modern rooms decked out in a Burmese theme (or is it an imperial Chinese?). Bathrooms are spacious with open-air showers. Unabashedly gaudy, but fun and comfortable.

✖ Eating & Drinking
Mae Sot is a culinary crossroads with a buffet of cuisines not seen in other Thai towns.

For a fun breakfast head to the area directly south of the Nurulislam Mosque, where several busy **Muslim restaurants** serve sweet tea, roti and *nanbya* (tandoor-style bread). The town's vibrant day market is the place to try Burmese dishes such as *mohinga* (Myanmar's unofficial national dish) or Burmese-style curries served over rice. Mae Sot's **night market** (Th Prasatwithi; mains 30-60B; ☺6-11pm) features mostly Thai–Chinese-style dishes.

The strip of Th Intharakhiri that runs west from Wat Aranyakhet has a handful of open-air bars.

Lucky Tea Garden   BURMESE $
(Th Suksri Rat-Uthit; mains 10-50B; ☺6am-6pm) For the authentic Burmese teashop experience without crossing over to Myawaddy, visit this friendly cafe equipped with sweet tea, tasty snacks and, of course, Burmese pop music.

Borderline Teashop   BURMESE $
(Borderline Shop, 674/14 Th Intharakhiri; mains 35-55B; ☺7.30am-9pm Tue-Sun; ✏) A cosy cafe with tasty Burmese-style salads, noodle dishes and sweets. If you like what you ate, consider enrolling in the linked cookery course (p275).

Phat Thai Mae Sot   THAI $
(Th Prasatwithi; mains 25-45B; ☺noon-9pm) This cosy place serves *pàt tai* with a local twist: toppings of pork rind and barbecued pork. There's no English-language sign; look for the rustic, semi-open-air wood building.

Casa Mia   INTERNATIONAL, THAI $
(Th Intharakhiri; mains 35-220B; ☺8am-10pm Sun-Fri; ✏) This simple restaurant serves what must be the cheapest homemade Italian pasta dishes in the universe. It also does Thai and Burmese, and some great desserts, including a decent banoffee pie.

★**Khaomao-Khaofang**   THAI $$
(www.khaomaokhaofang.com; 382 Rte 105; mains 120-490B; ☺11am-10pm; ✏) Like dining in a gentrified jungle, Khaomao-Khaofang replaces chandeliers with hanging vines, and interior design with orchids and waterfalls. Try one of the several delicious-sounding *yam* (Thai-style spicy salads) featuring ingredients ranging from white turmeric to local mushrooms.

The restaurant is north of town between the Km 1 and Km 2 markers on Rte 105, which leads to Mae Ramat.

Famous Ray's   AMERICAN $$
(Th Intharakhiri; mains 110-330B; ☺11.30am-10pm; ❄) The emphasis here is on burgers, including creative variations such as Thai (with *pàt tai* seasoning and sautéed morning glory) or Burmese (with curry spices and topped with Burmese-style tomato salad).

🔒 Shopping

Mae Sot is most famous for its gems trade and is the most important jade and gem centre along the border. Check out the hustle and bustle among the glittering treasures in the gem shops along Th Prasatwithi, just east of the morning market.

Municipal Market   MARKET
(off Th Prasatwithi; ☺6am-6pm) Mae Sot's municipal market is among the largest and most vibrant we've encountered anywhere in Thailand. There's heaps of exotic stuff from Myanmar, including Burmese bookshops, sticks of *thanaka* (the source of the yellow powder you see on many faces), bags of pickled tea leaves and velvet thong slippers from Mandalay.

Borderline Shop   ARTS & CRAFTS
(www.borderlinecollective.org; 674/14 Th Intharakhiri; ☺9am-7pm Tue-Sun) Selling arts and crafts made by refugee women, the profits from this shop go back into a women's collective and a child-assistance foundation. The upstairs gallery sells paintings, and the house is also home to a tea garden and cookery course.

WEAVE   ARTS & CRAFTS
(www.weave-women.org; 656 Th Intharakhiri; ☺9am-5pm Mon-Sat) One of two branches in northern Thailand, this shop specialises in bright hand-crafted cloth goods created by displaced women from Burma.

Walking Street   MARKET
(Soi Rong Chak; ☺5-9pm Sat) Every Saturday evening the small street by the police station is closed to traffic, and in its place are vendors selling handicrafts, clothes and food.

ℹ Information

Several centrally located banks have ATMs.

There is no official tourist office in Mae Sot, but **Khrua Canadian** (www.facebook.com/

kruacanadianrestaurant; 3 Th Sri Phanit; dishes 40-280B; ⊗7am-3pm & 7-10pm; 🛜 ✐) is a good source of local information.

Immigration (☑ 055 563000; Rte 12/AH1; ⊗8.30am-4.30pm) Located next to the Friendship Bridge, this office can do visa extensions.

Maesot General Hospital (☑ 055 531229; 175/16 Th Sri Phanit; ⊗24hr) Mae Sot's main hospital.

Pawo Hospital (☑ 055 533912; off Th Chid Lom; ⊗24hr)

Police Station (☑ emergency 191; Th Intharakhiri; ⊗24hr)

Tourist Police (☑ emergency 1155; Rte 12/AH1; ⊗24hr) Located near the Friendship Bridge.

❶ Getting There & Away

Mae Sot's tiny **airport** (☑ 055 563620; Rte 12/AH1) is about 2km west of town. At research time, **Nok Air** (☑ Mae Sot 055 563883, nationwide 1318; www.nokair.co.th; Mae Sot Airport, Rte 12/AH1; ⊗9am-5.30pm), with four daily flights to/from Bangkok's Don Muang International Airport (from 1649B, 65 minutes), was the only airline operating out of Mae Sot.

All long-distance sŏrng·tăa·ou, minivans and buses leave from Mae Sot's **bus station** (☑ 055 563435; Rte 12/AH1), located 1.5km west of town; a motorcycle taxi to/from here should cost about 50B.

❶ Getting Around

Most of central Mae Sot can be navigated on foot. Motorcycle taxis and săhm·lór (three-wheeled pedicabs) charge 40B for trips within the centre of town. Mae Sot also has a **taxi service** (☑ 055 030357, 09 8101 9345; www.facebook.com/taximaesot); service between the airport and town costs 60B.

Sŏrng·tăa·ou (Th Suksri Rat-Uthit) to the Friendship Bridge leave from a stop on Th Chid Lom (20B, 15 minutes, frequent from 6am to 6pm).

There are car-hire outlets at Mae Sot's airport, and many guesthouses hire motorbikes for around 250B for 24 hours.

Mae Sot to Um Phang

Rte 1090 goes south from Mae Sot to Um Phang, 150km away. This stretch of road used to be called the Death Highway because of the guerrilla activity in the area that hindered highway development. Those days ended in the 1980s, but lives are still lost because of brake failure or treacherous turns on this steep, winding road through incredible mountain scenery.

Along the way there are two waterfalls, **Nam Tok Thararak** (น้ำตกธารารักษ์; Rte 1090;

TRANSPORT TO/FROM MAE SOT

Buses

DESINATION	FARE (B)	DURATION (HR)	FREQUENCY
Bangkok	290-580	7-8	frequent 8am-9.50pm
Chiang Mai	290	5-6	6.15am & 10pm
Chiang Rai	374	9	7am
Lampang	223	4	6am, 7am & 10am
Mae Sai	416	12	7am
Phitsanulok	172	4	4 departures 7am-2.40pm
Sukhothai	133	3	4 departures 7am-2.40pm

Minivans & Sŏrng·tăa·ou

DESTINATION	FARE (B)	DURATION (HR)	FREQUENCY
Kamphaeng Phet	140	3	hourly minivans 8am-4pm
Mae Sariang	200	6	hourly sŏrng·tăa·ou 5.45am-noon
Um Phang	130	4	hourly sŏrng·tăa·ou 7.30am-3.30pm

ⓘ GETTING TO MYANMAR: MAE SOT TO MYAWADDY

The 420m Friendship Bridge links Mae Sot and Myawaddy, in Myanmar's Kayin State.

Getting To The Border *Sŏrng·tǎa·ou* make frequent trips between Mae Sot and the Friendship Bridge from 6am to 6pm (20B).

At The Border Immigration procedures are taken care of at the **Thai immigration booth** (☑ 055 563004; Rte 12/AH1; ⊙ 5.30am-8.30pm) at the Friendship Bridge. Cross to the **Myanmar immigration booth** (☑ 95 0585 0100; Bayint Naung Rd; ⊙ 5am-8pm (Myanmar time)), where, if you've already procured a Myanmar visa in Bangkok or elsewhere, you'll be allowed to stay overnight or proceed to other destinations. Otherwise you must pay a fee of 500B for a temporary ID card at the Myanmar immigration booth, which allows you to stay in Myawaddy until 8pm the same day; your passport will be kept at the border.

Myawaddy is a fairly typical Burmese town, with a number of monasteries, schools, shops and so on. The most important temple is **Shwe Muay Wan** (Dar Tu Kalair St) a traditional bell-shaped *chedi* gilded with many kilos of gold and topped by more than 1600 precious and semi-precious gems. Another noted Buddhist temple is **Myikyaun-gon** (Nat Shin Naung St), called Wat Don Jarakhe in Thai and named for its gaudy, crocodile-shaped sanctuary. Myawaddy's 1000-year-old earthen city walls, probably erected by the area's original Mon inhabitants, can be seen along the southern side of town.

Moving On About 200m from the border, on the corner with Pattamyar St, is a glut of white share taxis (called 'vans' by the Burmese). Destinations include Mawlamyine (10,000K, four to six hours, frequent departures from 6am to 4pm) and Hpa-an (9000K, six hours, hourly from 6am to 9pm). There are vans (K25,000, 14 hours, frequent 6am to 5pm) to Yangon, and a daily bus departs from a small office on Pattamyar St (15,000K, 14 hours, 5am).

⊙ 6am-6pm) **FREE**, 26km from Mae Sot, and **Nam Tok Pha Charoen** (น้ำตกพาเจริญ; Rte 1090; 200B; ⊙ 6am-6pm), 41km from Mae Sot. Nam Tok Thararak streams beside a picturesque *chedi* and over limestone cliffs and calcified rocks with a rough texture that makes climbing the falls easy. It's been made into a park of sorts, with benches right in the stream at the base of the falls for cooling off and a couple of outhouse toilets nearby; on weekends food vendors set up here. The turn-off isn't clear; look for the sign indicating Chedi Kho.

Just beyond Ban Rom Klao 4 – roughly midway between Mae Sot and Um Phang – is **Um Piam**, a very large Karen and Burmese refugee village with around 20,000 refugees who were moved here from camps around Rim Moei. There are also several Hmong villages in the area.

Sŏrng·tǎa·ou to Um Phang depart from Mae Sot's bus station hourly from 7.30am to 3.30pm (130B, four hours).

Um Phang & Around   อุ้มผาง

Sitting at the junction of Mae Nam Klong and Huay Um Phang, Um Phang is a remote village populated mostly by Karen. Many of the Karen villages in this area are quite traditional, and elephants are a common sight, especially in **Palatha**, a traditional Karen village 25km south of Um Phang. *Yaeng* (elephant saddles) and other tack used for elephant wrangling can be seen on the verandahs of the houses in this village.

Yet the majority of visitors come to Um Phang for nature, not culture. The area borders the Um Phang Wildlife Sanctuary (p280), a popular destination for rafting and hiking that is also home Nam Tok Thilawsu, the largest waterfall in Thailand.

⊙ Sights

Nam Tok Thilawsu   WATERFALL
(น้ำตกทีลอซู) Located in the Um Phang Wildlife Sanctuary (p280), this waterfall is Thailand's largest, measuring an estimated

Um Phang

Um Phang

200m high and up to 400m wide during the rainy season.

Thais, particularly fanatical about such things, consider Nam Tok Thilawsu to be the most beautiful waterfall in the country. There's a shallow cave behind the falls and several levels of pools suitable for swimming. The best time to visit is after the rainy season (November and December) when the 200m to 400m limestone cliffs alongside Mae Nam Klong are streaming with water and Nam Tok Thilawsu is at its wettest.

The easy 1.5km path between the sanctuary headquarters and falls has been transformed into a **self-guided nature tour**. Surrounding the falls on both sides of the river are some of Thailand's thickest stands of natural forest, and the hiking in the vicinity of Nam Tok Thilawsu can be superb. The forest here is said to contain more than 1300 varieties of palm; giant bamboo and strangler figs are also commonplace.

You can **camp** (30B) at the sanctuary headquarters, although you'll have to bring your own tent, and it's best to book ahead from November to January. This is also the only time of year the sanctuary's basic restaurant is guaranteed to be open.

The vast majority of people visit the falls as part of an organised tour, but it's also possible to go more or less independently. If you've got your own wheels, take the turn-off to Rte 1167 just north of Um Phang. After 12km, turn left at the police checkpoint onto Rte 1288. Continue 6km until you reach the sanctuary checkpoint, where you're expected to pay the entry fee (200B plus 30B per car). It's another 25km along a mostly paved road to the sanctuary headquarters.

It's easy to book a truck just about anywhere in Um Phang (round trip around 2000B). Alternatively, you can take a Poeng Kloeng–bound sŏrng·tăa·ou to the sanctuary checkpoint (30B, hourly from 6.30am to 3.30pm) and organise transport from there (round trip around 1800B).

Um Phang
Wildlife Sanctuary   NATURE RESERVE
(เขตรักษาพันธุ์สัตว์ป่าอุ้มผาง; ☎ 088 427 5272, 055 577318; 200B, plus car 30B; ⊗ 8am-4.30pm) The Nam Tok Thilawsu falls (p279) are near the headquarters of the Um Phang Wildlife Sanctuary, which is about 50km from Um Phang, towards Sangkhlaburi in Kanchanaburi Province.

The wildlife sanctuary links with the Thung Yai Naresuan National Park and Huay Kha Kaeng Wildlife Sanctuary (another Unesco World Heritage Site), as well as Khlong Lan and Mae Wong National Parks to form Thailand's largest wildlife corridor and one of the largest intact natural forests in Southeast Asia.

Tham Ta Khu Bi   CAVE
(ถ้ำตะโค๊ะบิ) FREE From Ban Mae Klong Mai, just a few kilometres north of Um Phang via the highway to Mae Sot, Rte 1167 heads

BORDER VILLAGES

Route 1288, which leads to the checkpoint for Um Phang Wildlife Sanctuary, continues for more than 70km, terminating in **Poeng Kloeng** (บ้านเปิงเคลิง), a Karen, Burmese, Talaku and Thai trading village on the Myanmar border.

Poeng Kloeng is a pretty nondescript border town where the main occupations appear to be selling black-market cigarettes from Myanmar and the production of betel nut, but the real reason to make the schlep here is to visit the neighbouring village of **Letongkhu** (เลตองคุ).

Located 12km south of Poeng Kloeng along a rough uphill track, according to what little anthropological information is available, the villagers belong to the Lagu or Talaku sect, said to represent a form of Buddhism mixed with shamanism and animism. Each village has a spiritual leader called a *pu chaik* (whom the Thais call *reu·sĕe* – 'rishi' or 'sage') who wears his hair long – usually tied in a topknot – and dresses in white, yellow or brown robes, depending on the subsect.

If visiting Letongkhu, take care not to enter any village structures without permission or invitation. Likewise, do not take photographs without permission. Overnight stays are not generally permitted.

From the *sŏrng·tăa·ou* station in Um Phang there are five daily *sŏrng·tăa·ou* to Poeng Kloeng hourly from 6.30am to 3.30pm (100B, 2½ hours). There's no regular transport to Letongkhu, but if you're not willing to walk from Poeng Kloeng or organise a guided visit to the village, a 4WD will do the trip from Um Phang for about 5000B.

southwest along the Thai–Myanmar border. Along the way is the cave system of Tham Ta Khu Bi, which in Karen allegedly means 'Flat Mango'. There are no guides here, so be sure to bring your own torch.

🏃 Activities

Virtually every guesthouse in Um Phang can arrange combination trekking and rafting trips, which start at about 4000B per person (for two people) for an all-inclusive three-day excursion. Only a handful of guides speak English. Elephant rides are a popular optional activity, but we don't recommend these.

Rafting trips range from one-day excursions along Mae Klong, from Um Phang to Nam Tok Thilawsu, to three-day trips from Palatha to Nam Tok Thi Lo Re, another impressive waterfall. Most rafting is only possible between November and January.

Another area for rafting is Um Phang Khi, northeast of Um Phang. Officially there are 47 (some rafting companies claim 67) sets of rapids rated at class III (moderate) and class IV (difficult) during the height of the rainy season. The rafting season for Um Phang Khi is short – August to October only.

Trekker Hill — TREKKING, RAFTING
(☑ 055 561090; Soi 2, Th Pravatpriwan) This recommended outfit has the greatest number

of English-speaking guides and offers a variety of treks running from two to three days.

Boonchuay Tour — TREKKING, RAFTING
(☑ 081 379 2591, 055 561020; Th Pravatpriwan; ☉ 1-6pm) Mr Boonchuay offers a variety of treks and rafting trips led by guides who can speak English and have experience in dealing with foreign trekkers.

Napha Tour — TREKKING, RAFTING
(☑ 081 867 0231, 055 561287; Soi 2, Th Pravatpriwan) Napha has an emphasis on rafting and offers a variety of programs and English-speaking guides.

🛏 Sleeping

Most places in Um Phang cater to large groups of Thai visitors, so individual foreign travellers can be met with a bit of confusion. Many rooms in town are designed for four or more people, but singles or couples can usually negotiate lower rates, especially in the wet season.

K & K Guest House — GUESTHOUSE $
(☑ 087 846 1087; Th Sukhumwattana; r 350-500B; ※ ⓐ) Eight spacious rooms with decent-sized beds in a modern shophouse right in the middle of the hustle and bustle of 'downtown' Um Phang. All are equipped with TV and hot water, and the price

depends on whether you opt to go with fan or air-conditioning.

Comesing Homestay GUESTHOUSE $
(📋 081 813 9742; off Th Pravatpriwan; r 300B) The eponymous guide has opened his rambling wooden home to visitors. The three fan-cooled rooms are simple and share communal areas with the family, although bathrooms are en suite. Pay another 100B and breakfast is thrown in; 200B gets you a home-cooked breakfast.

Se Heng Chai Resort HOTEL $
(📋 055 561605; Rte 1090; r 500B; ❋ 🗑) Just west of town, this 'resort' has 13 clean, modern rooms in a two-storey building. There's no English-language sign, but it's the tallest building on the hill.

Tu Ka Su Cottage HOTEL $$
(📋 055 561295; www.tukasu.webs.com; off Rte 1090; r 800-1500B; ❋ 🗑) This is the most comfortable and best-run accommodation in Um Phang. The attractive collection of brick-and-stone cottages is surrounded by flowers and exotic fruit gardens, and all rooms come equipped with air-con, hot water, TV, fridge and semioutdoor bathrooms.

Ban Phurkchaya HOTEL $$
(📋 055 561308, 089 268 7976; Rte 1090; r incl breakfast 700-1000B; ❋ 🗑) A compound of cutesy rooms in and around a modern villa, all of which appear clean and comfortable. There's no English sign here, but you'd struggle to miss the huge flower-decked letters out front.

Garden Huts HOTEL $$
(📋 055 561093, 087 073 7509; Rte 1090; r incl breakfast 300-1500B; 🗑) Operated by a sweet older lady, this collection of budget bungalows of varying degrees of comfort and size and a new building front the river. It features pleasant sitting areas and a well-cared-for garden.

✖ Eating & Drinking

Wae Kam Der THAI $
(Rte 1090; mains 30-120B; ⊘10am-8pm) One of the better eateries in town, the ladies here do a couple kà·nŏm·jeen (fresh rice noodles served with curry) dishes du jour, as well as a menu of Thai-style salads. Look for the semi-open structure with clay pots.

Evening Market THAI $
(Soi 9, Th Pravatpriwan; mains 20-60B; ⊘ 3-9pm Fri & Sat Nov-Feb) On Friday or Saturday evenings during the tourist season (approximately November to February), there's a small but good evening market.

Ban Kru Sun CAFE
(Th Sukhumwattana; ⊘6.30am-8.30pm; 🗑) Owned by a Thai musician, this souvenir shop also does decent coffee and other drinks.

ℹ Information

There are now two large banks and four ATMs in Um Phang.

Government Savings Bank (Th Pravatpriwan; ⊘8.3am-3.30pm Mon-Fri) A bank with ATM.

Hospital (off Th Ratpattana; ⊘24hr)

Police Station (📋 emergency 191; Th Sukhumwattana; ⊘24hr)

ℹ Getting There & Away

Sŏrng·tăa·ou to Mae Sot (Th Pravatpriwan) depart from a stop at the northern end of Th Pravatpriwan (130B, four hours, hourly from 6.30am to 12.30pm). **Sŏrng·tăa·ou to Poeng Kloeng** (Th Ratpattana) depart from a stop on Th Ratpattana, near the hospital (100B, 2½ hours, hourly from 6.30am to 3.30pm)

Mae Sot to Mae Sariang

Route 105 runs north along the Myanmar (Burma) border from Mae Sot all the way to Mae Sariang (226km) in Mae Hong Son Province. The winding, paved road passes through the small communities of **Mae Ramat**, **Mae Salit**, **Ban Tha Song Yang** and **Ban Sop Ngao** (Mae Ngao). The thick forest in these parts still has a few stands of teak, and the Karen villages continue to use the occasional work elephant.

Nam Tok Mae Kasa, between the Km 13 and Km 14 markers, is an attractive waterfall fronting a cave. There's also a hot spring in the nearby village of Mae Kasa.

In Mae Ramat, don't miss **Wat Don Kaew**, behind the district office, which houses a large Mandalay-style marble Buddha.

At Km 58, after a series of roadblocks, you'll pass **Mae La**, where it's estimated that 60,000 Burmese refugees live. The village is at least 3km long and takes a couple of minutes to drive past, bringing home the significant refugee issue that Thailand faces.

There are extensive limestone caverns at **Tham Mae Usu**, at Km 94 near Ban Tha Song Yang (not to be confused with the village of the same name further north). From the highway it's a 2km walk to Tham Mae Usu; note that it's closed in the rainy season, when the river running through the cave seals off the mouth.

At the northern end of Tak Province, you'll reach **Ban Tha Song Yang**, a Karen village attractively set at the edge of limestone cliffs by Mae Nam Moei. This is the last significant settlement in Tak before you begin climbing uphill and into the dense jungle and mountains of Mae Ngao National Park, in Mae Hong Son Province.

Ban Sop Ngao, little more than a roadside village that is home to the park headquarters, is the first town you'll come to in Mae Hong Son. From there it's another 40km to Mae Sariang, where there's ample food and accommodation.

ⓘ Getting There & Away

Sŏrng·tăa·ou to Mae Sariang depart from Mae Sot's bus station (200B, six hours, hourly 5.45am to noon).

MAE HONG SON PROVINCE จังหวัดแม่ฮ่องสอน

Accessible only by vomit-inducing windy mountain roads or a dodgy flight to the provincial capital, Mae Hong Son is arguably Thailand's remotest province. Thickly forested and mountainous, and far from the influence of sea winds, the temperature seldom rises above 40°C, while in January the temperature can drop to 2°C. The air is often misty with ground fog in the winter and smoke from slash-and-burn agriculture during the hot season. Mae Hong Son's location along the border with Myanmar means that it is also a crossroads for ethnic minorities (mostly Karen, with some Hmong, Lisu and Lahu), Shan and Burmese immigrants.

Although the province is firmly on the tourist trail, with many resorts opening in the area around the capital, the vast majority of visitors don't seem to make it much further than Pai.

Mae Hong Son Province

Pai ปาย

🎵 053 / POP 2000

Spend enough time in northern Thailand and eventually you'll hear the comparisons between Pai and Bangkok's Khao San Road. Although the comparisons are definitely a stretch, over the last decade the small town has started to resemble something of a Thai island getaway – without the beaches. Guesthouses appear to outnumber private residences in the 'downtown' area, a trekking agency or restaurant is never more than a few steps away and the nights buzz with the sound of live music and partying.

Despite all this, the town's popularity has yet to negatively impact its nearly picture-perfect setting in a mountain valley. There's heaps of quiet accommodation outside the main drag, a host of natural, lazy activities to keep visitors entertained and a vibrant art scene. And the town's Shan roots can still be seen in its temples, quiet backstreets and fun afternoon market.

◎ Sights

Most of Pai's sights are found outside the city centre, making hiring a motorcycle a necessity.

Pai

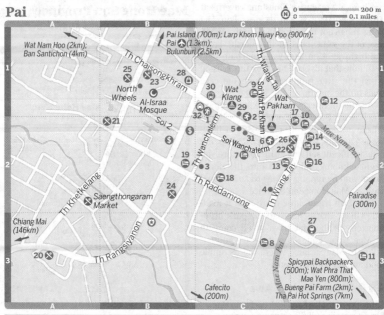

NORTHERN THAILAND PAI

Pai

Wat Phra That Mae Yen BUDDHIST TEMPLE
(วัดพระธาตุแม่เย็น; ⊙ daylight hours) This temple sits atop a hill and has terrific views overlooking the valley. To get there, walk 1km east from the main intersection in town to get to the stairs (353 steps) that lead to the top. Or, if you've got wheels, take the 400m sealed road that follows a different route.

Pai Canyon NATURE RESERVE
(กองแลนปาย; Rte 1095; ⊙ daylight hours) FREE Located 8km from Pai along the road to Chiang Mai, a paved stairway here culmi-

nates in an elevated lookout over high rock cliffs and the Pai valley. The latter can be followed by a dirt trail, but lacking shade, is best tackled in the morning or afternoon.

Tha Pai Hot Springs HOT SPRINGS
(บ่อน้ำร้อนท่าปาย; adult/child 300/150B; ⊙7am-6pm) Across Mae Nam Pai and 7km southeast of town via a paved road is this well-kept local park. Through it flows a scenic stream, which mixes with the hot springs in places to make pleasant bathing areas. The water is also diverted to a couple of nearby spas.

Wat Nam Hoo BUDDHIST TEMPLE
(วัดน้ำฮู; Ban Nam Hoo; ⊙daylight hours) **FREE** Wat Nam Hoo is about 2km west of Pai and houses a sacred Buddha image said to have once emitted holy water from its head. The place is popular with visiting Thais and there's a small market on the grounds.

Memorial Bridge LANDMARK
(สพานประวัติศาสตร์ท่าปาย; Rte 1095) To us it may look like an antiquated bridge, but to the thousands of Thais who stop here during the tourist season, it's one of several crucial photo ops along the '762 curves' to Pai. Located 9km from Pai along the road to Chiang Mai, the bridge was originally built by Japanese soldiers during WWII.

Waterfalls
There are a few waterfalls around Pai that are worth visiting, particularly after the rainy season (October to early December). The closest and the most popular, **Nam Tok Mo Paeng** (น้ำตกหมอแปง), has a couple of pools that are suitable for swimming. The waterfall is about 8km from Pai along the road that also leads to Wat Nam Hoo – a long walk indeed, but suitable for a bike ride or short motorcycle trip. Roughly the same distance in the opposite direction is **Nam Tok Pembok** (น้ำตกแพมบก), just off the road to Chiang Mai. The most remote is **Nam Tok Mae Yen** (น้ำตกแม่เย็น), a couple of hours' walk down the rough road east of Pai.

🏃 Activities
Rafting & Kayaking
Rafting along Mae Nam Pai during the wet season (approximately June to October) is a popular activity here. The trip runs from Pai to Mae Hong Son, which, depending on the amount of water, can traverse rapids from class 1 to class 5. Rates are all-inclusive

SHORT TREK
Don't have the time for a trek in Mae Hong Son? A taste of the area's natural beauty can be had by tackling the **Mae Sakut Nature Trail** (20B; ⊙8am-5pm), part of Nam Tok Mae Surin National Park. In a relatively easy 5km loop, you'll pass through bamboo forests, teak woods, waterfalls, wildflower fields (in season) and viewpoints.

The trailhead is about 7km north of Mae Hong Son town, along the same road that leads to Fern Resort; proceed about 200m past the resort to the roadblock where you're expected to park your vehicle and pay the entry fee.

(rafting equipment, camping gear, dry bags, insurance and food) and run around 2000B per person for a one-day trip and to around 3500B per person for two days.

Thai Adventure Rafting RAFTING
(☑053 699111; www.thairafting.com; Th Chaisongkhram; ⊙10am-9pm) This experienced, French-run outfit leads one- and two-day rafting excursions. On the way, rafters visit a waterfall, a fossil reef and hot springs; one night is spent at the company's permanent riverside camp.

Pai Adventure RAFTING
(☑053 699326; http://paiadventures.com; 28 Th Chaisongkhram; ⊙10am-10pm) The one- or two-day white-water rafting trips offered by this recommended outfit can be combined with hiking and other activities. Also offers a jungle-survival course upon request.

Trekking
Guided treks cost about 1000B per person per day in groups of two or more, and prices are all-inclusive. Most treks focus on the Lisu, Lahu and Karen villages in and around neighbouring Soppong (Pangmapha). Treks can be booked through guesthouse-based agencies or through specific outfitters.

Duang Trekking TREKKING
(☑053 699101; Duang Guesthouse, Th Chaisongkhram; ⊙7am-9pm) A established local agency for trekking and day trips around town.

Massage & Spas
There are plenty of traditional Thai massage places charging from around 150B an hour.

Reiki, crystal healing, acupuncture, reflexology and other non-indigenous methods of healing are also available; keep your eyes open for signs or refer to the monthly *Pai Events Planner*. In addition to these, a few local businesses, all of which are located approximately 1.5km northwest of Tha Pai Hot Springs (p285), have taken advantage of the area's thermal waters.

Pai Traditional
Thai Massage   HEALTH & WELLBEING
(PTTM; ☑083 577 0498; 68/3 Soi 1, Th Wiang Tai; massage per 1/1½/2hr 200/300/380B, sauna per visit 100B, 3-day massage course 3000B; ⊙9am-9pm) This long-standing and locally owned outfit offers very good northern Thai massage, and a sauna (cool season only) where you can steam yourself in medicinal herbs. Three-day massage courses begin every Monday and Friday and last three hours per day.

Pai Hotsprings Spa Resort   SPA
(☑053 065748; www.paihotspringsparesort.com; 84-84/1 Mu 2, Ban Mae Hi; thermal water soak 100B, 1hr massage 350B) A resort-style hotel that also offers massage (8am to 5pm) and thermal water soaks (7am to 7pm).

Spa Exotic   SPA
(☑053 065722; www.spaexotic.com; 86 Mu 2, Ban Mae Hi; thermal water soak 120B; ⊙8am-11pm) This resort channels the hot water from Tha Pai Hot Springs into its bungalow bathrooms and an open-air pool; the latter is open to the public.

🐎 Courses

The curriculum of courses available in Pai ranges from drumming to circus arts; check listings publications such as the *Pai Events Planner* (PEP) or the *Pai Explorer* (www.paiexplorer.com) to see what's on when you're in town.

Pai Cookery School   COOKING
(☑081 706 3799; Th Wanchalerm; lessons 600-750B; ⊙lessons 11am-1.30pm & 2-6.30pm) With a decade of experience, this outfit offers a variety of daily courses covering three to five dishes. The afternoon course involves a trip to the market for ingredients. Contact a day in advance.

Xhale Yoga Pai   HEALTH & WELLBEING
(www.xhaleyogapai.com; 5 days from 12,500B) Need some time out? Sign up for a five-night

yoga retreat (Monday to Saturday) in the foothills outside Pai. Courses suit beginners to intermediates and include accommodation, standout meals, yoga and meditation classes, plus an excursion to a nearby hot spring. Instructor Bhud is all smiles, laughter and sunshine, and the vibe is welcoming and non-competitive.

No drop-ins; pick-up from Pai's bus stop is provided.

Savoei (A Taste of Pai)   COOKING
(☑085 620 9918; Th Chaisongkhram; lessons 700-750B; ⊙lessons 9.30am-1.30pm & 4-8pm) The half-day classes here involve a visit to the fresh market and instruction in four dishes.

🛏 Sleeping

Despite several years of growth, Pai's accommodation expansion has slowed only slightly and the town is allegedly home to more than 500 hotels, guesthouses and resorts. Although 'downtown' Pai has seen relatively little change in this respect, new resorts continue to spring up in an approximate 3km circle around the town.

🛏 In Town

Pai's popularity, particularly among domestic tourists, has resulted in a glut of mid-range and upscale places. But there are still some cheap rooms just outside the centre of town, which is where you should base yourself if you're coming to Pai with preconceived notions of an idyllic, rural stay.

Pai Country Hut   HOTEL $
(☑087 779 6541; www.paicountryhut.com; Ban Mae Hi; bungalows incl breakfast 400-650B; 🛜) The bamboo bungalows here are utterly simple, but they're tidy and most have en suite bathrooms and inviting hammocks. Although it's not exactly riverside, it's the most appealing of several similar budget places close to the water.

Tayai's Guest House   GUESTHOUSE $
(☑053 699579; off Th Raddamrong; r & bungalows 400-700B; ❋🛜) Simple but clean fan and air-con rooms and bungalows in a quiet, leafy compound just off the main drag. The friendly elderly hosts here make the decision easy.

Pai Fah   HOTEL $$
(☑095 165 8945; 77 Th Wiang Tai; r 600-1200B; ❋@🛜) This self-professed 'boutique house'

takes the form of 14 simple but bright and clean rooms in a two-storey villa steps from all the action. Rooms with air-con are more expensive.

Baankanoon GUESTHOUSE **$$**
(☑ 053 699453; 33 Soi Wanchalerm; r 500-800B; ❄ 🛜) Consisting of bright duplex bungalows encircling a 100-year-old *kà·nǔn* (jackfruit) tree, this locally owned place is quiet, clean and cosy. The more expensive rooms have air-con.

TTK GUESTHOUSE **$$**
(☑ 053 698093; 8/10 Th Raddamrong; r 900-1200B; 🛜) Set behind the Israeli restaurant of the same name, the rooms here lack both natural light and interior design but are spotless and conveniently located.

Breeze of Pai Guesthouse HOTEL **$$**
(☑ 081 998 4597; www.facebook.com/breezeofpai; Soi Wat Pa Kham; r 600B, bungalows 800B; ❄ 🛜) This well-groomed compound near the river consists of nine plain but clean and spacious rooms and six A-frame bungalows. It's close to the action without the noise pollution. A loyal customer base means you'll probably have to book ahead.

★**Pai Village Boutique Resort & Farm** HOTEL **$$$**
(☑ 053 698152; www.paivillage.com; 88 Th Wiang Tai; bungalows incl breakfast 2700-5800B; ❄ @ 🛜) This well-maintained place has a collection of 38 wooden bungalows set among winding garden pathways. The rooms don't leave heaps of space to stretch, but they do have floor-to-ceiling sliding windows, large and quite plush bathrooms, and spacious terraces with rattan mats and axe cushions to best enjoy the greenery. Huge off-season discounts available.

★**Baantawan Guest House** HOTEL **$$$**
(☑ 053 698 116; www.baantawanpai.com; 117 Th Wiang Tai; incl breakfast r 1800B, bungalows 2000-3000B; ❄ @ 🛜) The older and more charming riverside bungalows made with salvaged teak are the reason to stay here, but there are also spacious (and less expensive) rooms in a large two-storey building. Service is first rate, and the hotel is located on a relatively isolated (read: quiet) stretch of the river.

Hotel des Artists HOTEL **$$$**
(☑ 053 699539; www.hotelartists.com; 99 Th Chaisongkhram; r incl breakfast 4000-4800B; ❄ 🛜)

WORTH A TRIP

CHINESE VILLAGE

The cheesy photo ops, piped-in music, restaurants serving Yunnanese food, tea tastings, pony rides, tacky re-creation of the Great Wall of China and **mountain-top viewpoint** (ทิวทัศน์บ้านสันติชล; 20B; ⊙ 4.30am-6pm) can make parts of **Ban Santichon** (บ้านสันติชล; Ban Santichon) seem like a Chinese-themed Disneyland. But get past these and you'll find a living, breathing Chinese village, one well worth exploring. Located about 4km west of Pai.

This former Shan mansion has been turned into one of the most charming boutiques in town. The 14 slightly crowded rooms mingle pan-Asian and Western design elements in a tasteful, attractive package. Twin beds are on an elevated platform, and all rooms have balconies, those with riverside views being slightly larger and more expensive.

Pai Vimaan Resort HOTEL **$$$**
(☑ 053 699403; www.paivimaan.com; 73 Th Wiang Tai; incl breakfast r 2500-3000B, bungalows 5000-6000B; ❄ 🛜) The highlight here is the five riverside tented bungalows. Huge and equipped with air-con, jacuzzi, TV and other modern amenities, they redefine camping. The resort's two-storey bungalows are bright and airy, with the top-floor rooms allowing great views of the river, and there are also rooms in the main wooden structure.

Rim Pai Cottage HOTEL **$$$**
(☑ 053 699133; www.rimpaicottage.com; 99/1 Th Chaisongkhram; bungalows 2500-4200B; ❄ 🛜 ♨) The home-like bungalows (which include breakfast from October to February) are spread out along a secluded and beautifully wooded section of Nam Pai. There are countless cosy riverside corners to relax in and a palpable village-like feel about the whole place. Tip: opt for one of the original wooden bungalows, as the newer concrete ones have markedly less charm.

Pai RiverCorner HOTEL **$$$**
(☑ 053 699049; www.pairivercorner.com; 94 Th Chaisongkhram; r incl breakfast 3500-4500B; ❄ 🛜 ♨) A no-brainer for the design-conscious traveller, the nine rooms here include beautiful Thai furniture, gorgeous colours and lots of deluxe details. The more

expensive rooms have river-facing balconies, lounges and interior spa pools.

🛏 Outside Town

If you've got your own wheels, you'll find many options outside the centre of Pai. Most are targeted at domestic rather than foreign tourists, which means they fall in the mid- and upper range of the price spectrum, and typically take the form of air-con-equipped bungalow compounds.

Spicypai Backpackers   HOTEL $

(☎ 088 294 2004; Mae Yen; dm 180B; 🖥) The impressive but exceedingly basic bamboo dorms here look like they could have featured in an episode of *Survivor*. Communal areas ranging from a kitchen to a fire pit continue the rustic feel, and correspondingly beds are little more than a mat on a bamboo frame.

It's about 750m east of Mae Nam Pai, just off the road that leads to Thai Pai Hot Springs.

★ Bueng Pai Farm   GUESTHOUSE $$

(☎ 089 265 4768; www.paifarm.com; Ban Mae Hi; bungalows 1000-2000B; 🖥🏊) In a rural setting about 2.5km east of Pai, the 12 spacious, fan-cooled bungalows here are strategically and attractively positioned around a vast pond stocked with freshwater fish. There's a campfire during the winter months, and a pool, communal kitchen and fishing equipment available year-round.

Located off the road that leads to Tha Pai Hot Springs; look for the sign.

★ Pairadise   HOTEL $$

(☎ 053 698065; www.pairadise.com; Ban Mae Hi; bungalows 900-1300B; 🌐🖥🏊) This neat resort looks over the Pai Valley from atop a ridge just outside town. The bungalows are stylish and spacious and include gold-leaf lotus murals, beautiful rustic bathrooms and terraces with hammocks. All surround a spring-fed pond that's suitable for swimming.

You'll find it about 750m east of Mae Nam Pai; look for the sign just after the bridge.

PuraVida   HOTEL $$

(☎ 089 635 7556; www.puravidapai.com; Wiang Nua; bungalows incl breakfast 1430B; 🌐🖥) A friendly Dutch-Thai couple look after these eight cute bungalows on a well-manicured hillside in the quiet Wiang Nua area. All rooms are equipped with air-con, TV, fridge and hot water; the honeymoon bungalow offers a bit more privacy.

PuraVida is about 4km from the centre of town off the road to Mae Hong Song; look for the well-posted turn-off about 1km from Pai.

Pai Chan   HOTEL $$

(☎ 081 180 3064; www.paichan.com; Ban Mae Hi; bungalows incl breakfast 500-1400B; 🖥🏊) Pai Chan doesn't look like much from the car park, but a closer look reveals eight attractive and comfortable heavy wooden bungalows that lack modern amenities (including air-con), but make up for this with balconies overlooking rice fields or an inviting pool.

It's about 200m east of Mae Nam Pai.

Sipsongpanna   HOTEL $$

(☎ 053 698259; www.facebook.com/paisipsongpanna; Wiang Nua; bungalows incl breakfast 1000-1500B; 🌐🖥) The five adobe-style riverside bungalows here are rustic and quirky with a mix of bright colours, beds on elevated platforms and sliding-glass doors opening to wide balconies. If you prefer to keep it old-school, there are also three original wooden bungalows.

The hotel is about 2.5km from the centre of town off the road to Mae Hong Son; look for the well-posted turn-off, about 1km from Pai.

Bulunburi   HOTEL $$

(☎ 053 698302; Ban Pong; bungalows incl breakfast 750-3000B; 🌐@🖥🏊) Set in a tiny secluded valley of rice fields and streams, the seductively bucolic location is as much a reason to stay here as the attractive accommodation. The 11 bungalows, which range from tight fan-cooled rooms to huge two-bedroom houses, are well equipped and stylish.

Bulunburi is about 2.5km from the centre of town along the road to Mae Hong Son; look for the well-posted turn-off, about 1km from Pai.

Pripta   HOTEL $$$

(☎ 053 065750; 90 Mu 3, Mae Hi; bungalows incl breakfast 3800-5000B; 🌐🖥) This hillside compound features 12 chic bungalows perched at the edge of the Pai Valley. Rooms are huge, with tall ceilings, and feature vast balconies with outdoor tubs using water supplied by the nearby hot springs.

It's about 7km from Pai, between Tha Pai Hot Springs and Rte 1095.

Pai Treehouse
HOTEL **$$$**

(☎081 911 3640; www.paitreehouse.com; Mae Hi; bungalows incl breakfast 1000-7500B; ✳️ 🖥️ 🛜) Even if you can't score one of the three treehouse rooms here (they're popular), there are several other attractive bungalows, many near the river. On the vast grounds you'll also find elephants and floating decks on Mae Nam Pai, all culminating in a family-friendly atmosphere.

The resort is 6km east of Pai, just before Tha Pai Hot Springs.

Phu Pai
HOTEL **$$$**

(☎053 065111; www.phupai.com; Mae Na Theung; bungalows incl breakfast 3300-5250B; ✳️ 🛜 🛁) This self-professed 'art resort' is an attractive, remote-feeling gathering of 40 locally styled, luxury bungalows. Views are the focus here, with most bungalows edging rice fields, and an infinity pool framing the Pai Valley.

The hotel is about 4km from the centre of town off the road to Mae Hong Son; look for the well-posted turn-off just after the airport runway, about 1.3km from Pai.

Pai Island
RESORT **$$$**

(☎053 699999; www.paiislandresort.com; bungalows incl breakfast 5000-6500B; ✳️ 🛜 🛁) This quirky and popular resort intertwines Pacific Island and African themes. Accommodation takes the form of 10 free-standing, private-feeling luxury villas located on islands connected by bridges, each equipped with jacuzzi and expansive semi-outdoor bathrooms.

It's located about 700m north of town, along the road that leads to Mae Hong Son.

✖️ Eating

At first glance, Pai has a seemingly impressive range of restaurants, but a few meals will reveal that the quality of food is overwhelmingly mediocre.

Every evening during the tourist season (approximately November to January) several vendors set up along Th Chaisongkhram and Th Rangsiyanon, selling all manner of food and drink from stalls and refurbished VW vans.

⭐ Larp Khom Huay Poo
NORTHERN THAI **$**

(Ban Huay Pu; mains 50-100B; ⏱️9am-8pm) Escape the wheatgrass-and-tofu crowd and get your meat on at this unabashedly carnivorous local eatery. The house special (and

the dish you must order) is '*larp moo kua*', northern-style *lâhp* (minced pork fried with herbs and spices). Accompanied by a basket of sticky rice, a plate of bitter herbs and an ice-cold beer, it's easily the best meal in Pai.

It's located about 1km north of town, on the road to Mae Hong Son.

Baan Benjarong
THAI **$**

(179 Th Rangsiyanon; dishes 90-170B; ⏱️11am-9pm) Emulate local families and come to this classy home-based restaurant at the edge of a rice field. Menu items such as stewed salted crabs in coconut milk and a salad of banana flower, shrimp and chicken culminate in some of the better Thai food in town.

Phat Thai Na-Win
THAI **$**

(Th Khetkelang; mains 50-150B; ⏱️10am-8pm) Forget the gloopy stuff for sale at Pai's night market; for real *pàt tai*, head a couple blocks west to this old wooden house. In addition to the eponymous fried noodles, you'll find a sizeable English-language menu of Thai standards. There's no Roman-script sign; look for the bright yellow sign opposite North Wheels.

Witching Well
INTERNATIONAL **$**

(www.witchingwellrestaurant.com; 97 Th Wiang Tai; mains 75-195B; ⏱️8am-10pm; 🛜 ✏️) This buzzy foreigner-run place is where to come if you're looking for authentic sandwiches, pasta, cakes and pastries. It also does good coffee and the kind of sophisticated breakfasts you're not likely to find elsewhere in Pai.

Om Garden Cafe
INTERNATIONAL **$**

(off Th Raddamrong; mains 60-120B; ⏱️8.30am-5pm Tue-Sun; ✏️) Fresh-pressed juices, meat-free takes on international dishes, barefoot and/or flute-playing patrons: basically everything you'd expect at a place called Om Garden, except that the food is actually good. Dishes range from Middle Eastern *meze* to breakfast burritos, as well as a good selection of salads and pastries.

Khanom Jeen Nang Yong
THAI **$**

(Th Chaisongkhram; mains 25-30B; ⏱️7am-10pm) This place specialises in northern Thai-style *kà·nǒm jeen* (thin rice noodles served with a your choice of a curry-like broth). It's located in the same building as Pai Adventure Rafting. There's no Roman-script sign.

Good Life
INTERNATIONAL $

(Th Wiang Tai; mains 50-220B; ⊘8am-11pm; 🛜📵) Kefir, kombucha, beet juice and wheatgrass are indicators of the vibe of this eclectic and popular cafe. But don't fear: coffee and soft drinks are available, as is a thick menu of Thai and international dishes, many of which are meat-free.

Evening Market
NORTHERN THAI $

(Th Raddamrong; mains 30-60B; ⊘3-7pm) For tasty take-home, local-style eats, try the market that unfolds every afternoon from about 3pm to sunset.

Cafecito
TEX-MEX $

(www.facebook.com/cafecitopai; mains 90-190B; ⊘9am-6pm Fri-Wed; 📵) Tacos, burritos and quesadillas: Cafecito serves the Tex-Mex staples, all overseen by an American. This is Pai, so there are lots of meat-free options and it also doubles as a cafe.

It's located about 600m south of Th Rangsiyanon, on the unmarked street adjacent to Pai's police station.

Nong Beer
THAI $

(cnr Th Khetkalang & Th Chaisongkhram; mains 60-250B; ⊘8am-8pm; 📵) A long-standing go-to for cheap and authentic Thai eats, ranging from *kôw soy* (curried noodles) to curries ladled over rice, including quite a few meat-free options.

Maya Burger Queen
AMERICAN $

(www.facebook.com/mayaburgerqueen; Th Wiang Tai; mains 90-165B; ⊘1-10pm; 📵) Burgers are a big deal in Pai, and our arduous research has concluded that Maya does the best job. Everything is homemade, from the soft, slightly sweet buns to the rich garlic mayo that accompanies the thick-cut fries.

TTK
ISRAELI $

(The Thai Kebab; Th Raddamrong; mains 60-195B; ⊘8.30am-9.30pm; 🛜📵) The expansive menu here spans Israeli dishes from standards to surprises, with a few breakfast options thrown in for good measure. Lots of meat-free options.

🍷 Drinking & Nightlife

As a general guide to downtown Pai's drinking scene, most of the open-air and VW van-based cocktail bars are found along Th Chaisongkhram; Th Wiang Tai is where you'll find Pai's highest concentration of bars, many with a reggae vibe; Th Rangsiyanon is where most of the guesthouse-style restaurant-bars with a diverse soundtrack and a dinner menu are located; and a knot of open-air, reggae-style bars can be found at the eastern end of Th Raddamrong, just across the bridge.

Don't Cry
BAR

(Th Raddamrong; ⊘6pm-late) Located just across the river, this is the kind of reggae bar you thought you left behind on Ko Phangan. Soporifically chilled out, featuring both live music and a club, it's open until the last punter goes home.

Shopping

Walking Street
MARKET

(Th Chaisongkhram & Th Rangsiyanon; ⊘6-10pm) Every evening during the tourist season, from November to February, a Walking Street forms in the centre of town.

ℹ️ Information

Several exchange booths and ATMs can be found along Th Rangsiyanon and Th Chaisongkhram.

The *Pai Events Planner* (PEP) is a free monthly newsletter that covers cultural events, travel destinations and some restaurant and bar openings; you can find it around town.

ℹ️ Getting There & Away

Pai's tiny **bus station** (Th Chaisongkhram) is the place to catch slow, fan-cooled buses:

DESTINATION	PRICE (B)	DURA-TION (HR)	FREQUENCY
Chiang Mai	80	3-4	noon
Mae Hong Son	80	3-4	11am
Soppong (Pangmapha)	80	1½	11am

More frequent and efficient minivans to Chiang Mai and destinations in Mae Hong Son also depart from here:

DESTINATION	PRICE (B)	DURA-TION (HR)	FREQUENCY
Chiang Mai	150	3	hourly 7am-5pm
Mae Hong Son	150	2½	8.30am
Soppong	100	1	8.30am

DON'T MISS

PANGMAPHA CAVES

The 900-sq-km area of Pangmapha district is famous for its high concentration of cave systems, where more than 200 have been found. Apart from Tham Lot, one of its most famous is **Tham Nam Lang**, which is 20km northwest of Soppong near Ban Nam Khong. It's 8.5km long and thought to be one of the largest caves in the world in terms of volume.

Many of the caves are essentially underground river systems, some of which boast waterfalls, lakes and sandy 'beaches'. *Cryptotora thamicola*, an eyeless, waterfall-climbing troglobitic fish that forms its own genus, is found in only two caves in the world, both of which are in Pangmapha. Other caves contain little or no life, due to an abundance of noxious gases or very little oxygen.

More than 85 of the district's 200 limestone caverns are known to contain ancient teak coffins carved from solid teak logs. Up to 9m long, the coffins are typically suspended on wooden scaffolds inside the caves. The coffins have been carbon-dated and shown to be between 1200 and 2200 years old. The ends are usually carved and Thai archaeologists have identified at least 50 different design schemes. The local Shans know these burial caves as *tâm pěe* (spirit caves) or *tâm pěe maan* (coffin caves). It is not known who made them or why they were placed in the caves, but as most caves have fewer than 10 coffins it's thought that only select individuals were accorded such an elaborate burial. Similar coffins have been found in karst areas west of Bangkok and also in Borneo, China and the Philippines, but the highest concentration of coffin caves from this period is in Pangmapha.

The easiest coffins to visit are in the **coffin cave** (ถ้ำผีแมน; Rte 1095; 20B; ⊙8.30am-5pm) just past Pangmapha Hospital, 2km west of Soppong, and the coffin caves in **Tham Lot** (p292), 9km northeast of Soppong. Several caves that scientists are investigating at the moment are off limits to the public, but John Spies at **Cave Lodge** (p293) may know which caves are possible to explore. His book, *Wild Times*, is also a great informal guide to the area's caves.

Aya Service (☑053 699888; www.ayaservice. com; 22/1 Th Chaisongkhram; motorcycles per 24hr 100-200B; ⊙7am-10pm) and **Du-an-Den** (☑053 699966; 20/1 Th Chaisongkhram; motorcycles per 24hr 100-250B; ⊙7am-9pm) also run air-con minivan buses to Chiang Mai (150B to 200B, three hours, hourly 7am to 5.30pm).

ⓘ Getting Around

Most of Pai is accessible on foot. Motorcycle taxis wait at the **taxi stand** (Th Chaisongkhram) across from the bus station. Sample fares are 50B to Ban Santichon village and 100B to Nam Tok Mo Paeng waterfall.

For local excursions you can hire bicycles or motorcycles in town.

Soppong   สบป่อง

Soppong (also sometimes known as Pangmapha, actually the name of the entire district) is a small market village a couple of hours northwest of Pai and about 70km from Mae Hong Son. There's not much to see in town, but the surrounding area is defined by dense forests, rushing rivers and dramatic limestone outcrops and is *the* place in northern Thailand for caving. The most accessible cave in the area is Tham Lot (p292).

There are also several Shan, Lisu, Karen and Lahu villages that can easily be visited on foot.

⊙ Sights & Activities

The best source of information on caving and trekking in the area is the owner of Cave Lodge (p293). Experienced local guides and recommended kayaking, hiking and caving trips in the area can be arranged here. It's located near Tham Lot, the most accessible cave in the area, 9km from Soppong.

⨳ Sleeping & Eating

There's little in the way of food in Soppong, but virtually every guesthouse has a restaurant attached.

★ **Soppong River Inn** HOTEL $$
(☑ 053 617107; www.soppong.com; Rte 1095; r
& bungalows 500-2450B; ✳@☎) Combining
rooms in a couple of rambling riverside
structures and a handful of free-standing
basic bungalows, this is the most attractive
place in Soppong. Set among lush gardens
with winding paths, the rooms have heaps
of character and are all slightly different; the
River Rim Cottage, with a private balcony
situated right over the river, is our fave.

It's at the western edge of town, within
walking distance of the bus station.

Baan Cafe Nature Resort HOTEL $$
(☑ 053 617081; khunjui@yahoo.com; Rte 1095;
r 600B, bungalows 1200B; ☎) Located near
the bridge, about 750m west of Soppong's
bus stop, this place combines spotless, fan-
cooled rooms and house-like bungalows in
a park setting by Nam Lang. The bungalows
include fireplaces, have balconies looking
over the river and are terrific value. Baan
Cafe is also one of the better restaurants
here (open 7.30am to 7.30pm) and serves locally grown coffee.

The Rock RESORT $$
(☑ 053 617134; Rte 1095; r & bungalows 800-
1500B; ✳☎) Located about 1.5km west of
town, you can't miss this place. The bunga-
lows are scattered across a manicured river-
bank pockmarked with rock formations, and
there are also a few rooms equipped with
TV, fridge and air-con. A suspension bridge
links the grounds with adjacent flower gar-
dens. Rock is geared towards Thai tourists,
and communicating in English might be a
problem.

Little Eden Guesthouse HOTEL $$
(☑053 617054; www.littleeden-guesthouse.com;
Rte 1095; r & bungalows 400-1700B; ✳@☎≋)
The five A-frame bungalows around a
pleasant pool are well maintained and include hot showers. The four rooms in the
new building are spacious and attractive.
But it's the beautiful two-storey 'houses'
that make this place special. Perfect for

families or a group of friends, they are stylishly decorated with living rooms, interesting nooks and crannies, and terraces with
hammocks.

Lemonhill Garden GUESTHOUSE $$
(☑ 089 757 9555; Rte 1095; r & bungalows 500-
1500B; ✳☎) Due to its location across from
the town bus stop, this guesthouse is prob-
ably the most popular spot in town, though
it must be said that there are nicer places to
stay. There's a mishmash of accommodation
ranging from fan-cooled rooms to air-con
bungalows – check out a few before coming
to a decision – and a restaurant (open 7am
to 6pm).

ⓘ Information

There are a couple ATMs in the centre of town
near the petrol station.

ⓘ Getting There & Around

Motorcycle taxis stationed in front of the 7-Elev-
en in Soppong will take passengers to Tham Lot
or the Cave Lodge for 70B per person; private
pick-up trucks will take you and up to five other
people for 300B.

Minivans stop near the town's market, roughly
opposite the petrol station.

Motorcycles can be hired at **Castrol Bike
Point** (☑ 053 617185; Rte 1095; ☉7am-6pm),
at the western edge of town, for 200B or 250B
per day.

Around Soppong

Tham Lot ถ้ำลอด

About 9km north of Soppong is **Tham Lot**
(from 150B; ☉ 8am-5.30pm) – pronounced *tâm
lôrt* and also known as *tâm nám lôrt* – a
large limestone cave with impressive sta-
lagmites, 'coffin caves' and a wide stream
running through it. Along with Tham Nam
Lang further west, it's one of the largest
known caves in Thailand. The total length
of the cave is 1600m, and the stream runs
through it for 600m.

MINIVANS TO/FROM SOPPONG

DESTINATION	FARE (B)	DURATION (HR)	FREQUENCY
Chiang Mai	250	5	hourly 8am-6pm
Mae Hong Son	100	1½	hourly 9.30am-6.30pm
Pai	100	1	hourly 8am-6pm

At the entrance, you must hire a gas lantern and guide for 150B (one guide leads up to three people) to take you through the caverns; visitors are not permitted to tour the caves alone. Rafts (up to three people, one-way 300B) from the entrance to the exit take in the Column Cavern, Doll Cave and Coffin Cave. If going one way, you can walk back from outside the cave (20 minutes), but only during the dry season (approximately November to May). In the dry season it may be possible to wade to the Doll Cave and then take a raft through to the exit (200B). Try to be at the exit at sunset, when hundreds of thousands of swifts pour into Tham Lot and cling to their bedtime stalagmites.

Apart from the main chamber there are also three side chambers – Column Cavern, Doll Cave and Coffin Cave – that can be reached by ladders. It takes around two hours to explore the whole thing. Access to parts of the cave may be limited between August and October because of water levels.

A **Nature Education Centre** (ศูนย์ศึกษา ธรรมชาติและสัตว์ป่าถ้ำน้ำลอด; ⊙8am-5.30pm) on the grounds has basic displays on the area as well as displays of pottery remains found in the cave.

🛌 Sleeping & Eating

A row of **outdoor restaurants** (mains 20-60B; ⊙9am-6pm) outside the Tham Lot park entrance offer simple Thai fare.

⭐ **Cave Lodge**　　　　GUESTHOUSE **$$**
(☑053 617203; www.cavelodge.com; dm 120B; r 400-1200B, bungalows 400-950B; 🛜) Open since 1986, this is one of the more legendary places to stay in northern Thailand (and probably the first guesthouse in Mae Hong Son). Run by John Spies, the unofficial expert on the area, the 20 fan-cooled rooms here are rustic but unique and varied.

The setting on a wooded hillside above Nam Lang is beautiful, and options for adventure abound.

Choose from caving and kayaking trips (the latter possible from approximately February to May), guided or unguided hikes (good maps are available) or just hang out in the beautiful communal area. The traditional Shan herbal sauna is an experience, and the custom ovens bake bread and other treats. Tham Lot is a short walk away.

Mae La-Na　　　　　แม่ละนา

Set in a picturesque mountain valley located 6km off Rte 1095, Mae La-Na, a tiny, remote Shan village, feels like a lost corner of the world. The surrounding area is home to several caves and an established homestay programme.

◎ Sights & Activities

The most famous local attraction is **Tham Mae La-Na**, a 12km-long cavern with a stream running through it. Although local guides are willing to take people inside, in reality the cave lacks the appropriate infrastructure to support visitors, who run a serious risk of permanently damaging delicate cave formations and disturbing the habitat of sensitive cave fish. A better bet is to check out the nearby **Tham Pakarang** (Coral Cave) and **Tham Phet** (Diamond Cave), both of which feature good wall formations. Guides (200B) can be arranged at the main village shop and petrol station. Some of the caves may not be accessible during the rainy season.

Mae La-Na is also a good base for some inspiring walks. Some of Mae Hong Son's most beautiful scenery is within a day's ramble, and there are several Red and Black Lahu villages nearby. It's also possible to walk a 15km half-loop all the way from Mae La-Na to Tham Lot. Khun Ampha at Maelana Garden Home can provide a basic map.

🛌 Sleeping & Eating

There are no restaurants or stalls in Mae La-Na, and eating is done at your homestay or at Maelana Garden Home.

Maelana Garden Home　　GUESTHOUSE **$**
(☑081 706 6021; r & bungalows 300-600B; 🛜) At the edge of town towards Tham Mae La-Na, this beautiful farm-like compound combines basic rooms in two wooden houses and a few A-frame bamboo bungalows. Authentic Shan meals can be prepared for 100B per person. Call ahead – transport can be arranged from Rte 1095 (150B) or Soppong (400B) – or ask for Khun Ampha at the village shop/petrol station.

Homestay Programme　　GUESTHOUSE **$**
(Ban Mae La-Na; per person per night 100B) Two dozen homes in Mae La-Na have collaborated to form a homestay program; fees go back into a community fund. Meals can be

prepared for 100B per person. Inquire at the sporadically staffed wooden office at the entrance to town or at any home with a 'homestay' sign.

ℹ Getting There & Away

The Mae La-Na junction is 13km west of Soppong, but no public transportation reaches the village. A motorcycle taxi here from Soppong costs 200B.

Mae Hong Son แม่ฮ่องสอน

📞 053 / POP 7000

With its remote setting and surrounding mountains, Mae Hong Son fits many travellers' preconceived notion of how a northern Thai city should be. A palpable Burmese influence and a border-town feel don't clash with this image and, best of all, there's hardly a túk-túk or tout to be seen. This doesn't mean Mae Hong Son is uncharted territory – tour groups have been coming here for years – but the city's potential as a base for activities, from boat trips to trekking, ensures that your visit can be quite unlike anyone else's.

History

Mae Hong Son has been isolated from Thailand geographically, culturally and politically for most of its relatively short existence. The city was founded as an elephant-training outpost in the early 19th century, and remained little more than this until 1856, when fighting in Burma caused thousands of Shan to pour into the area. In the years that followed, Mae Hong Son prospered as a centre for logging and remained an independent kingdom until 1900, when King Rama V incorporated the area into the Thai kingdom.

◉ Sights

With their bright colours, whitewashed stupas and glittering zinc fretwork, Mae Hong Son's Burmese- and Shan-style temples will have you scratching your head wondering which country you're in.

★ Wat Phra That Doi Kong Mu   BUDDHIST TEMPLE

(วัดพระธาตุดอยกองมู; ⊙ daylight hours) Climb the hill west of town, Doi Kong Mu (1500m), to visit this temple compound, also known as Wat Plai Doi. Two Shan *chedi*, erected in

1860 and 1874, enshrine the ashes of monks from Myanmar's Shan State. Around the back of the wát you can see a tall, slender, standing Buddha and catch views west of the ridge. There's also a cafe and a small tourist market.

The view of the sea of fog that collects in the valley each morning is impressive; at other times you get wonderful views of the town and surrounding valleys.

On Th Pha Doong Muay Do is a long stairway leading to the top of Wat Phra That Doi Kong Mu (it's easier than it might appear); otherwise a motorcycle taxi costs 120B return.

Wat Jong Klang   BUDDHIST TEMPLE

(วัดจองกลาง; Th Chamnansatit; ⊙ daylight hours) Wat Jong Klang houses 100-year-old glass *jataka* paintings and a museum. The temple is lit at night and is reflected in Nong Jong Kham – a popular photo op for visitors. Wat Jong Klang has several areas that women are forbidden to enter – not unusual for Burmese-Shan Buddhist temples.

Wat Jong Klang Museum   MUSEUM

(พิพิธภัณฑ์วัดจองกลาง; Wat Jong Klang, Th Chamnansatit; admission by donation; ⊙ 8am-6pm) This museum in Wat Jong Klang houses 150-year-old wooden dolls from Mandalay that depict some of the more gruesome aspects of the wheel of life.

Wat Jong Kham   BUDDHIST TEMPLE

(วัดจองคำ; Th Chamnansatit; ⊙ daylight hours) Next door to Wat Jong Klang, this temple was built nearly 200 years ago by Thai Yai (Shan) people, who make up about half of the population of Mae Hong Son Province.

Wat Phra Non   BUDDHIST TEMPLE

(วัดพระนอน; Th Pha Doong Muay Do; ⊙ daylight hours) Wat Phra Non is home to the largest reclining Buddha in town.

Wat Kam Kor   BUDDHIST TEMPLE

(วัดกำก่อ; Th Pha Doong Muay Do; ⊙ daylight hours) This Burmese-style temple is known for its unique covered walkway.

🏃 Activities

Trekking

Mae Hong Son's location at the edge of mountainous forest makes it an excellent base for hikes into the countryside. Trekking here is not quite the large-scale industry it is elsewhere, and visitors willing

Mae Hong Son

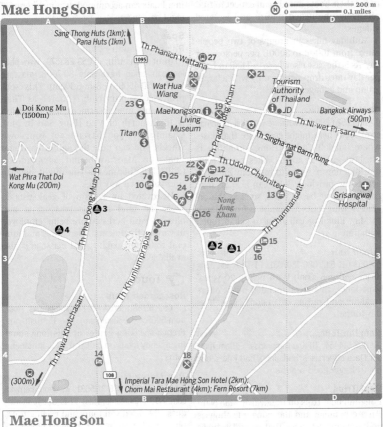

Mae Hong Son

◎ Sights
1	Wat Jong Kham	C3
2	Wat Jong Klang	C3
	Wat Jong Klang Museum	(see 2)
3	Wat Kam Kor	B2
4	Wat Phra Non	A3

◎ Activities, Courses & Tours
5	Friend Tour	C2
6	Nam Rin Tour	B2
7	Rosegarden Tours	B2
8	Tour Merng Tai	B3

⊜ Sleeping
9	Baan Mai Guest House	D2
10	Baiyoke Chalet Hotel	B2
11	Coffee Morning	D2
12	Friend House	C2
13	Jongkham Place	C2
14	Mountain Inn & Resort	B4
15	Palm House	C3
16	Romtai House	C3

⊗ Eating
17	Fern Restaurant	B3
18	little good things	B4
19	Maesribua	C2
20	Morning Market	C1
21	Night Market	C1
22	Salween River Restaurant & Bar	C2

◎ Drinking & Nightlife
23	Crossroads	B1
24	Sunflower	B2

⊜ Shopping
25	Manerplaw/Ethnic Echoes	B2
26	Walking Street	C3

⊙ Transport
27	Sŏrng·tǎa·ou to Mae Aw (Ban Rak Thai) & Ban Ruam Thai (Pang Ung)	C1

NORTHERN THAILAND MAE HONG SON

to get their boots muddy can expect to find relatively untouched nature and isolated villages.

Multiday hikes in groups of two people range from 1000B to 3000B per person, per day. As is the case elsewhere in Thailand, the per-day rates drop significantly with a larger group and a longer trek.

★ **Nature Walks** TREKKING
(☑ 089 552 6899; www.naturewalksthai-myanmar. com) Treks here might cost more than elsewhere, but John, a Mae Hong Son native, is the best guide in town. Hikes range from day-long nature walks to multiday journeys across the province. John can also arrange custom nature-based tours, such as the orchid-viewing tours he conducts from March to May. Email or call John to get in touch with him.

Friend Tour TREKKING
(☑ 053 611 647, 086 1807031; 21 Th Pradit Jong Kham; ⊙ 8am-6.30pm) With nearly 20 years' experience, this recommended outfit offers trekking and rafting excursions, as well as day tours.

Nam Rin Tour HIKING
(☑ 053 614454; Th Khunlumprapas; ⊙ 9am-7pm) Mr Dam advertises 'bad sleep, bad jokes', but his treks get good reports.

Boat Trips

Long-tail boat trips on the nearby Mae Nam Pai are popular, and the same guesthouses and trekking agencies that organise hikes from Mae Hong Son can arrange river excursions. The most common trip sets off from Tha Pong Daeng, 4km southwest of Mae Hong Son. Boats travel 15km downstream to the 'long-neck' village of Huay Pu Keng (700B, one hour) or all the way to the border outpost of Ban Nam Phiang Din (800B, 1½ hours), 20km from the pier, before return-

ing. Boats can accommodate a maximum of eight passengers.

Spas

Phu Klon Country Club SPA
(ภูโคลน คันทรีคลับ; ☑ 053 282579; www.phuk lon.co.th; mud treatments 80-700B, massage per hr 250-450B; ⊙ 8am-6.30pm) This self-professed country club is touted as Thailand's only mud treatment spa. Phu Klon is 16km north of Mae Hong Son in Mok Champae. If you haven't got your own wheels, you can take the daily Ban Ruam Thai- or Mae Aw-bound *sŏrng·tăa·ou* (25B), but this means you might have to find your own way back.

Discovered by a team of geologists in 1995, the mud here is pasteurised and blended with herbs before being employed in various treatments. There's thermal mineral water for soaking, and massage is also available.

☞ Tours

Rosegarden Tours TOURS
(☑ 053 611681; 86/4 Th Khunlumprapas; tours from 600B; ⊙ 8.30am-9pm) The English- and French-speaking guides at this long-standing agency focus on cultural and sightseeing tours.

Tour Merng Tai TOURS
(☑ 053 611 979, 086 3115631; www.tourmerngtai. com; 89 Th Khunlumprapas) This outfit mostly does city-based van tours and cycling tours, but can also arrange treks. Free city tours, led by student interns, are available here.

✸ Festivals & Events

Poi Sang Long Festival RELIGIOUS
(⊙ Mar) Wat Jong Klang and Wat Jong Kham are the focal point of this March festival, where young Shan boys are ordained as novice monks in the ceremony known as *bòdat lôok gâaou*. As part of the Shan custom, the boys are dressed in ornate costumes (rather than simple white robes) and wear flower headdresses and facial make-up.

Jong Para Festival RELIGIOUS
(⊙ approx Oct) An important local event, this festival is held towards the end of the Buddhist Rains Retreat around October – it's three days before the full moon of the 11th lunar month, so it varies from year to year.

The festival begins with local Shan bringing offerings to monks in the temples

---

STEAMY SPRINGS

Eleven kilometres south of the capital in the Shan village of Pha Bong is **Pha Bong Hot Springs** (บ่อน้ำร้อนผาบ่อง; Ban Pha Bong; private bath/bathing room 50/400B; ⊙ 8am-sunset), a public park with hot springs. You can take a private bath or rent a room, and there's also massage (per hour 150B). The springs can be reached on any southbound bus.

LONG-NECKED KAYAN VILLAGES

These villages are Mae Hong Son's most touted – and most controversial – tourist attraction. The 'long-necked' moniker originates from the habit of some Kayan women (sometimes also referred to as Padaung, a Shan term) of wearing heavy brass coils around their necks. The coils depress the collarbone and rib cage, which makes their necks look unnaturally stretched. A common myth claims that if the coils are removed, a woman's neck will fall over and she will suffocate. In fact the women attach and remove the coils at will and there is no evidence that this practice impairs their health at all.

Nobody knows for sure how the coil custom got started. One theory is that it was meant to make the women unattractive to men from other tribes; another story says it was so tigers wouldn't carry the women off by their throats. Most likely it is nothing more than a fashion accessory. Until relatively recently, the custom was largely dying out, but money from tourism, and undoubtedly the influence of local authorities eager to cash in on the Kayan, have reinvigorated it.

Regardless of the origin, the villages are now on every group tour's itinerary, and have become a significant tourist draw for Mae Hong Son. The villages are often derided as human zoos, and there are certainly elements of this, but we find them more like bizarre rural markets, with the women earning much of their money by selling souvenirs and drinks. The Kayan we've talked to claim to be happy with their current situation, but the stateless position they share with all Burmese refugees is nothing to be envied, and these formerly independent farmers are now reliant on aid and tourists to survive.

Any of the three Kayan settlements outside Mae Hong Son can be visited independently, if you have transportation, or any travel agency in Mae Hong Son can arrange a tour. The most-touted Kayan village is **Huai Seua Thao**, about 7km from Mae Hong Son. More remote, but definitely not off the beaten track, is **Kayan Tayar**, near the Shan village of Ban Nai Soi, 35km northwest of Mae Hong Son. Another 'long-necked' community is based at **Huay Pu Keng** and is included on long-tail boat tours departing from Tha Pong Daeng. All collect an entry fee from non-Thais of 250B per person.

in a procession marked by the carrying of models of castles on poles. Folk theatre and dance, some of it unique to northwest Thailand, is performed on wát grounds.

Loi Krathong CULTURAL
(⊘Nov) During this national holiday in November – usually celebrated by floating *grà·tong* (small lotus floats) on the nearest pond, lake or river – Mae Hong Son residents launch balloons called *grà·tong sà·wăn* (heaven *grà·tong*) from Doi Kong Mu.

🛏 Sleeping

Mae Hong Son generally lacks inspiring accommodation, although there are a couple of standout midrange options located outside the centre of town. Because it's a tourist town, accommodation prices fluctuate with the seasons, and outside the high season (November to January) it's worth pursuing a discount.

🛏 In Town

Baan Mai Guest House GUESTHOUSE $
(☑080 499 1975; www.facebook.com/baanmai guesthouse; 26/1 Th Chamnansatit; r incl breakfast 300B) The three simple fan-cooled rooms in a cosy wooden house near Nong Jong Kham have an authentic homestay feel.

Palm House GUESTHOUSE $
(☑053 614022; 22/1 Th Chamnansatit; r 300-700B; ❄🛜) The original building here offers several characterless but large, clean rooms with TV, fridge, hot water and fan/air-con. A new annexe offers much of the same, but in a much more modern, spacious and attractive package. The helpful owner speaks English and can arrange transport.

Friend House GUESTHOUSE $
(☑053 620119; 20 Th Pradit Jong Kham; r 150-500B; 🛜) The super-clean though characterless rooms here run from the ultra-basic (think mattress on the floor), which share hot-water bathrooms, to larger rooms with private bathrooms. All rooms are fan-cooled.

Jongkham Place GUESTHOUSE $$

(☑ 053 614294; 4/2 Th Udom Chaonited; r 500-
800B, bungalows 800B, ste 1200-1500B; ❄ 🛜)
This exceedingly tidy, family-run place by
the lake has a few rooms, four attractive
wooden bungalows and two penthouse-like
suites. Most accommodation includes TV,
fridge and air-con.

Mountain Inn & Resort HOTEL $$

(☑ 053 611803; www.mhsmountaininn.com; 112/2
Th Khunlumprapas; incl breakfast r 1200-1500B,
ste 4500B incl breakfast; ❄ @ 🛜 ⛶) Clean, cosy,
if somewhat aged rooms with decorative
Thai touches, air-con, TV and fridge are the
standard here. Rooms look over a pretty
courtyard garden with small ponds, a pool,
and benches and parasols. Superior rooms
are a better deal than the deluxe as they include a terrace overlooking the pool.

Coffee Morning HOTEL $$

(☑ 053 612234; 78 Th Singha-nat Barm Rung; r
600B; @🛜) This old wooden house unites
a cafe-bookshop and three basic rooms.
Considering that bathrooms are shared, the
rates aren't exactly a steal, but easy access
to coffee and an artsy atmosphere make up
for it.

Romtai House GUESTHOUSE $$

(☑ 053 612437; Th Chamnansatit; r 600-700B,
bungalows 1000B; ❄🛜) Hidden behind both
the lakeside temples and a bland-looking
reception area, this place has a huge variety
of accommodation ranging from plain but
spacious, clean rooms to more attractive
bungalows looking over a lush garden with
fishponds.

Baiyoke Chalet Hotel HOTEL $$$

(☑ 053 613132; www.baiyokehotel.com; 90 Th
Khunlumprapas; r incl breakfast 1380-1800B; ❄🛜)
This place intertwines convenient location
and comfortable lodging. As established in
the lobby, the rooms are tastefully outfitted in hardwood and subtle local themes.
A downside is that the restaurant-lounge
downstairs can get quite loud, so request a
room away from the street or on an upper
level. Low-season rates are almost 50% less.

🛏 Outside Town

★ Sang Tong Huts HOTEL $$

(☑ 053 611680; www.sangtonghuts.org; Th Maka
Santi; bungalows 1200-2500B; @🛜⛶) This
clutch of rustic, fan-cooled, TV-free binga-

lows in a wooded area just outside town is
one of Mae Hong Son's more character-filled
places to stay. Accommodation is spacious,
comfortable and well designed, and the tasty
baked goods and pool make up for the relative distance from the town centre.

It's popular among repeat visitors to Mae
Hong Son, so it pays to book ahead. Sang
Tong Huts is about 1km northeast of Th
Khunlumprapas, just off Th Maka Santi – if
going towards Pai, turn left at the intersection before the town's northernmost stoplight and follow the signs.

Pana Huts GUESTHOUSE $$

(☑ 053 614 331; 293/9 Th Maka Santi; r & bungalows 600-750B; 🛜) Set in a wooded area
outside town, the five bamboo huts here
all have hot-water bathrooms and terraces.
The inviting communal area is equally rustic, with its thatched teak-leaf roof, wooden
benches and enclosed campfire for chilly
nights.

Pana Huts is about 1km northeast of Th
Khunlumprapas, just off Th Maka Santi; if
going towards Pai, turn left at the intersection just before the town's northernmost
stoplight and follow the signs.

★ Fern Resort RESORT $$$

(☑ 053 686110; www.fernresort.info; off Rte 108;
bungalows incl breakfast 2500-3500B; ❄ @ 🛜 ⛶)
This long-standing resort is one of the more
pleasant places to stay in northern Thailand. The 35 wooden bungalows are set
among tiered rice paddies and streams and
feature stylishly decorated interiors. There's
no TV, but dogs, a pool, pétanque court and
the nearby nature trails at the adjacent Mae
Surin National Park are more than enough
to occupy you.

The only downside is that the resort is
7km south of town, but free pick-up is available from the airport and bus terminal, and
regular shuttles run to/from town, stopping
at Fern Restaurant.

Imperial Tara Mae
Hong Son Hotel HOTEL $$$

(☑ 053 684444-9; www.imperialhotels.com; Rte
108; r incl breakfast 3800B, ste incl breakfast 5000-
6600B; ❄ @ 🛜 ⛶) Rooms in this upmar-
ket, 104-room hotel all have wooden floors
and balconies and are tastefully decorated.
French windows that open onto a terrace
make a pleasant change from the standard

business hotel layout. Facilities include a sauna, swimming pool and fitness centre.

It's located about 2km south of town.

✗ Eating & Drinking

Mae Hong Son is home to several tourist-oriented restaurants and stalls, but to experience the town's unique and delicious Shan-style food, it's necessary to stick to less formal establishments such as the town's morning market and **night market** (Th Phanich Wattana; mains 20-60B; ⊙4-8pm).

★ Morning Market   THAI $
(off Th Phanich Wattana; mains 10-30B; ⊙6-9am) Mae Hong Son's morning market is a fun place to have breakfast. Several vendors at the northern end of the market sell unusual fare such as *tòo·a poo ùn*, a Burmese noodle dish supplemented with thick split pea porridge and deep-fried 'Burmese tofu'.

★ little good things   THAI, INTERNATIONAL $
(www.facebook.com/littlegoodthings; off Th Khunlumprapas; mains 30-70B; ⊙9am-3pm Wed-Mon;) In a town with such unique and tasty local food, we were reluctant to risk a meal at this new vegan cafe/restaurant. But 'little good things' is probably one of the better restaurants in town. A short menu lists appetising breakfast options and light, Thai-influenced meals, all of which are meat-free, wholesome, embarrassingly cheap and, most importantly, delicious.

Chom Mai Restaurant   THAI $
(off Rte 108; mains 40-290B; ⊙8.30am-3.30pm;) The English-language menu here is limited, but don't miss the deliciously rich *kôw soy* (northern-style curry noodle soup) or *kôw mòk gài* (the Thai version of biryani).

Chom Mai is located about 4km south of Mae Hong Son, along the road that leads to Tha Pong Daeng – there's no Roman-script sign, but look for the Doi Chaang coffee sign.

Salween River
Restaurant & Bar   INTERNATIONAL, THAI $
(23 Th Pradit Jong Kham; mains 40-330B; ⊙8am-10pm;) Salween is your typical traveller's cafe: a few old guidebooks, free wi-fi and a menu ranging from burgers to Burmese. Yet unlike most traveller's cafes, the food here is good; don't miss the Burmese green tea salad.

Fern Restaurant   INTERNATIONAL, THAI $
(Th Khunlumprapas; mains 65-180B; ⊙10.30am-10pm;) Fern is almost certainly Mae Hong Son's most upscale restaurant, but remember, this is Mae Hong Son. Nonetheless, service is professional and the food is decent. The expansive menu covers Thai and local dishes, with quite a few meat-free options. There is live lounge music some nights.

Maesribua   THAI $
(cnr Th Pradit Jong Kham & Th Singha-nat Barm Rung; mains 20-40B; ⊙8am-1pm) Like the Shan grandma you never had, Auntie Bua prepares a generous spread of local-style curries, soups and dips on a daily basis. There's no English-language menu here; simply point and choose what looks tasty.

Crossroads   BAR
(61 Th Khunlumprapas; ⊙8am-1am;) This friendly bar-restaurant is a crossroads in every sense, from its location at one of Mae Hong Son's main intersections to its clientele that ranges from wet-behind-the-ears backpackers to hardened locals. And there's steak (180B to 250B).

Sunflower   BAR
(Th Pradit Jong Kham; ⊙7.30am-10pm) Technically a restaurant (mains 50B to 320B), Sunflower's draught beer, live lounge music, views of the lake and tacky artificial waterfall also make it a passable bar.

MINIVANS TO/FROM MAE HONG SON

DESTINATION	FARE (B)	DURATION (HR)	FREQUENCY
Chiang Mai	250	6	hourly 7am-3pm
Mae Sariang	200	3½	2pm
Pai	150	2½	hourly 7am-3pm
Soppong (Pangmapha)	100	1½	hourly 7am-3pm

LIVE LIKE A LOCAL

For the last decade, the residents of Muang Pon, a picturesque and tradition-al Shan village just south of Khun Yuam, have collaborated in the **Muang Pon Homestay Program** (☑ 084 485 5937; per night incl breakfast & dinner 350B). Ap-proximately 15 households are involved, and the fee includes breakfast and din-ner, and involvement in daily activities such as making traditional handicrafts, cooking local-style sweets, taking part in agriculture and sightseeing.

The locals are welcoming and eager to share their knowledge but be aware that few speak much English.

Muang Pon is about 12km south of Khun Yuam; any Mae Sariang- or Chiang Mai-bound bus can drop you off here.

🛍 Shopping

A few well-stocked souvenir shops can be found near the southern end of Th Khunlumprapas.

Walking Street   MARKET
(Th Pradit Jong Kham; ⊘ 5-10pm Oct-Feb) From October to February the roads around Jong Kham Lake become a lively Walking Street market, with handicrafts and food vendors.

Manerplaw/Ethnic Echoes   ARTS & CRAFTS
(Th Khunlumprapas; ⊘ 10am-10pm) These linked shops specialise in locally produced hill-tribe garb.

ℹ Information

Most of the banks at the southern end of Th Khunlumprapas have ATMs.

Maehongson Living Museum (27 Th Singha-nat Barm Rung; ⊘ 8.30am-4.30pm; 📶)
An attractive wooden building – formerly Mae Hong Son's bus depot – has been turned into a museum on local culture, food and architec-ture, though the bulk of information is only in Thai. There are a few maps and brochures in English, free wi-fi and a free city tour every day at 4pm.

Srisangwal Hospital (☑ 053 611378; Th Singha-nat Barm Rung) Mae Hong Son's main hospital.

Tourism Authority of Thailand (TAT; ☑ 053 612982, nationwide 1672; www.tourismthai land.org/Mae-Hong-Son; Th Ni-wet Pi-sarn; ⊘ 8.30am-4.30pm) Basic tourist brochures and maps can be picked up here.

Tourist Police (☑ 053 611812, nationwide 1155; Th Singha-nat Barm Rung; ⊘ 8.30am-4.30pm)

ℹ Getting There & Away

Remote Mae Hong Son is connected to Chiang Mai by bus and air, and to Bangkok by bus.

For many people the time saved flying from Chiang Mai to Mae Hong Son versus bus travel is worth the extra baht. There are two flights daily to/from Chiang Mai (from 990B, 35 minutes), operated by **Bangkok Airways** (☑ 053 611426; www.bangkokair.com; Mae Hong Son Airport; ⊘ 8am-5.30pm). A túk-túk into town costs about 80B.

BUS

Mae Hong Son's bus and minivan station is 1km south of the city; a túk-túk or motorcycle ride to/from here costs 60B.

DESTINATION	FARE (B)	DURA-TION (HR)	FREQUENCY
Bangkok	675-1050	15	3pm, 4pm & 4.30pm
Chiang Mai	185-450	8-9	8am, 8pm & 9pm
Khun Yuam	43-200	2	8am, 8pm & 9pm
Mae Sariang	97-250	4	8am, 8pm & 9pm

ℹ Getting Around

The centre of Mae Hong Son can easily be covered on foot, and is one of the few towns in Thailand that doesn't seem to have a motorcycle taxi at every corner. A few can be found near the en-trance to the morning market, and charge 20B to 40B for trips within town. There are also a few túk-túk who charge from 40B per trip within town.

Because most of Mae Hong Son's attractions are outside town, renting a motorcycle or bicycle is a wise move.

Around Mae Hong Son

Mae Aw (Ban Rak Thai) & Around   แม่ออ

A worthwhile day trip from the provincial capital is to Mae Aw, an atmospheric Chi-nese outpost right at the Myanmar border, 43km north of Mae Hong Son. Established by Yunnanese KMT fighters who originally fled from communist rule in 1949, decades later the town's population and architecture remain very Chinese. The main industries are tourism and tea, and there are numerous places to taste the local brew, as well as several restaurants serving Yunnanese cuisine.

The road to Mae Aw is a beautiful route that passes through tidy riverside Shan villages such as **Mok Champae** before suddenly climbing through impressive mountain scenery. Stops can be made at **Pha Sua Waterfall**, about 5km up the mountain, and **Pang Tong Summer Palace**, a rarely used royal compound a few kilometres past the waterfall.

For an interesting detour, at Ban Na Pa Paek take a left and continue 6km to the Shan village of **Ban Ruam Thai**. There are several basic places to stay and eat here, and the road ends 500m further at **Pang Ung**, a peaceful mountain reservoir surrounded by pines that is immensely popular among Thai day-trippers in search of a domestic Switzerland.

From Ban Na Pa Paek it's 6km further to **Mae Aw**. There's a brief dirt road to a border crossing (for locals only), but it's not advisable to do any unaccompanied hiking here, as the area is an occasional conflict zone and an infamous drug smuggling route.

🛏 Sleeping & Eating

Mae Aw and Ban Ruam Thai are easily approached as day trips, but if you like what you see, each of the villages has a spread of basic accommodation.

Mae Aw is home to several restaurants and stalls serving delicious Chinese-Yunnanese cuisine.

Ping Ping Guest House　　GUESTHOUSE $
(☑ 084 4481 9707; Mae Aw (Ban Rak Thai); r 300-400B) This place and other similar outfits ringing Mae Aw's reservoir offer basic accommodation in adobe-style bungalows.

Guest House & Home Stay　　GUESTHOUSE $$
(☑ 083 571 6668; Ban Ruam Thai; r 400-2500B) The first guesthouse in Ban Ruam Thai (there are now numerous 'homestays' offering accommodation from 200B to 400B), this place consists of several simple brick huts positioned on a slope surrounded by coffee plants, tea plants and fruit trees.

★**Gee Lee Restaurant**　　CHINESE $$
(Mae Aw (Ban Rak Thai); mains 60-180B; ⊙8am-7pm; ☑) This was one of the first places in Mae Aw to serve the town's Yunnanese-style Chinese dishes to visitors. Stewed pork leg and stir-fried local vegies are the specialities. There's no Roman-script sign, but it's at the corner of the lake, just before the intersection that leads to the centre of the village.

❶ Getting There & Away

There are four daily *sŏrng·tăa·ou* that head towards Mae Aw from Mae Hong Son, all of which depart from a **stall** (Th Phanich Wattana) opposite the market. Two head to Ban Ruam Thai (80B, one hour, 9am and 3.30pm), while two terminate in Mae Aw (80B, one hour, noon and 3pm). The latter depart only when full, which can sometimes be a couple of hours after the scheduled departure time. Because of this, it's probably worth getting a group of people together and chartering a vehicle; the *sŏrng·tăa·ou* drivers we talked to quoted from 1200B to 1600B for either destination, while any tour agency in Mae Hong Son will arrange a vehicle for around 1500B. Heading back to Mae Hong Son, *sŏrng·tăa·ou* leave Ban Ruam Thai at 5.30am and 11am, and Mae Aw at 8am.

Alternatively, the route also makes a brilliant motorcycle ride – just make sure you have enough petrol, as the only station is in Ban Na Pa Paek, at the end of a very long climb.

Tham Pla National Park

The most touted attraction of **Tham Pla National Park** (อุทยานแห่งชาติถ้ำปลา; Rte 1095; adult/child 100/50B; ⊙8am-6pm) is Tham Pla (or Fish Cave), a water-filled cavern where hundreds of soro brook carp thrive. A 450m path leads from the park entrance to a suspension bridge that crosses a stream and continues to the cave. The park is 16km north of Mae Hong Son and can be reached by hopping on any northbound bus.

A statue of a Hindu *rishi* (sage) called Nara, said to protect the holy fish from danger, stands near the cave. The fish grow up to 1m long and are found only in the provinces of Mae Hong Son, Ranong, Chiang Mai, Rayong, Chanthaburi and Kanchanaburi. They eat vegetables and insects, although the locals believe them to be vegetarian and feed them only fruit and vegetables, which can be purchased at the park entrance.

It's all a bit anticlimactic, but the park grounds are a bucolic, shady place to hang out. Food and picnic tables are available.

Khun Yuam ขุนยวม

📞 053 / POP 7000

Between Mae Sariang and Mae Hong Son, where all northbound buses make their halfway stop, is the quiet hillside town of Khun Yuam. There are a couple of places to stay and a few notable sights, and this little-visited town is a nice break from more 'experienced' destinations nearby.

⊙ Sights

Most of Khun Yuam's sights are located outside of town and you'll need private transport to reach them.

Thai-Japan Friendship Memorial Hall
MUSEUM

(อนุสรณ์สถานมิตรภาพไทย-ญี่ปุ่น; Rte 108; adult/child 100/50B; ⊙8am-4.30pm) At the northern end of town is the recently renovated Thai-Japan Friendship Memorial Hall. After watching a brief film on the history of Khun Yuam, you'll find displays and artefacts that document the period when the Japanese occupied Khun Yuam in the closing weeks of the war with Burma, as well as local history and culture.

Some of the Japanese soldiers stayed in Khun Yuam and married; the last Japanese soldier who settled in the area died in 2000.

Wat To Phae
BUDDHIST TEMPLE

(วัดต่อแพ; ⊙daylight hours) About 6km to the west of Khun Yuam, the atmospheric Wat To Phae sits alongside a rural stream and boasts a Mon-style *chedi* (stupa) and an immaculate Burmese-style *wí·hǎhn* (sanctuary). Inside the latter, take a look at the large, 150-year-old Burmese *kalaga* (embroidered and sequined tapestry) that's kept behind curtains to one side of the main altar.

Ban Mae U Khaw
VILLAGE

(บ้านแม่อูคอ) On the slopes of Doi Mae U Khaw, 25km from Khun Yuam via Rte 1263, is the Hmong village of Ban Mae U Khaw. During late November the area blooms with scenic Mexican sunflowers, known locally as *dòrk boo·a đorng*. This event is popular among Thais and accommodation in the town is booked out.

Nam Tok Mae Surin
WATERFALL

(น้ำตกแม่สุรินทร์; 200B) Approximately 50km from Khun Yam is the 100m-high Nam Tok Mae Surin, part of Mae Surin National Park and reportedly Thailand's highest waterfall.

🛏 Sleeping & Eating

In Khun Yuam you'll find a collection of modest rice and noodle shops along the east side of Rte 108, towards the southern end of town. Most of these close by 5pm or 6pm.

Mithkhoonyoum Hotel
HOTEL $

(📞053 691057; Rte 108; r 400-600, bungalow 1200B; ❄) On the main road through the town centre, this long-standing place has simple, clean rooms with fans and private bathrooms, the more expensive of which boast air-con, were recently renovated and look better than ever.

Ban Farang
HOTEL $$

(📞053 622086; www.banfarang-guesthouse.com; 499 Th Ratburana; incl breakfast dm 200B; r & bungalows 600-1200B; ❄🛜) Off the main road towards the northern end of town (look for the signs near the bus stop), the exceedingly tidy bungalows here are set on a wooded hillside. The cheaper fan rooms are plain and dark but have a terrace, while the more expensive ones come with air-con, fridge and TV.

Yoont
HOTEL $$

(📞053 691531; yoontkhunyuam@hotmail.com; Rte 108; r incl breakfast 700-1200B; ❄@🛜) Yoont comprises 12 rooms in a tall concrete building located in the middle of Khun Yuam's main strip. Rooms are relatively spacious and stylish – if slightly overpriced – and there's an inviting rooftop chill-out area.

ⓘ Information

There are a couple of banks with ATMs along the main strip.

ⓘ Getting There & Away

Buses stop regularly at Khun Yuam on their runs between Mae Sariang and Mae Hong Son. The bus station is at the northern end of town.

In addition to the buses below, minivans go to Chiang Mai (300B, 5½ hours, five departures from 6am to 6pm), Mae Hong Son (100B, one hour, 8.30am) and Mae Sariang (150B, 1½ hours, six departures from 6am to 6pm).

DESTINATION	FARE (B)	DURA-TION (HR)	FREQUENCY
Chiang Mai	150-350	7-8	10am, 9.30pm & 10.30pm
Mae Hong Son	50	1½	4pm
Mae Sariang	60-250	2	10am, 9.30pm & 10.30pm

Mae Sariang   แม่สะเรียง

☎ 053 / POP 20,000

Little-visited Mae Sariang is gaining a low-key buzz for its attractive riverside setting and potential as a launching pad for sustainable tourism and hiking opportunities. There are several hill-tribe settlements in the greater area, particularly around Mae La Noi, 30km north of the city, and the area south of Mae Sariang is largely mountainous jungle encompassing both Salawin and Mae Ngao National Parks.

⊙ Sights

Wat Jong Sung
& Wat Si Bunruang   BUDDHIST TEMPLE
(วัดจองสูง/วัดศรีบุญเรือง; off Th Wiang Mai; ⊙daylight hours) These two adjacent Burmese-Shan temples, Wat Jong Sung and Wat Si Bunruang, are located just off Mae Sariang's main street. Built in 1896, Wat Jong Sung is the more interesting of the two and has slender, Shan-style *chedi* (stupas) and wooden monastic buildings.

Phra That Jom Thong   BUDDHIST TEMPLE
(พระธาตุจอมทอง; off Rte 105; ⊙daylight hours) You may have spotted this giant, golden hilltop Buddha statue, from where there are great views over Mae Sariang. It's located about 3km south of town, just off the road that leads to Mae Sot.

🏃 Activities & Tours

The area surrounding Mae Sariang is probably one of the best in northern Thailand for trekking, nature tours and other outdoor pursuits. This is due not only to the area's natural beauty and cultural diversity, but also because of a new breed of responsible and community-based touring and hiking outfits that have sprung up here. Prices range from 1500B to 5000B per day, per person, for groups of at least two people.

NG River Guides   RAFTING
(☎089 756 6443, 053 681139; www.ng-river-guides.com; 258/1 Th Mae Sariang; ⊙9am-5pm) Bobby, the local behind this outfit, conducts rafting and kayaking excursions along Mae Nam Yuam at its wet peak from October to December. Half-day trips, descending from Mae La Noi to Mae Sariang, start at 1200B per day per person in groups of two or more. Greater distances and overnight trips can also be arranged.

Bobby also leads catch-and-release fly-fishing expeditions in Mae Ngao and Mae La Noi; prices start at 9000B per day per person in groups of two or more.

Mae Sariang
Tours 1980   TREKKING, RAFTING
(☎088 404 8402; maesariang.man@gmail.com) Mae Sariang Man, as the owner of this company prefers to be known, is an experienced trekker who leads environmentally conscious and community-based treks and rafting trips in the jungles and national parks surrounding his native city, in Sop Moei and even into Myanmar.

Dragon Sabaii Tours   TREKKING
(☎085 548 0884; www.thailandhilltribeholidays.com; Th Mongkolchai) This outfit emphasises eco- and cultural tourism primarily in the Mae La Noi area just north of Mae Sariang. Activities range from non-intrusive tours of hill-tribe villages to homestays, 'volunteerism', and cooking and farming with hill tribes, all of which are designed to directly benefit local communities.

Piak Private Tours   TREKKING
(☎093 179 9786; piak1003@hotmail.com) An independent, experienced guide, Piak gets positive feedback for his tours and treks. Call or email to arrange an excursion

🛏 Sleeping

Northwest Guest House   GUESTHOUSE $
(☎098 368 3867; patiat_1@hotmail.com; 81 Th Laeng Phanit; r 250-350B; ✳@🛜) The seven rooms in this cosy wooden house are mattress-on-the-floor simple, and only half have en suite bathrooms, but they get natural light and are relatively spacious. Trekking and other excursions can be arranged here.

Mae Sariang

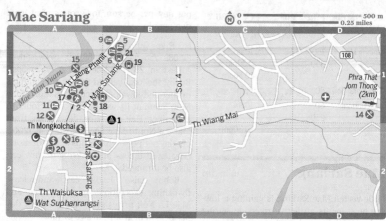

Mae Sariang

◎ Sights
1 Wat Jong Sung & Wat Si
 Bunruang B1

🏆 Activities, Courses & Tours
2 Dragon Sabaii Tours A1
3 NG River Guides A1

🛏 Sleeping
4 Above The Sea A1
5 Chok Wasana B1
6 Huen-Kham-Kong B1
7 Mae Loe Gyi B1
8 Northwest Guest House A1
9 River Bank Guest House B1
10 Riverhouse Hotel A1

11 Riverhouse Resort A1

🍴 Eating
12 Coriander in Redwood A1
13 Intira Restaurant A2
14 Muu Thup D1
15 Sawaddee Restaurant & Bar A1
16 Sunday Market A2

ℹ Transport
17 Bike Rental Shop A1
18 Bus Station B1
19 Sombat Tour B1
20 Sŏrng·tăa·ou to Mae Sam Laep A2
21 Sŏrng·tăa·ou to Mae Sot B1

★ **Riverhouse Hotel**   HOTEL $$
(☎053 621201; www.riverhousehotels.com; 77
Th Laeng Phanit; r incl breakfast 1000-1300B;
❄@🛜) The combination of teak and stylish
decor – not to mention the riverside loca-
tion – makes this boutique hotel the best
spot in town. Rooms have air-con, huge
balconies overlooking the river, as well as
floor-to-ceiling windows. Guests here can
use the pool at the Riverhouse Resort, just
south on Th Laeng Phanit and run by the
same folks.

Huen-Kham-Kong   HOTEL $$
(☎053 682416; www.huenkhamkong.com; 102 Th
Laeng Phanit; bungalows 800-900B; ❄🛜) The
six cutesy bungalows here appear comfortable, come equipped with TV, fridge, air-con
and bicycle, and are looked after by some
friendly folks.

Chok Wasana   GUESTHOUSE $$
(☎053 682132; 104 Th Laeng Phanit; r incl break-
fast 800-1000B; ❄🛜) If you don't require riv-
er views, consider one of the six rooms in
this residential-feeling compound. They're
spacious and tidy and come equipped with
air-con, TV and large refrigerators.

**River Bank
Guest House**   GUESTHOUSE $$
(☎053 682787; Th Laeng Phanit; r 400-1500B;
❄🛜) Rooms in this attractive riverside
house are decked out in hardwood and have
lots of natural light. It's worth shelling out
200B more for the rooms on the upper floor
as the cheaper rooms feel cramped and have
comically small TVs. A highlight here is the
stylish and inviting riverside balcony.

Above The Sea HOTEL **$$**

(☑ 091 859 5264; www.abovetheseamaesariang. com; Th Laeng Phanit; r incl breakfast 1000-1500B; ✳ ☎ ☀) This place has nine rooms decked out in an industrial chic-artsy style, including one large 'family room' with more space and a basic kitchenette. In general the vibe is more bar/restaurant than hotel, and it's one of the few places in town with a swimming pool.

Mae Loe Gyi GUESTHOUSE **$$**

(☑ 086 363 8740; Soi 4, Th Wiang Mai; bungalows 800B; ✳ ☎) Four rather empty-feeling but bright and spacious bungalows in a quiet compound, each equipped with separate sleeping, TV and kitchen areas.

Riverhouse Resort HOTEL **$$$**

(☑ 053 683066; Th Laeng Phanit; r incl breakfast 1500-2800B; ✳ @ ☎ ☀) Located next door to Riverhouse Hotel, and run by the same people, this place is mostly similar but lacks its sister's charm. Ask for a river-view room as the town-side ones are the same price.

🍴 Eating & Drinking

Th Laeng Phanit, north of the junction with Th Mongkolchai, is home to a strip of ever-changing riverside bars.

★ Muu Thup NORTHERN THAI **$**

(Th Wiang Mai; mains 50-80B; ⊙ 8am-7pm) An authentic – and utterly delicious – northern Thai-style grilled meat shack. You can't go wrong with the eponymous *mŏo đúp* (pork that's been grilled then tenderised with a mallet). Located at the junction of the road that leads to Mae Sariang; there's no Roman-script sign, but look for the grill.

Intira Restaurant THAI **$**

(Th Wiang Mai; mains 50-200B; ⊙ 8am-10pm) Probably the town's best all-around restaurant, this place features a thick menu of dishes using unusual ingredients such as locally grown shiitake mushrooms and fish from Mae Nam Moei.

Sunday Market THAI **$**

(Th Wiang Mai; mains 20-60B; ⊙ 3-8pm) If you're in Mae Sariang on a Sunday, don't miss this tiny but worthwhile market, where you'll find an impressive selection of local-style dishes.

Sawaddee
Restaurant & Bar THAI **$**

(Th Laeng Phanit; mains 40-150B; ⊙ 5pm-midnight; ☎ ☀) Like a beachside bar, this is a great place to recline with a beer and watch the water (in this case Mae Nam Yuam). There's a lengthy menu with lots of options for vegetarians. Christian and Beng are good sources of information for small-but-fun destinations and activities in the area.

Coriander in Redwood THAI **$$**

(Th Laeng Phanit; mains 50-420B; ⊙ 10am-10pm Mon-Sat) The city's poshest restaurant, this attractive wooden structure makes a big deal of its steaks, but we'd suggest sticking with Thai dishes such as the various *nám prík* (chilli-based dips). There's also ice cream and iced coffee drinks for an afternoon cooler.

ℹ Information

Mae Sariang has several banks with ATMs, mostly along the western end of Th Wiang Mai.

Hospital (☑ 053 681 032; 74 Th Wiang Mai; ⊙ 24hr) Mae Sariang's main hospital.

Police Station (☑ emergency 191; Th Mae Sariang; ⊙ 24hr) Mae Sariang's main police station.

ℹ Getting There & Around

Mae Sariang's dusty **bus station** (Th Mae Sariang) handles buses within Mae Hong Son Province and to/from Chiang Mai. In addition to buses, there are also minivans to Chiang Mai (200B, 3½ hours, hourly 7am to 5pm) and Khun Yuam (150B, 1½ hours, four departures 10am to 4pm). Located a couple blocks north of the

BUSES TO/FROM MAE SARIANG

DESTINATION	FARE (B)	DURATION (HR)	FREQUENCY
Bangkok	536-834	12	4 departures 4-8pm
Chiang Mai	100-350	4-5	12.30am, 1am & 1pm
Khun Yuam	150	3	4 departures 10.30am-4.30pm
Mae Hong Son	150	4	4am & 5pm

WORTH A TRIP

SALAWIN NATIONAL PARK & MAE SAM LAEP

Covering 722 sq km of protected land in Mae Sariang and Sop Moei districts, **Salawin National Park** (อุทยานแห่งชาติสาละวิน; ☑ 053 071429; 200B) is heavily forested with teak and Asian redwood and is home to what is thought to be the second-largest teak tree in Thailand.

Within the park's bounds, nearly at the end of a 50km winding mountain road from Mae Sariang, is the riverside trading village of **Mae Sam Laep** (แม่สามแลบ). Populated by Burmese refugees, the town has a raw, border-town feel.

The village acts as a launching point for boat trips along Mae Nam Salawin. The trips pass through untouched jungle, unusual rock formations along the river and, occasionally, enter Myanmar. From the pier at Mae Sam Laep it's possible to charter boats south to Sop Moei (approximately 2000B, 1½ hours), 25km from Mae Sam Laep, and north to the Salawin National Park station at Tha Ta Fang (approximately 1500B, one hour), 18km north of Mae Sam Laep. There are passenger boats as well, but departures are infrequent and, unless you speak Thai, difficult to negotiate.

Sŏrng·tăa·ou from Mae Sariang to Mae Sam Laep (80B, 1½ hours, five departures from 7am to noon) depart from a stop on Th Laeng Phanit near the morning market.

bus station, **Sombat Tour** (☑ 053 681532; Th Mae Sariang; ☺ 8am-8pm) handles buses to Bangkok.

Yellow *sŏrng·tăa·ou* to Mae Sam Laep (80B, 1½ hours, five departures 7am to noon) depart from a stop on Th Laeng Phanit, while *sŏrng·tăa·ou* to Mae Sot (250B, six hours, hourly 6.30am to noon) depart from a covered stop across the street from Sombat Tour.

Motorcycles and bicycles are available for hire at the **bike rental shop** (☑ 084 485 2525; off Th Laeng Phanit; bike/motorcycle hire per 24hr 50/200B; ☺ 7am-7pm), as well as at **Northwest Guest House** (p303).

Chiang Mai Province

Best Places to Eat

➡ Lert Ros (p340)

➡ SP Chicken (p340)

➡ Talat Pratu Chiang Mai (p342)

➡ Rustic & Blue (p345)

Best Places to Stay

➡ Dhara Dhevi (p337)

➡ Baan Orapin (p339)

➡ Awana House (p335)

➡ Good Morning Chiang Mai Tropical Inn (p336)

Why Go?

Thailand's northern capital is an overnight train ride and light years away from the bustle of Bangkok. Wrestled from Burmese control by the kingdom of Siam, the former capital of the Lanna people is a captivating collection of glimmering monasteries, manic markets, modern shopping centres, and quiet residential streets that wouldn't look amiss in a country village.

It's more country retreat than mega-metropolis, but this beguiling city still lures everyone from backpacking teenagers to young families, round-the-world retirees and a huge contingent of tourists from China, who are redefining the traveller experience in the city.

Historic monasteries and cooking courses are just part of the picture. Get out into the surrounding province to find a jumble of forested hills, great for rafting, hiking, mountain biking and other adrenalin-charged activities. Most visitors will leave the city at least once to interact with elephants and wander around experimental farms and lush botanic gardens.

When to Go

➡ Chiang Mai is at its best during the cool season, roughly from November to February, when temperatures are mild and rain is scarce.

➡ The hot season runs from March until June, and the mercury regularly climbs above 35°C; pick a hotel with air-conditioning and a pool!

➡ Songkran in April is Chiang Mai's biggest festival – and biggest party – but book well ahead for transport and accommodation.

➡ Monsoon rains usually peak in August and September, making this the low season for tourism. Bring a rain poncho, a sense of adventure and a good book.

CHIANG MAI

เชียงใหม่

♪ 053 / POP 201,000

The former seat of the Lanna kingdom is a blissfully calm and laid-back place to relax and recharge your batteries. Yes you'll be surrounded by other wide-eyed travellers but that scarcely takes away from the fabulous food and leisurely wandering. Participate in a vast array of activities on offer, or just stroll around the backstreets, and discover a city that is still firmly Thai in its atmosphere, and attitude.

A sprawling modern city has grown up around ancient Chiang Mai, ringed by a tangle of superhighways. Despite this, the historic centre of Chiang Mai still feels overwhelmingly residential, more like a sleepy country town than a bustling capital. If you drive in a straight line in any direction, you'll soon find yourself in the lush green countryside and pristine rainforests dotted with churning waterfalls, serene wát and peaceful country villages – as well as a host of markets and elephant sanctuaries.

History

King Phaya Mengrai (also spelt Mangrai) is credited for founding the kingdom of Lanna in the 13th century from his seat at Chiang Saen, but his first attempt at building a new capital on the banks of Mae Ping at Wiang Kum Kam lasted only a few years: the city was eventually abandoned due to flooding.

In 1296 King Mengrai relocated his capital to a more picturesque spot between the river and Doi Suthep mountain and named the auspicious city Nopburi Si Nakhon Ping Chiang Mai (shortened to Chiang Mai, meaning 'New Walled City'). In the 14th and 15th centuries, the Lanna kingdom expanded as far south as Kamphaeng Phet and as far north as Luang Prabang in Laos, but it fell to Burmese invaders in 1556, starting an occupation that lasted 200 years.

After the fall of Ayuthaya in 1767 to the Burmese, the defeated Thai army regrouped under Phraya Taksin in present-day Bangkok and began a campaign to push out the occupying Burmese forces. Chao Kavila (also spelt Kawila), a chieftain from nearby Lampang principality, helped 'liberate' northern Thailand from Burmese control, and was appointed king of the northern states, placing Chiang Mai under the authority of the kingdom of Siam.

Under Kavila, Chiang Mai became an important trading centre, aided by its abundant supplies of teak, and monumental brick walls were built around the inner city. Many of the later Burmese-style temples were built by wealthy teak merchants who emigrated from Burma during this period. In their wake came missionaries and British teak concessionaires who built colonial-style villas around the old city.

The demise of the semi-autonomous Lanna state was only a matter of time. Bangkok designated Chiang Mai as an administrative unit in 1892 in the face of expanding colonial rule in neighbouring Burma and Laos, and the Lanna princess Dara Rasmi was sent to Bangkok to become one of the official consorts of King Rama V, cementing the ties between the two royal families.

The completion of the northern railway to Chiang Mai in 1922 finally linked the north with central Thailand and in 1933 Chiang Mai officially became a province of Siam. Even so, Chiang Mai remained relatively undeveloped until 2001, when prime minister and Chiang Mai native Thaksin Shinawatra sought to modernise the city by expanding the airport and building superhighways.

A high-speed rail link to Bangkok that will reduce travel time to 3½ hours is in planning stages but the date of construction has still not been set.

◎ Sights

◎ Old City

เมืองเก่า

Within the old city, temples dominate the skyline, orange-robed monks weave in and out of the tourist crowds and the atmosphere is more like a country town than a heaving modern city. However, the residential feel of the old city is changing as government offices move out, residents sell up and developers move in.

Wát & Religious Sites

The highlight of any visit to the old city is exploring the temples that burst out on almost every street corner, attracting hordes of pilgrims, tourists and local worshippers. For a calmer experience, visit late in the afternoon, when the tourist crowds are replaced by monks attending evening prayers. Visitors are welcome but follow the standard rules of Buddhist etiquette: stay quiet during prayers, keep your feet pointed away

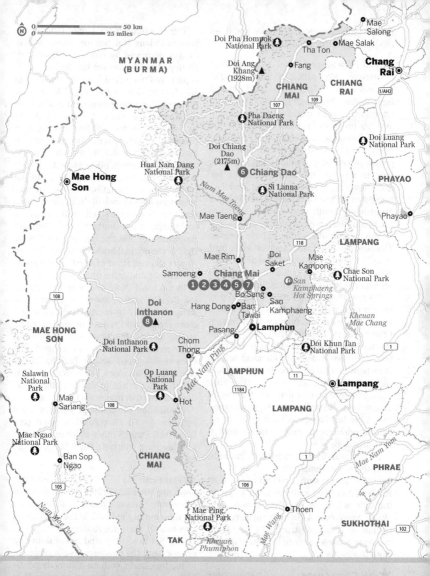

Chiang Mai Province Highlights

1 **Wat Phra Singh** (p310) Taking in Chiang Mai's finest temple.

2 **Chat with Monks** (p330) Discovering what motivates Chiang Mai's men in orange.

3 **Cooking Classes** (p330) Learning how to make the perfect green curry.

4 **Sunday Walking Street** (p350) Joining the human shopping parade.

5 **Talat Warorot** (p315) Plunging into Chiang Mai's time-capsule-like commercial beehive.

6 **Chiang Dao Cave** (p358) Exploring the mystical grotto and birdwatching in the jungle.

7 **Kao Soi Fueng Fah** (p341) Searching for your favourite *kôw soy*, Chiang Mai's signature curry noodle soup.

8 **Doi Inthanon National Park** (p363) Driving to Thailand's highest peak and trekking around plunging falls.

from Buddha images and monks, and dress modestly (covering shoulders and knees).

⭐**Wat Phra Singh**　　　BUDDHIST TEMPLE
(วัดพระสิงห์; Map p318; Th Singharat; 20B; ☺5am-8.30pm) Chiang Mai's most revered temple, Wat Phra Singh is dominated by an enormous, mosaic-inlaid *wí·hǎhn* (sanctuary). Its prosperity is plain to see from the lavish monastic buildings and immaculately trimmed grounds, dotted with coffee stands and massage pavilions. Pilgrims flock here to venerate the famous Buddha image known as **Phra Singh** (Lion Buddha), housed in Wihan Lai Kham, a small chapel immediately south of the *chedi* (stupa) to the rear of the temple grounds.

This elegant idol is said to have come to Thailand from Sri Lanka and was enshrined in 1367. The chapel is similarly striking, with gilded *naga* (serpent) gables and sumptuous *lai·krahm* (gold-pattern stencilling) inside.

Despite Phra Singh's exalted status, very little is known about the Phra Singh image, which has more in common with images from northern Thailand than with Buddha statues from Sri Lanka. Adding to the mystery, there are two nearly identical images elsewhere in Thailand, one in the Bangkok National Museum and one in Wat Phra Mahathat Woramahawihan in Nakhon Si Thammarat. Regardless of its provenance, the statue has become a focal point for religious celebrations during the Songkran festival.

As you wander the monastery grounds, note the raised temple library, housed in a dainty teak and stucco pavilion known as **Ho Trai**, decorated with bas-relief angels in the style of Wat Jet Yot. The temple's main *chedi,* rising over a classic Lanna-style octagonal base, was constructed by King Pa Yo in 1345; it's often wrapped in bolts of orange cloth by devotees.

⭐**Wat Chedi Luang**　　　BUDDHIST TEMPLE
(วัดเจดีย์หลวง; Map p318; Th Phra Pokklao; adult/child 40/20B; ☺7am-10pm) Wat Chedi Luang isn't as grand as Wat Phra Singh, but its towering, ruined Lanna-style *chedi* (built in 1441) is much taller and the sprawling compound around the stupa is powerfully atmospheric. The famed Phra Kaew (Emerald Buddha), now held in Bangkok's Wat Phra Kaew, resided in the eastern niche until 1475; today, you can view a jade replica.

This was possibly the largest structure in ancient Chiang Mai, but the top of the *chedi* was destroyed by either a 16th-century earthquake or by cannon fire during the recapture of Chiang Mai from the Burmese in 1775 (nobody knows for sure). Like most of the ancient monuments in Chiang Mai, Chedi Luang was in ruins when the city began its modern renaissance, but a restoration project by Unesco and the Japanese government in the 1990s stabilised the monument and prevented further degradation.

As you wander around the *chedi* you can easily spot the restoration work on the four *naga* stairways in each of the cardinal directions. The base of the stupa has five elephant sculptures on the southern face – four are reproductions, but the elephant on the far right is the original brick and stucco. The restorers stopped short of finishing the spire, as nobody could agree what it looked like.

In the main *wí·hǎhn* is a revered standing Buddha statue, known as **Phra Chao Attarot**, flanked by two disciples. There are more chapels and statues in teak pavilions at the rear of the compound, including a huge reclining Buddha and a handsome Chinese-influenced seated Buddha barely contained by his robes. The daily Monk Chat (p330) under a tree in the grounds always draws a crowd of interested travellers.

If you enter the compound via the main entrance on Th Phra Pokklao, you'll pass Wat Chedi Luang's other claim to fame, the **Làk Meuang** (หลักเมือง, City Pillar; ☺daylight hours).

⭐**Wat Phan Tao**　　　BUDDHIST TEMPLE
(วัดพันเตา; Map p318; Th Phra Pokklao; donations appreciated; ☺daylight hours) Without doubt the most atmospheric *wát* in the old city, this teak marvel sits in the shadow of Wat Chedi Luang. Set in a compound full of fluttering orange flags, the monastery is a monument to the teak trade, with an enormous prayer hall supported by 28 gargantuan teak pillars and lined with dark teak panels, enshrining a particularly graceful gold Buddha image.

The juxtaposition of the orange monks' robes against this dark backdrop during evening prayers is particularly sublime.

Above the facade is a striking image of a peacock over a dog, representing the astrological year of the former royal resident's birth. The monastery is one of the focal points for celebrations during the Visakha Bucha festival in May or June, when monks light hundreds of butter lamps around the pond in the grounds.

Wat Chiang Man BUDDHIST TEMPLE

(วัดเชียงมัน; Map p318; Th Ratchaphakhinai; donations appreciated; ☉ daylight hours) Chiang Mai's oldest temple was established by the city's founder, Phaya Mengrai, sometime around 1296. In front of the *ubosot* (ordination hall), a stone slab, engraved in 1581, bears the earliest-known reference to the city's founding. The main *wí·hăhn* also contains the oldest-known Buddha image created by the Lanna kingdom, cast in 1465.

Anusawari Sam Kasat
(Three Kings Monument) MONUMENT

(อนุสาวรีย์สามกษัตริย์; Map p318; Th Phra Pokklao) Marking the centrepoint of the old administrative quarter of Chiang Mai, the bronze Three Kings Monument commemorates the alliance forged between Phaya Ngam Meuang of Phayao, Phaya Mengrai of Chiang Mai and Phaya Khun Ramkhamhaeng of Sukhothai in the founding of the city. The monument is a shrine for local residents, who swing by after work to leave offerings.

Museums

The old city has three excellent historical museums in a series of Thai-colonial-style buildings that used to house the city administration. You can buy a single ticket covering all three, valid for a week, for 180/80B (adult/child).

★ Lanna Folklife Museum MUSEUM

(พิพิธภัณฑ์พื้นถิ่นล้านนา; Map p318; Th Phra Pokklao; adult/child 90/40B; ☉ 8.30am-5pm Tue-Sun) Set inside the Thai-colonial-style former Provincial Court, dating from 1935, this imaginative museum re-creates Lanna village life in a series of life-size dioramas that explain everything from *lai·krahm* pottery

---

SAY WÁT? SIGHTS AROUND TOWN

If you still have a taste for more Thai religious architecture, there are dozens more historic wát scattered around the old city and the surrounding streets. Here are some good places to start your explorations.

Wat Inthakhin Saduemuang (วัดอินทขิลสะดือเมือง; Map p318; donations appreciated; ☉ 6am-6pm) Marooned in the middle of Th Inthawarorot, this was the original location of the *làk meuang* (city pillar), and the gilded teak *wí·hăhn* is one of the most perfectly proportioned buildings in the city.

Wat Phan On (วัดพันอัน; Map p318; Th Ratchdamnoen; donations appreciated; ☉ 6am-5pm) Set with gilded Buddhas in alcoves decorated with *lai·krahm* (gold-pattern stencilling), the gold *chedi* at this prosperous wát is visited by scores of devotees after dark. The courtyard becomes a food court during the **Sunday Walking Street** (p350) market.

Wat Jet Lin (วัดเจ็ดลิน หรือ วัดหนองจลิน; Map p318; Th Phra Pokklao; donations appreciated; ☉ 4am-6pm) This friendly wát was used for the coronation of Lanna kings in the 16th century; today you can see a collection of giant gongs, a big old *mon·dòp*-style *chedi* and a large gilded Buddha with particularly graceful proportions.

Wat Lokmoli (วัดโลกโมฬี; Map p318; Th Chaiyaphum; donations appreciated; ☉ 6am-6pm) An elegant wooden complex dotted with terracotta sculptures. The *wí·hăhn* is topped by a dramatic sweeping three-tiered roof and the tall, barrel-shaped *chedi* still has some of its original stucco.

Wat Chomphu (วัดชมพู; Map p318; Soi 1, Th Chang Moi Kao; donations appreciated; ☉ 6am-6pm) Just north of Th Tha Phae, this calm monastery has a gorgeous gilded stupa with gold elephants, restored as a tribute to the king in 1999.

Wat Ou Sai Kham (วัดอู่ทรายคำ; Map p318; Th Chang Moi Kao; donations appreciated; ☉ 7am-6pm) This friendly neighbourhood wát has an impressive collection of jade Buddhas and jade and nephrite boulders in its main *wí·hăhn*.

Wat Mahawan (วัดมหาวัน; Map p318; Th Tha Phae; donations appreciated; ☉ 6am-6pm) A handsome, whitewashed wát that shows the obvious influence of the Burmese teak traders who used to worship here. The *chedi* and Burmese-style gateways are decorated with a stucco menagerie of angels and mythical beasts.

Chiang Mai

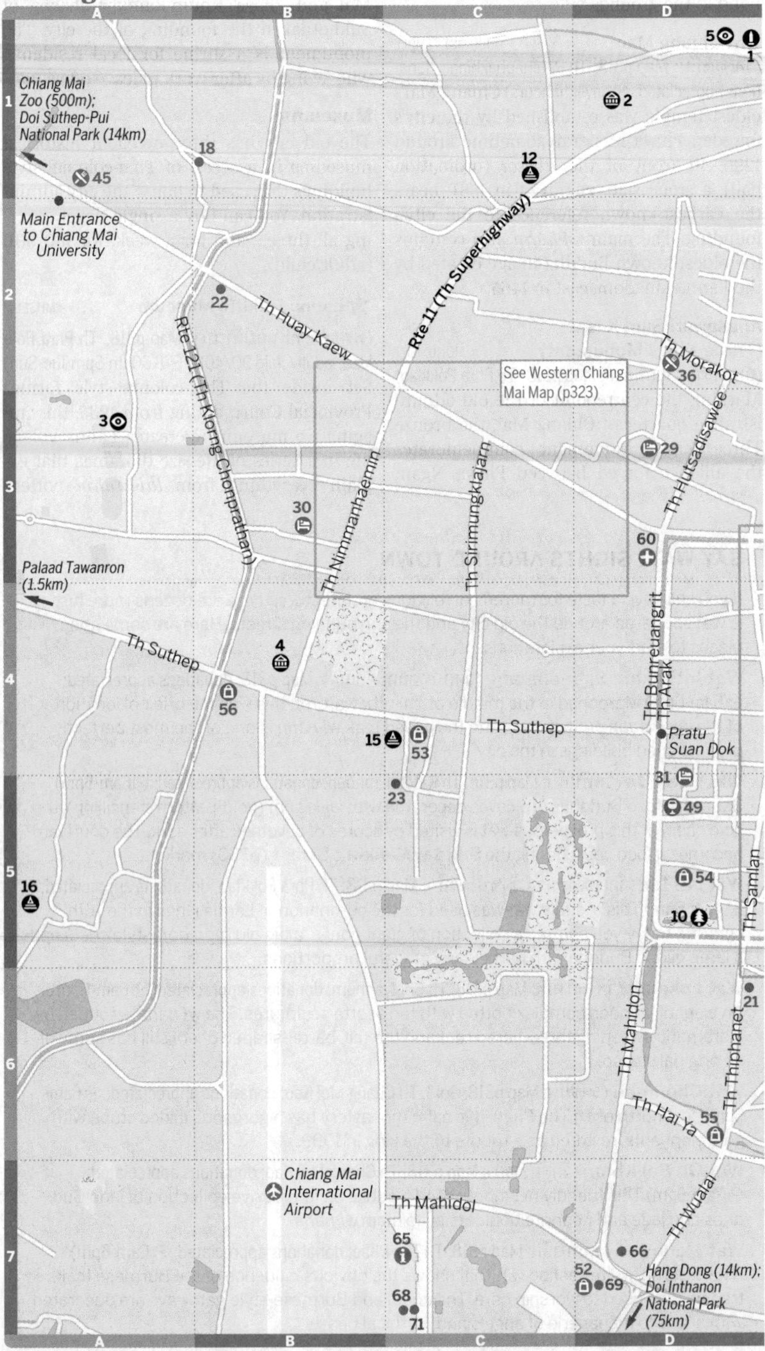

Chiang Mai
Zoo (500m);
Doi Suthep-Pui
National Park (14km)

5 ⊙   1

2

18

Main Entrance
to Chiang Mai
University

45

12

Th Huay Kaew

Rte 11 (Th Superhighway)

22

Th Morakot

36

Rte 121 (Th Klorng Chonprathan)

See Western Chiang
Mai Map (p323)

3 ⊙

29

Th Hatsadisawee

30

Th Nimmanhaemin

Th Sirimungklajarn

60

Palaad Tawanron
(1.5km)

Th Suthep

Th Bunreuangrit

Th Arak

4

56

Th Suthep

Pratu
Suan Dok

15

53

31

23

49

54

10

Th Samlan

16

21

Th Mahidon

Th Thiphanet

Th Hai Ya

55

Chiang Mai
International
Airport

Th Mahidol

Th Wualai

65

66

Hang Dong (14km);
Doi Inthanon
National Park
(75km)

52

69

68

71

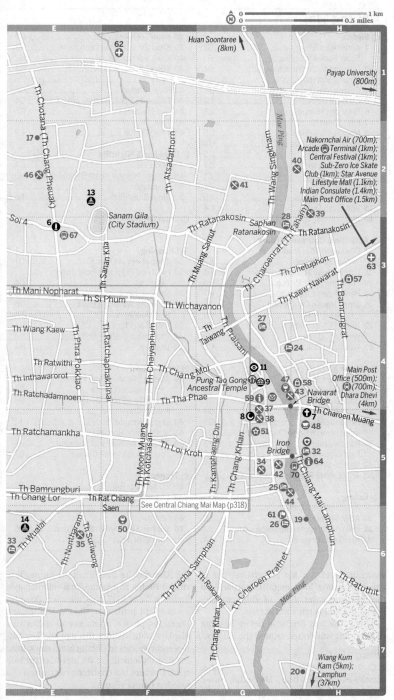

Chiang Mai

stencilling and *fon lep* (a mystical Lanna dance featuring long metal fingernails) to the intricate symbolism of different elements of Lanna-style monasteries.

This is the best first stop before heading to the many *wát* dotted around the old city.

Chiang Mai City Arts & Cultural Centre
MUSEUM
(หอศิลปวัฒนธรรมเชียงใหม่; Map p318; www.cmocity.com; Th Phra Pokklao; adult/child 90/40B; ⊗8.30am-5pm Tue-Sun) Set in the former Provincial Hall, a handsome Thai-colonial-style building from 1927, this museum provides an excellent primer on Chiang Mai history. Dioramas, photos, artefacts and audiovisual displays walk visitors through the key battles and victories in Chiang Mai's story, from the first settlements to the arrival of the railroad. Upstairs is a charming re-creation of a wooden Lanna village.

Chiang Mai Historical Centre
MUSEUM

(หอประวัติศาสตร์เมืองเชียงใหม่; Map p318; Th Ratwithi; adult/child 90/40B; ⊙8.30am-5pm Tue-Sun) Housed in an airy Lanna-style building behind the Chiang Mai City Arts & Cultural Centre, this appealing museum covers the history of Chiang Mai Province, with displays on the founding of the capital, the Burmese occupation and the modern era of trade and unification with Bangkok. Downstairs is an archaeological dig of an ancient temple wall.

Treasury Pavilion Coin Museum
MUSEUM

(ศาลาธนารักษ์; Map p318; Treasury Pavilion, Th Ratchadamnoen; ⊙8.30am-noon & 1-4.30pm) **FREE** It's worth ducking into this small government museum to see the bizarre shapes that Thai money has taken over the years, from hammered coins to round silver balls and ingots.

Museum of World Insects & Natural Wonders
MUSEUM

(พิพิธภัณฑ์แมลงโลกและสิ่งมหัศจรรย์ธรรมชาติ; Map p318; www.thailandinsect.com; Th Ratchadamnoen; adult/child 100/70B; ⊙9.30am-4.30pm) Thailand's giant butterflies and creepy crawlies are showcased at this little museum operated by a malaria researcher and his entomologist wife. As well as pinned and mounted specimens, there are info panels on insect-borne diseases and surreal paintings of nudes with mosquitoes. There's a small **branch** (Map p323; Soi 13; adult/child 200/100B; ⊙9am-5pm Mon-Sat, to 4pm Sun) in the Th Nimmanhaemin zone.

⊙ East of the Old City

Beyond Pratu Tha Phae is Chiang Mai's traditional commercial quarter, with sprawling bazaars and old-fashioned shophouses running down to the riverbank.

★Talat Warorot
MARKET

(ตลาดวโรรส; Map p318; cnr Th Chang Moi & Th Praisani; ⊙6am-5pm) Chiang Mai's oldest public market, Warorot (also spelt Waroros) is a great place to connect with the city's Thai soul. Alongside souvenir vendors you'll find numerous stalls selling items for ordinary Thai households: woks, toys, fishing nets, pickled tea leaves, sticky-rice steamers, Thai-style sausages, *kâab mŏo* (pork rinds), live catfish and tiny statues for spirit houses.

It's easy to spend half a day wandering the covered walkways, watching locals browsing, and haggling for goods that actually have a practical use back home.

You'll know you've arrived at the market when traffic comes to a standstill and carts laden with merchandise weave between the cars. The location by the river is no coincidence; historically, most of the farm produce sold in Chiang Mai was delivered here by boat along Mae Ping.

Immediately adjacent to Talat Warorot is Talat Ton Lam Yai, the city's main flower market, and to the south are more bazaars, full of 'wet and dry' foodstuffs, fabric vendors, Chinese goldsmiths and apparel stalls. The northern end of the bazaar area is thronged by fruit vendors selling bushels of lychees, longans, mangosteens and rambutans. Săhm·lór (three-wheel pedicabs; also spelt Săamláw) – now rarely seen in the city – wait to shuttle shoppers home with their produce.

Talat Ton Lam Yai
MARKET

(ตลาดต้นลำไย; Map p312; Th Praisani; ⊙24hr) Adjacent to Talat Warorot, Talat Ton Lam Yai morphs from a covered household market into an animated flower market (*gàht dòrk mái*), flanking the river on Th Praisani. Florists here are almost architects, assembling blooms and banana leaves into fantastically elaborate sculptures for festivals and home shrines.

The smell of jasmine floats like perfume along the passageways, and drivers stop outside day and night to purchase strings of miniature roses and jasmine blossoms to sweeten their cabs. Though the market is open 24/7, the bulk of its trade takes place after dark, away from the wilting daytime heat. The market goes into overdrive for big festivals such as Loi Krathong and the Flower Festival.

Wat Bupparam
BUDDHIST TEMPLE

(วัดบุปผาราม; Map p318; Th Tha Phae; 20B; ⊙6am-6pm) This highly ornate temple shows the clear influence of the Burmese teak merchants who immigrated to Chiang Mai during the 19th century. The eye-catching dharma hall has a *mon·dòp* (library) downstairs and a large prayer room above, but the most striking feature is the gorgeous, wonky *wí·hăhn,* built from teak inlaid with mirror mosaics in the classic Lanna style.

The *chedi* at the rear of the compound is in the Burmese Mon style, with four stucco *singha* (lions) around the base.

Talat Muang Mai   MARKET
(ตลาดเมืองใหม่; Map p318; Th Praisani; ◷24hr)
Chiang Mai's main wholesale fruit market
is a riot of activity every morning, when
enormous cargoes of mangoes, durians,
rambutans, longans, watermelons, Malay
apples, passionfruit and just about any other tropical fruit you could mention (and that
are in season) are unloaded from trucks
along the east bank and sold on to juice-
stand owners and market traders.

Chinatown   AREA
(Map p318; Th Chang Moi) The area dominated by the Warorot and Ton Lam Yai markets doubles as the city's small Chinatown,
marked by a flamboyant **Chinese welcome
gate** (Map p318) across Th Chang Moi. Dotted around the bazaar area are several small
Confucian temples, a handful of Chinese
apothecaries and lots of Chinese jewellery
shops, decorated in brilliant red, a symbol
of good fortune.

◉ South of the Old City

The main highway running southwest from
the old city, Th Wualai is famous for its **silver shops** and the entire street reverberates
to the sound of smiths hammering intricate
religious designs and ornamental patterns
into bowls, jewellery boxes and decorative
plaques made from silver, or, more often,
aluminium. This is also the location for the
energetic Saturday Walking Street market
(p350).

Wat Srisuphan   BUDDHIST TEMPLE
(วัดศรีสุพรรณ; Map p312; Soi 2, Th Wualai; donations appreciated; ◷6am-6pm) It should come
as no surprise that the silversmiths along Th
Wualai have decorated their patron monastery with the same fine artisanship shown
in their shops. The 'silver' *ubosot* is covered
with silver, nickel and aluminium panels,
embossed with elaborate repoussé-work designs. The effect is like a giant jewellery box,
particularly after dark, when the monastery
is illuminated by coloured lights.

Wat Srisuphan was founded in 1502, but
little remains of the original *wát* except for
some teak pillars and roof beams in the
main *wí-hǎhn*. The murals inside show an
interesting mix of Taoist, Zen and Theravada Buddhist elements. Note the gold
and silver Ganesha statue beneath a silver
chatra (umbrella) by the *ubosot*, a sign of
the crossover between Hinduism and Buddhism in Thailand.

Because this is an active ordination hall,
only men may enter the *ubosot*.

Wiang Kum Kam   HISTORIC SITE
(เวียงกุมกาม; Rte 3029; tours by horse cart/tram
300/400B; ◷8am-5pm) The first attempt at
founding a city on the banks of Mae Ping,
Wiang Kum Kam served as the Lanna capital for 10 years from 1286, but the city was
abandoned in the 16th century due to flooding. Today, the excavated ruins are scattered
around the winding lanes of a sleepy village
5km south of Chiang Mai.

The centuries haven't been kind to Wiang
Kum Kam, but the brick plinths and ruined
chedi give a powerful impression of its former magnificence.

The landmark monument of the ruins
is **Wat Chedi Liam**, with a soaring stucco
chedi divided into dozens of niches for Buddha statues, an architectural nod to India's
famous Mahabodhi Temple. In fact, this
spire was created as part of a rather fanciful restoration by a Burmese trader in 1908.
Over 1300 inscribed stone slabs, bricks, bells
and *chedi* have been excavated at the site
and some pieces are displayed at the visitor
centre. The most important archaeological
discovery was a four-piece stone slab, now
housed at the Chiang Mai National Museum, inscribed with one of the earliest known
examples of Thai script.

Most people explore the ruins by horse
cart or tram, starting from the visitor centre on Rte 3029; if you come with your own
transport via Th Chiang Mai–Lamphun (Rte
106), follow the signed road past a small
roundabout with a fountain and turn left at
the T-junction to reach Wat Chedi Liam.

◉ West of the Old City

Modern Chiang Mai has sprawled west
from the old city towards Doi Suthep and
the Chiang Mai University, but there are a
few historic sites dotted around the streets.
The main attraction here is the Neimman-
haemin area with its trendy restaurants and
shops.

Wat U Mong   BUDDHIST TEMPLE
(วัดอุโมงค์; Map p312; Soi Wat U Mong, Th Khlong
Chonprathan; donations appreciated; ◷daylight
hours) Not to be confused with the small Wat
U Mong in the old city, this historic forest

wát is famed for its sylvan setting and its ancient *chedi,* above a brick platform wormholed with passageways, built around 1380 for the 'mad' monk Thera Jan. As you wander the arched tunnels, you can see traces of the original murals and several venerated Buddha images.

The scrub forest around the platform is scattered with centuries' worth of broken Buddha images. The attendant monks raise cows, deer, chickens and, curiously, English bull terriers, and in the grounds is a pretty artificial lake, surrounded by *gù·đì* (monks' quarters). Check out the emaciated blackstone Buddha in the Burmese style, behind the *chedi.*

Wat U Mong is 600m south of Th Suthep near Chiang Mai University; be sure to ask the driver to take you to 'Wat U Mong Thera Jan' so you end up at the right monastery. If coming with your own transport, look for signs to Srithana Resort on Th Suthep.

★**Wat Phra That Doi Suthep**   BUDDHIST TEMPLE
(วัดพระธาตุดอยสุเทพ; Th Huay Kaew, Doi Suthep; 30B; ⊙6am-6pm) Overlooking the city from its mountain throne, Wat Phra That Doi Suthep is one of northern Thailand's most sacred temples, and its founding legend is learned by every schoolkid in Chiang Mai. The wát is a beautiful example of northern Thai architecture, reached via a 306-step staircase flanked by *naga* (serpents); the climb is intended to help devotees accrue Buddhist merit.

The monastery was established in 1383 by King Keu Naone to enshrine a piece of bone said to be from the shoulder of the historical

SACRED MOUNTAINS

Often bearing a crown of clouds, sultry **Doi Suthep** (1676m) and **Doi Pui** (1685m) are two of northern Thailand's most sacred peaks. A dense cloak of jungle envelops the twin summits, which soar dramatically on the fringes of Chiang Mai. A 265-sq-km area on the slopes of the mountains, encompassing both summits, is preserved as **Doi Suthep-Pui National Park** (อุทยานแห่งชาติดอยสุเทพ – ปุย; ☑053 210244; Th Huay Kaew; adult/child 200/100B, car 30B, 2-person tent 150B, bungalows 400-2500B; ⊙8am-sunset).

It attracts hordes of nature-lovers, and legions of pilgrims who come to worship at **Wat Phra That Doi Suthep**.

As you climb, lowland rainforest gives way to cloud forest, full of mosses and ferns, providing a haven for more than 300 bird species and 2000 species of ferns and flowering plants. The park is also a renowned destination for mountain biking, and several Chiang Mai–based agencies run technical mountain-biking tours along trails that were once used as hunting and trade routes by hill-tribe villagers.

The park accommodation makes a comfortable base from which to explore and a trail runs for 2km from the campground to the summit of Doi Suthep, though the only view is of eerie mists swirling between the trees.

As with other national parks in the area, Doi Suthep is blessed with many thundering waterfalls, including **Nam Tok Monthathon**, about 2.5km off the paved road, which surges into a series of pools that hold water year-round. Swimming is best during or just after the monsoon, but you'll have to pay the national park fee to visit. Closer to the start of the road to Doi Suthep, **Nam Tok Wang Bua Bahn** is free, and full of frolicking locals, although this is more a series of rapids than a proper cascade.

Above the Bhubing Palace (p321) are a couple of Hmong villages. **Ban Doi Pui** is off the main road and is basically a tourist market at altitude; it's more interesting to continue to **Ban Kun Chang Kian**, a coffee-producing village about 500m down a dirt track just past the Doi Pui campground (ask the park staff for directions). *Rót daang* (literally 'red trucks') run from the Wat Phra That Doi Suthep parking lot to both Ban Doi Pui (60B) and Ban Kun Chang Kian (200B return).

The entrance to the park is 16km northwest of central Chiang Mai. Shared *rót daang* leave from Chiang Mai University (Th Huay Kaew entrance) to various points within the national park. One-way fares start at 40B to Wat Phra That Doi Suthep and 70B to Bhubing Palace. You can also charter a *sŏrng·tăa·ou* (passenger pick-up truck) for a half-day of exploring for 500B to 600B.

Central Chiang Mai

21

Th Mani Nopharat

94 **98**

Pratu Chang Pheuak

Th Si Phum

111

Soi 4

17

61

143

42

81

37

Th Wiang Kaew

Th Singharat

Th Phra Pokklao

Former Chiang Mai Women's Prison

Th Ratwithi

Lanna
1 Folklife
Museum

108

91

45

8

7 **6**

137

105

Th Inthawarorot

88 **19**

Wat Umongmahatherachan

28

38

51

29 Soi 5

93

55

120 **15**

70

Wat Phra
5 Singh

102

39

74

129

106

54

96

121

Th Ratchadamnoen

13

107

12

140 **86**

25

83

30

Th Jhaban

Wat Phan Tao **4**

89

20

Wat Chedi
3 Luang

46 Soi 8

11

87

Th Ratchamankha

50

44

Th Samlan

Soi 7

Soi 6

115 **57**

132

60

62

Soi 5

31

84

135

52

47 Soi 1

139 **99**

Th Bamrungburi

Th Chang Lor

Chinese
Consulate

Pratu
Chiang Mai

Th Wualai

Th Ratchaphakhinai

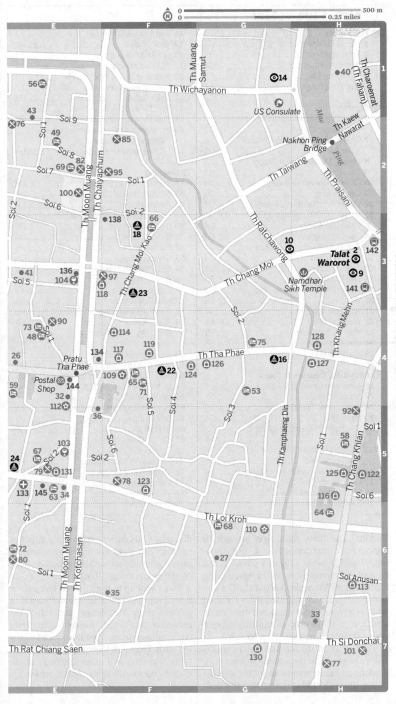

Central Chiang Mai

Buddha. The bone shard was brought to Lanna by a wandering monk from Sukhothai and it broke into two pieces at the base of the mountain, with one piece being enshrined at Wat Suan Dok (p322). The second fragment was mounted onto a sacred white elephant that wandered the jungle until it died, in the process selecting the spot where the monastery was later founded.

The terrace at the top of the steps is dotted with breadfruit trees, small shrines, rock gardens and monuments, including a statue of the white elephant that carried the Bud-

dha relic to its current resting place. Before entering the inner courtyard, children pay their respects to a lizard-like guardian dragon statue known as 'Mom'.

Steps lead up to the inner terrace, where a walkway circumnavigates the gleaming golden *chedi* enshrining the relic. The crowning five-tiered umbrella marks the city's independence from Burma and its union with Thailand. Pilgrims queue to leave lotus blossoms and other offerings at the shrines surrounding the *chedi*, which are

CHIANG MAI PROVINCE CHIANG MAI

studded with Buddha statues in an amazing variety of poses and materials.

Within the monastery compound, the Doi Suthep Vipassana Meditation Center (p332) conducts a variety of religious outreach programs for visitors.

Rót daang run to the bottom of the steps to the temple from several points in Chiang Mai, including from in front of the zoo (40B per passenger) and in front of Wat Phra Singh (50B per passenger), but they only leave when they have enough passengers. A charter ride from the centre will cost 300B, or 500B return. Many people cycle up on mountain-biking tours from Chiang Mai, and you can also walk (p333) from the university.

Bhubing Palace   GARDENS
(พระตำหนักภูพิงค์, Phra Tamnak Bhu Bing; www.bhubingpalace.org; Th Huay Kaew, Doi Suthep; 50B; ⊙8.30-11.30am & 1-3.30pm) The serene grounds of the royal family's winter palace are open to the public (when the royals aren't visiting). The unusually strict dress code requires bottoms below mid-calf and

DON'T MISS

HIKING IN CHIANG MAI

Thousands of visitors trek into the hills of northern Thailand each year hoping to see fantastic mountain scenery, interact with traditional tribespeople and meet elephants. A huge industry has grown up to cater to this demand, but the experience is very commercial and may not live up to everyone's notion of adventure.

The standard package involves a one-hour minibus ride to Mae Taeng or Mae Wang, a brief hike to an elephant camp, bamboo rafting and, for multiday tours, an overnight stay in or near a hill-tribe village. Many budget guesthouses pressure their guests to take these trips because of the commissions paid, and may ask guests to stay elsewhere if they decline. Note that they also arrange elephant rides, though these are not recommended as rides can be detrimental to the health of the animals.

While these packages are undeniably popular, they may visit elephant camps that have a questionable record on elephant welfare. Hill-tribe trips can also disappoint, as many of the villages now house a mix of tribal people and Chinese and Burmese migrants and have abandoned many aspects of the traditional way of life. Rafting can also be a tame drift on a creek, rather than an adrenalin-charged rush over white water.

If you crave real adventure, you'll have to be a bit more hands-on about organising things yourself. To get deep into the jungle, rent a motorcycle and explore the national parks north and south of Chiang Mai; Chiang Dao is an excellent place to base yourself for jungle exploration. To see elephants in natural conditions, spend a day at **Elephant Nature Park** (p328), then raft real white water with **Siam River Adventures** (p326). To encounter traditional hill-tribe culture, you'll need to travel to more remote areas than you can reach on a day trip from Chiang Mai; your best bet is to travel to Tha Ton (p360) and book a multiday trek from there.

shoulders covered – no scarves. The mountain's cool climate allows the royal gardeners to raise 'exotic' species such as roses, attracting lots of Thai sightseers.

Wat Suan Dok
BUDDHIST TEMPLE

(วัดสวนดอก; Map p312; Th Suthep; donations appreciated; ☉daylight hours) Built on a former flower garden in 1373, this important monastery enshrines one half of a sacred Buddha relic; the other half was transported by white elephant to Wat Phra That Doi Suthep (p317). The main *chedi* is a gilded, bell-shaped structure that rises above a sea of white memorial *chedi* honouring the Thai royal family, with the ridge of Doi Suthep soaring behind.

The hangar-like main *wí·hǎhn* contains a huge standing Buddha statue that almost touches the ceiling. Take some time to wander the memorial garden of whitewashed *chedi* in front of the monastery, which contain the ashes of generations of Lanna royalty.

Mahachulalongkorn Buddhist University is located on the same grounds and foreigners often join the popular Monk Chat (p330) and English-language meditation retreats.

Chiang Mai University
UNIVERSITY

(มหาวิทยาลัยเชียงใหม่, CMU; Map p312; www. cmu.ac.th; Th Huay Kaew & Th Suthep; adult/child 60/30B; ☉9am-5pm) The main campus of Chiang Mai's famous public university occupies a 2.9-sq-km wedge of land about 2km west of the city centre, partly covered by forest and open greenery. The required tram ride – introduced after Chinese tourists started dressing up in school uniforms and sneaking into classes! – starts at the Information Center near the Th Huay Kaew entrance.

Chiang Mai University Art Museum
GALLERY

(หอศิลปมหาวิทยาลัยเชียงใหม่; Map p312; www. finearts.cmu.ac.th; Th Nimmanhaemin; ☉9am-5pm Tue-Sun) **FREE** The Faculty of Fine Arts displays temporary exhibitions of contemporary Thai and international artists at its own gallery near the Th Nimmanhaemin/Th Suthep junction, but there's no permanent collection. Some shows take place at the Baan Tuek Art Center (ศูนย์ศิลปะบ้านตึก; Map p312; ☉3-8pm Tue-Sun) **FREE** on Th Tha Phae.

Royal Park Rajapruek
GARDENS

(ลานมหกรรมพืชสวนโลก; www.royalparkrajapruek. org; Rte 121, Mae Hia; adult/child 100/50B; ☉8am-

Western Chiang Mai

Western Chiang Mai

6pm) This sprawling formal garden has 21 themed gardens donated by international governments as part of Chiang Mai's International Horticultural Exposition in 2006.

It sounds a bit corporate on paper, but the complex is actually lush, green and peaceful, with a vast wát-shaped central pavilion full of

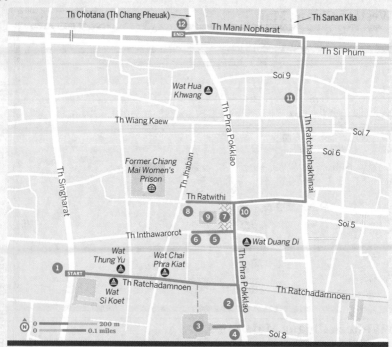

🚶 City Walk
Old City Temple Tour

START WAT PHRA SINGH
END TALAT PRATU CHANG PHEUAK
LENGTH 2.5KM; FIVE HOURS

No visit to Chiang Mai is complete without a temple tour. Start with the best, **1 Wat Phra Singh** (310), home to the city's most revered Buddha image, the Lion Buddha, then stroll down Th Ratchadamnoen and turn right onto Th Phra Pokklao. In swift succession, you'll get to the gorgeous teak *wí·hǎhn* of **2 Wat Phan Tao** (p310), which deserves a good wander, and the looming mass of **3 Wat Chedi Luang** (p310), the largest and grandest Lanna *chedi* in the city. Perform a ceremonial circumambulation clockwise around the stupa, then duck into the **4 Làk Meuang** (p310; if you're a man – Buddhist rules dictate that women are not allowed to enter) to view the revered city pillar.

Turn on your heels now and follow Th Phra Pokklao north to the junction with Th Inthawararot, where you'll see the postcard-perfect *wí·hǎhn* of **5 Wat Inthakhin**

Saduemuang (p311), which enshrined the city pillar in medieval times, perched surreally in the middle of the road. This is a good time to pause for lunch at the ever-popular **6 Kiat Ocha** (p340) for some *kôw man gài* (Hainanese-style boiled chicken). Post lunch, walk another block north on Th Phra Pokklao to the **7 Anusawari Sam Kasat** (p311), and pay your respects to the three Lanna kings who founded Chiang Mai.

You are now in the perfect location to take in Chiang Mai's trinity of excellent city museums, the airy, Lanna-style **8 Chiang Mai Historical Centre** (p315), the large **9 Chiang Mai City Arts & Cultural Centre** (p314) in a 1927 colonial building, and the **10 Lanna Folklife Museum** (p311), which is arguably the best museum in town. Continue north along Th Ratchaphakhinai to reach atmospheric and ancient **11 Wat Chiang Man** (p311), the oldest *wát* in a city awash with ancient temples. To finish, walk on to the moat and enjoy the Cowboy Hat Lady's fabulous *kôw kǎh mǒo* (slow-cooked pork leg with rice) at **12 Talat Pratu Chang Pheuak** (p342).

TEAK-ERA CHIANG MAI

Chiang Mai was never colonised by European powers, but the city has many of the hallmarks of European influence, dating back to the time when teak concessionaires from Britain and the US built fortunes on the timber being hauled from the surrounding forests.

One of the most striking colonial relics is the weatherboard **First Church** (คริสตจักร ที่ ๑ เชียงใหม่; Map p312; Th Chiang Mai-Lamphun), just south of Nawarat Bridge on the east bank, founded by the Laos Mission from North Carolina in 1868. Just south of here, the Iron Bridge was built as a homage to the demolished Nawarat Bridge, whose steel beams were fabricated by engineers from Cleveland in England. Local folklore states that the famous memorial bridge in Pai is not a WWII relic but a 1970s fake, built using reclaimed beams from Chiang Mai's Nawarat Bridge.

If you head in the other direction along the west bank, you'll pass the colonial-style former **Main Post Office**, which now houses a small **philatelic museum** (พิพิธภัณฑ์ ตราไปรษณียากร; Map p312; Th Praisani; ☉9am-4pm Tue-Sun) [FREE]. Similar Thai-Colonial administrative buildings spread out around the junction of Th Ratwithi and Th Phra Pokklao in the old city, where the former **Provincial Hall**, now the **Chiang Mai City Arts & Cultural Centre** (p314), and **Provincial Courthouse**, now the **Lanna Folklife Museum** (p311), show the clear influence of the British 'gentlemen foresters' who controlled 60% of Chiang Mai's teak industry in the 19th and 20th centuries.

Many of the teak concessionaires' mansions have fallen into disrepair, but the colonial style of architecture was adopted by the Lanna royal family. One of the most impressive surviving teak-era mansions is the **Lanna Architecture Center** (ศูนย์สถาปัตยกรรม ล้านนา; Map p318; www.lanna-arch.net; 117 Th Ratchadamnoen; ☉8.30am-4.30pm Mon-Fri) [FREE], formerly owned by prince Jao Maha In, built between 1889 and 1893; it displays some interesting models showing the changing face of Lanna architecture through the centuries. The former British Consulate, now the **Service 1921 restaurant** (p344) at the Anantara Resort, the central building at **137 Pillars** (p339), and the **Dara Pirom Palace** (p357) in Mae Rim are also fine examples of this hybrid style.

slightly over-the-top displays honouring the Thai royal family.

Wat Phra That Doi Kham BUDDHIST TEMPLE
(วัดพระธาตุดอยคำ; Mae Hia; donations appreciated; ☉6am-6pm) Reached via a steep *naga* stairway through the forest, this handsome wát looms above the city from the hillside above Royal Park Rajapruek. With its gilded *chedi,* super-sized Buddha statues and panoramic city views it's an attractive and quieter alternative to Wat Phra That Doi Suthep.

The easiest way to get here is by rented motorcycle or chartered *rót daang;* follow the signs for Royal Park Rajapruek from Rte 121 and go right at the roundabout before the entrance.

⊙ North of the Old City

From Pratu Chang Pheuak (White Elephant Gate), it's a short walk north to the **Elephant Monument** (อนุสาวรีย์ช้าง; Map p312), whose twin elephant statues in stucco pavil-

ions are said to have been erected by King Chao Kavila in 1800.

Wat Jet Yot BUDDHIST TEMPLE
(วัดเจ็ดยอด; Map p312; Rte 11/Th Superhighway; donations appreciated; ☉8.30am-5pm) This wát still has much of its original stucco intact, and gives an impression of what other wát in the city would have looked like in their heyday. The monastery was built to host the eighth World Buddhist Council in 1477, and its historic *wí·hǎhn* is decorated with time-worn stucco bas-reliefs of *deva* (angelic Buddhist spirits).

Topped by *jèt yôrt* (seven spires), representing the seven weeks Buddha spent in Bodhgaya in India after his enlightenment, the old *wí·hǎhn* is believed to be a replica of Bodhgaya's Mahabodhi Temple, but scholars believe that the plans were copied from a clay votive tablet showing the temple in distorted perspective.

Dotted around the compound are more chapels and *chedi,* as well as lots of mature ficus trees propped up with wooden stakes by devotees seeking merit.

Wat Ku Tao
BUDDHIST TEMPLE

(วัดกู่เต้า; Map p312; Soi 6, Th Chotana/Th Chang Pheuak; donations appreciated; ⊙6am-6pm) Behind the Muang Chiang Mai sports stadium, photogenic, 1631 Wat Ku Tao incorporates many Burmese and Confucian elements. The distinctive *chedi* is said to resemble a stack of watermelons, hence the name (*tao* means 'melon' in the northern Thai dialect). Contained inside are the ashes of Tharawadi Min, son of the Burmese king Bayinnaung, who ruled over Lanna from 1578 to 1607.

Chiang Mai National Museum
MUSEUM

(พิพิธภัณฑสถานแห่งชาติเชียงใหม่; Map p312; ☑ 053 221308; Rte 11/Th Superhighway; ⊙9am-4pm Wed-Sun) FREE Operated by the Fine Arts Department, this museum is the primary caretaker of Lanna artefacts and northern Thai history. But when we stopped by all the galleries were closed for refurbishment, and had been for a few years. When the museum reopens, expect the old admission fee of 100B to be reinstated.

Bags and cameras must be left in the free lockers by the ticket desk. To make a visit more worthwhile, combine your trip with a visit to Wat Jet Yot and the Chinese cemetery.

Chinese Cemetery
CEMETERY

(สุสานจีน; Map p312; Soi 1, Th Chotana/Th Chang Pheuak; ⊙6am-6pm) Tucked away on a quiet *soi* behind the National Museum, this peaceful cemetery is lined with elegant Chinese gravestones, whose level of ornamentation provides a good indication of the former wealth of their occupants. Nearby are the curious Anusawari Singh (p334), two stucco lions said to have been erected by King Chao Kavila himself.

🏃 Activities

Outdoor escapes are easy in Chiang Mai, with tropical rainforests, looming mountains, rushing rivers, hill-tribe villages, and sanctuaries and camps full of elephants all within an hour's drive of the city. Dozens of operators offer adventure tours, exploring the forested mountains and waterways on foot, or by bike, raft, all-terrain-vehicle and even zipline.

Adventure Sports

⭐ **Flight of the Gibbon** ZIPLINING
(Map p318; ☑ 053 010660; www.treetopasia.com; 29/4-5 Th Kotchasan; day tours 4000B; ⊙9.30am-6.30pm) Much copied but never equalled, this adventure outfit started the zipline craze, with nearly 5km of wire strung up like spiderwebs in the gibbon-populated (you may see some) forest canopy near Ban Mae Kampong, an hour's drive east from Chiang Mai. The day-tour includes an optional but highly recommended village visit, waterfall walk and delicious lunch cooked by the community.

As well as day trips, it offers multiday, multiactivity tours that include a night at a village homestay.

⭐ **Green Trails** ADVENTURE
(☑053 141356; www.green-trails.com; treks for 2 people from 2900B) A very reliable, eco and socially responsible outfit which can arrange trekking trips to Doi Inthanon, overnight trips to Ban Mae Kampong, specialty responsible elephant encounters and much more.

Chiang Mai Rock Climbing Adventures
ADVENTURE
(CMRCA; Map p318; ☑ 053 207102; www.thailandclimbing.com; 55/3 Th Ratchaphakhinai; climbing course from 5000B) CMRCA maintains many of the climbs at the limestone Crazy Horse Buttress, with bolted sport routes in the French 6a to 7a+ range. As well as climbing and caving courses for climbers of all levels, it runs a shuttle bus to the crag at 8am (300B return; book one day before). Very experienced and passionate owner.

You can rent all the gear you need here, either piece by piece, or as a 'full set' for two climbers (1875B).

Siam River Adventures
RAFTING
(Map p318; ☑089 515 1917; www.siamrivers.com; 17 Th Ratwithi; rafting per day from 1800B; ⊙8am-8pm) In operation since 2000, this outfit running white-water-rafting and kayaking trips has a good reputation for safety and professionalism. The guides have specialist rescue training and additional staff are located at dangerous parts of the river with throw ropes. Trips can be combined with elephant encounters and overnight village stays.

Chiang Mai Mountain
Biking & Kayaking   MOUNTAIN BIKING
(Map p318; ☑053 814207; www.mountainbiking
chiangmai.com; 1 Th Samlan; tours 1250-2700B;
⊘8am-8pm) This specialist operator offers
recommended kayaking trips on Mae Ping
and full-day guided mountain-biking tours
(using imported bikes) to Doi Suthep-Pui
National Park and further afield, including
the popular ascent to Wat Phra That Doi
Suthep.

Peak Adventure Tour   ADVENTURE
(Map p312; ☑053 800567; www.thepeakadven
ture.com; 302/4 Th Chiang Mai-Lamphun; tours
1600-2800B) The Peak offers a variety of adventure trips, including quad biking, abseiling, trekking, white-water rafting and rock
climbing, as well as photography tours of
Chiang Mai by sǎhm·lór.

Elephant Interactions
Chiang Mai is one of Thailand's most famous destinations for elephant encounters, with more elephant camps opening
by the day it seems, though many still offer
packages of non-bareback elephant rides,
circus-like sideshows and buffalo cart
rides or bamboo rafting on the nearest river. Better camps offer interaction in place
of exploitation: visitors walk with, feed
and wash the elephant herds, but avoid
activities that are harmful to the animals'
welfare.

CHIANG MAI PROVINCE CHIANG MAI

❶ ETHICAL ELEPHANT INTERACTIONS

Elephants have been used as beasts of burden in Thailand for thousands of years, hauling logs from the teak forests and transporting the carriages of Thai royalty. The ele-
phant-headed deities Erawan and Ganesha are revered by Buddhists and Hindus alike,·
and even the outline of Thailand resembles an elephant's head, with its trunk extending
down into the isthmus.

With the nationwide ban on logging in 1989, thousands of working elephants suddenly
found themselves out of a job, and herders and mahouts (elephant drivers) looked for
new ways to generate revenue from their animals. So were born Chiang Mai's elephant
camps, where former logging herds now entertain visiting tourists with circus-style displays and rides through the forest. However, growing awareness of animal welfare issues
is shining a new spotlight on this industry and its practices.

Elephant rides are particularly problematic, with just one of the many issues including
the fact that the howdahs (carriages) used to carry tourists place severe strain on elephants' spines and can cause debilitating damage over time. Circus-like performances
also put elephants at risk of injury, many camps keep their elephants chained and
segregated, and traditional ankus and similar types of metal hooks are used to control
the animals. Government regulations offer little to no oversight, as they still classify
elephants as modes of transport, and many animals show clear signs of psychological
damage, which has manifested itself in attacks on humans.

There are alternatives. Ideally, activist groups state, elephants should be left un-
chained and allowed to form their own social groups in sprawling compounds (although
there is rarely enough land for this). In place of rides, visitors walk around the grounds
with elephants and their mahouts, feeding the animals by hand with fruit and vegetables
and helping out at bath-time in the creek.

Increasingly, you can contribute to elephant conservation without the uncomforta-
ble feeling that you are contributing to the problem. The reality is that most elephants
cannot be returned to the wild and tourist dollars are often the only way to finance their
ongoing care. The scientific community stresses that the best camps should have a dedicated veterinary station where the animals can be treated for injuries and medical conditions. If rides are offered, bareback riding, where the rider sits on the elephants' shoulders, is less harmful than rides in wooden howdahs, though many animal welfare experts
insist that rides should be avoided altogether because elephants undergo brutal abuse
to 'learn' how to accept riders. Groups such as the ACEWG (Asian Captive Elephant
Working Group) are working with communities to encourage kinder training techniques
and insight into how humans and elephants can better work together.

DON'T MISS

CRUISING MAE PING

Before the construction of the roads and railways, Mae Ping was the main route of transit for goods coming into Chiang Mai. The markets along the riverbank are where the Lanna kingdom came to trade with the rest of Thailand, and via the Silk Route, with the rest of Asia. The river was used to transport everything from fruit and vegetables to the giant trunks of teak trees, but trade on the river slowly died after the arrival of the railways in 1922.

Mae Ping still traces a lazy passage through the middle of Chiang Mai, but few vessels ply its waters today, with the exception of tour boats, which provide an excellent vantage point from which to view the city. The longest-established operator is **Scorpion Tailed River Cruise** (Map p318; ☑ 081 960 9398; www.scorpiontailedrivercruise.com; Th Charoenrat; cruise 500B), which runs river tours in covered long-tailed boats from a pier by Wat Srikhong (just north of the Nakhon Ping bridge). Tours pass through peaceful countryside en route to a country farm, where passengers get a snack of mango and sticky rice. **Mae Ping River Cruise** (Map p312; ☑ 081 884 4621; www.maepingrivercruise.com; Wat Chaimongkhon, 133 Th Charoen Prathet; 2hr cruise from 550B; ⊙ 8.30am-5.30pm) offers similar trips starting from Wat Chaimongkhon, south of the centre on Th Charoen Prathet, as well as longer cruises to **Wiang Kum Kam** (p316).

If you don't mind paddling yourself, **Chiang Mai Mountain Biking & Kayaking** (p327) offers guided kayak tours along Mae Ping, visiting forested stretches north of the city.

Thai Elephant Care Center
ELEPHANT INTERACTION

(☑ 053 206247; www.thaielephantcarecenter.com; Mae Sa; half-/full day 2000/3000B) This small centre at Mae Sa, about 25km northwest of Chiang Mai, was set up to provide care for elderly elephants retired from logging camps and elephant shows. There are no rides and visitors feed the old-timers with ground grass, herb balls and bananas and help out at bath-time, and visit the cemetery for elephants who have died of old age.

Patara Elephant Farm
ELEPHANT INTERACTION

(☑ 081 992 2551; www.pataraelephantfarm.com; half-/full day 3800/4800B) At this camp 30km west of Chiang Mai, visitors become 'elephant owners' for a day and help with health inspections, feeding and bathing. Bareback riding is offered: animal welfare groups argue that this is harmful to elephants so you could consider avoiding these. The camp has one of the best veterinary stations, however, which makes it a favourite of many wildlife scientists and veterinarians.

Most interactions are one guest to one elephant and elephant trainer.

Elephant Nature Park
ELEPHANT INTERACTION

(Map p318; ☑ 053 818754, 053 272850; www.elephantnaturepark.org; 1 Th Ratchamankha; 1-/2-day tours 2500/5800B) 🐾 One of the first sanctuaries for rescued elephants in Chiang Mai, Elephant Nature Park has led the movement to abandon rides and shows and put elephant welfare at the top of the agenda, under the guidance of founder Sangduen (Lek) Chailert. Visits are focused on interaction – the day is spent wandering with mahouts and their charges, helping feed and wash elephants.

As is the case with all of the better elephant camps, the elephants here have been rescued from logging camps and tourist shows. The most rewarding experience is seeing the interaction between the elephants, with baby elephants having trunk tug-of-wars, families enjoying shared mud baths and older elephants taking care of blind and disabled members of the herd.

The main park is in the Mae Taeng valley, 60km from Chiang Mai, and day trips include a vegetarian buffet lunch. Longer volunteering packages are also available.

Elephant Retirement Park
ELEPHANT INTERACTION

(Map p318; ☑ 081 961 9663; www.elephantretirementpark.com; 5 Kotchasarn Soi 5; half-/full-day tours from 1500/2600B) An ethical operator at Mae Taeng offering walking, feeding and bathing encounters with elephants, but no rides; the herd are allowed to maintain their own family units.

Thai Massage

Once upon a time in Chiang Mai, massage parlours offered little more than a mattress and a vigorous pummelling for a modest fee, but these days the focus has shifted to lavish spas, which strive to re-create the elegant lifestyle of Lanna royalty, with massage tables set in lush gardens full of birdsong and the sound of trickling water.

If you fancy a massage in Chiang Mai, we recommend going to one end of the spectrum or the other. If you don't fancy a lavish pampering at a posh spa, head instead to the very inexpensive, informal massage pavilions inside some of Chiang Mai's wát or the massage services run as rehabilitation schemes for the blind and for former prison inmates.

★ Zira Spa
SPA

(☏ 053 222288; www.ziraspa.com; 8/1 Th Rajvithi; treatments 700-6000B; ⏰ 10am-10pm) Located on one of the main streets in the centre of Chiang Mai, Zira Spa offers some of the best spa treatments and massages in the region, all for a decent price. You need to book in advance for the larger spa packages, but same-day service is available for one or two of the 30-, 60- or 90-minute treatments.

Vocational Training Centre of the Chiang Mai Women's Correctional Institution
MASSAGE

(Map p318; ☏ 053 122340; 100 Th Ratwithi; foot or traditional massage from 200B; ⏰ 8am-4.30pm Mon-Fri, 9am-4.30pm Sat & Sun) Offers fantastic massages performed by female inmates participating in the prison's job-training rehabilitation program. The cafe next door is a nice spot for a post-massage brew.

Lila Thai Massage
MASSAGE

(Map p318; ☏ 053 327043; www.chiangmaimassage.com; Th Phra Pokklao; standard/herbal massage from 300/400B; ⏰ 10am-10pm) Established by the former director of the Chiang Mai women's prison, Lila Thai offers post-release employment for graduates from the prison's massage training program. There are five branches in the old city, including a **Th Ratchadamnoen branch** (Map p318; ☏ 053 327243; standard/herbal massage from 200/350B; ⏰ 10am-10pm).

Ban Hom Samunphrai
MASSAGE

(☏ 053 817362; www.homprang.com; 93/2a Mu 12, Tawangtan, Saraphi; steam bath 200B, massage

---

CHIANG MAI FOR KIDS

Chiang Mai is very popular with families, both for its easygoing vibe and for the massive range of activities on offer. As a sensible first step, pick a hotel with a pool and plan out your days to avoid overload; chartering a *rót daang* (literally 'red truck') or *túk-túk* (motorised three-wheel taxi; pronounced dúk dúk) will give you the independence to come and go as you please. **Suan Buak Hat** (สวนสาธารณะหนองบวกหาด; Map p312; Th Bamrungburi; ⏰ 5am-9pm) has the most convenient playground in the old city. At meal times you can find familiar Western food in the old city and shopping centres.

Set aside one day for an elephant interaction – **Patara Elephant Farm** gets the balance of conservation and interaction just right – and another day for a paddle, swim and picnic at the **Mae Sa waterfalls** (p356). Kids six and up will adore ziplining with the very well run **Flight of the Gibbon** (p326). Wát trips are popular with kids and the compounds are green, calm and mostly traffic free; **Phra That Doi Suthep** (p317), **Suan Dok** (p322), **U Mong Thera Jan** (p316), **Chedi Luang** (p310) and **Phra Singh** (p310) have the most going on to keep small sightseers entertained. The three old-city museums (p311) have plenty of modern, kid-friendly displays, and zoo-style wildlife encounters are possible at the **Chiang Mai Zoo** (สวนสัตว์เชียงใหม่; www.chiangmaizoo.com; 100 Th Huay Kaew; adult/child 150/70B, combined zoo & aquarium ticket 520/260B; ⏰ 8am-4.30pm; 🚗) and **Chiang Mai Night Safari** (เชียงใหม่ไนท์ซาฟารี; ☏ 053 999000; www.chiangmainightsafari.com; Rte 121; tours adult/child 800/400B; ⏰ 11am-10pm; 🚗).

For days when the temperature rises to unbearable levels, all the big shopping centres have icy air-con, multi-screen cinemas and kids' activities; Central Festival has the **Sub-Zero ice-rink** (☏ 053 288868; www.subzeroiceskate.com; 3rd fl, Central Festival Mall; per hour adult/child 250/200B; ⏰ 11am-10pm Mon-Fri, 10am-10pm Sat & Sun), complete with 'walkers' for first-time skaters. **Grand Canyon Water Park** (☏ 061 796 3999; www.facebook.com/Grandcanyonwaterpark; 202 Mu 3 Namprae, Hang Dong; adult/child 350/300B; ⏰ 9am-7pm) is another great escape especially for older kids and teens who like adrenalin-charged water fun.

> **LOCAL KNOWLEDGE**
>
> ## CHATTING WITH MONKS
>
> If you're curious about Buddhism, many Chiang Mai temples offer popular Monk Chat sessions, where novice monks get to practise their English and tourists get to find out about the inner workings of monastery life. It's a fascinating opportunity to discover a little more about the rituals and customs that most Thai men undertake for at least a small portion of their lives. Remember to dress modestly as a sign of respect: cover your shoulders and knees. Because of ritual taboos, women should take care not to touch the monks or their belongings, or to pass anything directly to them.
>
> **Wat Suan Dok** (p322) Has a dedicated room for Monk Chats from 5pm to 7pm Monday, Wednesday and Friday.
>
> **Wat Srisuphan** (p316) Holds its sessions from 5.30pm to 7pm just before a meditation course.
>
> **Wat Chedi Luang** (p310) Has a table under a shady tree where monks chat from 9am to 6pm daily.
>
> **Wat Pha Khao** (วัดผ้าขาว; Map p318; Th Ratchmankha; donations appreciated; ⊙ daylight hours) Holds a low-key session from 5pm to 9pm on Saturday and Sunday.

800-1600B) Teacher Maw Hom ('Herbal Doctor') comes from a long line of herbalists and massage therapists; as well as traditional Thai massage here, you can try a traditional herbal steam bath. It's 9km from Chiang Mai near the McKean Institute; check the website for directions. It also runs recommended massage courses.

Thai Massage Conservation Club MASSAGE
(Map p318; ☑ 053 904452; 99 Th Ratchamankha; massage 200-350B; ⊙ 8am-9pm) A collective of traditional Thai massage practitioners, the Thai Massage Conservation Club employs all blind masseuses, who are considered to be expert practitioners because of their heightened sense of touch.

Thai Boxing (Moo·ay tai)

Chai Yai Muay Thai MARTIAL ARTS
(☑ 082 938 1364; www.muaythaicampsthailand.com; Th Sunpiliang, Nong Hoi; day/week/month 600/1900/5500B) 🏋 This school has been training Thai and foreign fighters of all levels for 30 years. It's southeast of the city, off Rte 11 near the Chiang Mai 700 Years Park.

Santai Muay Thai MARTIAL ARTS
(☑ 082 528 6059; www.muay-thai-santai.com; 79 Mu 9, San Kamphaeng; day/week/month 600/3000/10000B) Run by former prize fighters, with a focus on reaching competition standard. The gym is east of town.

Lanna Muay Thai Boxing Camp MARTIAL ARTS
(Map p312; ☑ 053 892102; 161 Soi Chang Khian, Th Huay Kaew; day/week/month 400/2200/8000B)

Offers instruction to foreigners and Thais. The gym is famous for having trained the title-winning, transgender boxer Parinya Kiatbusaba.

Volunteering

Burma Study Center VOLUNTEERING
(Map p323; www.burmastudy.org; 302/2 Soi 13, Th Nimmanhaemin; ⊙ 11.30am-8pm Mon-Fri, to 6pm Sat) This nonprofit community centre conducts classes in English for Burmese migrants living in Thailand. Many of the students are young, low-wage workers whose education has been disrupted by political instability in Myanmar or dislocation from their home communities. It also maintains an outreach to educate the international community about Burmese-related issues through its lending library, book discussions and film screenings.

Cultural Canvas Thailand VOLUNTEERING
(www.culturalcanvas.com; Chiang Mai University) Places volunteers in migrant learning centres, art programs and other social-justice projects in northern Thailand.

🎓 Courses

Cooking

Chiang Mai is the most popular place in the country to learn Thai cooking, with well over a dozen schools competing for the honour of teaching you how to prepare your own curry pastes, Thai soups, stir-fries, curries and Thai puddings. Courses are typically based around one-day modules that you can bolt together to learn an entire Thai menu over a week, though some short half-day and evening courses are available.

All the courses will teach you about the ingredients as well as the techniques, with trips to local markets to buy herbs and spices, or walks around the herb garden. The best courses take place at bespoke communal kitchens at country farmhouses around Chiang Mai. Along the way, you get to eat the Thai food you make and you'll leave with a recipe booklet so you can create the same magic back home.

★ **Small House Chiang Mai Thai Cooking School** COOKING
(Map p312; ☎ 095 674 4550; www.chiangmaithai cooking.com; 19/14 Th Thipanet; 1-day/evening-only classes 1500/1300B) Arm teaches Thai cookery at the eponymous dwelling outside Chiang Mai. Courses include transport, a visit to a local market, and span northern Thai dishes. The small two- to four-person classes are intimate and the experience feels more local than touristy. She also offers day-long private classes from 3500B.

Asia Scenic Thai Cooking COOKING
(Map p318; ☎ 053 418657; www.asiascenic.com; 31 Soi 5, Th Ratchadamnoen; half-day courses 800-1000B, full-day courses 1000-1200B; ⊘ half-day courses 9am-1pm & 5-9pm, full-day courses 9am-3pm) On Khun Gayray's cooking courses you can study in town or at a peaceful out-of-town farm. Courses cover soups, curries, stir-fries, salads and desserts, so you'll be able to make a three-course meal after a single day.

Thai Farm Cooking School COOKING
(Map p318; ☎ 081 288 5989; www.thaifarmcooking. com; 38 Soi 9, Th Moon Muang; courses 1500B) Cooking classes at a beautiful and serene organic farm, 17km outside of Chiang Mai; includes return transport from Chiang Mai.

Chiang Mai Thai Cookery School COOKING
(Map p318; ☎ 053 206388; www.thaicookery school.com; 47/2 Th Moon Muang; courses from 1450B) One of Chiang Mai's first cooking schools, run by TV chef Sompon Nabnian and his team. Classes are held in a rural setting outside of Chiang Mai, and there's a special evening masterclass led by the founder, with northern Thai delicacies.

Baan Thai COOKING
(Map p318; ☎ 053 357339; www.baanthaicookery. com; 11 Soi 5, Th Ratchadamnoen; day/evening course 1000/800B) With a handy in-town location, this school offers all-day and evening classes.

Meditation

Several temples offer vipassana meditation courses and retreats, but most have strict rules and participants should dress in modest white clothes, which can typically be purchased from the temple. There is usually no set fee but donations are appropriate.

CHIANG MAI PROVINCE CHIANG MAI

THE PLIGHT OF CHIANG MAI'S MIGRANT WORKERS

Over the past three decades, an estimated 200,000 people have fled from Myanmar to Chiang Mai Province, escaping political violence, economic hardship and oppression in bordering Shan state. While some of these migrants have found sanctuary and opportunity in Thailand, others have found exploitation, working in almost slave-like conditions with little security or protection from abuse. Many of the 'long-necked' Padaung tribespeople put on display in tourist camps around Chiang Mai are actually indentured workers, working off fees charged by people-smugglers to bring them across the border.

Facing growing international and domestic pressure, the Thai government is taking steps to reduce the influx, tightening border controls, raiding people-smuggling camps, and introducing a nationality verification process, which qualifies migrants for legal status and a minimum wage. However, allegations that the police turn a blind eye to and even participate in exploitation are widespread.

In response to this situation, a number of nongovernmental organisations are working with the Burmese migrant community in Chiang Mai, providing health care, education and legal support for displaced people. If you are interested in contributing or volunteering, contact Chiang Mai's **Burma Study Center**, an umbrella for projects working with the Burmese refugee community.

Wat Suan Dok Meditation Retreat
HEALTH & WELLBEING

(Map p312; ☑084 609 1357; www.monkchat. net; Wat Suan Dok, Th Suthep; 2-day retreats 500B; ☉ Tue & Wed) The Buddhist university affiliated with Wat Suan Dok (p322) conducts a two-day meditation retreat at an affiliated forest wát. Register in advance for more information.

Doi Suthep Vipassana Meditation Center

(☑053 295012; www.fivethousandyears.org; Wat Phra That Doi Suthep, Th Huay Kaew; by donation) Set within the grounds of Wat Phra That Doi Suthep (p317), this centre offers meditation training retreats for all levels, lasting from four to 21 days.

Wat Srisuphan
HEALTH & WELLBEING

(Map p312; ☑053 200332; 100 Th Wualai; ☉5.30-9pm Tue, Thu & Sat) The silver temple south of the old city offers an introduction to meditation using the four postures: standing, walking, sitting and lying down.

Thai Massage

Chiang Mai has many massage schools, from tourist-focused courses that teach the basics to full government-accredited vocational programs.

Art of Massage
HEALTH & WELLBEING

(Map p318; ☑083 866 2901; www.artofmassage. webs.com; Soi 3, Th Loi Kroh; courses 1500-3000B) Khun Wanna gets rave reviews for her practical training sessions, limited to a maximum of two people, lasting two to three days.

Chetawan Thai Traditional Massage School
HEALTH & WELLBEING

(Map p312; ☑053 410360; www.watpomassage. com; 7/1-2 Soi Samud Lanna, Th Pracha Uthit; general courses 9500B) Bangkok's respected Wat

Pho massage school established this Chiang Mai branch outside of town near Rajabhat University.

Thai Massage School of Chiang Mai
HEALTH & WELLBEING

(TMC; ☑053 854330; www.tmcschool.com; 203/6 Th Chiang Mai-Mae Jo; basic courses from 8500B) Northeast of town, this well-known school offers a government-licensed massage curriculum. There are three foundation levels and an intensive teacher-training program.

Jack Chaiya
HEALTH & WELLBEING

(Map p318; ☑083 154 6877; www.jackchaiya. com; 74/3 Th Wiang Kaew; 3- to 5-day courses from 7000B) Jack Chaiya was trained by his mother in *jàp sên* (literally 'nerve touch'), a northern Thai massage technique akin to acupressure, and is passing on the wisdom at this small massage school near Wat Phra Singh.

Language

Being a university town, Chiang Mai is a popular place to learn the Thai language and there are also opportunities to train up as a TEFL (Teaching English as a Foreign Language) teacher.

American University Alumni
LANGUAGE

(AUA; Map p318; ☑053 214120; www.learnthai inchiangmai.com; 73 Th Ratchadamnoen; group courses 5300B) Conducts 60-hour Thai courses, with two hours of classes daily, Monday to Friday. Private instruction is also available.

Easy Study Thai
LANGUAGE

(Map p318; ☑089 429 9872; www.easystudythai. com; 3rd fl, Pantip Plaza, Th Chang Khlan; courses from 2500B) Upstairs in the Pantip Plaza shopping centre; offers a wide range of courses in Thai, from month-long beginner packages to year-long courses. Also offers classes via Skype if you want to practice pre–Thailand arrival.

UniTEFL International
LANGUAGE

(Map p312; ☑053 400001; www.unitefl.com; P & S Bldg 3, 213/2 Th Huay Kaew; TEFL courses from US$345) Offers TEFL certificate courses ranging from 60 to 120 hours, with post-qualification placements, as well as one-year Thai-language courses.

SONGKRAN IN CHIANG MAI

The traditional Thai New Year (13 to 15 April) is celebrated in Chiang Mai with infectious enthusiasm that's made it one of the best places in the country to be for the occasion. Thousands of revellers line all sides of the moat to throw water on passers-by and each other, while more restrained Songkran rituals are held at Wat Phra Singh.

☞ Tours

★ Chiang Mai on Three Wheels TOURS
(www.chiangmaionthreewheels.com; Don Kaeo, Saraphi; 4hr tours for 2 people 1700B) 🏍 There are few better ways to tour Chiang Mai than by slow, quiet, culturally immersive săhm·lór (three-wheel pedicabs; also spelt Săamláw). This organisation helps promote this dying industry by connecting tourists with the often non-English-speaking drivers and pairs you with an English-speaking guide. Profits go entirely to the drivers and to support their industry.

**Chiang Mai Street
Food Tours** FOOD & DRINK
(📱085 033 8161; www.chiangmaistreetfoodtours.com; tours 850B) These foodie trips through the city's morning and night markets are a great introduction to northern Thai cuisine.

Spice Roads CYCLING
(Map p318; 📱053 215837; www.spiceroads.com; 1 Soi 7, Th Moon Muang; day/multiday tours from 3850/16,250B) Offers a wide range of cycling tours, using impressively maintained, imported bicycles, from half-day trips around Chiang Mai city to serious mountain-biking trails in the surrounding countryside.

Click and Travel CYCLING
(📱053 281553; www.chiangmaicycling.com; half/full/multi-day tours from 950/1500/5350B; 🚲) Click and Travel offers family-friendly pedal-powered tours with a cultural focus, visiting temples and attractions in and outside of the city centre.

🎊 Festivals & Events

Flower Festival CULTURAL
(⊙early Feb) A riot of blooms, held over a three-day period. There are flower displays, cultural performances and beauty pageants, plus a floral parade from Saphan Nawarat to Suan Buak Hat.

Chiang Mai Chinese New Year NEW YEAR
(⊙Feb) The city's Chinese inhabitants herald the New Year in February with Chinese festival food, lion dances and the like.

Poy Sang Long (Poy Luang) RELIGIOUS
(⊙usually Apr) In this three-day ordination ceremony, novices at Wat Pa Pao, Wat Ku Tao and Wat Srisuphan are dressed in make-up and garish costumes representing Buddha's early life as a pampered prince.

STUDENT SPIRITUALITY

At the start of every academic year in July, the entire first-year class from Chiang Mai University embarks on a pilgrimage on foot to Wat Phra That Doi Suthep, to introduce new students to the spirit of the city, believed to reside in the mountain. More ambitious students make the ascent via a muddy footpath, which starts close to the TV tower near the back entrance to Chiang Mai Zoo and continues through the grounds of Wat Phalad. To get to the start of the path, go to the end of the university perimeter wall on Th Suthep and then follow the signposted road on the right towards Palaad Tawanron to reach the back entrance to the zoo; bear left at this fork and you'll reach the TV tower and a brown sign showing the start of the trail.

Inthakhin Festival RELIGIOUS
(⊙mid-May) Held at Wat Chedi Luang, this religious festival propitiates the city's guardian deity, who resides in the city pillar, ensuring that the monsoon will arrive on time.

Loi Krathong RELIGIOUS
(⊙Oct/Nov) Also known as Yi Peng, this lunar holiday is celebrated along Mae Ping with the launching of small lotus-shaped boats honouring the spirit of the river, and the release of thousands of illuminated lanterns into the night sky.

**Chiang Mai Red Cross
& Winter Fair** CULTURAL
(⊙Dec-Jan) This 10-day festival feels a bit like a country fair, with cultural performances and food hawkers doing a lively trade in northern Thai cuisine. The main venue is the Chiang Mai City Arts & Cultural Centre.

🛏 Sleeping

Make reservations far in advance if visiting during Chinese New Year, Songkran and other holiday periods.

Accommodation prices in the city are slowly creeping up, but you can still find a respectable air-con room from 650B.

🛏 Old City & Around

There are literally hundreds of places to stay in the old city. Go for the quieter ones

ONE MILLION RICE FIELDS

Once upon a time, northern Thailand was as separate and foreign to Bangkok as Cambodia or Laos is today. The northern kingdom of Lanna (meaning 'one million rice fields') had its own dialect, writing system, religious and social customs and tribal ethnicity. A concerted effort to create a unified 'Thai' identity began after WWII, and Lanna traditions declined in the face of massive influence from the south. Nevertheless, if you scratch the surface, you can still find traces of Lanna identity and even glimmers of Lanna national pride.

Carved crossed gables known as *kalae* (a legacy of animist tribal cults) still adorn buildings across Chiang Mai, and the northern Thai dialect continues to be spoken by millions of *kun meu·ang* (people of the north). Religious festivals in Chiang Mai erupt in a riot of noise and colour, as *piphat* bands strike up traditional tunes and devotees perform Lanna dances in outrageously colourful costumes. **Songkran** (p128), a festival introduced to Thailand from the north, is celebrated with particular aplomb in Chiang Mai.

More tantalising glimpses of old Lanna can be seen at **Anusawari Singh** (อนุสาวรีย์ สิงห์; Map p312; Soi 1, Th Chotana/Th Chang Pheuak), just beyond Hwy 11 in the north of the city, where Chao Kavila built two stucco lions on an artificial island to scare off would-be Burmese invaders. The lions are the focus of boisterous celebrations as part of the Suep Jata Muang festival in June, when older residents of Chiang Mai dance and make offerings to Chiang Mai's guardian spirits. Chao Kavila is also credited with building the stucco guardian elephants in the **Elephant Monument** (p325) by the bus station on Th Chotana (Th Chang Pheuak).

The animist origins of the Lanna kingdom are even more tangible at the **Pu Sae Ya Sae festival**, held 10 days after Suep Jata Muang at Mae Hia in the forest below **Wat Phra That Doi Kham** (p325). According to legend, Doi Kham mountain was once the domain of two evil giants known as Pu Sae and Ya Sae, but Buddha appeared to the giants and convinced them to pursue a life of dharma, saving the people of Mae Hia. To invoke blessings from the giants, a water buffalo is sacrificed and skinned by a village shaman, who becomes possessed by the spirit of Pu Sae.

dotted around the tiny lanes linking the main streets.

★ Diva Guesthouse
GUESTHOUSE $

(Map p318; ☑ 053 273851; www.divaguesthouse. com; 84/13 Th Ratchaphakhinai; dm 120-180B, r 300-800B; ❋ @ ⟨⟩) An energetic, vaguely bohemian spot on busy Th Ratchaphakhinai, Diva offers the full backpacker deal – dorm beds, budget boxrooms, adventure tours, net access, ambient tunes and fried rice and *sà·dé* (grilled meat with peanut sauce) in the downstairs cafe. Accommodation ranges from dorms to family rooms and comes with either fan or air-con.

60 Blue House
GUESTHOUSE $

(Map p318; ☑ 053 206120; www.60bluehouse. com; 32-33 Th Ratchaphakhinai; dm 250B, s/d from 350/400B; ❋ ⟨⟩) This appealing, clean and colourful hostel has one eight-bed dorm and clean private rooms with shared bathroom. Owner Khun Tao is a mine of local information, so guests always know where to go and what to do. A great bargain for high standards.

Banjai Garden
GUESTHOUSE $

(Map p318; ☑ 085 716 1635; www.banjai-garden. com; 43 Soi 3, Th Phra Pokklao; r with fan 450B, with air-con 550-1400B; ❋ ⟨⟩) Set in an orderly wooden house, Banjai Garden has a calm air and a pleasant garden for hanging out. Take your pick from simple but clean and great-value fan rooms or better air-con rooms. Staying here feels a little like staying in a Thai home.

Gap's House
GUESTHOUSE $

(Map p318; ☑ 053 278140; www.gaps-house.com; 3 Soi 4, Th Ratchadamnoen; r incl breakfast 420-1000B; ❋ ⟨⟩) The overgrown garden at this old backpacker favourite is a veritable jungle, providing plenty of privacy in the relaxing communal spaces. Modest budget rooms are set in old-fashioned wooden houses, and the owner runs cooking courses and dishes up a delicious vegetarian buffet from Monday to Saturday (closed June). No advance reservations.

Julie Guesthouse
HOSTEL $

(Map p318; 📞053 274355; www.julieguesthouse. com; 7 Soi 5, Th Phra Pokklao; dm 100-150B, r with/without bathroom from 260/150B; 🛜) Julie is perennially popular, though this is as much about budget as facilities. For not much more than the price of a fruit smoothie you can get a basic dorm bed, and tiny boxrooms cost only a little more. In the evenings travellers congregate on the covered roof terrace.

There's a **Th Ratchamankha branch** (Map p318; 📞094 628 1991; 11 Th Ratchamankha; dm 120-180B) with dorms only.

Smile House 1
GUESTHOUSE $

(Map p318; 📞053 208661; www.smilehouse chiangmai.com; 5 Soi 2, Th Ratchamankha; r with fan/air-con 350/700B; ❄️🛜🏊) There's a hint of the 1950s motel about this popular and friendly guesthouse, with a splash pool for kids and a bigger pool for grown-ups. It's very relaxed and the simply furnished rooms (with big windows) offer good value for money.

According to local folklore, the old house once served as the 'safe house' of Kun Sa, the infamous Shan-Chinese opium warlord.

★ Awana House
HOTEL $$

(Map p318; 📞053 419005; www.awanahouse.com; 7 Soi 1, Th Ratchadamnoen; r with fan 500B, with air-con 700-1000B; ❄️@🛜🏊) The pick of the guesthouses around the medieval city gate of Pratu Tha Phae, with rooms for every budget – all kept spotless – and a mini swimming pool under cover on the ground-floor terrace. Rooms get more comfortable and better decorated as you move up the price scale and there's a rooftop chill-out area with views across old Chiang Mai.

Staff are delightful and go the extra mile for children, so it's a big hit with families; book ahead.

★ Baan Hanibah
Bed & Breakfast
HOTEL $$

(Map p318; 📞053 287524; www.baanhanibah.com; 6 Soi 8, Th Moon Muang; s/d from 1000/1400B; ❄️🛜) Protected by a garden of fragrant frangipani trees, Baan Hanibah is a relaxed boutique escape on a quiet lane in the heart of the old city. Behind an ornate gateway, in a converted teak house, you'll find small, quite stylish rooms with floaty drapes and Thai trim.

Thapae Gate Lodge
GUESTHOUSE $$

(Map p318; 📞053 207134; www.thapaegatelodge. com; 38/7 Soi 2, Th Moon Muang; r from 800B; ❄️🛜) An upgrade of a typical Thai house, with simple but good-value backpacker rooms, some quite large and/or with balconies. It was purchased and remodelled by new beer-loving owners in 2017 who offer an array of craft Thai choices in the on-site bar that can be hard to find elsewhere. Delicious breakfasts are worth the extra 100B.

Hostel by Bed
HOSTEL $$

(Map p318; 📞053 217 215; www.hostelbybed.com; Th Singharat; dm 450-700B, d from 1250B; @🛜) Although you can find a room in Chiang Mai for the same price as these dorm beds, you get a lot of flashy facilities for your baht here, including a good breakfast, a chic kitchen, high cleanliness standards and a big bed with a curtain. Common areas inspire meeting people and it's in a decent location near cheap street food.

Baan Pordee Guesthouse
GUESTHOUSE $$

(Map p318; 📞083 764 8008; www.baanpordee. com; 6 Soi 12, Th Phra Pokklao; r from 1100B; ❄️🛜) A huge, open, airy balcony sets the scene at this calm, quiet guesthouse in an altogether lovely modern home, tucked away in an ideal location behind Wat Duang Di. Spotlessly tidy rooms face onto the garden.

★ Tamarind Village
HOTEL $$$

(Map p318; 📞053 418896-9; www.tamarindvillage. com; 50/1 Th Ratchadamnoen; incl breakfast r from 5200B, ste 8200-10,700B; ❄️🛜🏊) Effortlessly refined, this atmospheric Lanna-style property sprawls across the grounds of an old tamarind orchard in a prime location off Th Ratchadamnoen. Walkways covered by tiled pavilions lead to secluded and beautiful spaces, and tall mature trees cast gentle shade around the huge pool and gardens. Design-magazine-worthy rooms are full of gorgeous tribal fabrics and artefacts.

There's a babysitting service for children aged one year or older.

The Ruen Tamarind restaurant (p343) serves beautifully presented Thai dishes and there's an opulent spa offering the full range of treatments.

★ Sri Pat Guest House
HOTEL $$$

(Map p318; 📞053 218716; www.sri-patguesthouse. com; 16 Soi 7, Th Moon Muang; r 1500-2000B; ❄️🛜🏊) A standout flashpacker guesthouse with all the trimmings: wi-fi, pool, wood-decked communal areas, scattered Buddha carvings and smart tiled rooms with flat-screen TVs and little Thai details. You get plenty of personality for your baht and staff members are cheerful and friendly.

⭐ **Tri Yaan Na Ros** BOUTIQUE HOTEL **$$$**
(Map p312; ☑ 053 273174; www.triyaannaros. com; 156 Th Wualai; r incl breakfast 2300-2500B; ❄🏠🏊) South of the main tourist bustle on Th Wualai, and tucked away behind a restaurant, this charming boutique hotel features elegant period decor – perhaps the best re-creation of a traditional Thai home in Chiang Mai. Rooms come with four-poster beds, flowing drapes, oodles of dark timber and antique Buddhas. There's also a peaceful courtyard pool.

The location means you'll be in pole position for the Saturday Walking Street (p350) market.

⭐ **Good Morning**
Chiang Mai Tropical Inn HOTEL **$$$**
(Map p318; ☑ 086 922 3606; www.goodmorning chiangmai.com; 29/5 Soi 6, Th Ratchamankha; r incl breakfast 1500-2300B; ❄🏠🏊) A saltwater pool, superior breakfasts and a tranquil location south of Wat Phra Singh all score points for this comfortable guesthouse in a vaguely Spanish-style villa. Rooms full of natural timber come with crisp linen and vast, tasteful bathrooms. Excellent value.

BED Phrasingh Hotel BOUTIQUE HOTEL **$$$**
(Map p318; ☑ 053 271 009; www.bed.co.th; Sam-lan Soi 1; d from 2250B; ❄🏠🏊) This is our fa-vourite of the near identical, towering black, sleekly modern hotels in this small chain now in four locations in Chiang Mai. Hid-den behind vines on a small lane only a few minutes' walk from some of the city's most splendid, glittering sights and local food, it's insanely popular so book ahead.

Rachamankha HOTEL **$$$**
(Map p312; ☑ 053 904111; www.rachamankha. com; off Soi 1, Th Samlan; incl breakfast r 9800-11,200B, ste 23,700B; ❄@🏠🏊) Entering Ra-chamankha is like walking into an ancient monastery or a medieval village. Interlinked courtyards lead past perfectly manicured gardens to shady terracotta-tiled pavilions boasting statues and ancient artwork. The rooms continue the opulent theme with one-of-a-kind antiques, four-poster beds and an understated elegance.

Villa Duang Champa HOTEL **$$$**
(Map p318; ☑ 053 327199; www.duangchampa. com; 82 Th Ratchadamnoen; r incl breakfast 1800-3000B; ❄🏠) In a prime piece of real estate for the Sunday Walking Street (p350) market, the airy rooms here have polished-concrete floors, antique wooden French doors, ec-lectic furniture, lots of colonial charm and small nooks that catch the sun. The staff are exceptionally friendly and helpful, which only brightens the space more.

Vieng Mantra HOTEL **$$$**
(Map p318; ☑ 053 326640; www.viengmantra.com; 9 Soi 1, Th Ratchadamnoen; r incl breakfast 2400-2900B; ❄@🏠🏊) A proper hotel tucked into winding Soi 1, Vieng Mantra creates a little oasis with its courtyard pool and land-scaped gardens. Rooms range from simple standards to swanky deluxe-plus accommo-dation with circular divans and plump silk cushions. Balconies have built-in seats with a view over the electric-blue pool.

Buri Gallery GUESTHOUSE **$$$**
(Map p318; ☑ 053 416500; www.burigallery.com; 102 Th Ratchamankha; r 1500-2800B; ❄🏠🏊) Seconds from Wat Phra Singh, Buri Gallery is a perfect base for exploring the old city. Rooms, set around a lovely pool that's ideal for families, are tucked away behind the cof-feeshop and garden in a series of converted teak buildings. Although pricey, the villas have bits and bobs of Lanna art and the best have balconies where you can sit and enjoy the sunset.

Baan Huenphen BOUTIQUE HOTEL **$$$**
(Map p318; ☑ 053 281100; www.baanhuenphen. com; 117/1 Th Ratchamankha; incl breakfast r 2850-5500B, ste 5500B; ❄🏠🏊) Near the northern Thai restaurant of the same name, this up-graded Thai house has large, comfy rooms with immaculate bathrooms, and sit-on balconies out front. There's a small but love-ly swimming pool and lots of Hang Dong crafts and antiques in the communal areas downstairs.

3 Sis HOTEL **$$$**
(Map p318; ☑ 053 273243; www.the3sis.com; 1 Soi 8, Th Phra Pokklao; r incl breakfast 1700-2500B; ❄🏠) Facing the gates to Wat Chedi Luang, 3 Sis offers large, airy rooms set around a huge open atrium, behind a very busy street-side restaurant. The front building has fair-ly standard hotel rooms but with a dash of flair; the 'Vacation Lodge' at the back has

SEVEN SOOTHING COUNTRYSIDE RESORTS

For those who find downtown Chiang Mai too hectic, there are many scenic country resorts just beyond the superhighways where you can surround yourself with misty mountains, green fields and tropical forests. The following are less than two hours' drive from Chiang Mai.

Proud Phu Fah (☑ 053 879389; www.proudphufah.com; Rte 1096, Km 17; r incl breakfast 5500-15,000B; ❋◉☎❋) Designer chic in the jungle, this elegant country resort offers the most atmospheric accommodation on the Mae Sa–Samoeng Loop.

Tharnthong Lodges (p365) An eclectic chalet-style jungle resort close to Mae Kampong, with trickling brooks, scattered statues and rabbits leaping around the lawns.

Four Seasons Chiang Mai (☑053 298181; www.fourseasons.com; Th Mae Rim-Samoeng Kao, off Rte 1096; r from 17,000B; ❋◉☎❋) Ultra-upmarket, but beautifully executed, with lodges scattered through rainforests and fields still tilled by local farmers, close to Mae Rim.

Dhara Dhevi (☑ 053 888888; www.dharadhevi.com; 51/4 Th Chiang Mai-San Kamphaeng, off Rte 1006; r from 17,600B; ❋◉☎❋) Chiang Mai's most elegant address, this lavish resort re-creates a medieval Lanna village, right down to the farmers toiling on rice terraces between the villas. It's 5km east of the city.

Kaomai Lanna Resort (☑ 053 834470; www.kaomailanna.com; Th Chiang Mai-Hot/Rte 108, San Pa Thong; r 2000-8000B; ❋❋) This resort is set in a series of converted tobacco-curing sheds, redeveloped as swish hotel rooms. The resort can arrange tours to nearby handicraft villages and the outdoor restaurant serves superb Thai food.

Rabeang Pasak Tree House (☑ 087 660 1243; www.chiangmaitreehouse.com; Rd 4031, Baan Pasak Ngam, Doi Saket; r from 2500B; ☎) Grown-up tree houses among the branches. Lodging is simple but far from ordinary.

Chai Lai Orchid (☑ 086 923 0867; www.chailaiorchid.com; 202 Moo 9, Tambon Mae Win, Mae Wang; r 800-3240B; ❋❋) This collection of comfortable jungle huts is planted in the middle of the forest, reached via a suspended footbridge across Mae Wang.

CHIANG MAI PROVINCE CHIANG MAI

much more attractive rooms with wooden floors and extra comforts.

Charcoa House
HOTEL $$$

(Map p318; ☑ 053 212681; www.charcoa.com; 4 Soi 1, Th Si Phum; r 1440-2000B; ❋☎) Like a dainty petit four, this boutique hotel is run with precision by friendly staff, who also run the attached bakery and cafe. The decor falls somewhere between Spanish villa and Swiss B&B. It's worth staying just for the breakfast pastries.

East of the Old City

While it isn't as quaint as the old city, Th Tha Phae is just as convenient for sightseeing and nightlife and is even closer to the Night Bazaar.

Virgo Hostel
HOSTEL $

(Map p318; ☑ 053 234292; www.hit-thapae.com; Soi 2, Th Tha Phae; dm 350B; ❋☎) One of a cluster of spick-and-span backpacker hostels just east of the old city walls, Virgo has neat dorms with lockers, towels and a rooftop cafe. There's a women-only dorm on the 2nd floor.

SoHostel
HOSTEL $

(Map p318; ☑053 206360; sohostel.chiangmai@gmail.com; 64/2 Th Loi Kroh; dm/r from 219/1500B; ❋☎) Loi Kroh is better known for girlie bars than backpacker bunks, but this huge modern hostel is a good deal, just an easy stroll from the old city and the Night Bazaar. The two-tone red-and-white dorms (with six to 12 beds) are better value than the somewhat overpriced private rooms.

Nat Len Boutique Guesthouse
GUESTHOUSE $$

(Map p318; www.natlenboutiqueguesthouse.com; 2/4 Soi Wat Chompu, Th Chang Moi; r 750-1200B; ❋☎❋) Quirky rooms are spread over several colourful houses at this low-key guesthouse just outside the city walls. Our favourite feature is the pale blue pool with its bubbling whirlpools, and there are lots of interesting wát in the surrounding alleyways. It's a five-minute walk to Thapae Gate.

Baan Kaew Guest House
GUESTHOUSE $$

(Map p312; ☑ 053 271606; www.baankaew-guest-house.com; 142 Th Charoen Prathet; r from 700B; ❄ 🗟) This two-storey, apartment-style place is a good honest deal on the quiet west bank, but not too far from the Night Bazaar. Clean tiled rooms with immaculate white linen open onto a balcony with views across the spacious garden.

Thapae Boutique House
HOTEL $$

(Map p318; ☑ 053 284295; www.thapaebou tiquehouse.com; 4 Soi 5, Th Tha Phae; r/ste from 750/1200B; ❄ 🗟) This friendly, ageing hotel has enough murals, Thai textiles and wooden trim to justify the boutique tag, and the location is handy for both the old city and the Night Bazaar. Rooms are a little past their prime but have some character and rates include breakfast.

★ Banthai Village
HOTEL $$$

(Map p318; ☑ 053 252789; www.banthaivillage. com; 19 Soi 3, Th Tha Phae; r incl breakfast 3600-4800B, ste 5800-7800B; ❄ @ 🗟 ☒) True to its name, Banthai does indeed resemble a country village transported to the modern city. The hotel sprawls over a series of wooden buildings with broad balconies, surrounding an idyllic pool and gardens overflowing with birds-of-paradise flowers. Rooms do the heritage thing, but subtly, with low wooden beds, dark-wood furniture and scattered cushions and traditional triangular Thai pillows.

★ Mo Rooms
HOTEL $$$

(Map p318; ☑ 053 280789; www.morooms.com; 263/1-2 Th Tha Phae; r incl breakfast 2800-3900B; ❄ @ 🗟 🗟) Mo Rooms is designer in the urban mould, all exposed concrete and sculptural timbers juxtaposed with natural materials. Each of the Chinese-zodiac-themed rooms was decorated by a different Thai artist, ensuring some unique visions in interior decor – our top picks are 'Monkey' with its woven pod bed and 'Horse' with its surreal bed-tree.

DusitD2 Chiang Mai
HOTEL $$$

(Map p318; ☑ 053 999999; www.dusit.com; 100 Th Chang Khlan; r from 3550B; ❄ @ 🗟 ☒) DusitD2 is a slice of modern minimalism in the chaos at the Night Bazaar. The dominant orange colour scheme spills over from the lobby into the designer rooms, and hotel facilities run to a pool and a fitness room with city views.

Le Meridien Chiang Mai
HOTEL $$$

(Map p318; ☑ 053 253666; www.lemeridien chiangmai.com; 108 Th Chang Khlan; r from 4800B; ❄ @ 🗟 ☒) This corporate hotel delivers a sleek modern package on the doorstep of the Night Bazaar. Cool, silent corridors open onto spacious, contemporary rooms with bathrooms linked to the bedrooms by glass walls to bring in natural light. For our money, the infinity pool with mountain views is a better place to be seen! Cheaper walk-in rates are often available.

🛏 Riverside

The neighbourhoods on either bank of the riverside are less touristy, but are handy for

---

GALLOPING CHINESE ON THE SILK ROAD

In ancient times, Chiang Mai straddled one of Asia's famous crossroads: the southern spur of the Silk Road. Chinese-Muslim traders from Yunnan Province (China) drove their horse-drawn caravans south through the mountains to the Indian Ocean to trade with the merchant ships of seafaring powers. To the Thais of Chiang Mai, these caravans were a strange sight and the traders were nicknamed *jeen hor* (galloping Chinese), a reference to their strange beasts of burden.

The focus for this horse-trading was the market district known as **Ban Haw**, near the present Night Bazaar, where you'll still find a thriving Yunnanese Muslim community. Traders worship at the 100-year-old **Matsayit Ban Haw** (มัสยิดบ้านฮ่อ, Hedaytul Islam Mosque; Map p312; Soi 1/Th Charoen Prathet), founded by later arrivals from China. Along Halal St are a number of simple restaurants selling Thai-Muslim-style food, including excellent *kôw soy* (curried chicken and noodles), *kôw mòk gài* (chicken *biryani*) and *néu·a òp hŏrm* ('fragrant' dried beef).

the night market and the riverside eateries on the east bank.

Hollanda Montri
GUESTHOUSE $

(Map p312; ☑ 053 242450; www.hollandamontri. com; 365 Th Charoenrat/Th Faham; r with fan/air-con from 550/750B; ❄️ 🛜) A good-value alternative to the old-city backpacker places, within walking distance of the riverside restaurants and a half-hour walk to the old-city walls. Rooms are super basic and the riverbank location is quiet. Bike and motorcycle hire can be arranged.

★ Riverside House
GUESTHOUSE $$

(Map p312; ☑ 053 241860; www.riverside house-chiangmai.com; 101 Th Chiang Mai-Lamphun; r incl breakfast 800-1500B; ❄️ @ 🛜 ⛱️) Plain yet spotless and rather large rooms are spread across three blocks; you pay top dollar for the central block, by the pool and away from the traffic noise, but all the rooms are good for the money. It's great value and a fine choice for families. Note that despite the name and location, there are no river views.

★ Baan Orapin
GUESTHOUSE $$$

(Map p312; ☑ 053 243677; www.baanorapin.com; 150 Th Charoenrat/Th Faham; r incl breakfast 1800-4000B; ❄️ 🛜 ⛱️) Set in a tranquil private garden surrounding a stately teak house, Baan Orapin is a family affair. The owner's family have lived here since 1914, and guest rooms are in elegant villas dotted around the grounds and full of graceful furniture and fabrics. Design fans can find their own swish homewares in the posh boutiques along Th Charoenrat.

137 Pillars
BOUTIQUE HOTEL $$$

(Map p312; ☑ 02 079 7137; www.137pillarshotels. com; Wat Ket Soi 1; r from 9700B; ❄️ ⛱️) This elegant resort is built around Baan Borneo, an old teak house once managed by Louis Leonowens, Rajah Brook and others as a timber trading centre. Rooms continue with the colonial luxury theme with lots of teak, period tile and spacious bathrooms. The grounds contain several towering trees, a chic pool, two restaurants and a small museum.

Anantara Resort & Spa
DESIGN HOTEL $$$

(Map p312; ☑ 053 253333; www.chiang-mai. anantara.com; 123 Th Charoen Prathet; r from 7900B; ❄️ @ 🛜 ⛱️) 🍸 Where James Bond would stay if he came to Chiang Mai; the Anantara sprawls across the grounds of the handsome former British Consulate, and it offers a perfect blend of cutting-edge modern design and period elegance. Rooms are simply gorgeous – natural timber in varied tones, floor-to-ceiling windows, flat-screens, balconies with divans – and all overlook the Zen-inspired grounds and river.

🛏️ West of the Old City

Staying west of the old city puts you close to Chiang Mai University and trendy Th Nimmanhaemin's bars and restaurants.

Bunk Boutique
HOSTEL $

(Map p323; ☑ 091 859 9656; bunkboutique@ hotmail.com; 8/7 Th Ratchaphuek; dm 250-500B, r 900-1200B; ❄️ 🛜) Bunk Boutique offers superior accommodation in four-bed dorms in a large apartment block behind Th Huay Kaew. Blonde-wood bunks have curtains for privacy and everyone gets a locker. You can rent a dorm as a private room if there's space.

International Hotel Chiangmai
HOTEL $

(Map p312; ☑ 053 221819; www.ymcachiangmai. org; 11 Soi Sermsak, Th Hutsadisawee; r 500-2000B; ❄️ @ 🛜 ⛱️) The main Chiang Mai YMCA has well-priced, if slightly worn, rooms, and the usual comfortingly institutional atmosphere. Although the decor is stuck in the 1980s, staff keep everything scrubbed clean and you'll get a mountain view from the upper floors.

Nimman Boutique Resort
HOTEL $$

(Map p323; ☑ 053 222638; www.nimmanresort. com; 29 Soi 17, Th Nimmanhaemin; r from 1000B; ❄️ 🛜) This ochre-yellow hotel with multi-coloured windows is a rare bargain in the Nimmanhaemin neighbourhood. Runners and cushions in Thai textiles add flair to the otherwise ordinary rooms, and there's a garden to relax in. Walk-in and low-season discounts can bring rates down to 650B.

Baan Say-La
GUESTHOUSE $$

(Map p323; ☑ 053 894229; www.baansaylaguest house.com; 4 Soi 5, Th Nimmanhaemin; r with fan/air-con 600/900B; ❄️ 🛜) Set in a Nimmanhaemin shophouse, this boutique guesthouse has stylish rooms in a mixture of styles – modernist, heritage, flowery colonial – and the owners keep the place looking immaculately clean and prim. Prices are as low as you'll find this close to the action.

Bunthomstan Guesthouse
GUESTHOUSE **$$**

(Map p323; ☑ 053 217768; www.bunthomstan. com; 7 Soi 5, Th Nimmanhaemin; r 1150-1550B; ❄️ 🛜) The owner of this comfy guesthouse in a modern Thai home has a 1950s thing going on (check out the vintage petrol pump in the drive). It's a peaceful haven with some of Chiang Mai's best eating on the doorstep. Rooms are homey, spacious and deliciously air-conditioned.

Sakulchai Place
HOTEL **$$**

(Map p323; ☑ 053 211982; www.sakulchaiplace. com; Soi Plubpueng, Th Huay Kaew; r 650-1100B; ❄️ 🛜) Hidden away down an anonymous lane north of Th Huay Kaew, this self-contained tower offers rooms that positively gleam. Reached via calm, cool corridors, rooms come with TVs and other modern essentials that cost twice the price in many other hotels in town. There's a decent house restaurant. Overall it's a boring choice but a really great deal.

Artel Nimman
BOUTIQUE HOTEL **$$$**

(Map p323; ☑ 053 213143; www.facebook.com/ theartelnimman; Soi 13, Th Nimmanhaemin; r incl breakfast 1400-2200B; ❄️ 🛜) We're suckers for hotels with slides, so the Artel delivers in spades. The modernist building is all round windows, polished concrete, geometric forms and juxtaposed materials, and the rooms are cool, calm, creative spaces. It's built mostly with upcycled materials and is as friendly as can be.

Kantary Hills
HOTEL **$$$**

(Map p312; ☑ 053 222111; www.kantarycollection. com; Soi 12, Th Nimmanhaemin; r 3800-7200B, apt per month from 50,000B; ❄️ 🛜 🌊) Immaculately turned out Kantary Hills offers stylish apartment-style rooms with kitchens in a vast, self-contained complex set back a bit from the Nimmanhaemin action. It's a favourite with the business and diplomatic set. The bland studios are overpriced but the one- and two-bedroom choices are quite luxurious.

Yesterday Hotel
BOUTIQUE HOTEL **$$$**

(Map p323; ☑ 053 213809; www.yesterday.co.th; 24 Th Nimmanhaemin; r incl breakfast from 1400B; ❄️ 🛜) In the heart of the action on Th Nimmanhaemin, Yesterday offers a quick trip back to the near past. Communal spaces are decorated with vintage prints, old phonographs, Bakelite phones and flashback

tube TVs, and the rooms have a more subtle mid-century mood.

 Eating
======

The city's fabulous night markets (p342), which sprawl around the main city gates and several other locations, offer the best food.

The Chinese-influenced love for pork is exemplified by the northern Thai speciality of *sâi òo·a* (pork sausage). A good-quality *sâi òo·a* should be zesty and spicy with subtle flavours of lemongrass, ginger and turmeric. Sample them at any food market.

✗ Old City & Around

The old city is crammed with traveller cafes but standards vary widely, and there are limited options for an upmarket dinner.

★Lert Ros
THAI **$**

(Map p318; Soi 1, Th Ratchadamnoen; mains 30-160B; ⊙noon-9pm) As you enter this local-style hole in the wall, you'll pass the main course: delicious whole tilapia fish, grilled on coals and served with a fiery Isan-style dipping sauce. Eaten with sticky rice, this is one of the great meals of Chiang Mai. The menu also includes fermented pork grilled in banana leaves, curries and *sôm·đam* (spicy green papaya salad).

★SP Chicken
THAI **$**

(Map p318; 9/1 Soi 1, Th Samlan; mains 50-170B; ⊙11am-9pm) Chiang Mai's best chicken emerges daily from the broilers at this tiny cafe near Wat Phra Singh. The menu runs to salads and soups, but most people just pick a half (90B) or whole (170B) chicken, and dip the moist meat into the spicy, tangy dipping sauces provided.

★Kiat Ocha
CHINESE, THAI **$**

(Map p318; Th Inthawarorot; mains 50-90B; ⊙6am-3pm) This humble Chinese-style canteen is mobbed daily by locals who can't get enough of the *kôw man gài* (Hainanese-style boiled chicken). Each plate comes with soup, chilli sauce and blood pudding and the menu also includes wok-fried chicken and pork and *sà·đé* (grilled skewers of pork or chicken). There's no English sign but you'll know it when you see it.

Huen Phen
THAI **$**

(Map p318; ☑ 053 277103; 112 Th Ratchamankha; mains lunch 30-100B, dinner 80-200B; ⊙9am-

4pm & 5-10pm) Huen Phen restaurant serves a comprehensive, and usually quite delicious, selection of northern Thai food in an antique bric-a-brac, plant-filled house that feels more like a garden. It's phenomenally popular, so come early or face a long wait for a table. We loved the 'Pork Curry in Burmese Style'.

AUM Vegetarian Food VEGETARIAN **$**
(Map p312; 1/4 Suriyawong Rd; mains 80-150B; ☺10.30am-8.30pm; 🍴) One of the original health-food peddlers, AUM (pronounced 'om') attracts crowds of veggie travellers and a few veggie-curious carnivores. The menu runs from vegetable maki rolls to blue sticky rice and delicious *sôm·dam* with cashews and carrot. They make their own mushroom-based stock.

Good Morning Chiang Mai INTERNATIONAL **$**
(Map p318; 29/5 Soi 6, Th Ratchamankha; breakfasts & mains 80-150B; ☺8am-8pm) A favourite among expats, this guesthouse cafe near Wat Phra Jao Mengrai serves big, international breakfasts, from pancake towers to continental spreads and *ðôm yam*–flavoured pasta. You can eat inside, in the movie-memorabilia-covered cafe, or in the garden by the pool.

Swan BURMESE **$**
(Map p318; 48 Th Chaiyaphum; mains 70-150B; ☺11am-11pm) This worn-looking restaurant just east of the old city offers a trip across the border, with a menu of tasty Burmese dishes such as *gaang hang lay* (dry, sour pork curry with tamarind and peanuts). The

backyard courtyard provides an escape from the moat traffic.

Party Buffet KOREAN **$**
(Map p318; Th Mani Nopharat; buffet 169B; ☺4pm-6am) Don't be put off by the name – this all-night Korean BBQ and hotpot buffet is where Chiang Mai's night owls come to play. It's all-you-can-eat, so pay once and feast at traditional mealtime or until the wee hours on boiled and barbecued meat, fish and veg.

Dash THAI **$**
(Map p318; 38/2 Soi 2, Th Moon Muang; mains 85-325B; ☺11am-11pm) A cut above the average traveller restaurant, Dash offers flavoursome Thai curries that are full of spice, served in a smart teak house or outside on the terrace. The chocolate brownie à la mode is nothing short of spectacular.

Blue Diamond VEGETARIAN **$**
(Map p318; 35/1 Soi 9, Th Moon Muang; mains 65-220B; ☺7am-9pm Mon-Sat; 🍴) Blue Diamond offers an adventurous menu of sandwiches, salads, curries, stir-fries and curious fusion dishes such as *ðôm yam* (Thai-style sour soup) macaroni. Packed with fresh produce, prepackaged spice and herb mixes, and freshly baked treats, it also feels a little like a wholefood store.

Dada Kafe VEGETARIAN **$**
(Map p318; Th Ratchamankha; mains 75-180B; ☺10am-9.45pm Mon-Sat, to 2.45pm Sun; 🍴) A tiny hole-in-the-wall that does a busy trade in vitamin-rich, tasty vegetarian health food

CHIANG MAI PROVINCE CHIANG MAI

KÔW SOY SAMPLER

Chiang Mai's unofficial city dish is *kôw soy (khao soi)*, wheat-and-egg noodles in a curry broth, served with pickled vegetables and sliced shallots, and garnished with deep-fried crispy noodles. The dish is thought to have its origins with the Yunnanese traders who came to Chiang Mai along the Silk Road, and the vendors along **Halal Street** (Soi 1, Th Charoen Prathet) near the Night Bazaar still serve some of the best in town. For our baht, **Kao Soi Fueng Fah** (Map p312; Soi 1, Th Charoen Phrathet; mains 40-60B; ☺7am-9pm) has the edge over other vendors, with its particularly flavourful bowls, but the more simple and salty broth at **Khao Soi Islam** (Map p312; Chang Moi Soi 1; mains from 50B; ☺8am-5pm) is more popular with locals.

Another great place to try *kôw soy* is around **Wat Faham** on Th Charoenrat (also known as Th Faham), north of the Th Ratanakosin bridge on the eastern bank of Mae Ping. Our top pick is **Khao Soi Lam Duan Fah Ham** (Map p312; 352/22 Th Charoenrat/Th Faham; mains from 40B; ☺9am-4pm), a modest-looking place that is packed to the rafters at lunchtime with hordes of locals slurping down bowls of deliciously rich *kôw soy*. Nearby **Khao Soi Samoe Jai** (Map p312; 391 Th Charoenrat/Th Faham; mains 50-70B; ☺8am-5pm) also cooks up a tasty soup.

DON'T MISS

CHIANG MAI'S FOOD MARKETS

Everyone knows that the best food in Chiang Mai is served on the street, and the city's night markets are fragrant, frenetic and fabulous. Every evening from around 5pm, hawker stalls set up in key locations around the old city, alongside smoothie stalls and beer and soft-drink vendors. Each stall has a speciality: you'll find everything from grilled river fish and *pàt gà prow* (chicken or meat fried with chilli and holy basil) to Western-style steaks, grilled prawns, and 'Tornado potato' (a whole potato, corkscrew sliced and deep fried).

The city's day markets are also thronged by food stalls and wholesale vendors, who pre-pare *gàp kôw* (pre-made stews and curries served with rice) and other take-home meals for busy city workers. And, of course, the Saturday and Sunday Walking Street markets (p350) are mobbed by food hawkers. Here's a guide to Chiang Mai's best market eats:

Talat Pratu Chiang Mai (Map p318; Th Bamrungburi; mains from 40B; ⊙4am-noon & 6pm-midnight) This heaving market sells foodstuffs and ready-made packed lunches by day and night-market treats after dark. It's mobbed nightly, particularly during Th Wualai's Saturday Walking Street.

Talat Pratu Chang Pheuak (Map p318; Th Mani Nopharat; mains from 30B; ⊙5-11pm) Sprawling west from the city's northern gate, this is one of Chiang Mai's most popular night markets, serving all the usual suspects, alongside the city's finest *kôw kăh mŏo* (slow-cooked pork leg with rice), prepared with a flourish by the 'Cowboy Hat Lady' – you can't miss her stall.

Talat Somphet (Map p318; Soi 6, Th Moon Muang; mains from 30B; ⊙6am-10pm) A small local food market north of Pratu Tha Phae that transforms into a night market after hours. Many of the cooking schools do their market tours here.

Talat Ton Phayom (Map p312; Th Suthep; ⊙8am-6pm) This local market off Th Suthep is a popular stop for visiting Thais who come to pick up authentic northern foodstuffs such as *kâap mŏo* (pork rinds).

Talat Warorot (p315) The grandmother of Chiang Mai markets has northern Thai food stalls (mains from 30B) tucked in all sorts of corners.

Talat Thanin (Siri Wattana; Map p312; mains from 30B; ⊙5am-7pm) North of the old city off Th Chotana (Th Chang Pheuak), this public market specialises in takeaway meals, with vendors serving fish stews, curries, stir-fries and spicy condiments from huge pans, vats and platters.

Talat Na Mor (Map p312; Malin Plaza, Th Huay Kaew; mains from 40B; ⊙5-10pm) A cheerful night market for the college set, with low prices and lots of choice; the student restaurants nearby on Th Huay Kaew are also worth investigating.

and smoothies. Wholesome ingredients such as pollen and wheatgrass are whisked into fruit shakes and the food menu includes veggie burgers, omelettes, salads, sandwiches and curries with brown rice.

Pak Do Restaurant THAI $
(Map p318; Th Samlan; mains 40-60B; ⊙7am-3pm) Across the street from Wat Phra Singh, Pak Do has no menu – instead, just peek inside the big metal bowls out front and pick whatever takes your fancy. Most days feature a dozen meat-based and vegetarian curries and stews, served over rice. The pork ribs in dry northern curry are superb!

Fern Forest Cafe CAFE $$
(Map p318; Th Singharat; mains 105-255B; ⊙8.30am-8.30pm) A garden cafe, with antique-looking wooden tables dotted around a brick courtyard full of shady trees, ferns, flowers and even a gurgling mini-waterfall. The Westernised menu has photo-worthy breakfasts, sandwiches, salads, cakes and ice creams.

Girasole ITALIAN $$
(Map p318; ✆053 276388; Kad Klang Wiang, Th Ratchadamnoen; mains 120-260B; ⊙11am-9pm) In the tidy little Kad Klang Wiang arcade, Girasole makes a convincing claim to offer the city's best pizzas, prepared using real pepperoni and other hard-to-find ingredi-

ents. There are several spaces for eating, both inside and outside, and the menu runs to superior pasta dishes and *secondi piatti*, plus tasty gelato for dessert.

New Delhi INDIAN $$
(Map p318; Th Ratwithi; mains 80-220B; ☺11am-10pm) OK, you don't get much atmosphere, but this straightforward place serves up some of Chiang Mai's best Indian food – lots of complex flavours and not too much oil and grease. Hit it up before or after the nearby bars.

Hot Chilli THAI $$
(Map p318; 71A Th Ratchadamnoen; mains 120-270B; ☺noon-midnight) The premium you pay at this trendy eatery on Th Ratchadamnoen is not for the Thai food, which is only so-so, but for the ambience. Diners sit in giant swings beneath flowing red drapes and cascades of artificial flowers. There are conventional tables inside for those who prefer not to swing and eat!

★**Ginger & Kafe @ The House** THAI $$$
(Map p318; ☎053 419011; www.thehousethailand.com; The House, 199 Th Moon Muang; mains 150-390B; ☺11am-11pm) Dining at the restaurant in the House boutique feels like eating in a posh Thai mansion, with antique furniture, soft sofas and fine china. The Thai food is delish and lavishly presented, but watch out for hidden prices in the menu – Massaman curry costs almost twice as much with lamb as with beef!

Ruen Tamarind THAI $$$
(Map p318; Tamarind Village, 50/1 Th Ratchadamnoen; mains 220-440B; ☺11am-10.30pm; ✐) For a sophisticated dinner, the restaurant at Tamarind Village (p335) serves superior northern Thai food in sleek surrounds overlooking the hotel pool. Dishes such as *yum tawai gài* (spicy chicken salad with tamarind dressing) are presented as works of art, and musicians serenade diners.

La Fourchette FRENCH $$$
(Map p318; ☎053 277482; Th Phra Pokklao; mains 280-630B; ☺6-11pm) Decked out like a 1920s living room, La Fourchette is owned by a jazz-bass-loving, French-trained Thai chef who is putting his education to excellent use in Chiang Mai. Come for French dishes that occasionally veer into Asian fusion.

✗ East of the Old City

In the early morning, vendors sell *nám đow·hôo* (soy milk) and baton-shaped *youtiao* (Chinese-style doughnuts) from stalls in Chiang Mai's small Chinatown (p316). For the very best *sâi òo·a* (pork sausage) seek out the stall known as **Dom Rong** inside the dried goods hall at Talat Warorot (p315).

Butter is Better Diner & Bakery DINER $
(Map p318; ☎053 820761; www.butterisbetterbakery.com; 189 Th Chang Khlan; items 85-200B; ☺8am-9pm Mon-Sat, 8am-4pm Sun; ✐) A retro '50s-style restaurant that serves some of the best American breakfasts, baked sweets and diner favourites in town. It has excellent sandwiches, outstanding gluten-free blueberry pancakes, and an amazing Armenian lentil soup that's not to be missed. Vegan and vegetarian options available.

★**Hideout** BREAKFAST $$
(Map p318; Th Sithiwongse; breakfasts 55-160B; ☺8am-5pm closed Mon) Hidden but found by expats looking for Western breakfast and coffee a cut above the rest, this place takes great care to serve perfectly cooked eggs, bacon fried to order, house-made muesli and yoghurt, creative sandwiches on fresh bread and the best banana bread we've eaten in Southeast Asia. The coffee is amazing too.

Seating is very limited so arrive early for a table.

Anusarn Food Center MARKET $$
(Map p312; Anusarn Night Bazaar, Th Chang Khlan; mains 60-350B; ☺5-10pm) Behind the Anusarn souvenir market, the Anusarn Food Center has a neat gaggle of hawker-style stalls selling Thai-Chinese standards, and a collection of restaurants serving live seafood cooked your way (grilled, fried, or steamed with ginger, sweet-and-sour sauce or sweet chilli). Seafood is usually priced by weight, so make sure you know what you're spending before you commit.

Whole Earth Restaurant THAI, INDIAN $$
(Map p318; 88 Th Si Donchai; mains 165-420B; ☺11am-10pm) Set in a sprawling garden, this beautiful teak-house restaurant wears a coat of hanging vines and orchids. It is the sort of place Thais take visitors for Indian and Thai dishes that sound exotic but won't blow the roof off your mouth with too much chilli. The setting and service is lovely but the food is average.

Chez Marco Restaurant & Bar FRENCH $$
(Map p318; 053 207032; 15/7 Th Loi Kroh; mains 150-290B; 5.30pm-midnight Mon-Sat) Despite the unpromising location in the midst of Loi Kroh's girlie-bar scene, Chez Marco cooks up convincing and wholesome French food with fresh ingredients and a bit of Gallic flair.

Riverside & Around

The east side of Mae Ping is a good hunting ground for upscale choices.

Khun Churn VEGETARIAN $
(Map p312; Th Muang Samut; buffet 164B; 8am-10pm;) Moved to a slightly inconvenient location about 1.5km northeast of the old city walls near Th Rattanakosin, Khun Churn is best known for its all-you-can-eat meatless buffet (11am to 2.30pm), with dozens of dishes, salads, herbal drinks and Thai-style desserts.

River Market THAI $$
(Map p312; 053 234493; Th Charoen Prathet; mains 165-500B; 11am-11pm) Trading on its location rather than its kitchen, River Market nevertheless scores romantic dinner points for the night-time views across the illuminated Iron Bridge. The menu covers all the usual Thai bases.

Huan Soontaree THAI $$
(053 872707; 208 Th Patan; mains 110-250B; 4-11pm Mon-Sat) Thai tourists eagerly make the pilgrimage 8km north of town to this rustic restaurant in the hope of hearing the dulcet tones of its owner, Thai chanteuse Soontaree Vechanont. She performs here from around 8pm. The menu is a pleasing

---

---

blend of northern, northeastern and central Thai specialities.

It's on the west side of the river, just south of Rte 11.

★ **Service 1921** SOUTHEAST ASIAN $$$
(Map p312; 053 253333; Anantara Resort, 123 Th Charoen Prathet; mains 290-2000B; 6am-11pm) The pan-Asian restaurant at the Anantara (p339) is elegance incarnate, with waitstaff in full 1920s garb and interior decor resembling the secret offices of MI6 – appropriate as the gorgeous teak villa housing the restaurant used to be the British Consulate. The food is made with top-notch ingredients, though some dishes have the spice dialled down to appeal to international palates.

West of the Old City

Th Nimmanhaemin and the surrounding soi excel in international cuisine, but restaurants and cafes appear and vanish overnight.

★ **I-Berry** ICE CREAM $
(Map p323; off Soi 17, Th Nimmanhaemin; single scoop 69B; 10am-10pm;) Mobbed day and night, this shop creates fantastic ice cream and sorbets using local fruits and creative ingredients such as black beans and sticky rice; the *saraka* (snake fruit) sorbet is quite possibly the best ice cream in Thailand. There are also fancy cakes and deserts. I-Berry is owned by Thai comedian Udom Taepanich (nicknamed 'Nose' for his signature feature).

★ **Pun Pun** VEGETARIAN $
(Map p312; www.punpunthailand.org; Wat Suan Dok, Th Suthep; mains 40-85B; 8am-4pm Thu-Tue;) Tucked away at the back of Wat Suan Dok, this studenty cafe is a great place to sample Thai vegetarian food prepared using little-known herbs and vegetables and lots of healthy whole grains grown on its concept farm, which doubles as an education centre for sustainable living.

There's a branch called **Imm Aim Vegetarian Restaurant** (Map p312; 10 Th Santhitham; mains 45-90B; 10am-9pm;) near the International Hotel Chiangmai.

Neau-Toon Rod Yam THAI $
(Map p323; Soi 11, Th Nimmanhaemin; mains 60-100B; 9am-8am Mon-Fri, to 6pm Sat & Sun) Build your own soup at this yummy corner-shop cheaply. Choose between rice or

several types of noodles, spice level, then meat, ranging from basic chicken to beef entrails. It also makes a decent *kôw soy* and hotpot.

Anchan Noodle
CHINESE $

(Map p323; Soi 9, Th Sirimungklajarn; mains 40-70B; ⊘9am-4pm) Students love this calm, basic cafe on a residential lane east of Th Nimmanhaemin for big bowls of Chinese-style pork, served with pretty blue noodles or sticky rice, dyed with flower petals.

Cherng Doi Roast Chicken
THAI $

(Map p323; Suk Kasame Rd; mains around 75B; ⊘11am-10pm, closed Mon) Famous for its crispy-skin slow-roasted chicken with spicy tamarind sauce, this place also serves an array of *sôm·đam*, soups, *lâhp* (minced meat 'salads') and pork dishes. We found the signature dish tasty but dry and a bit overrated. It's still worth a stop, however, for an inexpensive, quick meal in the Nimmanhaemin area.

Esan Cafe
THAI $

(Map p323; Th Nimmanhaemin; mains 75-140B; ⊘11am-10pm) A modern, bright cafe serving delicious Isan-style salads and grills. There are half a dozen variations on *sôm·đam* and the salad dressings are fiery and superb.

Salad Concept
INTERNATIONAL $

(Map p323; Th Nimmanhaemin; salads 115-170B; ⊘9am-9pm; 🛜✍) Build your own salad with a variety of fresh choices or choose one of the house specialty salads. There's also quinoa dishes, healthy breakfasts and green juices. All is served in a large, modern, air-conditioned space. You can also find a **branch** (Map p318; salads 115-170B; ⊘9am-9pm) on Th Chaiyaphum.

Ai Sushi
JAPANESE $

(Map p323; Th Huay Kaew; mains 90-210B; ⊘5-11.30pm) Students are the ones to follow when it comes to cheap eats in Chiang Mai and Ai Sushi pulls them in in droves. The pace gets furious in the evening as diners pack it out for fresh and delicious sushi, sashimi and sides.

★Rustic & Blue
INTERNATIONAL $$

(Map p323; ✆053 216420; www.rusticandblue. com; Soi 7, Th Nimmanhaemin; mains 180-360B; ⊘8.30am-9.30pm; ❄🛜) With an interior looking like a Pinterest spread of farmhouse-chic and an outdoor patio complete with hammocks, Rustic & Blue's photogenic,

farm-to-table dishes are in perfect harmony with the decor. Think eggs served with an array of greens, fresh breads like baguettes or croissants and granola bowls topped with seasonal local fruit.

Burgers and sandwiches at lunch are piled high with accoutrements, smoothies are served in mason jars and you can top it all off with homemade ice cream and baked deserts.

★Tong Tem Toh
THAI $$

(Map p323; Soi 13, Th Nimmamnhaemin; mains 50-170B; ⊘11am-9pm) Set in an unpretentious garden of a teak house, this trendy cafe serves deliciously authentic northern Thai cuisine. The menu roams beyond the usual to specialities such as *nám prík ong* (chilli paste with vegetables for dipping), *gaang hang lay* (Burmese-style pork curry with peanut and tamarind) plus a few more adventurous dishes using snake heads and ant eggs.

★Italics
ITALIAN $$

(Map p323; ✆05 321 6219; www.theakyra.com; 22/2 Nimmana Haeminda Soi 9; pizzas 260-550B; ⊘7am-11pm) Yes the modern black decor interspersed with gigantic, golden candelabra-style chandeliers is interesting, the pastas and mains are innovative and the cocktails are addictive, but it's the perfect pizzas here that makes this a top choice in Chiang Mai. We are still dreaming of the 'Akyra Pizza' with mozzarella, mushrooms, salami, bacon, blue cheese and truffle paste.

Royal Project Restaurant
THAI $$

(Krua Silapacheep; Th Huay Kaew; mains 90-220B; ⊘9am-5.30pm) 🌿 Products from the Queen's agricultural projects are whisked into delicious salads, soups, stews, stir-fries and other healthy Thai meals at this neat government-run restaurant near the zoo. Rainbow trout and seasonal northern Thai specialities spruce up the menu and there's an attached shop with Royal Project produce.

Smoothie Blues
INTERNATIONAL $$

(Map p323; 32/8 Th Nimmanhaemin; mains 60-200B; ⊘7.30am-8pm) This expat favourite is a top spot for breakfast – pancakes, sandwiches, granola, an array of egg dishes from egg-white-only omelettes to decadent Benedicts, you know the drill – plus, of course, smoothies and fresh juices.

Salsa Kitchen
MEXICAN $$

(Map p323; Th Huay Kaew; mains 100-240B; ⊙11am-11pm) This place serves some of the best US-style Mexican food in Chiang Mai. It's an expat favourite and it's often busy in the evening.

Tengoku
JAPANESE $$$

(Map p323; ☑053 215801; Soi 5, Th Nimmanhaemin; mains 200-1650B; ⊙11am-2pm & 5.30-10pm; ☜) Chiang Mai loves Japanese food, but Tengoku leaves everywhere else in town in the shade of Mt Fuji. This sleekly modern restaurant serves superior sushi, yummy yakitori, spectacular sukiyaki and wonderful wagyu steaks, plus cheaper bento box set meals.

Palaad Tawanron
THAI $$$

(☑053 216039; off Th Suthep; mains 160-380B; ⊙11.30am-midnight) Set into a rocky ravine near Doi Suthep, this restaurant inhabits a magical spot overlooking a forest reservoir, with the city lights twinkling below. The ambience and the ride here through the forest are great, the food only so-so.

Follow the signs from the end of the university compound on Th Suthep; if you reach the back entrance to the zoo, you're on the right track.

Drinking & Nightlife

Chiang Mai has three primary areas for watering holes: the old city, the riverside and Th Nimmanhaemin. Almost everyone ends up at either **Riverside** (Map p312; Th Charoenrat; ⊙10am-1am) or Good Vie on the east bank of Mae Ping at some point in their stay.

Old City

Mixology
BAR

(Map p312; 61/6 Th Arak; ⊙3pm-midnight Tue-Fri, 11am-midnight Sat & Sun) A tiny, eclectic bar with a huge selection of microbrews, a thick menu of fruity house drinks, burgers and northern Thai eats, and a lounging dog. Even if you drink too many chilli-infused 'prick me ups', you probably won't regret it the next day.

Kafe 1985
BAR

(Map p318; 127/3 Th Moon Muang; ⊙8.30am-midnight, closed Thu) Open since 1985, Kafe is nonetheless a timeless place to sip a Singha and dig into classic Thai-style drinking snacks (mains 60B to 150B) such as deep-fried fermented pork ribs.

Zoe in Yellow
BAR

(Map p318; 40/12 Th Ratwithi; ⊙11am-2am) Part of a complex of open-air bars at the corner of Th Ratchaphakhinai and Th Ratwithi, Zoe is where backpackers come to sink pitchers of cold Chang, sip cocktails from buckets, rock out to cheesy dance-floor fillers, canoodle and swap travel stories until the wee hours. There's also a few Indian food places between the bar joints.

Khun Kae's Juice Bar
JUICE BAR

(Map p318; Soi 7, Th Moon Muang; ⊙10.30am-7.30pm) Our vote for Chiang Mai's best juice shack. Tonnes of fresh fruit, heaps of delicious combinations, generous serves and all this for prices that are almost comically low (drinks from 40B).

Writer's Club & Wine Bar
BAR

(Map p318; 141/3 Th Ratchadamnoen; cocktails 150-190B; ⊙10am-midnight Sun-Fri; ☜) Run by a former foreign correspondent, this bar and restaurant is popular with expats, and travellers looking for a more low-key drinking experience, with wine by the glass (from 140B).

John's Place
BAR

(Map p318; Th Moon Muang; ⊙11am-midnight) This old-school traveller bar is a blur of neon lights and mismatched posters. It's far enough from the seedy Loi Kroh scene to be a convivial place to drink and the roof deck is a great spot to sip a cold beer above the commotion.

West of the Old City

Th Nimmanhaemin is popular with CMU students and hi-so (high society) Thais, and bars open and close here faster than you can order a cold bottle of Chang. Find the latest hot spots by cruising the soi and stopping wherever you find a crowd.

Warmup Cafe
CLUB

(Map p323; www.facebook.com/warmupcafe1999; 40 Th Nimmanhaemin; ⊙6pm-2am) A Nimmanhaemin survivor, cavernous Warmup has been rocking since 1999, attracting a young, trendy and beautiful crowd as the evening wears on. Hip-hop spins in the main room, electronic beats reverberate in the lounge, and rock bands squeal out solos in the garden.

CHIANG MAI'S COFFEE BUZZ

If you closed your eyes and started randomly walking in central Chiang Mai, chances are high you'd walk into a cafe – there are that many. While global chains are present, most places are local, selling coffee sourced from the hill tribes and forest communities around the city. The high-quality arabica beans grown here were introduced as a replacement crop for opium. Some cafes have started taking coffee culture even further by roasting their own beans and brewing cups that would fit right in in Melbourne or San Francisco.

Here are our picks for the most snob-worthy coffees in Chiang Mai:

Akha Ama Cafe (Map p318; www.akhaama.com; 175/1 Th Ratchadamnoen; ☺8am-6pm; 🤶) A cute local coffeeshop founded by an enterprising Akha who was the first in his village to graduate from college.

Ristr8to (Map p323; www.ristr8to.com; Th Nimmanhaemin; espresso drinks 88B; ☺8.30am-7pm, closed Tue) Inspired by Australian coffee culture with roasting skills learned in the US; drinks come with a caffeine rating and are often topped with award-winning latte art. There are two banches in the Nimmanhaemin area.

Khagee (Map p312; Chiang Mai-Lamphun Soi 1; espresso drinks 75B; ☺10am-5pm Wed-Sun; 🤶) A Japanese-style place that's insanely popular. Pair basic but near-perfect brews with its fresh breads and pastries.

Wawee Coffee (Map p318; www.waweecoffee.com; Th Ratchadamnoen, Kad Klang Wiang; drinks from 50B; ☺8am-9pm Mon-Sat, to 11pm Sun; 🤶) It's hard to go more than a few blocks in Chiang Mai without stumbling across an air-conditioned Wawee Coffee branch. If you're in a bind, this will do.

Beer Republic   BAR
(Map p323; www.beerrepublicchiangmai.com; Soi 11, Th Nimmanhaemin; ☺4pm-midnight) The 15 draught beers keep the hop-lovers happy at this European-style, plant-laden beer bar in the trendiest part of Nimmanhaemin.

Elsewhere in Chiang Mai

⭐**Good View**   BAR
(Map p312; www.goodview.co.th; 13 Th Charoenrat/ Th Faham; ☺10am-2am) Good View attracts plenty of locals, with a big menu of Thai standards and sushi platters (mains 100B to 250B) and a nightly program of bands with rotating line-ups (meaning the drummer starts playing guitar and the bass player moves behind the piano).

Pinte Blues Pub   BAR
(Map p312; www.bluespubchiangmai.wordpress. com; 9 Soi 1,Th Ratcha Chiangsaen; ☺4pm-midnight) A veteran blues bar (founded in 1986) that has hopscotched around the city and currently resides on a back lane south of the moat, it offers country blues in a country-style setting.

Raming Tea House   CAFE
(Map p318; Th Tha Phae; drinks 50-120B; ☺8.30am-5.30pm) This elegant Victorian-era cafe within the Siam Celadon (p349) shop serves Thai mountain teas alongside tasty Thai and Western food. It's a beautiful setting for a cuppa and a snack. Afternoon-tea spreads with snacks and desserts start at 190B.

☆ Entertainment

There are several dedicated music venues, plus cinemas and *moo·ay tai* stadiums.

Live Music

As well as the dedicated music venues, the Riversid and Good View bars host bands nightly.

Inter   LIVE MUSIC
(Map p318; 271 Th Tha Phae; ☺4pm-1am) This small wooden house packs in a lively line-up of local talent. It has that beach-shack vibe beloved by travellers everywhere and a popular pool table – though we recommend against challenging the multiple-trophy-winning lady who owns the place!

Sangdee Gallery LIVE MUSIC

(Map p323; www.sangdeeart.com; 5 Soi 5, Th Siri-mungklajarn; ◎3pm-midnight Tue-Sat) Part gallery, music club, bar and cafe, Sangdee is beloved by the art set, who gather here for live music, DJ sets and art shows. There's an open-mic night on Thursday.

North Gate Jazz Co-Op LIVE MUSIC

(Map p318; www.facebook.com/northgate.jazzcoop; 95/1-2 Th Si Phum; ◎7-11pm) This compact jazz club tends to pack in more musicians than patrons, but the music can be pretty hip.

Thai Boxing (Moo·ay Tai)

Chiang Mai has three *moo·ay tai* stadiums – **Thapae Boxing Stadium** (Map p318; ☑089 434 5553; Th Moon Muang; tickets 400-600B; ◎9pm-midnight Mon-Sat), **Loi Kroh Boxing Stadium** (Map p318; ☑094 606 8029; Th Kamphaeng Din; tickets 400-600B; ◎from 8.30pm) and **Kalare Boxing Stadium** (Map p312; ☑081 681 8029; Th Chang Khlan; tickets 400-600B; ◎from 9pm Mon & Fri) – showcasing a mixture of Thai and international fighters, but purists may find the scene a bit contrived compared to the real deal down south.

Cinemas

All the big shopping centres have flashy multiplex cinemas, screening the latest Thai and Hollywood blockbusters, with tickets from 100B up to 350B for deluxe seats with waitress service. Try the **Maya Lifestyle Shopping Center** (Map p323; Th Huay Kaew; ◎11am-10pm Mon-Fri, 10am-10pm Sat & Sun), **Central Airport Plaza** (Map p312; www.centralplaza.co.th; Rte 1141/Th Mahidol; ◎11am-9pm Mon-Fri, 10am-9pm Sat & Sun), **Central Festival** (www.central.co.th; Rte 11, Faham; ◎11am-9pm Mon-Thu, 11am-10pm Fri, 10am-10pm Sat & Sun), or the less flashy but cheaper **Kad Suan Kaew Shopping Center** (Map p323; www.kadsuankaew.co.th; Th Huay Kaew; ◎10am-9pm).

 Shopping

Chiang Mai is Thailand's handicraft centre, and an incredible volume and variety of crafts are produced and sold here, from

---

NOCTURNAL SHOPPING

At times, it can feel like the whole of Chiang Mai is an engine built to sell souvenirs, and nowhere is this feeling stronger than in the **Chiang Mai Night Bazaar** (Map p318; Th Chang Khlan; ◎7pm-midnight), between the river and the old-city walls. As the afternoon wears on, hundreds of hawkers fill the pavement on both sides of the street, selling silk boxer shorts, 'I Love Chiang Mai' T-shirts, miniature wooden spirit houses, hill-tribe silver, dried mango, carved soaps, wooden elephants, wire models of túk-túk, Buddha paintings, fabrics, teddy-bear dioramas and selfie sticks. This slightly frenetic shopping experience is the modern legacy of the Yunnanese trading caravans that stopped here along the ancient Silk Road, and you'll still need to haggle hard today.

Within the Night Bazaar are two large covered markets, signposted as **Night Bazaar** and **Kalare Night Bazaar**, selling more of the same, with an emphasis on wooden carvings, paintings and other handicrafts. The Kalare Night Bazaar is the more raucous of the two, with a blues bar on a raised podium in the centre.

South of Th Loi Kroh on Th Chang Khlan is the less claustrophobic **Anusarn Night Bazaar** (Map p318; Th Chang Khlan; ◎5-10pm), a semi-covered market filled with tables of vendors selling hill-tribe trinkets, wooden elephants, carved soap flowers and other cottage-industry goods. It's also good for dried mango and other local preserves. Fringing the market are numerous massage and fish-nibbling-your-feet places, and there's a tacky *gà·teu·i* (also spelt *kàthoey*) cabaret, which features cross-dresser or transgender performers.

For food, there are abundant fast-food joints, some excellent *kôw soy* canteens along Halal St (Soi 1, Th Charoen Prathet) and some touristy seafood places inside the **Anusarn Food Center** (p343). There's also a noisy open-air **night market** (Map p318; Th Chang Khlan; mains from 40B; ◎6-11pm) just north of Halal St on Th Chang Khlan, serving a good range of hawker favourites.

Túk-túk and *rót daang* loiter around the junction of Th Loi Kroh and Th Chang Khlan to transport you and your purchases home for a slightly elevated fare.

handwoven hill-tribe textiles to woodcarving, basketry and reproduction antiques (frequently sold without that disclaimer). The Saturday and Sunday Walking Street markets (p350) are Chiang Mai's most entertaining shopping experiences.

Old City

Mengrai Kilns
CERAMICS

(Map p312; www.mengraikilns.com; 79/2 Th Arak; ⊙8am-5pm) In the southwestern corner of the old city, Mengrai Kilns keeps the tradition of Thai celadon pottery alive, with cookware, dining sets, ornaments and Western-style nativity scenes.

HQ Paper Maker
ARTS & CRAFTS

(Map p318; www.hqpapermaker.com; 3/31 Th Samlan; ⊙9am-6pm) This intriguing shop sells reams of handmade mulberry paper *(săh)*, in a remarkable range of colours and patterns, including gorgeous marbled sheets that resemble the end leaves of bound 19th-century books. Ask about its low-key, three-hour paper-making course for 800B per person.

Chaitawat Bikeshop
SPORTS & OUTDOORS

(Map p318; 75/4 Th Ratchaphakhinai; ⊙9am-6pm Mon-Sat) Well-stocked bike shop with parts for all the big foreign brands.

Herb Basics
COSMETICS

(Map p318; www.herbbasicschiangmai.com; Th Ratchadamnoen; ⊙9am-6pm Mon-Sat, 2-9pm Sun) A great stop for fragrant herbal balms, scrubs, creams, soaps and shampoos, all made in Chiang Mai with natural ingredients. There's a branch (Map p318; ⊙9am-8pm Mon-Sat, noon-8pm Sun) on Th Tha Phae and a small shop at the airport.

Ginger
HOMEWARES, CLOTHING

(Map p318; www.thehousethailand.com; The House, 199 Th Moon Muang; ⊙10am-10.30pm) Designer-ethnic is the prevailing theme at this boutique on the edge of the moat, with rooms full of bright textiles and arty melamine homewares. There's a branch (Map p323; 6/21 Th Nimmanhaemin; ⊙9.30am-7pm) on Th Nimmanhaemin.

Ethnic Lanna
ARTS & CRAFTS

(Map p318; www.ethniclanna.com; Th Chaiyaphum; ⊙9am-6pm Mon-Sat) A good selection of tribal bags, trinkets and textiles, sold on a fair-trade basis.

East of the Old City

Th Tha Phae is lined with small shops selling antiques of sometimes questionable lineage, and lots of bijou emporiums selling jewellery, accessories, clothes and handicrafts.

For reed hats and basketware bits and bobs, try the specialist basket shops lined up along Th Chang Moi, just east of the city walls.

Siam Celadon
CERAMICS

(Map p318; www.siamceladon.com; 158 Th Tha Phae; ⊙8am-6pm) This long-established company sells fine cracked-glazed celadon ceramics in a lovely fretwork-covered teak building from the time of the British teak concessionaires. After browsing, stop for a cuppa at the attached Raming Tea House (p347).

Suriwong Book Centre
BOOKS

(Map p318; 54 Th Si Donchai; ⊙8am-8pm) A Chiang Mai institution, with a well-organised and well-stocked bookshop upstairs, and a magazine shop downstairs packed with international mags from *Elle* to *Wallpaper*.

KukWan Gallery
CLOTHING

(Map p318; 37 Th Loi Kroh; ⊙10am-7pm) Set slightly back from the road, this charming little shop sells scarves, runners, bedspreads and natural cotton and silk by the metre.

Backstreet Books
BOOKS

(Map p318; 2/8 Th Chang Moi Kao; ⊙8am-8pm) Backstreet, a rambling shop along 'book alley' (Th Chang Moi Kao), has a good selection of guidebooks and stacks of crime and thriller novels.

Nova
JEWELLERY

(Map p318; www.nova-collection.com; 201 Th Tha Phae; ⊙9am-8pm Mon-Sat, 10am-8pm Sun) Sleekly contemporary, this high-class jewellery studio makes top-quality rings, pendants and earrings using silver, gold and precious stones. It also runs one- to five-day jewellery-making workshops (1750B to 8200B).

Nakorn Kasem
ARTS & CRAFTS

(Map p318; 231-3 Th Tha Phae; ⊙9am-8pm Mon-Sat) One of a string of ma-and-pa antique shops selling ceramics, statues, carvings and bronzes of hard-to-determine age and authenticity. Pick something because you like it, rather than as an investment in an heirloom.

WEEKEND SHOPPING EXTRAVAGANZA

As Bangkok has Chatuchak Weekend Market, so Chiang Mai has its weekend 'walking streets' – carnival-like street markets that close off main thoroughfares in the city on Saturday and Sunday for a riot of souvenir shopping, street performances and hawker food.

As the sun starts to dip on Saturday afternoon, the **Saturday Walking Street** (ถนน เดินวันเสาร์; Map p312; Th Wualai; ☺4pm-midnight Sat) takes over Th Wualai, running southwest from Pratu Chiang Mai. There is barely space to move as locals and tourists from across the world haggle vigorously for carved soaps, novelty dog collars, woodcarvings, Buddha paintings, hill-tribe trinkets, Thai musical instruments, T-shirts, paper lanterns and umbrellas, silver jewellery, herbal remedies, you name it.

An eclectic soundtrack is provided by wandering street performers – blind guitar players, husband-and-wife crooners, precocious school children with headset microphones – and food vendors fill every courtyard and alleyway. There are more stellar street-food offerings at nearby **Talat Pratu Chiang Mai** (p342). To escape the crowds, duck into **Wat Srisuphan** (p316), whose silver *ubosot* is illuminated in rainbow colours after dark.

On Sunday afternoon, the whole shebang moves across the city to Th Ratchadamnoen for the equally boisterous **Sunday Walking Street** (ถนนเดินวันอาทิตย์; Map p318; Th Ratchadamnoen; ☺4pm-midnight Sun), which feels even more animated because of the energetic food markets that open up in wát courtyards along the route. If you went to Th Wualai on Saturday, you'll recognise many of the same sellers and buskers that you spotted the night before. The markets are a major source of income for local families and many traders spend the whole week hand-making merchandise to sell on Saturday and Sunday.

Praewphun Thai Silk   CLOTHING
(Map p318; 83-85 Th Tha Phae; ☺10am-6pm) This shop, opened since the 1960s, sells silks of all ilks, made both into clothing and loose by the metre.

Elements   JEWELLERY
(Map p318; 400-402 Th Tha Phae; ☺9.30am-9.30pm) An eclectic collection of sterling silver and stone jewellery, silk scarves and other trinkets fills this unsigned store near Pratu Tha Phae. It's good for eye-catching one-off pieces.

Kesorn Arts   ARTS & CRAFTS
(Map p318; 154-156 Th Tha Phae; ☺9am-6pm) The collector's best friend, this cluttered shop has been trading old bric-a-brac from the hills for years. It specialises mainly in textiles, lacquerware and jewellery.

🛍 Riverside

Sop Moei Arts   CLOTHING, HANDICRAFTS
(Map p312; www.sopmoeiarts.com; 150/10 Th Charoenrat/Th Faham; ☺9am-6pm) High-end hill-tribe crafts, from off-the-loom textiles to baskets, are sold at this economic-development shop, which provides assistance for Karen villagers in Mae Hong Son Province.

Thai Tribal Crafts
Fair Trade   CLOTHING, HANDICRAFTS
(Map p312; www.ttcrafts.co.th; 208 Th Bamrungrat; ☺9am-5pm Mon-Sat) Baskets and ornate needlework from the provinces are the offerings at this missionary-backed, fair-trade shop near the McCormick Hospital. There is a **branch** (Map p318; 25/9 Th Moon Muang; ☺9.30am-6pm Mon-Sat) by the moat in the old city.

Vila Cini   FASHION & ACCESSORIES
(Map p312; www.vilacini.com; 30-34 Th Charoenrat/Th Faham; ☺9.30am-10.30pm) Set in an atmospheric teak house with marble floors and a narrow, rickety staircase, Vila Cini sells high-end, handmade silks and cotton textiles that are reminiscent of the Jim Thompson brand.

🛍 West of the Old City

Around affluent Th Nimmanhaemin, trendy and cosmopolitan boutiques pop up like mushrooms after rain (and vanish just as quickly).

★ **Studio Naenna**   CLOTHING, HOMEWARES
(www.studio-naenna.com; 138/8 Soi Chang Khian; ☺9am-5pm Mon-Fri, plus Sat Oct-Mar only) The colours of the mountains have been woven into the naturally dyed silks and cottons

here, part of a project to preserve traditional weaving and embroidery. You can see the whole production process at this workshop.

Hill-Tribe Products
Promotion Centre CLOTHING, HANDICRAFTS
(Map p312; 21/17 Th Suthep; ⊙9am-5pm) Hill-tribe textiles, bags, boxes, lacquerware and other crafts are sold at this large store near Wat Suan Dok; profits go to hill-tribe welfare programs.

Doi Tung ACCESSORIES, HOMEWARES
(Map p323; www.doitung.org; Th Nimmanhaemin; ⊙10am-7pm) Part of a development project for rural communities in Chiang Rai Province, this very chic emporium is full of handmade scarves, tablecloths, clothing and men's ties made from graceful and very touchable textiles in understated, modern colours. Expect to pay around 3500B for a tablecloth.

Shinawatra Thai Silk CLOTHING
(Map p323; www.shinawatrathaisilk.co.th; 18 Th Huay Kaew; ⊙9am-6pm) This venerable family-owned silk shop was already a household name before the owners' nephew, Thaksin Shinawatra, became (now-exiled) prime minister. The range here is a little more dowdy and middle-aged than at the competition, but it's good for scarves, shirts, ties and the like.

Booksmith BOOKS
(Map p323; www.smithproject.co.th; 11 Th Nimmanhaemin; ⊙10.30am-8.30pm) This pocket-sized store is a great stop for books on the culture and customs of Thailand.

Chabaa CLOTHING
(Map p323; www.atchabaa.com; 14/32 Th Nimmanhaemin, Nimman Promenade; ⊙10am-9pm) Taking ethnic fashion uptown, Chabaa is a cavern of clothes, jewellery and accessories in radiant, room-filling primary colours, sourced from Thailand, India and worldwide.

ⓘ Information

DANGERS & ANNOYANCES
Compared to Bangkok, Chiang Mai is a breeze for tourists. There are few hassles or rip-offs to watch out for.

The biggest annoyances:

Traffic During rush hour, especially. Take care when crossing busy roads, as motorcyclists

and *rót daang* (literally 'red truck'; shared taxi) drivers rarely give way.

Haze In March and April, smoky, dusty haze can be a problem because of farmers burning off their fields.

Dengue fever Outbreaks are common in the monsoon; take steps to avoid being bitten by mosquitoes, especially in the daytime.

Grand Canyon Water Park A number of travellers have drowned after losing consciousness when hitting the water.

EMBASSIES & CONSULATES
Canadian Consulate (☑05 3850147; 151 Superhighway, Tambon Tahsala; ⊙9am-noon Mon-Fri)

Chinese Consulate (Map p318; ☑05 328 0618; http://chiangmai.china-consulate.org; 111 Th Chang Lor, Tambon Haiya; ⊙9-11.30am & 3-4pm Mon-Fri)

French Consulate (☑053 281466; 138 Th Charoen Prathet, Chiang Mai; ⊙10am-noon Mon-Fri)

Indian Consulate (☑05 324 3066; 33/1 Th Thung Hotel, Chiang Mai; ⊙9am-noon Mon-Fri)

UK Visa Application Centre (Map p323; 191 Siripanich Bldg, 6th fl, Th Huay Kaew; ⊙8.30am-2.30pm Mon-Fri, 9am-noon Sat) While there is currently no UK consulate in Chiang Mai (the nearest is in Bangkok), other nationals can apply for UK visas here.

US Consulate (Map p318; ☑05 3107700; https://th.usembassy.gov; 387 Th Wichayanon; ⊙8am-3.30pm Tue & Thu) Has murals on the outside walls honouring Thai and US friendship.

EMERGENCY
Tourist Police (Map p312; ☑053 247318, 24hr emergency 1155; 608 Rimping Plaza, Th Charoenraj; ⊙6am-midnight) Volunteer staff speak a variety of languages.

Police Station (Map p318; ☑053 276040, 24hr emergency 191; 169 Th Ratchadamnoen)

IMMIGRATION
Chiang Mai Immigration Office (☑053 142788; ground fl, Bldg A, Promenada Resort Mall, 192-193 Tambon Tasala; ⊙8.30am-4.30pm Mon-Fri) Chiang Mai's foreign services office had temporarily moved to this location while the government facility was being renovated. The Promenada Mall is outside of central Chiang Mai and requires private transport.

INTERNET ACCESS
Almost all hotels, guesthouses, restaurants and cafes in Chiang Mai have free wi-fi access. The city has excellent mobile-phone data coverage, but roaming charges for Thailand can be crippling.

MEDIA

➡ The weekly English-language *Chiangmai Mail* is a useful source of local news.

➡ Look out for the free tourist magazines *Citylife*, *Chang Puak* and *Chiang Mai Mag*; all have interesting articles as well as maps and blanket advertising.

MEDICAL SERVICES

There are English-speaking pharmacies along Th Ratchamankha and Th Moon Muang.

Center of Thai Traditional & Complementary Medicine (Map p318; ☑ 053 949899; ttcmmedcmu@gmail.com; 55 Th Samlan; ☺ 8am-8pm) Run by the Faculty of Medicine; offers Western medical check-ups, Thai herbal therapies and Chinese traditional medicine.

Chiang Mai Ram Hospital (Map p312; ☑ 053 920300; www.chiangmairam.com; 8 Th Bunreuangrit) The most modern hospital in town.

Lanna Hospital (Map p312; ☑ 053 999777; www.lanna-hospital.com; Rte 11/Th Superhighway) Modern well-equipped hospital.

McCormick Hospital (Map p312; ☑ 053 921777; www.mccormick.in.th; 133 Th Kaew Nawarat) Former missionary hospital; good for minor treatments.

Mungkala Traditional Medicine Clinic (Map p318; ☑ 053 278494; 21-27 Th Ratchamankha; ☺ 9am-12.30pm & 2-7pm Mon-Sat) Government-licensed clinic using acupuncture, massage and Chinese herbal remedies.

MONEY

All of the big Thai banks have branches and ATMs throughout Chiang Mai and most operate small exchange booths with ATMs in the old city.

POST

Main Post Office (☑ 053 241070; Mae Khao Mu Soi 4; ☺ 8.30am-4.30pm Mon-Fri, 9am-noon Sat & Sun) Other convenient branches on Th Samlan (Map p318; ☺ 9am-4pm Mon-Sat), Th Prasaini (Map p312; ☺ 9am-4pm Mon-Sat), Th Phra Pokklao (Map p318; ☺ 9am-4pm Mon-Sat), and at the airport and university.

Postal shop (Map p318; Th Ratchadamnoen; ☺ 8am-8pm) Charges Thailand Post rates; staff specialise in wrapping awkwardly shaped packages to send home.

TOURIST INFORMATION

Chiang Mai Municipal Tourist Information Centre (Map p312; ☑ 053 252557; Th Tha Phae; ☺ 8.30-11.30am & 1-4.30pm Mon-Fri) City-run tourist information centre near the Night Bazaar.

Tourism Authority of Thailand (TAT; Map p312; ☑ 053 248604; www.tourismthailand.org; Th Chiang Mai-Lamphun; ☺ 8.30am-4.30pm) English-speaking staff provide maps and advice on travel across Thailand.

Tourist Assistance Centre (Map p312; ☑ 053 281438; ☺ 7am-11pm) Tourist information in Chiang Mai International Airport.

Getting There & Away

AIR

Domestic and international flights arrive and depart from **Chiang Mai International Airport** (☑ 05 327 0222; www.chiangmaiairportthai.com), 3km southwest of the old city.

Schedules vary with the seasons and tourist demand. Tickets to Bangkok start at around 1200B. Heading south, expect to pay from 2400B to Phuket, 1650B to Surat Thani. The bulk of the domestic routes are handled by the following airlines:

Air Asia (Map p318; ☑ 053 234645, nationwide 02 515 9999; www.airasia.com; 416 Th Tha Phae; ☺ 10am-8.30pm)

Bangkok Airways (Map p323; ☑ 053 289338, nationwide 1771; www.bangkokair.com; Room A & B, Kantary Terrace, 44/1 Soi 12, Th Nimmanhaemin; ☺ 8.30am-noon & 1-6pm Mon-Sat)

Kan Air (Map p312; ☑ 053 283311, nationwide 02 551 6111; www.kanairlines.com; 2nd fl, Chiang Mai International Airport; ☺ 8am-5.30pm)

Nok Air (Map p312; ☑ 053 922183, nationwide 02 900 9955; www.nokair.com; ground fl, Central Airport Plaza; ☺ 8am-5pm)

Thai Airways International (THAI; Map p318; ☑ 023 561111, 053 211044; www.thaiair.com; 240 Th Phra Pokklao; ☺ 8.30am-4.30pm Mon-Fri).

Thai Smile (Map p318; ☑ nationwide 02 118 8888; www.thaismileair.com; 35-41 Th Ratchadamnoen; ☺ 9am-9pm)

Direct flights linking Chiang Mai to neighbouring nations are also expanding fast, with regular flights to Kuala Lumpur (Malaysia), Yangon (Myanmar) and destinations around China.

Lao Airlines (Map p323; ☑ 053 223401; www.laoairlines.com; ground fl, Nakornping Condominium, 2/107 Th Huay Kaew; ☺ 8.30am-5pm Mon-Fri, to noon Sat) has direct flights to Luang Prabang and Vientiane. Less frequent services include Dong Hoi (Vietnam, transfer to Ho Chi Minh City). To reach Cambodia, you'll have to go via Bangkok.

The airport has luggage storage (7am to 9pm, 200B per day), a post-office branch (8.30am to 8pm), banks, souvenir shops and a **tourist assistance centre** (p352). If you have time to kill, you could just stroll back down the highway to the large **Central Airport Plaza** (p348).

SM Travel (Map p318; ☑ 053 281045; www.yourtripthailand.com; 87-95 Th Ratchadamnoen; ☺ 8am-6pm) in the old city is a good place to book flights.

BUS

Chiang Mai has two bus stations, and *sŏrng·tăa·ou* (passenger pick-up trucks) run from fixed stops to towns close to Chiang Mai.

Arcade Bus Terminal

About 3km northeast of the city centre, near the junction of Th Kaew Nawarat and Rte 11, Chiang Mai's **main long-distance station** handles all services, except for buses to northern Chiang Mai Province. This is the place to come to travel on to Bangkok or any other major city in Thailand. A chartered *rót daang* from the centre to the bus stand will cost about 60B; a túk-túk will cost 80B to 100B. There are also two bus routes between the bus terminals and town: B1 makes stops at Chiang Mai's train station and Tha Phae Gate (15B, every 40 minutes from 6am to 6pm), and B2 makes stops at Tha Phae Gate and Chiang Mai International Airport (15B, every 40 minutes from 6am to 6pm).

There are two terminal buildings, with ticket booths for dozens of private and government bus companies. Nominally, **Building 2** is for towns north of Chiang Mai and **Building 3** is for towns south of Chiang Mai, but in practice buses leave from both terminals to most destinations. There is also a third depot behind Building 2 used exclusively by the private bus company **Nakornchai Air** (☑ 053 262799; www.nca.co.th), which has luxury buses to Bangkok and almost everywhere else in Thailand.

Facilities for travellers are a little lacklustre; there's a parade of local-style restaurants beside the two terminal buildings, and a left-luggage office (3am to 9pm, 20B per item). If you have time to burn, head over to the **Star Avenue Lifestyle Mall** (☉ 24hr) by Building 3, which has air-conditioned coffee shops and restaurants.

There is a regular international bus service linking Chiang Mai to Luang Prabang, via Bokeo, Luang Namtha and Udom Xai. You can also travel by bus across to Nong Khai (for Vientiane).

Chang Pheuak Bus Terminal

Just north of the old city on Th Chotana (Th Chang Pheuak), the **Chang Pheuak Bus Terminal** (Map p312) is the main departure point for journeys to the north of Chiang Mai Province. Government buses leave regularly to the following destinations:

Chiang Dao 40B, 1½ hours, every 30 minutes
Hot 50B, two hours, every 20 minutes
Samoeng 90B, two hours, six daily
Tha Ton 90B, four hours, seven daily

Local blue *sŏrng·tăa·ou* run to Lamphun (25B, one hour, every 20 minutes). Air-con minibuses to Chiang Dao (150B, two hours, hourly) leave from Soi Sanam Gila, behind the bus terminal.

ⓘ TÚK-TÚK OR SŎRNG·TĂA·OU?

Túk-túk are more expensive and their drivers are likely to rip you off, but they do offer a direct service and most drivers speak English. *Sŏrng·tăa·ou* drivers are cheaper and less inclined to rip off passengers (because many Thais use them too), but English can be a problem and routes are not always direct. Riding in a *sŏrng·tăa·ou* is an excellent way to meet local Thais.

Sŏrng·tăa·ou Stops

There are several stops for *sŏrng·tăa·ou* running to towns close to Chiang Mai. Fares range from 20B to 30B and services run frequently throughout the day.

Talat Warorot Sŏrng·tăa·ou Stop (Map p318; Th Praisani) Serves Lamphun, Bo Sang, San Kamphaeng and Mae Rim.

Saphan Lek Sŏrng·tăa·ou Stop (Map p312; Th Chiang Mai-Lamphun) Serves Lamphun and Lampang.

Pratu Chiang Mai Sŏrng·tăa·ou Stop (Map p318; Th Bamrungburi) Serves Hang Dong, Ban Tawai and points south.

Sŏrng·tăa·ou to San Kamphaeng (Map p318) also depart from Th Khang Mehn.

TRAIN

Run by the State Railway of Thailand, **Chiang Mai Train Station** (☑ 053 245363, nationwide 1690; Th Charoen Muang) is about 2.5km east of the old city. Trains run five times daily on the main line between Bangkok and Chiang Mai. The government has promised more investment in the railways in future, including the creation of a new high-speed rail link between Chiang Mai and Bangkok. The train station has an ATM, a left-luggage room (5am to 8.45pm, 20B per item) and an advance-booking counter (you'll need your passport to book a ticket).

There are four classes of train running between Chiang Mai and Bangkok's Hualamphong station: rapid, sprinter, express and special express. Most comfortable are the overnight special express services leaving Chiang Mai at 5pm and 6pm, arriving in Bangkok at 6.15am and 6.50am. In the opposite direction, trains leave Hualamphong at 6.10pm and 7.35pm. However, schedules change regularly, so see the State Railway of Thailand website (www.railway.co.th) for the latest information.

At the time of research, fares to Bangkok were as follows:

3rd class (bench seat) 231B to 271B
2nd class (reclining seat) 391B to 641B

2nd-class sleeper berth (fan cooled) 601B to 671B

2nd-class sleeper berth (air-con) 1071B to 1131B

1st-class sleeper berth (air-con) 1453B to 1903B

ℹ Getting Around

Both Uber and Grab exist in Chiang Mai and although there have been ongoing threats to limit or shut down services, at the time of research both were running strong and were the easiest and most affordable way to get around town. Rides within the city average 50B.

TO/FROM THE AIRPORT

Chiang Mai International Airport has a licensed airport taxi service operating from Arrivals Exit 9. It costs around 160B to the old town. Cheaper shuttle and minibus services charge 40B. An Uber or Grab car will cost around 60B.

BICYCLE

Cycling is a good way to get around Chiang Mai but be cautious on the ring roads circling the old city. Rickety sit-up-and-beg bikes can be rented for around 50B a day or 300B per week from guesthouses and shops around the old city. Check the bike carefully before you hire – brakes in particular can be very iffy.

If you want a superior bike, you can rent good-quality foreign-made road bikes (100B

TRANSPORT TO/FROM CHIANG MAI

DESTINATION	AIR	BUS	MINIVAN	TRAIN
Bangkok	from 1200B, 70min, frequent	488-759B, 9-10hr, frequent	N/A	231-1903B, 10-12hr, 5-6 daily
Chiang Khong	N/A	202-451B, 6½hr, 1 daily	N/A	N/A
Chiang Rai	N/A	166-288B, 3-4hr, frequent	N/A	N/A
Dong Hoi (Vietnam)	1895B	N/A	N/A	N/A
Khon Kaen	from 1000B, 70min, 1 daily	535B, 12hr, 5 daily	N/A	N/A
Khorat (Nakhon Ratchasima)	N/A	540-662B, 12hr, 11 daily	N/A	N/A
Lampang	N/A	66-143B, 2hr, hourly	73B, 1hr, hourly	N/A
Luang Prabang (Laos)	from 5000B, 1hr, 4 weekly	1200B, 20hr, 9am (Mon, Wed, Fri, Sat, Sun)	N/A	N/A
Mae Hong Son	from 1687B, 40min, 6 daily	192-346B, 8hr, 3 daily	250B, 5hr, 3 daily	N/A
Nan	from 1890B, 45min, 2 weekly	197-254B, 6hr, 6 daily	N/A	N/A
Nong Khai	N/A	820B, 12hr, 2 daily	N/A	N/A
Pai	from 1990B, 25min, 3 weekly	80B, 4hr, hourly	150B, 3hr, hourly	N/A
Phuket	from 2481B, 2hr, 4 daily	1646B, 22hr, 1 daily	N/A	N/A
Sukhothai	N/A	207B, 5-6hr, hourly	hourly	N/A
Ubon Ratchathani	from 1898B, 45min, 1 daily	872B, 12hr, 1 daily	N/A	N/A
Udon Thani	from 680B, 1hr, 1 daily	545-767B, 12hr, 3 daily	N/A	N/A
Vientiane (Laos)	from 3638B, 1hr, 1 daily	N/A	N/A	N/A

to 400B per day) and mountain bikes (250B to 1000B) from **Chiang Mai Mountain Biking & Kayaking** (p327) and **Spice Roads** (p333). Spare parts for foreign bikes are available at **Chaitawat Bikeshop** (p349).

Chiang Mai also has an under-utilised shared bike scheme, **Bike@Chiangmai** (☑ 085 139 2410; www.bike-at.com), with five stations in the old city – at Wat Phra Singh, in front of the Lanna Folklife Museum, at Pratu Tha Phae, at Pratu Chiang Mai and at Suan Buak Hat – and more across the city. Registration fees are 320B, and there's a minimum 100B credit on the card you use to access the bikes; rental fees start at 20B for an hour.

CAR & TRUCK

Cars and pick-up trucks can be hired from rental agencies throughout the city, particularly along Th Moon Muang, but stick to companies that offer full insurance (liability) coverage and breakdown cover, and check the terms so you're clear on what is and isn't included. Most companies ask for a cash deposit of 5000B to 10,000B.

Standard rental rates for small 1.5L cars start at 1000B per day; prices include unlimited kilometres but not petrol. Well-regarded agencies include the following:

Budget Car Rental (Map p312; ☑ 053 202871; www.budget.co.th; 201/2 Th Mahidol) Across from Central Airport Plaza.

North Wheels (Map p318; ☑ 053 874478; www.northwheels.com; 70/4-8 Th Chaiyaphum) Offers hotel pick-up and delivery, 24-hour emergency road service and comprehensive insurance.

Thai Rent a Car (Map p312; ☑ 053 904188; www.thairentacar.com; Chiang Mai International Airport)

MOTORCYCLE

Renting a motorcycle or scooter is an extremely popular option in Chiang Mai. Agencies and guesthouses rent out everything from 100cc automatic scooters (from 150B per day) to larger Honda Dream bikes (from 350B) and full-sized road and off-road bikes up to 650cc (700B to 2000B). Smaller bikes are fine for city touring but if you plan to attempt any of the mountain roads around Chiang Mai, pick a machine with an engine size of 200cc or more.

Mr Mechanic (Map p318; ☑ 053 214708; www.mr-mechanic1994.com; 4 Soi 5, Th Moon Muang; per day scooter/motorcycle/car from 150/500/1200B) is probably the best operator in town in terms of insurance and support, with a new, well-maintained fleet and comprehensive insurance. There are two other branches at 33 Th Ratchaphakhinai (Map p318) and 135/1 Th Ratchaphakhinai (Map p318).

Tony's Big Bikes (Map p318; ☑ 053 207124; www.chiangmai-motorcycle-rental.com; 17 Th

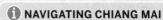

ⓘ NAVIGATING CHIANG MAI

When travelling in and beyond the old city, directions are often given in relationship to the old city's four cardinal gates.

Pratu Tha Phae (east) Head east from here along Th Tha Phae to reach the riverside, Talat Warorot and the Night Bazaar.

Pratu Chang Pheuak (north) Head north from here along Th Chotana (Th Chang Pheuak) to reach the Chang Pheuak Bus Terminal and Rte 107 to northern Chiang Mai Province.

Pratu Suan Dok (west) Head west from here along Th Suthep to reach Chiang Mai University, Doi Suthep, and the entertainment district of Th Nimmanhaemin.

Pratu Chiang Mai (south) Head southwest from here along Th Wualai for the Saturday Walking Street market and Rte 108 to southern Chiang Mai Province.

Ratchamankha; motorbike rental per day 500-3000B) rents well-maintained 125cc to 400cc motorbikes, and also offers riding lessons, gives touring advice and repairs motorcycles; rates are negotiable.

By law, you must wear a helmet, and police frequently set up checkpoints to enforce this. You should also carry photo ID and an International Driving Permit (IDP) to present at police checkposts. In practice, police are usually happy with foreign drivers' licences, but if you can't present a licence, you'll be fined.

Saving a few baht by renting without proper insurance could cost you dearly; stick to companies offering breakdown cover and full insurance. Most policies have a 1500B excess in case of accident and a 10,000B excess if the motorbike is stolen; use the chain and padlock provided!

Most bike-hire places will ask for your passport as a security deposit. While there are rarely any problems with this, better agencies will accept a cash deposit of 5000B to 10,000B as an alternative. This cannot be paid by credit card.

For tips on touring the countryside around Chiang Mai, check out the advice at Golden Triangle Rider (www.gt-rider.com).

LOCAL & CHARTERED TRANSPORT

Rót daang operate as shared taxis, and they roam the streets picking up passengers who are heading in the direction they are travelling.

DRIVING TOUR: MAE SA VALLEY & SAMOENG แม่สา/สะเมิง

Start Chiang Mai

End Chiang Mai

Length 80km

Your first stop should be **Nam Tok Mae Sa** (น้ำตกแม่สา; adult/child 100/50B; car 30B; ☉8am-4.30pm), a chain of cascades set in lush tropical forest on the fringes of Doi Suthep-Pui National Park, just 6km from the turn-off at Mae Rim. You should have no problem finding a pool to swim in, complete with waterfall-powered shower and rocky outcrop to picnic on. There are some simple food vendors by the car park.

About 6.5km along Rte 1096 are the **Queen Sirikit Botanic Gardens** (สวน พฤกษศาสตร์สมเด็จพระนางเจ้าสิริกิติ์; www.qsbg.org; Rte 1096; adult/child 100/50B, car/motorcycle 100/30B; ☉8.30am-4.30pm), where 227 hectares have been set aside for plantations, nature trails and vast greenhouses full of exotic and local flora. At the top of the ridge, the Natural Science Museum is an under-appreciated education centre, with lots of giant nature models and interactive displays for kids. The greenhouses shelter everything from jungle ferns to cacti and palms. Downhill is a canopy walkway through jungle trees.

After the botanic gardens the road climbs into a high-altitude basin that was once a major centre for opium poppy production. With sponsorship from the Thai royal family, local hill-tribe farmers have been persuaded to re-seed their terraced fields with vegetables, fruits and flowers.

To get a taste of the produce, turn off Rte 1096 at Ban Pong Yaeng and follow the steep concrete road uphill to the Hmong village of Nong Hoi. Above the village, you'll find the **Mon Cham** (Nong Hoi Mai; mains 60-180B; ☉7am-7pm; ☑) restaurant at the top of the ridge. Here you can sample tasty, freshly cooked Thai food, or just sip local fruit liqueurs in a series of bamboo pavilions with spectacular views over the surrounding valleys.

Further west, **Proud Phu Fah** (p337) is a stylish boutique hotel with elegant villas spread out along a brook, designed to give the illusion of sleeping in the great outdoors. The open-air restaurant serves healthy Thai food (mains 150B to 250B), with views across the lawns and mountains.

After Proud Phu Fah, the road swings around the mountain ridge, passing several spectacular viewpoints great for photos. There is less traffic on the return to Chiang Mai, which follows Rte 1269 all the way to Rte 121 on the outskirts of Chiang Mai.

There are no fixed routes so the easiest thing to do is to ask if the driver will take you where you want to go. Journeys start from 20B for a short trip of a few blocks and 40B for a longer trip (eg from the old city to Th Nimmanhaemin).

Drivers are also happy to hire out the whole vehicle for charter trips for a higher price, including day trips out into the countryside. If the vehicle is parked by the roadside instead of moving along the street, the driver is normally looking for a charter fare. Either way, there's little hassle involved; indeed, many *rót daang* are family businesses, with husbands driving and wives sitting alongside dealing with the money and route planning.

Túk-túk work only on a charter basis and are more expensive than *rót daang*, but they offer that energising wind-through-your-hair feeling and are faster in traffic. Rates start at 60B for short trips and creep up to 100B at night, although you'll probably have to bargain hard for these rates. Some drivers can be pushy and

may try to steer you towards attractions that pay commissions.

Chiang Mai still has a few săhm·lór, which offer short transfers around Talat Warorot for 20B or so.

TAXI

It is very rare to see a metered taxi to flag down in Chiang Mai, but you can call for a pick-up from **Taxi Meter** (☑ 053 244268, 053 241955; www.taxichiangmai.com) – fares within Chiang Mai are unlikely to top 160B.

NORTHERN CHIANG MAI PROVINCE

North of Chiang Mai, the land rucks up into forested mountains on either side of Mae Ping as northern Thailand merges into southeastern Myanmar. With a chartered *rót daang* or rented motorcycle (with sufficient horsepower) you can roam high into the hills, visiting national parks, spectacular viewpoints, Royal Project farms and hill-tribe villages. The website www.gt-rider.com has trip reports posted by motorcyclists who have made sorties through this region.

Mae Rim
แม่ริม

☑ 053 / POP 7476

The nearest town north of Chiang Mai, sleepy Mae Rim is an easy 30km ride from the city along Rte 107. Here you can visit the former palace of princess Dara Rasmee, and kick back at the Huay Teung Thao reservoir.

Most people stay in Chiang Mai and visit Mae Rim on a day trip.

◎ Sights

Dara Pirom Palace
MUSEUM

(พระตำหนักดาราภิรมย์; 20B; ⊘9am-5pm Tue-Sat) Dara Rasmee, the last princess of the Lanna kingdom, lived out her days in this handsome 19th-century residence, built in classic Thai-colonial style, with tall ceilings, elegant fretwork vents and timbered verandahs. Rooms full of heirlooms, photos and personal effects recall the princess's life and times.

The palace lies in the grounds of the Mae Rim police compound on the west side of Rte 107; turn right after the police station and follow the signs past the runway for the police helicopter.

Huay Teung Thao Reservoir
LAKE

(อ่างเก็บน้ำห้วยตึงเฒ่า; 20B; ⊘7am-7pm) For Thais, a reservoir is not just a water store, it's a place for some serious R&R. At this expansive body of water just west of town, families gather to swim or splash around by the beach and picnic by the water's edge in elevated bamboo cabins. It's like a day at the beach.

To get here, follow Rte 107 and turn southwest onto Rte 121, then turn right across the bridge by the Khuang Phra Chao Lanna shrine.

❶ Getting There & Away

Mae Rim is easily accessible by bus or *sŏrng·tăa·ou* (20B, 15 minutes) from Chiang Mai's Chang Pheuak Bus Terminal.

Chiang Dao
เชียงดาว

☑ 053 / POP 15,000

In a lush jungle setting in the shadow of a mighty limestone mountain, Chiang Dao is where expats and Chiang Mai's growing middle classes come to escape the heat of the plains. It gets cooler still as you leave the village and climb towards the summit of Doi Chiang Dao (2175m). The forest is a popular stop for birders and trekkers, and at the base of the mountain is a highly venerated *wát* marking the entrance to one of Thailand's deepest limestone caverns.

Buses to Chiang Dao stop in the modern village on the eastern side of Rte 107, but most travellers head to the nearby village of Ban Tham on the western side of the highway, where all the accommodation and the famous cave temple can be found.

◎ Sights & Activities

As well as exploring the cave temple, you can organise some impressive treks to birdlife hot spots, scattered hill-tribe villages and the lofty summit of Doi Chiang Dao. Lodges can arrange guides and camping equipment, but only from October to May, when the trails are dry enough to trek.

Hill-tribe villagers congregate for the bi-weekly **market** in Chiang Dao village, held on the first and third Tuesday of each month.

Doi Chiang Dao
Wildlife Sanctuary
NATURE RESERVE

(ดอยเชียงดาว, Doi Luang; ☑053 456623; 200B, vehicle 30B) Doi Chiang Dao rises dramatically above the surrounding plain, wrapped in a thick coat of tropical forest. This jungle wonderland is one of Thailand's top spots for birders, with more than 300 resident bird species, and is one of the best places in the world to see giant nuthatches and Hume's pheasants. It's a steep full-day hike to the summit, which offers spectacular views over the surrounding massifs; a one-day trip is 1000B per person, overnight costs 500B per person.

If you just want a taste of the marvellous scenery, take a right at the junction just before the cluster of lodges at Ban Tham and follow the gorgeously scenic, winding mountain road that climbs to the ridge through the forest. This is a challenging route and you'll need transport with sufficient power to handle the gradients.

Wat Tham Chiang Dao   CAVE

(ถ้ำเชียงดาว, Chiang Dao Cave; 40B, guide fee 100B; ⊙ 7am-5pm) Set in pretty grounds that teem with jungle butterflies, this forest wát sits at the entrance to **Chiang Dao Cave**, a chilly warren of passageways that extend more than 10km beneath the limestone massif of Doi Chiang Dao. For Buddhists, the cave is a meditation retreat, a sort of extension of the wát itself, and the twisting tunnels overflow with stalactites and stalagmites.

The chambers at the start of the network of tunnels – known as Tham Sua Dao and Tham Phra Non – are illuminated by electric lights, but the most interesting section of the cave system is unlit and you'll need to hire a guide with a gas lantern (100B) to explore, providing a living for a local villager in the process (they are actually volunteers so a 50B tip is appropriate and expected). The tour wriggles through narrow passageways to other large chambers – Tham Mah (735m), Tham Kaew (474m) and Tham Nam (660m) – and your guide will point out bat colonies and limestone features that have been named for their resemblance to animals. At the end of the illuminated section, you'll reach a small but highly revered sleeping Buddha in a small antechamber.

Local legend says that the cave was the home of a *reu·sĕe* (ascetic, holy man) who convinced the spirits to create several magic wonders inside the caverns: a stream flowing from the pedestal of a solid-gold Buddha, a storehouse of divine textiles, and a city of *naga* (mythical serpents). These miraculous features are said to be much deeper inside the mountain, beyond the last of the illuminated caverns.

Pha Daeng National Park   NATIONAL PARK

(อุทยานแห่งชาติผาแดง; ☑ 053 046370; www.dnp. go.th; Ban Muang Na; adult/child 100/50B, camping per person 30B) North of Doi Chiang Dao and reached by following Rte 1178, Pha Daeng National Park offers lush, jungle scenery and stunning bird life. Flanking the Myanmar border, the park is pockmarked by deep cave systems and has the usual full hand of scenic viewpoints, summit hikes and spurting waterfalls. Bungalow accommodation (600B to 2500B) is available at the park headquarters.

Wat Tham Pha Plong   BUDDHIST TEMPLE

(สำนักสงฆ์ถ้ำผาปล่อง; Ban Tham; donations appreciated; ⊙ daylight hours) This beautiful and serene forest wát lies on the edge of the Chiang Dao massif. A steep *naga* stairway climbs through the forest to the rocky crevice where the revered meditation master Luang Pu Sim once practised. You'll feel far, far away from the tourist crowd here. Continue on the road about a kilometre past the Chiang Dao lodges to reach the parking lot for temple.

🛏 Sleeping & Eating

The guesthouses are spread out along the road leading north from Wat Tham Chiang Dao on the edge of the forest. All can arrange tours, and rent bicycles and motorbikes.

The restaurants at Chiang Dao Nest and Chiang Dao Nest 2 are the area's undisputed culinary highlights, but all the lodges serve meals, and simple Thai restaurants cluster around the parking lot at Wat Tham Chiang Dao.

There is a **daily food market** off the main street through Chiang Dao.

Chiang Dao Hut   GUESTHOUSE $

(☑ 053 456625; r & bungalows 350-2500B; 🛜) This cute collection of rooms and bungalows in a glade that drops down to a stream is close to Wat Tham Chiang Dao, so you'll have extra choices for dinner. The cheaper accommodation has shared bathrooms with hot water, and the atmosphere is appropriately laid-back and unhurried.

Chiang Dao Roundhouses   BUNGALOW $$

(☑ 087 496 1571; www.chiangdao-roundhouses. com; bungalows incl breakfast 1300B; 🛜) This eye-catching collection of cap-shaped huts was fashioned using traditional techniques and materials such as recycled glass bottles, bamboo, rice husks, mud and straw. Bathrooms are partly open-air and the huts cluster around a breakfast room and yoga cave. It's down a small lane opposite the entrance to the Wat Tham Chiang Dao parking lot.

Malee's Nature Lovers Bungalows   GUESTHOUSE $$

(☑ 081 961 8387; www.maleenature.com; camping per person 100B, bungalows 500-2050B; 🛜🐾) Run by the orchid-obsessed and outrageously friendly Malee, this green-fingered spot on the road to Tham Pha Plong has simple, clean cottages with hot showers in an orchid-filled garden. The cheapest share bathrooms, while posher cabins have en suites. One is set high off the ground for birders to watch the canopy activity.

⭐ **Chiang Dao Nest 2**   BOUTIQUE HOTEL $$$
(www.chiangdaonest.com; bungalows 950-3500B; ❋🐾) Bamboo bungalows sit in a serene garden with views of the jungle-clad mountains. You'll feel like family here within minutes, and don't miss the world-class Thai cuisine in its chic patio restaurant overlooking flowers and greenery. There's also on-site massage service.

⭐ **Chiang Dao Nest**   GUESTHOUSE $$$
(📲 053 456242; www.chiangdaonest.com; bungalows 950-3500B; @🐾❋) The guesthouse that put Chiang Dao on the map is a charming country retreat, with comfortable, bamboo-weave bungalows scattered around a gorgeous tropical garden with plenty of shady gazebos where you can kick back with a book. There's a lovely, forest-flanked swimming pool with mountain views, and kids will love the wandering goats and toy pavilion.

🛍 Shopping

Morning Market   MARKET
(🕑 7am-noon 1st & 3rd Tue of month) The twice-monthly morning market has vendors selling hill-tribe handicrafts.

ℹ Getting There & Around

Chiang Dao is 72km north of Chiang Mai along Rte 107. It's a 100B motorcycle taxi or 150B *sŏrng·tăa·ou* ride from the bus stand in Chiang Dao village to the guesthouses near the cave temple. Buses travel to **Chiang Mai** (40B, 1½ hours, every 30 minutes) and **Tha Ton** (63B, 2½ hours, seven daily).

There are also air-conditioned minivans charging 150B to Chiang Mai.

Most of the lodges rent out mountain bikes (from 100B) and motorbikes (from 300B), or you can hire a *sŏrng·tăa·ou* for about 1000B a day to drive you around the area.

Doi Ang Khang   ดอยอ่างขาง
📲 053

Pushed up against the border with Myanmar, the mountain valleys around Doi Ang Khang are known locally as 'Little Switzerland' thanks to the cool climate, which gets cold enough for frost in January, but really the resemblance ends there. Instead of chalets and yodelling you'll find peaceful green valleys full of temperate flowers and plantations of 'exotic' – to the Thais at least – fruit, such as apples, pears and strawberries, tucked into the middle of a crown-shaped circle of forested mountains.

Today, people come here to enjoy the climate and explore the peaceful **Royal Agricultural Station** (สถานีเกษตรหลวง; 📲 053 969489; www.angkhangstation.com; 50B, car 50B; 🕑 6am-9pm), which sprawls out from the village of Ban Khum in the centre of the basin. Many staff here are villagers from the mixed Yunnanese, Burmese and hill-tribe villages of Pang Ma, Ban Luang, Ban Khob Dong and Ban Nor Lae, which circle the station and are also worth a visit.

Visitors can wander through the plantations and orchards – growing everything from peaches and plums to blueberries and kiwifruit – and into the villages themselves, which are working communities with none of the human-zoo atmosphere that you'll encounter on many hill-tribe treks in the area.

Dotted around the grounds are a string of pretty gardens and workshops where fruit is sorted, tea is processed and herbal remedies and beauty products are mixed and tested. Start at the outdoor garden and glasshouses by the entrance then continue to the bonsai garden and the gorgeous rose and flower gardens around the station restaurant and accommodation.

🛏 Sleeping & Eating

Accommodation is available at the Royal Agricultural Station (dorms 75B; bungalows 650 to 3500B). Most of the roomy bungalows have terraces where you can soak up the scenery.

There's more accommodation in Ban Khum village, the best choice being the rather lovely **Angkhang Nature Resort** (📲 053 450110; www.mosaic-collection.com/angkhang; bungalow incl breakfast 1800-3680B; ❋@).

The main station restaurant – a colonial-style space with waiters in flowery pyjamas – cooks up good lowland Thai food and Northern specialities, prepared using ingredients from the Royal Project.

ℹ Getting There & Away

To reach Doi Ang Khang, follow the looping hairpin turns of Rte 1249, which branches off Rte

CHIANG MAI PROVINCE DOI ANG KHANG

DON'T MISS

STEAMY HOT SPRINGS

About 10km west of Fang at Ban Meuang Chom, near the agricultural station, the serene **Doi Pha Hompok National Park** (อุทยานแห่งชาติดอยผ้าห่มปก, Doi Fang/Mae Fang National-al Park; ☑ 053 453517; www.dnp.go.th; adult/child 300/150B, car/motorbike/bike 30/20/10B, camping per person 30B, bungalows 1000-2000B; ☺ 7am-7pm) is part national park and part public spa, with a gorgeous hot-springs complex (*bor náam hórn* in northern Thai) set in a forest. Find everything from private mineral bathhouses (adult/child 50/20B) to a public pool (20/10B) and a sauna (30/10B); masseurs complete the package.

To get here, turn off Rte 107 onto Rte 5054 and follow the signs.

The springs are wonderfully peaceful and the setting is sublime, with steam vents blasting up from a meadow crossed by boardwalks and dotted with almost boiling hot springs. The exception is at weekends, when *sŏrng·tăa·ou* (passenger pick-up trucks) full of Thai picnickers head out from Fang to boil eggs and bathe in the springs. Accommodation is in simple but comfortable bungalows and there's a campsite with equipment for rent.

Beyond the hot-springs complex, the rest of the park is a ruckus of forested mountains, with lots of hiking trails and forest campsites. The most popular destination is the 2285m summit of Doi Pha Hompok, Thailand's second-highest peak. Most trekkers camp below the summit and leave early to reach the top at sunrise for an epic view over the surrounding countryside. At the top of the mountain, average temperatures are a mere 2°C during winter and 14°C during summer.

107 about 13km south of Fang. There's no public transport but you can reach the station by chartered *sŏrng·tăa·ou* or with a rented motorcycle, though a bike with less than 250cc will struggle.

Leaving the mountain, consider taking the scenic back route via Rte 340 and Rte 1178, snaking through the forest and emerging in Pha Daeng National Park near Chiang Dao.

Tha Ton
ฝาง/ท่าตอน

☑ 053 / POP 19,900

The northernmost town in Chiang Mai Province feels a long way from the provincial capital. This jungle outpost was once a key staging point for opium ferried across the border by Burmese warlord Khun Sa, but there's no legal border crossing now, and modern Tha Ton is a quiet backwater that sees just a trickle of tourists headed downriver towards Chiang Rai.

The trip downstream is possible from July to December – at other times, you may be the only foreigner in town. Nevertheless, there are some interesting detours in the area, including boat trips up to the Myanmar border and road trips to Mae Salong or the hot springs at Doi Pha Hompok National Park. The town has a sizeable population of Yunnanese migrants, who worship at the small Chinese-style mosque just south of the boat jetty.

Watch out for aggressive packs of dogs as you wander around.

◉ Sights & Activities

Resorts in Tha Ton can arrange **treks** and **rafting trips** to a string of hill-tribe villages inhabited by Palaung, Black Lahu, Akha, Karen and Yunnanese villagers. These are more traditional than the tribal villages close to Chiang Mai. Expect to pay around 1000B per person for a day trek, and from 2500B for a two-day rafting tour (October to February).

Wat Tha Ton BUDDHIST TEMPLE
(วัดท่าตอน; ☑ 053 459309; www.wat-thaton.org; Rte 107; donations appreciated; ☺ daylight hours) Just south of the bridge, this intriguing monastery complex sprawls west from Tha Ton over a series of forested hills. The *wát* buildings are spread over nine levels and each comes with its own collection of supersize statues and stunning views north towards Myanmar or east across the Tha Ton plain.

The first level has a statue of Kuan Yin, the Chinese goddess of compassion; level three has a portly Chinese Buddha and a towering white seated Buddha in the Thai style; level four has a huge seated Buddha with a *naga* (serpent) cowl; level eight crowns the hilltop, with a three-story, colourful stupa and a museum inside known as Chedi Kaew; and there's a huge golden standing Buddha holding a cauldron-sized begging bowl on level nine (reached via a road running across the saddle behind the *chedi*). Look out for helicopter-like dipterocarp seeds spiralling down from the canopy as you wander. Allow at least two hours to explore on foot or an hour by motorbike.

Chiang Rai Boat Trip — BOATING

(☑ 053 053727; per person 400B; ⊘ departs 12.30pm) During the rainy season and for as long as water levels stay high (July to December), long-tail boats make the journey between Chiang Rai and Tha Ton daily. It's a scenic trip, passing tracts of virgin forest, riverside monasteries, and villages of thatched huts with fishers casting nets in the shallows.

The travel time is anywhere from three to five hours, depending on river conditions and on how many stops are taken along the way. Each boat takes six to 12 passengers, but operators may be reluctant to depart if there are insufficient passengers; chartering the whole boat costs 2000B. You can also make the trip (much more slowly) upriver from Chiang Rai.

🛏 Sleeping & Eating

Tha Ton's guesthouses are strung out along both sides of the river by the bridge, and most can arrange treks, boat trips, and motorcycle and bicycle hire. Note that some resorts close during the quiet season (January to June), when the river is too low for boat trips. Almost all guesthouses have riverside restaurants, but there are several coffee-shop eateries on the main road south of the bridge and some backpacker cafes around the jetty.

Apple Resort — RESORT $$

(☑ 053 373144; applethaton@yahoo.com; off Rte 107; r & bungalows 500-1200B; ❄ 🛜) Popular Apple makes the most of its setting, facing the boat jetty from the north bank, with budget fan-cooled bungalows in the garden and much more welcoming riverfront bungalows with fantastic front porches facing the water. There's a friendly riverside restaurant (closed in low season) for enjoying Tha Ton's best feature: the river by moonlight.

Garden Home Nature Resort — RESORT $$

(☑ 053 373015; gardenhome14@hotmail.com; r with fan from 300B, with air-con 800-1500B; ❄ 🛜) Neat thatch-roofed bungalows are dotted around a calm, green compound full of lychee trees and bougainvillea at this tranquil riverside spot. There are also a few stone bungalows, and three larger, more luxurious bungalows on the river with TVs, fridges and lovely verandahs.

★ Old Tree's House — RESORT $$$

(☑ 085 722 9002; www.oldtreeshouse.net; Rte 107; bungalows incl breakfast 1200-2800B; ❄ 🛜 ❄) After an uninspiring approach beside a cement works, you'll struggle to suppress the oohs and aahs as you reach the tropical garden at this French-Thai operation on the hillside. From the restaurant overlooking the valley to the immaculate bamboo-weave bungalows and postcard-pretty palm-fringed pool, Old Tree's doesn't put a foot wrong. Look for the turn-off 400m past Tha Ton.

Saranya River House — HOTEL $$$

(☑ 053 373143; www.thatonthailand.com; r incl breakfast 1450-3200B; ❄ 🛜 ❄) A stylish, comparatively modern place off Rte 107 just across the boat jetty, with a pool out the back and tasteful Thai-meets-art-deco interiors.

Laap Lung Pan — THAI $

(Rte 107; mains 30-60B; ⊘ 7am-8pm) The go-to place in Tha Ton for Northern Thai–style eats. There's no English-language menu; simply point to whatever pot or item on the grill looks tasty. Nor is there an English-language sign; look for the Coke ad roughly across from the entrance to Wat Tha Ton.

Sunshine Cafe — CAFE $

(mains 60-110B; ⊘ 8am-3pm) This is the place to come for freshly brewed coffee in the morning. It also does a wide selection of Western breakfasts, including muesli, fresh fruit and yoghurt. It's located on the main road, just before the bridge.

❶ Information

There are a couple of ATMs in town.

All of Tha Ton's hotels and guesthouses offer wi-fi.

❶ Getting There & Around

The main bus stand in Tha Ton is a long hike south along the highway, but buses also swing in at the parking lot just north of the bridge. Services include the following:

Bangkok 600B to 720B, 14 hours, three daily

Chiang Dao 63B, 2½ hours, seven daily

Chiang Mai 90B, four hours, seven daily

To reach Chiang Rai by road, take a *sŏrng·tăa·ou* to Mae Salong (60B, 1½ hours, three daily).

With your own car or motorcycle, you can continue to Mae Salong along Rte 107, turning off onto Rte 1089, following a fully paved but sometimes treacherous mountain road and passing scattered Lisu and Akha villages.

Local guesthouses rent out motorcycles for 350B per day.

SOUTHERN CHIANG MAI PROVINCE

To the immediate south of Chiang Mai is the Ping Valley, a fertile agricultural plain that runs out to densely forested hills. Southwest is Thailand's highest peak, Doi Inthanon (2565m).

San Kamphaeng & Bo Sang สันกำแพง/บ่อสร้าง

📞 052 / POP 33,000

About 14km southeast of Chiang Mai along Rte 1006, the town of San Kamphaeng was once famous as a production centre for cotton, silk and other handicrafts, but many of the small factories have relocated and those remaining seem a little down on their luck. *Sŏrng·tăa·ou* and *rót daang* drivers in Chiang Mai push trips to San Kamphaeng quite heavily, steering tourists towards factories and workshops that pay a commission, but it's easy to get here by public transport, so there's no particular need to pay into this system if you don't want to. Most people stay in Chiang Mai and visit on a day trip.

The most engaging option is the 'umbrella village' of Bo Sang, just west of San Kamphaeng, with a string of souvenir shops, showrooms and workshops, most devoted to the production of paper and bamboo umbrellas and parasols. However, prices aren't especially cheap and you'll find similar items in Chiang Mai's night market.

In late January the surprisingly untouristy **Bo Sang Umbrella Festival** features a colourful umbrella procession along Bo Sang's main street.

ⓘ Getting There & Away

White *sŏrng·tăa·ou* to San Kamphaeng town (20B, 30 minutes) leave Chiang Mai frequently during the day from the lane south of Talat Warorot market; white *sŏrng·tăa·ou* to Bo Sang (20B, 25 minutes) leave from the riverside on Th Praisani.

San Kamphaeng Hot Springs

About 36km east of Chiang Mai, these **hot springs** (📞 053 037101; adult/child 100/50B; ⊙ 7am-8pm) are a delight. Set in a meandering country garden are public and private bathhouses, massage pavilions and a hot lazy river where you can soak away the tiredness from your calves.

Locals flock here at weekends to picnic and boil eggs in the hot vents, which emerge from the ground at a scorching 100°C. During the week, however, things are calm and peaceful, apart from the whoosh of steam roaring out of the steam vents. If you want the full-immersion experience, a dip in the public mineral pool costs 50/30B (adult/child), while a private bathhouse costs 60B for 15 minutes. Simple but comfortable rooms (from 1000B, with bathhouse from 1300B) are available and there's a campsite

CRAFTY SOUVENIRS

About 2km east of Hang Dong, **Ban Tawai Tourism Village** (www.ban-ta-wai.com; ⊙ 9am-6pm Mon-Sat) is a vast, pedestrian-friendly tourist market, with hundreds of small shops selling handicrafts and knick-knacks to spruce up your interiors back home. This vast enterprise was kicked off by local woodcarvers, who are famous for their artistry and prodigious output.

Today, carvings are produced on an industrial scale by workshops such as Sriboonmuang in Zone 5. It's all very commercial, but you'll find the same kinds of handicrafts and souvenirs that you see in Chiang Mai's walking street markets, spread out across six covered 'zones'. Signs saying 'antiques made to order' should make you question the origins of anything purporting to be old.

You can reach Ban Tawai by *sŏrng·tăa·ou* from Pratu Chiang Mai (20B, 20 minutes) but if you charter a *rót daang* you can also visit nearby Hang Dong.

(50B per person) and several restaurants serving Thai meals.

For a posher stay, the clean and comfortable bungalows at **Roong Aroon Hot Spring Resort** (☑ 053 939128; r Mon-Fri from 1600B, Sat & Sun 2000B), have access to its own set of hot springs. It's a few kilometres beyond the main springs.

Hang Dong หางดง

☑ 053 / POP 83,300

About 15km south of Chiang Mai on Rte 108, the village of Hang Dong built its fortune on the production and sale of furniture, woodcarving, antiques (both real and imitation) and handicrafts. Hang Dong's 'furniture highway' – Th Thakhilek – runs east from Rte 108 towards Ban Tawai; look for the turn-off just south of the market. Lined up along the road are dozens of antique and handicraft dealers, selling everything from elaborate antique Chinese wedding beds (with astronomical price tags) to gigantic Buddhist woodcarvings, Burmese lacquer boxes and cheaper and more portable Thai knick-knacks. Alongside are numerous shipping companies who will ship your purchases worldwide.

Good places to browse include: **De Siam** (☑053 441254; www.desiam-antiques. com; ⊙8.30am-5.30pm) for extravagant antique beds and cabinets; **Mandala** (☑081 490 9251; www.mandalaantiques.com; ⊙10am-5pm Mon-Sat) for Japanese heirlooms; **Siripat Antique** (☑053 433246) for reproduction antiques and enormous wood carvings; **Chilli Antiques & Arts** (☑053 433281; http://asian-antiques-arts.com; ⊙8.30am-5.30pm) for top-notch Thai and Burmese Buddhas; **World Port Services** (☑053 434200; www.legends collection.com; ⊙8am-5pm Mon-Sat) for portable handicrafts and Burmese lacquerware; and **Crossroads Asia** (☑053 434650; www.crossroadsasia.com; ⊙8.30am-5.30pm) for ethnic art and textiles spanning 26 countries.

ⓘ Getting There & Away

It is possible to reach Hang Dong by *sŏrng·tăa·ou* from Pratu Chiang Mai (20B, 20 minutes) but it's easier to come with a chartered *rót daang* so you can also visit nearby Ban Tawai and cart your purchases home.

Doi Inthanon National Park อุทยานแห่งชาติดอยอินทนนท์

Thailand's highest peak, Doi Inthanon soars to 2565m above sea level, an impressive altitude for the kingdom. Surrounding this granite massif is a 1000-sq-km national park, dotted with hiking trails and waterfalls and enveloped in an impenetrable curtain of jungle. When the heat of Chiang Mai gets too much, locals decamp to Doi Inthanon for day trips, especially during the New Year holiday when there's the rarely seen phenomenon of frost at the summit.

⊙ Sights & Activities

The whole point of the park is to get as high as you can to experience life in a colder climate.

At the summit of Doi Inthanon, the forest is dank and chilly, and often partly obscured by swirls of mist due to the condensation of warm humid air from lower down the mountain. It's otherworldly, and at times a little spooky. Do as Thai visitors do and bring a jacket and an umbrella or rain poncho in case of sudden showers.

The summit itself is reached via a 50m trail near the radar station, just beyond Doi Inthanon's twin *chedi*. At the end is a 'Highest Point in Thailand' sign, and a shrine to one of the last Lanna kings (Inthawichayanon). Don't expect a rewarding view; you'll see more from the terraces of the two *chedi*. The tiny cafe by the boardwalk is frequented by laughing thrushes and other exotic birdlife.

About 3km before the summit, set amid lush tropical gardens, the twin **stupas** (Km 41-42; admission to both 40B; ⊙6am-6pm) of Phra Mahathat Naphamethanidon and Phra Mahathat Naphapholphumisiri were built by the Royal Thai Air Force to commemorate the king's and queen's 60th birthdays in 1989 and 1992, respectively.

Most visitors charge straight to the stupas and summit. The only easy access into the forest is via the slippery **Ang Ka trail** (a 360m-long boardwalk) into the cloud forest, near the Km 48 marker. A more ambitious jungle walk is the **Kew Mae Pan Nature Trail** (admission & guide fee 300B; ⊙Oct-Jun) near the Km 42 marker. The trail snakes for nearly 3km, passing a string of viewpoints and a pretty waterfall; a guide is compulsory and should be arranged at the park head-

FLORA & FAUNA IN DOI INTHANON

The mist-shrouded upper slopes produce abundant orchids, lichen, moss and epiphytes, and 385 bird species make a home in the canopy, more than in any other habitat in Thailand. Keep an eye out for flashes of colour in the forest as electric-blue niltavas, yellow-cheeked tits and green-tailed sunbirds fly by. The best birdwatching season is from February to April, with the best chance of sightings at the *beung* (bogs) below the summit. The mountain is also home to Assamese macaques, Phayre's leaf monkeys, gibbons, Indian civets, barking deer and giant flying squirrels – around 75 mammal species in all.

quarters. The views are best in the cool dry season from November to February.

Also in the park are a few hill-tribe villages surrounded by rice terraces, which are rather picturesque. Most tribal people now work at farms and flower nurseries on the lower slopes. Near the national park headquarters, the Hmong village of **Ban Khun Klang** is worth visiting for its views of the Siriphum waterfall.

Waterfalls

During the wet season, the highlands collect rain like a sponge, sending it surging down towards the plains in raging torrents over eight dramatic waterfalls. Although swimming is discouraged because of the risk of flash floods, the falls are wonderfully scenic and spectacular after rain.

The most accessible cascade is **Nam Tok Mae Klang**, near the Km 8 marker, close to the turn-off from Rte 108 (take the signposted road just before the national park entrance), but the falls can get crowded with picnickers and coach tours at weekends. Reached via a side-road near the Km 21 marker and tucked into a forested basin, **Nam Tok Wachirathan** has a huge frothy mane that plummets 50m and after heavy rain it can be as loud as an AC/DC concert. There's an enticing collection of food vendors by the parking lot. Near the Km 30 marker, **Nam Tok Siriphum** is a delicate ribbon of silver when viewed from nearby Ban Khun Klang village.

🛏 Sleeping & Eating

Park accommodation is available in comfortable bungalows located next to the national park information centre at Ban Khun Klang village, near the Km 31 marker; the best ones overlook the water. Nearby is a roadside restaurant complex with several hawker-style eateries, and there are more food vendors at Nam Tok Wachirathan. Camping is also possible (with your own equipment) at Nam Tok Mae Pan.

One of the best options if you want to stay near the park entrance is a homestay in the rice-paddy-encircled Karen village of Ban Mae Klang Luang. Perched over the rice terraces, the clean, polished wood cabins at **Mae Klang Luang View** (☑ 086 189 4075; bungalows 1000B) are our favourite, although there are plenty of other options with prices hovering more around 500B.

There are some OK places to stay at the bottom of the mountain about 40km from the summit, near the junction of Rte 1009 and Rte 108; the nicest is the colonial-feeling **Inthanon Highland Resort** (www.inthanonhighlandresort.com; bungalows 1500-8500B; ❋ 🛜) on sprawling gardens next to a serene lake. Further on, only about 29km from Chiang Mai proper, is the stunning and tranquil boutique resort, Kaomai Lanna (p337).

ℹ Getting There & Away

Most visitors come with private transport or on a tour from Chiang Mai; if coming by motorcycle or moped from Chiang Mai allow 2½ hours each way.

To reach the park via public transport, you first need to take a bus from Chiang Mai to Chom Thong (60B) on Rte 108. There are occasional public *sŏrng·tăa·ou* into the park from the highway junction, but these will only take you to the summit and back. Considering the risk of getting marooned, it makes more sense to charter a whole *sŏrng·tăa·ou* for the round-trip (about 1000B).

Mae Kampong   แม่กำปอง

☑ 053 / POP 400

About 50km northeast of Chiang Mai, hidden away in the emerald jungles above Rte 1317, the pocket-sized village of Ban Mae Kampong has become an offbeat retreat for travellers looking to escape the commercialism of Chiang Mai and rediscover the village way of life. Most visitors are introduced to the area on zipline tours with Flight of the Gibbon, but it's worth coming under your own steam to explore the village and the surrounding jungle.

Perched at an altitude of about 1300m, Ban Mae Kampong is locally famous as a centre for the production of *mêeang* (pickled tea leaves), and local coffee is sold at many small coffeeshops dotted along the road through the village. The steep road continues through the forest into **Chae Son National Park** (อุทยานแห่งชาติแจ้ซ้อน; ☑054 380000; adult/child 200/100B), where you'll find waterfalls, hot springs and cottages in the woods.

🛏 Sleeping & Eating

The Community Ecotourism Committee provides local **homestays** (☑089 559 4797; r 600B); you can find a room just by asking at houses displaying a 'homestay' sign, or Green Trails (p326) or Flight of the Gibbon

(p326) in Chiang Mai can arrange overnight trips by minibus.

An alternative overnight stop is **Tharnthong Lodge** (☑081 961 538; www.tharnthong-lodge.com; r 1200-4000B), an appealing *Swiss Family Robinson* affair a few kilometres downhill from Ban Mae Kampong. It has wooden villas strewn over a jungle garden dotted with statues – including an incongruous Easter Island head. There's a superior restaurant overlooking a pebble stream (try the pie) and the resort is a popular centre for yoga training.

If you aren't staying at the lodge, meals are taken with local families.

ℹ Getting There & Away

There is no public transport from Chiang Mai, but the village is easy to reach with a decent-sized motorcycle or by chartered *rót daang* – just follow Rte 1317 from the city past Mae On to Ban Huai Kaew, and follow the signed road on the right.

Northeastern Thailand

Best Places to Eat

➡ Pa Ouan 2 (p437)

➡ Rung Roj (p428)

➡ Samuay & Sons (p390)

➡ Surin Green Market (p422)

Best Places to Stay

➡ Baan Chang Ton (p421)

➡ Bouy Guesthouse (p386)

➡ Mekong Riverside Resort & Camping (p377)

➡ Mut Mee Garden Guesthouse (p382)

Why Go?

The northeast is Thailand's forgotten backyard. Isan (*ee·săhn*), as it's usually called, offers a glimpse of the Thailand of old: rice fields run to the horizon, water buffalo wade in muddy ponds, silk weavers work looms under their homes, and pedal-rickshaw drivers pull passengers down city streets. If you have a penchant for authentic experiences, it will surely be satisfied here.

Spend even just a little time here and you'll discover as many differences as similarities to the rest of Thailand. The language, food and culture are more Lao than Thai, with hearty helpings of Khmer and Vietnamese thrown into the mix. And spend time here you should, because it's home to some of Thailand's best historic sites, national parks and festivals. Thailand's tourist trail is at its bumpiest here (English is rarely spoken), but the fantastic attractions and daily interactions could end up being highlights of your trip.

When to Go

➡ The weather is best during the cool season from November to February. It almost never rains, and temperatures, while still warm, are not as high as the rest of the year.

➡ The hot season from March to May sees temperatures soar to the high 30s and stay there. Any rain that falls at this time is a real blessing. Travelling can be exhausting, but some of the best festivals are held during this time.

➡ Isan is at its most beautiful during the rainy season (June to October) because the forests and rice paddies turn green and the waterfalls run wild. And it generally only rains for less than an hour in the late afternoon, so it's not much of a hindrance.

History

The early social history of the Isan region remains a mystery. Ancient rock paintings are widespread, and while they could be up to 10,000 years old, dating is not possible. It appears that the Ban Chiang culture, and closely related ones around them, began making bronze tools about 2000BC, well before the Bronze Age began in China.

Dvaravati kingdoms, about which very little is known, held sway here from somewhere between the 7th and 10th centuries, and traces of the culture can be found at Phu Phrabat in Udon Thani and Muang Sema in Nakhon Ratchasima.

The Khmer arrived in the 9th century and occupied most of the region for more than 400 years, though for much of this time it was in partnership with rather than dominion over local leaders. Hundreds of their iconic temples remain over most of Isan, most notably at Phimai in Nakhon Ratchasima and Phanom Rung in Buriram. After the Khmer empire waned, Isan was under the thumb of Lan Xang and Siam kings, but remained largely autonomous.

As the French staked out the borders of colonial Laos, Thailand was forced to define its own northeastern boundaries. Slowly but surely, for better and worse, Isan fell under the mantle of broader Thailand. Long Thailand's poorest region, the Thai government, with considerable help (and most of the money) coming from the US, only began serious development here in the 1960s as a way to counter the communist threat. There was also a dedicated program to make Isan more 'Thai' in the interests of national solidarity. The result was an improved economy and increased opportunity, but the per capita income here remains only one-third the national average.

Language & Culture

Isan is a melting pot of Thai, Lao and Khmer influences. The Isan language, still a more common first tongue than Thai, is a dialect of Lao. In fact, there are probably more people of Lao heritage in Isan than in Laos. Many villages in the far south still maintain Khmer as their primary language. The people of Isan are known by other Thais for their friendliness, work ethic and sense of humour: flip through radio stations and you'll hear DJs laughing at their own jokes.

Respect and hospitality towards guests is a cornerstone of Isan life, and most villagers, plus plenty of city folk, still pride themselves on taking care of others before themselves. Isan people are far less conservative than most Thais, but short shorts and spaghetti-strap tops will earn more stares than other places in Thailand because of the scarcity of tourists here.

Though this is by far Thailand's poorest region, historically, surveys show that the people of the northeast are generally the happiest because of their strong sense of community and close family ties. In the villages it's often hard to tell who is rich or poor because big homes and fancy clothes garner little respect. Modern culture, however, is changing this in the minds of many young people. Additionally, the massive influx of Western men marrying local women has brought changes too, and these days many Isan village women and their families work hard towards the goal of landing a foreign husband.

LOEI PROVINCE

Loei (meaning 'to the extreme') is a diverse, beautiful province mostly untouched by mass tourism, despite all it has to offer. It's hotter than elsewhere in Thailand during the hot season, yet it's also one of the few provinces in Thailand where temperatures drop below 0°C.

The majority of the people are Tai Loei, thought to have migrated from Luang Prabang via Chiang Mai.

Loei ‌ ‌ ‌ ‌ ‌ ‌ เลย

042 / POP 22,700

Loei is a relatively small provincial capital and easy to get around. It doesn't have anything that will wow tourists, and most foreigners visit just briefly while on their way to the province's national parks and small towns, though good accommodation options make longer stays pleasant if you want to use it as a base for your Loei exploration.

◉ Sights

Phu Bo Bit Forest Park ‌ ‌ ‌ VIEWPOINT
(วนอุทยานภูบ่อบิด; Rte 2138; ⊘5am-7.30pm)
FREE If you want to harden up your legs for

Northeastern Thailand Highlights

1 Pha Taem National Park (p434) Broadening your horizons with amazing views and ancient art.

2 Khao Yai National Park (p413) Spotting elephants, gibbons, deer and birds.

3 Phanom Rung (p417) Climbing an extinct volcano to a towering Khmer ruin.

4 Red Lotus Sea (p393) Boating through a field of flowers.

5 Phimai Historical Park (p411) Marvelling at impressive art in Thailand's largest Khmer ruin.

6 Wat Phu Thok (p397) Challenging your vertigo on the rickety walkways clinging to the side of the mountain.

7 Ban Ta Klang (p423) Meeting elephants with one of the ethical voluntourism programs.

8 Phu Phrabat Historical Park (p394) Exploring the mystical, beautiful landscape.

9 Nong Khai (p379) Chillin' along the Mekong River.

10 Rocket festivals (p443) Celebrating the height of the hot season.

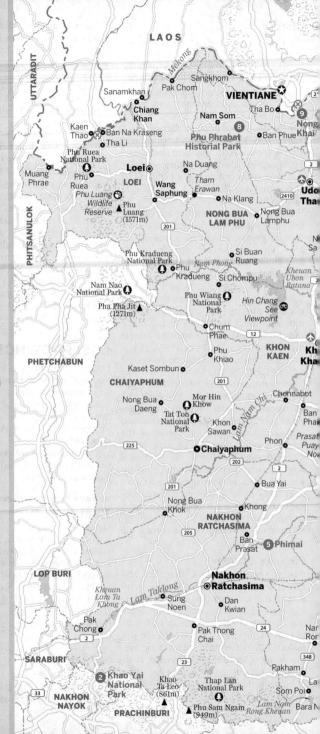

Loei Province

Loei's national parks, Phu Bo Bit gives you about 1400 steep steps to practise on, and rewards your effort with great 360-degree views of the town and surrounding mountains. The climb, which passes a Buddha cave on the way up, can be done in an hour and a half return.

The park is about 3km from the town centre along Rte 2138. You can get a túk-túk there and back for about 250B, including wait time. Many locals come up here at sunset and stay till after dark to see the lights of Loei. Lighting along the steps is supposedly turned off at 8pm, but locals advised us that sometimes it's switched off early, so plan to be down by 7.30pm.

Museum of Art & Culture Loei

MUSEUM

(ศูนย์วัฒนธรรมจังหวัดเลย; ☑ 042 835223; Rte 201; ⊙ 8.30am-4.30pm) **FREE** This little museum is 5km north of town at Rajabhat University.

The first gallery has an animatronic dinosaur (fossilised footprints have been found nearby) and the second has a few displays about the culture of the Tai Loei people, including the Phi Ta Khon (p376) festival. Check in at the office down below and they'll open the museum for you.

🖝 Tours

Sugar Guesthouse, Stay Guesthouse and freelance guide **Poppy** (☑ 088 698 3995; borntobe_travel@hotmail.com) all lead reasonably priced day trips to Suan Hin Pha Ngam (p381) and elsewhere in Loei Province.

🛏 Sleeping

★ Sugar Guesthouse

GUESTHOUSE **$**

(☑ 089 711 1975; sugarhuesthouse@gmail.com; Soi 2, Th Wisut Titep; s with fan 200-270B, d with aircon 380B; P ⊖ ✳ @ 중) This guesthouse has simple (the fan rooms share a bathroom), spotless rooms, and the friendly owner, Pat, speaks good English. There's bike and motorcycle hire and tours to sites around the province.

Stay Guesthouse   GUESTHOUSE $
(☑095 620 7570; www.thestayguesthouse.com; 91/6 Th Wisut Titep; r with fan 275B, air-con 399-699B; [P][☀][❋][☎]) Not exactly a guesthouse, rather there are some rooms for travellers in an older apartment complex. But what it lacks in style it makes up for in service. John and Tai are patient, hands-on owners with lots of helpful advice about the region, and tours to many attractions around Loei Province are available. The rooms are very clean, all with refrigerators and kettles.

It's north of town, 2km to Kut Pong Lake, but there are free bikes and motorcycles (250B per 24 hours) for hire.

Loei Village   HOTEL $$
(☑042 833599; www.loeivillages.com; Soi 3, Th Nok Kaew; r incl breakfast 990-1500B; [P][☀][❋][☎]) Starting with a cool welcome drink as you walk in the door, the focus is on service at this stylish hotel. The decor is smart, and little extras such as free minibar snacks and a good buffet breakfast make this one of the city's top choices. There are also bikes for guests' use. Staff are especially helpful.

King Hotel   HOTEL $$
(☑042 811225; kinghotel.loei@hotmail.com; Th Chumsai; r incl breakfast 600-800B; [P][❋][☎]) Fit for a king? No; though a thorough modernisation of this old classic has given the rooms a simple but attractive style and made it a pleasant place to stay. The rooms surround a courtyard and it's quiet here, despite the city-centre location.

Loei Palace Hotel   HOTEL $$$
(☑042 815668; www.mosaic-collection.com/loeipalace; Th Charoenrat; incl breakfast r 1600-3000B, ste 3500-5000B; [P][☀][❋][@][☎][❋]) Loei's flagship hotel sports some wedding-cake architecture, large renovated rooms with attractive wooden furnishings, nice views from upper floors, bikes (50/100B per half-/full day) for guests, and usually a high vacancy rate; so ask about discounts. Check out the flood photo in the lobby to see what the city suffered in May 2017.

✖ Eating & Drinking

A handful of bars on Th Ruamphattana comprise Loei's attempt at a trendy nightlife scene.

★Khao Tom Raeng Ngan   THAI $
(☑042 033050; Th Sert-Si; mains 60-300B; ⊙5pm-3am; [☎]) As busy as the street it sits on, this place serves not only the rice soup (*kôw đôm*) it's named after, but hundreds of other dishes, and the place is happy to improvise if what you want isn't on the menu. The service is quick and friendly, and the food won't disappoint.

Noi Tam Suea @ Loei   THAI $
(Th Sert-Si; mains 35-170B; ⊙9am-8pm; [☎]) This popular restaurant has all the expected Isan foods including *plah pŏw* (grilled fish) and duck *lâhp*, plus several less common options including *sôm·đam* made with *đôrng dêng* noodles, a super-thick version of the typical *kà·nŏm jeen* noodles. This is an English-free zone, but there are some pictures on the menu to help with ordering.

Walking Street   THAI $
(Th Ruamjit; ⊙4pm-11pm) Not to be confused with an actual Walking Street market (which takes place in front of the post office on Saturday nights), this is just a typical night market. It has all the expected Thai and Isan dishes.

Outlaw Brewing   CRAFT BEER
(☑096 695 8784; Th Sert-Si; ⊙7pm-midnight Wed-Sun) Loei is the unexpected home of one of Thailand's most serious brewmasters. Stop by this little spot for some of his own craft brews (perhaps a durian IPA) and some from elsewhere.

ℹ Information

Krung Thai Bank (Th Oua-Aree; ⊙9am-5pm) The only bank in the city centre that's open extended hours.

Loei Hospital (☑042 862123; Th Maliwan) The top hospital in Loei.

Tourism Authority of Thailand (TAT; ☑042 812812; tatloei@tat.or.th; Th Charoenrat; ⊙8.30am-4.30pm) Provides a good map of the province and has helpful staff.

Tourist Police (☑042 867364, nationwide 1155)

Loei

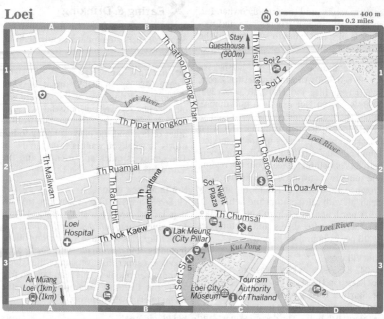

Loei

🛏 Sleeping
1. King Hotel C3
2. Loei Palace Hotel D3
3. Loei Village... B3
4. Sugar Guesthouse...............................C1

🍴 Eating
5. Khao Tom Raeng Ngan B3

Noi Tam Suea @ Loei..................... (see 5)
6. Walking Street C3

🍷 Drinking & Nightlife
7. Outlaw Brewing C3

ℹ Getting There & Away

AIR

Nok Air (☏ 088 874 0883, nationwide 02 900 9955; www.nokair.com; Loei Airport; ⊙ 6am-4pm) and **Air Asia** (☏ 042 844629, nationwide 02 515 9999; www.airasia.com; Loei Airport; ⊙ 9am-5pm) both connect Loei to Bangkok's Don Mueang Airport. Together there are three daily flights, with prices starting at around 900B.

A taxi into town from the **airport** (☏ 042 811520) runs to 150B.

BUS

Loei's **bus terminal** (☏ 042 833586; Th Maliwan) is south of town. **Air Muang Loei** (☏ 042 832042; Loei bus terminal) has good VIP service to Bangkok. Note that *sŏrng·tăa·ou* (pick-up minibuses) to Chiang Khan take you to near the city centre, while buses leave you pretty far away.

ℹ Getting Around

Sŏrng·tăa·ou (10B) run from the bus station into the centre of town, or you can take a túk-túk for 50B to 60B. Loei also has a few taxis. They park at the bus station and airport, and do not use their meters. Stay (p371) and Sugar (p370) guesthouses hire bikes (50B per day) and motorcycles (250B per day).

Chiang Khan   เชียงคาน

☏ 042 / POP 6100

What was once a sleepy, little-known Mekong-side town full of traditional timber shophouses became a trendy destination for Thais and is now full of gift shops and places for taking selfies. That said, Chiang Khan is far from spoiled and is still a good place to visit: it's just no longer great. The

BUSES TO/FROM LOEI

DESTINATION	FARE (B)	DURATION (HR)	FREQUENCY
Bangkok	360-560	9-10	hourly 6am-10.35pm
Chiang Khan	34	1	9 departures 6.30am-11.45pm
Chiang Khan (sǒrng·tǎa·ou)	35	1½	every 30min 5.30am-7.45pm
Chiang Mai	436-570	10	3.30pm, 8.30pm, 9.30pm, 11.30pm
Dan Sai	60-134	1½-2	10am, noon, 2.20pm, 3.30pm, 8.30pm, 9.30pm, 11.30pm
Khon Kaen	125	4	every 30min 3.45am-6.10pm
Nakhorn Ratchasima	252-342	7	hourly 5.30am-4.30pm
Nong Khai	140	7-8	6am
Pak Chom (sǒrng·tǎa·ou)	60	2½	hourly 6am-5pm
Phitsanulok	202-266	5	10am, noon, 2.20pm, 3.30pm, 8.30pm, 9.30pm, 11.30pm
Udon Thani	90-115	2½	every 30min 4am-5pm

photogenic views of the river and the Lao mountains beyond are still there, as are the old buildings, and things remain peaceful in the daytime before the evening shopping stampede begins. Every evening Th Chai Khong turns into a busy Walking Street market with buskers, artists and street-food vendors. Chiang Khan is less busy in the hot and rainy seasons – April to September.

○ Sights

Wat Si Khun Mueang   BUDDHIST TEMPLE
(วัดศรีคุณเมือง; Th Chai Khong; ☉daylight hours)
FREE The *bòht* (ordination hall) at Wat Si Khun Mueang, which probably dates to the Rama III era, is mostly Lao-style (in particular, note the sweeping roof), but it also freely mixes central (the lotus pillars) and northern (guardian lions) Thai styling. It's fronted by a superb mural of the *Jataka* tales.

Phu Thok   VIEWPOINT
(ภูทอก) In the cool season, people head to nearby Phu Thok mountain for sunrise and 'sea of fog' views. If you don't have your own vehicle, ask your hotel to arrange a ride. Túk-túk charge 100B per person and then you have to ride a *sǒrng·tǎa·ou* (25B per person) to the top.

Kaeng Khut Khu   NATURAL FEATURE
(แก่งคุดคู้) With the mountains making an attractive backdrop, this famous bend in the Mekong, and its small set of rapids, is a popular stop for visitors. It's 5km downstream from town; túk-túk drivers charge 100B per person there and back.

Activities

Many guesthouses arrange boat trips to Kaeng Khut Khu or further afield, and the mountain scenery makes them highly recommended, especially at sunset. Rates vary according to the price of petrol, but the typical one-hour trip costs around 800B for up to 15 people. If you enjoy paddling, another option from October to April is to kayak the river (1500B per person, minimum four) with **Mekong Culture & Nature** (☑089 569 3470; Rte 2195; kayaking trip per person 1500B, minimum 4).

✿ Festivals & Events

Phi Kon Nam   CULTURAL
(Ban Na Sao; ☉May or Jun) The little-known Phi Kon Nam festival in Ban Na Sao, 7km south of Chiang Khan, is part of the village's rain-inducing Bun Bang Fai (rocket festival; p443) and coincides with Visakha Bucha. Locals believe that the souls of their departed cows and buffaloes wander around the village so, as a show of their respect, the villagers don wild bovine-inspired masks and colourful costumes to commune with them.

Chiang Khan

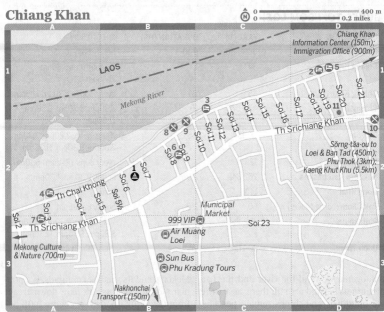

LAOS

Mekong River

Chiang Khan
Information Center (150m);
Immigration Office (900m)

Th Srichiang Khan

Sŏrng·tăa·ou to
Loei & Ban Tad (450m);
Phu Thok (3km);
Kaeng Khut Khu (5.5km)

Th Chai Khong

Th Srichiang Khan

Mekong Culture
& Nature (700m)

Municipal
Market

Soi 23

999 VIP

Air Muang
Loei

Sun Bus

Phu Kradung Tours

Nakhonchai
Transport (150m)

Chiang Khan

⊙ Sights
1 Wat Si Khun Mueang............................B2

⊙ Sleeping
2 Chiang Khan Guesthouse......................D1
3 Huean Yai Bab Pa C1
4 Norn-Nab-Dao.......................................A2
5 Old Chiangkhan Boutique Hotel D1
6 Poonsawasdi B2
7 Soi 3 Homestay......................................A3

⊗ Eating
8 Jer Loei B2
9 Rabiang Rim Khong...............................B2
10 Ting Song Tam......................................D2

⊙ Transport
11 Triple Z Hostel......................................D1

🛏 Sleeping

Chiang Khan's popularity means hotel owners don't need to price their rooms reasonably. Low-season (April to September) discounts can be as much as 50%, but even then rooms are pricier than most elsewhere in Isan. You can usually save money by staying on a *soi* (Sois 9,11 and 17 each have many to choose from) rather than along the river.

Soi 3 Homestay
GUESTHOUSE **$**
(📞 085 7614031; Soi 3; r 400B; 🅿 ❄ 🛜) If you want to trade charm for a low price, these eight, simple windowless rooms next to the friendly owner's home will do the trick. Given they have air-con and en-suite bathrooms, the price is very low by Chiang Khan standard. Guests can use bikes for free.

Chiang Khan Guesthouse
GUESTHOUSE **$**
(📞 086 325 7958; guesthouse.ck@gmail.com; 282 Th Chai Khong; r with fan/air-con 200/500B; ❄ ❄ 🛜) This traditional-style place is all creaking timber and tin roofing, and it's the inescapable wear-and-tear that makes it so cheap. But on the plus side the terrace sits really close to the river and the ever-smiling owner Ong will make you feel at home.

Poonsawasdi
HOTEL **$$**
(📞 042 821114; 251/2 Soi 9; r 800-1100B; ❄ @ 🛜) The oldest hotel in Chiang Khan, opened in 1950, has been modernised with air-con and en-suite bathrooms, but the seven upstairs rooms do a pretty good job of hanging onto their historic ambience. The cheaper ones don't have windows.

Norn-Nab-Dao   HOTEL **$$**
([☑]086 792 0215; Soi 3; incl breakfast d & tw 1700-220B, q 2900B; [P][😊][❄][📶]) This hotel isn't all timber, but it has charm nonetheless. The cutely painted rooms lie around an airy central courtyard, and there are great river views from the four end rooms. It's one of the best choices within the city for people who don't need luxury, but don't want to put up with the particular quirks of most Chiang Khan accommodation.

★**Huean Yai Bab Pa**   HOTEL **$$$**
([☑]042 821705, 089 694 3336; 340 Th Chai Khong at Soi 11; incl breakfast d 1800-2200B; f 3600-4500B; [😊][❄][📶]) The friendly owners of this seven-room spot have mixed historic touches from the family's 1925 home with modern stylings, and the results are impressive. More than any other place we've seen in Chiang Khan, it exudes a back-in-the-day vibe. One of the family rooms is a loft room in the building next door.

🍴 Eating

★**Ting Song Tam**   THAI **$**
([☑]088 0298251; Th Srichiang Khan at Soi 21; mains 30-100B; [⏰]8.30am-6pm) One of our favourite restaurants in Loei Province. There's a full Isan menu but its speciality is *dôrng dêng* noodles (a super-thick version of *kà·nŏm jeen*), which are made fresh when you order. Add them to your *sôm·đam* or eat with chilli sauce and vegetables, a Chiang Khan speciality called *kôw pûn rórn* that pairs well with *gài yâhng* grilled chicken.

There's no English sign, but it's the restaurant with the washing machines at the front of the dining area.

★**Rabiang Rim Khong**   THAI **$**
(Th Chai Khong at Soi 10; mains 60-250B; [⏰]10.30am-9.30pm) This place has been popu-

MORNING ALMS

Buying a tray of food to *dàk baht* (give food to the monks on their morning alms round) has become big business in Chiang Khan, particularly with visitors from Bangkok. We suggest giving it a pass since it runs counter to the local tradition of putting only sticky rice in the monks' bowls – other food should be taken to the temple and donated there. The Dos and Don'ts signs along Th Chai Khong include this request, along with no littering or making loud noises.

lar with locals since long before the tourism boom. The prices have risen a bit since those good old days and the building has changed, but the quality has not dropped.

Jer Loei   THAI **$**
(เจอเลย; 379 Th Chai Khong at Soi 9; mains 80-150B; [⏰]5pm-midnight; [📶]) From the decor to the music, this is a full-on Thai 'indy' place, and the seating is close enough to the river to catch a sunset view. The small menu is big on Thai-style salads and Isan *đôm sâep* soups. There's no English sign: look for the yellow and white circular sign in front.

ℹ️ Information

Chiang Khan Information Center (Th Chai Khong at Soi 25; [⏰]10am-5pm) Has little in the way of information.
Immigration Office ([☑]042 821911; Th Chai Khong at Soi 26; [⏰]8.30am-noon & 1-4.30pm Mon-Fri) For visa extensions.

ℹ️ GETTING TO LAOS: THA LI TO KAEN THAO

Foreigners can get Lao visas at the seldom-used Thai–Lao Nam Heuang Friendship Bridge in Amphoe Tha Li, 60km northwest of Loei.

Getting to the border An international bus runs daily from Loei to Luang Prabang in Laos (700B, 10 hours) via Sainyabuli (500B, seven hours). Buses leave Loei at 8am. There's no other public transport to the Thai border here.

At the border The border is open from 8am to 6pm and it's never busy.

Moving on If you somehow get to the border on your own, rather than using the international bus, you can take a túk-túk (50B) between the two border posts, but you'll find very little onward transport from Kaen Thao.

ℹ Getting There & Away

AIR

Air Asia and Nok Air have fly-and-ride service to Bangkok's Don Muang Airport via Loei Airport. Air Asia's meeting point is the **Old Chiangkhan Boutique Hotel** (☑ 088 340 3999; Soi 20, Th Chai Khong; r incl breakfast 1600-1800B; 🅿 😐 ❄ 🛜) and Nok Air uses **Triple Z Hostel** (☑ 097 319 9097; Soi 20).

BUS

Sŏrng·tǎa·ou to Loei (35B, 1½ hours) depart about every 30 minutes from a stop on Th Sri-chiang Khan (at Soi 26). They drive down Soi 21 and past the market before hitting Hwy 201 and

will pick up passengers on the way. Buses to Loei (34B, one hour, hourly 6.30am to 3.30pm) leave from the **Nakhonchai Transport** (☑ 042 821905; Rte 201) terminal. They continue to Khorat (283B, seven hours).

No transport runs direct to Nong Khai. The quickest way there is via Loei and Udon Thani, but for the scenic river route take a Loei-bound sŏrng·tǎa·ou south to Ban Tad (20B, 30 minutes), where you can catch the 6am bus from Loei to Nong Khai or one of the Loei–Pak Chom sŏrng·tǎa·ou.

Four companies, departing from their own offices, make the run to Bangkok (10 to 11 hours) in the morning and early evening: **Air Muang**

DAN SAI & THE PHI TA KON FESTIVAL

For 362 days a year, Dan Sai (ด่านซ้าย) is an innocuous little town. For the remaining three days, however, it's the site of one of the country's liveliest and loudest festivals, **Phi Ta Khon**. Combining a Buddhist festival (called Phra Wet) with Bun Bang Fai (the rocket festival), it produces a curious cross between the drunken revelry of Carnival and the spooky imagery of Halloween. The origins of the festival are shrouded in ambiguity, but some aspects appear to be related to tribal Tai (possibly Tai Dam) spirit cults. The dates for the festival (usually June) are divined by Jao Phaw Kuan, a local spirit medium who channels the information from the town's guardian deity (you can contact the tourist office in Loei (p371) for dates). Locals don wild costumes and masks for two days of dancing that's fuelled by lôw kŏw (rice whisky), before launching the rockets and heading to the temple.

At its normal peaceful self, the town won't appeal to everyone, but for people who appreciate slow travel and want a good look at local life, Dan Sai delivers in spades. The **Phi Ta Khon Museum** (พิพิธภัณฑ์ผีตาโขน; Th Kaew Asa; ⊙ 8.30am-4.30pm) **FREE** has a collection of costumes worn during the Phi Ta Khon celebrations and a display showing how the masks are made. It's also worth visiting **Wat Neramit Wiphatsana** (วัดเนรมิต วิปัสสนา; Rte 2013; ⊙ daylight hours) **FREE**, a gorgeous meditation temple featuring buildings made of unplastered laterite blocks, on a wooded hill just outside town. The most highly revered stupa in Loei Province is also here: **Phra That Si Songrak** (พระธาตุศรีสอง รัก; Rte 2113; ⊙ 7am-5pm) **FREE** is a whitewashed Lao-style chedi standing 20m high, built in 1560–63 on what was then the Thai–Lao border as a gesture of unity.

If you want to stay overnight, **Baan Chan Bhu** (☑ 081 561 7530, 042 891072; Rte 2013; r 600B; ❄ 🛜) is plain but kept very clean, while the Dan Sai **homestay** (☑ 042 892339, 086 862 4812; dm/tw & d 200/550B; 🅿) program gives a great opportunity to stay with Thai families (mostly teachers who can speak a bit of English). The crafts shop **Kawinthip Hattakham** (กวินทิพย์หัตถกรรม; ☑ 086 862 4812, 042 892339; Th Kaew Asa; ⊙ 8am-7pm), which sells Phi Ta Khon masks and other festival paraphernalia and also hires bikes, has details. For something a little more plush, luxury-meets-organic **PhuNaCome Resort** (☑ 042 892005; www.phunacomeresort.com; Rte 2013; r incl breakfast 4200-6500B; 🅿 ❄ @ 🛜) 🍃 has standard hotel rooms and wood-and-thatch Isan-inspired cottages.

Two bus companies stop near the junction of Kaew Asa road and Rte 2013, and of the seven total buses between Loei (60B to 134B, 1½ to two hours) and Phitsanulok (64B to 90B, three hours), most going east toward Loei pass through during the night. Two minivans (80B, 1½ hours, 11am and 3pm) to Lomsak, where you can easily catch a connection west to Phitsanulok or east to Khon Kaen, park across from the 7-Eleven near the municipal market. There are also four buses to Bangkok (342B, nine hours, 8am, 12.30pm, 8.30pm and 10pm) via Lomsak starting across the road from the PT gas station on Rte 2013 west of the junction.

Loei ([phone] 082 642 1629; Th Srichiang Khan Soi 23), **999 VIP** ([phone] 089 893 2898; Soi 9), **Phu Kradung Tours** ([phone] 089 842 1524; petrol station, Rte 201) and **Sun Bus** (Rte 201). Tickets range from 419B to 652B; 999 and Sun Bus have the best VIP service.

❶ Getting Around

Most hotels have free bikes for their guests, but if yours is an exception they can be hired all around town for 50B per day. Soi 9 is the locus of motorcycle rental (250B per day), with three companies based there.

Pak Chom ปากชม

Around 70km east of Chiang Khan along the Mekong is the dusty town – just an overgrown village really – of Pak Chom. It's a regional market centre with no attractions other than the spectacular river views that far exceed those of its more well-known sibling. And because of the beauty, there are some outstanding resorts that make this a place worth visiting if you're looking for rustic relaxation and natural charm.

🛏 Sleeping & Eating

Despite its remoteness – actually in large part because of it – there's excellent accommodation around Pak Chom for all budgets. There are several restaurants in town, but most people eat at their resort.

★ Rim Nam Kong Homestay & Camping
HOMESTAY $$

([phone] 099 125 0461; Hwy 211; r incl breakfast 600-900B, camping per person with own/hired tent 150/200B; P ⊖ ✳ ⊚ 🛜) Charming, friendly and attractively decorated, it's like a little bit of Chiang Khan plopped down in the countryside. Excellent English is spoken, and the family are great hosts. All rooms have private bathrooms, though the one with the best river view requires a walk outdoors. It's 1km west of town; staff will pick you up at the bus station.

★ Mekong Riverside Resort & Camping
RESORT $$

([phone] 082 272 7472; www.mekongriverside.com; Hwy 211; r incl breakfast 1390B, camping with/without own tent 300/350B; P ⊖ ✳ 🛜) This delightful spot, nestled up against a postcard-worthy view of the Mekong, is popular with travellers. Owner Khun Ben and her husband Mike are founts of knowledge on the local

THE GARDEN OF ISAN

The Phu Ruea region is famous for its flower farms, and there's a riot of colours along the roadside. The cool, dry climate allows farmers to grow a variety of crops not common elsewhere in Isan, such as strawberries, coffee (the Coffee Bun chain is based here, and its blend includes Loei-grown beans), macadamia nuts, petunias and persimmon.

If you have realistic expectations of the wine, you might find **Chateau de Loei** (ชาโต้เดอเลย; [phone] 089 944 2616; www.chateaudeloei.com; Rte 21, Km 61; ⊙ 8am-5pm) worth a visit. It released the first commercially produced Thai wine in 1995. It's a penny-ante operation compared to the attractive and well-managed wineries around Khao Yai, but visitors are welcome to have a peek in the utilitarian main building way to the back (where in the cool season they might have some available for tasting) or buy some bottles in the roadside gift shop.

area and can give good tips on activities and places to go. The four rooms are simple but tastefully designed and comfortable. Reservations are highly recommended.

Mekong Villas
RESORT $$$

([phone] 022 221290; www.mekongvillas.com; Hwy 211; incl breakfast 1-bedroom villa 3400-4900B, 3-bedroom villa 12,000B; P ⊖ ✳ ⊚ 🛜) This stunning retreat earns kudos not only for its middle-of-nowhere location on the Mekong, providing sweeping views across to Laos, but also for the splendid villas assembled from traditional Thai stately homes that retain their original ambience. The spot is very private and quiet, ideal for idling, though staff can set you up on road and boat trips.

❶ Getting There & Away

Pak Chom's bus stop is at the market, 500m east of the junction. Large *sŏrng·tǎa·ou* depart to Loei (60B, 2½ hours) hourly from 5.50am to noon and then once more at 4pm. There's no public transport between Pak Chom and Chiang Khan. Instead, take the Loei-bound *sŏrng·tǎa·ou* to Ban Tad (45B, 1½ hours) and change to another for Chiang Khan (20B, 30 minutes). To Nong Khai (80B, four hours) there are non-air-con buses at 5am, 10am and 3pm.

Phu Ruea National Park อุทยานแห่งชาติภูเรือ

Phu Ruea means 'Boat Mountain', a moniker stemming from a cliff jutting out of the peak that's sort of in the shape of a Chinese junk. The 121-sq-km Phu Ruea National Park isn't one of Isan's more impressive preserves, but it does offer a respite from the heat, as well as vast views from the summit (1365m), reached by either a *sǒrng·tǎa·ou* (10B per person) or a 1km footpath. For a longer hike to the top, take the easy (but seldom used) 2.5km trail from the lower visitor centre to 30m-tall Nam Tok Huai Phai, perhaps the park's most scenic waterfall, and then keep going another 6km.

🛏 Sleeping & Eating

In the park are five modern **bungalows** (☑ 042 810965; http://nps.dnp.go.th/reservation. php; 4/6 people 2000/3000B; P) and two cold-shower campsites; **upper** (☑ 042 810965; 3-person tent hire 405B, own tent 30B; P) and **lower** (☑ 042 810965; 3-person tent hire 405B, own tent 30B; P 🛜). Night-time temperatures can drop to near freezing in December and January, so come prepared. Below the park, along the entrance road, are many small resorts: **Suganya Resort** (☑ 042 899606, 081 042 6298; Phu Ruea National Park Rd; d 1000-2000B, f 3000-6500B; P ❄ 🛜) is one of the better ones.

There are small restaurants at the visitor centre and the upper campsite, but they are only open in the October-to-February high season.

ℹ Information

Phu Ruea National Park Visitor Center (☑ 042 810965; ⊙ 8am-4.30pm) Has maps and information about the park. Check in here before walking any of the hiking trails.

ℹ Getting There & Away

The park is 50km west of Loei city on Rte 21, and public transport (a mix of buses, minivans and *sǒrng tǎa ou* – mostly travelling in the morning) can drop you in the town of Phu Ruea (80B, one hour), where you'll have to hitch or charter a truck (around 900B, including a few hours' wait) to the park itself. The summit is 8km from the highway.

Phu Kradueng National Park อุทยานแห่งชาติภูกระดึง

Phu Kradueng National Park is one of the most popular national parks in Thailand, and spending the night atop its eponymous peak is something of a rite of passage for many students in the region. The park covers a high-altitude plateau cut through with trails and peppered with cliffs and waterfalls. Rising to 1316m, Thailand's second national park is always cool at its highest reaches (average year-round temperature is 20°C), where its flora is a mix of pine forest and savannah. Various forest animals, including elephants, Asian jackals, Asiatic black bears, sambar deer, serows and white-handed gibbons, inhabit the 348-sq-km park.

The park gets unbelievably crowded during school holidays (March to May and especially New Year) and it's closed June to September.

◉ Sights & Activities

The trail that passes six waterfalls in a forested valley is the most beautiful destination, even after November, when the water has largely dried up. There are also many clifftop viewpoints, some ideal for sunrise and sunset, scattered around the mountain.

The main trail scaling **Phu Kradueng** (อุทยานแห่งชาติภูกระดึง; ☑ 042 810833; 400B; ⊙ trail to summit 7am-2pm Oct-May) is 5.5km in length and takes about three to four hours to climb. It's strenuous, but not too challenging (except when it's wet) since there are steps at most of the steep parts. The hike is quite scenic and there are rest stops with food vendors about every 1km. Once on top, it's another 3km to the main visitor centre. There's a small **visitor centre** (☑ 042 810833; ⊙ 7am-5pm) at the base of the mountain, but almost everything else is up top. You can hire porters to carry your gear balanced on bamboo poles for 30B per 1kg.

🛏 Sleeping & Eating

Atop the mountain there's space for 5000 people to **camp** (☑ 042 810833; per person with own tent 30B, 1-to-5 person tent hire 100-800B) and some family-sized **bungalows** (☑ 042 810833; http://nps.dnp.go.th/reservation. php; bungalows 900-3600B). If you're arriving late, there's also camping and bungalows at the bottom. Restaurants at the top stay

Around Nong Khai

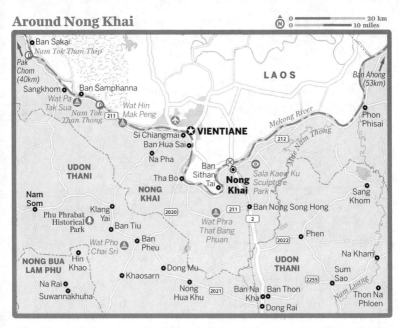

open late into the night, as long as there are customers.

ℹ️ Getting There & Away

Buses between Loei (49B, 1½ hours, every 30 minutes) and Khon Kaen (83B, 2½ hours) stop in Phu Kradueng town where *sŏrng·tăa·ou* (30B per person, charters 300B) take people to the base of the mountain, 10km away.

Nok Air (p372) has a fly-and-ride service from Bangkok direct to the park once a day.

NONG KHAI PROVINCE

Occupying a narrow sweep along the banks of the Mekong, beautiful Nong Khai Province is one of northeastern Thailand's most popular destinations.

Nong Khai   หนองคาย

📞 042 / POP 47,600

Just across from Vientiane in Laos, Nong Khai has been popular with travellers for years. Its popularity is about more than just its proximity to Vientiane and its bounty of banana pancakes, though. Seduced by its dreamy pink sunsets and sluggish pace of life, many visitors who

mean to stay one night end up bedding down for many more.

History

For most of its modern existence, this territory fell within the boundaries of the Vientiane (Wiang Chan) kingdom, which itself vacillated between independence and tribute to Lan Xang and Siam. In 1827 Rama III gave a Thai lord, Thao Suwothamma, the rights to establish Meuang Nong Khai at the present city site, which he chose because the surrounding swamps (*nong*) would aid in the city's defence.

When western Laos was partitioned off from Thailand by the French in 1893, the French demanded that Thailand have no soldiers within 25km of the river, and so the soldiers and administrators moved south and created Udon Thani, leaving Nong Khai's fortunes to fade.

One hundred and one years later, the opening of the US$30 million, 1174m-long Saphan Mittaphap Thai–Lao (Thai–Lao Friendship Bridge) marked a new era of development for Nong Khai as a regional trade and transport centre, though it remains a small town at heart.

Central Nong Khai

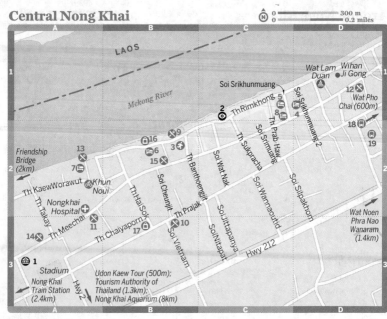

LAOS

Mekong River

Soi Srikhunmuang

Friendship Bridge (2km)

Khun Noui

Nongkhai Hospital

Th KaewWorawut

Th Takay

Th Meechai

Th Chaiyaporn

Th HaiSok

Th Banthoengjit

Th Prajak

Th Rimkhong

Th Sukpracha

Th Prab-Haw

Th Srimuang

Soi Srikhunmuang 2

Soi Wannaoutid

Soi Silpakhom

Hwy 212

Wat Lam Duan

Wihan Ji Gong

Wat Pho Chai (600m)

Wat Noen Phra Nao Wanaram (1.4km)

Stadium

Nong Khai Train Station (2.4km)

Udon Kaew Tour (500m); Tourism Authority of Thailand (1.3km); Nong Khai Aquarium (8km)

Central Nong Khai

Sights

★ **Sala Kaew Ku**   SCULPTURE

(ศาลาแก้วกู่, Wat Khaek; 20B; ⏱ 7am-6pm) One of Thailand's most enigmatic attractions, Sala Kaew Ku can't fail to impress. Built over 20 years by Luang Pu Boun Leua Sourirat, a mystic who died in 1996, the park features a weird and wonderful smorgasbord of bizarre cement statues of Buddha, Shiva, Vishnu and other celestial deities. The main shrine building is packed with hundreds of smaller sculptures of various description and provenance, photos of Luang Pu at various stages throughout his life, and his corpse lying under a glass dome ringed by flashing lights.

As he told his own story, Luang Pu tumbled into a hole as a child and met an ascetic named Kaewkoo who introduced him to the manifold mysteries of the underworld and set him on course to become a Brahmanic-yogi-priest-shaman. Shaking up his own unique blend of Hindu and Buddhist philosophy, Luang Pu developed a large following on both sides of the Mekong in this region. In fact, his original project was on the Lao side of the river, where he had been living until the 1975 communist takeover in Laos.

Some of the sculptures are quite amusing. If you're travelling with kids, they'll enjoy the serene elephant wading through a pack of anthropomorphic dogs (which teaches people to not be bothered by gossip). The tallest sculpture, a Buddha seated on a coiled *naga* (serpent deity) with a spectacular seven-headed hood, is 25m high. Also not to be missed is the Wheel of Life, which you enter through a giant 'mouth'. An explanation is available on the back side of the handy map of the sculpture park provided by Mut Mee Garden Guesthouse (p382).

All buses headed east of Nong Khai pass the road leading to Sala Kaew Ku (10B). It's about a five-minute walk from the highway. Chartered túk-túk will probably cost 250B return with a one-hour wait. You can reach it by bike in about 30 minutes; the Mut Mee map shows the scenic route.

Wat Pho Chai
BUDDHIST TEMPLE

(วัดโพธิ์ชัย; Th Phochai; ⊙ daylight hours, ubosot 6am-6.30pm) FREE Luang Po Phra Sai, a large Lan Xang–era Buddha image awash with gold, bronze and precious stones, sits at the hub of Nong Khai's holiest temple. The head of the image is pure gold, the body is bronze and the ùt·sà·nít (flame-shaped head ornament) is set with rubies. Due to the great number of miracles attributed to it, this royal temple is a mandatory stop for most visiting Thais.

Nong Khai Aquarium
AQUARIUM

(พิพิธภัณฑ์สัตว์น้ำจังหวัดหนองคาย; ☎ 083 459 4477; www.nongkhaiaquarium.com; off Rte 2; 100B; ⊙ 9am-5pm Tue-Sun) Although it's looking a little shabby these days, this large aquarium offers an interesting collection of freshwater and ocean-dwelling fish from Thailand and beyond. The highlight is the 'Big Tank', which features Mekong River species, including giant Mekong catfish, and has a walk-through tunnel. There's a scuba feeding performance daily at 2pm and also at 11am on Saturday, Sunday and public holidays. The aquarium is far out of town, on the Khon Kaen University campus off Rte 2, and not served by public transport.

Tha Sadet Market
MARKET

(ตลาดท่าเสด็จ; Th Rimkhong; ⊙ 8.30am-6pm) The most popular destination in town. Almost everyone loves a stroll through this covered market despite it being a giant tourist trap. It offers the usual mix of clothes, electronic equipment, food and assorted bric-a-brac, most of it imported from Laos and China, but there are also a few shops selling quirky and quality stuff.

THE KUNMING OF THAILAND

Locally billed as Kunming Mueang Thai, 'Thailand's Kunming', due to a slight resemblance with the Stone Forest in Kunming, China, **Suan Hin Pha Ngam** (สวนหินผางาม; ☎ 094 514 9231; tour per person 50B, tractor ride per person 20B; ⊙ visitor centre 8am-5.30pm, last departure to the mountain 4.30pm) is a beautiful trip. But Kunming it isn't, so if you just ride a tractor up to the easy-to-reach viewpoint for a quick look, you might be disappointed. The real highlight is a guided walk through the labyrinthine paths in the heart of the forest. Two kilometres north of the Suan Hin Pha Ngam visitor centre, at the end of the paved road, is **Namtok Phiang Din** (น้ำตกเพียงดิน; ⊙ daylight hours) FREE, the area's biggest waterfall.

A more adventurous destination is **Suan Sawan** (สวนสวรรค์; ☎ 096 727 5952; tour per group 100B, tractor ride per person 20B; ⊙ departures 8am-4.30pm). The walking path through 'Heavenly Garden' requires a little climbing over rocks and through some caves and it crosses several metal walkways. The guided trip takes about 90 minutes and you should bring a torch, though you can get through without one. If no one is around when you arrive, ask someone in the village to call a guide.

If you want to stay the night, **Chatikorn Resort** (☎ 086 249 0946; d/f 900/2500B; P ❄ ✳), along the main road just before the turn to Suan Hin Pha Ngam, has seven tidy, widely spaced bungalows.

Wat Noen Phra Nao Wanaram
BUDDHIST TEMPLE

(วัดเนินพระเนาวนาราม; Hwy 212; ☉daylight hours) **FREE** This forest wát on the south side of town is a respected *vipassana* (insight meditation) centre on pleasant, tree-shaded grounds. Most of the extremely ornate temple architecture, covered with stencil and mosaic, stands in contrast with the usual ascetic tone of forest monasteries. There are many Vietnamese graves here, and some of the statuary would fit right in at Sala Kaew Ku (p380).

Nong Khai Museum
MUSEUM

(พิพิธภัณฑ์ทั้งหวัดหนองคาย; Th Meechai; ☉8.30am-4pm Mon-Fri) **FREE** This small museum in the former city hall has little more than old photographs, but there's just enough English labelling to make it worth a few minutes of your time, and the price is right.

🏃 Activities

Healthy Garden
MASSAGE

(☎042 423323; Th Banthoengjit; Thai/foot massage per hour 170/200B; ☉8am-8pm) For the most effective treatment in Nong Khai, this place has foot massage and traditional Thai massage in air-conditioned rooms.

Pantrix Yoga
HEALTH & WELLBEING

(www.pantrix.net; Soi Mutmee) Pantrix offers week- and month-long yoga courses (they are not live-in) for serious students by experienced teachers. There's also a free daily yoga session from 2pm to 3pm.

✸ Festivals & Events

During **Songkran** (☉mid-Apr) the priceless image of Luang Po Phra Sai from Wat Pho Chai is paraded around town.

Like many other cities in the northeast, Nong Khai has a **rocket festival** (*bun bâng fai;* ☉late May/early Jun), which begins on Visakha Bucha day.

At the end of Buddhist Lent (Ork Phansaa) in late October/early November, there are **long-boat races** on the Mekong. These correspond with the October full moon, which is when naga fireballs can be seen.

One particularly fun event is Nong Khai's version of the **Chinese Dragon Festival** (☉usually Nov), held over 10 days, with dragon dancing, acrobatics, Chinese opera and lots of firecrackers.

The **Anusahwaree Prap Haw Festival** (☉5-15 Mar) boasts the city's biggest street fair.

🛏 Sleeping

Catering to the steady flow of backpackers, Nong Khai's budget lodging selection is the best in Isan, and there are many good midrangers too.

E-San Guesthouse
GUESTHOUSE $

(☎086 242 1860; 538 Soi Srikhunmuang; r with fan & shared bathroom 250B, with air-con 450B; **P** ❄ 🖥) Just off the river in a small, beautifully restored wooden house ringed by a long verandah, this is an atmospheric place for backpackers to stay. The air-con rooms in a new building are fine, though they lack the character of the original house. Bikes are free. There are two other wooden guesthouses on the same street.

Khiangkhong Guesthouse
HOTEL $

(☎042 422870; Th Rimkhong; r with fan/air-con 400/500B; **P** ❄ 🖥) Catch a refreshing breeze and snag some river views from the 3rd-floor terrace (and some of the rooms) at this family-run concrete tower that falls between guesthouse and hotel. Bicycles are free.

Sawasdee Guesthouse
GUESTHOUSE $

(☎042 420259, 081 596 2924; www.sawasdeeguesthouse.com; 402 Th Meechai; d & tw 500-550B, with fan & shared bathroom 280B; **P** ❄ @ 🖥) If you could judge a hotel by its cover, this charismatic guesthouse in an old Franco-Chinese shophouse would come up trumps. The rooms lack the oldschool veneer of the exterior and lobby, but they're tidy and fairly priced. Rooms are set around an open courtyard that's great for lounging. Bicycles are 40B per day, motorbikes 250B.

★ Mut Mee

Garden Guesthouse
GUESTHOUSE $$

(☎042 460717; www.mutmee.com; Soi Mutmee; r 200-1650B; ❄ 🖥) Nong Khai's budget classic has a riverfront garden so relaxing it's intoxicating, and most nights it's packed with travellers. Mut Mee caters to many budgets, with a huge variety of rooms (the cheapest with shared bathroom, the most expensive with an awesome balcony) clustered around a thatched-roof lounge, where owner Julian freely shares his wealth of knowledge about the area.

Ban Sai Thong
GUESTHOUSE $$

(☎081 975 6451; Soi Srikhunmuang 2, Th Rimkhong; r incl breakfast 600B; **P** ❄) Though it's a modern building, the all-wood construction

GREAT BALLS OF FIRE

Methane gas? Drunken Lao soldiers? Clever monks? Or perhaps the fiery breath of the sacred *naga*, a legendary serpent-like being that populates waterways throughout Southeast Asia. The sighting of the *bâng fai pá·yah·nâhk* (loosely translated, '*naga* fireballs') is an annual event along the Mekong River. Sometime in the early evening, at the end of the Buddhist Rains Retreat (usually October), small, reddish balls of fire shoot from the Mekong River and float 100 or so metres into the air before vanishing without a trace.

There are many theories about the fireballs. One, which aired on a Thai exposé-style TV program, claimed that Lao soldiers taking part in festivities on the other side of the Mekong were firing their rifles into the air. (The reaction to the TV program was a storm of protest from both sides of the river.) One bizarre suggestion is that a mixture of methane gas and phosphine, trapped below the mud on the river bottom, reaches a certain temperature at exactly that time of year and is released. Many simply assume that some monks have found a way to make a 'miracle'.

Curious Thais from across the country converge at various spots on the banks of the Mekong for the annual show. Special buses make the return trip to Nong Khai city during the event, and several hotels run their own buses, on which you'll get a guaranteed seat.

If you don't come with the right mindset, you'll likely be disappointed. The fireball experience is more than just watching a few small lights rise from the river; it's mostly about watching Thais watching a few small lights rise from the river. And even if the *naga* doesn't send his annual greeting on the day you come (it's sometimes delayed by a day due to the vagaries of calculating the arrival of the full moon), it'll be an interesting experience.

and large tiled roof give this nine-room hotel a bit of a historic atmosphere. The rooms are spacious and have verandahs with sitting areas in front. Bikes are free.

★**Pimali** RESORT $$$
(☏042 089725; www.pimali.org; s/d incl breakfast 1500/2000B; P❋🛜) 🍴 Pimali is a nonprofit organisation providing training for poor local youths (mostly orphans) in the hospitality industry. Its students manage four plush, fully stocked bungalows overlooking rice paddies, and a white-linen restaurant serving Thai, Isan and European food. It's deep in the countryside, 20km from the city; a one-way transfer costs 200B.

🍴 Eating

There are many restaurants in the Tha Sadet Market, and elsewhere along the promenade, that offer big river views.

Mae Ut VIETNAMESE $
(Th Meechai; mains 30-50B; ⊙10am-6pm) This little place, serving just four items, including fried spring rolls and *khâo gee·ab þahk mŏr* (fresh noodles with pork), is essentially grandma's kitchen. Look for the green building with tables under a silver awning and lots of potted plants. English is limited.

Daeng Namnuang VIETNAMESE $
(Th Rimkhong; mains 50-250B; ⊙8am-8pm; 🛜) This massive river restaurant has grown into an Isan institution, and hordes of out-of-towners head home with car boots and carry-on bags (there's an outlet at Udon Thani's airport) stuffed with their *năam neu·ang* (DIY pork spring rolls).

Sweet Cake & Coffee THAI $
(Th Meechai; mains 40-150B; ⊙6am-9pm; 🖉) It's hard to categorise this place, run by a sweet old lady who makes standard Thai dishes and also many international favourites such as baked cakes and banana pancakes. Enjoy the homely atmosphere for breakfast, lunch or dinner, or just a coffee (instant, brewed or traditional Thai).

Saap Lah THAI $
(Th Meechai; mains 25-150B; ⊙8.30am-7.30pm) For excellent *gài yâhng* (grilled chicken), *sôm·đam* (spicy green-papaya salad) and other Isan foods, follow your nose to this no-frills shop.

Hospital Food Court THAI $
(Th Meechai; mains 40-80B; ⊙6am-3pm) Don't be put off by the name – it isn't 'hospital food'. Located across from the hospital, this food court whips up Thai standards at low

prices. The food is delicious, there's plenty of choice and it's conveniently located near the most popular guesthouses in town.

★ Dee Dee Pohchanah   THAI $$

(1155/9 Th Prajak; mains 60-425B; ⊙11am-2am; 🛜) How good is Dee Dee? Just look at the dinner-time crowds. But don't be put off by them: despite having a full house every night, this open-air place is a well-oiled machine and you won't be waiting long.

Nakawari   THAI $$

(📞081 975 0516; Th Rimkhong; mains 50-480B; ⊙10am-9pm) Docked down below Mut Mee Garden Guesthouse (p382), this floating restaurant specialises in Thai and Isan fish dishes, and though the prices are a bit high, the quality is good. There's a one-hour sunset cruise most nights (80B; at least 10 guests needed before the cruise will go ahead) around 5pm or 5.30pm; order food at least 30 minutes before departure.

Drinking & Nightlife

There are several small bars along the river between Mut Mee Garden Guesthouse and Tha Sadet Market that cater to travellers and expats. For something truly Thai, follow the Mekong-hugging Th Rimkhong east past Tha Sadet Market and you'll pass a bevy of restaurants and bars, some earthy, some fashionable, churning out dinner and drinks. They're less convenient, but much better.

Shopping

Nong Khai Walking
Street Market   MARKET

(⊙4pm-10pm Sat) This weekly street festival featuring music, handmade items and food takes over the promenade every Saturday night. It's smaller, but far more pleasant than the similar Walking Street markets in Chiang Mai.

Village Weaver
Handicrafts   ARTS & CRAFTS

(📞042 422651; 1020 Th Prajak; ⊙8.30am-6pm) This place sells high-quality, handwoven fabrics and clothing (ready-made or made to order) that help fund development projects around Nong Khai. The *mát·mèe* cotton is particularly good here.

ⓘ Information

There are banks with extended opening hours at **Asawann** (Hwy 2) shopping centre.

Immigration (📞042 990935; Rte 2; ⊙8.30am-noon & 1-4.30pm Mon-Fri) One kilometre south of the Friendship Bridge. Offers Thai visa extensions.

Tourism Authority of Thailand (TAT; 📞042 421326; tat_nongkhai@yahoo.com; Hwy 2; ⊙8.30am-4.30pm) At the time of writing it was temporarily located in front of the old provincial hall at the end of Hwy 2, but was expected to return to its inconvenient location outside town in early 2018.

ⓘ GETTING TO LAOS: NONG KHAI TO VIENTIANE

Getting to the border If you already have your Lao visa, the easiest way to Vientiane is the direct bus from Nong Khai's bus terminal (55B, 1½ hours, six daily from 7.30am to 6pm). There's also a bus to Vang Vieng (270B, six hours, 9.40am). There's a 5B surcharge for tickets to Laos on weekends, holidays and the 7.30am and 6pm weekday services.

If you plan to get your visa at the border (6am to 10pm), take a túk-túk there – expect to pay 100B from the bus station or 60B from the town centre. Unless you're travelling in a large group, there's no good reason to use a visa service agency, so don't let a driver take you to one.

You can also go to Laos by train (there are immigration booths at both stations), though it doesn't go through to Vientiane, so this is not recommended. The 15-minute ride (20B to 30B, departs 7.30am and 2.45pm) drops you in Thanaleng (aka Dongphasay) station just over the bridge, leaving you at the mercy of túk-túk drivers who charge extortionate prices.

At the border After getting stamped out of Thailand, you can take the buses (15B to 20B) that carry passengers across the bridge to the hassle-free, but sometimes busy, Lao immigration checkpoint, where 30-day visas are available.

Moving on It's about 20km to Vientiane. Plenty of buses, túk-túk and taxis will be waiting for you, and it's easy to find fellow travellers to share the costs.

Nongkhai Hospital (☎ 042 413456; Th Meechai; ☺24hr) Has a 24-hour casualty department.

ℹ Getting There & Away

AIR

The nearest airport is 55km south in Udon Thani. **Udon Kaew Tour** (☎ 042 411530; Th Pranang Cholpratan; ☺8.30am-5.30pm) travel agency runs minivans (200B per person) to/from the airport. Coming into town it'll drop you at your hotel or the bridge; going back you need to get yourself to its office. It's best to buy tickets in advance.

BUS

Nong Khai bus terminal (☎ 042 421246) is located just off Th Prajak, about 1.5km from the main pack of riverside guesthouses. Although there's only one direct bus to Nakhon Phanom, you can also get there in stages via Bueng Kan or Udon Thani.

There are also vans departing from the border/bridge (they park next to the 7-Eleven) to Udon Thani (50B, hourly, 7am to 7pm): some go to the old bus station and some go to Central Shopping Mall.
Nakhonchai Air (☎ 042 420285) has the best bus service between Nong Khai and Bangkok.

TRAIN

One daytime and three evening express trains connect Bangkok (3rd/1st-class seats from 223/607B, 1st-class sleeper upper/lower 1157/1357B, 11½ hours) and **Nong Khai train**

station (☎042 411637, nationwide 1690; www.railway.co.th), which is 2km west of the city centre.

ℹ Getting Around

Nong Khai is a great place for cycling due to the limited traffic and the nearby countryside. Many guesthouses let you use their bikes for free. If you need to hire one, **Khun Noui** (☎081 975 4863; Th Kaew Worawut; ☺8am-4pm), who sets up on the roadside across from the entrance to **Mut Mee** (p382), has reliable bikes (50B per day) and motorcycles (200B); if he's not there, any of the túk-túk drivers parked nearby will give him a call and he'll be right over.

You can find metered taxis at the bus station and the bridge. Generally, people agree on a price rather than use the meter. A túk-túk between the Mut Mee area and the bus station or the bridge will cost about 60B and 100B respectively for two people.

Sangkhom
สังคม

POP 3500

The little town of Sangkhom, facing the Lao island of Don Klang Khong, makes a great rest stop for those following the Mekong between Nong Khai and Loei. Staring at the lovely scenery tends to dominate visitors' time here, but there are also some wonderful attractions around town.

NORTHEASTERN THAILAND SANGKHOM

BUSES TO/FROM NONG KHAI

DESTINATION	FARE (B)	DURATION (HR)	FREQUENCY
Bangkok	329-658	10-11	frequent in late afternoon & early evening, hourly during the day
Bangkok (Suvarnabhumi International Airport)	428	9-10	8pm
Bueng Kan (van)	140	2½	every 45min 6am-5.50pm
Chiang Mai	750-820	12	7pm
Kanchanaburi	495	12	7pm
Khon Kaen	120-155	3½-4	hourly 7am-6pm
Loei	140	7-8	7.30am
Nakhon Phanom	200	7-8	11am
Nakhon Ratchasima	257-409	6	hourly 6am-8.45pm
Sangkhom	60	3	7.30am, 11am, 3pm
Udon Thani (van)	50	1	frequent 5.30am-7pm

◉ Sights

There are some beautiful waterfalls in the surrounding area. Three-tiered **Nam Tok Than Thip** (น้ำตกธารทิพย์; ⊘daylight hours) **FREE**, 13km west of Sangkhom (2km off Rte 211), is the largest waterfall in the area. The lower level drops 30m and the second level, easily reached on stairs, falls 100m. The 70m top drop is barely visible through the lush forest. **Nam Tok Than Thong** (น้ำตกธารทอง; Rte 211; ⊘daylight hours) **FREE**, 12km east of Sangkhom, is a waterfall with a wide short drop and a swimmable pool at the bottom. Than Thong (near the highway) is more accessible than Than Thip, but can be rather crowded on weekends and holidays. Bear in mind that, like most Isan waterfalls, these are seasonal. Both are at full flow around July to September and dry up by February.

Wat Pha Tak Sua
BUDDHIST TEMPLE

(วัดผาตากเสื้อ; off Rte 211; ⊘6am-6pm) **FREE**
The forest wát peering down on the town lies just 2km away as the crow flies, but it's 19km to drive. Once a very serious meditation temple, it's now highly commercialised, with crowds coming up for the amazing Mekong views, which can be seen from a glass-bottomed 'sky walk.' In the cold season you might see the valley filled with fog early in the morning.

An overgrown footpath once used by the monks every morning to collect alms (they're now driven to town) begins east of town just before the Km 81 pillar. Follow Soi 5 past the last house, then veer right by the mango and papaya trees.

Din Phiang Cave
CAVE

(ถ้ำดินเพียง; per group 100B; ⊘6am-6pm) Thirteen kilometres past the road to Wat Pha Tak Sua is an interesting cave that many locals believe is the home of a *naga* king. If you can speak Thai you'll hear some fanciful stories. Guides lead a 30-minute route with lights or a two-hour route (not possible in the rainy season) using torches (flashlights). On both you'll need to manoeuvre through some small, wet passages – and you can't wear shoes.

⊨ Sleeping & Eating

As a growing tourist destination, Sangkhom has several decent places to sleep, some good restaurants, and plenty of street food.

Bouy Guesthouse
GUESTHOUSE $

(☏042 441065, 091 050 7426; toy_bgh@hotmail.com; Rte 211; r with fan/air-con 250/500B; P✳@✿) As the ever-smiling owners will tell you, Sangkhom's veteran lodge has just a few 'simple huts', but they're popular for good reason. The thatch-built fan-cooled ones come with hammocks and wooden decks, and the riverside location just west of town is wonderfully relaxing. The air-con bungalows in front lack charm and a view, but are priced fairly.

Bike/motorbike hire costs 50/200B and there's a restaurant, though it's not always open. River trips are available.

Sangkhom River View
HOTEL $$

(☏042 441088; Rte 211; r 600-1500B; P✳✿) This attractive set-up, featuring wooden walkways and decorative stonework, will satisfy those who demand a certain level of comfort. Many rooms have river views, and the restaurant is good. It's 1.5km east of the town centre.

Tantawan
THAI, INTERNATIONAL $

(Rte 211; mains 40-250B; ⊘8am-9pm; ✿) The first choice for many visitors to Sangkhom because of the good food and big views. It offers all the expected Thai and Isan dishes (the Mekong River fish *lâhp* is recommended) plus a page of pastas.

ⓘ Getting There & Away

There are three rickety fan buses a day from Nong Khai (60B, three hours); the earliest of those, arriving in Sangkhom around 10.30am, continues to Loei (70B, four hours). There's no bus stop in town; wave buses down when they pass.

UDON THANI PROVINCE

Udon Thani Province is dominated by its flashy, congested and rather nondescript capital. It's the World Heritage–listed Ban Chiang, amazing Red Lotus Sea and mysterious Phu Phrabat that makes it a fascinating destination.

Udon Thani
อุดรธานี

POP 143,390

Udon Thani is a big, brash city with one of the largest expat populations in Thailand. The city boomed on the back of the Vietnam

War as the site of a large US airbase, and it subsequently became the region's primary transport hub and commercial centre. The town itself doesn't have any must-see attractions, but there are some tremendously interesting spots around it.

◉ Sights

Nong Prajak Park   PARK
(สวนสาธารณะหนองประจักษ์) Udon's most popular park starts to rev up as the afternoon winds down. It's home to many colourful attractions such as a giant Ban Chiang–style pot and a huge floating rubber ducky that has become an Udon icon. A lot of action takes place along Th Thesa on the sunset-watching side of the lake where there are many restaurants, paint-your-own-pottery shops, and streetside **massage** (Th Thesa; per hour 180B; ⊘ 8am-10pm) artists. There's a bike-hire (p392) shop on the northeast shore.

Sanjao Pu-Ya   TEMPLE
(ศาลเจ้าปู่ย่า; Th Nittayo; ⊘ daylight hours) FREE This large Chinese temple on the southern shore of Nong Bua lake attests to the wealth of the local Thai-Chinese community. At its heart, the Pu-Ya Shrine houses small images of the Chinese gods Pu (Grandpa) and Ya (Grandma).

The **Udon Thani Thai-Chinese Cultural Center** (ศูนย์วัฒนธรรมไทย-จีน; Th Nittayo; ⊘ 9am-7pm) FREE is in front of the temple.

Udon Sunshine Orchid Farm   GARDENS
(สวนกล้วยไม้อุดรซันไฌน์; ☎ 085 747 4144; Th Gamon Patana; ⊘ 8am-5pm Mon-Sat, 3-5pm Sun) FREE The Udon Sunshine Orchid Farm, just northwest of town, earned fame for producing the first orchid-based perfume. It has since developed a hybrid of *Codariocalyx motorius ohashi leguminosae*, a succulent that 'dances' to music. If you sing or talk to the plant in a high-pitched voice (saxophone or violin works even better), a few of its smaller leaves will shift back and forth. It's no hype; we've seen it ourselves, although it's more of a waltz than a jig.

The plants are most active from November to February and from 7am to 9.30am and 4.30pm to 6.30pm. The plants aren't for sale, but you can buy Udon Dancing Tea (now very popular for its supposed medical benefits; each batch sells out quickly), made from the plant, along with the Miss Udon Sunshine orchids and perfumes. The nursery also makes Udon Toob Moob Maeng

Kaeng, a perfume derived from brown stink bugs.

To get here, go under the 'Welcome to Nongsamrong Community' sign on Rte 2024, then after 150m follow the 'Udon Sunshine Fragrant Orchid' sign. *Sŏrng·tǎa·ou* 6 and the Yellow Bus get you close to it. A round-trip túk-túk ride from Udon's city centre should cost about 150B.

Ho Chi Minh Historical Site   MUSEUM
(แหล่งประวัติศาสตร์โฮจิมินห์; ⊘ 8am-4pm) FREE During 1928 and 1929, Ho Chi Minh used the jungle around Nong Hang village as one of his bases to train soldiers and rally Isan's sizeable Vietnamese community for his resistance against the French occupation of Vietnam. This is a replica of his thatched-roof, mud-wall house, plus a very modest museum about his life.

✯ Festivals & Events

For the first 15 days of December, Udon celebrates the **Thung Si Meuang Fair**, with Isan cultural performances and all the usual shopping and eating. The Pu and Ya statues from Sanjao Pu-Ya spend the first 10 days in a temporary temple in Thung Si Meuang park. The transfers on 1 and 10 December are grand processions accompanied by a 99m-long dragon. There's also dragon dancing on 5 December.

🛏 Sleeping

Oldie & Sleepy Hostel   HOSTEL $
(☎ 088 697 9406; oldie.sleepy.hostel@gmail.com; Th Adunyadet; dm incl breakfast 200-250B; ❄ 🛜) The rooms are simple, as you'd expect at this price, but the whole package combines to make a fantastic place to stay. Pear and Thong's hospitality, and chill nights hanging out in the eclectic, jazz-infused lounge lead some guests to extend their stays. There's a kitchen and free-flowing travel advice.

Pakdee House   HOTEL $
(☎ 080 461 9600; Th Thepburi; r 400B; 🅿 ❄ 🛜) A clean, well-run place that's the clear pick of the pack of several other similarly priced hotels in this area. And though it's not exactly central, one of its best features is the neighbourhood full of university students and local restaurants.

Ban Pannarai   HOTEL $
(☎ 042 304001; Th Poniyom; r with fan/air-con 300/440B; 🅿 ❄ 🛜) In contrast to most

Udon Thani

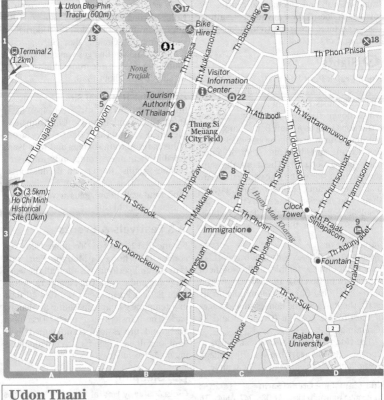

NORTHEASTERN THAILAND UDON THANI

cheapie hotels in Thailand, this bright yellow building set back off the street has some

actual character. It could use some new mattresses, but if you want to stay near the lake

random splashes of colour to craft a unique design. The backyard restaurant and pool area is another nice touch. There's free airport pick-up and drop-off.

Centara
HOTEL $$$

(☏042 343555; www.centarahotelsresorts.com; Th Prajak Sinlapacom; incl breakfast r 2270-3370B, ste 4770-8400B; P❋@❡☀) This large, full-service hotel makes a good impression with an attractive lobby and attentive staff. The quality continues in the rooms (except for the terrible 'standard' rooms, which are windowless and musty), which are stationed around a cavernous courtyard that is eerily quiet and strangely attractive, almost like a set from a sci-fi movie.

✘ Eating

Udonites take their night markets very seriously. The three adjoining markets in front of the train station, **Centre Point** (⊙4pm-10pm), **Preecha** (⊙4pm-10pm) and UD Bazaar, offer an impressive spread of food. Also, the sheer number of expats means there's a lot of Western food available in town.

★ UD Bazaar
THAI, INTERNATIONAL $

(Th Prajak Sinlapacom; ⊙11am-11pm) This lively place is the largest of Udon Thani's many night markets, and also the one offering the most varied cuisine. There's a stage for live music as well. A few shops serve lunch, but most get going about 4pm.

Phetkasem
THAI $

(Th Adunyadet; mains 78-358B; ⊙6pm-midnight; ❡) This garden restaurant is the kind of place where groups of friends come to eat, drink and eat some more. The menu covers the usual Thai and Isan options plus some less common ones like *plah nêung búay* (steamed fish in Chinese plum sauce) and *lâhp mah·mâh*, a fun version of this classic Isan dish using instant noodles instead of the usual meat.

Desserts
THAI $

(Th Naresuan; mains 55-95B; ⊙9am-3pm; ❡) This is not your ordinary Thai restaurant. Dishes such as *kôw klúk gà·pì* (rice with shrimp paste) and massaman curry are done with no short-cuts or skimping. It also does salads, and *kŏrng wăhn ruam·mít* for dessert; go to the counter and choose up to five ingredients to put in chilled coconut milk.

on a budget, this is a good choice. Bicycles for hire cost 20B per hour.

★ Jamjuree Home
GUESTHOUSE $$

(☏042 241727, 087 951 7940; 10/9 Benjang Rd; r incl breakfast 950-1290B; P❂❋@❡) The home part of the name is literally true as your hosts live on the ground floor of this fantastic four-room guesthouse. Rooms are modern and cosy and solid contenders for cleanest in all of Thailand. The two largest have kitchenettes. Though it's not the most tourist-friendly location, there are many good restaurants around and it's only a 10-minute walk to Nong Prajak lake (p387). Free bikes are available.

Much-che Manta
HOTEL $$

(☏042 245222; www.much-chemanta.com; Th Makkang; r incl breakfast 900-5000B; P❂❋ @❡☀) A lovely boutique hotel that uses creative lighting, plenty of real wood and

WORTH A TRIP

RIVERSIDE VILLAGE

If you're travelling from Nong Khai to Bueng Kan, Ban Ahong, a pretty riverside village 20km before Bueng Kan, makes a nice stop along the way. **Wat Ahong Silawat** (วัดอาฮงศิลาวาส; Rte 212; ⊙daylight hours) FREE, 20km west of the capital along Rte 212, is built amid ruddy boulders at a river bend known as Sàdeu Námkong (the Mekong River's Navel) because of the whirlpools that spin here from June to September. A 7m-tall copy of Phitsanulok's Chinnarat Buddha gazes over the Mekong from next to the simple little bòht (ordination hall). This is considered a highly auspicious spot to spend the evening of wan òrk pan·săh, the end of the Buddhist Rains Retreat, because bâng fai pá·yah·nâhk (naga fireballs) were first reported here. Legend claims it's the deepest spot along the river, and there are many stories about underwater caves where the naga live.

⭐ **Samuay & Sons**　　　　THAI $$
(Th Phon Phisai; mains 79-280B; ⊙11am-2.30pm & 5-9.30pm Tue-Sun; 🖥) This small chef-driven, open-kitchen place is Isan's version of a trendy Soho bistro. It does some Thai and Isan standards like panang curry and om curry with algae, but sets itself apart with fusion dishes and modern twists on old recipes such as tapioca shrimp balls and coconut milk duck confit with mango jam.

⭐ **Grey Cabin**　　　INTERNATIONAL, THAI $$
(Th Sinchaithani; mains 80-285B; ⊙10am-9pm; 🖥) There are many restaurants serving fa·ràng food in the Central Plaza/Soi Farang area, but we far prefer this small mother-and-daughter operation 2km south of Nong Prajak lake. The varied options, all fresh and delicious, include maple mustard glazed salmon, chicken pesto pasta, apple and brie salad, an artery-clogging three-cheese grilled cheese, seafood ramen and Thai mushroom salad.

⭐ **Rabiang Phatchanee**　　　THAI $$
(Th Suppakitchanya; mains 60-380B; ⊙10am-11pm; ❄🖥) This place on the lake's east shore offers all the usual Thai dishes, but also many you've probably never tried, such

as fish-stomach salad, and fried duck with crab in gravy. Eat outdoors on the deck or in air-conditioned dining rooms. When ordering, take note that many of the menu prices are 'per 100g' (ขีดละ).

Good Everything　　　INTERNATIONAL, THAI $$$
(Th Poniyom; mains 170-690B; ⊙10am-10pm; 🖥🚲) This white cottage and surrounding garden feels transported from the English countryside. It features fresh and healthy cuisine, such as salmon with spinach, roasted pumpkin soup, and fa·ràng-style salads, plus quality coffees and teas. It's one of Udon's most expensive restaurants, but the many regulars consider it money well spent.

🍷 Drinking & Nightlife

Udon has the largest and most in-your-face sex-tourism scene in Isan, and the Th Sampanthamit area (sometimes called 'Soi Falang') is rather sleazy at night – even in the day you'll have to endure 'Hallo, massaaaage'. That said, there are several foreigner-focused businesses here that are not a part of this scene.

Udon Thani's busiest nightlife area fronts the train station. Many of the bars here are sleazy, but far from all. Nearby Phetkasem (p389) is a chill alternative. Also, the three night markets offer a range of diversions besides dining. You can shop for clothes, sing karaoke, play snooker, get a tattoo, have your fortune told and listen to live bands.

🔒 Shopping

Udon's biggest shopping centre is **Central Plaza** (Th Prajak Sinlapacom; ⊙10.30am-9pm Mon-Fri, 10am-9pm Sat & Sun), but strolling the open-air **UD Town** (Th Thongyai; ⊙8am-11pm) is more fun.

Udon Bho-Phin Trachu　　　ARTS & CRAFTS
(📞 042 245618; www.udonbhophin-thaisilk.com; Th Poniyom; ⊙7.30am-6pm) There's a great selection of silk and cotton, including some natural-dyed fabrics, at this large spot northwest of Nong Prajak Lake. Look for the big sign with the wooden roof.

Udon City Walking Street　　　MARKET
(Th Athibodi & Th Panpraw; ⊙5pm-10pm Fri & Sat) With just a handful of the hundreds of vendors selling handmade items, Udon's Walking Street doesn't rise to the level of the markets in Chiang Mai and Khon Kaen that

inspired it, but it's still fun and it has good food

ⓘ Information

The free *Udon Thani Map* (www.udonmap.com) and its companion magazine, the *Udon Thani Guide*, are mostly geared towards expats, but are helpful for travellers, too. They're available free at hotels, the airport and *fa·ràng*-focused businesses.

Immigration (☑ 042 249982; Th Phosri; ☉8.30am-noon & 1-4.30pm Mon-Fri) Does visa extensions.

Visitor Information Center (☑ 085 010 3837; ☉8am-5pm Sun-Thu, to 6pm Fri & Sat; ☎) Has information for all of Udon Thani province.

Bangkok Hospital (☑ 042 343111; Th Thong-yai; ☉24hr) The best medical facility in Udon Thani.

Central Plaza and **UD Town** have extended-hour banks.

Tourist Police (☑ 042 211291; Th Naresuan)

ⓘ Getting There & Away

AIR

THAI Smile (☑ 042 246697, nationwide 1181; www.thaismileair.com; ☉7.30am-7pm) connects Udon Thani to Bangkok through Suvarnabhumi airport, while **Air Asia** (☑ nationwide 02 515 9999; www.airasia.com; ☉7am-9pm), **Thai Lion Air** (☑ 025 299999; www.lionairthai.com; ☉6am-8pm) and **Nok Air** (☑ nationwide 02 900 9955; www.nokair.com; ☉6.15am-7.30pm) use Don Muang Airport. Each flies four or five times daily and prices start around 900B one way. There are also daily direct flights to Chiang Mai (Nok), Hat Yai (Thai Lion), Phuket (Air Asia) and Pattaya (Air Asia). Buy tickets at **On Time**

(☑ 042 247792; ontimethailand@gmail.com; Th Sai Uthit; ☉8am-5pm Mon-Sat, 9am-3pm Sun), one of several travel agencies near Bus Terminal 1.

Some hotels pick guests up at the airport for free; otherwise shuttle vans to the city centre cost 80B per person; tickets are sold at the 'Limousine Service' counter.

Despite the name, there are no international flights at **Udon Thani International Airport** (☑ 042 244426), but there's talk of flights to China coming soon.

BUS

Most buses and minivans use Udon's slightly chaotic **Bus Terminal 1** (☑ 042 221916; Th Sai Uthit) in the heart of town. **Nakhonchai Air** (☑ 1624) has the best VIP service to Bangkok. For Nong Khai, note that some minivans departing here go to the bus station, while others go to the border bridge. Also, most Nong Khai vehicles stop to pick up passengers at Rangsina Market north of downtown on their way out of Udon. For the buses to Laos, you must already have a Lao visa to buy a ticket, and there's a 5B surcharge for the 6pm weekday departure and for all buses on weekends and holidays.

Almost next door to Bus Terminal 1 is the **Central Plaza Van Station** (Th Prajak Sinlap-acom), with minivans to Nong Khai (50B, one hour, every 30 minutes 6am to 8pm), Bueng Kan (190B, 3½ hours, every 30 minutes 5am to 7pm) and Roi Et (150B, four hours, every 30 minutes 5am to 5.40pm) via Khon Kaen (80B, two hours), and buses to Chiang Mai (545B, 12 hours, 12.45pm, 5.45pm, 6.45pm, 8.45pm), Nakhon Phanom (221B, three hours, 5.15am, 5.30am, 10pm) and Roi Et (139B to 150B, 4½ hours, every 30 minutes 6am to 5pm) via Khon Kaen (76B to 80B, 2½ hours).

BUSES & MINIVANS TO/FROM UDON THANI (TERMINAL 1)

DESTINATION	FARE (B)	DURATION (HR)	FREQUENCY
Bangkok	454-605	8-10	every 30min
Bueng Kan	208	4	hourly 4.10am to 4.10pm
Khon Kaen	76-120	2½	frequent 5am to 4.50pm
Khon Kaen (minivan)	80	2	frequent 6am to 8pm
Nakhon Phanom	147-200	4	every 45min 4.30am to 4.20pm
Nong Khai (minivan)	50	1	every 30min 6am-8pm
Pattaya	441-636	11	hourly 4.30am-9pm
Suvarnabhumi Airport	392	8	9pm
Vientiane (Laos)	80	2	8 departures 8am-6pm
Vang Vieng (Laos)	320	7	8.30am

BAN CHIANG CRAFTS

Rice farming remains Ban Chiang's primary livelihood, but selling souvenirs now comes a close second. Some of the items, including Ban Chiang–style pottery, are made in the area. Walk down the road facing the museum or the little Soi OTOP market just east of the museum to find a couple of **pottery painting workshops**, though they don't keep regular hours. Just south of the **Tai Phuan House** (บ้านไทพวน) is a small **women's weaving group** (กลุ่มทอผ้าฝ้ายย้อมครามบ้านเชียง ส.หงษ์แดง; ☑ 086 221 2268; ⊗ 9am-5pm) **FREE** that mostly weaves indigo cotton.

Bus Terminal 2 (☑ 042 214914) on the western ring road has few buses, mostly only for western cities such as Loei (90B to 115B, 2½ hours, every 30 minutes 4.50am to 5.50pm), Phitsanulok (311B to 493B, seven hours, every two hours 7.30am to 8.50pm) and Chiang Mai (760B, 12 hours, 7.15am, 2.30pm, 7.15pm, 8.30pm).

TRAIN

There are four daily trains between Bangkok (seat 95B to 457B, 1st-class sleeper upper/lower 1117/1317B, 9½ to 11 hours) and **Udon Thani train station** (☑ 042 222061), three departing in the early evening and one in the early morning. Five trains head to Nong Khai (11B to 48B, 45 minutes to one hour) throughout the day.

ⓘ Getting Around

Sŏrng·tăa·ou (10B) run regular routes across town. Route 6 (white) is handy since it runs up and down Th Udondutsadi (with a convenient detour to the Th Prajak-Surakarn junction), past Rangsina Market and out to Bus Terminal 2. There are also two infrequent city buses (10B). The White Bus follows Th Udondutsadi, while the Yellow Bus tracks Th Phosri-Nittayo, connecting the two bus terminals in the process. The *Udon Thani Map* (www.udonmap.com) shows all bus and *sŏrng·tăa·ou* routes.

You can rarely flag a **taxi** (☑ 042 244554, 042 343239) down on the street, but they park at Bus Terminal 1, Central Plaza and the airport. Drivers don't use meters. Túk-túk (called 'skylab' here) are seemingly everywhere. The cost from Central Plaza to Nong Prajak Park is usually 60B.

Lek Car Rental (☑ 086 059 3028; www.lekcarrentaludonthani.com) is a reputable local company, and there are many smaller ones around Central Plaza. **Avis** (☑ 089 969 8678;

www.avisthailand.com; Udon Thani International Airport; ⊗ 7am-9pm), **Thai Rent A Car** (☑ 082 668 5057; www.thairentacar.com; Udon Thani International Airport; ⊗ 6.30am-9pm) and the other big-name car-hire companies have branches at the airport.

Bike hire (1-/2-/3-seater per hour 20/40/50B; ⊗ 10am-8pm Mon-Fri, 8am-8pm Sat-Sun) is available on the northeast shore of the lake in Nong Prajak Park.

Ban Chiang บ้านเชียง

POP 5049

What's now one of Southeast Asia's most important archaeological finds, Ban Chiang was brought to the world's attention accidentally in 1966 when a sociology student from Harvard tripped while walking through the area and found the rim of a buried pot right under his nose. Looking around he noticed many more and speculated that this might be a burial site. He was right. Serious excavations began soon after and a treasure trove of artefacts and dozens of human skeletons were unearthed. The museum is one of Thailand's best and one excavation site is left open.

Ban Chiang was declared a Unesco World Heritage site in 1992.

⊙ Sights

Ban Chiang National Museum MUSEUM
(พิพิธภัณฑสถานแห่งชาติบ้านเชียง; 150B; ⊗ 9am-4pm Tue-Sun) This excellent museum, developed with some assistance from the Smithsonian Institution, exhibits a wealth of pottery from all Ban Chiang periods, plus myriad spearheads, sickles, fish hooks, ladles, neck rings and other metal objects. The displays (with English labels) offer excellent insight into the region's distant past, though note that dates shown have all been revised to more recent ones by archaeologists based on new information, and the museum has chosen not to fix them.

**Wat Pho Si Nai
Burial Site** ARCHAEOLOGICAL SITE
(หลุมขุดค้นทางโบราณคดีวัดโพธิ์ศรีใน; Included with museum ticket, free on Mondays; ⊗ 8.30am-6pm) One kilometre east of the Ban Chiang National Museum, this is the largest of the burial grounds excavated in the town and the only one kept open for tourism. It has a cluster of 52 individual bodies, most from the late period (300BC–200AD), buried with

pottery. Due to flooding, the whole site is now a replica (the skeletons are made of resin) but they did an excellent job and you probably wouldn't know it if we hadn't told you.

Sleeping & Eating

Lakeside Sunrise Guesthouse GUESTHOUSE $
(📞080 433 4300; banmai167@hotmail.com; r with/without bathroom 500/400B; 🅿🌀🛜) In a countryside setting, yet within easy striking distance of the museum, this old wooden house is reason enough to spend the night in town. The six simple rooms share a spacious verandah. Reservations are rarely needed, but it's best to call ahead to be sure the joyful owner, who speaks good English, will be at home when you arrive.

Krua Fah Nao THAI $
(mains 35-120B; ⊘8am-4pm) The 'Cold Sky Kitchen', just west of the museum entrance, does Thai standards quite well.

ⓘ Getting There & Away

From Udon Thani, take a bus bound for Sakon Nakhon or Nakhon Phanom and get off at Ban Nong Mek (35B, 45 minutes, every 30 minutes), where túk-túk charge 200B to take one or two people the 8km to Ban Chiang and come back.

Red Lotus Sea ทะเลบัวแดง

Really, it's a pink water lily lake, but you'll see pictures of the **Red Lotus Sea** (Kumphawapi District) all over Udon. It's now one of Isan's top attractions, but few Westerners make it there. You need to hire a boat (300B to 500B for up to 10 people) to go out into the middle of the lake to see the bloom, and the earlier the better as the flowers start to close up around 10.30am and are completely shut by noon.

The season depends on Mother Nature, but it generally starts late October and lasts to the end of February; January is often, but not always, the peak time. The main access point to Nong Han, the lake's actual name, is 40km southeast of Udon city in Ban Diam; there are so many road signs for it that it's impossible for drivers not to find it. There's no public transportation, but half-day trips (499B per person) depart from McDonald's at UD Town (p390) at 6.30am. Confirm details at your hotel or call the local **TAT office** (📞042 240616; tatu-

don@tat.or.th; Th Thesa; ⊘8.30am-4.30pm) for information as details change year to year.

SPECTACULAR CAVE SHRINE

High up in a beautiful karst mountain, directly on the Loei–Nong Bualamphu border, **Tham Erawan** (ถ้ำเอราวัณ; ⊘8am-5pm) is an amazing cave shrine reached by a steep but easily climbed stairway of 600 steps. The cave, with a big Buddha statue at its mouth, is very large and a line of lights leads you through the massive chamber and out the other side of the mountain.

From roughly 11am to noon and again around 2pm to 3pm, a hole in the roof of the cave lets down shafts of sunlight, making for a spectacular atmosphere. Don't linger late in the afternoon as the monks are punctual about turning out the lights – we speak from experience.

Buses from Loei (42B, 1¼ hours, every 30 minutes) to Udon Thani will drop you at Ban Pha Wang on Rte 210, 2.5km away from the temple. No túk-túk park here, but it's a fairly pleasant walk.

Ban Na Kha บ้านนาข่า
POP 6364

Na Kha village, 16km north of Udon city, is an excellent fabric-shopping destination. There's a **covered market** (⊘7am-6pm) running through the centre of the village selling silk and cotton from here and beyond. **Mae Bah Pah Fai** (📞042 206104; ⊘8am-5.30pm), across from Wat Na Kha Taewee's entrance, has as good a selection as any, including some century-old *kít* hanging in the back.

The village also has two temples worth a peek. **Wat Na Kha Taewee** (วัดนาคาเทวี; ⊘daylight hours) FREE was established by a wandering monk who found a hole from which bellowed the sound and smoke of a *naga*. He plugged the hole with a rock and decided to settle here. The hole, sandwiched between the *ubosot* and the stupa, is now an important local shrine. Pottery and human skeletons unearthed during various construction projects at the temple are on display under the giant Buddha. **Wat Tung Toomkam** (วัดทุ่งตูมคำ; ⊘daylight hours) FREE, 700m southeast of the village, features some

---

WORTH A TRIP

TEMPLE DAY-TRIP

With brightly painted statuary that's even more bizarre than Nong Khai's **Sala Kaew Ku** (p380), **Wat Pho Chai Sri** (วัดโพธิ์ชัยศรี; ⊙daylight hours) is a perfect add-on to **Phu Phrabat** if you have your own transportation. The life-size figures around the temple grounds are acting out scenes from Isan fables and demonstrating the punishments awaiting the wicked in the Buddhist hell.

Also known as Wat Ban Waeng, the temple is about 5km out of Ban Phue. A túk-túk from town costs about 100B round-trip with waiting time.

The temple is also home to Luang Po Naak, a very holy 1200-year-old Buddha image shaded by a seven-headed *naga* that locals believe is responsible for many miracles. A giant version of it was under construction at the time of writing.

---

curious Buddhist art, including many Buddhas covered with coins.

A few vendors in the market sell local snacks such as grilled yam and *kôw jèe* (grilled sticky rice in an egg batter), but there's no lodging in the village.

Sŏrng·tăa·ou 3 (15B, 30 minutes) runs along Th Udondutsadi in Udon Thani city and up to Ban Na Kha, as does the much less frequent White Bus. Minivans headed between Udon Thani and Nong Khai will also drop you here, but you have to pay the full 50B fare.

Phu Phrabat Historical Park
อุทยานประวัติศาสตร์ภูพระบาท

No one really knows the history of this mysterious, mystical **park** (☑ 042 219837; 100B; ⊙ 8.30am-4.30pm) peppered with bizarre rock spires, whale-sized boulders and improbably balanced rocks. Phu Phrabat Historical Park is one of Isan's most compelling sights and experiences. In prehistoric times many of the rock formations were modified to form various religious functions. Buddhist *sema* stones from the Dvaravati era, presumably about 1000 to 1200 years ago, are plentiful, and the ground under some rocky overhangs has been painstakingly carved into smooth platforms. The Khmer later added some Hindu elements to the site.

In addition, prehistoric paintings on several rock overhangs, best seen at side-by-side Tham Wua and Tham Khon, show this was probably regarded as a holy site perhaps 3000 years ago.

⊙ Sights

The park's highlight is **Hor Nang Usa**, an overturned-boot-shaped outcrop with a shrine built into it. Nearby is **Bo Nang Usa**, a man-made reservoir carved 5m deep into solid rock. Many of these rock formations are signposted with names that allude to the local legend of Princess Nang Usa and Prince Tao Baros – you can read the tale online at www.timsthailand.com/nang-usa-story.

A climb beyond the rock formations to **Pha Sa Dej** cliff ends with vast views of the farms and forest beyond. A web of trails meanders past the many sites and you can see them all in a leisurely two hours, but it's worth spending several more. The remote northern trail loop has fewer sites along it.

South of the entrance is **Wat Phra Phutthabaht Bua Bok**, with its namesake Lao-style *chedi* covering a Buddha footprint. It also has rocks like those in the park, though not as big or interesting.

🛏 Sleeping & Eating

There are no longer any rooms available for the public, but **camping** (per person with own tent 20B, tent hire 50B) is still allowed. There's a simple noodle and rice shop at the site and a good Isan restaurant in Ban Tiu, the village at the base of the hill.

ℹ️ Getting There & Away

The park is 65km from both Udon Thani and Nong Khai and can be visited as a day trip from either city.

Sŏrng·tăa·ou from Nong Khai's bus station to Ban Phue (60B, 1½ hours, 7.30am, 8am, 8.30am) travel via Tha Bo. Vehicles from Udon's Rangsina Market continue past Ban Phue to Ban Tiu (*sŏrng·tăa·ou*/minivans 35/100B, two hours/1½ hours, hourly starting at 6am), the village at the base of the hill, from where a motorcycle taxi costs 100B return for the final 5km climb; it can take a while to find one.

Túk-túk from Ban Phue cost around 350B return and motorcycle taxis about half as much. The last vehicle back to Nong Khai leaves at 4pm and the last to Udon a little after 5pm.

BUENG KAN PROVINCE

Thailand's newest province split off from Nong Khai in 2011. It's remote and often lovely territory, and though most people travelling along the Mekong River out of Nong Khai head west, there are some real rewards for bucking the trend and heading east, including one of Thailand's most amazing temples.

Bueng Kan   บึงกาฬ

POP 4850

Little Bueng Kan city is a workaday town and most travellers only stop long enough to catch connecting transport to Wat Phu Thok (p397). The only thing that qualifies as an attraction is the **Thai-Lao Market** (ตลาด ไทย-ลาว; Soi Buengkan; ◑ 4am-1pm Tue & Fri). It's mostly the same goods found in regular Thai markets, but some Lao vendors bring forest products such as mushrooms and herbal remedies.

If you do decide to stay, quiet **Rachawadee Hotel** (◑ 042 492119; www.rachavadee hotel.com; Th Bungkan; r 450B; ⓟ ⊛ ❋ ⓦ), a block from the riverfront promenade, has the best budget rooms in town. Out on the highway, **The One** (◑ 042 492234; www.theone hotel-bk.com; Hwy 212; r incl breakfast 790-1700B, ste 2500B; ⓟ ⊛ ❋ @ ⓦ ⛾) offers excellent value and service for the price. There are many restaurants along the riverfront road.

Bueng Kan functions as the transport hub for the province, and its oversized **bus station** (◑ 042 491302; Hwy 212) is out on the highway east of town. Although there's only one direct bus to Nakhon Phanom each day (130B, four hours, 2pm), you can also make the trip in stages. Buses also reach Bangkok (511-804B, 13 hours, 6.30am & 7am, 12 departures 4.30-6.15pm), Nong Khai (120B, 2½-3 hours, 3pm) and Udon Thani (208B, four hours, hourly 5am-3pm). Regular minivans also travel to Nong Khai (140B, 2½ hours, every 40min 5.50am-5pm) and Udon Thani (190B, 3½ hours, every 30min 5am-7pm).

Phu Wua Wildlife Sanctuary   เขตรักษาพันธุ์สัตว์ป่าภูวัว

The 186-sq-km **Phu Wua Wildlife Sanctuary** (เขตรักษาพันธุ์สัตว์ป่าภูวัว; ◑ 081 260 1845; 100B) is one of Isan's biggest and best wildlife reserves. With lots of exposed bedrock and some tall hills, it has a rugged beauty. The forest has several large waterfalls only active during or just after the rainy season (July–September mainly) and more than 40 elephants. The elephants are rarely encountered by visitors, though chances are best near Ban Kham Pia village in the rainy season. There are also monkeys, barking deer and a fair number of bird species.

The biggest waterfalls, Namtok Chet Si ('Seven Colours Waterfall') and Namtok Tham Phra ('Monk Cave Waterfall'), are both east of Rte 3024, near Wat Phu Thok. Tham Phra waterfall is reached by a boat (8am to 4pm, per person 30B), and foreigners pay the inflated entry fee of 200B.

🏃 Activities

While the various waterfalls signposted from surrounding roads can be visited independently, going elsewhere requires a guide. The best way to do this is through **Bunloed's Huts** (◑ 087 861 0601; www.bunloedhuts. jimdo.com; s/d bungalows 300/360B, without bathroom 200/260B, s/d in tent 80/100B, meals 60-100B; ⓟ ⓦ), since not only are their trips good, but permission to hire park rangers as guides begins with getting a letter of permission from the Department of National Parks, Wildlife and Plant Conservation in Bangkok.

🛏 Sleeping & Eating

There's no visitor accommodation at Phu Wua. The village of Ban Kham Pia has a welcoming homestay very near the eastern edge of the reserve, and the nearby town of Bung Khla on a gorgeous stretch of the Mekong has some proper hotels, including **Mon Prasit Resort** (◑ 042 499147; r with fan 300B, with air-con 350-600B; ⓟ ❋ ⓦ). Bueng Kan is near enough to also serve as a base for a Phu Wua visit.

Food is available in any of the gateway towns, but not in the reserve itself, except for a few food vendors at Namtok Chet Si and Namtok Tam Phra in the rainy season.

ℹ Getting There & Away

Unless you're visiting while staying at Bunloed's Huts at Ban Kham Pia, you'll need your own transportation to visit Phu Wua, and formal motorcycle rental isn't available at either Bung Khla or Bueng Kan. It is available at Bunloed's.

The easiest way to get to Ban Kham Pia is the daily bus between Nong Khai (100B, 3½ to four hours) and Nakhon Phanom (130B, three to four hours), which will drop you at Ban Don Chik, 3km away. There are also hourly Bueng Kan–Ban Phaeng minivans (100B, 5.30am to 3.30pm) so you can get to Ban Kham Pia, which is halfway between the two, from Nong Khai in stages. Coming the other way, start with a minivan from Nakhon Phanom to Ban Phaeng (60B, 2½ hours, 12.30pm, 1.30pm, 2.30pm, 4pm).

NAKHON PHANOM PROVINCE

Lao and Vietnamese influences are strong in Nakhon Phanom, a province bordered by the Mekong and full of highly revered temples. It's a region of subtleties rather than can't-miss attractions, but there are plenty of fine river views and interesting historic sites, and the colossal Wat Phra That Phanom is one of the icons of Isan culture.

Nakhon Phanom   นครพนม

☑ 042 / POP 22,710

Nakhon Phanom means 'City of Mountains', but the undulating sugarloaf peaks all lie across the river in Laos, so you'll be admiring rather than climbing them. The views are fantastic, though, especially during a hazy sunrise.

Nakhon Phanom's temples have a distinctive style. This was once an important town in the Lan Xang Empire and, after that, Thai kings sent their best artisans to create new buildings. Later a vivid French influence crossed the Mekong and jumped into the mix.

◎ Sights & Activities

Ho Chi Minh House   MUSEUM
(บ้านโฮจิมินห์; ☑ 042 522430; Ban Na Chok; donations appreciated; ☺ daylight hours) FREE The best of the three Ho Chi Minh–related attractions in Ban Na Chok village, this is a replica of the simple wooden house where 'Uncle Ho' sometimes stayed in 1928 and 1929 while planning his resistance movement in Vietnam. A few of the furnishings are believed to be originals. It's a private affair in the back of a family home and they're very proud of it.

Former Governor's
Residence Museum   MUSEUM
(จวนผู้ว่าราชการจังหวัดนครพนม (หลังเก่า); Th Sunthon Wijit; adult/child 50/20B; ☺ 9am-5pm Wed-Sun) Museum Juan, as it's also known, fills

a beautiful restored 1925 mansion with photos of old Nakhon Phanom, many labelled in English. Out the back are detailed displays about the illuminated boat procession (Lai Reua Fai) and cooking utensils in the old kitchen. Bai-Tong, the gift shop's owner and artist, speaks excellent English and is a great source of local advice.

Ho Chi Minh Museum   MUSEUM
(พิพิธภัณฑ์ประธานโฮจิมินห์; Ban Na Chok; ☺ 7am-4pm) FREE This is the least visited but most educational of the three Ho Chi Minh–related attractions in Ban Na Chok village. Covering his whole life, it's mostly just pictures, but many have English labels. It's located at the cultural centre up behind the Ho Chi Minh Memorial.

Ho Chi Minh Memorial   MEMORIAL
(อนุสรณ์สถานประธานโฮจิมินห์; Ban Na Chok; ☺ 8am-5pm) FREE Aiming for the tour bus crowd, there's a tasteful shrine at the centre of this walled complex in Ban Na Chok village, but the fake mountain, souvenir shops and piped-in Vietnamese music lend a theme-park feel. And the replica of the house where 'Uncle Ho' stayed in 1928 and 1929 is far inferior to the village's other replica house.

Wat Okat   BUDDHIST TEMPLE
(วัดโอกาส; Th Sunthon Wijit; ☺ daylight hours) FREE Predating the town, Wak Okat is home to Phra Tiow and Phra Tiam, two sacred wooden Buddha images covered in gold that sit on the highest pedestal in the wíhăhn (sanctuary). The current Tiam (on the right) is a replica because the original was stolen in 2010. The amazing modern murals showing the story of Phra Tiow and Phra Tiam floating across the Mekong from Laos are among our favourites – see if you can find the backpackers.

Thesaban Sunset Cruise   BOATING
(☑ 086 230 5560; Th Sunthon Wijit; per person 50B) The city runs this hour-long Mekong River cruise on creaky old Thesaban, which docks across from the Indochina Market. Departure is about 5pm. Snacks and drinks are available.

✲ Festivals & Events

Nakhon Phanom is famous for its illuminated boat procession, Lai Reua Fai (☺ late Oct/early Nov). A modern twist on the ancient tradition of sending rafts loaded with food,

WAT PHU THOK วัดภูทอก

With its network of rickety staircases and walkways built in, on and around a giant sandstone outcrop, **Wat Phu Thok** (⊗ 6am-5pm, closed 10-16 Apr) FREE is one of the region's wonders. The precarious paths lead past shrines and *gù·dì* (monk's huts) that are scattered around the mountain on cliffs and in caves and provide fabulous views over the surrounding countryside. A final scramble up roots and rocks takes you to the forest on the summit, which is considered the 7th level. If you hustle and take all the short-cuts you can be up and down in about an hour, but we advise against it: this is a climb that should be savoured.

The quiet isolation entices monks and *mâa chee* (nuns) from all over Thailand to come and meditate here, so remember to be quiet and respectful as you explore.

Monastery founder Luang Pu Juan died in a plane crash in 1980, along with several other highly revered forest monks who were flying to Bangkok for Queen Sirikit's birthday celebration. A marble *chedi* containing Luang Pu Juan's belongings, some bone relics and fantastic exterior sculptures sits below the mountain amid a lovely garden.

Túk·túk in Bueng Kan ask 1000B (this is negotiable) for the return journey to Wat Phu Thok, including a few hours of waiting time. It's cheaper to take a bus from Bueng Kan to Siwilai (20B to 30B, 45 minutes), where túk·túk drivers will do the trip for 400B. If you catch an early bus to Bueng Kan, Wat Phu Thok can be visited as a day trip from Nong Khai, although there's no need to backtrack since you could also just catch one of the vans or buses running from Bueng Kan to Udon Thani.

If you're driving or cycling, continue past Bueng Kan for 27km until you reach Chaiyaphon, then turn right at Rte 3024, the road signed for Chet Si and several other waterfalls; these are in the **Phu Wua Wildlife Sanctuary** (p395) and make worthy detours, as much for the weird rocky landscape as for the cascades (there's only water mid-May through December). After 17.5km make a right and continue 4km more.

flowers and candles down the Mekong as offerings for the *naga*, today's giant bamboo rafts hold up to 20,000 handmade lanterns, and some designers add animation to the scenes. Boat races, music competitions and other festivities run for a week, but the boats are launched only on the night of the full moon.

🛏 Sleeping

More than most cities of its size, Nakhon Phanom has a lot of quality midrange hotels. In part due to gamblers playing their luck in Laos, it can sometimes be hard to snag a room on weekends.

SP Residence HOTEL $
(☑042 513505; Th Nittayo; r 450-800B; P🌸@🛜) Plain but modern, the rooms here are less institutional than the exterior and hallways would lead you to believe, and it's set back from the road, keeping it quiet, even though it's in the heart of town. And despite its age, it's in better shape than some newer hotels.

★**River Hotel** HOTEL $$
(☑042 522999; www.therivernakhonphanom. com; Th Sunthon Wijit; r 790-1490B, ste 2490B; P🛜🌸🛜) Nakhon Phanom's best hotel is on the riverfront about 1km south of the city. Stylish and modern, the River has plush rooms, solid service and big views. The quality-to-price ratio is higher here than anywhere else in town.

777 Hometel HOTEL $$
(Tong Jed Hometel; ☑042 514777; www.777home tel.com; Th Tamrongprasit; r incl breakfast 590-790B; P🌸@🛜) Don't let the boxy exterior put you off – inside are some fairly stylish rooms. It's well managed, priced right and has some of the friendliest staff in town.

Fortune View Kong Hotel HOTEL $$
(☑088 557 4996; www.fortunevk.com; Th Sunthon Wijit; r with city/river view incl breakfast 850/950B, ste 2900B; P🛜🌸🛜) The town's former chart-topping hotel has been remodelled and rebranded and, though it's far from fancy, it sits right up against the Mekong, and if you take a river-view room on an upper floor you'll probably be happy here. There's a terrace overlooking the river and it

Nakhon Phanom

Nakhon Phanom

has karaoke, massage and other things Thai travellers need.

✗ Eating & Drinking

Nakhon Phanom has some excellent Vietnamese food and is home to a great **night market** (Th Fuang Nakhon; ⏰ 4-10pm). It also has a daily sunset **dinner cruise** (📞 089 780 7179; Th Sunthon Wijit; adult/child 200/100B).

Sam Anong   THAI $

(Th Samut Bunhan; mains 40-250B; ⏰ 8am-8pm; ❄🛜) A modern, comfortable choice for down-home Isan food with what must be a contender for best *gài yâhng* (grilled chicken) in Nakhon Phanom. And as a bonus, you can choose regular or black sticky rice.

Phornthep Naem Nueang   VIETNAMESE **$**
(Th Si Thep; mains 40-200B; ⏰6am-4pm) Classic, chaotic place with a full selection of Vietnamese dishes including the titular *năam neu·ang* (assemble-it-yourself pork spring rolls). Come in the morning for *khài gràtá* (a mini-skillet of eggs topped with sausages). There's no Roman-script sign, but it's located directly across from the old movie theatre next to Srithep Hotel.

Ohio   THAI **$$**
(Th Fuang Nakhon; mains 59-349B; ⏰5pm-4am; 🛜) This popular restaurant has gone through many incarnations during its 25 years – the current is colourful and classy and it feels more Bangkok than Nakhon Phanom – but it has always turned out good food. Though the menu is mostly Thai, with fish featuring prominently, there are some Isan and Western dishes too.

P Cafe   COFFEE
(Th Si Thep; espresso 40B; ⏰7.30am-7.30pm; 🛜) Coffee, tea, Italian sodas, smoothies, brownies and as much style as you are going to find in Nakhon Phanom. Old photos, big chairs and a piano make this a lovely and relaxing spot.

ⓘ Information

Bangkok Bank (Tesco-Lotus, Th Nittayo; ⏰10.30am-7pm) The nearest bank with evening and weekend hours in the city centre.
Immigration Office (☏042 532644; www.nakhonphanom-imm.com; Th Sunthon Wijit; ⏰8.30am-noon & 1-4.30pm Mon-Fri) For visa extensions.
Nakhon Phanom Hospital (☏042 511422; www.nkphospital.go.th; Th Apibanbuncha) The city's best medical facility.
Tourism Authority of Thailand (TAT; ☏042 513490; tatphnom@tat.or.th; Th Sunthon Wijit; ⏰8.30am-4.30pm) Covers Nakhon Phanom, Sakon Nakhon and Mukdahan provinces.

ⓘ Getting There & Away

AIR
Nahon Phanom's airport is located 20km west of town. **Nok Air** (☏082 790 7961, nationwide 02 900 9955; www.nokair.com; ⏰8am-8pm) and **Air Asia** (☏042 531571, nationwide 02 515 9999; www.airasia.com; ⏰8am-5pm) fly several times daily from Bangkok's Don Mueang Airport, with one-way prices typically costing 1100B. **Nakhon Phanom Travel Centre** (☏042 520999; Th Apibanbuncha; ⏰8.30am-6pm

WORTH A TRIP

BAN NA CHOK

Second to the lovely views, Nakhon Phanom is best known for its Ho Chi Minh connection. Ban Na Chok village, about 3.5km west of Nakhon Phanom, is one of a dozen places where 'Uncle Ho' stayed in Thailand between 1928 and 1930 while planning his resistance movement against the French in Vietnam.

The village remains mostly ethnically Vietnamese today and has embraced its former neighbour – he stayed here at various points in 1928 and 1929 – and there are now three Ho Chi Minh tourist sites. The faithful replica of the house (p396) where he stayed is the best, the memorial (p396) is aimed at tour buses and the museum (p396) is the least visited but most educational.

Ho Chi Minh's birthday is celebrated here every 19 May.

Túk-túk drivers usually ask 200B for the return trip from Nakhon Phanom, although you might get a taxi to do it for less.

Mon-Sat) sells tickets. For a taxi from the airport into town, expect to pay 150B to 200B.

BUS
Nakhon Phanom's **bus terminal** (☏042 513444; Th Fuang Nakhon) is west of the town centre. From here buses head to the following:
➡ Nong Khai (200B, seven to eight hours, 11am)
➡ Udon Thani (147B to 200B, four hours, every 45 minutes from 7.15am to 5pm)
➡ Khon Kaen (212B, five hours, 13 departures from 5.50am to 9.30pm)
➡ Ubon Ratchathani (155B to 200B, 4½ hours, 7am, 8.30am and 2pm)

Most people use minivans for Ubon Ratchathani (182B, four hours, hourly from 5.45am to 4pm) and Mukdahan (80B, 2½ hours, frequent from 5.30am to 6pm), all of which stop in That Phanom (40B, one hour). There are frequent buses to Bangkok (554B to 862B, 11 to 12 hours) between 4.30pm and 7.30pm plus two in the morning (7.30am, 7.45am) and three to Chiang Mai (737B, 14 to 15 hours, 9am, 3pm and 5pm).

Sŏrng·tăa·ou (passenger pick-up trucks) to That Phanom (40B, 1½ hours, frequent 7am to 5pm) park next to Kasikornbank in the city centre.

ℹ️ Getting Around

Túk-túk drivers expect 40B for one or two people from the bus station to most places in town, and 200B for the return trip to Ban Na Chok (p399). Nakhon Phanom also has a **taxi** (☏ 080 903 7222) service; drivers park at the bus station and they don't use meters.

Sŏrng·tǎa·ou to Na Kae depart from next to Kasikornbank and pass in front of **Mekong Underwater World** (โลกของปลาแม่น้ำโขง; ☏ 042 530780; Rte 2033; 30B; ⊙ 8.30am-4pm) (20B, 20 minutes) and within 1km of Ho Chi Minh's House (15B, 10 minutes).

Avis (☏ 062 597 3611, nationwide 02 2511131; www.avisthailand.com; Nakhon Phanom Airport; ⊙ 8am-7.30pm), **Budget** (☏ 042 531592, nationwide 02 203 9222; www.budget.co.th; Nakhon Phanom Airport; ⊙ 8am-6pm) and **Thai Rent A Car** (☏ 042 530681, nationwide 1647; www.thairentacar.com; Nakhon Phanom Airport; ⊙ 9am-7pm) offer car hire at Nakhon Phanom's airport and **River Hotel** (p397) also does car hire. The price of a car alone is about 1200B per day and a driver will cost 500B. River Hotel and **777 Hometel** (p397) have motorcycle hire for 250B per day.

Nakhon Phanom's sparse traffic and riverside bike trail, which takes you all the way north to the bridge, makes it a great place for cycling. Most hotels have free bikes for their guests, but if yours doesn't you can rent from another one such as 777 Hometel.

ℹ️ GETTING TO LAOS: NAKHON PHANOM TO THA KHAEK

Getting to the border Passenger ferries cross the Mekong to Tha Khaek in Laos, but they're for Thai and Lao only. All other travellers must use the Third Thai-Lao Friendship Bridge, north of the city. The easiest way to cross is to take the bus directly to Tha Khaek from Nakhon Phanom's bus station (70/75B weekdays/weekends, eight departures from 8am to 5pm).

At the border The Thai border is open from 6am to 10pm. All immigration formalities, including getting Lao visas, are handled at the bridge. Things get pretty chaotic when droves of Vietnamese workers are passing through.

Moving on The bus tends to wait a long time at the bridge, so total travel time to Tha Khaek can take more than two hours.

That Phanom ธาตุพนม

☏ 042 / POP 11,680

Towering over the small, peaceful town of That Phanom, the spire of the colossal namesake *chedi* at Wat Phra That Phanom is one of the region's most emblematic symbols and one of the great pillars of Isan identity. Some historic buildings in the Mekong-hugging half of town can round out a pleasant visit.

◉ Sights

Wat Phra That Phanom BUDDHIST TEMPLE
(วัดพระธาตุพนม; Th Chayangkun; ⊙ 5am-9pm) **FREE** This temple is a potent and beautiful place – even if you're feeling templed out, you'll likely be impressed. At its hub is a stupa *(tâht)*, more impressive than any in present-day Laos and highly revered by Buddhists from both countries. It's 53.6m high, and a 16kg real-gold umbrella laden with precious gems adds 4m more to the top. A visit in the evening is extra-special.

The local legend tells that the Lord Buddha travelled to Thailand and directed that one of his breast-bone relics be enshrined in a *chedi* to be built on this very site; and so it was in 535 BC, eight years after his death. Historians, on the other hand, assume the first construction (there's a **replica** (พระธาตุองค์เดิมจำลอง) **FREE** of how this short stupa may have looked on an island in front of the temple) was around the 9th century AD, and modifications have been routine since then. In 1690 it was raised to 47m and the current design went up in 1941, but it toppled during heavy rains in 1975 and was rebuilt in 1978. You'll find replicas of both the present and the previous designs all over Isan.

Behind the surrounding cloister is a shady little park with more statuary and a **museum** (พิพิธภัณฑสถานวัดพระธาตุพนมโมลีศรีโคตรบูรณ์; ⊙ 8.30am-4pm) **FREE**. To the north is what was once the largest gong in Thailand, and to the south is a market with food and handicrafts for all the Thai tourists visiting.

Tai-Lao Open-Border Market MARKET
(ตลาดนัด ไทยลาว; Th Rimkhong; ⊙ 5am-2pm Mon & Thu) This busy market running along the river takes place every Monday and Thursday. It's mostly the same fresh food and household goods found in other Thai markets, but some Lao traders come over to sell herbs, roots, mushrooms, bats and other forest products.

✨ Festivals & Events

Visitors descend from all over Thailand and Laos during the **That Phanom Festival** (⏱ late Jan/early Feb), to make merit and pay respect to the *tâht*. The streets fill with market stalls, many top *mŏr lam* troupes perform and the town hardly sleeps for nine days.

🛏 Sleeping

During the That Phanom Festival, rates soar and rooms are booked out well in advance.

Baan Ing Oon Guesthouse   HOTEL **$**
(📞 042 540111; baaningoonguesthouse2@gmail.com; Th Phanom Phanarak; r 500-800B; 🅿 ➖ ❄ 🛜) This place, a block off the river, offers cleanliness and comfort for a good price. The building is new, but has the classic French-Indochina style (the building next door is a genuine original) and a pleasant vibe. The family who runs it speaks little English, but is very friendly and helpful. Guests can use bikes for free.

Kritsada Rimkhong Hotel   HOTEL **$**
(📞 083 005 8621; Th Rimkhong; r incl breakfast 500-600B; 🅿 ❄ @ 🛜) There is a mix of rooms here, some older than others, but it's all about the pair of 2nd-storey river-view rooms. If the friendly English-speaking owner is around when you call, he'll pick you up at the bus station for free. Free bikes may or may not be available for use.

That Phanom Riverview Hotel   HOTEL **$$**
(📞 042 541555; www.thatphanomriverviewhotel.com; Th Rimkhong; r incl breakfast 850-1300B; 🅿 ❄ @ 🛜) Rooms at That Phanom's biggest and best lodge are pretty plain for the price, but being large and bright helps compensate, and the service and amenities are what you'd expect. Note that despite the name, most rooms have little or no view. There are free bicycles for guests' use.

That Phanom Place   HOTEL **$$**
(📞 042 532148; thatphanomplace@gmail.com; Th Chayangkun; d/tw incl breakfast 790/890B; 🅿 ➖ ❄ 🛜) There's a lot to like about this friendly place. You get a quality room, designed to catch a breeze, at a fair price and grade A service, often in English. If only it were by the river instead of 500m away along the highway. There are free bikes for guests' use, plus a good restaurant out front.

That Phanom

⊙ Sights

1 Kong Gate	B2
2 Replica Stupa	A2
3 Tai-Lao Open-Border Market	B1
4 That Phanom Museum	A2
5 Wat Phra That Phanom	A2

🛏 Sleeping

6 Baan Ing Oon Guesthouse	B3
7 Kritsada Rimkhong Hotel	B1
8 That Phanom Place	A3
9 That Phanom Riverview Hotel	B1

🍽 Eating

Krua Kritsada Rimkhong	(see 7)
10 Night Market	B2
11 Pugtukhong	B2

ℹ Transport

Pugtukhong	(see 11)

🍴 Eating & Drinking

The restaurants along the river are good places to lounge with a beer or *lôw kŏw* (local whiskey) at night. There are also a few retro-trendy bars just north of the **arch** (ประตูโขง) and some modern bars by the junction of Chayangkun and Chayangkun 2 roads south of the *tâht*.

Pugtukhong
THAI $

([☎] 091 057 0351; Th Rimkhong; mains 40-180B;
[⊙] 9am-9pm; [🛜]) Khun Maew, who speaks
English, **hires bikes** (per day 100B) and is
a good source of local info, serves heaping
plates of delicious Thai and Isan standards
with a river view.

Krua Kritsada Rimkhong
THAI $

(Th Rimkhong; mains 40-200B; [⊙] 9am-10pm; [🛜])
The food here, with an emphasis on Mekong
River delicacies, is consistently delicious,
and it's usually quieter than most of the
town's many other riverside restaurants,
although there is a seldom-used karaoke
machine.

Night Market
THAI $

([⊙] 3.30pm-9.30pm) Isan food predominates
at That Phanom's night market, but there's
also Thai and Vietnamese. It's all served for
takeaway.

ⓘ Information

There are several regular banks in the centre
of town. For weekends and evenings, there's a
Bangkok Bank ([⊙] 10.30am-7pm) north of town
in the Tesco-Lotus shopping centre.

ⓘ Getting There & Away

From That Phanom's new **bus station** (Rte
2030), inconveniently located west of town (a
túk-túk to the river should cost 30B to 40B),
there are buses to Ubon Ratchathani (162B,
4½ hours, seven daily), Udon Thani (160B to
180B, five hours, four daily) and Bangkok (473B
to 753B, 11 to 12 hours, 7.20am, 8am, and 11
between 5pm and 7pm), and minivans to Nakhon
Phanom (40B, one hour, frequent 6am to 6pm)
and Ubon Ratchathani (145B, four hours, hourly
6.30am to 5pm) via Mukdahan (40B, one hour).

Most people, however, don't use the bus
station since the minivans also stop just south
of the *tâht* on **Chayangkun road** (Th Chanyang-
khun), and for Nakhon Phanom you can take one
of the **sŏrng·tǎa·ou** (Rte 212) (40B, 1½ hours,
frequent 7am to 4pm) that depart from the highway 300m north of the *tâht*.

Air Asia (p399) has fly-and-ride service using
Nakhon Phanom's airport. It drops off and picks
up at a little blue **bus shelter** (Th Chayangkun)
just north of the *tâht*.

ⓘ Getting Around

You can walk everywhere in That Phanom, but a
bike is great for riding along the river. Most hotels have them available for guests, and you can
also hire them from **Pugtukhong**.

MUKDAHAN PROVINCE

Mukdahan is an often overlooked province.
It's capital city is a low-key hard sell, but
there's some beautiful scenery and historic
temples along the Mekong River.

Mukdahan
มุกดาหาร

[☎] 042 / POP 34,294

On the banks of the Mekong, directly
opposite the Lao city of Savannakhet,
Mukdahan – just plain *múk* to locals – sees
few visitors despite being the home of the
Thai–Lao Friendship Bridge 2 connecting
Thailand to Laos and Vietnam by road. It's
not an exciting place, but there's enough of
interest to fill a relaxing day, and the vibe
is friendly.

⦿ Sights

Hor Kaew Mukdahan
MUSEUM

(หอแก้วมุกดาหาร; Th Samut Sakdarak; 50B;
[⊙] 8am-6pm) This eye-catching 65m-tall
tower was built for the 50th anniversary of
King Rama IX's ascension to the throne. The
nine-sided base has a good museum with
displays (labelled in English) on the eight
ethnic groups of the province. There are
great views and a few more historical displays in 'The 360° of Pleasure in Mukdahan
by the Mekong' room, up at the 50m level.
The ball on the top holds a locally revered
Buddha image believed to made of solid
silver.

Talat Indojin
MARKET

(ตลาดอินโดจีน; Th Samran Chaikhongtai; [⊙] 8am-
5pm) Among Thais, Mukdahan is most
famous for this riverside market, which
stretches along and under the promenade.
Most Thai tour groups on their way to Laos
and Vietnam make a shopping stop for
cheap food, clothing and assorted trinkets –
much of it from China and Vietnam – plus
silk and cotton fabrics made in Isan.

Wat Pa Silawiwek
BUDDHIST TEMPLE

(วัดป่าศิลาวิเวก; Th Damrongmukda; [⊙] daylight
hours) **FREE** It's the resident monkeys rather
than anything religious or artistic that make
this forest temple on the edge of town worth
a visit. They reside in the far back of the temple and are most active in the early morning.

Phu Manorom
VIEWPOINT

(ภูมโนรมย์; [⊙] 4am-7pm) **FREE** You can get an
impressive view of Laos and the Mekong

Mukdahan

⬆ N 0 _____ 200 m
    0 _____ 0.1 miles

Mukdahan

from this mountain south of the city. The temple here has a small garden and an 84m-tall Buddha image is under construction. It's a popular place for photo ops, and while it's promoted as a sunrise-watching spot, odds are it will just be you and the monks at that time.

🎊 Festivals & Events

Held in the field fronting the provincial hall (*săh·lah glahng*), **Mukdahan Thai Tribal Festival** (Red Cross Fair; ⊘9-17 Jan) features dancing and other cultural activities from Mukdahan's eight ethnic groups.

🛏 Sleeping

Riverview Maekhong Hotel   HOTEL $
(☑087 945 4949; Th Samran Chaikhongtai; r 450-750B; 🅿❄🛜) This funky place just south of the centre has a great waterfront location, and the spacious layout means the river breezes are fully taken advantage of. The rooms are a little faded, but this is made up for by the friendly staff, free bikes, terrace overlooking the river and riverfront restaurant. The river-view rooms all have their own balconies.

Huanum Hotel   HOTEL $
(☑042 611137; Th Samut Sakdarak; d/tw with fan & cold-water shared bathroom 200/350B, d/tw 350/450B; 🅿❄🛜) This Mukdahan classic is a friendly, reliable and clean old-timer that has been pleasantly spruced up recently. It's the first choice of most backpackers.

Hotel de Ladda   HOTEL $$$
(☑042 611499; www.hoteldeladda.com; Th Samran Chaikhongtai; incl breakfast r 2100-3750B, ste 8000B; 🅿❄🛜🏊) The new best address in Mukdahan offers large, plush rooms with European-inspired style right up against the Mekong. Every room has a river view and a balcony. There's also a swimming pool, a fitness centre and a small spa.

🍴 Eating & Drinking

Most city-centre restaurants shut their doors early, but many along the river north and south of town, and also out along Th Phithak Phanomkhet, keep the woks sizzling late into the night.

Simple riverside bars are the best of Mukdahan's nightlife scene.

★ Bao Pradit   THAI $
(Th Samran Chaikhongthi; mains 30-300B; ⊘11am-10pm; 🛜) It's a bit of a trek south of the centre, but this is a real Isan restaurant with dishes such as *gŏry kài mót daang* (raw meat 'salad' with red ant eggs) and *gang wǎi* (rattan curry). Though the English menu is mysterious (it translates *yam*, Thai-style tangy salads, as 'review', and Bao Pradit doesn't really serve python), it's rare that a restaurant of this sort has any English at all.

Mukdahan Night Market   THAI, VIETNAMESE $
(Th Song Nang Sathit; ⊘4-9pm) Mukdahan's night market has all the Thai and Isan classics, but it's the Vietnamese vendors that set it apart. A few sell *băhn dah* (they'll tell

you it's 'Vietnamese pizza'), which combines soft noodles, pork, spring onions and an optional egg served on a crispy cracker.

Wine Wild Why? THAI $
(Th Samran Chaikhongtai; mains 80-150B; ⊙5-10pm; 🛜) Housed in an atmospheric wooden building next to the river, this relaxing spot has bags of character and delicious Thai and Isan food. The wine selection is small, and available by the bottle only.

Khrua Chow Wang THAI, INTERNATIONAL $$
(Th Samran Chaikhongnua; mains 65-545B; ⊙10am-10pm; 🛜) The menu is mostly Thai with lots of Mekong River fish on offer – the chuchi curry with catfish is one of the house specialities. There are several Isan and European dishes, including an unexpectedly good wood-fired pizza.

Goodmook* INTERNATIONAL, THAI $$
(🖉 042 612091; Th Song Nang Sathit; mains 80-400B; ⊙9am-5pm Tue-Sun; ❄🛜) This delightful place has a cool, retro theme and a mix of Thai and international food (expensive but good), art on the walls, chill music, and good coffee. It's a great place to drop in and meet other travellers, both Thai and Western.

ℹ Information

Krung Thai (Th Song Nang Sathit; ⊙10am-6pm Mon-Fri) in the city centre stays open late on weekdays, but for weekend banking you'll need to hit up one of the shopping malls along the highway north of the bus station.

Mukdahan Immigration Office (🖉042 674072; ⊙8.30am-noon & 1-4.30pm Mon-Fri) is north of town by the bridge. It's in a hard-to-find spot south of the large border gate.

Mukdahan International Hospital (🖉042 611 222; www.mukinter.com/en/; Th Samut Sakdarak; ⊙24hr) is a good private hospital.

ℹ Getting There & Away

AIR

Mukdahan does not have an airport, but **Air Asia** (🖉045 255762, nationwide 02 515 9999; www.airasia.com; Ubon Ratchathani Airport; ⊙7am-7pm) and **Nok Air** (p204) have daily fly-and-ride services using both Nakhon Phanom and Ubon Ratchathani airports. Air Asia departs from and drops at **Riverfront Hotel** (🖉042 633348; www.riverfrontmukdahan.com; Th Samran Chaikhongtai; r incl breakfast 850-2000B; P❄❄@🛜), while Nok Air uses the Ploy Palace Hotel. Also at Ploy Palace Hotel, **Ploy Travel** (🖉042 614599; ⊙8am-5pm) sells tickets and arranges van transport to Ubon's airport for other flights.

BUS

Mukdahan's **bus terminal** (🖉042 611207) is on Rte 212, west of town. Yellow *sŏrng·tăa·ou* (10B, 6.30am to 5pm) run north along Th Samut Sakdarak and west along Th Phithak Phanomkhet and end up at the station. Túk-túk there cost 50B from the city centre. **Sŏrng·tăa·ou** to Don

BUSES TO/FROM MUKDAHAN

DESTINATION	FARE (B)	DURATION (HR)	FREQUENCY
Bangkok	439-717	10-11	hourly in the morning, frequent 5-8pm
Khon Kaen	161-214	4½	hourly 3.30am-4pm
Khon Kaen (minivan)	240	4½	every 45min 4am-6pm
Nakhon Phanom (minivan)	80	2½	frequent 5.30am-6pm
Nakhon Ratchasima	272	7	hourly 5.45am to 6.30pm
That Phanom (minivan)	40	1	frequent 5.30am-6pm
Ubon Ratchathani	100-135	2½	hourly 11am-3.45pm
Ubon Ratchathani (minivan)	111	2½	every 30min 6am-5pm
Udon Thani	175-200	5	hourly 8.45am-3.30pm
Udon Thani (minivan)	180	5	hourly 6.30am-5.30pm
Yasothon	95	2½	every 2hr 5.45am-4pm
Yasothon (minivan)	84	2	every 30min 5.30am-6.10pm

Tan, for going to Phu Pha Thoep National Park, depart from in front of Pornpetch Market.

🛈 Getting Around

Mukdahan is a great place for a bike ride. Not the town itself, so much, but following the Mekong River north along various little roads takes you past historic temples, scenic rapids and deep countryside. Also, there's a proper bike path leading most of the way to Phu Pha Thoep National Park south of the city. **Nikorn Bike** (☑ 086 994 6669; Th Samut Sakdarak; mountain bikes per day 150B; ☉ 9am-9pm) between River City and Ban Rim Suan hotels hires good-quality mountain bikes. **Goodmook*** restaurant has little bikes for the same price, which are fine if you aren't planning to go far.

Ying Mongkhon Motor (☑ 086 428 1338, 042 613993; Th Samut Sakdarak; motorcycle hire per day from 200B; ☉ 8am-5pm Mon-Fri, to 4.30pm Sat), which has signs at many hotels using the name Tony Rental, hires motorcycles.

Rides with **Taxi Mukdahan** (☑ 042 613666; ☉ 6am-midnight) have a 60B flagfall plus the meter, although sometimes the price is just negotiated.

Phu Pha Thoep National Park อุทยานแห่งชาติภูผาเทิบ

Despite only covering 48 sq km, hilly Phu Pha Thoep National Park has a host of beautiful attractions – most famously, large mushroom-shaped rock formations. The main rock group sits right behind the visitor centre, and wildflowers bloom there October through December. Besides the weird rocks there are several clifftop viewpoints and Nam Tok Phu Tham Phra, a scenic waterfall (May to November only) with a grotto atop it holding hundreds of small Buddha images. It only takes a few hours and about 4km on the well-marked trails to see all these sights. Tham Fa Mue Daeng, a cave with ancient

hand paintings, is an 8km drive from the main park area and then a 1.5km walk.

🛏 Sleeping & Eating

For accommodation, there's **camping** (per person with own tent 30B, 4-person tent hire 300B) and a three-bedroom **bungalow** (☑ 094 289 2383; http://nps.dnp.go.th/reservation.php; bungalow 1800B) right by the visitor centre.

There's an Isan restaurant at the visitor centre serving *gài yâhng* (grilled marinated chicken), *sôm·đam* (spicy papaya salad) and *þlah pŏw* (grilled fish). Typically last order is 6pm, but go no later than 5pm to be safe. There are also a couple of shops with instant noodles and snacks.

🛈 Information

The **Visitor Center** (☑ 094 289 2383; ☉ 8.30am-4pm) has helpful staff. Hire rangers for visiting Tham Fa Mue Daeng here.

🛈 Getting There & Away

The park is 15km south of Mukdahan via Rte 2034. A bike path separated from the highway makes riding there safe and easy.

Sŏrng·tăa·ou (20B, 30 minutes, every 30 to 45 minutes) to Don Tan, departing from Pornpetch Market, 300m north of Hor Kaew Mukdahan, pass the turn-off to the park. Hitching the last 1.3km to the visitor centre isn't tough, or you can ask drivers to detour off the route and take you; they'll probably do it for 100B. Buses to Ubon Ratchathani from the bus station also pass the same junction. Be back at the junction by 4.30pm to guarantee finding a bus or *sŏrng·tăa·ou* back to town.

NAKHON RATCHASIMA PROVINCE

If you had just a single day to experience Thailand, Khorat, the original and still most commonly used name for Thailand's largest

🛈 GETTING TO LAOS: MUKDAHAN TO SAVANNAKHET

Getting to the border Thai and Lao citizens can use the boats that cross the Mekong from Mukdahan's city centre, while everyone else must use the bridge. The easiest way to cross is with the direct buses to Savannakhet (45B to 50B, hourly 7.30am to 7pm) from Mukdahan's bus station. There's a 5B fee during weekend, holidays and non-business hours.

At the border The border is open from 6am to 10pm. The crossing to Savannakhet can take from one to two hours, depending on the length of the immigration queues. There's time enough at the border to get a Lao visa.

Moving on From Savannakhet there are buses to various points in Laos, as well as Vietnam.

Nakhon Ratchasima (Khorat)

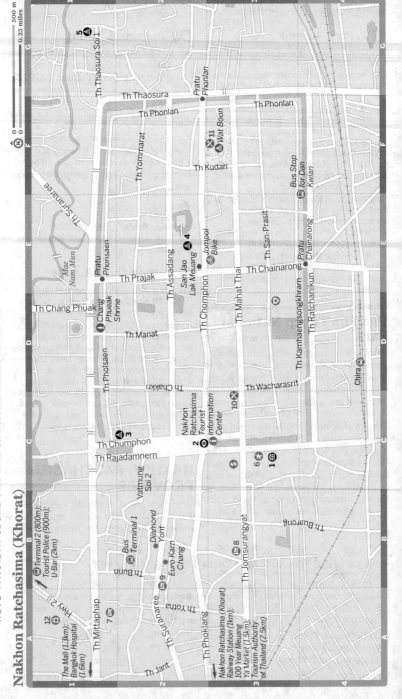

500 m
0.25 miles

Th Suranaree

Mae
Nam Mun

Th Thaosura Soi 1

5

Th Thaosura

Th Phonlan

Pratu
Phonlan

Th Phonlan

Th Yommarat

Wat Boon 11

Th Kudan

Bus Stop
for Dan
Kwian

Th Prajak

Pratu
Phonsaen

Th Assadang

San Jao
Lak Meuang 4

Jompol
Bike

Th Chomphon

Th San-Prasit

Pratu
Chainarong

Th Chainarong

Chang
Phueak
Shrine 1

Th Chang Phuak

Th Prajak

Th Mahat Thai

Th Kamhaengsongkhram

Th Ratchanikun

Th Manat

Th Pholsaen

Th Chakkri

Th Wacharasrit

10

Chira

3

Th Chumphon

Nakhon
Ratchasima
Tourist
Information
Center

2

Th Rajadamnern

$

6

1

Vatmung
Soi 2

Diamond
Yont

Th Buarong

Bus
Terminal 1

8

Euro Karn
Chang

Th Jomsurangyat

Th Burin

9

Th Yotha

7

Th Mittaphap

Th Suranaree

Th Phoklang

Th Jant

Hwy 2

12

Terminal 2 (800m);
Tourist Police (900m);
U-Bar (2km)

The Mall (1.3km);
Bangkok Hospital
(1.6km)

Nakhon Ratchasima (Khorat)
Railway Station (1km);
100 Year Meuang
Ya Market (1.5km);
Tourism Authority
of Thailand (2.5km)

Nakhon Ratchasima (Khorat)

province, would be a great place to spend it. Most visitors are here to jump into the jungle at Khao Yai, Thailand's oldest national park and newest Unesco World Heritage site. Its large size and easy access make it one of the best wildlife-watching sites in Thailand.

While Khao Yai is the soaring pinnacle of the province's tourist industry, silk and stone are solid cornerstones. Fashionistas should hit the shops in Pak Thong Chai, home of the region's silk-weaving industry, while history aficionados can soak up an evocative glimpse of the Angkor era's heyday at the restored ruins at Phimai.

Khorat city offers little as a destination, but with a solid selection of hotels and restaurants, it makes a good base for your Isan sojourn.

Nakhon Ratchasima (Khorat)

📞 044 / POP 151,450

Nakhorn Ratchasima is a big, busy city with little in the way of sights, but one that for many travellers serves as the gateway to Isan. Khorat (โคราช), as most people call the city, has a strong sense of regional identity (people call themselves *kon koh·râht* instead of *kon ee·săhn*) and is at its best in its quieter nooks, such as inside the eastern side of the historic moat, where local life goes on in a fairly traditional way and you are more likely to run into a metre-long monitor lizard than another traveller.

◉ Sights & Activities

Thao Suranari Monument　　　SHRINE
(อนุสาวรีย์ท้าวสุรนารี; Th Rajadamnern; ⊙ 24hr)
FREE Thao Suranari, wife of the assistant governor during Rama III's reign, is some-

thing of a Wonder Woman in these parts. Ya Mo ('Grandma Mo'), as she's affectionately called, became a hero in 1826 by organising a successful prisoner revolt after Chao Anou of Vientiane had conquered Khorat during his rebellion against Siam. One version of the legend says she convinced the women to seduce the Lao soldiers (another says she got them drunk) and then the Thai men launched a surprise attack, saving the city.

Wat Salaloi　　　BUDDHIST TEMPLE
(วัดศาลาลอย; Soi 1, Th Thaosura; ⊙ daylight hours) The city's most interesting temple was supposedly founded by local heroine Thao Suranari and her husband in 1827. Half of her ashes are interred in a small stupa (the other half are at her monument) and there are also singing troupes on hire to perform for her spirit here. A small statue of the heroine sits praying in the pond in front of the temple's award-winning *bòht* (ordination hall).

Maha Viravong National Museum　　　MUSEUM
(พิพิธภัณฑสถานแห่งชาติมหาวีรวงศ์; Th Rajadamnern; 50B; ⊙ 9am-4pm Wed-Sun) Though the collection at this seldom-visited museum is very small, it's very good. There's prehistoric pottery (don't miss sneaking a peek at what's stored in the back), Khmer bronze statues and a variety of Buddha images spanning the Dvaravati to Rattanakosin eras.

Wat Phra Narai Maharat　　　BUDDHIST TEMPLE
(วัดพระนารายณ์มหาราช; Th Chomphon; ⊙ daylight hours, Naranya Shrine 10am-6pm) **FREE** This large temple is of interest primarily for three holy Khmer sandstone sculptures that were unearthed here – Vishnu (Phra Narai in Thai) is the holiest. To see them, follow the signs with red arrows back to the Naranya Shrine at the southeast corner. The

DON'T MISS

PÀT MÈE KOH·RÂHT

One speciality you must try once is *pàt mèe koh·râht*. It's similar to *pát tai*, but boasts more flavour, has chilli pepper, and is made with a local style of soft rice noodle *(mèe koh·râht)*. It's widely available in Nakhon Ratchasima Province but very rare everywhere else.

building is not always open. There are some enormous monitor lizards living in the pond near here.

Wat Phayap BUDDHIST TEMPLE
(วัดพายัพ; Th Pholsaen; ⊙ daylight hours, cave shrine 8am-5pm) FREE When the abbot of Wat Phayap learned that blasting for a quarry in Saraburi Province was destroying a beautiful cave, he rescued pieces of it and plastered the stalactites, stalagmites and other incredible rocks all over a room below his residence, creating a shrine like no other.

Rajadamnern Nuat Pheua Sukhaphap MASSAGE
(☑ 092 969 6447; 768 Th Rajadamnern; Thai massage per hour 200B, with oil 400B; ⊙ 10am-10pm) This soothing place is nicely decked out and has lilting Thai music to calm the nerves. It's a genuine massage facility using various traditional Thai techniques, as well as herbs.

✦ Festivals & Events

Khorat explodes into life during the **Thao Suranari Festival** (⊙ 23 Mar-3 Apr), when the city celebrates the eponymous heroine. It features parades, theatre and other events along Th Rajadamnern. During Khao Phansaa, the beginning of Buddhist Lent, Khorat has a **candle parade** (⊙ Jul).

🛏 Sleeping

Sansabai House HOTEL $
(☑ 044 255144; www.sansabai-korat.com; Th Suranaree; r with fan 300B, with air-con 500-800B; P ❄ ❆ �) Long the best budget beds in Khorat, this clean, quiet and friendly place now brands itself as a 'vintage and boutique hotel'. But the only thing that has changed is the silly slogan. Rooms have good mattresses, mini-fridges and little balconies.

⭐ **Rom Yen Garden Place** HOTEL $$
(☑ 044 260116; www.romyenhotel.com; Th Jomsurangyat; r 1090-1290B; ste 2500B; P ⊖)

❄ � ⊠) With a very modern, welcoming feel, this stylish hotel is a great addition to Khorat's accommodation roster. The comfy, attractive rooms are good value and there's a pool, a fitness centre and a large deck in front. It's set back off the road, so noise isn't much of an issue.

Fortune Rajpruek Hotel HOTEL $$$
(☑ 044 079900; www.fortunehotelgroup.com/; Th Mittaphap; d incl breakfast 1800-2500B; P ❄ @ � ⊠) Refurbished and rebranded in 2017, this veteran hotel feels new. Rooms are spacious and comfortable, though on the expensive side. However, it regularly offers big discounts, in which case it's priced right.

🍴 Eating & Drinking

100 Year Meuang Ya Market MARKET $
(Th Mukhamontri; ⊙ 5pm-midnight) This night market is full of antiques and kitsch, but it's also a serious dining destination with dozens of restaurants (Thai, Isan and more) under a big roof.

Wat Boon Night Bazaar THAI $
(Th Chomphon; ⊙ 5-9.30pm) This is the largest night market inside the old town. All the usual Thai and Isan dishes are available for takeaway.

RN Yard THAI, ISAN $
(www.rnyard.com; Th Suranari; ⊙ 4-10pm; �) With both variety (Thai, Isan and more) and quality, many locals consider this Khorat's best night market. Most customers are here for take-home, but there's a two-level seating area in the back. Night Baan Koh (NBK) across the road is a poor man's Chiang Mai Walking Street. It's just north of the Dusit Princess Hotel.

Wan Warn THAI $$
(Th Mahat Thai; mains 45-250B; ⊙ 11am-9pm Mon-Sat) Peering through the window, you would be forgiven for thinking this wasn't a restaurant, because it really is just a few tables in a cluttered family home. It serves classic Thai recipes plus a few local dishes. Note that given the informality, things on the menu are often not available.

U-Bar CLUB
(Hwy 2; ⊙ 8am-2pm) For more than a decade this has been the most popular dance floor for students. It gets hopping around 10pm.

ℹ Information

Bangkok Bank (Th Jomsurangyat; ☺10.30am-7pm) in Klang Plaza mall, just south of the **Thao Suranari Monument** (p406), is the only city-centre bank open evenings and weekends. There are many more in **The Mall** (www.themall.co.th; Th Mittaphap; ☺10am-10pm) and **Terminal 21** (www.terminal21.co.th/korat; Th Mittaphap; ☺10am-10pm; 🛜).

Immigration (☎044 375138; ☺8.30am-noon & 1-4pm Mon-Fri) Located in Dan Kwian village, 15km southeast of the city.

Nakhon Ratchasima Tourist Information Center (Th Rajadamnern; ☺9am-5pm) The city-run, sometimes unstaffed, booth is by the Thao Suranari Monument.

Tourism Authority of Thailand (TAT; ☎044 213666; tatsima@tat.or.th; 2102-2104 Th Mittaphap; ☺8.30am-4.30pm) Khorat's branch of TAT is inconveniently located outside the centre of town next to the Sima Thani Hotel.

Police Station (☎044 242010; Th San Prasit; ☺24hr)

Tourist Police (☎044 370356; Hwy 2)

ℹ Getting There & Away

BUS

Khorat has two bus terminals. **Terminal 1** (bor kör sör nèung; ☎044 242899; Th Burin) in the city centre serves Bangkok (191B, 3½ to four hours, frequent) and most towns within the province, including Pak Chong (56B to 72B, 1½ to

BUSES & MINIVANS TO/FROM NAKHON RATCHASIMA (TERMINAL 2)

DESTINATION	FARE (B)	DURATION (HR)	FREQUENCY
Aranya Prathet (border with Cambodia)	150	4	7 departures 5.30am-6pm
Ayuthaya (minivan)	132	3½-4	frequent 5.40am-6.20pm
Bangkok	148-508	4	frequent
Bangkok (minivan)	171	4	frequent 6.30am-7.30pm
Chiang Mai	526-613	13	7 departures 3am-8.30pm
Khon Kaen	146-220	3½-4	frequent
Khon Kaen (minivan)	126	3-3½	every 40min 6.40am-6.30pm
Krabi	1168	16	4.50pm
Loei	252-342	7	hourly 5am-midnight
Lopburi	149	4-4½	6am, 10.45am, 1.30pm
Lopburi (minivan)	130	3½-4	every 40min 4.50am-6.30pm
Nang Rong	60-95	2	hourly
Nang Rong (minivan)	64	2	every 30min 4.30am-8.10pm
Nong Khai	257-409	6	11 departures, mostly in the afternoon
Mukdahan	272	7-8	hourly
Phimai	50	1½	every 30min 5am-10pm
Phimai (minivan)	50	1	hourly 10am-5.30pm
Surin	115-218	4	every 30min
Trat	297-409	8-9	7 departures
Ubon Ratchathani	248-386	7-8	hourly
Udon Thani	178-300	5½	frequent
Vientiane (must already have Lao visa)	900	6	11.30am

two hours, frequent 5.30am to 6.30pm) and Pak Thong Chai (21B, one hour, frequent). Minivans to Pak Chong (66B, 1½ hour, frequent 6.30am to 8pm) also leave from this terminal. Buses to most other destinations, plus more Bangkok buses and minivans, use the confusing and chaotic **Terminal 2** (bor kŏr sŏr sŏng; ☑ 044 256007; Hwy 2), north of the centre. For **Dan Kwian** (14B, 30 minutes), frequent buses leave from inside the old city, east of Chainarong Gate.

TRAIN

Many trains pass through **Khorat Train Station** (☑ 044 242044), but buses are much faster to most destinations. Ten daily trains go to/from Bangkok (50B to 425B, five to seven hours), via Ayuthaya. There are also nine trains to Ubon Ratchathani (58B to 453B, five to six hours) and four to Khon Kaen (38B to 295B, 3½ hours). Khorat's smaller **Chira Train Station** (Jira Train Station; ☑ 044 242363) is closer to the old city, so it may be more convenient to get off there.

ⓘ Getting Around

There are fixed *sŏrng·tăa·ou* (8B) routes through the city, but even locals find it hard to figure them out because of their dizzying array of numbers and colours. Most pass the junction of Th Suranaree and Th Rajadamnern, so if you want to go somewhere, just head there and ask around. Heading west on Th Suranaree, yellow *sŏrng·tăa·ou* 1, with white and green stripes, will take you past the train station, the tourism office and The Mall, while the white 1 with yellow and green strips also passes the train station. Heading north on Rajadamnern, the white 6 with red and yellow stripes passes The Mall more directly. Also going north on Rajadamnern, the white and blue 7 with no stripes, the white 10 with red and yellow stripes and the white 15 with purple stripes all go to Bus Terminal 2. The white and blue 7 also passes in front of Chira train station.

Túk-túk cost between 50B and 80B to most places in town. Motorcycle taxis and *săhm·lór* (pedicabs; also spelt săamláw), both of which are common, always cost less. Metered **taxis** (☑ 095 602 3636; ⊙ 24hr) pretty much only park at Bus Terminal 2 and **The Mall** (p409), so you'll need to call. There's almost no chance of getting drivers to use the meter.

Motorcycles can be hired at **Euro Karn Chang** (☑ 088 355 9393; 241 Th Suranaree; ⊙ 8am-5pm Mon-Sat) and **Diamond Yont** (☑ 081 878 7367; 100 Th Suranaree; ⊙ 8.30am-4pm Mon-Sat) from 250B per day for use within Khorat province. **Jompol Bike** (☑ 044 244015; 400 Th Chomphon; ⊙ 9am-7pm) hires bicycles for 100B per day.

Around Nakhon Ratchasima

Ban Prasat   บ้านปราสาท

☑ 044 / POP 1589

About 3000 years ago a primitive agricultural culture, closely related to Ban Chiang, put down roots at Ban Prasat, near the banks of the Than Prasat River. It survived around 1500 years, planting rice, domesticating animals, fashioning coloured pottery, weaving cloth and forging metal tools. The secrets of this early civilisation were revealed during extensive excavation digs completed in 1991; some of the excavation pits have been left open as tourist attractions, and a museum houses some of the discoveries.

South of the museum, one family still does silk weaving and they welcome visitors to come by for a look.

◉ Sights

Three **excavation pits** (แหล่งโบราณคดีบ้าน ปราสาท; ⊙ daylight hours) **FREE** are on display in the village, and artefacts are displayed in the small but good **museum** (พิพิธภัณฑ์บ้าน ปราสาท; ⊙ 8am-4.30pm) **FREE**.

🛏 Sleeping & Eating

The only accommodation in Ban Prasat is the excellent **homestay** (☑ 081 725 0791; per person incl 2 meals 400B) program.

The homestay program includes breakfast and dinner; for lunch there are a couple of *gŏo·ay dĕe·o* carts in town, including one across the road from the museum. A petite **night market** (⊙ 3-6pm Fri) takes over the bridge on Friday nights.

ⓘ Getting There & Away

Ban Prasat is 45km northeast of Khorat and 1.5km off Hwy 2. Buses (35B, one hour) heading to points north will drop you at the junction. A motorcycle taxi will zip you around to all the sites for 60B per person, but note that often only one driver is working.

Muang Sema Historical Site   โบราณสถานเมืองเสมา

Roughly halfway between Khorat and Pak Chong, little is known about the ancient city of Muang Sema, though it was clearly important in its day. It began as a Dvaravati outpost in the 7th or 8th century BC, during which it is presumed to have been the capital city of a small kingdom. Later, probably in the 10th century, it was occupied by the Khmer, although Mahayana Buddhism continued alongside Hinduism. Many artefacts found here are on display at the Phimai National Museum.

Other than one evocative reclining Buddha, it's mostly ruined foundations and a pair of moats. While Muang Sema isn't spectacular, what you get here is a sense of being off the beaten track. Beyond the **temple** (วัดธรรมจักรเสนาราม; ☉daylight hours) FREE, there's no tourist infrastructure other than a few explanatory signs, and you'll most likely have the place to yourself.

❶ Getting There & Away

Muang Sema is 37km from Khorat. Minivans between Khorat and Pak Chong will stop along the highway, 8km away, from where you can hire a motorcycle taxi to take you around the site for about 150B, though it may take a while to find one. A few buses (22B, 45 minutes) from Terminal 1 and local trains (6B to 63B, 30 minutes) run from Khorat to Sung Noen city, 4.5km away from the sites, where finding a motorcycle taxi is usually easier.

Phimai   พิมาย

POP 9768

The otherwise mundane little town of Phimai has one of Thailand's finest surviving Khmer temple complexes right at its heart. The architectural inspiration for Cambodia's Angkor Wat, Prasat Phimai once stood on an ancient highway linking the Khmer capital of Angkor with the northern reaches of the realm.

Being located smack in the centre of this small and pleasant town, Phimai is not just one of the most impressive ancient monuments in Thailand, it's also one of the most accessible. Phimai is an easy day trip out of Khorat, but if you prefer the quiet life, you could always make Khorat a day trip out of Phimai instead.

◎ Sights

⭐**Phimai Historical Park**   HISTORIC SITE
(อุทยานประวัติศาสตร์พิมาย; ☎044 471568; Th Ananthajinda; 100B; ☉7am-6pm, visitor centre 8.30am-4.30pm) Prasat Phimai is one of the most impressive Khmer ruins in Thailand, both in its grand scale and its intricate details. Though built as a Mahayana Buddhist

temple, the carvings feature many Hindu deities, and many design elements – most notably the **main shrine**'s distinctive *prang* tower – were later used at Angkor Wat. There has been a temple at this naturally fortified site since at least the 8th century, though most of the existing buildings were erected in the late 11th century by Khmer king Jayavarman VI.

You enter over a cruciform **naga bridge**, which symbolically represents the passage from earth to heaven, and then through the **southern gate** of the outer wall, which stretches 565m by 1030m. The orientation to the south (though not due south) is unusual since most Khmer temples face east. It's often written that Phimai was built facing south to align with the capital, though historians reject this theory since it doesn't face Angkor directly.

A raised passageway, formerly covered by a tiled roof, leads to the inner sanctum and the 28m-tall main shrine built of white sandstone and covered in superb carvings. Inside the adjacent **Prang Brahmathat** is a replica stone sculpture of Angkor King Jayavarman VII sitting cross-legged and looking very much like a sitting Buddha. The original is in the Phimai National Museum.

Knowledgeable local students sometimes act as guides, but few speak English. Luckily, various signs and a free brochure provide a basic overview of the complex.

Phimai National Museum   MUSEUM
(พิพิธภัณฑสถานแห่งชาติพิมาย; ☎044 471167; Th Tha Songkhran; 100B; ☉9am-4pm) One of the biggest and best museums in Isan, the Phimai National Museum is well worth a visit. Situated on the banks of Sa Kwan, a 12th-century Khmer reservoir, the museum consists of two spacious buildings housing a fine collection of Khmer sculptures from not just Phimai but also many other ruins from around Isan. Though the focus is on the Khmer era, there are also artefacts from Muang Sema, distinctive trumpet-mouthed and black Phimai pottery from Ban Prasat and Buddha images from various periods.

Sai Ngam   PARK
(ไทรงาม; ☉daylight hours) FREE A bit east of town is Thailand's largest and oldest banyan tree, a 350-plus-year-old giant spread over an island. The extensive system of interlocking branches and gnarled trunks

Phimai

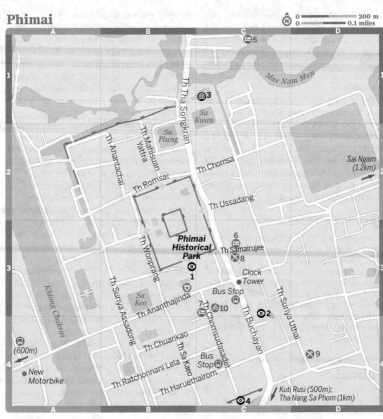

Phimai

◉ Top Sights
1 Phimai Historical Park B3

◎ Sights
2 Meru Bhramathat C3
3 Phimai National Museum C1
4 Pratu Chai C4

🛏 Sleeping
5 Moon River Resort Phimai C1

6 Phimai Paradise Hotel C3
7 Phimai Paradise House C3

✖ Eating
8 Rabiang Mai C3
9 Talat Jae Jae D4

ⓘ Transport
10 Boonsiri Guesthouse C3

makes the 'Beautiful Banyan' look like a small forest.

Other Historic Sites

Meru Bhramathat (เมรุพรหมทัต; Th Buchayan) is a toppled brick stupa dating back to the late Ayuthaya period (18th century). Its name is derived from a folk tale that refers to it as the cremation site of King Bhramathat.

Built by King Jayavarman VII, the most noteworthy of Phimai's three surviving 13th-century city gates is **Pratu Chai** (ประตู ชัย, Victory Gate) **FREE**, because it served the road to Angkor. Also built in the 13th century was **Kuti Rusi** (กุฏิฤาษี; ☉ daylight hours) **FREE**, the temple for a health centre, and **Tha Nang Sa Phom** (ท่านางสระผม; ☉ daylight hours) **FREE**, a 13th-century pier constructed out of laterite, now on the grounds of the Fine Arts Department compound.

✯ Festivals & Events

Staged in mid-November (usually the second weekend), the **Phimai Festival** celebrates the town's history with cultural performances, sound-and-light shows (tickets 200B to 600B) and long-boat races.

🛏 Sleeping

Moon River Resort Phimai   GUESTHOUSE $
(📞085 633 7097; www.moon-river-resort-phimai.com; Soi 2, Ban Sai Ngam Patana; r/f 600/1200B; 🅿😕❄🛜) This Thai-German-run guesthouse is in an almost-rural location on the north bank of the river (where you can swim) and features simple but good wooden and concrete cabins. They're surrounded by greenery and connected by a cool boardwalk. It's just outside town off the road to Khorat, 1km from the historical park entrance. Guests can hire bikes and motorcycles.

Phimai Paradise House   HOTEL $
(📞086 468 8402, 044 471918; www.phimaiparadisehotel.com; Th Chomsudasadet; dm 200B, incl breakfast tw 500B, d 600-800B; 🅿😕❄@🛜) Tops in the atmosphere category, this renovated wooden house is polished to a gloss and the rooms have a hint of history. The main drawback is that while each room gets its own bathroom, they are separate from the room. Guests can use the swimming pool at the **Phimai Paradise Hotel** (📞044 287565, 086 468 8402; www.phimaiparadisehotel.com; Th Chomsudasadet; incl breakfast d 450-600B, tr 700B; 🅿😕❄@🛜🏊), and bicycle hire costs 100B per day.

🍴 Eating & Drinking

Talat Jae Jae   MARKET $
(ตลาดเจแจ; Th Suriya Uthai; ⏰5-8am) This small morning street market is a good place to look for some breakfast.

Rabiang Mai   THAI $
(Th Samairujee; mains 50-250B; ⏰5pm-midnight; 🛜) This semi-fancy place is a tad on the pricey side, but the food (mostly Thai, plus some Isan and *fa·ràng* options) is quite good. It's also a bar with live music most nights starting 8.30-ish.

ℹ️ Information

Tourist Police (📞1155) Phimai's little tourist police box is often unstaffed.

ℹ️ Getting There & Around

Buses (50B, 1½ hours) and minivans (50B, one hour) to Phimai leave Khorat's Bus Terminal 1 about every 30 minutes throughout the day. All buses heading in and out of town pass official stops near **Pratu Chai** (Th Haruethairom) and the **clock tower** (Th Buchayan) and will also stop anywhere along the road north of town, such as the museum. Minivans only use Phimai's inconvenient **bus station**. If you're heading to somewhere north of Phimai, take the bus to Tala Khae (13B, 15 minutes) and catch a connection there; you may have to wait a while.

Phimai is small enough to stroll, but to travel further, hire a bike from **Boonsiri Guesthouse** (📞044 471159; Th Chomsudasadet; per half-/full day 40/80B) or **Phimai Paradise House**, or a motorcycle from **New Motorbike** (📞044 481880; Th Ananthajinda; per day 300B; ⏰8am-5pm Mon-Sat) for 300B per day.

Khao Yai National Park

Up there on the podium with some of the world's greatest parks, Khao Yai (อุทยานแห่งชาติเขาใหญ่) is Thailand's oldest and most visited national park. Covering 2168 sq km, Khao Yai incorporates one of the largest intact monsoon forests remaining in mainland Asia, which is why it was named a Unesco World Heritage site (as part of the Dong Phayayen–Khao Yai Forest Complex). But despite its size, it's one of the easiest national parks in Thailand for independent travellers to visit.

👁 Sights & Activities

Hiking

There are five hiking trails through the forest that visitors can walk on their own. All other forest hiking requires a guide. Park rangers can be hired as guides (500B to 1000B per group depending on the time) through the visitor centre. They can also lead you on longer off-trail treks, but only if they speak English or you speak Thai, so deep forest exploration is best done with a private guide arranged through local tour companies or hotels.

No matter where you hike, you should wear boots and long trousers. During the rainy season leeches are a problem. Mosquito repellent helps keep them away, but

DON'T MISS

ISAN'S CULINARY CREATIONS

Isan's cuisine is a blend of Lao and Thai cooking styles. The holy trinity of northeastern cuisine – *gài yâhng* (grilled marinated chicken), *sôm·đam* (spicy papaya salad) and *kôw něe·o* (sticky rice) – is integral to the culture. Also crucial are chillies – a fistful of potent peppers find their way into most dishes. Outsiders, including most other Thais, are rarely fans of *plah ráh*, an earthy fermented fish sauce, but Isan people consider it almost essential.

Fish dominates Isan menus, with *plah dùk* (catfish), *plah chôrn* (striped snake-head) and *plah boo* (sand goby) among the most popular, although farmed tilapia *plah nin* is now the most common. Insects traditionally comprised a large part of the typical family's diet and are still very common as snacks. Purple lights shining out in the countryside are for catching giant water bugs *(maang dah)*, which make a fragrant chilli paste *(prík maang dah)*.

Trying the following dishes will provide a well-rounded introduction to Isan food.

lâhp Thailand's famous 'minced-meat salad', as it's usually called, is actually an Isan dish and, when eaten here, it's one of the spiciest foods in the country. Sometimes the meat is raw, but this is not recommended due to bacteria and parasites.

nám dòk Essentially the same as *lâhp*, but with the meat sliced and grilled rather than diced and boiled.

đôm sâap The Isan version of *đôm yam*. Usually full of innards and tendons, the soft parts of an animal left over after making *lâhp*.

súp nòr mái Sometimes translated as 'bamboo shoot salad', *súp* is really more of a dipping sauce. It's usually less spicy than most other Isan foods.

gaang òrm This prototypical Isan curry is heavy on herbs and only mildly spicy. As with all Isan curries, there's no coconut milk.

gaang hèt This 'mushroom curry' often has tamarind to make it a little sour.

sâi gròrk ee·săhn 'Isan sausage' uses fermented pork for a sour taste. Sticky rice, garlic and salt also go inside the skin.

plah pŏw Grilled fish coated in salt with its stomach stuffed with pandanus leaves and lemongrass.

---

the leech socks sold in the visitor centre work much better.

Trail 1 (1.2km) The Kong Kaew Waterfall Nature Trail is a paved loop starting at the suspension bridge behind the visitor centre. It's not difficult, but it does have some steep spots.

Trail 2 (3km) This easy trail connects **Haew Suwat** (น้ำตกเหวสุวัต; ⊙7am-5pm) and Pa Kluai Mai waterfalls. Crocodiles are often seen in the river a short way past the latter falls. This trail was closed at the time of research, so check in at the visitor centre before hitting the trailhead.

Trail 3 (3.3km) This mildly challenging walk to the Nong Phak Chi observation tower starts at a small parking area by the Km 33 pillar. This is one of Khao Yai's best wildlife- and bird-watching areas. It's used

by many tour groups. Combine with Trail 5 to walk back to the visitor centre.

Trail 4 (2.7km) An easy, relatively little-travelled trail to a viewpoint of the Sai Sorn Reservoir.

Trail 5 (5km) Starting not too far south of the visitor centre, this is a good wildlife-watching trail that ends at the Nong Phak Chi observation tower. Makes a good combination with Trail 3.

Trail 6 (8km) The longest marked trail in the park goes from the visitor centre to Haew Suwat waterfall. It used to be open to independent trekking, but it's not well-trodden so many people got lost; some were even forced to sleep in the forest overnight. Now guides are required. Overall it's not too difficult, though there are a few rough spots and big hills.

Wildlife Watching

Around 200 elephants tramp the park's boundaries. Other mammals include tigers, leopards, bears, gaur, barking deer, otters, various gibbons and macaques, plus some rather large pythons. Khao Yai's bird list boasts 392 species, and one of Thailand's largest populations of hornbills lives here, including the great hornbill (*nók gòk* or *nók gah·hang*).

There are several viewpoints and salt licks (sometimes attracting elephants in the late afternoon and early morning) along the roads through the park. The best chance for seeing elephants is during a night safari (☑086 092 6529; per vehicle up to 10 people 500B; ⊙7pm & 8pm), where you also stand a good chance of seeing porcupines and jackals. You'll probably hear gibbons in the morning, but seeing them will require some walking – Trail 1 is a good place to try. You'll have to be very lucky (like lottery-winner lucky) to see a tiger. You will, however, surely see sambar deer, which congregate around the visitor centre and the Lam Tha Khong Campground in the morning and afternoon, and macaques, which roam park roads all day.

The Nong Phak Chi observation tower overlooks a little lake and a salt lick, and is one of the best wildlife-spotting sites in the park. The shortest way (900m) to the tower is a wide, easy path starting 1.8km north of the visitor centre, but two park hiking trails also go there.

☞ Tours

Three established companies – Greenleaf Guesthouse & Tour (☑089 424 8809; www.greenleaftour.com; Th Thanarat, Km 7.5), Khao Yai Garden Lodge and Bobby's Apartments & Jungle Tours (☑086 262 7006; www.bobbysjungletourkhaoyai.com; off Mittaphap Rd, Pak Chong) – have pretty much cornered the budget group-tour market, though the lodging is mostly aimed at backpackers and is not right for everyone. The typical trip runs one and a half days and costs 1500B (Khao Yai Garden Lodge charges 1600B) per person, though many people do just the full-day portion. Lunch, snacks, water and 'leech socks' are always included, and free pick-up in Pak Chong town might be.

Khao Yai and Beyond (☑089 946 1906; www.khaoyaiandbeyond.com) is a small company whose speciality is remote overnight trips with camping in the forest; all camping equipment is provided. Two noted bird-watching guides are Tony, who owns Khao Yai Nature Life Resort (☑096 565 5926; www.khaoyainaturelifetours.com), and Nang (☑089 427 1823; www.thailandyourway.com), one of Khao Yai's few female guides. Both also lead standard park tours.

The park offers one-hour night safaris, using spotlights to look for animals.

🛏 Sleeping & Eating

There are campsites and a variety of rooms and bungalows around the park; none have air-con. Note that you must book from the annoying national park website (http://nps.dnp.go.th/reservation.php; requires advanced payment) or in person at the park; phone reservations aren't allowed. Lodging is often fully booked except for low-season weekdays. Tent rental is almost always available.

Khao Yai Garden Lodge HOTEL **$**
(☑094 191 9176, 044 936352; www.khaoyaigardenlodge.com; Th Thanarat, Km 7; tw/tr with fan and shared bathroom 350/450B, incl breakfast d & tw with air-con 1150-2450B; P☺❅@?≋) One of Khao Yai's veteran resorts, this vast place is in need of TLC. For midrange rooms you can do better elsewhere, but these are just about the only truly budget rooms between Pak Chong city and the park that you can take without having to join a tour – although most do join because its tours are very good.

San Khao Yai Guesthouse GUESTHOUSE **$$**
(☑098 210 5098; www.sankhaoyaitour.com; Th Thanarat; bungalows 800B; P❅?) These colourful cottages just 100m from the park entrance are basic but very clean and a step up from most other budget lodging in the area. And there's no better place to be if you want to stay outside the park but get an early start on your wildlife-watching. It also hires motorcycles, arranges tours and serves food.

★Hotel des Artists HOTEL **$$$**
(☑044 297444; hoteldesartists@gmail.com; Th Thanarat, Km 22; incl breakfast r/villa 4600/7500B; P☺❅@?≋) This tasteful hotel goes for French-colonial chic rather than a nature theme, though with its mountain views out the back you won't forget where you are. The rooms are gorgeous, though small, and the villas sit right by the large swimming pool.

WORTH A TRIP

WINE COUNTRY

Thailand is the pioneer of 'New Latitude Wines' and, with over a dozen wineries in the region, the Khao Yai area is now the epicentre of this increasingly respected industry. Two of the leaders, **PB Valley** (พีบีวัลเล่ย์ เขาใหญ่ไวน์เนอรี่; ☑ 081 733 8783; www.khaoyaiwinery.com; tastings from 150B, tours 300B; ⊙tours 9am, 10.30am, noon, 1.30pm & 3.30pm) which corked its first bottle in 1998, and **GranMonte** (กราน-มอนเต้; ☑ 044 009543; www.granmonte.com; tastings/tours250/300B; ⊙tours 10am, 11.30am, 1.30pm, 3pm & 4.30pm Sat, Sun & holidays, 10.30am, 11.30am, 1.30pm & 3pm week-days), which got into the game three years later and is under the watch of Thailand's first female oenologist – lie along Muak Lek-Khao Yai road (exit Hwy 2 at Km 144), the direct route from Bangkok to the national park. Both are scenically set and offer tours (book in advance), tastings, gourmet gift shops, luxury lodging and classy restaurants for lunch and dinner. They're 22.5km and 16km respectively from the national park gate.

Roma Sausage   THAI, INTERNATIONAL $$
(Km 18, Th Thanarat; mains 80-850B; ⊙10.30am-9.30pm Sun-Tue & Thur, 10.30am-11pm Fri-Sat; 🖻) This casual alfresco spot on one of the busiest stretches of Th Thanarat manages to succeed at both Thai (yellow curry with mackerel and crispy tofu *lâhp*) and European (smoked chicken wings, duck confit and ultra-thin pizzas) food.

❶ Information

Khao Yai National Park Visitor Centre
(☑ 086 092 6529; ⊙6am-9pm, staffed from 8am) The staff here are friendly and knowl-edgeable and many speak good English. There are also displays giving a quick overview of the park's ecology.

❶ Getting There & Away

Sŏrng·tǎa·ou (Th Mittaphap) travel the 30km from Pak Chong down Th Thanarat to the park's northern gate (40B, one hour) every 30 minutes from 6am to 5pm. They start their journey from near the 7-Eleven by the artis-tic deer (they look like giraffes) statue. It's

another 14km to the visitor centre, and park guards are used to talking drivers into hauling people up there. The last *sŏrng·tǎa·ou* from the park gate back to Pak Chong departs around 3pm.

Pak Chong does not have a bus station: all departures are from the centre of town along the main road. Frequent minivans (66B, 1½ hours) and occasional 2nd-class buses (56B, two hours) to Khorat use a **bus stop** about 500m northeast of the deer statue near *dà·làht kàak* market between 5am and 6pm. Minivans to Bangkok (160B, three hours, every 30 minutes) depart from both sides of the road near the deer statue. First-class buses to both Bangkok (133B, three hours) and Khorat (72B, 1½ hour) stop at **Ratchasima Tour** (☑ 044 312131; Th Mitthap-hap) across the highway from the deer statue; the last departure to Bangkok is 8pm. You can also catch minivans (departing from Khorat) to Ayuthaya (100B, 2½ hours) and Lopburi (80B, two hours) directly across the street from *dà·làht kàak* (wait at the benches in the traffic island), if they have empty seats when they pass through, which they usually do.

You can also get to Pak Chong by **train** (☑ 044 311534) from Bangkok and Khorat, but it's much faster to go by bus or minivan. Ayuthaya, on the other hand, has no direct bus service and not many minivans, so the train (23B to 363B, two to three hours, 10 daily) can be a good option.

If you are driving from Bangkok, there's a second, seldom-used southern entrance in Prachinburi Province.

❶ Getting Around

The sights and the services are quite spread out, so you limit yourself by visiting without a vehicle, but not as much as you might think since it's really quite easy to catch a lift in the park during the day. However, getting a ride is never a sure thing so you shouldn't come without wheels if you aren't willing to walk.

Motorcycle is a good way to visit the park and they can be hired from **San Khao Yai Guest-house** (☑ 098 210 5098; www.sankhaoyaitour.com; 24hr 500B) near the park gate or from several shops on the main thoroughfare through Pak Chong, including **Thai Yen** (☑ 044 315536; Th Mittaphap, at Th Tesabarn 14; per day 300B; ⊙8am-5pm Mon-Sat), which is across from the road to the train station.

Bicycles are available for rent in the park **visitor centre** for 50/200B per hour/day. But remember, the park name means 'Big Mountain' and there are a lot of ups and downs between destinations.

BURIRAM PROVINCE

The city of Buriram is a friendly place, but lacks much of interest to travellers. The southern reaches of the province, on the other hand, have some of Thailand's must-see Khmer relics. The countryside is peppered with dozens of ancient ruins, the crowning glory of which is Phanom Rung, a beautifully restored complex climbing to the summit of an extinct volcano.

Nang Rong
นางรอง
☑ 044 / POP 20,920

The workaday city of Nang Rong is the most convenient base for visiting Phanom Rung Historical Park, and a full range of services and a good selection of hotels make it a friendly and comfortable one.

🛏 Sleeping & Eating

P California Inter Hostel
GUESTHOUSE $

(☑ 081 808 3347; www.pcalifornianangrong.webs.com; Th Sangkakrit; dm 150B, r 250-650B; P ❀ ⊖ ☎ 중) This great place on the eastern side of town offers bright, nicely decorated rooms with value in all price ranges. The cheapest rooms have fans while the more expensive options have living areas with sofas – all are cosy. English-speaking owner Khun Wicha has a wealth of knowledge about the area and leads low-priced tours. Bikes are free.

A motorcycle taxi/taxi from the bus station costs 50/60B.

Socool Grand Hotel
HOTEL $$

(☑ 044 632333; www.socoolgrand.com; Th Sapakitkoson; r incl breakfast 900-2100B; P ❀ ⊖ 중 ⊠) A new hotel with attractive black-and-white decor, Socool is now top of the heap in Nang Rong. Rooms are large and comfortable and there's a large pool-fitness complex in front. The prices would surely be higher if it wasn't in out-of-the-way Nang Rong.

Cabbages & Condoms
HOTEL $$

(☑ 044 657145; Hwy 24; r incl breakfast 560-1500B; P ❀ 중) ✐ This bizarrely named Population & Community Development Association-run resort, set in beautifully shaded grounds 6.5km west of town, is a pleasant place to stay. The rooms are large, with stone floors in most, and are very homey. There's a clothing factory on-site, opened to bring work normally found in the city to the villages.

As you might expect, condoms are a theme here.

Laksana Restaurant
THAI $

(Rte 24; mains 60-250B; ⊙ 7am-8pm; 중) A spot renowned for a rather sweet version of the city's famous *kăh mŏo nang rong* (stewed pork leg) – available in several styles including 'volcano' (*poo kŏw fai*), in which the pork is fried and served with pineapple and sweet and sour sauce – but there are also Thai salads, soups and stir-fries. It's near the road to the bus station.

❶ Getting There & Around

Nang Rong's **bus station** (☑ 044 631517) is on the western side of town and sees buses to/from all big cities in southern Isan including Surin (80B to 100B, two hours, every 30 minutes), Ubon Ratchathani (144B to 265B, six hours, 12 daily), Khorat (60B to 95B, two hours, hourly), and Pak Chong (125B, three hours, hourly), plus Bangkok (231B to 275, 5½ to six hours, hourly).

P California Inter Hostel hires motorcycles for 250B to 300B per day. Nang Rong **taxis** (☑ 093 551 4175, 092 478 0529) park at the bus station; a return trip to Phanom Rung and Muang Tam should run to about 1000B.

Phanom Rung Historical Park

The most spectacular Khmer monument in Thailand, Prasat Phanom Rung ('Big Mountain Temple') sits on the summit of a spent volcano 200m above the paddy fields. The dramatic entrance and beautiful design make it a must-visit attraction for anyone in the area.

Down below is the wonderful but often overlooked Prasat Muang Tam ('Lower City Temple'), which is also part of the historical park. It's smaller and less complete, but the peaceful setting – you'll often have it to yourself – and unique design make many people prefer it over its more famous neighbour.

◉ Sights

★ Prasat Phanom Rung
RUINS

(ปราสาทเขาพนมรุ้ง; ☑ 044 666251; 100B, combined ticket with Prasat Muang Tam 150B; ⊙ 6am-6pm) Prasat Phanom Rung has a knock-you-dead location. Crowning the summit of a spent volcano, this sanctuary sits 200m above the paddy fields below. To the southeast you can see Cambodia's Dongrek Mountains, and it's in this direction

PRASAT MUANG TAM

In the little village of Khok Meuang, the restored Khmer temple of **Prasat Muang Tam** (ปราสาทเมืองต่ำ; ☑ 044 666251; 100B, combined ticket with Prasat Phanom Rung 150B; ◷ 6am-6pm) is an ideal bolt-on to any visit to Phanom Rung, which is only 8km to the northwest. Dating back to the late 10th or early 11th century, this is generally considered Isan's third-most-interesting temple complex in terms of size, atmosphere and the quality of restoration work, but because so few people visit (you might have it all to yourself) it is some people's favourite.

The whole complex, built as a shrine to Shiva, has an unusual layout. Most significantly, the five towers (the main one could not be rebuilt) are grouped three in front and two in back rather than the expected quincunx cross shape. And Muang Tam is the only Khmer temple to have four L-shaped ponds at each corner.

Begin your visit across the road in the small **information centre** (◷ 8am-4.30pm) **FREE**, next to Baray Muang Tam (a 510m-by-1090m Khmer-era reservoir), which has good displays about the site.

Motorcycle-taxi drivers will add Muang Tam onto a trip to Phanom Rung for another 100B to 150B.

that the capital of the Angkor empire once lay. The temple was erected as a Hindu monument to Shiva between the 10th and 13th centuries, the bulk of it during the reign of King Suriyavarman II (r AD 1113–50).

Below the main sanctuary, above the long row of gift shops, an **information centre** (◷ 8.30am-4.30pm) **FREE** houses artefacts found at the site and displays about both the construction and the restoration, which took 17 years. You can pick up a free informative brochure or arrange a Thai-speaking guide (price is negotiable) here. Those who don't want to climb can use an upper parking lot (50B per car), but the brochure usually isn't available there.

One of the most remarkable aspects of Phanom Rung is the **promenade** leading to the main gate. It begins on a slope 400m east of the main tower with three earthen **terraces**. Next comes a cruciform base for what may have been a wooden pavilion. To the right of this is the **Phlab Phla**, assumed to be where royalty bathed and changed clothes before entering the temple complex. You then step down to a 160m-long **processional walkway** flanked by sandstone pillars with early Angkor-style lotus-bud tops. This walkway ends at the first and largest of three **naga bridges**, flanked by 16 five-headed *naga* in the classic Angkor style. As at all Khmer temples, these symbolic 'bridges' represent the passing from the earthly realm to the heavenly.

At the top, the magnificent **east gallery** leads into the main sanctuary. The **main tower** has a gallery on each of its four sides, and excellent sculptures of Shiva and Vaishnava deities can be seen in the lintels and pediments over the doorways and in various other key points on the exterior. On the eastern portico of the **mandapa** (hall in front of the main tower) is a Nataraja (Dancing Shiva) and the well-known Narai Bandhomsindhu lintel, which represent the destruction and rebirth of the universe respectively, while on the southern entrance are the remains of Shiva and Uma riding their bull mount, Nandi. The central cell of the main tower contains a Shivalingam (phallus image), and in front of it is an evocative Nandi statue.

⚜ Festivals & Events

Phanom Rung Festival   CULTURAL
(◷ Apr) Phanom Rung faces east, and four times a year the sun can be seen through all 15 sanctuary doorways. The correct solar alignment happens during sunrise from 3 to 5 April and 8 to 10 September and sunset from 5 to 7 March and 5 to 7 October (some years are one day earlier). The park extends its hours during these events, and locals celebrate the Phanom Rung Festival around the April alignment with ancient Brahman ceremonies and modern sound-and-light shows.

🛏 Sleeping & Eating

The only accommodation in the immediate area of the temple complexes is **Thanyaporn Homestay** (☑ 087 431 3741; r incl breakfast 500-

800B; P ✉ ❄ 🛜), a great budget guesthouse near Prasat Muang Tam. Most people spend the night in Nang Rong, though there's now decent accommodation in most of the other surrounding towns.

There are daytime-only food stalls at Prasat Phanom Rung and Prasat Muang Tam, plus a few simple restaurants (all closing early) in Ban Khok Meuang, the village next to Muang Tam.

★ **Baan Bong Pha Om**   GUESTHOUSE $$
(📱 084 236 5060, 095 620 5932; r incl breakfast 400-1200B; P ❄ 🛜) Bringing artistic flair and fantastic value to the rice fields of rural Buriram, this family-run place is fun, attractive and utterly relaxing. Many of the 14 creative rooms are up on stilts, with balconies and open-air showers. Some are in converted shipping containers, while the best – the House rooms (590B) and the Big Room (1200B) – are borderline luxurious and worth the extra baht.

❶ Getting There & Away

There's no public transport to Phanom Rung or Muang Tam. The best budget option is hiring a motorcycle from **P California Inter Hostel** (p417) in Nang Rong. You can also go by motorcycle-taxi (600B return) or car and driver (1000B) from Nang Rong. It costs 100/200B for the motorcycle/car to add Muang Tam.

P California Inter Hostel's standard one-day tour (2340B for four people) is a good choice because as well as Phanom Rung, Muang Tam and Wat Khao Angkhan you'll get to visit a silk-weaving village.

Otherwise you can take a bus from Nang Rong to the busy Ban Tako (20B to 30B, 20 minutes, every 30 minutes) junction 14km east of town, where motorcycle taxis usually charge 300B to Phanom Rung, including waiting time, but they sometimes demand more from non-Thai speakers. Buses from further afield (Pak Chong, Surin etc) also stop here, so if you are only visiting as a day trip you don't need to go into Nang Rong first. There are no longer motorcycle taxis in Ban Ta Pek, the village nearest to Phanom Rung.

Around Phanom Rung

For those with an insatiable appetite for Khmer ruins, the area around Phanom Rung offers a smorgasbord of lesser-known sites that, taken together, create a picture of the crucial role this region once played in the Khmer empire. Most people find these places of only minor interest, but driving

MOUNTAIN TEMPLE

Although peaceful **Wat Khao Angkhan** (วัดเขาอังคาร; ⏱ daylight hours) atop an extinct volcano has an ancient past, as evidenced by the 8th- or 9th-century Dvaravati sandstone boundary markers, it's the modern constructions that make Wat Khao Angkhan worth a visit. The *bòht* and several other flamboyant buildings were erected in 1982 in an unusual nouveau-Khmer style that sort of harks back to the age of empire. Inside the *bòht*, the *Jataka* murals, painted by Burmese artists, have English captions.

The temple also hosts a Chinese-style pagoda, a 29m reclining Buddha and beautiful views of the surrounding mountains.

The temple is about 20km from either Nang Rong or Phanom Rung, and there's no public transport. The route is pretty well signposted.

through this rice-growing region offers an unvarnished look at village life and will surely make for an enlightening trip. All of the following sites, restored to some degree by the Fine Arts Department, are free of charge and open during daylight hours.

Kuti Reusi Nong Bua Rai sits right below Phanom Rung to the east, and the similar but more atmospheric **Kuti Reusi Khok Meuang** is just northwest of Prasat Muang Tam across the road from the baray.

Little of **Prasat Khao Plaibat** is left standing, but the adventure of finding it, along with cool views of Phanom Rung and the Dangrek Mountains on the Cambodian border, makes it worth seeking out. The seldom-used trail starts at Wat Khao Plaibat, 3km from Prasat Muang Tam. Pass the gate (even though there's a 'monk zone, no entry' sign in Thai on the gate, we have been assured that it's okay to use this path to visit the ruin) behind the giant Buddha image, veer right at the *gù·dì* (monks' quarters) and slip through the barbed-wire fence. From here take the path to the right, and then a quick left up the hill and follow the strips of orange cloth tied to trees. The walk up the hill should take less than 30 minutes if you don't get lost along the way, though it's likely you will. Just keep aiming for the top of the hill and you'll eventually get there.

Around Phanom Rung

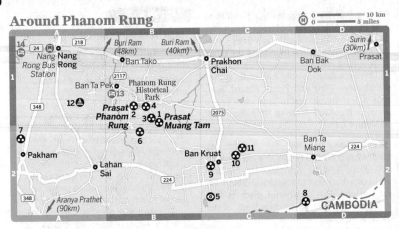

Prasat Khok Ngio, 3km before Pakham, has a small, dirty museum with old pots, human bones and Buddha images unearthed at and near the temple.

Prasat Thong (aka Khok Prasat), near the market in the middle of Ban Kruat town, is small and the three towers have lost their tops, but it's worth a stop if you're passing through.

The sandstone used to build these ancient structures came from the widely scattered **Lan Hin Dtat Ban Kruat** (Ban Kruat quarry), which is best seen at Wat Lan Hin Dtat, southwest of Ban Kruat town. Several cutting sites can be seen along a 1km-long surfaced path that starts east of the parking lot. The biggest cutting site is 100m down a side branch of this path: from the parking lot take the trail to the right after the Buddha statue and it's just past the last *gù·dì*.

Also near Ban Kruat are **Tao Nai Chian** and the larger **Tao Sawai**, two kilns that supplied pottery to much of the Khmer empire between the 9th and 13th centuries. Today they're little more than piles of dirt and brick with protective roofs over them.

You can easily add Surin Province's Prasat Ta Meuan (p424) to your trip around this region. It's 55km from Phanom Rung.

SURIN & SI SAKET PROVINCES

Surin and Si Saket Provinces are full of Angkor-era Khmer ruins. Most are rather modest and of interest only to those with a history habit. On the other hand, the artwork at Sikhoraphum is outstanding, and Prasat Ta Meuan, out in the jungle, is very evocative.

Besides the ruins, Surin Province is famous for the elephant round-up and is home to Ban Ta Klang elephant village, as well as some famous craft centres, while Si

Saket can offer Wat Lan Khuat, one of Thailand's most unusual Buddhist temples.

Sights

★ Wat Lan Khuat
BUDDHIST TEMPLE

(วัดล้านขวด; ⊙daylight hours) FREE Officially it's Wat Pa Maha Chedi Kaeo, but these days nearly everyone calls it Wat Lan Khuat, the 'Million Bottle Temple'. In 1982 the abbot dreamt of a *prah·sàht* in heaven made of diamonds and gems. Realising that this symbolised the need for clarity of purpose in one's life, he decided to replicate the idea as best he could on earth by covering nearly every surface of every building of his temple with glass bottles.

The more you look around, the less the name seems like an exaggeration. He took the theme one step further by using bottle caps to create much of the adornment. It's in Khun Han, 11km south of Hwy 24 via Rte 2111. Turn west at the roundabout in the centre of town.

Surin
สุรินทร์

📞 044 / POP 40,100

Surin city doesn't have much to say for itself until November, when the provincial capital explodes into life for the Surin Elephant Round-up, during which it hosts giant scrums of both pachyderms and tourists. It does, however, make the most comfortable base for exploring the sites further afield.

Sights

Surin National Museum
MUSEUM

(พิพิธภัณฑสถานแห่งชาติสุรินทร์; 📞 044 153054; Th Surin-Prasat; ⊙8.30am-4.30pm Wed-Sun) FREE Displays at this well-executed museum focus on the province's Khmer ruins and Surin's three ethnic groups: Lao, Khmer and Suai, the region's renowned elephant herders. It's 4km south of town on Rte 214. Several *sŏrng·tăa·ou* (10B) pass it. The most frequent are the orange ones going to Prasat that park in front of the fresh market (*dà·làht sòt*), west of the clock tower. Another is the pink 1 that passes in front of the bus station and then the clock tower.

Queen Sirikit Sericulture Center Surin
ARTS CENTRE

(ศูนย์หม่อนไหมเฉลิมพระเกียรติสมเด็จพระนางเจ้าสิริกิติ์ พระบรมราชินีนาถ (สุรินทร์); 📞 044 511393; Rte 226; ⊙8am-4pm) FREE You can see the entire silk-making process, from larva to loom, at this research centre 4km west of town. The displays (with very limited English) can be seen any time, though the weavers only work on weekdays.

Sleeping

Prices skyrocket during November's Elephant Round-up and hotels fill up fast, so book as far in advance as possible if you're visiting at that time.

★ Baan Chang Ton
HOMESTAY $

(📞 087 459 8962; www.baanchangton.com; Th Suriyarart; r incl breakfast 400-500B; P❈@🔊) The friendly owners here have rescued an old wooden house and created one of Isan's most charming places to stay. It's quite simple (shared bathrooms, mattresses on the floor and air-con in only one room) but the atmosphere makes it special. Guests can use the kitchen or, if arranged in advance, join the family for dinner. There are also free bikes to use.

Maneerote Hotel
HOTEL $

(📞 044 539477; www.maneerotehotel.com; Soi Poi Tunggor, Th Krungsri Nai; r 450-500B; P❈@🔊) This quiet hotel southwest of the fresh market is hands-down the best-value place in town. Rooms are clean and modern and there's an attached restaurant and coffee shop.

Surin Majestic Hotel
HOTEL $$

(📞 044 713980; www.surinmajestic.com; Th Jitrbumrung; r incl breakfast 1200-2200B; ste 4500B; P❈@🔊☲) The rooms here are clean and bright, though overall nothing special. But they can fetch these prices because they're the best in town and there are plenty of extras, including a big swimming pool and a fitness room. It's in the heart of town next to the bus station.

ℹ ELEPHANT FESTIVAL

Surin celebrates its famous and controversial **Elephant Round-up** for 11 days in mid-November. The main attraction is a 300-elephant battle re-enactment. Elephant 'shows' of all kinds are contentious because the elephants are forced to undergo torturous training to become tame enough. Consider this if you are thinking of attending.

Eating

⭐ Surin Green Market
THAI

(Th Jitrbumrung; ⊘5am-noon Sat-Sun) Foodies in town on a weekend should make this popular market their breakfast destination. Although there's a variety of food available, Isan dishes are the most common. This is one place to sample the local speciality, *gòp yát sài* (herb-stuffed frog). Silk fabric and other handicrafts are sold here too.

On Saturday the market is in the city centre at the OTOP shop and on Sunday it moves south of town to the entrance of Rajamangala University.

⭐ Som Tam Petmanee 2
THAI $

(Th Murasart; mains 30-100B; ⊘8am-4pm) AKA Som Tom Mae Pet, this simple Isan restaurant by Wat Salaloi (there's no Roman-script sign, but look for the large chicken grill) is Surin's most famous purveyor of *sôm·đam* (spicy green-papaya salad) and *gài yâhng* (grilled chicken). The *súp nòr mái* (bamboo-shoot dipping sauce) is good, too. Little English is spoken or written, but the food is so good it's worth stumbling through an order.

Surin Pochana
THAI $

(Th Tanasan; mains 60-250B; ⊘4pm-2am) A Surin classic, this simple place has served delicious Thai fare, including a good *đôm yam* and fried frog with basil, since 1943. It's between the train station and the fountain.

Kit Teung Bakery & Coffee
BAKERY, COFFEE $

(☑086 468 9414; Th Sanit Nikomrat; cakes 80B; ⊘7am-8pm; ☎) This bright, modern place just southeast of the train station has some of the best coffee in town, but it really sets itself apart with a fun selection of Thai baked goods.

Sydney Canale
INTERNATIONAL, THAI $$

(☑089 428 4711; 349/4 Th Tesabam 1; mains 90-690B; ⊘10am-3pm & 5-10pm; ☎) Filling big premises beside a section of the old outer moat, this is the top choice for *fa·ràng* (Western) food in Surin's city centre. It has air-con and open-air sections. The Australian-trained chef does a variety of dishes including fish and chips, pizza and duck breast fillet with orange sauce, plus a pretty mean crème caramel and some Thai and Japanese, too.

Shopping

OTOP
ARTS & CRAFTS

(Th Jitrbumrung; ⊘8am-4pm Mon-Sat) Across from the Provincial Hall, this shop has the broadest selection of crafts in town, including lots of silk fabric.

ⓘ Information

Banks in the **Surin Plaza** (Th Thesaban 1) mall, 250m west of the fountain, are the only ones in the city centre open evenings and weekends.

Ruampaet Hospital (☑044 513192; Th Tesabarn 1) Large full-service hospital in central Surin.

Tourism Authority of Thailand (TAT; ☑044 514447; tatsurin@tat.or.th; Th Tesabarn 1; ⊘8.30am-4.30pm)

ⓘ Getting There & Away

BUS

In addition to buses to distant cities, *sŏrng·tăa·ou* and minivans to local destinations such as Ban Ta Klang (50B, two hours, hourly 6am to 4pm) and Chong Chom (for the Cambodian border; 45B, 1½ hours, frequent from 5.30am to 6.30pm) depart from Surin's **bus terminal** (☑044 511756; Th Jitrbumrung).

BUSES TO/FROM SURIN

DESTINATION	FARE (B)	DURATION (HR)	FREQUENCY
Bangkok	275-353	7-8	hourly 7.30am-11pm
Khon Kaen	160-205	5	every 45min 3.30am-3pm
Nakhon Ratchasima (Khorat)	115-218	4	every 30min 3.30am-8pm
Nang Rong	80-100	2	every 30min 3.30am-8pm
Roi Et	90	2½	hourly 5am-5pm
Ubon Ratchathani	130-202	3½	12 departures 3.20am-10.30pm

ⓘ GETTING TO CAMBODIA: SURIN & SI SAKET

Chong Chom to O Smach

Getting to the border Because of the casino, there are plenty of public minibuses (45B, 1½ hours, frequent from 5.30am to 6.30pm) from Surin's bus terminal to the border at Chong Chom.

At the border The Cambodian border is open from 7am to 10pm and visas are available on the spot. There's a 5B fee at Thai immigration on weekends and early mornings/late afternoons.

Moving on There are two buses from O Smach to the City Angkor Hotel in Siem Reap (350B, three hours, 8am, 5pm). Chartering a 'taxi' (drivers wait at the border looking for passengers) for the drive to Siem Reap should cost 2000B or less, and you can wait for others to share the costs, though this is generally only possible in the morning.

Chong Sa-Ngam to Choam

This border crossing in Si Saket Province sees very little traffic, despite the road to Siem Reap being in excellent shape, because the route isn't serviced by public transport. Lots of private minivans shuttle gamblers from Si Saket and Ubon Ratchathani cities, so you could check with a travel agent about joining one.

Nakhorn Chai Air (☑ 044 515151) has the best service to Bangkok.

TRAIN

Surin train station (☑ 045 511295) is on the line between Bangkok (73B to 1186B, seven to nine hours, nine daily) and Ubon Ratchathani (31B to 382B, two to four hours, 12 daily).

ⓘ Getting Around

Surin is very convenient for travellers; virtually everything you'll want or need is within a few blocks of the bus and train stations. If you don't want to walk, túk-túk charge 40B to 60B for a trip within the centre and pedicabs a bit less. Surin also has a few taxis; they park at the bus station and don't use their meters.

Saren Travel & Tour (☑ 090 273 5665, 044 513828; 282/33 Th Surinpakdee; ⊗8am-5pm Mon-Fri, 9am-4pm Sat) and **Surin Chai Kit restaurant** (☑ 086 876 3559, 088 714 4456; 297 Th Tanasarn; mains 30-55B; ⊗7am-3pm Mon-Sat; 🛜) have car hire, with or without drivers. The latter also hires motorcycles (per day 300B), as does **Farang Connection**, an expat bar behind the bus station. Pirom, of **Pirom-Aree's House** (044 515140, 089 355 4140; r 200B; 🅿 ➌ 🛜), does expensive but excellent tours.

Around Surin

Ban Ta Klang
บ้านตากลาง

☑ 044 / POP 903

The little Suai village of Ban Ta Klang and its neighbours, where people and pachyderms

live side by side, are a bit of a mixed bag. Its main attraction, mostly for Thai tourists, is the only elephant camp in Isan, and it is focused on rides and an old-fashioned 'talent show'. On the other hand, the modern ethical elephant encounter programs, where the elephants are well cared for and there is no riding or tricks, are among the best in Thailand.

🏃 Activities

While the **Elephant Study Centre** (☑ 044 145050) made Ban Ta Klang famous, three separate but affiliated ethical elephant encounter programs are making it great. The veteran **Surin Project** (☑ 084 482 1210; www.surinproject.org; Ban Ta Klang) 🌿 and the new **Surin Elephant Homestay** (☑ 081 199 7659; www.elephantnaturepark.org; Ban Ta Klang) 🌿 and **Elephant Lover Home** (☑ 081 618 5232; www.elephantnaturepark.org; Ban Ta Klang) 🌿, all supported by Chiang Mai's renowned Save Elephant Foundation (p755), are not elephant rescue sanctuaries; rather they provide employment for local mahouts so their elephants don't need to do tricks, give rides or spend their days chained up (p754).

All three programs are essentially the same, with a mix of walking and swimming with the elephants, working alongside the mahouts to care for them, and various cultural activities. And, unlike the typical Thai elephant program, here you are staying in a village.

WORTH A TRIP

TEMPLES OF SI SAKET

If you're headed to Khao Phra Wihan, you may pass through Si Saket. There's not a whole lot to do but there are a couple of fine temples hereabouts.

Thirty kilometres west of Si Saket via Rte 226 in Amphoe Uthumphon Phisai, **Prasat Wat Sa Kamphaeng Yai** (⊙ daylight hours) **FREE**, built as a shrine to Shiva, features four 11th-century *prang* and two 'libraries' built of sandstone and brick. The *prang* have lost their tops, but many lintels and other carvings remain. A new museum has been built, but it remains empty for the foreseeable future. Minivans from Surin (60B, 1½ hours, frequent) to Si Saket can drop you very close.

Also worth a visit is the 'Million Bottle Temple', **Wat Lan Khuat** (p421) – the name makes sense when you see it. It's in Khun Han, 11km south of Hwy 24 via Rte 2111. Turn west at the roundabout in the centre of Si Saket town.

They offer week-long full-board programs which can be booked through the Save Elephant Foundation's website (www.elephantnaturepark.org/enp). Shorter visits are possible when space is available; call the projects directly about this. The minimum age is 16.

🛏 Sleeping & Eating

The three ethical elephant projects (p423) operating in the area include lodging and meals as part of the program. There's also a **hotel** (☑087 248 8355; Ban Ta Klang; d/tw 500/700B; ▣ 🖻) and a **homestay** (☑053 272855; Ban Ta Klang; per person 200B, meals 50-100B; ▣), of sorts, in Ban Ta Klang village.

Ban Ta Klang has a few restaurants, open for breakfast, lunch and dinner, facing the Elephant Study Centre. Even though most customers are tourists, the food is uncompromised and delicious.

❶ Getting There & Away

Sŏrng·tăa·ou run to Ban Ta Klang from Surin's bus terminal (50B, two hours, hourly), with the last one usually returning at 5pm, though plan to leave by 4pm, just to be safe. The *sŏrng·tăa·ou* don't park in the village, they just circle through, passing in front of the Elephant Study Centre.

Craft Villages

There are many craft villages within easy striking distance of Surin city and many of the products, including *pâh hohl* (a geometric pattern that bears a slight resemblance to *mát·mèe* but isn't tie-dyed) fabric, have a Cambodian influence. Surin silks aren't readily available in other parts of Thailand, and prices are much cheaper here.

The most famous weaving centre is **Chansoma** (จันทร์โสมา; ☑081 726 0397; ⊙8am-5pm) **FREE** in Ban Tha Sawang village. Two other good ones are **Ban Khwao Sinarin** and **Ban Chok**, next-door neighbours 18km north of Surin, that are known for silk (now mostly synthetic) and silver. One of the weaving specialities is *yók dòrk,* a simpler brocade style than what's made by Chansoma, but it still requires up to 50 foot-pedals on the looms. The best place to see it is the Mu 2 neighbourhood. The silver standout is *prà keuam,* a Cambodian style of bead brought to Thailand by Ban Chok's ancestors many centuries ago. You can see it, and other jewellery, being made in the little **OTOP handicrafts mall** at the eastern end of the villages or at some homes to the south. Big blue *sŏrng·tăa·ou* to Ban Khwao Sinarin (30B, two hours, hourly in the morning) depart from Surin's bus station and a few others from an unnamed *soi* just south of the train station – look for the blue Philips sign. The last one leaves Ban Khwao Sinarin at 3pm.

Prasat Ta Meuan   ปราสาทตาเมือน

The most atmospheric of Surin's Khmer ruins is a series of three sites in the forest on the Cambodian border known collectively as **Prasat Ta Meuan** (⊙9am-3pm) **FREE**. They line the ancient Khmer road linking Angkor Wat to Phimai (p411).

The first site, **Prasat Ta Meuan** proper, was built in the Jayavarman VII period (AD 1181–1210) as part of a rest stop for travellers. It's a fairly small monument with a two-door, five-window sanctuary constructed completely of laterite blocks. One sandstone lintel, of a meditating Buddha, remains.

Just 300m south, **Prasat Ta Meuan Toht**, which was the chapel for a 'healing station', is a bit larger. Also built by Jayavarman VII, the ruins consist of a *gopura, mon·dòp* and main *prang,* all surrounded by a laterite wall.

Nearly 1km further on, next to the army base at the end of the road, is the largest site, **Prasat Ta Meuan Thom**. This Shiva shrine, built around a natural rock linga, pre-dates the others by as much as two centuries. Despite a somewhat haphazard reconstruction (and major damage from when it was occupied by the Khmer Rouge in the 1980s), this one justifies the effort it takes to get here. Three *prang* and a large hall are built of sandstone blocks on a laterite base, and several smaller buildings still stand inside the boundary wall. No significant carvings remain. A stairway on the southern end (like Phimai, this temple faces south) drops to Cambodian territory, which begins at the tree line.

The sites begin 10.3km south of Ban Ta Miang (on Rte 224, 23km east of Ban Kruat) via a winding road used more by cows than cars. You need your own transport to get here, and a visit is just as convenient from Phanom Rung (p417) as from Surin city. Note the closing time: because of its proximity to the border, the times were chosen for security reasons, though there's no actual risk here as long as you don't wander into the forest.

Other Khmer Temple Ruins

The 11th-century **Prasat Ban Phluang** (ปราสาทบ้านพลวง; 50B; ⊙7am-6pm) `FREE`, 33km south of Surin, is just a solitary sandstone *prang* (Hindi/Khmer-style stupa) without its top, but the wonderful carvings (including Indra riding his elephant Airavata – Erawan in Thai – with just a single head rather than the usual three) make it worth a stop. The site sits 600m off Rte 214; the turn-off is 2.5km south of Hwy 24. Any vehicle from Surin bound for Kap Choeng or the border can drop you nearby (25B to 30B, 30 minutes).

Prasat Sikhoraphum (ปราสาทศีขรภูมิ; 50B; ⊙7.30am-6pm) is a larger and more rewarding Khmer site 30km northeast of Surin. Built in the 12th century, Sikhoraphum features five brick *prang* (Hindi/Khmer-style stupas), two of which still hold their tops (these were later modified by Lao

people who controlled this area after the Khmer), including the 32m-tall central one. Only one lintel remains, but it's a stunner. Located off Rte 226, Sikhoraphum can be reached by minivan (30B, one hour, frequent) or train (7B to 30B, 30 minutes, seven during the daytime) from Surin city. Sikhoraphum, incidentally, is well known for its *gah·lá·maa*, the Thai version of caramel. A shop (look for the elephant sign) near the ruins makes and sells it.

If you happen to be driving to Sikhoraphum you may as well take a 400m detour off Rte 226 for a peep at **Prasat Muang Thi** (ปราสาทเมืองที; ⊙daylight hours) `FREE`. The three remaining brick *prang* are in sad shape (one looks as though it's ready to topple), but they're so small they're kind of cute.

UBON RATCHATHANI PROVINCE

Little-visited Ubon Ratchathani is one of Thailand's most interesting provinces. The capital city has plenty of history and charm, and Pha Taem National Park has so much to see that it warrants a couple of days. Even more remote is the jungle-clad intersection of Thailand, Laos and Cambodia, now known as the 'Emerald Triangle'.

Ubon Ratchathani อุบลราชธานี

☑045 / POP 86,800

Few cities in Isan reward aimless wandering as richly as Ubon Ratchathani. Survive the usual knot of choked access roads, and the 'Royal City of the Lotus' will reveal an altogether more attractive face. Racked up against Mae Nam Mun, Thailand's second-longest river, the historic heart of the city, south of Th Kueuan Thani, has a sluggish character rarely found in the region's big conurbations. And throughout the city there are many interesting temples beckoning cultural travellers.

Ubon grew prosperous as a US airbase during the Vietnam War and is now a financial, educational and agricultural market centre. It's not a busy tourist destination, but the nearby Thai–Lao border crossing at Chong Mek generates a small but steady stream of travellers who by and large enjoy their visit.

Ubon Ratchathani

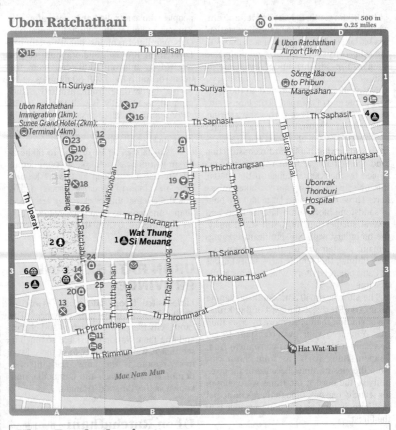

Ubon Ratchathani

◎ Top Sights
1 Wat Thung Si Meuang............................ B3

◎ Sights
2 Thung Si Meuang................................... A3
3 Ubon Ratchathani National
   Museum.. A3
4 Wat Si Pradu... D1
5 Wat Sri Ubon Rattanaram.................... A3
6 Wat Sri Ubon Rattanaram Museum..... A3

◈ Activities, Courses & Tours
7 Ubonvej Thai Massage.......................... B2

◉ Sleeping
8 28 Rachabutr.. A4
9 Outside Inn... D1
10 Phadaeng Hotel.................................... A2
11 Sri Isan Hotel....................................... A4
12 T3 House... A2

◉ Eating
13 Gway-tiao Gai Boran A3

14 Night Market.. A3
   Outside Inn....................................(see 9)
15 Peppers.. A1
16 Porntip Gai Yang Wat Jaeng................ B1
17 Rung Roj... B1
18 Sam Chai Cafe...................................... A2

◉ Drinking & Nightlife
19 U-Bar...B2

◉ Shopping
20 Again Please... A3
21 Camp Fai Ubon..................................... B2
22 Khampun... A2
23 Punchard... A2
24 Walking Street Market........................ A3

◉ Information
25 Tourism Authority of Thailand.............. A3

◉ Transport
   Outside Inn Motorcycle Hire.........(see 9)
26 Sakda Travel World.............................. A2

Sights

★ Wat Thung Si Meuang BUDDHIST TEMPLE
(วัดทุ่งศรีเมือง; Th Luang; ☉ daylight hours) FREE
Built during the reign of Rama III (1824–51), Wat Thung Si Meuang has a classic *hŏr đrai* (Tripitaka hall) in excellent shape. Like many *hŏr đrai,* it rests on stilts in the middle of a pond to protect the precious scriptures (written on palm-leaf paper) from termites. It's kept open so you can look inside. The original murals in the little *bòht* beside the *hŏr đrai* show life in that era and are in remarkably good condition.

Wat Phra That Nong Bua BUDDHIST TEMPLE
(วัดพระธาตุหนองบัว; Th Thammawithi; ☉ daylight hours, chedi 7am-7pm) FREE This spectacular, gleaming gold-and-white *chedi* is sure to dazzle. It loosely resembles the Mahabodhi stupa in Bodhgaya, India (where the Buddha reached enlightenment), and inside is another beautiful golden *chedi*. The latter was built in 1956 in honour of the 2500th anniversary of Buddhism, and the 55m-tall exterior went up over it 12 years later.

The temple is on the outskirts of town, reached by *sŏrng·tăa·ou* 10.

Wat Ban Na Meuang BUDDHIST TEMPLE
(วัดบ้านนาเมือง; ☉ daylight hours) FREE This temple, also known as Wat Sa Prasan Suk, stands out from other temples in many ways. Most famously, the *bòht* sits on a boat: a ceramic-encrusted replica of the late King Rama IX's royal barge *Suphannahong*, complete with crew. The *wí·hăhn* also has a boat-shaped base, this one resembling the second-most-important royal barge, *Anantanagaraj*; and it's surrounded by an actual pond.

Wat Si Pradu BUDDHIST TEMPLE
(วัดศรีประดู่; Th Buraphanok; ☉ daylight hours) FREE This temple's lovely, modern *bòht* has a soaring wing-shaped design that creates a striking scene inside. The delightful murals cover many subjects including the *Jataka* (past life stories of the Buddha) and feature many brightly coloured creatures from the mythical Himmapan forest.

A neighbourhood women's group does various handicrafts in a couple of buildings on the grounds.

Wat Sri Ubon Rattanaram Museum MUSEUM
(พิพิธภัณฑ์วัดศรีอุบลรัตนาราม; Th Uparat; ☉ 9am-4pm Wed-Sun) FREE The temple (วัดศรีอุบล รัตนาราม; Th Uparat; ☉ daylight hours) FREE has turned a beautiful old wooden *săh·lah* (hall) into a museum of religious items. The highlight is the collection of 18th-century *đoô prá đraiþìdòk*, cabinets used for storing sacred palm-leaf texts.

Ubon Ratchathani National Museum MUSEUM
(พิพิธภัณฑสถานแห่งชาติอุบลราชธานี; Th Kheuan Thani; 100B; ☉ 9am-4pm Wed-Sun) Occupying the former city hall (built 1918), this is a very informative museum with plenty on show, from Dvaravati-era Buddhas and 2000-year-old Dong Son bronze drums to Ubon textiles and clever little animal traps. The museum's most prized possession is a 9th-century Khmer Ardhanarisvara, a composite statue combining Shiva and his consort Uma into one being. It's one of just two ever found in Thailand.

Activities

Ubonvej Thai Massage MASSAGE
(☏ 045 260345; www.ubonvej.com; 113 Th Thepyothi; 2hr massage 250B; ☉ 10am-10pm) The front door declares boldly 'No Sex', but step inside this classy place and this would never be in doubt. There are many different kinds of massage to choose from besides just the standard Thai, and some English is spoken.

Legacy Gym MARTIAL ARTS
(☏ 089 627 8423, 045 264708; www.legacygym.com; Th Srisangthong; half-/full-day sessions 400/700B, training with accommodation per month from 12,500B) This gym is run by Ole Laursen, a Filipino-Danish former professional *moo·ay tai* (Thai kickboxing) fighter now living in Ubon. It's well set up for Westerners and offers accommodation and training packages. Women and men train here (although there's no 'women-only' session) and it's suitable for both serious fighters and those just wanting to train in fitness.

Festivals & Events

Candle Parade CULTURAL
(Kabuan Hae Tian; ☉ usually Jul) Ubon's famous Candle Parade began during the reign of King Rama V, when the appointed governor decided the rocket festival (p443) was too dangerous. The original simple designs have since grown (with the help of internal frames) to gigantic, elaborately carved wax sculptures. The parade is part of Khao Phansaa (the start of Buddhist Lent).

Lai Reua Fai CULTURAL

(⊙late Oct/early Nov) Ubon has a modest Lai Reua Fai (illuminated boat procession) during Ork Phansaa (the end of Buddhist Lent).

🛏 Sleeping

Phadaeng Hotel HOTEL $

(📞045 254600; thephadaen@gmail.com; Th Phadaeng; r 500B; P❄@⑦) One of the best-value hotels in Ubon, the Phadaeng has well-maintained rooms (they look almost brand new) with good furnishings including large TVs and desks. It's a good location just minutes from Thung Si Meuang park, and the large parking area separates it from street noise. The hotel is livened up with copies of classic paintings. Bike hire costs 50B per day.

28 Rachabutr GUESTHOUSE $

(📞089 144 3789; 28 Th Ratchabut; dm 180-230B, r with fan 280-380B, with air-con 430B; ❄⑦) Friendly and welcoming with a great location, this home turned guesthouse is very backpacker-friendly. Rooms are simple (the dorms have just thin mattresses on the floor) with shared bathrooms, but they have character and some have river views, as do the terraces in back. It's potentially quite communal, though this being Ubon, there aren't always other travellers here.

★ Outside Inn GUESTHOUSE $$

(📞088 581 2069; www.theoutsideinnubon.com; 11 Th Suriyat; r incl breakfast 650-799B; P❄@⑦) A nice little garden lounge area sets the relaxed, communal vibe here. The rooms are large, comfy and fitted with tastefully designed reclaimed-timber furnishings. Owners Brent and Tun are great hosts, cook some good **food** (Th Suriyat; mains 50-225B; ⊙11am-2.30pm & 5-9pm Wed-Mon; ⑦🍴), and have lots of advice on what to see and do in the area.

It's a long walk to the town's main attractions, but there are bikes (free for guests; 50B per day for others) and motorcycles (p430), and *sŏrng·tăa·ou* 10 can deliver you from the bus station.

T3 House HOTEL $$

(📞045 244911; t3house.ubon@gmail.com; Soi Saphasit 1, Th Saphasit; r 600-700B; P❄❄⑦) A solid option at this price, with a modern look and quality all around including rain showers, fast internet and excellent mattresses. It's tucked down a small *soi* so it's quite quiet. It's such a good bargain that it's often full.

Sunee Grand Hotel HOTEL $$$

(📞045 352900; www.suneegrandhotel.com; Th Chayangkun; incl breakfast r 1800-3200B, ste 3600B; P❄❄@⑦❄) Although it's not truly 'grand', this is Ubon's best hotel. From the stylish light fixtures to the at-a-snap service, it will meet expectations. There's a piano in the lobby, airport pick-up and a spa, and the adjacent shopping mall has a cinema and a kid-sized rooftop water park.

🍴 Eating

★ Rung Roj THAI $

(Th Nakhonban; mains 50-290B; ⊙9.30am-8.30pm Mon-Sat) An Ubon institution serving excellent food using family recipes and only fresh ingredients. Many people swear by the ox-tongue stew. From the outside it looks more like a well-to-do house than a restaurant, and inside it has 1950s and '60s classic rock 'n roll music and decor to match.

Gway-tiao Gai Boran THAI $

(Th Phrommarat; mains 35-40B; ⊙8.30am-3pm Mon-Sat) Yes, the *gŏo·ay·dĕe·o* (noodle soup) here is delicious, but we also love this place for its old-time feel. It's part of the revival of the old city centre.

Porntip Gai Yang Wat Jaeng THAI $

(Th Saphasit; mains 40-130B; ⊙8am-6pm) It looks like a tornado has whipped through this no-frills spot, but the chefs cook up a storm of their own. This is considered by many to be Ubon's premier purveyor of *gài yâhng* (grilled chicken), *sôm·đam* (spicy green-papaya salad), sausages and other classic Isan foods.

Night Market THAI, VIETNAMESE $

(Th Kheuan Thani; ⊙4.30-11pm) Though it's smaller than you'd expect, Ubon's city-centre night market makes an excellent dining destination, especially when paired with the weekend Walking Street Market. Vendors sell Thai, Isan and Vietnamese food.

Sam Chai Cafe THAI $

(Th Phadaeng; mains 30-70B; ⊙5.30am-1.30pm) Not really a cafe, this bustling popular breakfast stop serves *kôw đôm* (rice soup), *gŏo·ay dĕe·o* (noodle soup), *kài gà·tá* (pan egg with sausage) and traditional Thai coffee. The service is lightning-fast and the owner sometimes keeps order in a *Seinfeld*-esque 'Soup Nazi' style. It's a great local experience.

Peppers INTERNATIONAL, BAKERY **$$**
(297/2-3 Uppalisan Rd; mains 80-495B; ⊘8am-9pm; ☏) Peppers, popular with both *fa·ràng* and Thai, features a broad international menu with everything from nachos to schnitzel to pizza to *ɖôm yam gûng* and all-day breakfast. The bakery offerings, its real speciality, are downright delicious. There are also wines and international beers.

🍷 Drinking & Nightlife

As with any relatively large provincial capital, Ubon has a decent spread of bars and clubs. **U-Bar** (Th Thepyothi; ⊘8pm-2am) is perennially the nightclub of choice because it gets the best bands from Bangkok. For something low-key, hit the stretch of open-air, youthful bars that set up riverside along Th Rimmun between Luang and Ratchawong roads.

🛍 Shopping

Isan may be silk country, but Ubon is a cotton town and there are several good shops selling handwoven fabric, clothing, bags etc, many of them coloured with natural dyes.

Punchard ARTS & CRAFTS
(☑089 719 9570; www.punchard.net; Th Phadaeng; ⊘9am-6.30pm Thu-Tue) Though pricey, this is the best all-round handicrafts shop in Ubon. It specialises in silks and home-decoration products; many of its products merge old methods and modern designs.

Khampun ARTS & CRAFTS
(☑045 424121; Th Phadaeng; ⊘9am-6pm) Ubon's most famous silk specialist makes some exquisite fabrics, often with original patterns not found elsewhere. For two days before the Candle Parade (p427), the owner hosts a mini cultural festival at his gorgeous home-workshop just outside town.

Walking Street Market MARKET
(Th Srinarong; ⊘6-10.30pm Fri-Sun) This fun, youthful market takes over Th Srinarong and part of **Thung Si Meuang** (ทุ่งศรีเมือง) park on weekends.

Again Please ARTS & CRAFTS
(Th Kheuan Thani; ⊘10am-7pm Mon-Thu, to 9pm Fri-Sun) Specialising in locally themed cotton goods, the former Rawang Thang sells fun and funky shirts, pillows, postcards, picture frames and assorted bric-a-brac, most made and designed by the friendly husband-and-wife owners. They can fill you in on all things Ubon.

Camp Fai Ubon ARTS & CRAFTS
(Th Thepyothi; ⊘8.30am-5pm) You'll find a good assortment of clothing, bags and fabric (much of it coloured with natural dyes) at this shop, which is signed as Peaceland. It also has a branch at the airport.

ℹ Information

The little **SK Park** (Th Ratchathani) mall, near Rajabhat University, has the extended-hours banks nearest to the city centre.

Tourist Police (☑045 251451; Hwy 217) The tourist police office is well out of the city on the road to Phibun Mangsahan.

Tourism Authority of Thailand (TAT; ☑045 243770; tatubon@tat.or.th; 264/1 Th Kheuan Thani; ⊘8.30am-4.30pm) Has helpful staff and a free city map.

Tourist Assistance Center (☑086 361 4291) Run by the Ministry of Tourism and Sport, there are branches at the bus station, the train station and the airport.

Ubon Ratchathani Immigration (☑045 312133; Rajabhat University; ⊘8.30am-noon & 1-4.30pm)

Ubonrak Thonburi Hospital (☑045 429100; Th Phalorangrit) The best private hospital in Ubon, it has a 24-hour casualty department.

ℹ Getting There & Away

AIR

Together **Air Asia** (p404), **Nok Air** (☑nationwide 02 900 9955; www.nokair.com; ⊘7am-7pm) and **Thai Lion Air** (☑nationwide 02 529 9999; www.lionairthai.com; ⊘6am-7pm) fly to/from Bangkok's Don Mueang Airport (one hour) a dozen times daily, with prices well under 1000B usually available. **THAI Smile** (☑087 776 2266, nationwide 1181; www.thaismileair.com; ⊘7am-7.30pm) has four flights to/from Bangkok's Suvarnabhumi Airport (one hour) for a little bit more. Air Asia also has one daily flight each to Pattaya and Chiang Mai.

Sakda Travel World (☑045 254333; www.sakdatour.com; Th Phalorangrit; ⊘8.30am-6pm Mon-Sat) sells plane tickets, hires out cars and leads tours.

BUS

Ubon's **bus terminal** (☑045 316085; Hwy 231) is north of town; take *sŏrng·tăa·ou* 2, 3 or 10 to the city centre. The best service to Bangkok is with **Nakhonchai Air** (☑045 955999), which has its own station across the road from the main bus station, but also sells tickets and picks up passengers at the main station.

The early-morning **sŏrng·tǎa·ou** from Ubon Ratchathani to Phibun Mangsahan park in front of Ban Du market.

TRAIN

Ubon's **train station** (☑ 045 321004; Th Sathani) is in Warin Chamrap; take sŏrng·tǎa·ou 2. There are 10 daily trains between Ubon and Bangkok (3rd/1st-class seat 95/460B, 1st-class sleeper upper/lower 1200/1320B, 8½ to 12 hours), with the best sleeper service departing at 7pm. All these trains also stop in Si Saket, Surin and Khorat.

❶ Getting Around

Numbered *sŏrng·tǎa·ou* (10B) run throughout town. TAT's free city map marks the routes, most of which pass near its office. A túk-túk trip within the centre should cost about 50B. Metered **taxis** (☑ 045 265999; www.taxiubon.co.th) (flagfall 40B, call fee 20B) park at the bus and train stations and the airport and aren't too hard to find driving around town. Drivers usually use their meters.

The **Sri Isan** (☑ 045 261011; hotelsriisan@gmail.com; 62 Th Ratchabut), **Phadaeng** (p428) and **Outside Inn** (p428) hotels hire bikes for 30B, 50B and 50B respectively per day.

Ubon's airport is home to large car-hire companies including **Avis** (☑ 090 197 2262, nationwide 02 251 1131; www.avisthailand.com; ☉7am-8pm), **Budget** (☑ 081 261 4360, nationwide 02 203 9222; www.budget.co.th; ☉7am-8pm), **Hertz** (☑ 092 509 1441, nationwide 02 266 4666; www.hertzthailand.com; ☉8am-8pm), **Sixt** (☑ 092 223 1296, nationwide 1798; www.sixtthailand.com; ☉7am-8pm) and **Thai Rent A Car** (☑ 092 284 0220, nationwide 1647; www.thairentacar.com; ☉7am-8pm) and several local companies including **Chow Watana** (☑ 045 242202; ☉7.30am-7.30pm). Outside Inn can arrange cars with drivers for a good price, and is also reliable place for **motorcycle hire** (☑ 088 581 2069; www.theoutsideinnubon.com; 11 Th Suriyat; per day 250B), with discounts for long-term rentals.

BUSES TO/FROM UBON RATCHATHANI

DESTINATION	FARE (B)	DURATION (HR)	FREQUENCY
Bangkok	414-556	10	hourly 4am-midnight, frequent 4-8pm
Chiang Mai	707-790	12-14	7.30am, 12.45pm, 1.45pm, 2.45pm, 3.45pm, 5.45pm, 6.30pm
Chong Mek (Lao border)	100	2	every 30min 5am-6pm
Khon Kaen	176-244	4½-5	every 30min 5.30am-5.40pm
Mukdahan	130	2½	5.45am, 7.30am, 8.40am, 11.30am, 1pm
Mukdahan (minivan)	111	2½	every 30min 6am-5.30pm
Nakhon Ratchasima (Khorat)	248-386	7-8	hourly 5am-8pm
Nang Rong	144-265	5-6	hourly 5am-8pm
Pakse (Laos)	200	3	9.30am & 2.30pm
Rayong	515-801	13	7am, 7.15am, 5pm, 6pm, 7.30pm, 7.45pm, 8pm, 8.15pm
Surin	130-202	3½	hourly 5am-8pm
Udon Thani	284-332	7	every 30min 5.30am-5.40pm
Yasothon	66-99	2	hourly 5.30am-5.30pm
Yasothon (minivan)	80	2	hourly 5.30am-5.30pm

Ban Pa-Ao

♪ 045 / POP 1405

Ban Pa-Ao (บ้านปะอาว) village is famous for producing brass and bronze items using a unique lost-wax casting method involving long strands of wax. You can see ancient products using the same method in many museums, including at Ban Chiang, and this is the last place in Thailand that still does it.

Ban Pa-Ao is also a silk-weaving village and there's a **silk centre** (ศูนย์ทอผ้าไหมบ้าน ปะอาว; ♪ 082 153 7364; ⊙ 8am-4.30pm) **FREE** at the entrance to the town with a shop (the quality of the *mát·mèe* here is excellent) and a few looms.

◎ Sights

★ **Ban Pa-Ao**
Brassware Center   HANDICRAFTS
(Soon Thorng Leuang Ban Pa-Ao, ศูนย์ทองเหลือง บ้านปะอาว; ♪ 094 505 6292; ⊙ 8am-4.30pm) **FREE** Come here to see Ban Pa-Ao's famous brass artists using a unique lost-wax casting method. Workers here create bells, bowls and more on-site, although not every step is done daily, so what you'll see is a bit up to luck. A sign with photos and English text explains the entire process. The centre is on the far side of the village, on the edge of the forest.

Wat Burapa Pa-Ao Nuea Museum   MUSEUM
(พิพิธภัณฑ์วัดบูรพาปะอาวเหนือ; ⊙ 8am-5pm) **FREE** A surprising find in such a far-flung village, this gorgeous museum in Wat Burapa Pa-Ao Nuea holds various historical artefacts (in particular pottery, ancient coins and Dong Son bronze drums) and local handicrafts. It's kept locked, so you'll need to get the key from a monk.

🛏 Sleeping & Eating

There are no hotels or guesthouses in Ban Pa-Ao, but there is a village **homestay** (♪ 085 613 4713; per person including breakfast & dinner 310B) program available if anyone in your group can speak some Thai. There are a few simple restaurants in the village.

ℹ Getting There & Away

Ban Pa-Ao is 3.5km off Hwy 23. Minivans from Ubon to Maha Chana Chai pass the turn-off (30B, 20 minutes, every 30 minutes 6.30am to 5.30pm), and a motorcycle taxi from the highway costs 20B each way.

Phibun Mangsahan   พิบูลมังสาหาร

♪ 045 / POP 10,890

Thais often stop in the dusty town of Phibun Mangsahan to see a set of rapids called Kaeng Sapheu, just downstream of the Mun River bridge. The rocky islets make 'Python Rapids' rise between February and May, but the shady park here is a pleasant stop year-round.

The tile-encrusted *bòht* at **Wat Phu Khao Kaew** (วัดภูเขาแก้ว; ⊙ daylight hours) **FREE**, on the west side of town, is covered with Khmer symbols, including apsara (female spirits) and dancing Shivas on the outside, while the interior walls have reliefs of important stupas from around Thailand. Villages past the bridge as you drive toward Khong Jiam are famed for forging iron and bronze gongs, both for temples and classical Thai-music ensembles. You can watch the gong-makers hammering the metal discs and tempering them in rustic fires at many roadside workshops. People make drums, bells and cymbals here, too.

Phibun is famous for *sah·lah·pow* (Chinese buns; 5B each). Three ramshackle shops near the bridge sell them, as do many imitators out on the highway. The town is just a quick stopover on the way to or from Khong Jiam, but if you want to stay overnight, friendly and clean **Phiboonkit Hotel** (♪ 081 547 9207; Th Phiboon; r with fan 250B, with air-con 300-350B; 🅿🌐🛜) is your usual, slightly chaotic, old-time budget hotel.

ℹ Getting There & Away

Minivans run every 30 minutes between Ubon (40B, one hour) and Chong Mek (80B, one hour) via Khong Jiam (40B, 30 minutes), with a stop at the foot of the Mun River bridge in Phibun. There are also three early-morning *sŏrng·tăa·ou* (40B, 1½ hours, 6am, 7am, 8am) from Ban Du Market in Ubon Ratchathani's city centre to Phibun's bus stop behind the market.

Kaeng Tana National Park   อุทยานแห่งชาติแก่งตะนะ

Along the road to Khong Jiam you can cross the Pak Mun Dam to **Kaeng Tana National Park** (♪ 045 252722; 200B). After circling thickly forested Don Tana (Tana Island), linked to the mainland by two long suspension bridges, the Mun River roils

FOREST TEMPLES

When the Buddha set out on his quest for enlightenment 2500 years ago, he took to the forests, the traditional abode of ascetics and truth-seekers in India at the time. The first disciples were all accepted into the monkhood and lived and practised in forests.

As the teaching spread and the order of monks increased in size, some of the monks began setting up dwellings in towns. Over time these became known as the *gamavasi* (the town dwellers), while the monks who preferred to live in the forest were called *aranyavasi* (forest dwellers).

Forest-dwelling monks were disappearing from the landscape in Thailand until Venerable Ajahn Mun Bhuridatto (1870–1949) instigated a revival of the tradition. After his passing away, his legacy lived on in the remarkable number of students he left behind, many of whom became famous teachers in their own right.

Nowadays, forest teachers are sought after by Bangkok elites, intelligentsia and faithful farmers alike, as well as truth-seeking Westerners. Forest temples aren't tourist attractions, but the following have become places of spiritual pilgrimage and so are worth adding to your itinerary, with the exception of Wat Pa Nanachat, which is exclusively for sincere practitioners.

Wat Nong Pa Pong (วัดหนองป่าพง; ⊙ daylight hours, museum 8am-4.30pm) `FREE` The temple of renowned meditation teacher Ajahn Chah, who spent a brief but enlightening period with Ajahn Mun.

Wat Pa Nanachat (วัดป่านานาชาติ; www.watpahnanachat.org; ⊙ daylight hours) `FREE` Branch monastery of Wat Nong Pa Phong, established specifically for non-Thais.

Wat Phu Thok (p397) One of the most spectacular monasteries in Thailand, built by Ajahn Mun disciple Ajahn Juan.

Wat Hin Mak Peng (วัดหินหมากเป้ง; Rte 211; ⊙ daylight hours) `FREE` Overlooking the Mekong, this is the temple founded by senior Ajahn Mun disciple Luang Pu Thet.

through the park's beautiful namesake rapids (unseen below the surface in the rainy season) and passes below some short but photogenic cliffs. Towards the end of the dry season, large naturally eroded holes in the rock emerge.

There are several good short walks from the **visitor centre** (⊙ 8am-4pm): the 1.5km clifftop trail to Lan Pha Phueng viewpoint is especially serene. Nam Tok Tad Ton is a wide and lovely waterfall in the far south of the park, just 300m off the main road.

There are **bungalows** (☑ 045 406888; http://nps.dnp.go.th/reservation.php; 5/10 people 1000/2000B; P) and **camping** (per person with own tent 30B, 2-/3-/5-person tent hire 150/250/300B; P) available near the visitor centre. The simple cook-to-order restaurant by the visitor centre opens early and closes depending on the number of customers. There's also a small shop selling snacks and instant noodles.

❶ Getting There & Away

By road, the park is 14km from Khong Jiam. There's no public transport, but boats in town will take you upriver and drop you at the park for a look around for 800B.

Khong Jiam
โขงเจียม

☑ 045 / POP 6487

Khong Jiam, often spelled Khong Chiam, sits on a picturesque peninsula at the confluence of the reddish-brown Mekong and bluish-brown Mun rivers. It's known as Mae Nam Song Si (Two-Colour River) because of the contrasting colours at the junction. The multicoloured merger is usually visible from the shore, but it's best seen from a boat. When the rivers are high (June to October) the blending waters create small whirlpools and a strange bubbling that resembles boiling lava, though the colour divide is less distinct at this time.

❂ Sights & Activities

Wat Tham Khuha Sawan   BUDDHIST TEMPLE
(วัดถ้ำคูหาสวรรค์; Rte 222; ⊙ daylight hours) `FREE`
The views from this busy temple above the town (best seen from atop the bell tower or

the unfinished building next to it) are alone worth the trip, but it also has a beautiful nine-pointed *chedi*, an all-white *bòht* (ordination hall), an orchid garden (blooming in the cold season), one of the biggest gongs in Thailand, and the body of late abbot Luang Pu Kam covered in gold leaf on display in a glass case on a flamboyant altar.

Once Upon A Time ARTS CENTRE
(กาลครั้งหนึ่ง; ☎045 210324; www.experience khongchiam.com; Th Kaewpradit; ☺8am-5pm) **FREE** Indigo cotton weaving is the focus of the beautiful and inviting '*gah·lá krang neung*' arts centre, and you can watch, and usually try, each step in the process. Those wishing to dive in fully can take formal classes on weaving and natural dyeing as well as cooking (Thai or Isan food, per person 1000B), bamboo weaving and more.

River Tours BOATING
(☎081 999 0298, 090 234 5511) Half-hour tours on a sun-shaded 10-person boat are de rigueur in Khong Jiam. You'll find boat owners (or they'll find you) at the row of restaurants along the Mekong River. Expect to pay 500B for the trip, unless you can talk the boat driver down to something more reasonable. They'll also do longer trips such as Kaeng Tana (p431) and Pha Taem (p434) National Parks.

Sleeping & Eating

Khong Jiam doesn't get many *fa·ràng* visitors, but it's popular with Thais, so there's an abundance of lodging. In the high season, booking ahead on weekends is wise.

In addition to the usual bunch of food stalls and basic restaurants along the main road, there are several eateries near the Mae Nam Song Si, including some floating on the Mekong. You pay a premium for the views, but it's worth it.

Once Upon A Time GUESTHOUSE $
(กาลครั้งหนึ่ง; ☎045 210324; www.experience khongchiam.com; Th Kaewpradit; incl breakfast r per person with fan & private bathroom/with aircon & shared bathroom 300/350B; P❋✿) Billing itself as an 'edu-stay', '*gah·lá krang neung*' arts centre has four simple rooms in an old wooden house, though you don't need to partake in its classes and activities to stay here. The old-timey decor lends a grandma's house feel to the rooms and there's a cool 2nd-floor lounge in the front. The **food** (mains 70-100B; ☺7.30am-8.30pm; ✿) is good too.

★**Tohsang Khongjiam Resort** HOTEL $$$
(☎045 351174; www.tohsang.com; r incl breakfast 2500-3890B, villas 2500-7060B, Sedhapura pool villas 15,000-18,000B; P❋❋@✿) This place oozes understated class and capitalises on its prime location right on the banks of the Mun River. While its upmarket nature seems a little incongruous for this stretch of rural Thailand, it's not flashy and blends in well with the rustic surrounds. The ambience is totally restful. The open-air restaurant has spectacular views.

ⓘ GETTING TO LAOS: CHONG MEK TO VANGTAO

Getting to the border Almost every traveller uses the direct Ubon Ratchathani–Pakse buses (200B, three hours, 9.30am and 2.30pm), which wait long enough for you to buy Lao visas at the border. Otherwise, Chong Mek's little bus terminal serves minivans to/from Ubon Ratchathani (120B, two hours, every 30 minutes) via Khong Jiam and Phibun Mangsahan, and buses for Bangkok (484B to 638B, 12 hours, five daily). It's 600m from the bus station to the border: motorcycle taxis charge 20B.

At the border The border is open from 6am to 8pm and the crossing, involving walking though an underground tunnel, is largely hassle-free. Although it seems like a scam, there is a legitimate overtime fee on the Laos side after 4pm weekdays and all day on weekends and holidays. The real scam is that the officials ask for 100B even though the actual price is 10,000 Lao kip (about 40B). Just tell them you want a receipt and you'll pay the correct price. They sometimes ask for this at other times, but they're usually not too insistent.

Moving on Pakse is about an hour away in one of the frequent minivans (20,000K, 45 minutes) or *sŏrng·tǎa·ou* that park in a dusty/muddy parking area about 500m from the Lao immigration office.

There's a spa, and bikes and kayaks are available. It's 3.5km from town, on the south bank of the river.

ℹ️ Getting There & Away

All transport to town stops at the highway junction. **Minivans** go every 30 minutes all day long to Ubon Ratchathani (80B, 1½ hours), Phibun Mangsahan (40B, 30 minutes) and Chong Mek (40B, 30 minutes) at the Lao border. There are also **buses to Bangkok** (484B, 10 hours, 7.30am and 4.30pm).

ℹ️ Getting Around

Once Upon A Time has bike hire for 200B per day and also leads half-day bike tours for 650B per person – with a three-person minimum. Just down the road, **Apple Guesthouse** (☑ 045 351160; per day 50B) hires bikes for 50B per day and **Baan Steak** (☑ 081 2998980; motorcycles 300B per day; ⊙ 6am-9pm) restaurant has motorcycles for 300B per day. Some hotels, including **Ban Pak Mongkhon** (☑ 045 351352; Th Kaewpradit) and **Tohsang**, can also arrange a car with driver.

Pha Taem National Park อุทยานแห่งชาติผาแต้ม

A long cliff named Pha Taem is the centrepiece of awesome but unheralded **Pha Taem National Park** (☑ 045 252581; 400B, car/motorcycle 30/20B), which covers 340 sq km along the Mekong River. From the top you get a bird's-eye view across the Mekong into Laos, and down below a trail passes prehistoric rock paintings.

The wilderness north of the cliff holds more ancient art, some magnificent waterfalls (all flowing June to December) and scattered scattered rock fields known as Sao Chaliang, which are oddly eroded mushroom-shaped stone formations.

Many Thais come here for the sunrises. Pha Cha Na Dai cliff, which requires a high-clearance vehicle to reach, serves Thailand's first sunrise view of each day. But Pha Taem cliff is only about one minute behind.

◉ Sights & Activities

The **visitor centre** (⊙ 5am-6pm) contains exhibits pertaining to the park's ancient paintings and local ecology. This is the spot to pick up a free park map and arrange guides for treks, although it's best to call and reserve in advance if you want to do anything other than a short walk.

Pha Taem   NATURAL FEATURE
(ผาแต้ม) These ancient rock paintings, which are at least 1000 years old but probably much older, sit on a cliff down below the visitor centre. Subjects include *plah bèuk* (giant Mekong catfish), elephants, human hands, geometric designs and fish traps that look much like the huge ones still used today. The second viewing platform fronts the most impressive batch. It's only a short, though steep, walk down to the paintings; but you can also continue past the paintings and complete a 4.3km loop.

Nam Tok Saeng Chan   WATERFALL
(น้ำตกแสงจันทร์) One of the most amazing waterfalls you'll ever see, Saeng Chan ('Moonbean') flows through a hole cut naturally into the overhanging rock. There's water from June to December, but it's at its best when rain is actually falling.

Namtok Soi Sawan   WATERFALL
(น้ำตกสร้อยสวรรค์) Nam Tok Soi Sawan is a 25m-tall waterfall flowing from June to December. It's a 19km drive from the visitor centre and then a 500m walk, or you can hike with a ranger (must be arranged in advance) for about 15 largely shadeless kilometres along the top of the cliff.

What the park calls Thailand's largest **flower field** blooms from October to January (November and December are best) next to the falls.

🛏️ Sleeping & Eating

Pha Taem has **campsites** (per person with own tent 30B, 4-person tent hire 225B; 🅿) and **bungalows** (☑ 045 252581; http://nps.dnp.go.th/reservation.php; bungalows 6-person with fan 1200B, 5-person with air-con 2000B; 🅿). There's also a collection of uninspiring 'resorts' on the road to the park and along the Mekong below the park.

There are several restaurants across the parking area from the visitor centre. Only one stays open in the rainy season, and it usually closes before sunset. You can get instant noodles, snacks and coffee behind and below the visitor centre.

ℹ️ Getting There & Away

Pha Taem is 18km from Khong Jiam along Rte 2112. There's no public transport, so many people hire vehicles from Khong Jiam. Túk-túk ask 600B for the return trip.

KHON KAEN PROVINCE

Khon Kaen Province, the gateway to Isan for many people arriving from northern Thailand, serves up an interesting mix of old and new. Farming and textiles still dominate life in the countryside, while things are booming in the increasingly modern capital city.

Khon Kaen
ขอนแก่น

☑ 043 / POP 122,370

As the site of the northeast's largest university and an important hub for all things commercial, Khon Kaen is youthful, educated and on the move. While it's the kind of city that's more likely to land on a best-places-to-live list than a traveller's itinerary, there are more than enough interesting attractions and good facilities to make a stop rewarding.

◉ Sights

★ Wat Nong Wang   BUDDHIST TEMPLE
(วัดหนองแวง; Th Robbung; ⊙ daylight hours, stupa 6am-6pm) FREE Down at the south end of the lake, **Phra Mahathat Kaen Nakhon**, the gorgeous nine-storey stupa at the heart of this important temple, makes Wat Nong Wang Khon Kaen's one must-see attraction. It features enlightening modern murals depicting Isan culture and Khon Kaen's history; various historical displays, including a collection of rare Buddha images on the 4th floor; and a 9th-floor observation deck. The monks open the door to the upper floors when they are ready, which is roughly 7.30am to 5pm.

★ Walking Street Market   MARKET
(ถนนคนเดิน; Th Na Sunratchakan; ⊙ 5pm-10pm Sat) In the spirit of Chiang Mai's weekend street markets (but not touristy like them), hundreds of vendors take over Th Na Sunratchakan. Many of them sell handbags, T-shirts, postcards, picture frames and other handmade products. Dancers, musicians and other buskers work strategic corners, and the whole place is festooned with Chinese-style lanterns, adding to the festive atmosphere.

Bueng Kaen Nakhorn   LAKE
FREE This 100-hectare lake is the most pleasant place in town to spend some time, and the paths hugging its shore link quite a few interesting places. There's bike hire (p441) near the evening Rim Bueng Market.

Wat Pho Ban Nontan   BUDDHIST TEMPLE
(วัดโพธิ์บ้านโนนทัน; Th Pho Thisan; ⊙ daylight hours) FREE Just off the lake, this peaceful tree-filled temple and noted meditation centre pre-dates the city and has a *săh·lah* like no other in Thailand. The ground floor is covered with sculpted trees, animals and village scenes of people acting out old Isan proverbs. There's also a small museum under the *bòht*, and this temple is a great place for a Thai massage.

Rim Bueng Market   MARKET
(ตลาดริมบึง; Th Robbung; ⊙ 4pm-9pm) This fun little market, in the shadow of **Wat That** (วัดธาตุ; Th Robbung; ⊙ daylight hours, chedi 8am-6pm) FREE, features food, second-hand clothing and paint-your-own pottery stalls. During the day there are paddleboats for hire (40B per half-hour after 4.30pm, 50B for any length of time that ends before 4.30pm).

Khon Kaen National Museum   MUSEUM
(พิพิธภัณฑสถานแห่งชาติขอนแก่น; Th Lang Sunratchakan; 100B; ⊙ 9am-4pm Wed-Sun) This collection of artefacts spans prehistoric times to the present. Highlights are Ban Chiang–era pottery and a beautiful Dvaravati *bai săir·mah* (temple boundary marker) depicting Princess Pimpa cleaning Lord Buddha's feet with her hair. The household and agricultural displays shed light on what you'll see out in the countryside. Unfortunately, the English labelling is not very good.

🏃 Activities & Tours

Centrum Health Massage   MASSAGE
(☑ 089 711 8331; veenasspa@gmail.com; Soi Supatheera) Located at Khon Kaen Centrum (p437) hotel, Veena teaches Thai massage in English and Thai, and another masseur can teach in Japanese.

Isan Explorer   CULTURAL
(☑ 085 354 9165; www.isanexplorer.com) Isan Explorer specialises in slow-travel, cultural tours across the entire Isan region. Elephant encounters have a focus on the animals' welfare (no riding and no chains), and the company also does birdwatching and trekking tours in the mountains west of Khon Kaen.

Khon Kaen

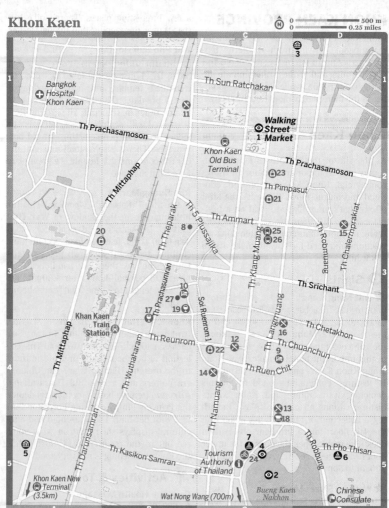

Thai Dream Tours   MEDITATION, CULTURAL
(☏ 089 711 8331; www.thaidreamtours.com; Soi Supatheera) Gregarious owner-guide Veena, who also runs Centrum Health Massage, organises all kinds of tours, but has made her speciality individually tailored meditation tours to forest meditation temples around Isan. Also on offer is a short, casual cooking class (1250B for two people) and Thai massage instruction.

✷ Festivals & Events

The **Silk Fair** and **Phuk Siaw Festival** are held simultaneously over 12 days starting in late November. Centred on the provincial hall (*săh·lah glahng*), the festival celebrates and seeks to preserve the tradition of '*pòok sèeo*' (friend bonding), a ritual union of friends during which *făi pòok kăan* (sacred threads) are tied around one's wrists. Other activities include a parade, Isan music and lots of shopping.

🛏 Sleeping

Khon Kaen has the best selection of accommodation of any city in Isan, especially in the midrange and top-end categories.

Khon Kaen

Charoenchit House HOTEL $

(☑ 043 227300; www.chousekk.com; Th Chuan-chun; r incl breakfast 500-600B; 🅿🕸🛜) A solid budget choice with a good location just north of the lake. It's clean and the rooms have a fair amount of va-va-voom for the price, making it quite popular.

Khon Kaen Centrum HOTEL $$

(☑ 081 574 0507; Soi Supatheera; incl breakfast d 650-750B, tr 850-1250B; 🅿😀🕸🛜) What seems like an ordinary small Thai hotel sets itself apart in the details. The rooms are fairly striking in their white-themed decor and have high-quality furnishings. The owner, who lives on-site, is serious about service and cleanliness. And it's quiet because it's built at the back of the block. Guests can rent bikes and motorcycles.

Hotel la Villa HOTEL $$

(☑ 043 336433; www.hotellavilla.in.th; Th Chatapa-dung; r incl breakfast 850-1300B; 🅿😀🕸🛜🏊) A bit out of the city centre, but still convenient if you have your own transport, Hotel la Villa ticks all the boxes for quality and service. Most of the large, comfortable rooms are around a small garden swimming pool.

Pullman Raja Orchid HOTEL $$$

(☑ 043 913333; www.pullmankhonkaen.com; off Th Prachasumran; incl breakfast r 2465-3360B, ste 4700B; 🅿😀🕸@🛜🏊) A stunning lobby sets the tone for Khon Kaen's top hotel. In the heart of the city it has plenty of razzle-dazzle, including a luxurious spa, pool and gym, a German microbrewery and well-equipped rooms. There are several restaurants to choose from, and the service is thorough and attentive, although English is spoken less than you would expect.

✖ Eating

Khon Kaen is a great dining destination for Thai and especially Isan food. Besides many excellent restaurants, Khon Kaen has some great **night markets** (Th Ruenrom; ⌚5pm-midnight).

★ Pa Ouan 2 THAI $

(Th Robbung; mains 40-280B; ⌚9am-8pm; 🛜) This popular Isan restaurant between Wat Nong Wang and Bueng Kaen Nakhon has a larger than normal menu spanning the expected *gài yâhng* and duck *lâhp* to sel-dom-encountered foods such as lotus stalk ('*lai bua*') *sôm·đam*, one of the 19 kinds of

PHU CHONG NAYOI NATIONAL PARK อุทยานแห่งชาติภูจองนายอย

Sitting at the heart of the 'Emerald Triangle' (a meeting of the Thai, Lao and Cambodian borders) is 686-sq-km **Phu Chong Nayoi National Park** (☎ 045 210706; admission 400B, car/motorcycle 30/20B), one of Thailand's wildest corners and healthiest forests. Resident fauna includes Malayan sun bears, barking deer, gibbons, black hornbills and endangered white-winged ducks, though you won't likely see them.

The primary attraction is **Namtok Huay Luang**, a 45m-tall waterfall with at least some water all year. You can walk down 274 steps to the bottom, where you can swim, though the water dries up around March. About 150m downstream is **Namtok Praon La-or**, also a pretty picture. Between the waterfall and the **visitor centre** (⊙ 8.30am-4pm) is **Palan Pachad**, a rocky field that features many wildflowers in November and December. There's more to see in the northern reaches of the park, but you must go with a ranger (arrange in advance) due to the risk of land mines and poachers.

Stargazing is superb here, so consider spending the night. There are three well-worn **bungalows** (☎ 045 210706; http://nps.dnp.go.th/reservation.php; 3-/6-person bungalows 600/1200B; P) plus a **campsite** (per person with own tent 30B, 2-person tent hire 150B; P). There are a few rice and noodle shops by the visitor centre and an Isan restaurant (grilled fish and spicy papaya salad) at Huay Luang Waterfall. These all typically open 8am to 4pm, though those at the visitor centre might stay open later.

There's no public transport to the park and not much traffic inside it, so you'll need your own wheels to get here.

sôm·đam available. There's also plenty of Thai food, and even a few fusion dishes such as fried frog with garlic.

★ **Gai Yang Rabeab** THAI $
(☎ 043 243413; Th Theparak; whole chickens 160B; ⊙ 9am-3pm) Many Thais believe Khon Kaen Province makes Thailand's best *gài yâhng* (marinated grilled chicken), and this simple joint, serving an all-Isan menu, gets the most nods as best of the best in the city.

Somtom Internet THAI $
(Soi Namuang 19; mains 30-60B; ⊙ 7.30am-8pm, dining room closes 6pm) This rustic spot is always busy for good reason – there's no better *sôm·đam* in Khon Kaen. It also does grilled chicken and fried fish. It's an English-free zone, but it doesn't matter much because everything available is laid out on a table in front, so you can just point.

Turm-Rom THAI $
(Th Chetakhon; mains 49-199B; ⊙ 5.30pm-1am; 🛜) This superb place combines one of the best kitchens in town with a covered garden to create the perfect place for a night out, rain or shine. The *pá·sá plah chôrn* (a hot and sour curry with snakehead fish) and *đam tùa mŏo gròrp* (spicy long bean salad with fried pork) are especially good, but in our many visits we've never had a dud dish.

Tawan Thong VEGAN $
(☎ 043 330389; Th Ammart; mains 25-40B; ⊙ 6am-2pm; 🛜 🚲) Tawan Thong is a large, all-vegie health-food buffet. The food is both good and cheap enough to attract some non-vegetarian diners.

🍷 Drinking & Nightlife

Some chill, open-air, Thai-style pubs have sprung up around the intersection of Th Ruenrom and Th Prachasumran. The Lang Mor neighbourhood, way out of town behind Khon Kaen University, has more of the same, with a mostly student clientele.

★ **Slove U Coffee** COFFEE $
(☎ 095 651 7121; Th Sri Nual; green-tea latte 45B, fruit smoothies 90B; ⊙ 8am-8pm; 🛜) Khon Kaen's youthful population has spawned many good coffee shops, and this friendly, attractively cluttered one is one of our favourites. They roast their own beans, have a couple of bikes to use, run a **hostel** (☎ 094 530 202; per person 150B; 🚲 🛜) upstairs and occasionally lead low-priced trips around Khon Kaen.

Rads CLUB
(Th Prachasumran; ⊙ 8pm-2am) The exuberant anchor of Khon Kaen's nightlife, this is a multifaceted place with live music, DJs,

karaoke, a wine bar and 'coyote' dancers. It gets going about 9pm.

U-Bar
CLUB

(Soi Khlong Nam; ☺8pm-2am) U-Bar packs them in with live music, often big-name bands from Bangkok. It's mostly a younger crowd than Rads.

☆ Entertainment

Central Plaza
CINEMA

(Th Srichant) Khon Kaen's glossiest shopping mall screens some movies in their original English or with English subtitles. There's also a large arcade/play area for kids.

🛍 Shopping

Because of the variety available, Khon Kaen is arguably the best place to buy Isan handicrafts.

Prathammakhant
ARTS & CRAFTS

(☑043 224080; Th Ruenrom; ☺9am-6.30pm) There's an impressively large selection of silk here, both fabric and finished clothing, plus plenty of other souvenirs. Combined with the adjoining **Thammoo Art-Decor**, (☑085 000 1548; Th Ruenrom; ☺9am-5.30pm) it makes a perfect one-stop shop.

Naem Lablae
FOOD

(Th Klang Muang; ☺6.30am-9pm) Few Thai visitors leave Khon Kaen without stuffing their suitcase full of local foods: *gun chee·ang* (red pork sausages) are especially popular, and this family-owned shop has been making its own for decades. *Kà·nŏm tùa* (sweets made with peanuts) and *kà·nŏm tan·yá·pêut* (sweets made with seeds) are other delicious local specialities available here.

Sueb San
ARTS & CRAFTS

(21/2 Th Klang Muang; ☺8am-6.30pm Mon-Sat) A small shop behind a pan-pipe arch stocking a few natural-dyed fabrics plus some creative handmade notebooks, postcards, bags and other souvenirs.

Ton Tann Green Market
MARKET

(Hwy 2; ☺5-10.30pm) Ton Tann is an attractive open space where some of vendors sell modern handmade crafts. There's also a fashion zone, an **art gallery** (หอศิลป์ใต้นต่าล; Hwy 2; ☺4.30-10pm) FREE and many restaurants.

Central Plaza
SHOPPING CENTRE

(Th Srichant; ☺10.30am-9pm Mon-Fri, 10am-9pm Sat-Sun) One of the biggest shopping malls in Isan. Has a branch of the English-language Asia Books.

ℹ Information

EMBASSIES & CONSULATES

Chinese Consulate (Th Robbung; ☺9am-noon Mon-Fri) Tourist visas are available only for Thai citizens and residents.

Lao Consulate (☑043 393402; Hwy 2; ☺8am-noon & 1-4pm Mon-Fri) Well north of the city, across from Raja City housing estate. Visas require one photo and are ready in about 10 minutes. Payment is by baht only, and at a poor exchange rate, so it's cheaper to pay in dollars at the border.

Vietnamese Consulate (☑043 242190; Th Chatapadung; ☺9-11.30am & 2-4.30pm Mon-Fri) Visas require one photo and are ready in one hour. It's 400m north of the stoplight on Th Srichant by Khon Kaen Hospital.

EMERGENCIES

Tourist Police (☑043 465385; Hwy 2) Just north of the immigration office.

MEDICAL SERVICES

Bangkok Hospital Khon Kaen (☑043 042888; www.bangkokhospitalkhonkaen.com; Th Maliwan) The top private hospital in the city. Has a 24-hour casualty department.

MONEY

Khon Kaen's three largest shopping malls, **Central Plaza**, TukCom and Fairy Plaza, have extended-hours banks.

TOURIST INFORMATION

Immigration (☑043 465242; Hwy 2; ☺8.30am-noon & 1-4.30pm Mon-Fri) North of town, near the eastern entrance to Khon Kaen University.

Tourism Authority of Thailand (TAT; ☑043 227714; tatkhkn@tat.or.th; Th Robbung; ☺8.30am-4.30pm) Distributes maps of the city and can answer questions about surrounding provinces too.

TRAVEL AGENCIES

Très Bien Travel (☑043 322338; Pullman Raja Orchid; ☺8.30am-5.30pm Mon-Fri, to 2pm Sat) A reliable spot for booking plane tickets.

THAI Airways Khon Kaen Sales Office (☑043 227701; www.thaiairways.com; Pullman Raja Orchid; ☺8am-5pm Mon-Fri) Sells tickets for THAI Smile's Khon Kaen flights, and also handles THAI Airways flights worldwide.

BUSES TO/FROM KHON KAEN
Old Bus Terminal

DESTINATION	FARE (B)	DURATION (HR)	FREQUENCY
Bangkok	365-427	7-8	every 30min 7.45am-12.45am
Chiang Mai	410-739	12	5am, 7am, 7.30am, 9am, 11am, 4pm, 7pm
Khorat	116	3½	every 30min 5.10am-7pm
Loei	125	4	every 30min 3.40am-6.30pm
Mukdahan	161-214	6	hourly 4.40am-5.30pm
Mukdahan (minivan)	240	6	every 45min 4am-6pm
Nakhon Phanom	212	5	hourly 7.30am-5pm
Nong Khai	120-155	3½-4	12.30pm, 1.10pm, 1.30pm, 2.30pm, 3.30pm
Phitsanulok	247-354	6	hourly 5am-7pm
Roi Et	73	2	every 30min 5.20am-7.30pm
Surin	160-205	5	every 45min 4am-3.30pm
Ubon Ratchathani	176	5	every 30min 5.30am-7pm
Udon Thani	76-120	2½	5am-5.40pm (frequent)
Udon Thani (minivan)	84	2	every 45min 6am-6pm

New Bus Terminal

DESTINATION	FARE (B)	DURATION (HR)	FREQUENCY
Bangkok	365-487	7	6.30am-1am (frequent)
Chiang Mai	410-739	12	4.20am-9pm (14 departures, most 6-9pm)
Khorat	146	3½	3.30am-1am (frequent)
Khorat (minivan)	126	3	every 45min 6.40am-6pm
Nong Khai	120-155	3½-4	hourly 7am-3pm
Phitsanulok	192-247	6	4.20am, 6.20am, 10.30am, 6pm, 7pm
Roi Et	92-107	2	hourly 5.30am-4pm
Surin	205	5	every 2hr 4am-4pm
Suvarnabhumi Airport	317	6½	10.50pm
Ubon Ratchathani	244	4½-5	hourly 5.30am-4pm
Udon Thani	95	2½	every 30min 5.30am-8pm
Udon Thani (minivan)	80	2	5am-7.15pm (frequent)
Vientiane (Laos; must have Lao visa)	180-185	4	8.15am & 3pm

ℹ Getting There & Away

AIR

Flights to **Khon Kaen** (☑043 468173; www.khonkaenairport.net) have expanded greatly in the past few years, which helps keep prices to Bangkok low; even on short notice, you can usually find a ticket for under 1000B. **THAI Smile** (☑nationwide 1181; www.thaismileair.com; ⊙7am-9pm) has seven daily flights using Suvarnabhumi Airport, while **Air Asia** (☑02 515 9999; www.airasia.com; ⊙5.30am-8.30pm), **Nok Air** (☑nationwide 02 900 9955; www.nokair.com; ⊙6am-8pm Apr-Sep, 7am-10pm Oct-Mar) and **Thai Lion Air** (☑nationwide 02 529 9999; www.lionairthai.com; ⊙7.30am-6.30pm Mon-Sat, 9am-8pm Sun) each have several daily flights to Don Muang Airport. Air Asia also operates a daily Chiang Mai and Hat Yai service.

Several hotels, including the Pullman, send shuttles (around 100B per person) to meet flights at Khon Kaen Airport, and you don't need to be staying at the hotels to use them. Taxis at the airport use the meter, but you must pay a 50B airport surcharge.

BUS

Khon Kaen is a busy bus transport hub – you can ride directly to nearly all cities in Isan and many beyond. The biggest, busiest bus station is the city-centre **Old Bus Terminal** (bor kor sŏr gòw; ☑043 237472; Th Prachasamoson), which serves all destinations within Khon Kaen, and many other cities. It's slated to be closed down but there's no way of predicting when.

All service will be moving to the **New Bus Terminal** (bor kor sŏr mài; ☑043 471562; Th Liang Muang Khon Kaen) out on the ring road, which has already been open for years and already handles most Bangkok and other long-distance buses. The best service to Bangkok is with **Nakhonchai Air** (☑02 939 4999, nationwide 1624; www.nakhonchaiair.com), departing about every 30 minutes throughout the day with six '1st-Class' VIP buses.

Nakhonchai Air still has a sales office at the defunct **Old Air-Conditioned Bus Terminal** (Th Klang Muang) (as do a few other companies) and runs an hourly shuttle to the New Bus Terminal for its customers. Another company, Chan Tour, parks its buses across the road so you can unofficially still begin a trip to Bangkok here.

While most minivans use the regular bus terminals, they also depart from the Old Air-Conditioned Bus Terminal every 30 minutes to Udon Thani (80B, two hours, 5.30am to 7.30pm) and Khorat (126B, three hours, 6.30am to 5.20pm), and from **Central Plaza** (Hwy 2) shopping mall every 30 minutes to Udon Thani (80B, two hours, 6.30am to 7.30pm) and Roi Et (120B, two hours, 6.30am to 6.30pm).

TRAIN

There's one morning and three evening express trains (seat 77B to 368B, 1st-class sleeper upper/lower 1008/1208B, eight to nine hours) between Bangkok and **Khon Kaen train station** (☑043 221112). There are also four trains to Nakhon Ratchasima (38B to 170B, 3½ hours) and five (though only two in the daytime) to Nong Khai (35B to 290B, two to three hours).

ℹ Getting Around

Sŏrng·tăa·ou (9B) ply regular routes across the city. Some of the handiest (all of which pass the Old Air-Conditioned Bus Terminal on Th Klangmuang) are line 4, which passes immigration and the Lao consulate; line 8, which goes to Wat Nong Wang and also northwest through the university; line 10 (going north), which passes near and sometimes in front of the Vietnamese consulate; and line 21, which goes out to the National Museum. There's also the new 24-hour Khon Kaen City Bus (15B), which starts at the New Bus Terminal and circles through the city up to the Old Bus Terminal and back, with some clearly labelled buses going all the way to the airport.

For individual rides, túk-túk are the most expensive way to get around (50B to 70B to most places in the centre), but they're the method most people use because it's rare to find **metered taxis** (☑043 342800, 043 465777; flagfall 30B, call fee 20B) on the street, and when you call for one you sometimes have to wait a while. About the only places in the city you're likely to find a taxi or motorcycle taxi (within town 30B to 40B) parked are the bus stations, airport and Central Plaza, and the taxis parked at the bus station won't use their meters.

There are many car-hire outlets around Tuk-Com. Big names like **Thai Rent A Car** (☑043 468178; www.thairentacar.com; ⊙7am-7.30pm) and **Budget** (☑043 345460; www.budget.com; ⊙7am-8pm) have outlets at the airport. **Khun Wanchai** (☑089 984 5503) is a taxi driver who speaks good English and charges 2500B (including fuel) per day within Khon Kaen province, and only a little more to go further afield. **Bueng Kaen Nakhon Bike Hire** (Th Robbung; per hour 30B, per day 100-150B; ⊙noon-8pm) has a variety of bikes available including two- and three-seaters.

Chonnabot ชนบท

☑043 / POP 3999

The little town of Chonnabot is at the heart of one of Thailand's most successful silk-weaving regions and is famous for producing top-quality *mát·mèe*. Located 55km southwest of Khon Kaen, it's a major

ELEPHANT-RUBBING ROCK

The core attraction of Nam Phong National Park, and the nearest nature to Khon Kaen city, the **Hin Chang Si** ('Elephant-Rubbing Rock'; จุดชมวิวหินช้างสี; ☏096 739 7920; 100B, car/motorcycle 30/20B; ⊘6am-5pm) area is full of oddly eroded house-sized rocks scattered around a scraggy forest. There are some wonderful viewpoints of Ubonrat Reservoir and the Phu Wiang Mountains. It's worth spending at least an hour roaming around here, and you could easily do more if you follow the trail northeast along the top of the cliff (you're supposed to hire a ranger for this).

A small rock-climbing community (www.khonkaenclimbing.com) is active here and hosts a bouldering festival in January. **Isan Explorer** (p435) has a trekking trip that takes you from the top of the mountain down to the lake below.

It's 50km from the city and there's no public transport anywhere near it.

shopping destination and there are many small stores selling fabrics (both silk and cotton) and finished clothes on Th Sriboonruang, aka Silk Rd. The small **Sala Mai Thai** (Thai Silk Exhibition Hall; ☏043 286160; ⊘8am-5pm Mon-Fri, 9am-5pm Sat & Sun) FREE museum outside town has displays with all the equipment used to make silk fabric, though it's more enjoyable to watch weavers working their looms at their homes. Just wander west or north of Silk Rd and you'll find some.

Chonnabot warrants just a short visit, and most people come here from Khon Kaen city. There are a few simple restaurants and a couple of coffee shops around town.

Khon Kaen tour companies run tours to Chonnabot, and you can also go by public transport if you're in no rush. Take a bus (35B, one hour, every 30 minutes) or train (9B to 39B, 30 minutes, 8am and 9.10am) to Ban Phai, from where you can get a *sŏrng·tăa·ou* to Chonnabot (13B, 20 minutes, every 30 minutes from 7am to 5pm).

Phu Wiang National Park อุทยานแห่งชาติภูเวียง

A geologist looking for uranium discovered a giant patella bone here in 1976, and the palaeontologists who were called to investigate then unearthed a fossilised 15m-long herbivore. It was later named *Phuwiangosaurus sirindhornae*, after Princess Sirindhorn. Dinosaur fever followed (explaining the myriad model dinosaurs in Khon Kaen city), more remains were uncovered and Phu Wiang National Park was born.

The park covers a strange horseshoe-shaped mountain that has just a single pass to its interior. Wiang Kao, the district inside the mountain, is a fruit-growing area and is a good place to explore by car if you want to look at traditional village life.

◉ Sights & Activities

Most people are here to see the dinosaur fossils left exposed in some **excavation sites** (⊘8.30am-4.30pm). The northern section has a new road, making it easy to see the **dinosaur footprints** (รอยเท้า ไดโนเสาร์ หินลาดป่าชาด) and Phu Wiang's biggest and best **waterfall** (น้ำตกตาดฟ้า).

Outside the park is the **Phu Wiang Dinosaur Museum** (พิพิธภัณฑ์ไดโนเสาร์ภูเวียง; ☏043 438206; adult/child 60/30B; ⊘9am-5pm Tue-Sun) and the photogenic **Si Wiang Dinosaur Park** (⊘daylight hours) FREE.

🛌 Sleeping & Eating

Phu Wiang is usually visited as a day trip from Khon Kaen, but it doesn't need to be. There are some hotels and village homestays (which must be arranged in advance through a tour company) outside the park and two rough campsites inside it. If you're camping, check in at the visitor centre first, and bring your own food.

Pruksa Garden House HOTEL $
(☏043 291639; http://pruksagardenhouse.com/; Phu Wiang-Nong Kae Rd; r incl breakfast 350-900B; P🐕❄🛜) The best hotel in the Phu Wiang National Park area lies away from the mountain in Phu Wiang city. The various sizes of bungalow are all good value and the setting is peaceful.

Tat Fa Campsite CAMPGROUND $
(☏043 358073; per person with own tent 30B, 3-person-tent hire 325B; P) The better of Phu

Wiang National Park's two campsites is up near Tat Fa Waterfall. Facilities are basic, though the remoteness is a bonus.

ℹ Getting There & Away

The park entrance is 90km west of Khon Kaen. Minivans (100B, two hours, six daily from 8.10am to 6.20pm) from Khon Kaen's old bus terminal go all the way to the national park, passing the **Phu Wiang Dinosaur Museum** on the way.

Nam Nao National Park

อุทยานแห่งชาติน้ำหนาว

One of Thailand's most valuable nature preserves, Nam Nao National Park covers 966 sq km across the Phetchabun Mountains west of Khon Kaen. With an average elevation of 800m, temperatures are fairly cool year-round (*nám nŏw* means 'water that feels cold') and frost can occur in December and January. There are evergreen and deciduous forests mixed with vast bamboo groves.

Nam Nao lies within the Western Isaan Forest Complex, a 6000-sq-km block of eight connected preserves, and wildlife is abundant. Elephant encounters are common enough that there's an electric fence around the campground and bungalows. Lucky visitors might also spot Malayan sun bears, gaur (wild cattle), Asian jackals, barking deer, gibbons and pangolins. There are even a few tigers. More than 200 species of birds, including great hornbill and silver pheasant,

fly through the forest, and the exceptional visibility makes this one of Thailand's best birdwatching sites.

◉ Sights & Activities

A good system of marked hiking trails branches out from the visitor centre through a variety of habitats. You'll need to hire a ranger to walk anywhere else in the park, including the best wildlife-spotting area south of the highway. **Spotlighting** trips (800B per truck) can be arranged at the visitor centre.

Phu Khor Viewpoint   VIEWPOINT
(Hwy 12, Nam Nao National Park) A gorgeous view at any time, Phu Khor is mostly visited at sunrise. The big mountain on the horizon is **Phu Kradueng** (p378). Phu Khor is 5km west of the visitor centre, a five-minute climb from the highway. Pick-up trucks deliver people to the viewpoints for 50B per person or 600B per truck; reserve a seat at the visitor centre.

**Haew Sai &
  Sai Thong Waterfalls**   WATERFALL
(Hwy 12, Nam Nao National Park) Namtok Haew Sai, about 900m from the roadside parking area, is a beautiful waterfall dropping about 20m over naturally layered rock. Further down the same trail is smaller Namtok Sai Thong. They're really only worth seeing during or just after the rainy season, but the walk is pleasant any time.

NORTHEASTERN THAILAND NAM NAO NATIONAL PARK

ROCKET FESTIVALS

Thailand's Isan region erupts into festival mode in the hot season, culminating in the riotous rocket festival celebrations held in the sixth lunar month (May and June). The festivals aren't just a chance to get drunk, dance bawdily in the street and tempt fate by firing huge homemade rockets into the sky, they're a reminder to Phaya Taen, a pre-Buddhist god, that it's time for him to send rain.

While just about every Isan village will launch at least one rocket, many places make it into a huge event. Without a doubt the most raucous and famous is the **Yasothon Rocket Festival** (Bun Bâng Fai; ⊙ 2nd weekend in May), which is heavily promoted by the Tourism Authority of Thailand.

Most big rocket festivals fall on weekends, with parades taking place on Saturday and the rocket launches on Sunday. The floats are big and elaborate and usually feature gold paint and a *naga* head on the rocket itself.

The rockets themselves were traditionally made of bamboo shafts stuffed with gunpowder, but nowadays PVC pipe is the vessel of choice. The largest can reach 3m in length and hold 120kg of gunpowder. Add to that the large amount of alcohol being consumed and you have a saucy recipe for danger. Accidents, some fatal, do happen. If you go, keep your wits about you and don't necessarily take your safety cues from the locals.

EPIC KHMER RUIN

The 12th-century **Prasat Puay Noi** (ปราสาทเปือยน้อย; ☉daylight hours) `FREE` is the largest and most interesting Khmer ruin in northern Isan. About the size of Buriram's Prasat Meuang Tam, but far less intact, the east-facing monument comprises a large central sandstone sanctuary surmounted by a partially collapsed prang and surrounded by laterite walls with two major gates. There are still some excellent carvings intact, including Shiva riding his bull Nandi on the pediment on the back of the 'library'. It's no longer accessible by public transport. If you have your own wheels, head east of Ban Phai on Hwy 23 for 11km to Rte 2301. Follow it and Rte 2297 for 24km.

🛏 Sleeping & Eating

The accommodation at Nam Nao is above average for Thai national parks. The cheapest **bungalows** (☑081 962 6236; http://nps.dnp.go.th/reservation.php; 4-12 person bungalows 1000-4000B; P) (sleeping from four to 30 people) are pretty old, but the more expensive ones are large, modern and very comfortable. The **campsite** (☑081 962 6236; per person with own tent 30B, camping set (tent, sleeping bags, pillows & ground mats) for 2 people 250B; P) is good too.

There are two very good restaurants (usually open from about 6am to 8pm) serving Thai and Isan food, plus a little convenience store for snacks next to the visitor centre. You can order in the afternoon for evening delivery to your room or campsite.

ℹ Getting There & Away

Most buses heading west to Lom Sak or Phitsanulok from either of Khon Kaen's bus terminals (the old bus terminal has the most departures) will stop at the park entrance (102B to 160B, 2½ hours). The visitor centre is 1.5km from the highway.

Roi Et   ร้อยเอ็ด

☑ 043 / POP 34,285

At one point in its past, legend says, Roi Et had 11 city gates. In ancient writing '11' was expressed as '10-plus-1' and somehow this morphed into the city's name, which means '101'. Except for extensive stretches of an ancient moat, Roi Et's long history hasn't followed it into the 21st century. Still, the city retains a charm and sense of identity all its own. You can't call Roi Et sleepy, but it is a pleasant place that does seem to move to its own urban beat.

⊙ Sights

★ Wat Pa Non Sawan   BUDDHIST TEMPLE

(วัดป่าโนนสวรรค์; ☉daylight hours) `FREE` Wat Pa Non Sawan is home to hundreds of colourful sculptures ranging from merely peculiar to 'what the...?!' Whether it's the immense dragons, waving turtles, Hindu gods, gruesome scenes of hell or the lonely polar bear, this place is sure to make you think as well as smile, which is exactly the point of it all.

Be sure to say sà·wàt·dee to Lungpu Khampan, the octogenarian abbot who inspired it all. He lives and greets visitors on the ground floor of the tower, inside Hanuman's mouth.

The temple is 30km east of Roi Et, and buses to Selaphum can drop you at the Thung Khao Luang junction (25B, 45 minutes), 8km from the temple, where a motorcycle taxi will charge 200B for a two-hour round trip.

Wat Klang Ming Muang   BUDDHIST TEMPLE

(วัดกลางมิ่งเมือง; Th Phadung Phanit; ☉daylight hours) `FREE` The first thing most people notice about this old temple, which dates to the late Ayuthaya era, is the unusual four-storey stupa at the back, but the real gem is the old Lan Xang–style bôht. It has a wide roof and gorgeous facade, and the exterior walls are covered with restored Isan-style paintings, which mostly recount the Jataka tales.

Wat Burapha   BUDDHIST TEMPLE

(วัดบูรพา; Th Phadung Phanit; ☉daylight hours) `FREE` The enormous standing Buddha towering above Roi Et's squat skyline is Phra Phuttha Ratana Mongkon Mahamuni (Luang Po Yai for short). Despite being of little artistic significance, it's hard to ignore. Head to toe he stands 59.2m, and from the ground to the tip of the ùt·sà·nít it's 67.8m. You can climb up the stairs behind him.

Roi Et

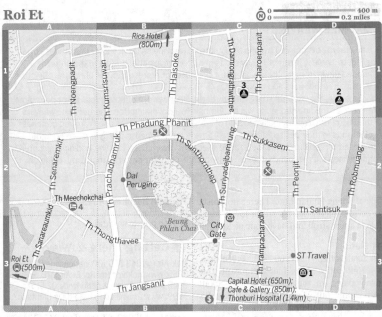

Rice Hotel
(800m)

Th Haisoke

Th Damrongrathwithee

Th Charoenpanit

3
Wat Klang Ming Muang

2
Wat Burapha

Th Noengpadit

Th Kumsrisuwan

Th Phadung Phanit

5
Elefin

Th Sunthornthep

Th Sukkasem

Th Senaremkit

Th Prachadhamruk

Th Suriyadejbamrung

6
Night Market

Th Peonjit

Th Robmuang

*Dal
Perugino*

Th Meechokchai

4
City Home Place

*Beung
Phlan Chai*

Th Santisuk

Th Sanareaumkid

Th Thongthavee

City
Gate

Th Prampracharadh

Roi Et
(500m)

ST Travel

1
Roi Et National Museum

Th Jangsanit

Capital Hotel (650m);
Cafe & Gallery (850m);
Thonburi Hospital (1.4km)

Roi Et

⊙ Sights

🛏 Sleeping

✖ Eating

Roi Et National Museum   MUSEUM
(พิพิธภัณฑสถานแห่งชาติร้อยเอ็ด; Th Peonjit; 100B;
⊙9am-4pm Wed-Sun) This interesting museum gives equal billing to ancient artefacts
and Isan culture. The 3rd floor features silk
weaving, including a good display showing
the materials used to produce natural-dye
fabrics. There are also some Lopburi-era
Khmer pieces.

🛏 Sleeping

City Home Place   HOTEL $
(☏043 516079; Th Thongthavee; d/tw 400/440B;
P❄🖥) The rooms here have hard mattresses and the feel of a student dorm, but
they're spotlessly clean and OK for the price.
City Home's best feature, however, is being

the only hotel right near the lake that isn't
old and run down.

Rice Hotel   HOTEL $$
(☏043 519999; Hwy 214; d/tw/ste incl breakfast
700/750/1500B; P⊖❄🖥) Though it only
just rises above the budget level, this newly
built hotel's bright, comfortable rooms are
the best that Roi Et has to offer. The only
negative is that it's in a somewhat isolated
area 750m north of the moat.

Capital Hotel   HOTEL $$
(☏043 519935; The_Capital_Roiet@hotmail.com;
Th Suriyadejbamrung; d/tw/ste incl breakfast
600/650/1200B; P❄🖥) There are some
scuffs and scratches, but due to limited competition, this is still one of Roi Et's best hotels. The rooms are large and the mattresses
are good, and it has the bonus of being located within the city. Note that some of the
suites are oddly placed outside fronting the
parking lot; inside is better.

✖ Eating & Drinking

Roi Et's nightlife zone, with several large
pubs and clubs, begins just north of the
moat along Th Haisoke.

There are some low-key bars and restaurants – both Thai and *fa·ràng* – on the west

LOCAL KNOWLEDGE

MÁT-MÈE WEAVING

Isan *mát·mèe* is one of Thailand's best-known weaving styles. It's a tie-dye process (*mát* is 'tie' and *mèe* is 'strands') that results in a geometric pattern. Most of the patterns, handed down from mother to daughter, are abstract representations of natural objects such as trees, flowers and birds.

To begin, the weavers string their thread (silk or cotton) tightly across a wooden frame as wide as the finished fabric will be. Almost always working from memory, the weavers then tie plastic (traditionally the skin of banana-plant stalks was used) around bunches of strands in their desired design. The frame is then dipped in the dye, which grips the exposed thread but leaves the wrapped sections clean. The wrapping and dipping continues for multiple rounds, resulting in intricate, complex patterns that come to life on the loom.

side of Bueng Phalan Chai. There's no sunset to be seen here, but it's still a lovely view. Take a short stroll and have your pick.

★ **Elefin** THAI, COFFEE $

(Th Sunthornthep; mains 60-150B; ⏲9am-8pm; 📶) Half coffee shop, half restaurant, this lovely place on the lake is serious about both beans (all Thai-grown) and rice. It's in a restored building, and the lovely tiles and wooden cabinets make it almost museum-like. Prices are high, but the quality justifies it.

Cafe & Gallery COFFEE $

(Th Ronnachai Chanyut; cappuccino 35B; ⏲9am-6.30pm; 📶) Owned by a photographer, and full of his framed prints (all for sale), this small coffee shop brings a welcome bit of culture to Roi Et. If coffee's not your thing, you can enjoy a strawberry smoothie or chocolate brownie. It's 1km south of the lake, across the street from Roi Et Hospital.

Night Market THAI $

(Th Prampracharadh; ⏲3-10pm) By day this big roof hosts Roi Et's municipal market, and at night it shifts gears to become the city's main night market. And it's a good one, with a mix of Thai and Isan, though seating is very limited as it's mostly bagged up for take-home.

ℹ Information

Banks are scattered around the centre. There are several at the north end of Th Suriyadet Bamrung, while on the south end of this road **Bangkok Bank** (Th Suriyadejbamrung; ⏲9am-6pm) is the only city-centre bank open evenings and weekends.

Thonburi Hospital (☎043 518200; www.thonburihospital.com; Th Prachadhamruk) Roi Et's top private hospital.

ℹ Getting There & Away

Nok Air (☎043 650500, nationwide 02 900 9955; www.nokair.com; Roi Et Airport; ⏲8am-9pm) and **Air Asia** (☎nationwide 02 515 9999; www.airasia.com) have daily flights to/from Bangkok's Don Muang Airport, with fares from about 1000B. **ST Travel** (☎043 512469; s.t_travel@hotmail.com; Th Peonjit; ⏲8.30am-6pm Mon-Sat) sells tickets. Roi Et Airport is 13km north of town; expect to pay about 200B for a taxi to the city.

Buses depart at least hourly from Roi Et's **bus terminal** (☎043 511939; Th Jangsanit), 1km west of the city centre, to Bangkok (360B to 552B, eight hours, 6.30am to 11pm), Khon Kaen (bus and minivan 73B to 107B, 2½ hours, every 30 minutes 5am to 7.20pm), Ubon Ratchathani (106B to 155B, three hours, every 30 minutes 8.30am to 6pm) and Surin (90B, 2½ hours, hourly 8am to 7pm). **Nakhonchai Air** (☎043 518095, nationwide 1624; Roi Et Bus Terminal) has VIP service to Bangkok.

ℹ Getting Around

Central Roi Et is very walkable, though there are lots of túk-túk (40B to 60B anywhere within the centre, including to/from the bus station) and a few pedal săhm·lór around. Roi Et also has some **taxis** (☎098 104 0930, 064 672 6941), which park at the bus station and airport. **Avis** (☎062 603 2937, nationwide 022 511131; www.avisthailand.com; ⏲7am-8.30pm) and a few local car hire companies have airport offices.

Expat bar-restaurant **Dal Perugino** (☎092 216 3542; Th Sunthornthep; per day 150B; ⏲10am-10pm) has motorcycle hire.

Yasothon ยโสธร

☐ 042 / POP 20,675

Yasothon has little to offer visitors outside the official whizz-bang rocket festival (p443) period of mid-May. Cultural travellers, however, will appreciate this detour from the fast track to check out a slice of Thailand that few people (including other Thais) ever see. Besides some historical sites in the city, people looking to nose deep into Isan culture will want to take a peek at **That Khang Khao Noi** (ธาตุก่องข้าวน้อย; ⊙ daylight hours) FREE and purchase some pillows in **Ban Si Than** (บ้านศรีฐาน) which, along with the rocket festival, compose a trifecta of Isan icons.

🛏 Sleeping & Eating

BM Grand   HOTEL $
(☐ 045 712333; Th Rattanakhet; d/tw 450/500B;
P ⊖ ✳ 🛜) This city-centre place near the night market has nicely decorated and well-appointed rooms that provide the best value in town.

⭐**Hippy Cafe**   THAI $
(Th Rattanakhet; mains 60-120B; ⊙ 9.30am-8pm;
🛜 🍴) This Thai-trendy cafe in the old bus station (by the clock tower) surprises with delicious Thai dishes, fresh salads and good coffee. We really like its tofu *lâhp* ('spicy tofu salad' on the menu), though you'll have to insist that they make it spicy.

❶ Getting There & Around

Yasothon's **bus terminal** (☐ 045 712965; Th Arunprasert) is north of the city on the bypass road. Bangkok (303B to 566B, eight to nine hours) buses leave approximately hourly during the day, and frequently from 7pm to 10.30pm. There are VIP buses with **999** (☐ 045 714933; Th Arunpraser). The other main destinations are Ubon Ratchathani (66B to 99B, two hours, every 30 minutes 8am to 7pm), Khorat (168B to 190B, four hours, hourly 7.35am to 7.50pm), Mukdahan (minivans 84B, two hours, every 30 minutes 5.30am to 6.10pm; buses 95B, 2½ hours, every two hours 10.35am to 10.40pm) and Khon Kaen (66B to 166B, 3½ hours, every 30 minutes 7am to 7.10pm) via Roi Et (47B to 69B, one hour).

Nok Air (p204) has twice-a-day fly-and-ride service from Bangkok's Don Muang Airport via Ubon Ratchathani Airport.

Yasothon has no túk-túk or taxis, only motorcycle taxis. From the bus station to the city centre they cost 60B, and it's best to get your driver's phone number for the return trip because finding a motorcycle taxi in town is difficult.

Ko Chang &
the Eastern Seaboard

Best Places to Eat

➡ Mantra (p459)

➡ Chanthorn (p470)

➡ Blues Blues Restaurant (p483)

➡ Namchok (p473)

➡ Pan & David Restaurant (p454)

Best Places to Stay

➡ Baan Luang Rajamaitri (p469)

➡ Baan Rim Nam (p480)

➡ Bann Makok (p486)

➡ Mangrove Hideaway (p482)

➡ Rabbit Resort (p458)

Why Go?

Two islands – Ko Samet and Ko Chang – are the magnets that draw travellers to the eastern seaboard. The mainland has plenty of its own attractions, particularly the charismatic, old-world charm of Trat and Chanthaburi.

Ko Samet, the nearest major island to Bangkok, is a flashpacker fave where visitors sip from vodka buckets and admire the fire jugglers or head for the quieter southern coves. Further down the coast is Ko Chang, Thailand's second-largest island. Spend your days diving, chilling on the westcoast beaches or hiking through dense jungle – then recover in time to experience the island's vibrant party scene.

Fewer travellers make it to Si Racha or Bang Saen, though their seafood restaurants and the latter's long beach make them worth a stopover. Less serene is the raucous resort of Pattaya, with its hedonistic nightlife and family-friendly attractions.

When to Go

➡ The best time to visit is the end of the rainy season (usually around November) but before the start of high season (December to March), when the weather is cool, the landscape green and rates reasonable. Peak season on Ko Chang is the Christmas and New Year holiday period. Crowds thin in March, the start of the hot season.

➡ The rainy season runs from May to October, though there are often days or weeks with no rain at all. A few businesses on Ko Chang and Ko Kut close, and Ko Mak and Ko Wai go into hibernation with many places shut. Your best bet during monsoon is Ko Samet, which enjoys its own microclimate and stays relatively dry.

Si Racha ศรีราชา

📞 038 / POP 80,000

Si Racha (pronounced 'see-ra-cha') is the gateway to the worthwhile little island of Ko Si Chang. Colourful, creaking fishing boats and squid rigs are still moored in Si Racha, but these days they share the water with giant container ships. Similarly, a building boom is overshadowing the traditional low-rise centre.

Sushi restaurants and karaoke bars cater for the hundreds of Japanese employees who work at nearby industrial estates, giving the town centre a Little Tokyo vibe. The real heart of Si Racha, though, is the waterfront, with rickety stilt guesthouses, a peaceful health park and a busy pier.

👁 Sights

Ko Loi ISLAND

(เกาะลอย) Attached to the mainland via a road, this rocky island hosts a **Thai-Chinese temple** (วัดเกาะลอย; ⏺ daylight hours) FREE and a viewing area for the impressive sunsets. Below the temple is a giant pond, where behemoth turtles can be fed squid. At time of last research, the bridge to the island was under major renovation and everything was closed down until completion.

🛏 Sleeping

The most authentic places to stay are the wooden hotels on the piers, which offer plenty of character, though the cheaper ones are very basic.

Samchai Resort GUESTHOUSE, HOSTEL $

(📞 081-963 1855; Soi 10, Th Jermjompol; dm 275B, r 350-900B; ❄🛜) There's plenty of character at this sprawling pier guesthouse that has a helpful English-speaking owner and a wide range of rooms, from functional windowless boxes to air-con sea-view suites. There's a great spot to sit at the end of the pier and gaze out across the water. Cheaper rooms are fan-only.

Triple B HOTEL $$

(📞 092 897 7881; www.triplebhotel.com; 119/1 Mu 2, Surasak Subdistrict; d incl breakfast 700-1000B; 🅿❄🛜⬚) Handy if you're arriving by minibus, this hotel offers comfortable, spacious rooms with some attractive design features. A few things don't quite work as they should, but it's a good deal at this price. The breakfast room overlooks the small plunge pool; the best rooms are on the top floor, with more of an outlook.

🍴 Eating & Drinking

There's a lively knot of Thai bars along Th Thetsaban. Northwest of here is a solid grid of karaoke bars.

My One VIETNAMESE $

(📞 089 693 3270; 14/10 Th Surasak 1; mains 50-160B; ⏺9am-9pm) This simple Thai-Vietnamese restaurant has a variety of fresh, healthy dishes, including rice paper rolls and salads. Look for the coffee cart out front.

Labubon Sriracha THAI $

(📞 087 748 1696; Th Si Racha Nakorn; mains 60-160B; ⏺8.30am-10pm) This open-plan barn of a spot offers reliably good eating; it's an Isan place with yummy *nám đòk mǒo* (spicy pork salad) and some great fish dishes that would serve two.

Mum Aroi SEAFOOD $$

(📞 038 771555; Soi 8, Th Jermjompol; mains 160-450B; ⏺11am-10pm; 🛜) Mum Aroi delivers on its name, 'delicious corner'. This is *the* place to enjoy a seafood meal with views of the squid rigs, with its tiers of terraces giving most diners a shot at a water vista. It is north of the town; head for Samitivej Sriracha Hospital; look opposite it for the tank with the 2m fish out front.

Teab Ta CRAFT BEER

(www.facebook.com/teabtasriracha; Soi 16, Th Jermjompol; ⏺5pm-midnight Mon-Fri, 4pm-midnight Sat & Sun; 🛜) On the long pier, Teab Ta has a

---

LOCAL KNOWLEDGE

HOT STUFF

Given that 'Sriracha' chilli sauce is hot stuff in the USA and elsewhere, you may expect it to be celebrated in its eponymous home town. But no. The sauce is thought to have been created in Si Racha decades ago, but it was a Vietnamese immigrant living in Los Angeles who launched the company with the rooster logo and made his sauce famous.

Thailand does have its own version (*nám prík sěe rah·chah*). It is usually eaten as a dip with *kài jee·o* (omelette) and *hǒy tôrt* (fried mussel omelette), and is sweeter than the more famous rooster brand.

Ko Chang & the Eastern Seaboard Highlights

1 **Ko Chang** (p474) Snorkelling and jungle trekking on this sizeable island that offers something for everyone.

2 **Ko Kut** (p485) Floating the day away at the marvellous beaches of this southeastern island.

3 **Ko Wai** (p488) Swimming with the fishes in gin-clear waters at this diminutive favourite near Ko Chang.

4 **Ko Samet** (p461) Walking between pretty coves on lovely Ko Samet.

5 **Chanthaburi** (p467) Strolling through the old waterfront community of this historic riverside town.

6 **Trat** (p471) Kicking back in the old-time atmosphere of this pleasing town's wooden shophouse quarter.

7 **Ko Si Chang** (p453) Taking a day trip on the ferry from pleasant Si Racha to peaceful Ko Si Chang.

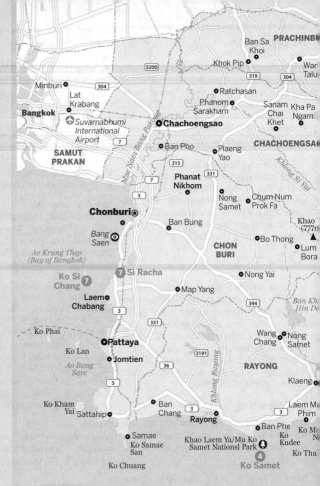

Si Racha

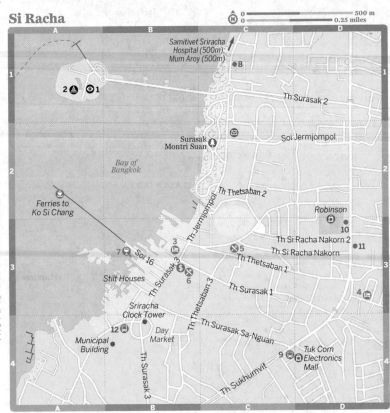

Si Racha

⊚ Sights
1 Ko Loi..A1
2 Wat Ko Loi......................................A1

⊝ Sleeping
3 Samchai Resort.............................B3
4 Triple B..D3

⊗ Eating
5 Labubon Sriracha..........................C3
6 My One...B3

⊝ Drinking & Nightlife
7 Teab Ta..B3

ℹ Information
8 Immigration Office.........................C1

ℹ Transport
9 Buses to Bangkok..........................C4
10 Minivans to Bangkok.....................D3
11 Minivans to Pattaya and Rayong....D3
12 Sŏrng·tăa·ou to Pattaya & Bang
     Saen..B4

fabulous selection of craft beer from around the world and various northern European brewing masterpieces, all at northern European prices. It's a great spot for a sundowner on the deck over the water: a lovely outlook. There's a reasonably priced menu of bar snacks and simple dishes plus a carefully curated modern indie soundtrack.

ℹ Information

Immigration Office (☏ 038 312571; www.immchonburi.go.th; 3/1 Th Jermjompol; ☺ 8.30am-4.30pm Mon-Fri)

Krung Thai Bank (www.ktb.co.th; cnr Th Surasak 1 & Th Jermjompol; ☺ 8.30am-4.30pm Mon-Fri) Has an ATM and exchange facilities.

Post Office (Th Jermjompol; ⊘8.30am-4.30pm Mon-Fri, to 12.30pm Sat) Opposite the municipal park.

Samitivej Sriracha Hospital (☎ 038 320300; www.samitivejhospitals.com; Soi 8, Th Jermjompol)

❶ Getting There & Around

Minivans, including services to **Bangkok**, **Pattaya and Rayong**, leave from Th Sukhumvit (Hwy 3) near **Robinson department store** (☎ 037 771001; www.robinson.co.th; 90/1 Th Sukhumvit; ⊘10.30am-9pm Mon-Fri, 10am-9pm Sat & Sun), and both **buses** and minivans leave from the nearby IT mall, **Tuk Com** (☎ 038 773619; www.tukcom.com; Th Sukhumvit; ⊘10.30am-9pm Mon-Fri, 10am-9pm Sat & Sun).

White *sŏrng·tăa·ou* (passenger pick-up trucks) leave from near Si Racha's **clock tower** for Pattaya's Naklua market (40B, 45 minutes, 6am to 6pm); red *sŏrng·tăa·ou* go to Bang Saen (15B, 20 minutes, 6am to 6pm).

Motorbike taxis zip around town for 30B to 40B.

Ko Si Chang   เกาะสีชัง

☎ 038 / POP 5000

Once a royal beach retreat, Ko Si Chang has a fishing-village atmosphere and enough attractions to make it a decent day's excursion from Si Racha, or a fine overnight stop for those who want to chill out. It gets busier at weekends, when Thais come to eat seafood, snap selfies by the sea and make merit at the local temples.

The island's one small settlement faces the mainland and is the terminus for the ferry. A bumpy road network links the village with the other sights.

◉ Sights & Activities

Several locals run **snorkelling** trips to nearby Ko Khang Khao (Bat Island), which has a good beach, or you can take a speedboat (400B) there from the main pier. **Kayaks** are available (200B per hour) on **Hat Tham Phang** (หาดถ้ำพัง, Fallen Cave Beach), the only sandy beach on the island. You paddle to Ko Khang Khao in 45 minutes.

Phra Chudadhut Palace   HISTORIC SITE
(พระจุฑาธุชราชฐาน; ⊘9am-5pm) **FREE** This former royal palace was used by Rama V (King Chulalongkorn) over the summer months, but was abandoned when the French briefly occupied the island in 1893. The main throne hall – a magnificent golden teak structure known as Vimanmek Teak Mansion – was moved to Bangkok in 1910. What's left are subdued Victorian-style buildings set in gardenlike grounds. It's a 15-minute stroll from the ferry. The museum buildings are closed Monday.

San Chao Pho Khao Yai   BUDDHIST TEMPLE
(ศาลเจ้าพ่อเขาใหญ่) **FREE** The most imposing sight on the island, this ornate dragon-infested temple dates back to the days when Chinese traders anchored in the sheltered waters. During New Year in February, the island is overrun with Chinese tourists. There are shrine caves, multiple platforms and a good view of the island and sea. It's just north of the main town.

TRANSPORT TO/FROM SI RACHA

DESTINATION	BUS	MINIVAN	TRAIN
Bangkok's Eastern Bus Terminal (Ekamai)	103B, 1½hr, hourly 5am-8pm	N/A	N/A
Bangkok Hualamphong	N/A	N/A	from 28B, 3¼ hr, 1 daily Mon-Fri
Bangkok's Northern Bus Terminal (Mo Chit)	113B, 2hr, hourly 5am-7.30pm	N/A	N/A
Bangkok Suvarnabhumi International Airport	110B, 1hr, hourly 5.10am-8pm	N/A	N/A
Bangkok's Victory Monument	N/A	110B, 1½hr, every 30min 5am-8pm	N/A
Pattaya	N/A	40B, 30min, frequent	from 5B, 30 minutes, 1 daily Mon-Fri

Sichang Healing House MASSAGE
(☎081 572 7840; off Th Makham Thaew; ⏰9am-4pm Thu-Tue) The charming, English-speaking owner of this leafy haven offers a range of excellent massages (300B to 600B). She also sells homemade health products and has modest bamboo rooms for rent (300B).

Sleeping & Eating

Charlie's Bungalows GUESTHOUSE $$
(☎061 749 4242; www.kosichang.net; Th Makham Thaew; r 1000-1100B; P❄📶) Bright, fresh, all-white bungalows set around a garden. All come with TVs and DVD players. Friendly and helpful staff. Book ahead at weekends and public holidays.

Somewhere Ko Sichang BOUTIQUE HOTEL $$$
(☎038 109400; www.somewherehotel.com; 194/1 Mu 3, Th Thewawong; r incl breakfast 2600-3600B; P❄🏊) White, modern and charming, this place occupies a very central but secluded location. Rooms have loads of space and a breezy maritime feel to the decor; most have balconies and sea views. The restaurant area is handsome and staff are eager to please. A relaxing and stylish retreat.

FlowerBlue CAFE $
(☎081 305 5544; www.facebook.com/flowerblue.coffee; mains 70-190B; ⏰7am-10pm; ❄📶) Popular with the Bangkok set, who appreciate the air-con and fair prices, this trendy cafe is always busy. It does breakfasts, burgers, speciality coffees and more in the attractive space, festooned with real plants and other botanical iconography.

★Pan & David Restaurant INTERNATIONAL, THAI $$
(☎038 216629; www.ko-sichang.com; 167 Mu 3, Th Makham Thaew; mains 170-300B; ⏰10am-10.30pm Mon-Fri, 8.30am-10pm Sat & Sun; 📶🖋) With free-range chicken, homemade ice cream, a reasonable wine list, excellent Thai dishes and an Italian touch, you can't go wrong here. It also has a series of rooms and bungalows available in spacious grounds (750B to 1800B), which include characterful converted fishing boats in dry dock.

Pee Noi SEAFOOD $$
(Th Makham Thaew; mains 100-350B; ⏰11am-9pm) This eat-on-the-street and takeaway restaurant is a favourite with locals thanks to its great seafood options. Look for the blue tables and umbrellas.

Information

Pan & David's website (www.ko-sichang.com) is an excellent source of local information.

Kasikornbank (99/12 Th Atsadang; ⏰8.30am-3.30pm) Has an ATM and exchange facilities.

Post Office (Th Atsadang; ⏰8.30am-4.30pm Mon-Fri, to 12.30pm Sat)

Getting There & Around

Boats to Ko Si Chang leave hourly from 7am to 8pm from the end of the main jetty in Si Racha (one way 50B, 45 minutes), dodging around the plethora of cargo ships unloading in the bay. From Ko Si Chang boats shuttle back hourly from 6am to 7pm. Outward ferries stop at little Ko Karm en route.

Motorbike taxis wait at the pier and will take you anywhere for 30B to 50B, and souped-up *săhm·lór* (three-wheel pedicabs; also spelt *săamláw*) do tours of the main spots for 250B.

Motorbikes are available to rent on the pier (80B hourly, 250B per day, 300B for 24 hours). **Bikes** (☎089 747 9097; per day/24hr 120/160B) are also available.

Bang Saen บางแสน

☎038 / POP 45,000

As the closest beach to Bangkok, Bang Saen is a weekend favourite for those wanting to escape city life. A handsome palm-lined beachfront and a huge quantity of accommodation have boosted its popularity. During the day, the 4km-long promenade is packed with tandem bicycles and seafood stalls. By night, the string of hip restaurants and bars facing the sea draws a studenty crowd. While there are cleaner strips of sand in Thailand,

OFF THE BEATEN TRACK

SECRET MANGROVE FOREST

The **Mangrove Forest Conservation Centre** (ศูนย์ศึกษาธรรมชาติและอนุรักษ์ป่าชายเลนเพื่อการท่องเที่ยว; ☎038 398268; Ang Sila; ⏰8.30am-6.30pm) is such a well-kept secret, many locals don't even know it's here. A 2km-long wooden walkway runs a circuit around the mangrove forest. Look out for crabs, cockles and mudfish and enjoy the sounds and smells.

It's in Ang Sila, 6km north of Bang Saen.

if swimming isn't a priority, then this is a great spot to get a feel for a beach break, Thai style.

👁 Sights

Nezha Sathaizhu Temple BUDDHIST TEMPLE
(ศาลเจ้าหน่าจาซาไท้จื้อ, Wihahn Tepsatit Pra Giti-chairloem; Ang Sila; ☺8am-5pm) FREE This opulent four-storey Chinese temple is fronted by an enormous heaven-earth pole and filled with intricate paintings and magnificent sculptures. Dragons and bats (which signify fortune) feature heavily in the decor. Locals regularly come to make merit, and temple volunteers are happy to explain the rituals if you want to make your own offerings. The temple is on the main road in Ang Sila, about 5km north of Bang Saen beach.

Khao Sam Muk HILL
(เขาสามมุข, Monkey Mountain; ☺road open 5am-11pm) Hundreds of rhesus monkeys with greedy eyes and quick hands live on this small hill (avoid feeding them, as this just makes them more aggressive).

🛏 Sleeping & Eating

Running back from the beach, Soi 1 is wall-to-wall budget guesthouses, with rooms available from 200B upward. Some more upmarket choices are dotted northward along the coast. **KT Guesthouse** (☎096 747 6711; 197/10 Th Long Had Bang Saen; r without breakfast 500-600B; 🖲 🛜) is handy for the bar strip and close to the beach – all rooms have modern furnishings and some have balconies. **Song Row Guesthouse** (☎038 193545; Soi 1, Bang Saen Sai 1; r without/with bathroom 300/400B) offers spotless family-run rooms both with and without bathroom. Using hot water and air-con costs an extra 50B. There's no English sign, look for the red and white lozenge tiles.

Nibble lemon tart or waffles at **Summer's Corner** (☎090 970 6403; www.facebook.com/summerscorner193; 193/25 Th Long Had Bang Saen; mains 100-170B; ☺11am-10pm Thu-Tue; 🖲 🛜), or head to **Andy's Seafood** (Bang Saen Sai 1 near Soi 1; mains 120-350B; ☺5pm-midnight) to feast on steamed sea bass as you watch palms wave in the evening breeze. Th Long Had Bang Saen has a string of popular bars/nightclubs with boisterous student crowds, live music at deafening volumes and outdoor seating.

ℹ Getting There & Away

Minivans and buses leave from either side of Th Sukhumvit, close to the main turn-off into Bang Saen. Red *sŏrng·tǎa·ou* go to Si Racha (15B, 20 minutes, 5.30am to 9pm), while blue ones on Line 1 connect Bang Saen with Ang Sila.

DESTINATION	BUS	MINIVAN
Bangkok's Eastern Bus Terminal (Ekamai)	86B; 1hr; hourly	N/A
Bangkok's Northern Bus Terminal (Mo Chit)	99B; 1½hr; hourly	120B; 1½hr; hourly; 5am-8.30pm
Bangkok Suvarnabhumi International Airport	110B; 1hr; hourly	N/A
Bangkok Victory Monument	110B; 1½ hr; hourly	N/A
Ban Phe (for Ko Samet)	N/A	190B; 2hr; 8am-5pm

Pattaya เมืองพัทยา
☑038 / POP 300,000

Multicultural Pattaya boasts some excellent places to stay and eat, and the area is also a family-friendly resort coast. Nevertheless, the city itself is no tropical paradise; its reputation as a sex capital is totally deserved, with hundreds of beer bars, go-go clubs and massage parlours. Much of the rest is dedicated to mass-market sun-seeking tourism, with a huge retired expat population, and enormous tour groups hurried through town in an almost constant stream. For a relaxing stay in Pattaya, base yourself outside the central area.

The city is built around **Ao Pattaya**, a wide, crescent-shaped bay that was one of Thailand's first beach resorts in the 1960s when American GIs came for some R & R. North Pattaya (Pattaya Neua) is more upmarket while Pattaya South (Pattaya Tai) remains the nightlife hub. Further south **Jomtien** is a laid-back resort, while to the north **Naklua** is also quieter, with some top-end resorts at Wong Amat.

👁 Sights & Activities

Rats on the beach and fuel from the numerous parked boats makes swimming in the centre of town a distinctly unappetising

Pattaya

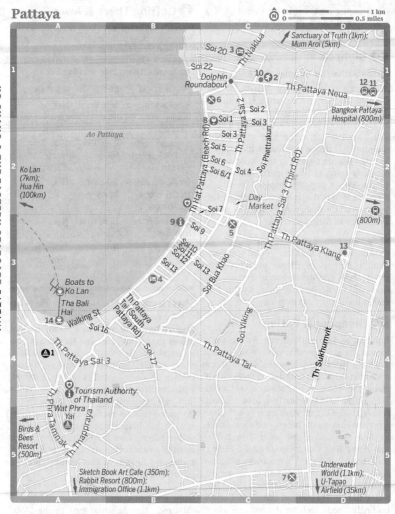

Pattaya

prospect. Better is Jomtien, which has a gay-friendly beach at Hat Dongtan, while to the north Naklua is appealing.

Around 20km south of Pattaya, there's a good scene at Bang Sare, a resort area with a long, narrow beach.

The best beaches in the area are on Ko Samae San, a tiny island with good snorkelling, and the navy-run Hat Nahng Ram, both 35km south of Pattaya.

Sanctuary of Truth   BUDDHIST MONUMENT

(ปราสาทสัจธรรม; ☏ 038 367229; www.sanctuary oftruth.com; Soi Naklua 12; adult/child 500/250B; ☺8am-6pm) Made entirely of wood (without any metal nails) and commanding a celestial view of the ocean, the Sanctuary of Truth is best described as a visionary environment: part art installation, religious shrine and cultural monument. Constructed in four wings dedicated to Thai, Khmer, Chinese and Indian religious iconography, its architecture and setting is impressive.

The ornate temple-like complex was conceived by Lek Viriyaphant, a Thai millionaire who spent his fortune on this and other heritage projects (such as Ancient City near Bangkok) that revived and preserved ancient building techniques and architecture in danger of extinction. In this case, the building continues to support hand-hewn woodworking skills as it's been under construction since 1981 and still isn't finished.

Every part of the 105m-tall building is covered with wood carvings of Hindu and Buddhist gods and goddesses – an artistic consolidation of centuries of religious myths under one unifying roof.

Compulsory tours are led through the building every 30 minutes. Thai dancing is at 11.30am and 3.30pm. The sanctuary is 1km down Soi 12 off Th Naklua, about 3km from the centre of town.

Anek Kusala Sala   MUSEUM

(Viharn Sien; อเนกกุศลศาลา/วิหารเซียน; ☏ 038 235250; off Th Sukhumvit; 50B; ☺8am-5.30pm) A popular stop for tour groups, this museum contains more than 300 impressive pieces of Chinese artwork, mainly bronze and brass statues depicting historical figures as well as Buddhist, Confucian and Taoist deities. Founded by Sa-nga Kulkobkiat, a Thai national who grew up in China, the museum was intended as a friendship-building project between the two countries.

The 1st floor is a crowded pavilion of Chinese immortals, from Pangu, the cosmic

> ### ISLAND DAY TRIP
>
> The small island of **Ko Lan** (เกาะล้าน), 7km offshore from central Pattaya, is an easy day trip. On weekends, its five beaches entertain thousands of visitors and the aquamarine sea is busy with banana boats and other marine merriment. Ferries leave Pattaya's Bali Hai pier (30B, 45 minutes, 11 daily) at the southern end of Walking St. Some go to the main village, while others go to Tawaen beach. You can also charter speedboats from along Beach Rd (think 2500B). The last boat back is at 6pm.

giant, to Guan Yin, the goddess of mercy. The 2nd-floor terrace is the museum's most dramatic, with larger-than-life-sized statues of Shaolin monks depicting different martial-arts poses. Nearby is a touching collection of daily life statues (a fortune teller, dress maker, liquor seller) that visitors place 1B coins on.

The museum is 16km south of central Pattaya; take a Pattaya–Sattahip *sŏrng·tăa·ou* (25B) to the Wat Yangsangwaram turn-off. Hire a passing motorbike to go the final 5km to the museum. Ask the driver to stick around, as a lift back is hard to find. Private transport is 1500B.

Khao Phra Tamnak   BUDDHIST TEMPLE

(เขาพระตำหนัก; ☺4am-10pm) **FREE** This hill has a modest Buddhist temple as well as a much-revered memorial to the admiral who founded the modern Thai navy. There are marvellous views over the Pattaya bay and a little cafe terrace from which to enjoy them. Sunset is a particularly spectacular time to be here, but you won't be alone. You can walk here from the southern end of Walking St.

Underwater World Pattaya   AQUARIUM

(อันเดอร์วอเตอร์เวิลด์ พัทยา; ☏ 038 756879; www. underwaterworldpattaya.com; 22/22 Mu 11, Th Sukhumvit; adult/child 500/300B; ☺9am-6pm; 🅿) The area's largest aquarium is particularly child-friendly, with touch pools and koi feeding sessions. The long viewing tunnel is the highlight. It's on the main road about 4km south of Pattaya.

Ramayana Water Park   WATER PARK

(☏ 033 005929; www.ramayanawaterpark.com; adult/child 1190/890B; ☺10am-6pm) This sizeable water park is excellent fun for the whole family, with a huge array of slides and pools. It's about 20km southeast of Pattaya, with packages that include transport available via the website. Towels and lockers are available there.

Flight of the Gibbon   ADVENTURE SPORTS
(☑ 053 010 660; www.treetopasia.com; tours from 3600B) This zipline course extends 3km via 26 platforms through the forest canopy of Khao Kheow Open Zoo, between Pattaya and Bangkok. It is an all-day tour with additional add-on activities, like a jungle obstacle course and a visit to the neighbouring zoo. Children 1m tall and over can do the zipline independently, while nippers can ride tandem with adults.

🛏 Sleeping

Accommodation in Pattaya is pricey by Thai standards. Rooms around central or south Pattaya tend to be cheaper but closer to the noisy nightlife. North Pattaya and parts of Naklua host the signature hotels, while Soi Bua Khao and Jomtien have budget options.

Jomtien Hostel   HOSTEL **$**
(☑ 038 233416; www.jomtienhostel.com; Soi Sarita Hotel, near Soi 12, Hat Jomtien; dm 300B, r 600-900B; ❇@⊛) A couple of kilometres south of the heart of Jomtien, this excellently maintained place has air-conditioned dorms

---

PATTAYA: EXPAT CENTRAL

Ever since the first US servicemen started arriving in the 1960s for some R & R, hedonism has been a permanent guest. But while Pattaya is known for sleaze, there is another side to the city. Thousands of expats live here, many attracted by the quality of life, relatively low cost of living and amenities – the area has some of Thailand's finest golf courses.

There's a large Russian population; many Brits have businesses here; there is a thriving Arab community centred on Soi 16 at the south end of Walking St; and Naklua is popular with the German crowd. Specialist shops offer everything from South American coffee to French cheese. An estimated 50,000 foreigners live in Pattaya, with many more spending part of the year here, and those numbers are likely to rise.

---

with good bedding and privacy curtains. It's all spotless, and private rooms are a great deal. It's 300m from the beach; lockers are available. Rates drop in low season.

Nonze Hostel   HOSTEL **$**
(☑ 038 711112; www.nonzehostel.com; Th Hat Pattaya; s/tw 650/1400B; ❇⊛) Very stylish industrial chic in a seafront building with views over the water makes this an appealing location. The rooms are capsules – tiny boxes stacked up like building blocks – but offer plenty of interest and are sweet if you're not a claustrophobe. Twin rooms give you a bit more breathing space. Bathrooms are shared but good.

Garden Lodge Hotel   HOTEL **$$**
(☑ 038 429109; www.gardenlodgepattaya.net; cnr Soi 20 & Th Naklua; r/bungalow/ste 1200/1700/3000B; P❇⊛⊛) A favourite among German tourists; the rooms here are old-fashioned but surrounded by landscaped gardens and a large swimming pool. It's in the salubrious end of Pattaya and a decent option for families.

★**Rabbit Resort**   RESORT **$$$**
(☑ 038 251730; www.rabbitresort.com; Hat Dongtan, Jomtien; r incl breakfast 6800-9000B; P❇@⊛⊛) On a different qualitative planet to most Pattaya accommodation, Rabbit Resort has stunning, stylish and secluded bungalows and villas that showcase Thai design and art, all set in peaceful beachfront greenery hidden between Jomtien and Pattaya Tai. With two pools (one designed for families) and superb service, the resort is an excellent option. The upstairs rooms are particularly luminous and appealing.

Birds & Bees Resort   RESORT **$$$**
(☑ 038 250556; www.cabbagesandcondoms.com; Soi 4, Th Phra Tamnak; r 4500-11,000B; P❇@⊛⊛) 🏊 As well as being a tropical garden resort with two pools and good-sized rooms, this place helps fund the work of the PDA, a notable rural development charity. Cheaper rooms have no views. The complex itself is delightful, with meandering pathways signposted with quirky, thought-provoking comments about the state of things. There's direct beach access, with the restaurant overlooking it.

🍴 Eating & Drinking

It can be pretty hard to find a bad meal in much of Thailand, but it's very easy in

Pattaya, particularly in the overpriced night-life area. Other parts of town and outside of the city, however, are a few excellent establishments. Bang Sare, busy at weekends, has a trendy international and Thai dining scene.

Walking St is a centre of sleaze but its profusion of bars are more fun for those just interested in a night out. The tawdrier red-light zone is a block back from the beach.

Leng Kee
CHINESE $
(Th Pattaya Klang; mains 100-300B; ⏱24hr) Duck dishes rule the roost in this well-established Thai-Chinese restaurant, though the seafood dishes are also tasty. It's very reasonably priced for the quality, though the unromantic setting reminds you that you're not paying for the decor.

Thepprasit Market
MARKET $
(cnr Th Thepprasit & Th Sukhumvit; snacks 30-80B; ⏱4-10pm Fri-Sun) As well as intriguing knick-knacks and endless clothes stalls, this thriving weekend market has a great range of smoothies, noodles and Thai snacks.

Mum Aroi
SEAFOOD, THAI $$
(☑038 223252; 83/4 Soi 4, Th Naklua; mains 150-420B; ⏱11am-11pm) This long-established restaurant is perched beside the sea in the fishing-village end of Naklua. Old fishing boats sit marooned offshore and crisp sea breezes envelop diners as they devour fantastic Thai food. Try *sôm·đam ƥoo* (spicy papaya salad with crab) and *ƥlah mèuk nêung ma-now* (squid steamed in lime juice).

Sketch Book Art Cafe
INTERNATIONAL, THAI $$
(☑038 251625; 478/938 Mu 12, Th Tha Phraya; mains 120-300B; ⏱8.30am-9pm) This gorgeous, leafy art cafe offers pleasant respite from the normal Pattaya vibe. It's surrounded by a sprawling garden, and the restaurant's walls are covered with the owner's artwork. Smoothies are lush and the Thai food, once you've selected from the telephone book of a menu, is fresh. Painting material is on sale if you feel inspired.

Glass House
THAI $$
(☑081 266 6110; www.glasshouse-pattaya.com; Soi Najomtien 10, Hat Jomtien; mains 170-380B; ⏱11am-midnight; 🛜) Diners at this all-white beachfront spot plunge their toes into the warm sand as waiters deliver seafood, pizza and steak. The quality of the Thai dishes in particular is excellent, and the atmosphere

romantic. It's about 9km south of central Pattaya.

★Mantra
THAI, INTERNATIONAL $$$
(☑038 429591; www.mantra-pattaya.com; Th Hat Pattaya; mains 350-1100B; ⏱5pm-1am daily, plus 11am-3pm Sun; 🛜) One of Pattaya's top restaurants, Mantra is fun even if you can only afford a classy cocktail (from 180B). The building and interior are sumptuous; try for a seat upstairs where you can overlook proceedings or nestle in a cosy booth. The menu has a range of international cuisines, but the Thai dishes are sensational, and beautifully presented.

Gulliver's
BAR
(www.gulliverbangkok.com; Th Hat Pattaya; ⏱3pm-2am; 🛜) The rather grand neo-colonial facade and mini Statue of Liberty belies the fairly standard sports bar inside this beach-road spot. Decent beer and service, air-conditioning and an absence of bar girls can make it an attractive option.

ℹ Information

DANGERS & ANNOYANCES
➤ Most problems in Pattaya are alcohol-induced, especially bad driving and fights.
➤ Leave valuables in your room to be on the safe side.
➤ Avoid renting jet skis as scams involving fictional damage are common.

EMERGENCY
The tourist police **head office** (☑emergency 1155; tourist@police.go.th) is beside the Tourism Authority of Thailand office on Th Phra Tamnak, with police boxes along **Pattaya** and Jomtien beaches.

IMMIGRATION
Immigration Office (☑038 252750; www.immigration.go.th; Soi 5, Hat Jomtien; ⏱8.30am-noon & 1-4.30pm Mon-Fri)

MEDICAL SERVICES
Bangkok Pattaya Hospital (☑038 259999; www.bangkokpattayahospital.com; 301 Mu 6, Th Sukhumvit, Naklua; ⏱24hr) For first-class health care.

MONEY
There are banks and ATMs throughout the city.

TOURIST INFORMATION
Tourism Authority of Thailand (TAT; ☑038 428750; www.tourismthailand.org; 609 Th Phra Tamnak; ⏱8.30am-4.30pm) Located at the

northwestern edge of Rama IX Park. Helpful staff have brochures and maps.

Tourist Information Kiosk (⏰ 8am-6pm)

WEBSITES

Pattaya Mail (www.pattayamail.com) One of the city's English-language weekly newspapers.

Pattaya One (www.pattayaone.news) Offers an intriguing insight into the darker side of the city.

Getting There & Away

AIR

Pattaya's airport is **U-Tapao** (UTP; ☎ 038 245595; www.utapao.com), 33km south of town. Make sure taxi drivers know it's this airport you want, or they may assume you're going to Bangkok.

Destinations around Thailand are served from here daily by **Bangkok Airways** (☎ 038 412382; www.bangkokair.com; Fairtex Arcade, Th Pattaya Neua), **Air Asia** (www.airasia.com) and **Kan Airlines** (www.kanairlines.com).

Air Asia also has international flights, as do a couple of other airlines.

There are also regular charter flights here.

BOAT

A new fast catamaran service across the Gulf of Thailand between Pattaya and Hua Hin had recently launched at time of research. Despite some problems coping with choppy conditions, the service, run by **Royal Ferry Group** (☎ 038 488999; www.royalferrygroup.com), seemed to be established, charging 1250/1550B for standard/business class for the two-hour crossing, which slashes the normal travel time...for a

price. At time of writing there was one service daily, but that was set to increase.

The same operator was mooting a service to Ko Chang from Sattahip, 30km south of Pattaya; don't bet on this getting off the ground.

BUS & MINIVAN

The main **bus station** is on Th Pattaya Neua. Services to Bangkok leave from here, as well as buses to Bangkok's Suvarnabhumi Airport (250B, 1½ to two hours, seven daily) run by **Bell Travel Service** (☎ 084 427 4608; www.bell travelservice.com; Th Pattaya Neua), which does hotel pick-ups if you prebook. **Roong Reuang Coaches** (www.airportpattayabus.com) run from Th Tha Phraya in Jomtien, near the corner of Th Thep Prasit, to Suvarnabhumi airport and vice versa for a much cheaper 120B.

Minivans heading north to Bangkok leave from the corner of Th Sukhumvit and Th Pattaya Klang. Minivans heading for the Cambodian border leave from the junction of Th Sukhumvit and Th Pattaya Tai. Downtown travel agents can book minivan services to Ko Chang (550B), Ko Mak (750B) and Ko Kut (800B).

TRAIN

Pattaya Train Station (☎ 038 429285) is off Th Sukhumvit east of town.

ⓘ Getting Around

Locally known as 'baht buses', *sŏrng·tăa·ou* do a loop along the major roads; just hop on and pay 10B when you get off. If you are going all the way to or from Naklua, you will have to change vehicles at the **Dolphin Roundabout** (Th Naklua & Th Pattaya Neua) in Pattaya Neua. Baht buses run to the bus station from the Dolphin

TRANSPORT TO/FROM PATTAYA

DESTINATION	BUS	MINIVAN	TRAIN
Aranya Prathet (for Cambodia)	N/A	260B, 5hr, hourly 4am-6pm	N/A
Bangkok's Eastern Bus Terminal (Ekamai)	108B, 2hr, every 30min 4.30am-11pm	130B, 2hr, frequent	N/A
Bangkok Hualamphong	N/A		from 31B, 4hr, 1 daily Mon-Fri
Bangkok's Northern Bus Terminal (Mo Chit)	117B, 2½hr, every 40min 4.30am-9pm	150B, 2½hr, frequent	N/A
Bangkok's Southern Bus Terminal	119B, 3hr, every 2hr 6am-6.30pm	150B, 2½hr, hourly	N/A
Hua Hin	389B, 6hr, 1 daily		N/A
Ko Samet	N/A	160B, 1hr, hourly	N/A
Rayong	N/A	100B, 1½hr, frequent	N/A
Si Racha	N/A	40B, 50min, frequent	from 5B, 30 minutes, 1 daily Mon-Fri

Roundabout as well. If you are going further afield, you can charter a baht bus; establish the price beforehand.

Motorbikes can be hired for 200B a day.

Rayong & Ban Phe ระยอง/บ้านเพ

♪ 038 / POP 70,000

You are most likely to transit through these towns en route to Ko Samet. Rayong is a sizeable, sprawling city with frequent bus connections to elsewhere. The little port of Ban Phe, 18km east, has ferry services to Ko Samet and quite a decent beach. Blue *sŏrng·tăa·ou* link the two towns (25B, 45 minutes, every 15 minutes). If you're spending time in Rayong, have a wander around its picturesque old town, south of the main road.

🛏 Sleeping & Eating

Rayong has a wide range of hotel accommodation, though most of it isn't particularly central. Ban Phe is well-stocked with mostly downmarket guesthouses and a string of eateries on its waterside road, including the impressive rainforest-style resort restaurant **Tamnanpar** (✆038 652884; www.tamnanpar -rayong.com; 167/6 Mu 7; mains 150-300B; ⏰10am-10pm; 📶).

La Paillote   GUESTHOUSE $$
(✆038 651625; www.lapaillotebanphe.com; Ban Phe; r 700-900B; 🕸📶) A decent budget option in Ban Phe itself, handy for the piers and beach. It offers welcoming staff, simple but comfortable rooms with decent facilities and an on-site outdoor restaurant and bar. There are good family options.

Rayong President Hotel   HOTEL $$
(✆038 622771; www.rayongpresidenthotel.com; Soi Klongkhud, off Th Sukhumvit, Rayong; r 700-850B; 🅿🕸📶) Rayong has better hotels than this, but they are all quite a way from the centre; this is one of the few within walking distance of the central bus station. Rooms have been somewhat renovated and offer OK value. Cheaper no-breakfast rates are also available.

ℹ Getting There & Around

Rayong has a central **bus station**, Number 1, and a **new one** 7km northwest of downtown (Number 2). All long-distance services now use the new one. The two are connected by very regular *sŏrng·tăa·ou* (15B, 20 minutes).

Minivans from Rayong's bus station 2 go to Bangkok's eastern (Ekamai) and northern (Mo Chit) bus terminals (both 160B, 3½ hours, hourly 4.40am to 8pm); these can also drop you off at the AirportLink station one stop away from Suvarnabhumi airport. There are also minivans to Pattaya (100B, 1½ hours, frequent), Chanthaburi (120B, two hours, frequent) and Trat (200B, three hours, frequent).

Ban Phe has regular boats and speedboats to Ko Samet. Buses opposite Ban Phe's Nuanthip pier go to/from Bangkok Ekamai (166B, four hours, every two hours, 7am to 6pm).

Ban Phe also has minivan services to Laem Ngop for boats to Ko Chang (250B, three hours, three daily) and overpriced services to Pattaya (200B, two hours, hourly) and Bangkok's Victory Monument (200B, four hours, every 40 minutes).

From Rayong's central bus station 1, there are frequent *sŏrng·tăa·ou* to Ban Phe (25B, 30 minutes).

From Ban Phe, catch them outside the main piers.

Ko Samet เกาะเสม็ด

Once the doyen of backpacker destinations, today Ko Samet shares its charms with a wider audience. The sandy shores, cosy coves and aquamarine waters attract ferryloads of Bangkokians looking to party each weekend, while tour groups pack out the main beach and many resorts. Fire-juggling shows and beach barbecues are nightly events on the northern beaches, but the southern parts of the island are far more secluded and sedate.

Despite being the closest major island to Bangkok, Ko Samet remains surprisingly underdeveloped, with a thick jungle interior crouching beside the low-rise hotels.

◉ Sights & Activities

On some islands you beach-hop, but on Ko Samet you cove-hop. The coastal footpath traverses rocky headlands, cicada-serenaded forests and one stunning bay after another, where the mood becomes successively more mellow the further south you go.

Various activities like kayaking, parasailing, diving, snorkelling and stand-up paddleboarding (SUP) are available on the island. Squid-fishing and other angling trips are another option. **Seaddict** (✆085 397 2716; www.facebook.com/s3addict; Ao Hin Khok) on the main road, hires out SUPs, skimboards and windsurfing rigs, and offers lessons.

Ko Samet

Laem Noi Na

Laem Phra

Ban Phe
(7km)

Ao Wiang
Wan

Ao Noi

Ao Kham

Sŏrng·tăa·ou Stop

Ao Noi Na
Ao Klang

Na Dan Pier

34

Na Dan

Khao Laem Ya/
Mu Ko Samet
National Park

31

15

3

Ao Prao

8

See Enlargement

33

Laem
Yai

Ao Hin Khok
Ao Hin Khok

Ao Phai
Ao Phai

2
23

Ao Phutsa
(Ao Tub Tim)

10

Laem Rua Taek

Ao Nuan

Ao Cho

National
Parks Office

7
6
14

13

Ao Wong Deuan

Gulf of
Thailand

4

Ao Thian

24
22

Ao Lung Dam

11

Gulf of Thailand

20
5

Ao Wai

Ao Kiu Na Nai

18

Ao Kiu Na Nok

17

Laem Khut

Ao Karang

12

Ko Samet
Health
Centre

29
25

30
16

National Parks
Main Office

Taxi
Stop

27
28
7

19
9
26
32

1
21

Ao
Hin Khok

Ko Samet

🧭 Tours

Ko Samet, along with nine neighbouring islands, is part of the **Khao Laem Ya/Mu Ko Samet National Park** (อุทยานแห่งชาติเขาแหลมหญ้า-หมู่เกาะเสม็ด; ☑038 653034; www.dnp.go.th; adult/child 200/100B). While there is some development on the other islands, most visitors come for day trips. **Ko Kudee** has a small, pretty sandy stretch, clear water for decent snorkelling and a nice little hiking trail. Ko Man Nai is home to the **Rayong Turtle Conservation Centre**, which

is a breeding place for endangered sea turtles, and has a small visitor centre. Agents for boat tours can be found on the popular beaches and have a couple of different boat trips on offer (from 500B per person).

🛌 Sleeping

A word of caution to early risers: Hat Sai Kaew, Ao Hin Khok, Ao Phai and Ao Wong Deuan are the most popular beaches and host well-amplified night-time parties.

Hat Sai Kaew & Na Dan

In the island's northeastern corner near the ferry pier, Hat Sai Kaew (หาดทรายแก้ว), the 'town beach', is the island's widest, dirtiest and wildest stretch of sand. The beach can feel totally overrun and the scene is lively at night, too.

Mossman House GUESTHOUSE **$**
(☑038 644017; r 1200-1500B; ✳🖥) On the main street, just before the national park ticket office, is this sound guesthouse, with large, comfortable rooms along a shared veranda and leafy grounds. Choose a spot at the back for some quiet as the bar opposite stays open late. Off-season rooms go for around 800B.

Baan Minnie GUESTHOUSE, APARTMENT **$$**
(☑086 691 9662; www.facebook.com/baanminnie; Silver Park Ave, Na Dan; d 1200-1700B; P✳🖥) There are several places to stay in these rows of terraced accommodation behind the main strip in Ko Samet's capital village. Rooms have firm, comfortable mattresses and attractive modern decor; some have a patio seating area. There are also 'houses' which are well-kept apartments, some duplex, sleeping up to six. It's pretty casual; you're left to your own devices.

Ao Hin Khok & Ao Phai อ่าวหินโขก/อ่าวไผ่

Less frenetic than Hat Sai Kaew, Ao Hin Khok and Ao Phai are two gorgeous bays separated by rocky headlands. The crowd here tends to be younger than in Hat Sai Kaew; these two beaches are the island's traditional backpacker party centres.

Silver Sand RESORT **$$**
(☑038 644300; www.silversandsamed.com; Ao Phai; r incl breakfast 2500-2800B; P✳@🖥) An ever-expanding empire, Silver Sand is

a miniresort, complete with a restaurant, shops and a lively LGBT-friendly bar. It's a little impersonal but the rooms are decent quality and the place is set on a super strip of beach.

Samed Pavilion Resort　　　　RESORT **$$$**
(☑038 644420; www.samedpavilionresort.com; Ao Phai; d incl breakfast 3500-5500B; P❄@🛜🏊) This handsome boutique resort has elegant, spacious rooms in an upstairs-downstairs configuration tightly set around a sociable pool. It's a good spot for families, with lots of dedicated rooms for them, beach access and removal from the road. Rates are usually best online, but it has off-season promotions for direct bookings. It's substantially cheaper midweek.

🛏 Ao Phutsa & Ao Nuan

South of Ao Hin Khok and Ao Phai is cute, sandy Ao Phutsa (อ่าวพุทรา), which strikes a good balance, being relatively accessible but generally not too crowded.

★ Ao Nuan Bungalows　　　BUNGALOW **$$**
(☑081 781 4875; Ao Nuan; bungalows with fan 800-1200B, with air-con 1500-3000B; ❄🛜) Samet's one remaining bohemian bay is tucked off the main road down a dirt track. Running down a jungle hillside to the sea are cute wooden bungalows ranging from simple fan-cooled affairs with shared cold-water bathroom to romantic air-conditioned retreats with elegant deck furniture.

There's a bar and simple restaurant; if you need more action, Tubtim beach is a few minutes' stroll.

Tubtim Resort　　　　　　RESORT **$$**
(☑038 644025; www.tubtimresort.com; Ao Phutsa/Ao Tub Tim; r incl breakfast fan 700-1400B, air-con 2200-3700B; P❄🛜) A well-organised place with great, nightly barbecues and a range of solid, spacious bungalows of varying quality close to the beach. Confusingly, the best are in the 'N' zone, right by the sand with a great outlook from bed, desk and deck. 'A' zone sea-view rooms are older and set back a little, but still pleasant.

🛏 Ao Wong Deuan & Ao Thian　　อ่าววงเดือน/อ่าวเทียน

Ao Wong Deuan, meaning 'crescent moon bay', is Samet's second-busiest beach, with a range of resorts and more modest guesthouses. It's a wide, flat arc with a shallow gradient that's good for kids. Ao Thian (Candlelight Beach) is one of Samet's most easygoing beaches, punctuated by big boulders that shelter small sandy spots.

Apaché　　　　　　　　BUNGALOW **$**
(☑081 452 9472; Ao Thian; r 800-1500B; ❄🛜) Apaché's eclectic, quirky decorations and cheerfully random colour scheme add character to this super-chilled spot at the southern end of a tranquil strip. Bungalows are basic but adequate. The on-site restaurant on stilts is well worthwhile.

Blue Sky　　　　　　　BUNGALOW **$**
(☑089 936 0842; Ao Wong Deuan; r 800-1200B; ❄🛜) A rare budget spot on Ao Wong Deuan, Blue Sky has beaten-up bungalows set on a rocky headland at the north end of the beach. It's run by a friendly couple but they are a bit cagey about advanced bookings, so you'll probably have to turn up and see.

★ Viking Holidays Resort　　BUNGALOW **$$**
(☑038 644354; www.vikingholidaysresort.com; Ao Thian; r incl breakfast 1500-1800B; P❄🛜) One of a line of casual bungalow complexes on this tranquil beachside, Viking is well run and has pretty, compact rooms with carpet and strings of seashells for decoration. Staff are particularly helpful and friendly and good English is spoken. Unlike many Ko Samet bungalows, you can book online (and pick your bungalow location).

Ton Had Bungalow BUNGALOW $$
(☎081 435 8900; Ao Thian; r incl breakfast 1200-1800B) Simple bungalows decorated with seashells and offering both fan and air-con make for a peaceful sleep at this sweet family-run spot at Ao Thian. It's located on the short rocky shore between two beaches: views are great but you've got an almost two-minute stroll to the sand. Things are tough here.

La Lune Beach Resort HOTEL $$$
(☎Koh Samet 089 892 9690, reservations Bangkok 02 260 3592; www.lalunebeachresort.com; Ao Wong Deuan; r incl breakfast 3000-4500B; P ❄ ᯤ ≋) Meet the new face of Samet. Stylish, chic resorts like this are becoming more common. The 40 rooms, all with stressed wood underfoot and a soft greeny-grey-and-white theme, are set around a central pool in a three-level U-shape that opens onto the beach. The three grades of room differ only by outlook, which isn't so different.

Ao Wai อ่าวหวาย

Ao Wai is a lovely beach far removed from everything else (though in reality it's only 1.5km from Ao Thian).

Samet Ville Resort RESORT $$
(☎038 651682; www.sametvilleresort.com; standard r incl breakfast fan/air-con 1400/2000B, superior r 2300-5000B; P ❄ ᯤ ≋) Spread over two bays – Ao Wai and Ao Hin Kleang – this leafy, 4.5-hectare resort is secluded and soporific. The rooms, of which there are several types, are all a few steps from the excellent beach. For this price, though, they are badly in need of a touch-up and the lackadaisical management could do with the same sort of treatment.

Ao Prao อ่าวพร้าว

On the west coast, Ao Prao (Coconut Beach) is one of the island's prettiest beaches. It's secluded but backed by three high-end resorts, so it still gets quite busy.

Lima Coco Resort RESORT $$$
(☎Bangkok 02 129 1140; www.limaresort.co.th; r incl breakfast 3000-8900B; ❄ ᯤ ≋) Ao Prao, on Samet's west coast, has three fancy resorts. Lima Coco, in the middle, is the cheapest of these, with compact whitewashed rooms in a variety of categories climbing up the hill behind the beach. It's a little down at heel but offers energetic staff, beachside massages and other facilities.

Ao Pakarang & Ao Kiu

The southernmost tip of the island has an exclusive, discreet feel.

Paradee Resort RESORT $$$
(☎038 644283; www.samedresorts.com/paradee; Ao Kiu; r incl breakfast 25,000-35,000B; P ❄ ᯤ ≋) Exclusive and offering excellent privacy, this sleek resort near the southern end is one of the island's most luxurious. Golf carts hum about among discreetly screened thatched villas, most of which have their own jacuzzi. The lovely beach is effectively private and, across the road, a bar deck lets you appreciate the sunset views from the island's western shore.

Nimmanoradee Resort RESORT $$$
(☎038 644271; www.nimmanoradee.com; Ao Pakarang; r incl breakfast 3000-5800B; P ❄ ᯤ) The southernmost resort on the island, Nimmanoradee offers tranquillity, plenty of space and cheerfully coloured octagonal bungalows. There's good swimming here and a pretty little boutique promontory. Kayaks and snorkels are on hand to explore the area, staff are friendly and the very pleasant open-air restaurant serves decent food at fair prices.

Eating

Along the beaches are strung restaurant and bars, while many hotels and guesthouses have restaurants that do beach barbecues at night. There are cheapie Thai places along the main road in Na Dan.

GIGANTIC WELCOME

The imposing statue of a topless female giant at Na Dan pier is impossible to miss (although at time of last research she was modestly wearing a wrap). She is an allusion to Ko Samet's most famous son, the poet Sunthorn Phu, and his famous story *Phra Aphaimani*. In the tale, a prince is exiled to an undersea kingdom ruled by the lovesick female giant. A mermaid helps the prince escape to Ko Samet, where he defeats the giant by playing a magical flute. You can see mermaid and prince together at the western end of Hat Sai Kaew.

Banana Bar
THAI $

(☑ 038 644033; Na Dan; mains 80-150B; ⊙ 11am-11.30pm) Casual and relaxed, this somewhat ramshackle yet oddly attractive main street spot is a good choice for well-priced Thai food. Run by a staunch motherly figure, it offers smallish portions of Thai curries, salads and Isan dishes; it's all very tasty.

Jep's Restaurant
INTERNATIONAL $

(☑ 038 644 112; www.jepsbungalows.com; Ao Hin Khok; mains 70-200B; ⊙ 7am-11pm; ☑) Canopied by the branches of an arching tree decorated with pendant lights, this pretty place right on the sand does a wide range of international, and some Thai, dishes. Leave room for dessert.

Red Ginger
INTERNATIONAL, THAI $$

(☑ 084 383 4917; www.redgingersamed.com; Na Dan; mains 120-565B; ⊙ 11am-10pm; ☎☑) An atmospheric main-street eatery that feels like an extension of this Canadian-Thai family's lounge room: expect cheery informality, quirks and chatting over a drink with the personable owner. The menu is short but tasty, with authentic, flavoursome Thai dishes complemented by a handful of international offerings. Excellent oven-baked ribs slathered in barbecue sauce are the highlight.

Kitt & Food
SEAFOOD, THAI $$

(☑ 038 644087; Hat Sai Kaew; mains 120-400B; ⊙ 11am-10.30pm) Better than most of the beachfront restaurants, this is a romantic place for dinner, with tables almost lapped by the waves. Don't plough too deep into the phonebook of a menu – seafood is the speciality here. Various fresh fish (mostly farmed) are arrayed; pick one and decide how you want it done. Baked in salt takes a while but is great.

Ploy Talay
SEAFOOD, THAI $$

(☑ 038 644212; Hat Sai Kaew; mains 110-400B; ⊙ 11am-11pm; ☎) The busiest of the string of mediocre beach restaurants on Hat Sai Kaew, this packs out for its nightly 8.30pm fire show, which is quite a sight (and smell). You can see it from the beach too, but people enjoy their leisurely (the service will ensure that) seafood dinners here. The location is better than the quality, but the food is OK.

🍸 Drinking & Nightlife

On weekends, Ko Samet is a boisterous night owl with tour groups crooning away on karaoke machines and the young ones slurping down beer and buckets to a techno beat. There is usually a crowd on Hat Sai Kaew, Ao Hin Khok, Ao Phai and Ao Wong Deuan.

Audi Bar
BAR

(☑ 084 418 8213; Na Dan; ⊙ 4pm-4am; ☎) Sharing an upstairs main-street space with a gym, this bar offers good people-watching from its high vantage point, the Samet-standard Day-Glo graffiti and a couple of pool tables. It's notably welcoming – staff want you to enjoy yourself – and serves as a one-last-drink venue for those straggling back from the beach dance floors.

Talay Bar
BAR

(☑ 083 887 1588; Hat Sai Kaew; ⊙ 2pm-midnight; ☎) Cheerily fronted by burning torches and Thai flags, this is at the eastern end of the island's busiest beach, away from the most crowded parts. It's an upbeat, enthusiastic spot with space to lounge on the sand and kick back with a cocktail or beer bomb from the unfeasibly large (size-wise) menu.

Naga Bar
BAR

(Ao Hin Khok; ⊙ 3pm-late) This busy beachfront bar is covered in Day-Glo art and run by a friendly bunch of locals who offer good music, lots of whisky and vodka/Red Bull buckets. It gets lively later on, with dance-floor action.

Breeze
BAR

(☑ 038 644100; www.samedresorts.com; Ao Prao Resort, Ao Prao; ⊙ 7am-10.30pm; ☎) On the sunset side of the island, this is a lovely sea-view restaurant perfect for a sundowner. You will need private transport to reach it, or it's a 2.5km walk from Hat Sai Kaew.

❶ Information

There are plenty of ATMs on Ko Samet, including some near the Na Dan pier, outside the 7-Eleven behind Hat Sai Kaew, and at Ao Wong Deuan, Ao Thian and Ao Phutsa, as well as at several resorts.

There are tourist police points at both the **main village** (☑ 24hr 1155) and **Ao Wong Deuan** (☑ 24hr 1155).

The **Ko Samet Health Centre** (☑ 038 644123; ⊙ 24hr) and **International Clinic Ko Samet** (☑ 038 644414, emergency 086 094 0566; www.sametclinic.in.th; ⊙ 8am-6pm, emergencies until midnight), both in the village near Na Dan pier, offer health services. The nearest full-service hospital is in Rayong.

ℹ️ Getting There & Away

Ko Samet is accessed via the mainland piers in Ban Phe. There are many piers, each used by different ferry companies, all of which charge the same fares (one-way from mainland/return/one-way from island 70/100/50B, 40 minutes, hourly, 8am to 5pm) and dock at **Na Dan** (usage fee 20B), the main pier on Ko Samet. The last boat back to the mainland leaves at 6pm.

If you are staying at Ao Wong Deuan or further south, catch a ferry from the mainland directly to the beach (one-way/return 90/140B, one hour, two to three daily departures).

Speedboats charge 200B to 500B one-way and will drop you at the beach of your choice, but only leave when they have enough passengers. Otherwise, you can charter one for around 1500B.

Ticket agents at the Ban Phe piers will often try to rip you off on tickets for both ferries and speedboats and will try and pressure you to take a speedboat by saying that there are no slow boats for the next few hours etc.

From Bangkok, head to Rayong. You'll arrive at bus station 2; there are some minibuses from here to Ban Phe, but it'll usually be quicker to catch a *sŏrng·tăa·ou* to bus station 1, then another from there to Ban Phe. There is no Rayong service from Suvarnabhumi airport; either head to Pattaya and change there or head into Bangkok's Ekamai bus station and catch Rayong- or Ban Phe–bound transport from there.

From the island, it's easy to arrange minibus transfers to Bangkok (250B), Suvarnabhumi airport (500B), Ko Chang piers (250B) and elsewhere.

ℹ️ Getting Around

Ko Samet's small size makes it a great place to explore on foot. A network of roads connects most of the island.

Green *sŏrng·tăa·ou* meet boats at the pier and provide drop-offs at the various beaches (20B to 200B, depending on the beach and number of passengers). Chartering one ('taxi') costs 150B to 700B on the official rate sheet, but you can usually negotiate a discount. Taxis also congregate at a stop (Hat Sai Kaew) by the national park entrance.

You can rent motorcycles nearly everywhere along the northern half of the island for 100/300B per hour/day. The road is good, but be careful on steep descents. It's 7km by road from the ferry pier to the southern tip of the island. For those who prefer four wheels, golf carts are also available for hire.

Chanthaburi
จันทบุรี

🕿 039 / POP 120,000

Chanthaburi is proof that all that glitters is not gold. Here, gems do the sparkling, with precious stones ranging from sapphires to emeralds traded every weekend in a bustling street market. Nearby, wonderfully restored waterfront buildings in a charming historic quarter are evidence of how the Chinese, French and Vietnamese have influenced life – and architecture – here.

Vietnamese Christians fled persecution from Cochin China (southern Vietnam) in the 19th century and came to Chanthaburi. The French occupied Chanthaburi from

---

OFF THE BEATEN TRACK

ROAD-TRIPPING THE CHANTHABURI COAST

Little visited by island-hungry foreigners, the coast near Chanthaburi is a rewarding day trip from the city or a scenic diversion en route to/from Rayong. It's within bicycle reach of the city and is a popular cycling circuit for Thais. All the beaches mentioned here offer places to stay and eat.

At **Laem Sing**, some 20km from Chanthaburi by road, the river estuary, spanned by a bridge, is wide and handsome. There's a fishing fleet here, an offshore island and a long beach backed by a park.

From here, Rte 4036 heads northwestish, passing turn-offs to a handful of quiet beach villages before reaching more developed **Hat Chao Lao**. Close by is **Hat Laem Sadet**, with medium-market resort hotels, a beach and a bay, Ao Khung Kraben. A mangrove reserve lets you explore the estuarine ecosystem on wooden boardwalks.

The last of the beaches on this stretch, some 15km beyond Chao Lao and Laem Sadet, is **Hat Khung Wiman**, with a nice narrow beach and pleasant westerly outlook. The road through the village loops round to a fishing village on the bay side; there are good places to snack on simple seafood here.

Chanthaburi

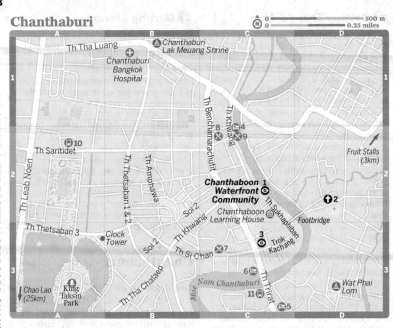

Chanthaburi

1893 to 1905 due to a dispute over the border between Siam and Indochina. More Vietnamese arrived in the 1920s and 1940s as they fled French rule, then a third wave followed in 1975 after the communist takeover of southern Vietnam.

The surrounding area has waterfall-heavy national parks and charming beach villages to discover.

⊙ Sights

★ Chanthaboon Waterfront Community
HISTORIC SITE

(ชุมชนริมน้ำจันทบูร; Th Sukhaphiban) 🌿 Hugging the banks of Mae Nam Chanthaburi is this charismatic part of town, filled with restored houses and elderly residents sitting around reminiscing with each other about their Chanthaburi tales. The **Learning House** (ศูนย์เรียนรู้ประชาชนริมน้ำจันทบูร; ☑ 081 945 5761; 69 Th Sukhaphiban; ⊙ 10am-4pm) **FREE** displays neighbourhood photos, paintings and architectural designs, including upstairs drawings of intricate ventilation panels that feature Chinese characters and French fleurs-de-lis.

Gem Market
MARKET

(ตลาดพลอย; Th Si Chan & Trok Kachang; ⊙ 9am-6pm Fri-Sun) Every weekend, the normally quiet streets near Th Si Chan (or 'Gem Road') burst into life as gem traders arrive to bustle and bargain. It's incongruously humble considering the value of the commodities on offer, as people cluster around makeshift tables examining small piles of unset stones.

Cathedral of the Immaculate Conception
CATHEDRAL

(อาสนวิหารพระนางมารีอาปฏิสนธินิรมล; ⊙8.30am-4.30pm) FREE Thailand's largest cathedral, on the east bank of Mae Nam Chanthaburi, started life as a modest chapel in 1711. Since then there have been four reconstructions and the current Gothic-style structure includes some impressive stained-glass windows and an upstairs gallery that gives the interior the feel of a medieval hall. The statue of the Virgin Mary at the front is bedecked with more than 200,000 sapphires – a fitting link between religion and the city's famous gem trade.

🛏 Sleeping

River Guest House
GUESTHOUSE $

(☑092 717 1470; www.facebook.com/theriver guesthouse; 3/5-8 Th Si Chan; s 170-250B, d 300-350B; ❄🕸) Right by the river, albeit next to a noisy bridge, is this friendly guesthouse with a range of simple rooms, some of which are tiny. Beds are basic but the riverside seating area compensates for this. The cheapest rooms have a shared bathroom; rooms with hot water and air-con cost a little more. It hires bikes and mopeds.

★ Baan Luang Rajamaitri
HISTORIC HOTEL $$

(☑088 843 8516; www.baanluangrajamaitri.com; 252 Th Sukhaphiban; r incl breakfast 1250-1900B, ste 3100-3300B; ❄🕸) 🌿 Community-owned and named after a local philanthropist, this expertly restored historic hotel has wonderfully characterful elegant rooms in the heart of the riverfront district. Dark wooden furniture, creaky floorboards and a great waterside deck make for excellent atmosphere. The cheapest rooms are small with a comfortable bunk bed and little terrace. Quirky antique touches abound; it's a top spot.

Chernchan Hostel
HOSTEL $$

(☑065 573 8841; www.facebook.com/ chernchan2017; 43/11-13 Th Tirat; dm 450B, r 900-1500B; ❄🕸) On a quiet lane close to the river, this boutique hostel has eye-catching modern design and helpful staff. Dorms and rooms are compact but comfortable; downstairs in the cafe an abundant breakfast is

---

WORTH A TRIP

NATIONAL PARKS NEAR CHANTHABURI

Two small national parks are easily reached from Chanthaburi, and make good day trips. Both are malarial, so take the usual precautions.

Khao Khitchakut National Park (อุทยานแห่งชาติเขาคิชฌกูฏ; ☑039 452074; http://nps. dnp.go.th; 200B; ⊙8.30am-4.30pm) is 28km northeast of town. Though it's one of Thailand's smallest national parks (59 sq km), it's bordered by wildlife sanctuaries and harbours wild elephants. The cascade of Nam Tok Krathing is only impressive just after the rainy season. Another attraction atop a hill is a temple where, by an enormous boulder, Buddha is believed to have left a footprint. To get to Khao Khitchakut, take a *sŏrng·tăa·ou* (passenger pick-up truck) from next to the post office, near the northern side of the market in Chanthaburi (35B, 45 minutes). The *sŏrng·tăa·ou* stops 1km from the park headquarters on Rte 3249, from which point you will have to walk. Returning transport is scarce so expect to wait.

Namtok Phlio National Park (อุทยานแห่งชาติน้ำตกพลิ้ว; ☑039 434528; http://nps.dnp. go.th; 200B; ⊙8am-6pm), off Hwy 3, is 14km to the southeast of Chanthaburi and is much more popular. A pleasant short nature trail loops around the waterfalls, which writhe with soro brook carp; you can bathe here. Also on display are the strikingly mossy Phra Nang Ruar Lom stupa (c 1876) and Along Khon *chedi* (c 1881). To get to the park, catch a *sŏrng·tăa·ou* from the northern side of the market in Chanthaburi to the park entrance (50B, 30 minutes). You will get dropped off about 1km from the entrance. Private transport is 1500B.

Accommodation is available at both parks; book with the **park reservation system** (☑02 562 0760; www.dnp.go.th).

ⓘ GETTING TO CAMBODIA: BAN PAKARD TO PAILIN

Getting to the border In Chanthaburi, minivans (☎ 092 037 6266) depart from a stop across the river from the River Guest House (p469), where you can book your spot, to Ban Pakard (180B, 1½ hours, 10am and noon). There are also *sŏrng·tăa·ou* from the bus station (100B, two hours) that tend to leave early.

At the border This is a far less busy and more pleasant crossing than Poipet further north. You need a passport photo and US$30 for the visa fee. Cambodian e-visas aren't officially accepted here, though some travellers have reported getting through. Demanding US$35 for the visa is standard practice here.

Moving on Hop on a motorbike taxi to Pailin in Cambodia. From there, you can catch frequent shared taxis (US$5 per person, 1½ hours) to scenic Battambang. After that, you can move on to Siem Reap by boat, or Phnom Penh by bus.

served (included in room but not dorm rates). It rents bikes.

🍴 Eating

Chanthaburi is famed for its fruit. You can taste why at the various **fruit stalls** (fruit 20-80B; ☺8am-9pm; 🖉) that line Th Sukhumvit, 8km northeast of the city (you pass them on the way into Chanthaburi), which sell a range of rambutans, bananas, mangosteens and more. The annual **Fruit Festival** (☺May or Jun) is an even better excuse to sink your teeth into the region's superbly sticky, juicy produce...including the ever-pungent durian.

Crab noodles and pork with *chamung* leaf are also local specialities. A string of eateries can be found on Th Sukhaphiban and there are lots of options around the centre in general. Across the other side of the river are some open-air spots that look across to Chanthaboon.

786 Muslim Restaurant   INDIAN $
(☎081 353 5174; Th Si Chan; mains 50-80B; ☺9.30am-6pm) In among all the Chanthaburi gem dealers, this restaurant run by Thai Muslims is worth a stop for its excellent *paratha, biryani,* curries, meatballs and chai tea.

★Chanthorn   THAI $$
(102/5-8 Th Benchamarachutit; mains 120-250B; ☺9am-9pm; 🖉) This welcoming family-run restaurant in the centre near the waterfront is a great place to try local specialities; the *chamung* leaves with pork and Chanthaburi crab noodles are particularly good, but it's all really excellent quality. It's a fairly early closer at dinner time.

Tamajun Restaurant   THAI $$
(☎039 311977; www.tamajunhotel.com; Th Sukhaphiban; mains 140-260B; ☺food 4-11pm; 🖻) The most sophisticated of the riverside restaurants, Tamajun has elegant vintage-style decor and excellent tables hanging over the water. Live crooner bands operate at night, when tasty dishes that pack a serious spice punch cover prawn and pork specialities as well as other fare.

TRANSPORT TO/FROM CHANTHABURI

DESTINATION	BUS	MINIVAN
Bangkok's Eastern Bus Terminal (Ekamai)	184B, 4hr, 25 daily	210B, frequent
Bangkok's Northern Bus Terminal (Mo Chit)	187B, 4hr, 4 daily	215B, frequent
Nakhon Ratchasima (Khorat)	279B, 4hr, every 2 hours	
Rayong		120B, 2hr, hourly
Sa Kaew	145B, 2hr, every 2 hours	
Trat		52-70B, 1hr, frequent

❶ Information

Banks with change facilities and ATMs can be found across town.

Chanthaburi Bangkok Hospital (☑039 319888; www.chanthaburihospital.com; Th Tha Luang; ☺24hr) is central and has 24-hour emergency service.

❶ Getting There & Around

Chanthaburi's bus station (Th Saritidet) is west of the river. Minivans also leave from the bus station. Motorbike taxis charge 20B to 40B for trips around town.

Trat
ตราด

☑039 / POP 22,000

Trat is a major transit point for Ko Chang and coastal Cambodia, and worth a stop anyway for its underappreciated old-world charm. The guesthouse neighbourhood occupies an atmospheric wooden shophouse district, bisected by winding sois and filled with typical Thai street life: children riding bikes, homemakers running errands and small businesses selling trinkets and necessities.

◉ Sights

Walk down Th Lak Meuang and you will see that the top floors of shophouses have been converted into **nesting sites** for birds that produce the edible nests considered a Chinese delicacy. Swiflets' nests were quite rare (and expensive) in the past because they were only harvested from precipitous sea caves.

In the 1990s entrepreneurs figured out how to replicate the cave atmosphere in multistorey shophouses.

Indoor Market　　　　MARKET

(ตลาดกลาง; Soi Sukhumvit; ☺6am-5pm) The indoor market sprawls east from Th Sukhumvit to Th Tat Mai and has a little bit of everything, especially all the things that you forgot to pack. Without really noticing the difference you will stumble upon the day market (p473), selling fresh fruit, vegetables and takeaway food.

🛏 Sleeping

Trat has many budget hotels in traditional wooden houses on and around Th Thana Charoen.

KO CHANG & THE EASTERN SEABOARD TRAT

★**Ban Jai Dee Guest House**　GUESTHOUSE $
(☑039 520678, 083 589 0839; banjaideehouse@ yahoo.com; 6 Th Chaimongkol; s/d 250/300B; ☞) This relaxed traditional wooden house has simple rooms with shared bathrooms (hot-water showers). Paintings and objets d'art made by the artistically inclined owners decorate the beautiful common spaces. There are only seven rooms and an addictively relaxing ambience so it can fill fast. The owners are full of helpful information and understand a budget traveller's needs.

Yotin Guest House　　GUESTHOUSE $
(☑089 224 7817; Th Thana Charoen; r 350-600B; ❄☞) Backing a typically venerable building in Trat's lovely old quarter are pretty, inviting refurbished rooms with colourful linen and comfortable mattresses. Cheaper rooms are compact and either share a bathroom or have a very tight en suite; higher grade rooms have more space. The couple that run the place are thoughtful and helpful: it's a very sound base. You can hire bikes here.

★**Rimklong
Boutique Hotel**　　BOUTIQUE HOTEL $$
(☑039 523388; www.facebook.com/Rimklong -Boutique-Hotel-trat-127177424027071/; 194 Th Lak

Trat

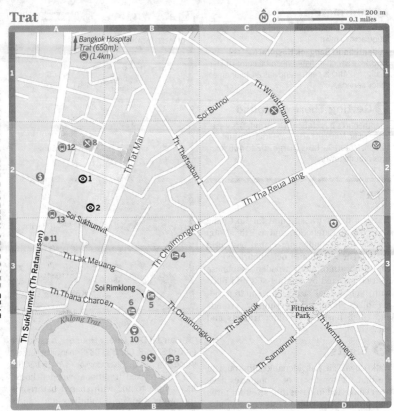

Trat

⊙ Sights
1 Day Market A2
2 Indoor Market A2

🛏 Sleeping
3 Artist's Place B4
4 Ban Jai Dee Guest House B3
5 Rimklong Boutique Hotel................... B3
6 Yotin Guest House................................ B3

⊗ Eating
7 Namchok... C1

8 Night Market A2
9 Pier 112 .... B4

🍸 Drinking & Nightlife
10 Cafe Oscar... B4

ℹ Transport
11 Family Tour A3
12 Sŏrng·tăa·ou to Bus Station &
    Laem Sok... A2
13 Sŏrng·tăa·ou to Ko Chang
    ferries... A2

Meuang; s 650B, d 950-1100B, ste 1300B; P ❈ 🛜)
Run by refined and helpful Mr Tuu, this hotel offers compact, sparkling rooms in the
heart of the old part of town. It's well worth
booking ahead, as it's often full, and understandably so. Prices are very reasonable for
this quality of accommodation; some rooms

are in an annexe a few paces down the soi.
Out front it does real espresso and cocktails.

Artist's Place   GUESTHOUSE $$
(📞 082 469 1900; pier.112@hotmail.com; 132/1 Th
Thana Charoen; r incl breakfast 300-1100B; P ❈ 🛜)
The individually decorated rooms, and piec-
es of art dotted around the adjoining garden,

come courtesy of the owner, Mr Phukhao. Cheaper rooms with fans share bathrooms, but are dark and lack the same character. Check in at Pier 112 restaurant opposite.

🍴 Eating & Drinking

Trat is all about market eating: head to the **day market** (ตลาด; Th Tat Mai; ⊙ 6am-5pm) for *gah·faa bohrahn* (ancient coffee), the **night market** (off Th Sukhumvit; mains from 30B; ⊙ 5-9pm), or the indoor market (p471) for lunchtime noodles. Food stalls line Th Sukhumvit come nightfall.

⭐ Namchok   THAI $$
(Th Wiwatthana; mains 100-250B; ⊙ 10am-10pm) This uncomplicated open-walled restaurant is deservedly a local favourite, with some excellent seafood dishes and well-meaning service from an army of young helpers. The unpriced English menu could be better translated, but they get ostrich right, and there are some other intriguing dishes: try the raw softshell crab salad. It's only signposted in Thai: look for the Coke and Chang logos.

Pier 112   THAI $$
(132/1 Th Thana Charoen; mains 80-250B; ⊙ 10.30am-9pm; 🛜 🍴) In the old town by the river, Pier 112 has a large selection of vegetarian dishes, as well as reliable curries. You can eat outside in a plant-festooned garden.

Service can be on the slow side, but what's the hurry?

Cafe Oscar   BAR
(Th Thana Charoen; ⊙ 4.30pm-late) An eclectic crew of locals and expats gather at this cubbyhole corner bar, with wooden furniture and a retro 1970s and '80s soundtrack. In high season it opens during the day too.

ℹ️ Information

Th Sukhumvit runs through town, though it is often called Th Ratanuson. This is where you'll find the bulk of banks and ATMs.

Bangkok Hospital Trat (🕿 039 552777; www.bangkoktrathospital.com; 376 Mu 2, Th Sukhumvit; ⊙ 24hr) Located 400m north of the town centre, this hospital offers the best health care in the area.

Krung Thai Bank (Th Sukhumvit; ⊙ 8.30am-4.30pm Mon-Fri) Has an ATM and currency-exchange facilities.

Police Station (🕿 24hr 1155; cnr Th Santisuk & Th Wiwatthana) A short walk from Trat's centre.

Post Office (Th Tha Reua Jang; ⊙ 8.30am-4.30pm Mon-Fri, 9am-noon Sat & Sun) East of Trat's commercial centre.

ℹ️ Getting There & Away

AIR

Bangkok Airways (🕿 039 525767; www.bangkokair.com; Trat Airport; ⊙ 8.30am-6.30pm) operates three daily flights to/from Bangkok's Suvarnabhumi International Airport (one hour).

BUSES FROM TRAT

Trat's bus station is 2km out of town, and serves the following destinations:

DESTINATION	FARE (B)	DURATION (HR)	FREQUENCY
Bangkok Eastern (Ekamai) Bus Terminal	256	4½	hourly 6am-11.30pm
Bangkok Northern (Mo Chit) Bus Terminal	265	5½	4 daily
Bangkok Suvarnabhumi International Airport	245	4-4½	5 daily
Chanthaburi	70	1	every 2hr 8.15am-6pm

There are also minivans to the following destinations:

DESTINATION	FARE (B)	DURATION (HR)	FREQUENCY
Bangkok Eastern (Ekamai) Bus Terminal	280	4	every 2hr 8.30am-4.30pm
Bangkok Northern (Mo Chit) Bus Terminal	280	4	every 2hr 8.30am-4.30pm
Chanthaburi	70	50min	frequent 6am-6pm
Hat Lek (for the border with Cambodia)	120	1½	hourly 5am-6pm
Pattaya	300	3½	every 2hr 8am-6pm
Rayong/Ban Phe (for Ko Samet)	200	3½	every 2hr 8am-6pm

Trat's airport is 40km from town, and taxis into town cost 600B; try to hail a *sŏrng·tǎa·ou*.

BOAT

To/from Ko Chang

The piers that handle boat traffic to/from Ko Chang are located west of Laem Ngop, about 30km southwest of Trat. There are three piers, each used by different boat companies, but the most convenient services are through **Koh Chang Ferry** (☑ 039 555188; Laem Ngop; adult/child/car one way 80/30/120B; ⏱ 6.30am-7pm), from Tha Thammachat, and **Centrepoint Ferry** (☑ 039 538196; Laem Ngop; adult one way/return 80/150B, child one way/return 40/70B, car one way/return 100/180B; ⏱ hourly 6am-7.30pm, to 7pm May-Oct), from Tha Centrepoint.

Sŏrng·tǎa·ou (Th Sukhumvit) to Laem Ngop and the piers (50B to 60B per person, 300B for the whole vehicle, 40 minutes) leave from Th Sukhumvit, just past the market. It should be the same charter price if you want to go directly from Trat's bus station to the pier.

From Bangkok, you can catch a bus from Bangkok's Eastern (Ekamai) station all the way to Tha Centrepoint (250B, five hours, three morning departures). This route includes a stop at Suvarnabhumi (airport) bus station as well as Trat's bus station. In the reverse direction, buses have two afternoon departures from Laem Ngop.

To/from Ko Kut

Ferries to Ko Kut run from the pier at **Laem Sok** (p487), 22km southeast of Trat, the nearest bus transfer point. If you prebook, the boat operators offer free transport from central Trat or its bus station (but not the airport) to the pier.

There's no public transport between Laem Ngop and Laem Sok piers; think 400B to 500B for a taxi. In high season, you won't need this option, as you can travel directly between Ko Chang and Ko Kut.

BUS

A useful minivan operator is **Family Tour** (☑ 081 940 7380; Th Sukhumvit), with services to Bangkok, as well as to Phnom Penh and Siem Reap.

❶ Getting Around

Motorbike taxis charge 20B to 30B for local hops.

Local *sŏrng·tǎa·ou* leave from **Th Sukhumvit** near the market for the bus station (20B to 60B, depending on the number of passengers). Chartering one to the airport costs 600B.

Motorbikes can be rented for 150B to 200B a day along Th Sukhumvit near the guesthouse area.

HAT MAI RUT

The sliver of Trat Province that extends southeast towards Cambodia is fringed by sandy beaches. One of the easiest beaches to reach is Hat Mai Rut, roughly halfway between Trat and the border crossing of Hat Lek. Nearby is a traditional fishing village filled with colourful wooden boats and the sights and smells of a small-scale industry carried on by generations of families. **Mairood Resort** (☑ 089 841 4858; www.mairoodresort.com; 28 Mu 6, Khlong Yai; bungalows incl breakfast 1650B-2250B, huts 750B; P❄@🖥🌊🐕) is a lovely spot to stay overnight, with cottages by the sea and in the mangroves.

You can get to Hat Mai Rut from the Trat bus station via Hat Lek–bound *sŏrng·tǎa·ou*. The resort is 3km from the Km 53 highway marker.

Around 7km beyond here, Hat Ban Chun has several resorts and hotels.

Ko Chang เกาะช้าง

☑ 039 / POP 10,000

With steep, jungle-covered peaks, picturesque Ko Chang (Elephant Island) retains its remote and rugged spirit – despite the transformation of parts of it into a package-tour destination. Sweeping bays are sprinkled along the west coast; most have superfine sand, some have pebbles. What it lacks in sand it makes up for in an unlikely combination: accessible wilderness with a thriving party scene.

Because of its relative remoteness, it is only in the last 20 years or so that tourists have arrived. Today, it is still a slog to get here, but the resorts are now busy with package tourists, Cambodia-bound backpackers and island-hopping couples funnelling through to more remote islands in the marine park. Along the populous west coast are sprawling minitowns that have outpaced the island's infrastructure. For a taste of old-school Chang, head to the southeastern villages and mangrove forests of Ban Salak Phet and Ban Salak Kok.

ℹ️ GETTING TO CAMBODIA: HAT LEK TO CHAM YEAM

Getting to the border From Trat, the closest Thai–Cambodia crossing is from Hat Lek to the Cambodian town of Cham Yeam, and then on to Ko Kong. Minivans run to Hat Lek hourly from 5am to 6pm (120B, 1½ hours) from Trat's bus station.

At the border Attempts to overcharge for the Cambodian visa (officially US$30) at this border are common; they may quote the e-visa rate (US$36) or demand payment in Thai baht at an unfavourable exchange rate. You will need a passport photo too. To avoid the hassle, you may feel that just getting an e-visa beforehand is worthwhile. Avoid anyone who says you require a 'medical certificate' or other paperwork. The border opens at 7am and closes at 8pm.

Thai visas can be renewed at this border, but note that visas at land borders are now limited to two a year. They'll give you 30 days.

Moving on Take a taxi (US$10), túk-túk (US$5) or *moto* (motorcycle taxi; US$3) to Ko Kong where you can catch onward transport to Sihanoukville (four hours, one or two departures per day) and Phnom Penh (five hours, two or three departures until 11.30am).

⊙ Sights

👁 West Coast

The west coast is by far the most developed part of Ko Chang, thanks to its beaches and bays. Public *sŏrng·tăa·ou* (passenger pickup trucks) make beach-hopping easy and affordable. Some beaches are rocky, so it's worth bringing swim booties for children. Most of the time the seas are shallow and gentle but be wary of rips during storms and the rainy season (May to October).

The longest, most luxurious stretch of sand on the island is **Hat Sai Khao** (หาด ทรายขาว; White Sands Beach), packed with package-tour hotels and serious sunbathers. Head to the north section of the beach to find the more secluded backpacker spot. Meanwhile **Lonely Beach** (หาดท่าน้ำ) is anything but: this is Ko Chang's backpacker enclave and the liveliest place to be after dark when vodka buckets are passed around and speakers are turned up. **Hat Kai Mook** (หาดไข่มุก) means 'pearl beach', although the 'pearls' here are really just large pebbles that culminate in fish-friendly headlands. Swimming and sunbathing are out but there's good snorkelling.

Ao Khlong Prao (อ่าวคลองพร้าว; Khlong Prao) is a pretty sweep of sand pinned between hulking mountainous headlands and bisected by two estuaries. At low tide, beachcombers stroll the rippled sand eyeing the critters left naked by the receding water. Its companion beach is **Hat Kaibae** (หาดไก่แบ้), a slim strip of sand that unfurls around an island-dotted bay and is a good spot for families and thirty-something couples.

Ban Bang Bao VILLAGE
(บ้านบางเบ้า) At this former fishing community built in the traditional fashion of interconnected piers, the villagers have swapped their nets for renting out portions of their homes to souvenir shops and restaurants. Most visitors come for the excellent seafood and shopping.

👁 East Coast

You will need private transport to explore the peaceful, undeveloped east coast.

Ban Salak Phet VILLAGE
(บ้านสลักเพชร) To discover what Ko Chang was like before the tourists came, visit Ban Salak Phet, in the far southeastern corner. This sleepy community is full of stilt houses, fishing boats and yawning dogs who stretch out on the roadside; it also provides access to some good treks.

Ao Salak Kok BAY
(อ่าวสลักคอก) The dense tangle of mangroves here is protected by a group of fisherfolk who recognise its ecological importance. Mangroves are the ocean's nurseries, fostering the next generation of marine species, as well as resident birds and crustaceans, and this bay is now Ko Chang's prime ecotourism site. Villagers operate an award-winning program to preserve the environment and traditional way of life. They rent kayaks through the Salak Kok Kayak Station (p478) and run an affiliated restaurant.

Ko Chang

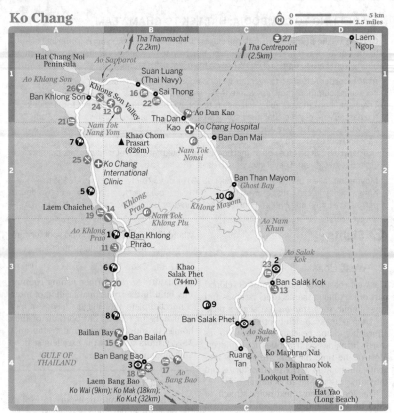

Nam Tok Khiri Phet
WATERFALL

(น้ำตกคีรีเพชร) This small waterfall, 2km from Ban Salak Phet, is a 15-minute walk from the road and rewards you with a small, deep plunge pool. It is usually less crowded than many of the larger falls and is easily reached if you are in the neighbourhood of Ao Salak Phet.

Nam Tok Than Mayom
WATERFALL

(น้ำตกธารมะยม; park fee 200B; ⊙8am-5pm) A series of three falls along the stream of Khlong Mayom can be reached via the park office near Nam Tha Than Mayom. The view from the top is superb and nearby there are inscribed stones bearing the initials of Rama V, Rama VI and Rama VII.

🏃 Activities

Numerous operators offer boat cruises, often with a glass-bottom option and snorkelling stops. Most of these leave from Bang Bao.

Diving & Snorkelling

The dive sites near Ko Chang offer a variety of coral, fish and beginner-friendly shallow waters.

The seamounts off the southern tip of the island within the Mu Ko Chang National Marine Park are reached within a 30-minute cruise. Popular spots include **Hin Luk Bat** and **Hin Rap**, rocky, coral-encrusted seamounts with depths of around 18m to 20m. These are havens for schooling fish and some turtles. In 2013, near Hin Rap, a 30m gunship was deliberately sunk and now lies on its side.

By far the most pristine diving in the area is around **Ko Rang**, an uninhabited island protected from fishing by its marine park status. Visibility here is much better than near Ko Chang and averages between 10m and 20m. Everyone's favourite dive is **Hin Gadeng** – spectacular rock pinnacles with coral visible to around 28m. On the eastern

Ko Chang

side of Ko Rang, **Hin Kuak Maa** (also known as Three Finger Reef) is another top dive spot and is home to a coral-encrusted wall sloping from 2m to 14m and attracting swarms of marine life.

Ko Yak, **Ko Tong Lang** and **Ko Laun** are shallow dives perfect for both beginners and advanced divers. These small rocky islands can be circumnavigated and have lots of coral, schooling fish, pufferfish, morays, barracuda, rays and the occasional turtle.

About 7km offshore from Ban Bang Bao there's a popular dive to the wreck of the **HTMS Chang**, a 100m-long former Thai naval vessel purposely sunk in 2012 to form an artificial reef that now sits 30m beneath the surface.

Reef-fringed Ko Wai (p488) features a good variety of colourful hard and soft corals and is great for snorkelling. It is a popular day-tripping island but has simple overnight accommodation for more alone time with the reef.

The snorkelling on **Ko Mak** is not as good, but the island offers some decent dives,

even if the reefs don't see as many fish as elsewhere.

One-day diving trips typically start at 3000B. Think 15,000B per person for PADI or other certification. Many dive shops remain open during the rainy season (May to October) but visibility and sea conditions are generally poor.

BB Divers   DIVING
(☏ 039 558040; www.bbdivers.com; Bang Bao; 2 boat dives 3000B) Based at Bang Bao, this well-run diving outfit has branches in Lonely Beach and Hat Sai Khao, as well as outposts on Ko Kut and Ko Mak (high season only).

Scubadawgs   DIVING
(☏ 080 038 5166; www.scuba-dawgs.com; Bang Bao; 2 boat dives 3000B) This upbeat outfit is helpful and customer focused. It does PADI and RAID certification.

Scandinavian Chang Diving Centre   DIVING
(☏ 039 619022; www.changdiving.com; Ban Khlong Prao) Professional diving set-up with excellent instructors and equipment, offering a

good range of excursions and courses, including some aimed at families and kids.

Kayaking

Ko Chang cuts an impressive and heroic profile when viewed from the sea aboard a kayak. The water is generally calm and offshore islands provide a paddling destination that is closer than the horizon. Many hotels rent open-top kayaks (from 300B per day) that are convenient for near-shore outings and noncommittal kayakers; some provide them for free. Contact **KayakChang** (☑097 182 8319; www.kayakchang.com; Emerald Cove Resort, Khlong Prao; kayaks per day from 1000B) for more serious apparatus.

Salak Kok Kayak Station   KAYAKING
(Chang Spirit Club; ☑087 748 9497; Baan Salak Kok; kayak rental per hour 200B) 🏊 On the east side of the island, explore the mangrove swamps of Ao Salak Kok while supporting an award-winning ecotour program. Salak Kok Kayak Station rents self-guided kayaks and is a village work project designed to promote tourism without affecting the traditional way of life. They can also help arrange wooden-boat trips with a guide (200B), village homestays and hiking tours.

Hiking & Ziplining

Ko Chang isn't just about the beaches. The island has a well-developed trekking scene, with inland routes that lead to lush forests filled with birds, monkeys and flora. A handful of English-speaking guides grew up near the jungle and are happy to share their secrets.

Though the inadequate national park map shows a walking trail traversing the island, this is long overgrown: don't try it without a guide.

Mr Tan   HIKING
(☑089 645 2019; hikes 600-1400B) A hiking guide with good English, Mr Tan offers ascents of Khao Chom Prasart, full-day treks to and around the Khlong Prao waterfall and easier family-friendly routes.

Jungle Fever   HIKING
(☑081 588 3324; www.junglefever.in.th) Jungle Fever offers half-day (700B) and full-day (1200B) treks, including the waterfall-to-waterfall island traverse. It also offers ascents of the island's principal mountains and has dedicated walks for birdwatchers.

Evolution Tour   TREKKING
(☑039 557078; www.evolutiontour.com) If you're interested in hiking in the island's interior, you can arrange guides with this agency as the ranger stations around the island aren't very useful for solo trekkers.

Tree Top Adventure Park   ADVENTURE SPORTS
(www.treetopadventurepark.com; Ao Bailan; 1100B; ⊙9am-5pm) Swing through the jungle like Tarzan, walk the rope bridges, or ride the ziplines, flying skateboards and bicycles at this popular attraction. Close to Bailan Bay, this is a two-hour adventure. Add on 150B for transport there and back. All tour agencies around Ko Chang can book it. No flip-flops or under sevens.

Volunteering

Koh Chang Animal Project   VOLUNTEERING
(☑089 042 2347; www.kohchanganimalproject.org; Ban Khlong Son) 🏊 Abused, injured or abandoned animals receive medical care and refuge at this nonprofit centre. With local people it also works on general veterinary services and spaying and neutering. Volunteers and donations are welcome. Travelling vets and vet nurses often drop by, while

---

HOW TO SPEND A WEEK ON KO CHANG

First day just lie on the beach, rotate your body and repeat, with occasional forays into the ocean. On day two, rouse yourself out of your sun-induced stupor to explore the island. Do a day hike through the jungle or view the island from aboard a kayak. Catch a *sŏrng·tăa·ou* (passenger pick-up truck) to Ban Bang Bao (p475) for lunch or an early dinner, followed by souvenir shopping. The next day rent a motorbike and explore the mangrove forest and fishing villages of the east coast (p475). On day four, hit the beach again or go diving (p476).

Head to Ko Mak (p487) for some snorkelling or across to Ko Wai (p488) for powder-soft sands, or devote a day or two to giving back to the island by lending a hand at the Koh Chang Animal Project.

nonvets are needed to help with numerous odd jobs. Call to make an appointment.

Most *sŏrng·tăa·ou* drivers know how to get here; tell them you are going to 'Ban Lisa' (Lisa's House) in Khlong Son. If you have a bike, turn off the main road in Ban Khlong Son at the 7-Eleven; the project is 1.5km down the road.

Massage

Sima Massage MASSAGE
(☑ 081 489 5171; Khlong Prao; massage per hour 250-400B; ⊙ 8am-10pm) Sima is regarded by locals as the best massage on the island – quite an accolade in a place where a massage is easier to find than a 7-Eleven. It's on the main drag through Khlong Prao.

🡒 Courses

Koh Chang Thai Cookery School COOKING
(☑ 039 557243; www.kohchangcookery.com; Blue Lagoon Bungalows, Khlong Prao; courses 1500B) Break up your lazy days with classes designed to enhance mind and body. Classes are typically five hours and include a market tour; book ahead. Slices, dices and sautés are performed in a shady open-air kitchen beside the estuary.

🛌 Sleeping

In general, rates have risen while quality has not, partly because hotels catering to group tours are guaranteed occupancy and don't have to maintain standards to woo repeat visitors or walk-ins. There is also a lot of copy-cat pricing, giving value-oriented visitors little choice.

On the west coast, Lonely Beach is still the best budget option, Hat Kaibae is the best-value option and Hat Sai Khao is the most overpriced.

Lonely Beach

One of the cheapest places to sleep on the island, though budget spots smack on the beach are harder to find. Ignored by the flashy resorts, the streets are filled with grungy bars and cheap guesthouses.

★ **Paradise Cottage** BUNGALOW $
(☑ 081 773 9337; www.paradisecottageresort.com; 104/1 Mu 1; r basic/fan/sea view 450/990/1700B; P ☀ 🛜) With house music as a backdrop, hammock-clad pavilions facing the sea and compact, handsome rooms, well-run Para-

dise Cottage is a gloriously relaxing retreat. The sea-view rooms have air-con and a marvellous outlook, while the cheapest ones have fans but lack hot water and sockets. At low tide a sandbank just beyond the rocks can be reached. Off-season prices are great.

Little Eden BUNGALOW $
(☑ 084 867 7459; www.littleedenkohchang.com; Soi 3; r with fan/air-con 950/1500B; P ☀ 🛜) On the quiet side of the main road, but still close to the beach, Little Eden has a series of wooden bungalows, all connected by an intricate lattice of wooden walkways. Rooms are comfortable with a terrace, wooden floors and mosquito nets: expect plenty of chirping noise from forest critters.

There are good breakfasts and other meals, a pleasant communal area and friendly staff.

BB Lonely Beach HOSTEL $
(☑ 089 504 0543; www.bblonelybeach.com; dm 250B, r with fan 500-700B; 🛜 ❄) One of the only dorms within reach of the beach, this has basic and stuffy – but decent – shared and private rooms at bargain rates. There's plenty to do here, with a dive school, a gym, Belgian beers and a pool: it's a great spot to meet fellow travellers.

It's surrounded by bars so this is definitely one for party folk.

Oasis Koh Chang BUNGALOW $$
(☑ 081 721 2547; www.oasis-kohchang.com; 4/28 Mu 1; r 550-1600B; P ☀ 🛜) Literally the top place in Lonely Beach – largely due to its hillside location – Oasis has great sea views, and the scene from its 12m-tall tree house is even more impressive. Run by a friendly Dutch couple, it has roomy, midrange bungalows in four categories. Cheaper rooms are fan-only.

Warapura Resort HOTEL $$
(☑ 039 558123; www.warapuraresort.com; 4/3 Mu 1; r incl breakfast 1700-3300B; P ☀ @ 🛜 ❄) Right by the sea, Warapura has a series of excellent rooms lightly decorated with rustic furniture and a white colour scheme with turquoise trim. Higher-priced rooms are larger and closer to the sea, with great balconies and huge bathrooms. Though the beach isn't really swimmable just here, the sound of the waves and the decent pool make up for it.

Hat Kaibae

Hat Kaibae has some of the island's best variety of accommodation, from boutique hotels to budget huts and midrange bungalows. The trade-off is that the beach is only sandy in parts.

Porn's Bungalows
BUNGALOW $

(☑ 080 613 9266; www.pornsbungalows-kohchang. com; r 600-1600B; P 🛜) This is a very chilled spot at the far western end of Kaibae beach, with a popular on-site restaurant. All of the wooden bungalows are fan-only. The beachfront bungalows are larger, have a great outlook, and are a fab deal at around 1000B. They can't be booked ahead, so you might have to find somewhere else first in busy periods.

Garden Resort
HOTEL $$

(☑ 039 557260; www.gardenresortkohchang. com; 98/22 Mu 4; r incl breakfast 2200-3500B; P ✳ @ 🛜 ≋) Just off the main road and yet secluded, Garden Resort has large, rather charming bungalows dotted either side of a shady garden pathway that leads to a pleasant swimming pool area. The bar and restaurant at the front are popular hang-outs. It's a short stroll to a sandy stretch of beach.

Green Resort
BUNGALOW $$

(☑ 097 110 7094; www.thegreen-kohchang.com; 51/3 Mu 4; r 1200B; P ✳ 🛜) Just off the strip in Hat Kaibae, this resort nevertheless achieves tranquillity with its pleasingly attractive, if darkish, modern rooms around a lawn. Staff are friendly and helpful and the rooms are well-equipped, with decent wi-fi, cable TV and fridges.

Chill
RESORT $$$

(☑ 039 552555; www.thechillresort.com; r incl breakfast 5250-14,400B; P ✳ @ 🛜 ≋) Cleverly designed, with all ground-floor rooms opening onto one of three pools, Chill has contemporary, bright rooms with loads of space and bags of facilities. It's right on the beach and has good family-friendly features and very helpful staff.

Khlong Prao

Ao Khlong Prao is dominated by high-end resorts, with a few budget spots peppered in between.

★ Pajamas Hostel
HOSTEL $

(☑ 039 510789; www.pajamaskohchang.com; Khlong Prao; dm/r incl breakfast 570/2600B; P 🛜 ≋) A couple of kilometres north of the main Khlong Prao strip and by the beach, this superb hostel oozes relaxation, with an open-plan lounge and bar overlooking the swimming pool. Good modern air-con dorms are upstairs, while the private rooms are really excellent, with platform beds, a cool, light feel and your own terrace/balcony. It's all spotless, and exceedingly well run.

★ Baan Rim Nam
GUESTHOUSE $$

(☑ 087 005 8575; www.iamkohchang.com; Khlong Prao; r 1000-1900B; ✳ 🛜) This marvellously converted fishers house is right over the mangrove-lined river estuary and makes a supremely peaceful place to stay. Cool, appealing rooms open onto a wonderful waterside deck. The owner is a mine of information and keen that visitors enjoy what the region has to offer. Free kayaks and canoes are provided – the beach is a three-minute paddle away.

Blue Lagoon Bungalows
BUNGALOW $$

(☑ 089 515 4617; www.kohchang-bungalows-blue-lagoon.com; Ban Khlong Phrao; bungalows 800-2000B; P ✳ 🛜) Set beside a scenic estuary, Blue Lagoon has an eclectic bunch of bungalows and rooms arrayed in a rustic manner across a riverside mangrove with a walkway to the beach. They all have different layouts and design schemes; check out the elephant dung family room.

Dewa
RESORT $$$

(☑ 039 557341; www.thedewakohchang.com; Khlong Prao; r incl breakfast 5100-12000B; P ✳ @ 🛜 ≋) The top luxury pad in these parts, everything about Dewa is chic, from the dark-bottomed 700-sq-metre pool to the contemporary Thai-style rooms that are a design dream. Expect big discounts if booking early.

Ban Bang Bao & Around

Accommodation options are mainly converted pier houses overlooking the sea, with easy access to departing interisland ferries and lovely Khlong Kloi beach just east. Night owls should hire a motorbike or stay elsewhere, as sŏrng·tăa·ou become rare and expensive after dinnertime.

---

❶ DON'T FEED THE ANIMALS!

On many of the around-the-island boat tours, operators amaze their guests with a stop at a rocky cliff to feed the wild monkeys. It seems innocent enough, and even entertaining, but there's an unfortunate consequence. The animals become dependent on this food source and when the boats don't come as often during the low season the young and vulnerable ones are ill-equipped to forage in the forest.

The same goes for the dive or boat trips that feed the fish leftover lunches, or bread bought on the pier specifically for this purpose. It might be a fantastic way to see a school of brilliantly coloured fish, but they then forsake the coral reefs for an easier meal, and without the daily grooming efforts of the fish the coral is soon overgrown with algae and will eventually suffocate.

Cliff Cottage BUNGALOW **$**
(☑ 080 823 5495; www.cliff-cottage.com; Ban Bang Bao; bungalows 950-1100B; 🌐 🗑) Partially hidden on a verdant hillside west of the pier are a few dozen simple, comfortable huts overlooking a rocky cove with water on both sides. Most have sea views and a couple offer spectacular vistas.

⭐**Buddha View** GUESTHOUSE **$$**
(☑ 039 558157; www.thebuddhaview.com; Ban Bang Bao; r 800-1400B; 🌐 🗑) This swish pier guesthouse is very easy on the eye. There are just seven thoughtfully designed, all-wood rooms, four of which come with private bathrooms (the shared ones are excellent anyway). The restaurant is great too: sit at the cutaway tables and dangle your feet over the water and sculptures below.

⭐**Bang Bao Beach Resort** BUNGALOW **$$**
(☑ 093 327 2788; www.bangbaobeachresort.com; Hat Khlong Koi; r 1700-2500B) Very sprucely set along green lawn right on super Khlong Koi beach, just east of Bang Bao, this is a marvellous spot. Old and new bungalows are available; both are attractively wooden and air-conditioned. It's a very efficiently run spot with easy access to beach bars and restaurants alongside. Walk along the beach from the canal bridge or drive the long way round.

El Greco GUESTHOUSE **$$**
(☑ 086 843 8417; elgrecoloungebar@gmail.com; Ban Bang Bao; r 1400-1600B; 🌐 🗑) Run by a genial family, this has an excellent location halfway along Bang Bao pier. Rooms are simple but attractive, with mosquito nets, balconies and slightly hard beds. The on-site Greek restaurant is worth a look.

🛏 Hat Sai Khao

The island's prettiest beach is also its most expensive. Close to the finest sand, the northern and southern extremities have some budget and midrange options. There's a groovy backpacker enclave north of KC Grande Resort, accessible only via the beach.

Independent Bo's GUESTHOUSE **$**
(☑ 039 551165; r 300-800B; 🗑) Quirky and enchanting, this is an old-school bohemian budget place right on the sand. It's a striking sight and experience: a warren of driftwood cabins, common areas and quirky signs with a communal, hippie feel and the sea at your feet. The fan-only rooms are simple and mostly rather charming; bathrooms range from extremely basic to modernised. No reservations (and no children).

Starbeach Bungalows GUESTHOUSE **$**
(☑ 089 574 9486; www.starbeach-kohchang.com; bungalows 600-750B; 🗑) Right on the prime part of the beach, this ramshackle-looking spot is a glorious place for no-frills sand-and-sea sleeping. Fan-cooled rooms are simple but decent and all look out towards the water. There's a friendly on-site bar and restaurant. No reservations: text to see if there's a vacancy. Head towards the beach down the side of the 7-Eleven and turn right.

Rock Sand Resort GUESTHOUSE **$$**
(☑ 084 781 0550; www.rocksand-resort.com; r incl breakfast with fan/air-con 1000/3500B; 🅿 🌐 🗑) Touting itself as a flashpacker destination, this is the most upmarket of the knot of places at the north end of White Sand Beach, but feels overpriced in summer. The sea-view rooms are, however, decent and share a balcony. Cheaper rooms are plain. Waves

---

ℹ PEAK SEASON PRICES

During the wet season (May to October) rates drop precipitously, although many places close altogether. Consider booking ahead and shopping for online discounts during peak season (November to March), weekends and holidays.

---

beat against the foundations; be prepared to wade here at high tide. You can get a vehicle here via the scarily steep road to White Sand Beach Resort.

Arunee Resort GUESTHOUSE **$$**
(☑ 086 111 9600; aruneeresorttour@hotmail.com; r incl breakfast with fan/air-con 500/1500B; ❄ ✈) Recent renovations mean the super-cheap rooms have been replaced by bright and breezy ones. Arunee is set back from the main road and is a 50m-walk to the beach. It's not flash, but the price is OK for this location.

🛏 Interior & East Coast

You will likely need your own transport to not feel lonely out in the less developed parts of the island, but you'll be rewarded with a quieter, calmer experience.

★ Mangrove Hideaway GUESTHOUSE **$$**
(☑ 080 133 6600; www.themangrovehideaway. com; Ban Salak Phet; r 1900-2700B; ❄ ✈) 🌿 Facing the mangrove forest, this environmentally friendly guesthouse is a fabulous spot. Crisp, attractive rooms face the verdant front garden, while the sumptuous superior suites have gorgeous wooden floors and overlook the dining area and mangroved river estuary. There's an open-air jacuzzi and massage area upstairs; the resort was made using locally sourced wood and employs local villagers.

Serenity Resort HOTEL **$$**
(☑ 088 092 4452; www.serenity-koh-chang.com; Ao Dan Kao; r 2800-3200B; P ❄ ✈) Not far from the ferries, on the peaceful east side of the island, this well-presented spot has serene, cool white rooms with impressive towel-folding skills on show, even by Thai standards. Friendly, modern and spotless, the complex is right on the beach, where there's a bar and pool. Kayaks and SUPs are on hand.

Amber Sands HOTEL **$$$**
(☑ 039 586177; www.ambersandsbeachresort. com; Ao Dan Kao; r 3250-5250B; ☉ mid-Oct–Aug; P ❄ ✈ ✈) Right on a quiet orangey-red sand beach, this is an impeccably run place set around a beautifully kept garden. Rooms have wonderful wooden floors, elegant furnishings and are very easy on the eye. The outlook is perfect for relaxation. The restaurant opens to nonguests at mealtimes. It feels a world away but is close to the ferries; they'll arrange pick-up for you.

Spa Koh Chang Resort RESORT **$$$**
(☑ 083 115 6566; www.thespakohchang.com; Ao Salak Kok; r incl breakfast 2150-4000B; P ❄ ✈ ✈) Specialising in health-care packages, including fasting, yoga and meditation, this resort has lush, peaceful surroundings that almost touch the bay's mangrove forests. Elegantly decorated bungalows scramble up a flower-filled hillside providing a peaceful getaway for some quality 'me' time. The restaurant has vegan and veggie options. The 'hill' options are far lighter than the 'oriental' rooms. There's no beach access.

🍴 Eating & Drinking

Virtually all of the island's accommodation choices have attached restaurants with adequate but not outstanding fare. It's usually worth seeking places outside; there's some very decent eating to be done on the island.

Parties abound on the beaches and range from the more mature, restrained scene on Hat Sai Khao, to the younger and more frenetic one on Lonely Beach.

🍴 West Coast

Porn's Bungalows Restaurant THAI **$**
(Hat Kaibae; mains 80-180B; ☉ 11am-11pm; ✈) This laid-back, dark-wood restaurant is the quintessential beachside lounge. Great barbecue. Feel free to have your drinks out-size your meal and don't worry about dressing up for dinner.

★ Phu-Talay SEAFOOD **$$**
(☑ 039 551300; 4/2 Mu 4, Khlong Prao; mains 120-320B; ☉ 10am-10pm) A beautiful place right on the *klorng*, Phu-Talay has cute wooden-floored, blue-and-white decor, a picturesque deck and its own boat (for pick-up up from nearby accommodations). It specialises in seafood, with standout softshell crab,

prawns and other fish dishes. It's far more reasonably priced than many other seafood places.

★ **Barrio Bonito** MEXICAN $$
(☎080 092 8208; www.barriobonito.com; Hat Kaibae; mains 160-280B; ☺5-10pm Jul-late May; 🛜🍴) Fab fajitas and cracking cocktails are served by a charming French-Mexican couple at this roadside spot in the middle of Kaibae. Offering authentic, delicious, beautifully presented food and stylish surroundings, this is one of the island's finest places to eat.

Saffron on the Sea THAI $$
(☎039 551253; Hat Kai Mook; mains 120-350B; ☺8am-10pm; 🛜) Owned by an arty escapee from Bangkok, this friendly little boutique bungalow complex has a beautiful seafront dining area and a relaxed, romantic atmosphere. All the Thai dishes are prepared in the island style, more sweet than spicy. The menu is somewhat reduced off-season. The rooms (1200B to 1500B in high season) are attractive too; all face the front.

Baanta THAI $$
(www.facebook.com/baantaorchidrestaurant; Khlong Prao; mains 120-320B; ☺noon-10pm; 🛜) Baanta is an attractive main-road spot offering personable service and a wide choice of dishes, from Thai classics to regional specialities, seafood blowouts and a range of Western dishes and Japanese-influenced salmon plates. It's a reliably pleasant spot.

Oodie's Place INTERNATIONAL, THAI $$
(☎039 551193; www.facebook.com/oodies.place; Hat Sai Khao; mains 80-390B; ☺11am-midnight) Local musician Oodie runs a nicely diverse operation with excellent French food, tasty Thai specialities, pizzas and live blues music from 10pm. After all these years, it is still beloved by expats.

Paul's Restaurant GERMAN, THAI $$
(☎039 551499; www.topresort-kohchang.com; Hat Sai Khao; mains 140-330B; ☺6am-10pm; 🛜) Quality cooking in big portions is served up at this clifftop hotel restaurant, along side orders of sarcasm from the entertaining owner. The menu covers both German and Thai bases. You'll need to book ahead in high season, as it's deservedly popular.

Ka-Ti Culinary THAI $$
(☎081 903 0408; www.facebook.com/katikhrua thai; Khlong Prao; 160-510B; ☺noon-10pm Mon-

Sat, 5-10pm Sun; 🛜) Seafood, a few Isan dishes and their famous, homemade curry sauce are the best bets here. The menu features creative smoothies, featuring lychee, lemon and peppermint, and there's a children's menu. Daily specials might feature whole steamed snapper and other fishy delights.

Up2You THAI $$
(Khlong Prao; mains 120-300B; ☺10am-10pm; 🛜) With a nice line in seafood, this main-road spot near the 7-Eleven offers solid value and a welcoming atmosphere. Tasty scallop stir-fries and prawn dishes are highlights, but it's all pretty flavourful. Portion sizes aren't huge.

Interior & East Coast

★ **Blues Blues Restaurant** THAI $
(☎087 144 6412; Ban Khlong Son; mains 80-170B; ☺9am-9pm) Through the green screen of tropical plants is an arty stir-fry hut that is beloved for its expertise, efficiency and economy. The owner's delicate watercolour paintings are on display too. Take the road to Ban Kwan Chang; it's 600m ahead on the right.

★ **Shambhala** BAR
(☎098 579 4381; www.shambhalabeachbar.com; Siam Royal View, Ao Khlong Son; ☺11am-10pm or later Thu-Tue) Perched at the top of the island, this poolside bar has some excellent, fairly priced cocktails and a magnificent outlook across green lawn to a secluded golden sweep of beach and forested peninsula. It's the perfect spot for a sundowner; there are also quality Thai and international dishes. Enter via the southernmost 'Marina' entrance to the Siam Royal View complex.

ℹ️ Information

DANGERS & ANNOYANCES

➡ Take extreme care when driving from Ban Khlong Son south to Hat Sai Khao, as the road is steep and treacherous, with several hairpin turns. There are mud slides and poor conditions during storms. If you do rent a motorbike, ride carefully between Hat Kaibae and Lonely Beach, especially in the rainy season. Wear protective clothing when riding on a motorcycle.

➡ The police conduct regular drug raids on the island's accommodation. If you get caught with narcotics, you could face heavy fines or imprisonment.

➡ Be aware of the cheap minibus tickets from Siem Reap to Ko Chang; these usually involve some sort of time- and money-wasting commission scam.

➡ Ko Chang is considered a low-risk malarial zone, meaning that liberal use of mosquito repellent is probably an adequate precaution.

EMERGENCY

Head to the **tourist police station** (☏1155; Khlong Prao) in Khlong Prao for any need.

MEDICAL SERVICES

Bang Bao Health Centre (☏039 558086; Ban Bang Bao; ☺8.30am-4pm) For the basics. On the pier.

Ko Chang Hospital (☏039 586131; Ban Dan Mai) Public hospital with a good reputation and affordably priced care; south of the ferry terminal.

Ko Chang International Clinic (☏039 551555; www.bangkoktrathospital.com; Hat Sai Khao; ☺24hr) Related to the Bangkok Hospital Group; accepts most health insurance and has expensive rates.

MONEY

There are banks with ATMs and exchange facilities along all the west-coast beaches.

POST

Ko Chang Post Office (☏039 551240; Hat Sai Khao; ☺9am-5pm) At the far southern end of Hat Sai Khao.

TRAVEL AGENCIES

Nuttakit Tour (☏092 647 3009; nuttakittour@gmail.com; Bang Bao) The first agency on the right after entering Bang Bao's pier itself, this is a step ahead of the rest, with helpful English-speaking staff who can arrange tailored boat trips as well as the usual excursions.

TOURIST INFORMATION

➡ The free magazine *Koh Chang Guide* (www.koh-chang-guide.com) is widely available on the island and has handy beach maps.

➡ The comprehensive website I Am Koh Chang (www.iamkohchang.com) is a labour of love from an irreverent Brit living on the island. It's jam-packed with opinion and information.

❶ Getting There & Away

Whether starting from Bangkok or Cambodia, it is an all-day haul to reach Ko Chang. Overnighting in Trat is a pleasant way to break the journey.

Ferries from the mainland (Laem Ngop) leave from either Tha Thammachat, operated by Koh Chang Ferry (p474), or Tha Centrepoint with Centrepoint Ferry (p474). Boats from Tha Thammachat arrive at Tha Sapparot, Centrepoint ferries at a pier 3km further south. The Koh Chang ferries are faster and a little better.

Bang Bao Boat (☏084 567 8765; www.kohchangbangbaoboat.com; Ban Bang Bao; ☺Nov-Apr) runs an interisland ferry that connects Ko Chang with Ko Mak and Ko Wai (with a speedboat connection from there to Ko Kut) during the high season. Boats leave from Bang Bao in the southwest of the island.

Speedboats travel between the islands during high season from both Bang Bao and Hat Kaibae.

It is possible to go to and from Ko Chang from Bangkok's Eastern (Ekamai) bus terminal via Chanthaburi and Trat; there are also direct bus and minibus **services** (☏083-794 2122; www.

TRANSPORT TO/FROM KO CHANG

DEPARTS	DESTINATION	BOAT	BUS
Bangkok's Eastern Bus Terminal (Ekamai)	Tha Thammachat (Laem Ngop)	N/A	269B, 6hr, 2 daily
Ko Chang	Bangkok's Suvarnabhumi International Airport	N/A	single/return 600/900B, 6-7hr, 2-3 daily
Ko Chang	Ko Kut	speedboat 900B, 2½hr, 3 daily; wooden boat plus speedboat 700B, 5hr, 1 daily	N/A
Ko Chang	Ko Mak	speedboat 600B, 1hr, 3 daily; wooden boat 400B, 2hr, 1 daily	N/A
Ko Chang	Ko Wai	speedboat 400B, 30min, 3 daily; wooden boat 300B, 1hr, 1 daily	N/A
Tha Centrepoint (Laem Ngop)	Ko Chang	80B, 40min, hourly 6am-7.30pm	N/A
Tha Thammachat (Laem Ngop)	Ko Chang	80B, 30min, every 45min 6.30am-7pm	N/A

bussuvarnabhumikohchang.com) from Bangkok's Suvarnabhumi International Airport.

The closest airport is in Trat. **Ko Chang Minibus** (☑ 087 785 7695; www.kohchangminibus. com) offers a variety of transfer packages from airport to beach.

ℹ Getting Around

Shared *sŏrng·tăa·ou* meet arriving boats to shuttle passengers to the various beaches (Hat Sai Khao 100B, Khlong Prao 150B and Lonely Beach 200B). Hops between neighbouring beaches range from 50B to 200B but prices rise dramatically after dark, when it can cost 500B to travel from Bang Bao to Hat Sai Khao.

Motorbikes can be hired from 200B per day. Ko Chang's hilly and winding roads are dangerous; make sure the bike is in good working order.

Hiring a car is also a decent option. **Sawadee Koh Chang Travel** (☑ 086 712 6804; sawadee-kohchang@hotmail.co.th; Hat Kaibae; car per day from 1200B; ⊙ 8am-8.30pm) is one of a couple of places on the island to do so.

Ko Kut   เกาะกูด

☑ 039 / POP 2100

Ko Kut is often feted as the perfect Thai island, and it is hard to argue with such an accolade. The supersoft sands are like talcum powder, the water lapping the bays is clear and there are more coconut palms than buildings.

Unlike its larger neighbour Ko Chang, here you can forget about any nightlife or noise – this is where you come to do almost nothing. If you can be roused from your hammock, kayaking and snorkelling are the main activities (nearby Ko Rang is particularly good for fish-gazing).

Half as big as Ko Chang and the fourth-largest island in Thailand, Ko Kut (also known as Koh Kood) has long been the domain of package-tour resorts and a seclusion-seeking elite. But the island is becoming more egalitarian, and independent travellers, especially families and couples, will find a base here.

◎ Sights & Activities

With its quiet rocky coves and mangrove estuaries, Ko Kut is great for snorkelling and kayaking. Most resorts have equipment on offer.

White-sand beaches with gorgeous aquamarine water are strewn along the western side of the island. **Hat Khlong Chao** is the island's best and could easily compete with Samui's Hat Chaweng in a beach beauty contest. **Ao Noi** is a pretty boulder-strewn beach with a steep drop-off and steady waves for strong swimmers. **Ao Prao** is another lovely sweep of sand.

There is no public transport on Ko Kut, though taxi services exist and you can rent motorbikes for exploring the west-coast beaches. The road is mostly paved from Khlong Hin in the southwest to Ao Noi in the northeast.

Nam Tok Khlong Chao   WATERFALL

(น้ำตกคลองเจ้า) Two waterfalls on the island make good destinations for a short hike. The larger and more popular Nam Tok Khlong Chao is wide and pretty with a massive plunge pool. It is a quick jungle walk to the base from the end of the road, or you can kayak up Khlong Chao. Further north is **Nam Tok Khlong Yai Ki**, which is smaller but also has a large pool to cool off in.

🛏 Sleeping & Eating

During low season many boats stop running and some bungalow operations close altogether. On weekends and holidays during the high season, holidaying Thais fill the resorts. Call ahead to book so you can be dropped off at the appropriate pier by the speedboat operators or transfer drivers.

Most guesthouses have on-site restaurants but there are also lots of independent places, mainly specialising in seafood.

Mangrove Bungalow   BUNGALOW **$**

(☑ 089 936 2093; www.kohkood-mangrove.com; Hat Khlong Chao; r incl breakfast with fan 700-1000B, with air-con 1500B; ❄ 🛜) With a mangrove forest on one side and the beach a short walk away, this collection of wooden bungalows is immersed in nature. Khlong Chao waterfall is in easy striking distance by kayak or on foot. Rooms are clean and neat and there's a restaurant.

Cozy House   GUESTHOUSE **$**

(☑ 089 094 3650; www.kohkoodcozy.com; Hat Khlong Chao; r incl breakfast 600-1200B; ❄ 🛜) The go-to place for backpackers, Cozy is a 10-minute walk from delightful Hat Khlong Chao. There are cheap and cheerful fan rooms and more comfortable wooden bungalows with air-con.

Ko Mak & Ko Kut

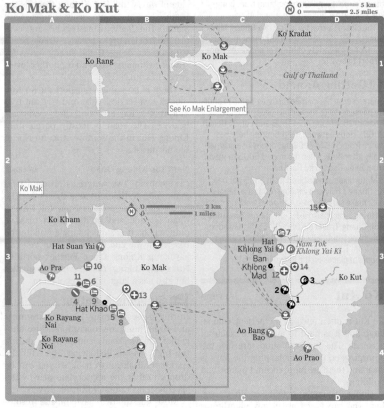

Ko Mak & Ko Kut

★ **Bann Makok** HOTEL **$$**
(📞 088 203 0699; www.facebook.com/bannmakok; Khlong Yai Ki; r incl breakfast 3200-3800B; 🅿 ❄ @ 🛜) 🕭 This boutique hotel, tucked into the

mangroves, uses recycled timbers painted in vintage colours to create a maze of eight rooms that resembles a traditional pier fishing village. Common decks and reading nooks provide peaceful spaces to listen to birdsong or get lost in a book.

Kokut Coconut
Garden Resort
BUNGALOW $$

(Suan Maprao; 086 833 7999; www.facebook.com/Suan-Maprao-Ko-Kut-Resort-1533121720312175; Ao Ngam Kho; r 1500B; P ✳ 🛜) You'll get a genuine smile and welcome at this place just off the southern beach road (opposite the seaplane). Excellent modern huts are simple and stylish, with timber cladding and smoothed concrete interiors. They sit a short walk from the beach amid towering coconut palms. It's a lovely spot and is fronted by a decent restaurant.

Tinkerbell Resort
RESORT $$$

(081 826 1188; www.tinkerbellresort.com; Hat Khlong Chao; r incl breakfast 9800-12,000B; P ✳ @ 🛜 ⛱) Natural materials, like bamboo privacy fences and thatched-roof villas, sew this resort (one of a group of four Peter Pan-named ones) seamlessly into the landscape. The terracotta-coloured bungalows open right onto a postcard-perfect beach; the villas behind come with plunge pools. The bar is a great spot for a sundowner. Expect 40% discounts in low season.

Ra Beang Mai
THAI $$

(Hat Khlong Chao; mains 100-180B; ⊙ 8am-10pm; 🛜) Handy for the cluster of accommodation near Khlong Chao beach, this restaurant is cordially family-run and attractive, with a covered area plus pleasant outdoor seating on rustic wooden furniture. Dishes include plump prawn salads, seafood curries and international favourites and come bursting with flavour. It's a lovely spot.

ℹ Information

There is one ATM on Ko Kut but it's best not to rely on it. Major resorts can exchange money.

Almost all hotels and guesthouses have wi-fi.

A small **hospital** (039 525748; ⊙ 24hr) at Ban Khlong Mad can handle minor emergencies. **Police Station** (039 525741; ⊙ 24hr) Near the hospital at Ban Khlong Dam.

ℹ Getting There & Away

Ko Kut is accessible from the mainland pier of **Laem Sok**, 22km southeast of Trat, the nearest bus transfer point. Three boat services as well as a speedboat service run from adjacent piers. Boat services offer free transport from Trat guesthouses and the bus station but not from the airport.

Speedboats will drop you off at your resort if possible; normal boats offer free land transfer on your arrival at **Ao Salad Pier** to your destination.

Koh Kood Princess (086 126 7860; www.kohkoodprincess.com) runs an air-con boat (350B, 1¾ hours, 12.30pm) that docks at Ao Salad, in the northeastern corner of the island.

Ko Kut Express (09-0506 0020; www.kokutexpress.in.th) runs an air-con fast ferry (350B, 1¼ hours, 1pm) to Ao Salad. It also runs a twice-daily speedboat service from November to April (600B, one hour, 10.30am and 2.30pm), dropping to weekends-only (and weather-permitting) off-season.

Boonsiri (085 921 0111; www.boonsiriferry.com) has a catamaran (500B, 1¼ to 1¾ hours, 10.45am and 2.20pm) that runs from Laem Sok to Ao Salad. The afternoon departure goes via Ko Mak. From mid-May to mid-October there's only one departure, at 1.30pm (and no Ko Mak link), with an extra 10.45am boat on Fridays. The company runs a direct bus service from Bangkok to meet the boats (850B including boat, five hours).

Two companies run speedboats from Ko Chang to Ko Kut (900B, 2½ hours) via Ko Wai and Ko Mak. The cheapest way to do this is to book a through-trip with Bang Bao Boat (p484) via Ko Mak, with the first section by wooden boat and the second by speedboat (700B).

ℹ Getting Around

Ko Kut's roads are steep, which rules out renting a push bike unless you are a champion cyclist.

Motorbikes can be rented for 200B to 300B per day.

Ko Mak
เกาะหมาก

039 / POP 600

Little Ko Mak measures only 16 sq km and doesn't have any speeding traffic, wall-to-wall development, noisy beer bars or crowded beaches. The palm-fringed bays are bathed by gently lapping water and there's a relaxed vibe. It's a sweet place, despite sand flies and rubbish being a pain on some beaches, with a local movement that tries to keep the impact of tourism sustainable. The interior is a utilitarian but peaceful landscape of coconut and rubber plantations.

Visiting the island is easier in the high season (December to March); during the low season (May to September) many boats stop running.

KO WAI

Stunning Ko Wai (เกาะหวาย) is teensy and primitive, but endowed with gin-clear waters, excellent coral reefs for snorkelling and a handsome view across to Ko Chang. Expect to share the bulk of your afternoons with day trippers but have the remainder of your time in peace.

Overnight in simple wooden bungalows at **Ko Wai Paradise** (☏ 081 762 2548; r 300-500B; ⊙ Oct–mid-May), on a postcard-perfect beach on the western side of the north coast. Equally good value is **Good Feeling** (☏ 081 850 3410; r 400-600B; ⊙ Oct–mid-May), whose 12 wooden bungalows (all but one with private bathroom) are spread along a rocky headland with good snorkelling nearby. More upscale is **Koh Wai Beach Resort** (☏ 081 306 4053; www.kohwaibeachresort.com; r incl breakfast 2100-3400B; ⊙ Oct–mid-May; ✹ 🛜) on the southern side of the island, with all mod cons and just a few steps from the beach.

Note that all budget bungalows on Ko Wai close from May to September when seas are rough and flooding is common, and power is rationed and intermittent except at the resorts. There are no banks or ATMs, so stock up on cash before visiting the island.

Boat services run to Ko Wai from November to April; outside of this time (when most accommodation is closed anyway) you can ask for the reduced Ko Mak services to stop at Ko Wai. Speedboats (one-way 450B, 50 minutes) from Laem Ngop will drop you off at the nearest pier to your guesthouse; otherwise you'll have to walk 15 to 30 minutes along a narrow forest trail. From Ko Chang, speedboats (400B, 15 minutes, three daily) and the wooden Bang Bao (p484) ferry (300B, 45 minutes, one daily) head to Ko Wai, continuing to Ko Mak (wooden/speedboat 200/400B) and back. Speedboats head on to Ko Kut (700B).

◉ Sights & Activities

The best beach on the island is **Ao Pra** in the west, but it is undeveloped and hard to reach. For now, swimming and beach strolling are best on the northwestern bay of **Ao Suan Yai**, which is a wide arc of sand and looking-glass-clear water that gets fewer sandflies than the southern beaches. It is easily accessible by bicycle or motorbike if you stay elsewhere.

Depending on winds, all beaches can suffer from quantities of rubbish washing up, much of it generated by the fishing boats.

Offshore is **Ko Kham**, a private island that was sold in 2008 for a reported 200 million baht. It used to be a popular day trippers' beach; today it's a resort island. You can still use the beach, but they'll ask you to pay a fee.

Koh Mak Divers DIVING
(☏ 083 297 7724; www.kohmakdivers.com; Ao Khao; 2-dive trips from 2500B) Runs dive trips to the Mu Ko Chang National Marine Park, about 45 minutes away. Its office is on the road near Baan Koh Mak.

🛏 Sleeping & Eating

Most budget guesthouses are on Ao Khao, a decent strip of sand on the southwestern side of the island, while the resorts sprawl out on the more scenic northwestern bay of Ao Suan Yai. Most bungalow operations and resorts open year-round, but a few still close from May to September.

Beachside restaurants exist at nearly every guesthouse and resort, and there's a handful of family-run restaurants on the main road between Monkey Island and Makathanee Resort.

SPEEDBOATS TO/FROM KO MAK

DESTINATION	FARE (ONE WAY)	DURATION	FREQUENCY
Ko Chang	600B	1hr	3 daily
Ko Kut	400B	45min	3 daily
Ko Wai	400B	30min	3 daily
Laem Ngop (mainland pier)	450B	1hr	8 daily

Monkey Island
BUNGALOW **$**

(☑ 085 389 0949; www.monkeyislandkohmak.com; Ao Khao; fan r with/without bathroom 600/400B, air-con r incl breakfast 1300-2000B; P ✱ @ 🛜 🏊) Monkey Island has earthen or wooden bungalows in three creatively named models – Baboon, Chimpanzee and Gorilla – which range from very basic to beachfront villa chic. All have fun design touches and the hip restaurant does respectable Thai cuisine in a leisurely fashion. There's also a small children's pool.

Seavana
RESORT **$$**

(☑ 090 864 5646; www.seavanakohmak.com; Ao Suan Yi; r 2900-5800B; P ✱ 🛜 🏊) Stylish, wine-coloured buildings overlook garden, coconut palms and white sand at this top-drawer set-up near the northern pier. Staff are cordial and competent and the range of rooms is excellent. We especially like the upstairs ones with their own seaview jacuzzi, perfect for quality time with someone special or stoking social media envy.

Lazy Day Resort
BUNGALOW **$$**

(☑ 081 882 4002; www.kohmaklazyday.com; Ao Khao; r incl breakfast 2700-3000B; ☺ Oct-May; ✱ 🛜) At the end of the sweep of Ao Khao, this professionally run operation has a dozen big white raised bungalows stationed around an attractive garden. The beach here is pretty but can suffer from plastic debris. Service is excellent, with a genuine welcome and relaxation guaranteed.

Baan Koh Mak
BUNGALOW **$$**

(☑ 089 895 7592; www.baan-koh-mak.com; Ao Khao; r 1800-2600B; P ✱ 🛜) Each of the slick bungalows here comes with heaps of natural light, arty features and a rakishly angled roof. The price goes up as you get closer to the beach. There's a decent restaurant and a beachside bar where fire twirlers heat up the revelry.

Ao Kao Resort
BUNGALOW **$$$**

(☑ 080 567 0197; www.aokaoresort.com; Ao Khao; r 4500-5000B; P ✱ 🛜) 🏊 In a pretty crook of the bay, Ao Kao has an assortment of stylish concrete bungalows with fab roof terraces offering thatched shade, hammocks and sea views. All have easy beach access. There are lots of amenities including sports options and a massage pavilion.

❶ Information

There are no banks or ATMs on the island, so stock up on cash before visiting.

Ball Cafe (☑ 081 925 6591; Ao Khao; ☺ 8am-9pm; 🛜) Khun Ball runs his coffee shop and information centre in a spot just behind Baan Koh Mak; he's an active island promoter and runs www.kohmak.com as well as environmental initiatives. You can rent bikes (100B for 24 hours) and scooters (250B) here.

Ko Mak Health Centre (☺ 8.30am-4.30pm) Can handle basic first-aid emergencies and illnesses. It is on the cross-island road near Ao Nid Pier.

Police Station (☑ 1155) Small station in the centre of the island.

❶ Getting There & Around

Speedboats (450B one way, one hour) from Laem Ngop arrive at the pier on Ao Suan Yai, at Ao Nid or at Makathanee Resort on Ao Khao. The Ko Kut–bound Boonsiri (p487) ferry also stops in here once daily in high season (from mainland 400B).

In low season only one or two boats a day run from the mainland. Guesthouses and hotels pick people up free of charge.

From Ko Chang, speedboats (600B, one hour, three daily) and the wooden Bang Bao (p484) ferry (400B, two hours, one daily) head to Ko Mak via Ko Wai (wooden/speedboat 200/400B) and back. Speedboats head on to Ko Kut (400B).

Once on the island, you can pedal (40B per hour) or motorbike (200B per day) your way around.

Hua Hin & the Upper Gulf

Best Places to Eat

➡ Cicada Market (p500)

➡ In Town Seafood (p514)

➡ Jek Pia (p504)

➡ Koti (p505)

➡ Sôm·dam Tanontok 51 (p504)

Best Places to Stay

➡ Baan Bayan (p504)

➡ Centara Grand Beach Resort & Villas (p504)

➡ La a natu Bed & Bakery (p509)

➡ Salsa Hostel (p518)

➡ The Theatre Villa (p517)

Why Go?

The upper gulf has long been the favoured playground of the Thai elite due to its proximity to Bangkok. Following in the footsteps of the royal family – every Thai king from Rama IV on has spent his summers at a variety of regal holiday homes here – they in turn have inspired countless domestic tourists to flock to this stretch of coast in pursuit of fun and fine seafood.

A winning combination of outdoor activities and culture is on offer here, with historic sites, national parks and long sandy beaches ideal for beachcombing (the swimming isn't all that great at most) also drawing an increasing number of expats for the twin delights of an unspoiled coastline and the relaxed pace of provincial life. There's not much diving or snorkelling, but kiteboarders will be in paradise as this part of the gulf is by far the best place in Thailand to ride the wind.

When to Go

➡ The best time to visit is during the hot and dry season (February to June).

➡ January through March is the best time to learn how to kiteboard, as the water is usually smooth.

➡ October is the rainiest month, but stays drier than rest of country so there's no need to stay away.

➡ November to March is the coolest time of year – visit to see the 'sea of fog' at Kaeng Krachan National Park.

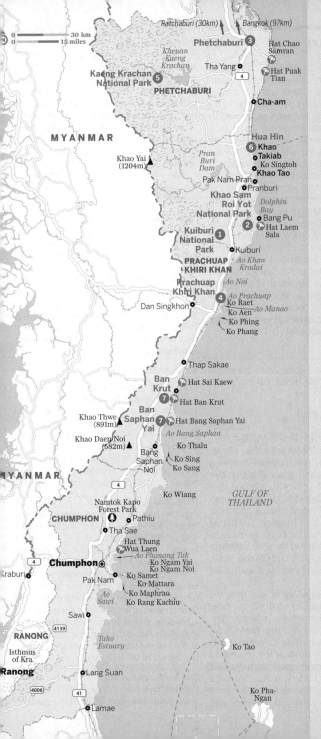

Hua Hin & the Upper Gulf Highlights

1 Kuiburi National Park (p508) Spotting wild elephants.

2 Khao Sam Roi Yot National Park (p510) Making the pilgrimage to see the illuminated cave shrine of Tham Phraya Nakhon.

3 Phetchaburi (p492) Exploring the hilltop palace and underground caves while dodging monkeys.

4 Prachuap Khiri Khan (p511) Motorcycling between curvaceous bays and limestone peaks.

5 Kaeng Krachan National Park (p496) Escaping into the depths of this national park, spotting tropical birds, swinging gibbons and the sea of fog.

6 Hua Hin (p500) Dining out in Hua Hin, home to countless good restaurants, both Thai and international.

7 Ban Krut & Bang Saphan Yai (p516) Stepping off the backpacker trail on your own secluded strip of sand.

Phetchaburi เพชรบุรี

☑ 032 / POP 23,200

An easy escape from Bangkok, Phetchaburi should be on every cultural traveller's itinerary. It has temples, palaces and cave shrines, and is a convenient stop on your way to the beach. Best of all, Phetburi, as it's usually called, remains an untouched and largely untouristed provincial town, complete with riverside markets and old teak shophouses. It's a great place for random wandering.

Historically, Phetchaburi is a visible timeline of kingdoms that have migrated across Southeast Asia. During the 11th century the Khmer empire settled in, although their control was relatively short-lived. As Khmer power diminished, Phetchaburi became a strategic royal fort during the Thai-based Sukhothai and Ayuthaya kingdoms and in the 17th century it flourished as a trading post between Myanmar (Burma) and Ayuthaya. The town is often referred to as a 'Living Ayuthaya' because while the great temples of the former capital were destroyed, smaller but similar ones here live on.

⊙ Sights

Phetchaburi thrived in the Ayuthaya era, so almost every temple in the city has something interesting to see.

★ Phra Nakhon Khiri Historical Park
HISTORIC SITE

(อุทยานประวัติศาสตร์พระนครคีรี; ☑ 032 401006; 150B, cable car return 50B; ⊙ park 8.30am-4.30pm, museum 9am-4pm) This national historical park sits regally atop Khao Wang (Palace Hill), surveying the city with subdued opulence. Rama IV (King Mongkut) built the palace and dozens of surrounding structures in 1859 as a retreat from Bangkok. The hilltop location allowed the king to pursue his interest in astronomy. Parts of the palace, made in a mix of European, Thai and Chinese styles, are now a museum furnished with royal belongings.

Rolling cobblestone paths lead from the palace through the forested hill to three summits, each topped by a stupa. The 40m-tall white spire of Phra That Chom Phet skewers the sky from the central peak. You can climb up through the interior to its waist. The western peak features Wat Phra Kaew Noi (Little Wat Phra Kaew), a small building slightly resembling one from Bangkok's most important temples, and

Phra Prang Daeng stupa with a Khmer-influenced design.

There are two entrances to the site. The east (front) entrance is across from Th Ratwithi and involves a not-too-strenuous footpath. The west entrance on the opposite side of the hill has a cable car (closed for 15 days each June for regular maintenance and a few other days during the year to change the cable) that glides up and down to the summit. At both, keep a leery eye on the troops of unpredictable monkeys (p493).

This place is a popular school-group outing and you'll be as much of a photo op as the historic buildings.

★ Wat Mahathat Worawihan
BUDDHIST TEMPLE

(วัดมหาธาตุวรวิหาร; Th Damnoen Kasem; ⊙ daylight hours) FREE Centrally located, gleaming white Wat Mahathat is one impressive temple. The showpiece is a 42m-tall five-tiered Ayuthaya-style *prang* (corn-cob shaped stupa) decorated in stucco relief, a speciality of Phetchaburi's local artisans you'll see all over town, while inside the *wí·hǎhn* (sanctuary) that fronts it are important, though highly damaged, early 20th-century murals.

Tham Khao Luang
CAVE

(ถ้ำเขาหลวง; ⊙ 8am-4pm Mon-Fri, 8am-5pm Sat & Sun) FREE About 4km north of town is Khao Luang Cave, a dramatic stalactite-stuffed cavern that's one of Thailand's most impressive cave shrines, and a favourite of King Rama IV when he was a monk. Accessed via steep stairs, it's lit by a heavenly glow every morning (clouds permitting) when sunbeams filter in through the natural skylight.

Phra Ram Ratchaniwet
HISTORIC SITE

(พระรามราชนิเวศน์, Ban Peun Palace; Th Damnoen Kasem; 50B; ⊙ 8.30am-4pm Mon-Fri, 8.30am-4.30pm Sat & Sun) Construction of this elegant summer palace, an incredible art nouveau creation, began in 1910 at the behest of Rama V (who died just after the project was started) and finished in 1916. It was designed by German architects who indulged the royal family's passion for all things European with a Poseidon statue, badminton court, ceramic cherubs lining the double spiral staircase and a state-of-the-art, for the time, adjustable shower in the king's bathroom.

Wat Yai Suwannaram
BUDDHIST TEMPLE

(วัดใหญ่สุวรรณาราม; Th Phongsuriya; ⊙ bòht 7am-6pm, săh·lah 8am-5pm) FREE This expansive temple, founded in the late Ayuthaya era, holds quite a bit of history. Foremost are the faded murals inside the beautiful *bòht* (ordination hall), which date back to about 1700, making them some of the oldest Thai-temple murals still in existence. Mostly they're rows of various deities though the entrance wall vividly shows the demon Mara and his army trying to stop the Buddha from reaching enlightenment.

Shadow Puppet Museum
MUSEUM

(พิพิธภัณฑ์หนังใหญ่ วัดพลับพลาชัย; Th Damnoen Kasem; ⊘9am-5pm) FREE Not a fully fledged museum, rather there are 32 large *nǎng yài* shadow puppets, made by the former abbot, displayed on light boxes in Wat Plabplachai's old *bòht*. It's not kept open; you'll need to find a monk across the road to get a key. This temple also has a lot of masterful historic stucco work on the buildings.

Wat Phra Phuttaya Saiyat
(Wat Phra Non)
BUDDHIST TEMPLE

(วัดพระพุทธไสยาสน์ วัดพระนอน; Th Khiriataya; ⊘daylight hours) FREE The main attraction at this temple, also known as Wat Phra Non (the Reclining Buddha Temple), is 43m long. It's almost as big as the famous Wat Pho (p69) in Bangkok, but without the crowds.

Tham Khao Bandai-It
CAVE

(ถ้ำเขาบันไดอิฐ; Rte 3171; ⊘8am-5pm) FREE This hillside monastery, 2km west of town, sprawls through several large caverns converted into simple Buddha shrines and meditation rooms. There are some natural formations and skylights, and one chamber contains quite a few bats, but it's not nearly as beautiful as Tham Khao Luang (p492). It's well-lit and the floor is concrete throughout, so the kids who want to guide you aren't necessary; but if you do go with them, they expect a tip.

🎊 Festivals & Events

Phra Nakhon Khiri Fair
CULTURAL

(งานพระนครคีรี-เมืองเพชร) Centred on Khao Wang hill, this provincial-style celebration lasts 10 days and usually takes place in February. Phra Nakhon Khiri Historical Park (p492) is festooned with lights, and there are traditional dance performances, craft and food displays, fireworks and a beauty contest.

🛏 Sleeping

⭐ 2N Guesthouse
GUESTHOUSE $

(☎085 366 2451; two_nguesthouse@hotmail.com; 98/3 Mu 2, Tambol Bankoom; d & tw/q incl breakfast 580/850B; P ❄ 🛜) In a generally quiet neighbourhood 1.5km north of the city centre, the six rooms here are big and bright, and great for the price. The English-speaking owners do everything themselves and are really dedicated to pleasing their guests. They have free bicycles and can help with travel planning.

Ferngully Hostel
HOSTEL $

(☎085 369 4692; www.ferngullyhostel.com; Th Chisa-In; dm incl breakfast 300B, q 700B; ❄ 🛜) Owner Fern has spruced up an older building with a few guest rooms and lots of social space. A traveller herself, she's a good source of advice about Phetchaburi. The hostel is right next to Phra Nakhon Khiri Historical Park (p492) and the caged rooftop lounge allows close encounters with monkeys and good views of Phra That Chom Phet stupa.

Sabaidee Resort
GUESTHOUSE $

(☎086 344 4418; sabai2505@gmail.com; 65-67 Th Klongkrachang; r 350-500B; ❄ 🛜) It doesn't look like much at first, but step inside and you'll find good rooms around a little garden and shady terrace right on the river. There are modern concrete rooms and bamboo

---

ℹ MONKEY BUSINESS

Phetchaburi is full of macaque monkeys who know no shame or fear. Having once just congregated on Khao Wang hill (Phra Nakhon Khiri Historical Park; p492), they have now spread to the surrounding buildings, and there are additional troops at Khao Luang (p492), Tham Khao Bandai-It and other forested places. There, they lurk by food stands, or eye-up passing pedestrians as potential mugging victims. These apes love plastic bags – regarding them as a signal that you're carrying food – and beverages, so be wary about displaying them. Keep a tight hold on camera bags, too. It's not just enough to heed the signs and don't feed or tease them, you should be on guard any time they are near. They do bite.

Phetchaburi (Phetburi)

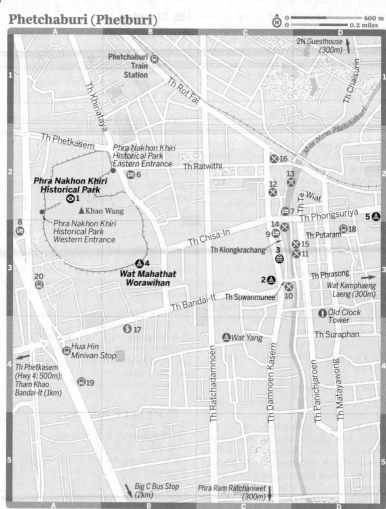

cottages, all with private bathrooms – the latter have cold showers. The pleasant owners can arrange Thai cooking classes, and bikes (50B) and scooters (300B) can be hired.

★ White Monkey Guesthouse
GUESTHOUSE $$
(☏ 092 840 1633; whitemonkey.guesthouse@gmail.com; 78/7 Th Klongkrachang; tw/d/f 500-650/900/1500; P❋@❋) Excellent guesthouse with bright, spacious, spick-and-span rooms (the cheapest with shared bathrooms and no air-con) and a great location. There's views of Phra Nakhon Khiri Historical Park

(p492) and Wat Mahathat Worawihan (p492) from the rooftop terrace and helpful English-speaking staff who can organise trips in the area. Bikes are free.

Sun Hotel
HOTEL $$
(☏ 032 401000; www.sunhotelthailand.com; Th Rim Khao Wang; r incl breakfast 850-950B; P❋@❋) Sitting opposite the cable car entrance to Phra Nakhon Khiri Historical Park (p492), the Sun Hotel has helpful staff and large, uninspiring rooms that are fine, but should be a little cheaper. There's a pleasant cafe downstairs and bikes are free.

Phetchaburi (Phetburi)

HUA HIN & THE UPPER GULF PHETCHABURI

While the location might sound good, it's actually pretty isolated from everything except the historical park.

✖ Eating

Surrounded by palm-sugar plantations, Phetchaburi is famous for its sweet concoctions, including *kà·nŏm môr gaang* (egg custard) and various 'golden' desserts made from egg yolks and sugar. They're sold in most markets, as is the raw sugar.

Nearby fruit orchards produce refreshingly aromatic *chom·pôo phet* (Phetchaburi rose apple – the fruit that adorns many street signs), pineapples and *nám wáh* bananas.

Rabieng Rimnam THAI, INTERNATIONAL $
(☏ 032 425707; rabieng@gmail.com; 1 Th Chisa-In; mains 50-120B; ⊙ 8am-midnight; 🛜) This riverside restaurant serves up a real bygone-days atmosphere from an 1897 wooden home perched over the river and usually some good food, too – try the sugar palm tree fruit curry with prawn. English-speaking owners Nid and Tom will often join you for a chat about Thailand and share their decades of travel advice.

Talat Taa Rot Tua MARKET $
(Th Ratwithi; ⊙ 4-9pm) Big and bustling from the late afternoon, head to this covered night market for all the standard Thai favourites plus Phetchaburi's famous *kà·nŏm jeen tôrt man* (fresh rice noodles with curried deep-fried fishcake). There's lots of seating available.

Cucina THAI $
(Th Suwanmunee; mains 50-390B; ⊙ 10.30am-9pm; 🛜✏) Hidden down a little passageway

in front of Wat Mahathat (p492), this small restaurant has a big menu ranging from green curry fried rice to chicken teriyaki to waffle sandwiches. There's a few fun fusion foods like the *đôm yam* fish salad and 'cucina pizza', which is pizza with instant noodles as the crust.

Phetchaburi Walking Street MARKET $
(Th Chaisurin; ⊙ 4-9pm Sat) Unlike a typical walking street market, almost every vendor here is selling food and you can easily snack yourself full.

Kow Chae Mae Awn THAI $
(ข้าวแช่แม่อร; Th Panichjaroen; 15B; ⊙ 9am-4pm; ✏) Mae Awn sells her famous *kôw châe* (moist chilled rice) with a choice of fish, shrimp or pickled daikon radish along the walkway at the southeast corner of the **Rim Nam Market** (⊙ 5-11am). She has just two tables, but does a brisk take-away business.

Ney & Neyn THAI $
(Th Damnoen Kasem; mains 30-120B; ⊙ 8am-4pm) Great soups served in clay bowls are the signature dishes at this casual place. The *gŏo·ay đĕe·o gài* (chicken noodles) comes southern style with a whole chicken drumstick. There's no English sign, but just look for the stacks of clay bowls.

ℹ Information

There's no formal information source in town, but the guesthouses can provide up-to-date travel tips. The **Tourism Authority of Thailand's office in Cha-am** (TAT; ☏ 032 471005; tatphet@tat.or.th; Th Phetkasem; ⊙ 8.30am-4.30pm) handles all of Phetchaburi Province.

Kasikorn Bank (Th Bandai-It; ⏱11am-7pm) at Phetpaiboon Plaza shopping centre is the nearest extended hours bank to the city centre.

ⓘ Getting There & Away

The train is usually the most convenient and comfortable way to travel, and Phetchaburi's **train station** (☏ 032 425211; Th Rot Fai) is within walking distance of most guesthouses.

There are no longer any buses to Bangkok originating or finishing in Phetchaburi, only minivans. These use the new **Wat Tham Kaew Minivan Station** (Th Bandai-It; sà·tǎh·nee bor kǒr sǒr wát tâm gâaou), as do minibuses to Kaeng Krachan National Park. Most guesthouses can call to have the Kaeng Krachan minivans pick you up at their door for an extra 50B per person.

Minivans to Hua Hin, Cha-am and Prachuap Khiri Khan are 500m south of the minivan station on the side of the road next to Phetcharat Hospital and they also pick up further south in front of the Big C shopping centre. Some long-distance buses passing through town (going both north and south) will also stop by Big C, but if you want to try it, be prepared for a long wait. For Chumphon and southern cities, there's a small **southern bus stop** (Phetkasem Hwy) 300m south of the hospital. Another option is to Hua Hin and Cha-am are the **ordinary buses** that depart from the town centre next to Wat Potaram.

ⓘ Getting Around

Motorcycle taxis go anywhere in the town centre for 20B to 40B. Phetchaburi's four-wheel túk-túk (locally called rót léng) cost just a little more. You can also hire them for the day for about 700B to 800B.

All the guesthouses hire out bicycles (50B per day) and motorbikes (150B to 250B); Rabieng Rimnam (p495) charges the least. Reserve a motorcycle when you reserve a room because many guesthouses get them from outside sources and you may have to wait a while to get one if you just ask at the desk.

Kaeng Krachan National Park
อุทยานแห่งชาติแก่งกระจาน

Wake to an eerie symphony of gibbon calls as the early-morning mist floats through the forest canopy, and then hike through lush forests in search of elephant herds and other wildlife. Thailand's largest (2915 sq km) national park is surprisingly close to civilisation but shelters an intense tangle of wilderness that sees relatively few tourists.

Despite the park having a poaching problem, animal life includes wild elephants, tigers, leopards, tapir, gaur (wild cattle), white-handed gibbons, dusky langurs and black giant squirrels. This park also occupies an interesting, overlapping biozone for birds as the southernmost spot for northern species and the northernmost for southern species. The result is a bird list that exceeds 400 species, including blue pitta, ratchet-tailed

TRANSPORT TO/FROM PHETCHABURI

DESTINATION	BUS	MINIVAN	TRAIN
Bangkok Hualamphong	N/A	N/A	34-388B, 3-3½hr, 12 daily
Bangkok Southern & Northern (Mo Chit) Bus Terminals	N/A	100B, 2hr, frequent 3.30am-7.30pm	N/A
Bangkok Thonburi	N/A	N/A	31B, 4hr, 7.16am, 12.56pm
Cha-am	30B, 1hr, hourly 5.40am-4.30pm (from Wat Potaram)	50B, 45min, frequent 5am-6.20pm	8-38B, 40min, 5 daily
Chumphon	328-500B, 6hr, hourly 6.30am-8pm, frequent 8-10pm	N/A	58-455B, 5½-6½hr, 11 daily
Hua Hin	40B, 1½hr, hourly 5.40am-4.30pm (from Wat Potaram)	80B, 1hr, frequent 5am-6.20pm	14-341B, 1hr, 12 daily
Kaeng Krachan National Park	N/A	120B, 1hr, hourly 7.30am-6.30pm	N/A
Prachuap Khiri Khan	150-200B, 2½hr, hourly 6.30am-8pm, frequent 8-10pm	150B, 2½hr, every 40min 5am-6.20pm	31-382B, 2-3hr, 11 daily

treepie, banded broadbill, great slaty wood-pecker and great hornbill.

The park, except for the scenic reservoir by the headquarters and **Pa La-U Waterfall** (น้ำตกป่าละอู; ⊙8am-5pm), closes to the public from August to October. The best, and also busiest, months to visit are between November and March, though only weekends and holidays see crowds. Independent visits without a vehicle are possible, though take some patience, and 4WD is required for some parts.

⊙ Sights & Activities

There are two main spots to visit in the heart of the park. The wildlife-rich **Ban Krang** area has a nice 2.5km nature trail and is really good for birdwatchers. It's another 15km up a 4WD-only road to Panoen Thung Viewpoint. The park's **visitor centre** (☑032 772311; Rte 3432; ⊙8am-4pm) at the main entrance, next to the photogenic **Kaeng Krachan Reservoir**, is a one-stop shop for park information and assistance.

In particular, this is where you hire drivers to go up into the park proper. Some staff speak English.

★**Panoen Thung Viewpoint**   VIEWPOINT
(จุดชมวิวพะเนินทุ่ง) Up at the end of the 4WD-only road, Panoen Thung is refreshingly cool at 960m above sea level. Most visitors are here to see the fantastic mountain overlooks that are ideal for the early-morning 'sea of fog' (*tá·lair mòrk*) views. They can happen year-round, but are most common in the November to March cool season. If you're coming up in the morning, you'll need to leave headquarters at 5.30am to arrive in time to see it.

Also here is a 4km trail to **Nam Tok Tho Thip**, a nine-tiered waterfall, though you can only see five of them and you need to do the walk with a ranger.

🛏 Sleeping & Eating

There are simple **bungalows** (☑032 772311; http://nps.dnp.go.th/reservation.php; Kaeng Krachan National Park; bungalows 1200-3000B) and a **campsite** (per person with tent/tent hire 30/200-300B; 🅿) by the reservoir at the entrance to the park, though you won't see much wildlife here other than birds.

There are also campsites deep in the forest at **Ban Krang** (per person with tent/tent hire 30/200-300B; 🅿) and **Panoen Thung** (per person with tent/tent hire 30/200-300B; 🅿), and

in the far south near **Pa La-U** (per person with tent/tent hire 30/200-300B; 🅿) waterfall. Camping equipment can be hired at each. The bungalows at Pa La-U are undergoing renovations.

There's a fast food noodle and rice restaurant at each of the campsites. Those up on the mountain (Ban Krang and Panoen Thung) generally serve from 8am to 6pm, though it will depend on the number of customers. Those at the headquarters and Pa La-U waterfall normally close at 4pm. There are also restaurants just outside the park entrance if you want a little more choice.

🛈 Getting There & Away

Kaeng Krachan is 52km southwest of Phetchaburi and 68km from Hua Hin. Tours are available from both towns, though they're pretty infrequent, especially from Phetchaburi, unless you pay for a private trip.

You can reach the headquarters by minivan from Phetchaburi and Bangkok, but in both cases be sure the driver knows you are going to Kaeng Krachan National Park and not just Kaeng Krachan town. In Petchaburi minivans leave hourly between 7.30am and 6.30pm and cost 120B; for an extra 50B per person, your guesthouse can have the van pick you up.

In Bangkok, minivans leave from the old Southern Bus Terminal (*sǎi đâi gòw*) hourly between 9am and 5pm for 250B and take 3½ hours hours. If you're travelling from Hua Hin, you can go to Tha Yang by a north-bound minivan and catch a Kaeng Krachan minivan (assuming seats are available) there instead of going all the way to Phetchaburi.

🛈 Getting Around

There's one road through the main section of the park. Regular cars can drive 35km up to the Ban Krang Campsite, but beyond this the road requires 4WD. There's no public transport and motorcycles and bicycles are not allowed (except for Pa La-U Waterfall) because of the danger of wild animals. Hitching requires patience.

There are drivers with 4WD trucks at headquarters and Bang Krang. The round-trip cost per truck (up to 10 people) per day from the visitor centre to Ban Krang Campsite is 1200B and it's 1600B to Panoen Thung Campsite; add 200B if you spend the night and come back the next morning. You can often, but not always, find other people at headquarters to share the costs. The road is so narrow that there are scheduled times for going up and going down. Vehicles can begin driving up from 5.30am to 7.30am and 1pm to 3pm, and begin the drive down from 9am to 10am and 4pm to 5pm.

Cha-am
ชะอำ

☑ 032 / POP 35,600

Cheap and cheerful, Cha-am is a popular beach getaway for working-class families and Bangkok students. On weekends and public holidays, neon-painted buses (called *chìng·chàp tua*), their sound systems pumping, deliver groups of holidaymakers. It's a very Thai-style beach party, with eating and drinking marathons held around umbrella-shaded beach chairs and tables. Entertainment is provided by the banana boats that zip back and forth, eventually making a final jack-knife turn that throws the passengers into the sea.

Cha-am doesn't see many foreigners: visitors are usually older Europeans who winter here instead of more expensive Hua Hin. Like Hua Hin, the shallow sea is better for strolling and sunbathing than swimming, but unlike its southern neighbour, there isn't much else to do here beyond the beach and the gibbon-filled **forest park** (วนอุทยาน ชะอำ; Phetkasem Hwy; ⊙ daylight hours). That said, the seafood is superb, the weekend people-watching entertaining and the prices are some of the most affordable anywhere on the coast.

✪ Festivals & Events

Gin Hoy, Do Nok, Tak Meuk　FOOD & DRINK
(⊙ Sep) You really can do it all at this annual festival held in September. The festival's English name is 'Shellfish Eating, Bird Watching & Squid Catching' and is a catchy slogan for some of Cha-am's local attractions and traditions. Mainly it's a food festival showcasing a variety of seafood, but there are also bird-watching events at nearby sanctuaries and nightly concerts.

Thailand International Kite Festival　ART
(⊙ Mar) Most years, but not every, artistic kites from around the world take to the skies over the beach for a long weekend.

🛏 Sleeping

Cheap, charmless guesthouses in narrow concrete shophouses near the beach remain Cha-am's bread and butter. Avoid staying on seedy Soi Bus Station unless you're not planning to sleep much. Expect significant weekday discounts.

Pa Ka Ma　GUESTHOUSE $$
(☑ 032 433504; Soi Cay-ben Tee-wee; r 1000B; ❄ 🛜) Probably the best low-cost guesthouse

in Cha-am, and only a little more expensive than the average. It's attractively designed – each room has its own individual style and the rooms at the back have little balconies. The bathrooms are good too, though hot water can take a long time to arrive. Not much English is spoken.

It's on an unsigned soi between Sois 1 and 2 North. There are a few other good choices nearby if it's full.

Cha Inn @ Cha-Am　HOTEL $$
(☑ 032 471879; www.chainn-chaam.com; 274/34 Th Ruamjit; r incl breakfast 1200-2000B; P ❄ 🛜) The owners have creatively and beautifully adapted this old building into a stylish hotel that's refreshingly out of the ordinary for Cha-am. There's a restaurant on the ground floor and an airy lounge up above. And then there are the 17 rooms; large, comfortable and full of the same subtle design found in the public areas.

Dream Boutique Hotel　HOTEL $$
(☑ 032 470896; 235/35 Soi Anatachai; d 800-1200, f 1800B; ❄ @ 🛜) There's nothing boutique about it, but the misnomer is the only knock on a very well-run, impeccably clean hotel. Rooms aren't fancy, but they're fully kitted out and have balconies, plus guests can lounge on the roof. There's bike and motorcycle hire and you'll get picked up when you arrive in town.

It lies between Sois 1 and 2 South, which is actually the third soi south of Th Narathip.

Bann Pantai Resort　HOTEL $$$
(☑ 032 470155; www.bannpantai.com; Th Ruamjit; r incl breakfast 4000-6000B; P ❄ 🛜 ≋) Rather more upmarket than most hotels in Cha-am, this beautiful, family-friendly place has a huge pool and small fitness centre, and the beach is just across the road.

Rooms are big with great beds and terraces in front.

🍴 Eating & Drinking

From your deckchair you can wave down vendors selling plastic-wrapped meals, or order from the many nearby beachfront restaurants and they'll deliver.

The top seafood restaurants are found at the far northern end of the beach by the fishing pier.

The main expat enclave, full of cold beer, pool tables, TV sports, massage and *masaaaage,* is Soi Bus Station, the first street south of Th Narathip. You can also follow the lead of some Thai visitors and just stay in your beach chair with a bottle, even after the sun goes down.

Khrua Rua Makham
THAI **$$**

(Th Ruamjit; mains 60-420B; ⏱7am-7pm Sun-Thu, 7am-8pm Fri & Sat; 🛜) This alfresco restaurant serves mostly a regular Thai menu such as garlic fried chicken, green curry and the like. But there's also a good seafood selection, with grilled squid being a local speciality. The food probably won't wow you, but it won't let you down either.

Krua Medsai Seafood
THAI **$$**

(Off Th Ruamjit; mains 40-450B; ⏱10am-10pm) Massive Medsai is one of dozens of seafood spots next to Cha-am's fishing port. While some of the smaller restaurants out here have more character, few others can offer this big a selection or provide a properly translated English menu.

ℹ️ Information

Phetkasem Hwy runs through Cha-am's busy town centre, which is about 1km away from the beach via Th Narathip. This is where you'll find banks, the fresh market, the train station and most bus stops.

There are plenty of ATMs and a few extended-hours exchange booths along Th Ruamjit.

ℹ️ Getting There & Away

There's a little minivan station for **Hua Hin-Pran Tour** (☑ 032 511654; Th Sasong) at the Soi Bus Station with departures to Bangkok (Southern and Mo Chit terminals) every half-hour from 7am to 5.30pm. All other public road transport stops on Phetkasem Hwy at the intersection with Th Narathip. Mostly it's minivans, since very few buses from Hua Hin or other southern towns stop to pick up passengers in Cha-am. The **Airport Hua Hin Bus** (☑ 084 697 3773; www.airporthuahin-bus.com; Th Phetkasem, next to Hua Hin Airport) from Hua Hin to Bangkok's Suvarnabhumi Airport stops specifically in front of the Government Savings Bank while Shinnakeart Korat, with buses to Bangkok, Nakhon Ratchasim (328B, eight hours, 10.30am, 9.30pm) and Ubon Ratchathani (609B, 15 hours, 6.30pm), are also here.

The **train station** (☑ 032 471159; Th Narathip) is west of Phetkasem Hwy at the end of Th Narathip and is not served by any express trains. Note that Cha-am is listed in the timetable as 'Ban Cha-am'.

You can hire a taxi (any private car available for hire) along the beach. The fare is 500B to Hua Hin.

ℹ️ Getting Around

From the city centre to the beach it's a quick motorcycle (40B) or taxi (100B) ride.

You can hire bicycles (100B per day) and motorcycles (200B to 250B) all along Th Ruamjit.

TRANSPORT TO/FROM CHA-AM

DESTINATION	BUS	MINIVAN	TRAIN
Bangkok Don Mueang International Airport	N/A	180B, 4hr, every 40min 6.30am-6.30pm	N/A
Bangkok Hualamphong	N/A	N/A	40-143B, 4-4½hr, 1.40am, 4.55am, 2.33pm
Bangkok Southern and & Northern (Mo Chit) Bus Terminals	241B, 4½hr, 9.30am, 12.30pm, 2.40pm, 5.30pm	160B, 3½hr, frequent 4.30am-7.30pm	N/A
Bangkok Suvarnabhumi International Airport	269B, 4hr, every 90min 6.20am-6.20pm	N/A	N/A
Bangkok Thonburi	N/A	N/A	38B, 4hr, 6.41am, 12.13pm
Hua Hin	20B, 30min, hourly 6.30am-5.30pm	30B, 30min, frequent 6am-7.30pm	6-33B, 30min, 5 daily
Kanchanaburi	N/A	200B, 3½hr, hourly 6.40am-5.40pm	N/A
Phetchaburi	30B, 1hr, hourly 6.30am-4.30pm	50B, 45min, frequent 6am-7.30pm	8-38B, 40min, 5 daily

Hua Hin
หัวหิน

☑ 032 / POP 59,369

Thailand's original beach resort is no palm-fringed castaway island and arguably is the better for it. Instead, it's a refreshing mix of city and sea with an almost cosmopolitan ambience, lively markets, good golf courses and water parks, international cuisine and excellent accommodation. In fact, many visitors never even step foot on the sand.

Hua Hin traces its aristocratic roots to 1911 when the railroad arrived from Bangkok and some in the royal family built vacation homes here. By the mid-1920s it was a full-fledged resort town for the Bangkok-based nobility with a golf course and a seaside hotel featuring a European restaurant manager. Even Kings Rama VI and VII built summer palaces here. The latter's **Phra Ratchawang Klai Kangwon** (พระราชวังไกลกังวล; Th Phetkasem; Far from Worries Palace) remains a royal residence today and was the full-time home of King Rama IX for many of his later years.

There's a lot of money swirling around Hua Hin, but it's still a good budget destination: seafood is plentiful and cheap, there's convenient public transport and it takes a lot less time and effort to get here from Bangkok than to the southern islands.

◉ Sights

A former fishing village, Hua Hin's old town retains links to its past with an old teak shophouse district bisected by narrow winding sois, fronted by pier houses that hold restaurants and guesthouses, and punctuated with a busy fishing pier still in use today. Along the shore beyond, especially to the north, there are still many historic wooden summer residences.

Hua Hin Beach (หาดหัวหิน) is a pleasant but not stunning stretch of fine white powder lapped by calm grey-green waves, made for strolling and sunbathing, not swimming. Watch out for jellyfish, especially in the wet season.

★ Cicada Market
MARKET

(ตลาดจั๊กจั่น; ☑ 080 650 4334; www.cicadamarket. com; Soi Hua Thanon 23, Th Phetkasem, South Hua Hin; ☺ 4-11pm Fri-Sun) FREE Vastly better than the city-centre Hua Hin Night Market (p506), this popular place 3.5km to the south is a fun mix of food, shopping and performing arts. It's not a high-sell environment, rather it's a very relaxed shopping experience. Many artists come to sell their handmade home decor and clothes, and there's food from Thailand and beyond. Live entertainment hits the stage from 8.30pm and there are buskers all around.

The last green *sǒrng·tǎa·ou* back to the city passes about 9pm.

Mrigadayavan Palace
HISTORIC BUILDING

(พระราชนิเวศน์มฤคทายวัน; ☑ 032 508443; www. mrigadayavan.or.th; 30B; ☺ 8.30am-4.30pm Thu-Tue, last tickets sold at 4pm) With a breezy seaside location 12km north of Hua Hin, this summer palace – Phra Ratchaniwet

---

WORTH A TRIP

BEACH-HOPPING NEAR HUA HIN

South of Hua Hin are a series of beaches framed by dramatic headlands that make great day trips when Hua Hin beach feels too urban.

Khao Tao (Turtle Mountain) protects an idyllic little cove where **Hat Sai Noi Beach** drops off quickly into the sea, providing a rare opportunity for deep-water swimming. A small resort (p504) and a couple of restaurants operate here and while weekends bring the expected crowds, it's quiet on weekdays – if you're lucky you could have it all to yourself.

Wat Tham Khao Tao, on the north side of the hill, has quite a bit of Buddhist and other statuary in a concrete 'cave' in front of a small real cave. Keep walking further back to see even more colourful shrines and climb stairs up to the Buddha on the hill. If you're walking or on a motorcycle just follow the base of the hill from the beach to the temple, but if you're driving a car you need to go the long way around the reservoir.

To get to the beach, take a Pranburi-bound bus from Hua Hin and ask to be dropped off at Ban Tao village (20B). From here a motorbike taxi (there aren't many, so you might have to wait a while) can take you to the beach (30B). Take the driver's phone number for getting back. Hitching would be very difficult.

Hua Hin

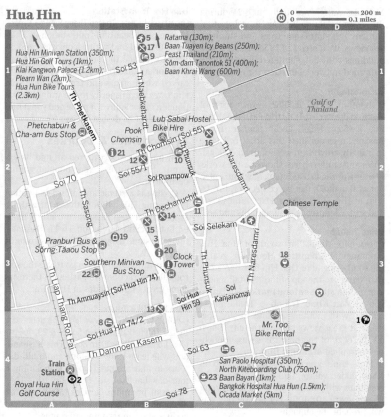

HUA HIN & THE UPPER GULF HUA HIN

Mrigadayavan – was built in 1924 during the reign of Rama VI. Set in a beautiful garden with statuesque trees and stunning sea views, it's a series of 18 interlinked teak buildings with tall, shuttered windows and patterned fretwork built upon stilts.

Baan Silapin GALLERY
(บ้านศิลปิน; ☏ 086 1620162; www.huahinartist village.wordpress.com; Th Hua Hin-Pa Lu-U; ⊙ 10am-5pm Tue-Sun) FREE Local painter Tawee Kasangam established this artist collective in a shady grove 4km west of town. The galleries and studio spaces showcase the works of over a dozen artists, many of whom opted out of Bangkok's fast-paced art world in favour of Hua Hin's more relaxed atmosphere and scenic landscape of mountains and sea.

Khao Takiab HILL
(เขาตะเกียบ) About 7km south of Hua Hin, monumental Chopstick Mountain guards the southern end of Hua Hin beach. A steep road curves to the top of the 77m-tall mountain, passing the **seafood market**, and takes you to **Wat Khao Takiab**, a Thai-Chinese temple with nothing architecturally special, but great views back to the city. Down on the edge of the beach is a large, much-photographed **standing Buddha**.

Hua Hin's green *sŏrng·tăa·ou* stop in Khao Takiab village, 1km away, but you can negotiate with the drivers to go to the temple; an extra 50B-100B per person one-way will probably be enough.

Hua Hin Train Station HISTORIC SITE
(สถานีรถไฟหัวหิน; Th Liap Thang Rot Fai) Probably the most beautiful train station in Thailand, this red-and-white icon was built in 1926 to replace the original station. It has a Victorian gingerbread design with lots of carved wood pillars and trim. Because Hua Hin owes its prosperity to the train, the station is a major source of pride and you'll find imitations of its design all over town.

🏃 Activities & Courses

With nine courses scattered around its environs, Hua Hin is a very popular golfing destination.

Cycling is a scenic and affordable option for touring Hua Hin's outlying attractions, especially on weekdays when traffic is lighter. But be extra careful on Th Phetkasem – there are some truly terrible drivers going at high speeds.

Tours are a good way to go to see the surrounding attractions. In particular, there are some great biking guides in Hua Hin.

Hua Hin Bike Tours CYCLING
(☏ 081 173 4469; www.huahinbiketours.com; 15/120 Th Phetkasem, btwn Soi 27 & 29; full-day tours from 2950B; ⊙ 10am-8pm) This husband-and-wife team leads day-long and multi-day tours in and around Hua Hin, including a four-day Bangkok to Hua Hin trip. They also rent premium bicycles (500B per day, discount for longer rentals) for independent cyclists and can recommend routes.

DON'T MISS

ELEPHANT REFUGE

You don't have to spend long in Thailand to understand how little regard is given towards animal welfare. One of the most active groups trying to improve the situation, the Wildlife Friends Foundation Thailand, runs a **wildlife rescue centre** (มูลนิธิเพื่อนสัตว์ป่า; ☏ 032 458135; www.wfft.org; full-access tours incl lunch half-/full-day 1100/1800B) 🦮, 45km west of Hua Hin, that adopts and cares for abused, injured and abandoned animals that cannot be released back into the wild.

The centre cares for over 500 animals, including bears, tigers, gibbons, macaques, loris and birds. There's also an affiliated elephant rescue program where the elephants live out their lives chain-free. A visit here is a great day out – far better than the elephant and tiger tourist traps featured on many tours out of Hua Hin. The centre offers full-access tours introducing animals and discussing rescue histories. The full-day option includes walking and bathing elephants. Drop-in visits are not allowed.

Hotel transfer from Hua Hin or Cha-am costs 200B per person and there's also a small lodge (4000B per night including meals) on-site. Those looking for a more in-depth experience can **volunteer** (☏ 032 458135; www.wildlifevolunteer.org) 🦮 at the centre.

They also lead the long-distance **Tour de Thailand** (www.tourdethailand.com) charity bike tours across Thailand.

North Kiteboarding Club　　KITESURFING
(☑083 438 3833; www.northkiteboardingclub.com; 113/5 Th Phetkasem, at Soi 67, South Hua Hin; 3-day beginner course 11,000B; ☉9am-9pm) Based in Hua Hin, but with outlets in Chumpon and Phuket, this is a well-established company offering lessons and a large store.

Hua Hin Golf Centre　　GOLF
(☑032 530476; www.huahingolf.com; Th Selakam; ☉noon-8.30pm) The friendly staff at this pro shop run by **Hua Hin Golf Tours** (☑032 530119; Soi 41; ☉6.30am-10pm), can steer you to the most affordable, well-maintained courses where the monkeys won't try to run off with your balls.

This company organises golf tours and rents sets of quality clubs (500B to 700B per day) to their customers.

Thai Massage by the Blind　　MASSAGE
(☑081 944 2174; The Naebkenhardt; Thai massage 200B; ☉7am-9pm) Traditional head, foot and body massages by blind masseuses, plus some other treatments like herbal wraps. There are two other locations further out from the city centre.

Thai Cooking Course Hua Hin　　COOKING
(☑081 572 3805; www.thai-cookingcourse.com; Soi 19, Th Phetkasem; courses 1500B) Aspiring chefs should sign up for a one-day cooking class here that includes a market visit, making five dishes and a recipe book to take home. The course runs only if there are a minimum of three people and hotel pick-up is provided.

🕝 Tours

Feast Thailand　　FOOD
(☑095 461 0557, 032 510207; www.feastthailand. com; Th Naebkehardt, inside Raruk Hua Hin market; from 1350B; ☉8.30am-4pm Mon-Sat) A small company with highly regarded half-day food tours. You pick your tour – either sample Thai cuisine basics or dive into some less-common foods – and they pick you up at your hotel. Join-in tours are sometimes available.

Hua Hin Adventure Tour　　ADVENTURE
(☑032 530314; www.huahinadventuretour.com; Th Naebkehardt; ☉9am-6pm Mon-Sat) Hua Hin Adventure Tour offer active excursions, including kayaking trips in the Khao Sam Roi Yot

National Park (p510) and wildlife watching in Kaeng Krachan National Park (p496).

⚑ Festivals & Events

Hua Hin Jazz Festival　　MUSIC
In honour of King Rama IX's personal interest in the genre, the city that hosts royal getaways also hosts an annual jazz festival featuring Thai and international performers. All events are free. It takes place in a new month each year and the dates are usually not announced very far in advance.

🛏 Sleeping

The city's character suddenly becomes more local and less boisterous north of Th Chomsin. Focused on Th Naebkehardt and Soi 51, this is the neighbourhood of choice for Bangkok's trendy youth.

If sun and surf are your main reasons for coming here, stay south where the beach is fairly quiet and mostly tout-free.

Chanchala Hostel　　HOSTEL $
(☑086 331 6763; www.chanchalahostelhuahin. com; 1/5 Th Sasong; dm incl breakfast 340B; ❄🎧) This spick and span three-room dorm five minutes walk from the train station does things right. Each bed in the six- and eight-bed rooms (one for women only) comes with its own locker, reading light and power outlet. Guests mingle with the friendly staff in the coffee shop and with each other at the rooftop lounge.

★King's Home　　GUESTHOUSE $$
(☑089 052 0490; www.huahinkingshome.blog-spot.com; off Th Phunsuk; r 750-950B; ❄🎧⛱) Family-run guesthouse with great prices and loads of character – you're greeted at the front door by a crystal chandelier and a statue of a German Shepherd wearing a floral lei on its head. The rest of the house, including the six small guestrooms, are also crammed with antiques and kitsch providing a real homely atmosphere.

Big Apple　　GUESTHOUSE $$
(☑089 686 1271; www.bigapplehuahin.com; Soi Hua Hin 83, Th Phetkasem, South Hua Hin; r/apt 1200/1800B; 🅿❄🎧⛱) This small, immaculate guesthouse (or Bed & Pool, as they call it) is in a soi between the beach and the massive Bluport shopping mall. There are five regular rooms and three apartments with small kitchens next to a playful garden with a big swimming pool. Book well in advance

during the high season. There's a two-night minimum stay.

Hua Hin Place
GUESTHOUSE $$

(☑ 032 516640; www.huahin-place.com; 43/21 Th Naebkehardt; d & tw 400-1500 f 1200-1500B; ❄ 🤖) Straddling a fine line between hotel and guesthouse, this fairly large place still falls into the latter thanks to the breezy ground-floor lounge – full of a museum's worth of shells, photos and other knick-knacks – where you can chat with the charming owner and other guests.

Love Sea House
GUESTHOUSE $$

(☑ 080 079 0922; siamozohlie@hotmail.com; 35 Th Dechanuchit; r 700-800B; ❄ 🤖) Pleasant, family-run guesthouse decked out in a blue-and-white nautical theme. The English-speaking elderly owners keep the good-sized rooms impressively clean. It's very near Hua Hin's party zone, but it's not an appropriate place for those planning to partake in it.

Baan Somboon
GUESTHOUSE $$

(☑ 032 511538; 13/4 Soi Hua Hin 63, Th Damnoen Kasem; r 800B; ❄🤖) With framed photos decorating the walls, polished wooden floors and a compact garden, this place on a very quiet centrally located soi is like staying at your favourite Thai auntie's house. Rooms are small and dated, but it's probably the homiest guesthouse in Hua Hin.

★ Centara Grand Beach Resort & Villas
HOTEL $$$

(☑ 032 512021; www.centarahotelsresorts.com; 1 Th Damnoen Kasem; r incl breakfast 8700-14,000B; P ❄ @ 🤖 🏊) The historic Railway Hotel opened in 1922 and was Hua Hin's first hotel. It's been updated and expanded over the decades, but hasn't lost its genteel aura – no other local resort can match the ambience here. The rooms are large, the facilities fantastic and the staff on the ball, plus the vast gardens are full of frangipani and trimmed topiary.

★ Sanae Beach Club
HOTEL $$$

(☑ 032 900971; www.sanaebeachclub.com; Hat Sai Noi; r incl breakfast 3700-4700B; P ❄ 🤖 🏊) The main thing about this small resort is that it's the only lodging right on gorgeous Hat Sai Noi (p500). The beach is nearly deserted on weekdays though it's very busy on weekends, and their 300B daily access pass means it's not just the beach that gets busy.

Rooms are large and comfortable, although the all-white interior is a bit jarring.

★ Baan Bayan
HOTEL $$$

(☑ 032 533540; www.beachfronthotelhuahin.com; Th Phetkasem, at Soi 69, South Hua Hin; r incl breakfast 4000-13,000B; P ❄ 🤖 🏊) Centred on a beautiful teak house built in the early 20th century, Baan Bayan is perfect for travellers seeking a luxury experience without big resort overkill. The hotel is airy, with high-ceilinged rooms and attentive staff, and the location is absolute beachfront. Most of the rooms were added in modern times but share the same historic quality as the three originals.

✖ Eating

Hua Hin is famous for its seafood, but locals prefer the simple restaurants in Ban Takiab south of the city, some of which do 400B buffets.

★ Baan Khrai Wang
THAI, COFFEE $

(Th Naebkehardt; mains 65-285B; ⊙9am-6pm) The palm trees, flower garden, historic wooden beach homes and the sound of the surf make the setting at 'The House Near the Palace' pretty much perfect. For many, it's a place to lounge with coffee and coconut cake, but there's also a small menu of massaman curry, crab fried rice, *kôw châe* and Caesar salad wrap.

★ Jek Pia
THAI $

(51/6 Th Dechanuchit; mains 35-150B; ⊙6.30am-12.30pm & 5.30-8pm) Once just a coffee shop, this 50-plus-year-old restaurant is one of Hua Hin's top culinary destinations. The late mother of the current owner invited her favourite cooks to come join her and it's now a gourmet food court of sorts, hence the stack of menus you get when you arrive.

★ Sôm·dam Tanontok 51
THAI $

(Th Damrongraj/Soi 51; mains 40-190B; ⊙10am-8pm; 🤖) A stand-out restaurant in a great dining neighbourhood, this is real Isan food (p414) cooked by a family from Khorat. There's everything you'd expect to find including grilled catfish, *gaang orm* (coconut-milk-less herbal curry) and many versions of *sôm·dam* other than papaya, including cucumber and bamboo shoot. It also does a squid *lâhp*.

KITE CRAZY

Hua Hin is Thailand's kiteboarding capital, blessed with strong, gusty winds, shallow water and a long, long beach off which to practise your moves. Hua Hin even hosted the Kiteboarding World Cup in 2010.

From here down to Pranburi the winds blow from the northeast October to December, usually with lots of waves, and then from the southeast January to May usually with smooth water. Even during the rainy months in between there are plenty of days when the wind is fine for taking to the waves.

This is also one of the best places in Thailand to *learn* how to kiteboard, with a number of schools in Hua Hin offering lessons. Generally after three days with them you can be out on your own. January to March is the best time since the sea is less choppy. The schools also cater for more advanced students, and you can qualify as an instructor here.

Hua Hin Vegan Cafe
VEGAN, THAI $

(Th Phetkasem; mains 100-250B; ⊙9.30am-9pm; 🛜🖋) 🖉 Except for the lack of animal products, this modern place has nothing in common with the typical Thai 'jae' vegan restaurant: there's wine, garlic, air-con, jazz, organic ingredients and creative cooking. There's lots of Thai – traditional and otherwise (quinoa *lâhp,* for example), but the menu knows no borders: pulled jackfruit teriyaki burgers, lentil tacos and West African peanut soup.

Chomsin-Naebkehardt Junction Street Food
STREET FOOD $

(cnr Th Chomsin & Th Naebkehardt; ⊙6am-midnight) These noted street-food spots are a three-for-one deal and though the setting is humble, there's some excellent Thai food here. The action starts early each morning on Th Naebkehardt about 50m south of Chomsin and gradually more street carts start serving both here and across the road at the junction. Both spots sit under roofs for comfortable daytime dining.

At about 5pm the *dtôo rûng lék* (Little Night Market) takes over Soi 55/1 until late. It adds a little Isan food to the mix.

Baan Tuayen Icy Beans
THAI $

(Th Naebkehardt; mains 55-145B; ⊙7am-10pm; 🛜) A hipster hang-out that draws the crowds with three different menus for breakfast, lunch and dinner. There are dishes such as green curry with braised pork, but as the name suggests, desserts are the real stars; try the ice cream with red-bean sauce or red-bean smoothies.

Velo Cafe
COFFEE $

(Th Naebkehardt; coffee from 50B; ⊙7.30am-5.30pm; 🛜) Coffeeshops are everywhere in Hua Hin, but few are as serious as this little one, which roasts its own beans. It also makes very good sandwiches.

★Ratama
THAI $$

(12/10 Th Naebkehardt; mains 50-200B; ⊙8.30am-3.30pm) This restaurant's menu runs Thai omelettes to spicy seafood curries to a great panang curry, but it's famous for duck served in many forms including a bowl of *gŏo·ay đĕe·o* noodle soup and a plate of fried beaks.

We also recommend trying the *súpêr đeen gài* (chicken-feet *đôm yam*), and if you ask they'll substitute duck feet.

The English-script sign is very hard to spot so look for the giant duck statue.

★Koti
CHINESE, THAI $$

(☏032 511252; 16/1 Th Dechanuchit; mains 40-400B; ⊙11am-10pm) This Thai-Chinese restaurant, opened in 1932, is a national culinary luminary. Thais adore the stir-fried oyster with flour and egg, while foreigners frequently aim for the *đôm yam gûng.* Everyone loves the *yam tá-lair* (spicy seafood salad) and classic green curry. Be prepared to wait for a table.

The Social Salad
INTERNATIONAL $$

(1/8 Th Chomsin; mains 85-280B; ⊙8am-10pm; 🛜🖋) 🖉 This simple but nicely decorated place attracts many repeat customers for its 190B make-your-own salads – choose from a long checklist of fresh organic ingredients. Anti-salad folks can choose from a few pastas or fish and chips. Ten percent of proceeds go to tree-planting programs.

🍷 Drinking & Nightlife

Drinking destinations in Hua Hin's tourist zone are virtually all stuck in a time warp of sports bars or hostess bars. Try the posh hotels if you want something more sophisticated.

White Lotus Sky Bar

BAR

(Th Naresdamri; beers from 200B; ☉6pm-midnight; 🛜) Up atop the Hilton Hotel, on the 17th floor, this classy lounge has inspiring views and refreshing breezes. And though it faces east, come early and you can watch an obstructed-view sunset. There's also a fancy Chinese restaurant here.

🛍 Shopping

Plearn Wan

MARKET

(เพลินวาน; ☑032 520311; www.plearnwan.com; Th Phetkasem btwn Soi 38 & Soi 40; ☉9am-9pm Sun-Thu, 9am-10pm Fri & Sat) One of Hua Hin's top destinations for Thai travellers, Plearn Wan ('Lose Yourself In The Past') is a retro-themed market with small stalls designed to resemble the old shophouses of Thai-Chinese neighbourhoods in Bangkok and Hua Hin. It's full of old photos, vintage furniture and Thais posing for photos.

Hua Hin Night Market

MARKET

(Th Dechanuchit; ☉5pm-midnight) An attraction that rivals the beach in popularity, Hua Hin's two-block-long night market is full of tourists every night. There's all the standard knock-off clothes and cheap souvenirs, plus dozens of very annoying restaurant hosts waving menus in your face from the middle of the road.

For what it's worth, Lung Ja seems to be the only restaurant here that Thai visitors eat at; locals don't eat here at all. The market's off-street section in the southeast, known as Chatsila, is mostly more of the same, but does has a few shops selling actual art.

ℹ Information

There are exchange booths open into the evening and ATMs all around the tourist centre, in particular on Th Naresdamri and Th Damnoen Kasen streets. For full service banking head to

---

> ### ℹ HUA HIN ONLINE
>
> **Hua Hin Today** (www.huahintoday.com) Expat-published newspaper. A paper version (50B) is printed monthly.
>
> **Tourism Hua Hin** (www.tourismhuahin.com) Decent coverage of the city and the outlying area.

Th Phetkaksem and for banks open evenings and weekends head to a shopping mall.

Bangkok Hospital Hua Hin (☑032 616800; www.bangkokhospital.com/huahin; Th Phetkasem at Soi 94) An outpost of the well-regarded national hospital chain in south Hua Hin.

Immigration Office (☑032 905111; Th Phetkasem, at Soi 100, South Hua Hin; ☉10am-6pm Mon-Fri) In the basement level of Bluport shopping mall. You can extend tourist visas here.

Municipal Tourist Information Office (☑032 611491; Th Naebkehardt; ☉9am-4.30pm Mon-Fri, 9am-5pm Sat & Sun) Has a good free map of the city and surrounding area and can answer basic questions.

San Paolo Hospital (☑032 532576; www.sanpaulo.co.th; 222 Th Phetkasem, South Hua Hin) A small private hospital south of town at Soi 86; it's a good option for ordinary illnesses and injuries.

Tourism Authority of Thailand (TAT; ☑032 513854; www.tourismthailand.org/hua-hin; 39/4 Th Phetkasem, at Soi 55; ☉8.30am-4.30pm) Staff here speak English and are quite helpful, though they rarely open on time.

Tourist Police (☑032 516219; Th Damnoen Kasem) At the eastern end of the street just before the beach.

ℹ Getting There & Away

The train is the most pleasant way to get to or leave Hua Hin, but minivan is the most popular. If you prefer to get between Hua Hin and Bangkok as quickly (as little as three hours) and comfortably as possible, private cars start at 1600B.

BOAT

Lomprayah (☑032 532761; www.lomprayah.com; Th Phetkasem; ☉8am-10pm) offers a bus-boat combination from Hua Hin to Ko Tao (1050B, six to nine hours), as well as to Ko Pha-Ngan (1300B, nine to 12 hours) and Ko Samui (1400B, 10 to 13 hours) with departures from its office at 8.30am and 11.30pm.

There's also now a **passenger ferry** (☑093 495 9499; www.royalferrygroup.com; Soi Ao Hua Don 3; economy/first-class/8-person VIP room 1250/1550/14,000B; ☉ departs Pattaya/Hua Hin 10am/1pm) between Hua Hin and Pattaya allowing you to skip Bangkok.

BUS & MINIVAN

Minivans going north (including Phetchaburi, Kanchanaburi and many destinations in Bangkok) use the new **Hua Hin Van Station** (Soi 51) while minivans (and the occasional bus) going south stop in the road next to the clock tower. Service runs frequently from about 6am to most places (4am for Bangkok and Phetchaburi) until the early evening.

The quiet little **Hua Hin Bus Station** (Th Phetkasem, at Soi 96) south of the city has a few buses (most going between Bangkok and the south don't come into town) to Bangkok, Chiang Mai, Nakhon Ratchasima (Khorat), Phuket and Ubon Ratchathani. Tickets should be bought a day in advance.

A more convenient place to get a bus to Bangkok (Southern Bus Terminal) is with Hua Hin-Pran Tour (p499) on Th Sasong near the night market, though the buses are old. Also, there's Airport Hua Hin Bus (p499) going from Hua Hin Airport to Bangkok's Suvarnabhumi International Airport and Pattaya. If you use this bus, they have a shuttle to your hotel for 100B, which is cheaper than what a túk-túk will charge to take you into town. The green sŏrng·tăa·ou don't go quite this far.

Ordinary (fan) buses go to Pranburi from Th Sasong by the night market and to Cha-am and Phetchaburi about hourly all day from Th Phetkasem across from the Esso petrol station.

ⓘ Getting Around

Green sŏrng·tăa·ou (10B) depart from the corner of Th Sasong and Th Dechanuchit, by the night market. They travel from 6am to 9pm along Th Phetkasem south to Khao Takiab (turning east

TRANSPORT TO/FROM HUA HIN

DESTINATION	BUS	MINIVAN	TRAIN
Bangkok Don Mueang International Airport	N/A	200B, 4½hr, every 40min	N/A
Bangkok Ekkamai (Eastern Bus Station)	N/A	180B, 4½hr, hourly	N/A
Bangkok Hualamphong	N/A	N/A	44-402B, 3½-4½hr, 12 daily
Bangkok Northern (Mo Chit) Bus Terminal	241B, 4½hr, 9am, noon, 1.30pm, 3pm	180B, 4hr, frequent	N/A
Bangkok Southern Bus Terminal	155B, 4½hr, 3am, 10am, noon daily & 4pm, 9pm Fri-Sat	180B, 4hr, frequent	N/A
Bangkok Suvarnabhumi International Airport	269B, 4½hr, every 90min 6am-6pm	N/A	N/A
Bangkok Thonburi	N/A	N/A	42-96B, 4½hr, 2 daily
Cha-am	20-30B, 30-45min, hourly 6am-4pm	30B, 30min, frequent	6-33B, 30min, 5 daily
Chiang Mai	735-980B, 13hr, 5.30pm, 6pm, 6.15pm	N/A	N/A
Chumphon	328B, 5hr, noon	N/A	49-423B, 4-5hr, 12 daily
Kanchanaburi	N/A	220B, 4hr, hourly	N/A
Nakhon Ratchasima (Khorat)	347-518B, 6-7hr, 10am, 6pm, 9pm, 11pm	N/A	N/A
Pattaya	389B, 5hr, 11am	N/A	N/A
Phetchaburi	40B, 1½hr, hourly 6am-4pm	80B, 1hr, frequent	14-341B, 1hr, 12 daily
Phuket	587-913B, 10-11hr, 10am, 12.30pm, 7pm, 8.30pm, 9pm, 10.30pm, midnight	N/A	N/A
Prachuap Khiri Khan	N/A	80B, 1½hr, frequent	19-353B, 1-1½hr, 11 daily
Pranburi	20B, 30min, every 30min 7am-3pm	30B, 30min, frequent	5-31B, 30min, 3 daily
Ubon Ratchathani	628-868B, 12-13hr, 6pm, 9pm, 11pm	N/A	N/A

on Th Damnoen Kasem on the way) and north to the airport.

Four-wheeled túk-túk fares start at a whopping 100B for short trips. Motorcycle taxis are much more reasonable (30B to 50B) for short hops.

Many shops around town hire motorcycles (200B to 250B per day) and a few have bicycles (100B to 200B per day). Damnoen Kasem, Naebkehardt and Chomsin streets have several shops each. Hua Hin Bike Tours (p502) and **Velo Thailand** (☑ 032 900392; www.velothailand. com; Th Phetkasem; ☉ 8am-6pm Sun-Thu, 8am-9pm Fri & Sat) rent top-of-the-line bikes.

There are roadside tables arranging taxis (any vehicle that you can charter, including pick-up trucks and túk-túk) all around the city centre. Prices are mostly fixed, but it's worth haggling. Don't agree to anything without knowing exactly what vehicle you are getting. Booking through your hotel or a tour company may cost a little more than doing it yourself.

Thai Rent A Car (☑ 083 887 5454; www. thairentacar.com; Th Phetkasem at Soi 84, South Hua Hin; ☉ 8.30am-6.30pm) is a professional Thailand-based car-rental agency with competitive prices, a well-maintained fleet, hotel drop-offs and one-way rentals.

Pranburi & Around   ปราณบุรี
☑ 032 / POP 24,800

Half an hour south of Hua Hin is the country 'suburb' of Pranburi district, which serves as a quiet coastal alternative. There are many expensive boutique resorts ideal for anyone looking to escape the crowds without travelling too far from civilisation.

The core area is the small town of **Pak Nam Pran** (mouth of the Pranburi River), which has the biggest resorts but not much beach. Though tourism is growing here, fishing is still the key to the economy and most Thai visitors return home with some dried squid.

South of Pak Nam Pran there's a sandy shore and the coastal road provides a quick pleasant trip to **Khao Kalok** (Skull Mountain), a mammoth, oddly eroded headland that shelters the most, and pretty much only, attractive beach in the area. It's signed as Thao Kosa Forest Park, but locals and road signs all call it Khao Kalok.

◉ Sights & Activities

Pak Nam Pran and points south have the same great kiteboarding winds as Hua Hin. For lessons and rentals there's **Yoda Kite School** (☑ 087 017 6428; www.pudla0.wixsite. com/yodakiteschool; Beach Rd, Pak Nam Pran; ☉ 10am-6pm) or talk to Karl Tindell at Beach House Bistro (p509) or at his new Beach House Bar, 250m south of Yoda.

★ **Kuiburi National Park**   NATIONAL PARK
(อุทยานแห่งชาติกุยบุรี; ☑ 085 266 1601; Rte 4024; adult/child 200/100B, wildlife-spotting trip per truck 850B; ☉ wildlife trips 2-6pm) Who doesn't want to see herds of wild elephants roaming through the forest or enjoying an evening bath? At Kuiburi National Park's *hôoay léuk* unit, up near the border with Myanmar, it's almost guaranteed. Wildlife-watching drives in the back of pick-up trucks (with bench seating for up to 10) go through forest and reclaimed farm fields where about 240 elephants live. They're used to seeing vehicles, so they pay them little mind, making this almost like an African safari experience.

There are also plenty of gaur (wild cattle) and they're seen fairly often. Most of the spotters don't speak English, but they know some relevant vocabulary. Avoid Saturdays if possible, as the park gets very busy. It's 45 minutes west of Khao Sam Roi Yot National Park (p510) – follow the national park signs for 'wildlife watching' – and the two make an ideal combo visit.

Pranburi Forest Park   NATURE RESERVE
(วนอุทยานปราณบุรี, Wana-Utthayan Pranburi; ☑ 032 621608; ☉ 6am-6pm) Just north of the Pranburi River is an extensive natural mangrove forest. A 1km-long boardwalk with interpretive signs, some in English, lets you explore it from the perspective of a mud-dweller, while an observation tower gives you a bird's-eye view. At high tide fishermen will take visitors on 45-minute boat trips (500B) along the river and small canals.

You'll see hundreds of crabs, and usually a fair number of birds, mudskippers and water monitors. In some areas you'll hear snapping shrimp. There's quite a bit of variety within this forest – the ecosystem is different enough from the young, replanted mangrove across the river at **Sirinart Rajini Mangrove Ecosystem Learning Center** (ศูนย์ศึกษาเรียนรู้ระบบนิเวศป่าชายเลนสิรินาถราชินี; Pak Nam Pran; ☉ 8.30am-4.30pm) FREE that nature lovers will appreciate visiting both.

It's a 14km drive from Pak Nam Pran via Rte 1019, passing very near Hat Sai Noi (p500) on the way. A more direct route half this length is shown on many maps, but it's not passable any more.

🛏 Sleeping

Not all of the beach resorts earn the price tag so be discerning when making online reservations. As at Hua Hin, there are big weekday discounts.

Thongsuk Mini Resort   HOTEL **$$**

(📞 098 423 2661; jamsawang38@gmail.com; r 850B; P ❄ 🛜) Not the cheapest address in Pak Nam Pran, but for about 100B extra than most others, these nine white bungalows are a good budget option. There are free bikes and though the owners speak little English they're very eager to please. It's a two-minute walk from the squid roundabout where the minivans stop.

★ La a natu
Bed & Bakery   BOUTIQUE HOTEL **$$$**

(📞 032 689941; www.laanatu.com; south of Khao Kalok; r/fm incl breakfast & afternoon tea 5500-16,000/11,000B; P ❄ 🛜 ≋) Turning the humble Thai rice village into a luxury living experience is what La a natu does and it does it with panache. The blissfully remote thatched-roof villas rising on stilts are full *Gilligan's Island* outside with a touch of luxury inside, and real rice paddies below.

🍴 Eating & Drinking

The obligatory seafood restaurants are up at the top of Pak Nam Pran town, near the river's mouth. The biggest **night market** (Beach Rd; ⊙ 5-9.30pm) takes place on the coastal road while there's also the much smaller 'Roundabout Market', **Talat Wong-Wian** (Th Pasukwanich at Soi 10; ⊙ 5-9pm), in the centre of town.

There are scattered bars, mostly occupied by expats and long-term guests, along the coastal road in Pak Nam Pran continuing down south to Khao Kalok.

★ Krua Renu   THAI **$**

(Th Pak Nam Pran; mains 40-120B; ⊙ 7am-10pm Thu-Tue) There are both budget and beautiful restaurants along the coastal road, but some of the best food in Pak Nam Pran is in the town at this tall restaurant 200m east of the squid roundabout. Go with the standard *dôm yam* or try the *gaang pàh hâang* (dried jungle curry).

Beach House Bistro   INTERNATIONAL **$$**

(📞 095 549 0206; Th Pak Nam Pran-Khao Kalok; mains 80-365B; ⊙ 9am-10pm; 🛜) Though it's 1km from the sea, this small place does have a beach vibe. It does a little of everything – Italian, Mexican, baguette sandwiches, wine,

South of Hua Hin

Thai and a 265B Sunday roast – with all the quality of the four-star resorts, but at half the price.

ℹ Getting There & Around

Pak Nam Pran is about 25km south of Hua Hin. Ordinary buses (20B, 30 minutes, every 30 minutes 7am to 3pm), minivans (30B, 30 minutes, frequent 6am to 7pm) and trains (5B to 31B, 30 minutes, 11.47am, 5.50pm, 8.10pm) will drop you off in Pranburi town, 10km from Pak Nam Pran and taxi drivers charge 200B between the two. There are also minivans (60B, one hour, frequent 5am to 6.40pm) and trains (14B to 62B, one hour, 4.51am, 10.03am, 2.26pm) from Prachuap Khiri Khan.

There's a direct minivan service from Pak Nam Pran (at the squid roundabout on the south side of town) every 30 minutes from early morning to late afternoon to Bangkok's Mo Chit and Southern bus terminals (200B, five hours). These vans also stop in Phetchaburi (140B, two hours), but do not stop in Hua Hin.

If you want to explore the area, you'll probably want to rent a motorbike as public transport isn't an option. They can be hired from Beach House Bistro (p509) or **Luang Utane** (☑ 084 080 4023; Th Pak Nam Pran; ⊙ 8.30am-5pm) for 200B per day. A car and driver can be arranged through any hotel or there's **Cosmo Car** (☑ 080 139 6665) rental in Pranburi town that's reliable and cheap, though limited English is spoken.

Khao Sam Roi Yot National Park อุทยานแห่งชาติเขาสามร้อยยอด

Towering limestone outcrops form a rocky jigsaw-puzzled landscape at 98-sq-km Khao Sam Roi Yot National Park, whose name means Three Hundred Mountain Peaks. There are also caves, beaches and wetlands to explore for outdoor enthusiasts and birdwatchers.

With its proximity to Hua Hin, the park is well travelled by day trippers and contains a mix of public conservation land and private shrimp farms which have replaced most of the natural mangrove forest. Almost all visitors are here to see Tham Phraya Nakhon, one of the most spectacular and, for Thais, famous caves in Thailand.

Although the birdwatching is excellent, there's not a lot of other wildlife here besides the obligatory macaques. Mainland serow, similar to goats, are shy so sightings are rare. The adorable dusky langur is easy to find at Tham Phraya Nakhon and the visitor centre.

There's no park gate. Admission tickets are sold and checked, and maps provided at each of the park's attractions.

◎ Sights & Activities

At the intersection of the East Asian and Australian migration routes, the national park hosts over 300 migratory and resident bird species, including yellow bitterns, purple swamphens, ruddy-breasted crakes, bronze-winged jacanas, black-headed ibises, great spotted eagles and oriental reed warblers. The park is one of the few places in Thailand where purple heron and Malaysian plover breed.

Most birders come here for waterbirds, which are most commonly seen in the cool season from November to March. The beach east of the headquarters and the marsh to the west are two hot spots. **Thai Birding** (www.thaibirding.com) provides in-depth information.

★ **Tham Phraya Nakhon & Hat Laem Sala** CAVE

(ถ้ำพระยานคร/หาดแหลมศาลา; parking 30B; ⊙ daylight hours) The park's most-visited attraction is this revered cave sheltering a royal *săh·lah* (often spelt *sala*) built for Rama V in 1890. Scenes of this **Khuha Kharuehat Pavilion** bathed in streams of morning light (usually starting at about 10.30am) are widespread making this place famous across the kingdom. Even more interesting is the cave itself. The roof has collapsed in both of the large chambers allowing small forests to grow, adding an otherworldly ambience.

The trail to the cave is a 430m-long, steep and rocky stairway built into the hill. You'll almost certainly meet macaques and dusky langur on the way up. The path begins at picturesque **Laem Sala Beach**, flanked on three sides by limestone hills and shaded by casuarina trees. It can get busy here on weekends, but it's always peaceful at night and in the early morning.

There's no road access to the beach. Most people ride a boat (200B one-way) from the fishing village of Bang Pu. Note that these are wet landings, but in shallow water. Alternatively, you can follow the steep footpath from Bang Pu for a 1km hike to the beach. A boat ride to Laem Sala from the Hat Sam Roi Yot resort area costs 1200B and for an extra 200B they throw in a 'monkey island'.

A leisurely visit to Tham Phraya Nakhon will take at least three hours, but it could easily be extended into a full day with time on the beach, or even an overnight if you camp (p511).

Khlong Khao Daeng RIVER

(คลองเขาแดง; ☑ 062 479451; Rte 4020; up to 6 people 500B; ⊙ 8am-5.45pm) You can hire a covered boat at Wat Khao Daeng for a one-hour scenic cruise along this stream. There are great mountain views and you'll also see birds, macaques, water monitors and mudskippers. The guides don't speak much English, but they know some relevant vocabulary.

Tham Kaew CAVE

(ถ้ำแก้ว; ⊙ daylight hours, begin walk no later than 3.30pm) Though it's on the way to Tham Phraya Nakhon, few people visit this beautiful cave where the stalactites and flowstone glitter with calcite crystals; hence the name, 'Jewel Cave'. You enter the cavern down a ladder after a quite steep and rough 130m trail

DON'T MISS

DOLPHIN BAY

Hat Sam Roi Yot, aka Dolphin Bay as occasionally dolphins and porpoises can be spotted far offshore, is a 15-minute drive from Bang Pu, the primary entry point of Khao Sam Roi Yot National Park. Resorts are value-oriented, traffic is minimal and nightlife is nearly non-existent. The wide strip and powdery sand is not an inviting swimming beach, but it's a great place to sit and stare at the sculpted, jungle-covered islands to the south and the jagged coast to the north. There are kayaks for hire for 100B per hour, though some guesthouses have them free for guests.

Want to splash around for more than just a day? **Dolphin Bay Resort** (☑ 032 825190; www.dolphinbayresort.com; Th Liap Chai Tale, Hat Sam Roi Yot; r 4590-13,680B, f 1690-2790; P ✳ @ 🖥 🗙) is a family-friendly retreat with a variety of standard-issue, value-oriented rooms and villas, plus two big pools, a playground and a toy room.

up the mountain. Inside you can walk pretty easily for about 200m to see the natural wonder and beyond that are more chambers that require getting dirty.

🛏 Sleeping & Eating

The **Laem Sala Beach Campground** (☑ 032 821568; per person with tent 30B, 2-person tent hire 150B), not accessible by road, is an attractive peaceful place to spend the night. **Thung Sam Roi Yot** (☑ 032 821568; per person with tent 30B) and **Sam Phraya Beach** (☑ 032 821568; per person with tent 30B, 3-person tent hire 150B) also have campgrounds. The bungalows at Khao Daeng aren't very pleasant. Many people stay just outside the park at Hat Sam Roi Yot beach.

There are restaurants, open 6am to 6pm, at Bang Pu where you start and end visits to Tham Phraya Nakhon. Restaurants at Laem Sala beach, Sam Phraya beach and Thung Sam Roi Yot generally open at 8am and close at 5.30pm, 8pm and 8pm, respectively.

ℹ Information

The Hat Sam Roi Yot tourist zone has ATMs and small shops.

Khao Sam Roi Yot Visitor Center (☑ 032 821568; Rte 4020; ⊙ 8am-4.30pm) The park's main visitor centre has friendly, helpful staff, but there's generally no need to visit since tickets are sold and maps provided at all of the park attractions. There used to be a 900m boardwalk through the mangrove forest behind the visitor centre; it may reopen someday.

ℹ Getting There & Away

The park is around 50km from both Hua Hin and Prachuap Khiri Khan. There's no public transport to or within the park, so you need to come with your own wheels. Hiring a car and driver for the day from Hua Hin and Prachuap will cost about 1800B to 2000B including petrol while it's as little as 1200B from Hat Sam Roi Yot. Some people charge extra to include Thung Sam Roi Yot. Many people combine a morning visit to Khao Sam Roi Yot with afternoon elephant watching at Kuiburi National Park (p508). Most Hua Hin tour companies have day trips here, but they only visit Tham Phraya Nakhon.

Motorcycles (250B to 350B per day) and bikes (100B to 200B) can be hired at Dolphin Bay Resort and some other spots in Hat Sam Roi Yot.

A taxi from the train station or bus stop in Pranburi to Hat Sam Roi Yot is a fixed 400B. No public transport comes here any more.

Prachuap Khiri Khan   ประจวบคีรีขันธ์

☑ 032 / POP 33,500

A sleepy seaside town, Prachuap Khiri Khan is a delightfully relaxed place; the antithesis of Hua Hin. The broad bay is a tropical turquoise punctuated by bobbing fishing boats and overlooked by honeycombed limestone mountains – scenery that you usually have to travel to the southern Andaman to find.

In recent years, foreigners have discovered Prachuap's charms and some Bangkokians drive past Hua Hin for their weekends away, but their numbers are still very small compared to better-known destinations.

◉ Sights & Activities

Th Suseuk south of the Municipal Market 1 still has lots of old wooden houses and makes a great walk day and night. It hosts the **Suseuk Culture and Fun Street Market** with food, crafts, music and more food the first weekend of each month.

Prachuap Khiri Khan

Ao Prachuap
BAY

(อ่าวประจวบ) The town's crowning feature is Ao Prachuap (Prachuap Bay), a gracefully curving bay outlined by an oceanfront promenade and punctuated by dramatic headlands at both ends. The sunrise is superb and an evening stroll along the promenade and pier is a peaceful delight.

North of **Khao Chong Krajok** (เขาช่อง กระจก), over the bridge, the bay stretches peacefully to a toothy mountain, part of **Khao Ta Mong Lai Forest Park** (วนอุทยาน เขาตาม่องล่าย; ☏ 081 378 0026; ⊙ daylight hours). The long sandy beach running parallel with the road before the forest park only sees people on weekends and even then not very many, making it a fine place to idle and beachcomb at any time. It's deep enough for swimming, but not very clean.

Wat Ao Noi
BUDDHIST TEMPLE

(วัดอ่าวน้อย; ⊙ daylight hours) **FREE** Leaving Ao Prachuap behind, turn north for 2.5km, passing the fishing village of **Ban Ao Noi**, where some of the larger boats dock and unload, to this large temple linking two bays: Ao Noi and Ao Khan Kradai. It features a lovely *bòht* constructed entirely of teak without nails, and the murals, mostly telling the Buddha's life story, are composed of framed painted wood carvings. The pond in front is filled with fish, eager to be fed by merit-makers.

Ao Manao
BEACH

(อ่าวมะนาว; ⊙ beach zone 5am-7pm, mountain zone 6am-6pm) On weekends, locals head to Ao Manao, an island-dotted bay ringed by a curving beach within Wing 5 Thai Air Force base – the only beach where locals go swimming as both the water and sand are clean. There are the usual seaside amenities: restaurants, beach chairs, umbrellas and inner tubes, plus some dry-land diversions including quad-bike rides and a petting zoo. It's packed on weekends but can be nearly deserted on weekdays.

You need to register at the base entrance, at the end of Th Salacheep. Normally no passport is necessary, but best to bring it in case you're asked. From here it's 2.5km to the beach. Across the bay from the public beach is Khao Lammuak (p513).

Sunset Cruise
CRUISE

(☑ 080 110 8277; www.samaowtour.com; Th Chai Thaleh; 300B) Sam Aow Princess Tour has a short sunset cruise in Prachuap Bay starting around 5.30pm or 6pm nightly, if there are enough passengers. Drinks are sold.

🛏 Sleeping

This is a town where you don't want to be far from the sea. The closest you can get to luxury are some decent midrange places. There are lots of small homestays and guesthouses in the city centre near the sea. Book ahead on high-season weekends.

🛏 In Town

Safehouse Hostel
HOSTEL $

(☑ 087 909 4770; 28 Soi 6, Th Salacheep; dm 250, r 450-650B; ❄ 🛜) With fairly frumpy though very tidy rooms, the host Sherry is the real reason this small hostel has become popular. She goes out of her way to please guests and leads good tours to Kuiburi National Park (p508) and elsewhere. There's a communal kitchen.

Yutichai Hotel
HOTEL $

(☑ 032 611055; yutichai_hotel@hotmail.com; 115 Th Kong Kiat; r with fan 220-450, air-con 500-550B;

❄ 🛜) A bit of history right near the train station, this old wooden hotel is properly maintained and the prices are right. Most rooms (including those with air-con, private bathrooms and hot water) are in a more modern, but still classic concrete building at the back. Light sleepers will want to stay at the back, or elsewhere.

★ Prachuap Beach Hotel
HOTEL $$

(☑ 032 601288; www.prachuapbeach.com; 123 Th Suseuk; d & tw 800-900, tr 1200B; P ❄ 🛜) The best located, and possibly quietest, hotel in the city is near lots of good restaurants, opens up to the promenade and has great views from upper floors. The 2nd-floor rooms are cheapest, but it's worth paying the extra 100B to be up higher – the 5th floor is the top.

The rooms are old-fashioned, though very good for the price.

★ Grandma's House
BOUTIQUE HOTEL $$

(☑ 089 526 6896; grandmaprachuap@gmail.com; 238 Th Suseuk; r incl breakfast 700-900B; ❄ 🛜) Up above its popular vintage-themed café (mains 39-159B, coffee from 30B; ⊘ 7.30am-6pm; 🛜), these three solid wooden rooms (two small and one large) are decorated with some actual antiques. They share two modern bathrooms.

You'll need to endure street noise, but there's normally not too much at night.

> **WORTH A TRIP**
>
> ### WORLD WAR II MONUMENTS
>
> Prachuap was one of seven points on the gulf coast where Japanese troops landed on 8 December 1941 during their invasion of Thailand. The Air Force base at Ao Manao was the site of fierce skirmishes – the Japanese didn't fully capture the town until the next day after the Thai government ordered its soldiers to stop fighting since an armistice had been arranged.
>
> Forty-one soldiers and civilians who died in the battle are memorialised at **Khao Lammuak** (เขาล้อมหมวก; ⊘ 6am-6pm, museum 9am-3pm Sat & Sun), a soaring limestone mountain marking the southern end of Ao Prachuap. Several street names around town also refer to the battle such as Phitak Chat (Defend Country), Salacheep (Sacrifice Life) and Suseuk (Fight a Battle). About 400 Japanese also died.
>
> About 400m in front of the mountain, three attractive monuments and the **Wing 5 Museum** commemorate the battle. You need to register at the Wing 5 Thai Air Force base entrance, at the end of Th Salacheep, and again at a second checkpoint. Bring your passport in case you're asked. It's 4.3km to the mountain from the entrance; follow the 'Historical Park' signs.
>
> At the mountain's rocky summit are a Buddha footprint and fantastic views. However, because of many accidents, the climb, requiring pulling yourself up with ropes at some points, is now only allowed on long holiday weekends.

OFF THE BEATEN TRACK

MYANMAR (BURMA) BORDER MARKET

A mere 12km west of Prachuap Khiri Khan is the Myanmar border and for many years there has been talk of foreigners being able to cross 'in the near future'. Don't hold your breath. In the meantime, you can still visit the town of Dan Singkhon on the Thai side of the border, 20km drive from the city. There's a Saturday-morning border market for Burmese traders to come across and sell to Thais. Its former exotic appeal has been washed away by modern construction and few people now consider it worth the trip unless they're shopping for wooden furniture or orchids. Many of the people selling these products are here the rest of the week too. Minivans (100B, 30 minutes) make the trip from Prachuap Khiri Khan's minivan station (p516), but only depart when there are enough passengers.

🛏 Out of Town

★ **Khao Ta Mong Lai**
Forest Park Campsite   CAMPGROUND $
(📱081 378 0026; with tent 50B, 3-person tent hire 200B) There's a shady, seldom-used campground in this park (p512) with some of the cleanest facilities in Thailand. There are simple bungalows too, but they're intended for large groups. Since it's across the bay from the city centre, you get some great sunsets.

Golden Beach Hotel   HOTEL $$
(📱032 601626; www.goldenbeachboutique.com; 113 Th Suanson; d & tw 1100-2500, f 1400-1800B; ₱❄🛜) After a full renovation, these large rooms are now some of Prachuap's best, if you don't mind being about 2km from the city centre. The higher prices get the biggest sea views, but the scenery is preferable from the cheapest rooms at the back, which have river and ocean views together. The beach is across the road.

🍴 Eating

Restaurants in Prachuap are known for cheap and excellent seafood, while Western options are easy to find. The **Municipal Market 1** (Th Maitri Ngam; ⊙4am-4pm) is the place to get pineapples fresh from the orchards;

ask the vendor to cut it for you. There are a pair of small **night markets** (Th Kong Kiat; ⊙4.30pm-2am) in the city centre.

Krua Chaiwat   THAI $
(Th Salacheep; mains 40-160B; ⊙9am-3pm & 4.30-8pm Mon-Sat; 🛜🖊) With good food at low prices, this small restaurant serves a mix of locals and expats. While Thai food is its strength – the *dôm yam* and *mêe·ang kam* (an assemble-it-yourself snack with wild pepper leaves) are quite good – there's also steaks and a few fusion foods like the stir-fried spaghetti with salted mackerel.

Ty I-House   BAKERY $
(235 Th Suseuk; bakery 30B; ⊙8am-5pm Mon-Sat; 🛜) Khun Suchada took an early retirement and has turned her hobby into a small business. She bakes what she feels like, only having a few things available at any one time, and sells it from a small table. Her chocolate brownie is excellent.

Som Tam Baa Nook   THAI $
(Th Suseuk; mains 30-90B; ⊙7am-4pm) Baa Nook is a transplant from Isan and she serves real-deal northeastern fare from this rough-and-tumble street-food shop. The *sôm·đam* (spicy papaya salad) is excellent – she has the *plah ráh* (fermented fish sauce) shipped down from her family back in Buriram – and there's chicken *lâhp,* grilled catfish and more.

Rim Taley Market   MARKET $
(Th Chai Thaleh; ⊙4-8.30pm Mon-Thu, 4-9pm Fri & Sat) The 'Oceanside Market' isn't very large, but it makes an ideal dinner destination because you can eat your food on the promenade or pier. On Friday and Saturday the few dozen regular vendors are joined by about 200 more as the market morphs into **Walking Street**, though there's little in the way of artistic or handmade goods on sale.

★ **In Town Seafood**   THAI $$
(Th Chai Thaleh; mains 50-350B; ⊙3-11pm) A go-to place for discerning locals, here you can eat streetside under a utilitarian tent while gazing at the squid boats in the bay. Great range of fresh seafood on display – barracuda, crab and shellfish – so you can point and pick if you don't recognise the names on the menu. Service can be slow.

Ciao Pizza   ITALIAN $$
(Th Suseuk; mains 160-280B; ⊙11am-3pm & 4-10pm; 🛜🖊) Ciao Pizza is Italian-owned; come here for fine pizzas, pastas and gelato,

as well as fresh bread baked daily and a take-away selection of cheese and salami. There's a quiet dining area hidden at the back.

Rop Lom
SEAFOOD **$$**

(Th Suanson; mains 70-190B; ⊙10am-9pm; 🔊) Popular with the locals, the *pàt pŏng gà·rèe bŏo* (crab curry) comes with big chunks of sweet crab meat and the *yam tá-lair* (seafood salad) is spicy and zesty. On the non-oceanic side of things there's *yam dòk·· kaa* (sesbania flower salad).

Drinking & Nightlife

The beach road is the place to be. There's a small bunch of low-key bars north of the Prachuap Beach Hotel; it's absolutely nothing like the loud sleazy bar scene in Hua Hin.

Maggie's Wine Garden
BAR

(Th Chai Thaleh; slushy cocktails 200B; ⊙4-11pm Sat-Thu; 🔊) Just a few doors down from her

guesthouse
(📋087 597 9720; Th Chai Thaleh; r 250-600B; ❄@🔊), Maggie has a cosy bar with a big liquor list and a little food. The slushy margaritas and pineapple mojitos are more fitting of the vibe than the shiraz. There's a stage with instruments waiting for willing open-mike musicians.

Top Deck
BAR

(53 Th Chai Thaleh; beers/cocktails from 65/130B; ⊙1.30-11pm Thu-Tue; 🔊) At the Top Deck you can sip a libation until relatively late while gazing out at the winking lights of the fishing boats in the bay. Also does surprisingly good Thai plus a little Western food (80B to 300B).

Information

There are lots of banks and ATMs in the city centre. The nearest banks that are open evenings and weekends are in the Tesco-Lotus shopping mall out on the highway, 3km west of the city centre.

TRANSPORT TO/FROM PRACHUAP KHIRI KHAN

DESTINATION	BUS	MINIVAN	TRAIN
Ban Krut	70B, 1hr, 3 daily (to the town)	70-90B, 1hr, every 30min 5.40am-7pm (to the Hwy)	13-339B, 1hr, 8 daily
Bang Saphan Yai	80B, 1½hr, 10 daily (to the town)	80-100B, 1½hr, every 30min 5.40am-7pm (8 to the town, all others to the Hwy)	16-347B, 1¼hr, 9 daily
Bangkok Hualamphong	N/A	N/A	168-455B, 4½-5½hr, 9 daily
Bangkok Northern (Mo Chit) Bus Terminal	240B, 6-7hr, 3.30pm	220B, 5hr, every 45min 1.30am-7.30pm	N/A
Bangkok Southern Bus Terminal	200B, 6-7hr, every 90min 7.30am-9pm	200B, 5hr, every 45min 3am-7pm	N/A
Bangkok Thonburi	N/A		56-130B, 6hr, 1.05pm
Cha-am	N/A	120B, 2hr, frequent 5am-6.40pm	54-85B, 2hr, 4 daily
Chumphon	220B, 4hr, hourly 11am-midnight	180B, 3½hr, every 50min 6am-7pm	16-347B, 2½-3hr, 10 daily
Hua Hin	N/A	80B, 1½hr, frequent 5am-6.40pm	19-353B, 1-1½hr, 11 daily
Phetchaburi	150B, 2½hr, hourly 7.30am-9pm	150B, 2½hr, every 40 min 3am-7pm	31-382B, 2-2½hr, 11 daily
Phuket	587-913B, 9-10hr, 11am & every 30min 8pm-midnight	N/A	N/A
Pranburi	N/A	60B, 1hr, frequent 5am-6.40pm	14-62B, 1hr, 3 daily
Ranong	N/A	250B, 4½hr, 8am, 10am, 1pm, 3.30pm	N/A

Tourist Office (☏ 032 604143; Th Chai Taley; ⏰ 8.30am-noon & 1-4.30pm Mon-Fri) At the foot of the pier, has free city maps and the staff speak English.

❶ Getting There & Around

Most buses do not come into town, they just park along the Phetkasem Hwy (Hwy 4) at an area known as 'sà·tăh·nee dern rót', 4km northwest of the city centre. Tickets are sold on the northbound side of the road; to be sure you get a seat, buy your ticket the day before because often buses are full when they pass Prachuap. The exception are the four daily air-conditioned buses to Bangkok's Southern Bus Terminal (200B, 9am, 11am, 1pm, 1am) and Phetchaburi (150B, two hours) from a small **bus stop** on Th Phitak Chat. Minivans form the backbone of Prachuap transportation and they all depart from **kew rót đòo** (Th Prachuap Khiri Khan/Rte 326) minivan station at the junction of Rte 326 and Hwy 4 near the main bus stop. The **train station** (☏ 032 611175; Th Maharat) is a 15-minute walk to the main accommodation area.

Prachuap is small enough to get around on foot, but you can hop on a motorcycle taxi to most places for 30B; 50B out to the bus stop and minivan station. Most hotels have motorcycle hire for 200B to 250B per day. A few also do bicycles for 50B.

Ban Krut & Bang Saphan Yai

☏ 032 / POP 4200 & 15,100

While calling Ban Krut and Bang Saphan Yai beaches idyllic is a bit of a stretch, they're no slouches in the beauty department. Around 65km and 90km south of Prachuap Khiri Khan, most people don't come here for the scenery, they come because so few others choose to come. There are no high-rises, no late-night bars and no speeding traffic to distract you from a serious regimen of reading, swimming, eating and biking. You'll often be all on your lonesome as you sit or stroll between the coconut trees and the crystalline blue sea that laps the long sandy coastline. There's a November to March high season, though it's a wonderfully meagre one.

◉ Sights & Activities

Ban Krut has a string of resorts, restaurants and inner-tube rental shops sitting across the road from the sea. Families park their cars and spend the day eating, drinking and watching their kids splash around. That said, it's still much more subdued than a typical tourist beach as you don't need to go very far south to score a private patch of sand, even on holiday weekends.

Topping **Khao Thong Chai**, the headland north of Ban Krut beach, is a beautiful and unusually wide, 50m-tall stupa, **Phra Mahathat Chedi Phakdi Praka** (พระมหาธาตุเจดีย์ภักดีประกาศ; Rte 1029; ⏰ 8am-5pm) **FREE**. The main room has modern murals painted in traditional Thai style showing local festivals and ceremonies from around Thailand. Down below, beautiful coastal views form alongside the 10m-tall seated Buddha statue.

Bang Saphan Yai still clings to that famous beach cliché: Thailand 20 years ago before pool villas and package tourists pushed out all the beach bums. Much of the lodging is right on the beach itself (called Hat Suan Luang) and hawkers are rare. Islands off the coast, including **Ko Thalu** with its natural rock arch, offer good snorkelling and diving from March to October, with March and April being the best months. Although they're near Bang Saphan Yai, trips to these islands can also be arranged from Ban Krut.

🛌 Sleeping

Most places are pretty much empty on weekdays and are only really busy on holiday weekends when Bangkokians are willing to take the time to drive past Hua Hin.

🛏 Ban Krut   บ้านกรูด

Most accommodation is in the busy core beach area that begins 1km from the tiny and timeless wooden shophouse-filled village. To the north of the temple-topped headland (this beach is called Hat Sai Kaew) and to the south it quickly turns remote and private with only a few scattered resorts in between coconut groves.

Siripong Guesthouse   GUESTHOUSE **$**
(☏ 032 695464; Hat Ban Krut; r with fan 250-300, air-con 400B; P🕸❄️) The region's cheapest lodging is pretty bare-bones, but the rooms are actually better than the dishevelled exterior would lead you to believe, and it's right at the junction, slightly away from the busiest parts of the beach. All showers are cold water and the fan rooms have either bucket-dump toilets in the rooms or shared bathrooms.

Proud Thai Beach Resort
GUESTHOUSE **$$**

(✆089 682 4484; www.proudthairesort.com; Hat Ban Krut; r 800B; P❋≋) Eight wooden bungalows, all with terraces, sit under the shade of trees across the road from the beach. They're old, but well-maintained by the English-speaking owner.

Bayview Beach Resort
HOTEL **$$$**

(✆032 695566; www.bayviewbeachresort.com; Ban Krut; incl breakfast r 1900-2300, f 3500-4800B; P❋❋≋) Bayview has handsome bungalows with large verandas, set amid shady grounds on a barely inhabited stretch of beach well north of the main tourist strip. There's a beachside pool with a kid-friendly wading pool, as well as a small playground. The resort also offers snorkelling and diving trips, and rents kayaks, motorcycles and bikes.

🛏 Bang Saphan Yai บางสะพานใหญ่

The beach is 6km south of Bang Saphan Yai town. There are a handful of small flash resorts here and also a row of basic, budget bungalows with direct beach access to the north of the Why Not Bar.

Ploy Bungalows
BUNGALOW **$**

(✆032 817119; r 500-700B; P❋❋) A quiet, casual place with brightly painted concrete bungalows. As a bonus to backpackers, all bungalows that are right up on the beach are the 500B fan variety. There are several other places of similar style along this road. There's no food here, so you'll have to walk a bit to eat.

⭐ The Theatre Villa
HOTEL **$$**

(✆085 442 9150; www.thetheatrevilla.com; r incl breakfast 1350-2100B; P❋❋) Quiet even by Bang Saphan standards, this small hotel sits on a great piece of beach and is meticulously cared for. Rooms are bright and very comfortable and come in three varieties: hotel-like rooms at the back, more expensive bungalows in the middle and two sea-view rooms at the front. It's west of the main road.

Coral Hotel
HOTEL **$$$**

(✆032 817121; www.coral-hotel.com; incl breakfast r 3400, f 4940-6700B; P❋❋≋) Catering mostly to French tourists – the restaurants are decent – this upmarket hotel is right on the beach and has all the resort amenities, including organised diving and snorkelling tours, trips to the national parks and Thai cooking classes. The

tastefully decorated rooms are very comfortable and the pool is big.

🍴 Eating & Drinking

Locals eat almost exclusively along the road to town where there are a few regular restaurants, coffee shops and a mini night market (3pm to 9pm) next to Tesco-Lotus Express. Bang Saphan Yai has a few foreigner-focused restaurants.

There are bars in both towns. Ban Krut's cheapest beers are sold informally along the beach across from Siripong Guesthouse – a mix of locals and expats lounge here. Kasama's has a good liquor list.

Bang Saphan Yai has a few popular expat watering holes. **Why Not Bar** is on the beach and **Blue Bar**, with pool table, is up almost at the highway junction. There's often live music at both.

Kasama's Pizza
ITALIAN **$$**

(✆081 139 0220; www.kasamapizza.com; Rte 1029, Hat Ban Krut; mains 45-355B; ⊙10am-10pm, reduced hours in low season; ☎) A friendly spot and one of the longest-running restaurants in Ban Krut, Kasama's has substantial sandwiches, all-day breakfasts, pizzas and real chocolate milkshakes. And it delivers, even to the beach.

It's located off the access road, behind the 7-Eleven.

ℹ Information

Ban Krut Info (www.bankrutinfo.com) Local information on the area.

Bang Saphan Guide (www.bangsaphanguide. com) Local information on the area.

Bankrut Tour & Travel (✆081 736 3086; www. bankrut.co.th; Hat Ban Krut; ⊙8am-8pm) This is a friendly and reliable, full-service agency inside Na Nicha Bankrut Resort, just before the beach. Staff arrange day trips, including snorkelling at Ko Thalu, and onward travel, including ferry tickets for the southern islands.

ℹ Getting There & Away

Both towns have train stations. All 11 trains from Bangkok's Hualamphong to the far south stop at **Bang Saphan Yai Train Station** (✆032 691552; Soi Bang Saphan), 179B to 480B, five to seven hours, and seven of these also stop at **Ban Krut Train Station** (✆032 695004). Most of these trains arrive deep into the night. There's also a 7.30am ordinary train from Bangkok's Thonburi station (67B to 155B, 7½ hours). You can also get to both by rail from Prachuap Khiri Khan (16B to

347B, one hour), Chumphon (20B to 355B, 1½ to two hours) and Hua Hin (33B to 386B, two hours).

From Bangkok's southern terminal, buses go to Bang Saphan Yai (273B, six hours, hourly) about every two hours between 7.30am and midnight, and three of these stop in Ban Krut. Heading north, these buses will stop in Prachuap Khiri Khan (80B, one hour) and Phetchaburi (173B, 3½ hours), but not Hua Hin. Both bus stops are just a short distance south of the train stations. For a small fee you can get tickets through your resort or Bankrut Tour & Travel (p517).

Minivans (Rte 3169) from Bang Saphan Yai depart from the highway in front of Sweet Home Bakery in the heart of town. They go to Prachuap Khiri Khan (100B, one hour, eight daily from 6.20am to 4.50pm) and Chumphon (80B, two hours, 7am). The minivans to Prachuap pick up in Ban Krut. The Chumphon van normally doesn't pick up in Ban Krut, but Bankrut Tour & Travel can arrange it with the cost rising to 400B.

Other buses and minivans stop along the highway, about 10km west of both towns, rather than coming into town. Most buses that travel this route stop at Bang Saphan Yai, though few stop at Ban Krut and you risk waiting a long time if you try it there. In both cases, it's about a 100B motorcycle taxi ride to the town, more to the beach.

ℹ️ Getting Around

All but some of the cheapest resorts will pick you up in town and send you back for free, but all charge for going out to the Phetkasem Hwy.

The beach at Bang Saphan Yai is 6km south of the town via Rte 3374 – you can't miss the turnoff as there's a mass of resort signs. Ban Krut is 1km to the beach, though most of the accommodation is spread out far from the junction. Moto-taxis from Bang Saphan Yai to the beach cost 100B, from Ban Krut it's 20B to 30B.

In Ban Krut, Siripong Guesthouse (p516) and Bankrut Tour & Travel (p517) rent motorcycles for 200B per day, as do several other nearby shops around the junction. Several shops at Bang Saphan Yai's beach also hire motorcycles for 250B to 350B. Another option is to hire them in town at **Tae's Restaurant** (☑ 087 919 2910; Soi Bang Saphan; ⊙ 2pm-1am), just down from the train station for 200B to 250B, though this is a very casual operation and they're often not available.

Chumphon ชุมพร

☑ 077 / POP 33,500

A transit town funnelling travellers to and from Ko Tao or southwards to Ranong or Phuket, Chumphon is where the south of

Thailand starts proper; Muslim headscarves are a common sight here.

While there's not a lot to do in town while you wait for your ferry, it's not an unpleasant place and the surrounding beaches are alternative sun and sand stops far off the backpacker bandwagon. Beautiful **Hat Thung Wua Laen** (Fast Running Cow Beach), 15km northeast of town and full of traveller amenities, is the best known and during the week you'll have it mostly to yourself. On weekends it will be rocking.

👁️ Sights

It's not one of Thailand's biggest or best national museums, but the prehistoric pottery, axes and jewellery displayed in **Chumphon National Museum** (พิพิธภัณฑสถานแห่งชาติ ชุมพร; ☑ 077 504105; 100B; ⊙ 9am-4pm Wed-Sun) will appeal to history buffs. Also worth a browse is Chumphon's main **fresh market** (ตลาดสดชุมพร; Th Pracha Uthit; ⊙ midnight-3pm), the main source of meat, fruit and veggies for most of the city's restaurants. It's at its busiest very early in the morning.

🎉 Festivals & Events

Usually in mid-March, **Chumphon Marine Festival** (⊙ Mar) takes place at the seaside town of Paknam, 13km southeast of Chumphon city. There are four days of sea-related events, including boat trips, sand sculpture and underwater rubbish pick up.

To mark the end of Buddhist Lent (Ork Phansaa), which usually occurs in October, traditional long-tail boats race each other on the Lang Suan River about 60km south of Chumphon. Unlike long-tail boat races everywhere else in Thailand, here the winner must have someone hang on the bow of the boat and snatch a flag.

🛏️ Sleeping

As most people overnighting in Chumphon are backpackers, there's a lot of accommodation serving them. **Th Tha Taphao** is the local Th Khao San, with cheap older guesthouses. Some newer flashier hostels are found east of the train station along Th Krumluang Chumphon. If you prefer sea to city, there's lodging up at **Hat Thung Wua Laen**, 15km northeast of town.

★ **Salsa Hostel** HOSTEL $
(☑ 077 505005; www.salsachumphon.com; 25/42 Th Krumluang Chumphon; incl breakfast dm 300-330, tw/d 650/750B; ❄️@🛜) East of the train

Chumphon

Chumphon

◉ Sights
1 Chumphon Fresh Market.....................B3

🛏 Sleeping
2 Fame Guesthouse.................................B2
3 Loft Mania..D3
4 Salsa Hostel..C1

🍽 Eating
5 Kook Noy Kitchen C2
6 Night Market..C1
7 Prikhorm A3

🍷 Drinking & Nightlife
8 Aeki's Bar B1

ℹ Information
9 New Infinity Travel B2
10 Ocean Shopping Mall...........................C1

ℹ Transport
11 Affiliated Bus..A1
12 Bang Saphan Yai Minivan
Stop..A2
13 Choke Anan Tour.................................C3
14 San Tavee New Rest Home................A2
15 San Tavee New Rest Home................B2
16 Surat Thani & Prachuap
Khiri Khan Minivan Stop...................C2

station near the night market, this is one of the best addresses in Chumphon. It's clean, friendly, not too big and a reliable source of local info in excellent English. The private rooms are some of the best in town, regardless of the price.

Fame Guesthouse GUESTHOUSE **$**
(☎077 571077; www.chumphon-kohtao.com; 188/20-21 Th Sala Daeng; r with shared/private bathroom 150-200/300B; @🛜) A *fa·ràng* depot, Fame does a little bit of everything, from providing clean basic rooms for people

overnighting (or just resting during the day) to booking tickets and renting motorbikes. The attached restaurant is a key backpacker hang-out, and offers a wide range of Thai, Indian and Western food.

Chumphon Cabana Resort & Diving Centre HOTEL **$$**
(☎077 560245; www.chumphoncabanaresort.com; Hat Thung Wua Laen; r incl breakfast 1000-1500B; P❄🛜♨) 🌿 Away from the road and on a great piece of beach, this is *the* place to stay at Hat Thung Wua Laen as long as you

JUNGLE GETAWAY

Only 4km from Chumphon, but deep in the countryside, **Villa Varich** (☑ 086 964 7123; www.villavarich.com; Soi Wat Bangmak; incl breakfast r 700-900, ste 1600B; P ✹ ☎) is unlike any other Chumphon hotel. The large rooms, half sitting along the jungle-clad Tha Taphao River, are comfortable and attractive, and you'll wake to bird song. Tang and Khom are great hosts. There are free bikes, and kayaks and motorcycles cost 200B. A túk-túk from the train station should cost 200B. Booking ahead is recommended.

don't need full-on luxury. The rooms have verandas for lounging and while an upgrade is in order, they're still plenty comfortable. A transfer from Chumphon costs 300B.

Loft Mania HOTEL $$
(☑ 077 501789; loftmania.bh@gmail.com; Th Suksamur; r/ste 1300/4000B; P ✹ ☎ ⛱) The closest thing to luxury in Chumphon city, this popular hotel has quality rooms, industrial-chic design, helpful staff and a medieval coat of arms to greet you at the door. Guests get a pool, fitness centre and free bikes.

✖ Eating & Drinking

Chumphon's main **night market** (Th Krumluang Chumphon; ◷ 4pm-midnight) has a big variety of food options and good people-watching. There's more evening street food at the south end of Th Tha Taphao and south of the train station.

★ Kook Noy Kitchen THAI $
(Th Suksamur; mains 40-180B; ◷ 4pm-4am Mon-Sat; ☎) Just a concrete floor, a corrugated roof and a chaotic kitchen turning out central and southern Thai dishes you know like *dôm yam* with free-range chicken and crab fried rice, plus many you probably don't, including fried ducks beak and *pàt pèt gòp* (curry fried frog).

Prikhorm THAI $$
(32 Th Tha Taphao; mains 95-450B; ◷ 11am-10pm; ☎ ☑) This wannabe fancy place has dishes from across the kingdom, from southern *gaang sôm* fish curry to northeastern mushroom *lâhp*, one of many vegetarian dishes.

Aeki's Bar BAR
(Soi Rot Fai 1; beer/cocktails from 65B/100B; ◷ 3pm-late; ☎) This bar across from the train station has an island vibe and hosts a lot of travellers. There's a pool table, *moo·ay tai* (Thai boxing) ring, Thai and international food, live reggae and a friendly welcome from the owner.

❶ Information

There are several banks open evenings and weekends in the **Ocean Shopping Mall** (Th Krumluang Chumphon) across from the night market.

Immigration Office (☑ 077 630282; Rte 41, in Chumphon bus station; ◷ 8.30am-noon & 1-4.30pm Mon-Fri) Can do extensions of stays for tourists. It's next to the bus station.

New Infinity Travel (☑ 077 570176; new_infinity@hotmail.com; 68/2 Th Tha Taphao; ◷ 8.30am-9pm; ☎) A great travel agency that can help you out in excellent English. Also has a very good selection of second-hand books in many languages. Closing hours vary.

Tourism Authority of Thailand (TAT; ☑ 077 502775; tatchumphon@tat.or.th; Soi 1, Th Tawee Sinka; ◷ 8.30am-4.30pm) You can probably get all the information you need from your guesthouse, but if not, this office is helpful. And it gives out a good free map of Chumphon.

Virajsilp Hospital (☑ 077 542555; Th Poramin Mankha) Privately owned; handles emergencies.

❶ Getting There & Away

For a transit hub, Chumphon is surprisingly unconsolidated – there's no single bus station and the ferry pier for boats to Ko Tao, Ko Pha-Ngan and Ko Samui are some distance from town. But travel agencies and guesthouses can point you to the right place, and sell tickets for all ferries, flights and many buses.

AIR
Chumphon's airport is nearly 40km from the centre of town and Nok Air, the only airline flying here, has one flight to Bangkok's Don Mueang Airport in the early morning and another in the late afternoon. Fame Guesthouse (p519) has an airport shuttle for 150B per person.

BOAT
There are essentially two options for getting to Ko Tao. **Lomprayah** (☑ City 081 956 5644, Pier 077 558214; www.lomprayah.com; Th Krumluang Chumphon; ◷ 4.30am-6pm) and **Songserm** (☑ 077 506205; www.songserm. com) have modern ferries sailing during the day. Lomprayah is the best and most popular; Songserm has a reputation for being poorly

TRANSPORT TO/FROM CHUMPHON

DESTINATION	BOAT	BUS	MINIVAN	TRAIN	AIR
Bang Saphan Yai	N/A	N/A	80B, 2hr, 2pm, 3.30pm	20-355B, 1½-2hr, 12 daily	N/A
Bangkok Don Mueang International Airport	N/A	N/A	N/A	N/A	from 1200B, 1hr, 2 daily
Bangkok Hualamphong	N/A	N/A	N/A	seat/sleeper 192-510/620-1194B, 6½-8hr, 11 daily	N/A
Bangkok Southern Bus Terminal	N/A	155-510B, 8hr, 11 daily 9am-10pm	N/A	N/A	N/A
Bangkok Thonburi	N/A	N/A	N/A	80-383B, 9½hr, 7.30am	N/A
Chiang Mai	N/A	1385B, 18hr, 6pm	N/A	N/A	N/A
Hat Yai	N/A	328-355B, 7hr, 8 daily 7am-midnight	N/A	79-502B, 8-10½hr, 7 daily	N/A
Hua Hin	N/A	N/A	N/A	49-423B, 4-5hr, 12 daily	N/A
Ko Pha-Ngan (Lomprayah)	1000B, 3¼-3¾hr, 7am, 1pm	N/A	N/A	N/A	N/A
Ko Pha-Ngan (Songserm)	900B, 4½hr, 7am	N/A	N/A	N/A	N/A
Ko Samui (Lomprayah)	1100B, 3¾-4¼hr, 7am, 1pm	N/A	N/A	N/A	N/A
Ko Samui (Songserm)	1000B, 6¼hr, 7am	N/A	N/A	N/A	N/A
Ko Tao (car ferry)	400B, 6hr, 11pm Mon-Sat	N/A	N/A	N/A	N/A
Ko Tao (Lomprayah)	600B, 1¾hr, 7am, 1pm	N/A	N/A	N/A	N/A
Ko Tao (Songserm)	500B, 2¾hr, 7am	N/A	N/A	N/A	N/A
Ko Tao (Sunday night boat)	450B, 6hr, midnight Sun	N/A	N/A	N/A	N/A
Nakhon Si Thammarat	N/A	N/A	300B, 5½hr, every 2hr 8am-2pm	N/A	N/A
Phetchaburi	N/A	328-500B, 6hr, hourly 7am-10pm	N/A	58-455B, 5½-6½hr, 11 daily	N/A
Phuket	N/A	350-600B, 6-7hr, 7 daily 5am-2.30pm	N/A	N/A	N/A
Prachuap Khiri Khan	N/A	220B, 4hr, hourly 7am-10pm	180B, 3½hr, every 50min 5.30am-6pm	16-347B, 2½-3hr, 10 daily	N/A
Ranong	N/A	120B, 2½hr, 4 daily	120B, 2½hr, hourly 6am-5pm	N/A	N/A
Surat Thani	N/A	N/A	170B, 3½hr, hourly, 6am-5.30pm	34-388B, 2-3hr, 12 daily	N/A

organised and not providing promised transfers on its bus-boat combo tickets (though this isn't an issue when beginning in Chumphon). These boats also serve Ko Pha-Ngan and Ko Samui.

The other option is night boats operated by a variety of companies. From Monday to Saturday there are car ferries that have air-conditioned rooms with beds – essentially a dorm on the sea – while Sunday is a regular wooden boat with mattresses on the floor and only fans, no air-con.

Boats leave from different piers and transfer costs 50B to 100B. Sometimes tickets are sold that include the transfer, sometimes not – be sure you have a ticket for both the bus and the boat.

BUS

Chumphon's main **bus station** (☑ 077 576 796; Rte 41) is on the highway, an inconvenient 12km from Chumphon. It's not used much – many ticket offices are unstaffed for much of the day – since the main bus companies have their own stops in town.

Choke Anan Tour (☑ 077 511480; off Soi 1, Th Pracha Uthit), near the main market, has the most buses to Bangkok (via Phetchaburi and Prachuap Khiri Khan) and Phuket (via Ranong) plus one to Hat Yai. **Minivans to Ranong** leave from Th Tha Taphao across from New Infinity Travel and **minivans to Surat Thani and Prachuap Khiri Khan** (Th Krumluang Chumphon) leave from Chumphon Night Bazaar, 500m down Th Krumluang Chumphon from the train station near Salsa Hostel.

Other services are along Th Nawamin Ruamjai south of the train station. **Suwannatee Tour** (☑ 077 504901), running five buses to Bangkok including one cheap second-class bus, plus **minivans to Nakhon Si Thammarat** (☑ 077 506326) are across the river, about 1km away.

Affiliated Bus (☑ 082 284 6462) serves Hat Yai (plus a night bus to Bangkok) from its office next to the petrol station and **minivans to Bang Saphan Yai** are at the covered minivan stop that has a yellow sign, 400m south of the petrol station.

For the few services that do use the station, like Chiang Mai, you can buy tickets at guesthouses and travel agencies. Note that there's no scheduled direct service to Hua Hin, you'll need to change at Prachuap Khiri Khan.

TRAIN

There are frequent services between Bangkok and the far south stopping in Chumphon. Make reservations as far in advance as possible. Second-class sleepers are often available day of departure, but first-class rarely is.

❶ Getting Around

Motorcycle taxis (20B to 30B per trip) are seemingly everywhere in town while the more expensive four-wheeled túk-túk are much less common, though there are always some parked at the train station.

Motorcycles can be rented through many guesthouses for 200B to 300B per day. Besides motorcycles, **San Tavee New Rest Home** (☑ 089 011 1749; Soi Sala Daeng 3) also hires bicycles for 100B.

Yellow *sŏrng·tăa·ou* to Hat Thung Wua Laen (30B, 30 minutes, frequent 5.30am to 6pm) leave from the Chumphon Fresh Market on Th Pracha Uthit and then follow Th Sala Daeng north. Little white *sŏrng·tăa·ou* to the main bus station and immigration (25B, 30 to 45 minutes, frequent 7am to 5pm) depart from Th Phinit Khadi next to the City Pillar Shrine. A túk-túk to the bus station will cost upwards of 300B from the city centre. There's an airport shuttle (150B per person) from Fame Guesthouse (p519).

Ko Samui
& the Lower Gulf

Best Places to Eat

➡ Dining On The Rocks (p538)

➡ Pepenero (p538)

➡ Fisherman's Restaurant (p558)

➡ Barracuda (p573; Ko Tao)

➡ Barracuda (p537; Ko Samui)

Best Places to Stay

➡ Six Senses Samui (p538)

➡ Four Seasons Koh Samui (p529)

➡ Kupu Kupu Phangan Beach Villas by l'Occitane (p553)

➡ Jamahkiri Resort & Spa (p572)

Why Go?

The Lower Gulf features Thailand's ultimate island trifecta: Ko Samui, Ko Pha-Ngan and Ko Tao. This family of spectacular islands lures millions of tourists every year with their powder-soft sands and emerald waters. Ko Samui is the oldest sibling who made it big, where high-class resorts operate with Swiss efficiency as uniformed butlers cater to every whim. Ko Pha-Ngan is the slacker middle child with tangled dreadlocks and a penchant for hammock-lazing and all-night parties. Meanwhile Ko Tao is the outdoorsy, fun-loving kid with plenty of spirit and energy – the island specialises in high-adrenalin activities, including world-class diving and snorkelling.

The mainland coast beyond the islands sees few foreign visitors, but is far more authentic Thailand. From the pink dolphins and waterfalls of sleepy Ao Khanom to the Thai Muslim flavours of beach-strolling Songkhla and the charm of Nakhon Si Thammarat, this region is stuffed with off-the-beaten-track wonders.

When to Go

➡ Visit from February to April to celebrate endless sunshine after the monsoon rains have cleared.

➡ June through August are the most inviting months, with relatively short drizzle spells, conveniently coinciding with the Northern Hemisphere's summer holidays.

➡ Expect torrential monsoon rains to rattle on hot tin roofs from October to December; room rates (excluding Christmas) drop significantly.

Ko Samui & the Lower Gulf Highlights

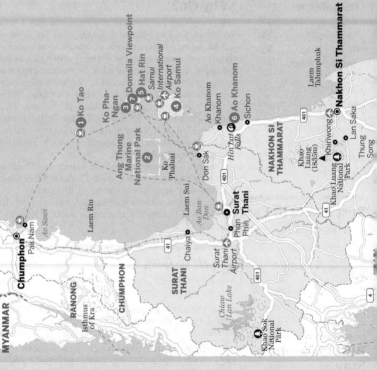

1 Ko Tao (p563) Finding Nemo in this technicolour dive kingdom.

2 Ang Thong Marine National Park (p577) Paddling to hidden bleach-blond beaches.

3 Ko Pha-Ngan (p545) Stringing up a cotton hammock and toeing the curling tide along a secluded beach on the east coast.

4 Ko Samui (p526) Enjoying five-star international cuisine and sipping fancy sunset cocktails.

5 Full Moon Party (p560) Joining the masses of party pilgrims and trancing the night away at Hat Rin on Ko Pha-Ngan.

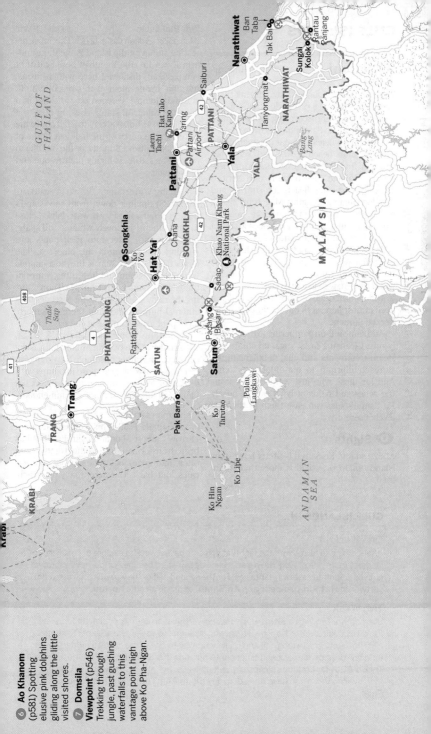

GULF OF
THAILAND

408
41
Krabi
TRANG
Trang
KRABI
4
Rattaphum
PHATTHALUNG
Thale
Sap
Pak Bara
Ko
Tarutao
SATUN
Satun
Padang
Besar
Ko Hin
Ngam
Ko Lipe
Pulau
Langkawi
ANDAMAN
SEA
Songkhla
Ko
Yo
Hat Yai
Chana
SONGKHLA
42
Sadao
Khao Nam Khang
National Park
MALAYSIA
Laem
Tachi
Hat Talo
Kapo
Taning
Pattani
Pattani
Airport
Saiburi
42
PATTANI
Yala
YALA
Bang
Lang
Narathiwat
Tak Bai
Ban
Taba
Saiburi
Tanyongmat
NARATHIWAT
Sungai
Kolok
Rantau
Panjang
MALAYSIA

6 Ao Khanom
(p581) Spotting
elusive pink dolphins
gliding along the little-
visited shores.

7 Domsila
Viewpoint (p546)
Trekking through
jungle, past gushing
waterfalls to this
vantage point high
above Ko Pha-Ngan.

GULF ISLANDS

Ko Samui
เกาะสมุย

POP 62,000

Whether you're sun-seeking, dozing in a hammock, feasting on world-class cuisine, beach partying or discovering wellness in an exclusive spa, Ko Samui has it covered.

Ko Samui's beaches are a diverse bunch: roll up your beach towel and see what you can find. Make it Coco Tam's in Fisherman's Village for cocktails and serious relaxing, Chaweng Beach for sunrise and people-watching, lengthy Mae Nam Beach for peace, or napping under a coconut tree before giving in to a west-coast sunset across seas shimmering with bronze. Dining is Samui's other top indulgence. The island is stuffed with *kôw gang* (rice and curry) shops, often a flimsy wooden shack serving southern Thai–style curries. Follow locals to the food markets for pointers, but if you need atmosphere, seek out romantic, sunset-flecked dinners.

Add some full-on pampering to the leisurely mix. Cleansing fasts, yoga, tai-chi, herbal steam treatments and chakra-balancing restore equilibrium to out-of-kilter systems. And for those who just want to ease away the aches and pains of lying on the beach, Ko Samui's spas can ease them to the next level of serenity.

◉ Sights

At 229 sq km, Ko Samui is pretty large – the island's main ring road is more than 50km total.

Wat Plai Laem BUDDHIST TEMPLE
(Map p528; ☉ dawn-dusk) FREE The most arresting statue on the island is the thousand-arm Kwan Im (the Buddhist bodhisattva of compassion), displayed here with 18 arms, in a fan arrangement at this recently built, stunning temple. Perched on an island in a lake, the colourful statue rises up next to a temple hall – similarly constructed above the water. To the north of the hall is a statue of the jovial Maitreya Buddha, or the Buddha to come. The setting is highly picturesque and photogenic.

Na Muang Waterfalls WATERFALL
(Map p528) Spilling down from the island's highest points, these two waterfalls – close to each other – are lovely when in full spate, pouring frigid water into rock pools and gushing down towards the blue sea. The larger of the two, at 30m, is the most famous waterfall on Samui and lies in the centre of the island about 12km from Na Thon. During the rainy season, the water cascades over ethereal purple rocks, and there's a superb, large pool for swimming at the base.

Na Muang Waterfall 2 (Map p528) FREE, the smaller of the two Na Muang falls, is accessed via the rather miserable Na Muang Safari Park, where you can pose for snaps with a tiger or leopard, or feed an elephant bananas (all for a fee, and not recommended).

Fisherman's Village VILLAGE
(Map p541; Bo Phut) This concentration of narrow Chinese shophouses in Bo Phut has been transformed into some trendy (and often midrange) boutique hotels, eateries, cafes and bars. The accompanying beach,

---

GULF ISLANDS IN...

One Week

After coming to terms with the fact that you only have a week to explore these idyllic islands, start on one of **Ko Pha-Ngan's** secluded western beaches or journey east to live out your ultimate castaway fantasies. For the second half of the week choose between partying in **Hat Rin**, pampering on **Ko Samui** or diving off little **Ko Tao**.

Two Weeks

Start on **Ko Tao** with a 3½-day Open Water certification course, or sign up for a few fun dives. Slide over to **Ko Pha-Ngan** and soak up the sociable vibe in party-central Hat Rin. Then, grab a long-tail and make your way to one of the island's hidden coves for a few days of detoxing and quiet contemplation. **Ko Samui** is next on the agenda. Try **Bo Phut** for boutique sleeps or live it up like a rock star on Chaweng or Choeng Mon beach. And, if you have time, do a day trip to **Ang Thong National Marine Park**.

particularly the eastern part, is slim and coarse but becomes whiter and lusher further west. The combination of pretty sands and gussied-up old village is a winner, but it can get busy during peak season. Off-season, it's lovely, quiet and elbow-free.

Ban Hua Thanon
AREA

(Map p528; Ban Hua Thanon) Just south of Hat Lamai, Hua Thanon is full of photo ops and home to a vibrant Muslim community; its anchorage of high-bowed fishing vessels by the almost deserted beach through the palm trees at the end of the community is a veritable gallery of intricate designs, though it's a shame about all the rubbish on the sand. Look out for the green, gold and white **mosque** in the village, along the main drag.

Wat Racha Thammaram
BUDDHIST TEMPLE

(Wat Sila Ngu; Map p536; off Rte 4169; ☉dawn-dusk) This temple (the name means Snake Stone Temple) on the south side of Rte 4169 has a recently built red-clay temple hall, decorated with a fascinating display of bas-relief designs and statues. It's an astonishing sight against the blue sky. A golden pagoda contains relics of Sakyamuni, and a sacred bodhi tree also grows within the grounds. From the pagoda, steps head down to a collection of stupas, commemorating former monks.

Hainan Temple
TEMPLE

(Hailam Nathon Shrine; 海南公所; Map p528; Na Thon; ☉dawn-dusk) FREE Fronted by a pair of golden Chinese lions, adorned with coiling dragons and pretty much the most colourful Chinese temple (and guildhall) on the island, this shrine was set up by Thai-Chinese who originated from the island of Hǎinán in the far south of China. You can find signs to it pointing off Rte 4169.

Hin-Ta & Hin-Yai
LANDMARK

(Map p536; Lamai) At the south end of Hat Lamai, you'll find these infamous genitalia-shaped stone formations (also known as Grandfather and Grandmother Rocks) that provide endless mirth for giggling Thai tourists.

🏃 Activities

Ko Samui offers many activities geared towards kids and teenagers. Be wary of 'ecotourism' tours on the island – many are just commercial operations with little concern for what they may appear to promote.

DON'T MISS

KO TAN

Tired of tours and busy beaches? For the intrepid DIY traveller there's no better way to spend a day on Ko Samui than with a trip to the white sands of Ko Tan. Hire a long-tail boat from the boatmen who beach their boats alongside the strip of seafood restaurants on Hat Thong Tanot on Ko Samui's south coast; a boat for up to six people should cost 1500B to 2000B for a four-hour trip. The island itself is only about 15 minutes from Ko Samui. While the snorkelling isn't that great, the white-sand beach is empty aside from the occasional visit by charter boats and local fishermen, and the views and swimming are sublime.

★ Red Baron
CRUISE

(Map p541; contact@redbaron-samui.com; Hat Bang Rak; from 2500B) With day-long cruises around Ko Samui (9.30am Tuesday), brunch trips to Ko Pha-Ngan (11am Wednesday and Sunday), sunset dinner cruises to Ko Som (4.30pm, Monday and Friday) and journeys over the waves to Ang Thong Marine Park (8.30am, Thursday), Red Baron is a traditional and very popular sailing junk moored at Bangrak. Meals and drinks provided. Private charters also available.

Samui Dog & Cat Rescue Centre
VOLUNTEERING

(Map p531; ☎081 893 9443; www.samuidog.org; Soi 3, Chaweng Beach Rd; ☉9am-6pm) Donations of time and/or money are hugely appreciated at the aptly named Samui Dog & Cat Rescue Centre. Volunteers are always needed to take care of the animals at their kennel/clinic in Ban Taling Ngam (but not at the smaller Hat Chaweng branch). Call the centre for volunteering details or swing by for additional info. Check the website for directions.

Coco Splash Waterpark
WATER PARK

(Map p536; ☎081 082 6035; www.samuiwaterpark.com; Ban Lamai; over/under 1.5m 349/329B, under 0.9m free; ☉10.30am-5.30pm) Kids under 10 will love this small park of painted concrete water slides. Towel hire is 60B (200B deposit) and there's a restaurant (open till 10pm). Note that if you're planning on watching the kids and not going in the water yourself, you get in for free. Those under 1.5m get a T-shirt thrown in; if you're over 1.5m, it's a cocktail.

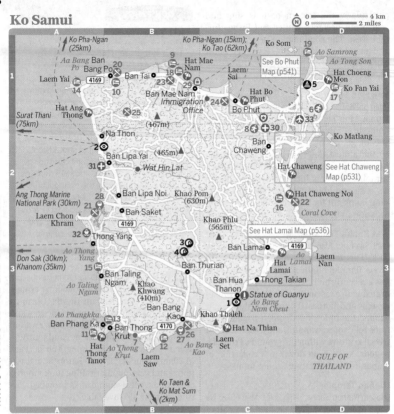

Koh Samui Rum
DISTILLERY

(Map p528; ☑ 091 816 7416; www.rum-distillery.com; Ban Bang Kao; tasting shots 50-75B; ⊗ 9am-6pm) The only rum distillery in Thailand produces Caribbean agricole-style spirits (distilled from fresh, fermented sugarcane juice) in a variety of all natural flavours, including a delectable coconut rum obtained from soaking coconut meat in the rum for several months. There's a video about the production process, a tasting area, an excellent French-Thai restaurant and a shop in beautiful palm-shaded surrounds.

Kiteboarding Asia
WATER SPORTS

(Map p528; ☑ 083 643 1627; www.kiteboardingasia.com; Na Thon; 1-/3-day course 4000/11,000B; ⊗ 9am-6pm) This pro place will get you kitesurfing on flat shallow water. The Na Thon location on the west side is for December to March winds (another in Hua Thanon in the south of the island is for April to October gusts).

Diving

If you're serious about diving, head to Ko Tao and base yourself there. If you're short on time and don't want to leave Samui, there are plenty of operators who will take you to the same dive sites (at a greater fee, of course). Try to book with a company that has its own boat (or leases a boat) – it's slightly more expensive, but you'll be glad you did it. Companies without boats often shuttle divers on the passenger catamaran to Ko Tao, where you board a second boat to reach your dive site. These trips are arduous, meal-less and rather impersonal.

Certification courses tend to be twice as expensive on Ko Samui as they are on Ko Tao, due largely to use of extra petrol, since Ko Tao is significantly closer to the preferred diving locations. You'll spend between 14,000B and 22,000B on an Open Water certification, and figure on between 4500B and 6200B for a

Ko Samui

diving day trip including two dives, depending on the location of the site.

Ko Samui's **hyperbaric chamber** (Map p541; ☑ 077 427427, emergency 081 081 9555; www.sssnetwork.com/our-chambers-and-medical-clinics/koh-samui-thailand; Big Buddha Beach; ⊙24hr) is at Big Buddha Beach (Hat Bang Rak).

★**100 Degrees East**   DIVING
(Map p541; ☑ 077 423936; www.100degreeseast.com; Hat Bang Rak; ⊙9am-6.30pm Dec-Oct) Highly professional and recommended, with a dedicated team, for excellent and excellent diving and snorkelling expeditions to Ang Thong Marine National Park, Ko Tao, Sail Rock and other sites.

★**The Life Aquatic**   DIVING
(Map p541; ☑ 086 030 0286; www.thelifeaquatic.asia; The Wharf, Fisherman's Village) Overseen by friendly and very competent and experienced instructors, this first-rate dive operation offers a range of SSI & PADI dive courses, dive

trips to Ko Tao as well as snorkelling trips and accommodation.

Spas & Yoga

Competition between Samui's five-star accommodation is fierce, meaning spas are of the highest calibre. The Spa Resort (p532) in Lamai is the island's original health destination, and is still known for its effective 'clean me out' fasting regime.

Yoga is offered at many hotels and is also big business. Ko Pha-Ngan is perhaps more the place for the hard-core, but you won't have a problem finding classes on Ko Samui – try Samahita Retreat (p530) or Absolute Sanctuary (p530).

★**Spa at the Four Seasons**   SPA
(Map p528; ☑ 077 243000; www.fourseasons.com/kohsamui/spa; Bang Po) The luxury **Four Seasons** on a rocky peninsula in the northwest corner of Ko Samui has one of the best spas around, with a heady range of therapies

to pamper body and soul, from chakra-balancing to body-wraps and coconut pedicures. Emerge transformed.

★**Absolute Sanctuary** YOGA, SPA
(Map p528; ☑ 077 601190; www.absolutesanctuary.com; Choeng Mon) Detox, spa, yoga, Pilates, fasting, lifestyle and nutrition packages, in an alluring Moroccan-inspired setting.

Samahita Retreat YOGA, SPA
(Map p528; ☑ 077 920090; www.samahitaretreat.com; Laem Sor Beach) Secreted away along the southern shores, Samahita Retreat has state-of-the-art facilities and a dedicated team of trainers for the growing band of therapeutic holidaymakers, wellness seekers and serious detoxers. Accommodation is in a comfy apartment block up the street, while yoga studios, wellness centres and a health-food restaurant sit calmly along the shore.

Tamarind Springs MASSAGE
(Map p536; ☑ 080 569 6654; www.tamarindsprings.com; off Rte 4169; spa packages from 1500B) Tucked far away from the beach within a silent coconut-palm plantation, Tamarind's small collection of villas and massage studios is seamlessly incorporated into nature: some have granite boulders built into walls and floors, while others offer private ponds or creative outdoor baths. There's also a superhealthy restaurant and packages for three-night or longer stays in the elegant villas and suites.

🎓 Courses

★**Samui Institute of Thai Culinary Arts** COOKING
(SITCA; Map p531; ☑ 077 413172; http://sitca.com; Chaweng Beach Rd; courses 1850B) For Thai cooking skills, SITCA is the place to do it, with daily Thai cooking classes and courses in the aristocratic Thai art of carving fruits and vegetables into intricate floral designs. Lunchtime classes begin at 11am, while dinner starts at 4pm (both are three-hour courses with three or more dishes).

★**Lamai Muay Thai Camp** HEALTH & WELLBEING
(Map p536; ☑ 087 082 6970; www.lamaimuaythaicamp.com; 82/2 Moo3, Lamai; day/week training sessions 300/1500B; ⏰7am-8pm) The island's best *moo·ay tai* (Thai boxing) training (for the seriously serious) is at this place, which caters to beginners as well as those wanting to hone their skills. There's also a well-equipped gym for boxers and nonboxers

who want to up their fitness levels, plus accommodation and breakfast (and all-meals-included) packages.

Hemingway's on the Beach COOKING
(Map p528; ☑ 088 452 4433; off 4170, Ao Thong Krut; per person 1500B; ⏰10.30am-12.30pm) During the week, this restaurant on the southern sands of Thong Krut hosts a Thai cookery school – you get to select three dishes from the menu and learn how to cook it all up in a two-hour class. There's a minimum of two and a maximum of four people per class.

Mind Your Language LANGUAGE
(Map p528; ☑ 077 962088; www.mindyourlanguagethailand.com; 142/7 Mu 1, Bo Phut) With lessons from 600B per hour, this accessible and professional language school in Bo Phut can gear you up with classes in Thai, including intensive programs.

🛏 Sleeping

There is no shortage of top-end resorts sporting exclusive bungalows and pampering spas. Bo Phut, on the northern coast, has attractive boutique lodgings for midrange travellers. Backpack-lugging visitors may have to look harder, but budget digs pop up periodically along all beaches.

🛏 Hat Chaweng

Busy, throbbing, commercial Chaweng is packed with accommodation, from cheap backpackers to futuristic villas with swimming pools. The northern half of the beach is the biggest party zone, and nearby resorts are in ear-shot of Ark Bar at the centre of it all. If you're hoping for early nights, pick a resort to the south or bring earplugs.

Samui Hostel HOSTEL $
(Map p531; ☑ 089 874 3737; Chaweng Beach Rd; dm 200-300B, d 850B; ✳@) It doesn't look like much from the front, but this neat, tidy, friendly and popular place is very central, with clean fan and air-con dorm rooms and spruce air-con doubles on the nonbeach side of the road. Service is a cut above the rest and there's a popular room at the front with wooden tables for lounging and chatting.

Pott Guesthouse GUESTHOUSE $
(Map p531; Chaweng Beach Rd; r with fan/air con from 300/600B; ✳☏) The big, bright cement rooms all with attached hot-water bathrooms and balcony in this nondescript

Hat Chaweng

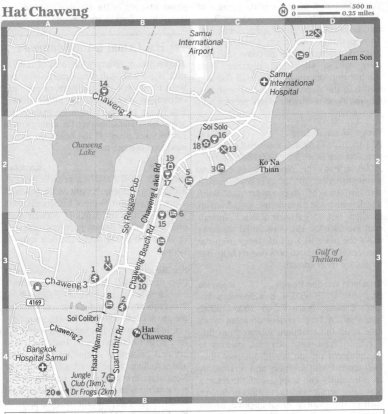

Hat Chaweng

KO SAMUI & THE LOWER GULF KO SAMUI

apartment block are a steal, but that's about it. Reception is at an unnamed restaurant on the main drag right opposite across the alley.

Ark Bar Beach Resort RESORT $$$
(Map p531; ☎ 077 961333; www.ark-bar.com; Chaweng Beach Rd; r from 2000B; ❄️📶🏊)

You'll find two of every party animal at clean and well-tended 328-room Ark Bar – frat boys, chilled-out hippies, teenagers, 40-somethings and so on. Contemporary, brightly painted rooms all come with balcony, within staggering distance from the bar that pumps out music all day and well into the night, along with fire shows. Ground-floor rooms have less privacy and are noisier.

Tango Beach Resort
RESORT $$$

(Map p531; ☑ 077 300451; www.tangobeachsamui.com; Chaweng Beach Rd; r 2200-2800, ste 3800-7500B; ※ 🛜 🌊) The colourful lobby suggests a youngish vibe, but Tango is really more a standard string of bungalows arranged along a teak boardwalk meandering away from an excellent but busy stretch of beach, though staff are friendly. The dark tinted windows make the place look a little tacky from the outside (and the dated pool doesn't help) but rooms are fresh enough.

Chaweng Garden Beach
RESORT $$$

(Map p531; ☑ 077 960394; www.chawenggarden.com; Chaweng Beach Rd; r 3600-33,000B; ※ @ 🛜 🌊) A huge variety of room types hide amid the abundant foliage, from fine if rather bland standards with balcony to an indulgent private beachfront pool villa. Well tended with greenery and serviced by an extrasmiley and helpful staff, the resort's best-value accommodation awaits in choices such as the modern Asian-inspired 'Shino' rooms and polished wood bungalows.

★ Buri Rasa Village
RESORT $$$

(Map p531; ☑ 077 956055; www.burirasa.com; Chaweng Beach Rd; r 4850-8900B; ※ 🛜 🌊) This Zen-like place is beautifully landscaped with palms and frangipani. It's central, well priced and on a good stretch of busy beach, but the real reason to stay here is the bend-over-backwards friendly and helpful service, while Thai-style wooden doors lead to private villa patios and simple yet elegant rooms.

★ Library
RESORT $$$

(Map p531; ☑ 077 422767; www.thelibrary.co.th; Chaweng Beach Rd; studio/ste incl breakfast from 11,900/13,600B; ※ @ 🛜 🌊) This library is too cool for school. The entire resort is a sparkling white mirage accented with black trimming and slatted curtains. Besides the futuristic iMac computer in each page (rooms are 'pages' here), our favourite feature is the large monochromatic wall art – it

glows brightly in the evening and you can adjust the colour to your mood.

📑 Hat Lamai & the Southeast

The central, powdery white area of Hat Lamai is packed with sunburned souls, but head to the grainier northern or southern extremities and things get much quieter. Ban Lamai runs back from the main beach area. Unlike Hat Chaweng, the main party in Lamai takes place off the beach, so accommodation is more tranquil.

New Hut
BUNGALOW $

(Map p536; ☑ 077 230437; Lamai North; huts 250-800B; 🛜) A-frame huts right on the beach all share a big, clean block of bathrooms, with a lively restaurant, friendly enough staff, one of the simplest and happiest backpacker vibes and pretty much the best value in Lamai.

Spa Resort
BUNGALOW $$

(Map p536; ☑ 077 230855; www.thesparesorts.com; Lamai North; bungalows 720-1200B; ※ 🛜 🌊) Programs at this friendly, practical and simple spa include colonics, massage, aqua detox, hypnotherapy and yoga, just to name a few. With rattan furniture, traditional wall art and balconies, rooms are comfortable and excellent value, but book up quickly. Nonguests are welcome to partake in the spa programs and dine at the excellent (and healthy) open-air **restaurant** (Map p536; off Rte 4169; meals 100-400B; ⊙ 7am-10pm; 🛜 🖉) by the beach.

★ Rocky's Resort
RESORT $$$

(Map p536; ☑ 077 418367; www.rockyresort.com; off Rte 4169; r 8000-20,000B; ※ 🛜 🌊) With a supremely calm reception area and two swimming pools, Rocky effortlessly finds the right balance between an upmarket ambience and an unpretentious, sociable vibe. During quieter months prices are a steal, since ocean views abound, and each room (some with pool) has been furnished with beautiful Thai-inspired furniture that seamlessly incorporates a modern twist.

Samui Jasmine Resort
RESORT $$$

(Map p536; ☑ 077 232446; www.samuijasmineresort.com; 131/8 Moo 3, Lamai; r & bungalows 4600-12,000B; ※ 🛜 🌊) Smack dab in the middle of Hat Lamai, varnished-teak yet frilly Samui Jasmine is a great deal. Go for the lower-priced rooms – most have excellent views of the ocean and the crystal-coloured lap pool.

Bo Phut & the Northeast

The point of focus is Fisherman's Village, with a fine selection of accommodation. Things get very busy during peak season, but during the low season, prices are down and it can be particularly quiet and inviting.

Castaway Guesthouse   GUESTHOUSE $$
(Map p541; ☑ 081 968 5811; www.castawaysamui. com; Fisherman's Village; r with fan/air-con 650-1500B; ※ ⑦) A block away from the beach, Castaway's 15 rooms are all clean, bright and cheery.

Eden   BUNGALOW $$$
(Map p541; ☑ 077 427645; www.edenbungalows. com; Fisherman's Village; bungalows 1500-2300B; ※ ⑦ ☑) A short walk from the beach, the 10 bungalows and five rooms here are all tucked away in a lovely tangle of garden with a small pool at its centre. Cheaper options are rather shabby but an upgrade gets you a more stylish suite with yellow walls and naturalistic wood furniture; for families, there's a 100-sq-m apartment with kitchenette too.

Hacienda   GUESTHOUSE $$$
(Map p541; ☑ 077 960827; www.samui-hacienda. com; Fisherman's Village; r 2500-4800B; ※ ⑦ ☑) Polished terracotta and rounded archways lend the entrance a Spanish mission motif. Similar decor permeates the adorable rooms, which sport touches such as pebbled bathroom walls and translucent bamboo lamps. Hacienda Suites, the overflow property a few doors down, has the smaller and cheaper rooms which are mostly windowless, but still clean and comfortable. The tiny rooftop pool has gorgeous ocean views.

★ Samui Honey Cottages Resort   RESORT $$$
(Map p528; ☑ 077 427093; www.samuihoney.com; Choeng Mon; r incl breakfast 3500-6500B; ※ ⑦ ☑) At the quieter southern part of the beach, this small resort (with an equally small pool) isn't anything that special, but it's nicer than some of the other mediocre offerings in this price range on this beach. Expect attractive, classic Zen-style rooms.

★ Scent   RESORT $$$
(Map p541; ☑ 077 960123; www.thescenthotel. com; Off Beach Rd; ste 8500-10,500B) Seek out the taste (and scent if you light your complimentary incense) of Indo-China at this tranquil gem that recreates the elegance of 1940s and '50s colonial Asia. The tall grey concrete structure is cut by elongated teak-framed windows and surrounds a courtyard swimming pool and ornamental trees and plants.

★ W Retreat Koh Samui   RESORT $$$
(Map p541; ☑ 077 915999; www.wretreatkohsamui. com; Mae Nam; r from 20,000B; ※ @ ⑦ ☑) A be-jewelled 'W' welcomes guests on the curling road to the lobby, beyond which glittering infinity pools lead to an endless horizon. The trademark 'W glam' does its darnedest to fuse an urban vibe with tropical serenity throughout. Do note, though, that this hotel is on a hill and not on a beach, though it does have its own length of sand.

Mae Nam & the North Coast

Mae Nam has some excellent accommodation choices, especially in the top end, but budget-seekers can find some excellent value bungalows too.

Shangri-la   BUNGALOW $
(Map p528; ☑ 077 425189; Mae Nam; bungalows with fan/air-con from 500/1300B; ※ ⑦) A backpacker's Shangri La indeed – these are some of the cheapest huts around and they occupy a sublime stretch of the beach. Grounds are sparsely landscaped but the basic concrete bungalows, all with attached bathrooms (only air-con rooms have hot water), are well kept and the staff are pleasant.

★ Code   HOTEL $$$
(Map p528; ☑ 077 602122; www.samuicode.com; Mae Nam; ste 3300-11,100B; ※ ⑦ ☑) Sleek modern lines and dust-free white contrast against the turquoise sea and the hotel's large infinity pool, making for a stunning piece of architecture. The all-ocean-view suites are spacious and efficient, and the service is just as neat. Of course, everything you require is there at your fingertips, including a gym, spa, steam room, tennis court and restaurant.

Coco Palm Resort   BUNGALOW $$$
(Map p528; ☑ 077 447211; www.cocopalmbeach resort.com; Mae Nam; bungalows 3000-9450B; ※ ⑦ ☑) The huge array of bungalows at well-tended Coco Palm have been crafted with hardwood, bamboo and rattan touches, with a palm-fronted rectangular pool the centrepiece along the beach, facing the sea. The cheapest choices are the furthest

MOUNTAIN-TOP RETREAT

The perilous drive up the road from Chaweng is totally worthwhile once you take in the incredible views from **Jungle Club** (Map p528; ☑ 081 894 2327; www.jungleclubsamui.com; huts 800-1800B; houses 2700-4500B; ✳@🛜🏊). With a relaxed back-to-nature vibe, this isolated mountain getaway is a huge hit among locals and tourists alike. Guests chill around the stunning horizon pool or catnap under the canopied roofs of an open-air *săh·lah*. Even if you don't stay here, it's worth a trip for a drink overlooking the views from the **bar** (☉9am-9.30pm). Jungle Club can arrange pick up from Chaweng for 400B, or you can get a taxi for a similar fare.

from the sand, but even these are comfy. If you want to make a real splash, aim for the beachfront pool villas.

★ **Belmond Napasai**   RESORT $$$
(Map p528; ☑077 429200; www.napasai.com; Bang Po; r 15,800-80,800B; ✳@🛜🏊) Gorgeously manicured grounds welcome weary travellers as they glide past grazing water buffalo and groundsmen donning cream-coloured pith helmets. A generous smattering of villas dot the expansive landscape – all sport traditional Thai-style decorations, from the intricately carved wooden ornamentation to streamers of luscious local silks and bamboo interiors, as well as sumptuous views over the Gulf of Thailand from the lovely balconies.

Na Thon & the West

Na Thon itself has few hotels of merit, though it's a handy hub for getting on or off the boat. Further south you'll find two of the island's best hotels: the Conrad Koh Samui and the Intercontinental Samui Baan Taling Ngam Resort.

Chytalay Palace Hotel   HOTEL $$
(Map p528; ☑077 421079; 152 Nathon Moo 3; d 400-950B, tr 800-1000B; ✳🛜) This quiet hotel on the beachfront road a short walk south from the pier has very good, spacious rooms with balcony overlooking the sea and some delightful sunsets. The lower-floor rooms have electricity cables partially blocking the view but are 400B less than the newer rooms

upstairs. Cheaper doubles are fan only. All rooms have attached showers. Service is pleasant.

★ **Conrad Koh Samui**   RESORT $$$
(Map p528; ☑077 915888; www.conradkohsamui.com; villas 45,000-126,000B; ✳🛜🏊) The 81 exceptionally neat-lined, contemporary and gorgeous villas of the sumptuous Conrad gaze out over an azure sea, by way of their very own infinity pools. Everything is simply state of the art, the bathrooms are marbled perfection and the full-on sunsets quite unforgettable. Four restaurants, a wine cellar and a superb spa round off a handsome and tempting picture.

★ **Intercontinental Samui Baan Taling Ngam Resort**   RESORT $$$
(Map p528; ☑077 429100; www.samui.intercontinental.com; Taling Ngam; r from 12,000B; ✳🛜🏊) This 79-room resort on the west coast whisks you from the crowded east coast and ushers you into sunset-drenched luxury, with views out over to Ang Thong Marine National Park. Rooms are beautifully presented with dark-wood furnishings, while the resort boasts seven swimming pools. The beachfront pool villas come with plunge pools, while dining and drinking choices are simply superb.

South Coast

Easy Time   BUNGALOW $$$
(Map p528; ☑077 920111; www.easytimekohsamui.com; Bang Kao; villas 2300-4000B; ✳@🛜🏊) Safely tucked away from the throngs of tourists, this little haven – nestled a few minutes' walk to the beach around a serene swimming pool – doesn't have well-oiled service so be prepared to be master of your own off-the-beaten-path getaway. Duplex villa units and a chic dining space create an elegant mood that is refreshingly unpretentious.

Elements   RESORT $$$
(Map p528; ☑077 914678; www.kosamui.com/elements-boutique-resort; Ao Phang Ka; r incl breakfast 7400-24,000B; ✳@🛜🏊) Peaceful Elements occupies a lonely strand of palm-studded sand with views of the stunning Five Islands, and is the perfect place for a meditative retreat or quiet couples' romantic getaway. Chic rooms are arranged in condo-like blocks, while hidden villas dot the path down to the oceanside lounge area. Free kayaks and bikes plus excellent service add to the calm.

✖ Eating

The island enjoys an ample supply of fresh seafood as well as the various culinary influences of southern Thai cuisine: Malay, Indian, Chinese and Indonesian ingredients, flavours and dishes have found a place here. You'll find that curries are spicier than their central Thailand counterparts and are often seasoned with turmeric, which imparts a yellowish hue. Cloves, cinnamon and cardamom are some of the spices from Indonesia and India that are fed into the aromatic make-up of local dishes such as gang *mát·sà·màn* (Muslim curry) and *kôw mòk gài* (chicken biryani).

✖ Hat Chaweng

Scores of restaurants on the 'strip' serve a mixed bag of local bites, international cuisine and fast food. Competition sees new arrivals all the time and a gradual raising of the bar. To escape the eardrum-piercing noise of the *moo·ay tai* (Thai boxing) vans at night, flee to the beach, where many bungalow operators set up tables on the sand.

Laem Din Market   MARKET $
(Map p531; Chaweng; dishes from 35B; ⊗4am-6pm, night market 6pm-2am) A busy day market, Laem Din is packed with stalls that sell fresh fruits, vegetables and meats and stock local Thai kitchens. Pick up a kilo of sweet green oranges or wander the stalls trying to spot the ingredients in last night's curry. For dinner, check out the adjacent night market to sample tasty southern-style fried chicken and curries.

Tuk Tuk Backpackers   CAFE $
(Map p531; ☑087 268 2575; Chaweng Beach Rd; mains from 120B; ⊗10am-2am) This full-on, no-holds-barred, high-impact, brazen and voluminous saloon-style Western cafe/restaurant/bar on Chaweng Beach Rd does good hangover-cure brekkies, with multiple TV screens, pool tables and all the usual trappings.

Hungry Wolf   BURGERS $$
(Map p531; ☑094 408 2243; Chaweng Beach Rd; mains from 220B; ⊗10am-10pm) With fun, vibrantly designed and catchy murals revolving around British culinary idioms, this neat Polish-run Chaweng restaurant does a good trade in juicy burgers, steaks, ribs, pizza and a whole variety of other delicious fare. It's not big, and attracts considerable custom, but

the capable and enthusiastic owner makes everyone feel at home.

★ Dr Frogs   STEAK $$$
(Map p528; ☑077 448505; www.drfrogssamui.com; Rte 4169; mains from 480B; ⊗7am-11pm) Perched atop a rocky overlook, Dr Frogs combines beautiful ocean vistas with delicious international Italian grills, seafood, pasta, pizza and Thai favourites. Delectable steaks and crab cakes, and friendly owners, make it a winner. It's a romantic setting, and for harassed parents there's a kids' playground in the front garden. Live guitar music on Mondays and Wednesdays at 7.30pm.

★ Page   FUSION $$$
(Map p531; ☑077 422767; www.thelibrarysamui.com/the-page; dishes 300-1650B; ⊗7am-midnight; ☎) If you can't afford to stay at the ultra-swanky Library (p532), have a meal at its beachside restaurant instead. It's not cheap, but lunch is a bit more casual and affordable, although you'll miss the designer lighting in the evening. Sunrise breakfasts are lovely.

★ Larder   EUROPEAN $$$
(Map p531; ☑077 601259; www.thelardersamui.com; Chaweng Beach Rd; mains 300-820B; ⊗noon-11pm Mon-Sat; ☎) This restaurant/bar/gastro-pub pulls out the stops in an invigorating menu of classic fare in a relaxing and tasteful setting, supported by a strong selection of wines and zesty cocktails. It's a winning formula, with dishes ranging from slow-cooked lamb spare ribs to fish and chips.

✖ Hat Lamai & the Southeast

As Samui's second-most populated beach, Hat Lamai has a surprisingly limited assortment of decent eateries when compared to Hat Chaweng next door. The **Lamai Walking Street Night Market** (Map p536; Lamai; ⊗4-10pm Sun) is excellent for street food, but turn on your pickpocket radar.

Hua Thanon Market   MARKET $
(Map p528; Ban Hua Thanon; dishes from 30B; ⊗6am-6pm) Slip into the rhythm of this village market slightly south of Lamai; it's a window into the food ways of southern Thailand. Vendors shoo away the flies from the freshly butchered meat, and housewives load bundles of vegetables into their baby-filled motorcycle baskets. Follow the market road to the row of food shops delivering edible Muslim culture: chicken biryani, fiery

Hat Lamai

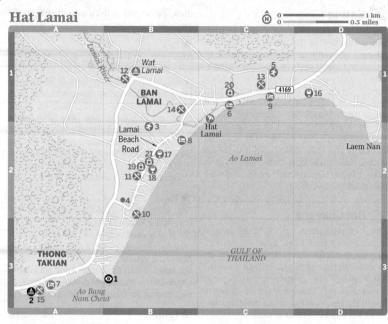

Hat Lamai

⊙ Sights

⊕ Activities, Courses & Tours

⊜ Sleeping

⊗ Eating

⊙ Drinking & Nightlife

⊟ Shopping

curries or toasted rice with coconut, bean sprouts, lemon grass and dried shrimp.

Pad Thai
THAI $

(Map p536; ☎077 458560-4; www.manathai.com/samui/phad-thai; Rte 4169; mains from 70B; ☺11am-9.30pm) On the corner of the huge Manathai hotel by the road, this highly affordable, semi-alfresco and smart restaurant is a fantastic choice for stir-fried and soup noodles, rounded off with a coconut ice cream.

Kangaroo
THAI $

(Map p536; Lamai Beach Rd; mains from 120B; ☺1-11pm) Colourful, efficient and friendly Kangaroo serves excellent Thai and Western dishes, and a wealth of succulent seafood, including shark steak, barracuda steak and blue crab as well as more standard chicken curries, sizzling platters, fried rice dishes and pasta.

★ La Fabrique
BAKERY **$$**

(Map p536; ☎ 077 961507; Rte 4169; set breakfasts from 120B; ⏱ 6.30am-10.30pm; 🛜) Ceiling fans chop the air and service is snappy and helpful at this roomy French-style boulangerie/patisserie away from the main drag, near Wat Lamai on Rte 4169. *The* place for brekkie, select from fresh bread, croissants, gratins, baguettes, meringues, yoghurts, pastries or unusually good set breakfasts that include fresh fruit. Wash down with a decent selection of coffees or teas.

★ Baobab
FRENCH **$$**

(Map p536; ☎ 084 838 3040; Hat Lamai; mains 150-380B; ⏱ 8am-6pm) Grab a free beach towel and crash out on a sun lounger after a full meal at breezy Baobab, or have a massage next door, but seize one of the beach tables (if you can). You'll need two hands to turn over the hefty menu, with its all-day breakfasts, French/Thai dishes, grills, pastas and popular specials, including red tuna steak (350B).

Tandoori Nights
INDIAN **$$**

(Map p536; ☎ 091 161 7026; Lamai; mains from 150B; ⏱ 11am-11pm) The set meals at this welcoming Indian restaurant will only set you back 190B for a vegetable curry, soft drink and a papadum; otherwise select your spice level from the à la carte menu or take a deep breath and order the eye-watering lamb vindaloo (290B), quenched with a chilled beer.

★ The Dining Room
FRENCH **$$$**

(Map p536; www.rockyresort.com; off Rte 4169; dishes 300-950B; ⏱ lunch & dinner) The signature beef Rossini at this fantastically positioned beachfront restaurant at Rocky's Resort (p532) is like sending your taste buds on a Parisian vacation as the views pop you into seventh heaven.

🍴 Bo Phut & the Northeast

Fisherman's Village has the nicest setting and a bounty of choice, including the busy Friday Walking Street market, plus heaps of well-priced options on the road leading inland towards the main road. Choeng Mon's lively main drag is well provided with eating options, although price tags are high and there's no beach view. There are several decent restaurants and cafes around Big Buddha Beach, west of Choeng Mon.

Ninja Crepes
THAI **$**

(Map p541; 4171 Beach Rd, Bo Phut; mains from 80B; ⏱ 9am-9pm) The owners of this great place were recently turfed out of their lucrative Chaweng restaurant, but the pay-off is fine sea views; the location sees less custom, but that makes it quieter too. Expect Thai seafood, curries, crepes, soups and sticky desserts.

★ Salefino
MEDITERRANEAN **$$**

(Map p541; ☎ 091 825 2190; www.salefinosamui.com; Hat Bang Rak; ⏱ 1-3pm & 5-9pm Mon-Fri, 5-10.30pm Sat) This new restaurant (sister establishment of Pepenero; p538) serves delightful seafood, pasta and tapas dishes with a strong tilt towards Italian, with a fine selection of wines and a lovely setting by the sea, all viewed from a rustic chic setting; dinner is particularly charming, with sunset.

Leonardo Gelateria Italiana
GELATO **$$**

(Map p541; ☎ 092 847 7385; Wat Phra Yai; from 150B; ⏱ 9am-6pm) This small gelateria is not cheap – it's 150B for one cup of ice cream or sorbet – but there's a tempting range of 25 flavours and it stands out among the disappointing selection of eateries at Wat Phra Yai. Choose from lime, mango, tiramisu, pistachio, coconut, blackberry, passion fruit, black chocolate and more.

★ Barracuda
MEDITERRANEAN **$$$**

(Map p541; ☎ 077 430003; www.barracuda-restaurant.com; The Wharf, Fisherman's Village; mains from 575B; ⏱ 6-11pm) Abounding in alluring Mediterranean culinary inflections, but only open come evening, Barracuda is one of the island's best dining options. The romantic and seductive night-time environment is almost as delightful as the menu: expect to be charmed and well fed on a diet of seared scallops, yellowfin tuna, rack of lamb, Norwegian salmon, delectable pasta dishes and fine service.

★ Chez François
FRENCH **$$$**

(Map p541; ☎ 096 071 1800; www.facebook.com/chezporte; 33/2 Mu 1, Fisherman's Village; set meal 1700-1950B; ⏱ 6-11pm Tue-Sat) With no à la carte menu, but a reputation for outstanding cuisine that has sent waves across the culinary map of Ko Samui, Chez Francois serves a three-course surprise meal. Book ahead – and if you're only on Ko Samui for a few days, book early to get a table. It's tiny (and cash only).

CRAZY FOR COCONUTS

It's no surprise that Samui's most famous natural produce finds its way into a medley of dishes. There's sweet coconut jam to spread on your croissants in the morning. *Wai kôo·a* is a spicy and sour coconut-based curry featuring octopus. *Tom Kha* is a flavoursome chicken soup made with coconut milk, lemongrass, lime juice, ginger, fish sauce and chilli paste. Usually made with chicken, beef or lamb, Massaman curry also employs coconuts – the meat is simmered in spices and coconut milk to soften it up after frying. You'll also see seafood being barbecued over coals of coconut husks.

Chez Francois is hidden away behind a wooden door near a pharmacy.

★ **Zazen Restaurant**　　　FUSION $$$
(Map p541; 077 425085, 098 015 8986; dishes 540-900B; set menu from 1300B; ⏱ lunch & dinner) This superb romantic dining experience at the **Zazen Resort** (www.samuizazen.com) comes complete with ocean views, dim candle lighting and soft music. Thai dancers animate things on Thursday and Sunday nights from 8pm. Reservations recommended.

★ **Dining On The Rocks**　　　FUSION $$$
(Map p528; 077 245678; www.sixsenses.com/resorts/samui/dining; Choeng Mon; set menus from 2800B; ⏱ 5-10pm) At the isolated **Six Senses Samui**, the island's ultimate dining experience takes place on nine cantilevered verandahs yawning over the gulf. After sunset (and wine), guests feel like they're dining on a barge set adrift on a starlit sea. Each dish on the set menu is the brainchild of cooks experimenting with taste, texture and temperature.

🍴 Mae Nam & the North Coast

Mae Nam has lots of eating options, from beachside, palm-thatch and driftwood affairs serving a mix of Thai, Western and seafood dishes to classier places tucked along the inland, lily-pad-pond-dotted tangle of roads. It's a lovely place to wander and find your own surprises. Don't overlook Mae Nam's **Walking Street** (Map p528; Mae Nam; ⏱ from 5pm Thu), on Thursday evenings.

★ **Fish Restaurant**　　　INTERNATIONAL $
(Map p528; 087 472 4097; Rte 4169, Mae Nam; mains from 50B; ⏱ 11am-11pm) With elegant Thai tablecloths and a well-priced, tasty menu of Thai seafood and pan-Asian dishes and international appetisers, this popular wood-floored eatery pulls in a regular stream of diners for its charming setting, winning spring rolls, gorgeous seafood curries, steamed sea bass and much more.

Bang Po Seafood　　　SEAFOOD $$
(Map p528; Bang Po; dishes from 100B; ⏱ dinner) A meal at Bang Po Seafood is a test for the taste buds. It's one of the only restaurants that serves traditional Ko Samui fare: recipes call for ingredients such as raw sea urchin roe, baby octopus, sea water, coconut and local turmeric.

★ **Pepenero**　　　ITALIAN $$
(Map p528; 077 963353; www.pepenerosamui.com; Mae Nam; mains from 250B; ⏱ 6-10pm Mon-Sat) Pepenero continues to cause a stir on Ko Samui, moving to this more accessible Mae Nam location. What this excellent and neatly designed Italian restaurant lacks in views is more than made up for by a terrific menu (including cutting boards with cheese and cold cuts) and the care and attention displayed to customers by the very sociable, hard-working hosts. Put this one in your planner.

Gaon Korean Restaurant　　　KOREAN $$
(Map p528; Mae Nam; mains from 180B; ⏱ 3-11pm) Right in China Town in Mae Nam, this excellent restaurant offers barbecued meat, grilled fish and steamed seafood sets, as well as Korean staples such as delicious *bulgogi* (marinated beef with mushroom and carrot on a hot plate), kimchi pancake, Korean ice cream, a kids' menu and a range of sizzling choices for vegetarians.

John's Garden Restaurant　　　THAI $$
(Map p528; 077 247694; www.johnsgardensamui.com; Mae Nam; mains from 160B; ⏱ 1-10pm) This delightful garden restaurant is a picture, with tables slung out beneath bamboo and palms and carefully cropped hedges. It's particularly romantic when lantern-lit at night, so reserve ahead, but pack some mosquito repellent (which is generally provided, but it's good to have backup). The signature dish on the Thai and European menu is the excellent massaman chicken.

★ **Farmer** INTERNATIONAL $$$
(Map p528; ☑ 077 447222; www.farmersboutique
resort.com/restaurant; Mae Nam; mains 300-
1500B; set lunch 250-340B; ⊙ 7am-10.30pm)
Magically set in front of a photogenic rice
field with green hills in the distance, fantas-
tic Farmer – within the boutique resort of
the same name – is a choice selection, es-
pecially when the candlelight flickers on a
starry night. The mostly European-inspired
food is lovely and well-presented, there's a
free pick-up for nearby beaches, and service
is attentive.

✗ Na Thon & the West

The quiet west coast features some of the
best seafood on Samui as well as some of the
best views, especially come sunset. Na Thon
has a lot of choice, but the restaurants don't
really stand out, although there's a giant day
market on Th Thawi Ratchaphakdi.

Lucky INTERNATIONAL $$
(Map p528; ☑ 077 420392; Na Thon; 100-250B;
⊙ 8am-9pm Mon-Sat, noon-9pm Sun; 🛜) This
restaurant facing the sea serves tasty and
filling enough Western and Thai food, and
it's convenient if you're off the boat or travelling up the west coast, but it's the sunset

views and friendly service that nudge it into
the recommended bracket. Good choice of
vegetarian dishes too.

Big John's Seafood Restaurant SEAFOOD $$
(Map p528; ☑ 077 485775; Lipa Noi; mains 150-
300B; 🛜) This friendly restaurant is a pop-
ular west-coast seafood choice for sunset
dining, with live evening entertainment.

Phootawan Restaurant THAI $$
(Map p528; ☑ 081 978 9241; mains from 150B;
⊙ 9am-8.30pm) Getting up the hill to this
restaurant is a struggle on a scooter, but it's
worth the effort to be rewarded with ranging, glorious views over the trees, rather than
just for the serviceable food. To enjoy the visuals at their best, sunset is the time to arrive.

✗ South Coast

Sweet Sisters Cafe CAFE $
(Map p528; Bang Kao; ⊙ 11am-9pm; 🛜) Charming, cosy and with an enticing interior, this
roadside cafe down in the quiet south of Ko
Samui, just before the turn off for Ao Bang
Kao, is a welcoming place for shots of caffeine, juices and snacks as you explore the
beaches, bays and pagodas of the southern
shore.

KO SAMUI & THE LOWER GULF KO SAMUI

SALT & SPICE IN SOUTHERN THAI CUISINE

Southern Thai cooking is undoubtedly the spiciest regional style in a land of spicy regional cuisines. The food also tends to be very salty, and seafood, not surprisingly, plays
an important role, ranging from fresh fish that is grilled or added to soups, to pickled or
fermented fish, and fish served as sauces or condiments.

Two of the principal crops are coconuts and cashews, both of which find their way
into a variety of dishes. Nearly every meal is accompanied by a platter of fresh herbs and
vegies, and a spicy 'dip' of shrimp paste, chillies, garlic and lime.

Dishes you are likely to come across in southern Thailand include the following:

Gaang đai þlah An intensely spicy and salty curry that includes đai þlah (salted fish
stomach) – much tastier than it sounds.

Gaang sôm Known as gaang lěu·ang (yellow curry), this sour/spicy soup gets its hue
from turmeric.

Gài tôrt hàht yài The famous deep-fried chicken from the town of Hat Yai gets its rich
flavour from a marinade containing dried spices.

Kà·nŏm jeen nám yah This dish of thin rice noodles served with fiery curry-like sauce is
accompanied by fresh vegetables and herbs.

Kôo·a glîng Minced meat fried with curry paste is a southern staple.

Kôw yam A popular breakfast, this dish includes rice topped with sliced herbs, bean
sprouts, dried prawns, toasted coconut and powdered red chilli, served with a sour/
sweet fish-based sauce.

Pàt sà·đor This stir-fry of 'stink beans' with shrimp, garlic, chillies and shrimp paste is
pungent and spicy.

★ Hemingway's on the Beach   THAI **$$**

(Map p528; ☑ 088 452 4433; off Rte 4170, Ao Thong Krut; mains from 175B; ☺ 10am-8pm Sat, Mon, Tue & Thu, 10am-6pm Sun) With appetising Thai dishes – and popular cookery courses too – this beachside choice on Rte 4170 as it loops into Thong Krut is an excellent reason to escape to the southwest corner of Ko Samui; tuck into fresh seafood and bask in the views, especially come sundown. Hemingway's also arranges long-tail and speedboat island tours, while massage is at hand for post-meal relaxation.

 Drinking & Nightlife

A recent ruling that all bars need to close by 1am means the island is quieter at night than it once was. Samui's biggest party spot is brash and noisy Hat Chaweng. Lamai and Bo Phut come in second and third respectively, while the rest of the island is generally quiet, with drinking usually focused on resort bars. For sunset cocktails, hit the west coast, or parts of the north coast.

Hat Chaweng

★ Drink Gallery   COCKTAIL BAR

(Chaweng Beach Rd; Map p531; ☺ 4pm-1am) Part of the Library hotel (p532), this highly stylish bar along Chaweng Beach Rd has top design and some excellent cocktails. It's a place to be seen in, and a place to people-watch from or

DON'T MISS

'WALKING STREET' NIGHT MARKETS

These food-filled markets occur at least weekly, offering you the chance to sample local delicacies, shop for gifts and mingle with tourists and locals. They start at around 4pm and run until around midnight. To avoid the crowds arrive before 6pm or after 10pm. Pickpockets can be prevalent.

This was the schedule at the time of research, but some are considering opening more frequently:

Ban Chaweng Monday to Thursday and Saturday

Ban Lamai Sunday

Ban Meanam Thursday

Bo Phut (Fisherman's Village) Friday

Ban Choeng Mon Friday

just admire the interior artwork, while nibbling on tapas-style Thai bites.

Bees Knees Brewpub   BREWERY

(Map p531; ☑ 085 537 2498; www.samuibrew. pub; Chaweng Lake Rd; ☺ 3pm-1am) The rather charmless interior decor and downcast service wins no prizes, but the beer (from 120B) – brewed on-site – gets serious accolades and big thumbs-up. Choose from five beers (wheaty bee, summer bee, black bee, bitter bee or black-and-tan) and enjoy some deeply rich and thorough flavours. The brewery is right next to the bar, visible through glass.

Sawasdee Bar   BAR

(Map p531; Chaweng Beach Rd; ☺ 5pm-midnight Mon-Fri) This bright-blue converted Volkswagen camper van sets up five days a week, serving outdoor cocktails (99B), beers (80B), cocktail buckets (450B) and spirits (140B) with servings of fun live music.

Ark Bar   BAR

(Map p531; ☑ 7am-1am; www.ark-bar.com; Hat Chaweng) Drinks are dispensed from the multicoloured bar to an effusive crowd, guests recline on loungers on the beach, and the party is on day and night, with fire shows lighting up the sands after sundown and DJs providing house music from the afternoon onwards.

Pride Bar   GAY & LESBIAN

(Map p531; ☑ 088 753 2921; Chaweng Beach Rd; ☺ 5pm-2am) At the heart of Chaweng, this easygoing place attracts a mixed crowd of Thais and foreigners.

Hat Lamai & the Southeast

Lamai doesn't have the same range of bars or quality as nearby Chaweng, but it's a much more pleasant place for a drink for those who want more peace. There are far fewer girlie bars as well, and prices are a little lower, but overall, the bars have less character.

Bear Cocktails   BAR

(Map p536; Lamai Beach Rd; ☺ 5pm-2am) It's not a traditional bar, but a fun, open-air cocktail stall on the road run by some friendly girls (Bear and Lek); buy a strawberry daiquiri, grab a plastic seat and chat to whoever's at hand. It's not far from the McDonald's; cocktails are 79B.

Lava Lounge   BAR

(Map p536; ☑ 080 886 5035; Hat Lamai; ☺ 4pm-2am) One of the better bars in Hat Lamai, Lava Lounge is a chilled-out spot with an

Bo Phut

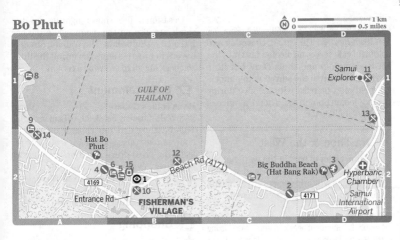

Bo Phut

invigorating menu of cocktails (99B to 150B), and a happy hour that runs from 4pm to 9pm, which includes a spirit with mixer for 79B.

Beach Republic   BAR
(Map p536; ☎077 458100; www.beachrepublic.com; 176/34 Mu 4, Hat Lamai; ☺7am-11pm) Recognised by its yawning thatch-patched awnings, Beach Republic could be the poster child of a made-for-TV, beachside, booze-swilling holiday. There's a wading pool, comfy lounge chairs, an endless cocktail list and even a hotel if you never, ever want to leave the party. The Sunday brunches (11.30am to 3.30pm) here are legendary.

🍸 Bo Phut & the Northeast

★**Woobar**   BAR
(Map p541; ☎077 915999; Bo Phut; ☺11am-midnight; ☏) With serious wow factor and 270-

degree panoramas, the W Retreat's signature lobby bar gives the word 'swish' a whole new meaning, with cushion-clad pods of seating plonked in the middle of an expansive infinity pool that stretches out over the infinite horizon. This is, without a doubt, the best place on Samui for sunset cocktails blended with cool music mixes.

★**Coco Tam's**   BAR
(Map p541; Fisherman's Village; ☺1pm-1am) Grab a swing at the bar or plop yourself on a beanbag on the sand, order a giant cocktail served in a jar and take a toke on a shisha (water pipe; 500B). It's a bit pricey, but this boho, beach-bum-chic spot oozes relaxation, it's lovely when the sun goes down and the coconut milkshakes are to die for. Fire dancers perform most nights.

Chez Isa   CAFE
(Map p541; 082 423 9221; Wat Phra Yai; ⏰9.30am-7pm; 🛜) This small, charming and colourful cafe serves no alcohol (as Wat Phra Yai is alongside) and shuts early, but it's a lovely spot to catch the sunset with a mocktail held aloft or relax with a coffee during the day, looking out to sea. There's a range of jewellery for sale too.

🍷 Na Thon & the West

There aren't a lot of bars in the west, but the ones you can find are pretty dapper. Their forte is the westerly perspective, facing straight into fiery sunsets over the gulf.

 Air Bar   BAR
(Map p528; Intercontinental Samui Baan Taling Ngam Resort, Taling Ngam; ⏰5pm-midnight) Toast the setting sun as it sinks into the golden gulf from this magnificent outside bar perched above a cliff at this swanky resort (p534). There's an excellent menu of tapas and snacks if you simply can't pull yourself away and want to make a meal of it. This is pretty much the top romantic choice on the island.

Nikki Beach   BAR
(Map p528; ☎077 914500; www.nikkibeach.com/kohsamui; Lipa Noi; ⏰11am-11pm; 🛜) The acclaimed luxury brand brings international flair to the secluded west coast of Ko Samui. Think haute cuisine, chic decor, gaggles of jet-setters and killer sunsets. Themed brunch and dinner specials keep the masses coming throughout the week, and sleek villa accommodation is also on offer.

Max Murphys   BAR
(Map p528; Na Thon) This fun Irish pub offers all the usual ingredients of a fun night: Premier League fixtures, Western and Thai pub grub, draught beer (Guinness, Kilkenny, Hoegaarden), a few craft beers, cocktails and obliging staff. It's as Irish as a bowl of tom yam soup, but after a few pints, you won't care.

🍷 South Coast

Buffalo Baby   BAR
(Map p528; Bang Kao) Way down on the south shore at Ao Bang Kao, this fun beachside bar (run by the affable Maurice) really comes alive on Saturdays at 5pm when the Bang Kao Walking Street, a buzzing market set to live music on a stage right on the sand, takes off.

Occasional fire shows lighting up the sands are also on the menu, while the bar has a DJ on Saturdays. The Walking Street is a work in progress and growing all the time, so check ahead to see what's cookin'.

⭐ Entertainment

Paris Follies Cabaret   CABARET
(Map p531; Chaweng Beach Rd; ⏰8pm-midnight) This dazzling and fun cabaret offers one-hour *gà·teu·i* (also spelled *kàthoey*) cabaret featuring cross-dresser and/or transgender performers every night at 8pm, 9pm, 10pm and 11pm and attracts a mixed clientele of both sexes. Admission is free, but you need to buy a drink (from around 300B).

🛍 Shopping

 Central Festival   SHOPPING CENTRE
(Map p531; Chaweng Beach Rd; ⏰11am-11pm) This bright, shiny and huge monster-mall is stuffed with shops, cafes and restaurants and legions of Chinese shoppers. There's a terrific range of shopping options, and some of the dining choices are excellent too. There's a bouncy slide for kids.

Fisherman's Village Walking Street   MARKET
(Map p541; Fisherman's Village; ⏰5-11pm Fri) Every Friday night, this busy and colourful Walking Street transforms Fisherman's Village into a forest of sharp elbows, market stalls, street food, handicrafts, T-shirts and cheap cocktails.

Thanon An Thong   STREET
(Map p528; Na Thon) Just a block inland from the pier, this pretty street is lined with wooden shophouses, Chinese lanterns and caged singing birds, with souvenir shops plying goods and gifts you can pick up more cheaply and with less pushing and shoving than in Chaweng.

Island Books   BOOKS
(Map p536; ☎061 193 2132; www.island-books-samui.com; off Rte 4169; ⏰9am-7pm) Tucked away on a lane off the 4169 and run by Liverpudlian Paul, Island Books on the main drag past Lamai has the largest selection of used books – in pretty much every language – on the island. There's another smaller branch (⏰9am-7pm) in Lamai village itself.

ℹ Information

DANGERS & ANNOYANCES
The repetitive scream of ambulances racing up and down the island's roads is a sure sign that

the road accident fatality rate on Ko Samui is high. This is largely due to the significant number of (inexperienced) tourists who rent motorcycles and scooters only to find out that the winding roads, sudden tropical rains, frenzied traffic and sand on the roads can be lethal.

Look out for glass on less-visited beaches – it's incomprehensible how much broken glass can just lie on the sands. Parts of the beach in Na Thon have a lot of broken glass on them, but you'll also find potentially dangerous shards on lengths of sand such as the sandbar leading to Ko Ma in the northwest of the island. Tread carefully and keep a look-out at all times.

The seas of Samui can be rough, even for strong swimmers, and drownings do occur, especially in Chaweng and Lamai, which experience strong currents and rip tides. Hotels will usually post warnings of swimming hazards and conditions on a beach board or warning flags. If you are caught in a rip tide (a strong surface current heading seaward), swim parallel to the shore to exit the current or float along with it until it dissipates in deeper water and you are deposited.

Beach vendors are registered with the government and should all be wearing a numbered jacket. No peddler should cause an incessant disturbance – seek assistance if this occurs.

EMERGENCY

Tourist Police (Map p528; ☑ 077 430018; www.samui-tourist-police.com) Useful for contacting either for advice or if you are arrested.

INTERNET ACCESS

Wi-fi is widespread at effectively all accommodation choices, restaurants and bars. You may have to pay for wi-fi access at some high-end hotels, but it is generally provided free at most midrange and budget places.

LEGAL MATTERS

The Thai police tend to leave foreigners alone, but the laws regarding drugs can be rigidly enforced and the penalties for possession of drugs can be severe.

If arrested for any offence, the police will allow you to make one phone call. If arrested, being confrontational will make things worse for you.

Make sure you carry a copy of your passport or ID as the police can ask to see it. While you will see many drivers not wearing one, a helmet is required by law if you are driving a motorbike or scooter.

The Tourist Police can be of great help in any situation regarding the law.

MEDICAL SERVICES

Ko Samui has four private hospitals, located near Chaweng's Tesco Lotus supermarket on the east coast (where most of the tourists tend to gather). The government hospital (Samui Hospital) in Na Thon has seen significant improvements in the past couple of years but the service is still a bit grim because funding is based on the number of Samui's legal residents (which doesn't take into account the many illegal Myanmar workers).

Bangkok Hospital Samui (Map p531; ☑ 077 429500, emergency 077 429555; www.bangkok hospitalsamui.com) Centrally located, internationally accredited hospital in Chaweng. Your best bet for just about any medical problem.

Bandon International Hospital (Map p528; ☑ 077 245236; www.bandonhospitalsamui. com; off route 4169) A private hospital offering international standards of healthcare.

Ko Samui Hospital (Map p528; ☑ 077 913200; www.samuihospital.go.th/weben; Na Thon; ⊙24hr) Public, government hospital located in the south of Na Thon.

Samui International Hospital (Map p531; ☑ 077 300394; www.sih.co.th; Chaweng Beach Rd; ⊙24hr) International hospital in Chaweng. Emergency ambulance service is available 24 hours and credit cards are accepted.

MONEY

ATMs are widely available. Credit cards are accepted in most hotels and restaurants.

POST

In several parts of the island there are privately run post-office branches charging a small commission. You can almost always leave your stamped mail with your accommodation.

TOURIST INFORMATION

There is no official tourist office on the island. Tourist information is largely provided by hotels and travel agents.

Siam Map Company (www.siammap.com) Puts out quarterly booklets including a Spa Guide, Dining Guide and an annual directory, which

> ### 🛈 DOG WARNING
>
> Dogs are everywhere on the island – they breed like rabbits and may bite. The Samui Dog & Cat Rescue Centre (p527) has the job of looking after and neutering/spaying stray dogs and controlling rabies (largely under control, but check with a health professional if bitten), and they have their work cut out for them. You may find menacing dogs at temples or sitting around the beaches in packs; exercise caution and don't stroke them.

lists thousands of companies and hotels on the island. Its *Samui Guide Map* is fantastic, free and easily found throughout the island.

VISA EXTENSIONS

The new **Immigration Office** (Map p528; ☎ 077 423440; Soi 1 Mu 1, Mae Nam; ⊙ 8.30am-4.30pm Mon-Fri) is located south of Rte 4169 in Mae Nam. Officials here tend to issue the minimum rather than maximum visa extensions. It's better located and bigger than the former offices in Na Thon, but you may still be denied an extension for no particular reason.

Don't overlook the option to join a three-month to one-year Thai language course with a school on the island, which would qualify you for a student visa to cover the length of the course.

ℹ Getting There & Away

AIR

Ko Samui Airport (www.samuiairportonline. com) is in the northeast of the island near Big Buddha Beach.

Bangkok Airways (www.bangkokair.com) operates flights roughly every 30 minutes between Samui and Bangkok's Suvarnabhumi International Airport (65 minutes). Bangkok Airways also flies direct from Samui to Phuket, Pattaya, Chiang Mai, Singapore, Kuala Lumpur, Hong Kong and other cities in Southeast Asia. Bangkok Airways also flies to Chéngdū and Guǎngzhōu in China. There is a **Bangkok Airways Office** (Map p531; ☎ 077 420512, 077 420519; www.bangkok air.com) in Hat Chaweng and another at the airport. The first (at 6am) and last (10pm) flights of the day are always the cheapest.

During the high season, make your flight reservations far in advance as seats often sell out.

ℹ MOTORBIKE RENTAL SCAMS

Even if you escape unscathed from a motorbike riding experience, some shops will claim that you damaged your rental and will try to extort some serious cash. The best way to avoid this is to take copious photos of your vehicle (cars included) at the time of rental, making sure the person renting you the vehicle sees you do it (they will be less likely to make false claims against you if they know you have photos).

If they still make a claim against you, keep your cool. Losing your temper won't help you win the argument and could significantly escalate the problem.

If things get really bad call the tourist police (p543), not the regular police.

If the Samui flights are full, try flying into Surat Thani from Bangkok and taking the short ferry ride to Samui instead. Flights to Surat Thani are generally cheaper than a direct flight to the island, although they involve much more hassle.

BOAT

To reach Samui, the main piers on the mainland are Ao Ban Don, Tha Thong, Don Sak and Chumphon – Tha Thong (in central Surat) and Don Sak being the most common. On Samui, the three most used ports are Na Thon, Mae Nam and Big Buddha Beach. Expect complimentary taxi transfers with high-speed ferry services.

To The Mainland

There are regular boat departures between Samui and Don Sak on the mainland.

High-speed **Lomprayah** (☎ 077 4277 656; www.lomprayah.com) departs from Na Thon (400B; 8am, 9.45am, 12.45pm & 3.30pm) and takes just 45 minutes; some departures can connect with the train station in Phun Phin (600B) for Surat Thani.

There's also the slower but regular **Raja** (Map p528; ☎ 022 768211-2, 092 274 3423-5; www. rajaferryport.com; adult 130B) car ferry (130B; 90 minutes) to Don Sak, which departs from Thong Yang. The slow night boat to Samui (300B) leaves from central Surat Thani each night at 11pm, reaching Na Thon around 5am. It returns from Na Thon at 9pm, arriving at around 3am. Watch your bags on this boat.

Lomprayah ferries also depart from Pralarn Pier in Mae Nam for Chumphon (1100B; 8am and 12.30pm; 3¾ hours).

To Ko Pha-Ngan & Ko Tao

There are almost a dozen daily departures between Ko Samui and Thong Sala on the west coast of Ko Pha-Ngan, and many of these continue on to Ko Tao. These leave from Na Thon, Pralarn Pier in Mae Nam or Big Buddha Beach pier, take from 20 minutes to one hour and cost 200B to 300B to Ko Pha-Ngan, depending on the boat.

To go directly to Hat Rin, the *Haad Rin Queen* goes back and forth between Hat Rin and Big Buddha Beach four times a day (the first boat leaves Hat Rin at 9.30am and departs Big Buddha Beach at 10.30am), with double the number of sailings the day after the Full Moon Party and an extra trip laid on at 7.30am the same day. The voyage takes 50 minutes, costs 200B and the last boat leaves Big Buddha Beach at 6.30pm.

Also for Hat Rin and the more remote east coast beaches of Ko Pha-Ngan, the small and rickety *Thong Nai Pan Express* runs once a day at noon from Mae Hat on Ko Samui to Hat Rin and then up the east coast, stopping at all the beaches as far as Thong Nai Pan Noi. Prices range from 200B to 400B, depending on the destination. The boat won't run in bad weather.

BUS & TRAIN

A bus-ferry combo is more convenient than a train-ferry package for getting to Ko Samui because you don't have to switch transportation in Phun Phin. However, the trains are much more comfortable and spacious – especially at night. If you prefer the train, you can get off at Chumphon and catch the Lomprayah catamaran service the rest of the way.

Several services offer these bus-boat combo tickets, the fastest and most comfortable being the Lomprayah, which has two daily departures from Bangkok, at 6am and 9pm, and two from Samui to Bangkok, at 8am and 12.30pm. The total voyage takes between 11 and 14 hours and costs between 1400B and 1450B.

ⓘ Getting Around

Note that once you're in the Ko Samui sticks, you'll see signs everywhere for this or that bar, this or that restaurant or hotel, with a distance inscribed. As a rough guide, 300m on these signs equals 1km.

CAR & MOTORBIKE

You can rent motorcycles and scooters from almost every resort on the island. The going rate for a scooter is 150B to 200B per day, but for longer periods try to negotiate a better rate. You'll generally need to hand over your passport as a deposit (but you may need it if moving hotel, so plan ahead). You'll see petrol for sale in bottles at 40B at litre, but it's much cheaper at petrol stations.

If you decide to rent a motorcycle, protect yourself by wearing a helmet, and ask for one with a plastic visor; keep to driving slowly. If you rent a motorbike or scooter, be warned that if you don't have an international driving licence, you may have problems in the event of an accident and your insurer might not cover you.

MINIBUSES

Drivers of *sŏrng·tăa·ou* (pick-up minibuses) love to try to overcharge you, so it's always best to ask a third party for current rates, as they can change with the season. These vehicles run regularly during daylight hours. It's about 50B to travel between beaches, and no more than 100B to travel halfway across the island. Figure about 20B for a five-minute ride on a motorcycle taxi.

TAXIS

Taxi service is quite chaotic due to the plethora of cabs, and fares are ridiculously inflated compared to Bangkok. Taxis typically charge around 500B for an airport transfer. Some Hat Chaweng travel agencies can arrange minibus taxis for less.

Ko Pha-Ngan   เกาะพะงัน

POP 12,500

In the late 1970s, Ko Pha-Ngan was a pristine paradise that beckoned the intrepid. Its innocent days may be long gone, but don't let that deter you: this gulf isle offers much more than the Full Moon parties that made it famous.

Choose quieter days in the lunar calendar, or the smaller but still-raucous half-moon party periods, and the island's charms are brought to the fore. It's easier to get a room, prices are more reasonable and far fewer people are on the island, meaning more solitude and tranquillity. Even Hat Rin – party central when the moon is round – is quiet and relaxing during other periods, and the beaches are kept clean.

The quietest months are April to June, when the island is in low gear – an ideal time to visit for low accommodation prices, fewer elbows per square kilometre and safer roads.

◉ Sights

Beyond Full Moon wild partying, this large jungle island boasts many overlooked, spectacular natural features to explore, including tree-clad mountains, waterfalls, unspoiled forest and national park land as well as some of the most spectacular beaches in all of Thailand. Also remember that, outside the Full Moon, the island is a largely peaceful and serene place.

Remember to change out of your beach clothes when visiting one of the 20 wát on Ko Pha-Ngan. Most temples are open during daylight hours.

Hat Than Sadet   BEACH

(Map p546) Fronted by a fringe of coconut trees, the lovely beach of Hat Than Sadet rewards the scooter journey from Thong Sala, Ao Thong Nai Pan or Ban Tai. Explore up and down the delightful beach, and consider crossing the bridge at the south end to the Mai Pen Rai bungalows and following the rocks around the headland to the beach at Hat Thong Reng. The swimming is good at both beaches.

Hat Thong Reng   BEACH

(Map p546) The smaller, very secluded sibling of Hat Than Sadet, Hat Thong Reng on Ao Thong Reng is located around the headland to the south of its big brother. It is a lovely beach, with good swimming. Follow the huge

Ko Pha-Ngan

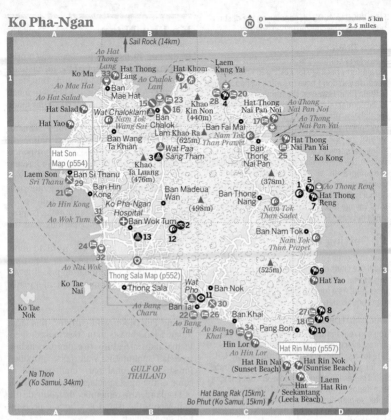

rocks around the south of Hat Than Sadet to reach the beach, but watch your step.

Nam Tok Phaeng   WATERFALL
(Map p546) Nam Tok Phaeng is protected by a national park; this waterfall is a pleasant reward after a short but rough hike. After the waterfall (dry out of season), it's a further exhilarating 15-minute climb up a root-choked path (along the Phaeng-Domsila Nature Trail) to the fantastic **Domsila Viewpoint** (Map p546), with superb, ranging views. The two- to three-hour trail then continues on through the jungle in a loop, past other waterfalls before bringing you back. Take water and good shoes.

Ko Pha-Ngan's
Tallest Yang Na Yai Tree   LANDMARK
(Map p546) Thrusting into the heavens near Wat Pho, Ko Pha-Ngan's tallest Yang Na Yai (dipterocarpus alatus; ยางนา) is an astonishing sight as you veer round the bend for the

diminutive Wat Nok temple, a small shrine tucked away in the greenery beyond. These giants grow to over 50m in height and, for tree lovers, are real beauties. This imposing specimen is often garlanded with colourful ribbons.

Hat Khuat   BEACH
(Bottle Beach; Map p546) This lovely stretch of sand overlooked by green hills is a superb choice for a relaxing day of swimming and snorkelling, and the bungalow operations along the beach beckon would-be overnighters. There's a great hike from Ban Chalok Lam, the fishing village in the island's north, but take enough water and follow the bottles on poles that should mark the way; the usual way to the beach is by beach taxi from Ban Chalok Lam or Thong Nai Pan.

Deang Waterfall   WATERFALL
(Map p546) Than Sadet has a string of waterfalls down to the beach at Ao Thong Reng,

Ko Pha-Ngan

and this is the best. Deang features a sequence of falls, a pool for swimming in and lots of rock-clambering opportunities. You may even find someone slumped in the main flow, cooling off on the rocks in the gush of the water. Look for the signs.

Secret Beach
BEACH
(Hat Son; Map p554) Not so secret, this palm-fringed, soft-sand cove (aka Hat Son) down a steep road in the northwest of the island is a gorgeous choice for sunset, but any time of day will do. To fully get in the mood, check into the Haad Son Resort (p553), or sink a twilight cocktail at the Secret Beach Bar (p560). Swimming here is generally very good.

Hat Wai Nam
BEACH
(Map p546) A small white-sand beach slung out between Hat Thian and Hat Yao on the more remote east coast, titchy Hat Wai Nam can be reached on foot from Hat Rin along the path up the mountain, but that's the long way round (you'll need four hours or more), and getting here by long-tail boat is advised. Expect a secluded beach with ravishing waters.

Hat Thian
BEACH
(Map p546) Hat Thian is a pretty, relatively empty, back-to-nature beach on the east of the island, accessible either by boat or on foot trekking from Hat Rin (p548). You can walk here from **Hat Yuan** (Map p546) in under 10 minutes via the rocky outcrop. The longer trek from Hat Rin (the mountain path leading here goes from north of Hat Rin Nok) takes just over two hours, but it can be hot going so load up on fluids.

Hat Yao (East)
BEACH
(Map p546) This lovely white-sand beach can only be reached on foot or by boat, lending it a gorgeous sense of seclusion. Most visitors arrive by boat, as the walk is a good four- to five-hour hike along the 7km-long mountain path from Hat Rin, which shouldn't be attempted if it's getting dark.

Guanyin Temple
BUDDHIST TEMPLE
(Map p546; 40B; ⊘7am-6pm) Signposted as the 'Goddess of Mercy Shrine Joss House', this fascinating Chinese temple is dedicated to Guanyin, the Buddhist Goddess of Mercy. The temple's Chinese name (普岳山) on the entrance gate refers to the island in China

that is the legendary home of the goddess. The main hall – the Great Treasure Hall – is a highly colourful confection, containing several bodhisattvas, including Puxian (seated on an elephant) and Wenshu (sitting on a lion).

Hat Rin Nok
BEACH

(Sunrise Beach; Map p557) Aka Sunrise Beach, aka Full Moon Party Beach, this is astonishingly (you may think) one of Ko Pha-Ngan's cleanest and most pleasant beaches. This is where much of the money goes from the monthly partying admission charge – to cleaning the sand and returning it to an attractive state. Its reputation as party central keeps many people away, so it can be surprisingly crowd-free at times.

Wat Phu Khao Noi
BUDDHIST TEMPLE

(Map p546; ⊙dawn-dusk) The oldest temple on the island is Wat Phu Khao Noi, near the hospital in Thong Sala. While the site is open to visitors throughout the day, the monks are only around in the morning.

🏃 Activities

Ko Pha-Ngan is stuffed with activities, from diving to trekking, kayaking, snorkelling, swimming and beyond.

Hiking and snorkelling day trips to Ang Thong Marine National Park generally depart from Ko Samui, but tour operators shuttle tourists from here too.

Many larger accommodation options can sort out jet skis and kayaks.

Diving & Water Sports

There's a more laid-back diving scene on Ko Pha-Ngan than on nearby Ko Tao, but there's no shortage of professional, competitively priced dive operations with courses from novice to instructor level as well as free-diving.

A drop in Open Water certification prices has also made local rates competitive with Ko Tao. Group sizes tend to be smaller on Ko Pha-Ngan since the island has fewer divers in general. Recommended dive outfits include **Haad Yao Divers**, **Lotus Diving**, **Chaloklum Diving**, and **Apnea Koh Pha Ngan** for free-diving.

Like the other islands in the Samui Archipelago, Pha-Ngan has several small reefs dispersed around the island. The clear favourite snorkelling spot is **Ko Ma**, a small island in the northwest connected to Ko Pha-Ngan by a charming sandbar. There are also some rock reefs of interest on the eastern side of the island.

A major perk of diving from Ko Pha-Ngan is the proximity to **Sail Rock** (Hin Bai), the best dive site in the Gulf of Thailand and a veritable beacon for whale sharks. This large pinnacle lies about 14km north of the island. An abundance of corals and large tropical fish can be seen at depths of 10m to 30m, and there's a rocky vertical swim-through called **The Chimney**.

Dive shops on Ko Tao also visit Sail Rock; however, the focus tends to be more on shallow reefs (for newbie divers) and the deep-dive waters at Chumphon Pinnacle. The most popular trips departing from Ko Pha-Ngan are three-site day trips which stop at Chumphon Pinnacle, Sail Rock and one of the other premier sites in the area. These three-stop trips cost from around 3650B to 4000B and include a full lunch. Two-dive trips to Sail Rock will set you back around 2500B to 2800B.

Apnea Koh Pha Ngan
DIVING

(Map p546; ☑092 380 1494; www.apneakohphangan.com; Chalok Lam; from 1600B) Free-diving has taken off on Ko Pha-Ngan and this is the best-known operator on the island, with courses run on Sail Rock. A one-day intro course costs 4000B (taking you down to a maximum 12m), while the standard two-day course is 7000B (taking you down to a maximum 20m). The instructor-level course is 35,000B.

Sail Rock Divers
DIVING

(Map p546; ☑077 374321; www.sailrockdivers resort.com; Ban Chalok Lam; from 3500B) Equipped with its own lovely 3m-deep pool, bungalow accommodation (900B to 1600B) and restaurant in Chalok Lam, Sail Rock Divers is a very popular and professional choice, with courses from beginner to advanced.

Chaloklum Diving
DIVING

(Map p546; ☑077 374025; www.chaloklum-diving. com; from 1000B; ⊙6am-8pm) One of the longer-established dive shops on the island, these guys (based on the main drag in Ban Chalok Lam) have quality equipment and provide high standards in all that they do, whether scuba-diving, free-diving, night diving or snorkelling trips.

Haad Yao Divers
DIVING

(☑086 279 3085; www.haadyaodivers.com; from 1400B) Established in 1997, this dive operator has garnered a strong reputation by maintaining European standards of safety and customer service. Prices start at 1400B for a beach dive at Hat Yao, but there's a huge selection of courses and options.

Wake Up
WATER SPORTS
(☑ 087 283 6755; www.wakeupwakeboarding.com; from 1200B; ☺ Jan-Oct) Jamie passes along his infinite wakeboarding wisdom to eager wannabes at his small water sports school in Chalok Lam. Fifteen minutes of 'air time' will set you back 1200B, which is excellent value considering you get one-on-one instruction. Kneeboarding, wakeskating, wakesurfing and waterskiing sessions are also available.

Trekking
Almost 90% of Ko Pha-Ngan is made up of unspoiled tropical forest, with a whopping 40% protected national park land harbouring an abundance of wildlife. If trekking along more isolated areas, make sure you take loads of sunscreen and water.

Popular hikes include the Chalok Lam to Bottle Beach Trek, and the hilly hike from Hat Rin to Hat Yuan, Hat Thian and on to Hat Yao (east). The hike up to the Domsila Viewpoint, and beyond, above Nam Tok Phaeng is another excellent hike, don't miss it. From here it's also possible to continue up to Khao Ra, the highest mountain on the island at 625m. Switch your flip-flops for decent walking shoes.

Chalok Lam to Bottle Beach Trek
HIKING
(Map p546) Long-tail boats run east from Chalok Lam to Bottle Beach, but you can also hike the 5km distance, though it's advisable to go early in the morning to avoid the midday sun. Look for the trail marked with bottles, just beyond the end of the road from Chalok Lam, which heads up the hill. The trek takes around an hour, but avoid the hike in wet weather, when things can get slippery.

Check on conditions at shops in Chalok Lam before setting out. At the other end, long-tail boats return to Chalok Lam, or you can continue by boat to Thong Nai Pan.

🥢 Courses

The Phangan Thai Cooking Class
COOKING
(Map p552; ☑ 087 278 8898; Thong Sala; 1200-1500B) Located along the main road in Thong Sala, this fun school – run by likeable chef Oy – takes you to a market for supplies before knuckling down to the serious business in the kitchen.

C&M
Vocational School
LANGUAGE, HEALTH & WELLBEING
(Map p554; ☑ 077 349233; http://thaiculture.education; Ban Sri Thanu) Bridging the yawning experiential gulf between yelping at the full Ko Pha-Ngan moon and Thai culture, this large vocational school runs classes and courses in Thai language, cuisine, yoga and massage.

🛏 Sleeping

Ko Pha-Ngan's legendary history of laid-back revelry solidified its reputation as *the* stomping ground for the gritty backpacker lifestyle, even though many local mainstays have collapsed their bamboo huts in favour of newer, sleeker accommodation.

But backpackers fear not – it will still be a while before the castaway lifestyle vanishes.

Many operations have a minimum three-, four- or five-night stay during the Full Moon, Christmas and New Year periods.

🛏 Hat Rin

The thin peninsula of Hat Rin features three separate beaches: beautiful blond Hat Rin Nok (Sunrise Beach) is the epicentre of Full Moon tomfoolery; Hat Rin Nai (Sunset Beach) is the much less impressive stretch of sand on the far side of the tiny promontory; and Hat Seekantang (also known as Hat Leela), just south of Hat Rin Nai, is a smaller, lovely white and more private beach. The three beaches are linked by Ban Hat Rin (Hat Rin Town) – an inland collection of restaurants, hotels and bars. It takes only a few minutes to walk from one beach to another.

Hat Rin sees Thailand's greatest accommodation crunch during the Full Moon festivities. At this time, bungalow operations expect you to stay for a minimum number of days (usually five). If you plan to arrive the day of the party (or even the day before), we strongly suggest booking a room in advance, or else you'll probably have to sleep on the beach (which you might end up doing anyway, either intentionally or not). Some cattle-car-style dorms stack and cram a seemingly impossible number of beds into dark small rooms, and shared toilets are few.

Full Mooners can also stay on Ko Samui or other beaches on Ko Pha-Ngan and take speedboat shuttles to access the festivities – prices will depend on how far away you're staying, but the money you'll save on staying anywhere besides Hat Rin itself will probably make it worth it. With gory and often fatal accidents on a monthly basis, driving on Ko Pha-Ngan during the festivities is an absolutely terrible idea.

Expect room rates to increase by 20% to 300% during Full Moon.

Seaview Sunrise
BUNGALOW $

(Map p557; ☑ 077 375160; www.seaviewsunrise.com; Hat Rin Nok; r 500-1400B; ❋ 🛜) Budget Full Moon revellers who want to sleep inches from the tide should apply here (but note the minimum five-day policy during the lunar lunacy). Some of the options back in the jungle are sombre and musty, but the solid beachfront models have bright, polished wooden interiors facing onto a line of coconut trees and the sea.

Same Same
GUESTHOUSE $

(Map p557; ☑ 077 375200; www.same-same.com; Ban Hat Rin; dm 400B; r 650B; ❋ 🛜) Run by two Danish backpackers (Christina and Heidi), this sociable spot offers simple but bright rooms and plenty of party preparation fun for the Full Moon beach shenanigans; it's very lethargic outside lunar-lunacy periods, but that's a good time to pitch up. The restaurant and bar is a solid choice.

Lighthouse Bungalows
BUNGALOW $

(Map p557; ☑ 077 375075; www.lighthousebungalows.com; Hat Seekantang; bungalows 400-1000B; ❋ 🛜) This remote outpost perched on the rocks south of Hat Rin has simple, good-value fan options and air-con bungalows with sweeping views of the sea; plus there's a cushion-clad restaurant/common area and high-season yoga classes. To get there, follow the wooden boardwalk southeast from Hat Leela. Beware the monthly techno parties, unless that's on your wishlist.

Tommy Resort
RESORT $$

(Map p557; ☑ 077 375215; www.tommyresort.com; Hat Rin Nok; r incl breakfast 2200-8500B; ❋ 🛜 ≋) This trendy address at the heart of Hat Rin strikes a balance between chic boutique and carefree flashpacker hang-out, with standard rooms, bungalows and pool villas. Wander down to a lovely strip of white sand, past flowering trees, to a resort with an azure slab of a pool at the heart of things and helpful, obliging staff. Rooms come with air-con, fridge and safe.

Delight
GUESTHOUSE $$

(Map p557; ☑ 077 375527; www.delightresort.com; Ban Hat Rin; r 800-6400B; ❋ 🛜 ≋) Slap bang in the centre of Hat Rin, friendly Delight offers decent lodging in a Thai-style building that comes with subtle designer details (such as peacock murals), sandwiched between an inviting swimming pool and a lazy lagoon peppered with lily pads.

Pha-Ngan Bayshore Resort
RESORT $$$

(Map p557; ☑ 077 375224; Hat Rin Nok; r 2300-6000B; ❋ @ 🛜 ≋) This neat and well-maintained hotel-style operation soaks up an ever-increasing influx of Hat Rin flashpackers. Staff are on the ball and welcoming, while sweeping beach views and a giant swimming pool nudge it into one of the top addresses on Sunrise Beach, especially if you can nab one of the special promotions.

Sarikantang Resort & Spa
RESORT $$$

(Map p557; ☑ 077 375055; www.sarikantang.com; Hat Seekantang; bungalows incl breakfast from 2400B; ❋ 🛜 ≋) Cream-coloured cabins, framed with teak posts and lintels, are sprinkled among swaying palms and crumbling winged statuettes on one of Hat Rin's best stretches of beach, with a spa at hand for some sunset pampering.

❶ BOX JELLYFISH

There are several species of venomous jellyfish in the waters off Ko Pha-Ngan, Ko Samui and Ko Tao, including scyphozoans, hydrozoans and box jellyfish. The most notorious is the box jellyfish, a cnidarian invertebrate whose sting – which contains a potent venom that attacks the nervous system, heart and skin cells – can result in death. Growing up to 3m in length and named after the box-like appearance of its bell, the box jellyfish's sting can be so painful the swimmer can enter a state of shock and drown before reaching the shore. The jellyfish is more prolific in sea waters after heavy rain.

Ko Pha-Ngan and Ko Samui have the highest incidence of fatal and near-fatal box jellyfish stings in the whole of Thailand. Some beaches, such as Hat Rin Nok, are equipped with stations warning of the danger of jellyfish, as well providing a cylinder containing standard household vinegar, which should be poured onto the area affected by the sting for 30 seconds. Avoid the inclination to rub or scratch the stung area.

The Coast
RESORT **$$$**

(Map p557; 077 951567; www.thecoastphangan. com; Hat Rin Nai; 3700-10,800B; ❄ 🛜 ☀) This dark grey, sharp-angled and stylish resort leads to a slim but OK stretch of beach away from the party hub. Swanky room interiors feature polished cement and beds topped with white duvets, while an infinity pool overlooks the sea, and service pulls out the stops. Hip, cool and minimalist, but comfy.

Ban Khai to Ban Tai

The waters at Ban Tai tend to be shallow and opaque, especially during low season, but lodging options are well priced compared to other parts of the island, and you're close to Thong Sala and not too far from Hat Rin.

As with Ban Tai, Ban Khai's beaches aren't the most stunning, but the accommodation is cheap and there are beautiful views of Ang Thong Marine National Park (p577) in the distance.

These beaches are where many of the moon-but-not-full-moon parties happen so even if your resort seems quiet, there's probably some boozed-up action nearby.

Boom's Cafe Bungalows
BUNGALOW **$**

(Map p546; 081 979 3814; www.boomscafe.com; Ban Khai; 600-1000B; ❄) Staying at Boom's is like visiting the Thai family you never knew you had. Superfriendly and helpful owner Nok takes care of all her guests and keeps things looking good. No one seems to mind that there's no swimming pool, since the curling tide rolls right up to your doorstep. At the far eastern corner of Ban Khai, near Hat Rin.

V-View Beach Resort
BUNGALOW **$$**

(Map p552; 077 377436; Bantai Rd; r 600-2100B; ❄ 🛜 ☀) An effortless air of seclusion settles over this quiet beach resort, and although the sea can be a bit swampy, there are hammocks galore and a fine pool, decent bungalows and a helpful owner.

★ Divine Comedie
RESORT **$$$**

(Map p546; 077 377869, 080 885 8789; www. divinecomedyhotel.com; Ban Tai; r 2700-4300B; ste 4500-5600B; ❄ 🛜 ☀) A stunning mix of 1920s Chinese and perhaps Mexican hacienda architecture with a colour palette that shifts from mint to ochre, this 15-room (10 bungalows and five bedrooms) boutique oasis not only works, it's beguiling. Junior suites have rooftop terraces, while standard rooms have modest balconies, and the elongated infinity pool runs to the slim beach. No kids under 12.

Bay Lounge & Resort
RESORT **$$$**

(Map p546; 077 377892; www.thebayphangan. com; Ban Khai; bungalows incl breakfast 1800-3200B; ❄ 🛜 ☀) On a private white nugget of beach sandwiched by jungle-topped boulders, this intimate, chic choice has bungalows that mingle with the natural surroundings, while inside it's all urban, with distressed concrete and bright modern art. It's midway between Hat Rin's Full Moon Party and the Half Moon Party in Ban Khai – the resort offers transport to each. Check-out time is late at 1pm.

Milky Bay Resort
RESORT **$$$**

(Map p552; 077 332762; www.milkybaythailand. com; Ban Tai; bungalows 1800-13,200B; ❄ @ 🛜 ☀) A delightful picture in Ban Tai, with covered swimming pool, a sauna, gym, table tennis and comfy tree-bark and wood-chip shavings along the paths, accommodation at this tempting choice is a variety of minimalist-chic bungalows with dark tinted glass hidden in the shade of tall stands of bamboo.

Mac Bay
BUNGALOW **$$$**

(Map p546; 077 238443; Ban Khai; bungalows 1200-8500B; ❄ 🛜 ☀) Home to the Black Moon Party (another lunar excuse for Ko Pha-Ngan to go wild), pleasant Mac Bay is a sandy slice of Ban Khai where even the cheaper bungalows are spic and span. At beer o'clock, grab a shaded spot on the sand and watch the sun dance amorphous shadows over the distant islands of Ang Thong Marine National Park.

Thong Sala

Thong Sala's beach is really just an extension of Ban Tai but the beaches are a bit wider up this way and have the advantage of being walking distance to Ko Pha-Ngan's main town, its restaurants and services.

★ Coco Garden
BUNGALOW **$**

(Map p552; 077 377721, 086 073 1147; www.co-cogardens.com; Thong Sala; bungalows 450-1100B; ❄ 🛜) One of the best budget hang-outs along the southern coast and superpopular with the backpacker set, fantastic Coco Garden one-ups the nearby resorts with well-manicured grounds and 25 neat bungalows plus a funtastic beach bar, where hammocks await and a beachfront restaurant supplies breakfast, lunch and dinner with views.

Thong Sala

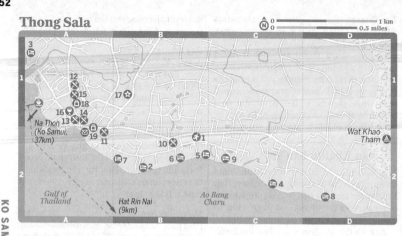

Thong Sala

Hacienda Resort
BUNGALOW $

(Map p552; ☎077 238825; www.beachresort hacienda.com; Thong Sala; dm 300B, r 500-1500B; ❄🛜🏊) With good-looking blue-and-white painted bungalows, rooms in two-storey blocks further down and beachfront air-con dorms, the Hacienda is a spruce and efficient outfit, although the poolside bar can get noisy at night. There's a Phangan International Diving School office and an open-air gym.

Lime n Soda
RESORT $$

(Map p552; ☎077 332721; www.limesodathailand. com; Thong Sala; bungalows 700-2300B; ❄🛜🏊) This solid and decent Thong Sala choice offers clean and simple tiled bungalows in the shade of bamboo and coconut palms along a breakwater above the beach.

Baan Manali Resort
BUNGALOW $$$

(Map p552; ☎077 377917; www.baan-manali.com; Thong Sala; bungalows 2000-3300B; ❄🛜🏊) Quiet, clean and attractively laid out among the coconut trees, 14-bungalow Baan Manali is a convenient, relaxing and well-run choice with infinity pool and excellent restaurant, close to the action at Thong Sala, with a variety of room and bungalow choices.

Charu Bay Villas
VILLA $$$

(Map p552; ☎084 242 2299; www.charubayvillas. com; Ao Bang Charu; villas & studios 1490-9900B; ❄🛜) These fully equipped villas on the bay of Ao Bang Charu, just southeast of Thong Sala, are good value (especially if you're a group), and there's a modern garden self-catering seaside studio too, plus a two-bedroom garden-view villa with rooftop terrace. The Beachfront Villa is a three-bed with large jacuzzi, big enough to sleep up to 10.

B52 Beach Resort
BUNGALOW $$$

(Map p552; www.b52-beach-resort-phangan.info; Thong Sala; bungalows 1500-5000B; ❄ 🛜 ≋) B52's campus of Thai-styled bungalows sports plenty of thatch, polished concrete floors and rustic tropical tree trunks that lead down to the sea. It's all a bit Flintstones, staff are pleasant to boot and there's a pool.

🛏 Ao Nai Wok to Ao Sri Thanu

Close to Thong Sala, the resorts peppered along this breezy west-coast strip mingle with small beaches between patches of gnarled mangroves. There is a lack of sand, but the prices are cheap and the sunsets can be fantastic.

Loyfa Natural Resort
BUNGALOW $$

(Map p546; ☎077 349022; www.loyfanatural resort.com; Ao Sri Thanu; r 750B, bungalows 1300-3100B, villas from 3825B; ❄ 🛜) Loyfa scores high marks for its friendly, congenial French-speaking Thai staff, charming gardens, sturdy huts guarding sweeping ocean views and two pools (one for sunrise, the other for sunset). Modern bungalows tumble down the promontory onto an exclusively private sliver of ash-coloured sand. Cheapest rooms are in a hotel block.

Chills Resort
RESORT $$

(Map p546; ☎089 875 2100; www.chillsresort. hotel.phanganbungalows.com; Ao Sri Thanu; r 1000-2300B; ❄ 🛜 ≋) Set along a stunning and secluded stretch of stony outcrops north of Ao Hin Kong, Chills' cluster of delightfully simple but modern rooms all have peaceful ocean views letting in plenty of sunlight, sea breezes and gorgeous sunset views.

★Kupu Kupu Phangan Beach Villas & Spa by l'Occitane
RESORT $$$

(Map p546; ☎077 377384; www.kupuphangan. com; Ao Nai Wok; villas from 8500B; ❄ 🛜 ≋) This supreme Balinese-style resort is one of the island's most swoon-worthy, with lily ponds, tall palms, a swimming pool straight from a luxury magazine centrefold, spa, rocky boulders that meet the sea and glorious west-coast sunsets. The delightful wooden villas boast dipping pools and spacious, elegant interiors.

Paragon Spa Resort
BUNGALOW $$$

(Map p554; ☎090 982 5276; www.paragonspa resort.com; Ban Sri Thanu; bungalows 1750-12,000B; ❄ @ 🛜 ≋) A tiny hideaway with just seven rooms – each one different – the Paragon has decor that incorporates stylistic elements from ancient Khmer, India and Thailand, without forfeiting any modern amenities. Rooms upstairs have balconies.

🛏 Hat Yao & Hat Son

One of the busier beaches along the west coast, Hat Yao sports a swimmable beach, numerous resorts and a few extra services such as ATMs and convenience stores. With a delightful sense of seclusion, Hat Son is a quiet, much smaller beach that feels like a big secret.

Shiralea
BUNGALOW $

(Map p554; ☎080 719 9256; www.shiralea.com; Hat Yao; dm 275B, bungalows 645-1400B; ❄ 🛜 ≋) The fresh-faced poolside bungalows are simple but the air-con dorms are great, and the ambience, with an on-site bar with draught beer, is fun and convivial. It's about 100m away from the beach and it fills up every few weeks with Contiki student tour groups.

Haad Son Resort & Restaurant
RESORT $$

(Map p554; ☎077 349104; www.haadsonresort. net; Hat Son; bungalows 1875-6750B; ❄ @ 🛜 ≋) There's a mixed bag of rooms here, from big, older wooden bungalows with terraces on the hillside to polished-cement suites and rooms along the beachfront. The secluded beach setting is spectacular and is highlighted by one of the most beachy-chic restaurants on the island on a jungle- and boulder-clad peninsula overlooking the sea. During Full Moon, it's a three-night minimum stay.

Tantawan Bungalows
BUNGALOW $$

(Map p554; ☎077 349108; www.tantawanbunga low.com; Hat Son; bungalows 600-2500B; ❄ ≋) This relaxed, chilled-out 11-bungalow (fan and air-con) teak nest, tucked among jungle foliage, is attractive, with fantastic views and a fine pool, but it's a bit of a steep climb with luggage.

Haad Yao High Life
BUNGALOW $$$

(Map p554; ☎077 349114; www.haadyaohighlife. com; Hat Yao; air-con bungalows 1500-3200B; ❄ 🛜 ≋) With dramatic ocean views from the infinity-edged swimming pool, High Life has 25 bungalows, of various shapes and sizes, on a palmed outcropping of granite soaring high above the cerulean sea. Staff are polite and responsive.

Hat Son

N 0 ___ 1 km
0 ___ 0.5 miles

GULF OF
THAILAND

Ao Hat Salad

Hat Salad

Hat Yao

Hat Son

Hat Chaophao

Haad Yao Bay View Resort   RESORT **$$$**
(Map p554; ☑ 077 349141; www.haadyao-bayview
resort.com; Hat Yao; r & bungalows incl breakfast
from 1500-4000B; ❊@☎☒) This blend of
bungalows and hotel-style accommodation
looks like a tropical mirage on Hat Yao's
northern headland. There's a huge array of
options, but we recommend the tiny but
good-value rooms that hover right over the
sea. For more luxe head up to the hillside
sea-view bungalows.

🛏 Hat Salad

This slim, pretty beach on the northwest
coast is fronted by shallow blue water – a
clutch of photogenic long-tail boats tend
to park at the southern end. It's slightly
rustic, with local Thai fishermen coming
out to throw their nets out at sunset, yet
with plenty of amenities and comfortable
accommodation.

Cookies Salad   RESORT **$$$**
(Map p554; ☑ 083 181 7125, 077 349125; www.
cookies-phangan.com; Hat Salad; bungalows 1700-
3300B; ☎☒) Sling out on a hammock at this
resort with private Balinese-style bungalows
on a steep hill, orbiting a two-tiered lap
pool tiled in various shades of blue. Shaggy
thatching and dense tropical foliage give the

place a certain rustic quality, although you
won't want for creature comforts. It's super-
friendly and books up fast.

Salad Hut   BUNGALOW **$$$**
(Map p554; ☑ 077 349246; www.saladhut.com;
Hat Salad; bungalows 2200-5000B; ❊@☎☒)
Totally unpretentious despite sharing a
beach with some distinctly upscale options,
this small clutch of a dozen Thai-style bun-
galows sits a stone's throw from the rolling
tide, though the pool is rather small. The per-
spective on the sun dipping below the golden
seas from your lacquered teak porch or the
beach bar is a major pull.

Green Papaya   BUNGALOW **$$$**
(Map p554; ☑ 077 374230; www.greenpapaya
resort.com; Hat Salad; bungalows 4100-10,400B;
❊@☎☒) With its tranquil, elegant setting,
Green Papaya and its polished wooden bungalows are a clear, albeit pricey, standout
along the lovely beach at Hat Salad.

🛏 Ban Chalok Lam (Chaloklum) & Hat Khom

In the north of the island, the small and quiet
fishing village at Ban Chalok Lam is a con-
glomeration of teak shanties and huts, slowly
being infiltrated by the occasional European-
style bakery, authentic Italian restaurant or
Russian-owned cafe. *Sŏrng·tăa·ou* ply the

route from here to Thong Sala for around 150B per person.

Fantasea   BUNGALOW $

(Map p546; ☎089 443 0785; www.fantasea -resort-phangan.info; Chalok Lam; bungalows with fan/air-con from 600/1200B; 🛜) This friendly place far from the Full Moon mayhem on the other side of the island is one of the better of a string of family-run bungalow operations along the quiet eastern part of Chalok Lam, with a thin beach out front, OK swimming and an elevated Thai-style restaurant area to chill out in.

Mandalai   HOTEL $$$

(Map p546; ☎077 374316; www.mandalaihotel. com/web2014; Chalok Lam; r 2000-3000B; ❄ @ ❄) This lovely small 'room-only' boutique hotel (with spa) quietly towers over the low-lying form of Chalok Lam, with floor-to-ceiling windows commanding views of tangerine-coloured fishing boats in the bay, and a small but inviting pool in the main courtyard, mere steps from the sand.

🛏 Hat Khuat (Bottle Beach)

This isolated dune in the north of the island has garnered a reputation as a low-key get-away, so it's pretty popular. Grab a long-tail taxi boat from Chalok Lam for 100B to 150B (depending on the boat's occupancy), or tackle the hike (but stay on the path and avoid the midday sun). The trek takes around two hours; follow the bottles on trees marking the way, take water and insect repellent and ensure you don't end up trekking back in darkness.

Smile Bungalows   BUNGALOW $

(Map p546; ☎085 429 4995; www.smilebungalows. com; Hat Khuat; bungalows 520-920B; ⊘closed Nov) For real remoteness and seclusion, it's hard to beat this place at the far western corner of Bottle Beach. Family-run Smile features an assortment of all-fan wooden huts climbing up a forested hill: the two-storey bungalows (920B) are our favourite.

Bottle Beach II   BUNGALOW $

(Map p546; ☎081 537 3833; Bottle Beach/Hat Khuat; bungalows 500-1500B; ⊘closed Nov; 🛜) At the far eastern corner of the beach, this double string of very basic, turquoise bungalows is the ideal place to chill out – for as long as you can – if you don't need many creature comforts, though there are some

new modern family bungalows too, and the restaurant is a decent choice.

🛏 Thong Nai Pan

The pair of rounded bays in the northeast are some of the most remote yet busy beaches on the island. Ao Thong Nai Pan Yai (*yai* means 'big') is the southern half that has some excellent budget and midrange options, and Ao Thong Nai Pan Noi (*noi* means 'little') is Ko Pha-Ngan's most upscale beach, curving just above. Both bays are great for swimming and hiking. A taxi between the two is around 100B. The road from Thong Sala to Thong Nai Pan is now excellent.

Longtail Beach Resort   BUNGALOW $

(Map p546; ☎077 445018; www.longtailbeach resort.com; Thong Nai Pan; bungalows with fan/air-con from 690/990B; ❄ 🛜) Tucked away by the forest at the lovely southern end of Thong Nai Pan – and a long way from Full Moon Ko Pha-Ngan madness – Longtail offers backpackers charming thatch-and-bamboo abodes that wind up a lush garden path; there's plenty of choice, too, for larger groups and families. The sand is fantastic and the lush, green setting is adorable.

Anantara Rasananda   RESORT $$$

(Map p546; ☎077 956660; http://phangan-ras ananda.anantara.com; Ao Thong Nai Pan Noi; villas from 11,000B; ❄ @ 🛜 ❄) Blink and you'll think you've been transported to Ko Samui. This five-star luxury resort is a sweeping sand-side property with a smattering of semi-detached villas – many bedecked with private plunge pools. A savvy mix of modern and traditional styling prevails, and superb Anantara management assures service is polished.

🛏 East Coast

Both Hat Thian and Hat Yuan, near the southeastern tip of the island, have a few bungalow operations, and are quite secluded. You can walk between the two in less than 10 minutes via the rocky outcrop that separates them.

To get here hire a long-tail from Hat Rin (300B to 400B) or organise a boat pick-up from your resort. A dirt road to Hat Yuan has been cleared for 4WDs, but is only passable in the dry season; even then the voyage by sea is much easier.

Bamboo Hut BUNGALOW $
(Map p546; 087 888 8592; Hat Yuan; bungalows 400-1000B;) Beautifully lodged up on the bouldery outcrops that overlook Hat Yuan and the jungle, groovy, friendly, hippie-village Bamboo Hut is a favourite for yoga retreats, meditative relaxation and some serious chilling out. The dark wood bungalows are small, with terraces, while the restaurant serves up superb views and reasonable food.

Barcelona BUNGALOW $
(Map p546; 077 375113; Hat Yuan; bungalows 400-700B) At the south end of Hat Yuan, these old, rickety wood fan bungalows with balconies – some with hammocks – climb up the hill on stilts behind a palm garden, looking onto decent vistas. Price depends on the view, but there's not a huge amount of variation between bungalows apart from size, so grab a cheap one.

Mai Pen Rai BUNGALOW $$
(Map p546; 093 959 8073; www.thansadet.com; Than Sadet; bungalows 683-1365B;) By the river at the south end of leisurely Than Sadet, this lovely, secluded retreat elicits sedate smiles. Bungalows – some temptingly right on the rocks by the sea – also mingle with Plaa's next door on the hilly headland, and sport panels of straw weaving with gabled roofs. Family bungalows are available and a friendly on-site restaurant rounds out an appealing choice.

★ Sanctuary BUNGALOW $$$
(Map p546; 081 271 3614; www.thesanctuarythailand.com; Hat Thian; 2000-7300B) A friendly, forested enclave of relaxed smiles, the Sanctuary is a haven of splendid lodgings, yoga classes and detox sessions. Accommodation, in various manifestations of twigs, is scattered along a tangle of hillside jungle paths, while Hat Thian is wonderfully quiet and is great for swimming. Note that payment is cash only.

Pariya Resort & Villas RESORT $$$
(Map p546; 087 623 6678; www.pariyahaadyuan.com; Hat Yuan; villas 8000-17,000B;) The smartest option on gloriously soft sands of Hat Yuan has a large choice of very spacious and comfortable villas, but they're not cheap. It's remote and quiet, but getting about is hard and you're pretty isolated, which is perfect for some, but not for others.

Eating

Most visitors quickly adopt the lazy lifestyle and wind up eating at their accommodation,

which is a shame as Ko Pha-Ngan has some excellent restaurants scattered around the island; at the very least, it's another reason to get exploring.

Hat Rin

Hat Rin has a large conglomeration of restaurants and bars on the island, yet many of them are pretty average so it's not worth coming here for the food alone.

Palita Lodge SEAFOOD $
(Map p557; Hat Rin Nok; mains from 100B) The front restaurant of the Sunrise Beach bungalows outfit of the same name offers up tasty Thai seafood and set meals with views overlooking a beach that's pretty serene outside of the Full Moon period.

Lazy House INTERNATIONAL $$
(Map p557; Hat Rin Nai; dishes 90-270B; lunch & dinner) Back in the day, this joint was the owner's apartment – everyone liked his cooking so much that he decided to turn the place into a restaurant and hang-out spot. Today, Lazy House is one of Hat Rin's best places to veg out in front of a movie with a scrumptious shepherd's pie.

Monna Lisa ITALIAN $$
(Map p557; 084 441 5871; Hat Rin Nai; pizza & pasta from 200B; 3-11pm) Travellers still rave about the pizza here, and the pasta gets a thumbs-up as well. It's run by a team of friendly Italians and has a basic, open-air atmosphere. There's another branch in Thong Sala too.

Om Ganesh INDIAN $$
(Map p557; Hat Rin Nai; mains from 100B; 9am-11pm;) Seasoned old-timer Om Ganesh sees a regular flow of customers for its north Indian curries, biryani rice, roti and lassis, with a token spread of Chinese dishes for good measure. Set meals start at 300B.

Southern Beaches

In recent years Thong Sala has attracted many new excellent restaurants, so spend some time dining here. There are also some well-established cafes that do excellent business and are among the best places on the island for breakfast. There are some superb restaurants and cafes dotted along the road between Thong Sala and Hat Rin.

On Saturday evenings from 4pm to 10pm, a side street in the eastern part of Thong

Hat Rin

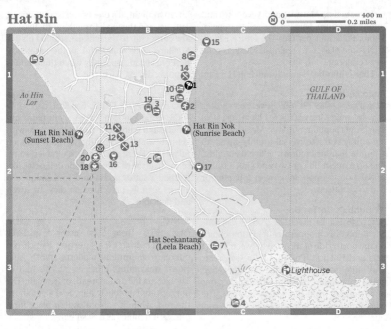

Hat Rin

Sala becomes a fun **Walking Street** – a bustling pedestrian zone mostly filled with locals hawking their wares to other islanders. There's plenty on offer, from clothing to food.

★ Food Market   MARKET $
(Map p552; Thong Sala; dishes 25-180B; ⊙ 1-11pm)
A heady mix of steam and snacking locals, Thong Sala's terrific food market is a must for those looking for doses of culture while nibbling on low-priced snacks. Wander the stalls for a galaxy of Thai street food, from vegetable curry puffs to corn on the cob, spicy sausages, kebabs, spring rolls, Hainanese chicken rice or coconut ice cream.

★ Nira's   BAKERY $
(Map p552; Thong Sala; snacks from 80B; ⊙ 7am-7pm; 🛜) With lots of busy staff offering outstanding service, a big and bright interconnected two-room interior, scrummy baked goodies, tip-top coffee (and exotic

rarities such as Marmite and Vegemite) and trendy furniture, Nira's is second to none in Thong Sala, and perhaps the entire island. This is *the* place for breakfast. Music is cool, jazzy chill-out.

There's another (small) branch in Hat Rin.

Ando Loco
MEXICAN $

(Map p552; ☑085 791 7600; www.andoloco.com; Ban Tai; mains from 50B; ⊘1-10pm Wed-Mon) This superpopular outdoor Mexican hangout still gets the universal thumbs-up. Grab a jumbo margarita, down a 'drunken fajita', line up a quesadilla or two and sink a round of balls on the pool table with a tequila or two to go with it.

★ Bubba's Coffee Bar
CAFE $

(Map p546; Ban Tai; mains 120-220B; ⊘7am-5pm; 🛜) Bubba's is a superb caffeination choice on the north side of the road between Thong Sala and Hat Rin. Pull in, find a seat, relax and enjoy some fine coffee and the easygoing atmosphere (despite attracting legions of customers from the nearby hostels). The wholesome menu is lovely too, as is the cool interior.

★ Fat Cat
CAFE $

(Map p552; Thong Sala; breakfast from 70B, mains 90-195B; ⊘9am-3pm Mon-Sat; 🛜) This small, charming, colourful and busy – with staff rather run off their feet – Portuguese-run cafe does wholesome breakfasts and lovely coffees through the day. It's a very enjoyable place for a wake-up meal first thing in the morning, or any other time.

★ Dots
CAFE $

(Map p552; Thong Sala; snacks from 60B; ⊘8.30am-9pm Mon-Sat, 9am-6pm Sun; 🛜) Light, bright and spacious, Dots is a welcome addition to Thong Sala's cafe culture, with a modern and chilled vibe. Pretty much right next to the Food Market, it's a sharp-looking spot for a slice of carrot cake, frappé, full-flavoured coffee, hot choc or a croissant for brekkie.

Satimi
ICE CREAM $

(Map p552; Thong Sala; per scoop 30-40B; ⊘10.30am-6.30pm Tue-Sun) The small and enterprising back-street gelateria sells homemade ice-cream and sorbets, using natural and locally sourced ingredients.

★ Fisherman's Restaurant
SEAFOOD $$

(Map p546; ☑084 454 7240; Ban Tai; dishes 50-600B; ⊘1.30-10pm) Sit in a long-tail boat looking out over the sunset and a rocky pier.

Lit up at night, it's one of the island's nicest settings, and the food, from the addictive yellow curry crab to the massive seafood platter to share, is as wonderful as the ambience. Reserve ahead, especially when the island is hopping during party time.

Fabio's
ITALIAN $$

(Map p546; ☑077 377180; Ban Khai; dishes 150-400B; ⊘6-10pm Mon-Sat) An intimate, authentic and truly delicious Italian place with golden walls, cream linens and bamboo furniture. There are only seven tables, so reserve in advance. House-made delicacies like seafood risotto, pizzas and iced limoncello are as artfully presented as they are fresh and delicious.

SOHO
BURGERS $$

(Map p552; Thong Sala; mains from 180B; ⊘9.30am-midnight) This terrific British-run burger restaurant is modern, stylish, spacious, welcoming, efficient, at the hub of Thong Sala life and a breath of fresh air. The burgers are fabulously juicy and a cut above the rest, while it's also a superb place for a pint as it doubles as a flash bar.

🍴 Other Beaches

JJ's Restaurant
THAI $

(Map p546; Ao Wok Tum; mains from 80B; ⊘9am-9pm) Drop off at scenically situated JJ's come sunset to swoon in front of stirring visuals over the young, replanted mangrove trees at Ao Wok Tum while devouring tasty treats from the kitchen and toasting it all with a chilled beer.

Pura Vida
CAFE $

(Map p554; ☑095 034 9372; Hat Yao; mains from 120B; ⊘8.30am-3pm Mon-Sat) Hobbled only by short opening hours, this charming and bright Portuguese cafe is an alluring choice as you head up the west coast. Breakfasts are excellent, especially the pancakes and natural yoghurt, but you can go the whole hog with a full brekkie, and delicious burgers, sandwiches and paninis are also served. Love the 'Eat Well, Travel Often' campervan painting.

Bamboo Hut
WESTERN, THAI $

(Map p546; Hat Yuan; dishes 100-300B; ⊘breakfast, lunch & dinner; 🛜🍴) Lounge on a Thai-style cushion or sit at a teak table that catches sea breezes and looks over infinite blue. There are plenty of options, from vegetarian specialities and fresh juices for those coming off a fast or cleanse, to classic, very well-prepared Thai dishes with all assortments of beef, chicken and prawns.

★ Peppercorn
STEAK $$

(Map p554; ☑087 896 4363; www.peppercorn phangan.com; Hat Salad; mains 160-400B; ⊗4-10pm Mon-Sat; ☑) Escargot, succulent steaks and schnitzel in a rickety jungle cottage? You bet! Peppercorn may be tucked in the brush away from the sea, but that shouldn't dissuade foodies from seeking out some of Ko Pha-Ngan's best international cuisine, with a fine selection of good vegetarian dishes to boot, and mango cake for dessert. No MSG or artificial ingredients.

★ Crave
BURGERS $$

(Map p546; ☑098 838 7268; www.cravekohphang an.com; Sri Thanu; mains from 200B; ⊗6-10pm Wed-Mon; ☞) Attractively bedecked with glowing lanterns at night, this excellent, very popular and atmospheric choice in Sri Thanu puts together some fine burgers in a cosy and charming setting. Cocktails are great too, starting at 170B. Shame it's only open evenings.

Sanctuary
HEALTH FOOD $$

(Map p546; www.thesanctuarythailand.com; Hat Thian; mains from 130B; ☞) The restaurant at the Sanctuary resort (p556) proves that wholesome food (vegetarian and seafood) can also be delicious. Enjoy a tasty parade of plates – from massaman curry to crunchy Vietnamese spring rolls. Don't forget to wash it all down with a blackberry, soya milk and honey immune booster. No credit cards.

🍷 Drinking & Nightlife

Every month, on the night of the full moon, pilgrims pay lunar tribute to the party gods with trance-like dancing, wild screaming and glow-in-the-dark body paint. For something mellower, the west coast has several excellent bars, where you can raise a loaded cocktail glass to a blood-orange sunset from a hilltop or over mangrove trees at the water's edge. Thong Sala has as a couple of decent bars too.

🍷 Hat Rin

Hat Rin is the beating heart of the legendary Full Moon fun. When the moon isn't lighting up the night sky, party-goers flock to other spots on the island's south side. Most party venues flank Hat Rin's Sunrise Beach from south to north.

Rock
BAR, CLUB

(Map p557; ☑093 725 7989; Hat Rin Nok; ⊗8am-late) The superb views of the party from the elevated terrace – and excellent panoramas at all other times – on the far south side of the beach are matched by super cocktails and a mixed menu of plates for just about all palates.

Tommy
BAR, CLUB

(Map p557; Hat Rin Nok) One of Hat Rin's largest venues lures the masses with loungers, low tables, black lights and blaring Full Moon trance music. Drinks are dispensed from a large ark-like bar.

Palms Cafe
BAR

(Map p557; Hat Rin; ⊗10am-late; ☞) This smart cafe/bar and environmentally inclined restaurant near Hat Rin Nai is a good-looker – with its lovely poolside location – and provides a perfect escape from Hat Rin's noisier, rougher and busier backstreets. There's a good choice of cocktails and an experimental approach to all manner of protein shakes and health drinks.

Sunrise
BAR, CLUB

(Map p557; ☑077 375144; Hat Rin Nok) A spot on the sand where trance beats shake the graffitied walls, with drum 'n bass coming into its own at Full Moon.

Mellow Mountain
BAR

(Map p557; Hat Rin Nok; ⊗24hr; ☞) Also called 'Mushy Mountain' (you'll know when you get there), this trippy hang-out sits at the northern end of Hat Rin Nok, delivering stellar views of the shenanigans below.

🍷 Southern Beaches

Hub
PUB

(Map p552; ☑088 825 4158; Thong Sala; ⊗8am-midnight; ☞) With chatty staff and a prime location on the corner straight down from the pier, cavernous wood-floored Hub is the sports bar of choice for those crucial Premier League fixtures, draft beer, cider and excellent pub fare. They also rent out scooters and motorbikes.

Viewpoint Bar
BAR

(Map p546; Ban Khai; ☞) If you're heading back from Hat Rin to Thong Sala or Ban Tai, park up your scooter and head into this bar at the Viewpoint Hotel, with a terrific perch over the gulf from a high spot off this side of the road. The views are simply fantastic.

DON'T MISS

FULL MOON PARTIES

No one knows exactly when or how the wild **full-moon parties** (Map p557; Hat Rin Nok; 100B; ☾ full moon, dusk till dawn) started – most believe they began in 1988, but accounts of the first party range from an Australian backpacker's going-away bash in August to a group of hippies escaping Samui's 'electric parties' in October. None of that is relevant now: today, thousands of bodies converge monthly on the kerosene-soaked sands of **Hat Rin Nok** (aka Sunrise Beach; p548) for an epic dusk-until-dawn trance-a-thon.

The pounding heart of the Full Moon action, Sunrise Beach sees crowds swell to an outrageous 40,000 party-goers during high season, while the low season still sees a respectable 8000 wide-eyed pilgrims. To take a break, head to the Rock (p559) bar at the south end or Mellow Mountain (p559) at the north end and chill out. You'll be knocking into stalls selling buckets of alcohol – vodka, gin, rum, whisky, mixed with coke and red bull – all along the beach, but go easy, you can quickly end up downing more than you think. Try to leave them until late.

Flaming among the thumping bass-lines and flashing neon are the petrol-drenched fire ropes where dancers are invited to hop over a swinging line of fire (burns are generally the order of the day on that one). Some critics claim the party is starting to lose its carefree flavour, especially given increasing violence and the fact that the island's government now charges a 100B entrance fee to party-goers (the money goes towards much-needed beach cleaning and security).

Have your accommodation sorted way in advance – if you turn up on the day, you won't find a bed for the night in Hat Rin, though you can always do an in-and-out from Ko Samui.

Other Beaches

★ Belgian Beer Bar BAR

(Map p554; www.seetanu.com; Ban Sri Thanu; ☾ 8am-10pm) Run by the affable Quentin, this enjoyable bar defies Surat Thani's appropriation by yogis and the chakra-balancing crowd with a heady range of Belgian beer, the most potent of which (Amber Bush) delivers a dizzying 12.5% punch. If the yogic flying doesn't give you wings, this might.

★ Secret Beach Bar BAR

(Map p554; Hat Son; ☾ 9am-7pm) There are few ways better to unwind at the end of a Ko Pha-Ngan day than watching the sun slide into an azure sea from this bar on the northwest sands of the island. Grab a table, order up a mojito and take in the sunset through the palm fronds.

Amsterdam BAR

(Map p546; ☏ 089 072 2233; Ao Plaay Laem; ☾ noon-midnight) Near Ao Wok Tum on the west coast, hillside Amsterdam attracts tourists and locals from all over the island, seeking a superchilled spot to catch a Ko Pha-Ngan sunset and totally zone out.

Flip Flop Pharmacy BAR

(Map p546; Thong Nai Pan; ☾ noon-1am; 🛜) With flip-flops on the wall, this popular beach bar on the sands of Thong Nai Pan has a fine beach perspective (and a pool table) and a terrific setting.

Three Sixty Bar BAR

(Map p546; Ban Mae Hat; ☾ 8am-midnight) High up a road east of Ko Ma, the Three Sixty Bar does what it says on the packet, with splendid, wide-angle views – sunset time is killer.

Shopping

★ Thong Sala Walking Street MARKET

(Map p552; Taladkao Rd, Thong Sala; ☾ 4-10pm Sat) Thong Sala's Walking Street market kicks off every Saturday from around 4pm, with a terrific choice of street food, souvenirs, gifts, handicrafts and clothes. It's the best time to see Thong Sala at its liveliest.

★ Lilawadee CLOTHING

(Map p552; ☏ 630 920327; Thong Sala; ☾ 10.30am-1.30pm & 5-9pm Fri-Wed) This neat and idiosyncratic shop stocks a sparkling range of customised, head-turning glitter motorbike helmets, stacked temptingly on shelves at the rear, fashion, art and clothing. If it's raining, expect hours to be reduced to noon to 8pm.

ℹ Information

DANGERS & ANNOYANCES

Some of your fondest holiday memories can hatch on Ko Pha-Ngan; just be mindful of the following situations where things can go pear-shaped:

Drugs There have been instances of locals approaching tourists and attempting to sell them drugs at a low, seemingly enticing, price. Upon refusing the offer, the vendor may drop the price even more. Once purchased, the seller informs the police, which lands said tourist in the local prison to pay a wallet-busting fine. If you're solicited to buy drugs, stand your ground and maintain refusal. This may happen frequently on Ko Pha-Ngan, so be aware and avoid the scenario if you suspect it happening. Another important thing to remember: your travel insurance does not cover drug-related injuries or treatment. Drug-related freak-outs *do* happen – we've heard first-hand accounts of party-goers slipping into extended periods of delirium. Suan Saranrom (Garden of Joys) Psychiatric Hospital in Surat Thani has to take on extra staff during Full Moon to handle the number of *fa·ràng* (Westerners) who freak out on magic mushrooms, acid or other abundantly available hallucinogens.

Women Travellers Female travellers should be particularly careful when partying on the island. We've received numerous reports about drug- and alcohol-related rape (and these situations are not limited to Full Moon parties). Women should also take care when accepting rides with local motorcycle taxi drivers. Several complaints have been filed about drivers groping female passengers; there are even reports of severe sexual assaults.

Motorcycles & Scooters Ko Pha-Ngan has more motorcycle accidents than injuries incurred from Full Moon tomfoolery, although bad motorcycle driving coincides with the Full Moon revelries. Nowadays there's a decent system of paved roads (extended to Than Sadet), but some tracks remain rutted dirt-and-mud paths and the island is also hilly, with some steep inclines. The island has a special ambulance that trawls the island helping injured bikers. If you don't have an international driving licence, you will also be driving illegally and your insurance may not cover you in the event of an accident, so costs could pile up fast.

Drowning Rip currents and alcohol don't mix well. Drownings are frequent; if swimming, it's advisable to be clear-headed rather than plunging into the sea on a Full Moon bender.

Dodgy Alcohol This is a common scam during the Full Moon mania at the bucket stalls on the beach and along the road. Buckets may be filled with low-grade moonshine rice whisky, or old bottles filled with homemade alcohol. Apart from obvious health risks, dodgy alcohol is also a prime mover in incidents from motorcycle accidents to drownings, fights and burns from jumping fire ropes.

Glass on the Beach Beware nasty cuts from broken glass in the sand – wear good footwear.

The last time we visited, the southern reaches of the beach at Thong Sala (and other beaches) were full of broken bottles, just left there.

EMERGENCY

Main Police Station (Map p546; ☏191, 077 377114; Thong Sala) Located about 2km north of Thong Sala. Come here to file a report. You might be charged between 110B and 200B to file the report, which is for insurance, and refusing to pay may lead to complications. If you are arrested you have the right to an embassy phone call; you don't have to accept the 'interpreter' you are offered. If you have been accused of committing serious offence, do not sign anything written only in Thai, or write on the document that you do not understand the language and are signing under duress.

LAUNDRY

If you get fluorescent body paint on your clothes during your Full Moon revelry, don't bother sending them to the cleaners – it will never come out. Trust us, we've tried. For your other laundry needs, there are heaps of places that will gladly wash your clothes. Prices hover around 40B per kilo, and express cleanings shouldn't be more than 60B per kilo.

MEDICAL SERVICES

Be wary of private medical services in Ko Pha-Ngan, and expect unstable prices. Many clinics charge a 3000B entrance fee before treatment. Serious medical issues should be dealt with on nearby Ko Samui, which has superior facilities.

Ko Pha-Ngan Hospital (Map p546; ☏077 377034; ⊙24hr), about 2.5km north of Thong Sala, is a government hospital that offers 24-hour emergency services.

MONEY

Thong Sala, Ko Pha-Ngan's financial 'capital', has plenty of banks, currency converters and several Western Union offices. Hat Rin also has numerous ATMs and a couple of banks at the pier. There are also ATMs in Hat Yao, Chalok Lum and Thong Nai Pan.

WORTH A TRIP

CINEMA ESCAPISM

Set in a seductive garden-meets-jungle setting, the **Moonlight Cinema** (Map p552; ☏093 638 5051; www.moonlight-phangan.com; Thong Sala; 150B; ⊙3pm-1am Tue-Fri, 1pm-1am Sat & Sun; 🖥) has a huge screen, great smoothies, a bar, fantastic vegan food and some excellent films (with headphones provided). It's fun, atmospheric and highly relaxing.

POST

Main Post Office (Map p552; Thong Sala; ⊙ 8.30am-4.30pm Mon-Fri, 9am-noon Sat)
Post Office (Map p557; Hat Rin)

TOURIST INFORMATION

There are no government-run Tourist Authority of Thailand (TAT) offices on Ko Pha-Ngan; instead tourists get their information from local travel agencies and brochures. Most agencies are clustered around Hat Rin and Thong Sala. Agents take a small commission on each sale, but their presence helps to keep prices relatively stable and standardised. Choose an agent you trust if you are spending a lot of money – faulty bookings do happen on Ko Pha-Ngan, especially since the island does not have tourist police.

Several mini-magazines also offer comprehensive information about the island's accommodation, restaurants, activities and Full Moon parties. Our favourite option is the pocket-sized quarterly Phangan Info (www.phangan.info), also available as a handy app.

Phanganist (www.phanganist.com) is an online resource that's full of insider tips for all things Ko Pha-Ngan.

At the time of writing, the enterprising Backpackers Information Centre (www.backpacker sthailand.com) had shut, but may have reopened by the time you read this.

ⓘ Getting There & Away

As always, the cost and departure times for ferries are subject to change. Rough waves are sometimes known to cancel ferries between November and December.

AIR

Ko Pha-Ngan's airport plans are on hold, so watch this space. At the time of writing, there were issues relating to the airport encroaching on land belonging to Than Sadet-Koh Phangan National Park, so everything was still in the air, so to speak.

BOAT

To Bangkok, Hua Hin & Chumphon

The **Lomprayah** (Map p552; www.lomprayah. com) and **Seatran Discovery** (www.seatrandis covery.com) services have bus-boat combination packages (Lomprayah from around 1300B, Seatran from 1000B) that depart from the Th Khao San area in Bangkok and pass through Hua Hin and Chumphon. The whole voyage takes between 10 and 17½ hours.

It is also quite hassle-free (unless your train breaks down, which happens a lot) to take the train from Bangkok or Hua Hin to Chumphon and switch to a ferry service. In this case expect to pay 300B for a second-class seat on a train from Bangkok to Chumphon (about 8½ hours); Lomprayah boats from Chumphon to Ko Pha-Ngan take around 3 to 3¾ hours and costs 1000B.

To Ko Samui

There are around a dozen daily departures between Thong Sala on Ko Pha-Ngan and Ko Samui. These boats leave throughout the day from 7am to 6pm, take from 20 minutes to an hour and cost 200B to 300B depending on the boat.

The **Haad Rin Queen** (Map p557; ☑ 077 484668) goes back and forth between Hat Rin and Big Buddha Beach four times a day (the first boat leaves Hat Rin at 9.30am and departs Big Buddha Beach at 10.30am), with double the number of sailings the day after the Full Moon Party and an extra trip laid on at 7.30am the same day. The voyage takes 50 minutes, costs 200B and the last boat leaves Big Buddha Beach at 6.30pm.

The **Thong Nai Pan Express** (Map p557) is a wobbly old fishing boat (not for the faint-hearted) that runs once a day from Mae Nam on Ko Samui to Hat Rin on Ko Pha-Ngan and then up the east coast, stopping at all the beaches as far as the **pier** (Map p546) at Thong Nai Pan Noi. Prices range from 200B to 400B depending on the destination. The boat won't run in bad weather.

To Ko Tao

Ko Tao-bound **Lomprayah** ferries (500B to 600B) depart from Thong Sala on Ko Pha-Ngan at 8.30am, 1pm and 5.30pm and arrive at 9.30am, 2.15pm and 6.30pm. The **Seatran** service (450B, 90 mins) departs from Thong Sala at 8.30am, 1.30pm and 5pm daily. Taxis depart Hat Rin for Thong Sala one hour before the boat departure. The cheaper and slower **Songserm** (350B) leaves Ko Pha-Ngan at 12.30pm and alights at 2pm, before continuing to Chumphon.

To Surat Thani & The Andaman Coast

There are four daily **Lomprayah** (550B, 2¾ hours) services to Don Sak (for Surat Thani), both travelling via Ko Samui. These boats leave from Thong Sala from 7.20am to 2.30pm. One **Seatran** (www.seatrandiscovery.com) boat (700B) also leaves daily from Thong Sala for Surat Thani at 10.30am, with a bus connection to Phun Phin train station outside the city. Every night, depending on the weather, a night boat runs from Surat Thani (400B, seven hours), departing at 11pm. Boats in the opposite direction leave Ko Pha-Ngan at 10pm.

Combination boat-bus tickets are available at any travel agency. Simply tell them your desired destination and they will sell you the necessary links in the transport chain. Most travellers will pass through Surat Thani as they swap coasts.

ℹ️ Getting Around

Bicycle rentals are not such a great idea unless you're fit enough to take on the Tour de France.

Pick-up trucks and *sŏrng·tăa·ou* chug along the island's major roads, and the riding rates double after sunset. Ask your accommodation about free or discount transfers when you leave the island. The trip from Thong Sala to Hat Rin is 100B; further beaches will set you back around 150B to 200B. From Hat Rin, **sŏrng·tăa·ou** (Map p557) bound for Thong Sala depart from west of Hat Rin Nok.

Long-tail boats depart from Thong Sala, **Chalok Lam** (Map p546) and Hat Rin, heading to far-flung destinations such as **Hat Khuat** (Map p546; Bottle Beach) and **Hat Than Sadet** (Map p546). Expect to pay anywhere from 50B for a short trip, and up to 300B for a lengthier journey. You can charter a private boat ride from beach to beach for about 150B per 15 minutes of travel.

You can rent motorcycles all over the island for 200B to 250B per day; it's cheaper if you book for several days. Always wear a helmet – it's the law on Ko Pha-Ngan, and local policemen are starting to enforce it. But whatever the law, without a helmet, if you come off even at quite a low speed and hit your head, you can sustain serious injuries. Check that the motorcycle has enough space in the under-seat compartment to store your helmet. If you plan on riding over dirt tracks it is imperative that you rent a bike comparable to a Honda MTX125 – gearless scooters cannot make the journey. Avoid driving on the roads during any Full Moon.

Ko Tao   เกาะเต่า

POP 2032

The baby of the Samui–Pha-Ngan–Tao trio, Ko Tao may still be the smallest in size but in many other ways it's all grown up. The island is consistently gaining in popularity and going more upscale, but for now this jungle-topped cutie has the busy vibe of Samui mixed with the laid-back nature of Pha-Ngan.

But Tao also has its wild card, something the others don't: easy-to-get-to, diverse diving right off its shores. Cavort with sharks and rays in a playground of tangled neon coral, toast the day with sunset cocktails on a white beach, then get up and do it all over again.

But even though the island is synonymous with diving, there is much more to the place. Hikers and hermits can re-enact an episode from *Lost* in the dripping coastal jungles. And

when you're Robinson Crusoe-ed out, hit the pumpin' bar scene that rages on until dawn.

👁️ Sights

⭐ Ao Tanot   BEACH
(Map p564) With crystal-clear waters and superb snorkelling, pretty Ao Tanot on the east coast also affords excellent rock-jumping opportunities from the huge rock in the bay. If diving or snorkelling, look out for angelfish, coral trout and bannerfish. There's a sunken catamaran in the bay. There are five resort and bungalow operations here if you want to overnight and catch the splendid sunrise.

⭐ Laem Thian Beach   BEACH
(Map p564) In the lee of the headland, this secluded and sheltered little white-sand beach in the middle of the east coast, north of Ao Tanot, is a delightful place with excellent snorkelling, excellent rock jumping and very clear waters. It's quite a hike to get here along a dirt track; otherwise it's reachable by long-tail boat. There's the shell of an old resort here, crumbling away and covered in graffiti. If you hike, take loads of water and sunscreen.

Ko Nang Yuan   ISLAND
(Map p564; 100B; ⊙10am-5pm) These three lovely islands off the northwest coast of Ko Tao are linked together by a sandbar, with superb view from the island highpoints. Boats run from the Lomprayah pier in Mae Hat.

🏃 Activities

Diving
If you've never been diving before, Ko Tao is *the* place in Thailand to lose your scuba virginity. The shallow bays scalloping the island are perfect for newbie divers to take their first stab at scuba; the waters are crystal clear, there are loads of neon reefs and the temperatures are bathwater warm. With many sheltered dive sites, waters around Ko Tao can be dived all year round; it's only during the monsoon months that diving may stop for a day or two if the waters are too choppy, but this is actually quite rare.

The best dive sites are found at offshore pinnacles within a 20km radius of the island, but seasoned scubaholics almost always prefer the top-notch sites along the Andaman coast. The local marine wildlife includes groupers, moray eels, batfish, bannerfish, barracudas, titan triggerfish, angelfish, clownfish (Nemos), stingrays, reef sharks and frequent visits by mighty whale sharks.

Ko Tao

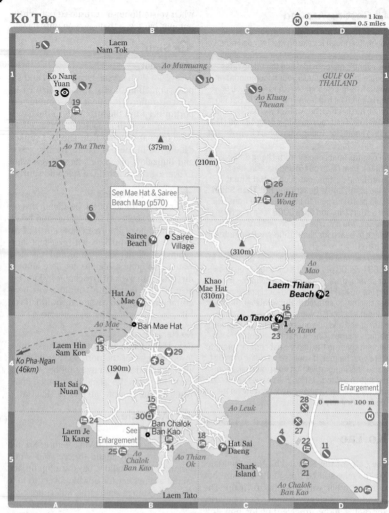

KO SAMUI & THE LOWER GULF KO TAO

Onshore, scores of dive centres are ready to saddle you up with gear and teach you the ropes in a 3½-day Open Water certification course. The intense competition among scuba schools means that certification prices are unbeatably low and the standards of service top-notch; dozens of dive shops vie for your baht, so be sure to shop around. The island issues more scuba certifications than anywhere else in the world.

★ Apnea Total
DIVING

(Map p570; ☎ 081 956 5430, 081 956 5720; www.apneatotal.com; Sairee Beach; one-/two-day course 3500/5500B) The capable, outgoing and enthusiastic staff at Apnea Total, which has earned several awards in the free-diving world, possess a special knack for easing newbies into this awe-inspiring sport. The student-teacher ratio of three to one also ensures plenty of attention to safety. The standard intro course is over two days, getting you (potentially) down to 20m.

★ Crystal Dive
DIVING

(Map p570; ☎ 077 456106; www.crystaldive.com; Mae Hat) This award-winning school (and resort) is one of the largest operators on the

Ko Tao

island (and around the world), but high-quality instructors and intimate classes keep the school feeling quite personal. Multilingual staff members, air-conditioned classes and two on-site swimming pools sweeten the deal. Crystal also puts considerable energy into marine conservation projects on Ko Tao. Highly recommended.

New Heaven DIVING
(Map p564; ☑077 457045; www.newheavendiveschool.com; Chalok Ban Kao) The owners of this diving operation dedicate considerable time to preserving the natural beauty of Ko Tao's underwater sites with regular reef checks, and also contribute to reef restoration efforts. A special CPAD research diver certification program is available in addition to the regular programs and fun dives, as well as free-diving. Instructors are friendly, reassuring and encouraging.

ACE Marine Expeditions DIVING
(Map p570; ☑077 456547; www.divephotothai.com; Sairee Village) The luxe choice: entry level to advanced, plus courses for kids. Zip out on the James Bond–worthy speedboat and reach sites in a fraction of the time. Sunset cruises also offered to add a further golden sheen to your holiday.

Big Blue Diving DIVING
(Map p570; ☑077 456050; www.bigbluediving.com; Sairee Beach) If Goldilocks were picking a dive school, she'd probably go for Big Blue – this midsize operation (not too big, not too small) is popular for fostering a sociable vibe while maintaining high standards of service. Divers of every ilk can score accommodation across the budget ranges, from backpacker dorms up to top-notch family villas at their resort.

Ban's Diving School DIVING
(Map p570; ☑077 456466; www.bansdivingresort.com; Sairee Beach) A well-oiled diving machine that's relentlessly expanding, Ban's is one of the world's most prolific diver certification schools yet it retains a five-star feel. Classroom sessions tend to be conducted in large groups, but there's a reasonable amount of individual attention in the water. A breadth of international instructors means that students can learn to dive in their native tongue.

Buddha View DIVING
(Map p564; ☑077 456074; www.buddhaview-diving.com; Chalok Ban Kao; from 1000B; ☉7am-6.30pm) One of several of the big dive operations on Ko Tao, Buddha View offers the standard fare of certification for around 2000B and special programs for technical diving (venturing beyond the usual parameters of recreational underwater exploration). Discounted accommodation is available at its friendly resort.

Snorkelling

Snorkelling is a popular alternative to diving, and orchestrating your own snorkelling adventure here is simple, since the bays on the east coast have small bungalow operations offering equipment rental for between 100B and 200B per day.

Most snorkel enthusiasts opt for the do-it-yourself approach on Ko Tao, which involves swimming out into the offshore bays or hiring a long-tail boat to putter around further out. Guided tours are also available and can be booked at any local travel agency. Tours range from 500B to 800B (usually including gear, lunch and a guide/boat captain) and stop at various snorkelling hotspots around the island.

Laem Thian is popular for its small sharks, **Shark Island** has loads of fish (but ironically no sharks), **Ao Hin Wong** is known for its crystalline waters, and Lighthouse Bay (p567), in the north, offers a dazzling array of colourful sea anemones. Ao Tanot (p563) is also a popular snorkelling spot.

Dive schools will usually allow snorkellers on their vessels for a comparable price – but it's only worth snorkelling at the shallower sites such as Japanese Gardens (p567). Note that dive boats visit the shallower sites in the afternoons.

Free-Diving

With a large number of fully qualified free-divers on the island, many traditional dive operators now offer free-diving (exploring the sea using breath-holding techniques rather than scuba gear). Apnea Total (p564) has earned several awards in the free-diving world and possesses a special knack for easing newbies into this heart-pounding sport. The student-teacher ratio of three to one also ensures plenty of attention to safety. Also worth a special mention is the highly capable **Blue Immersion** (Map p570; ☑ 081 188 8488; www.blue-immersion.com; Sairee Beach; from 3000B). Free-diving prices are pretty much standardised across the island – a 2½-day SSI beginner course will set you back 5500B.

Technical Diving & Cave Diving

Well-seasoned divers and hardcore Jacques Cousteaus should contact **Tech Dive Thailand** (www.techdivethailand.com) or one of a handful of other tech-diving schools if they want to take their underwater exploration to the next level and try a technical dive. Technical diving exceeds depths of 40m and requires stage decompressions, and a variety of gas mixtures are often used in a single dive. You must be a certified tech diver to undertake tech dives; training courses are available at many schools on the island, offering various tech-diving certifications.

For wreck exploration, the gulf has long been an important trading route, and new wrecks are being discovered all the time, from old Chinese pottery wrecks to Japanese *marus* (merchant ships). The HTMS *Sattakut* wreck and deeper pinnacle dive sites are also good for tech diving, and Tech Dive Thailand has a complete online database of dozens of wrecks.

Cave diving has taken Ko Tao by storm, and the most intrepid scuba buffs are lining up to make the half-day trek over to Khao Sok National Park. Beneath the park's main lake lurks an astonishing submarine world filled with hidden grottos, limestone crags and skulking catfish. In certain areas divers can swim near submerged villages that were flooded in order to create a reservoir and dam. Most cave-diving trips depart from Ko Tao on the afternoon boat service and return to the island on the afternoon boat service of the following day. Overnight stays are arranged in or near the park.

Underwater Photography & Videography

If your wallet is already full of diving certification cards, consider renting an underwater camera or enrolling in a marine videography course. Many scuba schools hire professional videographers to film Open Water Diver certifications, and if this piques your interest, you could potentially earn some money after completing a video internship. Your dive operator can put you in touch with any of the half-dozen videography crews on the island. We recommend **ACE Marine Images** (Map p570; ☑ 077 457054; www.acemarineimages.com; Sairee Beach), one of Thailand's leading underwater videography studios. An introductory course including camera, diving and instruction is 4500B and can also be used towards an Advanced PADI certification. **Crystal Images** (Map p570; ☑ 092 476 4110; www.crystalimageskohtao.com; Mae Hat) and **Oceans Below** (Map p570; ☑ 086 060 1863; www.oceansbelow.net; Sairee Village) offer videography courses and internships; each have their own special options.

Other Activities

★ **Flying Trapeze Adventures** ACROBATICS (FTA; Map p570; ☑ 080 696 9269; www.goodtimethailand.com; Sairee Beach; ⊙ 4-8pm, lessons 3.30-5.30pm) Test your vertigo and find if you're a great catch with a fun 90-minute small-group beginner trapeze lesson (1500B). Courses are taught by a superfriendly posse of limber sidekicks, who take you from circus neophyte to soaring savant in four jumps or fewer. There are occasional nightly shows, involving audience participation. Class times vary depending on sundown; reserve ahead.

★**Goodtime Adventures** HIKING, ADVENTURE SPORTS
(Map p570; ☎ 087 275 3604; www.gtadventures. com; Sairee Beach; ☺ noon-late) Dive, hike through the island's jungle interior, swing from rock to rock during a climbing and abseiling session, or unleash your inner daredevil cliff-jumping or throw yourself into multisport or powerboat handling. Alternatively, take a shot at all of them on the full-day Koh Tao Adventure (3300B).

★**Shambhala** YOGA
(Map p570; ☎ 084 440 6755; www.shambhala yogakohtao.com; Sairee Beach; ☺ 10am-noon & 6-7.30pm Mon-Sat, 10am-noon Sun) Ko Tao's leading yoga centre – making students supple for two decades – is housed in beautiful wooden

---

DIVE SITES AT A GLANCE

In general, divers don't have much of a choice as to which sites they explore. Each dive school chooses a smattering of sites for the day depending on weather and ocean conditions.

Deeper dive sites such as Chumphon Pinnacle are usually visited in the morning. Afternoon boats tour the shallower sites such as Japanese Gardens. There are two large sunken vessels off the coast, providing scubaphiles with wreck dives.

Divers hoping to spend some quality time searching for whale sharks at Sail Rock should join one of the dive trips departing daily from Ko Pha-Ngan.

Chumphon Pinnacle (36m maximum depth), 11km northwest of Ko Tao, has a colourful assortment of sea anemones along the four interconnected pinnacles. The site plays host to schools of giant trevally, tuna and large grey reef sharks. Whale sharks are known to pop up once in a while.

Green Rock (Map p564; 25m maximum depth) is an underwater jungle gym featuring caverns, caves and small swim-throughs. Rays, grouper and triggerfish hang around. It's a great place for a night dive.

Japanese Gardens (Map p564; 12m maximum depth) between Ko Tao and Ko Nang Yuan, is a low-stress dive site perfect for beginners. There's plenty of colourful coral, and turtles, stingray and pufferfish often pass by.

Mango Bay (Map p564; 16m maximum depth) might be your first dive site if you are putting on a tank for the first time. Lazy reef fish swim around as newbies practise their skills on the sandy bottom.

Lighthouse Bay (Gluay Teun Bay; Map p564; 14m maximum depth), also excellent for snorkelling, this shallow dive site on the northeastern tip of the island sports some superb coral. Look out or yellowtail barracuda, parrotfish and bannerfish.

Sail Rock (40m maximum depth), best accessed from Ko Pha-Ngan, features a massive rock chimney with a vertical swim-through, and large pelagics like barracuda and kingfish. This is one of the top spots in Southeast Asia to see whale sharks; in the past few years they have been seen year-round, so there's no clear season.

Southwest Pinnacle (28m maximum depth) offers divers a small collection of pinnacles that are home to giant groupers and barracudas, and whale sharks are sometimes spotted.

Tanot Bay (p563; 18m maximum depth) is suitable for every level of diver. It's pretty shallow and a superb snorkelling site. Look out for angelfish, coral trout, bannerfish and the sunken catamaran.

White Rock (Map p564; 29m maximum depth) is home to colourful corals, angelfish, clownfish and territorial triggerfish, and is a popular spot for night divers.

HTMS Sattakut (Map p564) In 2011, HTMS *Sattakut* was sunk southeast of Hin Pee Wee at a depth of 30m and has become one of the most popular wreck-diving sites.

TAKING THE PLUNGE: CHOOSING YOUR KO TAO DIVE SCHOOL

When you alight at the pier in Mae Hat, swarms of touts will try to coax you into staying at their dive resort. But there are dozens of dive centres on Ko Tao, so it's best to arrive armed with the names of a few reputable schools and go from there. If you're not in a rush, consider relaxing on the island for a couple of days before making any decisions – you will undoubtedly bump into swarms of scubaphiles and instructors who will offer their advice and opinions.

Remember: the success of your diving experience will largely depend on how much you like your instructor. Other factors to consider are the size of your diving group, the condition of your equipment and the condition of the dive sites, to name a few.

For the most part, diving prices are standardised across the island, so there's no need to spend your time hunting around for the best deal. A **PADI** (www.padi.com) Open Water Diver (OWD) certification course costs 9800B; an **SSI** (www.ssithailand.com) OWD certificate is slightly less (9000B) as the PADI teaching materials, which include the certification, command a higher price, which is passed on to students. Increasingly popular across the island, a **RAID** (www.diveraid.com) OWD course is 8500B. An **Advanced Open Water Diver** (AOWD) certification course will set you back 8500B, a rescue course is 9500B and the Divemaster program costs a cool 35,000B (which includes the divemaster pack which everyone requires). Fun divers should expect to pay roughly 1000B per dive, or around 7000B for a 10-dive package. These rates include all dive gear, boat, instructors/guides and snacks. Discounts are usually given if you bring your own equipment. Be wary of dive centres that offer too many price cuts – safety is paramount, and a shop giving out unusually good deals is probably cutting too many corners. The market is easy to enter as there are no barriers to access, meaning cheap and poorly run places pop up offering superb deals.

Most dive schools will hook you up with cheap or even free accommodation. Almost all scuba centres offer gratis fan rooms for anyone doing beginner coursework. Expect large crowds and booked-out beds throughout December, January, June, July and August, and a monthly glut of wannabe divers after every Full Moon Party on Ko Pha-Ngan.

săh·lah on the forested grounds of Blue Wind Resort. Led by experienced teachers, the two-hour classes cost 300B (10 classes 2500B). No need to book ahead, just drop by.

★ **Monsoon Gym & Fight Club** MARTIAL ARTS (Map p570; ☑ 086 271 2212; www.monsoongym. com; Sairee Beach) This popular club combines *moo·ay tai* (Thai boxing) programs and air-con dorm accommodation (300B) for students signed up to get to grips with the fighting art. It's an excellent and exhilarating way to spend time in Ko Tao, if diving isn't your scene. The well-equipped concrete gym is right alongside the Thai boxing ring. Drop-in fight training costs 300B, six sessions is 1500B and monthly unlimited use is 7000B.

Ko Tao Leisure Park BOWLING, MINIGOLF (Map p564; ☑ 077 456316; ⊙ noon-midnight) On the main road between Mae Hat and Chalok Ban Kao, this place has homemade bowling lanes where the employees reset the pins after every frame (300B per hour). The 18-hole minigolf course has a landmark theme – putt your ball through Stonehenge or across the Golden Gate Bridge. There are also *pétanque* courts, table tennis and a big outdoor screen.

🛏 Sleeping

If you are planning to dive while visiting Ko Tao, your scuba operator will probably offer you free or discounted accommodation to sweeten the deal. Some schools have on-site lodging, while others have deals with nearby bungalows. It's important to note that you only receive your scuba-related discount on the days you dive.

🏖 Sairee Beach

Giant Sairee is the longest and most developed strip on the island, with a string of dive operations, bungalows, travel agencies, minimarkets and internet cafes. The northern end is the prettiest and quietest, while there's more of a party scene and noise from the bars to the south. For most people, this is the choice beach to stay since it has a great blend of scenery and action and the sunsets are serene.

Spicytao Backpackers HOSTEL $

(Map p570; ☑ 082 278 7115; www.spicyhostels.com/Home.html; Sairee Village; dm 230-280B; ❉ ⊚) With bargain prices, no-frills Spicytao is like your own supersocial country hangout; it is hidden off the main drag in a rustic garden setting. Backpackers rave about the ambience and staff who are always organising activities. Book in advance!

★ Ban's Diving Resort RESORT $$

(Map p570; ☑ 077 456466; www.bansdivingresort.com; Sairee Beach; r 700-10,000B; ❉ @ ⊚ ⊜) This dive-centric party palace offers a wide range of quality accommodation, from basic backpacker digs to sleek hillside villas, and it's growing all the time. Post-scuba chill sessions take place on Ban's prime slice of beach or at one of the two swimming pools tucked within the strip of jungle between the two-storey, pillared and terraced white hotel blocks.

Big Blue Resort BUNGALOW $$

(Map p570; ☑ 077 456050; www.bigbluediving.com; Sairee Beach; dm 400B, r 1500-10,000B; ❉ @) This scuba-centric resort has a summer-camp vibe – diving classes dominate the daytime, while evenings are spent en masse, grabbing dinner or watching fire twirling. There are basic six-bed fan dorms, air-con bungalows and villas as well as luxury family villas. Some rooms and accommodation options are only available if you are diving with Big Blue (p565).

★ Place RESORT $$$

(Map p570; www.theplacekohtao.com; villas 8000-9000B; ❉ ⊚) About a 15-minute walk or five-minute taxi ride from its hilltop location to Sairee Beach, this romantic boutique choice has nine private luxury villas nestled in leaf-clad hills with sweeping ocean views. Honeymooners will rejoice: a private plunge pool is standard, and private chef services satisfy those who choose to remain in their nuptial nest instead of venturing out for sustenance.

Seashell Resort BUNGALOW $$$

(Map p570; ☑ 077 456271; www.seashell-kohtao.com; Sairee Beach; r 1950-4500B, villa 2680-12,500; ❉ ⊚ ⊜) A huge mix of lodging, from simple wood fan bungalows to hotel-style rooms in a block and plush villas, this is a busy resort with nicely tended grounds, but prices are rather out of whack with what you can find elsewhere. It's a good backup, however, that welcomes divers and nondivers.

Palm Leaf Resort BUNGALOW $$$

(Map p570; ☑ 077 456731; www.kohtaopalmleaf.com; Sairee Beach; bungalows 2000-4500B; ❉ ⊚ ⊜) Palm Leaf bungalows and villa rooms are good though nothing spectacular, but the location, at the quieter northern section of silky Sairee Beach simply can't be beaten.

🛏 Mae Hat

All ferry arrivals pull into the pier at the busy village of Mae Hat. As such this isn't the best beach for a tranquil getaway, although it's a good hub if your main goal is diving. The more charming options extend in both directions along the sandy beach, both north and south of the pier.

Ko Tao Central Hostel HOSTEL $

(Map p570; ☑ 077 456925; www.kohtaohostel.com; Mae Hat; dm 310B; ❉ ⊚) Identified by its London Underground–style logo and decorated with Banksy murals and Tube-line stripes, this clean, central and friendly hostel has good 14-bed dorms, if all you need is a handy bed near to the pier. Check out is at 11am. Reception is in Island Travel next door; no towel service, so bring your own.

Captain Nemo Guesthouse GUESTHOUSE $$

(Map p570; www.captainnemo-kohtao.com; Mae Hat; d 890-2850B; ❉ ⊚) With only five rooms, this popular, small choice a short walk from the pier is nearly always full, so book upfront. The owners are responsive, friendly and helpful, and everything is kept clean.

Ananda Villa HOTEL $$

(Map p570; ☑ 077 456478; www.anandavilla.com; Mae Hat; r 600-1800B; ❉ ⊚) This friendly, two-storey cream-and-white hotel with verandahs and lined with decorative palms and plumeria has a colonial feel, a short walk north of the jetty. The cheapest bungalows are fan only, with hot water, in the garden on the far side of the road.

Nadapa Resort RESORT $$

(Map p570; ☑ 077 456495; www.nadaparesort.com; Mae Hat; tw & d 1500B; ❉ ⊚) It's not really a resort and it's not the choice if what you want is a pool and a beach front, but reliable Nadapa is bright, clean and comfortable, with colour-coded rooms in a block with balcony and bungalows, amid a riot of fun, cartoonish statuettes. Away from, but not far from, the action and close to the pier.

Mae Hat & Sairee Beach

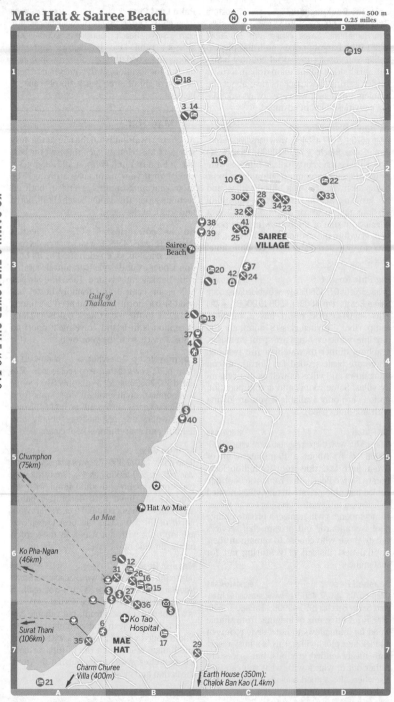

0   500 m
0   0.25 miles

19

18

3 14

11

10

30 28 34 23
32
38 41
39 25

SAIREE
VILLAGE

22

33

Sairee
Beach

20 7
1 42 24

2 13
37
4
8

40

9

Gulf of
Thailand

Chumphon
(75km)

Ko Pha-Ngan
(46km)

Hat Ao Mae

Ao Mae

Surat Thani
(106km)

5
12
31 26 16
27 15
6 36

Ko Tao
Hospital

35

17

29

MAE
HAT

21

Charm Churee
Villa (400km)

Earth House (350m);
Chalok Ban Kao (1.4km)

Mae Hat & Sairee Beach

Charm Churee Villa RESORT $$$
(Map p564; ☑ 077 456393; www.charmchureevilla.com; Mae Hat; bungalows 3600-39,100B; ❋ ☎ ☀) Tucked under sky-scraping palms on a 48-hectare jungle plot away from the bustle of the pier, the luxuriant villas of Charm Churee are dedicated to the flamboyant spoils of the Far East. Staircases, chiselled into the rock face, wind their way down a palmed slope revealing teak huts strewn across smoky boulders. The villas' unobstructed views of the swishing waters are beguiling.

Sensi Paradise Resort RESORT $$$
(Map p570; ☑ 077 456244; www.sensiparadiseresort.com; Mae Hat; r 3300-15,000B; ❋ ☎ ☀) 'Natural chic' on the prettiest stretch of Mae Hat proper, right up against some boulder outcrops. You won't escape the noise of the pier, however, and rooms on the hillside are rather worn (and not worth the price), while newer models closer to the beach are attractive and comfy. Friendly caretakers and several airy teak săh·lah add an extra element of charm.

🛏 Chalok Ban Kao

Ao Chalok Ban Ko, about 1.7km south of Mae Hat by road, has one of the largest concentra-

tions of accommodation on Ko Tao. This is a slim stretch of sand in a scenic half-circle bay framed by boulders at either end. The milky-blue water here is quite shallow and at low tide a sandbar is exposed that's fun to wade out to for prime sunbathing.

Tao Thong Villa BUNGALOW $
(Map p564; ☑ 077 456078; Ao Sai Nuan; bungalows 500-2000B; ❋ @ ☎) Popular with long-termers seeking peace and quiet, these no-frills bungalows have killer views. Tao Thong straddles two tiny beaches on a craggy cape about halfway between Mae Hat and Chalok Ban Kao. To reach it, grab a boat taxi for a short ride from the Mae Hat pier.

★ Dearly Koh Tao Hostel HOSTEL $$
(Map p564; ☑ 077 332494; www.thedearlykohtaohostel.com; 14/55 Mu 3, Chalok Ban Kao; dm 600-700B, d 1700-3000B, tr 2400B; ☎ ☀) Located on the road that leads inland from Chalok Ban Kao, this new hostel has all the right ingredients: clean, comfortable, contemporary (but also traditional) rooms, bubbly and friendly staff, rattan furniture and a rooftop terrace. There's a mix of dorms and private rooms, and a swimming pool was going in when we visited. Breakfast is included.

Koh Tao Tropicana Resort GUESTHOUSE $$

(Map p564; ☑ 077 456167; www.koh-tao-tropicana
-resort.com; Chalok Ban Kao; r 820-2500B) This
friendly place offers basic, low-rise units peppered across a sandy, shady garden campus
with fleeting glimpses of the blue ocean between fanned fronds and spiky palms.

New Heaven Resort BUNGALOW $$

(Map p564; ☑ 077 456422; www.newheavendive
school.com; Chalok Ban Kao; dm 300B; r & bungalows 800-3500B; ❈ 🌐) New Heaven – part
of the diving operation of the same name –
delivers colourful huts perched on a hill
over impossibly clear waters, air-con beachfront rooms, family sea-view bungalows and
budget dorm beds.

★ View Point Resort RESORT $$$

(Map p564; ☑ 091 823 3444; www.viewpoint
resortkohtao.com; Chalok Ban Kao; bungalows incl
breakfast 2700-18,000B; ❈ 🌐 🏊) Near Saan
Jao beach, lush grounds of ferns and palms
meander across a boulder-studded hillside
offering stunning views over the sea and the
bay. All options – from the exquisite private
suites that feel like Tarzan and Jane's love
nest gone luxury to the huge, view-filled bungalows – use boulders, wood and concrete
to create comfortable, naturalistic abodes.
Rates include taxi transfer.

Ko Tao Resort RESORT $$$

(Map p564; ☑ 077 456133; www.kotaoresort.
com; Chalok Ban Kao; r & bungalows 2100-9500B;
❈ @ 🌐 🏊) Rooms at this resort are split between 'pool side' and 'paradise zone' – all are
well furnished, water-sports equipment is on
offer, and there are several bars primed to
serve an assortment of fruity cocktails. Views
of the milky-blue waters are gorgeous.

Chintakiri Resort RESORT $$$

(Map p564; ☑ 077 456133; Chalok Ban Kao; r & bungalows 3200-6200B; ❈ @ 🌐 🏊) Perched high
over the gulf waters overlooking Chalok Ban
Kao, Chintakiri is one of Ko Tao's more luxurious properties. Rooms are spread around
the inland jungle and boast crisp white walls
with lacquered finishing.

🛌 Hin Wong

This boulder-strewn bay on the serene east
side of the island has crystal-clear waters
and it's a picture. The road to Hin Wong is
paved in parts, but sudden sand pits and
steep hills can toss you off your motorbike,
so take it easy. The walk is a steep but enjoyable workout.

Hin Wong Bungalows BUNGALOW $

(Map p564; ☑ 077 456006; Hin Wong; bungalows
400-700B; 🌐) Above boulders strewn to the
sea, these decent enough but basic corru-
gated roof huts are scattered across a lot of
untamed tropical terrain. A rickety dock,
jutting out just beyond the breezy restaurant, is the perfect place to dangle your legs
and watch schools of black sardines slide
through the cerulean water; or why not hop
in with a snorkel?

View Rock BUNGALOW $

(Map p564; ☑ 077 456549, 077 456548; viewrock@
hotmail.com; Hin Wong; bungalows 500-2000B;
❈ 🌐) Coming down the dirt road into Hin
Wong, follow the signs north past Hin Wong
Bungalows. View Rock is precisely that:
views and rocks; the hodgepodge of wood-
en huts, which resembles a secluded fishing
village, is built into the steep crags, offering
stunning views of the bay. Bungalows are
simple and modest, but clean enough. Wi-fi
in the restaurant only.

🛌 Ao Tanot (Tanote Bay)

Boulder-strewn Ao Tanot is more populated
than some of the other eastern coves, but it's
still rather quiet and picturesque and has
some great rocks in the sapphire water for
leaping from. This is also excellent snorkelling and shallow-diving territory.

Poseidon BUNGALOW $

(Map p564; ☑ 077 456735; poseidonkohtao@hot-
mail.com; Ao Tanot; bungalows 800-1500B; 🌐)
Poseidon keeps the tradition of the budget
bamboo bungalow alive with basic but
sleepable fan huts scattered near the sand.
There's a reasonable restaurant here which
is also a good spot for a drink.

Family Tanote BUNGALOW $$

(Map p564; ☑ 077 456757; Ao Tanot; bungalows
1000-3800B; ❈ @ 🌐) This family-run scatter
of hillside bungalows is a so-so choice for
solitude-seekers. Strap on a snorkel mask
and swim around with the fish at your doorstep, or climb up to the restaurant for a tasty
meal and beautiful views of the bay.

🛌 Ao Leuk & Ao Thian Ok

★ Jamahkiri Resort & Spa RESORT $$$

(Map p564; ☑ 077 456400; www.jamahkiri.com;
Ao Thian Ok; bungalows incl breakfast 8400-
30,000B; ❈ @ 🌐 🏊) Wooden gargoyle masks
and stone fertility goddesses abound amid

swirling mosaics and multi-armed statues at this whitewashed estate. Hoots from distant monkeys confirm the jungle theme, as do the thatched roofs and tiki-torched soirees. There are lots of steps, but views are drop-dead gorgeous, the spa is top of the range and the dive centre is excellent.

Ko Nang Yuan

Photogenic Ko Nangyuan, just off the north-west coast of Ko Tao, is easily accessible by the Lomprayah catamaran, and by water taxis that depart from Mae Hat and Sairee (100B each way). There's a 100B tax for all visitors to the island.

Ko Nangyuan Dive Resort   BUNGALOW $$$
(Map p564; ☑ 077 456088; www.nangyuan.com; Ko Nangyuan; bungalows incl breakfast 1500-9000B; ✷ ☎) The rugged collection of wood and aluminium bungalows winds its way across three coolie-hat-like conical islands connected by an idyllic beige sandbar. Yes, this is a private-island paradise but note it gets busy with day-trippers. The resort also boasts the best restaurant on the island (more precisely, the only place to eat). Prices include round-trip to Ko Tao.

✗ Eating

With supersized Ko Samui lurking on the horizon, it's hard to believe that quaint little Ko Tao holds its own in the gastronomy category. Most resorts and dive operators offer on-site dining, and stand-alone establishments are multiplying at lightning speed in Sairee Beach and Mae Hat. The diverse population of divers has spawned a broad range of international cuisine dining options, including Mexican, French, Italian, Chinese, Indian and Japanese.

✗ Sairee Beach

★ 995 Roasted Duck   CHINESE $
(Map p570; Sairee Village; mains from 70B; ⊘ 9am-9pm) You may have to queue a while to get a seat at this glorified shack and wonder what all the fuss is about. The fuss is excellent roast duck, from 70B for a steaming bowl of roasted waterfowl with noodles to 700B for a whole bird, served in a jiffy. You'd be quackers to miss out.

Su Chili   THAI $
(Map p570; Sairee Village; dishes 85-225B; ⊘ 10am-10.30pm) Inviting and bustling, Su

Chili serves fresh and tasty Thai dishes, with friendly staff always asking how spicy you want your food and somehow getting it right. Try the delicious northern Thai specialities or Penang curries. There's a smattering of Western comfort food for homesick diners.

Oishi Kaiso   JAPANESE $
(Map p570; ☑ 080 041 7263; Sairee Village; mains from 90B; ⊘ 11.30am-10.30pm; ☎) This neat and very slim establishment the size of a *gyoza* (Japanese dumpling) is often full, doing a brisk trade in *nigiri, sashimi* and *maki,* while maintaining a poised equilibrium, but it's a great bolthole if you miss rush hour. A couple of Thai dishes are thrown in for good measure, but you can find them elsewhere and the *gyoza* are very tempting indeed.

Bang Burgers   BURGERS $
(Map p570; ☑ 081 136 6576; Sairee Village; mains from 130B; ⊘ 10am-10pm) You may have to dig your heels in and wait in line at this terrific burger bar that does a roaring trade in Sairee. There's around a half-dozen burgers (cheese, double cheese, red chilli cheese) on the menu, including a vegie choice for meat-free diners; chips are 50B.

★ Barracuda Restaurant & Bar   FUSION $$
(Map p570; ☑ 080 146 3267; www.barracuda kohtao.com; Sairee Village; mains 240-380B; ⊘ 6-10.30pm; ☎) Sociable chef Ed Jones caters for the Thai princess when she's in town, but you can sample his exquisite cuisine for mere pennies in comparison to her budget. Locally sourced ingredients are turned into creative, fresh, fusion masterpieces. Try the seafood platter, pan-fried barracuda fillet or vegetarian falafel platter – then wash it down with a passionfruit mojito.

★ The Gallery   THAI $$
(Map p570; ☑ 077 456547; www.thegallerykohtao. com; Sairee Village; mains 120-420B; ⊘ noon-10pm) One of the most pleasant settings in town, the food here is equally special. The signature dish is *hor mok maprao on* (chicken, shrimp and fish curry served in a young coconut; 420B) but the white snapper fillet in creamy red curry sauce is also excellent and there's a choice of vegetarian dishes.

Taste of Home   INTERNATIONAL $$
(Map p570; ☑ 086 012 0727; Sairee Village; mains 120-250B; ⊘ 10am-1pm & 5-10pm; ☎) German-run and serving a bit of everything (Swedish meatballs, Turkish kofta, Hungarian goulash and Wiener schnitzel to name a few), but

it is all delicious and prepared with heart. It's a small, simple setting popular with expats. Don't forget to finish your meal with the owner's homemade whiskey-and-cream liqueur!

Farango's PIZZA $$
(Map p570; ☑ 077 456205; www.farangopizzeria. com; Sairee Village; dishes 80-230B; ⊘ 11am-midnight; 🛜) Things are cookin' at this busy pizzeria doing a fine trade in Sairee Village, with decent pizzas and other signature Italian fare. Payment is cash only.

✗ Mae Hat

Zest Coffee Lounge CAFE $
(Map p570; Mae Hat; dishes 70-200B; ⊘ 6am-4pm; 🛜) All brick and wood with a scuffed floor, Zest pulls out the stops to brew up some excellent coffee and wake up sleepyheads at brekkie time. Eggs Benedict gets the morning off on the right foot, while idlers and snackers can nibble on ciabatta sandwiches or sticky confections while nursing their creamy caffe latte. There's a second branch in Sairee (8am to 5pm), although we prefer this location.

Pranee's Kitchen THAI $
(Map p570; Mae Hat; dishes 50-150B; ⊘ 7am-10pm; 🛜) An old Mae Hat fave, Pranee's serves scrumptious curries and other Thai treats in an open-air pavilion sprinkled with lounging pillows, wooden tables and TVs. English-language movies are shown nightly at 6pm.

Safety Stop Pub INTERNATIONAL $
(Map p570; ☑ 077 456209; Mae Hat; mains 60-250B; ⊘ 7am-11pm; 🛜) A haven for homesick Brits, this pier-side restaurant and bar feels like a tropical beer garden. Stop by on Sundays to stuff your face with an endless supply of barbecued goodness; and the Thai dishes also aren't half bad.

Cappuccino CAFE $
(Map p570; ☑ 077 456870; Mae Hat; dishes from 30B; ⊘ 7am-6pm; 🛜) With marble tabletops, wall mirrors and good grooves, chirpy Cappuccino's decor falls somewhere between the New York deli on *Seinfeld* and a French brasserie – it's a fine place to grab some caffeine and prepare for your Ko Tao day over croissants and cappuccino foam.

Greasy Spoon BREAKFAST $
(Map p570; Mae Hat; breakfast 140B; ⊘ 6.30am-3pm; 🛜) Bringing a tear to the eyes of homesick Brits, Greasy Spoon stays true to its name by offering a variety of heart-clogging English breakfast fare: black pudding, eggs, sausage, hash browns, chips (and vegie options). The only thing missing is the free copies of the *Sun* and the *Daily Mirror*.

★ **Whitening** INTERNATIONAL $$
(Map p570; ☑ 077 456199; Mae Hat; dishes 160-480B; ⊘ 1pm-1am; 🛜) This starched, white, beachy spot falls somewhere between being a restaurant and a chic seaside bar – foodies will appreciate the tasty twists on indigenous and international dishes. Dine amid dangling white Christmas lights while keeping your bare feet tucked into the sand. And the best part? It's comparatively easy on the wallet.

Café del Sol INTERNATIONAL $$
(Map p570; ☑ 077 456578; www.cafedelsol.ws; Mae Hat; mains from 100B; ⊘ 8am-10.30pm; 🛜) This corner cafe a few steps away from the pier is an excellent choice to down a French, full English or diver's breakfast and watch the morning Ko Tao world go by. Lunch and dinner dishes range from hearty pepper hamburgers to homemade pasta, though prices can be quite inflated.

The cafe also has rooms from 1200B.

✗ Chalok Ban Kao

South Beach Cafe CAFE $
(Map p564; ☑ 094 369 1979; Chalok Ban Kao; mains from 100B; ⊘ 6am-10pm) Service is rather slack, but the coffee is good, as are the breakfasts at this fresh, spruce and handsome addition to Chalok Ban Kao. The menu spans paninis, salads, pizzas, burgers, vegan dishes, cheesecake and glasses of house wine (99B), plus the obligatory full English breakfast (plus a full vegan), an early kick-off and a long day.

I (Heart) Salad CAFE $$
(Map p564; Chalok Ban Kao; mains from 120B; ⊘ 8am-9pm; 🛜) This rustic choice offers a healthy array of salads using fresh ingredients, with a good supply of vegetarian and vegan dishes and sticky desserts to follow. There are also real fruit juices and healthy egg-white-only breakfasts.

Viewpoint Restaurant INTERNATIONAL $$$
(Map p564; ☑ 077 456444; Chalok Ban Kao; 250-1100B; ⊘ 7.30am-10pm) On a beautiful wood deck overlooking Ao Chalok Ban Kao, this is one of the most romantic settings on the island. The food is also the most upscale and holds its own against Ko Samui's best – try

the braised pork belly or the whole tuna from the oven. Apart from the Australian beef dishes, prices are reasonable.

Drinking & Nightlife

★ Lotus Bar
BAR

(Map p570; ☑ 087 069 6078; Sairee Beach) Lotus is the leading late-night hang-out spot along the northern end of Sairee; it also affords front-row seats to some spectacular sunsets. Muscular fire-twirlers toss around flaming batons, and the drinks are so large there should be a lifeguard on duty.

★ Fizz
BAR

(Map p570; Sairee Beach; ⊗ 8am-1am) Come sunset, sink into a green beanbag, order up a designer cocktail and let the hypnotic surf roll in amid a symphony of ambient sounds. Fantastic.

★ Earth House
BEER GARDEN

(Map p564; www.theearthhousekohtao.com; ⊗ noon-midnight Mon-Sat) This relaxing, secluded and rustic spot serves up a global selection of 40 beers, craft labels and ciders in a dreamy garden setting. With its own relaxing treehouse, there's also a restaurant for bites (9am to noon and 1pm to 6pm Monday to Saturday) – and there are bungalows alongside for going prone if you overdo it on the Green Goblin (cider).

Earth House is on the road to Ao Tanot, just before the turn-off for Ao Leuk.

Fishbowl Beach Bar
BAR

(Map p570; ☑ 062 046 8996; Sairee Beach; ⊗ noon-2am) This buzzin' and hoppin' bar gazes out at sunset onto killer views; with fire shows, live music kicking off from 8pm and DJs casting their spell.

Maya Beach Club
BAR

(Map p570; ☑ 080 578 2225; www.mayabeachclub kohtao.com; Sairee Beach; ⊗ noon-9pm Sat-Thu, to 2am Fri) Rivalling Fizz for its entrancing sunset visuals and relaxing mood, Maya has nightly DJs and party nights. Make a move for a beach lounger and stay put.

☆ Entertainment

★ Queen's Cabaret
CABARET

(Map p570; ☑ 087 677 6168; Sairee Village) Every night is different at this intimate bar where acts range from your standard sparkling Abba to steamy topless croons. If you're male, note you may get 'dragged' into the performance if you're sitting near the front.

The show is free but it's expected that you will purchase a (pricey) drink – which is totally worth it. Show starts at 10.15pm.

Shopping

Although most items are cheap when compared to prices back home, diving equipment is a big exception to the rule. On Ko Tao you'll be paying Western prices plus shipping plus commission on each item so it's better to shop at home or online.

Pharmacies charge unnaturally high prices for imported sunscreen, shampoos, mosquito repellent and other items, including paracetamol and aspirin; check branches of 7-Eleven for better-priced equivalents.

★ Hammock Cafe Plaeyuan
HOMEWARES

(Map p564; ☑ 082 811 4312; ⊗ 9am-6pm Sun-Fri) This small French- and Thai-run cafe with tables out front on the road to Chalok Ban Kao doubles as a hammock shop, selling a fantastic selection of brightly coloured Mlabri hand-woven hammocks, some with up to 3km of fabric. Prices start at around 1700B for a sitting hammock, up to 5000B for the most elaborate. Attractive handmade jewellery is also for sale.

Chez Albert
FOOD & DRINKS

(Map p570; ☑ 077 332577; Sairee Village; ⊗ 1.30pm-late Mon-Sat) Principally selling wine, this enterprising shop feeds expat palates with coffee, cheese, cold cuts and other imported desirables and gastronomic necessities.

ⓘ Information

DANGERS & ANNOYANCES
While hiring a scooter is extremely convenient, this is really not the place to learn how to drive: the roads on Ko Tao are being paved but some remain treacherous. The island is rife with abrupt hills and sudden sand pits along gravel trails as well as trenches in the road; if driving a scooter, stick to good roads and if you are unsure, turn back. Wear a helmet at all times.

EMERGENCY
Police Station (Map p570; ☑ 077 456631) Between Mae Hat and Sairee Beach along the rutted portion of the beachside road.

INTERNET ACCESS
Wi-fi is widely available at resorts, bars and restaurants.

MEDICAL SERVICES
There are several walk-in clinics and mini-hospitals scattered around Mae Hat and Sairee,

ⓘ DENGUE FEVER

Be aware that mosquito-borne dengue fever is a real and serious threat. The virus can spread quickly due to tightly packed tourist areas and the small size of the island.

There is currently no widely available vaccine for dengue; the best precaution is to avoid being bitten by mosquitoes: use insect repellent and wear loose but protective clothing.

but all serious medical needs should be dealt with on Ko Samui.

Ko Tao Hospital (Map p570; ☎ 077 456490; ⊕ 24hr) For general medical and dental treatment.

MONEY

There are several **banks** (Map p570) in Mae Hat, at the far end of town along the island's main inland road. Most dive schools accept credit cards for a 3% handling fee.

There is a money exchange window at Mae Hat's pier and a second location near Chopper's in Sairee Beach.

There are 24-hour ATMs at the island's 7-Elevens and also a cluster orbiting the ferry docks at Mae Hat. Most will will charge you a 200B or so fee for withdrawing money, so figure than into your calculations.

ATMS (Map p570) are located near the pier in Mae Hat and by Sairee Beach.

POST

Post Office (Map p570; ☎ 077 456170; Mae Hat; ⊕ 9am-5pm Mon-Fri, 9am-noon Sat) A 10- to 15-minute walk from the pier; at the corner of Ko Tao's main inner-island road and Mae Hat's 'down road'.

TOURIST INFORMATION

There's no government-run TAT office on Ko Tao. Transportation and accommodation bookings can be made at most dive shops or at any of the numerous travel agencies, all of which take a small commission on services rendered.

WEBSITES

Koh Tao Complete Guide (www.kohtao completeguide.com) Handy website and an excellent quarterly free hard copy guide in book form.
Koh Tao Online (www.kohtaoonline.com) An online version of the Koh Tao Info booklet.

ⓘ Getting There & Away

Costs and departure times are subject to change. Rough waves are known to cancel fer-ries between October and December. When the waters are choppy we recommend taking the Seatran rather than the Lomprayah catamaran if you are prone to seasickness. The catamarans ride the swell, whereas the Seatran cuts through the currents as it crosses the sea. Note that we highly advise purchasing your boat tickets *several* days in advance if you are accessing Ko Tao from Ko Pha-Ngan after the Full Moon Party.

AIR

Nok Air (www.nokair.com) jets passengers from Bangkok's Don Mueng airport to Chumphon once or twice daily in each direction. Flights to/ from Bangkok are usually around 3000B. Upon arriving in Chumphon, travellers can make a seamless transfer to the catamaran service bound for Ko Tao.

BOAT

Boat services are rarely disrupted by the weather, but you may get some days of cancellations during the monsoon months, if waves are too high.

To Ko Pha-Ngan

The **Lomprayah** (Map p570) catamaran offers a thrice-daily service (500B to 600B), leaving Ko Tao at 6am, 9.30am and 3pm and arriving on Ko Pha-Ngan around 7am, 10.45am and 4pm. The **Seatran** (Map p570) Discovery Ferry (430B) offers a similar service, but its earliest boat departs at 6.30am. The **Songserm** (Map p570) express boat (350B) departs daily at 10am and arrives on Ko Pan-Ngan at 11.30am. Hotel pick-ups are included in the price.

To Ko Samui

The Lomprayah catamaran offers a twice-daily service (600B), leaving Ko Tao at 9.30am and 3pm and arriving at Mae Nam on Ko Samui via Ko Pha-Ngan, around 11.20am and 4.40pm. An earlier boat (700B) at 6am goes to Na Thon on Ko Samui, arriving at 7.50am. The Seatran Discovery Ferry (600B) offers a similar service, with departures at 6.30am, 9am and 3pm. The Songserm express boat (500B) departs daily at 10am and arrives on Samui (again via Ko Pha-Ngan) at 1.15pm. Hotel pick-ups are included in the price.

To Surat Thani & the Andaman Coast

Many travellers head to Surat Thani via Ko Pha-Ngan or Ko Samui. Otherwise, board a Surat Thani-bound Lomprayah catamaran (800 to 1000B), then transfer to a bus upon arrival.

To Chumphon

Songserm boats leave for Chumphon (500B) at 2.30pm, arriving at 5.30pm. Lomprayah cata-marans (600B) leave for Chumphon at 10.15am and 2.45pm, arriving at 11.45am and 4.15pm.

BUS

Bus-boat package tickets to/from Bangkok are available from travel agencies all over Bangkok and the south; tickets cost around 1000B and the whole voyage takes around 12 hours. Buses switch to boats in Chumphon, and Bangkok-bound passengers can choose to disembark in Hua Hin (for the same price as the Ko Tao–Bangkok ticket).

TRAIN

Travellers can plan their own journey by taking a boat to Chumphon, then making their way to Chumphon's town centre to catch a train up to Bangkok (or any town along the upper southern gulf); likewise in the opposite direction. A 2nd-class ticket to Bangkok will cost around 300B and the trip takes around 8½ hours.

From Ko Tao, the high-speed Lomprayah catamaran departs for Chumphon at 10.15am and 2.45pm (600B, 1½ hours), and a Songserm express boat makes the same journey at 2.30pm (500B) arriving at 5pm. There may be fewer departures if the swells are high.

ℹ️ Getting Around

If you know where you intend to stay, we highly recommend calling ahead to arrange a pick-up. Many dive schools offer free pick-ups and transfers as well.

MOTORBIKE

Renting a motorcycle can be a dangerous endeavour if you're not sticking to the main, well-paved roads. Daily rental rates begin at 150B for a scooter, with larger bikes starting at 350B. Discounts are available for weekly and monthly rentals. Be wary of renting all-terrain vehicles (ATVs) or jet skis – accidents are not uncommon. Most of the bottles of petrol on sale by the wayside cost 50B (on Ko Samui they are 40B).

SŎRNG·TĂA·OU

In Mae Hat *sŏrng·tăa·ou* (pick-up minibuses and motorbikes) crowd around the pier as passengers alight. If you're a solo traveller, you will pay 200B to get to Sairee Beach or Chalok Ban Kao. Groups of two or more will pay 100B each. Rides from Sairee to Chalok Ban Kao cost 150B per person, or 300B for solo tourists. These prices are rarely negotiable, and passengers will be expected to wait until their taxi is full unless they want to pay an additional 200B to 300B. Prices double for trips to the east coast, and the drivers will raise the prices when rain makes the roads harder to negotiate.

WATER TAXI

Boat taxis depart from Mae Hat, Chalok Ban Kao and the northern part of Sairee Beach (near Vibe Bar). Boat rides to Ko Nang Yuan will set you back at least 100B. Long-tail boats can be chartered for around 1500B per day, depending on the number of passengers carried.

Ang Thong Marine National Park อุทยานแห่งชาติหมู่เกาะอ่างทอง

The 40-something jagged jungle islands of **Ang Thong Marine National Park** (adult/child 300/150B) stretch across the cerulean sea like a shattered emerald necklace – each piece a virgin realm featuring sheer limestone cliffs, hidden lagoons and perfect peach-coloured sands. These dream-inducing islets inspired Alex Garland's cult classic novel *The Beach*.

February, March and April are the best months to visit this ethereal preserve of greens and blues; crashing monsoon waves mean that the park is almost always closed during November and December.

⊙ Sights

Every tour stops at the park's head office on **Ko Wua Talap**, the largest island in the archipelago. The naturally occurring stone arches on **Ko Samsao** and **Ko Tai Plao** are visible during seasonal tides and in certain weather conditions. Because the sea is quite shallow around the island chain, reaching a maximum depth of 10m, extensive coral reefs have not developed, except in a few protected pockets on the southwest and northeast sides.

There's a shallow coral reef near Ko Tai Plao and Ko Samsao that has decent but not excellent snorkelling. There are also several novice dives for exploring shallow caves and colourful coral gardens, and spotting banded sea snakes and turtles. Soft powder beaches line **Ko Tai Plao**, **Ko Wuakantang** and **Ko Hintap**.

Viewpoint   VIEWPOINT
(Ko Wua Talap) This viewpoint might just be the most stunning vista in all of Thailand. From the top, visitors will have sweeping views of the jagged islands nearby as they burst through the placid turquoise water in easily anthropomorphic formations. The trek to the lookout is an arduous 450m trail that takes roughly an hour to complete. Hikers should wear sturdy shoes and walk slowly on the sharp outcrops of limestone.

A second trail leads to **Tham Bua Bok**, a cavern with lotus-shaped stalagmites and stalactites.

Emerald Lagoon   LAKE

(Ko Mae Ko) With an ethereal minty tint, the Emerald Sea (also called the Inner Sea) on Ko Mae Ko is a large lake in the middle of the island that spans an impressive 250m by 350m. You can look but you can't touch: the lagoon is strictly off limits to the unclean human body. A dramatic **viewpoint** can be found at the top of a series of staircases nearby.

🐾 Tours

The best way to experience Ang Thong is by taking one of the many guided tours departing Ko Samui and Ko Pha-Ngan. The tours usually include lunch, snorkelling equipment, hotel transfers and (fingers crossed) a knowledgeable guide. If you're staying in luxury accommodation, there's a good chance that your resort has a private boat for providing group tours. Some midrange and budget places also have their own boats, and if not, they can easily set you up with a general tour operator. Dive centres on Ko Samui and Ko Pha-Ngan offer scuba trips to the park, although Ang Thong doesn't offer the world-class diving that can be found around Ko Tao and Ko Pha-Ngan.

Tour companies tend to come and go like the wind. Ask at your accommodation for a list of current operators.

🛌 Sleeping & Eating

Ang Thong does not have any resorts; however, on Ko Wua Talap the national park has set up five bungalows, each housing between two and eight guests (500B to 1400B). Campers are also allowed to pitch a tent in certain designated zones. Online bookings are possible, although customers must forward a bank deposit within two days of making the reservation. For advance reservations contact the National Parks Services.

Food is generally provided by tours whisking visitors to and from the Marine National Park. A restaurant can be found at the park head office.

ℹ️ Information

National Parks Services (📞 077 286025; www.dnp.go.th)

ℹ️ Getting There & Around

The best way to reach the park is to take a private day tour from Ko Samui or Ko Pha-Ngan (28km and 32km away, respectively). The islands sit between Samui and the main pier at Don Sak; however, there are no ferries that stop off along the way.

SURAT THANI PROVINCE

Surat Thani   อำเภอเมืองสุราษฎร์ธานี

📞 077 / POP 128,990

Known in Thai as 'City of Good People', Surat Thani was once the seat of the ancient Srivijaya empire. Today, this typical Thai town is a busy transport hub moving cargo and people around the country. Travellers rarely linger here as they make their way to the popular islands of Ko Samui, Ko Pha-Ngan and Ko Tao, but it's a great stop if you enjoy real Thai working cities, good southern-style street food and nosing around colourful Chinese temples and Chinese shopfronts.

Looking down from its elevated position is a vast **Statue of Guanyin** (Kwan Im; Th Na Muang), the Buddhist bodhisattva of compassion (more associated with the Mahayana tradition). It stands next to a temple and charity dedicated to the goddess, equipped with its own ambulance that runs the streets.

🛌 Sleeping

Prices are low – you get a lot for relatively few baht. If you're on a very tight budget, consider zipping straight through town and taking the night ferry to reach your island destination.

My Place @ Surat Hotel   HOTEL $

(📞 077 272288; 247/5 Th Na Muang; d 490-590B; f 620B; ❄️📶) All smiles and nary a speck of dust, this excellent central hotel offers spacious, clean rooms, bright paint, colourful throw cushions, modern art on the walls, power showers and value for money. It may be budget, but it doesn't seem that way and will suit almost anyone. Breakfast is served in the so-so cafe next door.

Wangtai Hotel   HOTEL $$

(📞 077 283020; 1 Th Talad Mai; r 800-2000B; ❄️@📶♨️) Across the river from the TAT office (p580), the 230-room Wangtai is a smart, marbled choice in the centre of town, offering pleasant and comfortable, if rather generic, rooms with good views of the city.

Surat Thani

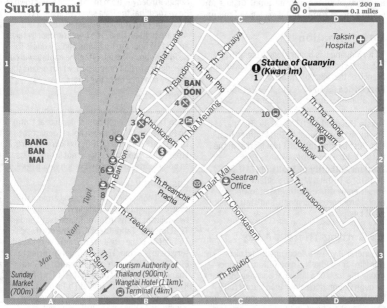

Surat Thani

✕ Eating & Drinking

Surat Thani is packed with delicious street food for lunch and dinner. Aside from the central night market, stalls near the departure docks open for the daily night boats to the islands, and there's an afternoon **Sunday market** (⊙4-9pm) near the TAT office. During the day, many food stalls near the downtown bus terminal sell *kôw gài òp* (marinated baked chicken on rice).

Surat Thani doesn't have a great choice of bars and is rather a quiet city come sundown.

Sweet Kitchen   INTERNATIONAL $
(mains from 80B) With easy-going music and a charming, unhurried interior, this restaurant also tempts with a fine menu and polite service. Dishes range from excellent seafood chowder through pasta to beef stroganoff and pages of Thai staples, with a decent selection of vegetarian choices too.

Night Market   MARKET $
(Sarn Chao Ma; Th Ton Pho; dishes from 35B; ⊙6-11pm) A smorgasbord of food including masses of melt-in-your-mouth marinated meats on sticks, fresh fruit juices, noodle dishes and desserts.

Milano   PIZZA $$
(☎084 011 2709; Th Bandon; pizza from 190B; ⊙noon-10pm) Often surprisingly busy, this Italian restaurant near the pier bakes up a tasty selection of pizza, while pasta and

a choice of other international dishes and comfort food round out a very good menu.

ℹ Information

Th Na Meuang has banks along its length in the heart of downtown, including a convenient branch at the heart of the action.

Post Office (☑ 077 272013, 077 281966; ⊙ 8.30am-4.30pm Mon-Fri, 9am-noon Sat & Sun)

Taksin Hospital (☑ 077 273239; Th Talat Mai) The most professional of Surat's three hospitals. Just beyond the Talat Mai Market in the northeast part of downtown.

Tourism Authority of Thailand (TAT; ☑ 077 288818; 5 Th Talat Mai; ⊙ 8.30am-4.30pm) This friendly office southwest of town has useful brochures and maps, and staff speak good English.

ℹ Getting There & Away

In general, if you are departing Bangkok or Hua Hin for Ko Pha-Ngan or Ko Tao, consider taking the train or a bus-boat package that goes through Chumphon rather than Surat. You'll save time, and the journey will be more comfortable. Travellers heading to/from Ko Samui will most likely pass through town.

AIR

Around 18km due west of the centre of town, Surat Thani International Airport has daily shuttles to Bangkok on Thai Air Asia (www.airasia.com), Thai Smile, Thai Lion Air and Nok Air (www.nokair.com). Although flights from Bangkok to Surat Thani are cheaper than the flights to Samui, it takes quite a bit of time to reach the gulf islands from the airport. Air Asia offers a convenient bus and boat shuttle with their flights that can alleviate some of the stress.

BOAT

Various ferry companies offer services to the islands. Try **Lomprayah** (p544), **Seatran Discovery** (☑ 077 275063; www.seatrandiscovery.com) or **Songserm** (☑ 077 377704; www.songserm-expressboat.com).

Bus-Boat Combination Tickets

In the high season travellers can usually find bus-boat services to Ko Samui and Ko Pha-Ngan directly from the Phun Phin train station (14km west of Surat). These services don't cost any more than those booked in Surat Thani and can save you some serious waiting time.

There are also several ferry and speedboat operators that connect Surat Thani to Ko Tao, Ko Pha-Ngan and Ko Samui. Most boats – such as the Raja and Seatran services – leave from Don Sak (about one hour from Surat; bus transfers are included in the ferry ticket) although the

Songserm leaves from the heart of Surat town. Be warned that the Raja service can be a very frustrating experience, especially for travellers who are tight on time. The boat trip usually takes around 1½ hours to Ko Samui and 2½ hours to Ko Pha-Ngan, although often the captain will cut the engines to half propulsion, which means the journey can take up to five hours.

Night Ferry

From the centre of Surat there are nightly ferries to **Ko Tao** (600B, eight hours, departs at 11pm), **Ko Pha-Ngan** (400B, seven hours, departs at 11pm) and **Ko Samui** (300B, six hours, departs at 11pm). These are cargo ships, not luxury boats, so bring food and water and watch your bags.

BUS & MINIVAN

The most convenient way to travel around the south, frequent buses and minivans depart from two main locations in town: Talat Kaset 1 and Talat Kaset 2. **Talat Kaset 1**, on the north side of Th Talat Mai (the city's main drag) offers speedy service to Nakhon (120B, 1½ hours). Buses to Phun Phin – the nearest train station to Surat Thani – also leave from Talat Kaset 1. At **Talat Kaset 2**, on the south side of Th Talat Mai, you'll find buses to Phuket and Hat Yai, and regular minibuses to Khanom (100B, 90 minutes, hourly).

The 'new' bus terminal (actually quite a few years old now, but still referred to as new by the locals) is 7km south of town on the way to Phun Phin. This hub services traffic to and from Bangkok (380B to 800B, 11 to 14 hours).

Buses & Minivans From Surat Thani

DESTINATION	FARE	DURATION
Bangkok	425–860B	10hr
Hat Yai	165–300B	5hr
Khanom	100B	1hr
Krabi	170B	2½hr
Phuket	270B	6hr
Trang	180B	2hr 10min

TRAIN

When arriving by train you'll actually pull into Phun Phin, a nondescript town 14km west of Surat. From Phun Phin, there are buses to Phuket, Phang-Nga and Krabi – some via Takua Pa, a junction for Khao Sok National Park. Transport from Surat moves with greater frequency, but it's worth checking the schedule in Phun Phin first – you might be lucky and save yourself a slow ride between towns.

If you plan on travelling during the day, go for the express train. Night travellers should opt for the air-con couchettes. Trains passing through Surat stop in Chumphon and Hua Hin on their way up to the capital, and in the other direction you'll call at Trang, Hat Yai and Sungai Kolok before hopping across the border into Malaysia. The train station at Phun Phin has a 24-hour left-luggage room that charges around 20B a day. The advance ticket office is open from 6am to 6pm daily (with a nebulous one-hour lunch break somewhere between 11am and 1.30pm). The trip to Bangkok takes more than 8½ hours and costs 297B to 1379B depending on class.

ⓘ Getting Around

Air-conditioned vans to/from Surat Thani airport cost around 100B per person and they'll drop you off at your hotel.

To travel around town, a *sŏrng·tăa·ou* will cost 10B to 30B (it's around 30B to reach Tesco Lotus from the city centre).

Fan-cooled orange buses run from Phun Phin train station to Surat Thani every 10 minutes (15B, 25 minutes). For this ride, taxis charge a cool 200B for a maximum of four people, while share taxis charge 100B per person. Other taxi rates are posted just north of the train station (at the metal pedestrian bridge).

NAKHON SI THAMMARAT PROVINCE

Home to south Thailand's highest peak – Khao Luang (1835m), surrounded by the majestic forests of Khao Luang National Park – Nakhon Si Thammarat Province is best known to travellers for stunning Wat Phra Mahathat Woramahawihaan in the province's namesake main town. More than the sum of its parts, the provincial capital is a likeable place, especially if you have recently pitched up from Ko Samui, Ko Pha-Ngan or Ko Tao in search of some genuine Thai flavour.

Ao Khanom   อ่าวขนอม

Pretty and placid Ao Khanom, halfway between Surat Thani and Nakhon Si Thammarat, quietly sits along the blue gulf waters. Overlooked by tourists who flock to the jungle islands nearby, this pristine region, simply called Khanom, is a worthy choice for those seeking a serene beach setting unmarred by enterprising corporations. The waters are free of jet skis to protect the local pink dolphins, making the region quiet and undisturbed. Tours whisk visitors off to view the dolphins in their natural environment.

The beach area is long and comprises two beaches: the main, long Hat Nadan and the smaller and more remote Hat Nai Plao beyond. Beyond Hat Nai Plao is very quiet Hat Thong Yi at the end of the road, which is well worth a journey for its castaway feel. This area is also home to a variety of pristine geological features, including waterfalls and caves.

⊙ Sights

Pink Dolphins

The most special feature of Khanom is the pink dolphins – a rare albino breed with a stunning pink hue. They are regularly seen from the old ferry pier and the electric plant pier around dawn and dusk, and resorts are now offering full-day tours (from 1700B) that include viewing the dolphins by boat and a car tour to the area's caves and waterfalls.

If you just want to see the dolphins you can hire a boat for a few hours (for up to six people) for 1200B. Enquire at your hotel.

Caves

There are two beautiful caves along the main road (Hwy 4014) between Khanom and Don Sak. **Khao Wang Thong** has a string of lights guiding visitors through the network of caverns and narrow passages. A metal gate covers the entrance; stop at the house at the base of the hill to retrieve the key (and leave a small donation). Turn right off the main highway at Rd 4142 to find **Khao Krot**, with two large caverns (bring a torch).

Other Sights

⭐**Hat Thong Yi**   BEACH

For a real escape, head as far down the main beach road as you can, till it joins the 4073, and turn left to follow the coast further south past Hat Nai Plao. Keep going as far as you can and the road will end at lovely and often deserted Hat Thong Yi, with its splendid views back down the bay. A beachside restaurant can get you a drink and food.

Dat Fa Mountain   MOUNTAIN

(Khao Dat Fa) For splendid postcard-worthy vistas of the undulating coastline, head to Dat Fa Mountain (Khao Dat Fa; 732m), about 5km west of the coast along Hwy 4014 (look out for the sign). The area has not been developed for tourism and the hillside is usually deserted, making it easy to stop along the way to snap some photos.

Samet Chun Waterfall   WATERFALL

This is the largest waterfall in the area, with tepid pools for cooling off, and superb views of the coast. To reach the falls, head south from Ban Khanom and turn left at the blue Samet Chun sign. Follow the road for about 2km and, after crossing a small stream, take the next right and hike up into the mountain following the dirt road. After about a 15-minute walk, listen for the waterfall and look for a small trail on the right.

Hin Lat Falls
WATERFALL

The scenic Hin Lat Falls south of Hat Nai Plao is the smallest of the cascades in the area, but the easiest to reach. There are pools for swimming and several huts providing shade.

🛏 Sleeping

Khanom's beaches remain a very low-key and quiet retreat. Many resorts see very few customers, and irregular use may mean that some rooms can be a bit dank. In general, it's advisable to stay away from the large hotels and stick to beachside bungalow operations. It's not like Ko Samui: options are spaced far apart so you'll need wheels to get about.

Suchada Villa
BUNGALOW $

(☑ 075 528459; Hat Naiplau; bungalows incl breakfast 800-1000B; ❄ 🛜) Right off the main road and a five-minute walk to the beach, Suchada offers a cache of brightly coloured, quite cute bungalows.

Sea Breeze House
BUNGALOW $$

(☑ 081 276 1457; www.naiplao.com; Hat Nai Plao; r 850-1650B; 🛜) With a very secluded location, this lovely Swiss-owned choice has excellent beach-front rooms, including a large suite. If you seek peace and tranquillity, plus splendid views of the sunrise and a chance to see pink dolphins, it's excellent, but you'll need wheels to get about to find places to dine.

Talkoo Beach Resort
BUNGALOW $$

(☑ 089 871 4442; www.talkoobeachresortkhanom. com; Hat Nadan; bungalows 1000-1500B; ❄ 🛜 ▦) Talkoo has a range of beachfront bungalows in a garden by the sand and cheaper ones across the main road in a more dry, sparse area. All are in good shape, spacious, comfortable and include charming touches like naturalistic bathrooms and traditional art.

Racha Kiri
RESORT $$$

(☑ 075 300245; www.rachakiri.com; bungalows 3550-7150B; ❄ 🛜 ▦) With spa, pool and elegant rooms, Khanom's upscale retreat is a beautiful campus of rambling villas. The big price tag deters the crowds and the location is serene. Rooms come with terrace.

Khanom Hill Resort
BUNGALOW $$$

(☑ 081 956 3101; www.khanom.info; Hat Naiplau; bungalows incl breakfast 2900-3900B; ❄ 🛜 ▦) Travellers love this spot on a small hill leading to a half-circle of dreamy white beach. Choose from modern, concrete villas with thatched roofs, cheaper models with Thai-style architecture or big family-sized apartments; all are clean and comfy.

🍴 Eating & Drinking

For cheap eats, head to Hat Kho Khao at the end of Rte 4232 where you'll find a steamy jumble of barbecue stands offering tasty favourites such as *mǒo nám đòk* (spicy pork salad) and *sôm·đam* (spicy green papaya salad). There are markets further inland on Wednesday and Sunday; and the coast road is dotted with a variety of Thai and Western restaurants, all looking out on to the sea.

Many of the restaurants down the beach double as bars come evening.

★ Le Petit Saint-Tropez
INTERNATIONAL $$

(☑ 093 727 0063; mains from 300B; ⊘ 8am-9.30pm) With an open and breezy setting, this charming restaurant faces out onto the sea, serving delightful French and Thai fare.

CC Beach Bar & Bungalows
INTERNATIONAL $$

(☑ 087 893 8745; www.ccbeachbarthai.wordpress. com; mains 100-300B; ⊘ 9am-midnight) With a splendid perspective onto the bay over the sands, this beach bar and restaurant is a good choice for its mixed menu of Thai and Western food. English breakfasts, fish and chips, vegetable curry, pizza and fried catfish salad are all on the menu. It doubles as a bar in the evening.

ℹ Information

There's a 7-Eleven with an ATM in the heart of Khanom town.

The police station is just south of Ban Khanom at the junction leading to Hat Kho Khao.

The hospital is just south of Ban Khanom at the junction leading to Hat Kho Khao.

ℹ Getting There & Away

Minivans from both Surat Thani and Nakhon leave every hour on the hour from 5am to 5pm daily and drop passengers off in Khanom town, which is several kilometres from the beach.

A taxi to/from Don Sak pier for the gulf islands is 1000B and a motorcycle taxi is around 300B.

ℹ️ Getting Around

From Khanom town you can hire motorcycle taxis out to the beaches for about 25B to 100B depending on the distance you're going. If you've booked in advance your hosts may offer to pick you up in Khanom town for free.

Once at your lodging you'll be stranded unless you hire your own transport or take a tour with your hotel, so the best approach is to hire a scooter. There's a rental operator at the bus drop off from Surat Thani who charges around 150B a day.

Nakhon Si Thammarat
อำเภอเมืองนครศรีธรรมราช

☑ 075 / POP 120,836

With one of the most significant temples in the kingdom, the historic city of Nakhon Si Thammarat (usually shortened to 'Nakhon') is a natural and rewarding stop between Hat Yai and Surat Thani.

Hundreds of years ago, an overland route between the western port of Trang and the eastern port of Nakhon Si Thammarat functioned as a major trade link between Thailand and the rest of the world. This ancient influx of cosmopolitan conceits is still evident today in the local cuisine, and housed in the city's temples and museums.

👁️ Sights

South of the clock tower is the city's magnificent Wat Mahathat, while tantalising remains of the historic red-brick city walls stand near the park and public square of Sanam Na Muang. Note also the gold-coloured statues of the 12 animals of the Thai zodiac atop lamp-posts along Th Ratchadamnoen, each representing one of the 12 city states that were tributary to the Nakhon Si Thammarat kingdom.

★ Wat Phra Mahathat Woramahawihaan TEMPLE
(Th Si Thamasok; ⊘ 8.30am-4.30pm) FREE The most important wát in southern Thailand, stunning Wat Phra Mahathat Woramahawihaan (simply known as Mahathat) boasts an imposing 77m white *chedi* (stupa) crowned by a gold spire piercing the sky. According to legend, Queen Hem Chala and Prince Thanakuman brought relics to Nakhon more than 1000 years ago, and built a small pagoda to house the precious icons. The temple has since grown into a huge site, and today

crowds gather daily to purchase the popular Jatukham amulets.

Shadow Puppet Museum MUSEUM
(Th Si Thamasok Soi 3; ⊘ 9am-4.30pm) FREE There are two styles of local shadow puppets: *năng đà·lung* and *năng yài*. At just under 1m tall, the former feature movable appendages and parts; the latter are nearly life-sized, and lack moving parts. Both are intricately carved from cow hide. Suchart Subsin's puppet house has a small museum where staff can demonstrate the cutting process and put on performances for visitors (50B).

National Museum MUSEUM
(☑ 075 341075; Th Ratchadamnoen; 150B; ⊘ 9am-4pm Wed-Sun) When the Tampaling (also known as Tambralinga) kingdom traded with merchants from Indian, Arabic, Dvaravati and Champa states, the region around Nakhon became a melting pot of crafts and art. Today, many of these relics are on display in this absorbing national museum.

Old City Walls RUINS
The intriguing and well-kept remains of the historic red-brick city walls can be seen in several sections close to one another along the Khlong Na Meuang canal near the park and public square of Sanam Na Muang on either side of Th Ratchadamnoen.

🛏️ Sleeping

As an authentic Thai city, Nakhon has a particular and genuine charm about it, although accommodation diversity is not a forte. Nonetheless, you can find several decent enough options not far from the train station – just don't expect your hotel to be the highlight of your stay.

Thai Hotel HOTEL $
(☑ 075 341509; fax 075 344858; 1375 Th Ratchadamnoen; r with fan/air-con 350/450B; ❄️ 🅿️) The most central sleeping spot in town, not far from the train station, the Thai Hotel is a semi-smart bargain and is perfectly acceptable. Walls may be a bit thin and the wi-fi twitchy, but rooms are clean and a good deal, each with a TV – and the higher floors have good views of the urban bustle – while staff are lovely.

Nakorn Garden Inn HOTEL $
(☑ 075 323777; 1/4 Th Pak Nakhon; r 445B; ❄️ 🅿️) There's a lovely forested setting here that's more like a shady jungle than the centre of town, but sadly most of the bare-brick rooms

KHAO LUANG NATIONAL PARK

Known for its beautiful mountain and forest walks, cool streams, waterfalls and orchards, **Khao Luang National Park** (อุทยานแห่งชาติเขาหลวง; 075 300494; www.dnp.go.th; adult/child 400/200B) surrounds the 1835m peak of Khao Luang. A soaring mountain range covered in virgin forest and a habitat for a plethora of bird species, it's a good spot for any ornithologist. There are more than 300 species of orchid in the park, some of which are found nowhere else on earth. Camping is permitted, and there are **bungalows** (075 300494; www.dnp.go.th; per night 600-2000B) (from 600B). There's also a restaurant at park HQ.

To reach the park, take a *sǒrng·tǎa·ou* (pick-up minibus) for around 40B from Nakhon Si Thammarat to Lan Saka; drivers will usually take you the extra way to park headquarters. The entrance to the park and the offices of the Royal Forest Department are 33km from the centre of Nakhon on Rte 4015, an asphalt road that climbs almost 400m in 2.5km to the office and a further 450m to the car park. Plenty of up-to-date details are available on the park's website.

are rather gloomy, although they come with air-con, TV, hot water and fridge. It's a nice rustic change from a cement block, though, and prices are a steal, although English is not spoken.

Twin Lotus Hotel HOTEL **$$$**
(075 323777; www.twinlotushotel.net; 97/8 Th Phattanakan Khukhwang; r 1500-2500B; ❄ 🐕 🛜 🏊) The 401-room, 16-storey Twin Lotus is still a good choice to go a little more upscale when in Nakhon; rooms are OK, but it's ageing. It's 2km southeast of the city centre, with a Tesco right across the road.

Eating

Nakhon is a great place to sample cuisine with a distinctive southern twist. In the evening, Muslim food stands sell delicious *kôw mòk gài* (chicken biryani), *má·dà·bà* (murdabag; Indian pancake stuffed with chicken or vegetables) and roti. A good hunting ground is along Th Neramit, which turns into Th Pak Nakhon – the street bustles with food stalls every night.

★**Krua Talay** THAI **$**
(1204/29-30 Th Pak Nakhon; dishes 50-300B; 4-10pm) Opposite the Nakorn Garden Inn (p583) and overseen by an all-seeing, all-knowing matriarch, this restaurant serves simply awesome seafood dishes. Take a seat in the lovely rear garden area and order up fried prawn cake, crispy catfish with hot & spicy salad or stir-fried vegetables in oyster sauce, and make a meal of it.

Hao Coffee CAFE **$**
(075 346563; Bovorn Bazaar; dishes 30-60B; 7am-4pm) This charming, shuttered and well-staffed cafe is always stuffed with talkative locals and decorated with an eclectic array of collectibles and knick-knacks, from pith helmets to hunting rifles, ancient ceramics and wall clocks. It's a great place for a scrambled-eggs breakfast, a larger meal or a caffeine fix, either inside or out front.

★**Pixzel Caffe** CAFE **$$**
(086 682 5471; pizza from 120B; 9am-7pm) The blurb says open 'eight days a week', pointing to a Beatles leaning at this arty, thin-crust pizza-serving, coffee-brewing place in a traditional-style wooden house just across the way from Wat Phra Mahathat. It's a popular and very cosy spot and makes an excellent break if you're templed out.

Glur House CAFE **$$**
(Th Ratchadamnoen; mains 60-260B; 8am-7pm; 🛜) A neat addition to town and decorated with smashed skateboards, this cool rough-concrete cafe is a decent place to hang out with a mocha latte, a mint latte, a caramel macchiato, an Italian soda, a hot dog, banana waffle, a brownie or even a waffle pizza (why not?).

ℹ Information

Several banks and ATMs hug Th Ratchadamnoen in the northern end of downtown.
Police Station (1155; Th Ratchadamnoen)
Post Office (Th Ratchadamnoen; 8.30am-4.30pm Mon-Fri, 9am-noon Sat & Sun)
Tourism Authority of Thailand (TAT; 075 346515; 8.30am-4.30pm) Housed in a fine 1926-vintage building in the northern end of the Sanam Na Muang (City Park), this office has some useful brochures, but spoken English is limited.

ℹ Getting There & Away

AIR

Several carriers such as Nok Air, Air Asia and Thai Lion Air fly from Bangkok Don Mueang International Airport to Nakhon every day. There are about six daily one-hour flights, with one-way fares around 1500B.

BUS

Ordinary buses to Bangkok leave from the main **bus station** off Rte 4016 in the west of town, a good 25-minute walk from the centre. The journey takes 12 hours and costs 426B to 851B depending on the class of bus. Minibuses also run from the station to Hat Yai (140B), Surat Thani (120B) and Khanom (80B), and buses run to Phuket (350B).

When looking for minivan stops to leave Nakhon, keep an eye out for small desks along the side of the downtown roads (minivans and waiting passengers may or may not be present nearby). It's best to ask around as each destination has a different departure point. Krabi and Don Sak minivans are grouped together – just make sure you don't get on the wrong one. Stops are scattered around Th Jamroenwithi, Th Wakhit and Th Yommarat.

TRAIN

There are two daily train departures (1pm and 3pm) to Bangkok from Nakhon (133B to 652B; stopping at Hua Hin, Chumphon and Surat Thani along the way). In the other direction, trains leave Bangkok at 5.35pm and 7.30pm. It's 15 hours in either direction, so they are night trains. These trains continue on to Hat Yai and Sungai Kolok.

ℹ Getting Around

Sŏrng·tǎa·ou run north–south along Th Ratchadamnoen and Th Si Thammasok for 10B (a bit more at night). Motorcycle-taxi rides start at 30B and cost up to 50B for longer distances. A motorbike from the centre of town to the bus station is 40B.

SONGKHLA PROVINCE

Songkhla Province's two main commercial centres, Hat Yai and Songkhla, are less affected by the political turmoil plaguing the cities further south, although some state travel advisories warn against travel here. You won't be tripping over foreign backpackers, but you'll see a fair number of tourists drawn to wandering through local markets, savouring Muslim-Thai fusion cuisine, relaxing on breezy beaches and tapping into Hat Yai's fun and eclectic urban vibe.

Songkhla & Around   สงขลา

🎵 074 / POP 90,780

'The great city on two seas' is photogenic in parts; however, slow-paced Songkhla doesn't see much in the way of foreign tourist traffic. Although the town hasn't experienced any of the Muslim separatist violence plaguing the provinces further south, it's still catching the same bad press.

The population is a mix of Thais, Chinese and Malays, and the local architecture and cuisine reflect this fusion at every turn.

◉ Sights & Activities

★**National Museum**   MUSEUM

(พิพิธภัณฑสถานแห่งชาติสงขลา; Th Wichianchom; 150B; ⊙ 9am-4pm Wed-Sun, closed public holidays) This 1878 building was originally built in a Chinese architectural style as the residence of a luminary. This is easily the most picturesque national museum in Thailand and contains exhibits from all Thai art-style periods, particularly the Srivijaya. Walk barefoot on the wood floors to view elaborate wood carvings, historical photos and pottery salvaged from a shipwreck.

Hat Samila   BEACH

(หาดสมิหลา) Stroll this beautiful strip of white sand and enjoy the kite-flying (a local obsession); it's a gorgeous spot for a wander at sundown. A bronze **Mermaid sculpture**, in tribute to Mae Thorani (the Hindu-Buddhist earth goddess), sits atop some rocks at the northern end of the beach. Locals treat the figure like a shrine, tying the waist with coloured cloth and rubbing the breasts for good luck.

Don't expect to sunbathe here – the local dress code is too modest – but it's a wholesome spot to meet locals and enjoy a distinctly Thai beach scene.

Songkhla Aquarium   AQUARIUM

(สงขลาอะควาเรี่ยม; 🎵 088 788 1456; www.songkhlaaquarium.com; adult/child 300/200B; ⊙ 9.30am-4pm) Children will love seeking out the clownfish at this fun aquarium and watching the feeding show, performed by divers; there's also a go-kart track (from 400B). Adults can have their feet nibbled clean by garaa rufa fish (200B).

Singora Tram Tour

ACTIVITY

(⊘9am-3pm) **FREE** These free 40-minute tours (six daily) in an open-air tram leave from next to the National Museum. You'll be lucky if you get any English narration but you will get a drive through the old part of town past the Songkhla mosque, a Thai temple, Chinese shrine and then out to Hat Samila.

🛏 Sleeping & Eating

Hotels in and around Songkhla tend to be lower-priced than other areas in the gulf, which makes going up a budget level a relatively cheap splurge.

For quality seafood, head to the street in front of the BP Samila Beach Hotel – the best spot is the restaurant directly in the roundabout. If market munching is your game, you'll find a place to sample street food most days of the week. The best cafe in town is the excellent Blue Smile Cafe.

Sook Soom Boon 2

HOTEL $

(☑074 323809; 14 Th Saiburi; d 550-650B; ❄️🛜) The owner speaks good English and rooms are really decent value at this centrally located choice. It's nothing special, but it's serviceable, especially when compared to some less salubrious nearby choices.

BP Samila Beach Hotel

HOTEL $$

(☑074 440222; 8 Th Ratchadamnoen; r 1600-2500B; ❄️@🏊) This landmark hotel is a great deal – you'd pay nearly double for the same amenities on the islands. The beachfront establishment offers large rooms with fridges, satellite TVs and a choice of sea or mountain views (both are pretty darn good), although it's rather set in its ways and checking on wi-fi reception in your room first is prudent.

★ Blue Smile Cafe

CAFE $

(☑061 230 5147; 254 Th Nakhonnai; mains from 100B; ⊘3-11pm Mon, Tue, Thu & Fri, from 10am Sat & Sun) A fine place for a snack, coffee, some alcohol or cool beats, we're not sure what we like best at this Canadian-owned place: the excellent roof garden – fantastic at sunset – *The Blues Brothers* poster, the B52s and Bob Dylan pics, the live jazz (from 7.15pm Friday and Saturday) or the baked goodies.

Ong Heap Huad

CAFE

(☑081 690 6640; Th Nakhonnai; ⊘10am-6pm) This family-run curiosity shop-slash-cafe has a mesmerising museum-like collection of ancient Chinese and Thai shop signs, antiques, statuette, lamps, stuffed animal heads and more. It's an enchanting place for a glass of tea. Look for the shop with the urns and bric-a-brac outside and the Chinese shop sign saying 黃協發, opposite No 239.

🛈 Information

Banks can be found all over town.

Indonesian Consulate (☑074 311544; www.kemlu.go.id/songkhla; 19 Th Sadao)

Malaysian Consulate (☑074 311062; 4 Th Sukhum, Songkhla; ⊘8.15am-noon & 1-4pm Mon-Fri)

Police Station (☑074 321868; Th Laeng Phra Ram)

Post Office (Th Wichianchom)

🛈 Getting There & Away

BUS

The bus and minibus station is on Songkhla Plaza Alley (off Nakhonnok St) around 1km south of the **Blue Smile Cafe**. Three 2nd-class buses go daily to Bangkok (693B to 1080B), stopping in Nakhon Si Thammarat and Surat Thani, among other places. For Hat Yai, buses (21B) and minivans (30B to 40B) take around 40 minutes, and leave from Th Ramwithi. *Sŏrng·tăa·ou* also leave from here for Ko Yo.

TRAIN

From Songkhla you'll have to go to Hat Yai to reach most long-distance destinations in the south (trains no longer pass through town).

DON'T MISS

SONGKHLA LAKE ISLAND

A popular day trip from Songkhla is **Ko Yo** (เกาะยอ) island in the middle of Songkhla Lake, which is actually connected to the mainland by bridges and is famous for its cotton-weaving industry; a roadside market sells cloth and ready-made clothes at excellent prices.

If you visit Ko Yo, don't miss **Wat Phrahon Laem Pho**, with its giant reclining Buddha, and check out the **Thaksin Folklore Museum** (☑074 591618; 100B; ⊘8.30am-4.30pm), which actively aims to promote and preserve the culture of the region. The pavilions here are reproductions of southern Thai–style houses and contain folk art, handicrafts and traditional household implements.

Hat Yai   หาดใหญ่

♫ 074 / POP 191,696

Welcome to the urban hub of southern Thailand, where Western-style shopping malls mingle with wafts from busy street-food stalls as old Chinese men watch the world go by on rickety chairs outside junk shops. You'll notice that the town's tourism scene is still predominantly Malaysian mixed with a few Western expats. Hat Yai has a seamy side, popular with Malaysian men on weekend visits.

Those who explore will be rewarded with some of the region's best food and the dynamic flavour of southern Thailand's big smoke.

🛏 Sleeping

Hat Yai has dozens of business-style hotels in the town centre, within walking distance of the train station, as well as a hostel and several cheap options.

Hat Yai Backpackers   HOSTEL $
(www.hatyaibackpackershostel.com; 226 Th Niphat Uthit 1; dm 240B; 🛜) With four-bed female dorms and eight-bed mixed dorms, this central choice is a decent bet, and there are helpful staff at hand for Hat Yai pointers.

Red Planet   HOTEL $
(🖉 074 261011; www.redplanethotels.com; 152-156 Th Niphat Uthit 2; r from 900B; ❄🛜) In a very central location, this hotel offers cleanliness, affordability and decent service, with uncluttered, but modern, functional rooms. The atmosphere and theme are generically chain charmless; prices depend a lot on how far in advance you book.

Centara   HOTEL $$$
(🖉 074 352222; www.centarahotelsresorts.com; 3 Th Sanehanusorn; r/apt from 4000/5300B, ste 8500B; ❄🛜🏊) The centrally located, 244-room Centara is a particularly smart choice, with pool, excellent rooms, terrific service and some fine views from the upper floors. Evening live jazz in the foyer bar brings some style.

🍴 Eating & Drinking

The city is the unofficial capital of southern Thailand's cuisine, offering Muslim roti and curries, Chinese noodles, duck rice and dim sum, and fresh Thai-style seafood from both the gulf and Andaman coasts. Hawker stalls are everywhere, but a particularly good hunting ground is along Th Supasarnrang-san. Meals here cost between 25B to 80B.

As you'd expect from a city with a commercial sex side, Hat Yai's nightlife is rather tacky.

Night Market   MARKET $
(Th Montri 1) The night market boasts heaps of local eats including several stalls selling the famous Hat Yai-style deep-fried chicken and *kà·nŏm jeen* (fresh rice noodles served with curry), as well as a couple of stalls peddling grilled seafood.

Daothiam   CAFE $
(79/3 Thammanoonvithi Rd; mains from 60B; ⊙7am-7pm; 🛜) Serving Hat Yai patrons since 1959, this traditional Chinese cafe has framed banknotes on its walls, friendly staff, a reliable menu of Thai/Chinese dishes and fine breakfasts. Curiously, its name means 'Satellite'. It's opposite the Odean Shopping Mall.

Gedi Chadian   CHINESE $
(Ko Ti Ocha; 134-136 Th Niphat Uthit 3; mains from 50B) This big, open, spacious and very busy restaurant serves steaming bowls of scrumptious wonton noodles, chicken rice, *chā shāo* pork and other filling Chinese staples. The name in Chinese means 'Brothers Tea Shop'.

ⓘ Information

DANGERS & ANNOYANCES

The town is often said to be safe from the violent hullabaloo of the far south; however, it hasn't been ignored. The Lee Gardens Plaza Hotel was bombed in 2012, killing four people in a subsequent fire and injuring 400. Three bombs exploded in Hat Yai in 2014, injuring eight. In previous years pubs, malls, department stores and hotels have been targeted in other bombings.

It's up to you if you want to stop here, but changing transport shouldn't be too risky.

EMERGENCY

Tourist Police (Th Niphat Uthit 3; ⊙24hr)

TOURIST INFORMATION

Tourism Authority of Thailand (TAT; www.tourismthailand.org/hatyai; 1/1 Soi 2, Th Niphat Uthit 3; ⊙8.30am-4.30pm) The very helpful staff here speak excellent English and have loads of info on the entire region.

TRAVEL AGENCIES

Cathay Tour (🖉 086 488 0086; 93/1 Th Niphat Uthit 2; ⊙8am-6pm) Superfriendly staff and full range of services, from tickets to tours to visa runs.

THAILAND'S FORGOTTEN WAR

Just 300km or so south of the party islands of Ko Samui and Ko Pha-Ngan, a guerrilla war between ethnic Malay Muslims and the overwhelmingly Buddhist Thai state has claimed almost 6000 lives since 2004. Military convoys rumble through the villages and towns, checkpoints dominate the roads and residents are subject to compulsory DNA tests designed to make identifying suspected insurgents easier.

Around 80% of the 1.8 million people who live in Thailand's three southernmost provinces of Pattani, Narathiwat and Yala are ethnic Malay Muslims. They speak a Malay dialect and many want their own independent state, as the region once was hundreds of years ago.

For the estimated 12,500 to 15,000 separatist fighters here, the Deep South is 'Patani': the name given to the Qatar-sized sultanate during its glory days in the 14th and 15th centuries. The insurgents view the Thai government as a colonial power and Thai Buddhists as interlopers in their land.

Ranged against the separatists are around 150,000 soldiers, police and militias. Targeted in ambushes along the coconut-tree-lined roads of the region, or by increasingly sophisticated IEDs (improvised explosive devices), barely a week goes by without a member of the Thai security forces being killed or wounded.

At the same time, the insurgency has set neighbours against each other. Gruesome tit-for-tat killings occur, with both Buddhist and Muslim civilians being gunned down as they ride home on their motorbikes or beheaded in the rubber plantations that are the mainstay of the local economy. Bombs are planted outside shops and in the markets of the towns, claiming random victims.

The few remaining Buddhist monks in the region have to be escorted by the army when they collect alms every morning for fear they will be assassinated, while mosques are riddled with bullet holes.

The insurgents have resisted attacking targets outside the Deep South, a tactic that would do huge damage to the Thai psyche and would garner them far more attention around the world. Nor do they appear to be connected to the more extreme Islamic militants of Indonesia and the Philippines. There seems to be no common leader of the insurgent groups, which renders the sporadic peace talks with the Thai government meaningless.

While the insurgency kicked into life in earnest in 2004, after 32 suspected Muslim rebels were cornered in an ancient mosque in Pattani Town and brutally killed by the Thai army, its roots go back hundreds of years. From the 16th century on, the sultanate of Patani was unwillingly under Thai rule for brief periods. But it wasn't until the Anglo-Siamese Treaty of 1909 that the Deep South was absorbed into Thailand proper. Britain recognised Thai sovereignty over the region, in return for Bangkok abandoning its claims to other parts of what were then the British-ruled Malay states.

Since then, Thailand, the most populous Buddhist country in the world, has set about attempting to remake the Deep South in its own image. Muslim schools have been shut down and all children made to study in Thai, even though most of them speak it only as a second language. They are also forced to learn about Buddhism, a part of the Thai national curriculum, despite following Islam. Officials from other parts of the country are imported to run the region.

With the insurgency mostly confined to just three provinces, and a small part of neighbouring Songkhla Province, few Thais are even aware of why the fighting is taking place. Nor are they willing to contemplate giving in to the separatists' demands. Imbued with the nationalism taught in their schools, the idea that the Deep South should want to secede from Thailand is unthinkable, both to ordinary Thais and the authorities.

Yet, some form of autonomy for the region is likely the only way to end the violence. Until that happens, Thailand's forgotten war will carry on and the grim list of casualties will continue to grow.

VISA EXTENSIONS

Immigration Office (Th Phetkasem) Near the railway bridge, it handles visa extensions.

ℹ Getting There & Away

AIR

Hat Yai International Airport (☑ 074 227131; www.hatyaiairportthai.com) is around 14km southwest of town. Air Asia (www.airasia.com), Nok Air (www.nokair.com), Thai Lion Air (www.lionairthai.com) and **Thai Airways** (THAI; www.thaiairways.com; 182 Th Niphat Uthit 1) have daily flights to and from Bangkok. Thai Smile (www.thaismileair.com) flies to Bangkok Suvarnabhumi International Airport.

There's an **airport taxi service** (182 Th Niphat Uthit 1; 100B per person; ⏲ 6.30am-6.45pm) that runs to the airport six times daily (6.45am, 10am, 12.15pm, 1.45pm, 3pm and 6.15pm). A private taxi for this run costs 320B.

BUS

Most interprovincial buses and southbound minivans leave from the bus terminal 2km south-east of the town centre, while most northbound minivans now leave from a minivan terminal 5km west of town at Talat Kaset, a 60B túk-túk ride from the centre of town. Buses link Hat Yai to almost any location in southern Thailand.

Cathay Tour (p587) can also arrange minivans to many destinations in the south.

Buses From Hat Yai

DESTINATION	FARE (B)	DURATION (HR)
Bangkok	688–1130B	15hr
Krabi	182–540B	5hr
Nakhon Si Thammarat	140B	4hr
Pak Bara	130B	2hr
Phuket	370B	7hr
Songkhla	40B	1½hr
Sungai Kolok	220B	4hr
Surat Thani	240B	5hr
Trang	110B	2hr

TRAIN

Four overnight trains run to/from Bangkok each day (259B to 945B, 16 hours); trains go via Surat Thani (105B). There are also seven trains daily that run along the east coast to Sungai Kolok (92B) and two daily trains running west to Butterworth (332B) and Padang Besar (57B), both in Malaysia.

There is an advance booking office and left-luggage office at the train station; both are open 7am to 5pm daily.

ℹ Getting Around

Sŏrng·tăa·ou run along Th Phetkasem (10B per person). Túk-túk and motorcycle taxis around town cost 20B to 40B per person.

DEEP SOUTH

In the deep southern Thai provinces, the culture, language, religion and historical influences of Malaysia penetrate and a regional identity that traces itself back to the Malay sultanate of Patani asserts itself. Most inhabitants of the region speak a dialect of Malay, being ethnically closer to their Malay cousins over the border.

The tourist potential in this fascinating region is largely unexploited, put on the back foot by a long-simmering insurgency that pits Muslim separatists against the Thai state, with just a small trickle of visitors and consequently a paucity of infrastructure to cater to them.

Yala ยะลา

☑ 073 / POP 61,250

Landlocked Yala wiggles its way south to the Malaysian border, making it Thailand's southernmost province. Its eponymous capital appears very different from other Thai metropolises and feels distinctly Western, with big boulevards and a well-organised street grid set around a huge circular park. Around three-quarters of the population is Muslim and it is a university town, the educational centre of the Deep South.

◉ Sights

Yala's biggest attraction is **Wat Kuha Pi Muk** (Wat Khuhapimuk), one of the most important pilgrimage points in southern Thailand. Located 8km west of town on the road connecting Yala to Hat Yai (Rte 409), this Srivijaya-period cave temple (also called Wat Na Tham or Cave-front Temple) features a reclining Buddha that dates back to AD 757.

Further south, Betong is home to the largest **mail box** in Thailand, first built in 1924.

🛏 Sleeping & Eating

Yala is a pleasant place, but many of the city's cheapest lodgings double as unofficial brothels. There's not a great selection of places in town but the Yala Rama is a good choice.

ℹ️ TRAVEL IN THE DEEP SOUTH: SHOULD YOU GO?

No tourists, or indeed any Westerners, have been targeted by the insurgents. Yet, by nature insurgencies are unpredictable, and bombs kill indiscriminately. Explosive devices planted on parked motorbikes outside shops, or in markets, are a common tactic of the separatists and are frequently used in the city centres of Yala, Pattani, Narathiwat and Sungai Kolok.

It's best not to linger on the streets for too long; you could be in the wrong place at the wrong time. Nor is travel in the countryside in the early morning or after dark advisable. This isn't an area to be driving a motorbike in if you can't be identified as a foreigner.

The insurgency has stifled tourism to the extent that there is very little infrastructure for visitors. Travel between the major centres apart, you'll need private transport to get around. There are few hotels and restaurants, and almost no nightlife, while those beautiful beaches have absolutely no facilities.

If you do want to travel here, research the current situation carefully and take advice from your embassy.

There are excellent restaurants scattered around the park's perimeter.

Yala Rama HOTEL $
(☎ 073 212815; 21 Th Sri Bumrung; r 600B; ❄️ 🛜) Like most hotels in the region, this central and reputable nine-floor place, a short walk from the train station, would be more expensive if it weren't located in the Deep South. Clean, comfortable rooms and an OK attached restaurant.

ℹ️ Information

Betong functions as a legal, but inconvenient, border crossing to Malaysia; contact Yala's **immigration office** (☎ 073 231292; Betong; ⏱ 8.30am-4.30pm).

ℹ️ Getting There & Away

Yala's bus station is south of the city centre. There are three daily buses to and from Bangkok's southern bus terminal (783B to 1422B, 15 hours). The 4pm bus from Bangkok carries onto Betong.

Four trains a day run between Bangkok and Yala (18 hours). Two trains travel daily between Yala and Sungai Kolok (three to four hours). The train station is just north of the city centre.

Buses to Hat Yai (160B, 2½ hours) stop several times a day on Th Sirirot, outside the Prudential TS Life office.

Minivans to Betong and Sungai Kolok (100B, two hours) depart hourly from opposite the train station.

Pattani
ปัตตานี

☎ 073 / POP 44,234

Once the heart of a large Muslim principality that included the neighbouring provinces of Yala and Narathiwat, Pattani Province has never adjusted to Thai rule. Although today's political situation has stunted the area's development, Pattani Town has a 500-year history of trading with the world's most notorious imperial powerhouses. The Portuguese established a trading post here in 1516, the Japanese passed through in 1605, the Dutch in 1609 and the British flexed their colonial muscles in 1612.

Yet despite the city's fascinating past, there's little of interest in Pattani. There are some decent beaches nearby, but the ongoing insurgency has made most of these sandy destinations unsafe for the independent traveller.

◉ Sights

The Mae Nam Pattani (Pattani River) divides the older town to the east and the newer town to the west. Along Th Ruedi you can see what is left of old Pattani architecture – the Sino-Portuguese style that was once so prevalent in this part of southern Thailand. On Th Arnoaru there are several ancient but still quite intact Chinese-style homes.

Pattani could be one of the better beach destinations in the region. The coastline between Pattani Town and Narathiwat Province is stunning: untouched and deserted apart from fishing villages. But exploring much of this area independently is not a safe option at this time.

Matsayit Klang MOSQUE
(Th Naklua Yarang) One of Thailand's largest mosques, the Matsayit Klang is a traditional structure with a green hue and is probably still the south's most important mosque, dating to the 1960s. Non-Muslims can enter outside of prayer times.

🛏 Sleeping & Eating

Palace Hotel
HOTEL **$**

(📞 073 349171; 10-12 Pipit Soi Talattewiwat 2; r 180-350B; ❄) There's not a lot palatial about this place, but it's the only budget option in town for foreigners and close to the night market. Go for the air-con rooms with hot water.

CS Pattani Hotel
HOTEL **$$**

(📞 073 335093; www.cspattanihotel.com; 299 Moo 4, Th Nong Jik; r from 1400B; ❄ @ 🛜 ☝) The safest and best hotel in town, with soldiers outside and a metal detector in the lobby, this is where Thai politicians stay on their rare visits to the Deep South. The paucity of tourists means you get great rooms and facilities for a bargain price.

Night Market
THAI **$**

(Soi Talattewiwat; dishes from 25B; ⊙4-9pm) Pattani shuts down far earlier than most Thai towns, but the night market offers solid seafood, as well as southern Thai-style curries and the usual noodle and fried-rice options.

ℹ Information

There are several banks along the southeastern end of Th Pipit, near the Th Naklua Yarang intersection.

Pattani Hospital (📞 073 335135, 073 335134, 073 711010; Th Nong Jik)
Police Station (📞 073 349018; Th Pattani Phirom)

ℹ Getting There & Away

Minivans and buses depart from Pattani's bus station on the western fringes of town, with frequent daytime departures to Hat Yai (110B, 1½ hours), Narathiwat (110B, 1½ hours) and Sungai Kolok (150B, 2½ hours).

There are two daily buses to and from Bangkok's southern bus terminal (765B to 1250B, 14 hours).

ℹ Getting Around

Motorbike taxis charge 30B for hops around town, but they become very scarce after dark.

Narathiwat
นราธิวาส

📞 073 / POP 41,342

Sitting on the banks of the Bang Nara River, Narathiwat is probably the most Muslim city in Thailand, with mosques scattered around town. A few old Sino-Portuguese buildings line the riverfront (although blink and you'll miss them), and there some excellent beaches just outside town, but few tourists pass through, due to the security situation.

OFF THE BEATEN TRACK

GATEWAY TO MALAYSIA: SUNGAI KOLOK

It's not the most prepossessing place to enter or exit the 'Land of Smiles', but Sungai Kolok is the main gateway between Thailand and Malaysia. As such, it's a scuzzy border town best known for smuggling and prostitution. Less of a target than the other major towns in the region, the unstable situation in the Deep South has nevertheless severely diminished its 'sin city' reputation, with the Malaysian men who once came here for wild weekends now favouring safer Hat Yai. Fewer travellers, too, leave Thailand here now; more come in the opposite direction and immediately hop on a train heading north.

If you do pass through, **Merlin Hotel** (📞 073 611003; 68 Th Charoenkhet; r 600B; ❄ 🛜) is clean and handy for the train station while **Genting Hotel** (📞 073 613231; 250 Th Asia 18; r 700B; ❄ @ 🛜 ☝) has efficient security, though its midrange rooms are rather scuffed for the price; it's a few hundred metres east of the train station on the far side of the road. Reliable, Muslim-run **Kakyah Restaurant** (43/11 Th Charoenkhet; dishes from 30B; ⊙10am-10pm) offers decent Malaysian food. The long-distance **bus station** (Th Asia 18) is 2km west of the centre on Th Asia 18. There are four buses daily to and from Bangkok's southern bus terminal (707B to 1414B, 17 to 20 hours). Minivans to Hat Yai (200B, four hours) leave from here too.

There is an **immigration office** (📞 073 614114; Th Charoenkhet; ⊙8am-5pm Mon-Fri) opposite the Merlin Hotel with helpful, English-speaking staff. The Thai border (open 5am to 9pm) is about 1.5km from the centre of Sungai Kolok. Motorbike taxis charge around 30B. After completing formalities, walk across the Harmony Bridge to the Malaysian border post. Two-hundred metres beyond the post, you can catch shared taxis and buses to Kota Bharu, the capital of Malaysia's Kelantan State.

◉ Sights & Activities

Just 2km north of town is **Hat Narathat**, a 5km-long sandy beach fronted by towering pines, which serves as a public park for locals. Five kilometres south of town, **Ao Manao** is a superb strip of palm tree-fringed sand.

Wat Khao Kong   BUDDHIST TEMPLE

(⊙9am-5pm) FREE The tallest seated-Buddha image in southern Thailand is at Wat Khao Kong, 6km southwest of town on the way to the train station in Tanyongmat. Located in a park, the image is 17m long and 24m high, and made of reinforced concrete covered with tiny gold-coloured mosaic tiles that glint magically in the sun.

Matsayit Klang   MOSQUE

(Yum lyah Mosque) Towards the southern end of Th Pichitbumrung stands Matsayit Klang, a wooden mosque built in the Sumatran style and known locally as the 'old central mosque'. It was reputedly built by a prince of the former kingdom of Pattani more than a hundred years ago. Non-Muslims can enter outside of prayer times.

🛏 Sleeping & Eating

Most of the town's accommodation is located on and around Th Puphapugdee along the Bang Nara River.

The centre of town, near the river, is well provided with restaurants and cafes.

Ocean Blue Mansion   HOTEL $

(☑073 511109; 297 Th Puphapugdee; r 400-500B; ❄🛜) Decent-sized rooms have seen better days, but some have fine river views and this remains the best budget choice.

Tanyong Hotel   HOTEL $$

(☑073 511477; 16/1 Th Sophaphisai; r 690-890B; ❄🛜) This respectable, welcoming hotel has big, comfortable rooms and an OK attached restaurant, while staff speak some English.

Mangkorntong   THAI $

(☑073 511835; 433 Th Puphapugdee; dishes 55-200B; ⊙10am-10pm) Perched over the river, you have a choice of two terraces to dine on here, with a wide selection of seafood dishes available, as well as vegie options; alcohol is served.

ℹ Information

The **Tourism Authority of Thailand** (TAT; ☑Narathiwat 073 522411, nationwide call centre 1672) is located a few kilometres south of town, just across the bridge on the road to Tak Bai.

ℹ Getting There & Away

Air Asia (www.airasia.com) flies daily to and from Bangkok (from 1783B, 1½ hours), as does Thai Smile (www.thaismileair.com; from 1730B, 1½ hours).

Minivans and buses leave from Narathiwat's **bus terminal** (☑073 511552), 2km south of town on Th Rangae Munka. There are two daily buses to and from Bangkok's southern bus terminal (860B to 1350B, 15 to 17 hours).

Frequent minivans head to Hat Yai (170B, three hours), Pattani (100B, two hours), Sungai Kolok (70B, one hour) and Yala (100B, 1½ hours).

ℹ Getting Around

Narathiwat is small enough to navigate by foot. Motorcycle taxis charge 30B to get around.

Phuket & the Andaman Coast

Best Places to Eat

➡ Eat Bar & Grill (p644)

➡ Efe (p670)

➡ Krua Thara (p663)

➡ One Chun (p627)

➡ Pad Thai Shop (p644)

Best Places to Stay

➡ Rayavadee (p658)

➡ Castaway Resort (p699)

➡ Iniala Beach House (p613)

➡ Fin Hostel (p641)

➡ Amanpuri Resort (p647)

Why Go?

The Andaman is Thailand's dream coast: one of those places that you see on a postcard which make you want to quit your job and live in flip-flops...forever. And it is stunning. Pure-white beaches of soft sand, a turquoise sea, towering limestone cliffs and jungle-covered isles extend down the Andaman Sea from the border of Myanmar to Malaysia. Phuket is the glitzy show-stealer, but head north and you'll uncover world-class dive sites, little-visited islands, and the waterfalls and caves of Phang-Nga's national parks. To the south, you can lazily island-hop down to the Malaysian border.

The catch? The Andaman Coast is no secret and its beaches are increasingly crowded with backpackers, package tourists, high-end jet-setters and everyone in between. Flashy resorts are pushing out the bamboo shacks and Thai-Rasta bars and authenticity hides largely in the backwaters now. But if you're willing to search hard, your postcard dream is still here.

When to Go

➡ May is the start of the five-month-long rainy season. Some resorts close, others slash their prices.

➡ The Vegetarian Festival is held in Phuket and Trang in September. Expect pierced-faced worshippers and fantastic food.

➡ December is the beginning of peak tourist season and conditions are ideal for diving and snorkelling.

Phuket & the Andaman Coast Highlights

1 Trang Islands (p685) Buzzing across jade-green waters between white-sand beaches.

2 Ko Lipe (p697) Snorkelling over colourful corals and explore the untouched nearby islands.

3 Phuket (p618) Experiencing the heady mix of luxury lodgings, super spas and street-food treats.

4 Khao Sok National Park (p605) Hiking through a real-life Jurassic Park.

5 Railay (p656) Scaling limestone cliffs above blissful beaches.

6 Ko Phi-Phi (p664) Floating in a

ANDAMAN
SEA

GULF OF
THAILAND

MYANMAR

Kawthoung

Ko Tao

Chong Tao

Ko Pha-Ngan

Chong Phu-Ngan

Ko Samui

Chang Samui

Ang Thong
National
Marine Park

Ko Phaluai

Khanom

Sichon

Tha Sala

401

4014

Phi-Pun

4015

Wiang Sa

Na Doem

Ban Na
San

41

Chai
Buri

4110

Nakhon Si

Phrom
Khiri

Surat
Thani

Ao Ban
Don

Chaiya

4112

Khian Sa

Khirirathnikhom

SURAT
THANI

Surat
Thani
Airport

Tha Chang

Lamae

41

Ban
Takhun

Phanom

401

Khao Sok
National Park

Chiaw
Lan Lake

Klong Yan

RANONG

Ranong

Ranong
Airport

La-Un

Isthmus
of Kra

CHUMPHON

Pha To

4006

Kapoe

Laem Son
National
Park

Ao Sawi

Sawi

Ko Kula

Thung Tako

Laem Riu

Ko
Phayam

Ko Chang

Hat Bang
Ben

Ko Kam
Noi

Ko Kam
Yai

Hat Praphat

Ko Ra

Ngan
Yong

Khuraburi

4

Ko Phra
Thong

Ko Kho
Khao

Takua Pa

Kapong

PHANG-NGA

Meuang
Phang-Nga

Takua

420

Thap Put

KRABI

Plaiphaya

Thap Lamu

Thai

Hat Bang Sak

Hat Bang Niang

Hat Nang Thong

Hat Khao Lak

Khao Lak/Laem Ru
National Park

Surin Islands
Marine National Park

Surin
Islands

7

Ko Tachai

Ko Bon

Similan Islands
Marine National Park

7

Similan
Islands

cerulean sea by day, then dance the night away.

7 Similan (p611) & Surin Islands (p603) Diving with manta rays and whale sharks.

8 Ko Lanta (p672) Exploring the culturally rich old town or laze on the laid-back beaches.

9 Ao Phang-Nga (p615) Marvelling as you kayak into spectacular, semi-submerged caves.

10 Ko Phayam (p600) Embracing the mellow beach-bar vibe.

Map labels

NAKHON SI THAMMARAT

Na Bon

Ron Phibun

Thung Song

Thung Yai

Lam Thap

Khao Phanom

KRABI

Krabi Airport

Khao Phanom Bencha National Park

Ban Lam Kruat

Klong Thom

Ao Nang

Krabi

Hat Noppharat Thara-Mu Ko Phi-Phi National Park

Ao Nang

5 Ao Railay

Ko Jum (Ko Pu)

6 Ko Phi-Phi

Ko Raya Yai

Ko Raya Noi

National Park

Ko Yao Noi

9 Ao Phang-Nga Marine National Park

Ko Yao Yai

PHUKET

Phuket International Airport

Thalang

Kathu

3 Phuket

Patong

Phuket Town

Natai

Huat Yot

Siban Phot

Wang Wiset

TRANG

Trang

Trang Airport

Sikao

Hat Chang Lang

Pak Meng

Ko Ngai

Ko Muk

1 Trang Islands

Ko Kradan

Hat Chao Mai National Park

Kantang

Yan Ta Khao

Ban Ta Seh

Palian

Yong Sata

Mu Ko Phetra National Park

Ban Pa Bon Nua

PHATTHALUNG

Khao Chaison

Tha Mot

Phatthalung

Khuan Khanun

SONGKHLA

SATUN

Thung Wa

Pak Bara

Ko Bulon Le

Ko Lao Liang

Ko Libong

Ko Lanta Noi

8 Ko Lanta Yai

Mu Ko Lanta National Park

Ko Lanta

ANDAMAN SEA

Khuan Don

La-Ngu

Tha Phae

Satun

Tammalang

Thaleh Ban National Park

Ko Tarutao Marine National Park

Ko Tarutao

Ko Adang

Ko Rawi

Ko Butang

2 Ko Lipe

Khlong Lamini

Ko Phetra National Park

0   25 miles

0   50 km

N

RANONG PROVINCE

The Andaman's northernmost province is a whole different package to the white-sand, turquoise-sea paradise that is used to sell the Andamans on tourist brochures. Thailand's least populated and wettest region gets up to eight months of rain a year, so it's soggy, while beaches along the coast are scarce.

The upside is that Ranong's forests are lush and its smattering of beautiful islands – Ko Chang (p599) and Ko Phayam (p600) especially – remain *relatively* under the radar. Most visitors, though, come here to cross the border to Myanmar.

Ranong Town   ระนอง

077 / POP 17,500

On the eastern bank of Mae Nam Pak Chan's turbid, tea-brown estuary, Ranong lies just a 45-minute boat ride from Myanmar. This border town par excellence (shabby, frenetic, slightly seedy) has a thriving population from Myanmar, bubbling hot springs, crumbling historical buildings and some sensational street food.

Once a backwater, Ranong is increasingly busy with cross-border business and visitors heading to nearby Ko Phayam and Ko Chang, and has clearly benefitted from Myanmar's more stable political situation. Now, there are quirky boutique hotels and a style-conscious local scene (relatively speaking).

🏃 Activities

Diving

Liveaboard dive trips from Ranong to world-class bubble-blowing destinations, particularly the Burma Banks and the Surin and Similan Islands, are deservedly popular.

Andaman International Dive Center DIVING
(☑ 089 814 1092; www.aidcdive.com; Bus Terminal, Th Phetkasem; ☻Oct-Apr) Mainly focused on extensive excursions (six to 14 days) to the Mergui Archipelago in Myanmar, but also does a few trips to the Surin Islands. Four-day liveaboards 20,000B.

A-One-Diving DIVING
(☑ 077 832984; www.a-one-diving.com; 256 Th Ruangrat; ☻Oct-Apr) Specialises in liveaboards to the Surin Islands and Myanmar's Mergui Archipelago (from 34,900B), plus PADI diving certification courses.

Spas & Hot Springs

⭐ **Siam Hot Spa** SPA
(☑ 077 813551; 73/3 Th Phetkasem; treatments 300-750B; ☻11am-8pm) This is a highly recommended mineral bath experience, classier than the public hot springs opposite in Ranong Town. Soak in a private hot tub, then add a salt scrub or a classic Thai massage.

Rakswarin Hot Springs HOT SPRINGS
(Th Phetkasem; 40B; ☻5am-9pm) Ranong's healing waters bubble from a sacred spring hot enough to boil eggs (65°C), on the southeastern side of town. The riverside pools are blessed with chequered mosaic tiles, showers, towels and sunbeds. Just stretch out and let the heat work its natural magic.

🛏 Sleeping

Rueangrat Hotel HOTEL $
(☑ 092 279 9919; rueangratranong@gmail.com; 240/10 Th Ruangrat; r 690B; ❄ 🛜) Bright, shiny rooms set back from the road at this new place close to restaurants and shops. All come with fridges, TVs and decent bathrooms. There's free coffee in the lobby area, friendly staff and good wi-fi.

Ranong Backpacker's Hostel HOSTEL $
(☑ 091 041 7555, 077 983978; backpackers.rn@gmail.com; 240/9 Th Ruangrat; dm 320B; ❄ 🛜) Two eight-bed dorms here – one male, one female – with bunk beds and proper lockers. There's no real communal area, but it works if you're looking for a cheap and clean place to crash before or after crossing the border to/from Myanmar.

Luang Poj GUESTHOUSE $
(☑ 077 833377, 087 266 6333; www.facebook.com/luangpojhostel; 225 Th Ruangrat; r 600B; ❄ 🛜) This self-styled 'boutique guesthouse' is a cool remodel of a 1920s-era building that was Ranong's first hotel, decorated with mod-meets-vintage flair: Indian art, wall murals, one-of-a-kind light fixtures and retro photography. Rooms are spotless, comfy and cosy in signature colours (we like the hot orange). The drawback is that many rooms lack windows, while all share (clean) bathrooms.

The B BOUTIQUE HOTEL $$
(☑ 077 823111; Br.ranong@gmail.com; 295/1-2 Th Ruangrat; r 1300-2000B; ❄ 🛜 ☋) This good-value chunk of polished-concrete modernism is evidence of Ranong's rising fortunes. Stylish, comfy rooms have floating

Ranong

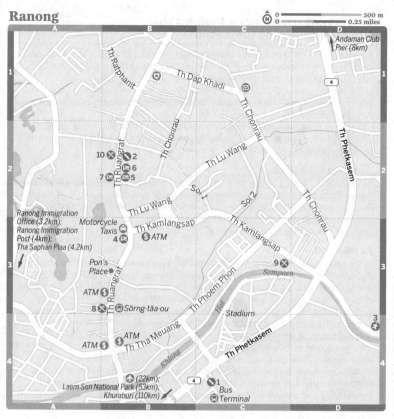

Ranong

beds, rain showers and tasteful, bright decor. Extra points for the snooker bar, the B restaurant and, particularly, the rooftop

infinity pool overlooking Ranong and the surrounding green hills.

✗ Eating & Drinking

Ranong's food markets are excellent value. The bubbly **day market** (Th Ruangrat; mains 40-70B; ⊙5am-midnight) offers delicious, inexpensive Thai and Burmese meals, while the **night market** (Th Kamlangsap, off Hwy 4; mains 30-70B; ⊙2-7pm), just northwest off the highway, sizzles up brilliant Thai dishes at killer prices. There are restaurants along Th Ruangrat.

After dark, Ranong has a lively, very local drinking scene involving lots of karaoke.

Ranong Hideaway   THAI, INTERNATIONAL **$$**
(☑077 832730; 323/7 Th Ruangrat; mains 110-480B; ⊙10am-11pm; ☎) A long-time favourite of expats and border businessmen, this small international eatery unfurls beneath a stilted bamboo roof, offering decent pastas,

ℹ GETTING TO MYANMAR: RANONG TOWN TO KAWTHOUNG (VICTORIA POINT)

Kawthoung, a dusty, bustling port on the southernmost tip of mainland Myanmar, was named Victoria Point by the British, but is known as Ko Song (Second Island) by Thais. Most travellers pop across just to renew their visas, but it's an interesting day trip.

Fishing and trade with Thailand keep things ticking over, but Kawthoung also churns out some of Myanmar's best kickboxers. Nearby isles are inhabited by chow lair (sea gypsies, also spelt *chao leh*).

The most hassle-free way to renew your visa is on one of the 'visa trips' (1300B) offered by Ranong travel agencies, including Pon's Place. But it's easy enough to do the legwork yourself.

Getting to the Border

As long as the Thailand–Myanmar border is open, boats to Kawthoung leave from Tha Saphan Plaa, 5km southwest of Ranong. Red *sŏrng·tăa·ou* 4 (pick-up minibus) goes from Ranong to the pier (20B), where long-tail captains lead you to the immigration post, then to their boat (one-way/return per person 100/200B). You'll need a photocopy of your passport, which you can get at the pier (5B).

At the Border

At the Kawthoung checkpoint, you must inform the authorities that you're a day visitor if you don't plan on staying overnight – in which case you'll pay a US$10 fee (it must be a crisp bill; long-tail captains can get this from harbour touts for 500B). The only hassle comes from 'helpers' on the Myanmar side, who ask for tips.

If you're just renewing your Thai visa, the whole process takes two hours. When returning to Thailand, bear in mind that Myanmar's time is 30 minutes behind Thailand's. This has previously caused problems for returning travellers who got through Myanmar Immigration before its closing time only to find the Thai immigration post closed. It's worth checking Thai immigration closing hours when leaving the country.

A quicker, easier and much more polished alternative is via the Andaman Club 8km northwest of town, off Rte 4004. At the terminal, you'll get your passport stamped immediately, and a Myanmar-bound speedboat (950B return, 15 minutes each way) leaves hourly from 8.30am to 3.30pm, docking at a flash casino. The whole trip takes one hour.

Moving On

It's possible to stay overnight in one of Kawthoung's overpriced hotels, but you'd probably rather not. If you have a valid Myanmar visa, which you'll have to apply for in advance at the Myanmar Embassy in Bangkok (or a third country), you'll be permitted to stay for up to 28 days and can exit anywhere you like.

There are daily flights from Kawthoung to Yangon.

---

pizzas, meaty mains, Thai curries and international breakfasts, along with beers and foreign liquor.

The B Restaurant THAI, INTERNATIONAL **$$**
(Th Ruangrat; mains 120-390B; ⏲7am-1am; ☎) The B now has two restaurants: an open-air rooftop restaurant in the hotel itself (p596) and this new place on the street which attracts upmarket locals. There's a good choice of Thai food, as well Western classics such as steaks, pizzas, pastas and sandwiches. Live music most nights and a well-stocked bar.

ℹ Information

ATMs are clustered around the intersection of Th Ruangrat and Th Tha Meuang.

EMERGENCY

Police Station (Th Dap Khadi) Ranong's main police station.

IMMIGRATION

Andaman Club Immigration Office (Off Rte 4004; ⏲7am-5pm) The Thai immigration office at the Andaman Club, 8km northwest of town.

Ranong Immigration Office (Th Chalermprakiat; ⏲8.30am-5pm) Main immigration office, 4km southwest of town; handles visa extensions.

Ranong Immigration Post (Tha Saphan Plaa; ⊙8am-5pm) If you're just popping in and out of Myanmar's Kawthoung, visiting this small immigration post, 5km southwest of town, is sufficient.

POST

Post Office (Th Chonrau; ⊙8.30am-4.30pm Mon-Fri, 9am-noon Sat & Sun) You can send mail overseas from here.

TRAVEL AGENCY

Pon's Place (📱081 597 4549; www.ponplace -ranong.com; Th Ruangrat; ⊙8am-7.30pm; 🛜) Friendly Pon's is Ranong's go-to spot for everything from wi-fi and European breakfasts to motorbike rental (200B to 250B), flight bookings, visa runs (1300B), airport pick-ups and bus schedules. You can also arrange a car for day trips to Laem Son National Park (2000B return).

❶ Getting There & Away

Ranong Airport is 22km south of town. Nok Air (www.nokair.com) flies twice daily to Bangkok (Don Mueang).

The **bus terminal** (Th Phetkasem) is 1km southeast of the centre. The blue *sŏrng·tăa·ou* 2 (passenger pick-up truck) passes the terminal. From here, minivans head to Surat Thani (200B, 3½ hours, 6am and 2pm) and Chumphon (160B, two hours, hourly 7am to 5pm).

❶ Getting Around

Motorcycle taxis (Th Ruangrat) cluster along Th Ruangrat and take you almost anywhere in town for 50B, including **Tha Saphan Plaa**, 5km southwest of the centre, for boats to Myanmar, and **Tha Ko Phayam**, 6km southwest of the centre, for Ko Chang and Ko Phayam. The red *sŏrng·tăa·ou* 4 stops near the piers (20B).

Pon's Place helps with motorcycle and car rentals and offers shuttle vans from its office/ the airport to the piers (70/200B).

Ko Chang   เกาะช้าง

The little-visited, rustic isle of Ko Chang is a long way (in every respect) from its much more popular Trat Province namesake. The speciality here is no-frills living, and electricity and wi-fi are still scarce. An all-pervading quiet lies over the island, with the hum of modern life replaced by the sound of the sea. Between May and October (low season) it's beyond mellow and many places shut down.

Wide west-coast **Ao Yai** has gorgeous marbled white-and-black sand in the south, which obscures the otherwise clear sea. White-sand snobs will be happiest on Ao Yai's north end. A short trail leads south over the bluff to **Ao Tadaeng**, a boulder-strewn beach and the island's best sunset spot.

Inland is the tiny village capital, cashew orchards and rubber plantations. Dirt trails wind around and across the island and if you're lucky, you'll spot sea eagles, Andaman kites and hornbills floating above the mangroves.

🏃 Activities

Aladdin Dive Safari   DIVING
(📱087 274 7601; www.aladdindivesafari.com; Cashew Resort, Ao Yai; 2 dives 5800B; ⊙10am-6pm Nov-May) A relatively flash, long-established liveaboard operation that runs day trips to the Surin and Similan Islands, Open Water Dive courses (18,700B to 19,800B) and liveaboards to Myanmar's Mergui Archipelago, the Surins, the Similans, Ko Phi-Phi, Hin Daeng and Hin Muang (15,800B to 19,800B).

BUSES FROM RANONG

DESTINATION	FARE (B)	DURATION (HR)	FREQUENCY
Bangkok	403-627	9-10	7.30am, 8.10am, 10.30am, 1.30pm, 3.30pm, 7.30pm, 8pm (VIP), 8.30pm (VIP)
Chumphon	150	2	hourly 7am-5pm
Hat Yai	380	7	6am, 10am, 8pm
Khao Lak	165	3½	hourly 6.30am-5.45pm
Krabi	210	6	7am, 10am, 2pm
Phang-Nga	180	5	7am, 10am, 2pm
Phuket	225	5-6	hourly 6.30am-5.45pm
Surat Thani	190	4-5	hourly 6am-4pm

Om Tao YOGA
(☑ 085 470 9312; www.omtao.net; Ao Yai; classes 300B) German-run studio with daily yoga (8.30am) November to April. Classes are by request at other times.

🛏 Sleeping & Eating

Simple bamboo huts are the norm. Expect a bed, mosquito net, basic bathroom, hammock, small balcony and little else. Most are only open from November to April. Electricity is limited; some places have solar and wind power.

Most lodgings are in Ao Yai or tucked away on Ao Tadaeng, immediately south. To really get away from it all, head to the northwest coast. The only restaurants are inside the resorts.

★ **Crocodile Rock** GUESTHOUSE $
(☑ 080 533 4138; tonn1970@yahoo.com; Ao Yai; bungalows 400-700B; ☉ Oct-Apr; 🛜) Simple metal-roofed bamboo bungalows with hammocks perched on Ao Yai's serene southern headland with superb bay views. The classy kitchen turns out homemade yoghurt, breads, cookies, good espresso, and a variety of veggie and seafood dishes. It's popular, so book ahead.

Sangsuree Bungalows BUNGALOW $
(☑ 081 2511 7726; bungalow.sangsuree@gmail.com; Ao Takien; bungalows 300-500B; 🛜) Ko Chang's northwest coast is dotted with hidden bays and Sangsuree's seven basic bungalows are positioned just above one of them commanding fine sea views. Run by a charming husband-and-wife team, this is a classic, old-school Thai island chill-out spot, with communal meals and much lazing around. It's a 10 minute walk to a sandy swimming beach.

Little Italy BUNGALOW $
(☑ 084 851 2760; daniel060863@yahoo.it; Ao Yai; r 400-500B; 🛜) Just three immaculate bungalows attached to a Thai-Italian restaurant amid the trees towards the southern end of Ao Yai. Two are stilted split-level concrete-and-wood jobs encircled by wraparound verandahs. The third concrete bungalow is back on earth, with a tiled bathroom. Book ahead in high season.

Sunset Bungalows BUNGALOW $
(☑ 084 339 5224; Ao Yai; bungalows 300-600B; ☉ Oct-mid-Apr) Sweet wooden bungalows with bamboo decks and attached Thai-style bathrooms sit back in the trees along Ao Yai's finest (northern) patch of beach. Staff are as friendly as they come.

ℹ Information

Wi-fi has arrived at a few places, including Koh Chang Resort (southern Ao Yai). Connections are weak.

There are no ATMs.

ℹ Getting There & Around

From the centre of Ranong, *sŏrng·tăa·ou* (20B) and motorcycle taxis (50B) go from Th Ruangrat to Tha Ko Phayam pier near Saphan Plaa, from where two daily long-tail boats (200B, two hours) leave for Ko Chang at 9.30am and 2pm. In high season, they stop at the west-coast beaches, returning at approximately 8.30am and 1pm. During the monsoon, only one long-tail runs, at 2pm, docking at the main pier on the northeast coast.

During the November–April high season, two daily speedboats (350B, 30 minutes, 8.30am and 10.30am) travel between Ranong's Tha Ko Phayam and Ko Chang's northeast-coast pier. In low season, only the 8.30am speedboat runs.

High-season Ko Phayam–Ranong speedboats often drop off and pick up passengers in Ko Chang (350B) on request, though they're unreliable; get your resort to make (and confirm) the booking. You can charter long-tails to Ko Phayam (2000B) through Koh Chang Resort.

Motorcycle taxis meet boats, charging 100B between the northeast-coast pier and Ao Yai.

Ko Phayam เกาะพยาม

Technically part of Laem Son National Park (p602), Ko Phayam is fringed with beautiful soft-white beaches and is becoming increasingly popular as a family destination. If you're coming from Phuket or Ko Phi-Phi, it'll feel refreshingly wild and dozy. The spectacular northwest and southwest coasts are dotted with rustic bungalows, small-scale resorts, breezy sand-side restaurants and barefoot beach bars. Fauna includes wild pigs, monkeys and tremendous bird life (sea eagles, herons, hornbills).

The island's one 'village' (on the east coast, beside the main pier) caters mostly to tourists. But hit it during a festival (say the February Cashew Festival) and you'll see that the locals still have a firm grip on their island.

Narrow motorcycle pathways, concrete roadways and dirt trails run across the island's wooded interior; some are rutted to the point of hazardous – drive slowly.

⊙ Sights & Activities

Ko Phayam is dotted with gorgeous blonde sands, but don't expect to have them to yourself between November and April.

The most impressive beaches are **Ao Yai** (Long Beach), to the southwest, where you can rent boogie boards and surfboards (150B per hour), and **Ao Khao Kwai** (Buffalo Bay) to the northwest, a golden cove with jungle-clad bluffs. **Ao Mea Mai**, south of the pier on the east coast, is OK for swimming and popular with families.

Ko Phayam's main drawback is that the snorkelling isn't great; high sea temperatures have killed off all the coral. But the Surin Islands are close, and you can hop on liveaboard dive expeditions or speedboat transfers. **Phayam Divers** (☑ 086 995 2598; www.phayamlodge.com; Ao Yai; 2 dives 4900B; ⊙ Nov-Apr) offers dive trips to the Surins, plus multiday liveaboards to the Surins, Ko Tachai and Ko Bon, as well as PADI Open Water courses (14,900B). Snorkellers are welcome too.

Wat Phayam   BUDDHIST TEMPLE
(วัดเกาะพยาม; ⊙ dawn-dusk) `FREE` Shrouded in jungle just north of the main pier, on Ko Phayam's east coast, you'll find a majestic golden Buddha flanked by a three-headed *naga* (serpent).

🛏 Sleeping & Eating

Many resorts stay open year-round. It's now more or less standard to have 24-hour power. The west-coast beaches are the most popular places to stay. The east coast is quieter and you're close to the village, but the beaches are not as good.

🛏 Ao Yai   อ่าวใหญ่

Frog Beach House   HOTEL $
(☑ 083 542 7559; www.frogbeachhouse.com; bungalows 500-1400B; 🛜) Well-kept, traditional Thai-style hardwood chalets at the north end of Ao Yai, with wooden floors, outdoor bathrooms, glass-bowl sinks and mosquito nets, line up behind a nice slab of sand beside a small stream.

Bamboo Bungalows   BUNGALOW $$
(☑ 077 820012; www.bamboo-bungalows.com; bungalows 750-2600B; 🛜) Smart, rustic bungalows come with indoor/outdoor bathrooms, some decoration and balconies with hammocks. All are scattered throughout a leafy garden set just back from the middle of lovely Ao Yai. The beachfront restaurant is pretty good and kayaks and boogie boards can be hired. It has 24-hour electricity in high season.

Aow Yai Bungalows   BUNGALOW $$
(☑ 098 313 1777; www.aowyaibungalows.com; bungalows 700-4000B; ❄🛜) This French-Thai operation is the thatched bamboo bungalow pioneer that kicked it all off two decades ago. Choose between decent, rustic small wooden-and-bamboo bungalows amid towering palms and pines, and larger beachfront wood models that sleep three or concrete bungalows. Only the most expensive have air-con. Located at the southeast end of Ao Yai.

Ban Nam Cha   INTERNATIONAL $$
(Ao Yai; mains 100-250B; ⊙ 9am-6.30pm) Twinkling lights, prayer flags and driftwood signs adorn this artsy, easygoing food shack. Tuck into fantastic homemade panini (garlic mushroom, cashew-nut pesto), sandwiches, cakes and a range of Burmese, European and vegetarian treats, and peruse a paperback from the lending library. It's 500m inland from central Ao Yai. Note that hours can vary.

🛏 Ao Khao Kwai   อ่าวเขาควาย

Mr Gao   BUNGALOW $$
(☑ 077 870222; www.mr-gao-phayam.com; bungalows 1000-1800B; @🛜) These sturdy, varnished wood-and-brick or bamboo bungalows are popular with activity-oriented couples and families and are decent-sized coming with mosquito nets, tiled bathrooms and front decks. The owner arranges kayak rental, snorkelling and multiday trips to the Surin Islands. Now has 24-hour electricity, while the most expensive rooms have air-con (you'll pay a hefty surcharge if you want to use it).

Baan Klong Kleng   BUNGALOW $$
(☑ 089 772 5090; www.baanklongkleng.com; r 1300-2000B; ⊙ mid-Oct–Apr; 🛜) Simple,

clean wooden bungalows cascade through trees to a luscious chunk of beach. They're comfy, if not overly exciting, with stylish ceramic-bowl sinks and semi-open bathrooms. The fabulous open-walled beachside **restaurant** (Ao Khao Kwai; mains 150–300B; ⊙8am-10pm mid-Oct-Apr; 🐾🍴) has a fun vibe, dishing up fragrant Thai curries (veg versions available), delicious breakfasts and fusion specials like green-curry pasta.

🏠 Ao Hin Khow อ่าวหินขาว

PP Land BUNGALOW $$
(📞082 806 0413; www.ppland-heavenbeach.com; bungalows 900-1400B; 🐾🖥) 🐾 The concrete bungalows at this Thai-Belgian–owned ecolodge are powered by wind and sun, with 24-hour electricity and hammocks on terraces overlooking the sea. The owners bake cakes, run an organic garden, treat sewage and make their own all-natural laundry detergent.

The drawback is that you're on the least impressive beach on Ko Phayam. The resort is also adults only.

ℹ️ Information

Most resorts have wi-fi, but signals are often weak. There are no ATMs; bring cash with you.

ℹ️ Getting There & Away

Two daily ferries at 9.30am and 2pm travel from Ranong's Tha Ko Phayam (p599), 6km southwest of town, to Ko Phayam (200B, two hours), returning at 8.30am and 3pm. During the November–April high season, speedboats (350B, 35 minutes) make the run almost hourly from 7.30am to 5.30pm, returning to the mainland at 8am, 9am, 9.30am, 11.30am, noon, 3.30pm, 4pm and 4.30pm.

High-season speedboats go from Ko Phayam to Ko Chang (350B, 20 minutes) en route to Ranong at 8.30am, 9am, noon, 12.30pm, 3pm and 3.30pm, though they aren't completely reliable.

ℹ️ Getting Around

Motorcycle taxis from the pier to Ao Khao Kwai/ Ao Yai cost 50/70B. Walking distances are long; it's about 45 minutes from the pier to Ao Khao Kwai, the nearest bay. You can rent motorbikes (around 250B) in the village (best) and from larger resorts; you'll need one to explore properly.

Laem Son National Park อุทยานแห่งชาติแหลมสน

This serene 315-sq-km **national park** (📞077 861431; www.dnp.go.th; adult/child 200/100B; ⊙8am-4.30pm) covers 60km of Andaman coastline (Thailand's longest protected shore) and over 20 islands, including increasingly popular Ko Phayam. It's 85% open sea. Much of the coast is fringed by mangroves and laced with tidal channels, home to fish, deer, macaques, civets, giant squirrels and over 100 bird species, including white-bellied sea eagles.

The most accessible beach is lovely, casuarina-backed 3km **Hat Bang Ben**, home to the park headquarters and accommodation. To the south, peninsulas jut out into the ocean concealing isolated coves accessible only by long-tail. All these beaches are allegedly safe for swimming year-round. From Hat Bang Ben you can see Ko Kam Yai, Ko Kam Noi, Mu Ko Yipun, Ko Khang Khao and, to the north, Ko Phayam. If there's a prettier sunset picnic spot in the northern Andaman, we missed it.

Hat Praphat, 56km south of Hat Bang Ben, is a turtle nesting ground.

Nature trails wind off from the park headquarters, where you can arrange one-day boat trips (2500B, maximum 10 people) to nearby islands. Turn left (south) towards the pier just before park headquarters to access the beach without paying park fees.

At **Wasana Resort** (📞077 861434; www.wasanaresort.org; Hat Bang Ben; bungalow fan/aircon 450/800B; ❄🐾), the welcoming Dutch-Thai owners make a gloriously authentic gado-gado, organise Laem Son day trips, lend bicycles and are full of fantastic ideas for exploring the park (ask about the stunning 10km trek around the headland). The national park offers simple air-conditioned concrete **bungalows and camping** (📞077 861431, in Bangkok 02 562 0760; www.dnp.go.th; Hat Bang Ben; r 1000-1800B, campsite per person 30B, with tent hire 270B; ❄).

ℹ️ Getting There & Away

The Laem Son National Park turn-off is 44km south of Ranong on the west side of Hwy 4, between the Km 657 and Km 658 markers. Buses heading south from Ranong will drop you here (ask for Hat Bang Ben; 50B, one hour). You'll have to flag down a vehicle going towards the park or grab a taxi (200B) at the roadside agency. It's 10km from Hwy 4 to the park entrance.

A return taxi from Ranong is 2000B. Pon's Place (p599) in Ranong can arrange one.

PHANG-NGA PROVINCE

Jungle-shrouded mountains carved up by thick rivers leading to aqua bays sprinkled with sheer limestone karsts and, below, some of Thailand's finest underwater treasures. This is national park territory, with four of Thailand's finest conservation areas in fairly close proximity.

Phang-Nga is very seasonal. From mid-October to mid-April, visitors flood in for the clear waters, snow-white beaches and colourful reefs. But far fewer arrive during the May–October monsoon, leaving you plenty of space.

Khuraburi   คุระบุรี

Blink and you'll miss it. But, if you keep your eyes wide open, you'll enjoy this soulful, dusty, roadside gateway to the Surin Islands. For local inhabitants, Khuraburi is a tiny market town relied on by hundreds of squid fishers. Until the Thai government started cracking down on people smuggling, the surrounding area had an unsavoury reputation as being a key entry point for people being trafficked or smuggled into Thailand from Myanmar.

Andaman Discoveries (☑087 917 7165; www.andamandiscoveries.com; 120/2 Mu 1, Th Phetkasem; 3-day trip per person 6000B; ☺8.30am-5.30pm Mon-Fri) runs award-winning, community-based tours, snorkelling trips to the Surin Islands with the *chow lair* ('sea gypsies'; also spelt *chao leh*), village homestays and ecotours to Khao Sok National Park (p605). It also manages community projects that take volunteers, and can rent bicycles for 150B per day.

If you're sticking around, **Boon Piya Resort** (☑081 752 5457; 175/1 Th Phetkasem; bungalows 650B; ❈🛜) offers spacious, sparkling-clean, modern concrete bungalows with tiled floors, hot-water bathrooms and little balconies. The helpful owner can book transport to/from the Surin Islands and Ko Phra Thong, as can **Tom & Am Tour** (☑086 272 0588; 298/3 Mu 1, Th Phetkasem; ☺24hr).

Don't miss the **morning market** (Th Phetkasem; mains 20-40B; ☺6-10am) at the north end of town: stallholders fry chicken, grill coconut waffles, and bubble kettles with Thai doughnuts to be dipped in thick, sugary green curry.

The small **night market** (Th Phetkasem; mains from 30B; ☺3pm-7.30pm), actually at its peak in the late afternoon, offers noodle dishes and good fried chicken. It's just to the side of the Chinese temple, a 10 minute walk south of town along the highway.

❶ Getting There & Away

Most buses running between Ranong (105B, two hours) and Phuket (150B, four hours) stop in Khuraburi. Take a Phuket-bound bus to Takua Pa (50B, 1¼ hours), 55km south, to transfer to further destinations including Khao Sok National Park.

The pier for the Surin Islands and Ko Phra Thong is 9km northwest of town. Whoever books your boat to the islands will arrange free pier transfer.

Surin Islands Marine National Park

อุทยานแห่งชาติหมู่เกาะสุรินทร์

The five gorgeous isles of the **Surin Islands Marine National Park** (☑076 491378; www.dnp.go.th; adult/child 500/300B; ☺mid-Oct–mid-May) sit 60km offshore, 5km from the Thailand–Myanmar marine border. Healthy rainforest, spectacular white-sand beaches in sparkling, sheltered bays, and rocky headlands that jut into the ocean characterise these granite-outcrop islands.

Superbly clear water in never-ending shades of jade and turquoise makes for easy marine-life spotting, with underwater visibility of up to 30m outside monsoon. These shielded waters attract *chow lair,* an ethnic group of Malay origin who live on Ko Surin Tai during the May–November monsoon. Here they're known as Moken, from the local word *oken* ('salt water').

Ko Surin Tai (south) and Ko Surin Neua (north) are the two largest islands. Park headquarters, an information office (p605) and all visitor facilities are at Ao Chong Khad on southwest Ko Surin Neua. Khuraburi is the park's jumping-off point.

⊙ Sights & Activities

Ban Moken   VILLAGE
(Ao Bon, Ko Surin Tai) Ban Moken on east Ko Surin Tai welcomes visitors. Post-tsunami, the Moken (from the Sea Gypsy ethnic group) have re-settled in this sheltered bay, where a major ancestral worship ceremony, **Loi Reua**, takes place each April. The colourfully carved bamboo poles dotted around embody Moken ancestors. This population experienced no casualties during the 2004 Boxing Day tsunami that wiped out the village, because they understood nature's signs and evacuated to the hilltop.

The Surin Islands Marine National Park runs two-hour trips from Ko Surin Neua to Ban Moken (150B per person, minimum five people). You'll stroll through the stilted village, where you can ask permission/guidance for hiking the 800m **Chok Madah trail** over the jungle-clad hills to an empty beach. Handicrafts for sale help support the local economy and clothing donations are accepted. Please refrain from bringing along alcohol and sweets; alcoholism is a growing problem among Moken.

Diving & Snorkelling

The park's dive sites include **Ko Surin Tai**, **Ko Torinla** (south) and **HQ Channel** between the two main islands. **Richelieu Rock**, a seamount 14km southeast, is also technically in the park and happens to be one of the Andaman's premier dive sites (if not the best). Manta rays pay visits and whale sharks are sometimes spotted here during March and April.

There's no dive facility inside the park, so dive trips (four-day liveaboards from 20,000B) must be booked through centres in Khao Lak, Phuket and Ranong. Transfers are usually included. There's a 200B park diving fee per day, plus the national park fee (adult/child 500/300B), which is valid for five days.

Though recent bleaching of hard corals means snorkelling isn't quite as fantastic as it once was, you'll still see plenty of colourful fish and soft corals. The most vibrant soft corals we saw were at **Ao Mai Yai**, off southwest Ko Surin Neua. There's good snorkelling at **Ao Sabparod** and **Ao Pak Kaad**, where you might spot turtles, off east and south Ko Surin Tai. More fish swim off tiny Ko Pajumba, but the coral isn't great. Ao Suthep, off north Ko Surin Tai, has hundreds of colourful fish.

The nearest decompression chamber is in Phuket. In the case of an accident, dive operators will contact the chamber's Khao Lak–based SSS Ambulance (p611), which meets boats and rushes injured divers south to Phuket.

Half-day snorkelling trips (150B per person, snorkel hire 160B) leave the island headquarters at 9am and 2pm. You'll be mostly in the company of Thais, who generally splash around semi-clothed in life jackets. For more serene snorkelling, charter a long-tail from the national park (3000B per day) or, better yet, directly from the Moken in Ban Moken.

Tour operators in Khuraburi and Khao Lak organise snorkelling day trips to the park (adult/child 3700/2450B).

Greenview Tour   OUTDOORS
(☑ 076 472070; www.toursurinislands.com; 140/89 Mu 3, Khuraburi; ⊙ 7.30am-9pm) Impressive in safety, service and value, Greenview runs excellent Surin Islands snorkelling day trips (adult/child 3500/2100B) with knowledgeable guides. Rates include transfers, snacks, equipment and a delicious lunch. Also organises multi-night stays in the Surins.

Wildlife-Watching & Hiking

Around park headquarters, you can explore the forest fringes and spot crab-eating macaques and some of the 57 resident bird species, including the beautiful Nicobar pigeon, endemic to the Andaman islands, and the elusive beach thick-knee. Along the coast you're likely to see Brahminy kites and reef herons. Twelve species of bat live here, most noticeably the tree-dwelling fruit bat (flying fox).

🛏 Sleeping & Eating

Ko Surin Neua is the only island it is possible to stay on. The **bungalows** (☑ 076 472145; www.dnp.go.th; Ko Surin Neua; r 2000-3000B; campsite per person 80B, with tent hire 300B; ⊙ mid-Oct–mid-May; ✷) are good enough, if over-priced for what you get, although it can feel seriously crowded when full (around 300 people). The clientele is mostly Thai, giving the place a lively holiday-camp vibe. You can also camp here (tents can be hired). Book well in advance.

The two park restaurants, where the accommodation is, serve reasonable Thai food; try **Ao Mai Ngam Restaurant** (Ko Surin

Neua; mains 80-180B, set menu 120-280B; ⊘7.30-9am, noon-2pm & 6.30-8pm).

ℹ Information

Surin Islands Marine National Park Office (Ko Surin Neua; ⊘7.30am-8.30pm mid-Oct–mid-May) Offers information on the islands and accommodation bookings.

ℹ Getting There & Away

If you're not visiting on an organised tour, tour operator speedboats (return 1800B, 1¼ hours one-way) leave around 9am, return between 1pm and 4pm and honour open tickets. Return whenever you please, but confirm your ticket with Ko Surin Neua's park office the night before.

Khao Sok National Park อุทยานแห่งชาติเขาสก

If you've had enough of beach-bumming, venture inland to the wondrous 738-sq-km **Khao Sok National Park** (📞077 395154; www.khaosok.com; Khao Sok; adult/child 300/150B; ⊘6am-6pm). Many believe this lowland jungle (Thailand's rainiest spot) dates back 160 million years, making it one of the world's oldest rainforests, and it's interspersed by hidden waterfalls and caves.

Khao Sok's vast terrain makes it one of the last viable habitats for large mammals. During rainy months you may spot bears, boars, gaurs, tapirs, gibbons, deer, marbled cats, wild elephants and perhaps even a tiger. And you'll find more than 300 bird species, 38 bat varieties and one of the world's largest (and smelliest) flowers, the increasingly rare *Rafflesia kerrii*, which, in Thailand, grows only in Khao Sok.

Animal-spotting aside, the best time to visit is the December–April dry season. During the June–October monsoon, trails get slippery and leeches come out in force. The upside is that the waterfalls are in full flow.

◎ Sights & Activities

Kayaking (800B) and tubing (500B; rainy season) are popular activities. We strongly suggest avoiding the elephant tour.

The road leading 1.8km northeast from Rte 401 to park headquarters (p607) is lined with guesthouses and travel agents offering park tours and guide services. We recommend a two-day, one-night canoeing and hiking trip (2500B; per person) to Chiaw Lan, where you sleep on the lake in floating huts. Book through the park headquarters or any tour agency: the price is the same everywhere.

Chiaw Lan Lake   LAKE
(เขื่อนเชี่ยวหลาน; day/overnight trip 1500/2500B) This stunning 165-sq-km lake sits 65km (an hour's drive) east of park headquarters (p607). It was created in 1982 by an enormous shale-clay dam called Ratchaprapha (Kheuan Ratchaprapha or Chiaw Lan). Limestone outcrops protruding from the lake reach up to 960m, over three times higher than Phang-Nga's formations. Most lake visits involve a day or overnight tour (including transfers, boats and guides).

Charter boats (2000B per day) from local fisherfolk at the dam's entrance to explore the coves, canals, caves and cul-de-sacs along the lakeshore.

Two caves can be accessed by foot from the southwestern shore. **Tham Nam Tha-lu** contains striking limestone formations and subterranean streams. Visiting during the rainy season isn't recommended; there have been fatalities. **Tham Si Ru** features four converging passageways used as a hideout by communist insurgents between 1975 and 1982.

Hiking

Khao Sok hiking is excellent. Most guesthouses and agencies arrange hiking tours (full day 1200B to 2000B); just ensure you find a certified guide (they wear official

---

VILLAGE OF THE DEAD

Ban Sok, the village on the banks of Mae Nam Sok, near the entrance to Khao Sok National Park, has a past so dark it had to rename itself. In the 1940s a vicious wave of smallpox swept through Takua Pa and Phuket, decimating populations. People escaped high into these limestone mountains. Sadly, death followed in such numbers that the village they settled in in 1944 became known as Ban Sop, Village of the Dead. By 1961, when Rte 401 was built to connect Surat Thani with Phang-Nga, the villagers had rebranded, naming their village Ban Sok, which technically means nothing at all.

badges). The park headquarters can also line you up with a reliable guide (1200B per day).

The park headquarters hands out basic hiking maps. You can hike independently from the headquarters to the waterfall at **Wing Hin** (2.8km); hikes to the waterfalls at **Bang Hua Rad** (3km), the 11-tiered waterfall at **Sip-Et Chan** (4km). **Than Sawan** (6km), the most impressive and least-visited waterfall, and **Than Kloy** (7km) require a guide.

🛏 Sleeping

All guesthouses have wi-fi, although connections aren't always great.

Jungle Huts BUNGALOW $
(☑ 077 395160; www.khaosokjunglehuts.com; 242 Mu 6, Khao Sok; r fan/air-con 400/1200B; ﹡ 🞉) This popular hang-out contains a collection of decent, individually styled bungalows, all with bathrooms and porches. Choose from plain stilted bamboo huts, bigger wooden editions, pink-washed concrete bungalows, or rooms along vertiginous walkways.

Tree Tops River Huts BUNGALOW $$
(☑ 081 747 3030; www.treetopsriverhuts.com; 54 Mu 6, Khao Sok; r 500-1200B; ﹡ 🞉) Clean and sturdy, if ageing, simply furnished pebble-dashed bungalows with porches and small bathrooms sit high on stilts in the trees at this riverside spot near the park headquarters. The cheapest are fan-only and more basic, but they do have hot water. The pleasant, semi-open restaurant overlooks the river.

Art's Riverview Jungle Lodge GUESTHOUSE $$
(☑ 090 167 6818; www.info@artsriverviewlodge. com; 54/3 Mu 6, Khao Sok; r 1200-2400B; 🞉) In a monkey-filled jungle bordering a rushing river with a limestone cliff-framed swimming hole, Art's enjoys Khao Sok's prettiest setting. Stilted brick, shingled and all-wood bungalows are spacious and comfy and come with balconies, many offering river views. There's a host of family-friendly activities. It's signposted 1.5km northeast off Rte 401.

Nonguests can visit the swimming hole here, which is also popular with locals and monkeys.

Jasmine Garden RESORT $$$
(☑ 082 282 3209; www.khaosokjasmine.com; 35/6 Mu 6, Khao Sok; d 3800B; ﹡ 🞉 🞉) Family-run Jasmine hosts some of Khao Sok's classiest non-luxury lodgings, plus cooking classes (800B). Five orange-toned concrete bungalows open onto roomy terraces overlooking a warm-blue pool with sensational cliff vistas. Delicate interiors involve wood-carved beds, Buddha paintings, tiled floors and plenty of teak. Book ahead.

★ Elephant Hills RESORT $$$
(☑ 076 381703; www.elephanthills.com; 170 Mu 7, Tambon Klong Sok; 3 days all-inclusive from 20,300B; 🞉 🞉) 🖉 Whether you're a five-strong family, honeymooning backpacker couple or a soloist, this resort makes everyone smile. Above Mae Nam Sok, at the foot of stunning limestone mountains draped in misty jungle, Khao Sok's only top-end tented camp offers rootsy Serengeti-style luxury. It's real glamping: the luxury tents have wood furnishings, full, big bathrooms, skylights and hammocks on porches.

All-inclusive prices cover meals, guided hikes and canoe trips downriver for a night at its elephant camp, where 12 lovely ladies (rescued from other camps where they were forced to carry tourists around) are treated kindly. You get to feed, bathe and spend quality time with them. It's a special experience. Another option is a night at their floating **Rainforest Camp** (Chiaw Lan Lake). Reservations only.

🍴 Eating

★ Pawn's Restaurant THAI $$
(Khao Sok; mains 110-250B; ☉ 9am-10pm; 🖉) A friendly all-female team runs this humble but deservedly popular open-sided eatery: your go-to spot for deliciously spiced curries, from searing red pumpkin-and-veg to beautifully creamy tofu or chicken massaman, and huge hearty breakfasts. It's 500m southwest of the national park headquarters.

Chao Italian Restaurant ITALIAN $$
(☑ 087 264 2106; Khao Sok; mains 100-320B; ☉ noon-10pm; 🞉) The go-to spot for fine,

wood-fired pizzas, cooked by a veteran of Italian restaurants on Phuket, as well pasta, salads and your usual Thai curries, all served by smiley staff underneath a high thatched roof. It's a couple of minutes south of the national park headquarters.

ℹ️ Information

Khao Sok National Park Headquarters

(☑ 077 395154; www.khaosok.com; ⏲ 6am-6pm) About 1.8km northeast off Rte 401, exiting near the Km 109 marker; helpful maps and information.

There are several ATMS along the road leading to the park headquarters.

ℹ️ Getting There & Away

From Surat catch a bus going towards Takua Pa; from the Andaman Coast, take a Surat Thani–bound bus. Buses stop on Rte 401, 1.8km southwest of the visitors centre. If touts don't meet you, you'll have to walk to your chosen guesthouse (50m to 2km). Most minivans will drop you at your accommodation.

There is a daily bus to Bangkok (1000B, 11 hours) at 6pm.

Daily minivan departures include the following:

DESTINATION	FARE (B)	DURATION (HR)
Khao Lak	200	1¼
Ko Lanta	800	5
Ko Tao	1000	8
Krabi	350	3
Phang-Nga	250	2
Surat Thani	200	1

Ko Phra Thong & Ko Ra เกาะพระทอง/เกาะระ

According to legend, pirates buried a golden Buddha beneath the sands at Ko Phra Thong (Golden Buddha Island) many centuries ago. The statue was never found, but the island's modern-day treasures are its endless sandy beaches, mangroves, vast bird life and rare orchids.

Home to around 300 people, this long, slender, wooded island is as quiet as a night on the open ocean. Fishing (squid, prawns, jellyfish) remains its main industry; the local delicacy is pungent gà·bì (fermented prawn paste). On the southern west coast lies 10km of virgin golden-sand beach kissed by blue sea.

Immediately north is barely inhabited Ko Ra, encircled by golden beaches and mangroves. This small isle is a mountainous jungle slab with impressive wildlife, including over 100 bird species, leopard cats, flying lemurs, wild pigs, monitor lizards, scaly anteaters and slow lorises.

🛏️ Sleeping & Eating

Mr Chuoi's   BUNGALOW $

(☑ 087 898 4636, 084 855 9886; www.mrchuoibarandhut.com; Ko Phra Thong; bungalows 500-750B; ☎) Simple, attractive, artsy wood-and-bamboo bungalows, on the island's northwest coast, with evening electricity. You'll also find a tame deer, a fun bar and a decent restaurant, enlivened by Mr Chuoi himself. Call ahead and he'll arrange transport to Ko Phra Thong.

Golden Buddha Beach Resort   BUNGALOW $$$

(☑ 081 892 2208, 081 895 2242; www.goldenbuddharesort.com; Ko Phra Thong; bungalows 3500-8500B; ⏲ Oct-May; ☎) The area's poshest resort attracts yogis, couples and families keen for a secluded getaway. Accommodation is in uniquely designed, naturalistic-chic, privately owned wooden houses, short- or long-term; there are big family-sized house options too. Rooms have open-air bathrooms, wood-carved interiors and glimpses of the fabulous 10km beach through surrounding forest and gardens. Everyone congregates at the mosaic-floored club house restaurant-bar (mains 220-400B; ⏲ 7.30am-9.30pm; 🍴).

Horizon   BUNGALOW $$$

(☑ 081 894 7195; www.horizonecoresort.com; Ko Phra Thong; bungalows 1300-1900B) 🌿 This northwest-beach ecolodge has seven roomy, shaggy-haired, wood-and-bamboo bungalows made from natural local products from renewable sources (wherever possible) and only use fans; they sleep two or four. Horizon organises hiking tours to neighbouring Ko Ra (1600B, minimum three people) and has the island's only dive school, Blue Guru (☑ 096 284 8740; www.blue-guru.org; Ko Phra Thong; 2 dives 4500-6500B; ⏲ Oct-May), ideally positioned for underwater explorations of the nearby Surin Islands.

🛈 Getting There & Away

You could theoretically charter a long-tail from the Khuraburi pier to Ko Phra Thong (return 1500B), but boatmen can be hard to find. For the same price, your accommodation on Ko Phra Thong, or tour operators and guesthouses in Khuraburi, will arrange your transport.

Khao Lak & Around เขาหลัก

When people refer to Khao Lak, they're usually talking about a series of beaches hugging Phang-Nga's west coastline, about 70km north of Phuket. With easy day trips to the Similan and Surin Islands, Khao Sok and Khao Lak/Lam Ru National Parks, or even Phuket, the area makes a central base for exploring the northern Andaman.

Southernmost **Hat Khao Lak** gives way to **Hat Nang Thong**, both within walking distance of Khao Lak proper (Khao Lak Town), a bland but convenient jumble of low-rise hotels, restaurants, bars, shops and tour and dive operators sited along grey Hwy 4.

About 2.5km north, **Hat Bang Niang** is a quieter version of sandy bliss with skinnier beaches. **Hat Pakarang** and **Hat Bang Sak**, 12km to 13km north of Hat Khao Lak, are a sleepy, unbroken sandy stretch surrounded by thick mangroves and rubber-tree plantations. You'll feel like you've really escaped it all there.

◉ Sights

Khao Lak/Lam Ru National Park NATIONAL PARK
(อุทยานแห่งชาติเขาหลัก-ลำรู่; ☑ 076 485243; www.dnp.go.th; adult/child 200/100B; ⊙ 8am-4.30pm) Immediately south of Hat Khao Lak, this vast 125-sq-km park is a collage of sea cliffs, 1000m-high hills, beaches, estuaries, waterfalls, forested valleys and mangroves. Wildlife includes hornbills, drongos, tapirs, serows, monkeys, Bengal monitor lizards and Asiatic black bears.

The park office and visitors centre, 3km south of Khao Lak proper off Hwy 4, has little printed information, but there's a scenic open-air **restaurant** (off Hwy 4, Khao Lak; mains 130-250B; ⊙ 8.30am-7pm) perched on a shady slope overlooking the sea. From here, there's a fairly easy 3km (one-hour) round-trip nature trail south along the cape to often-deserted **Hat Lek**.

🏃 Activities & Tours

Diving and snorkelling day excursions to the Similan and Surin Islands are immensely popular but, if you can, go for a liveaboard. The islands are around 70km from the mainland (1½ hours by speedboat), so liveaboards allow you a more relaxing trip sans masses of day trippers. Dive shops offer liveaboard package trips from around 19,000B for three days and 35,000B for six days, and day trips for 5000B to 6000B.

Day trips normally involve two dives. On the multiday trips, you'll sink below the sea's surface up to four times daily. While both the Similan and Surin Islands have experienced vast coral bleaching in recent years, Richelieu Rock (p604), just north of the Surin Islands, is still the crème de la crème of the region's dive sites, frequented by whale sharks from March to April. **Ko Bon** and **Ko Tachai** are rewarding Similan sites due to the traffic of giant manta rays. Most dive shops welcome snorkellers, and tour operators offer day trips from 3700B.

Open Water certification costs between 10,500B and 16,650B. Beginners can join one-day Similans Discover Scuba trips for around 6000B. Rates exclude the 700B national park diving fee.

The Similan and Surin dive seasons run from mid-October to mid-May, when the national parks are open. Trips in April and May are weather dependent.

★ Fantastic SNORKELLING
(☑ 076 485998; www.fantasticsimilan.com; adult/child 3200/2200B; ⊙ mid-Oct–mid-May) Fantastic is an over-the-top frolic of a Similans snorkelling tour featuring players from the local cross-dressing cabaret as guides. It's a trip duplicated nowhere else on earth; they get you to the prime snorkel sites too. Prices include hotel pick-ups from Phuket or Khao Lak. Bookings essential online or by phone.

★ Wicked Diving DIVING
(☑ 085 795 2221; www.wickeddiving.com; Th Nangthong, Khao Lak; 2 dives 5700B; ⊙ Oct-May) Out to change the world 'one dive at a time', Wicked is an exceptionally well-run, environmentally conscious outfit. It offers diving and snorkelling day and overnight trips (three-day Surin Islands snorkelling trip 12,300B), a range of liveaboards (three-day

Khao Lak

Boat 813 (1.5km); Takieng (1.5km);
International Tsunami Museum (1.6km);
Bed Hostel (1.8km);
Wicked Diving (1.8km);
Takua Pa (31km)

6

7

10

Bus Stop
(Northbound)

4

Khao Lak
Land Discovery

8

ATM

Bus Stop
(Southbound)

5

ANDAMAN SEA

13

Th Phetkasem

12

4

9

4

2

3

11

1

Sea Dragon Dive Centre DIVING
(☑ 076 485420; www.seadragondivecenter.com; Th
Phetkasem, Khao Lak; 2 dives 6000B; ☺9am-9pm)
Khao Lak's oldest dive centre, super-efficient
Sea Dragon maintains high standards, running snorkelling day trips (3500B), wreck
dives (2600B), Open Water Diver certification (10,500B to 15,000B) and an array
of Similan and Surin Islands liveaboards
(three-day trip from 10,500B). Look for the
small swimming pool outside its office.

Khao Lak Land Discovery ADVENTURE
(☑ 076 485411; www.khaolaklanddiscovery.com;
21/5 Mu 7, Th Phetkasem, Khao Lak; ☺8am-
8.30pm) This multilingual agency, one of
Khao Lak's most reliable, runs adventure-
activity day trips (adult/child 2200/1600B)
to Khao Lak/Lam Ru National Park, and
day and overnight excursions into Khao
Sok National Park (two-day trip adult/child
6700/4700B). It can also organise snorkelling trips to the Similan Islands (adult/child
3700/2450B).

🛏 Sleeping

Cheaper accommodation dominates Khao
Lak Town's congested centre, while three-
and four-star resorts line the coast. High-
end hotels dot Hat Pakarang and Hat Bang
Sak. Book ahead if you're planning to be
here in the November–April period.

Similans trip from 19,400B), conservation
trips and a range of dive courses (PADI Open
Water certification costs 16,500B).

Sea Bees DIVING
(☑ 076 485174; www.sea-bees.com; Th Phetkasem,
Khao Lak; 2 dives 2900-4900B; ☺11am-7pm)
Well-organised German-run dive operation
that offers two-dive Similan day trips, one-day
tasters (8500B), Open Water courses (16,650B)
and advanced diver courses, plus Similans
liveaboards (two day trip from 17,500B). Snorkellers can join day trips (2900B).

Walker's Inn　　　GUESTHOUSE **$**

(☎ 084 840 2689; www.walkersinn.com; 26/61 Mu 7, Th Phetkasem, Khao Lak; dm/r 250/600B; 🌣 🛜) A long-running backpacker fave, Walker's is looking its age these days. Rooms are old-fashioned and plain, if big, while the dorm is fan-only. But the price is right. The downstairs pub dishes up hearty breakfasts and Thai and Western classics. It rents motorbikes (200B per day).

Bed Hostel　　　HOSTEL **$**

(☎ 087 387 4050; krittayakorn.d@gmail.com; 6/3 Mu 5, Hat Bang Niang; dm fan/air-con 370/450B, r 1600B; 🌣 🛜) This modest, family-run hostel lacks a communal area, but the compact dorms are clean and come with lockers and it's fine if you just want a place to lay your head, after a day's diving or lazing on the sand. It's a 15-minute walk to the beach.

To Zleep　　　GUESTHOUSE **$$**

(☎ 076 485899; www.tozleep.com; Th Phetkasem, Khao Lak; r 700-1200B; 🌣 🛜) This chequered roadside block is a tasteful, hostel-feel guesthouse full of colourful wall murals and small, spotlessly smart rooms. Some have bunks, others doubles. All come coolly kitted out with minimalist furnishings, concrete floors and colour-on-white themes. It is worth spending more for the biggest and brightest rooms, which are corner mountain-view doubles.

Fasai House　　　GUESTHOUSE **$$**

(☎ 076 485867; www.fasaihouse.com; 5/54 Mu 7, Khao Lak; r 950B; 🌣 @ 🛜) One of Khao Lak's best budget choices, Fasai wins us over with its delightful staff and simple but immaculate, motel-style air-con rooms set in a warm yellow-washed block framing a little pool. It makes a good divers crash-pad. Look for the sign off Hwy 4 towards the northern end of Khao Lak.

Casa de La Flora　　　DESIGN HOTEL **$$$**

(☎ 076 428999; www.casadelaflora.com; 67/213 Mu 5, Hat Bang Niang; r incl breakfast 12,600-30,200B; 🌣 🛜 🏊) Folded into trim seaside grounds dotted with contemporary art, this sleekly modern, well-run belle is composed of smart cube-like glass-and-concrete villas and suites adorned with warm-wood-panelled walls, double-sided mirrors, chunky concrete bathtubs and private plunge pools. Thoughtful touches include iPod docks, in-room espresso machines, hairdryers and, of course, pillow menus. Pod-style lounge beds fringe the sea-view infinity pool.

🍴 Eating

Khao Lak Town and the neighbouring beaches aren't a culinary hot spot, but tourists congregate at a few local haunts to rehash the day's diving. Early-morning divers will struggle to find breakfast before 8.30am.

Go Pong　　　THAI **$**

(Th Phetkasem, Khao Lak; mains 50-140B; ⊙ 10am-11pm) Get a real taste of local flavours at this terrific streetside diner where they stir-fry noodles and sensational spicy rice dishes and simmer aromatic noodle soups that attract a loyal lunch following. Dishes are packed full of flavour.

Takieng　　　THAI **$$**

(26/43 Mu 5, Hat Bang Niang; mains 120-400B; ⊙ noon-10pm; 🛜) Of two open-air Thai

---

THE 2004 TSUNAMI

On 26 December 2004, an earthquake off the Sumatran coast sent enormous waves crashing into Thailand's Andaman Coast, claiming almost 5400 lives (some estimates have it much higher) and causing millions of dollars of damage.

In 2005, Thailand officially inaugurated a national disaster warning system. The public will be warned via the nationwide radio network, dozens of TV channels and SMS messages. For non-Thai speakers, there are warning towers along high-risk beachfront areas that will broadcast announcements in various languages, accompanied by flashing lights.

The wave-shaped **Tsunami Memorial Park** (Ban Nam Khem; ⊙ 24hr) **FREE** in Ban Nam Khem, a squid-fishing village 26km north of Hat Khao Lak that was nearly wiped out, was built to memorialise those who lost their lives. **Boat 813** (Bang Niang) lies 1km inland from Hat Bang Niang where it was deposited by the wave, just around the corner from the **International Tsunami Museum** (พิพิธภัณฑ์สึนามิระหว่างประเทศ; Hwy 4, Bang Niang; adult/child 200/100B; ⊙ 9am-9pm). The moving memorials augment what, for years, were unofficial pilgrimage sites for those who came to pay their respects.

restaurants beneath stilted tin roofs on Hwy 4, 2.5km north of Khao Lak Town, Takieng is the most popular and attractive. It steams fresh fish in sweet green curry, does a scintillating chicken or pork *lâhp*, bubbles up beautifully spiced curries, and fries squid in a delicious chilli paste. Service is impeccable.

Jumbo Steak & Pasta   ITALIAN **$$**
(☑ 098 059 8293; Th Phetkasem, Ban Khukkhuk; mains 80-280B; ⊙10am-10pm) A hole-in-the-wall joint on the west side of Hwy 4, 6km north of Khao Lak proper, launched by a former Le Meridien line chef who does beautiful pasta dishes in all kinds of flavours, plus a host of pizzas and terrific steaks. Dishes are great value in terms of quality, though portions aren't huge.

PhuKhaoLak   INTERNATIONAL, THAI **$$**
(☑ 076 485141; www.phukhaolak.com; Mu 7, Th Phetkasem, Khao Lak; mains 100-350B; ⊙7am-10pm Oct-May; 🛜🌙) With cloth tables spilling to the lawn edge at the south end of Khao Lak's highway strip, this place is hard to miss. And you shouldn't, because there's a never-ending, well-prepared Thai-European menu of fried/grilled/steamed fish, sirloin steaks, pastas and sandwiches, and a dedicated veg section featuring such delights as spicy tofu with peanut sauce.

ℹ Information

Wi-fi is widely available.

ATMs are spread along the coast, along with banks and money-change offices. There is an ATM in the centre of **Khao Lak Town**.

SSS Ambulance (☑ 076 209347, emergency 081 081 9000; ⊙24hr) For diving-related emergencies, the SSS Ambulance rushes injured persons down to **Phuket International Hospital** (Map p620; ☑ 076 361818, 076 249400; www.phuketinternationalhospital.com; 44 Th Chalermprakiat), and can also be used for car or motorcycle accidents.

ℹ Getting There & Around

Any bus between Takua Pa (60B, 45 minutes) and Phuket (120B, two hours) will stop at Hat Khao Lak if you ask. Both **northbound** and **southbound** buses stop and pick up on Hwy 4.

Minivans run daily to Ko Samui (850B, eight hours) at 9am. There are also hourly minivans to Krabi (350B, 3½ hours) from 8am to 4pm. They'll pick you up at your accommodation.

Khao Lak Land Discovery (p609) runs shared minibuses to Phuket International Airport

(600B, 1¼ hours). Alternatively, you can take **Cheaper Than Hotel** (☑ 085 786 1378, 086 276 6479; cheaperkhaolak1@gmail.com; Hwy 4) taxis to Phuket airport (1000B) and points south. Otherwise, taxis cost 1200B from Khao Lak to the airport. Or tell a Phuket-bound bus driver to drop you at the 'airport'; you'll be let off at an intersection from which motorcycle taxis usually take you to the airport (10 minutes, 100B).

Numerous travel agencies and guesthouses rent motorbikes by the day (200B to 250B).

Similan Islands Marine National Park อุทยานแห่งชาติหมู่เกาะสิมิลัน

Known to divers the world over, the beautiful 70-sq-km Similan Islands Marine National Park (☑ 076 453272; www.dnp.go.th; adult/child 500/300B; ⊙mid-Oct–mid-May) lies 70km offshore from Phang-Nga Province. Its smooth granite islands are as impressive above the bright-aqua water as below, topped with rainforest, edged with blindingly white beaches and fringed by coral reefs. Coral bleaching has killed off many hard corals, but soft corals are still intact and the fauna and fish are still there. However, the Similans are now on the tourist trail and many beaches and snorkel sites get packed out with day trippers.

You can stay on Ko Miang (Island 4) and Ko Similan. The park visitors centre (p613) and most facilities are on Ko Miang. The islands all have names, but are more commonly known by their numbers.

Hat Khao Lak is the park's jumping-off point. The pier and mainland national park headquarters (p613) are at Thap Lamu, 12km south (Hwy 4, then Rte 4147).

🏃 Activities

Diving & Snorkelling

The Similans offer diving for all levels, at depths from 2m to 30m. There are rock reefs at Ko Hin Pousar (Island 7) and dive-throughs at Hin Pousar (Elephant Head Rock), with marine life ranging from tiny plume worms and soft corals to schooling fish, manta rays and rare whale sharks. Ko Bon and Ko Tachai are two of the better diving and snorkelling areas. There are dive sites at each of the six islands north of Ko Miang. The park's southern section (Islands 1, 2 and 3) is an off-limits turtle nesting ground.

Similan Islands Marine National Park

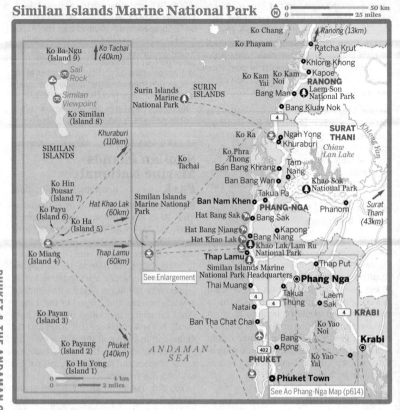

No facilities for divers exist in the national park, so you'll be taking a dive tour. Dive schools in Hat Khao Lak book day trips (two dives 6000B) and liveaboards (three-/six-day trip from around 19,000/35,000B), as do Phuket dive centres (two-dive day trip from 5600B, three-day liveaboard from 18,900B).

Agencies in Khao Lak offer snorkelling-only day trips that visit three or four sites from 3200B.

Wildlife-Watching & Hiking

The forest around Ko Miang's visitors centre has some walking trails and great wildlife. The fabulous Nicobar pigeon, with its wild mane of grey-green feathers, is common here. It's one of the park's 39 bird species. Hairy-legged land crabs and fruit bats (flying foxes) are relatively easy to spot in the forest, as are flying squirrels.

A small beach track, with information panels, leads 400m east from the visitors centre to a tiny snorkelling bay. Detouring from the track, the Viewpoint Trail, about 500m or 30 minutes of steep scrambling, has panoramic vistas from the top. A 500m (20-minute) walk west from the visitors centre leads through forest to smooth west-facing granite platform Sunset Point.

On Ko Similan, there's a 2.5km forest hike to a viewpoint, and a shorter, steep scramble off the north-coast beach to Sail Rock (Balance Rock), during daylight it's clogged with visitors.

🍴 Sleeping & Eating

You will need to book at least two to three months ahead to guarantee a bed or a tent.

A restaurant (Ko Miang (Island 4); mains 120-150B, lunch buffet 230B; ⏰ 7.30am-8.30pm) beside the park office on Ko Miang serves simple Thai food. There's another one on Ko Similan for those staying the night.

Similan Islands Marine National Park

Accommodation BUNGALOW **$$**

(✆076 453272, in Bangkok 02 562 0760; www.dnp.go.th; Ko Miang (Island 4); r fan/air-con 1000/2000B, campsite with tent hire 570B; ⊘mid-Oct–mid-May; ❀) On Ko Miang, there are 20 bungalows, the best with balconies, or tents. You are paying for the location: the bungalows are simple. During the day, many tour groups will drop by. Electricity operates 6pm to 6am.

Book ahead online, by phone or through the mainland park headquarters at Thap Lamu. If you are camping, bring repellent: the mosquitoes are ferocious.

❶ Information

Similan Islands Marine National Park Headquarters (✆076 453272; www.dnp.go.th; 93 Mu 5, Thap Lamu; ⊘8am-5pm mid-Oct–mid-May) You can book accommodation on the Similan Islands well in advance with this office south of Khao Lak.

Similan Islands Marine National Park Visitors Centre (Ko Miang (Island 4); ⊘7.30am-8pm mid-Oct–mid-May) Visitors centre on Ko Miang.

❶ Getting There & Away

There's no official public transport to the Similans. Theoretically, independent travellers can book return speedboat transfers (2000B, 1½ hours each way) with a Khao Lak day-trip operator, though they discourage independent travel. Most will collect you from Hat Khao Lak, but if you book through the national park you'll have to find your own way to the office in Thap Lamu and wait for a pier transfer.

Dive centres and tour agents in Hat Khao Lak and Phuket book day/overnight tours (from 4900/8500B), dive trips (three-day liveaboards from 10,500B to 19,000B) and multiday trips including park transport, food and lodging, which cost little more than what you'd pay getting to and staying on the islands independently.

Natai นาใต้

✆076

Officially in Phang-Nga Province, Natai's spiritual home is high-end Phuket, but reality it's even more flash and fabulous. Just 26km north of Phuket International Airport, this luxury bolt-hole lies within easier reach of Phuket than parts of Phuket itself. There's little else out here yet, apart from a delicious broad blonde beach that disappears into turquoise waters and which some of southern Thailand's most exclusive restaurants and lodgings gaze out upon. Don't bother turning up unless your pockets are very deep.

🛏 Sleeping & Eating

★**Iniala Beach House** DESIGN HOTEL **$$$**

(✆076 451456; www.iniala.com; 40/14 Mu 6, Ban Natai; d full-board US$2200-3100; ❀ 🛜 ❀) From expertly concocted passion-fruit welcome drinks to highly personal service, in-house dining and bold, one-of-a-kind futuristic design, Iniala oozes cool, creativity and sophistication. This is southern Thailand's most luscious design property. It took 10 designers to create the 10 uniquely fashioned rooms, tucked into three self-contained three-suite villas and a penthouse, with skinny dark-tiled infinity pools meandering to Natai's beautiful beach.

Aleenta BOUTIQUE HOTEL **$$$**

(✆in Bangkok 02 514 8112; www.aleenta.com; 33 Mu 5, Ban Natai; r incl breakfast 24,900-77,100B; ❀ 🛜 ❀) Sleek loft-style rooms spill out into shared infinity pools through floor-to-ceiling windows. Boardwalks criss-cross lily ponds to secluded, uber-chic villas and suites, where private pools reflect soaring palms. Split-level quadruples with kitchenettes are ideal for families. Swish cabanas dot the black-tiled seafront infinity pool and there's an elegant spa.

Esenzi SEAFOOD **$$$**

(✆076 451456; www.esenzirestaurant.com; 40/14 Mu 6, Ban Natai; mains 700-2000B; ⊘6pm-11pm Tue-Sat; 🛜) Seafood from around the world is the theme at Esenzi, the latest incarnation of the acclaimed restaurant at Iniala Beach House. The menu moves between Europe, Japan and the US, as well as Thailand. If you're feeling flush, the eight-course tasting menu (8000B) is the way to go. Super service and wine list.

❶ Getting There & Away

Taxis to/from Phuket airport cost 700B. Alternatively, you can rent a car at the airport (from 1454B per day) and drive here yourself.

Ao Phang-Nga

0 —— 10 km
0 —— 5 miles

PHANG-NGA · Thap Put · Phang Nga · Takua Thung · Tha Dan · Tha Surakul · Ao Luk · Ko Panyi · Laem Sak · Ko Khao Phing Kan (James Bond Island) · Ao Phang-Nga · Ao Luk · Ao Phang-Nga National Park · Ko Yao Noi · Ban Tha Khao · KRABI · Tha Manok · Tha Khao · Bang Rong · Tha Klong Hia · Ao Tha Len · Tha Len · Ao Nang · Tha Bang Rong · PHUKET · Ko Yao Yai · Phuket Town · Tha Rassada · ANDAMAN SEA · Ko Phi Phi Don

Ao Phang-Nga
อ่าวพังงา

Between turquoise bays peppered with craggy limestone towers, brilliant-white beaches and tumbledown fishing villages, Ao Phang-Nga is one of the Andaman's most spectacular landscapes. Little wonder then that it was here, among looming cliffs and swifts' nests, that James Bond's nemesis, Scaramanga (*The Man with the Golden Gun*), chose to build his lair. Modern-day wanted assassins with world-domination goals would doubtless skip the place, as it's swarming with tourists, motorboats and sea kayaks year-round.

Phang-Nga
พังงา

📞 076 / POP 10,800

Phang-Nga is an unremarkable small town set against sublime limestone cliffs. There isn't much to see or do unless you're here during the annual **Vegetarian Festival** (late September or October), and it's very much a staging post for people heading further north to Khao Lak (p608) or Khao Sok National Park (p607). Hotels and amenities are mostly on Th Phetkasem.

☞ Tours

Although it's fun to create your own Ao Phang-Nga itinerary by chartering a boat, it's easier (and cheaper) to join a tour with one of Phang-Nga's agencies, most of which are at the bus station. Quality varies, but all offer near-identical itineraries and prices.

Sayan Tours   BOATING
(📞090 708 3211, 076 430348; www.sayantour. com; Old Bus Station, off Th Phetkasem; half/full day 800/1100B; ⊗7am-9pm) A long-standing Ao Phang-Nga tour company offering day trips to Ko Panyi, Ko Phing Kan and Tham Lod (covered in stalactites), and overnight stays on Ko Panyi (1950B).

Mr Kean Tour   BOATING
(📞089 871 6092; Old Bus Station, off Th Phetkasem; half/full day 800/1100B; ⊗7am-6pm) Mr Kean has been running tours of Ao Phang-Nga for over 25 years. Half- and full-day tours include Tham Lod, Ko Phing Kan and Ko Panyi. You can add kayaking (300B per person) and trekking, or spend the night on Ko Panyi (1750B).

🛏 Sleeping & Eating

Several food stalls along Th Phetkasem sell delicious *kà·nŏm jeen* (thin wheat noodles) with chicken curry, *nám yah* (spicy ground-fish curry) or *nám prík* (spicy sauce). There's a small **night market** (Th Phetkasem; mains from 30B; ⊗4-9pm) on Th Phetkasem, beside the 7-Eleven.

Thaweesuk Hotel   GUESTHOUSE $
(📞076 412100; www.thaweesukhotel.com; 79 Th Phetkasem; r incl breakfast with fan/air-con 450/800B; ☀✻🤶) A friendly family-run place in a historic building with a colourful mosaic-floor lobby, on north Th Phetkasem. Ground-floor cold-water fan/air-con rooms are simple, compact and clean. Hot-water air-con pads on the first floor are rather more stylish with varnished-wood floors. There's also a four-bed family room. Breakfast is downstairs in the lounge-like lobby.

The Sleep   HOTEL $$
(📞076 411828; 144 Th Phetkasem; r 600-1000B; ✻🤶) This brand new hotel offers the most modern rooms in Phang-Nga, decked out in white and dark wood with comfortable beds, TVs and fridges, although the bathrooms are very tight. There's a terrace for free morning coffee.

ⓘ Getting There & Away

The nearest airport to Phang-Nga is in Phuket, a 1½-hour drive away.

Phang-Nga's **bus terminal** (Th Phetkasem) is 4km south of the town centre. Motorcycle taxis charge a flat 50B to/from the station.

Minivans run to Khao Sok National Park (250B, two hours) at 8.30am, 10.30am, noon, 2pm, 3.30pm and 5.30pm. They'll drop you at your accommodation.

Buses for Takua Pa (150B, 1½ hours), where you can connect for Khao Lak, as well as Ranong and Khao Sok National Park, leave at 8am, 10am, 11am, noon, 2pm and 5.20pm.

Ao Phang-Nga Marine National Park อุทยานแห่งชาติอ่าวพังงา

The classic karst scenery of the 400-sq-km **Ao Phang-Nga National Park** (☏ 076 481188; www.dnp.go.th; adult/child 300/100B; ⊙8am-4pm) was famously featured in the James Bond movie *The Man with the Golden Gun*. Huge vertical cliffs frame 42 islands, some with caves accessible only at low tide. The bay is composed of large and small tidal channels, which run north to south through Thailand's largest remaining primary mangrove forests.

Ao Phang-Nga's marine limestone environment conceals reptiles like Bengal monitor lizards, two-banded monitors, flying lizards, banded sea snakes, shore pit vipers and Malayan pit vipers. Mammals include serows, crab-eating macaques, white-handed gibbons and dusky langurs.

In high season (November to April) the bay becomes a clogged day-tripper superhighway. But if you visit in the early morning (ideally from the Ko Yao islands) or stay out later, you might just find a slice of beach, sea and limestone karst of your own. The best way to explore is by kayak.

⊙ Sights & Activities

You can charter boats to explore Ao Phang-Nga's half-submerged caves and oddly shaped islands from Tha Dan, 9km south of central Phang-Nga. Expect to pay 1500B to 2000B for a half-day tour.

Two- to three-hour tours (1000B per person) head to well-trodden **Ko Phing Kan** (เกาะเขาพิงกัน, James Bond Island), **Ko Panyi** (เกาะปันหยี) and elsewhere in the park. Tha Surakul, 13km southwest of Phang-Nga in Takua Thung, has private boats for hire at similar prices to tours. From the national park headquarters, you can hire boats (1400B, maximum four passengers) for three-hour islands tours. From Phuket, John Gray's Seacanoe (p625) is the top choice for Ao Phang-Nga kayakers.

🛏 Sleeping & Eating

Most people visit on day tours from either the Ko Yao islands, Phuket or Phang-Nga.

Ao Phang-Nga National Park Accommodation   BUNGALOW **$$** (☏ 076 481188, in Bangkok 02 562 0760; www.dnp. go.th; Rte 4144; bungalows 800-1000B) Simple air-con bungalows sleep two to three, in quiet shady grounds 8.5km south of central Phang-Nga. There's a basic waterside Thai restaurant.

ⓘ Getting There & Away

From central Phang-Nga, drive 7km south on Hwy 4, turn left onto Rte 4144 and travel 2.6km to the park headquarters in Tha Dan. Opposite the headquarters is the jetty where you can hire boats to explore the park. Otherwise take a *sǒrng·tǎa·ou* to Tha Dan (30B).

BUSES FROM PHANG-NGA

DESTINATION	FARE (B)	DURATION (HR)	FREQUENCY
Bangkok (VIP)	829	12	4pm, 5pm, 7pm, 8pm
Bangkok (1st class)	533-622	12	8.40am, 3pm, 4.30pm, 5.30pm, 6.30pm, 7.30pm
Hat Yai	265	6	8.50am, 9.50am, 10.50am, 12.50pm, 1.50pm
Krabi	80	1½	hourly 7.30am-6pm
Phuket	80	1½	hourly 5.30am-5.30pm
Ranong	170	5	10.15am
Surat Thani	150	4	9.30am, 11.30am, 1.30pm, 3.30pm
Trang	175	3½	hourly 8am-4.20pm

LOCAL KNOWLEDGE

ANCIENT ROCK ART

Many of Ao Phang-Nga's limestone islands have prehistoric rock art painted on or carved into cave walls and ceilings, rock shelters, cliffs and rock massifs. You can see rock art at Khao Khian, Ko Panyi, Ko Raya, Tham Nak and Ko Phra At Thao. Images at **Khao Khian** (the most visited cave-art site) contain human figures, fish, crabs, prawns, bats, birds and elephants, as well as boats, weapons and fishing equipment, seemingly referencing some communal effort tied to the all-important sea harvest. Most rock paintings are monochrome, though some have been traced in orange-yellow, blue, grey and black.

Ko Yao   เกาะยาว

With mountainous backbones, unspoilt shorelines, hugely varied birdlife and a population of friendly Muslim fisherfolk, Ko Yao Yai and Ko Yao Noi are relaxed vantage points for soaking up Ao Phang-Nga's beautiful karst scenery. The islands are part of Ao Phang-Nga National Park (p615), but can be accessed from Phuket and elsewhere easily.

Ko Yao Noi is the main population centre, despite being smaller than its neighbour, with fishing, coconut farming and tourism sustaining its small, year-round population. It's not a classic beach destination: bays on the east coast, where most resorts are, recede to mudflats at low tides. Nevertheless, **Hat Pasai** (Ko Yao Noi), on the southeast coast, and **Hat Paradise** (Ko Yao Noi), on the northeast coast, are both gorgeous.

Ko Yao Yai is twice the size of its sibling and wilder. The most accessible beaches are **Hat Lo Pared** (Ko Yao Yai), on the southwest coast, and powder-white **Hat Chonglard** (Ko Yao Yai) on the northeast coast.

🏃 Activities

One-day three-island snorkelling tours (2000B) of Ao Phang-Nga are easily arranged through guesthouses or at the piers.

Kayaks (500B per day) are widely available on Ko Yao Noi, including at Sabai Corner.

Amazing Bike Tours (p625) runs popular small-group day trips to Ko Yao Noi from Phuket. If you're keen to explore the numerous dirt trails on Ko Yao Noi or Ko Yao Yai independently, most guesthouses rent bikes (250B per day), though they're more readily available on Ko Yao Noi.

Elixir Divers   DIVING
(☎ 087 897 0076; www.elixirdivers.com; 2/3 Mu 3, Ko Yao Yai; 2 dives 2900-3900B; ⊙ Oct-Apr) Ko Yao Yai's only dive school is an on-the-ball operator covering a range of PADI courses, two-dive day trips locally and to Ko Phi-Phi, and liveaboards to Hin Daeng, Hin Muang and the Similans (22,900B), plus snorkelling excursions to Ao Phang-Nga, Krabi and Ko Phi-Phi.

If you're staying on Ko Yao Noi, they'll help with transfers.

Mountain Shop Adventures   CLIMBING
(☎ 083 969 2023; www.facebook.com/mountainshopadventures; Tha Khao, Ko Yao Noi; half-day 3200B; ⊙ 9am-7pm) There are over 150 climbs on Ko Yao Noi; Mountain Shop owner Mark has routed most of them himself. Trips range from beginner to advanced and many involve boat travel to remote limestone cliffs. His ramshackle office is just down the road from the Tha Kao pier. It's best to contact him in advance.

Island Yoga   YOGA
(☎ 087 387 9475; www.thailandyogaretreats.com; 4/10 Mu 4, Hat Tha Khao, Ko Yao Noi; classes 600B) This popular yoga school hosts daily drop-in classes at 10am, as well as scheduled classes at 7.30am and 4.30pm. Also does multiday yoga and tai chi retreats.

🛏 Sleeping & Eating

Almost all accommodation on Ko Yao Noi is on the east coast. The farther north you go, the wilder the roads get and shops and restaurants are very thin on the ground. Ko Yao Yai has fewer sleeping and eating choices.

🛏 Ko Yao Noi

Hill House   BUNGALOW $$
(☎ 089 593 9523; www.hillhouse-kohyaonoi.com; Hat Tha Khao, Ko Yao Noi; r 1100-1300B; 🐾) A friendly, simple hillside spot where well-kept, dark-wood, hot-water, fan-cooled bungalows are swathed in mosquito nets and have beautiful views through trees to Ao Phang-Nga's limestone karsts from hammock-loaded terraces.

Sabai Corner Bungalows GUESTHOUSE $$
(📞076 597497; www.sabaicornerbungalows.com; Hat Khlong Jark, Ko Yao Noi; bungalows 1000-1900B; 🛜) Pocketed into a rocky headland, these no-fuss bungalows with whizzing fans, mosquito nets and hammocks on terraces are blessed with gorgeous sea views. One oddity is that there are no connecting doors to the bathrooms; you have to go outside to reach them. The good, chilled-out waterside **restaurant** (mains 95-300B; ⊙8am-10pm; 🛜) is a bubbly place to hang out; kayaks for rent.

Ko Yao Island Resort RESORT $$$
(📞076 597474; www.koyao.com; 24/2 Mu 5, Hat Khlong Jark, Ko Yao Noi; villas 7400-19,900B; ❄@🛜≋) Open-concept thatched bungalows offer serene views across a palm-shaded garden and beach-facing infinity pool to a white strip of sand. We love the graceful, airy, safari-like feel of the villas, with their fan-cooled patios and indoor/outdoor bathrooms. There's a snazzy bar-restaurant area and service is stellar.

Suntisook BUNGALOW $$$
(📞075 582750, 089 781 6456; www.facebook.com/suntisookkoyaonoi; 11/1 Mu 4, Hat Tha Khao, Ko Yao Noi; r 2000-2200B; ❄🛜) Suntisook's comfy and fresh varnished-wood bungalows are sprinkled across an attractive garden just metres from a quiet beach. They're not huge, but all have spacious hammock-laden verandahs, fridges and pot plants. It's run efficiently by a helpful English-speaking Thai family, who offer a good authentic **restaurant** (mains 60-150B; ⊙7.30am-9pm; 🛜) and kayak hire. It sometimes closes for parts of the low season (May to October).

Chaba Café INTERNATIONAL $
(📞087 887 0625; Hat Khlong Jark, Ko Yao Noi; mains 80-220B; ⊙9am-5pm Mon-Sat; 🍴) Rustic-cute Chaba is a haven of pastel-painted prettiness, with driftwood walls, mellow music and a small gallery. Organic-oriented offerings include honey-sweetened juices, coconut-milk-and-avocado shakes, chrysanthemum tea and home-baked paninis, cookies and cakes, plus soups, pastas and Thai dishes. It's just beyond northern Hat Khlong Jark.

Pizzeria La Luna ITALIAN $$
(📞085 0689 4326; btwn Hat Khlong Jark & Hat Tha Khao, Ko Yao Noi; mains 170-320B; ⊙3pm-10pm;

🛜) There's a big range of wood-fired pizzas, including veggie choices, at this laid-back, semi-open-air roadside eatery, as well as homemade pasta, salads, cakes and antipasto in high season (October to May). It's an equally good place to sip a cocktail, with a proper wooden bar to sit at.

★**Rice Paddy** INTERNATIONAL, THAI $$$
(📞076 454255, 082 331 6581; Hat Pasai, Ko Yao Noi; mains 180-890B; ⊙noon-10pm & 6-10pm May-Oct; 🛜🍴) On the roadside corner at the southwest end of Hat Pasai, this sweet, all-wood, German-owned Thai-international kitchen is very special. Flash-fried *sôm·đam* (spicy green papaya salad), fantastic falafel and hummus, spicy, fruit enhanced curries served in clay pots and fresh salads are all delicious. They do excellent veggie dishes too, as well as decent cocktails.

At the time of research, there were rumours the restaurant would move to a new location on the island.

🛏 Ko Yao Yai

Thiwson Beach Resort BUNGALOW $$$
(📞081 956 7582; www.thiwsonbeach.com; 58/2 Mu 4, Hat Chonglard, Ko Yao Yai; r incl breakfast 2000-3600B; ❄🛜≋) Easily the sweetest of the island's humbler bungalow properties. Here are proper wooden thatch- or tin-topped huts with polished floors, outdoor bathrooms and wide patios overlooking the

---

SUSTAINABLE SPA

Need to get the rock climbing, kayaking and biking thoroughly massaged out of your system? Look no further than the back-to-nature elegance of **Six Senses Spa** (📞076 418500; www.sixsenses.com; 56 Mu 5, btwn Hat Khlong Jark & Hat Tha Khao, Ko Yao Noi; treatments 4200-25,000B; ⊙8am-9pm). Therapists at the stilted 'spa village' are trained in massage and organic-fuelled treatments from China, India and Thailand. Prolong the pampering with an overnight stay in one of the five-star property's 56 hillside **pool villas** (📞076 418500; www.sixsenses.com; 56 Mu 5, btwn Hat Khlong Jark & Hat Tha Khao, Ko Yao Noi; villa incl breakfast 35,000-66,000B; ❄🛜≋) 🍃. Bonus: the resort has impressive commitment to sustainability.

island's prettiest, northeast-coast beach, fronted by an aqua pool. Beachfront bungalows are biggest, but fan rooms are excellent low-season value.

Glow Elixir
RESORT $$$

(☎ 087 808 3838; www.glowhotels.com/elixir; 99 Mu 3, Prunai, Ko Yao Yai; bungalows incl breakfast 9100-23,200B; ✳@ ☎ ☳) Beside its own silky beach in the southwest corner of the island, the oldest of Yao Yai's four-star resorts offers tasteful beachfront and hillside peaked-roof villas steeped in classic Thai style: dark-wood floors, outdoor showers and fish-patterned ceramic-bowl sinks. Some have private pools. You'll also enjoy a high-season dive centre (p616), massage pagodas and spectacular sunsets over Phuket.

Koh Yao Yai Village
RESORT $$$

(☎ 076 363700; www.kohyaovillage.com; 78 Mu 4, Ko Yao Yai; r 4300-10,200B; ✳ ☎ ☳) This eco-friendly resort is upmarket without being over the top price-wise. It offers very big, light, elegantly furnished villas with outdoor bathrooms set high in the trees for spectacular sea views towards Phuket. There's also a tremendous infinity pool, spa, on-site restaurant and you're handily placed to access Hat Chonglard, the best beach on the island.

ⓘ Information

There are ATMs in Ta Khao, Ko Yao Noi's largest settlement, and a few more dotted along the east coast. There's also an ATM at Tha Bang Rong (p623) pier on Phuket, where boats to Ko Yao depart from.

On Ko Yao Yai, there are a handful of ATMs. It's wise to take money with you; otherwise you'll have to head back to Tha Bang Rong to cash up.

ⓘ Getting There & Away

TO/FROM AO NANG

From November to April, there's an 11am speed-boat from the pier at Hat Noppharat Thara to Ko Yao Noi and Ko Yao Yai (both 650B, 45 minutes). It continues to Phuket's Tha Bang Rong, returning at 3pm.

TO/FROM KO PHI-PHI

Three weekly speedboats run to/from Ko Phi-Phi (500B) and Ko Lanta (500B) from October to April.

TO/FROM KRABI

From 9am to 5.30pm daily, there are frequent long-tails (150B) between Ko Yao Noi's Tha

Khao and Krabi's Tha Len (33km northwest of Krabi Town). *Sŏrng·tăa·ou* (100B) run between Tha Len and Krabi's Th Maharat via Krabi's bus terminal.

TO/FROM PHANG-NGA

From Tha Dan in Phang-Nga there's a 1pm ferry to Ko Yao Noi (200B, 1½ hours), returning at 7.30am.

TO/FROM PHUKET

From Phuket's Tha Bang Rong, there are daily speedboats (200B, 30 minutes) to Ko Yao Noi at 7.50am, 8.40am, 9.15am, 9.50am, 10.30am, 11.30am, 1.30pm, 2.30pm, 5pm and 5.40pm, plus long-tails (120B, one hour) at 9.15am, 12.30pm and 5pm. Some stop en route at Tha Klong Hia on Ko Yao Yai (200B, 25 minutes). Boats return to Phuket between 6.30am and 4.40pm.

Taxis run from Tha Bang Rong to Phuket's resort areas for 600B to 800B, and *sŏrng·tăa·ou* (40B) leave for Phuket Town at 7am, 8.30am, 11am and 2.30pm daily.

ⓘ Getting Around

Frequent shuttle boats run from Ko Yao Noi's Tha Manok to Ko Yao Yai's Tha Klong Hia (50B). On the islands, *túk-túk* rides cost about 150B, and most guesthouses rent motorbikes (250B to 300B per day). It's 100B for *sŏrng·tăa·ou* transport to the resorts.

PHUKET PROVINCE

First, let's get the pronunciation right. The 'h' in Phuket (ภูเก็ต) is silent. And then remember that this is the largest Thai island, so you rarely feel surrounded by water. But that means there is space for everyone.

Phuket offers such a rich variety of experiences – beach-bumming, culture, diving, fabulous food, hedonistic or holistic pleasures – that visitors are spoilt for choice. Each beach is different, from the upmarket resorts of Surin and Ao Bang Thao to family-oriented Rawai, or the sin city of Patong, home of hangovers and go-go girls.

ⓘ ECOFRIENDLY TOURS

We recommend opting for a bike tour (p625) instead of supporting the questionable animal-welfare and environmental standards of Phuket's elephant ride and 4WD tour operators.

But there's also the culturally rich east-coast capital Phuket Town, as well as wildlife sanctuaries and national parks in the north.

 Activities

There's no shortage of adrenaline-fuelled activities on Phuket, from bungee jumps to zip lines. Equipment quality and safety levels vary, and there have been serious, even fatal, accidents. Ask for recommendations and don't proceed if you have any doubts.

Diving & Snorkelling

Phuket enjoys an enviable central location relative to the Andaman Sea's top diving destinations. The much-talked-about Similan Islands lie 100km northwest, while dozens of dive sites orbit Ko Phi-Phi and Ko Lanta, 40km and 72km southeast. Trips from Phuket to these awesome destinations cost slightly more than from places closer to the sites, as you'll be forking out extra baht for transport costs.

Most Phuket operators take divers to the nine decent sites orbiting the island, including **Ko Raya Noi** and **Ko Raya Yai** (Ko Racha Noi and Ko Racha Yai), but these spots rank lower on the wow-o-meter. The reef off the southern tip of Raya Noi is the best among them, with soft corals and pelagic fish species aplenty, though it's usually reserved for experienced divers. Manta and marble rays are frequently glimpsed here and, if you're lucky, you might spot a whale shark.

One-day, two-dive trips to nearby sites start at 3000B. Non-divers and snorkellers can usually tag along for a significant discount. Open Water Diver certification costs 11,480B to 18,400B for three days' instruction. Some schools charge 500B extra for equipment.

From Phuket, you can join a huge range of liveaboard diving expeditions to the Similan Islands (p611) and Myanmar's Mergui Archipelago.

Snorkelling isn't wonderful off Phuket proper, though mask, snorkel and fins (200B per day) are available for rent in most resort areas. As with diving, you'll find better snorkelling (with greater visibility and variety of marine life) along the shores of small outlying islands, such as Ko Raya Yai and Ko Raya Noi.

Like elsewhere in the Andaman Sea, the best diving months are November to April, when weather is good and seas smooth and clear, though most dive shops power on (weather permitting) through the low season, with good discounts.

Recommended dive schools have branches across Phuket, including in Patong (p635), Kata (p641) and Karon (p643).

Surfing

Phuket is an under-the-radar surf destination. With the monsoon's midyear swell, glassy seas fold into barrels. The best waves arrive between June and September, when annual competitions are held on Hat Kata Yai (p640), Phuket's most popular surf spot, and Hat Kalim, just north of Patong. Phuket Surf (p641) is based at the south end of Kata Yai near the best break, which tops out at 2m. **Hat Nai Han** (หาดในหาน; Map p633) gets bigger waves (up to 3m), in front of the yacht club. Both Kata and Nai Han have vicious undertows that can claim lives.

Hat Kalim is sheltered and has a consistent break that gets up to 3m. This is a hollow wave, and is considered the best break on the island. The northernmost stretch of Hat Kamala (p644) has a nice 3m beach break. **Laem Singh** (แหลมสิงห์), 1km north, gets very big and fast waves, plus it's sheltered from wind by a massive headland. Hat Surin (p645) gets some of Phuket's most challenging waves.

Hat Nai Yang (p649) has a consistent (if soft) wave that breaks more than 200m offshore. **Hat Nai Thon** gets better-shaped

PHUKET & THE ANDAMAN COAST AO PHANG-NGA

Phuket Province

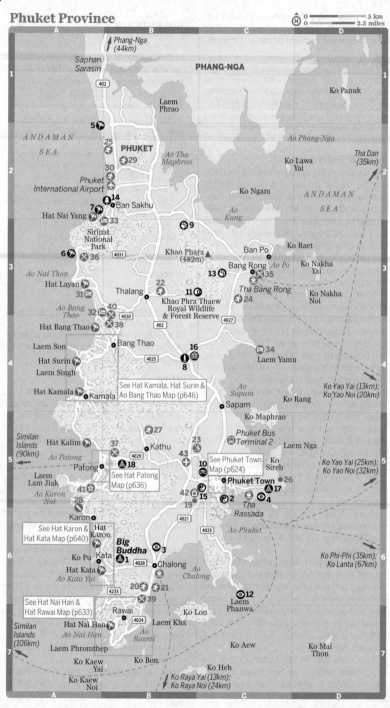

Phuket Province

PHUKET & THE ANDAMAN COAST AO PHANG-NGA

waves, with swells up to 3m high a few times per year.

In the low season, you can rent surfboards (150B to 300B per hour) on most of these beaches.

Sea Kayaking

Several Phuket-based companies offer canoe tours of spectacular Ao Phang-Nga, a collection of towering karst outcrops rising from the sea northeast of Phuket and close to the mainland. Kayaks can enter semi-submerged caves inaccessible to longtail boats. A day paddle (around 4000B per person) includes meals, equipment and boat transfer. Some outfits run all-inclusive, three-day (from 13,500B) or six-day (from 23,500B) kayaking and camping trips, covering Ao Phang-Nga and Khao Sok National Park. John Gray's Seacanoe (p625) is the island's star operator.

Kitesurfing

One of the world's fastest-growing sports is also among Phuket's latest addictions. The best kitesurfing spots are Hat Nai Yang (p649) from April to October and Rawai (p632) from mid-October to March. All listed kitesurfing outfitters are affiliated with the International Kiteboarding Organisation (www.ikointl.com).

Yachting

Phuket is one of Southeast Asia's main yachting destinations. You'll find all manner of craft anchored along its shores, from 80-year-old wooden sloops to the latest in high-tech motor cruisers.

Marina-style facilities with year-round anchorage are available at several locations. Marinas can advise in advance on the latest port-clearance procedures. Expect to pay from 11,300B per day for a high-season, bareboat charter.

Water Parks

Splash Jungle
WATER PARK

(Map p620; ☎ 076 372111; www.splashjunglewaterpark.com; 65 Mu 4, Soi 4, Mai Khao; adult/child 1450/700B; ☉10am-6pm) Within eyeshot of Phuket airport, this massive water park has a wave pool, a kids pool with water cannons, 12 multicoloured twisting water slides for all ages, a 'super-bowl' slide and...a bar for anyone craving a break. For an extra 400B per person you'll get picked up and returned to your hotel. Children under five get in free.

Phuket Wake Park
WATER SPORTS

(Map p620; ☎ 076 510151; www.phuketwakepark.com; 86/3 Mu 6, Th Vichitsongkram, Kathu; adult/child 2hr visit 750/350B, day pass 1250/650B; ☉9am-6pm; ⊛) Buzz Kathu's marvellous hill-backed lake on a wakeboard. This outfit, mostly aimed at teenagers and older kids, offers rides in two-hour blocks, by the day or as lessons (1000B per hour). Board rental is available (500B), as are hotel transfers.

Courses

Popular Thai cooking classes are held in Kata (p641), Phuket Town (p625), Ko Sireh (p631) and Patong (p635).

ℹ️ Information

DANGERS & ANNOYANCES

➥ Thousands of people are injured or killed every year on Phuket's highways. If you must rent a motorbike, make sure you at least know the basics and wear a helmet. Rental rarely includes insurance.

➥ Take special care on the roads from Patong to Karon and from Kata to the Rawai–Hat Nai Han area, where we've had reports of late-night motorbike muggings and stabbings.

➥ Women should think twice before sunbathing topless (a big no-no in Thailand anyway) or alone, especially on isolated beaches, as random sexual assaults can also happen.

➥ Avoid running alone at night or early in the morning.

MEDICAL SERVICES

Local medical care is generally good. Hospitals are equipped with modern facilities, emergency rooms and outpatient clinics.

Most diving emergencies are taken to **Phuket International Hospital** (p611), which has a hyperbaric chamber.

TOURIST INFORMATION

You can find **tourist information** (Map p624; Th Thalang; ☉9am-4.30pm) offices in Phuket Town. There are police stations at all the major beaches.

WEBSITES

Local English-language newspapers include the following:

FLIGHTS TO/FROM PHUKET

DESTINATION	FREQUENCY	FARE (B)	AIRLINE
Bangkok (Don Muang)	14 daily	1600	Air Asia
Bangkok (Don Muang)	8 daily	1680	Nok Air
Bangkok (Suvarnabhumi)	7-9 daily	1700	Bangkok Airways
Bangkok (Suvarnabhumi)	9-10 daily	2500	THAI
Chiang Mai	3 daily	2100	Air Asia
Dubai	1-2 daily	16,370	Emirates
Hat Yai	daily	1600	Bangkok Airways
Hong Kong	daily	3800	Air Asia
Ko Samui	4-5 daily	3300	Bangkok Airways
Kuala Lumpur	5 daily	2200	Air Asia
Seoul	daily	12,800	Korean Air
Shanghai	2 daily	7350	China Eastern
Singapore	daily	2000	Air Asia

Taxis remain seriously overpriced on Phuket. A 15-minute journey from, say, Hat Karon to Hat Patong will set you back 400B. Price boards outline *maximum* journey rates and drivers rarely budge from them.

Jot down the phone number of a metered taxi and use the same driver throughout your stay. The best way to do this is to take a metered taxi from the airport (the easiest place to find them) when you arrive. Metered taxis are 50m to the right as you exit airport arrivals. Set rates are 50B for the first 2km, 12B per kilometre for the next 15km and 10B per kilometre thereafter, plus a 100B 'airport tax'. That's no more than 700B to anywhere on the island from the airport.

For cheaper taxi options, the Grab app (www.grab.com/th) is increasingly popular in Thailand. Taxis booked via Grab use their meters and add a small pick-up charge on top, making them much cheaper than taxis hailed on the street. Your accommodation can also help book taxis (many hotel staff have Grab and are used to booking taxis for tourists with it).

Phuket Gazette (www.phuketgazette.net) Weekly information on island-wide activities, dining and entertainment, plus the latest scandals.
Phuket News (www.thephuketnews.com) Another source for up-to-date island news and local life.

ⓘ Getting There & Away

AIR
Phuket International Airport (☏ 076 632 7230; www.phuketairportthai.com; Phuket Airport) is 30km northwest of Phuket Town. It takes 45 minutes to an hour to reach the southern beaches from here. A number of carriers serve domestic destinations.

BUS & MINIVAN
Interstate buses depart from **Phuket Bus Terminal 2** (p630), 4km north of Phuket Town.

Phuket travel agencies sell tickets (including ferry fare) for air-con minivans to destinations across southern Thailand, including Krabi, Ranong, Trang, Surat Thani, Ko Samui and Ko Pha-Ngan. Prices are usually slightly higher than for buses.

FERRY & SPEEDBOAT
Phuket's **Tha Rassada** (Map p620; Tha Rassada), 3km southeast of Phuket Town, is the main pier for boats to Ko Phi-Phi, Krabi, Ao Nang, Ko Lanta, the Trang Islands, Ko Lipe and even as far as Pulau Langkawi in Malaysia (which has ferry connections to Penang). Additional services to Krabi and Ao Nang via Ko Yao leave from **Tha Bang Rong** (Map p620; Tha Bang Rong), 26km north of Tha Rassada.

ⓘ Getting Around

Local Phuket transport is terrible. The systems in place make tourists either stay on their chosen beach, rent a car or motorbike or take a

heavily overpriced taxi or túk-túk. *Sŏrng·tăa·ou* run from Phuket Town to the beaches, but often you'll have to go via Phuket Town to get from one beach to another (say Hat Surin to Hat Patong), which takes hours.

Phuket Town เมืองภูเก็ต

☏ 076 / POP 78,900

Long before flip-flops and selfie sticks, Phuket was an island of rubber trees, tin mines and cash-hungry merchants. Attracting entrepreneurs from the Arabian Peninsula, China, India and Portugal, Phuket Town was a colourful blend of cultural influences. Today, it stands as a testament to the island's history. Wander down streets lined with Sino-Portuguese architecture housing arty coffee shops, eccentric galleries, bright textiles stores and fantastic restaurants, and peek down alleyways to incense-cloaked Chinese Taoist shrines.

The Old Town is Phuket's hipster heart, attracting artists and musicians in particular. That has led to some startling gentrification. Century-old shophouses and homes are being restored and it can feel like every other building is now a trendy polished-concrete cafe or a quirky guesthouse. But Phuket Town is still a wonderfully refreshing cultural break from the island's beaches, all of which it is connected to via a network of *sŏrng·tăa·ou*.

◎ Sights

Phuket Thaihua Museum　　　　　MUSEUM
(พิพิธภัณฑ์ภูเก็ต ไทยหัว; Map p624; ☏ 076 211224; 28 Th Krabi; 200B; ⊙9am-5pm) Formerly a Chinese language school, this flashy museum

Phuket Town

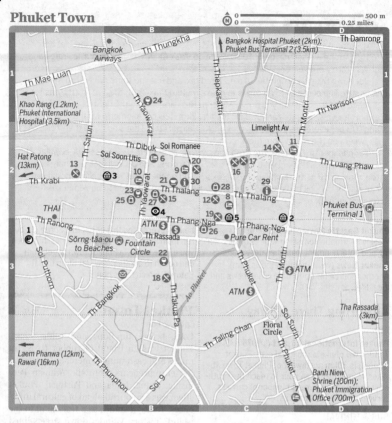

Phuket Town

is filled with photos and English-language exhibits on Phuket's history, from the Chinese migration (many influential Phuketian families are of Chinese origin) and the tin-mining era to local cuisine, fashion and literature. There's an overview of the building's history, which is a stunning combination of Chinese and European architectural styles, including art deco, Palladianism and a Chinese gable roof and stucco.

Shrine of the Serene Light SHRINE
(ศาลเจ้าแสงธรรม, Saan Jao Sang Tham; Map p624; Th Phang-Nga; ⊙8.30am-noon & 1.30-5.30pm) **FREE** A handful of Chinese temples pump colour into Phuket Town, but this restored shrine, tucked away up a 50m alley, is particularly atmospheric, with its Taoist etchings on the walls and the vaulted ceiling stained from incense plumes. The altar is always fresh with flowers and burning candles. The shrine is said to have been built by a local family in the 1890s.

Khao Rang VIEWPOINT
(เขารัง, Phuket Hill; Map p620) For a bird's-eye view of the city, climb (or drive) up Khao Rang, 3km northwest of the town centre. A new viewing platform has opened up the commanding panoramas across Phuket Town and all the way to Chalong Bay, Laem Phanwa and Big Buddha (p131). It's at its best during the week, when the summit is relatively peaceful. There are a few restaurants up here. It's about an hour's walk, but don't try it at night. A taxi up costs 700B.

🏃 Activities

★ John Gray's Seacanoe KAYAKING
(Map p620; ☑076 254505; www.johngray-sea canoe.com; 86 Soi 2/3, Th Yaowarat; adult/child from 3950/1975B) 🌊 The original, the most reputable and by far the most ecologically sensitive kayaking company on Phuket. The 'Hong by Starlight' trip dodges the crowds, involves sunset paddling and will introduce you to Ao Phang-Nga's famed after-dark bioluminescence. Like any good brand in Thailand, John Gray's 'Seacanoe' name and itineraries have been frequently copied. Located 3.5km north of Phuket Town.

Amazing Bike Tours CYCLING
(Map p620; ☑087 263 2031, 076 283436; www. amazingbiketoursthailand.asia; 32/4 Th Chaofa; half/full-day trip 1900/3200B) This highly popular adventure outfitter leads small groups on half-day bicycle tours through the villages of northeast Phuket, as well as on terrific full-day trips around Ko Yao Noi and more challenging three-day adventure rides around Khao Sok National Park (14,900B) and Krabi Province (15,900B). Prices include bikes, helmets, meals, water and national-park entry fees.

🎓 Courses

★ Suay Cooking School COOKING
(Map p624; ☑081 797 4135; www.suayrestaurant. com; 50/2 Th Takua Pa; classes per person 2500B) Learn from one of Phuket's top chefs at the most laid-back, soulful and fun cooking school around. Noy Tammasak leads visitors through the local market and teaches how to make three dishes, before cracking open a bottle of wine to enjoy with your culinary creations. Highly recommended; minimum three people.

Blue Elephant Cooking School COOKING
(Map p624; ☑076 354355; www.blueelephant cookingschool.com; 96 Th Krabi; half-day classes 3296B; ⊙Mon-Sun) Master the intricate art of royal Thai cooking in a stunningly restored Sino-Portuguese mansion. Options range from half-day (morning or afternoon) group lessons to private eight-dish vegetarian classes (7000B). Morning sessions visit the market. Book ahead.

🛏 Sleeping

Phuket Town is a treasure trove of affordable lodging, with hip hostels, guesthouses and boutique hotels spread across the Old Town.

Ai Phuket Hostel HOSTEL $
(Map p624; ☑076 212881; www.aiphukethostel. com; 88 Th Yaowarat; dm 299B, d 700-900B; ✳@ 🖥) Popular, well-organised hostel in the heart of town. Doubles are tight but come with wood floors, black-and-white photos and, for two rooms, private bathrooms. Not all have windows, something of an Old Town trait. Dorms lack windows also but are colourful and clean, sleeping six

---

TO MARKET, TO MARKET

A wonderful way to embrace Phuket Town's local flavour is by getting lost in its markets. The **Weekend Market** (Map p620; off Th Chao Fa West; ⊙4-10pm Sat & Sun) is the pick of the bunch.

DON'T MISS

SINO-PORTUGUESE ARCHITECTURE

Stroll along Ths Thalang, Dibuk, Yaowarat, Ranong, Phang-Nga, Rassada and Krabi for a glimpse of Phuket Town's Sino-Portuguese architectural treasures. The most magnificent examples are the **Standard Chartered Bank** (ธนาคารสแตนดาร์ดชาร์เตอร์ด; Map p624; Th Phang-Nga), Thailand's oldest foreign bank; the **THAI office** (Map p624; ☑ 076 360444; www.thaiairways.com; 78/1 Th Ranong, Phuket Town; ◷ 8am-4.30pm); and the **old post office building**, which now houses the **Phuket Philatelic Museum** (พิพิธภัณฑ์ตราไปรษณียากรภูเก็ต; Map p624; ☑ 076 211020; Th Montri; ◷ 9am-4.30pm Mon-Fri, to noon Sat) **FREE**. Some of the most colourfully revamped buildings line Soi Romanee, off Th Thalang, once home to brothels, gambling and opium dens.

The best-restored residential properties lie along Ths Thalang, Dibuk and Krabi. The fabulous 1903 **Phra Phitak Chyn Pracha Mansion** has been refurbished into the upscale **Blue Elephant restaurant** (Map p624; ☑ 076 354355; www.blueelephant.com; 96 Th Krabi; mains 420-980B; set menus 1150-2050B; ◷ 11.30am-2pm & 6.30-10pm; 🖱🖋) and **cooking school** (p625).

(women-only) to eight. All share polished-concrete hot-water bathrooms and a small downstairs hang-out lounge.

Art-C House
GUESTHOUSE $

(Map p624; ☑ 082 420 3911; ArtCphuket@hotmail.com; 288 Th Phuket; d 800B; 🖱) Not many guesthouses have their own climbing wall and a (smaller) bouldering wall inside. Art-C does, along with 10 tidy private rooms that are a good deal for pricey Phuket. There's a downstairs cafe and friendly staff; non-guests can access the climbing wall for 350B per day. There's no lift: you climb to your room (ropes provided free).

★ Casa Blanca
BOUTIQUE HOTEL $$

(Map p624; ☑ 076 219019; www.casablancaphuket.com; 26 Th Phuket; d 2300-2800B; 🖱🖋🖳) All whites and pastels, this elegantly revamped Sino-Portuguese beauty gets extra boutique spark from Moorish-themed touches such as patterned tiles and a plant-lined patio. Modern art adorns smart rooms, in soft greens and pale blues. Deluxe rooms have balconies with city panoramas; superior ones overlook the little pool. A teensy cafe doles out fresh-from-the-oven pastries in the bright lobby.

Tint @ Phuket Town
BOUTIQUE HOTEL $$

(Map p624; ☑ 076 217099; www.thetintphuket.com; 2/11 Th Dibuk; r 1600-3100B; 🖱🖋) The different floors at this newish, reasonably priced boutique place are colour-themed, with the compact, comfortable and modern rooms decked out in bright pastel colours, ranging from orange and pink to blue and sea green. All have TVs, fridges, desks and small balconies. Staff are efficient and welcoming. It's down a small lane off Th Dibuk.

RomManee
BOUTIQUE HOTEL $$

(Map p624; ☑ 089 728 9871; www.therommanee.com; Soi Romanee; d 1200B; 🖱🖋) On Phuket Town's prettiest street, this 'boutique guesthouse' has some style with its turquoise-toned exterior, varnished-concrete floors and wood-block reception bar. The four spacious rooms are competitively priced and have an arty modern feel: wood floors, flat-screen TVs, colour accent walls, neon-washed chairs and tasteful lighting. Stairs are steep and there's no lift. There's a less-stylish **branch** (Map p624; ☑ 076 214488; 4-6 Th Krabi; d 1200-1500B; 🖱🖋) a block away.

🍴 Eating

★ Abdul's Roti Shop
BREAKFAST $

(Map p624; Th Thalang; mains from 40B; ◷ 7am-4pm Mon-Sat, to noon Sun) Time to try Abdul's legendary, delicious *roti*. At 75-years-plus, Abdul has been cooking flaky *roti* at the front of his shop for years. Whether you're a fan of sweet or savoury, this place has it covered, with sticky banana *roti* or plain served with spicy chicken, beef or fish massaman (curry).

Kopitiam by Wilai
THAI $

(Map p624; ☑ 083 606 9776; www.facebook.com/kopitiambywilai; 18 Th Thalang; mains 95-180B; ◷ 11am-10pm Mon-Sat; 🖱) Kopitiam serves Phuket soul food in an atmospheric old shophouse setting. It does Phuketian *pàt tai* (thin rice noodles with egg, tofu and/or shrimp) with a kick, and a fantastic *mee sua*:

noodles sautéed with egg, greens, prawns, chunks of sea bass and squid. Wash it all down with fresh chrysanthemum or passionfruit juice.

Indy Market
MARKET $

(Map p624; Limelight Av; mains 30-100B; ◎4-10.30pm Wed-Fri) Local families, schoolkids and students flock to this smallish central market for the excellent array of food stalls, ranging from barbecue and dumplings to sushi and sweet snacks. There's also a couple of outdoor bars, live music and clothes and jewellery stalls.

★One Chun
THAI $$

(Map p624; ☑076 355909; 48/1 Th Thepkasattri; mains 90-350B; ◎10am-10pm; ☎) A sister restaurant to Raya (Map p624; ☑076 218155; rayarestaurant@gmail.com; 48/1 Th Dibuk; mains 180-650B; ◎10am-10pm), only the dishes here are cheaper and that's why the locals crowd it out every night. Superb seafood – the crab-meat curry in coconut milk is the best in Phuket Town – but also a great roasted-duck red curry. The atmospheric shophouse setting, with 1950s decor and tiled floors, adds to the experience.

★Torry's Ice Cream Boutique
ICE CREAM $$

(Map p624; ☑076 510888; www.torrysicecream. com; Soi Romanee; ice creams & desserts 60-200B; ◎11am-9.30pm Tue-Sun) You'll find gourmet ice cream, sorbets and Phuket-style desserts at this very popular cafe-style place on Phuket Town's most photogenic street. It's a swish setting – a chandelier dangles over the ice-cream counter – in a cool conversion of an old shophouse. Also does coffee, tea and juices.

Surf & Turf by Soul Kitchen
FUSION $$

(Map p624; ☑089 104 7432; 115 Th Phang-Nga; mains 240-420B; ◎5.30-10.30pm; ☎) This relaxed, stylish restaurant scores with its twist on European-Thai fusion food, such as homemade ravioli with a yellow curry sauce and thinly sliced Australian beef on a delicate bed of white risotto. The portions aren't huge, but they are full of flavour and nicely presented. Small but proper wine list.

★Suay
INTERNATIONAL, THAI $$$

(Map p624; ☑081 797 4135; www.suayrestaurant.com; 50/2 Th Takua Pa; mains 300-1000B; ◎5pm-midnight) Fabulous fusion at this converted house, just south of the Old Town proper. Prices have gone up, as the chef's fame has increased, but the food remains excellent. The grilled lemongrass lamb chops with a papaya salsa, the braised beef cheek massaman (curry) and sea bass steak in green curry rock, as do the many flavoursome salads.

🍷 Drinking & Nightlife

Phuket Town is where you can party like a local. Bars buzz until late, patronised almost exclusively by Thais and local expats.

★Bookhemian
CAFE

(Map p624; ☑098 090 0657; www.bookhemian. com; 61 Th Thalang; ◎9am-7pm Mon-Fri, to 8.30pm Sat & Sun; ☎) Every town should have a coffee house this cool, with a split-level design that enables it to be both a cafe and an art exhibition space. Used books (for sale) line the front room, bicycles hang from the wall, and the offerings include gourmet coffee, tea and cakes, as well as all-day breakfasts, salads, sandwiches and pasta.

PHUKET BEACH CLEAN-UP

Since 2014, there has been a crackdown on illegal construction and commercial activity on the island's overcrowded beaches. Initially, all rental sunbeds, deckchairs and umbrellas were banned, with thousands removed under the watch of armed soldiers. Illegally encroaching buildings were bulldozed, including well-established beach clubs and restaurants, and others dramatically reduced in size.

The positive side of the crackdown is the beaches are cleaner and less cluttered than before. Beach mats and umbrellas are still available to rent, in limited numbers and in allocated areas; sunbeds remain banned. Tourists may pitch their own umbrellas and chairs within the designated areas too. Jet skis, which were suspended to begin with, are still very much operating in Patong. Some businesses have simply moved to new locations.

It's a confusing, fluid and typically Thai situation, so things may change again.

VEGETARIAN FESTIVAL: BODY-PIERCING, FIRECRACKERS & FLAGELLATION

Deafening machine-gun-like popping sounds fill the streets, the air is thick with grey-brown smoke and men and women traipse along blocked-off city roads, their cheeks pierced with skewers and knives or, more surprisingly, lamps and tree branches. Some have blood streaming down their fronts or open lashes across their backs. No, this isn't a war zone, this is the **Vegetarian Festival** (www.phuketvegetarian.com; ☉ late Sep-Oct), one of Phuket's most important celebrations and centred on Phuket Town.

The festival, which takes place during the first nine days of the ninth lunar month of the Chinese calendar, celebrates the beginning of 'Taoist Lent', when devout Chinese abstain from meat, dairy and alcohol. Most obvious to outsiders are the fast-paced daily processions winding through town with floats of ornately dressed children and *gà·teu·i* (also spelt *kàthoey;* Thai transgender and cross-dressers), armies of flag-bearing, colour-coordinated young people and, most noticeably, men and women engaged in outrageous acts of stomach-churning self-mortification. Shop owners along Phuket Town's central streets set up altars in front of their shopfronts offering nine tiny cups of tea, incense, fruit, firecrackers, candles and flowers to the nine emperor gods invoked by the festival.

Those participating as mediums bring the nine deities to earth by entering a trance state, piercing their cheeks with an impressive variety of objects, sawing their tongues or flagellating themselves with spiky metal balls. The temporarily possessed mediums (primarily men) stop at shopfront altars to pick up the offered fruit and tea and bless the house. The shop owners and their families stand by making a *wâi* (palms-together Thai greeting) gesture out of respect. Frenzied, surreal and overwhelming barely describe it.

Phuket Town's festival focuses on five Chinese temples. **Jui Tui Shrine** (ศาลเจ้าจุ้ยตุ่ยเต้าโบ้เก้ง; Map p624; Soi Puthorn; ☉8am-8pm) FREE, off Th Ranong, is the most important, followed by **Bang Niew** (ศาลเจ้าบางเหนียว; Map p620; Th Ong Sim Phai; ☉6am-6pm) FREE and **Sui Boon Tong** (ศาลเจ้าซุ่ยบุ่นต๋อง; Map p620; Soi Lorong; ☉hours vary) FREE shrines. There are also events in nearby Kathu (where the festival originated) and Ban Tha Reua. If you stop by any procession's starting point early enough (around 6am), you may spot a surprisingly professional, latex-glove-clad crew piercing the devotees' cheeks (not for the faint-hearted). Other ceremonies include firewalking and knife-ladder climbing. At the temples, everyone wears white. Beyond the headlining gore, fabulous cheap vegetarian food stalls line the side streets; many restaurants turn veg-only for the festival.

Oddly enough, there is no record of these acts of devotion associated with Taoist Lent in China. Local Chinese claim the festival was started in 1825 in Kathu, by a theatre troupe from China which performed a nine-day penance of self-piercing, meditation and vegetarianism after becoming seriously ill for failing to propitiate the nine emperor gods of Taoism.

Phuket's **Tourism Authority of Thailand** (TAT; Map p624; ☎076 211036; www.tourismthailand.org/Phuket; 191 Th Thalang; ☉8.30am-4.30pm) prints festival schedules. The festival also takes place in Trang, Krabi, Phang-Nga and other southern towns.

Timber Hut
CLUB
(Map p624; ☎076 211839; 118/1 Th Yaowarat; ☉6pm-2am) Locals, expats and visitors have been packing out this two-floor pub-club nightly for 27 years, downing beers and whisky while swaying to live bands that swing from hard rock to pure pop to hip-hop. No cover charge.

Ka Jok See
CLUB
(Map p624; ☎076 217903; kajoksee@hotmail.com; 26 Th Takua Pa; ☉8pm-1am Nov-Apr, reduced hours May-Oct) Dripping with Old Phuket charm and the owner's fabulous trinket collection, this intimate, century-old house has two identities: half glamorous eatery, half crazy party venue. There's good Thai food (buffet 2500B per person), but once the tables are cleared it becomes a bohemian madhouse with top-notch music and – if you're lucky – some sensationally extravagant cabaret. Book a month or two ahead. There's no sign.

Rockin' Angels BAR

(Map p624; ☑089 654 9654; 55 Th Yaowarat; ◷6pm-1am Tue-Sun) This intimate Old Town bar is packed with biker paraphernalia and framed LPs. It gets loud when Patrick, the Singaporean-born owner, jams with his house blues band from around 9.30pm most nights. Beers are cold and you'll be surrounded by a good mix of Thais and local expats.

🔒 Shopping

There are bohemian-chic boutiques scattered throughout the Old Town selling jewellery, women's fashions, fabrics and souvenirs, as well as many whimsical art galleries and antique shops.

★Ranida ANTIQUES, FASHION

(Map p624; ☑076 214801; 119 Th Thalang; ◷10am-8pm Mon-Sat) An elegant antique gallery and boutique featuring antiquated Buddha statues and sculptures, organic textiles, and ambitious, exquisite high-fashion women's clothing inspired by vintage Thai garments and fabrics.

Drawing Room ART

(Map p624; ☑086 899 4888; isara380@hotmail. com; 56 Th Phang-Nga; ◷9am-6pm) With a street-art vibe reminiscent of pre-boom Brooklyn or East London, this wide-open cooperative is by far the stand-out gallery in a town full of them. Canvases might be vibrant abstract squiggles or comical pen-and-ink cartoons. Metallic furniture and bicycles line concrete floors. House music thumps at low levels.

Ban Boran Textiles TEXTILES

(Map p624; ☑076 211563; 51 Th Yaowarat; ◷10.30am-6pm) Shelves at this hole-in-the-wall shop are stocked high with quality silk scarves, Burmese lacquerware, sarongs, linen shirts, cute colourful bags and cotton textiles from Chiang Mai.

Oldest Herbs Shop FOOD & DRINKS

(Map p624; ☑099 359 9564; Th Thalang; ◷7.30am-6pm Mon-Sat, to 11.30am Sun) Craving ginseng or perhaps dried insects? You can't miss the wafting aromas of Phuket's oldest herbs shop as you stroll along Th Thalang. Stop here to stock up on Chinese herbal remedies or to simply watch portions of herbs being weighed on antique scales and mixed together ready for sale at this generations-old family business.

ℹ️ Information

There are numerous ATMs on Ths Phuket, Ranong, Montri and Phang-Nga. Wi-fi is everywhere.

ℹ️ Getting There & Around

TO/FROM THE AIRPORT

Despite what airport touts say, an hourly bright-orange government airport bus (www. airportbusphuket.com) runs between the airport and Phuket Town (100B, one hour) via the Heroines Monument (p652) from 8am to

BUSES FROM PHUKET BUS TERMINAL 2

DESTINATION	FARE (B)	DURATION (HR)	FREQUENCY	BUS TYPE
Bangkok	913	13	5pm, 6.30pm	VIP
	587	13-14	6.30am, 7am, 1.30pm, 3.30pm, 5.30pm, 6pm, 6.30pm	air-con
Chiang Mai	1646	22	12.30pm	VIP
Hat Yai	507	7	9.45pm	VIP
	326	7	hourly 7.30am-12.30pm, 7.30pm & 9.30pm	air-con
Ko Samui	450	8 (bus/boat)	9am	air-con
Ko Pha-Ngan	550	9½ (bus/boat)	9am	air-con
Krabi	140	3½	hourly 4.50am-7pm	air-con
Phang-Nga	80	2½	hourly 4.50am-7pm	air-con
Ranong	225	6	hourly 5.30am-6.10pm	air-con
Satun	329	7	8.15am, 10.15am, 12.15pm, 8.15pm	air-con
Surat Thani	195	5	8am, 10am, noon, 2pm	air-con
Trang	230	5	hourly 4.50am-7pm	air-con

8.30pm. Taxis from the airport to Phuket Town cost 650B.

CAR & MOTORCYCLE

Th Rassada has cheap car-rental agencies near **Pure Car Rent** (Map p624; ☑ 076 211002; www.purecarrent.com; 75 Th Rassada; ⊙ 8am-7pm), a good central choice. Cars cost around 1200B per day (including insurance), although you'll get them for more or less the same price through the big car-hire chains at Phuket airport.

You can rent motorcycles on Th Rassada, including at Pure Car Rent, or from many other places around town, for 200B to 250B per day.

BUS

Phuket Bus Terminal 1 is mostly used by min-ivans. A local bus (30B) and minivans (50B) head to Patong 7am to 5pm from here too.

Interstate buses depart from **Phuket Bus Terminal 2** (Map p620; Th Thepkrasattri), 4km north of Phuket Town and 100B by motorcycle taxi, or 300B in a taxi.

MINIVAN

From **Phuket Bus Terminal 1** (Map p624; Th Phang-Nga), 500m east of Phuket Town centre, minivans run to destinations across southern Thailand, including the following:

DESTINATION	FARE (B)	DURATION (HR)
Hat Yai	360	7
Ko Lanta	280	5
Krabi	140	3
Phang-Nga	100	2
Surat Thani	200	4

ⓘ BEACH SAFETY

During the May–October monsoon, large waves and fierce undertows can make swimming dangerous. Dozens of drownings occur every year on Phuket's beaches, especially Laem Singh, Kamala, Karon and Patong. Heed the red flags signalling serious rips.

At any time of year, keep an eye out for jet skis when you're swimming. Although the Phuket governor declared jet skis illegal in 1997 and they were re-banned again in 2014, enforcement of the rule is another issue. Long-tail boats can also be hazardous as they come in close to shore. Do not expect the boat-man to see you!

SŎRNG·TĂA OU & TÚK-TÚK

Large bus-sized *sŏrng·tăa·ou* run regularly from Th Ranong near the day market to Phuket's beaches (20B to 40B per person, 30 minutes to 1½ hours), from 7am to 5pm; otherwise you'll have to charter a túk-túk to the beaches, which costs 400B (Rawai, Kata and Ao Bang Thao), 500B (Patong, Karon and Surin) or 600B (Kamala). Beware of tales that the only way to reach beaches is by taxi.

For a ride around town, túk-túk drivers charge 100B to 200B and motorcycle taxis 50B.

Laem Phanwa   แหลมพันวา

An elongated jungle-covered cape jutting into the sea just south of Phuket Town, Laem Phanwa is an all-natural throwback. Some say this is the last vestige of Phuket as it once was. The biggest bloom of development is near the harbour at the cape's tip, 12km south of Phuket Town, where there are a number of high-end resorts and the Phuket Aquarium.

On either side of the harbour, the beaches and coves remain rustic, protected by rocky headlands and mangroves and reached by a dreamy, sinuous coastal road. This is very much a place for peace and quiet, with little or no nightlife.

⊙ Sights & Activities

Phuket Aquarium   AQUARIUM
(สถานแสดงพันธุ์สัตว์น้ำภูเก็ต; Map p620; ☑ 076 391126; www.phuketaquarium.org; 51 Th Sakdidej; adult/child 180/100B; ⊙ 8.30am-4.30pm) Get a glimpse of Thailand's wondrous underwater world at Phuket's popular aquarium, by the harbour on the tip of Laem Phanwa. It's not the largest collection of marine life, but there are useful English-language displays and captions.

Check out the blacktip reef shark, the tiger-striped catfish resembling a marine zebra, and the electric eel with a shock of up to 600V.

★ Cool Spa   SPA
(Map p620; ☑ 076 371000; www.coolspaphuket. com; Sri Panwa, 88 Mu 8, Th Sakdidej; treatments from 4500B; ⊙ 10am-9pm) One of the best spas on Phuket, this is an elegant wonderland of fruit-infused wraps, facials and scrubs, and hilltop ocean-view pools. Oh, and then there's the dreamy setting, on the southernmost tip of Phuket's Laem Phanwa.

CHALONG BAY RUM

When Marine Lucchini and Thibault Spithakis, each born into a prestigious French wine family, met and fell in love, they bonded over booze – fine rum, in particular. Which is why they became master distillers and launched their own distillery, **Chalong Bay Rum** (ฉลองเบย์รัม ดิสทิลเลอรี่; Map p620; ☑ 093 575 1119; www.chalongbayrum.com; 14/2 Mu 2, Soi Palai 2; tour 300B; ⊘ tours hourly 2-6pm).

They knew they wanted to make natural rum in the French style, the kind made in Martinique, which meant distilling sugar-cane juice, rather than molasses (as is used for most rum). Thailand is the world's fourth-largest sugar cane producer with over 200 varieties currently in cultivation and so, in 2012, the couple imported 40-year-old copper Armagnac stills and incorporated one of the world's great islands into their brand.

Chalong Bay Rum is white, has great flavour, took a gold medal at the 2015 San Francisco World Spirits Competition, and makes a mean mojito – which you'll be sipping as you tour the facility, learning way more about rum than you could ever imagine.

Book ahead, because you'll need directions. About 3km north of Chalong Circle, turn east at the signs to the zoo; it's signposted shortly after.

🛏 Sleeping & Eating

This is four- and five-star resort territory.

There are seafood restaurants along the harbour waterfront, where you can watch the fishing boats bobbing by.

★ Sri Panwa   RESORT $$$
(Map p620; ☑ 076 371000; www.sripanwa.com; 88 Mu 8, Th Sakdidej; d incl breakfast 29,700-279,000B; P ❀ 🛜 ☒) A genuine candidate for best hotel on Phuket, Sri Panwa is poised idyllically on the island's jungle-cloaked southernmost tip. Multi-room villas feature hot tubs, outdoor showers, private pools, personal sound systems and awesome sea views. More affordable digs are still wonderfully comfortable, with the solicitous staff claiming that when the guests see their rooms, 'they don't want to leave them'.

Panwa Boutique Beach Resort   RESORT $$$
(Map p620; ☑ 076 393300; www.panwaboutique beachresort.com; 5/3 Mu 8, Ao Yon; d incl breakfast 4300-15,600B; P ❀ 🛜 ☒) With its own exclusive stretch of beachfront and views of Chalong, Rawai and Big Buddha (p131), this slightly dated resort on the cape's west coast offers seclusion, sizeable rooms, a fantastic pool, three restaurants and four-star service without breaking the bank.

❶ Getting There & Away

From Th Ranong in Phuket Town, *sŏrng·tăa·ou* travel here from 7am to 5pm (30B); the last stop is the Phuket Aquarium. A taxi here will cost 400B.

Ko Sireh   เกาะสิเหร่

The tiny island of Ko Sireh, 4km east of Phuket Town and connected to Phuket by a bridge, is known for its hilltop reclining Buddha at **Wat Sireh** (วัดบ้านเกาะสิเหร่; Map p620; Th Sireh; ⊘ daylight hours) FREE and its *chow lair* **village** (หมู่บ้านชาวเล; Map p620).

Thailand's largest settlement of *chow lair* is little more than a cluster of stilted, metal-roofed shacks. The Urak Lawoi, the most sedentary of the three *chow lair* groups, live only between here and the Tarutao–Langkawi archipelago, and speak a mixture of Malay and Mon-Khmer.

A single road loops the island, passing a few villas, prawn farms, rubber plantations, a bit of untouched forest and east-coast **Hat Teum Suk** (หาดเติมสุข). Just south on a quiet seafront plot, **Phuket Thai Cookery School** (Map p620; ☑ 082 474 6592; www.phuketthaicook ery.com; Ko Sireh; 1-day course 2900B; ⊘ 8am-3pm, closed Wed) can get you acquainted with Thai spices on a market tour and cooking class (up to six hours). Round-trip transport is provided to most places in Phuket.

There are a few hotels and restaurants but most people visit on a day trip. *Sŏrng·tăa·ou* run here from Th Ranong in Phuket Town from 7am to 5pm (20B). A taxi here from Phuket Town is 300B.

Rawai ราไวย์

Rawai is a delightful place to stay or live, which is why this stretch of Phuket's south coast is teeming with retirees, artists, Thai and expat entrepreneurs, as well as a booming service sector.

The region is defined not just by its beaches but also by its lush coastal hills that rise steeply and tumble into the Andaman Sea, forming **Laem Phromthep** (แหลมพรหมเทพ; Map p633; Rte 4233). Phuket's beautiful southernmost point (for a more secluded sunset spot, seek out the **secret viewpoint** (มุมมอง; Map p633; Rte 4233) 1.5km north). These hills are home to pocket neighbourhoods and cul-de-sacs knitted together by just a few roads – although more are being carved into the hills each year and you can almost envision real-estate money chasing away all the seafood grills and tiki bars. Let's hope that's several decades off. Or at least one. Even with the growth you can still feel nature, especially when you hit the beach.

🏃 Activities

Rawai is the epicentre of Phuket's ever-growing *moo·ay tai* (Thai boxing, also spelt *muay Thai*) mania, home to half a dozen schools where students (of both sexes) live and train traditional-style in camps with professional *moo·ay tai* fighters.

Hat Rawai is an excellent place to arrange **boat charters** (Map p633; Hat Rawai) to neighbouring islands. Destinations include quiet Ko Bon (long-tail/speedboat 1200/2400B) and Coral Island (1800/3500B, maximum eight people) for snorkelling.

Kingka Supa Muay Thai   HEALTH & FITNESS
(Map p633; ☑ 076 226495; www.supamuaythai phuket.com; 43/42 Mu 7, Th Viset; per session/week 600/3000B; ☉ 7am-7pm Mon-Sat, 9am-6pm Sun) Strap up those wrists and get fired up at this Thai boxing gym opened by a former *moo·ay tai* champion (he doesn't teach here). People come from around the world to learn how to fight alongside seasoned professionals. A mix of Thais and foreigners live in on-site dorms, but tourists can join drop-in classes or try a taekwondo session (200B).

Sinbi Muay Thai   HEALTH & FITNESS
(Map p633; ☑ 083 391 5535; www.sinbi-muay-thai.com; 100/15 Mu 7, Th Sai Yuan; per session/week 400/3000B; ☉ 7.30am-7pm Mon-Sat) A

well-respected boxing training camp for both men and women.

Bob's Kite School   KITESURFING
(Map p620; ☑ 092 459 4191; www.kiteschool phuket.com; Rte 4024; 1hr lesson 1500B, 3-day course 11,000B; ☉ Nov-Apr) Phuket's very first, German-run kite school is still going strong with keen, friendly staff. From May to mid-October it operates on the northwest side of the island at Hat Nai Yang (p649). Equipment hire costs 1000B per hour.

Atsumi   SPA
(Map p620; ☑ 081 272 0571; www.atsumihealing. com; 34/18 Soi Pattana, Th Sai Yuan; massage 600-1000B, treatment 1200-1600B, detox package 5500-9100B; ☉ 9am-5pm) Phuket isn't all about boozing and gorging on cream-loaded curries. In fact, there's a flourishing wellness scene. At this earthy fasting-detox retreat, guests check in for days-long water, juice and/or herb fasts with massages. But non-dieters are also welcome for spa sessions, taking in traditional Thai, oil and deep-tissue treatments, plus signature Thaiatsu (Thai meets shiatsu) massages and yoga (300B).

🛏 Sleeping

Good 9 at Home   GUESTHOUSE $
(Map p633; ☑ 088 457 6969; www.facebook.com/ good9athome; 62 Mu 6, Soi Wassana, Hat Rawai; d 900B; ❄ 🤶) Set beside a cute patio, these seven fresh, gleaming contemporary-style rooms spiced up with colour accent walls, tiled bathrooms and the odd bit of artwork make for good-value digs, 300m up the street from **Hat Rawai** (หาดราไวย์; Map p633). The lime-green-and-grey house is kept clean, cosy and friendly, with a thoughtful little coffee corner thrown into the mix.

Phu Na Na   BOUTIQUE HOTEL $$
(Map p633; ☑ 076 226673; www.phunana-phuket. com; 43/234 Mu 7, Th Viset; d 1500-3900B; ❄ 🤶 🏊) Set around a pool, the smart rooms here are like mini-apartments with comfortable beds, fridges, microwaves, decent bathrooms and terraces, making them a reasonable deal for the price. All are well-maintained and you're walking distance from **Hat Friendship** (Hat Mittraphap, หาดมิตรภาพ; Map p633), or a short motorbike or túk-túk ride to Hat Rawai's restaurants.

Vijitt   RESORT $$$
(Map p633; ☑ 076 363600; www.vijittresort.com; 16 Mu 2, Th Viset; villas incl breakfast 6700-26,000B;

Hat Nai Han & Hat Rawai

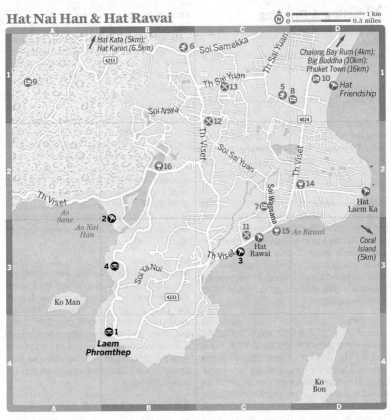

Hat Nai Han & Hat Rawai

◎ Top Sights
1 Laem Phromthep.................................. B4

◎ Sights
2 Hat Nai Han... B2
3 Hat Rawai... C3
4 Secret Viewpoint................................ B3

◔ Activities, Courses & Tours
Boat Charters................................(see 3)
5 Kingka Supa Muay Thai C1
6 Sinbi Muay Thai.................................... B1

⌂ Sleeping
7 Good 9 at Home................................... C2

8 Phu Na Na... D1
9 Sabai Corner.. A1
10 Vijitt D1

⊗ Eating
11 Flip Side C3
12 German Bakery C1
13 Rum Jungle C1

⊜ Drinking & Nightlife
14 Laguna Rawai..D2
15 Nikita's C3
16 Reggae Bar..B2

P ❅ ⌘ ⌖) Arguably the area's most elegant property, peaceful Vijitt is set around a garden sprinkled with frangipani trees. Deluxe villas boast limestone floors, large bathtubs, outdoor showers and gorgeous sea views from private terraces (some with their own pools). The stunning, multilevel, black-bottom infinity pool overlooks Hat Friendship.

✖ Eating & Drinking

Hat Rawai is lined with a dozen locally owned seafood grills sizzling fresh catch along the roadside (mains 90B to 300B), as well as a few international places.

German Bakery
EUROPEAN $

(Map p633; Th Viset; mains 80-200B; ⊙7.30am-4.30pm) This fun, friendly, semi-outdoor restaurant run by a German-Thai couple does the best pastries in the area and is deservedly popular. It makes fine brown bread, serves excellent breakfasts (try the pineapple pancakes), and has decent bratwurst and sauerkraut.

Som Tum Lanna
THAI $$

(Map p620; ☑081 597 0569; 3/7 Th Sai Yuan, Hat Rawai; mains 80-250B; ⊙9am-5pm Tue-Sun) When it comes to *sôm·đam* (spicy green papaya salad), order it mild – it'll still bring some serious heat. And while the fish at this Isan soul-food shack is good, its equal exists elsewhere. The chicken, on the other hand, is outstanding.

Flip Side
BURGERS $$

(Map p633; ☑090 869 5552; 469/4 Th Viset, Hat Rawai; mains 250-490B; ⊙11am-10.30pm, closed Tue; 🕏) This beachfront joint offers Western eats and beers for those looking for a break from Thai food. Gourmet burgers arrive on wooden platters and are succulent and satisfying. Chicken wings, fish and chips, salads, sandwiches and other bites are available too, and there's a big menu of Belgian, German and US craft beers. Service can be slack.

★ Rum Jungle
INTERNATIONAL $$$

(Map p633; ☑076 388153; www.facebook.com/Rum-Jungle-Cafe-Rawai-Phuket-173738946050909; 69/8 Mu 1, Th Sai Yuan; mains 280-620B; ⊙3-11pm Mon-Sat; 🖉) Perhaps Rawai's finest restaurant, this semi-open thatched-roof place with an exceptional world-beat soundtrack serves up classy Italian and international dishes in a laid-back, intimate setting. The New Zealand lamb shank is divine, as are the steamed clams, and the pasta sauces are all made from scratch. Tempting veggie choices include aubergine parmigiana and pasta Gorgonzola. Book ahead.

Nikita's
BAR

(Map p633; ☑076 288703; www.nikitas-phuket.com; Hat Rawai; mains 220-800B; ⊙10am-midnight; 🕏) This popular open-air hang-out gazes over the sea just west of Rawai's pier and offers reasonably priced beers and cocktails, as well as coffee, green tea and a good selection of shakes. A mango margarita, perhaps? If you're hungry, it also does decent wood-fired pizzas, Western mains and a lot of seafood.

Reggae Bar
BAR

(Map p633; Th Viset; ⊙noon-late, hours vary) Spilling out from an old wooden shed is this creatively cluttered, laid-back lounge bobbing to classic roots tunes. A leathersmiths by day, it hosts impromptu jams and erratic concerts, barbecues and parties, featuring local reggae bands and, occasionally, some of Thailand's most legendary Rastas. Leather belts dangle, art is plastered across walls, and blacklight graffiti covers every inch of space.

Laguna Rawai
CLUB

(Map p633; ☑098 031 2700; www.lagunarawai.com; 178/15 Th Viset; ⊙5pm-2am; 🕏) One of the few late-night spots in mellow Rawai, the Laguna club gets busy on weekend nights, attracting a mixed crowd of Thais, foreigners and bar girls. Opposite the club is a strip of bars where you can showcase your pool-playing skills. The club and bars are open until 2am, but sometimes run for longer than that.

ⓘ Getting There & Away

Rawai is 18km southwest of Phuket Town. *Sŏrng·tǎa·ou* run to Rawai (30B) from Phuket Town's Th Ranong between 7am and 5pm. Some continue to Hat Nai Han (40B), but not all, so ask first. Taxis from Rawai to Nai Han cost 200B.

Taxis go from Rawai and Hat Nai Han to Phuket airport (750B), Patong (700B) and Phuket Town (500B).

Hat Patong
หาดป่าตอง

☑07620,600 / POP 20,600

Patong (ป่าตอง) is a free-for-all and by far Phuket's most notorious and divisive destination. Almost anything is available for the right price and while that's true of other places in Thailand, Patong doesn't try to hide it. That doesn't mean you're going to like it. But despite the concrete, silicone and moral turpitude, there's something honest about the place.

Gaze out at the wide, white-sand beach and its magnificent crescent bay, and you'll understand how the whole thing started. Diving and spa options abound, along with upscale dining, street-side fish grills, extravagant cabaret, Thai boxing, dusty antique shops and, of course, the opportunity to party from dusk till dawn.

The sun-scorched Russians in bad knock-off T-shirts, the Chinese tour groups, the Western men turning the midlife crisis into a full-scale industry, and the overwhelming disregard for managed development meanwhile make Patong ripe with unintentional comedy.

⊙ Sights & Activities

Wat Suwan Khiri Wong (วัดสุวรรณคีรีวงศ์; Map p620; cnr Th Phra Barami & Th Phisit Karani; ⊙daylight hours) FREE, just off Th Phra Barami at the northeast end of Patong, is a welcome respite from the chaos outside. Less tranquil but worth a look is the **Good Luck Shrine** (ศาลเจ้าโชคดี; cnr Th Tawiwong & Th Phra Barami), a beautiful, golden Bodhisattva statue in the middle of a traffic circle, adorned with rainbow-coloured ribbons and guarded by carved elephants festooned with flowers, incense and candles.

⭐**Sea Fun Divers**   DIVING
(Map p620; ☑076 340480; www.seafundivers. com; 29 Soi Karon Nui; 2/3-dive trip 3900/4400B, Open Water Diver certification 18,400B; ⊙9am-6pm) An outstanding, very professional diving operation, with high standards, impeccable service and keen, knowledgeable instructors (though more expensive than other dive operators). Sea Fun is based at Le Meridien resort at the southern end of Patong; there's a second location (p641) in Kata Noi.

Nicky's Handlebar   ADVENTURE
(☑076 343211; www.nickyshandlebars.com; 41 Th Rat Uthit; half/full-day tour incl bike hire from 7000/9000B) The big-beast bikes here are begging to be taken for a spin, but they aren't for amateurs. Nicky has been leading Harley tours around Phuket for over a decade. Full-day itineraries tour Phang-Nga Province; there are half-day options too, plus Harley rentals for independent explorations (from 4800B). You'll need a big-bike license from home. Hit the bar (p639) for post-drive refreshments.

Pum Thai Cooking School   COOKING
(☑076 346269; www.pumthaifoodchain.com; 204/32 Th Rat Uthit; 3/5hr class 1700/3700B; ⊙11am-9pm) This restaurant/cookery school (with other branches in Thailand, as well as France and the UK) holds daily classes. Popular, five-hour 'Little Wok' classes include a market tour and a take-home cookbook.

🛌 Sleeping

If you can't score a bed in a hostel – be sure to book ahead – you'll struggle to find a room for under 1000B between November and April. Outside this time period rates drop by 40% to 60%.

⭐**Wire Hostel**   HOSTEL **$**
(☑076 604066; 66/10 Th Bangla; dm 340-550B; ❋@🛜) Patong's hostel of the moment is right in the belly of the beast: a minute's walk from the Bangla nightlife. There's some stylish design on display, three floors of dorms (none with doors but you can get a double bed if you fancy getting intimate in public). Downstairs bar, clean shared bathrooms but, unsurprisingly, it can get noisy. Book ahead.

ℹ️ TIGER KINGDOM

At some point during your stay, you'll likely be handed a brochure flaunting Phuket's controversial Tiger Kingdom. Launched in 2013, Tiger Kingdom Phuket (like its original in Chiang Mai) offers hundreds of daily visitors the chance to stroke, feed and pose over-enthusiastically with its 'domesticated' tigers.

Concerns about animal welfare and human safety abound, and there are constant reports about animals being maltreated, confined to small cages and sedated to keep them docile. Like the infamous Tiger Temple in Kanchanaburi, Tiger Kingdom denies all allegations that its tigers are mistreated.

In 2014, an Australian tourist was seriously mauled while visiting Tiger Kingdom. The tiger in question was 'retired'.

Given the significant animal-welfare issues involved, Lonely Planet does not recommend visiting Tiger Kingdom.

Hat Patong

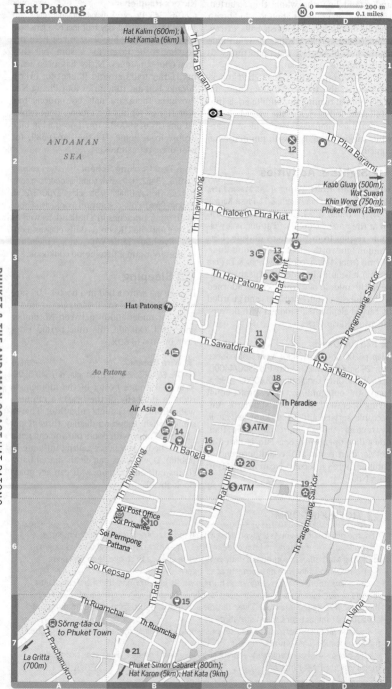

Hat Kalim (600m);
Hat Kamala (6km)

Th Phra Barami

ANDAMAN
SEA

Th Thawiwong

Th Chaloem Phra Kiat

Th Phra Barami

Kaab Gluay (500m);
Wat Suwan
Khin Wong (750m);
Phuket Town (13km)

Th Hat Patong

Th Rat Uthit

Hat Patong

Th Sawatdirak

Ao Patong

Th Sai Nam Yen

Th Paradise

Air Asia

Th Pangmuang Sai Kor

ATM

Th Bangla

Th Thawiwong

ATM

Th Rat Uthit

Soi Post Office
Soi Prisanee
Soi Permpong
Pattana
Soi Kepsap

Th Pangmuang Sai Kor

Th Nanai

Th Ruamchai

Sŏrng·tăa·ou
to Phuket Town

Th Rat Uthit

Th Ruamchai

La Gritta
(700m)

Th Prachanukro

Phuket Simon Cabaret (800m);
Hat Karon (5km); Hat Kata (9km)

0   200 m
0   0.1 miles

Hat Patong

Patong Backpacker Hostel   HOSTEL $

(☑076 341196; 140 Th Thawiwong; dm 300-550B; ✳🛜) This busy budget spot has a great location across the road from the beach, a communal lounge and eccentric but welcoming staff. Colourful dorms sleep three to 10 and come with good mattresses and small lockers. The top floor is brightest, but dorms on the lower floors each have their own attached bathrooms.

Lupta Hostel   HOSTEL $

(☑076 602462, 092 934 6453; www.luptahostel. com; 138 Th Tawiwong; dm/d 690/1390B; ✳@🛜) Just 100m from Th Bangla, this well-kept place offers compact and comfortable four- to eight-bed dorms in light woods and whites, although not all have windows. Each bed gets its own locker, plug socket and tiny shelf. There's a women-only dorm, a sole private room and a social lobby loaded with cushions, high stools and rattan lamps.

Priew Wan Guesthouse   GUESTHOUSE $$

(☑076 344441; info@priewwanguesthouse.com; 83/9 Th Rat Uthit; d 1600B; 🛜) This long-running and reliable family-run guesthouse is hidden down a mostly residential soi, but is still only a 10-minute walk to the northern end of Hat Patong. Clean, sizeable rooms come with balconies, safes, fridges and TVs and are a good deal. Friendly staff and great low-season (April to October) discounts.

★ BYD Lofts   APARTMENT $$$

(☑076 343024; www.bydlofts.com; 5/28 Th Hat Patong; apt 3600-9900B; ✳🛜🏊) Spread over four buildings, BYD feels like it's been torn straight out of an upmarket interior design magazine. Stylish and comfortable (and only a couple of minutes' walk from the beach), the apartments are coated in white and come with sharp lines and colourful art. Some rooms have private pools. For everyone else there's a turquoise rooftop pool.

Impiana Phuket Cabana   HOTEL $$$

(☑076 340138; www.impiana.com; 41 Th Thawiwong; d 12,000-27,000B; 🅿✳🛜🏊) Cabana-style and bang on the best (north) part of the beach, Impiana's rooms are laden with sophisticated creature comforts and still close to all the action. There's good Asian-Mediterranean fusion food at poolside Sala Bua (p638), while indulgent treatments at the on-site Swasana Spa (massage or treatment 1500-5900B; ⊙10am-7pm) see you nestled in a cool glass cube with ocean views.

✗ Eating

Bargain seafood and noodle stalls pop up at night. Try the sois around Th Bangla, and Patong Food Park (Th Rat Uthit; mains 50-200B; ⊙4.30pm-midnight) once the sun drops. The swishest restaurants sit above the cliffs on the north edge of town.

Chicken Rice Briley

THAI $

(☑ 081 597 8380; Th Rat Uthit, Patong Food Park; mains 50-200B; ☺ 6am-9pm) One of few places in Patong Food Park (p637) to offer sustenance while the sun shines. Steamed chicken breast is served on rice with a bowl of chicken broth with crumbled bits of meat; the chili sauce is fantastic for dipping. The stewed pork on rice, plus mango with sticky rice, is popular too. There's a reason it's perennially packed here.

★ Ella

INTERNATIONAL $$

(☑ 076 344253; 100/19-20 Soi Post Office; mains 150-400B; ☺ 9am-midnight; 🛜) This moulded-concrete, industrial-feel bistro-cafe is a lovely surprise. Inventive all-day breakfasts feature spicy Rajasthani scrambled eggs, massaman (curry) chicken tacos, omelettes stuffed with chicken and veg, and baguette French toast with caramelised banana. At night, it's also a bar and a cool spot for a cocktail.

There are similarly styled **rooms** (d 2200-4000B; 🗲 🛜) for rent upstairs.

★ No.9 2nd Restaurant

ASIAN $$

(☑ 076 624445; 143 Th Phra Barami; mains 165-800B; ☺ 11.30am-11.30pm, closed 5th & 20th of every month) Deceptively simple, with wooden tables and photo-strewn walls, this is one of the best, busiest restaurants in Patong, thanks to the inventive and delicious mix of Thai, Japanese and Western dishes. It's

---

GAY PRIDE IN PHUKET

Although Bangkok and Pattaya host big gay-pride celebrations, the **Phuket Gay Pride Festival** (www.phuket-pride. org; ☺ April) is widely considered the best in Thailand, possibly even in all of Southeast Asia. Though the date has changed several times since the festival's inception in 1999, it usually lands in late April. Whenever it blooms, (mostly male) revellers from all over the world flock to the island – to Patong, specifically, for a four-day weekend party.

For updates on future festivals and the local gay scene, check out Gay Patong (www.gaypatong.com).

At any other time of year, you'll find Phuket's gay pulse in the network of streets that link the Royal Paradise Hotel with Th Rat Uthit in Patong. It's a predominantly male scene.

---

a rare feat for a kitchen to be able to turn out authentic sushi, vegetarian versions of Thai curries and a lamb shank without any dip in quality.

★ Georgia Restaurant

GEORGIAN $$

(☑ 076 390595; 19 Th Sawatdirak; mains 200-390B; ☺ noon-10pm, closed Sun) The influx of Russian visitors to Patong has seen a corresponding rise in eateries catering to them. Georgia is the pick of the bunch, offering Russian salads and dumplings alongside delicious *khachapuri*, a cheese-filled bread; *ajapsandali*, a rich, vegetarian stew; and classic eastern European dishes such as *solyanka*, a spicy, sour meat soup served in a clay pot.

Kaab Gluay

THAI $$

(Map p620; ☑ 076 346832; 58/3 Th Phra Barami; mains 135-250B; ☺ 11am-2am; 🛜) Remodelled since our last visit, this busy, semi-open-air roadside eatery is a hit for its authentic, affordable Thai food, with switched-on staff and well-spelt (!) menus to match. Unpretentious dining under a huge roof with ceiling fans. Expect red-curry prawns, chicken satay, sweet-and-sour fish, deep-fried honeyed chicken, classic noodles and stir-fries, and 30-plus takes on spicy Thai salads.

Sala Bua

FUSION $$$

(☑ 076 340138; www.impiana.com; 41 Th Thawiwong; mains 220-610B; ☺ 11am-11pm) Asian-Mediterranean fusion cuisine in a classy seaside four-star resort setting. Start with smoked-salmon Caesar salad or rock lobster, avocado and roasted veg salad, then move on to wood-fired pizzas, seafood-packed spaghetti or *pá·naang* curry osso buco.

🍷 Drinking & Nightlife

Some visitors may find that Patong's bar scene puts them off their *pàt tai*, but if you're in the mood for plenty of banging bass, winking neon and short skirts, it's certainly an experience.

Illuzion

CLUB

(www.illuzionphuket.com; 31 Th Bangla; ☺ 9pm-late) Still the most popular of Patong's mega-aclubs, Illuzion is a multilevel mishmash of dance and gymnastics shows, international DJs, regular ladies' nights, all-night electronic beats, LED screens and more bars than you could ever count.

Craft Beer Lounge
BAR

(www.grandmercurephuketpatong.com; Soi 1, Th Rat Uthit, Grand Mercure Phuket Patong; ⊙10am-11pm) Tapping into one of the world's booze crazes, this sleekly contemporary boutique beer bar stocks more than 100 international draught and craft labels, mostly from the US, plus local brands. For 500B you get free-flowing Singha beer for an hour, but the bartenders also make proper cocktails. The lounge is tucked into the back of the Grand Mercure's lobby.

Nicky's Handlebar
BAR

(☑ 076 343211; www.nickyhandlebars.com; 41 Th Rat Uthit; ⊙7am-1am; 🛜) This fun biker bar welcomes all, wheels or no wheels. Once a bit of a dive, Nicky's has never looked better. There's a good selection of beers and the menu encompasses Western and Thai, including what the bar claims is Thailand's spiciest burger. You can get your own wheels here by asking about Harley tours (p635) and hire (from 4800B).

Zag Club
GAY, BAR

(123/8-9 Royal Paradise Complex; ⊙9pm-3am) Packed-out gay-scene favourite Zag Club hosts no less than three shimmering cabarets at 10.40pm, 11.40pm and 1.20am. In between, everyone drinks and dances to booming chart-toppers.

Aussie Bar
PUB

(www.phuketaussiebar.com; Th Bangla; ⊙9am-late; 🛜) Does what it says on the tin: Aussie sport on the many screens, Aussie food on the menu and lots of visiting Australians clutching beers. Also has pool tables and tabletop football, and it does provide an antidote to the surrounding go-go bars.

☆ Entertainment

Cross-dressing cabarets and Thai boxing are Patong's specialities.

Bangla Boxing Stadium
SPECTATOR SPORT

(☑ 076 273416; www.banglaboxingstadiumpatong. com; Th Pangmuang Sai Kor; stadium/ringside 1700/2500B; ⊙9pm Wed, Fri & Sun) A packed line-up of competitive *moo·ay tai* (Thai boxing) bouts featuring Thai and foreign fighters.

Phuket Simon Cabaret
CABARET

(Map p620; ☑ 076 342114; www.phuket-simon cabaret.com; 8 Th Sirirach; adult 800-1000B, child 600-800B; ⊙shows 6pm, 7.30pm & 9pm) About 500m south of town, Simon puts on fun, colourful trans cabarets that are wildly popular with Asian tourists. The 600-seat theatre is grand, the costumes are glittery, feathery extravaganzas, and the ladyboys are convincing. The house is usually full – book ahead.

Rock City
LIVE MUSIC

(www.rockcitypatong.com; 169 Th Rat Uthit; ⊙8pm-2am) On the corner of Th Bangla and Th Rat Uthit, this suitably dark and sweaty den of rock lives on the glory of AC/DC, Metallica and Guns N' Roses tribute bands and attracts a headbanging crowd of tourists and locals. The live music gets going around 9pm.

ℹ Information

There are ATMs, currency-exchange facilities and wi-fi across town.

ℹ Getting There & Away

Sŏrng·tăa·ou from Th Ranong in Phuket Town go to the south end of Hat Patong (40B) from 7am to 6pm. From here you can walk or hop on motorbike taxis (30B per ride) or túk-túk. After-hours túk-túk charters from Phuket Town cost 500B. A 'local bus' runs between Phuket Town's Bus Terminal 1 and Patong (30B) from 7am to 5pm, or you can catch minivans that leave when full from the same place (50B).

Taxis to/from the airport cost 800B. There's a shared minibus from the airport to Patong (180B per person, minimum 10 people).

ℹ Getting Around

A túk-túk will circle Patong for around 200B per ride. Numerous places rent motorbikes (250B); Nicky's Handlebar rents Harleys (from 4800B). The mandatory helmet law is strictly enforced in Patong, where roadblocks/checkpoints can spring up suddenly. **Avis** (☑ 062 604 0361; www.avisthailand.com; 239/1 Th Rat Uthit; ⊙7.30am-7pm) hires cars at the south end of town.

Hat Kata
หาดกะตะ

Classier than Karon and without Patong's seedy hustle, Kata (กะตะ) attracts travellers of all ages to its lively beach. While you won't bag a secluded strip of sand, you'll still find lots to do. A prime spot for surfing in the shoulder and wet seasons, Kata also has some terrific day spas, top-notch food and a highly rated yoga studio.

Hat Karon & Hat Kata

The golden-sand beach is carved in two by a rocky headland: **Hat Kata Yai** (หาด กะตะใหญ่; Map p640) lies on the north side; more secluded **Hat Kata Noi** (หาดกะตะน้อย; Map p640) unfurls to the south. The road between them is home to Phuket's original millionaire's row.

The main street, Th Kata, runs parallel to the beach. There are cheaper restaurants, bars and guesthouses on Th Thai Na, which branches inland just south of where Th Kata heads up over the hill into Karon.

◉ Sights & Activities

The small island of **Ko Pu** is just offshore, but be careful of rip currents, heed the red flags and don't go past the breakers in the rainy season unless you're a strong, experienced ocean swimmer.

Both of Kata's beaches offer decent surfing from April to November. Hiring stand-up paddle kit or kayaks costs 300/900B per hour/day. There's a branch of the highly rated Sea Fun Divers on Kata Noi.

Rumblefish Adventure   DIVING
(Map p640; ☏ 095 441 8665; www.rumblefish adventure.com; 98/79 Beach Centre, Th Kata, Hat

Kata; 2/3-dive day trip 3500/3900B; ⊙ 10am-7pm) A terrific boutique dive shop offering all the standard courses, day trips and liveaboards from its Beach Centre location in Kata. The PADI Open Water Diver certification course costs 12,500B. There's a small **hostel** (Map p640; ☑ 076 330315; www.rumblefishadventure. com; 98/79 Th Kata, Hat Kata; dm 300B, d 400-950B; ✸ 🛜) attached: divers get a free dorm bed if there's room. Book ahead.

Phuket Surf   SURFING

(Map p640; ☑ 063 870280; www.phuketsurfing. com; Hat Kata Yai; lessons 1500B, board rental per hour/day 150/500B; ⊙ 8am-7pm Apr-late Oct) Offers private 1½-hour surf lessons plus board rentals. Check the website for info on local surf breaks.

Sea Fun Divers   DIVING

(Map p640; ☑ 076 330124; www.seafundivers. com; 14 Th Kata Noi, Katathani; 2/3-dive day trip 3900/4400B; ⊙ 9am-6pm) An outstanding and very professional diving operation, albeit rather more expensive than the competition. Standards are extremely high; service is impeccable and instructors are keen and knowledgeable. Open Water Diver certification costs 18,400B. Sea Fun also has a branch (p635) at Le Meridien resort at the southern end of Patong.

Dive Asia   DIVING

(Map p640; ☑ 076 330598; www.diveasia.com; 24 Th Karon, Hat Kata; 2/3-dive day trip 3400/4900B; ⊙ 10am-9pm) This outfit runs an extensive range of PADI certification courses (Open Water Diver 11,480B) plus day-trip dives to Ko Phi-Phi and liveaboards to the Similan and Surin Islands (from 21,000B). There's another branch (p643) in Karon.

🍴 Courses

Kata Hot Yoga   YOGA

(Map p640; ☑ 076 605950; www.katahotyoga. com; 217 Th Koktanod, Hat Kata; 550B per class; ⊙ 9-10.30am, 5.15-6.45pm, 7.15-8.45pm) Craving more heat? At Kata Hot Yoga, Bikram's famous asana series is taught over 90 minutes in a sweltering room by the expert owner and an international roster of visiting instructors. All levels welcome; no bookings needed. Multi-class packages offer good deals.

Boathouse Cooking Class   COOKING

(Map p640; ☑ 076 330015; www.boathouse-phuket.com; 182 Th Koktanod, Hat Kata; classes 2570-4095B; ⊙ classes 10am Wed, Sat & Sun) Kata's top fine-dining **restaurant** (Map p640; ☑ 076 330015; www.boathouse-phuket.com; 182 Th Koktanod, Hat Kata; mains 470-1750B, tasting menus 1800-2200B; ⊙ 11am-10.30pm) offers fantastic one-day and two-day Thai cooking classes with its renowned chef.

🛏 Sleeping

Hostels and guesthouses cluster near the north of Hat Kata Yai: posher hotels and resorts can be found further south.

If you're stuck without shelter, you'll probably find a room at the Beach Centre, a complex of new-build townhouses packed with way too many guesthouses to list. From Th Kata, turn inland just south of the intersection with Th Thai Na; it's signposted.

★ Fin Hostel   HOSTEL $

(Map p640; ☑ 088 753 1162; www.finhostelphuket. com; 100/20 Th Kata/Patak West; dm/capsules/d 400/600/2000B; ✸ 🛜 🛏) This well-kept, efficient hostel, set back from the road, spreads across two buildings. Dorms are spotless with comfy mattresses. The capsules are a step up – curtained spaces with either single or double mattresses – while private rooms have some quirky decoration, beanbags, TVs and fridges.

There's a decent communal area, a small rooftop pool and you're walking distance to Kata beach.

Fantasy Hill Bungalow   BUNGALOW $

(Map p640; ☑ 076 330106; fantasyhill@hotmail. com; 8/1 Th Kata, Hat Kata; d 600-1200B; 🅿 ✸ 🛜) Tucked into a lush garden on a low-rise hill, long-standing Fantasy Hill is peaceful and central. The ageing but well-maintained bungalows and rooms are great value for the location (the cheapest are fan-only and compact) and staff are pleasant. Go for a corner air-con room with views across Kata and beyond.

Sabai Corner   BUNGALOW $$

(Map p633; ☑ 089 875 5525; www.facebook.com/ Sabai-Corner-150517525037992; Hat Kata, off Rte 4233; chalets 2000B; 🅿 🛜) No other rooms on the island offer the fabulous 270-degree ocean views available from these isolated hillside chalets. Each is a spacious independent studio with pebbled bathroom, canopied four-poster bed, wall-mounted TV, fridge, sofa and safe, as well as a large outdoor terrace with lounge chairs. Book ahead.

★**Kata Rocks**   DESIGN HOTEL **$$$**
(Map p640; ☑ 076 370777; www.katarocks.com; 186/22 Th Koktanod, Hat Kata; d 35,000-84,800B; P ❄ 🛜 ≋) A contemporary all-white beauty, poised on cliffs between Kata's two beaches. Villas are minimalist-chic apartments with iPad-controlled sound systems, full kitchens, Nespresso machines, private pools, hip contemporary artwork on the walls and electric blinds. Semi-submerged sunbeds dot the pale-turquoise sea-view infinity pool.

The innovative **Infinite Luxury Spa** (treatment 3600-9500B; ⊙ 10am-10pm) blends traditional therapies with bang-up-to-date technology such as anti-jetlag pods.

★**Sawasdee Village**   BOUTIQUE HOTEL **$$$**
(Map p640; ☑ 076 330979; www.phuketsawasdee.com; 38 Th Kade Kwan, Hat Kata; d 4800-15,000B; ❄ @ 🛜 ≋) This opulent boutique resort mixes classic Thai style with Moroccanesque flourishes, immersed in a lush tropical landscape laced with canals, waterfalls, Buddhist art installations and a stunning **spa** (treatment 1100-5000B; ⊙ 10am-10pm). Ornate, peaked-roof bungalows aren't huge but have super-comfy beds, wooden floors, beamed ceilings and lots of character. The villas are two-floor homes with direct access to one of two romantic pools.

✗ Eating

Kata Mama   THAI **$**
(Map p640; ☑ 076 284006; Hat Kata Yai; mains 100-200B; ⊙ 8am-10pm) Our pick of several cheapie seafood places at the southern end of Hat Kata Yai, long-standing Kata Mama keeps busy thanks to its charming management, reliably tasty Thai standards and low-key beachside setting.

★**Red Duck**   THAI **$$**
(Map p640; ☑ 084 850 2929; 88/3 Th Koktanod, Hat Kata; mains 240-380B; ⊙ noon-11pm Tue-Sun; 🛜 ☑) Dishes here are more expensive than at other Thai restaurants, but they're delicious, MSG-free and prepared with the freshest of ingredients. The seafood curries and soups are especially fine. There's also a big vegan selection of Thai classics, such as pineapple or coconut curry and a vegetable *larb*.

Eat inside or on the small outdoor terrace. Service is excellent.

★**Istanbul Restaurant**   TURKISH **$$**
(Map p640; ☑ 091 820 7173; www.istanbulrestaurantphuket.com; 100/87 Th Koktanod, Hat Kata; mains 210-320B; ⊙ 8am-10pm) This delightful, family-run place is the most popular foreign restaurant in Kata and for good reason. The food is simply splendid, ranging from big Western- or Turkish-style breakfasts to completely authentic and super-tasty mains such as *hünkar beğendi* (beef stew on a bed of eggplant puree), kebabs and Turkish-style pizza. Then there are the superb soups, salads and delectable desserts.

🍷 Drinking & Nightlife

★**Art Space Cafe & Gallery**   BAR
(Map p640; ☑ 090 156 0677; Th Kade Kwan, Hat Kata; ⊙ 11am-1am) Hands down the most fabulously quirky bar in Phuket, this trippy, multi-use space bursts with colour and is smothered in uniquely brushed canvases and sculptures celebrating, especially, the feminine form. It's the work of an eccentric creative and his tattoo-artist wife, who whip up both decent cocktails and veggie meals (160B to 400B). There's normally live music around 8pm.

★**Ska Bar**   BAR
(Map p640; www.skabar-phuket.com; 186/12 Th Koktanod; ⊙ 1pm-2am) Tucked into the rocks on the southernmost curl of Hat Kata Yai and seemingly intertwined with the trunk of a grand old banyan tree, Ska is our choice for seaside sundowners. The Thai bartenders add to the laid-back Rasta vibe, and buoys, paper lanterns and flags dangle from the canopy. There's normally a fire show on Friday nights.

After Beach Bar   BAR
(Map p640; ☑ 081 894 3750; Rte 4233; ⊙ 9am-11pm) It's impossible to overstate how glorious the 180-degree views are from this stilted, thatched reggae bar clinging to a cliff above Kata: rippling sea, rocky peninsulas and palm-dappled hills. Now put on the Bob Marley and you've got the perfect sunset-watching spot. When the fireball finally drops, lights from fishing boats blanket the horizon. Try the bursting-with-flavour *pàt tai*.

❶ Information

There are plenty of ATMs and wi-fi is available everywhere.

❶ Getting There & Around

Sŏrng·tăa·ou run from Th Ranong in Phuket Town to Kata (40B) from 7.30am to 6pm, stopping on Th Pak Bang (opposite Kata Beach Resort).

Taxis from Kata go to Phuket airport (1200B), Phuket Town (600B), Patong (500B) and Karon (300B). There's a minibus service from the airport to Kata (200B per person, minimum 10 people).

Motorbike rentals (250B per day) are widely available.

Hat Karon   หาดกะรน

Hat Karon is like the love child of Hat Patong and Hat Kata: chilled-out and starry-eyed but a tad sleazy. Despite the mega-resorts, there's still more sand space per capita here than at Patong or Kata. The further north you go the more beautiful the broad golden beach gets, culminating at the northern-most edge (accessible from a rutted road past the roundabout) where the water is like turquoise glass.

Within the inland network of streets and plazas you'll find a harmless jumble of good local food, more Russian signage than seems reasonable, low-key girly bars, T-shirt vendors and pretty Karon Park, with its artificial lake and mountain backdrop. The northern end of town, near the roundabout, is more package-touristy, while southern Karon blends into more sophisticated Kata.

🏃 Activities

During the April–October low season, you can take surf lessons (one hour 1200B) and rent surfboards/bodyboards (300/150B per hour) at the south end of **Hat Karon** (หาด กะรน; Map p640).

Kata-based Dive Asia has an office in south Karon.

Sunrise Divers   DIVING

(Map p640; ☑ 084 626 4646, 076 398040; www. sunrise-divers.com; 269/24 Th Patak East; 3-dive trip 3700-3900B, liveaboard from 12,900B; ◷ 9am-5pm) Managed by a long-time local blogger, Phuket's biggest liveaboard agent organises a range of budget to luxury multiday dives to the Similan and Surin Islands, Myanmar's Mergui Archipelago and Ko Phi-Phi. Also arranges day-trip dives, including to Ko Phi-Phi annad the Similans.

Dive Asia   DIVING

(Map p640; ☑ 076 396199; www.diveasia.com; Th Karon/Patak West; day trip 2950B) Runs a big range of PADI certification courses (Open Water Diver 14,900B) plus day-trip dives to Ko Phi-Phi and liveaboards to the Similan and Surin Islands (from 21,000B). The main branch (p641) is in Kata.

Dino Park   MINIGOLF

(Map p640; ☑ 076 330625; www.dinopark.com; Th Karon/Patak West; adult/child 240/180B; ◷ 10am-11pm) *Jurassic Park* meets minigolf at this bizarre fun park on the southern edge of Hat Karon. It's a maze of caves, waterfalls, lagoons, leafy gardens and dinosaur statues, all spread across 18 holes of putting greens. Kids will have a blast, but really it's for everyone. Adults also have the option of retreating to the *Flintstones*-esque bar at the entrance.

🛏 Sleeping

★**Doolay Hostel**   HOSTEL $

(Map p640; ☑ 062 451 9546; www.doolayhostel. com; 164 Th Karon/Patak West; dm 450-600B; ✴ 🛜) There are 40 beds spread across six compact, four- and eight-bed dorms at this newish place that's a mere stroll across the road to the sand. Mattresses are good and the bathrooms are clean. There's a nice communal area and, best of all, a long 2nd-floor seafront terrace strewn with bean bags that's fine for lounging. Helpful staff. Book ahead.

Pineapple Guesthouse   GUESTHOUSE $

(Map p640; ☑ 076 396223; www.pineapple phuket.com; 291/4 Karon Plaza; dm/d 300/1100B; ✴ @ 🛜) Pocketed away 400m inland from Hat Karon, Pineapple is a decent budget choice under warm Thai-English management. Rooms are old-fashioned, but clean and comfortable enough with colourful feature walls, fridges and, in some cases, small balconies. There's a simple 10-bed dorm (closed low season April to October) with its own bathroom and big lockers.

In On The Beach   HOTEL $$

(Map p640; ☑ 076 398220; www.karon-inonthe beach.com; 695-697 Mu 1, Th Patak West; d incl breakfast 3500-4800B; 🅿 ✴ 🛜 ☒) Steps from the northern end of Hat Karon, this hotel's slightly dated but comfortable cream-walled rooms set around a deep-blue pool were waiting for an upgrade at the time of research. Many have sea views, the staff are friendly and breakfast is served on the rooftop terrace. With substantial low-season discounts, it's an ideal surf lair.

Marina Phuket   RESORT $$$
(Map p640; ☑ 076 330625; www.marinaphuket.com; 47 Th Karon; d incl breakfast 6600-18,600B; ▣❈🛜⛱) Stilted boardwalks lead through lush, hushed gardens to comfy, secluded sea- and jungle-facing rooms decked out in classic Thai style. All enjoy breezy terraces, warm-wood decor, teak furniture and silk throws. Villas have hot tubs. There's a big pool, a spa and no fewer than four restaurants.

✕ Eating

There are reliable Thai and seafood places at the north end of Hat Karon and on the main road near south Hat Karon.

★ Pad Thai Shop   THAI $
(Map p640; Th Patak East; mains 50-80B; ⊙ 8am-7pm, closed Fri) This glorified roadside food shack makes rich, savoury chicken stew and absurdly good *kôw pàt boo* (fried rice with crab), *pàt see·éw* (fried noodles) and noodle soup. It also serves up some of the best *pàt tai* we've ever tasted: spicy and sweet, packed with tofu, egg and peanuts, and plated with spring onions, bean sprouts and lime.

Elephant Cafe   THAI, INTERNATIONAL $$
(Map p640; ☑ 076 398129; 489 Th Patak East; mains 80-390B; ⊙ 10am-11pm; ☑) Reliable and popular spot for both Thai and Western food. Dine on curries and spicy salads, or steaks, chops and pizza, in the enclosed, garden-like interior. Plenty of vegetarian choices too, as well as cakes and cocktails.

★ Eat Bar & Grill   GRILL $$$
(Map p640; ☑ 085 292 5652; www.eatbargrill.com; 250/1 Th Patak East; mains 200-800B; ⊙ 11am-10pm; 🛜) There's awesome burgers and superb steaks, a contender for the best on Phuket, at this laid-back place with a wooden bar and limited space (make sure to book ahead). The menu includes other dishes, including a great lamb shank, but beef is the thing here: prepared to your taste, stylishly presented and reasonably priced, given the quality. Proper cocktails too.

❶ Getting There & Around

Sǒrng·tǎa·ou run frequently from Th Ranong in Phuket Town to Hat Karon (30B) from 7.30am to 6pm.

Taxis from Karon go to Phuket airport (1000B), Phuket Town (550B), Patong (400B) and Kata (200B). A minibus runs from the airport to Karon (200B, minimum 10 people).

Motorbike rental costs 250B per day.

Hat Kamala   หาดกมลา

A chilled-out hybrid of Hat Karon and Hat Surin, Kamala lures in a mix of longer-term, low-key visitors, including families and young couples. The bay is magnificent and serene, with palms and pines mingling on its leafy, rocky northern end, where the water is a rich emerald green and the snorkelling around the rock reef is halfway decent. The entire beach is backed by a paved path and lush rolling hills, which one can only hope are left alone...forever. Flashy new resorts are carved into the southern bluffs and jet skis make an appearance, but the nightlife is serene and Kamala is quietish and laid-back by Phuket standards.

◉ Sights & Activities

During the May–October monsoon, you can hire surfboards (300B per hour) and take surf classes (1500B) on south Hat Kamala.

Tsunami Memorial   MEMORIAL
(อนุสรณ์สถานสึนามิ; Map p646) Kamala was one of Phuket's worst-hit areas during the 2004 Boxing Day tsunami. The Heart of the Universe Memorial pays tribute to lost loved ones with a moving, wave-inspired metallic oval created by prominent Thai artist Udon Jiraksa.

🛏 Sleeping

Baan Kamala   GUESTHOUSE $
(Map p646; ☑ 076 279053; www.baankamalaphuket.com; 74/42 Mu 3; dm 450-550B, d 2000B; ❈🛜) A cross between a guesthouse and a hostel, welcoming Baan Kamala offers big and light six-bed dorms for backpackers and a collection of individually designed private rooms for flashpackers. The concrete walls of the spacious rooms are livened up with paintings and beds are comfortable, although bathrooms are a little poky. The communal area features its very own long-tail boat.

Papa Crab BOUTIQUE HOTEL **$$**
(Map p646; ☑076 385315; www.phuketpapacrab.com; 93/5 Mu 3; d 2300B; ✳🖭) This elegant boutique guesthouse combines homey lodgings, a peaceful location and discreet, friendly service. A wooden bridge trails over the lobby's lily pond to tastefully styled terracotta-floor rooms with dark-wood beds and soothing lime-green-and-white colour schemes. It's better than many more-expensive nearby options. The hotel usually closes for August.

Cape Sienna HOTEL **$$$**
(Map p646; ☑076 337300; www.capesienna.com; 18/40 Mu 6, Th Nakalay; d 4600-16,650B; ✳🖭🏊) This flashy, romantic hotel sprawls up the southern headland offering magnificent azure bay views from the lobby, pool and every room. Rooms are bright, smart and modern, with all amenities and splashes of orange and turquoise. Deluxe rooms have balcony hot tubs. Up above is Kamala's breeziest cocktail bar, **Vanilla Sky** (Map p646; 18/40 Mu 6, Th Nakalay, Cape Sienna; ⊙5pm-midnight), and there's fine steaks at the on-site Plum steakhouse.

✗ Eating

Meena Restaurant THAI **$**
(Map p646; Hat Kamala; mains 80-150B; ⊙9am-5pm, closed May-Oct) This family-run beach-side shack with rainbow-striped and leopard-print sarongs for tablecloths is a real find. The owners couldn't be more welcoming. The tasty authentic Thai food is exceptional and so are the fresh fruit shakes. The rustic setting is exactly what you likely came to Kamala for. It's at the north end of the beach.

Isaan Popeye Thai Food THAI **$**
(Map p646; ☑089 056 9605; 74/43 Mu 3; mains 100-200B; ⊙9.30am-10pm) One of the few restaurants in Kamala where you'll find locals dining, thanks to the winning combination of authentic and spicy northeastern dishes, fresh seafood and classic stir-fries and noodles. It also does Western breakfasts. It's a five-minute walk inland from the beach.

★ Blue Manao THAI **$$**
(Map p646; ☑076 385783; 93/13 Mu 3, Th Hat Kamala; mains 130-530B; ⊙noon-11pm; 🖭) This relaxed, French-run eatery decked out in marine blue has rather more atmosphere

ⓘ PHUKET FANTASEA

It's impossible to ignore the brochures and touts flogging Phuket Fantasea, the US$60 million 'cultural theme park' located just east of Hat Kamala and relentlessly promoted as one of the island's top 'family-friendly' attractions. While it is very popular with Asian tourists, and some Westerners, we recommend reading up on the numerous animal-welfare issues associated with this Vegas-style spectacle, at which animals are forced to 'perform' daily, before choosing to support it.

than its nearby competitors, as well as a more individual menu. The seafood – barracuda, yellow curry squid – is an obvious draw, but the traditional Thai curries (whether meat, fish or vegetarian) are also excellent, as are the European desserts. It has a proper bar too.

Plum INTERNATIONAL **$$$**
(Map p646; ☑076 337300; 18/40 Mu 6, Th Nakalay, Cape Sienna; mains 500-5000B; ⊙6-11pm, closed Mon; 🖭) Part steakhouse, part European-style seafood emporium, Plum is dominated by its charcoal grill on which imported, melt-in-the-mouth cuts of beef are laid lovingly. But there's also a big seafood selection, pastas, risottos and salads, all generously served with beautiful beach and bay panoramas from up high. Book ahead to dine at an in-pool cabana table.

ⓘ Getting There & Away

Sŏrng·tăa·ou run between Phuket Town's Th Ranong and Kamala (40B) from 7am to 5pm. *Sŏrng·tăa·ou* also go from Kamala to Hat Surin (20B). Taxis to/from the airport cost 700B.

Hat Surin หาดสุรินทร์

With a wide, golden beach, water that blends from pale turquoise in the shallows to a deep blue on the horizon, and lush, boulder-strewn headlands, Surin (สุรินทร์) is as attractive a spot as anywhere in Phuket. It's also home to five-star spa resorts, stunning galleries and fabulous boutiques. These days, Surin is very much an upmarket destination, attracting cashed-up foreigners and Thais.

Hat Kamala, Hat Surin & Ao Bang Thao

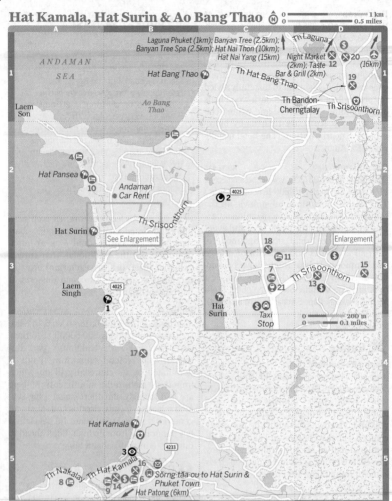

Phuket's crackdown on unlicensed beachfront restaurants and bars hit Surin particularly hard. All establishments on the sand have been cleared away, with some moving up the road to Ao Bang Thao (p648) and others just closing. As a consequence, there are rather fewer eateries and bars here than elsewhere on Phuket's west coast.

Despite this, Hat Surin remains welcoming and beautiful. North of here is small, secluded **Hat Pansea** (หาดพันซี), home to exclusive resorts.

Busy mosque **Masjid Mukaram Bang Thao** (มัสยิดมุการ์ร่ม บางเทา; Map p646; Rte 4025; ⊙ daylight hours) FREE provides a good insight into Phuket village life and makes an interesting change of scene from the beach.

🛏 Sleeping

Hat Surin hosts some of Phuket's classiest resorts, but little for those on a budget.

Benyada Lodge   HOTEL **$$**
(Map p646; ☑ 076 271777; www.benyadalodge-phuket.com; 106/52 Mu 3, Hat Surin; d incl

Hat Kamala, Hat Surin & Ao Bang Thao

breakfast 1500-3000B; ❄🛜) A reasonably priced option in a neigbourhood dominated by upmarket resorts and just a couple of minutes from the beach, Benyada has big, slightly old-fashioned but comfortable rooms. The best come with small balconies. Smiley service, and you can catch the sunset from the rooftop bar.

★ **Surin Phuket** RESORT $$$
(Map p646; ☎076 621580; www.thesurinphuket.com; 118 Mu 3, Hat Pansea; bungalows incl breakfast 14,600-34,400B; P❄🛜❄) Almost any establishment on a secluded beach this quiet and stunning would be a top pick. But the bungalows here, hidden beneath hillside foliage and overlooking Hat Pansea, up the ante with homey, earthy, luxurious interiors, and the six-sided sea-view pool is gorgeously abstract. It's quite a walk up hills and over wooden walkways to many of the 'cottages'.

★ **Amanpuri Resort** RESORT $$$
(Map p646; ☎076 324333; www.amanresorts.com; Hat Pansea; villas US$1000-3100; P❄🛜❄) Understated, luxurious and immensely peaceful, celebrity-magnet Amanpuri is one of Phuket's finest, most exclusive hotels. Graceful traditional-design bungalows are all about the location on quiet Hat Pansea, with sea-facing cabanas, warm-wood decor and enormous bathrooms; many have their own private pools. There's a huge array of activities on offer (yoga, kayaking, surfing), plus a jet-black pool and supreme service.

❌ Eating & Drinking

Surin's dining scene is now rather forlorn, with all the beachfront places ejected from

the area. Most restaurants can be found along Th Srisoonthorn or on the soi just back from the beach.

Blue Lagoon THAI $
(Map p646; ☎087 923 8235; Th Srisoonthorn; mains 80-180B; ⊙7.30am-11pm) One of a dwindling number of restaurants in Surin, following the crackdown on beachfront establishments, this family-run, semi-open-air joint serves up tasty versions of all your classic Thai dishes, as well as seafood and Western breakfasts. It's rather more down-to-earth than most Surin eateries.

Bocconcino DELI, ITALIAN $$$
(Map p646; ☎076 386531; www.bocconcinophuket.com; 8/71 Mu 3, Th Srisoonthorn; mains 320-520B; ⊙9am-10pm; 🛜) An Italian deli may not be what you came to Phuket for, but Bocconcino's homemade gelato is classic Surin: refined and refreshing. This elegant, expat-frequented eatery houses an Italophile's dream of wines, coffee, cakes, cheeses, cured meats, homemade pastas, pizzas and changing specials. For something lighter, try traditional salads such as tomato and mozzarella. It's 600m east of Hat Surin.

Oriental Spoon THAI, INTERNATIONAL $$$
(Map p646; ☎076 316500; 106/46 Mu 3, Hat Surin; mains 350-1300B; ⊙11am-11pm; 🛜) This big restaurant inside **Twin Palms** (Map p646; ☎076 316500; www.twinpalms-phuket.com; 106/46 Mu 3, Hat Surin; d incl breakfast 8900-26,100B; ❄@🛜❄) resort gets busy for its popular Sunday brunch (1990B), but it's also worth checking out its unusual selection of dishes that show a Peranakan flavour: a mix of Thai, Chinese and Malay influences.

Expect spicy and sour, with lots of tamarind and lemongrass. It also does Western mains and has a comprehensive wine list.

9th Glass Wine Bar & Bistro WINE BAR

(Map p646; ☑ 076 068 0068; www.the9thglass. com; 106/16 Mu 3, Hat Surin; ⊙ 4pm-midnight Mon-Sat) The widest choice of wine in Surin, with labels spanning Europe, Australia, New Zealand and South Africa, as well as properly mixed cocktails and a big liquor selection. This refined, intimate bar also offers tapas to nibble while you imbibe, or Western-style mains. It's as close to the beach as is now possible for a bar in Surin.

ℹ Information

There are ATMs along Th Srisoonthorn. All hotels have wi-fi.

ℹ Getting There & Away

Sŏrng·tăa·ou go from Phuket Town's Th Ranong to Hat Surin (40B) from 7am to 5pm, continuing to Hat Kamala; túk-túk charters and taxis cost 500B. Taxis to/from the airport cost 700B.

Ao Bang Thao หาดบางเทา

Stunning **Hat Bang Thao**, 8km of white-sand beach, is the glue that binds this area's disparate elements together. The southern half of the region is dotted with three- and four-star resorts, and a swanky beach club. Further inland you'll find an old fishing village laced with canals, a number of upstart villa subdivisions, stellar restaurants and signs of more development. More than anywhere else on Phuket, Ao Bang Thao is still being remodelled.

Smack in the centre of it all is the somewhat bizarre Laguna Phuket complex, a network of four- and five-star resorts tied together by an artificial lake (patrolled by tourist shuttle boats) and a paved nature trail. At the northern end of the region, mother nature reasserts itself, and a lonely stretch of powder-white sand and tropical blue sea extends past the bustle into the peaceful bliss you originally had in mind.

🛏 Sleeping

The Laguna Phuket complex includes seven luxury resorts. There are cheaper beach-front resorts in southern Ao Bang Thao.

★ **Anantara Phuket Layan** RESORT $$$

(Map p620; ☑ 076 317200; www.anantara.com; 168 Mu 6, Soi 4, Hat Layan; d 14,000B, villas 16,500-81,500B; [P ✿ ⊛ 🛜 ☲]) On its own secluded, wild-feel bay just north of Hat Bang Thao, this is an exquisite top-end choice. Chic, contemporary-Thai rooms come decked out with dark woods, marble floors, ceramic-bowl sinks and Apple gadgets. Villas have dark-tiled pools and 24-hour butlers. A laid-back lounge-bar overlooks the beachside pool. Dine at three excellent on-site restaurants or in a private beach cabana.

Banyan Tree RESORT $$$

(Map p620; ☑ 076 372400; www.banyantree.com; 33 Mu 4, Th Srisoonthorn, Laguna Phuket; d incl breakfast 17,900-31,500B; [P ✿ @ 🛜 ☲]) One of Phuket's finest hotels, and the first to introduce bungalows with their own personal pools, the sprawling Banyan Tree is a lushly shaded oasis of sedate, understated luxury. Accommodation is in sophisticated villas, with free-standing, open-air baths and private pools, and there's also an adults-only pool.

Don't miss the on-site **spa** (Map p620; www. banyantreespa.com; massage or treatment 3500-9500B; ⊙ 10am-10pm).

🍴 Eating

Some of Phuket's best international restaurants cluster in Ao Bang Thao. For cheap eats, head to the new **night market** (Map p620; Laguna Phuket, Ao Bang Thao; mains from 40B; ⊙ 5-10pm).

★ **Pesto** THAI, INTERNATIONAL $$

(Map p646; ☑ 082 423 0184; Th Bandon-Cherng-talay; mains 135-530B; ⊙ noon-11pm; 🖉) Mix a Paris-trained Thai chef with a simple street-side, semi-open-air location and you get delicious, wallet-friendly Thai and international food. Light pesto pasta and lobster lasagne whizz you to the Mediterranean. Otherwise, stay local with grilled tuna on Andaman seaweed, *đôm yam gûng* (spicy-sour prawn soup), deep-fried turmeric-spiced fish of the day and all your favourite curries.

Andaman Restaurant THAI $$

(Map p646; 82/9 Mu 3, Hat Bang Thao; mains 195-325B; ⊙ 8am-10pm; 🛜) Part of the **Andaman Bangtao Bay Resort** (Map p646; ☑ 076 314290; www.andamanresort.com; d incl breakfast 1900-5900B; [P ✿ 🛜 ☲]), this simple seaside restaurant has a laid-back castaway paradise feel with rustic bamboo lanterns and driftwood furniture. Dine on decent-enough BBQ seafood and Thai curries on a multi-level platform trickling down to the sand.

★**Bampot** INTERNATIONAL **$$$**

(Map p646; ☑ 093 586 9828; www.bampot.co; 19/1 Mu 1, Th Laguna; mains 500-1200B; ☺ 6pm-midnight) Cool-blue booths, dangling pans, black-topped tables and white brick walls hung with art set the scene for ambitious European-inspired meals (lobster mac and cheese, sea bass ceviche with pomelo) straight from the open-plan kitchen. Creatively concocted cocktails and international wines round things off.

★**Taste Bar & Grill** FUSION **$$$**

(Map p620; ☑ 087 886 6401; www.tastebargrill.com; 3/2 Mu 5, Th Srisoonthorn, Ao Bang Thao; mains 390-990B; ☺ noon-11pm Tue-Sun; ☏) Minimalist modern lines, top-notch service, a sophisticated but chilled-out vibe and delicious fusion food make this eatery an outstanding choice. The menu features Thai and Mediterranean influences, but the steaks are great too. You can't go wrong with the seafood, and there are excellent salads and a huge array of starters.

Tatonka INTERNATIONAL **$$$**

(Map p646; ☑ 076 324349; 382/19 Mu 1, Th Laguna; mains 350-790B; ☺ 6-10pm Mon-Sat; ☑) Tatonka bills itself as the home of 'globetrotter cuisine', which owner-chef Harold Schwarz has developed by combining local products with cooking learned in Europe, Colorado and Hawaii. The eclectic, tapas-style selection includes inventive vegetarian and seafood dishes and such delights as Peking duck pizza, green-curry pasta and eggplant 'cookies' with goat's cheese. Book ahead in high season.

❶ Getting There & Away

Sŏrng·tăa·ou run between Phuket Town's Th Ranong and Ao Bang Thao (30B) from 7am to 5pm. Túk-túk charters are 400B. Taxis to/from the airport cost 700B.

Sirinat National Park อุทยานแห่งชาติสิรินาถ

Comprising the exceptional beaches of Nai Thon, Nai Yang and Mai Khao, along with the former Nai Yang National Park and Mai Khao wildlife reserve, **Sirinat National Park** (Map p620; ☑ 076 328226, 076 327152; www.dnp.go.th; 89/1 Mu 1, Hat Nai Yang; adult/child 200/100B; ☺ 6am-6pm) encompasses 22 sq km of coastline and 68 sq km of sea, stretching from the north end of Ao Bang Thao to Phuket's northernmost tip. This is one of the sweetest slices of the island, with slightly less tourist traffic than elsewhere, especially on **Hat Mai Khao** (หาดไม้ขาว; Map p620), and a generally chilled vibe. Kitesurfers flock to **Hat Nai Yang** (หาดในยาง; Map p620) from May to October, which gives you something to look at while you laze on the sand, but this part of Phuket is pretty quiet in low season.

The whole area is 15 minutes or less from Phuket International Airport.

☍ Activities

During the May to October monsoon, Hat Nai Yang is great for kitesurfing. A number of schools, including **Kiteboarding Asia** (Map p620; ☑ 081 591 4594; www.kiteboardingasia.com; 116 Mu 1, Hat Nai Yang; 1hr lesson 2000B, 3-day course 11,000B; ☺ Apr-Oct), **Kite Zone** (☑ 083 395 2005; www.kitesurfthailand.com; Hat Nai Yang; 1hr lesson 1100B, 3-day course 10,000B; ☺ May-late-Oct) and Rawai-based Bob's Kite School (p632), teach budding kitesurfers.

Phuket's longest beach, Hat Mai Khao is a beautiful, secluded 10km stretch of sand extending from just south of the airport to the island's northernmost point. Sea turtles lay eggs here between November and February. Take care with the strong year-round undertow. Hat Nai Yang, 3km south of the airport, is sheltered by a reef that slopes 20m below the surface – which means good snorkelling in high season and fantastic kitesurfing during the monsoon. West-coast **Hat Nai Thon** (หาดในทอน; Map p620), 7km south of the airport, is a lovely arc of fine golden sand away from Phuket's busy buzz and good swimming (except at the height of the monsoon).

Phuket Riding Club HORSE RIDING

(Map p620; ☑ 081 787 2455; www.phuketridingclub.com; 60/9 Th Thepkasattri, Mu 3, Mai Khao; 1/2hr rides 1200/2200B; ☺ 7.30am-6.30pm) The perfect opportunity to live out that horse-riding-through-the-tropics dream. Phuket Riding Club offers fun one- or two-hour

VOLUNTEER WITH ANIMALS

About 2km from Hat Mai Khao, **Soi Dog** (Map p620; ☑ 081 788 4222; www.soidog. org; 167/9 Mu 4, Soi Mai Khao 10; admission by donation; ⏰ 9am-noon & 1-3.30pm Mon-Fri, tours 9.30am, 11am, 1.30pm & 2.30pm) is a nonprofit foundation that protects hundreds of cats and dogs (some rescued from the illegal dog-meat trade), focusing on sterilisation, castration, re-homing and animal-welfare awareness. Visits are by in-depth tour. The 'old dogs' enclosure can be upsetting, but they're in a happy home. Visitors can play with the animals, or become a dog-walking or long-term volunteer.

rides on the beaches and interior of northern Phuket. Book a day ahead.

🛏 Sleeping

There's a mix of accommodation here, with top resorts mingling with more affordable digs. If you want one of the cheaper places, reserve well in advance.

Pensiri House
GUESTHOUSE $

(Map p620; ☑ 076 327683; www.pensirihouse. com; 112 Mu 5, Hat Nai Yang; d 800-1200B; ❄ 🛜) 300m inland from Hat Nai Yang, this friendly place is the best budget option in the area. Rooms are spread across two buildings. The nicest are in the new block: sizeable, light, modern and with balconies. All come with TVs, fridges and safes.

Sirinat National Park
Accommodation
CAMPGROUND, BUNGALOW $

(Map p620; ☑ 076 327152, in Bangkok 02 562 0760; www.dnp.go.th; 89/1 Mu 1, Hat Nai Yang; camping per person 30B, bungalows 700-1000B) At the park headquarters at the north end of Hat Nai Yang you'll find campsites (bring your own tent) and large, concrete, air-con bungalows just back from the beach on a gorgeous, shady, white-sand bluff. Book ahead online or by phone.

Discovery Beach Resort
GUESTHOUSE $$

(Map p620; ☑ 082 497 7500; discovery-phuket@ hotmail.com; 90/34 Mu 5, Hat Nai Yang; d 1800-3200B; ❄ 🛜) Rooms at this amenable place are a little old-fashioned, but they're spotless and come with sofas, TVs and fridges,

while the beds are fine. It's nothing fancy, but the location – right on the beach – makes it great value.

⭐ Slate
RESORT $$$

(Map p620; ☑ 076 327006; www.theslatephuket. com; 116 Mu 1, Hat Nai Yang; d 7700-22,000B, villas 45,400-61,500B; ℗ ❄ 🛜 🏊) One of Phuket's most unique mega-resorts takes its design cues from the island's tin-mining history. Hardware (vices, scales and other mining tools) features in the delicate decor, while the doors to the swish, stylish, luxurious rooms and villas are distressed metal. The best rooms have their own plunge pools. There are three restaurants on-site, and the fantastic **Coqoon Spa** (Map p620; massage or treatment 2000-8000B; ⏰ 10am-8pm).

Pullman
RESORT $$$

(Map p620; ☑ 076 303299; www.pullmanphuket arcadia.com; 22/2 Mu 4, Hat Nai Thon; d 6500B, villas 24,400-32,400B; ℗ ❄ @ 🛜 🏊) With a spectacular setting high on cliffs above northern Hat Nai Thon, this big resort offers stunning sea views almost from the moment you cross the arched bridge to the lobby. A dreamy network of reflection pools extends out above the sea. Service is divine. All rooms and the villas are spacious, supercomfortable and come with balconies.

🍴 Eating

Mr Kobi
THAI $$

(Map p620; Hat Nai Yang; mains 150-350B; ⏰ 10am-11pm) The sign says 'Broken English spoken here perfect', but the ever-popular Mr Kobi speaks English very well. He handles the drinks, while Malee deals with the seafood and Thai faves served up in refreshingly unpretentious surroundings. One wall is dedicated to telling the story of the 2004 tsunami.

Coconut Tree
THAI $$

(Map p620; ☑ 098 364 6366; Th Hat Nai Thon, Hat Nai Thon; mains 100-300B; ⏰ 10am-10pm; 🛜) This friendly, relaxed spot towards the south end of the beach rustles up quality seafood dishes such as stir-fried crab with black pepper, and tiger prawns cooked in everything from yellow curry to bitter ginger, on a rustic semi-open verandah with a few pot-plants. Also does Western classics. The Andaman sparkles beyond soaring palms and casuarinas.

Elements　　　　　　　　THAI **$$$**
(Map p620; ☑ 076 303299; www.pullmanphuket
arcadia.com; 22/2 Mu 4, Pullman, Hat Nai Thon;
mains 270-1320B; ☺noon-10.30pm) Perched
high on the cliffs at the northern end of the
beach, Nai Thon's sleekest resort (p650) of-
fers sophisticated Thai food in a swish, spa-
cious indoor-outdoor dining room with huge
pillars, abstract modern art and beautiful
views across the bay. Lunch sees burgers and
sandwiches thrown into the mix, and on Fri-
days the restaurant fires up a seafood BBQ.

❶ Getting There & Away

Sŏrng·tăa·ou from Phuket Town to Hat Nai Yang
run between 7am and 5pm (40B). Taxis to/from

the airport cost 400B to 500B, depending which
beach you're on.

Thalang District　　อำเภอถลาง

Far from the beaches, untouristed Thalang
(ถลาง) is an area that people tend to pass
through while on their way somewhere
else. That's a shame, because there are
some intriguing cultural attractions here,
including the **Thalang National Museum**
(พิพิธภัณฑสถานแห่งชาติ ถลาง; Map p620; ☑ 076
379895; Th Srisoonthorn/Rte 4027; adult/child
200/100B; ☺9am-4pm). Most people visit en
route to the worthwhile and justifiably pop-
ular Phuket Elephant Sanctuary (p652).

WORTH A TRIP

KHAO PHRA THAEW ROYAL WILDLIFE & FOREST RESERVE　　อุทยานสัตว์ป่าเขาพระแทว

The **Khao Phra Thaew Royal Wildlife & Forest Reserve** (Map p620; off Rte 4027 &
Hwy 402; adult/child 200/100B) protects 23 sq km of virgin island rainforest (evergreen
monsoon forest) in north Phuket. Its royal status means it's better-maintained than the
average Thai national park, although the staff have a reputation for being unhelpful to-
wards visitors. The highest point is Khao Phra (442m).

Tigers, Malayan sun bears, rhinos and elephants once roamed here, but nowadays
residents are limited to humans, wild boar, monkeys, slow loris, langurs, gibbons, deer,
civets, flying foxes, cobras, pythons, squirrels and other smaller creatures.

Gibbon poaching is a big problem on Phuket, fuelled in no small part by tourism: cap-
tive gibbons are paraded around tourist bars. Financed by donations, the tiny **Phuket
Gibbon Rehabilitation Project** (โครงการคืนชะนีสู่ป่า; Map p620; ☑ 076 260492; www.
gibbonproject.org; off Rte 4027; admission by donation; ☺9am-4.30pm, to 3pm Sat) ✔ adopts
gibbons that were kept in captivity in the hope of reintroducing them to the wild. Swing
by around 9am to hear the gibbons' morning song. You can't get too close to the animals,
which may disappoint kids, but the volunteer work done here is outstanding.

Elsewhere, there are pleasant hill hikes and some photogenic waterfalls, including
Nam Tok Ton Sai (น้ำตกโตนไทร; Map p620; ☑ 076 311998; off Hwy 402; adult/child
200/100B) and **Nam Tok Bang Pae** (น้ำตกบางแป; Map p620; off Rte 4027; adult/child
200/100B), 300m along a jungle-fringed path from the Gibbon Project. The falls are
most impressive during the June–November monsoon. Park rangers may guide hikers
in the park on request: expect to pay around 1500B. Tucked into the hills behind a quilt
of pineapple fields, rubber plantations and mango groves is **Cable Jungle Adventure
Phuket** (Map p620; ☑ 081 977 4904; www.cablejunglephuket.com; 232/17 Mu 8, Th Bansu-
anneramit; without/with hotel pickup 2150/2300B; ☺9am-5pm), a maze of zip lines linking
ancient ficus trees. The zips range from 6m to 50m above the ground and the longest
run is 300m long. Closed-toe shoes are a must. Hotel pick up is available.

There is neither accommodation nor restaurants inside the park, but you're a taxi or
motorcycle ride away from the rest of Phuket.

To get to Khao Phra Thaew from Phuket Town, take Th Thepkasattri 13km north to
Thalang District. At the Heroines Monument (p652), drive 9km northeast on Rte 4027,
turn left (west) towards Nam Tok Bang Pae and after 1km you're at the Phuket Gibbon
Rehabilitation Project. A taxi will cost 800B. The reserve is also accessible off Hwy 402,
6km northwest of the Heroines Monument.

The district unfolds around the **Hero-ines Monument** (อนุสาวรีย์ท้าวเทพกษัตรีท้าว ศรีสุนทร; Map p620; Hwy 402), 13km north of Phuket Town, which while not exactly in the centre of Phuket, acts as the island's central roundabout where roads heading in all directions intersect.

🛏 Sleeping & Eating

⭐ Point Yamu by Como
RESORT $$$

(Map p620; ☑ 076 360100; www.comohotels.com/ pointyamu; 225 Mu 7, Pa Klok, Laem Yamu; d incl breakfast 10,200-51,000B; P ❄ ☎ ☲) Breeze into the soaring lobby, where white-mosaic pillars frame ponds reflecting encircling palms, and fall in love. This five-star stunner blends Thai influences (monk-robe orange, lobster traps as lamps) into a coolly contemporary, Italian-designed creation. An array of huge rooms, some with private pools, come in royal-blue or turquoise, intensifying the endless sea and Ao Phang-Nga panoramas from the property.

Bang Rong Seafood
THAI, SEAFOOD $$

(Map p620; ☑ 081 370 3401, 093 737 9264; Tha Bang Rong, off Rte 4027; mains 120-350B; ⏱ 10am-6pm) This rustic fish-farm-turned-restaurant sits on a floating pier amid the mangroves,

DON'T MISS

ELEPHANT REFUGE

The **Phuket Elephant Sanctuary** (Map p620; ☑ 094 990 3649; www.phuket elephantsanctuary.org; 100 Mu 2, Pa Klok, on 4027 Highway; adult/child 3000/1500B; ⏱ 9.30am-1pm & 2-5.30pm; 👶) is the island's only genuine refuge (beware of imitators) for pachyderms who have spent their lives being mistreated while working in the tourist and logging industries. It's a rare opportunity to get up close to these magnificent animals. Sadly, elephants are still being used to give tourists rides, or to perform for them, in Phuket and elsewhere in Thailand.

All tours here must be booked in advance. If you want to see more of the animals, the sanctuary accepts up to six volunteers at a time for week-long stays. The 16,000B fee goes directly to the care of the elephants and includes accommodation and three vegetarian meals a day.

accessed via a wooden boardwalk 750m east of Rte 4027. Your catch – red and white snapper, crab or mussels – is plucked after you order, so you know it's fresh. You can have everything steamed, fried, grilled, boiled or baked, but this is a Muslim enterprise so there's no beer.

⭐ Breeze Restaurant
INTERNATIONAL $$$

(Map p620; ☑ 081 271 2320; www.breezecape yamu.com; Laem Yamu; mains from 700B, tasting menus 2000-2150B; ⏱ noon-10pm Wed-Sun; ☎ ☲) Classy yet understated, one of Phuket's finest restaurants sits in glorious hilltop, sea-surrounded seclusion, 20km northeast of Phuket Town. Blue beanbags overlook pool and sea from the pillared open-walled dining hall. Menus that change weekly triumph with divine, inventive European-style dishes infused with local produce. Pair with classic cocktails given a Thai twist. Book ahead.

❶ Getting There & Away

Sŏrng·tăa·ou heading to Hat Surin and Ao Bang Thao from Phuket Town between 7am and 5pm pass by the Heroines Monument (30B), which is walking distance from the Thalang National Museum. To head anywhere else in the district you'll need private wheels or a taxi. A taxi from Phuket Town to the Phuket Elephant Sanctuary will cost 700B.

KRABI PROVINCE

When travellers talk dreamily about the amazing Andaman, they usually mean Krabi, with its trademark karst formations curving along the coast like a giant limestone fortress of adventure, or rising out of the islands and hanging over idyllic white-sand beaches. Rock climbers will find their nirvana in Railay, while castaway wannabes should head to Ko Lanta, Ko Phi-Phi or any of the other 150-plus islands swimming off this 120km-long shoreline.

Krabi Town
กระบี่

☑ 075 / POP 31,475

Bustling Krabi Town is majestically situated among impossibly angular limestone karst formations jutting from the mangroves, but mid-city you're more likely to be awestruck by the sheer volume of guesthouses and travel agencies packed into this compact

Krabi Town

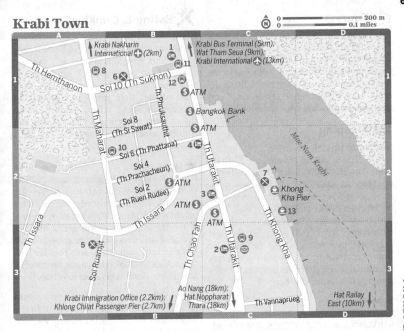

town. It's a key transport hub, around which a busy traveller scene continues to evolve. There's no shortage of restaurants, or gift shops selling the usual trinkets.

But hang around a while and you'll see that there's also a very real provincial scene going on beneath the tourist industry.

👁 Sights & Activities

⭐ Wat Tham Seua   BUDDHIST TEMPLE
(วัดถ้ำเสือ, Tiger Cave Temple; ⏱ dawn-dusk) This sprawling hill and cave temple complex 9km northwest of Krabi Town is an easy, worthwhile day trip. At the park entrance you'll come to a gruellingly steep 1260-step staircase leading to a 600m karst peak. After a 30- to 40-minute climb, the fit and fearless are rewarded with golden Buddha statues, a gilded stupa and spectacular views out to sea beyond Ao Nang. Start early and bring water; there are drinking taps at the top.

Sea Kayak Krabi   KAYAKING
(📱 089 724 8579, 075 630270; www.seakayak krabi.com) A wide variety of recommended sea-kayaking tours, including to Ao Tha Len (half/full day 900/1500B), which has looming sea cliffs; Ko Hong (full day 2200B), famed for its emerald lagoon; and Ban Bho

Tho (full day 2200B), which has karsts and sea caves with 2000- to 3000-year-old cave paintings. Rates include guides, transfers, lunch and water.

☞ Tours

Many companies offer day trips to Khlong Thom, 45km southeast of Krabi on Hwy 4, taking in hot springs and freshwater pools for around 1200B to 2000B, including transport, guides, lunch and beverages. Bring decent shoes. Various other 'jungle tours' and mangrove and island trips are available.

🛏 Sleeping

★ Pak-Up Hostel   HOSTEL $
(☏075 611955; www.pakuphostel.com; 87 Th Utarakit; dm/r 380/850B; ❄@🛜) Still the hostel of choice in Krabi, Pak-Up has contemporary, polished-cement air-con dorms with big wooden bunks built into the wall, each with its own locker. Massive, modern shared bathrooms have cold-water stalls and hot-water rain showers. The two doubles share bathrooms and women-only dorms are available. The bar gets busy and there's a young, fun-loving vibe here.

Seacation   HOSTEL $
(☏075 622828; www.seacationkrabi.com; 11/5 Soi 6 Th Maharat; dm/r 450/1200B; ❄@🛜) Brand-new and smart hostel, even if the design and long corridors make it feel a little institutional. Dorms are comfortable with decent beds and big lockers, while there's an impressive communal area with a pool table. Private rooms are compact. Affable staff and an ideal location.

Apo   HOTEL $$
(☏093 709 1811; www.apohotel.com; 189 Th Utarakit; r 1000-1700B; ❄🛜) The best-value of several fresh, modern guesthouses in this otherwise unremarkable block, Apo has big and bright, gleaming, minimalist-smart rooms decorated with a single colourful swirl and wall-mounted TVs, spread across two buildings. Some have river views from little balconies. The only drawback is that there's no lift.

Chan Cha Lay   GUESTHOUSE $$
(☏075 620952; www.lovechanchalay.com; 55 Th Utarakit; r fan 400-1400B; ❄🛜) The en-suite, air-con rooms at long-standing Chan Cha Lay, done up in Mediterranean blues and whites with white-pebble and polished-concrete open-air bathrooms, are among Krabi's most comfortable and charming for the price. There's a range of cheaper rooms with shared-bathroom, and fan or A/C, which are plain and compact but spotless.

✖ Eating & Drinking

Night Market   MARKET, THAI $
(Th Khong Kha; mains 30-70B; ⊘4-10pm) Beside Tha Khong Kha, this market is a popular place for an evening meal. Try authentic *sôm·dam* (spicy green papaya salad), wok-fried noodles, *đôm yam gûng* (prawn and lemon grass soup), grilled snapper and all things satay, plus creamy Thai desserts and freshly pressed juices. English menus are a bonus.

★ May & Mark's   INTERNATIONAL, THAI $$
(☏081 396 6114; 34 Th Sukhon; mains 75-250B; ⊘7am-10pm; 🛜) A classic travellers' meeting spot with a bold varnished-concrete coffee bar, May and Mark's is always busy. We love it for the excellent espresso and the big choice of delicious omelettes, pancakes and home-baked bread. It also does popular Thai meals, plus international salads, sandwiches and mains. Good vegetarian selection.

Gecko Cabane   THAI, FUSION $$
(☏081 958 5945; 1/36-37 Soi Ruam Jit, Th Maharat; mains 70-550B; ⊘11am-11pm; 🛜) Thai dishes with a twist and Western food served up with style in an eye-catching conversion of two traditional shophouses. Dine on the dark-wood terrace, or in the living-room-like interior. The slow-cooked massaman curry is especially fine, as is the lamb shanks with mash potato, but all the dishes here are decent and good value.

Playground   BAR
(www.facebook.com/krabiplaygroundbar; 87 Th Utarakit; ⊘7pm-2am; 🛜) This bar with a large outside area at Pak-Up Hostel keeps the island bar tradition alive on the mainland, with beer pong, open-mic nights and occasional live music. Happy hour runs until 9.30pm.

ℹ Information

All guesthouses and many restaurants offer free wi-fi.

Bangkok Bank (Th Utarakit; ⊘8.30am-3.30pm) Exchanges cash and travellers cheques and has ATMs.

Krabi Immigration Office (☏075 611097; 382 Mu 7, Saithai; ⊘8.30am-4.30pm Mon-Fri) Handles visa extensions. Around 4km southwest of Krabi,

Krabi Nakharin International Hospital (☏075 626555; www.krabinakharin.co.th; 1 Th Pisanpob) Located 2km northwest of town.

Post Office (Th Utarakit; ⏱ 8.30am-4.30pm Mon-Fri, 9am-noon Sat & Sun) You can send mail overseas from here.

ℹ️ Getting There & Away

AIR

The airport is 14km northeast of Krabi on Hwy 4. Most domestic carriers fly between Bangkok and Krabi. Bangkok Air (www.bangkokair.com) flies daily to Ko Samui and Air Asia (www.airasia.com) to Chiang Mai.

BOAT

Ferries to Ko Phi-Phi and Ko Lanta leave from the **Khlong Chilat Passenger Pier** (Tha Khlong Chilat), 4km southwest of Krabi. Travel agencies selling boat tickets include free transfers.

Hat Railay East Long-tail boats (150B, 45 minutes) leave from Krabi's **Tha Khong Kha** between 7.45am and 6pm. Boatmen wait until they have eight passengers before leaving; otherwise, you can charter the whole boat (1200B). Boats to Hat Railay West leave from Ao Nang.

Ko Jum From November to late April, Ko Lanta boats stop at Ko Jum (400B, one hour), where long-tails shuttle you to shore.

Ko Lanta From November to late April, one daily boat (400B, two hours) leaves at 11.30am. During the rainy season, you can only get to Ko Lanta by frequent air-con minivans (250B to 300B, 2½ hours), which also run in high season.

Ko Phi-Phi Year-round boats (300B to 350B, 1½ to two hours) leave at 9am, 10.30am, 1.30pm and 3pm, returning at 9am, 10am, 1.30pm and 3.30pm. Ferries don't always run every day between May and October.

Phuket & Ko Yao Islands The quickest route is with direct boats from the pier at Hat Noppharat Thara (p663), 19km southwest of Krabi. *Sǒrng·tǎa·ou* (50B) run between Krabi's Tha Khong Kha and the pier at Hat Noppharat Thara; taxis cost 600B. Boats also run several times daily to Ko Yao Noi from Tha Len (150B), 33km northwest of Krabi Town.

BUS

Krabi Bus Terminal (☎ 075 663503; cnr Th Utarakit & Hwy 4) is 4km north of central Krabi at Talat Kao, near theTh Utarakit and Hwy 4 junction.

MINIVAN

Travel agencies run air-con minivans and VIP buses to popular southern tourist centres, but you'll end up crammed cheek-to-jowl with other backpackers. Most offer combined minivan and boat tickets to Ko Samui (700B, five hours) and Ko Pha-Ngan (850B, seven hours). More (usually cheaper) minivans depart from the **bus terminal**. Departures from Krabi include the following:

DESTINATION	FARE (B)	DURATION (HR)
Hat Yai	230	4
Ko Lanta	250-300	2½
Phuket	140	2-3
Satun	200	4
Surat Thani	180	2½
Trang	100	2

SǑRNG·TǍA·OU

Sǒrng·tǎa·ou run from the bus station to the centre of Krabi Town (30B) and on to Hat Noppharat

BUSES TO/FROM KRABI

DESTINATION	FARE (B)	DURATION (HR)	FREQUENCY
Bangkok (VIP)	862	12	5pm
Bangkok (air-con)	587	12	8am, 8.20am, 4pm, 5pm, 6pm
Hat Yai	255	4½	hourly 8.30am-7.20pm
Phuket	140	3	every 30min 8.30am-7.20pm
Ranong	210	5	8.30am & noon
Satun	212	5	11am, 1pm, 2pm, 3pm
Surat Thani	150	2½	hourly 4.30am-4.30pm
Trang	110	2	every 30min 7.30am-5pm

Thara (50B), Ao Nang (60B) and the Shell Cemetery at Ao Nam Mao (70B) between 6am and 7pm, picking up passengers along the way.

The most convenient places to catch them in Krabi's town centre are Th Utarakit and Th Maharat. From Th Maharat, you can catch *sŏrng·tăa·ou* to **Ao Luk** (80B, one hour, 6am to 3pm), Ao Nang and **Hat Noppharat Thara**. From Th Utarakit, there is also a service to **Ao Nang** and **Hat Noppharat Thara**, as well as to **Ban Laem Kruat**. In the opposite direction, Th Utarakit is the best place to pick up a *sŏrng·tăa·ou* to the **bus station**.

In high season services run until 10pm, but less frequently and for a small surcharge.

ℹ Getting Around

You can explore central Krabi on foot. *Sŏrng·tăa·ou* between the bus terminal and Krabi stop on Th Utarakit, outside the River View Hotel. Most travel agencies and guesthouses, including Pak-Up Hostel, rent motorbikes (200B per day).

TO/FROM THE AIRPORT

Taxis between the airport and Krabi Town cost 350B; motorcycle taxis cost 200B. Agencies and Pak-Up Hostel (p654) can arrange seats on the airport bus (130B). Several international car-rental companies have offices at the airport (vehicle hire from 1100B).

Railay   ไร่เล

Krabi's fairytale limestone formations come to a dramatic climax at Railay (also spelt Rai Leh), the ultimate Andaman gym for rock-climbing fanatics. Monkeys frolic alongside climbers on the gorgeous crags, while down below some of the prettiest beaches in all Thailand are backed by proper jungle.

Accessible only by boat, but just a 15-minute ride from Ao Nang, the busiest parts of Railay are sandwiched between the scrappy, not good for swimming, beach of Hat Railay East and the high-end resorts and beautiful white sand of Hat Railay West and Hat Tham Phra Nang.

Railay is more crowded than it once was and sees many day trippers. Thankfully, though, it remains much less-developed than Ko Phi-Phi and if you head away from Hat Railay West and Hat Railay East the resorts disappear and the atmosphere is one of delightfully laid-back Thai-Rasta bliss.

◉ Sights

Tham Phra Nang   CAVE

(ถ้ำพระนาง, Princess Cave; Hat Tham Phra Nang) At the eastern end of Hat Tham Phra Nang is this important shrine for local fishermen (Muslim and Buddhist), who make offerings of carved wooden phalluses in the hope that the inhabiting spirit of a drowned Indian princess will provide a good catch. According to legend, a royal barge carrying the princess foundered here in a storm during the 3rd century BC. Her spirit took over the cave, granting favours to all who paid their respects.

Sa Phra Nang   LAGOON

(Holy Princess Pool) Halfway along the trail linking Hat Railay East to Hat Tham Phra Nang, a sharp 'path' leads up the jungle-cloaked cliff wall to this hidden lagoon. The first section is a steep 10-minute uphill climb (with ropes for assistance). Fork right for the lagoon, reached by sheer downhill climbing. If you fork left, you'll quickly reach a dramatic cliff-side viewpoint; this is a strenuous but generally manageable, brief hike.

🏃 Activities

Rock Climbing

With more than 1000 routes in 51 areas, ranging from beginner to challenging advanced climbs, all with unparalleled cliff-top vistas, it's no surprise that Railay is among the world's top climbing spots. You could spend months climbing and exploring – many people do. Deep-water soloing, where free-climbers scramble up ledges over deep water, is incredibly popular. If you fall you'll probably just get wet, so even daring beginners can try.

Most climbers start off at **Muay Thai Wall** and **One, Two, Three Wall**, at the southern end of Hat Railay East, which have at least 40 routes graded from 4b to 8b on the French system. The mighty **Thaiwand Wall** sits at the southern end of Hat Railay West, offering a sheer limestone cliff with some of the most challenging climbing routes, graded from 6a to 7c+.

Other top climbs include **Hidden World**, with its classic intermediate routes, **Wee's Present Wall** (Hat Railay West), an overlooked 7c+ winner, and **Diamond Cave** and **Ao**

Railay

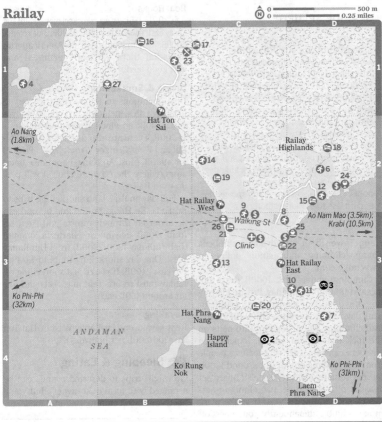

PHUKET & THE ANDAMAN COAST RAILAY

Railay

⊙ Sights
1 Sa Phra Nang	D4
2 Tham Phra Nang	C4
3 Viewpoint	D3

⊕ Activities, Courses & Tours
4 Ao Nang Tower	A1
5 Basecamp Tonsai	B1
6 Diamond Cave	D2
7 Hidden World	D4
8 Hot Rock	C3
9 King Climbers	C3
10 Muay Thai Wall	D3
11 One, Two, Three Wall	D3
12 Real Rocks	D2
13 Thaiwand Wall	C3
14 Wee's Present Wall	C2

⊟ Sleeping
15 Anyavee Railay Resort	D2
16 Chill Out	B1
17 Forest Resort	C1
18 Railay Cabana	D2
19 Railei Beach Club	C2
20 Rayavadee	C3
21 Sand Sea Resort	C3
22 Sunrise Tropical Resort	C3

⊗ Eating
23 Mama's Chicken	B1
Sunset Restaurant	(see 21)

⊜ Drinking & Nightlife
Chill Out	(see 16)
24 Last Bar	D2

⊕ Transport
25 Ferry Jetty	D3
Long-Tail Boats to Ao Nam Mao	(see 25)
26 Long-Tail Boats to Ao Nang	C3
27 Long-Tail Boats to Ao Nang	B1
Long-Tail Boats to Krabi	(see 25)

SEASIDE SPLURGE

Arguably one of Thailand's finest chunks of beachfront property, **Rayavadee** (☑ 075 620740; www.rayavadee.com; Hat Tham Phra Nang; pavilion incl breakfast 15,900-51,500B; villa incl breakfast 58,500-138,000B; ❄ ⚡ ☒) is an exclusive resort that sprawls across huge grounds filled with banyan trees, flowers and meandering ponds. The two-storey, mushroom-domed pavilions are packed with antique furniture, locally sourced spa products and every mod con (including butler service). Some have private pools. There's also a top-notch spa, gym and no less than four restaurants.

Nang Tower, both for advanced climbers. There's climbing information online at www.railay.com.

Climbing courses cost 1000B for a half day and 1800B for a full day. Private instruction runs 3000B for a half day and 4500B for a full day. Three-day courses (6000B) involve lead climbing, where you clip into bolts on the rock face as you ascend. Experienced climbers can rent gear sets for two people from the climbing schools for around 1200B per day (quality can vary); the standard set consists of a 60m rope, two climbing harnesses and climbing shoes. If you're planning to climb independently, you're best off bringing your own gear.

Basecamp Tonsai   CLIMBING
(☑ 081 149 9745; www.tonsaibasecamp.com; Hat Ton Sai; half/full day 800/1500B, 3-day course 6000B; ☺ 8am-5pm & 7-9pm) Long-established, laid-back climbing outfit. Big on deep-water soloing (700B).

King Climbers   CLIMBING
(☑ 081 797 8923; www.railay.com; Walking St; half/full day 1000/1800B, 3-day course 6000B; ☺ 8.30am-9pm Mon-Fri, to 6pm Sat & Sun) One of the biggest, oldest and most reputable climbing schools.

Hot Rock   CLIMBING
(☑ 085 641 9842; www.railayadventure.com; Hat Railay East; half/full day 1000/1800B, 3-day course 6000B; ☺ 9am-8pm) Owned by one of the granddaddies of Railay climbing, Hot Rock has a good reputation.

Real Rocks   CLIMBING
(☑ 080 718 1351; www.realrocksclimbing.com; Hat Railay East; half/full day 1000/1800B, 3-day course 6000B; ☺ 8am-10pm) A Thai-American–run operation that's efficiently managed and gets good feedback.

Diving & Snorkelling

Dive operations in Railay run trips out to local dive sites, including Ko Poda. Two dives cost 3700B; an Open Water dive course is 14,500B. There are also dive trips to Ko Phi-Phi and **King Cruiser Wreck** (Ko Phi-Phi Don) for 4900B. Most Ao Nang–based dive operators (where there's more choice) will pick up from Railay.

Full-day, multi-island snorkelling trips to Ko Poda, Ko Hong, Ko Kai and beyond can be arranged through resorts and agencies from 1200B, or you can charter a long-tail (half-/full-day 1800/2800B) from Hat Railay West. One-day snorkelling tours to Ko Phi-Phi cost 2400B. If you're just snorkelling off Railay, most resorts rent mask sets and fins for around 150B each.

Kayaking

Rent kayaks on Hat Railay West or Hat Ton Sai (200/800B per hour/day).

🛏 Sleeping & Eating

Overnight trips to deserted islands can be arranged with local boat owners, but you'll need your own camping gear and food.

🛏 Hat Railay East   หาดไร่เลย์ทิศตะวันออก

There are many midrange options around Hat Railay East and a fair few bars inland.

Anyavee Railay Resort   RESORT $$
(☑ 075 819437; www.anyaveerailay.com; Hat Railay East; r 3050-3600B; ❄ ⚡ ☒) This place is consistently one of the best midrange options on what is a pricey island. The rooms aren't the newest, but they are spacious and clean with large balconies, TVs, fridges and safety boxes. All are set around a real jungle garden – expect to see white-faced monkeys passing through – with an attractive pool and overlooked by karst cliffs.

Sunrise Tropical Resort   RESORT $$$
(☑ 075 819418; www.sunrisetropical.com; Hat Railay East; bungalows incl breakfast 3900-6300B; ❄ @ ⚡ ☒) Swish 'chalets' and 'villas' here

rival some of the finest on Hat Railay West but are priced for Hat Railay East – so we reckon this is one of the best deals in Railay. Expect soothing smart decor, hardwood floors, four-poster beds or wooden mattress-platforms, lush bathrooms with aqua-tiled floors and private balconies or patios.

🛏 Hat Railay West   หาดไร่เลย์ทิศตะวัน

Hat Railay West is home to upmarket resorts and the best beachfront restaurants.

★ Railei Beach Club   VILLA $$$

(☑ 086 685 9359; www.raileibeachclub.com; Hat Railay West; house 2900-28,800B; ❄ 🛜) At the northern end of the beach, hidden in forested grounds that stretch back to luscious limestone cliffs, is this collection of Thai-style homes for six to eight people, rented out on behalf of absent owners. They come with patios, kitchens and amenities, and there are also a few smaller but impeccably stylish dark-wood doubles. Only a few have air-con.

Sand Sea Resort   RESORT $$$

(☑ 075 819463; www.krabisandsea.com; Hat Railay West; bungalows incl breakfast 3000-6500B; ❄ @ 🛜 ⚓) The cheapest resort on this sublime beach offers everything from ageing 'superior' bungalows to newly remodelled cottages and smart, sparkly, contemporary rooms with every amenity. The grounds aren't as swanky as the neighbours', but rooms are comfy and there are two peaceful, foliage-enclosed pools, one with karst views, making this a reasonable deal for the location.

At the recommended beachfront **Sunset Restaurant** (Hat Railay West; mains 180-400B; ⏲ 11am-9pm; 🛜), red-shirted waiters take seafood-grill and Thai-curry orders on iPads.

🛏 Railay Highlands

There are many midrange accommodation options around the Railay Highlands.

Railay Cabana   BUNGALOW $

(☑ 084 534 1928, 075 621733; Railay Highlands; bungalows 800B) Superbly located in a bowl of karst cliffs, this is your tropical mountain hideaway. The creaky yet clean thatched-bamboo bungalows with 24-hour electricity were undergoing renovation at the time of research, so expect prices to rise, and are surrounded by mango, mangosteen, banana and guava groves. It's just north of Tham Phra Nang Nai, inland from Hat Railay East.

🛏 Hat Ton Sai   หาดต้นไทร

Hat Ton Sai, the most isolated beach, is where you'll find the best budget choices and a buzzing backpacker/climber scene. Cheap eats abound here, too. Note that on Hat Ton Sai, electricity runs only in the evening.

Forest Resort   BUNGALOW $

(☑ 081 149 9745; www.basecamptonsai.com; Hat Ton Sai; dm 200B, r & bungalows 400-800B) The bamboo bungalows are slightly less scruffy than the sparse three-person, concrete-floor cells which pass for dorms here. The best bet are the wood-and-brick bungalows with tiled floors, red-brick bathrooms, private porches and tin roofs. All are fan cooled when the electricity is running (6pm to 1am). If there's no one around, ask at Basecamp Tonsa, which manages the place.

Chill Out   BUNGALOW $$

(☑ 087 699 4527, 084 186 8138; www.chilloutkrabi. com; Hat Ton Sai; dm 300B, bungalows 600-1200B; 🛜) While no more luxurious than Ton Sai's other offerings, Chill Out's bungalows bring a sociable, laid-back atmosphere and a pinch more style. Vibrantly painted international flags are plastered across the doors of basic tin-topped, wood-floored huts, which have terraces, cold-water bathrooms and mosquito nets. The dorm is functional with bunk beds. The bar (p660) gets busy. Electricity and wi-fi in evenings only.

Mama's Chicken   THAI $

(Hat Ton Sai; mains 70-100B; ⏲ 7am-10pm; 🖉) Relocated to the jungle path leading inland to Hat Railay East and West, Mama's remains one of Ton Sai's favourite food stops for its international breakfasts, fruit smoothies and extensive range of cheap Thai dishes, including a rare massaman tofu and other vegetarian-friendly adaptations.

🍷 Drinking & Nightlife

There are a fair few bars inland from Hat Railay West and along Hat Railay East. Hat Ton Sai is reggae bar heaven.

★ Last Bar
BAR

(Hat Railay East; ⊗11am-late) A reliably packed-out multilevel tiki bar that rambles to the edge of the mangroves, with bunting, balloons and cushioned seats on one deck, candlelit dining tables on another, live music at the back and waterside fire shows.

Chill Out
BAR

(Hat Ton Sai; ⊗11am-late; 🛜) Kick back over cold beers, live music, DJ beats and frenzied fire shows at Ton Sai's top jungle reggae bar.

ℹ Information

There's lots of local information on www.railay.com. There are many ATMs along Hat Railay East and on the paths leading to Hat Railay West. Bigger resorts change cash. Wi-fi is widely available.

The **clinic** (☑ 084 378 3057; Railay Bay Resort, Hat Railay West; ⊗8am-10pm) treats minor injuries. For anything serious, head to Krabi or Phuket.

ℹ Getting There & Away

Long-tails run to Railay from Krabi's Tha Khong Kha and from the seafront at Ao Nang and Ao Nam Mao. To Krabi, **long-tails** (⊗7.45am-6pm) leave from Hat Railay East. Boats in both directions leave between 7.45am and 6pm when they have eight people (150B, 45 minutes). Chartering the boat costs 1200B.

Boats to Hat Railay West or Hat Ton Sai from the southeastern end of Ao Nang (15 minutes) cost 100B from 8am to 6pm or 150B from 6pm to midnight. Boats don't leave until eight people show up. Private charters cost 800B. Services stop as early as 5pm May to October. **Long-tails** (⊗8am-6pm) return to Ao Nang from Hat Railay West on the same schedule. **Boats** (⊗8am-6pm) from Hat Ton Sai are less frequent, as fewer people travel from there. It's often quicker to head to Hat Railay West for a ride.

During exceptionally high seas, boats from Ao Nang and Krabi stop running; you may still be able to get a **long-tail** (⊗8am-6pm) from Hat Railay East to Ao Nam Mao (100B, 15 minutes), where you can take a *sŏrng·tăa·ou* (50B) to Krabi or Ao Nang.

A year-round ferry runs to Ko Phi-Phi (400B, 1¼ hours) from the **ferry jetty** at Hat Railay East at 9.45am; long-tails motor over to meet it. Boats to Ko Lanta (500B, two hours, 10.45am daily) operate only during the October–April high season. For Phuket (650B, 2¼ hours), there's a year-round ferry at 3.15pm. Some ferries pick up off Hat Railay West.

Ao Nang
อ่าวนาง

First the hard truths. Thanks to its unchecked development huddled in the shadows of stunning karst scenery, Ao Nang is ugly-pretty. There's a slightly seedy undercurrent, too.

So, yes, it's a little trashy, but if you forgive that and focus on the beaches, framed by limestone headlands tied together by narrow strips of golden sand, there's plenty to like. In the dry season the sea glows a turquoise hue; during the monsoon, currents stir up the mocha shallows. If you're hankering for a snorkel in clearer waters, it's easy to get to the little islands that dot the horizon, which generally enjoy less murky water, at any time of the year. Divers too, are close to some prime spots for getting underwater. Above all, Ao Nang is a straightforward and compact, if blandly touristy, destination to visit and that's why people head here.

◎ Sights

Shell Cemetery
NATURE RESERVE

(สุสานหอย, Gastropod Fossil, Su-San Hoi; adult/child 200/100B; ⊗8am-6pm) About 8km east of Ao Nang at the eastern end of Ao Nam Mao is the Shell Cemetery: giant slabs formed from millions of tiny 75-million-year-old fossil shells. There's a dusty **visitors centre** (⊗8am-4.30pm), with mildly interesting geological displays, plus stalls selling snacks. *Sŏrng·tăa·ou* from Krabi/Ao Nang cost 70/50B.

🏃 Activities

Diving & Snorkelling

Ao Nang has numerous dive schools offering trips to 15 local islands, including Ko Si, Ko Ha, Ko Poda, Yava Bon and Yava Son. Ko Mae Urai is one of the more unique local dives, with two submarine tunnels lined with soft and hard corals. Expect to pay 3200B for two dives.

Other trips run further afield to King Cruiser Wreck (p658) or Ko Phi-Phi, for 3500B to 3900B, and Hin Daeng, Hin Muang and **Ko Haa** south of Ko Lanta for 5700B to 6600B. An Open Water course costs 14,900B. Most dive companies also arrange snorkelling trips (from 1800B).

The Dive
DIVING

(☑ 082 282 2537; www.thediveaonang.com; 249/2 Mu 2; 2 dives 3500B; ⊗11am-8pm) This keen diving team with an excellent reputation runs trips to Ko Phi-Phi (3500B), which snorkellers can join (2500B), and to Ko Haa (6200B). Open Water certification costs 14,900B.

Aqua Vision DIVING
(📞 086 944 4068; www.diving-krabi.com; 76/12 Mu 2; 2/3 dives 3600/4500B; ⏰ 9am-7pm) A reliable, well-informed dive school offering local dives, two-dive trips to Ko Phi-Phi, Open Water Diving courses (14,900B) and 'safaris' to Hin Daeng, Hin Muang and Ko Haa (5700B to 6600B), plus local snorkelling trips (1800B).

Kon-Tiki DIVING
(📞 075 637826; www.kontiki-krabi.com; 161/1 Mu 2; 2/3 dives 3200/4000B; ⏰ 9am-9pm) A well regarded, large-scale operation, Kon-Tiki does fun dives to Ko Phi-Phi (3900B) and Ko Haa (6300B), local after-dark dives (4800B), snorkelling 'safaris' (2700B) and Open Water courses (15,500B).

Cycling

Take a Tour de Krabi by hooking up with **Krabi Eco Cycle** (📞 081 607 4162, 075 637250; www.krabiecocycle.com; 309/5 Mu 5; half-/full-day tour 1500/3000B). The recommended full-day 15.5km pedal takes you through rubber plantations, small villages, hot springs and, finally, a cooler dip at the aptly named Emerald Pool. Lunch is included on all tours except the half-day bike-only tour.

Kayaking

Several companies offer kayaking tours to surrounding mangroves and islands from 1000B to 2500B, depending on the itinerary and whether you're travelling by speedboat. Popular destinations include the hidden lagoon at Ko Hong to view collection points for sea swallow nests (spurred by the ecologically dubious demand for bird's-nest soup). There are also trips to the lofty sea cliffs at Ao Tha Len and to the sea caves and 2000- to 3000-year-old paintings at Ban Bho Tho. Rates always include lunch, water, kayaks and guides.

👉 Tours

All agencies can book you on popular four- or five-island tours from 1400B to 2000B, depending on whether you choose long-tail or speedboat. **Ao Nang Long-Tail Boat Service** (Hat Ao Nang, northwestern end; ⏰ 8am-4pm,

to 2pm May-Oct) and **Ao Nang Long-Tail Boat Service Club** (Hat Ao Nang, southeastern end; ⏰ 8am-midnight, to 8pm May-Oct) offer private charters to Hong Island (2400B) and Bamboo Island (3800B), and half-day trips to Ko Kai (Chicken Island) and Ko Poda (1700B); maximum six people.

Tour agencies offer half-day tours to Khlong Thom (adult/child 1200/800B), including visits to freshwater pools and hot springs.

A speedboat tour to Ko Phi-Phi, including a stop at Bamboo Island is 2800B.

🛏 Sleeping

Ao Nang has a good mix of hostels, guesthouses, hotels and resorts, but the popular places fill up quickly in high season. Always book ahead. Prices drop by 50% during low season.

★ Glur HOSTEL **$**
(📞 075 695297, 089 001 3343; www.krabiglurhostel.com; 22/2 Mu 2, Soi Ao Nang; dm 600B, d 1300-1500B; 🅿 ❄ @ 🛜 🏊) A fabulous retreat of a hostel, designed, built, owned and operated by a talented Thai architect and his wife. The complex incorporates shipping containers, glass, and moulded and polished concrete to create sumptuous dorms, with curtained-off turquoise bunk beds, as well as private rooms (also equipped with bunk beds), all set in a lovely garden with a small pool.

It's a walkable 1.5km northeast of Ao Nang proper.

Anawin BUNGALOW **$$**
(📞 075 637664, 081 677 9632; www.anawinbungalows.com; 263/1 Mu 2; bungalows 1000-1600B; ❄ 🛜) Zingy-yellow collection of 10 clean concrete cabins with TVs and fronted by little verandahs, all tucked into a quiet flowery corner just 400m northeast of Ao Nang beach. Rooms are a little old-fashioned, but they're decent-sized and the owner is friendly.

Phra Nang Inn HOTEL **$$$**
(📞 075 637130; www.vacationvillage.co.th; Th Ao Nang; r incl breakfast 4000-8500B; ❄ 🛜 🏊) A thatched explosion of rustic coconut wood, shell curtains, bright orange and purple paint and elaborate Thai tiles with Mexico-inspired flair. Divided into two wings – there are also two pools – rooms aren't huge and some

could use a refresh (renovations were under way at the time of research), but the location is great and there's a beachfront bar.

Red Ginger Chic
HOTEL $$$

(📞 075 637999; www.redgingerchicresort.com; 168 Mu 3; r 5500-12,350B; ❋ 🛜 ☒) On a hotel-filled boulevard at the far western end of Ao Nang, Red Ginger is fashionable and colourful with detailed tiles, red paper lanterns, draped fabrics and a frosted glass bar in the lobby.

Spacious, smart rooms feature elegant wallpaper, modern furnishings and big balconies overlooking an expansive pool. Efficient staff.

✖ Eating & Drinking

Ao Nang has many mediocre restaurants serving Thai, Indian, Italian and Scandinavian food. By far the best restaurants are the seafood joints. For budget meals, stalls pop up in the evening on the road to Krabi (near McDonald's).

You'll find *roti* (pancakes), *gài tôrt* (fried chicken), hamburgers and the like, and around lunchtime street stalls set up just north of Krabi Resort.

Krua Ao Nang Cuisine
SEAFOOD $$

(📞 075 695260; Soi Sunset; mains 150-400B; ⊙ 10am-10pm) One of the best (and most popular) of several seafood restaurants with gorgeous sea vistas in this pedestrian-only alley at the western end of the beach. A model ice boat at the entrance shows off the day's catch (you pay by the kilo for seafood). It's a little more pricey than other options around Ao Nang; you're paying for the view.

Myeong Dong
KOREAN $$

(📞 075 813164; 345 Mu 2; mains 150-700B; ⊙ 11am-10pm; 🛜) If you want a change from seafood and mediocre Western cuisine, try this Korean barbecue place popular with Ao Nang's many Asian visitors. It offers classic Korean soups and stews, but the barbecue is the draw.

The grill is on your table, order your choice of meat; the veggies and side dishes come free.

Last Fisherman
BAR

(📞 081 267 5338; 266 Mu 2; ⊙ 10am-midnight) Sit at one of the breezy tables overlooking the beach, or perch at the long-tail boat-shaped bar, to enjoy your sundowner at this mellow but popular place at the southern end of Ao Nang.

❶ Information

All so-called 'tourist information' offices on the main drag through Ao Nang are private tour agencies.

There are many ATMs and foreign-exchange windows (open approximately 10am to 8pm).

❶ Getting There & Away

TO/FROM THE AIRPORT
White airport buses (150B) run hourly from 9am to 5pm, stopping outside McDonald's on the Krabi road. Private taxis (500B) and minivans (150B) go to/from the airport.

BOAT
Boats to Hat Railay West (15 minutes) are run by Ao Nang Long-Tail Boat Service (p661) and Ao Nang Long-Tail Boat Service Club (p661). Rates per person are 100B to 150B. Boats leave with eight passengers; you can charter the whole boat for the eight-person price.

CAR & MOTORCYCLE
Dozens of agencies along the main strip rent out motorcycles (200B to 250B). A number of places offer car hire from 1100B per day. Budget Car Hire (www.budget.co.th) has a desk at Krabi airport (vehicle rental per day from 1200B).

MINIVAN
Daily minivans (often combined boat-minivan tickets) go to destinations across southern Thailand.

DESTINATION	FARE (B)	DURATION (HR)
Khao Sok	400	3
Ko Lanta	400	3
Ko Lipe	1000	6
Ko Samui	700	4
Ko Tao	1100	7
Ko Pha-Ngan	850	5
Phuket	450	3

SŎRNG·TĂA·OU
Sŏrng·tăa·ou run to/from Krabi (60B, 30 minutes). The route goes from Krabi's bus terminal via Th Maharat to Krabi's Tha Khong Kha and on to Hat Noppharat Thara, Ao Nang and the Shell Cemetery. From Ao Nang to Hat Noppharat Thara or the Shell Cemetery costs 30B.

Hat Noppharat Thara   หาดนพรัตน์ธารา

North of Ao Nang, the golden beach turns more natural as it curves 4km around a less developed headland, until the sea eventually spills into a busy natural lagoon at **Hat Noppharat Thara-Mu Ko Phi-Phi National Park** (อุทยานแห่งชาติหาดนพรัตน์ธารา-หมู่เกาะพีพี; ☑ 075 661145; www.dnp.go.th; adult/child Ko Phi-Phi 400/200B, other islands 200/100B) headquarters. Its visitors centre has displays on coral reefs and mangrove ecology in Thai and English.

Hat Noppharat Thara is quieter and less built-up than Ao Nang. Several resorts here deceptively advertise a 'central Ao Nang' location, though you may well prefer ending up here anyway.

🛏 Sleeping & Eating

Several restaurants serving typical Thai snacks (fried chicken, papaya salad, noodles and stir fries) cluster near the national park headquarters and in a little enclave near the Sabai Resort. There are some decent seafood restaurants along the beachfront road.

Sabai Resort   HOTEL **$$**
(☑ 075 637791; www.sabairesort.com; 79/2 Mu 3; bungalows 1300-3500B; ❄@🛜🏊) The most professionally run of the area's bungalow properties. Tiled-roofed, mint-green, well-kept bungalows come in fan-cooled or air-con editions, with pebbled concrete patios overlooking a palm-shaded pool and flower-filled gardens. There are four-person family-sized rooms as well.

Hat Noppharat Thara-Mu Ko Phi-Phi National Park Accommodation   BUNGALOW, CAMPGROUND **$$**
(☑ 075 661145; www.dnp.go.th; camping per person 30B, bungalows 1000B; ❄) Rustic but well-maintained concrete, air-con, 24-hour-electricity bungalows, just over the road from the beach. No wi-fi. Note that while you can still camp here, just behind the park HQ, you will need your own tent as they're no longer available for rent. Book ahead online or at the visitors centre.

★ Krua Thara   SEAFOOD **$$**
(☑ 075 661166; 82 Mu 5; mains 150-250B; ⊙ 11am-10pm) This cavernous, tin-roofed delight is one of the best restaurants in southern Andaman and one of the finest seafood kitchens in southern Thailand. There's no pretension here, just the freshest fish, crab, clams, oysters, lobster, squid and prawns done dozens of ways. The steamed yellow conch (a local delicacy) and the crab stir-fried in yellow curry are especially memorable.

❶ Information

Hat Noppharat Thara-Mu Ko Phi-Phi National Park Visitors Centre (☑ 075 661145; www. dnp.go.th; ⊙ 8am-4.30pm) Offers information about the national park. You can also book the park accommodation here.

❶ Getting There & Away

BOAT
Boats leave from Hat Noppharat Thara's pier for the following destinations:

Ko Phi-Phi The *Ao Nang Princess* runs daily (450B, two hours) from around November to April, and on Wednesday, Friday and Sunday from May to October. Boats leave at 9.30am, returning from Ko Phi-Phi at 3.30pm, via Railay.

Ko Lanta A 10.30am *Ao Nang Princess* boat runs to Ko Lanta (550B, 2¾ hours).

Phuket From November to April, the fastest option to Phuket is the **Green Planet** (☑ 075 637488; www.krabigreenplanet.com) speedboat to Tha Bang Rong (1200B, 1¼ hours), via Ko Yao Noi and Ko Yao Yai (both 650B, 45 minutes). The boat leaves Hat Noppharat Thara's pier at 11am, returning from Phuket at 3pm; transport to your Phuket accommodation is included. There's also a 4pm *Ao Nang Princess* boat to Phuket (700B, three hours; reduced services May to October).

SÖRNG·TÄA·OU
Sörng·tăa·ou between Krabi (60B) and Ao Nang (30B) stop in Hat Noppharat Thara.

Ko Phi-Phi   เกาะพีพีดอน

With their curvy, bleached beaches and stunning jungle interiors, Phi-Phi Don and Phi-Phi Leh – collectively known as Ko Phi-Phi – are the darlings of the Andaman Coast. Phi-Phi Don is a hedonistic paradise where visitors cavort by day in azure seas and party all night on soft sand. In contrast, smaller Ko Phi-Phi Leh is undeveloped and hotel-free, its coral reefs and crystal-clear waters overseen by soaring, jagged cliffs, and visited only on day or sunset cruises.

Ko Phi-Phi Don

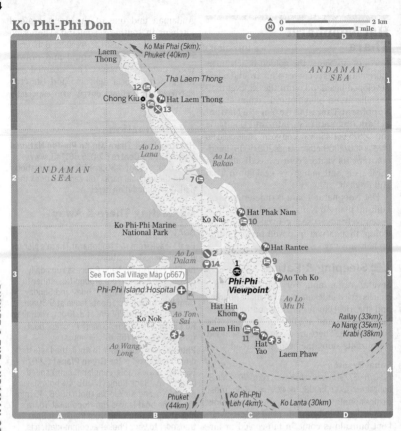

Ko Phi-Phi Don

Rampant development has rendered the centre of Ko Phi-Phi Don, as well as the two bays that flank it, a chaotic, noisy mess of hotels, restaurants, bars and shops. If you want tranquillity, head to the stunning white coves of the east coast, or less-developed Hat Yao in the south. Tread lightly, manage your expectations and Ko Phi-Phi may seduce you as it has so many other travellers. You might, equally, find you can't wait to leave.

⦿ Sights

★ Phi-Phi Viewpoint   VIEWPOINT
(จุดชมวิวเกาะพีพีดอน; Map p664; Ko Phi-Phi Don; 30B) The strenuous Phi-Phi-viewpoint climb is a steep, rewarding 20- to 30-minute hike up hundreds of steps and narrow twisting paths. Follow the signs on the road heading northeast from Ton Sai Village; most people will need to stop for a break (don't forget your water bottle). The views from the top are exquisite: Phi-Phi's lush mountain butterfly brilliance in full bloom.

🏃 Activities

Watersports Experience   WATER SPORTS
(☑ 096 924 4043; www.watersportsexperience. com; Ko Phi-Phi Don; per person without/with sports 1500/2500B; ⊙ tour 10am-6pm) Zip around in a speedboat and stand-up paddle board (SUP), wakeboard, water-ski, cliff-jump and snorkel the waters around Phi-Phi Don and Phi-Phi Leh. Anyone who doesn't fancy getting sporty is welcome to a discount. Book at any Ton Sai Village agency. Beers are included in the price.

Diving

Crystalline water and abundant marine life make the perfect recipe for top-notch scuba diving. Phi-Phi dive prices are fixed across the board. Open Water certification costs 13,800B, while standard two-dive trips cost 2500B to 3500B and Discover Scuba costs 3400B. Hin Daeng and Hin Muang, 60km south, are expensive ventures from Ko Phi-Phi (5500B); it's slightly cheaper to link up with a dive crew in Ko Lanta.

Blue View Divers   DIVING
(Map p664; ☑ 094 592 0184; www.blueviewdivers. com; Phi Phi Viewpoint Resort, Ao Lo Dalam, Ko Phi-Phi Don; 2 dives 2500B; ⊙ 10am-8pm) 🦋 Professional, well-organised outfit that focuses on community involvement, beach clean-ups and environmental conservation, with two-dive trips (2500B), night dives (1900B), Open Water courses (13,800B) and Discover Scuba (3400B).

Princess Divers   DIVING
(Map p667; ☑ 088 768 0984; www.princessdivers. com; Ton Sai Village, Ko Phi-Phi Don; ⊙ 9.30am-10pm) Recommended dive outfit that speaks multiple languages and uses big boats, rather than long-tails or speedboats. Offers Discover Scuba (3400B) and SSI/PADI Open Water courses (12,900/13,800B).

Snorkelling

Ko Mai Phai (Bamboo Island; Ko Phi-Phi Don), 6km north of Phi-Phi Don, is a popular shallow snorkelling spot where you may see small sharks. There's good snorkelling along the eastern coast of **Ko Nok** (near Ao Ton Sai), along the eastern coast of **Ko Nai**, and off **Hat Yao**. Most resorts rent out snorkel, mask and fins sets (200B per day).

PHUKET & THE ANDAMAN COAST KO PHI-PHI

BEST KO PHI-PHI DIVE SITES

Leopard sharks and hawksbill turtles are common on Ko Phi-Phi's dive sites. Whale sharks sometimes make cameo appearances around Hin Daeng, Hin Bida and Ko Bida Nok in February and March. November to February boasts the best visibility. Top dives around Ko Phi-Phi include the following:

DIVE SITE	DEPTH (M)	FEATURES
Anemone Reef	17-26	Hard coral reef with plentiful anemones and clownfish
Hin Bida Phi-Phi (Ko Phi-Phi Don)	5-30	Submerged pinnacle with hard coral, turtles, leopard sharks and occasional mantas and whale sharks
King Cruiser Wreck	12-30	Sunken passenger ferry (1997) with snappers, leopard sharks, barracudas, scorpionfish, lionfish and turtles
Kledkaeo Wreck (Ko Phi-Phi Don)	14-26	Deliberately sunk decommissioned Thai navy ship (2014) with lionfish, snappers, groupers and barracudas
Ko Bida Nok (Ko Phi-Phi Don)	18-22	Karst massif with gorgonians, leopard sharks, barracudas and occasional whale sharks and mantas
Phi-Phi Leh	5-18	Island rim covered in coral and oysters, with moray eels, octopuses, seahorses and swim-throughs

Snorkelling trips go from 600B to 1500B, not including national park fees, depending on whether you travel by long-tail or speed-boat. Snorkellers can tag along with dive trips.

Rock Climbing

Yes, there are good limestone cliffs to climb on Phi-Phi, and the views are spectacular. The main climbing areas are **Ton Sai Tower** (Map p664; Ko Phi-Phi Don), at the western edge of Ao Ton Sai, and **Hin Taak** (Map p664; Ko Phi-Phi Don), a short long-tail boat ride around the bay. Climbing operators, though, are in short supply, mostly congregating on nearby Railay. Ask the **Adventure Club** (Map p667; ☑081 895 1334; www.diving-in-thailand.net; 125/19 Mu 7, Ton Sai Village, Ko Phi-Phi Don; 2 dives 2500B; ⏱7am-10pm) 🛥 for a recommendation.

Courses

Pum Restaurant & Cooking School   COOKING (Map p667; ☑081 521 8904; www.pumthaifood chain.com; 125/40 Mu 7, Ton Sai Village, Ko Phi-Phi Don; ⏱classes 11am, 4pm & 6pm) Thai food fans can take highly recommended cooking courses ranging from two-hour sessions (1500B) to five-hour 'healthy lifestyle' extravaganzas and, the most expensive, a whole day class with Pum herself (7500B). You'll learn the secrets behind some of the excellent dishes served in Pum's Ton Sai Village restaurant and go home with a cookbook.

Tours

Ever since Leo (DiCaprio) smoked a spliff in the film rendition of Alex Garland's *The Beach*, Phi-Phi Leh has become a pilgrimage site. Aside from long-tail boat trips to Phi-Phi Leh and Ko Mai Phai on Phi-Phi Don, tour agencies organise sunset tours around Phi-Phi Leh that include Monkey Bay and the beach at Wang Long.

PP Original Sunset Tour   BOATING (Map p667; Ton Sai Village, Ko Phi-Phi Don; per person 900B; ⏱tours 1pm) A sensational sunset cruise that sees you bobbing around Phi-Phi Leh aboard a double-decker boat to mellow beats, snorkelling and kayaking between Ao Pi Leh's sheer-sided cliffs and dining on fried rice off Maya Beach, led by an enthusiastic, organised team. Bliss.

Maya Bay Sleepaboard   BOATING (Map p667; www.mayabaytours.com; Ton Sai Village, Ko Phi-Phi Don; per person 3500B) You

can no longer camp on Phi-Phi Leh's Maya Beach, but Maya Bay Sleepaboard can arrange for you to spend the night just offshore. Prices include food, sleeping bags and national park entry fees; tours depart at 3pm, returning at 10am the following morning. The same team runs the popular **Plankton Sunset Cruise** (www.mayabaytours. com; Ko Phi-Phi Leh; per person 1700B; ⏱3-8pm) to Phi-Phi Leh.

Captain Bob's Booze Cruise   BOATING (Map p667; ☑094 464 9146; www.phiphi boozecruise.com; Ko Phi-Phi Don; women/men 2500/3000B; ⏱tours 1-7pm) One of Phi-Phi's most popular excursions: we can't think why. Cruise the waters around Phi-Phi Don and Phi-Phi Leh, beverage in hand. There are rumours that the days of the booze cruises are numbered, with locals ticked off when smashed *fa·ràng* (Westerners) returning to town just at the time more sober tourists are going out for dinner.

🛏 Sleeping

On Ko Phi-Phi Don, expect serious room shortages and extortionate rates, especially at peak holiday times. Book ahead. Life is much easier in low season (May to October), when prices drop dramatically.

There is no accommodation on Ko Phi-Phi Leh. Nor can you camp here anymore. Your only option is to sleep on a boat offshore, which can be arranged with Maya Bay Sleepaboard.

Ton Sai Village & Ao Lo Dalam บ้านต้นไทร/อ่าวโละดาลัม

The flat, packed-out, hourglass-shaped land between Ao Ton Sai and Ao Lo Dalam is crammed with lodging options. Central Ton Sai is called the 'Tourist Village'.

Ao Lo Dalam is the traditional backpacker beach and there are many functional hostels here. Framed by stunning karst cliffs, it's arguably Phi-Phi's prettiest stretch of sand. But it's clogged with people, long-tail boats, many beach bars and day trippers. After 9pm, it turns into a vast open-air nightclub.

Rock Backpacker   HOSTEL $ (Map p667; ☑081 607 3897; Ton Sai Village, Ko Phi-Phi Don; dm 300B, r fan/air-con 900/2000B; ✳@🛜) A proper hostel on the village hill, with clean, big dorms lined with bunk beds, small private rooms, an

Ton Sai Village

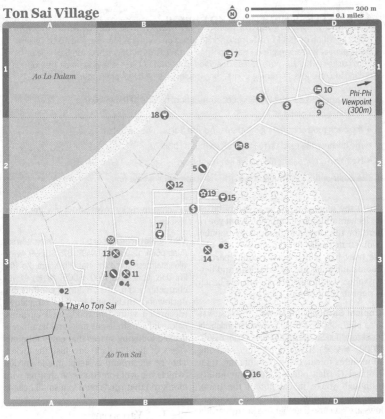

N 0 —————— 200 m
0 —————— 0.1 miles

inviting restaurant-bar and a rugged, graffiti-scrawled exterior. It's still one of Ton Sai's cheaper pads and there's a buzzing backpacker scene – just don't expect an effusive welcome. Walk-ins only.

Ibiza House HOSTEL, HOTEL **$$**
(Map p667; ☏ 080 537 1868, 075 601274; ibiza-houseppth@gmail.com; Ao Lo Dalam, Ko Phi-Phi Don; dm 1000-1500B; r incl breakfast 3500B; villas 5000-15,000B; ❄ ⊛ ⊠) The dorms here aren't

ℹ SLEEPLESS NIGHTS ON KO PHI-PHI

Noise pollution on Phi-Phi is terrible and focused on central Ao Ton Sai and Ao Lo Dalam. Don't expect an early night on Hat Hin Khom either. Bars in Dalam and Ton Sai have a 2am curfew (which is more or less observed), but that doesn't stop private parties, or inebriated revellers slamming doors, throwing up, falling down or wandering around cramped dorms at 4am.

For a shot at peaceful Phi-Phi accommodation, try one of the following:

➡ Phi-Phi's east coast

➡ the back road connecting southeast Ao Ton Sai with Ao Lo Dalam

➡ the hill near the road up to Phi-Phi Viewpoint (p665)

➡ Hat Yao (Long Beach; Map p664; Ko Phi-Phi Don)

The other option is to succumb to the inevitable and join the fun.

worth the money: bunk beds, safety boxes for lockers and shared bathrooms, but you're here for the large and perennially popular pool, strategically flanked on two sides by the busy bar, which hosts regular parties. Rooms and villas are big and clean and better value, if still over-priced. But the beach is right in front of you.

Tropical Garden Bungalows   BUNGALOW **$$**
(Map p667; ☑ 089 729 1436; www.thailandphiphi travel.com; Ton Sai Village, Ko Phi-Phi Don; r 1100-1800B; ❄ 🛜 🏊) If you don't mind walking 10 minutes to eat, drink or sunbathe, then Tropical Garden offers a little tranquillity (although you're in earshot of the bars). Near the viewpoint path, the simple bungalows are set close together in a shady garden and come with balconies and hammocks. The cheapest are fan-only.

There's a small flower-fringed pool with a swim-up bar.

Up Hill Cottage   BUNGALOW **$$$**
(Map p667; ☑ 075 601124; www.phiphiuphillcot tage.com; 140 Mu 7, Ton Sai Village, Ko Phi-Phi Don; r 2000-2500B; ❄ 🛜 🏊) These cream-painted, wood-panelled bungalows come in cute pastels offset by colourful bed runners and snazzily tiled bathrooms. Most enjoy island views (of varying beauty) from private balconies. It's *slightly* beyond the madness, at the eastern end of the main street heading north from Ton Sai Village. Small pool. Beware the hundreds of stairs.

🏖 Hat Hin Khom หาดหินคม

A 15-minute beach or jungle walk east of Ao Ton Sai, this area has a few small white-sand beaches in rocky coves and a few midrange resorts.

Viking Natures Resort   BUNGALOW **$$$**
(Map p664; ☑ 083 649 9492, 075 819399; www. vikingnaturesresort.com; Hat Hin Khom, Ko Phi-Phi Don; bungalows 1500-4500B; ❄ 🛜) If it's character you're after, Viking's comfortable dark-wood, thatch-and-bamboo bungalows (decorated with driftwood, shell curtains, colourful art, stone-cut sinks and hammock-decked lounging spaces that enjoy fabulous views of Phi-Phi Leh) are just the ticket. They're set around a steep, jungle garden (which you will sometimes be sharing with monkeys) that runs down to a small beach.

🏖 Hat Yao หาดยาว

This lively stretch of pure-white south-coast beach is perfect for swimming, but don't expect it to yourself. There are also midrange resorts here. You can walk here in 30 minutes from Ton Sai via Hat Hin Khom or take long-tails (100B to 150B) from Ton Sai pier.

Paradise Pearl Bungalow   RESORT **$$$**
(Map p664; ☑ 075 601248; www.phiphiparadise pearl.com; Hat Yao, Ko Phi-Phi Don; r incl breakfast 3000-5000B; ❄ 🛜) A sprawling complex of dark-wood Thai chalets, decked out with art, tucked into the rocky headland on the northern curl of Hat Yao. Delightfully old-fashioned beach-facing wooden 'houses' have four-poster beds, lace curtains and tea/coffee stands. The loungey **restaurant** (Map p664; Hat Yao, Ko Phi-Phi Don; mains 120-400B; ⏱7.30am-10pm; 🛜), typically packed with young couples, rambles to the edge of the sand.

Hat Rantee หาดรันตี

This small, low-key, remote, grey-gold eastern bay has midrange family bungalows and good snorkelling. Arrive by long-tail from Ton Sai's pier (700B; return 200B per person, minimum four people; resorts provide free pick up if you've booked) or via the strenuous 45-minute hike over the viewpoint.

Rantee View   BUNGALOW $$
(Map p664; ☏ 092 124 0599; Hat Rantee, Ko Phi-Phi Don; bungalows fan 1500B, air-con 2500-4500B; ❀ ☎) Basic, acceptable-enough woven bamboo bungalows and newer, clean, tiled concrete bungalows with air-con and wide porches overlooking a trim garden path that leads to the sand. No restaurant. Closes low season.

Hat Phak Nam หาดผักน้ำ

This gorgeous white-sand beach shares its bay with a small fishing hamlet, is quiet and has a few midrange places to stay. Charter a long-tail from Ao Ton Sai (1000B; 200B by shared taxi boat to return) or make the sweaty one-hour hike over the viewpoint.

Relax Beach Resort   BUNGALOW $$$
(Map p664; ☏ 089 475 6536; www.phiphirelax resort.com; Hat Phak Nam, Ko Phi-Phi Don; bungalows 2100-4600B; @ ☎) These 47 lacquered Thai-style bungalows, with wood floors, thatched roofs, two-tiered terraces with lounging cushions and mosaic bathrooms (in the best rooms), are rimmed by lush jungle. There's a good seafood-focused Thai/international **restaurant** (Map p664; mains 120-350B; ⏱ 7.30am-9pm; ☎) and breezy bar, and it's run by charming staff who treat guests like family.

Ao Lo Bakao อ่าวโละบาเกา

Ao Lo Bakao's fine stretch of northeastern palm-backed sand, ringed by dramatic hills, is one of Phi-Phi's loveliest, with offshore views over aqua bliss to Bamboo and Mosquito Islands. A long-tail charter from Ao Ton Sai costs 1000B.

Phi-Phi Island Village   BUNGALOW $$$
(Map p664; ☏ 075 628900; www.phiphiislandvil lage.com; Ao Lo Bakao, Ko Phi-Phi Don; r incl breakfast 7300-26,400B; ❀ ☎ ☒) This whopping resort – 201 wood-and-concrete bungalows

mostly set just back from the beach with palms swaying between them – is its own self-contained world with everything you'd need on site, including two pools, restaurant, coffee shop, spa, dive shop and tennis courts (as well as its own tsunami shelter). The resort arranges long-tail transfers to/from Ton Sai. Discounts if you book online.

Hat Laem Thong หาดแหลมทอง

Despite the upmarket resorts here, this northeastern white-sand beach is busy (it's a stop on day tours from Phuket) and has a small, rubbish-strewn *chow lair* settlement at its northern end. Long-tail charters from Ao Ton Sai cost 1200B; hotels arrange transfers.

★ Zeavola   HOTEL $$$
(Map p664; ☏ 075 627000; www.zeavola.com; Hat Laem Thong, Ko Phi-Phi Don; bungalows incl breakfast 11,100-22,100B; ❀ ☎ ☒) Hibiscus-lined pathways lead to shady teak bungalows with sleek, distinctly Asian indoor-outdoor floorplans. Each comes with floor-to-ceiling windows on three sides, beautiful 1940s fixtures and antique furniture, huge ceramic sinks, indoor/outdoor showers, tea/coffee pods on a private terrace and impeccable service. The finest villas enjoy their own infinity pools and there's a fabulous couples-oriented spa.

PP Erawan Palms Resort   HOTEL $$$
(Map p664; ☏ 075 627500; www.pperawanpalms. com; Hat Laem Thong, Ko Phi-Phi Don; r incl breakfast 4500-9000B; ❀ ☎ ☒) Step onto the grounds and let the stress fall away as you follow a meandering path through gardens to bright, spacious, modern yet traditional-feel 'cottages' and smaller rooms decorated with Thai art and handicrafts. Beds could be bigger and better, but there's an inviting pool bar plus friendly service.

✗ Eating

★ Esan Ganeang   THAI $
(Map p667; Ton Sai Village, Ko Phi-Phi Don; mains 70-150B; ⏱ 10am-midnight) On an alley jammed with hole-in-the-wall places favoured by the locals, family-run Esan Ganeang has fantastic and authentic dishes from the Isan region in northeast Thailand. Come here for fiery salads and soups, as well as more mild curries and noodle dishes packed with

flavour. Make sure to order sticky rice to accompany your meal.

Local Food Market
MARKET, THAI $

(Map p667; Ton Sai Village, Ko Phi-Phi Don; mains 60-80B; ⊙7am-10pm) Phi-Phi's cheapest, most authentic eats are at this market close to the pier. A handful of enthusiastic local stalls serve up scrumptious *pàt tai*, fried rice, *sôm·đam* (spicy green papaya salad) and smoked catfish.

★ Unni's
INTERNATIONAL $$

(Map p667; ☑091 837 5931; Ton Sai Village, Ko Phi-Phi Don; mains 140-600B; ⊙8am-11pm; 🛜) Swing by this local expat fave for homemade breakfast bagels topped with everything from smoked salmon to meatballs. or specials like avocado-and-feta toast, served in a bright and pleasant cafe-style atmosphere. Other excellent global treats include massive Greek salads, pastas, burritos, nachos, burgers, tapas, cocktails and more.

★ Efe
TURKISH $$

(Map p667; ☑095 150 4434; Ton Sai Village, Ko Phi-Phi Don; mains 170-640B; ⊙noon-10.30pm; 🛜) This Mediterranean newcomer has swiftly become the restaurant of choice for discerning travellers and expats, thanks to its super selection of kebabs served on sizzling plates, salads and wraps. Also does fine burgers and pizzas. It's a cosy place, with a few tables inside and a tiny patio, so expect to wait for a table during the dinner rush.

★ Jasmin
SEAFOOD $$

(Map p664; Hat Laem Thong, Ko Phi-Phi Don; mains 150-500B; ⊙10am-10pm) Break out of your posh resort to eat at this fine and relaxed, semi-open-air seafood place right in the middle of idyllic Laem Thong beach. The fresh fish (pay by the weight), lovingly grilled, is the draw, but it also whips up all your Thai classics, Western standards, sandwiches and breakfasts. Also does a reasonable cocktail.

Papaya Restaurant
THAI $$

(Map p667; ☑087 280 1719; Ton Sai Village, Ko Phi-Phi Don; mains 70-450B; ⊙8.30am-10pm) Cheap, tasty and spicy. Here's some real-deal Thai food served in heaping portions. It

---

ⓘ THEFT WARNING

Thefts can be a problem on Ko Phi-Phi Don. Watch your possessions and close windows and lock doors.

---

has your basil and chilli, all the curries, *sôm·đam* (spicy green papaya salad) and *đôm yam,* too.

🍷 Drinking & Nightlife

Buckets of cheap whisky and Red Bull and sickly sweet cocktails make this the domain of gap-year craziness and really bad hangovers. Be wary of anyone offering you drugs on the beaches: they may be setting you up for a visit from the local coppers.

Banana Bar
BAR

(Map p667; Ton Sai Village, Ko Phi-Phi Don; ⊙11am-2pm; 🛜) The 'alt' bar destination in Ton Sai Village, inland for those seeking to escape the house and techno barrage on the beach, Banana is spread over multiple levels. Climb to the rooftop, or lounge on cushions on the raised decks around the bar. Solid sounds and popular with people who like to roll their own cigarettes. Also does Mexican food.

Slinky
CLUB

(Map p667; Ao Lo Dalam, Ko Phi-Phi Don; ⊙9pm-2am) Still the best fire show on Ao Lo Dalam and still the beach dancefloor of the moment. Expect throbbing bass, buckets of liquor (from 350B) and throngs of tourists mingling, flirting and flailing to the music.

Relax Bar
BAR

(Map p667; Ton Sai Village, Ko Phi-Phi Don; ⊙noon-1am) The coldest beer on Phi-Phi, with a fridge chilled to Arctic temperatures, this intimate, mellow bar lives up to its name and is unusual for the island in attracting locals, as well as travellers and expats. Reasonably priced drinks and no wi-fi: you have to talk to each other here.

Sunflower Bar
BAR

(Map p664; Ao Lo Dalam, Ko Phi-Phi Don; ⊙11am-2am; 🛜) This ramshackle driftwood gem is one of Phi-Phi's most chilled-out bars and excellent for nursing a beer while the sun dips into the sea. Destroyed in the 2004 tsunami, it was rebuilt with reclaimed wood. The long-tail booths are named for the four loved ones the owner lost in the deluge.

Carlito's
BAR

(Map p667; Ao Ton Sai, Ko Phi-Phi Don; ⊙11am-1am; 🛜) For a more toned-down take on the fire-twirling madness that dominates Ao Lo Dalam, sit at one of the candlelit tables, or pull up a plastic chair on the sand, at this fairy-light-lit joint on Ao Ton Sai. There's a nightly fire show and live music, but it's a rather more refined and romantic venue than most of Phi-Phi's beach bars.

☆ Entertainment

Kong Siam   LIVE MUSIC
(Map p667; Ton Sai Village, Ko Phi-Phi Don; ⊙ 6pm-2am) Live music nightly at this popular place that draws Thais and *fa·ràng* (Westerners). The owner is a talented guitarist, and his mates and the other acts who play here aren't too shabby either.

❶ Information

ATMs are spread thickly throughout the Tourist Village on Ko Phi-Phi Don, but are non-existent on the eastern beaches and there are none on Ko Phi-Phi Leh. Wi-fi is everywhere.
Phi-Phi Island Hospital (Map p664; ☑ 075 622151) Emergency care at the west end of Ao Ton Sai. For anything truly serious, get on the first boat to Krabi, or better still, Phuket.
Post Office (Map p667; Ton Sai Village, Ko Phi-Phi Don; ⊙ 9am-5pm Mon-Fri & 9am-1pm Sat) You can send mail overseas from here.

❶ Getting There & Away

Ko Phi-Phi Don can be reached from Ao Nang, Krabi, Phuket, Railay and Ko Lanta. Most boats moor at **Ao Ton Sai** (Map p667; Ton Sai Village, Ko Phi-Phi Don), though a few from Phuket use isolated, northern **Tha Laem Thong** (Map p664). Ferries operate year-round, although not always every day.

There are also combined boat and minivan tickets to destinations across Thailand, including Bangkok (850B, 11 hours, 3.30pm), Ko Samui (500B, 6½ hours, 10.30am) and Ko Pha-Ngan (600B, seven hours, 10.30am).

You can travel to Ko Phi-Phi Leh on tours, or by long-tail boat (600B to 800B) and speedboat (2500B).

❶ Getting Around

There are no real roads on Ko Phi-Phi Don and while some locals do use motorbikes, foreigners can't hire them. Transport is by foot, or long-tails can be chartered at Ao Ton Sai for short hops around both islands.

Long-tails leave Ao Ton Sai pier for Hat Yao (100B to 150B), Hat Rantee (700B), Hat Phak Nam and Ao Lo Bakao (1000B), Laem Thong (1200B) and Viking Cave (on Ko Phi-Phi Leh; 600B).

Chartering a long-tail for three/six hours costs 1500/3000B; a half-day speedboat charter costs 5000B.

Ko Lanta   เกาะลันตา
☑ 075 / POP 26,800

Once the domain of sea gypsies, Lanta has morphed from a luscious Thai backwater into a getaway for both Asian and European, especially Scandinavian, visitors who come for the divine miles-long beaches (though the northern coast is alarmingly eroded) and nearby dive spots of Hin Daeng, Hin Muang and Ko Haa.

Charming Lanta remains more calm and real than its brash neighbour Ko Phi-Phi, although – whisper it quietly – the backpacker party scene is growing. Flatter than surrounding islands and with reasonable roads that run 22km from north to south, Lanta is easily toured on a motorbike, revealing a colourful crucible of cultures – fried-chicken stalls sit below slender minarets, stilted villages of *chow lair* cling to the island's east side, and small Thai *wát* hide within tangles of curling mangroves.

Ko Lanta is technically called Ko Lanta Yai. Boats pull into dusty Ban Sala Dan, on the northern tip of the island.

TRANSPORT TO/FROM KO PHI-PHI DON

DESTINATION	FARE (B)	DURATION (HR)	TO KO PHI-PHI	FROM KO PHI-PHI
Ao Nang	450	1¾	9.30am	3.30pm
Ko Lanta	350-600	1½	8am, 11.30am, 1pm, 4pm	11.30am, 3pm & 3.30pm
Krabi	350	1½-2	9am, 10.30am, 1.30pm, 3.30pm	9am, 10.30am, 1.30pm & 3.30pm
Phuket	350	1¼-2	9am, 11am, 1pm, 1.30pm, 3pm	9am,11am, 2pm, 2.30pm & 3.30pm
Railay	450	1¼	9.45am	3.30pm

Ko Lanta

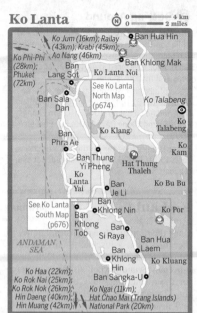

0 ————— 4 km
0 ————— 2 miles

Ko Jum (16km); Railay (43km); Krabi (45km); Ao Nang (46km)
Ban Hua Hin
Ko Phi-Phi (28km); Phuket (72km)
Ban Khlong Mak
Ban Lang Sot
Ko Lanta Noi
See Ko Lanta North Map (p674)
Ban Sala Dan
Ko Talabeng
Ko Talabeng
Ban Phra Ae
Ko Klang
Ban Thung Yi Pheng
Ko Kam
Hat Thung Thaleh
Ko Lanta Yai
Ban Je Li
Ko Bu Bu
See Ko Lanta South Map (p676)
Ban Khlong Nin
Ko Por
Ban Khlong Tob
Ban Si Raya
Ban Hua Laem
ANDAMAN SEA
Ban Khlong Hin
Ko Kluang
Ko Haa (22km); Ko Rok Nai (25km); Ko Rok Nok (26km); Hin Daeng (40km); Hin Muang (42km)
Ban Sangka-U
Ko Ngai (11km); Hat Chao Mai (Trang Islands) National Park (20km)

👁 Sights

⭐ Ban Si Raya   VILLAGE

(บ้านศรีรายา, Lanta Old Town; Map p676) Halfway down Lanta's eastern coast, Ban Si Raya was the island's original port and commercial centre, providing a safe harbour for Arab and Chinese trading vessels sailing between Phuket, Penang and Singapore. Known to the locals as Lanta Old Town, the vibe here is very different from the rest of the island, with wooden century-old stilt houses and shopfronts transformed into charming, characterful guesthouses. Pier restaurants offer fresh catch overlooking the sea, and there are some cute bohemian shops dotted around.

Tham Khao Maikaeo   CAVE

(ถ้ำเขาไม้แก้ว; Map p676; ☎089 288 8954; tours 300B) Monsoon rains pounding away at limestone crevices for millions of years have created this complex of caverns and tunnels. There are cathedral-size chambers, dripping with stalactites and stalagmites, tiny passages you have to squeeze through on hands and knees, and even a subterranean pool. A local family runs hourly treks to the caves (with headlamps). The full trip takes two hours; sensible shoes essential.

It's signposted off the main road from Hat Khlong Tob to the east coast. Phone ahead for timings.

Lanta Animal Welfare   ANIMAL SANCTUARY, VOLUNTEERING

(Map p674; ☎084 304 4331; www.lantaanimal welfare.com; 629 Mu 2, Ban Phra Ae; tours by donation; ☉10am-4pm) This long-standing animal rescue centre cares for around 30 dogs and 60 cats through feeding, sterilising and re-homing, and vaccination and local awareness campaigns. Visitors can join hourly 40-minute facilities tours and play with kittens. The centre also welcomes casual dog-walking visitors and volunteers for longer placements.

🏃 Activities

Diving & Snorkelling

Some of Thailand's top diving spots are within arm's reach of Lanta. The best diving can be found at the undersea pinnacles of Hin Muang and Hin Daeng, two hours away by boat. These lone mid-sea coral outcrops act as important feeding stations for large pelagic fish such as sharks, tuna, barracudas and occasionally whale sharks and manta rays. Hin Daeng is commonly considered to be Thailand's second-best dive site after Richelieu Rock (p604), near the Myanmar border.

The sites around Ko Haa have consistently good visibility, with depths of 18m to 34m, plenty of marine life (including turtles) and a three-chamber cave known as the 'Cathedral'. Lanta dive outfitters run trips up to King Cruiser Wreck (p658), Anemone Reef (Ko Phi-Phi Don) and several other Ko Phi-Phi dive sites.

Lanta's dive season is November to April, though some operators run weather-dependent dives during low season. Trips to Hin Daeng and Hin Muang cost 3600B to 4500B; Ko Haa dives are 3100B to 4000B. PADI Open Water courses cost 13,700B to 15,900B. Rates usually exclude national park fees.

From mid-October to April, agencies across Lanta offer four-island snorkelling and kayaking tours (1200B to 1900B) to Ko Rok Nok, the Trang Islands and other nearby isles.

Scubafish   DIVING

(Map p676; ☎075 665095; www.scubafish.com; Ao Kantiang; 2 dives 3500B; ☉8am-8pm) A long-running outfit based in the south of Lanta (closer to the dive sites) with a stellar reputation, Scubafish offers personable programs, including the Liquid Lense underwater photography courses, although it's pricier than other outfits. The three-day dive packages (9975B) are popular. One-day Discover Scuba is 5200B; Open Water certification costs 15,900B.

Lanta Diver　　　　　　　　　　DIVING
(Map p674; ☏ 075 668058; www.lantadiver.com; 197/3 Mu 1, Ban Sala Dan; 2 dives 3600B; ☉10am-6pm) A very professional Scandinavian-run operator, based near the pier and with smaller resort concessions. Two-dive day trips to Hin Daeng and Hin Muang run 3600B to 4100B; two-dive Discover Scuba is 4500B. Open Water certification is 14,400B.

Blue Planet Divers　　　　　　　DIVING
(Map p674; ☏ 075 668165; www.divinglanta.com; 3 Mu 1, Ban Sala Dan; 2 dives 3100B; ☉8.30am-9pm) The first Lanta school to specialise in free-diving instruction (from 2700B). Also does Open Water certification (13,700B), Discover Scuba (4300B) and snorkelling tours (1500B).

Go Dive　　　　　　　　　　　DIVING
(Map p674; ☏ 075 668320; www.godive-lanta. com; 6 Mu 1, Ban Sala Dan; 2 dives 3300B; ☉Oct-Apr) One of Lanta's newer outfitters. Fun dives (two for 4200B at Hin Daeng/Hin Muang), two-dive Discover Scuba (4400B) and Open Water certification (PADI/SSI 13,900/12,900B).

Yoga

Drop-in classes (250B to 400B) are offered during high season (November to April) at **Oasis Yoga** (Map p674; ☏ 085 115 4067; www. oasisyoga-lanta.com; Hat Khlong Dao) and **Relax Bay** (Map p674; ☏ 075 684194; www.relaxbay.com; Ao Phra Ae; r 1800-4900B; ❄️🛜🏊). Sri Lanta (p675) has classes year-round for 550B.

🎓 Courses

Time for Lime　　　　　　　COOKING
(Map p674; ☏ 075 684590; www.timeforlime. net; Hat Khlong Dao; ☉class 4pm) On south Hat Khlong Dao, this popular beachfront school-restaurant offers excellent cooking courses (2000B) in the high season with a slightly more exciting recipe selection than most Thai cookery schools. The five-hour courses can be adapted for vegetarians and there are multiple-class discounts. Profits finance Lanta Animal Welfare. Book ahead. The on-site restaurant offers a tasting menu from Monday to Saturday (540B).

🛏 Sleeping

Some resorts close for the May–October low season; others drop rates by 50%. Reservations are essential in high season.

🛏 Hat Khlong Dao หาดคลองดาว

Costa Lanta　　　　　　HOTEL $$$
(Map p674; ☏ 075 668186; www.costalanta.com; Hat Khlong Dao; r incl breakfast 7100-9700B; ❄️🛜🏊) These Zen-like standalone abodes are nestled in a coconut-palm garden laced with tidal canals at the north end of Hat Khlong Dao. Everything from the floors to the walls to the washbasins is polished concrete, and the barn doors of each minimalist-chic cabana open on two sides to maximise space and breezes. Big bathrooms.

Lanta Island Resort　　　BUNGALOW $$$
(Map p674; ☏ 075 684124; www.lantaislandresort. com; 10 Mu 3, Hat Khlong Dao; bungalows 1800-5300B; ❄️🛜🏊) Oldish concrete bungalows with white tiled floors, but they are sizeable and well-kept, dotted around a leafy garden and pool a few metres from the beach. The bungalows have some space between them, allowing for privacy. The resort's **Island Bar** (Map p674; 10 Mu 3, Hat Khlong Dao; ☉noon-late; 🛜) is an amenable spot for a sundowner and has live music in high season.

🛏 Hat Phra Ae หาดพระแอ

Chill Out House　　　　　　HOSTEL $
(Map p674; ☏ 082 183 2258; www.chillouthouse lanta.com; Hat Phra Ae; dm 220B, d 280-320B; ☉Sep-Apr; 🛜🏊) This buzzing backpacker 'treehouse community' set back from the beach has three different and simple dorms, shared bathrooms, chalkboard doors and rickety doubles with bathrooms. It's basic, but you can't beat the laid-back vibe (or the price): swings at the bar, a communal iPod dock, and a wonderful (yes) chill-out lounge heavy on hammocks.

Lanta Baan Nok Resort　　BUNGALOW $$
(Map p674; ☏ 075 684459; lantabaannokresort@ gmail.com; Hat Phra Ae; bungalows 1500B; ❄️🛜) New resort with eight spotless, comfortable bungalows with modern bathrooms, beds raised up off the floor on platforms, balconies with hammocks and an agreeably

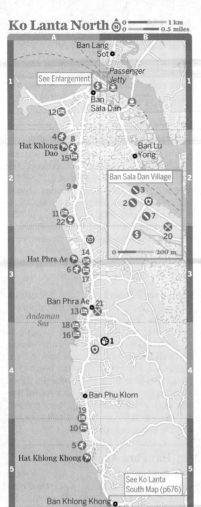

PHUKET & THE ANDAMAN COAST KO LANTA

Long Beach Chalet BUNGALOW **$$$**
(Map p674; ☑ 075 695668; www.longbeachchalet.
net; Hat Phra Ae; bungalows 3000-9000B; ☞☒)
Large wooden bungalows with balconies
raised up on concrete stilts surround a cool
pool and manicured garden a 200m walk
from the beach. The gimmick here is that
the bungalows are divided into two halves:
one houses the bedroom, the other the bath-
room. Efficient staff.

Lazy Days BUNGALOW **$$$**
(Map p674; ☑ 075 656291; www.lantalazydays.
com; Hat Phra Ae; bungalows 4200-5000B; ☒☞)
Lazy days indeed if you can score one of the
fine nine bungalows tucked away here in a
secluded spot at the end of Phra Ae beach.
The bungalows are bamboo with thatched
roofs and balconies; inside they are very
comfortable with great beds, decent bathrooms, hot water, TVs, fridges and safety
boxes. There's a restaurant too.

laid-back vibe. A decent deal for the price.
It's a short walk to the beach.

Hutyee Boat BUNGALOW **$$**
(Map p674; ☑ 083 633 9723; Hat Phra Ae; bun-
galows 600-1200B; ☞) A hidden, hippie par-
adise of big, basic, fan-only bungalows on
stilts with tiled bathrooms, mini fridges and
swinging hammocks in a forest of palms and
bamboo. It's just back from the beach (be-
hind Nautilus Resort) and run by a friendly
Muslim family.

Hat Khlong Khong หาดคลองโขง

★Bee Bee Bungalows
BUNGALOW **$$**

(Map p674; ☎081 537 9932; Hat Khlong Khong; bungalows 700-1000B; ⊙Oct-Apr; ☎) Bee Bee's is comprised of a dozen creative bamboo cabins managed by super-friendly staff. Each bungalow is unique; a few are stilted in the trees. The on-site restaurant has a library of tattered paperbacks to keep you occupied while you wait for your delicious Thai staples.

Where Else!
BUNGALOW **$$**

(Map p674; ☎092 942 6554, 093 293 6545; where-else-lanta@hotmail.com; Hat Khlong Khong; bungalows 600-1500B; ☎) One of Lanta's hippie outposts – think thatched bungalows with semi-outdoor cold-water bathrooms. If you're trying to avoid late-night parties and tropical critters look elsewhere. Still, the place buzzes with backpackers, the owner is cool and there's a fun barefoot-beach vibe centred on the popular Feeling Bar (p679). Pricier bungalows are multilevel abodes sleeping up to four.

Hat Khlong Nin หาดคลองนิน

Round House
GUESTHOUSE **$$**

(Map p676; ☎086 950 9424; www.lantaround house.com; Hat Khlong Nin; bungalows without/with bathroom 800/1500B, house 3000B; ❄☎) A cute multi-option find on the north end of the beach. Stilted bamboo-and-wood fan bungalows are simply styled the cheapest share hot-water bathrooms) and sit just behind the breezy beachfront restaurant. Also available is a cool two-person adobe round house, concrete rooms fronted by porches and an air-con beach house perfect for families. There's morning yoga classes, too (300B).

Sri Lanta
BOUTIQUE HOTEL **$$$**

(Map p676; ☎075 662688; www.srilanta.com; Hat Khlong Nin; r 3400-7400B; ❄☎☀) 🌿 At the southern end of the beach, this ecospot popular with Asian tourists consists of comfortable wooden villas with lots of light in gardens stretching from the beach to the hillside behind. There's a flower-fringed beachside area with two pools, restaurant and massage pavilions. The resort strives

---

❶ WHERE TO STAY IN KO LANTA

Ban Sala Dan There's decent budget accommodation in characterful Ban Sala Dan. It's also handy for local-flavoured seafood restaurants and boat arrivals/departures, but not on the beach.

Hat Khlong Dao (Map p674) Once an outstanding 2km white-sand stretch perfect for swimming, this beach has become so eroded that at high tide there's no sand at all.

Hat Phra Ae (Long Beach; Map p674) A large travellers' village has grown up along sandy Hat Phra Ae, 3km south of Ban Sala Dan. The beach has suffered erosion recently, but there's a nice stretch on its northern flank.

Hat Khlong Khong (Map p674) This is thatched-roof, Rasta-bar bliss and backpacker central with beach volleyball, moon parties and the occasional well-advertised mushroom shake, 9km south of Ban Sala Dan.

Hat Khlong Nin (Map p676) The main road heading south forks 13km south of Ban Sala Dan (after Hat Khlong Tob). The right-hand road hugs the coastline for 14km to Ko Lanta's southernmost tip. The first beach is lovely white-sand Hat Khlong Nin, which has lots of small, flashpacker-type guesthouses at its north end. Shop around.

Ao Kantiang (Map p676) This superb southwestern sweep of sand backed by mountains is also its own self-contained village with mini-marts, motorbike rental and restaurants.

Ao Mai Pai (Map p676) A lush nearly forgotten cove at the southwestern curve just before the cape, Ao Mai Pai is one of Lanta's finest beaches.

Laem Tanod (Map p676) The wild, jungled, mountainous southern tip of the island has sheer drops and massive views.

Ban Si Raya (p672) There are a handful of guesthouses in Lanta's oft-ignored, wonderfully dated and culturally rich east-coast Old Town, which has its own bohemian groove.

Ko Lanta South

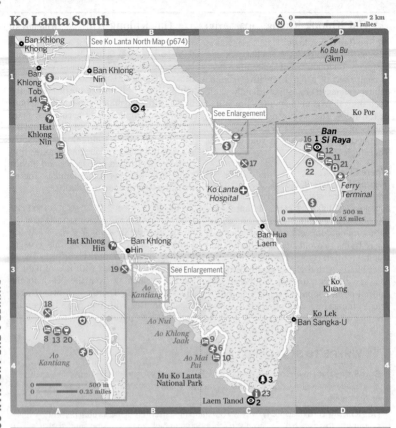

Ko Lanta South

for low environmental impact by using bio-degradable products and minimising energy use and waste.

Ao Kantiang อ่าวกันเตียง

Baan Laanta Resort & Spa HOTEL $$$
(Map p676; ☎075 665091; www.baanlaanta. com; Ao Kantiang; bungalows incl breakfast 4500-5500B; ❊ ☎ ⟁) Landscaped grounds wind around comfortable wooden bungalows with terraces and a sultry dark infinity pool refreshed by elephant fountains and surrounded by frangipani trees, all overlooking an idyllic white sandy beach. Fixtures are a little old-fashioned, but the bungalows are sizeable, with sofas and futon-style beds raised off the floor. The Scubafish (p672) dive school is on-site.

Phra Nang Lanta HOTEL $$$
(Map p676; ☎075 665025; www.vacationvillage. co.th; Ao Kantiang; r 4250-5252B; ❊ ☎ ⟁) These 15 gorgeous, Mexican-style, adobe-looking concrete studios are straight off the pages of an interiors magazine. Think: clean lines, hardwood and whites accented with vibrant colours, lounge cushions and ceramic sinks. Outside, flowers and foliage climb over bamboo lattice sunshades, and the pool and restaurant-bar look over the beautiful beach. Excellent low-season deals.

Ao Mai Pai อ่าวไม้ไผ่

★La Laanta BOUTIQUE HOTEL $$$
(Map p676; ☎087 883 9966, 087 883 9977; www. lalaanta.com; Ao Mai Pai; bungalows incl breakfast 2800-6200B; ❊ ☎ ⟁) Operated by a young English-speaking Thai-Vietnamese couple, this is one of the grooviest spots on Lanta. Thatched bungalows have polished-concrete floors, platform beds, floral-design murals and decks overlooking a sandy volleyball pitch, which blends into a rocky beach. The laid-back **restaurant** (Map p676; Ao Mai Pai; mains 120-350B; ⊗8am-9pm; ☎) does a tasty Thai menu with lots of veggie-friendly choices. It's the last turn before the national park, far from everything else.

Baan Phu Lae BUNGALOW $$$
(Map p676; ☎085 474 0265, 075 665100; www. baanphulaeresort.com; Ao Mai Pai; bungalows fan 1800B, air-con 2000-2400B; ⊗Oct-Apr; ❊ ☎) Set on secluded rocks at the northern end of the final beach before Lanta's southern cape, this collection of cute, canary-yellow

concrete fan and air-con bungalows have thatched roofs, colourful art, bamboo beds and private porches. Just behind stand stilt-ed, wooden, air-con bungalows. They also arrange diving and snorkelling trips, cooking classes, massages and transport.

Laem Tanod แหลมโตนด

Mu Ko Lanta National Park Accommodation BUNGALOW, CAMPGROUND $
(Map p676; ☎075 660711, in Bangkok 02 561 4292; www.dnp.go.th; Laem Tanod; bungalows 1500-3000B, campsite per person 40B, with tent hire 300B) Engulfed by craggy outcrops and the sound of crashing waves, the secluded national park headquarters grounds are a gloriously serene place to stay, in simple four- to eight-person bungalows or tents. There are toilets and running water, and there's also a shop but you'll need to bring your own food. You can also get permission for camping on Ko Rok here.

Ban Si Raya บ้านศรีราชา

Sriraya GUESTHOUSE $
(Map p676; ☎075 697045; punpun_3377@hot-mail.com; Ban Si Raya; r with shared bathroom 600B; ☎) Sleep in a simple but beautifully restored, thick-beamed Chinese shophouse with plenty of style and a friendly welcome. Walls are brushed in earth tones and sheets are bright. Go for the street-front balcony room overlooking the old town's character-ful centre. The restaurant does great food.

★Old Times GUESTHOUSE $$
(Map p676; ☎075 697255, 075 697288; www. theoldtimeslanta.com; Ban Si Raya; r 500-1700B; ❊ ☎) Tucked into two artfully revamped 100-year-old teak houses facing each other across the street, this is an excellent choice. Impeccably-styled rooms grace various sizes and budgets, under music-inspired names such as 'Yellow Submarine'. The best – bright and decked with black-and-white photos – jut out over the sea on the jetty, where there's a cushioned communal chill-out area. Fun, fresh and friendly.

★Mango House GUESTHOUSE $$$
(Map p676; ☎095 014 0658; www.mangohouses. com; Ban Si Raya; ste 2500-3000B, villas 4000-7000B; ☎) These century-old Chinese teak pole houses and former opium dens are stilt-ed over the harbour. The original time-worn wood floors are intact, ceilings soar and the

three, house-sized suites are kitted out with kitchenettes, satellite TVs, DVD players and ceiling fans. There are also new-build Old Town–style seafront villas sleeping two to six people. Rates drop by 50% in low season.

✕ Eating

The best-value places for seafood are along the northern edge of Ban Sala Dan, which offer fresh fish sold by weight (including cooking costs) on verandahs over the water.

Phad Thai Rock'n'Roll   THAI **$**
(Map p676; ☑ 080 784 8729; www.facebook.com/ phadthairock77; Ao Kantiang; mains 90-150B; ⊙ 11am-9pm) It's not every day you get your spiced-to-taste *pàt tai* whipped up streetside by a guitarist. Choose from just six options ('jazz' fried rice, 'blues' fried noodles, veg, chicken, pork or seafood), swiftly and artfully prepared in simple contemporary surrounds. With about as many tables as dishes, it's deservedly popular, so you may have to wait.

★ **Drunken Sailors**   INTERNATIONAL, THAI **$$**
(Map p676; ☑ 075 665076; www.facebook. com/drunkensailors; Ao Kantiang; mains 130-200B; ⊙ 9am-3pm & 6-10pm; ☎ ☑) This super-relaxed place features beanbags, hammocks and low-lying tables spilling out onto a terrace. The global, want-to-eat-it-all menu employs quality ingredients and roams from handmade pasta, baguettes and burgers to top-notch Thai, including perfectly spiced ginger stir-fries and red curries cooked to personal taste. Coffees, cakes and juices are also excellent. It closes for a couple of months in the low season.

★ **Kung Restaurant**   SEAFOOD **$$**
(Map p674; ☑ 075 656086; 413 Mu 1, Ban Sala Dan; mains 90-220B; ⊙ 5-11pm) Highly rated by both visiting Thais and locals, this Thai-Chinese place offers a delectable range of fresh fish (pay by the weight) in a simple setting close to the pier in Sala Dan. The sea bass, snapper and barracuda go quick, so get here early in the evening. There's also a large menu of Thai standards and some Chinese-style dishes.

Patty's Secret Garden   THAI **$$**
(Map p674; ☑ 098 978 8909; 278 Mu 2, Hat Phra Ae; mains 120-320B; ⊙ 9am-11pm; ☎ ☑) Not so secret now that more and more travellers are discovering this casual, family-friendly place set in a pleasant, plant- and flower-filled shaded garden. The menu mixes Thai favourites with Western standards, including a kids selection, and it's also good for breakfast.

Caoutchouc   INTERNATIONAL, THAI **$$**
(Map p676; ☑ 075 697060; Ban Si Raya; mains 150-300B; ⊙ 10am-9pm) For Thai-international flavours blended into delectable creative concoctions, hunt down this rustic-chic restaurant 800m south of the Old Town pier. The menu changes at the whim of the eccentric but friendly French owner. Normally,

---

WORTH A TRIP

MU KO LANTA NATIONAL PARK

Established in 1990, **Mu Ko Lanta National Park** (อุทยานแห่งชาติหมู่เกาะลันตา; Map p676; ☑ 075 660711, in Bangkok 02 561 4292; www.dnp.go.th; adult/child/motorbike 200/100/20B; ⊙ 8am-6pm) protects 16 islands in the Ko Lanta group, including the southern tip of Ko Lanta Yai. The park is increasingly threatened by the runaway development on west-coast Ko Lanta Yai, though other islands in the group have fared slightly better.

Ko Rok Nai (Ko Rok Nai) is still very beautiful, with a crescent-shaped bay backed by cliffs, fine coral reefs and a sparkling white-sand beach. Camping is permitted on adjacent **Ko Rok Nok** with permission from the park headquarters. On the eastern side of Ko Lanta Yai, **Ko Talabeng** (Map p672) has some dramatic limestone caves that you can visit on sea-kayaking tours (1300B). National park fees apply if you visit any of the islands. Ko Rok Nai, Ko Rok Nok and Ko Haa (p661) are off limits to visitors from 16 May to 31 October.

The national park headquarters and visitors centre are at Laem Tanod, on the southern tip of Ko Lanta Yai, reached by a steep paved road. There are some basic hiking trails, two twin beaches and a gorgeously scenic lighthouse, plus camping facilities and bungalows amid wild, natural surroundings.

though, you should be able to enjoy a deliciously fresh feta-and-rice or shrimp curry salad, served alongside mango or pineapple lassi.

Drinking & Nightlife

If you fancy a low-key bar scene with music wafting well into the night, Lanta has options on most beaches, and particularly around Hat Phra Ae. Things move around depending on the day, so check out posters island-wide for upcoming events. Low season (May to October) is very mellow.

★ Why Not Bar
BAR
(Map p676; Ao Kantiang; ⊙11am-2am; 🛜) Tap into Ao Kantiang's laid-back scene at this driftwood-clad beachfront hang-out. It keeps things simple but fun with a killer mix of fire twirlers, sturdy cocktails, bubbly bar-staff and fantastic nightly live music jams, best enjoyed at low-slung wooden tables on a raised deck.

Feeling Bar
BAR
(Map p674; Hat Khlong Khong; ⊙11am-late; 🛜) Joined to the rickety but much-loved Where Else! (p675) bungalows, Feeling keeps that original Lanta hippie-backpacker vibe alive with its 'Friday Feeling' beach parties. Three different bar counters and palm-thatched raised platforms to imbibe on.

Irie
BAR
(Map p674; ☑084 170 6673; ⊙11am-late) The Monday-night live reggae session (in high season) at this ramshackle joint has become famous across Lanta (they put on rock bands sometimes too), but Irie is a relaxed place for a drink at any time. Also does OK Thai food.

Shopping

★ Hammock House
HOMEWARES
(Map p676; ☑084 847 2012; www.jumbo hammock.com; Ban Si Raya; ⊙10am-6pm) For unique, quality, colour-bursting hammocks, crafted by rural villagers and threatened Mlabri tribespeople in northern Thailand, don't miss Hammock House. They sometimes close for part of low season (May to October).

★ Malee Malee
FASHION & ACCESSORIES
(Map p676; ☑075 697235; 55/3 Mu 2, Ban Si Raya; ⊙9am-9pm) A bohemian wonderland of quirky homemade goods, from silk-screened and hand-painted T-shirts and silk scarves

to journals, toys, baby clothes, paintings, jewellery and handbags. Prices are low, it's super fun to browse and a sweet cafe (coffees around 80B) sits on the doorstep.

❶ Information

There are ATMs all along the western coast. ATMs that take foreign cards can be found at **Ban Sala Dan** (Map p674; Ban Sala Dan), **Ban Si Raya** (Map p676; Ban Si Raya) and **Hat Khlong Nin** (Map p676; Hat Khlong Nin).

There are police stations at **Hat Phra Ae** (Map p674; Hat Phra Ae) and **Ban Sala Dan** (Map p674; ☑075 668192; Ban Sala Dan) and a **police outpost** (Map p676; Ao Kantiang) in the south of Lanta,

Ko Lanta Hospital (Map p676; ☑075 697017; Ban Si Raya) About 1km south of the Ban Si Raya Old Town.

Mu Ko Lanta National Park Headquarters (Map p676; ☑075 660711, in Bangkok 02 561 4292; Laem Tanod; ⊙8am-4pm) The national park HQ is in the far south of Lanta.

Mu Ko Lanta National Park Visitors Centre (Map p676; Laem Tanod; ⊙8am-6pm) The national park visitors centre is in the far south of Lanta.

The Lanta Pocket Guide (www.lantapocket guide.com) is a useful resource

Post Office (Map p674; Hat Phra Ae)

❶ Getting There & Away

Transport to Ko Lanta is by boat or air-con minivan. If arriving independently, you'll need to use the frequent **vehicle ferries** (motorcycle/pedestrian/car 20/20/200B; ⊙6am-10pm) between Ban Hua Hin and Ban Khlong Mak (Ko Lanta Noi) and on to Ko Lanta Yai.

BOAT

Ban Sala Dan has two piers. The **passenger jetty** (Map p674; Ban Sala Dan) is 300m from the main strip of shops; vehicle ferries leave from a **jetty** (Map p674; Ban Sala Dan) 2km east.

From mid-October to mid-April, the high-speed **Tigerline** (☑075 590490, 081 358 8989; www.tigerlinetravel.com) ferry runs between Phuket (1500B, two hours) and Ban Sala Dan (Ko Lanta) and on to Ko Lipe (1700B, five hours), via Ko Ngai (750B, one hour), Ko Kradan (850B, 1½ hours) and Ko Muk (850B, two hours). The service heads south at 10am, returning from Lipe at 10am the following day and stopping on Ko Lanta around 3pm before continuing north.

Ko Phi-Phi Ferries between Ko Lanta and Ko Phi-Phi run year-round. Boats leave Ko Lanta at 8am and 1pm (300B, 1½ hours), returning from Ko Phi-Phi at 11.30am and 3pm. There are also high-season speedboats between Lanta and Phi-Phi (700B to 800B, one hour).

Krabi From November to late April, boats leave Ko Lanta for Krabi's Khlong Chilat pier at 8.30am and 11.30pm (400B, two hours) and return from Krabi at 11.30am. During high season, they stop at Ko Jum (400B, one hour).

Phuket There are year-round ferries to Phuket at 8am and 1pm (500B), although you normally have to transfer boats at Ko Phi-Phi.

Trang Islands From November to early April, speedboats buzz from Ko Lanta to the Trang Islands, including the **Satun Pak Bara Speedboat Club** (Map p694; ☑ 099 404 0409, 099 414 4994; www.spcthailand.com) and **Bundhaya Speedboat** (☑ 075 668043; www.bundhayaspeedboat.com). Stops include Ko Ngai (650B, 30 minutes), Ko Muk (900B, one hour), Ko Kradan (1150B, 1¼ hours), Ko Bulon Leh (1600B, two hours) and Ko Lipe (1900B, three hours).

Ko Lanta Noi A **vehicle ferry** (Map p672; Ko Lanta Noi) and a **passenger ferry** (Map p672; Ko Lanta Noi) link Ko Lanta Noi to Ko Lanta Yai.

MINIVAN

Minivans are your easiest option from the mainland and they run year-round, but they're particularly packed in this region and traffic jams for vehicle ferries can cause delays. Most minivans offer pick ups from resorts. Frequency is reduced in low season.

Minivans to Krabi airport (300B, 2½ hours) and Krabi Town (300B, three hours) run hourly between 7am and 4pm in both directions. You can connect in Krabi for further destinations, including Khao Lak and Bangkok. Departures from Lanta include the following:

DESTINA-TION	FARE (B)	DURATION (HR)	FREQUENCY
Ko Pha-Ngan	750	8½	8am
Ko Samui	550	6½	8am
Phuket	500	6	8am & noon.
Trang	450	3	8am, 9am, 10.30am & 1pm

❶ Getting Around

Most resorts send vehicles to meet the ferries – a free ride to your resort. In the opposite direction expect to pay 100B to 400B. Alternatively, take a motorcycle taxi from outside 7-Eleven in Ban Sala Dan; fares run from 50B to 400B, depending on distance.

Motorbikes (250B per day) can be rented everywhere (without insurance), as can bicycles

(150B per day). Agencies in Ban Sala Dan rent out small 4WDs (1300B per day).

Ko Jum & Ko Si Boya เกาะจำ/เกาะศรีบอยา

Just north of Ko Lanta, Ko Jum and its low-lying neighbour Ko Si Boya are surprisingly undeveloped; what's there is tucked away in the trees. There's little more to do than wander the long beaches on Ko Jum (Ko Si Boya's beach is less impressive) and soak up the rustic beauty.

Ko Jum was once the exclusive domain of Lanta's *chow lair*, but ethnic Chinese began arriving after communist takeover of China in 1949. At the time there were no Thai people living here at all, but eventually the three cultures merged into one, a mix best sampled early in the morning amid the ramshackle poetry of Ban Ko Jum, the fishing village on the southeast side of the island.

Although technically one island, local people consider only the flatter southern part of Ko Jum to be Ko Jum. The northern hilly bit is Ko Pu.

🛏 Sleeping & Eating

🛏 Ko Jum

Accommodation is strung out along Ko Jum's west coast. Most resorts have on-site restaurants; some close for the May–October low season.

Bodaeng BUNGALOW $
(☑ 081 494 8760; Hat Yao, Ko Jum; bungalows 200-400B) An old-fashioned hippie vortex with very basic bamboo bungalows and a couple of newer wood huts with their own bathrooms, set in the trees behind Hat Yao. No fans – sea breezes only – no wi-fi and squat toilets in the shared bathrooms. Limited electricity sometimes. But the grinning matriarch owner is a charmer and you are right by the beach.

★**Woodland Lodge** BUNGALOW $$
(☑ 081 893 5330; www.woodland-koh-jum.com; Hat Yao, Ko Jum; bungalows 1300-1700B; 🛜) Tasteful, clean, fan-cooled bamboo huts with proper thatched roofs, polished wood floors and verandahs, spaciously laid out across shady grounds, make this our favourite spot on Ko Jum. Concrete-and-wood

family bungalows sleep three. The friendly British-Thai owners organise boat trips and run the excellent on-site **Fighting Fish Restaurant** (Hat Yao; mains 100-30B; ⊙ 8am-4pm & 6-10pm; 🐟).

★**Koh Jum Beach Villas** VILLA $$$
(📞 086 184 0505; www.kohjumbeachvillas.com; Hat Yao, Ko Jum; villas incl breakfast 12,000-32,000B; 🐟 🗙) 🔗 The poshest digs on Ko Jum. Huge and elegant wooden homes with their own living rooms and kitchens and sea views sprawl back among frangipani- and bougainvillea-filled gardens from a luscious golden beach. Some have romantic private infinity pools. The resort keeps things as environmentally and socially responsible as possible. Staff are delightful, the **restaurant** (Hat Yao; mains 250-900B; ⊙ 7.30am-10pm; 🐟) and bar scrumptious.

Koh Jum Lodge RESORT $$$
(📞 089 921 1621; www.kohjumlodge.com; Hat Yao, Ko Jum; bungalows incl breakfast 4500-7000B; ⊙ Nov-Apr; 🐟 🗙) An ecolodge with style: 19 spacious cottages with lots of hardwood and bamboo, gauzy mosquito netting, coconut palms, Thai carvings and silk throws. Then there are the manicured grounds, massage pavilions and a hammock-strewn curve of white sand out front. It strikes that hard-to-get balance of authenticity and comfort.

Hong Yong Restaurant THAI $
(Ban Ting Rai, Ko Jum; mains 70-100B; ⊙ 7.30am-9pm) Local food talk sends you inland to this makeshift village restaurant, where bubbly Rosa sizzles up delicious Thai curries, stir-fries and international breakfasts at bargain prices. Try the fragrant massaman curry or the seasonal seafood specials. Also known as Rosa's.

Ko Si Boya

Low-lying, rural Ko Si Boya has yet to garner more than a trickle of the annual tourism stream, and that's just fine with repeat visitors.

Siboya Bungalows BUNGALOW $$
(📞 081 979 3344; www.siboyabungalows.com; Ko Si Boya; bungalows 350B, house 500-1800B; 🐟) Ko Si Boya's beach isn't spectacular, but the mangrove setting is wild and full of life, the bungalows and private homes are large, stylish and affordable, and the excellent restaurant is wired with high-speed

internet. No wonder ever-smiling, secretive 50-somethings flock here like it's a retiree's version of Alex Garland's *The Beach*. There are family-friendly homes that sleep four people.

🛈 Getting There & Away

From November to May, the boat from Krabi to Ko Lanta will drop you at Ko Jum, for the full fare (400B, one hour, 11.30am); boats return from Lanta at 8.30am. In high season, daily boats run from Ko Jum to Ko Phi-Phi (600B, 1½ hours) at 8.30am, collecting guests from the Hat Yao resorts; boats return from Phi-Phi at 2pm.

There are year-round long-tails to Ko Jum from Ban Laem Kruat, 38km southeast of Krabi at the end of Rte 4036, off Hwy 4. Boats (100B, 30 minutes) leave at 9am, 10am, 11.30am, noon, 1pm, 2.30pm, 4pm, 5.30pm and 6.15pm, and return at 6.30am, 7.15am, 7.40am, 8am, 8.30am, 10.30am, 1.30pm, 2.30pm and 4pm.

If you're arriving on Ko Jum via Laem Kruat, note that boats run to three different piers; Ban Ko Jum and Mu Tu piers are the most convenient. Guesthouses will arrange transfers from the piers if you call in advance, otherwise you're relying on the kindness of strangers.

Daily boats to Ko Si Boya (50B, 15 minutes) run from Laem Kruat every hour between 8am and 5.30pm, returning hourly from 6.15am to 5pm. Call Siboya Bungalows to arrange transfer from the pier.

Sŏrng·tăa·ou meet boats at Laem Kruat and go to Krabi (100B), via Krabi airport and Nua Khlong (where you can connect for Ko Lanta).

🛈 Getting Around

Several places in Ban Ko Jum and some Ko Jum guesthouses rent bicycles (100B) and motorbikes (250B).

TRANG PROVINCE

South of Krabi, Trang Province has an impressive limestone-covered Andaman Coast with several sublime islands that see marginally fewer visitors than their nearby and better-known counterparts. For the adventurous, there's plenty of big nature to explore in the lush interior, including dozens of scenic waterfalls and limestone caves. And it's nowhere near as popular as Krabi, which means you're more likely to see working rubber plantations here than rows of T-shirt vendors. Transport links are good and during the high season (November to April) you can easily island-hop all the way to Malaysia.

Trang ตรัง

📞 075 / POP 60,000

Most visitors to Trang are in transit to near-by islands, but if you're an aficionado of culture, Thai food or markets, stay a day or more. Here is an easy-to-manage, old-school Thai town where you can get lost in wet markets, hawker markets and Chinese coffee shops. At nearly any time of year, there will be some minor festival that oozes local colour.

Most tourist facilities lie along Th Praram VI, between the clock tower and the train station.

◉ Sights & Activities

The lively, colourful **wet and dry markets** on Th Ratchadamnoen and Th Sathani are worth exploring.

Tour agencies around the train station and Th Praram VI offer boat trips to Hat Chao Mai National Park and the Trang Islands (850B, plus park fees), snorkelling trips to Ko Rok (per person 1700B) and private car trips to local caves and waterfalls (2000B, maximum four people).

Wat Tantayaphirom   BUDDHIST TEMPLE

(วัดตันตยาภิรมย์; Th Tha Klang) **FREE** Wat Tantayaphirom has a huge white-and-gold *chedi* (stupa) enshrining a footprint of the Buddha that's mildly interesting.

✦ Festivals & Events

★ Vegetarian Festival   CULTURAL

(⏰ Oct) As much a Buddhist festival as it is food heaven for veggies – by not eating meat participants gain merit for themselves – Trang celebrates this wonderful nine-day festival all over town to coincide with Phuket's Vegetarian Festival (p628) in the first two weeks of October.

🛌 Sleeping & Eating

The town is famous for its *mǒo yâhng* (crispy barbecued pork), spongy cakes, early-morning dim sum breakfasts and *ráhn go·pǐi* (coffee shops) that serve real filtered coffee. You can find *mǒo yâhng* in the mornings at some coffee shops or by weight at the wet market on Th Ratchadamnoen.

Yamawa Guesthouse   GUESTHOUSE $

(📞 099 402 0349, 075 290477; www.yamawaguesthouse.blog.com; 94 Th Visetkul; r fan/air-con 350/450B; 🌀🛜) Simple, spotless, old-fashioned fan or air-con rooms equipped with fridges that are decent value for the price. The sweet local owners hand out detailed Trang maps, sound advice and rent motorbikes (250B per day). Often full in high season (November to April), so book ahead.

Mitree House   GUESTHOUSE $$

(📞 075 212292; mitreehouse.trang@gmail.com; 6-8 Th Sathani; r 750-1050B; 🌀🌀🛜) New-ish, well-located guesthouse that has immaculate, modern rooms with comfy beds and reasonably sized bathrooms. The cheapest lack windows; the more expensive ones upstairs are big and bright. Communal areas on both floors, helpful staff and the price includes a simple breakfast. Motorbikes can be rented for 250B per day. Good wi-fi.

Rua Rasada Hotel   HOTEL $$$

(📞 075 214230; www.ruarasadahotel.com; 188 Th Phattalung; r incl breakfast 6000-60,000B; 🌀🛜🏊) Trang's slickest choice is this hulking monolith handily located opposite the bus station, a 10-minute (40B) motorbike ride northeast from the train station. From the outside it looks its age a bit, and inside it feels a little 1980s, too. But rooms are huge and comfortable, while the pool is massive. You can normally score 40% to 50% discounts in low season.

★ Night Market   MARKET $

(btwn Th Praram VI & Th Ratchadamnoen; mains from 40B; ⏰4-9pm) The finest night market on the Andaman Coast will have you salivating over bubbling curries, fried chicken and fish, deep-fried tofu, *pàt tai* and an array of Thai desserts. Go with an empty stomach and a sense of adventure. There's a second, equally glorious weekend **night market** (Train Station; mains from 40B; ⏰6-10pm Thu-Sun) opposite the train station.

Asia Ocha   THAI $

(Th Kantang; mains 25-200B; ⏰7am-5pm) Open for 60-plus years, this cool, old school Sino-Thai coffee shop has vintage marble-topped tables, helicopter fans and a menu that includes excellent soups, as well as delicious roast duck and crispy pork. It serves a few Western-style dishes too.

Khao Tom Kim   THAI $$

(50 Th Kantang; mains 60-200B; ⏰3.30pm-midnight) A popular spot with the locals and always lively, thanks to a solid selection of

Trang

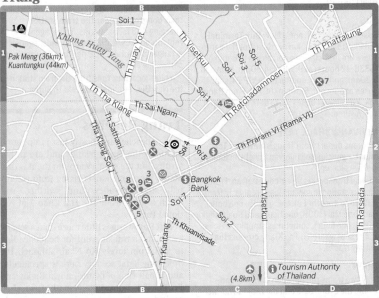

Trang

⊙ Sights
1 Wat Tantayaphirom............................A1
2 Wet & Dry Market B2

🛏 Sleeping
3 Mitree House..B2
4 Yamawa Guesthouse C2

⊗ Eating
5 Asia Ocha..B3
6 Khao Tom Kim......................................B2
7 Night Market...D1
8 Night Market...B2

ℹ Information
9 Trang Happy Trip & Tour B2

curries and seafood dishes. It stays open later than most Trang restaurants. Not much English spoken, but there is an English menu.

ℹ Information

ATMs and foreign-exchange booths line Th Praram VI. The following take foreign cards:

ATM (Th Praram VI)
Bangkok Bank (Th Praram VI)

There is also an **ATM on Th Ratchadamnoen** (Th Ratchadamnoen) that accepts foreign cards.

Post Office (cnr Th Praram VI & Th Kantang; ⊙8.30am-4.30pm Mon-Fri, 9am-noon Sat) You can send mail overseas from here.

Tourism Authority of Thailand (TAT; ☑ 075 211580, 075 215867; www.tourismthailand.org; 199/2 Th Visetkul; ⊙8.30am-4.30pm) Tourist information, although you're better off speaking to one of the many travel agencies that cluster close to the train station.

Trang Happy Trip & Tour (☑ 075 219757; www. facebook.com/tranghappytrip&tour; 22 Th Sathani; ⊙6.30am-10pm) Knowledgeable and reliable Sai and Jip run this travel agency close to the train station. They can arrange private cars, rent motorbikes, book minivan and boat tickets/transfers and run one-day tours around the Trang Islands.

ℹ Getting There & Away

AIR

The airport is 5km south of Trang. Air Asia (www.airasia.com) and Nok Air (www.nokair. com) fly here daily from Bangkok (Don Mueang).

Minivans to town (90B) meet flights. In the reverse direction, taxis, motorbike taxis or túk-túks (pronounced đúk đúks) cost 100B to 120B. Agencies at airport arrivals sell combined taxi-boat tickets to Trang's islands, including Ko Ngai (1000B).

BUS

Buses leave from Trang's **New Bus Terminal** (Th Phattalung), 3.5km northeast of the centre. There are first-class air-con buses to Bangkok (583B, 12 hours) at 9.30am, 4.30pm, 5pm and 5.30pm, and more comfortable VIP 24-seat buses at 5pm and 5.30pm (907B). From Bangkok, VIP/air-con buses leave between 6.30pm and 7.30pm.

MINIVAN & SHARE TAXI

Minivans depart from Trang's **New Bus Terminal**. Agencies sell minivan tickets including in-town pick-up.

Local transport is by air-con minivan. From the bus station, minivans leave regularly from 7.30am to 4pm for Pak Meng (80B, one hour), Hat Chao Mai (100B, one hour) and Kuantungku (100B, one hour), sometimes stopping in town just east of where Th Tha Klang crosses the railway tracks.

TRAIN

Only two trains run between Bangkok and Trang: the express 83 and the rapid 167, which leave from Bangkok's Hualamphong station at 5.05pm and 6.30pm and arrive in Trang the next morning at 8.05am and 10.30am respectively.

From Trang, trains leave at 1.30pm and 5.25pm, arriving in Bangkok at 5.35am and 8.35am the following morning. Fares are range from 245B for 3rd class to 1480B for 1st-class air-con sleeper.

❶ Getting Around

Túk-túks (pronounced *đúk đúks*) and motorbike taxis **congregate near the train station**, charging 40B for local trips. Travel agencies rent motorbikes (250B per day). Most agencies arrange car rental (200B per day). You can rent cars at the airport.

A blue 'local bus' runs from the train station to the New Bus Terminal (12B) via Th Sathani.

Trang Beaches

Trang's beaches are mostly just jumping-off points to the Trang Islands and are rather scruffy. But the scenery around them is dramatic: limestone karsts rising from steamy palm-studded valleys and swirling seas. Much of it is inside the Hat Chao Mai National Park.

Hat Pak Meng is little more than a scruffy beach and a transit point for boats heading to and from lovely Ko Ngai, although the limestone karst scenery here is spectacular and equals that of better-known Railay and Ko Phi-Phi. Immediately south, casuarina-backed **Hat Chang Lang** is a prettier beach, but still can't compare to the ones on the nearby islands. The Hat Chao Mai National Park headquarters is at the southern end of the beach.

◉ Sights & Activities

Pak Meng tour agencies organise one-day boat tours to Ko Muk, Ko Cheuk, Ko Ma

TRANSPORT FROM TRANG

Buses from Trang

DESTINATION	FARE (B)	DURATION (HR)	FREQUENCY
Hat Yai	120	3	every 30min 5.30am-5.30pm
Krabi	110	2	hourly 5.30am-6.30pm
Phang-Nga	170	4	hourly 5.30am-6.30pm
Phuket	230	5	hourly 5.30am-6.30pm

Minivan & Share Taxi from Trang

DESTINATION	FARE (B)	DURATION (HR)	FREQUENCY
Hat Yai	120	2	hourly 6am-6pm
Ko Lanta	250	2½	five daily 9.50am-4.30pm
Krabi	100	2	hourly 7am-5pm
Satun	120	2	every 40min 6am-6pm
Surat Thani	160	3	hourly 7am-5pm

Trang Province

and Ko Kradan, and snorkelling day tours, all including lunch (per person 750B, plus Hat Chao Mai National Park fees). Mask and snorkel sets and fins can be rented by the pier (50B each).

Hat Chao Mai National Park   NATIONAL PARK
(อุทยานแห่งชาติหาดเจ้าไหม; ☎ 075 203308; www. dnp.go.th; adult/child 200/100B; ⏱9am-4pm) This 231-sq-km park covers the shoreline from Hat Pak Meng to Laem Chao Mai, and encompasses the islands of Ko Muk, Ko Kradan and Ko Cheuk (plus a host of small islets). While touring the coast and islands, you may spot endangered dugongs and rare black-necked storks, as well as more common species like barking deer, sea otters, macaques, langurs, wild pigs, pangolins, little herons, Pacific reef egrets, white-bellied sea eagles and monitor lizards.

   Park headquarters (☎ 075 210 099; www. dnp.go.th; Hat Chang Lang; ⏱8am-4pm) are at

the southern end of Hat Chang Lang, just south of where the beachfront road turns inland.

🛏 Sleeping & Eating

Several seafood restaurants, popular with Thais on day trips or weekend getaways, can be found in Pak Meng, where Rte 4162 meets the coast.

Hat Chao Mai National Park
Accommodation   CAMPGROUND, BUNGALOW **$**
(☎ 075 203308; www.dnp.go.th; Hat Chang Lang; bungalows 800B, campsites per person 30B, with tent hire 225B) Simple fan-cooled cabins sleep two to six people or you can camp under the casuarinas. There's also a restaurant.

Anantara Si Kao   HOTEL **$$$**
(☎ 075 205888; www.sikao.anantara.com; Hat Chang Lang; r incl breakfast 4080-13,680B; P ❄ 🛜 🌊) Deluxe oceanfront rooms with

THE 50B SURCHARGE

Tigerline (p680) ferries and speedboats often stop off the Trang and Satun islands, rather than docking. There's a 50B surcharge for long-tail transfers on/off islands, which you'll be asked for once you're aboard the long-tail; boatmen usually refuse to continue until you pay up. Yes, it's frustrating, but it'll hardly ruin your trip, so keep your cool and change handy.

rich wood floors, floating desks and delicious views of Pak Meng's signature karsts bring Anantara's trendy glamour to northern Hat Chang Lang. Impressive timber columns and Balinese furnishings line the lobby, there's a host of activities on offer, and the sea-views from Italian restaurant **Acqua** (mains 300-1050B; ⏱6-10.30pm; 🖉) are jaw-dropping.

❶ Getting There & Away

Air-con minivans run regularly from Trang's New Bus Terminal (p684) to Hat Pak Meng (80B, one hour) and Hat Chao Mai (100B, one hour) between 7.30am and 4pm. Taxis from Trang cost 1000B.

Boats leave Pak Meng for Ko Ngai at noon daily (350B, one hour), returning to Pak Meng at 9am (350B, one hour). Long-tail charters cost 1500B.

The Hat Chao Mai National Park headquarters is 1km off the main road, down a clearly sign-posted track.

Trang Islands

Covered in verdant jungle and lined with pure white-sand beaches, the Trang Islands are less developed than other Andaman islands and have far smaller populations. This is real honeymooners territory – there's very little nightlife – so don't come here if you want to party all night long.

❶ Getting There & Away

Boats to the Trang Islands run from three different piers: Hat Yao, Kuantungku and Pak Meng, all an hour south of Trang. Regular minivans run to the piers (80B to 100B, one hour, 7.30am to 4pm). If you book your boat ticket with a travel agency in Trang, they will arrange the transfer to the boat.

From November to April, Tigerline (p679) and Satun Pak Bara (p680) speedboats connect Ko Muk, Ko Kradan and Ko Ngai with Phuket, Ko Phi-Phi, Ko Lanta and Ko Lipe.

There are regular minivans from Trang to Hat Chao Mai National Park (100B, one hour, 7.30am-4pm).

Ko Ngai   เกาะไหง (ไห)

Encircled by coral and clear waters, densely forested Ko Ngai (Ko Hai) is both the most family-friendly of the Trang Islands and prime honeymoon territory. The long blonde wind-swept beach on the eastern coast spills into turquoise water with a sandy bottom (perfect for children) that ends at a reef drop-off with good snorkelling. It's a stunning place and with no indigenous population on the island, the entire main beach is set up for your amusement.

Although technically part of Krabi Province, Ko Ngai's mainland link is with Pak Meng, 16km northeast.

🏃 Activities

Ko Ngai has a couple of dive centres (dives from 1300B). Resorts rent snorkel sets and fins (300B per day) and sea kayaks (150B per hour), or you can join half-day snorkelling tours of nearby islands (from 600B).

🛏 Sleeping & Eating

Thanya Resort   BUNGALOW $$$
(📞075 206 967, 086 950 7355; www.kohngai thanyaresort.com; r incl breakfast 3700-6900B; ❄@🛜🏊) Ko Ngai's Bali-chic choice has dark but stylish, spacious teak bungalow with indoor hot showers and outdoor country-style bucket showers (don't knock it until you've tried it). Laze in the gorgeous beachside pool and gaze across the frangipani-filled lawn rolling out towards the sand from your terrace. There's an on-site **dive centre** (📞085 056 3455; 1 dive 1300-1500B) plus a reasonably priced Thai **restaurant** (mains 150-300B; ⏱7am-8pm; 🛜). It's at the south end of main beach.

Coco Cottage   BUNGALOW $$$
(📞089 724 9225; www.coco-cottage.com; bungalows 3300-7900B; ⏱Oct-May; ❄🛜) These cottages are coconut thatched-roof extravaganzas with coconut-wood walls and coconut-shell lanterns, set in a jungle garden just back from the north end of the main beach. Wake up to twinkling Andaman

vistas through floor-to-ceiling windows in sea-view bungalows. Other perks include bamboo loungers, massage pavilions and a decent Thai/fusion beachfront **restaurant-bar** (mains 170-260B; ⊙7-10am, 11am-4pm & 6-9.30pm). It's at the north end of main beach.

Ko Hai Fantasy Resort & Spa   RESORT $$$
(☑075 210 317; www.kohhai.com; r 3300-17,200B; ❋ 🌐 ⚂) Well-kept, comfortable, modern, decent-sized rooms meander back from the southern end of the main beach and straggle around a neat garden and up the surrounding hillside. The seafront restaurant is reasonable, there's a mini-mart, and snorkelling and island trips can be arranged.

Talay Lounge
Restaurant   THAI, INTERNATIONAL $$
(Thapwarin Resort; mains 170-300B; ⊙7am-10pm mid-Jun–mid-May; 🌐) Catch evening fire shows beneath rubber trees at this beach-facing lounge bar and restaurant, which tackles everything from grilled snapper to pizza and pasta. It's part of **Thapwarin Resort** (☑081 894 3585; www.thapwarin.com; north end of main beach; garden/sea-view bungalow incl breakfast 4500/5500B; ⊙mid-Jun–mid-May; ❋ 🌐), at the northern end of Ko Ngai's main beach.

ⓘ Getting There & Away

There's a daily boat from Ko Ngai to Pak Meng (350B, one hour) at 9am, returning to Ko Ngai at noon. You can also charter long-tails to and from Pak Meng (1500B), Ko Muk (1500B), Ko Kradan (1500B) and Ko Lanta (2000B); enquire

at **Ko Ngai Seafood Bungalows** (☑095 014 1853; kob_1829@hotmail.com; middle of the main beach; bungalow 1500-1800B; ⊙year-round; 🌐). Most resorts arrange transfers to the mainland.

From mid-October to mid-April, **Tigerline** (p679) ferries stops just off Ko Ngai en route between Phuket and Ko Lipe. From November to early April, **Satun Pak Bara Speedboat Club** (p680) and **Bundhaya Speedboat** (☑074 750389, 074 750388; www.bundhayaspeedboat.com) offer faster and comfier island-hopping transport.

The pier is at Koh Ngai Resort, but long-tails usually drop you at your resort.

Ko Muk   เกาะมุก

Motoring toward jungle-clad Ko Muk is unforgettable, whether you land on sugary white eastern sand bar **Hat Sivalai**, on humble, local-flavoured **Hat Lodung** or on southwest **Hat Farang** (Hat Sai Yao, Charlie Beach), where jade water kisses a perfect beach.

The accommodation options here are improving all the time, the west-coast sunsets are glorious, it's an easy hop to most islands in the province, the principal village by the main pier remains more real than those on many tourist islands, and you'll be mixing with travellers who are more likely to relish the calm than party all night. The only drawback is that there's a steady stream of package tourists tramping Hat Sivalai and day-tripping over to Tham Morakot from Ko Lanta.

BOATS TO/FROM KO NGAI

DESTINATION	BOAT COMPANY	FARE (B)	DURATION
Ko Lanta	Tigerline	750	1hr
	Speedboat	650	30min
Ko Lipe	Tigerline	1600	4hr
	Speedboat	1300	2½hr
Ko Kradan	Tigerline	750	30min
	Satun Pak Bara Speedboat Club	400	25min
Ko Muk	Tigerline	750	1hr
	Speedboat	350	30min
Ko Phi-Phi	Tigerline	1350	2½hr
	Satun Pak Bara Speedboat Club	1350	2hr
Phuket	Tigerline	1800	3½hr
	Satun Pak Bara Speedboat Club	2150	3hr

◉ Sights & Activities

Between Ko Muk and Ko Ngai are two small karst islets, **Ko Cheuk** and **Ko Waen**, both with small sandy beaches and good snorkelling (though there's some coral damage).

Koh Mook Garden Beach Resort rents out bikes (150B per day) with self-guided maps, several resorts rent kayaks (100B to 300B per hour) and motorbikes (250B per day), and you can spend hours walking through rubber plantations and the island's devout Muslim sea shanty villages (remember to cover up).

Tham Morakot   CAVE

(ถ้ำมรกต, Emerald Cave) This beautiful limestone tunnel leads 80m into a cave on Ko Muk's west coast. No wonder pirates buried treasure here. You have to swim through the tunnel, part of the way in darkness, before exiting at a small white-sand beach surrounded by lofty limestone walls. A piercing shaft of light illuminates it around midday. National park fees (adult/child 200/100B) apply.

🛏 Sleeping & Eating

Hat Sivalai, a short walk from the main pier on the eastern side, has the poshest digs. Hat Lodung, west of the pier beyond a stilt village and mangroves, has cheaper options, but the beach isn't nearly as nice.

The sea is cleaner on crescent-shaped Hat Farang, where more budget-friendly resorts lie inland from the beach. It's a 10-minute motorbike taxi to/from the pier (50B).

Koh Mook Hostel   HOSTEL $

(☏089 724 4456; www.kohmookhostel.com; dm 380B; ✴🛜) The only hostel in the Trang Islands, this place is run by a friendly Muslim family and consists of two decent-sized and clean dorm rooms (one female-only). They're painted in breezy pastel colours, as is the communal area, while the attached bakery cafe serves up homemade bread, cakes and pizza. It's a 10-minute walk from lovely Hat Sivalai.

Koh Mook
Garden Beach Resort   GUESTHOUSE $$

(☏081 748 3849; DaDakohmook@gmail.com; Hat Lodung; r 1000-1500B; ✴🛜) Endearingly ramshackle and very laid-back, Garden Beach Resort stands out from the more anonymous (and professional) resort crowd thanks to its family feel. Bungalows, both

the older and basic bamboo ones and the newer, more comfortable concrete ones, are scattered around a garden leading to your own small section of Hat Lodung. The attached restaurant serves up tasty Thai food.

Phusambig Resort   HOTEL $$$

(☏09 1706 7727; cee210919@hotmail.com; r incl breakfast 1200-2700B; ✴🛜) Chilled-out and welcoming, Phusambig's bungalows lie in a garden 10 minutes' walk from Hat Farang. They come in a variety of guises and sizes – the cheapest are fan-only – but all are modern with OK bathrooms and are a step up from similarly priced digs elsewhere. During low season you'll be serenaded at night by the local bullfrogs.

Sivalai   HOTEL $$$

(☏089 723 3355; www.komooksivalai.com; Hat Sivalai; bungalows incl breakfast 5500-8500B; ✴🛜) Straddling an arrow-shaped white-sand peninsula framed by views of karst islands and the mainland, Sivalai wins the award for Ko Muk's most fabulous location. The elegant dark-wood bungalows are sizeable and tasteful; some have wraparound verandahs. There are two pools, a handy spa (massages from 700B) and the restaurant sits right at the tip of the peninsula.

★ Hilltop Restaurant   THAI $$

(mains 100-300B; ⏰9am-10pm) Still the most atmospheric place to eat on Ko Muk – a jungle-cloaked, garden setting – this welcoming, family-run operation serves up all your Thai favourites. The seafood curries are superb (spice levels are adjusted on request) and will have you returning for seconds, but all the dishes are prepared with love and care. It's about 800m inland from Hat Farang.

❶ Getting There & Away

Boats and long-tails to Ko Muk (120B to 250B, 30 minutes) leave daily from the pier at Kuantungku at noon, 1pm and 5pm November to April, returning to the mainland at 8am, 9am and 2pm. Services peter out in November and April, but the cheapest long-tail runs year-round at 1pm. Minibus-and-boat combo tickets take you to/from Trang (350B, 1½ hours) and Trang airport (500B, 1½ hours). You can also charter long-tails to/from Kuantungku (800B, 30 minutes).

From November to early April, Ko Muk is a stop on the Tigerline (p679) and Satun Pak Bara (p680) speedboats connecting Ko Lanta (950B, one hour), Ko Ngai (350B to 750B, 30 minutes) and Ko Lipe (1400B to 1600B, two hours).

Long-tail charters from Ko Muk to Ko Kradan (800B, 30 minutes), Ko Ngai (1000B, one hour) and Pak Meng (1500B, 45 minutes to one hour) are easily arranged on the pier or by asking at your accommodation.

Ko Kradan   เกาะกระดาน

Beautiful Ko Kradan is dotted with slender, silky, white-sand beaches, bathtub-warm shallows and dreamy views across the twinkling turquoise sea to Ko Muk, Ko Libong and limestone karsts from its main, east-coast beach. The water is clean, clear and inviting, and there's a small but lush tangle of jungle inland.

🏃 Activities

Hat South   SNORKELLING
Although some of Kradan's coral structure has been decimated, there's good snorkelling when the wind is calm off the island's south beach, which you can reach in a 10-minute walk along a jungly path from Paradise Lost guesthouse, signposted at the south end of the main beach.

Hat Sunset   BEACH
A short signposted track at the south end of the main beach leads past Paradise Lost guesthouse and over the ridge to sunset beach, a mostly wet and rocky patch of sand facing open seas – and a fun place to get a little beachside privacy over a flaming pink sunset.

🛏 Sleeping & Eating

Kalume   HOTEL $$
(📞080 932 0029; www.kalumekradan.com; r 1200-1800B; 🐾) The cheapest beachfront resort, Kalume has a collection of bamboo

and wooden bungalows set around a garden. None are very special or spacious, with minimal facilities inside, but you're steps away from Kradan's best beach, the staff are amenable and the laid-back bar and restaurant is a good place to while away the night.

Paradise Lost   GUESTHOUSE $$
(📞081 894 2874; www.kokradan.wordpress. com; dm 300B, bungalows 700-1200B) One of Kradan's first lodgings, this inland property is in walking distance of all three of Kradan's main beaches. There's an airy five-bed, fan-cooled dorm, but the bungalows are basic with the cheapest sharing bathrooms. The bigger and more expensive bungalows have their own bathrooms but are still only functional. Closed low season.

The open-plan **kitchen** (mains 140-350B; ⊙8am-9pm) dishes up tasty food in big portions.

Seven Seas Resort   HOTEL $$$
(📞075 2033 8990; www.sevenseasresorts.com; r incl breakfast 6000-12,000B; ❄️🖥🏊) This

PHUKET & THE ANDAMAN COAST TRANG ISLANDS

BOATS TO/FROM KO KRADAN

DESTINATION	BOAT COMPANY	FARE (B)	DURATION
Hat Yao (for Trang)	Tigerline	1050	1hr
Ko Lanta	Tigerline	950	1½hr
	Satun Pak Bara Speedboat Club	1150	1¼hr
Ko Lipe	Tigerline	1600	3½hr
	Satun Pak Bara Speedboat Club	1400	2hr
Ko Muk	Satun Pak Bara Speedboat Club	300	15min
Ko Ngai	Tigerline	750	30min
	Satun Pak Bara Speedboat Club	400	45min

KO SUKORN
เกาะสุกร

Little-visited Ko Sukorn is a natural paradise of tawny beaches, light-green sea, jungle-shrouded black-rock headlands, and stilted shack neighbourhoods home to 2600-odd mainly Muslim residents whose rice fields, watermelon plots and rubber plantations unfurl along narrow concrete roads.

With few hills, expansive panoramas, plenty of shade and lots of opportunities to meet islanders, Sukorn is best explored by rented bike (200B). The main beach, dotted with a few low-key resorts, extends along the island's southwestern coast. Cover up away from the beach.

Enjoy fiery pink sunsets over outlying islands from the gorgeous long beach at the front of **Yataa Island Resort** (☑089 647 5550; www.yataaresort.com; Ao Lo Yai Beach; bungalow incl breakfast 1400-6500B; ❋🛜🅿), whose green-roofed concrete air-con bungalows frame a cool blue pool. The restaurant is excellent, too. Alternatively, **Sukorn Cabana** (☑089 724 2326; www.sukorncabana.com; bungalow incl breakfast 900-1500B; ⊙ closed May; ❋🛜) has clean, if a little old, bungalows sporting thatched roofs, fridges, polished-wood interiors and plush verandahs.

The easiest way to get to Sukorn is by private transfers from Trang, arranged through your resort (per person 1900B). The cheapest way is to take a *sŏrng·tăa·ou* (pick-up minibus) from Trang to Yan Ta Khao (80B, 40 minutes), then transfer to Ban Ta Seh (50B, 45 minutes), from where long-tails to Ban Saimai (50B), Sukorn's main village, leave when full. Trang guesthouses and travel agents arrange *sŏrng·tăa·ou*-and-boat transfers (250B to 350B) to Ban Saimai via Ban Ta Seh, departing Trang at 11am daily.

Otherwise, book a taxi from Trang to Ban Ta Seh (900B). The resorts are a 3km walk or 100B motorcycle-taxi ride from Ban Saimai. You can charter long-tails directly to the beach resorts (400B).

---

boutique resort is by far the swishest and best option on Kradan. Super-sleek rooms draw many Scandinavian visitors with their terrazzo floors, indoor/outdoor bathrooms blending into tropical gardens, enormous low-slung beds and, for some, private cabanas. Hugging the jet-black infinity pool, the breezy **restaurant** (mains 200-1000B; ⊙7am-10pm; 🛜) serves pricey Thai/international dishes. Prime location halfway up Kradan's main beach.

❶ Getting There & Away

From November to April, daily boats to Kuantungku on the mainland leave at 8.30am and 1pm; tickets include connecting minibuses to Trang (450B) or Trang airport (550B). From Trang, combined minibus-and-boat services depart for Ko Kradan at 11am and 4pm. You can charter long-tails to/from Kuantungku (1500B, 45 minutes to one hour), Ko Muk (800B, 30 minutes) and Ko Ngai (1500B, 45 minutes).

The Phuket–Ko Lipe Tigerline (p679) stops off Ko Kradan from mid-October to mid-May. November to early April, Satun Pak Bara Speedboat Club (p680) offers faster and cheaper links.

Ko Libong
เกาะลิบง

Trang's largest island is just 30 minutes by long-tail from mainland Hat Yao. Less visited than neighbouring islands, it's a gorgeous, lush mountainous pearl, wrapped in rubber trees, thick with mangroves and known for its captivating flora and fauna (especially the resident dugongs and migrating birds) more than its thin gold-brown beaches. The island is home to a small Muslim fishing community and has a few west-coast resorts. With its scruffy sweetness and untouristy backwater charm, Libong has a way of drawing you in, if you let it.

◉ Sights

Libong Archipelago Wildlife Reserve   NATURE RESERVE

This large mangrove area on Ko Libong's east coast at Laem Ju Hoi is protected by the Botanical Department. The sea channels are one of the last habitats of the endangered dugong: over 100 graze on the sea grass that flourishes in the bay. Most of Ko Libong's resorts offer dugong-spotting boat tours, led by trained naturalists, for 1000B to 1500B.

🛏 Sleeping & Eating

Almost all of Ko Libong's lodgings are on the west coast, which has the nicest beaches.

Libong Beach Resort BUNGALOW $$
(☑ 084 849 0899; www.libongbeach-resort.com; bungalows 1000-2500B; ✷ 🛜) Cute spot with everything from bland slap-up shacks behind a murky stream to more upmarket varnished wood-and-thatch beachfront chalets with semi-outdoor bathrooms. It also offers wildlife-spotting trips, transport info and motorbike rental (250B per day). We love the restaurant; try the *pàt see·éw* (fried noodles) or the *đôm yam kà-mîn* (turmeric fish soup).

Libong Relax Beach Resort BUNGALOW $$$
(☑ 094 582 5113, 091 825 4886; www.libongrelax. com; r incl breakfast 1600-3700B; ✷ 🛜) Top choice at this friendly, laid-back resort are stylish wood bungalows with terracotta sinks, shiny floors and shuttered doors that open up to the sea. Fan-cooled bamboo cottages are more rustic, simple and compact but well-kept. The resort offers bird and dugong-spotting and snorkelling trips, plus kayak rental (200B per hour). The beachside **restaurant** (mains 120-350B; ⊙ 7.30am-3pm & 5-9pm; 🛜) does a good line in Thai staples.

❶ Getting There & Away

During daylight hours, long-tail boats to Ban Ma Phrao on Ko Libong's east coast leave when full from Hat Yao (per person 100B, 30 minutes). On Ko Libong, motorcycle taxis run across to the west-coast resorts (per person 100B). Chartered long-tails from Hat Yao to the resorts cost 900B. You can charter boats to Ko Kradan (1500B), Ko Muk (1500B) and Ko Ngai (2300B).

SATUN PROVINCE

Satun was until recently mostly overlooked, but that's all changed thanks to the dynamic white sands of Ko Lipe – a one-time backpacker secret turned mainstream beach getaway. The rest of the province passes by in the blink of an eye, as visitors rush north to Ko Lanta or south to Pulau Langkawi (Malaysia). Which means that they miss the untrammelled beaches and sea caves of Ko Tarutao, the rugged trails and ribbon waterfalls of Ko Adang, the rustic beauty of Ko Bulon Leh and easygoing Satun itself.

Largely Muslim in make-up, Satun has seen little of the political turmoil that plagues the fellow Muslim majority provinces of neighbouring Yala, Pattani and Narathiwat.

Satun   สตูล
☑ 074 / POP 23,800
Lying in a steamy jungle valley surrounded by limestone cliffs and a murky river, isolated Satun is a surprisingly bustling little city: the focal point of a province that's home to over 300,000 people. Few foreign visitors pass through, and most of them are heading to and from Malaysia, or are yachties dropping in for cheap repairs in Satun's acclaimed boat yard. If you do stick around you'll discover that Satun has some intriguing Sino-Portuguese and religious architecture, delicious food, lots of friendly smiles and plenty of authentic charm. The surrounding countryside is lovely and ripe for exploration.

⊙ Sights & Activities

Housed in a restored 1902 Sino-Portuguese mansion, Satun's excellent little **museum** (พิพิธภัณฑ์สถานแห่งชาติสตูล, Kuden Mansion; Soi 5, Th Satun Thanee; 50B; ⊙ 9am-4pm Wed-Sun) was originally constructed as a temporary home for King Rama V during a royal visit. Now, it features informative displays on local history, customs and Muslim life in southern Thailand.

Soak up Satun's beauty by hiking **Monkey Mountain**, a jungle mound of limestone teeming with macaques.

🛏 Sleeping & Eating

Quick, cheap Chinese and Muslim restaurants are on Th Burivanich and Th Samanta Prasit. Chinese food stalls specialise in *kôw mŏo daang* (red pork with rice); Muslim restaurants offer *roti* with southern-style chicken curry and the local version of biryani. There's a decent night market too.

Satun Tanee Hotel GUESTHOUSE $
(☑ 074 711010, 074 712309; www.satuntanee hotel.com; 90 Th Satun Thanee; r 300-570B; ✷ 🛜) Behind the lime-green-and-orange exterior lie reasonably sized, modern rooms with comfortable beds and wood-panelled floors, plus dingier, cheaper, unrenovated fan-only rooms on the top floor (no lift). It's a bit

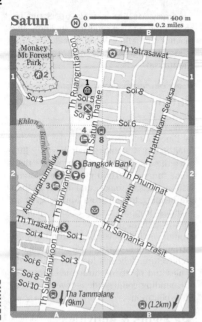

Satun

◎ Sights

◔ Activities, Courses & Tours

⌂ Sleeping

⊗ Eating

◷ Drinking & Nightlife

⊕ Information

⊕ Transport

institutional, but the updated rooms are good value and you get a warm welcome.

★ Night Market
MARKET **$**

(off Th Satun Thanee; mains from 40B; ⊙5-9pm) Satun's small but busy night market springs to life with flavour-packed *pàt tai*, fried fish, chicken satay and excellent, spicy, southern-style curries. There's a larger Saturday night market on Th Burivanich.

♟ Drinking & Nightlife

★ On's Living Room
BAR

(☑074 724133; 36 Th Burivanich; ⊙5pm-2am; ☏) Satun's only Western-style bar takes up the ground floor of an atmospheric, tastefully converted Sino-Portuguese-style shophouse. There's a fine long wooden bar, a pool table and plenty of space to lounge around. This is where you will find Satun's tiny foreign community, and any *fa·ràng* passing through town. Upstairs houses part of On's Guesthouse.

⊕ Information

Bangkok Bank (Th Burivanich; ⊙8.30am-3.30pm Mon-Fri) has a foreign-exchange desk and an ATM. ATMs line Th Burivanich.

Immigration Office (☑074 711080; Th Burivanich; ⊙8.30am-4.30pm Mon-Fri) Op-

posite the clocktower, this office handles visa issues and extensions. It's easier for tourists to exit and re-enter Thailand via the border checkpoint at Tha Tammalang.

Police Station Satun's main police station.

Post Office (cnr Th Satun Thanee & Th Samanta Prasit; ⊙8.30am-4.30pm Mon-Fri, 9am-noon Sat) Satun's main post office.

⊕ Getting There & Away

The nearest airport to Satun is at Hat Yai, a two-hour drive away.

BOAT

From Tha Tammalang (10km south of Satun), there are two ferries daily to Pulau Langkawi (10am and 3pm, 300B) in Malaysia. In the reverse direction, ferries leave Pulau Langkawi daily for Satun at 10.30am and 5.15pm (RM36).

BUS

Buses leave from **Satun Bus Terminal**, 2km south of town. **Buses to Trang** (100B, two hours, hourly 5am to 4.30pm) also pick up passengers on Th Satun Thanee by the 7-Eleven. Trang buses go via La-Ngu (50B), where you can hop a *sŏrng·tăa·ou* to Pak Bara (20B) for boats to Ko Lipe and other islands.

Departures include the following:

Bangkok – VIP (1042B, 14 hours, 4pm)

Bangkok – air-con (679B, 14 hours, 7am, 2.30pm, 3pm, 4.30pm)

Krabi (215B, five hours, 8.15am, 10.15am, 12.15pm, 8pm)

Phuket (329B, eight hours, 8.15am, 10.15am, 12.15pm, 8pm)

MINIVAN & SHARE TAXI

Minivans run from Satun Bus Terminal to Krabi (200B, five hours, 7am and 2pm), Trang (120B, two hours, hourly 5am to 5pm), Hat Yai (100B, two hours, 6am to 5pm) and Hat Yai airport (300B 2½ hours, 6am to 5pm), **Minivans to Hat Yai** also pick up passengers on Th Satun Thanee by the 7-Eleven. There are also minivans to Kuala Perlis in Malaysia (400B). They don't run every day and pick you up from your accommodation. **On's Guesthouse** (☏ 074 724133; onmarch13@hotmail.com; 36 Th Burivanich; dm 250B, r 350-600B; ✳ ☏) can organise tickets.

ℹ Getting Around

The centre of Satun is easily walkable, but you can rent bicycles (150B per day) and motorbikes (250B per day) from On's Guesthouse.

Sŏrng·tăa·ou to the bus station cost 40B per person. Orange *sŏrng·tăa·ou* to **Tha Tammalang** pick up passengers at the 7-Eleven on Th Su-lakanukoon. Motorcycle taxis run around town for 50B.

Pak Bara   ปากบารา

☏ 074 / POP 3000

Pak Bara, 60km northwest of Satun, is the main jumping-off point for the dazzling islands of the Ko Tarutao Marine National Park (p696). Facilities are slowly improving as Pak Bara becomes increasingly packed with tourists, although almost all are in transit to the islands.

The main road from La-Ngu (Rte 4052) terminates at the pier, which is basically a massive passenger terminal for Lipe- and Tarutao-bound speedboats. The Ko Tarutao Marine National Park **visitors centre** (Map p694; ☏ 074 783485; Pak Bara Pier; ◷ 8am-5pm) is by the pier. Local travel agents arrange one-day tours (2000B) to the parks' islands.

ℹ Getting There & Away

BUS

From Satun, take an ordinary Trang bus and get off at La-Ngu (50B, 30 minutes), continuing by *sŏrng·tăa·ou* to Pak Bara (20B, 20 minutes). A few minivans also make the run daily (60B). Pick up the bus and minivans outside the 7-Eleven on Th Satun Thanee.

BOAT

From mid-October to mid-May **speedboats** (p680) run from **Pak Bara's Ferry Terminal** (Map p694) to Ao Pante Malacca on Ko Tarutao (450B, 30 minutes), and on to Ko Lipe (650B, 1½ hours) at 11.30am. There are speedboats to Ko Tarutao (450B) only at 11am and 2.30pm October to May. Further speedboats run directly to Ko Lipe at 9.30am, 12.30pm, 1.30pm and 3.30pm. Boats return from Ko Lipe at 9.30am, 11.30am, 12.30pm, 1pm and 3.30pm.

For Ko Bulon Leh (450B, 30 minutes), boats depart at 12.30pm and buzz on to Ko Lipe. If you miss the Bulon boat, you can charter long-tails from local fishermen (2000B, 1½ hours). During low season, services to Ko Lipe are less frequent, but you can always count on the 11.30am boat from Pak Bara (weather permitting), returning at 9.30am.

MINIVANS TO/FROM PAK BARA

Air-con minivans run every 45 minutes between 7.30am and 6.30pm from Hat Yai to Pak Bara pier (120B, two hours). Minivan services may be reduced mid-May to mid-October.

Ko Tarutao Marine National Park   อุทยานแห่งชาติหมู่เกาะตะรุเตา

One of Thailand's most exquisite, unspoilt regions, **Ko Tarutao Marine National Park** (Map p694; ☏ 074 783485; www.dnp.go.th; adult/child 200/100B; ◷ mid-Oct–mid-May) encompasses 51 islands blanketed by well-preserved rainforest teeming with

MINIVANS TO/FROM PAK BARA

DESTINATION	FARE (B)	DURATION (HR)	FREQUENCY
Hat Yai	120	2	11.30am, 1.30pm, 3.30pm
Hat Yai Airport	200	2	11.30am, 1.30pm, 3.30pm
Ko Lanta	400	3	11.30am
Krabi	350	4	11.30am
Phuket	500	6	1.30am, 1pm
Trang	200	2	11.30am, 1pm, 2pm, 3pm

Ko Tarutao Marine National Park & Around

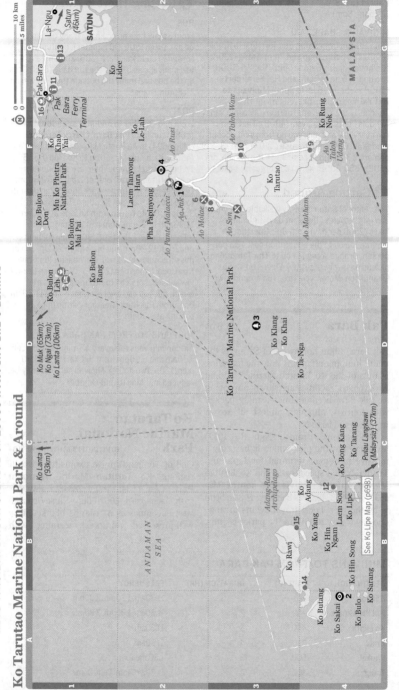

Ko Tarutao Marine National Park & Around

fauna, surrounded by healthy coral reefs and radiant white beaches. Within, you might spot dusky langurs, crab-eating macaques, mouse deer, wild pigs, sea otters, fishing cats, tree pythons, water monitors, Brahminy kites, sea eagles, hornbills, reef egrets and kingfishers.

Ko Lipe has become a high-profile tourist destination and it's where most travellers stay. It's exempt from national park rules governing development because it is home to communities of *chow lair*.

The only other islands you can stay on are Ko Tarutao, the biggest island and home to the park headquarters (p696), and Ko Adang.

Rubbish on the islands is a problem. Do your part and tread lightly. Apart from Ko Lipe, the park officially shuts from mid-October to mid-May.

Ko Tarutao   เกาะตะรุเตา

Most of Ko Tarutao's whopping 152 sq km is covered in jungle, rising sharply to the park's 713m peak, making this one of Thailand's wildest islands. Mangrove swamps and limestone cliffs circle much of it, while steep trails and rough roads lead through the interior, making this a great place for fit hikers and mountain bikers. Tarutao's beaches are less inviting, thanks to tidal garbage and cloudy water. If you're after idyllic

strips of sand and snorkelling, head to Ko Adang or Ko Rawi instead.

Ko Tarutao has a squalid past as a prison island: one of the reasons why it has never been developed.

The island closes officially from mid-May to mid-October.

Sights & Activities

With a navigable river and long paved roads, Tarutao is perfect for independent exploration. Hire kayaks (200/500B per hour/day) or mountain bikes (50/250B) from park headquarters.

Toe-Boo Cliff   VIEWPOINT
(จุดชมวิวผาโต๊ะบู; Map p694) Behind park headquarters at Ao Pante Malacca, on the northwest side of the island, a steep 500m (20-minute) trail winds through the jungle below a limestone karst dripping with precipitation, then climbs a series of stone-cut steps to this dramatic rocky outcrop with fabulous views across Ko Tarutao towards Ko Adang and other surrounding isles.

Tham Jara-Khe   CAVE
(ถ้ำจระเข้, Crocodile Cave; Map p694) The large stream flowing inland from **Ao Pante Malacca** (อ่าวพันเตมะละกา; Map p694; Ko Tarutao), on northwest Ko Tarutao, leads to Tham Jara-Khe, once home to deadly saltwater crocodiles. The cave is navigable for 1km at

POLITICAL PRISONERS

Between 1938 and 1948, more than 3000 Thai criminals, including 70 political rebels, were incarcerated on Ko Tarutao. Among them were So Setabutra, who compiled the first Thai–English dictionary while imprisoned on Tarutao, and Sittiporn Gridagon, son of Rama VII.

During WWII, food and medical supplies from the mainland were severely depleted and hundreds of prisoners died from malaria, starvation and maltreatment. Prisoners and guards allied and mutinied, taking to piracy in the nearby Strait of Malacca until they were suppressed by British troops in 1946.

The ruins of the political prisoners camp can be seen at Ao Taloh Udang. You can also visit Ao Taloh Waw, the east coast site of the camp for ordinary criminals, although there are no buildings left. The Ko Tarutao Visitors Centre has some displays about the island's prison past.

low tide and can be visited on long-tail tours (500B) from Ao Pante Malacca's jetty.

🛏 Sleeping & Eating

There are basic government-run bungalows at **Ao Pante Malacca** (Map p694; www.dnp.go.th; Ao Pante Malacca; r 600-1200B; ⊙mid-Oct–mid-May), **Ao Molae** (Map p694; www.dnp.go.th; Ao Molae; r 600B; ⊙mid-Oct–mid-May) and **Ao Son** (Map p694; www.dnp.go.th; Ao Son; r 350-550B; ⊙Nov–mid-May). Water is rationed, electricity runs from 6.30pm to 6am. You can also camp at Ao Molae, Ao Son, Ao Makham, Ao Taloh Waw and Ao Taloh Udang. Facilities are very basic and monkeys often wander into tents. Shut them tight.

Accommodation can be booked online or, more easily, at the park's visitors centre (p693) in Pak Bara.

There are simple canteens offering Thai food at **Ao Pante Malacca** (Map p694; Ao Pante Malacca; mains 80-180B; ⊙7.45am-2.30pm & 5.30-8.30pm), **Ao Molae** (Map p694; Ao Molae; mains 70-140B; ⊙7am-2pm & 5-9pm) and **Ao Son** (Map p694; Ao Son; mains 60-140B; ⊙7am-8pm).

ℹ Information

Ko Tarutao Marine National Park Headquarters (Map p694; Ao Pante Malacca, Ko Tarutao; ⊙8am-5pm)

Ko Tarutao Visitors Centre (Map p694; Ao Pante Malacca, Ko Tarutao; ⊙8am-5pm) Maps and local information.

There are ranger stations across the island, at **Ao Molae** in the northwest, **Ao Son** on the west coast, **Ao Taloh Udang** in the south and **Ao Taloh Waw** on the east of the island.

ℹ Getting There & Away

From mid-October to mid-May, there are three speedboats daily from Pak Bara to the **ferry terminal** (Map p694; Ao Pante Malacca, Ko Tarutao) at Ao Pante Malacca on Ko Tarutao (450B, 30 minutes). They leave at 11am, 11.30am and 2.30pm. During high season, you can also visit on speedboat day tours from Pak Bara (including park fees, lunch, drinks and snorkelling around 2000B).

If you're staying at Ao Molae, take a shared van from Ao Pante Malacca at 11am or 1pm daily (per person 50B; demand-dependent).

Ko Lipe   เกาะหลีเป๊ะ

Once a serene tropical paradise, Ko Lipe is now a poster child for untamed development on Thailand's islands. Blessed with two beautiful wide white-sand beaches separated by jungle-covered hills and close to protected coral reefs, the centre of Ko Lipe has been transformed into an ever-expanding maze of hotels, restaurants, cafes, travel agencies and shops. The biggest losers have been the 700-strong community of *chow lair,* whose ancestors were gifted Lipe as a home by King Rama V in 1909, but who sold it in the 1970s.

Despite all the development, there is still an awful lot to love about Lipe: those gorgeous, salt-white sand crescents for a start, sensational dive sites, a jungle interior, chilled-out reggae bars, a contagiously friendly vibe and a good few inhabitants keen to minimise their environmental impact. Just don't expect to have it to yourself.

🏃 Activities

Diving

Diving is outstanding when the visibility clarifies, somewhat counter-intuitively, in the early part of the wet season (mid-April to mid-June). There are some fun drift dives and two rock-star dive sites.

Eight Mile Rock is a deep pinnacle that attracts devil rays and (very) rare whale sharks. **Stonehenge** is popular because of its resident seahorses, rare leopard sharks and reef-top boulders. **Ko Sarang** (Map p694) has gorgeous soft corals, a ripping current and solar flares of fish that make it many people's favourite Lipe dive spot.

Ko Lipe Diving DIVING
(Map p698; ☑088 397 7749, 087 622 6204; www.kolipediving.com; Walking St; 1/2 dives 1700/2800B; ⊙8am-10pm) Well-organised, professional dive operator with consistently glowing reviews for its selection of special-ist courses and fun dives focused on diving education. Two-dive Discover Scuba costs 2800B; PADI certification is 14,500B.

Forra Dive DIVING
(Map p698; ☑084 407 5691; www.forradiv ing.com; Hat Sunrise; 1/2 dives 1500/2800B) French-owned Forra is one of Lipe's long-est running outfitters. It offers Discover Scuba (from 1500B) and Open Water Diver courses (14,500B), as well as more advanced qualifications.

Has another office on **Walking St** (Map p698; ☑084 407 5691; www.forradiving.com; Walking St; 1/2 dives 1500/2800B).

Davy Jones' Locker DIVING
(Map p698; ☑085 361 7923; www.scubadive kohlipe.com; Hat Pattaya; dives from 2500B) One-dive Discover Scuba sessions cost 2500B; PADI Open Water certification is 14,000B (including free accommodation at Ko Lipe Backpackers).

Snorkelling

There's good coral along the southern coast and around **Ko Kra** (Map p698) and **Ko Usen** (Map p698), the islets opposite Hat Sunrise (be careful with oncoming long-tails). Most resorts rent out mask-and-snorkel sets and fins (200B). Travel agents and some dive op-erators arrange four-point snorkel trips to Ko Adang, Ko Rawi and other coral-fringed islands from 450B per person.

Kitesurfing

It is possible to kitesurf on Lipe, but winds are variable. Forra Dive can rent you the requisite gear.

Yoga

Swing by Castaway Resort for beachfront yoga (400B; 7am, 9am and 4.30pm).

🛏 Sleeping

More and more Ko Lipe resorts are staying open year-round. A few humble bamboo bungalows still stand strong, but resorts are colonising, particularly on Hat Pattaya. If

---

ℹ GETTING TO MALAYSIA

Keep in mind that Malaysia is one hour ahead of Thai time.

Ko Lipe to Pulau Langkawi

From mid-October to mid-April, Tigerline (p680), Bundhaya Speedboat (p687) and Sat-un Pak Bara Speedboat Club (p680) run daily from Ko Lipe to Pulau Langkawi in Malay-sia (1000B to 1200B, 2½ hours). Departures are at 9.30am, 10.30am, 11am and 4pm. Head to the **immigration office** (Map p698; ⊙8am-6pm) in the centre of Hat Pattaya 1½ hours ahead to get stamped out. In reverse, boats leave Pulau Langkawi for Ko Lipe at 9.30am and 2.30pm Malaysian time.

Satun to Kuala Perlis or Pulau Langkawi

There are currently no speedboats or long-tail boats running from Satun to Pulau Lang-kawi in Malaysia.

It's possible to take a minivan from Satun to Kuala Perlis (400B) in Malaysia via the Wang Prajan/Wang Kelian border crossing, but they don't run every day. On's Guest-house (p693) sells tickets.

At The Border

Citizens of the US, EU, Australia, Canada and several other countries may enter Malaysia for up to 90 days without prior visa arrangements. If you have questions about your eligibility, check with the nearest Malaysian embassy or consulate and apply for a visa in advance.

Ko Lipe

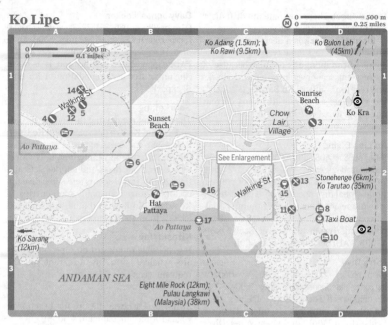

Ko Lipe

⊙ Sights
1 Ko Kra..D1
2 Ko Usen...D3

⊕ Activities, Courses & Tours
    Castaway Divers..........................(see 8)
    Davy Jones' Locker.......................(see 9)
3 Forra Dive..D1
4 Forra Dive..A1
5 Ko Lipe Diving....................................A1

⊜ Sleeping
6 Bila Beach..B2
7 Blue Tribes...A2
8 Castaway Resort.................................D2
9 Koh Lipe Backpackers Hostel.............B2

⊗ Eating
10 Serendipity.......................................D3
11 Barracuda..C2
12 Elephant Coffee House.....................A1
13 Nee Papaya......................................D2
14 Papaya Mom.....................................A1

⊙ Drinking & Nightlife
15 Pooh's Bar..C2

⊙ Information
16 Immigration Office.............................C2

⊙ Transport
17 Ferry Jetty..C2

you want tranquillity, head to less busy Hat Sunset. Book well ahead during high season and holidays, when prices skyrocket.

Koh Lipe Backpackers Hostel   HOSTEL $$
(Map p698; ☎085 361 7923; www.kohlipeback packers.com; Hat Pattaya; dm 500B, r 2500-3000B; ❈ ☎) There's a slightly random, spacey feel to Lipe's only hostel. Rooms and dorm are housed in a contemporary-style concrete block on west Hat Pattaya. Showers are shared, but you get private lockers, wi-fi,

the on-site Davy Jones' Locker dive school (p697) (divers get a discount) and the beach location is ace. Upstairs are simple but comfortable enough air-con private rooms.

Bila Beach   BUNGALOW $$
(Map p698; ☎087 570 3684; www.bilabeachre sort.com; Hat Sunset; bungalows 1500B) A killer bamboo reggae bar and beachfront restaurant lurk below stylish shaggy-haired cliffside bungalows set above a tiny, secluded white-sand cove, which is strewn with

boulders and adjacent to Hat Sunset. It's the perfect setting for your hippie honeymoon and a short sweaty walk over the hill from Hat Pattaya.

Blue Tribes
BUNGALOW $$$

(Map p698; ☑ 080 546 9464, 083 654 0316; www.bluetribeslipe.com; Hat Pattaya; bungalows 1800-3000B; ☎) Tucked into flower-filled gardens, Blue Tribes is one of Hat Pattaya's more laid-back resorts. The best choices are two-storey thatched wooden bungalows with downstairs living rooms and top-floor bedrooms that offer sea views. Other bungalows are simple and no frills, but they come with balconies and you're just steps from the beach. The attached restaurant is pretty good.

★ Castaway Resort
HOTEL $$$

(Map p698; ☑ 083 138 7472, 081 170 7605; www.castaway-resorts.com; Hat Sunrise; bungalows 2700-4750B; ☎) 🌿 Roomy dark-wood bungalows with hammock-laden terraces, cushions everywhere, overhead fans and fabulous, modern-meets-natural bathrooms embody Lipe at its barefoot-beach-chic best. This welcoming resort is also one of Lipe's most environmentally friendly, run on solar water heaters and lights (there's no AC). There's a super-chilled beachside cafe, plus high-season yoga classes (450B) and a good **dive school** (Map p698; ☑ 087 478 1516; www.kohlipedivers.com; Castaway Resort, Hat Sunrise; 1/2 dives 2500/3800B; ◷ 10am-8pm).

★ Serendipity
BUNGALOW $$$

(Map p698; ☑ 088 395 5158; www.serendipityresort-kohlipe.com; Hat Sunrise; r 6720-14,400B; ❋ ☎ ⌨) An exquisitely designed spot, delightfully isolated by draping itself up above the boulder-strewn southern point of Hat Sunrise and accessed via a wooden boardwalk. Spacious dark-wood thatched bungalows feature private patios offering super views, great beds and stylish bathrooms, while the most expensive have plunge pools. If you're feeling flush, go for the lavish 200 sq metre Big Lebowski suite.

Eating

There's some great seafood: the best places are mostly inland. Find cheap eats at the *roti* stands and small Thai cafes along Walking St. Please take advantage of the waste-reducing water refill points at many resorts and eateries.

★ Nee Papaya
THAI $

(Map p698; mains 80-150B; ◷ 9am-11pm) Delightful Nee offers an affordable fish grill nightly, all the standard curries (including a dynamite beef *pá·naang*), noodles and stir-fries (beef, chicken, seafood or veggie), along with an array of fiery Isan dishes. She'll tone down the chillis on request, but her food is best when spiced for the local palate, which is why she attracts many Thai tourists.

★ Barracuda
SEAFOOD $$

(Map p698; mains 80-250B; ◷ 9am-10pm) Every second restaurant on Lipe offers fresh seafood barbecue, but this is the one the locals patronise the most. The other dishes on the menu are also great, especially the salads. The ramshackle, slightly tucked away setting adds to the sense that you're eating at a place designed for Thais rather than foreigners.

Elephant Coffee House
INTERNATIONAL $$

(Map p698; ☑ 089 657 2178; www.facebook.com/ElephantKohLipe; Walking St; mains 120-420B; ◷ 8am-1am) The bar is a long-tail, second-hand books are for sale and black-and-white local-life photos are plastered across varnished-concrete walls. Pop into this coolly contemporary cafe for fabulous all-day breakfasts of thick French toast, excellent coffee and homemade muesli loaded with tropical fruit. Otherwise choose from fresh

---

BEACH VOLUNTEERS

Trash Hero (www.trashhero.org) The pioneering, increasingly successful brainchild of a Thai-Swiss duo, Trash Hero organises regular Monday volunteer clean-ups to preserve Lipe's beloved white-sand beaches and others in Ko Tarutao Marine National Park. The program launched in December 2013 with the straightforward aim of protecting the islands' beaches using only materials and people-power to hand. Local businesses quickly pledged support, supplying long-tails, food, drinks and rubbish bags.

Over 1000 volunteers (locals and tourists) have since removed 21,000kg of rubbish from local beaches. Trash Hero now runs weekly clean-ups at 11 official points across Thailand and Indonesia.

ℹ BEACH SAFETY

Keep your eyes open for long-tail boats while swimming, especially in low season. People have been run down before. Don't expect boats to see you.

Do not try to swim the narrow strait between Lipe and Adang at any time of year; currents are swift and can be deadly.

salads, sandwiches, burgers and pizzas. Also hosts live music most evenings.

Papaya Mom   THAI $$

(Map p698; Walking St; mains 90-500B; ⊙8am-10pm; ⊘) The big menu at this friendly place crosses regional Thai food boundaries, and offers some Western dishes, but it is the fiery and authentic Isan dishes from the northeast that draw in Thai travellers and many locals. Vegetarians can raid the luscious fruit stand, or order from the thoughtful veggie menu featuring a delicious bean-curd-and-bean-sprouts stir-fry.

🍷 Drinking & Nightlife

Coffee shops are sprinkled all over the island, especially on Walking St.

A few driftwood-clad Rasta bars can still be found on the beaches, especially Hat Pattaya and Hat Sunset.

Pooh's Bar   BAR

(Map p698; ☎089 463 5099, 074 750345; www.poohlipe.com; Walking St; ⊙1pm-1am; 🛜) This sprawling complex (which includes bungalows, a dive shop and several restaurants) was built by a Lipe pioneer and remains a popular local expat hang-out. Nightly films and sports are projected onto the big screen and there's often live music.

ℹ Information

Immigration Office (p697) Immigration now has its own official kiosk on the beach next to Bundaya Resort.

ℹ Getting There & Away

From mid-October to mid-May, speedboats run from Pak Bara to Ko Lipe via Ko Tarutao or Ko Bulon Leh at 9.30am, 11.30am, 12.30pm, 1.30pm and 3.30pm (650B, 1½ hours). Boats return to Pak Bara at 9.30am, 11.30am, 12.30pm, 1pm and 1.30pm. Low-season transport is weather dependent, but there's usually a direct

daily boat from Pak Bara to Lipe at 11.30am, returning at 9.30am.

From November to late April, the high-speed Tigerline (p679) ferry departs Ko Lipe at 10am for Phuket (2100B, eight hours), via Ko Phi-Phi (1750B, seven hours), Ko Lanta (1500B, five hours), Ko Muk (1400B, 3½ hours), Ko Kradan (1600B, 3½ hours) and Ko Ngai (1400B, 4½ hours).

From mid-November to late March, Bundhaya Speedboat (p687) and Satun Pak Bara Speedboat Club (p680) leave Ko Lipe at 9am for Ko Lanta (1900B, three hours), via Ko Bulon Leh (600B, one hour), Ko Kradan (1400B, two hours), Ko Muk (1400B, two hours) and Ko Ngai (1600B, 2½ hours). Speedboats return from Lanta at 10.30am.

Boats also run from Ko Lipe to Pulau Langkawi (1000B to 1200B, 2½ hours) in Malaysia, mid-October to mid-April.

No matter which boat you end up using, you'll have to take a 50B long-tail shuttle to/from the **floating ferry jetty** (Map p698) off Hat Pattaya, and pay a 20B 'entrance fee'. It's part of a local agreement to share the flow. Speedboats *may* drop you directly on Hat Pattaya. During low season (May–October), boats mostly dock at Hat Sunrise and there's no long-tail shuttle fee.

ℹ Getting Around

There are few experiences as relaxing as pottering between the jungle gems of Ko Rawi, Ko Adang and surrounding islets. The best way to see the archipelago is to hire a *chow lair* captain from the **Taxi Boat** (Map p698; Hat Sunrise) stand on Hat Sunrise. You can rent kayaks (250B per hour) across the island, including at Daya's.

Ko Adang & Ko Rawi   เกาะอาดัง/เกาะราวี

Ko Adang, the 30-sq-km island immediately north of Ko Lipe, is a former pirate haunt and has brooding, densely forested hills, white-sand beaches and healthy coral reefs. There's a *chow lair* village on the east coast, as well as an illegally built resort that has yet to open. It's possible to stay in national park accommodation, and to camp.

Ko Rawi, a rocky, 29-sq-km jungle-covered ellipse 1km west of Ko Adang, is almost completely uninhabited. There are fantastic beaches on both the north and south of the island and large coral reefs offshore, which make for excellent snorkelling.

Both islands are popular stops on day snorkelling tours from Ko Lipe.

◉ Sights & Activities

There are a few short jungle trails on Ko Adang that lead to small waterfalls. Great views can be had from Chado Cliff, a half-hour hike above the main beach. Ko Rawi has a few trails too.

There's fine snorkelling off both Ko Adang and Ko Rawi. Top spots include north Ko Yang, 1km south of Ko Rawi's southeastern end, and tiny Ko Hin Ngam, 3km further south, which has underwater fields of giant clams, vibrant anemones and striped pebble beaches.

⊨ Sleeping & Eating

You can stay in simple bungalows on Ko Adang or camp. Camping (per person 30B, tent hire 200B) at Ao Lik on Ko Rawi, close to the Ranger Station, is allowed, with park permission, but facilities are very basic.

There's a restaurant at the accommodation on Ko Adang, and a very simple one on Ko Rawi at the Ranger Station on the southeast coast.

Ko Tarutao Marine National Park Accommodation   BUNGALOW **$**
(Map p694; ☑ 089 736 9328; www.dnp.go.th; Ko Adang; d 600B, campsite per person 30B, with tent hire 280B; ☺ mid-Oct–mid-May) Ko Adang's park accommodation is near Laem Son ranger station in the island's southeast, set back from the beach. There are attractive but simple, fan-cooled doubles, as well as six-person family bungalows (1800B), all with attached cold-water bathrooms, plus camping facilities. Book ahead, online or at the Pak Bara park visitors centre (p693). A small restaurant provides good Thai meals.

ⓘ Information

There are no ATMs or shops on Ko Adang or Ko Rawi. Bring cash and everything you might need.

There are ranger stations near the accommodation on **Ko Adang** (Map p694), and on Ko Rawi's **southeast coast** (Map p694; Ko Rawi) and **southwest coasts** (Map p694; Ko Rawi).

ⓘ Getting There & Away

Long-tail boats from Ko Lipe take you to Ko Adang for around 400B or Ko Rawi for 600B, depending on your bargaining skills. Even a short stop on the islands will cost you the park entrance fee.

Ko Bulon Leh   เกาะบุโหลนเล

Gracious and peaceful Ko Bulon Leh, 23km west of Pak Bara, is surrounded by the Andaman's signature clear waters and has its share of faultless alabaster beaches with swaying casuarinas. This gorgeous island is in that perfect phase of being developed enough to offer some facilities, yet it's not so popular that you have to book weeks in advance (though bungalow numbers are on the rise).

The exceptional, main white-sand beach extends along the east coast from Bulone Resort, on the northeast cape, to Pansand Resort. In places it narrows, especially where buffered by gnarled mangroves and strewn with thick sun-bleached logs, making it easy to find a secret shady spot with dreamy views.

◉ Sights & Activities

The island's wild beauty is accessible on the northern coast at blue, coral-gravel-laden **Ao Panka Yai**, which has decent snorkelling. This bay is linked by a small paved path to **Ao Panka Noi**, a fishing village with a clutch of good, simple restaurants, on the eastern half of the northern coast. Follow a signposted trail nearby west through remnant jungle and rubber plantations to wind your way south to **Ao Muang** (Mango Bay), where there's an authentic *chow lair* squid-fishing camp.

There's good coral off **Laem Son** on the northeastern edge of the island and down the eastern coast. You can rent masks, snorkels and fin sets (200B) and kayaks (200B per hour) at Bulone Resort and Pansand Resort. Snorkelling is best at low tide.

Resorts can arrange guided snorkelling trips (1700B, four hours, maximum six people) to other islands. Tours usually take in the glassy emerald waters of **Ko Gai** and **Ko Ma**. But the most stunning sight is **White Rock**: bird-blessed spires shooting out of the open sea. Beneath the surface is a mussel-crusted rock reef teeming with colourful fish.

⊨ Sleeping & Eating

Most places close from mid-April to November. It's worth wandering over to Ao Panka Noi for food. There are a few local restaurants and shops in the Muslim village between Ao Panka Noi and Ao Panka Yai. All the resorts have their own restaurants.

Chaolae Homestay   BUNGALOW $
(Map p694; ☑ 086 290 2519, 086 967 0716; www. facebook.com/chaolae.homestay; Ao Panka Yai, Ko Bulon Leh; bungalows 600B; ☺ Dec-Apr) Simple bamboo-and-wood bungalows with cold water showers and squat toilets. It's a blissfully quiet, shady spot, close to the village and run by a welcoming *chow lair* family, and steps away from decent snorkelling at Ao Panka Yai.

The restaurant is OK too. No wi-fi.

Bulone Resort   HOTEL $$$
(Map p694; ☑ 081 897 9084; www.bulone-resort. com; Main Beach; bungalows incl breakfast 3000-4500B; ☺ Nov-Apr; ❄ 🐾) Perched on Bulon's northeast cape with access to two exquisite white-sand stretches, Bulone Resort steals the island's top location. Cute whitewashed-wood bungalows (some fan, some air-con) come with queen-sized beds, iron frames and ocean breezes. Huge alpine chalet-style air-con rooms tower behind on stilts, with glorious views.

Enjoy 24-hour electricity, a Thai-international **restaurant** (mains 180-350B; ☺ 7.30-10am & 6-10pm; 🐾) and a coffee corner.

Su's Corner   THAI, BREAKFAST $
(Map p694; ☑ 081 189 7183; Ao Panka Noi, Ko Bulon Leh; mains 80-140B; ☺ 7am-8pm) Anyone who can transform veggie fried rice into something magical deserves high praise. This simple open-air cafe, with only a few tables scattered under palms just inland from Ao Panka Noi, is deservedly popular for its baguettes, shakes, cakes and Thai staples done with flair.

ℹ Information

There are no ATMs on Ko Bulon Leh; the nearest are at Pak Bara. Bring cash. Wi-fi is available but signals are not always great.

ℹ Getting There & Away

From November to April, speedboats to Ko Bulon Leh (450B, 30 minutes) leave from Pak Bara at 12.30pm daily. Long-tail ship-to-shore transfers cost 50B; ask to be dropped off on the beach closest to your resort. In the reverse direction, **the boat** (Map p694) moors in the bay in front of Pansand Resort at 9am. You can charter long-tails to/from Pak Bara (2000B, 1½ hours).

From November to April, daily speedboats (600B, one hour) run from Ko Bulon Leh to Ko Lipe at 2pm, stopping in front of Pansand Resort. Boats originate in Ko Lanta (1600B, two hours) and make stops at Ko Ngai (1050B, 1½ hours), Ko Muk (900B, one hour) and Ko Kradan (900B, one hour), returning from Lipe at 9am.

Understand Thailand

Thailand Today

Many of the political loose ends that have caused instability and uncertainty in Thailand for nearly a decade reached a finale in 2016. The death of the revered king brought about a sense of national unity. The transfer of the crown from father to son occurred peacefully. And a new constitution cemented the role of the military in the government. These changes mark the end of an era for a democratic Thailand and Rama IX's reign. Stay tuned for the next chapter.

Best Books

Pisat (Evil Spirits) (Seni Saowaphong; 1957) Deals with conflicts between the old and new generations.

Lai Chiwit (Many Lives; Kukrit Pramoj; translation 1996) A collection of short stories featuring the lives of 11 different Thais.

A History of Thailand (Chris Baker & Pasuk Phongpaichit; 2009) The authoritative English-language guide to Thai history.

Bangkok Days (Lawrence Osborne; 2010) A witty and insightful account of living in Bangkok.

Best on Film

How to Win at Checkers (Every Time) (Josh Kim; 2015) Based on a short story by Rattawut Lapcharoensap, 11-year-old Oat deals with the military draft of his older (and gay) brother.

Tom-Yum-Goong (Prachya Pinkaew; 2005) Tony Jaa, the Jackie Chan of Thailand, stars in this martial arts movie, the most successful Thai film ever released in the US.

Last Life in the Universe (Pen-ek Ratanaruang; 2003) A lonely love story that established Thai new wave cinema.

Tropical Malady (Apichatpong Weerasethakul; 2004) This rural romance and drama won the Jury Prize at the Cannes Film Festival.

A Nation in Mourning

On 13 October 2016, the beloved King Bhumibol Adulyadej (Rama IX) passed away at the age of 88 after many years of failing health. With a 70-year reign, King Bhumibol was the world's longest-serving monarch and the only king that the majority of the Thai population had ever known. He was regarded as a national father figure and benevolent ruler, undertaking many poverty-alleviation programs during his lifetime.

The country entered into a state-mandated and personal grieving period. The government requested a month-long hiatus from 'joyful' events (concerts, parties, festivals, football matches and the like). Even Thailand's sex-tourism industry obliged, with curtailed hours and no scantily clad promoters. Civil servants were ordered to wear black clothing for one year. Large crowds collected in public spaces and in processions to express their grief. The demand for mourning clothes outpaced supply, and large bubbling vats for dyeing clothes popped up around Bangkok. The government also supplied eight million free black shirts to low-income people.

In October 2017, after Rama IX's body had been lying in state at Bangkok's Grand Palace for a year, one of the most lavish funerals in modern history was held. A 50m-high funeral pyre was built at Sanam Luang, and black-clad mourners from across the country lined the streets of the capital for the various ceremonies, which allegedly ran up a bill of US$90 million.

A New King

After a brief mourning period, the late king's son, the crown prince, ascended the throne as King Maha Vajiralongkorn (Rama X) on 1 December 2016. His first official act as monarch was to issue pardons or sentence reductions to 100,000 prisoners as an act of mercy.

Under Thailand's constitutional monarchy, the king oversees the Crown Property Bureau, which owns approximately US$50 billion in assets, and a regiment of the Royal Guard. There is also a close relationship between the palace and the Thai military, which has control over the government.

Prior to his coronation, the thrice-divorced king was not favourably viewed, due to a variety of personal scandals and a jet-setting lifestyle, such as spending much of his free time in Germany with his girlfriend – an arrangement that Thais weren't used to seeing from their king. But due to strict lèse-majesté laws, the Thai public were reluctant to express candid sentiments, remaining hopeful for stability and decorum.

A New Constitution

Thailand ratified a draft version of its 20th constitution on 7 August 2016 by popular vote. The new constitution dilutes democracy in the kingdom and gives formal governing powers to the military. The 250-member Senate (upper house) will be solely appointed, with no direct elections, and includes seats reserved for the military. There is also a provision for an unelected council to have authority to remove an elected government, and for the Senate to appoint a prime minister. The military-drafted constitution was described by the regime as a road map to democracy and a stable, corruption-free government.

At 55%, voter turnout was low but it passed with a 61% majority. Public information about the constitution was limited, and criticisms of the provisions were repressed by the ruling military junta. Some polled voters supported the measure because the military has brought about an end to street protests in Bangkok.

Prime minister Prayuth Chan-o-cha hinted at a general election in 2018, the first since the military coup in 2014.

POPULATION: **68.4 MILLION**

GDP: **US$390.6 BILLION**

GDP PER CAPITA: **US$16,800**

INFLATION: **0.2%**

UNEMPLOYMENT: **0.6%**

if Thailand were 100 people

94 would be Buddhist
5 would be Muslim
1 would be Christian

land use (%)

41 agricultural land

37 forest

22 other

population per sq km

THAILAND   USA

👤 ≈ 35 people

History

Thai history begins as a story of migrants heading into a frontier land claimed by distant empires for trade, forced labour and patronage. Eventually the country fused a national identity around language, religion and monarchy. The kings resist colonisation from the expansionist Western powers on its border only to cede their absolute grip on the country when challenged from forces within. Since the transition to a constitutional monarchy in 1932, the military predominantly rules the country with a few democratic hiccups in between.

Ancient History

Little evidence remains of the cultures that existed in Thailand before the middle of the 1st millennium AD. *Homo erectus* fossils in Thailand's northern province of Lampang date back at least 500,000 years, and the country's most important archaeological site is Ban Chiang, outside Udon Thani, which provides evidence of one of the world's oldest agrarian societies. It is believed that the Mekong River Valley and Khorat Plateau were inhabited as far back as 10,000 years ago by farmers and bronze-workers. Cave paintings in Pha Taem National Park near Ubon Ratchathani date back some 3000 years.

Early Empires

Starting around the 10th century, the 'Tai' people, considered to be the ancestors of the contemporary Thais, began migrating from southern China into present-day Southeast Asia. These immigrants spoke Tai-Kadai, said to be the most significant ethno-linguistic group in Southeast Asia. Some settled in the river valleys of modern-day Thailand while others chose parts of modern-day Laos and the Shan state of Myanmar.

They settled in villages as farmers, hunters and traders and organised themselves into administrative units known as *meu·ang,* under the rule of a lord, that became the building blocks of the Tai state. Over time, the Tai expanded from the northern mountain valleys into the central plains

TIMELINE	4000–2500 BC	6th–11th centuries	9th–13th centuries
	Prehistoric people develop pottery, rice cultivation and bronze metallurgy in northeastern Thailand.	Dvaravati establish city-states in central Thailand, develop trade routes and Mon culture and practise Theravada Buddhism.	Angkor extends control across parts of Thailand, building Hindu-Buddhist sanctuaries.

and northeastern plateau, where there existed several important trading centres ruled by various indigenous and 'foreign' empires, including the Mon-Dvaravati, Khmer (Cambodia) and Srivijaya (Malay).

Dvaravati

The Mon dominated parts of Burma (present-day Myanmar), western Thailand and into the central plains. In the 6th to 9th centuries, the Dvaravati culture emerged as a distinct Buddhist culture associated with the Mon people. Little is known about this period but it is believed that Nakhon Pathom might have been the centre, and that overland trade routes extended to Burma, Cambodia, Chiang Mai and Laos as evidenced by findings of distinctive Dvaravati Buddha images, temples and stone inscriptions in the Mon language.

The Dvaravati was one of many Indian-influenced cultures that established themselves in Southeast Asia, but scholars single out the Dvaravati because of its artistic legacy and the trade routes that might have provided an early framework for what would become the core of the modern-day Thai state.

Khmer

The Khmers were Southeast Asia's equivalent of the Roman Empire. This kingdom became famous for its extravagant sculpture and architecture and had a profound effect on the art and religion of the region. Established in the 9th century, the Khmer kingdom built its capital in Angkor (modern-day Cambodia) and expanded westward across present-day central and northeastern Thailand. Administrative centres anchored by Angkor-style temples were built in Lopburi (then known as Lavo), Sukhothai and Phimai (near Nakhon Ratchasima) and linked by road to the capital.

The Khmer's large-scale construction projects were a symbol of imperial power in its frontier lands and examples of the day's most advanced technologies. Khmer elements – Hinduism, Brahmanism, Theravada Buddhism and Mahayana Buddhism – mark this period in Thailand.

Srivijaya

While mainland Thailand was influenced by forces from the north and west, the Malay peninsula was economically and culturally fused to cultures further south. Between the 8th and 13th centuries, the Malay peninsula was under the sway of the confederation of the Srivijaya, which controlled maritime trade between the South China Sea and Indian Ocean. The Srivijaya capital is believed to have been in Palembang on Sumatra.

Ancient Sites

Ayuthaya Historical Park

Sukhothai Historical Park

Chiang Saen Historical Park

Lopburi Khmer ruins

Nakhon Si Thammarat National Museum

Phimai Historical Park

HISTORY EARLY EMPIRES

Relief carvings at Angkor Wat depict Tai mercenaries serving in Khmer armies. The Khmer called them 'Syam'. The name was transliterated to 'Siam' by the English trader James Lancaster in 1592.

10th century	**1240–1438**	**1283**	**1292**
Approximate arrival of Tai peoples in Thailand.	Approximate dates of Sukhothai kingdom.	Early Thai script invented by King Ramkhamhaeng of Sukhothai.	Chiang Mai becomes the capital of Lanna, the historic northern kingdom.

Of the series of Srivijaya city-states along the Malay peninsula, Tambralinga established its capital near present-day Nakhon Si Thammarat and adopted Buddhism in the 13th century, while the states further south adopted Islam, creating a religious boundary which persists to this day. Remains of Srivijaya culture can be seen around Chaiya and Nakhon Si Thammarat. Many art forms of the Srivijaya kingdom – such as *năng đà·lung* (shadow theatre) and *lá·kon* (classical dance-drama) – also persist today.

Emerging Tai Kingdoms

In the 13th century, the regional empires started to decline and prosperous Tai city-states emerged with localised power and military might. The competing city-states were ultimately united into various kingdoms that began to establish a Thai identity. Scholars recognise Lanna, Sukhothai and Ayuthaya as the unifying kingdoms of the period.

Lanna

The Lanna kingdom, based in northern Thailand, dates its formation to the upper Mekong River town of Chiang Saen in the middle of the 13th century by King Mengrai. He migrated south to Chiang Mai (meaning 'New City') in 1292, and four years later made it his capital. The king was a skilled diplomat and forged important alliances with potential rivals, such as King Ngam Muang of Phayao and King Ramkhamhaeng of Sukhothai; a bronze statue commemorating this confederation stands in Chiang Mai today. King Mengrai is also

---

RAMKAMHAENG'S STONE INSCRIPTION

In an inscription of 1292, King Ramkhamhaeng gives a picture of his kingdom as idyllic and free of constraints, and of himself as a benevolent patriarch:

In the time of King Ramkhamhaeng this land of Sukhothai is thriving. There are fish in the water and rice in the fields...whoever wants to trade in elephants, does so; whoever wants to trade in horses, does so;...if any commoner in the land has a grievance...it is easy; he goes and strikes the bell which the king has hung there; King Ramkhamhaeng...hears the call; he goes and questions the man, examines the case, and decides it justly for him.

Translation by AB Griswold and Prasert Na Nagara, *Journal of the Siam Society* (July 1971)

1351–1767	1511	1688	1700
Reign of Ayuthaya and rise of the Siamese.	Portuguese found foreign mission in Ayuthaya, followed by other European nations.	The death of pro-foreign King Narai is followed by the Palace Revolution and the expulsion of the French. As a result, Thailand's ties with the West are near-severed until the 1800s.	Ayuthaya's population is estimated to be one million, making it probably the largest city in the world at the time.

credited for successfully repulsing the Mongol invasions in the early 14th century.

The Lanna kingdom is recognised for its royal patronage of the Sinhalese tradition of Theravada Buddhism, now widely practised in Thailand, and of the distinctive northern Thai culture of the region. The Lanna kingdom didn't experience an extensive expansion period as it was plagued by dynastic intrigues and wars with rival powers.

Sukhothai

During the 13th century, several principalities in the central plains united and wrested control from the dying Khmer empire, making their new capital at Sukhothai (meaning 'Rising of Happiness'). Thais consider Sukhothai the first true Thai kingdom and the period is recognised as an artistic and cultural awakening.

The most revered of the Sukhothai kings was Ramkhamhaeng, who is credited with developing the modern Thai writing system, which is based on Indian, Mon and Khmer scripts. He also established Theravada Buddhism as the official religion.

In its prime, the Sukhothai kingdom extended as far as Nakhon Si Thammarat in the south, to the upper Mekong River Valley in Laos and to Bago (Pegu) in southern Burma. For a short period (1448–86) the Sukhothai capital was moved to Phitsanulok, but by that time another star was rising in Thailand, the kingdom of Ayuthaya.

Ayuthaya

In the mid-14th century, the Ayuthaya kingdom began to dominate the Mae Nam Chao Phraya basin during the twilight of the Khmer period. It survived for 416 years, defining itself as Siam's most important kingdom with an expansive sphere of influence (including much of the former Khmer empire) and a fundamental role in organising the modern Thai state and social structure.

With a strategic island location formed by encircling rivers, Ayuthaya grew wealthy through international trade during the 17th century's age of commerce and fortified itself with superior Portuguese-supplied firearms and mercenaries. The river system connected to the Gulf of Thailand and to the hinterlands as well.

This is the period when Western traders 'discovered' Southeast Asia, and Ayuthaya hosted many foreign settlements. Accounts by foreign visitors mention Ayuthaya's cosmopolitan markets and court. In 1690 Londoner Engelbert Campfer proclaimed, 'Among the Asian nations, the kingdom of Siam is the greatest'.

1767	1768	1782	1821
Ayuthaya is sacked by the Burmese.	King Taksin establishes a new capital in Thonburi.	Founding of the Chakri dynasty and Bangkok as the new capital.	A boatload of opium marks the visit of the first Western trader to Bangkok; the trade of this substance is eventually banned nearly 20 years later.

THE INTERNATIONAL KING

In the 1680s many foreign emissaries were invited to Ayuthaya by King Narai, who was keen to acquire and consume foreign material, culture and ideas. His court placed orders for spyglasses, hourglasses, paper, walnut trees, cheese, wine and marble fountains. He joined the French Jesuits to observe the eclipse at his palace in Lopburi and received a gift of a globe from France's King Louis XIV.

Narai's openness to foreign influence was tested as his health failed and rival factions competed for succession. One of his trusted advisers was the Greek adventurer Constantine Phaulkon, who was later accused of conspiring to overthrow the ailing king. Instead, the accusers led a coup, executed Constantine and closed off Siam from the Europeans.

Ayuthaya adopted Khmer court customs, honorific language and ideas of kingship. The monarch styled himself as a Khmer *devaraja* (divine king) rather than Sukhothai's *dhammaraja* (righteous king); and Ayuthaya continued to pay tribute to the Chinese emperor, who rewarded this ritualistic submission with generous gifts and commercial privileges.

The kingdom functioned according to a strict and complex hierarchy, much of which was defined by King Trailok (r 1448–88). Elaborate lists of official posts with specific titles and ranks were established. Individual social status was measured in numerical units of how much land one possessed. Fines and punishments were proportional to the person's rank. Ayuthaya society consisted of royalty, nobility and commoners. Commoners were further divided into freemen and slaves. Freemen were assigned to a royal or noble overseer. For six months of each year they owed labour to the ruling elite, doing personal errands, public works or military service. Despite the clear social hierarchy, social mobility was possible, depending on personal skills, connections (including marriage) and royal favour. These societal divisions are reflected in the feudal elements that persist in Thai society today.

The glories of Ayuthaya were interrupted by the expansionist Burmese. In 1569 the city had fallen to the great Burmese king, Bayinnaung, but regained independence under the leadership of King Naresuan. Then, in 1765, Burma's ambitious and newly established Kongbaung dynasty pushed eastward to eliminate Ayuthaya as a political and commercial rival. Burmese troops laid siege to the capital for a year before destroying it in 1767. The city was devastated, its buildings and people wiped out. The surrounding areas were deserted. So chilling was this historic sacking

King Naresuan is portrayed as a national hero and has become a cult figure, especially worshipped by the Thai army. His story inspired a high-budget, blockbuster film trilogy, *King Naresuan,* funded in part by the Thai government.

1826	1851–68	1855	1868–1910
Thailand allies with Britain during the first Anglo-Burmese War.	Reign of King Mongkut (Rama IV) and a period of Western influence.	Bowring Treaty concluded between Siam and Britain, stimulating the Thai economy and granting extraterritorial rights to British subjects in Siam.	Reign of King Chulalongkorn (Rama V) and increased European imperialism in neighbouring countries.

and razing of Ayuthaya that the perception of the Burmese as ruthless aggressors still persists in the minds of many Thais to this day.

The Bangkok Era

With Ayuthaya in ruins, the line of succession of the kings was broken and chaos ensued. A former general, Taksin, claimed his right to rule, defeated potential rivals and established his new capital in Thonburi, a settlement downriver from Ayuthaya with better access to trade. King Taksin, the son of a Chinese father and Thai mother, strongly promoted trade with China. After 15 years, the king was deposed in 1782 by the military.

One of the coup organisers, Chao Phraya Chakri, assumed the throne as King Yot Fa (Rama I) and established the Chakri dynasty, which still rules today. The new monarch moved the capital across Mae Nam Chao Phraya to modern-day Bangkok. The first century of Bangkok rule focused on rebuilding the cultural, political and military might of Ayuthaya. The new rulers extended their influence in every direction. Destroying the capital cities of both Laos and Cambodia, Siam contained Burmese aggression and made a vassal of Chiang Mai. Defeated populations were resettled and played an important role in increasing Siam's production of rice, much of which was exported to China.

Unlike the Ayuthaya rulers who identified with the Hindu god Vishnu, the Chakri kings positioned themselves as defenders of Buddhism. They undertook compilations and Thai translations of essential Buddhist texts and constructed many royal temples.

In the meantime, a new social order and market economy was taking shape in the mid-19th century. Siam turned to the West for modern scientific and technological ideas and reforms in education, infrastructure and legal systems. One of the great modernisers, King Mongkut (Rama IV; r 1851–68) never expected to be king. Before his ascension he had spent 27 years in the monastery, founding the Thammayut sect based on the strict disciplines of the Mon monks.

During his reign, Siam concluded treaties with Western powers that integrated the kingdom into the world market system, ceded royal monopolies and granted extraterritorial rights to British subjects.

Mongkut's son, King Chulalongkorn (Rama V), who ruled between 1868 and 1910, was to take much greater steps in replacing the old political order with the model of the nation-state. He abolished slavery and the corvée system (state labour), which had lingered on ineffectively since the Ayuthaya period. Chulalongkorn's reign oversaw the creation of a salaried bureaucracy, a police force and a standing army. His reforms brought uniformity to the legal code, law courts and revenue offices.

In 1868 King Mongkut (Rama IV) abolished a husband's right to sell his wife or her children without her permission. The older provision, it was said, treated the woman 'as if she were a water buffalo'.

HISTORY THE BANGKOK ERA

1874	1890	1893	1902
Slavery is abolished.	Siam's first railway connects Bangkok with Nakhon Ratchasima.	French blockade Mae Nam Chao Phraya (Chao Phraya River) over disputed Indochina territory, intensifying threat of colonisation.	Siam annexes Yala, Pattani and Narathiwat from the former sultanate of Patani.

**Landmarks
of the
Bangkok
Era**

....

Wat Arun

....

*Wat Phra Kaew &
Grand Palace*

....

Dusit Palace Park

Siam's agricultural output was improved by advances in irrigation techniques and increasing peasant populations. Schools were established along European lines.

Chulalongkorn relied greatly on foreign advisers, mostly British. Within the royal court, much of the centuries-old protocol was abandoned and replaced by Western forms. The architecture and visual art of state, like the new throne halls, were designed by Italian artists.

Like his father, Chulalongkorn was regarded as a skilful diplomat and is credited for successfully playing European powers off one another to avoid colonisation. In exchange for independence, Thailand ceded territory to French Indochina (Laos in 1893, Cambodia in 1907) and British Burma (three Malayan states in 1909). In 1902, the former Patani kingdom was ceded to the British, who were then in control of Malaysia, but control reverted back to Thailand five years later.

Defying old traditions, Chulalongkorn followed in his father's footsteps in allowing himself to be seen in public, photographed in peasant garb, and consented to his image being reproduced on coins, stamps and postcards. He was also well travelled and visited Europe, Singapore, Java, Malaya, Burma and India. He collected art and inspiration from these travels and built fanciful palaces as architectural scrapbooks.

Siam was becoming a geographically defined country in a modern sense. By 1902, the country no longer called itself Siam but Prathet Thai (the country of the Thai) or Ratcha-anachak Thai (the kingdom of the Thai). By 1913, all those living within its borders were defined as 'Thai'.

Democracy vs Military

In 1932 a group of young military officers and bureaucrats calling themselves Khana Ratsadon (People's Party) mounted a successful, bloodless coup which marked the end of absolute monarchy and introduced a constitutional monarchy. The leaders of the group were inspired by the democratic ideology they had encountered during their studies in Europe.

In the years after the coup, rival factions (royalists, military, civilians) struggled for the upper hand in the new power regime. Even the People's Party was not unified in its vision of a democratic Thailand, and before general elections were held the military wing of the party seized control of the government. The leader of the civilian wing of the People's Party, Pridi Phanomyong, a French-educated lawyer, was forced into exile in 1933 after introducing a socialist-leaning economic plan that angered the military generals. Thailand's first popular election was held in 1937 for half of the seats in the People's Assembly, the newly instated legislative

1909	1913	1914	1916
Anglo-Siamese Treaty outlines Siam's boundaries.	King Vajiravudh requires all citizens to adopt surnames.	Official opening of Don Mueang, Thailand's first international airport, which remained the country's main domestic and international airport until the opening of Suvarnabhumi in 2006.	The first Thai university, Chulalongkorn University, is established.

THE THAI MONARCHY

The country's last absolute monarch was King Prajadhipok (Rama VII), who accepted the 1932 constitution, abdicated the throne and went into exile. By 1935 the new democratic government reinstated the monarchy, appointing the abdicated king's 10-year-old nephew, Ananda Mahidol (Rama VIII), who was living in Europe at the time. In 1946, after the king came of age, he was shot dead under mysterious circumstances. In 1950, his younger brother was crowned King Bhumibol (Rama IX) and ruled until his death in 2016.

At the beginning of his reign, King Bhumibol was primarily a figurehead of national unity. The military dictator General Sarit (1958–63) supported the expansion of the king's role as a symbol of modern Thailand. An attractive royal couple, King Bhumibol and Queen Sirikit met Elvis and were portrayed in photographs in the same way as the US president John F Kennedy and his wife Jackie: fashionable models of the postwar generation. Through rural development projects the king became regarded as the champion of the poor. The Royal Project Foundation was created in 1969 and is credited with helping to eradicate opium cultivation among the northern hill tribes. During the 1970s protest movements, the king came to be a mediating voice, calling for peace between the military and the pro-democracy factions. During another political crisis in 1992, the king summoned the leaders of the political factions to the palace in an effort to quell street protests.

During the most recent political crisis of the 2000s, the ageing king's influence had less of a stabilising effect. Pro-royalist, anti-Thaksin supporters wore yellow in honour of the king and pro-democracy, pro-Thaksin supporters viewed the monarchy with suspicion. The king died on 13 October 2016 and is survived by his wife and adult children, including the new king, Maha Vajiralongkorn, who had assumed many of the royal duties during his father's illness. Princess Sirindhorn, a beloved member of the royal family, carries on her father's philanthropic endeavours.

body. General Phibul Songkhram, one of the military leaders, became prime minister, a position he held from 1938 to 1944 and again from 1948 to 1957.

Phibul's regime coincided with WWII and was characterised by strong nationalistic tendencies of 'nation' and 'Thai-ness'. He collaborated with the Japanese and allowed them to use Thailand as a staging ground for its invasion of other Southeast Asian nations. The Phibul government was hoping the allegiance would restore historical territory lost during France's expansion of Indochina. Thailand intended to declare war on the US and Britain during WWII. But Seni Pramoj, the Thai ambassador in Washington and a member of Seri Thai (the Thai Liberation Movement), refused to deliver the formal declaration of

1917	1932	1935	1939
Siam sends troops to join the Allies in WWI.	Bloodless coup ends absolute monarchy.	King Prajadhipok (Rama VII) becomes the only Thai king to abdicate. The government chooses Prince Mahidol to replace him.	The country's English name is officially changed from Siam to Thailand.

HISTORY MILITARY DICTATORSHIPS

LIBERAL COUNTERWEIGHT

Pridi Phanomyong (1900–83) was a French-educated lawyer and a civilian leader in the 1932 revolution and People's Party. His work on democratic reforms in Thailand was based on constitutional measures and attempts to restrict by law military involvement in Thai politics. He supported nationalisation of land and labour, state-led industrialisation and labour protection. In 1934, he founded Thammasat University. He also served as the figurehead of Seri Thai (the resistance movement against WWII Japanese occupation of Thailand) and was Thai prime minister (1946).

Though acknowledged as a senior statesman, Pridi Phanomyong was a controversial figure and a major foe of Phibul and the military regimes. He was accused of being a communist by his critics and forced out of the country under suspicion of regicide. Since the thawing of the Cold War, his legacy has been re-examined and recognised for its democratic efforts and the counterbalancing effects it had on military interests. He was named one of Unesco's great personalities of the 20th-century world in 2000.

war, thus saving Thailand from bearing the consequences of defeated-nation status. Phibul was forced to resign in 1944 and was tried for war crimes.

For a brief period after the war, democracy flourished: full elections for the People's Assembly were held and the 1946 constitution sought to reduce the role of the military and provide more democratic rights. And it all lasted until the death of King Ananda, the pretext the military used to return to power with Phibul at the helm.

Military Dictatorships

In 1957 Phibul's successor General Sarit Thanarat subjected the country to a true military dictatorship: abolishing the constitution, dissolving the parliament and banning all political parties. In the 1950s, the US partnered with Sarit and subsequent military dictators Thanom Kittikachorn and Praphat Charusathien (who controlled the country from 1964 to 1973), to allow the US military to develop bases in Thailand during the war in Vietnam in exchange for economic incentives.

By 1973, an opposition group of left-wing activists, mainly intellectuals and students, organised political rallies demanding a constitution from the military government. On 14 October that year the military brutally suppressed a large demonstration in Bangkok, killing 77 people and wounding more than 800. The event is commemorated by a monument on Th Ratchadamnoen Klang in Bangkok, near the Democracy Monu-

1941	1945	1946	1957
Japanese forces enter Thailand during WWII.	WWII ends; Thailand cedes seized territory from Laos, Cambodia and Malaysia.	King Bhumibol Adulyadej (Rama IX) ascends the throne; Thailand joins the UN.	Sarit Thanarat leads a coup that introduces military rule that lasts until 1973.

ment. King Bhumibol stepped in and refused to support further blood-shed, forcing Thanom and Praphat to leave Thailand.

In the following years, the left-oriented student movement grew more radical, creating fears among working-class and middle-class Thais of home-grown communism. In 1976 Thanom returned to Thailand (ostensibly to become a monk) and was received warmly by the royal family. In response, protesters organised demonstrations at Thammasat University against the perceived perpetrator of the 14 October massacre. Right-wing, anti-communist civilian groups clashed with the students, resulting in bloody violence. In the aftermath, many students and intellectuals were forced underground, and joined armed communist insurgents – known as the People's Liberation Army of Thailand (PLAT) – based in the jungles of northern and southern Thailand.

Military control of the country continued through the 1980s. The government of the 'political soldier', General Prem Tinsulanonda, enjoyed a period of political and economic stability. Prem dismantled the communist insurgency through military action and amnesty programs. But the country's new economic success presented a challenging rival: prominent business leaders who criticised the military's role in government and their now-dated Cold War mentality. Communists, they maintained, should be business partners, not enemies.

Business Interests

In 1988, Prem was replaced in fair elections by Chatichai Choonhavan, leader of the Chat Thai Party, who created a government dominated by well-connected provincial business people. His government shifted power away from the bureaucrats and set about transforming Thailand into an 'Asian Tiger' economy. But the business of politics was often bought and sold like a commodity and Chatichai was overthrown by the military on grounds of extreme corruption. This coup demarcated an emerging trend in Thai politics: the Bangkok business community and educated classes siding with the military against provincial business-politicians and their money politics.

In 1992, General Suchinda Kraprayoon inserted himself as prime minister. This was met with popular resistance and the ensuing civilian-military clash was dubbed 'Black May'. Led by former Bangkok mayor Chamlong Srimuang, around 200,000 protesters (called the 'mobile phone mob', representing their rising urban affluence) launched a mass demonstration in Bangkok that resulted in three nights of violence with armed soldiers. On the night of 20 May, King Bhumibol called an end to the violence.

1959	1965	1968	1973
The first tourism authority is created.	Thailand hosts US military bases during the Vietnam War.	Thailand is a founding member of the Association of Southeast Asian Nations (ASEAN).	Thai students, workers and farmers demonstrate for the re-installation of a democratic government.

Thaksin Shina-watra was the first prime minister in Thai history to complete a four-year term of office. His sister Yingluck managed three years in power before being deposed.

After Black May, a new wave of democracy activists advocated for constitutional reforms. For most of the 1990s, the parliament was dominated by the Democrat Party, which represented the urban middle class and business interests. Its major base of support came from the southern Thai population centres, formerly port towns now dominated by tourism and exports (rubber, tin and fishing). On the other side of the spectrum were the former pro-military politicians based in the central plains and the people of the agrarian northeast in new provincial towns who focused on state-budget distributions. These political lines still exist today.

In 1997, the boom years ended and the Asian economic crisis unfolded. The country's economy was plagued by foreign-debt burdens, a real-estate bubble and a devalued currency. Within months of the crisis, the Thai currency plunged from 25B to 56B per US$1. The International Monetary Fund (IMF) stepped in to impose financial and legal reforms and economic liberalisation programs in exchange for more than US$17 billion to stabilise the Thai currency.

In the aftermath of the crisis, the Democrats returned to power uncontested, but were viewed as ineffective as the economy worsened.

Thaksin Era & the 2006 Coup

In 2000, the economic slump began to ease. Thaksin Shinawatra, a telecommunications billionaire and former police officer, and his Thai Rak Thai (TRT or 'Thai Loving Thai') party won a majority in the elections of 2001. Self-styled as a CEO-politician, Thaksin swiftly delivered on his campaign promises for rural development, including agrarian debt relief, village capital funds and cheap health care.

Thanks to the 1997 constitutional reforms designed to strengthen the prime minister's position, his was one of Thailand's most stable elected governments. The surging economy and his bold, if strong-arm, leadership won an outright majority in 2005, introducing one-party

PROTESTERS FOR HIRE

It is common practice for both sides of the political divide to pay protestors for their time. During the tumultous street demonstrations following the 2006 coup, anti-government protestors (depending on who was in power) were labourers from the Thaksin-aligned north and northeast or anti-Thaksin-aligned south. After work, Bangkok-based supporters would join the party encampments.

1976	1979	1980	1988
Violent suppression of the student movement by the military.	After three years of military rule, elections and parliament are restored.	Prem Tinsulanonda's government works to undermine the communist insurgency movement and eventually ends it with a political solution.	Chatichai Choonhavan becomes the first elected PM since 1976.

THAILAND'S PARLIAMENT

Much of the country's political drama involves a long-standing debate about how to structure Thailand's legislative body and, ultimately, who gets greater control. Each constitution (or suspension of a constitution) results in a reshuffling of popularly elected versus appointed members. The current parliament, renamed the National Legislative Assembly of Thailand following the 2014 coup, has approximately 200 members (though the number fluctuates), the majority of whom are military (both active and retired). The remaining members are university rectors, police, former senators and business people. The 1997 constitution, dubbed the 'People's Constitution', called for both chambers to be fully elected by popular vote. This power to the people paved the way for Thaksin and his Thai Rak Thai party to gain nearly complete control. The military and the elites have since curtailed full democracy in Thailand.

rule. His popularity among the working class and rural voters was immense.

In 2006 Thaksin was accused of abusing his powers and of conflicts of interest, most notably in his family's sale of their Shin Corporation to the Singaporean government for 73 billion baht (US$1.88 billion), a tax-free gain thanks to legislation he helped craft. Demonstrations in Bangkok called for his ousting and on 19 September 2006, the military staged a bloodless coup that forced Thaksin into exile. General elections were held shortly thereafter, with Thaksin's political allies forming a government led by Samak Sundaravej.

This was an unsatisfactory outcome to the military and the anti-Thaksin group known as People's Alliance for Democracy (PAD), comprised of mainly urban elites nicknamed 'Yellow Shirts' because they wore yellow (the colour associated with the king's birthday). It was popularly believed that Thaksin was consolidating power during his tenure so that he could interrupt royal succession.

In September 2008, Samak Sundaravej was unseated by the Constitutional Court on a technicality: while in office, he hosted a TV cooking show deemed to be a conflict of interest. Concerned that another election would result in a Thaksin win, the Yellow Shirts seized control of Thailand's main airports, Suvarnabhumi and Don Mueang, for a week in November 2008, until the military manoeuvred a silent coup and another favourable court ruling that further weakened Thaksin's political proxies. Through last-minute coalition building, Democrat Abhisit Vejjajiva was elected in a parliamentary vote, becoming Thailand's 27th prime minister.

Voting in Thailand is compulsory for all eligible citizens, apart from monks and other religious figures who are barred from participating in elections.

1991–2	1997	2001	2004
General Suchinda attempts to seize power; King Bhumibol intervenes to halt civil turmoil surrounding 'Black May' protests.	Asian economic crisis; passage of historic 'people's constitution'.	Telecommunications tycoon Thaksin Shinawatra is elected prime minister.	Indian Ocean tsunami kills over 5000 people in Thailand and damages tourism and fishing industries; Muslim insurgency reignites in the Deep South.

Thaksin supporters organised their own counter-movement as the United Front for Democracy Against Dictatorship (UDD), better known as the 'Red Shirts'. Supporters hail mostly from the north and north-east, and include anti-coup, pro-democracy activists; anti-royalists; and die-hard Thaksin fans. There is a degree of class struggle, with many working-class Red Shirts expressing bombastic animosity towards the aristocrats.

The Red Shirts' most provocative demonstration came in 2010, when Thailand's Supreme Court ordered the seizure of US$46 billion of Thaksin's assets after finding him guilty of abusing his powers as prime minister. The Red Shirts occupied Bangkok's central shopping district for two months and demanded the dissolution of the government and reinstatement of elections. In May 2010 the military used force to evict the protesters, resulting in bloody clashes where 91 people were killed and shopping centres set ablaze (US$1.5 billion of crackdown-related arson damage was estimated).

Phibul Songkhram officially changed the name of the country in 1939 from 'Siam' to 'Prathet Thai' (or 'Thailand' in English); it was considered an overt nationalistic gesture intended to unite all the Tai-speaking people.

Democracy vs Military (Again)

In 2011, general elections were held and Thaksin's politically allied Puea Thai party won a parliamentary majority, with Thaksin's sister Yingluck Shinawatra elected as prime minister. Yingluck Shinawatra became both the first female prime minister of Thailand and the country's youngest-ever premier. But throughout her time in power, Yingluck faced accusations that she was just the proxy for her older brother Thaksin, who fled the country to avoid corruption charges following the 2006 coup. Accounts of his influence over the Yingluck government circulated in Bangkok, with Thaksin said to be joining cabinet meetings by Skype from his homes in London, Dubai and Hong Kong.

Trouble loomed for her administration due to the so-called rice-pledging scheme. Designed to boost the incomes of small farmers, the government would buy their rice at above market rates, stockpile it – forcing global prices up – and then sell it at a handsome profit. But the scheme went disastrously wrong, as India lifted its ban on rice exports and flooded the world market with grains. Thailand, the world's biggest rice exporter until 2012, could only watch as prices sank. The damage to the economy was huge, while millions of baht were alleged to have disappeared into the hands of the politicians and officials overseeing the policy. In May 2014, Yingluck was indicted on charges relating to the scheme; she was found guilty in 2017, but fled the country before she could be arrested.

The Democrat Party (Phak Prachathipat), founded in 1946, was the longest-surviving political party in Thailand.

Equally contentious was Yingluck's misguided attempt to introduce an amnesty bill that would have pardoned various politicians, including

2006	2008	2009	2010
King Bhumibol celebrates 60th year on the throne; Thaksin government overthrown in a coup and prime minister forced into exile.	Cambodia petitions Unesco to list Phra Wihan as a World Heritage Site, reigniting border tensions; Yellow Shirt, pro-royalist activists seize Bangkok's international airports, causing weeklong shutdown.	Red Shirt, pro-Thaksin activists force the cancellation of the Fourth East Asia Summit in Pattaya. A state of emergency is declared in Bangkok.	Red Shirts occupy central Bangkok for two months; military crackdown results in 91 deaths.

AN EU FOR SOUTHEAST ASIA

By the end of 2015, the ASEAN Economic Community (AEC) united the association's 10 Southeast Asian countries in a liberalised marketplace where goods, services, capital and labour are shared across borders with little or no country-specific impediments. In theory, the AEC will make it easier to buy and sell goods, hire non-nationals and invest within the ASEAN region. Implementation of the AEC goals has been slow due to the disparities and political interests of each member nation.

Thaksin. This was widely seen as the prelude to the return of Thaksin to Thailand. Street demonstrations against the government began in October 2013, led by former deputy prime minister Suthep Thaugsuban and his coalition of anti-government groups known as the People's Democratic Reform Committee. The group called for Yingluck and the government to step down and introduced yet another round of protest encampments and confrontations in Bangkok.

With sporadic violence between Yingluck's supporters and opponents breaking out, Yingluck and nine of her ministers were forced to step down by the Constitutional Court on 7 May 2014, followed by a military-led coup, the 13th time since 1932.

Return to Military Dictatorship

On 22 May 2014, the Thai military under General Prayuth Chan-o-cha overthrew the elected government and brought to an end months of political crisis. Prayuth said the coup was necessary to restore stability.

Prayuth's military government is known as the National Council for Peace and Order (NCPO). The NCPO set about restoring stability by implementing martial law and silencing critics. All media were under orders to refrain from dissent. Internet providers were ordered to block any content that violated the junta's orders. Even now, some websites, including the Thailand section of the Human Rights Watch website, remain inaccessible inside Thailand. In March 2015 Prayuth told journalists that he would execute those who did not toe the official line – the domestic media now self-censors its stories.

The crackdown extended into the civilian sphere as well. More than 1000 people – opposition politicians, academics, journalists, bloggers and students – have been detained or tried in military courts. In March 2015, the UN's High Commissioner for Human Rights claimed that the military was using martial law to silence opposition and called for freedom of expression to ensure genuine debate.

Thailand has had 20 constitutions, all rewritten following various miltary coups. A draft version of constitution number 20 was approved by popular referendum in 2016. Each new version redefines how much of the legislature will be popularly elected, who is eligible to be prime minister and how the PM will be selected.

2011	2012	2013	2013–2014
Yingluck Shinawatra becomes Thailand's first female prime minister; devastating floods inundate industrial region.	Multiple car bombings across the Deep South in March leave 16 people dead and over 300 injured.	Peace talks start then stall with southern militants.	Antigoverment protesters seize key sections of Bangkok; violent incidents lead to 825 injuries and 28 deaths.

IN MEMORY OF KING BHUMIBOL

King Bhumibol Adulyadej (Rama IX; 1927–2016) was born in the USA, where his father Prince Mahidol was studying medicine at Harvard University. He was fluent in English, French, German and Thai and ascended the throne in 1946. An ardent jazz composer and saxophonist, Rama IX hosted jam sessions with the likes of jazz greats Woody Herman and Benny Goodman. The king was also a sailor and a painter. He is credited for his extensive development projects, particularly in rural areas of Thailand. *King Bhumibol Adulyadej: A Life's Work* (Nicholas Grossman & Dominic Faulder eds; 2011) is the official biography of the king.

King Bhumibol and Queen Sirikit had four children: Princess Ubol Ratana (b 1951), King Maha Vajiralongkorn (b 1952), Princess Mahachakri Sirindhorn (b 1955) and Princess Chulabhorn (b 1957).

Along with nation and religion, the monarchy is very highly regarded in Thai society – negative comments about the king or any member of the royal family is a social as well as legal taboo.

In preparation for the inevitable transfer of the crown, the military also increased prosecution of the country's strict lèse-majesté laws. In August 2015 one man received a 30-year prison sentence for insulting the monarchy on his Facebook page after sharing a news article.

On 13 October 2016, at the age of 89, King Bhumibol, Thailand's – and the world's – longest-serving monarch, passed away. The occasion was marked by a year of mourning culminating in a funeral at Bangkok's Grand Palace that cost US$90 million. Power was passed to his son, Maha Vajiralongkorn, who had assumed many of the royal duties during his father's illness.

Although royal transition was smooth, the junta, at press time in power for more than four years, has failed to address Thailand's slumping economy. Foreign investment, exports and GDP all contracted after the coup. In 2016 a much-needed infrastructure investment plan was announced to help bolster the downturn. Tourism continues to be the bright spot in the economy.

The Buddhist clergy has had its share of scandals, but nothing like the 2017 standoff between the government and Wat Phra Dhammakaya. Followers have barricaded the temple from police intrusion in an effort to protect the abbot who is charged with money laundering and embezzlement.

2014	2015	2016	2017
The military stages its 13th coup since 1932, overthrowing Yingluck Shinawatra's Puea Thai government.	Terrorist bomb explosion at popular Bangkok Erawan Shrine kills 20 people.	King Bhumibol Adulyadej (Rama IX) dies; his son succeeds the throne. Military-backed constitution wins popular referendum.	Yingluck Shinawatra, the last democratically elected prime minister of Thailand, flees into exile to avoid appearing in court to hear a judgement on corruption charges.

Above Akha woman

People & Culture

Thailand's cohesive national identity provides a unifying patina for ethnic and regional differences that evolved through historical migrations and geographic kinships with ethnically diverse neighbours.

Ethnic Make-up

Some 75% of the citizens of Thailand are ethnic Thais, providing a superficial view of sameness. But subtle regional differences exist. In the central plains (Chao Phraya delta), Siamese Thais united the country through its historic kingdoms and promulgated its culture and language. Today the central Thai dialect is the national standard, and Bangkok exports unified culture through popular media and standardised education.

The northeast (Isan) has always stood apart from the rest of the country, sharing closer ethnic and cultural ties with Laos. In the northeastern provinces that border Cambodia, there is a distinct Khmer influence as many families migrated across the border during historical tumult. A tribe of minority people, known as Suay, live near Surin and Khorat (Nakhon Ratchasima), and are traditional elephant mahouts.

Thai Pak Tai people define the characteristics of the south. The dialect is a little faster than standard Thai and there is more mixing of Muslim folk beliefs into the regional culture thanks to the geographic proximity to Malaysia and the historic Muslim population.

If you were to redraw Thailand's borders according to ethnicity, northern Thailand would be united with parts of southern China and northern Myanmar. The traditional homeland of the Tai people was believed to be the Yúnnán region of China. There are also many sub-groups, including the Shan (an ethnic cousin to the Thais who settled in the highlands of Burma) and the Tai Lü (who settled in Nan and Chiang Rai province as well as the Vietnam highlands).

After the Thai Chinese – the most numerous ethnic minority in Thailand, with a population of just under 9.5 million – the second-largest group is the Malays (4.6%), most of whom reside in the provinces of the Deep South. The remaining minority groups include smaller percentages of non-Thai-speaking people such as the Vietnamese, Khmer, Mon, Semang (Sakai), Moken (*chow lair,* also spelt *chao leh;* 'people of the sea', or 'sea gypsies'), Htin, Mabri, Khamu and a variety of hill tribes. A small number of Europeans and other non-Asians reside in Bangkok and the provinces.

Thai Chinese

People of Chinese ancestry – second- or third-generation Hakka, Teochew, Hainanese or Cantonese – make up 14% of the population, the world's largest overseas Chinese population. Bangkok and the nearby coastal areas have a large population of immigrants from China who

---

MIGRANTS & ASYLUM SEEKERS

It is estimated that approximately three million migrant workers, mainly from Myanmar (an estimated two million) and to a lesser extent Laos and Cambodia, live and work in Thailand. The majority are low-skilled workers from economically depressed or politically unstable areas, with little to no formal education. Often in the country illegally and smuggled in by a broker, they frequently have no labour protections and are virtual modern-day slaves or indentured servants. Fisheries, garment factories, brothels and construction sites depend heavily on migrant labour.

Over the past 30 years, there has been an increasing exodus of Burmese to Thailand. Initially, ethnic groups living in Myanmar were forced out of tribal areas to refugee camps in Thailand, and there are currently more than 100,000 people living in a string of refugee camps along the border. In 2016 the Thai government began a pilot program to repatriate these families to Myanmar. The Rohingya people are the most recent ethnic minority to flee persecution in Myanmar. In 2015, the public learned that boats full of desperate Rohingya migrants were being pushed back to sea by the Royal Thai Navy. Mass graves of Rohingya people were found at human-trafficking camps, allegedly operating with cooperation from local authorities in southern Thailand.

Thailand has long struggled with immigration and the number of displaced people seeking refuge in the kingdom. With the slowing of the economy and the law-and-order policies of the military junta, there has been increased deportation of undocumented migrant labourers. The Thai government has also declared that by 2020 there will be no undocumented migrant children living in the kingdom. The International Organisation of Migration estimates that there are 375,000 migrant children in Thailand. In 2014, the military junta was accused of human rights violations by a Human Rights Watch report that documented the inhumane conditions of child detention centres.

Thai Muslim woman

came for economic opportunities in the early to mid-20th century. His-torically, wealthy Chinese introduced their daughters to the royal court as consorts, developing royal connections and adding a Chinese blood-line that extends to the royal family.

The mercantile centres of most Thai towns are run by Thai-Chinese families, and many places in the country celebrate Chinese festivals such as the annual Vegetarian Festival.

Chinese Buddhist temples, often highly colourful and displaying an allegiance again to southern Chinese folklore and belief, are widespread, especially in the south. Temples to Mazu (Tianhou; Tienhau) – the Queen of Heaven and goddess of fisherfolk and those who make their living from the sea – are common, and typical of the southern seaboard prov-inces of China from where many Thai Chinese can trace their ancestors. You will also encounter temples to Guandi, colloquially known as the God of War and frequently red-faced, as well as a host of other Taoist deities, some deeply obscure. Guanyin – the Buddhist Chinese Goddess of Mercy – is also widely venerated by the Thai Chinese, as are other bodhisattvas who enjoy similar adoration throughout China. Chinese guildhalls and ancestral halls are also plentiful.

Thai Muslims

At around 5% of the population, Muslims make up Thailand's largest re-ligious minority, living side by side with the Buddhist majority. Many of Thailand's Muslims reside in the south, but an ever greater number are scattered through the nation. Most of Thailand's southern Muslims are ethnically Malay and speak Malay or Yawi (a dialect of Malay written in the Arabic script) in addition to Thai. In northern Thailand there are also a substantial number of Chinese Muslims who emigrated from Yúnnán in the late 19th century.

Akha women, Chiang Rai

Hill Tribes

Ethnic minorities in the mountainous regions of northern Thailand are often called 'hill tribes', or in Thai vernacular, *chow kŏw* (mountain people). Each hill tribe has its own language, customs, mode of dress and spiritual beliefs.

Most are of semi-nomadic origin, having come from Tibet, Myanmar, China and Laos during the past 200 years or so. Or they were forced out of their traditional homeland in neighbouring countries due to conflicts with the national governments. They are 'fourth-world' people in that they belong neither to the main aligned powers nor to the developing nations. Language and culture constitute the borders of their world. The Tribal Research Institute in Chiang Mai recognises 10 different hill tribes but there may be up to 20. Hill tribes are increasingly integrating into the Thai mainstream and many of the old ways and traditional customs are disappearing. Due to urban migration, many hill-tribe villages now include a variety of ethnicities as well as Burmese migrants.

Many NGOs in Chiang Mai and Chiang Rai work with hill-tribe communities to provide education, health care and advocacy efforts.

Akha (I-kaw)

Population: 80,000
Origin: Tibet
Present locations: Thailand, Laos, Myanmar, Yúnnán (China)
Belief system: Animism with an emphasis on ancestor worship; some groups are Christian
Cultural characteristics: The Akha are among the poorest of Thailand's ethnic minorities and reside mainly in Chiang Mai and Chiang Rai provinces, along mountain ridges or steep slopes 1000m to 1400m in altitude. They're regarded as skilled farmers but are often displaced from arable land by government intervention. The

well-known Akha Swing Ceremony takes place from mid-August to mid-September, between rice planting and harvest time. Akha houses are constructed of wood and bamboo, usually on short wooden stilts and roofed with thick grass. At the entrance of every traditional Akha village stands a simple wooden ceremonial 'spirit gate' to which Akha shamans affix various charms made from bamboo strips to prevent malevolent spirits from entering. Standing next to each village gateway are crude wooden figures of a man and a woman, each bearing exaggerated sexual organs, in the belief that human sexuality is abhorrent to the spirit world. Akha are focused on family ties and will recite their personal genealogies upon first meetings to determine a shared ancestor. Their traditional clothing consists of a headdress of beads, feathers and dangling silver ornaments. With many different dialects, the tonal Akha language belongs to the Lolo branch of the Tibeto-Burman family.

Hmong (Mong or Maew)

Population: 151,000
Origin: South China
Present locations: South China, Thailand, Laos, Vietnam
Belief system: Animism
Cultural characteristics: Divided into two subgroups (White Hmong and Blue Hmong), the Hmong are Thailand's second-largest hill-tribe group and are especially numerous in Chiang Mai Province, with smaller enclaves in the other northern provinces. They usually live on mountain peaks or plateaus above 1000m. Kinship is patrilineal and polygamy is permitted. Hmong tribespeople wear simple black jackets and indigo or black baggy trousers with striped borders (White Hmong) or indigo skirts (Blue Hmong) and silver jewellery. Sashes may be worn around the waist, and embroidered aprons draped front and back. Most women wear their hair in a bun.

Thailand Demographics

⇒ Population: 68 million

⇒ Fertility rate: 1.41

⇒ Percentage of people 65 and older: 10%

⇒ Urbanisation rate: 2.97%

⇒ Life expectancy: 74.7 years

A MODERN PERSPECTIVE ON THE HILL TRIBES

Hill tribes tend to have among the lowest standards of living in Thailand. Although it could be tempting to correlate this with traditional lifestyles, their situation is compounded, in most cases, by not having Thai citizenship. Without the latter, they are technically illegal residents in the country of their birth and don't have the rights to own land, educate their children, earn a minimum wage or access health care.

In recent decades some hill-tribe groups have been issued Thai identification cards, which enable them to access national programs (in theory, though, extra fees might prevent families from being able to afford public schooling and health care). Other hill-tribe families have received residency certificates that restrict travel outside an assigned district, in turn limiting access to job opportunities associated with a mobile modern society. In 2015, the Thai government granted citizenship to 18,000 stateless people. This reduced the country's total to 443,862 and was part of an effort to end statelessness by 2024.

Furthermore, the Thai government has pursued a 30-year policy of hill-tribe relocation, often moving villages from fertile agricultural land to infertile land, removing the tribes from a viable subsistence system in which tribal customs were intact to a market system in which they can't adequately compete and in which tribal ways have been fractured.

In the past decade, the expansion of tourism into the mountainous regions of the north has presented a complicating factor to the independence of hill-tribe villages. City speculators buy land from hill-tribe farmers for fairly nominal sums only for it to be resold, usually to resorts, for much higher costs if the documentation of ownership can be procured. (In many cases the hill-tribe farmer doesn't own the land rights and has very little bargaining power when approached by outsiders.) The displaced farmer and his family might then migrate to the city, losing their connection to their rural and tribal lifestyle and with few resources to succeed in the lowland society.

Top Kayan woman

Bottom Hmong village

Karen (Yang or Kariang)

Population: 500,000
Origin: Myanmar
Present locations: Thailand, Myanmar
Belief system: Animism, Buddhism, Christianity, depending on the group
Cultural characteristics: The Karen are one of the largest hill-tribe groups in Thailand. They tend to live in lowland valleys and practise crop rotation rather than swidden (slash-and-burn) agriculture. Their numbers and proximity to mainstream society have made them the most integrated and financially successful of the hill-tribe groups. Karen homes are built on low stilts or posts, with the roofs swooping quite low. Many Karen also live in refugee camps along the Thai–Myanmar border, having been pushed out of tribal villages in Myanmar. There are four distinct Karen groups: the Skaw (White) Karen, Pwo Karen, Pa-O (Black) Karen and Kayah (Red) Karen. Thickly woven V-neck tunics of various colours are typically worn (though unmarried women wear white). Kinship is matrilineal and marriage is monogamous. Karen languages are tonal and belong to the Sino-Tibetan family.

The hill-tribe communities who lived at altitudes of 900m or above were once opium-poppy cultivators but the illicit cash crop was mostly eradicated through a royally sponsored crop substitution program and improved infrastructure.

Lahu (Musoe)

Population: 100,000
Origin: Tibet
Present locations: Southwest China, Thailand, Myanmar
Belief system: Theistic animism; polytheistic; some groups are Christian
Cultural characteristics: The Thai term for this tribe, *moo·seu*, is derived from a Burmese word meaning 'hunter', a reference to their skill in the forest. The Lahu, originating in the Tibetan plateau, tend to live at about 1000m in remote areas of the Chiang Mai, Chiang Rai and Tak provinces. They typically live in mixed ethnic villages and are an ethnically diverse group with five main subsets: Red Lahu (the most numerous Lahu group in Thailand), Black Lahu, White Lahu, Yellow Lahu and Lahu Sheleh. Houses are built of wood, bamboo and grass, and usually stand on short wooden posts. Lahu food is probably the spiciest of all the hill-tribe cuisines. Traditional dress consists of black-and-red jackets, with narrow skirts worn by women, and bright green or blue-green baggy trousers worn by men. The tonal Lahu language belongs to the Lolo branch of the Tibeto-Burman family.

Lisu (Lisaw)

Population: 55,000
Origin: Tibet
Present locations: Thailand, Yúnnán (China)
Belief system: Animism with ancestor worship and spirit possession
Cultural characteristics: Lisu villages are usually in the mountains at an elevation of about 1000m and occur in eight Thai provinces: Chiang Mai, Chiang Rai, Mae Hong Son, Phayao, Tak, Kamphaeng Phet, Sukhothai and Lampang. Patrilineal clans have pan-tribal jurisdiction, which makes the Lisu unique among hill-tribe groups (most of which have power centred with either a shaman or a village headman). Homes are built on the ground and consist mostly of bamboo and thatched grass. The women wear long multicoloured tunics over trousers and sometimes black turbans with tassels. Men wear baggy green or blue pants pegged in at the ankles. Closely related to Akha and Lasu, the tonal Lisu language belongs to the Lolo branch of the Tibeto-Burman family.

Mien (Yao)

Population: 30,000
Origin: Central China
Present locations: Thailand, south China, Laos, Myanmar, Vietnam
Belief system: Animism with ancestor worship, Taoism, Buddhism and Christianity
Cultural characteristics: The Mien are highly skilled at crafts such as embroidery and silversmithing. They settle near mountain springs at between 1000m and

Spirit house

1200m, with a concentration in Nan, Phayao and Chiang Rai provinces and a few communities elsewhere. Migration into Thailand increased during the American War when the Mien collaborated with the CIA against Pathet Lao; 50,000 Mien refugees were resettled in the US. The Mien are influenced by Chinese traditions and use Chinese characters to write their language, although a unified script was also developed in the 1980s. Kinship is patrilineal and marriage is polygamous. Houses are built at ground level, out of wood or bamboo thatch. Women wear trousers and black jackets with intricately embroidered patches and red fur-like collars, along with large dark-blue or black turbans. Men wear black tunics and black pants. Mien is a tonal language and belongs to the Hmong-Mien language family.

The Lahu people are known for their strict adherence to gender equality, the result of their society's dyadic worldview that emphasises pairs and cooperation.

Lifestyles in Thailand

Individual lifestyles vary according to family background, income and geography. In many ways Bangkok is its own phenomenon where upper- and middle-class Thais wake up to an affluent and modern lifestyle: smartphones, fast food, US hip-hop and fashion addictions. The amount of disposable income in Bangkok is unmatched elsewhere in the country, though affluence throughout the nation is on the rise.

There continues to be a migration from the countryside or small towns to the urban job centres. It was once standard for Thais to send a portion of their pay home to support their parents or dependent children left behind to be raised in the village. This still happens today in some socio-economic strata, but increasingly affluent parents don't need financial help from their adult children. In fact, an important social shift has occurred: parents continue to support their adult children with big-ticket purchases of cars and real estate that entry-level salaries can't afford. As a result, the older generation often criticises today's youth as having an inflated sense of entitlement.

In the provincial capitals, life is more traditional, relatively speaking. The civil servants – teachers and government employees – make up the backbone of the Thai middle class and live in nuclear families in terrace housing estates outside the city centre. Some might live in the older in-town neighbourhoods filled with front-yard gardens growing papayas, mangoes and other fruit trees. The business class lives in the city centre, usually in apartments above shops, making for an easy commute but a fairly urban life.

One of the best places to view the Thai 'lifestyle' is at the markets. Day markets sell kitchen staples as well as local produce and regional desserts. Night markets are good for dinner and people-watching, as few Thais bother to cook for themselves.

From a demographic perspective, Thailand, like most of Asia, is grey-ing. It is projected that 25% of the Thai population in 2040 will be over 60 years old. It is currently at 13%. Women are pursuing careers instead of husbands; unmarried women now comprise 30% of the population (plus they start to outnumber men in their 30s). Thailand's population growth rate is low, with a current growth rate of only around 0.35%. Successful government-sponsored family-planning efforts and profes-sional opportunities have reduced the fertility rate so successfully – from six children in the 1960s to 1.41 children today – that analysts are now warning of future labour shortages and over-extended pension systems.

The Thai Character

Much of Thailand's cultural value system is hinged upon respect for the family, religion and monarchy. Within that system each person knows his or her place, and Thai children are strictly instructed on the impor-tance of group conformity and suppressing confrontational views. In most social situations, establishing harmony often takes a leading role, and Thais take personal pride in making others feel at ease.

Sà·nùk

In general, Thais place high value on *sà·nùk*, which means 'fun'. It is often regarded as a necessary underpinning of anything worth doing. Even work and studying should have an element of *sà·nùk,* otherwise it automatically becomes drudgery. This doesn't mean Thais don't work, but they labour best as a group, so as to avoid loneliness and ensure an element of playfulness. Nothing condemns an activity more than *mâi sà·nùk* (not fun). Thais often mix their job tasks with a healthy dose of socialising, from the back-breaking work of rice farming to the tedium of long-distance bus driving.

Lifestyle Statistics

➡ Average marriage age for a Thai man/woman: 27/24 years

➡ Minimum daily wage: 300–310B

➡ Entry-level professional salary: 9000–12,000B per month

GUARDIAN SPIRITS

Many homes or inhabited dwellings in Thailand have an associated 'spirit house', built to provide a residence for the plot of land's *prá poom* (guardian spirits). Based on animistic beliefs that pre-date Buddhism, guardian spirits are believed to reside in rivers, trees and other natural features and need to be honoured (and placated). The guardian spirit of a particular plot of land is the supernatural equivalent of a mother-in-law, an honoured but sometimes troublesome family member. To keep the spirits happily distracted, Thais erect elaborate dollhouse-like structures where the spirits can 'live' comfortably separat-ed from humans. To further cultivate good relations and good fortune, daily offerings of rice, fruit, flowers and water are made to the spirit house. If the human house is enlarged, the spirit house must also be enlarged, so that the spirits do not feel slighted. Spirit houses must be consecrated by a Brahman priest.

Amphawa Floating Market (p148), Bangkok

Saving Face

Thais believe strongly in the concept of saving face, ie avoiding confrontation and endeavouring not to embarrass themselves or other people (except when it's *sà·nùk* to do so). The ideal face-saver doesn't bring up negative topics in conversation, doesn't express firm convictions or opinions and doesn't claim to have an expertise. Agreement and harmony are considered to be the most important social graces.

While Westerners might think of heated discussion as social sport, Thais regard any instance where voices are raised as rude and potentially volatile. Losing your temper causes a loss of face for everyone, and Thais who have been crossed may react in extreme ways. Minor embarrassments, such as tripping or falling, might elicit giggles from a crowd of Thais. In this case they aren't taking delight in your mishap, but helping you save face by laughing it off.

> The official year in Thailand is calculated from 543 BC, the beginning of the Buddhist Era, so that AD 2018 is BE 2561, AD 2019 is BE 2562 etc.

Status & Obligation

All relationships in traditional Thai society – and those in the modern Thai milieu as well – are governed by social rank defined by age, wealth, status and personal or political position. The elder position is called *pôo yài* (literally the 'big person') and is used to describe parents, bosses, village heads, public officials etc. The junior position is called *pôo nóy* (little person) and describes anyone who is subservient to the *pôo yài*. Although this tendency towards social ranking is to some degree shared by many societies around the world, the Thai twist lies in the set of mutual obligations linking the elder to the junior.

Pôo nóy are supposed to show obedience and respect towards the elder. Those with junior status are not supposed to question or criticise those with elder status. In the workplace, this means younger staff mem-

Novice monks at Wat Phra Puttachai (p179)

bers are not encouraged to speak during meetings and are expected to do their bosses' bidding.

In return *pôo yài* are obligated to care for or 'sponsor' the *pôo nóy*. It is a paternalistic relationship in which *pôo nóy* can ask for favours involving money or job access. *Pôo yài* reaffirm their rank by granting requests when possible; to refuse would risk a loss of face and status.

The protocol defined by the social hierarchy governs almost every aspect of Thai behaviour. Elected or appointed officials occupy one of the highest rungs on the social ladder and often regard themselves as caretakers of the people, a stark contrast to the democratic ideal of being the voice of the people. The complicated personal hierarchy in Thailand often prevents collaboration, especially between those with competing status. This is perhaps why Bangkok has several modern-art museums with somewhat anaemic collections rather than one consolidated powerhouse.

Most foreign visitors will interact with a simplified version of this elder-junior relationship in the form of *pêe* (elder sibling) and *nórng* (younger sibling). All Thais refer to each other using familial names. Even people unrelated by blood quickly establish who's *pêe* and who's *nórng*. This is why one of the first questions Thais ask new acquaintances is 'How old are you?'

Religion in Thailand

Colourful examples of daily worship can be found on nearly every corner. Walk the streets early in the morning and witness the solemn procession of Buddhist monks, with shaved heads and orange-coloured robes, engaged in *bin·tá·bàht*, the daily house-to-house alms food gathering.

Although the country is predominantly Buddhist, other religions often practise alongside one another. Beyond the substantial Muslim minority population of Thailand, there is also a community of around 70,000

MERIT-MAKING RITUALS

Pilgrimages to famous temples are an important feature of domestic tourism. During these visits, merit-making is an individual ritual rather than a congregational affair. Worshippers buy offerings such as lotus buds, incense and candles, and present these symbolic gifts to the temple's primary Buddha image. Other merit-making activities include offering food to the temple *sangha*, meditating (individually or in groups), listening to monks chanting *suttas* (Buddhist discourse), and attending a *têht* or *dhamma* talk by the abbot or another respected teacher. Though Thailand is increasingly secular, merit-making remains an important cultural activity often linked to wish fulfilment (finding love or academic success) rather than religious devotion.

Sikhs. More primordial animist beliefs, which long pre-date Buddhism and Hinduism, survive most noticeably in spirit houses (p729) but also in festivals such as animal sacrifice in the Pu Sae Ya Sae festival in Chiang Mai. Loi Krathong also has its origins in animist belief, honouring the spirit of the water.

Buddhism

Approximately 95% of Thai people are Theravada Buddhists, a branch of Buddhism that came from Sri Lanka during the Sukhothai period.

The ultimate end of Theravada Buddhism is *nibbana* ('nirvana' in Sanskrit), which literally means the 'blowing out' or extinction of all grasping and thus of all *dukkha* (suffering). Effectively, *nibbana* is also an end to the cycle of rebirths (both moment-to-moment and life-to-life) that is existence. In reality, most Thai Buddhists aim for rebirth in a 'better' existence rather than the supra-mundane goal of *nibbana*. The concept of rebirth is almost universally accepted in Thailand, even by non-Buddhists.

The idea of reincarnation also provides Thais with a sense of humility and interconnectedness. They might observe a creepy-crawly in the bushes and feel that perhaps they too were once like that creature, or that a deceased relative now occupies a non-human body. Reflecting Thailand's social stratification, reincarnation is basically a reward or punishment. This is essentially the Buddhist theory of karma, expressed in the Thai proverb *tam dee, dâi dee; tam chôoa, dâi chôoa* (good actions bring good results; bad actions bring bad results). A good person can improve his lot in life today and in future lives by making merit (*tam bun*).

The Buddhist hierarchy in Thailand is made up of the Triratana (Triple Gems) – the Buddha, the *dhamma* (teachings) and the *sangha* (Buddhist community). Historically the Thai king has occupied a revered position in Thai Buddhism, often viewed as semi-divine. Thai royal ceremonies remain almost exclusively the domain of Brahman priests, bestowed with the duty of preserving the three pillars of Thai nationhood, namely sovereignty, religion and the monarchy.

Thai Buddhism has no particular Sabbath day but there are *wan prá* (holy days), which occur every seventh or eighth day depending on phases of the moon. There are also religious holidays, typically marking important events in the Buddha's life.

Thais are fastidious in their personal appearance, often bathing twice a day, and wonder why seemingly wealthy foreigners can appear so unkempt.

Monks & Nuns

Socially, every Thai male is expected to become a monk (*bhikkhu* in Pali; *prá* or *prá pík·sù* in Thai) for a short period in his life, optimally between the time he finishes school and the time he starts a career or marries. A family earns great merit when one of its sons 'takes robe and bowl'.

New Year's Day offerings, Chiang Rai

Traditionally, the length of time spent in the wát is three months, during the *pan·sǎh* (Buddhist lent), which begins in July and coincides with the rainy season. However, nowadays men may spend as little as a week to accrue merit as monks. Most temporary ordinations occur under the age of 20, when a man may enter the *sangha* as a 10-vow novice *(nairn)*.

Monks are required to shave their heads, eyebrows and any facial hair during their residence in the monastery as a sign of renouncing worldly concerns. They are also required to live an ascetic life free of luxury and eat one meal per day (sometimes two, depending on the temple traditions). Monks who live in the city usually emphasise study of the Buddhist scriptures, while those who opt for the forest temples tend to emphasise meditation. Fully ordained monks perform funeral and marriage rites, conduct sermons and instruct monastic teachings.

The monastery sometimes still serves its traditional role as a social welfare institution. Male children can enter the monastery and receive a free education, a tradition that has been largely replaced by public schooling.

In Thai Buddhism, women who seek a monastic life are given a minor role in the temple that is not equal to full monkhood. A Buddhist nun is known as *mâa chee* (mother priest) and lives as an *atthasila* (eight-precept) nun, a position traditionally occupied by women who had no other place in society. Thai nuns shave their heads, wear white robes and take care of temple chores. Generally speaking, *mâa chee* aren't considered as prestigious as monks and don't have a function in the merit-making rituals of lay people. An increasing number of foreigners come to Thailand to be ordained as Buddhist monks and nuns.

Matsayit Klang (p590), Pattani

Islam

There are close to 3500 mosques in Thailand – more than 200 in Bangkok alone. Of these mosques, 99% are associated with the Sunni branch of Islam (in which Islamic leadership is vested in the consensus of the Ummah, or Muslim community), and 1% with the Shi'ite branch (in which religious and political authority is given to descendants of the Prophet Mohammed). As with other parts of Asia, Islam in Thailand is infused with aspects of Sufism.

Islam was introduced to Thailand's southern region between AD 1200 and 1500 through the influence of Indian and Arab traders and scholars.

Arts & Architecture

Thailand possesses an intensely visual culture, in which an appreciation of beauty and aesthetics infuses everything from extravagant temple buildings and humble old-fashioned houses to the high arts conceived for the royal court. Temple architecture and Buddhist sculpture define the bulk of Thailand's ancient arts, but the modern era has seen creativity express itself in multiple forms, from social commentary in contemporary paintings to sky-piercing towers in Bangkok. Musical traditions range from classical orchestras to teenage dance anthems.

Architecture

The most striking aspect of Thailand's architectural heritage is its frequently magnificent Buddhist temples (wát). One of the most distinctive features of Buddhist temple architecture is the *chedi* (stupa), a monument that pays tribute to the enduring stability of Buddhism. Many

Above Traditional Thai temple decoration

contain relics of important kings, the historical Buddha or the remains of notable monks or nuns. Thai temples freely mix different foreign influences, from the corn-shaped stupa inherited from the Khmer empire to the bell-shaped stupa of Sri Lanka.

Thai temples are replete with Hindu-Buddhist iconography. *Naga,* a mythical serpent-like creature who guarded Buddha during meditation, is often depicted in entrance railings and outlining roof gables. On the tip of the temple hall roof is the *chôr fáh*, a golden bird-shaped silhouette suggesting flight.

A venerated Buddhist symbol, the lotus bud is another sacred motif that often decorates the tops of temple gates, verandah columns and the spires of Sukhothai-era *chedi*. Images of the Buddha often depict him meditating on a lotus pedestal. The lotus carries with it a reminder of the tenets of Buddhism. The lotus can bloom even from the mud of a rancid pond, illustrating the capacity for religious perfection in a defiled environment.

Thais began mixing traditional architecture with European forms in the late 19th and early 20th centuries. The port cities, including Bangkok and Phuket, acquired fine examples of Sino-Portuguese architecture –

THAILAND'S ARTISTIC PERIODS

PERIOD	TEMPLE & CHEDI STYLES	BUDDHA STYLES	EXAMPLES
Dvaravati Period (7th–11th centuries)	Rectangular-based *chedi* (stupa) with stepped tiers	Indian-influenced; thick torso, large hair curls, arched eyebrows (like flying birds), protruding eyes, thick lips and flat nose	Phra Pathom Chedi, Nakhon Pathom; Lopburi Museum, Lopburi; Wat Chama Thewi, Lamphun
Srivijaya Period (7th–13th centuries)	Mahayana Buddhist-style temples; Javanese-style *chedi* with elaborate arches	Indian-influenced; heavily ornamented, human-like features and slightly twisted at the waist	Wat Phra Mahathat Woramahawihaan and National Museum, Nakhon Si Thammarat
Khmer Period (9th–11th centuries)	Hindu-Buddhist temples; corn-cob-shaped *prang* (Khmer-styled *chedi*)	Buddha meditating under a canopy of the seven-headed *naga* and atop a lotus pedestal	Phimai Historical Park, Nakhon Ratchasima; Phanom Rung Historical Park, Surin
Chiang Saen–Lanna Period (11th–13th centuries)	Teak temples; square-based *chedi* topped by gilded umbrella; also octagonal-based *chedi*	Burmese influences with plump figure, round, smiling face and footpads facing upwards in meditation pose	Wat Phra Singh, Chiang Mai; Chiang Saen National Museum, Chiang Saen
Sukhothai Period (13th–15th centuries)	Khmer-inspired temples; slim-spired *chedi* topped by a lotus bud	Graceful poses, often depicted 'walking', no anatomical human detail	Sukhothai Historical Park, Sukhothai
Ayuthaya Period (14th–18th centuries)	Classical Thai temple with three-tiered roof and gable flourishes; bell-shaped *chedi* with tapering spire	Ayuthaya-era king, wearing a gem-studded crown and royal regalia	Ayuthaya Historical Park, Ayuthaya
Bangkok-Ratanakosin Period (19th century)	Colourful and gilded temple with Western-Thai styles; mosaic-covered *chedi*	Reviving Ayuthaya style	Wat Phra Kaew, Wat Pho and Wat Arun, Bangkok

Wat Arun (p80), Bangkok

buildings of stuccoed brick decorated with an ornate facade – a style that followed the sea traders during the colonial era. It is locally known as 'old Bangkok' or 'Ratanakosin'.

Visual Arts

Much of Thailand's best ancient art is on display inside the country's myriad hallmark temples, while Bangkok's many national and commercial museums curate more contemporary collections.

Traditional Painting & Sculpture

Thailand's early artistic output was based almost entirely on religion, with Buddha sculptures and murals communicating a continuous visual language of the belief system.

The country first defined its own artistic style during the Sukhothai era, famous for its graceful and serene Buddha figures. Temple murals are the main form of ancient Thai art. Always instructional in purpose, murals often depict the *Jataka* (stories of the Buddha's past lives) and the Thai version of the Hindu epic *Ramayana*. Lacking the durability of other art forms, pre-20th-century religious painting is limited to very few surviving examples. The earliest examples are found at Ayuthaya's Wat Ratburana, but Bangkok is home to some of the best surviving examples.

The development of Thai religious art and architecture is broken into different periods defined by the patronage of the ruling capital. The best examples of a period's characteristics are seen in the variations of the *chedi* (stupa) shape and in the features of the Buddha sculptures, including facial features, the top flourish on the head, the dress and the position of the feet in meditation.

Silk weaver at work

Contemporary Art

Adapting traditional themes to the secular canvas began around the turn of the 20th century as Western influence surged in the region. In general, Thai painting favours abstraction over realism and continues to preserve the one-dimensional perspective of traditional mural paintings. There are two major trends in Thai art: the updating of religious themes, and tongue-in-cheek social commentary, with some artists overlapping the two.

Italian-born Corrado Feroci is often credited as the father of modern Thai art. He was invited to Thailand by Rama VI in 1923 and built Bangkok's Democracy Monument and other monuments in the city.

In the 1970s, Thai artists tackled the modernisation of Buddhist themes through abstract expressionism. Leading works include the colourful surrealism of Pichai Nirand and the mystical pen-and-ink drawings of Thawan Duchanee. Internationally known Montien Boonma uses the ingredients of Buddhist merit-making, such as gold leaf, bells and candle wax, to create installation pieces.

Politically motivated artwork defined a parallel movement in Thai contemporary art. In Thailand's rapidly industrialising society, many artists watched as rice fields became factories, the forests became asphalt and the spoils went to the politically connected. Manit Sriwanichpoom is best known for his Pink Man on Tour series, in which he depicted artist Sompong Thawee in a pink suit with a pink shopping cart amid Thailand's most iconic attractions. A graduate of the College of Fine Art in Bangkok, outspoken artist and poet Vasan Sitthiket is more blatantly controversial and uses mixed-media installations to condemn exploitation and corruption. His often powerful works have been banned in Thailand and criticised as anti-Thai.

In the 1990s there was a push to move art out of museums and into public spaces. Navin Rawanchaikul started his 'in-the-streets' collaborations in his hometown of Chiang Mai and then moved to Bangkok, where he filled the city's taxis with art installations, a show that literally went on the road. His other works have a way with words, such as the mixed-media piece *We Are the Children of Rice (Wine)* (2002) and his rage against the commercialisation of museums in his epic painting entitled *Super (M)art Bangkok Survivors* (2004).

Up-and-coming artists use a variety of media and take on more introspective topics, like Maitree Siriboon, who uses collage and photography to explore personal identity, sexuality and transformation. Born in 1979, Thai-Japanese artist Yuree Kensaku creates allegorical, sometimes surreal cartoon-like paintings with vivid pop-culture references.

Closely associated with Buddhist statuary, Thai sculpture is considered to be the strongest of the contemporary arts. Influenced by Henry Moore, who taught him, Khien Yimsiri created elegant human and mythical forms from bronze. Manop Suwanpinta moulds the human anatomy into fantastic shapes that often intersect with technology, such as hinged faces that open to reveal inanimate content. Kamin Lertchaiprasert explores the subject of spirituality and daily life in his sculptures. His *Ngern Nang (Sitting Money)* installation, made between 2004 and 2006, included a series of figures made from discarded paper bills from the national bank embellished with poetic instructions on life and love.

During the political turmoil of the past decade, artists channelled first-person experiences into multimedia installations. Tanks, guns, violence and protest imagery are woven together to express outrage, grief, anxiety and even apathy. In 2012 Vasan Sitthiket created a collection of colourful but chaotic collages in the series descriptively called *Hypocrisy*. Chulayarnnon Siriphol's short film *A Brief History of Memory* (2010) recounts one woman's experience of violent street protests.

In recent years, there's a growing sense that art is starting to move beyond purely intellectual, political or even artsy circles and into the mainstream. The number of galleries in Bangkok and elsewhere has increased immensely; in 2017, Kamin Lertchaiprasert was asked to create art that would decorate the trains of Bangkok's Skytrain/BTS network; and Thailand has been prepping for its first biennale, Bangkok Art Biennale 2018.

Music

Throughout Thailand you'll encounter a rich diversity of musical genres and styles, from the serene court music that accompanies classical dance-drama to the bass-heavy house music shaking dance clubs across the nation.

Best Arty Books

➡ *The Thai House* (Ruethai Chaichongrak; 2002)

➡ *The Arts of Thailand* (Steve Van Beek; 1998)

➡ *Flavours: Thai Contemporary Art* (Steven Pettifor; 2005)

➡ *Bangkok Design: Thai Ideas in Textiles and Furniture* (Brian Mertens; 2006)

➡ *Buddhist Temples of Thailand* (Joe Cummings; 2010)

REGIONAL HANDICRAFTS

Thailand has a long tradition of handicrafts, often region- or even village-specific. Thai ceramics include the greenish celadon products, red-earth clay pots of Dan Kwian, and central Thailand's *ben·jà·rong* ('five-colour' style), employing elaborate, multi-coloured enamels on white porcelain. Once exclusively manufactured for the royal court, *ben·jà·rong* is based on Chinese patterns, while celadon is of Thai origin.

Northern Thailand has long produced regionally distinctive lacquerware thanks to the influence of Burmese artisans.

Each region in Thailand has its own silk-weaving style. In ancient times woven textiles might have functioned much like business cards do today – demarcating tribal identity and sometimes even marriage status. Today village weaving traditions continue but have become less geographically specific.

Top Democracy Monument, Bangkok

Bottom Traditional Thai musicians

Köhn performer

Classical Music

The classical orchestra is called the *pèe pâht* and was originally developed to accompany classical dance-drama and shadow theatre, but these days can be heard in straightforward performances at temple fairs and tourist attractions. The ensemble can include from five to more than 20 players. Prior to a performance the players offer incense and flowers to the *dà·pohn* (or *thon*), a double-headed hand drum that sets the tempo for the entire ensemble.

The standard Thai scale divides the eight-note octave into seven full-tone intervals, with no semitones. Thai scales were first transcribed by the Thai-German composer Peter Feit (also known by his Thai name, Phra Chen Duriyang), who composed Thailand's national anthem in 1932.

Lôok Tûng & Mŏr Lam

The best-selling modern musical genre in Thailand is *lôok tûng* (literally 'children of the fields'), which dates to the 1940s. Roughly analogous to country and western music in the US, it appeals to working-class Thais. Traditional subject matter are tales of lost love, tragic early death, and the dire circumstances of struggling farmers. The plaintive singing style ranges from sentimental to anguish, and singers are often backed by Las Vegas–style showgirl dancers.

Mŏr lam is Thailand's blues; it's a folk tradition firmly rooted in northeast Thailand and Laos and is based on the songs played on the *kaan* (a wind instrument devised of a double row of bamboo-like reeds fitted into a hardwood soundbox). The oldest style is most likely to be heard at a village gathering and has a simple but insistent bass beat and is often sung in Isan dialect. With songs frequently dwelling on unrequited love and

Thai Hits
Deungdutjai
(http://deung-
dutjai.com) posts
Thai pop hits with
Thai and trans-
lated or translit-
erated lyrics.

The tuned gongs of the *kórng wong yài*

the hardships of life, *mŏr lam* has jumped the generational fence with an electrified pop interpretation and a seriously silly side.

As economic migrants moved from across the country to Bangkok, the two genres merged with each other as well as with other forms, leading to hybridisation and cross-pollination. Contemporary singers might sing about city woes, factory work or being too fat, often backed up by a dance beat.

Thailand's most famous *lôok tûng* singer was Pumpuang Duangjan, a vocalist who received a royally sponsored cremation and a major shrine at Suphanburi's Wat Thapkradan when she died aged just 30 in 1992. Gravelly voiced Siriporn Ampaipong helped carry the tradition afterwards and is still much loved. The new *lôok tûng* princesses are Yingli Sijumpon from Buriram, and Baitei R Siam, who has crossed over into sexy pop. Pai Pongratorn and Tai Orathai are other stalwarts while Auu Jeerawat has an acoustic take on the genre.

Thai Rock & Pop

The 1970s ushered in the politically conscious folk rock of the US and Europe, which the Thais dubbed *pleng pêu·a chee·wít* ('songs for life'). Chiefly identified with the Thai band Caravan, this style defined a major contemporary shift in Thai music, with political and environmental topics replacing the usual love themes. During the authoritarian dictatorships of the '70s many of Caravan's songs were officially banned. Another long-standing example of this style is Carabao, which mixed in rock and heavy metal and spawned a whole generation of imitators.

Thailand's thriving teen-pop industry – sometimes referred to as T-pop – first surfaced in the 1970s and '80s, and centred on artists chosen for their good looks, which often means they are half-Thai, half-*fa·ràng* and sport English names. Thailand's king of pop is Thongchai 'Bird' McIntyre (also known as Pi Bird). His first album hit the shelves in 1986 and he has followed up with an album almost every year since. With Elton George's staying power coupled with a nice-guy persona, he is highly popular with Thais in their 30s and 40s. A potential heir-apparent is Channakan Rattana-udom (Atom), a singer-songwriter who has had a string of sweet hits. The current crop of pop stars have amped up dance beats or are still tugging at the heartstrings. Ballads and booty-shaking always top the charts. An emerging rap scene has been gaining popularity.

The 1990s gave birth to an alternative pop scene – known as 'indie' – pioneered by the independent record label Bakery Music. During indie's heyday, Modern Dog, composed of four Chulalongkorn University graduates, orchestrated the generation's musical coming of age. Another indie fixture was Loso (from 'low society' as opposed to 'hi-so' or socialites), which updated Carabao's affinity for Thai folk melodies and rhythms. The noughties saw these bands move towards classic rock status, while Bakery Music was bought by a conglomerate.

The alt scene lives in a variety of forms – lounge pop, garage rock, shoegaze and electronica. The cast of characters changes as underground bands break through and then later break up. In the 2000s, Tattoo Colour, hailing from Khon Kaen, scored several hits from a small indie label. Electro-rock band Futon announced their arrival with a catchy version of The Stooges' 'I Wanna Be Your Dog' in 2003 and then later pursued solo careers. Endorphine was a feel-good noughties band led by sweet-faced Da with almost a decade's worth of hits; Da later went solo. The hip-hop band Thaitanium has been rapping since the millennium.

In more recent years there has been an increasingly perceptible move away from guitar-based rock and toward electronic music, with outfits like Clokue, Morg, Koichi Shimizu and Gorn Clw making noise and gaining praise.

Thailand Playlist

➡ *That Song* (Modern Dog)

➡ *The Sound of Siam: Leftfield Luk Thung, Jazz & Molam in Thailand 1964–1975* (Soundway Records compilation)

➡ *Made in Thailand* (Carabao)

➡ *Best* (Pumpuang Duangjan)

➡ *I Wanna Be Your Dog* (Futon)

➡ *Still Resisting* (Thaitanium)

ARTS & ARCHITECTURE THEATRE & DANCE

Theatre & Dance

Thailand's high arts have endured decline since the palace transitioned from a cloistered community, although some endangered art forms have been salvaged and revived for a growing tourist community. Folk traditions enjoy broader appeal, but the era of village stage shows is sadly long gone.

Thailand's most famous dance-drama is *kŏhn*, which depicts the *Ramakian*, the Thai version of India's *Ramayana*. The central story revolves around Prince Rama's search for his beloved Princess Sita, who has been abducted by the evil 10-headed demon Ravana and taken to the island of Lanka. Dancers are clothed in elaborate costumes, with some characters masked.

Every region has its own traditional dance style performed at temple fairs and provincial parades. Occasionally temples also provide shrine

TRADITIONAL INSTRUMENTS

þèe High-pitched woodwind, often heard at Thai-boxing matches.

rá·nâht èhk Bamboo-keyed percussion that resembles a xylophone.

kórng wong yài Tuned gongs arranged in a semicircle.

đà·pohn (thon) A double-headed hand-drum.

pĭn Four-stringed instrument plucked like a guitar.

sor Slender bowed instrument with a coconut-shell soundbox.

klòo·i Wooden flute.

dancers, who are commissioned by merit-makers to perform. School-aged children often take traditional Thai dance lessons.

Most often seen at Buddhist festivals, *lí·gair* is a gaudy, raucous theatrical art form thought to have descended from drama rituals brought to southern Thailand by Arab and Malay traders. It's a colourful mix of folk and classical music, outrageous costumes, melodrama, slapstick comedy, sexual innuendo and up-to-date commentary that's partly improvised.

Puppet theatre also enjoyed royal and common patronage. *Lá·kon lék* (little theatre) used marionettes of varying sizes for court performances similar to *kŏhn*. Two to three puppet masters are required to manipulate the metre-high puppets by means of wires attached to long poles. Stories are drawn from Thai folk tales, particularly *Phra Aphaimani,* and occasionally from the *Ramakian.*

Shadow-puppet theatre – in which two-dimensional figures are manipulated between a cloth screen and a light source at night-time performances – has been a Southeast Asian tradition for perhaps five centuries, originally brought to the Malay Peninsula by Middle Eastern traders. In Thailand it is mostly found in the south. As in Malaysia and Indonesia, shadow puppets in Thailand are carved from dried buffalo or cow hides (*năng*). The capital of shadow puppetry today is Nakhon Si Thammarat, which has regular performances at its festivals. While a dying art, the puppets are popular souvenirs for tourists.

Cinema

When it comes to Thai cinema, there are usually two concurrent streams: movies that are financially successful and films that are considered cinematically meritorious. Only rarely do they overlap. The proliferation of online streaming of movies has altered the once flourishing Thai cinematic new wave, but it has also given short-film makers access to larger audiences.

Popular Thai cinema ballooned in the 1960s and '70s, especially when the government levied a tax on Hollywood imports, kick-starting a homegrown industry. The majority of films were cheap action flicks that were typically dubbed *nám nôw* ('stinking water'), but the fantastic (even nonsensical) plots and rich colours left a lasting impression on future Thai film-makers.

Classic Thai Movies

➡ *6ixtynin9* (1997)

➡ *Yam Yasothon* (2005)

➡ *Ruang Rak Noi Nid Mahasan* (*Last Life in the Universe;* 2003)

➡ *Fah Talai Jone* (*Tears of the Black Tiger;* 2000)

➡ *Mekhong Sipha Kham Deuan Sip-et* (*Mekong Full Moon Party;* 2002)

➡ *Uncle Boonmee Who Can Recall His Past Lives* (2010)

KICK THE MACHINE: FILMS OF APICHATPONG WEERASETHAKUL

Bangkok-born independent film director Apichatpong Weerasethakul, winner of the Palme d'Or at the 2010 Cannes Film Festival for his *Uncle Boonmee Who Can Recall His Past Lives,* has made a point of ruffling feathers at home in defence of his art. Joint founder of the Free Thai Cinema Movement, formed to oppose the 2007 draft law devising ratings for films that encouraged censors to demand cuts to his film *Syndromes and a Century,* the enfant terrible of Thai movie-making has said he does not wish his latest feature-length film *Cemetery of Splendour* (2015) to be screened in Thailand, fearing calls for censorship. The film's theme – a group of soldiers receiving treatment in a clinic after suffering from a form of sleeping sickness – has been widely read as a metaphor for Thailand's dysfunctional political culture.

Of Thai Chinese stock and a prolific creator of short films, full-length films and installations, Weerasethakul first came to international attention with his 2002 erotic romance *Blissfully Yours*, which won the Un Certain Regard prize at Cannes in 2002, and *Tropical Malady,* which scooped the Prix du Jury at Cannes two years later, despite an opinion-dividing reception. Weerasethakul favours personal themes and social issues in his films (all produced by his film company, Kick the Machine), conveyed in an often hypnotic, dream-like and sometimes surreal form with a spiritual underlay.

Thai shadow-puppet theatre

Thai cinema graduated into international film circles in the late 1990s and early 2000s, thanks in part to the output of Pratt Institute–educated arthouse director and screenwriter Pen-Ek Ratanaruang and his gritty and engrossing oeuvre of films such as 2003's *Last Life In The Universe*. Apichatpong Weerasethakul (p744) is Thailand's leading cinéma-vérité director and has garnered three Cannes accolades, including the Palme d'Or (the festival's highest prize) for his *Uncle Boonmee Who Can Recall His Past Lives* (2010).

Modern life, with its myriad aggravations, represents a recent theme in Thai movies. Nawapol Thamrongrattanarit gained acclaim for his modern-girl-in-the-city screenplay *Bangkok Traffic Love Story* (2009) and followed up with his directorial debut *36* (2012), which uses 36 static camera shots to explore lost love and lost memories. His *Mary is Happy, Mary is Happy* (2013) was a film festival hit that adapted the Twitter feed of a Thai teen into a movie. In 2016 there were several Korean-Thai ventures, including *So Very, Very* (Park Jae-wook) and *How to Win at Checkers (Every Time)* (Josh Kim), highlighting a new pan-Asian collaboration. Cited as an inspiration by aspiring film-makers, *The Blue Hour* (2015), by Anucha Boonyawatana, merges a coming-out story with magic realism.

Film fest fare has been bolstered by independent film clubs and on-line streaming services. Short films and other DIY projects are how low-budget film-makers bypass the big studios, the ever-vigilant cinema censors and the skittish, controversy-averse movie theatres. Being censored by the film board may seem like the kiss of death, but it often guarantees indie success and cult status. Two political documentaries of 2013 challenged the board's sensitivities. Pen-Ek Ratanaruang's historical *Paradoxocracy* had to mute objectionable dialogue, while Nontawat Numbenchapol's *Boundary* was initially banned, though that was lifted after an appeal. The Thai horror *Arbat* was banned in 2015 because it depicted ~~'improper' conduct by Thai monks, which was considered a slur~~ against Buddhism.

The big studios prefer ghost stories, horror flicks, historic epics, sappy love stories and camp comedies. Elaborate historical movies and epics serve a dual purpose: they can be lucrative and they promote national identity. Criticised as a propaganda tool, the *Legend of King Naresuan* epic, which comprises four instalments, focuses on the Ayuthaya-era king who repelled an attempted Burmese invasion. Each chapter (five have been released so far) has been a box-office winner.

In recent years, and perhaps as a response to the military dictatorship that rules Thailand, there's been an increasing number of socially and politically themed films such as Pimpaka Towira's *The Island Funeral* (2016), which follows the journey of a Muslim woman in conflict-plagued Pattani, and Anocha Suwichakornpong's *By the Time it Gets Dark* (2016), which chronicles two students impacted by the 1976 massacre at Thammasat University.

Literature

The written word has a long history in Thailand, dating back to the 11th or 12th century when the first Thai script was fashioned from an older Mon alphabet. The 30,000-line *Phra Aphaimani*, composed by poet Sunthorn Phu in the late 18th century, is Thailand's most famous classical literary work. Like many of its epic predecessors around the world, it tells the story of an exiled prince who must complete an odyssey of love and war before returning to his kingdom in victory.

Of all classical Thai literature, however, *Ramakian* is the most pervasive and influential in Thai culture. The Indian source, *Ramayana,* came to Thailand with the Khmers 900 years ago, first appearing as stone reliefs on Prasat Hin Phimai and other Angkor temples in the northeast. Eventually the Thais developed their own version of the epic, which was first written down during the reign of Rama I (r 1782–1809). This version contained 60,000 stanzas and was a quarter longer than the Sanskrit original.

Although the main themes remained the same, the Thais embroidered the *Ramayana* with more biographical detail on arch-villain Ravana (called Thotsakan, or '10-necked' in the *Ramakian*) and his wife Montho. Hanuman, the monkey god, differs substantially in the Thai version in his flirtatious nature (in the Hindu version he follows a strict vow of chastity). One of the classic *Ramakian* reliefs at Bangkok's Wat Pho depicts Hanuman clasping a maiden's bared breast as if it were an apple.

Environment & Wildlife

Thailand spans a distance of 1650km from its northern tip to its southern tail, a distance that encompasses 16 latitudinal degrees and a variety of ecological zones, making it one of the most environmentally diverse countries in Southeast Asia.

The Land

Thailand's odd shape is often likened to the head of an elephant, with the trunk being the Malay peninsula and the head being the northern mountains. Starting at the crown of the country, northern Thailand is dominated by the Dawna-Tenasserim mountain range, a southeast-trending extension of the Himalaya. Dropping into the central region, the topography mellows into rice-producing plains fed by revered rivers. Thailand's most exalted river is Chao Phraya, which is formed by the northern tributaries of Ping, Wang, Yom and Nan – a lineage as notable as any aristocrat's. The country's early kingdoms emerged around the Chao Phraya basin, still the seat of the monarchy today. The river delta is in cultivation for most of the year.

Tracing the contours of Thailand's northern and northeastern border is another imposing watercourse: the Mekong. From its source in the Tibetan Plateau and then flowing through China's Yúnnán province as the Lancang River (Láncāng Jiāng), the Mekong courses through Myanmar, Laos, Thailand, Cambodia and Vietnam to the South China Sea. The Mekong both physically separates and culturally fuses Thailand with its neighbours. The river has been dammed for hydroelectric power, and swells and contracts based on seasonal rains. In the dry season, farmers plant vegetables in the muddy floodplain, harvesting crops before the river reclaims its territory.

The landscape of Thailand's northeastern border is occupied by the arid Khorat Plateau rising some 300m above the central plain. This is hardscrabble land where rains are meagre, soil is anaemic and red dust stains as stubbornly as the betel nut chewed by the ageing grandmothers.

The kingdom's eastern rivers dump their waters into the Gulf of Thailand, a shallow basin off the neighbouring South China Sea. The warm, gentle gulf is an ideal cultivation ground for coral reefs. Sliding further south is the Malay peninsula, a long trunk-like landmass. On the western side extends the Andaman Sea, a tropical setting of blue waters and limestone islands. Onshore, the peninsula is dominated by remaining stands of rainforest and ever-expanding rubber and palm-oil plantations.

Native Animals: A Rich Menagerie

In the northern half of Thailand, most indigenous species are classified zoologically as Indo-Chinese, referring to fauna originating from mainland Asia. Those of the south are generally Sundaic, typical of peninsular Malaysia, Sumatra, Borneo and Java. An overlap, starting in Uthai

---

Environmental Statistics

Thailand encompasses 514,000 sq km, slightly larger than Spain.

Bangkok sits at N14° latitude, level with Madras, Manila, Guatemala City and Khartoum.

Flowing through six nations, the Mekong River rivals the Amazon River in terms of biodiversity, and shelters endangered and newly discovered species, such as the Khorat big-mouthed frog, which catches prey with its fangs.

Thani and extending south to the gulf region around Prachuap Khiri Khan, provides habitat for wildlife from both zones.

Thailand is particularly rich in bird life, with over a thousand recorded resident and migrating species, approximately 10% of the world's bird species. The cool mountains of northern Thailand are populated by montane species and migrants with clear Himalayan affinities such as flycatchers and thrushes. The arid forests of Khao Yai National Park in northeastern Thailand are favourites for hornbills. Marshland birds prefer the wetlands of the central region, while Sundaic species such as Gurney's Pitta flock to the wetter climate of southern Thailand.

Thailand is home to five species of macaque, four species of the smaller leaf-monkey and three species of gibbon. Although they also face habitat loss, monkeys sometimes survive in varying states of domestication with humans. The long-armed gibbons were once raised alongside children in rural villages, and macaques can be found living in wooded patches or unused temples. Other species in parks and sanctuaries include gaur (Indian bison), banteng (wild cattle), serow (an Asiatic goat-antelope), sambar deer, muntjac (barking deer), mouse deer and tapir.

Thailand has six venomous snakes: the common cobra, king cobra, banded krait, green viper, Malayan viper and Russell's pit viper. Although the relatively rare king cobra can reach up to 6m in length, the nation's largest snake is the reticulated python, which can reach a whopping 10m.

The country's many lizard species include *đúk·gaa,* heard in the early evening coughing its name, and *jîng·jòk,* a spirited house lizard that is usually spotted on ceilings and walls chasing after bugs. The dinosaur-like black jungle monitor inhabits some southern forests.

The oceans are home to hundreds of species of coral, whose reefs support fish, crustaceans and tiny invertebrates. You can find some of the world's smallest fishes (the 1cm-long dwarf pygmy goby) and the largest cartilaginous fish (the 12m-long whale shark), plus reef denizens such as clownfish, parrotfish, wrasse, angelfish, triggerfish and lionfish. Deeper waters are home to grouper, barracuda, sharks, manta rays, marlin and tuna. You might also encounter turtles, whales and dolphins.

Endangered Animals

Thailand's most famous animals are also its most endangered. The Asian elephant, a smaller cousin to the African elephant, once roamed the forests of Indochina in great herds. But the wild elephant faces extinction due to habitat loss and poaching. According to statistics from the Thai Elephant Conservation Center, the population of wild elephants in Thailand is estimated between 2000 to 3000.

ILLEGAL WILDLIFE TRADE

Thailand is a signatory to the UN Convention on International Trade in Endangered Species (Cites), but the country remains an important transport link and marketplace for the global wildlife trade, the third-largest black-market activity after drugs and arms dealing. Endangered animals and animal parts are poached from local forests or smuggled from neighbouring countries through Thailand en route to the lucrative markets of China or the US.

Although the country's efforts to stop the trade are more impressive than those of its neighbours, corruption and weak laws hinder law enforcement. Thai law allows the trade of wild species bred in captivity, designed ostensibly to take the pressure off wild populations. This is especially problematic with elephants; criminal gangs steal baby elephants from wild herds or smuggle them across the Burmese borders and then forge registration papers so that the elephant appears to have been born to a captive mother and can be 'legally' sold to elephant camps (p754).

Reclusive wild tigers stalk the hinterlands between Thailand and Myanmar, but in ever-decreasing numbers. It is notoriously difficult to obtain an accurate count, but experts estimate that around 200 wild tigers remain in Thailand. Although tiger hunting and trapping is illegal, poachers continue to kill the cats for the overseas wildlife trade.

Weighing up to 1000kg, the rare dugong (also referred to as 'sea cows') – a herbivorous marine mammal once thought extinct in Thailand – survives in a few small pockets around Trang, but it is increasingly threatened by habitat loss and the lethal propellers of tourist boats.

Forests & Flora

Thailand's jungles can be divided into monsoon (with a distinct dry season of three months or more) and rainforest (where a rain falls more than nine months per year). The most heavily forested provinces are Chiang Mai and Kanchanaburi.

Northerly monsoon forests comprise deciduous trees, which are green and lush during the rainy season but dusty and leafless during the dry season. Teak is highly valued, but logging has been banned since 1989.

In southern Thailand, where rainfall is plentiful and distributed evenly throughout the year, forests are classified as rainforests with a few areas of monsoon forest. One remarkable plant found in some southern forests is *Rafflesia kerrii,* with a huge flower 80cm across.

Thailand is home to nearly 75 coastal mangrove species, small salt-tolerant trees that provide an incubator for many coastal fish and animal species. Reforestation programs of mangrove areas have gained popularity thanks to their protective role during the 2004 Asian tsunami.

Orchids are Thailand's most exquisite native flora. There are over 1100 native species: some ground dwellers, others high up in trees.

Environmental Issues

Coastal & Marine Degradation

It is estimated by the Department of Mineral Resources that approximately 5m per year of coastline is lost each year due to coastal development (construction of jetties, breakwaters, oceanfront hotels and roads), land subsiding (due to groundwater depletion) and rising sea levels. Accurate data is lacking on coastal water quality, but analysts admit that wastewater treatment facilities are outpaced by the area's population and that industrial wastewater is often insufficiently treated.

Another risk factor for Thailand's diverse sea environment is rising sea temperatures, associated with El Niño weather conditions, which cause coral bleaching and death. More than 10 dive sites in Thailand were closed in 2016 due to bleaching. Between 40% to 80% of the reefs on the Gulf and Andaman coasts were affected. A similar El Niño–related event occurred in 2010. It is estimated that about 50% of Thailand's coral reefs are classified as highly threatened, indicating a disproportionate number of dead coral to living coral, according to a World Bank 2006 environmental report.

An important part of the Thai economy, the overall health of the ocean is further impacted by large-scale fishing. Fisheries continue to experience declining catches as fish stocks plummet. The fishing industry is also under scrutiny for its exploitative labour practices; it is accused of using slave and child labour.

Deforestation

According to the World Bank, natural forest cover constituted about 32% of land area in 2016, compared to 53.5% in 1961. Depletion of forests coincided with industrialisation, urbanisation and commercial logging.

ENVIRONMENT & WILDLIFE FORESTS & FLORA

The Western Forest Complex in northeastern Thailand comprises approximately 18,000 sq km and 17 protected areas. It is considered a model for natural habitats and supports 500 tigers and other threatened species.

National Marine Parks

Ko Tarutao

Mu Ko Chang

Mu Ko Surin & Similan

Forest loss has slowed since the turn of the millennium to about 0.6% per year and total cover is up from 27.4% in 1990.

The Thai government created a large number of protected areas, starting in the 1970s, and establishing a goal of 40% forest cover by the middle of this century. In 1989 all logging was banned following disastrous mudslides in Surat Thani Province that buried villages and killed more than a hundred people. It is now illegal to sell timber felled in the country, but this law is frequently flouted.

Wildlife experts agree that the greatest danger faced by Thai fauna and flora is neither hunting nor the illegal wildlife trade, but habitat loss. Species that are notably extinct in Thailand include the kouprey (a type of wild cattle), Schomburgk's deer and Javan rhino.

A 2015 air quality index report found that Bangkok ranked better than Washington, DC, and San Francisco.

Energy Consumption

Thailand's increasingly affluent society is expected to consume 75% more energy in the forthcoming decades, according to the Oxford Business Group. Thailand is looking to increase and diversify its energy supply and production, by expanding oil and gas resources or developing alternative fuel sources, including nuclear. Currently, three quarters of Thailand's energy derives from natural gas. Most existing oil and gas fields are in the Gulf of Thailand in an area known as the Pattani Trough; the government is also working with Cambodia on the development of reserves in the upper Gulf of Thailand near the Thailand–Cambodia border.

Thailand also produces biofuels, including ethanols from molasses and cassava, and biodiesel from palm oil. Power generation, agriculture and industrial activity account for the largest proportion of the country's greenhouse gas emissions. While the energy sector searches for additional fuel supplies to feed the economy, the country received World Bank funds for a national carbon market with a mandatory trading scheme.

Thailand is aiming to boost its production of renewable energy but the military coup has stalled policy progress in pioneering industries. The first large-scale solar farm in Lopburi went online in 2011 and provides enough power for 70,000 households.

Flooding

Seasonal flooding is common in some parts of Thailand due to monsoon rains. But high-level, property-damaging floods have increased in recent years. The record-busting 2011 floods were unlike anything the country had ever experienced. Tropical storms brought an inundation of rain that triggered a domino flood effect spanning nearly three months. Of Thailand's 77 provinces, 65 were declared flood disaster zones; there were 815 deaths and an estimated US$45.7 billion worth of damages. It was one of the world's costliest natural disasters.

The 2011 flood trumped the previous year's record-setting event in which late-arriving rains transformed reservoirs in Nakhon Ratchasima Province from parched pits into overflowing disaster zones. There were 177 deaths in the 2010 floods, and a massive disaster relief response that lasted for several months. Another record flood occurred in 2006 with 46 affected provinces, mainly in the north, and again in 2008 along the Mekong.

Many environmental experts attribute human alteration of natural flood barriers and watercourses and deforestation as contributory factors. Increased flooding along the Mekong is often linked to upstream infrastructure projects, such as dams and removal of rapids for easier navigation, and increasing human populations that infringe on forested floodplains and wetlands. Another emerging and possibly crucial component is the role of climate change in the increase of seasonal rains.

Survival Guide

Responsible Travel

CULTURAL ETIQUETTE

The monarchy and religion (which are interconnected) are treated with extreme deference in Thailand. Thais avoid criticising or disparaging the royal family for fear of offending someone or, worse, being charged with a violation of the country's very strict lèse-majesté laws, which carry a jail sentence.

Buddha images are sacred objects. Thais consider it bad form to pull a silly pose in front of one for a photo, or to clamber upon them (in the case of temple ruins). Instead they would show respect by performing a *wâi* (a prayer-like gesture) to the figure no matter how humble it is. As part of their ascetic vows, monks are not supposed to touch or be touched by women. If a woman wants to hand something to a monk, the object is placed within reach of the monk or on the monk's 'receiving cloth'.

From a spiritual viewpoint, Thais regard the head as the highest and most sacred part of the body and the feet as the dirtiest and lowest. Many of the taboos associated with the feet have a practical derivation as well. Traditionally Thais ate, slept and entertained on the floor of their homes with little in the way of furniture. To keep their homes and eating surfaces clean, the feet (and shoes) contracted a variety of rules.

Shoes aren't worn inside private homes and temples, as a sign of respect and for sanitary reasons. Thais can kick off their shoes in one fluid step and many lace-up shoes are modified by the wearer to become slip-ons. Thais also step over – not on – the threshold, which is where the spirit of the house is believed to reside. On some buses and 3rd-class trains, you'll see Thais prop their feet up on the adjacent bench, and while this isn't the height of propriety, they always remove their shoes before doing so. Thais also take off their shoes if they need to stand on a chair or seat.

Thais don't touch each others' heads or ruffle hair as a sign of affection. Occasionally you'll see young people touching each others' heads, which is a teasing gesture between friends.

Social Conventions & Gestures

The traditional Thai greeting, known as *wâi*, is made with a prayer-like, palms-together gesture. The depth of the bow and the placement of the fingers in relation to the face is dependent on the status of the person receiving the *wâi*. Adults don't *wâi* children, and in most cases service people (when they are doing their jobs) aren't *wâi-ed*, though this is a matter of personal discretion.

In the more traditional parts of the country, it is not proper for members of the opposite sexes to touch one another, either as lovers or as friends. Hand-holding is not acceptable behaviour outside the major cities such as Bangkok. But same-sex touching is quite common and is typically a sign of friendship, not sexual attraction. Older Thai men might grab a younger man's thigh in the same way that buddies slap each other on the back. Thai women are especially affectionate with female friends, often sitting close to one another or linking arms.

Thais hold modesty in personal dress in high regard, though this is changing among the younger generation. The importance of modesty extends to the beach as well. Except for urbanites, most provincial Thais swim fully clothed. For this reason, sunbathing nude or topless is not acceptable and in some cases is even illegal. Remember that swimsuits are not proper attire off the beach; wear a cover-up in between the sand and your hotel.

RESPONSIBLE TOURISM

Most forms of tourism, despite the prevailing prejudices, have a positive economic effect on the local economy in Thailand, providing jobs for young workers and business opportunities

ESSENTIAL ETIQUETTE

Do

Stand respectfully for the national anthem It is played on TV and radio stations as well as in public and government places at 8am and 6pm.

Rise for the royal anthem It is played in movie theatres before every screening.

Smile a lot It makes everything easier.

Bring a gift if you're invited to a Thai home Fruit, drinks or snacks are acceptable; flowers are usually for merit-making purposes, not home decor.

Take off your shoes When you enter a home, temple building or wherever there are sandals piled up at the door.

Lower your head slightly When passing between two people having a conversation or when passing near a monk; it is a sign of respect.

Dress modestly for temple visits Cover to the elbows and ankles and always remove your shoes when entering any building containing a Buddha image.

Give and receive politely Extend the right hand out while the left hand gently grips the right elbow when handing an object to another person or receiving something – truly polite behaviour.

Respect all Buddha images and pictures of the monarchy Signs of disrespect can have serious consequences.

Sit in the 'mermaid' position inside temples Tuck your feet beside and behind you so that your feet aren't pointing at the Buddha image.

Don't

Get a tattoo of the Buddha (or display one you have) It is considered sacrilegious.

Criticise the monarchy The monarchy is revered and protected by defamation laws – more so now than ever.

Prop your feet on tables or chairs Feet are considered dirty and people sit on chairs.

Step on a dropped bill to prevent it from blowing away Thai money bears a picture of the king. Feet + monarchy = grave offence.

Step over someone or their personal belongings Aaah, attack of the feet.

Tie your shoes to the outside of your backpack They might accidentally brush against someone: gross.

Touch a Thai person on the head It is considered rude, not chummy.

Touch monks or their belongings Women are expected to step out of the way when passing one on the footpath and do not sit next to them on public transport.

---

for entrepreneurs. But in an effort to be more than just a consumer, many travellers look for opportunities to spend where their money might be needed, either on charitable causes or activities that preserve traditional ways of life. Thailand has done a good job at adapting to this emerging trend by promoting village craft programs and homestays. Unfortunately, much of this is aimed at the domestic market rather than international visitors. But more and more, foreign tourists can engage in these small-scale tourism models that offer an insight into traditional ways.

Diving & Snorkelling

Thailand's diving industry places immense pressure on fragile coral sites. To help preserve the ecology, adhere to these simple rules:

➡ Avoid touching living marine organisms, standing on coral or dragging equipment (such as fins) across reefs. Coral polyps can be damaged by even the gentlest contact.

➡ When treading water in shallow reef areas, be careful not to kick up clouds of sand, which can easily smother the delicate reef organisms.

➡ Take care in underwater caves where your air bubbles can be caught on the roof and leave previously submerged organisms high and dry.

➡ Join a coral clean-up campaign that's sponsored by dive shops.

➡ Don't feed the fish or allow your dive operator to dispose of excess food in the water.

Ethical Elephant Encounters

Throughout Thai history, elephants have been revered for their strength, endurance and intelligence, working alongside their mahouts harvesting teak, transporting goods through mountainous terrain or fighting ancient wars.

Many of the elephants' traditional roles have either been outsourced to machines or outlawed, leaving the 'domesticated' animals and their mahouts without work. Some mahouts turned to begging on the streets in Bangkok and other tourist centres, but most elephants find work in Thailand's tourism industry. Their jobs vary from circus-like shows to elephant camps giving rides to tourists, to 'mahout-training' schools, while sanctuaries and rescue centres provide modest retirement homes to animals that are no longer financially profitable to their owners.

It costs about 30,000B (US$1000) a month to provide a comfortable living for an elephant, an amount equivalent to the salary of Thailand's upper-middle class. Welfare standards within the tourism industry are not standardised or subject to government regulations, so it's up to the conscientious consumer to encourage the industry to ensure safe conditions for elephants.

With more evidence available than ever to support claims by animal welfare experts that elephant rides and shows are harmful to these gentle giants, who are often abused to force them to perform for humans, a small but growing number of sanctuaries offer more sustainable interactions, such as walking with and bathing retired and rescued elephants.

Lonely Planet does not recommend riding on elephants or viewing elephant performances. We also urge visitors to be wary of organisations that advertise as being a conservation centre but actually offer rides and performances.

Hill-Tribe Hikes

Though marginalised within mainstream society, Thailand's hill-tribe minorities remain a strong tourism draw, with large and small businesses organising 'trekking' tours (these can range from proper hikes to leisurely walks) to villages for cultural displays and interactions. Economically it is unclear whether hill-tribe trekking helps alleviate the poverty of the hill-tribe groups, which in turn helps to maintain their separate ethnic identity. Most agree that a small percentage of the profits from trekking filters down to individual families within hill-tribe villages, giving them a small source of income that might prevent urban migration.

In general, the trekking business has become more socially conscious than in past decades. Most companies now tend to limit the number of visits to a particular area to lessen the impact of outsiders on the daily lives of ordinary villagers. But the industry still has a long way to go. It should be noted that trekking companies are Thai owned and employ Thai guides, another bureaucratic impediment regarding citizenship for ethnic minorities. Without an identification card, guides from hill tribes do not qualify for a Tourist Authority of Thailand (TAT) tour guide license and so are less than desirable job candidates.

Trekkers should also realise that the minority tribes maintain their own distinct cultural identity and many continue their animistic traditions, which define social taboos and conventions. If you're planning on visiting hill-tribe villages on an organised trek, talk to your guide about acceptable behaviour.

VOLUNTEERING

There are myriad volunteer organisations in Thailand to address both the needs of the locals and visitors' desires to help. A regularly updated resource for grassroots-level volunteer opportunities is Volunteer Work Thailand (www.volunteerworkthailand. org). Be aware, though, that so-called 'voluntourism' has become a big business and that not every organisation fulfils its promise of meaningful experiences. It is essential that you do your own thorough research before agreeing to volunteer with any organisation.

Humanitarian & Educational Work

Northern Thailand, especially Chiang Mai and Chiang Rai, has a number of volunteer opportunities working with disadvantaged hill-tribe groups. Chiang Mai, Mae Sot and Sangkhlaburi have distressed communities of Burmese refugees and migrants. There are also many volunteer teaching positions in northeastern Thailand, the country's agricultural heartland.

When looking for a volunteer placement, it is essential to investigate what your chosen organisation does and, more importantly, how it goes about it. If the focus is not primarily on your skills and how these can be applied to help local people, that should ring alarm bells. Any organisation that promises to let you do any kind of work, wherever you like, for as long as you like, is unlikely to be putting the needs of local people first.

For any organisation working with children, child protection is a serious concern, and organisations that do not conduct background checks on volunteers should be regarded with extreme caution.

Some reliable and/or long-running organisations include:

Baan Unrak (บ้านอุ่นรัก; www.baanunrak.org) ✐ A home and school that cares for over 150 orphaned or abandoned children. Regardless of their religion, the children follow a neohumanist philosophy of vegetarianism (volunteers must also during their stay), meditation and universal love.

Cultural Canvas Thailand (www.culturalcanvas.com; Chiang Mai University) Places volunteers in migrant learning centres, art programs and other social-justice projects in northern Thailand.

Open Mind Projects (☎042 413578; www.openmindprojects.org) Offers volunteer positions in IT, health care, education and community-based ecotourism throughout Thailand.

Starfish Ventures (www.starfish-adventure.com) Places volunteers in building, health care and teaching programs throughout Thailand.

Volunthai (www.volunthai.com) A family-run operation that places volunteers in teaching positions at rural schools with homestay accommodation.

Animal Welfare & Environment

A number of NGOs undertake local conservation efforts and run rescue and sanctuary centres for wild animals that have been adopted as pets or veterinarian clinics that tend to the domesticated population of dogs and cats.

Elephant Nature Park (Map p318; ☎053 818754, 053 272850; www.elephantnaturepark.org; 1 Th Ratchamankha, Chiang Mai; 1-/2-day tours 2500/5800B) ✐ This popular and well-run elephant sanctuary offers seven-day volunteer programs at several sister organisations such as Surin Project in the Isan region and Elephant Haven in Kanchanaburi.

Highland Farm Gibbon Sanctuary (☎081 727 1364; www.gibbonathighlandfarm.org; Mae Sot) Gives a permanent home

TOP HOMESTAYS

Muang Pon Homestay Program (☎084 485 5937; per night incl breakfast & dinner 350B) Dive headfirst into Shan life in this charming village in Mae Hong Son.

Mae Kampong Homestay Program (☎089 559 4797; r 600B) The homestay that Thai tourists are drawn to.

Bunloed's Huts (☎087 861 0601; www.bunloedhuts.jimdo.com; s/d bungalows 300/360B, without bathroom 200/260B, s/d in tent 80/100B, meals 60-100B; P⑤) Near the Phu Wua Wildlife Sanctuary, a stay here blends culture and nature.

Ban Na Ton Chan Homestay (☎089 885 1639; http://homestaynatonchan.blogspot.com; per person incl breakfast & lunch 700B) This picture-perfect northern village has opened its doors to visitors.

Dan Sai Homestay (☎042 892339, 086 862 4812; dm/tw & d 200/550B; P) Crash with friendly villagers during this community's famous festival.

to orphaned, abandoned and mistreated gibbons. Volunteers are asked for a one-month commitment and to help with daily farm chores.

Koh Chang Animal Project (Map p476; ☎089 042 2347; www.kohchanganimalproject.org; Ban Khlong Son) ✐ Travelling vets and vet nurses often drop by to volunteer here, while non-vets are needed to help with numerous odd jobs. Call to make an appointment.

Lanta Animal Welfare (Map p674; ☎084 304 4331; www.lantaanimalwelfare.com; 629 Mu 2, Ban Phra Ae; tours by donation; ☺10am-4pm) This centre on Ko Lanta welcomes both casual dog-walking visitors and volunteers for longer placements.

Phuket Elephant Sanctuary (Map p620; ☎094 990 3649; www.phuketelephantsanctuary.org; 100 Mu 2, Pa Klok, on 4027 Highway; adult/child 3000/1500B; ☺9.30am-1pm & 2-5.30pm; ♿) Takes up to six volunteers at a time for week-long stays.

Samui Dog & Cat Rescue Centre (Map p531; ☎081 893 9443; www.samuidog.org; Soi 3, Chaweng Beach Rd; ☺9am-6pm) Donations of time and/or money are hugely appreciated at this centre. Volunteers are always needed to take care of the animals

at its kennel/clinic in Ban Taling Ngam (but not at the smaller Hat Chaweng branch). Call the centre for volunteering details or swing by for additional info. Check the website for directions.

Soi Dog (Map p620; ☎081 788 4222; www.soidog.org; 167/9 Mu 4, Soi Mai Khao 10; admission by donation; ☺9am-noon & 1-3.30pm Mon-Fri, tours 9.30am, 11am, 1.30pm & 2.30pm) This Phuket centre welcomes visitors to play with the animals, or become a dog-walking or long-term volunteer.

Trash Hero (www.trashhero.org) A volunteer outfit that runs weekly clean ups at 11 official points across Thailand.

Wild Animal Rescue Foundation (WARF; ☎02 712 9715; www.warthai.org) Operates the Phuket Gibbon Rehabilitation Project (where volunteers can help with cleaning cages, feeding and tracking released gibbons), as well as several other programs across the country.

Wildlife Friends Foundation Thailand Rescue Centre and Elephant Refuge (มูลนิธิเพื่อนสัตว์ป่า; ☎032 458135; www.wfft.org; full-access tours incl lunch half-/full-day 1100/1800B) ✐ Puts volunteers to work caring for sun bears, macaques, gibbons and elephants at its animal rescue centre in Phetchaburi, 45km northwest of Hua Hin.

Directory A–Z

Accommodation

Finding a place to stay in Thailand is easy. For peace of mind, book a room for your arrival night; after that, you can wing it. Bear in mind, vacancies can become scarce during certain holidays and peak travel periods.

Hostels & Guesthouses

In big cities and expensive islands, European-style hostels offer the best budget option. Most hostels have both shared and private sleeping quarters with various amenities, and strive for a hip communal vibe.

Once upon a time, most budget accommodation in Thailand took the form of a guesthouse: a simple room with shared bathroom in an enterprising Thai family's home. In popular destinations, such as Bangkok and the islands, most guesthouses have expanded into mini-hotels or 'flashpacker' hotels with more style, comfort and midrange rates.

In small provincial towns, guesthouses continue to

reign. There are still some budget cheapies with shared bathroom and a rickety fan, but private en suite facilities, air-con and a TV are becoming the norm. Many budget places make their bread and butter from their on-site restaurants, which serve the classic backpacker fare (banana pancakes and fruit shakes).

Homestays

A visit to a homestay is one of the best ways to experience Thailand's rural culture, not to mention a way to ensure that your baht are going directly to locals. More popular with domestic tourists, homestays differ from guesthouses in that visitors are welcomed into a family's home, typically in a small village that isn't on the tourist trail. Accommodation is basic: usually a mat or foldable mattress on the floor, or occasionally a family will have a private room. Rates include lodging, meals with the family and cultural activities that highlight the region's traditional way of life, from rice farming to silk weaving. English fluency varies, so homestays are also

an excellent way to exercise your spoken Thai.

Hotels

With the increase in domestic tourism and the expanding international traveller's budget, hotels have graduated from musty concrete boxes to designer 'experiences'. These boutique hotels are good value for comfort and character. It is standard in most midrange hotels for rooms to come with air-con, fridge, hot water, TV and wi-fi. Add-ons include breakfast, which can range from 'buffets' based around toast and oily fried eggs (often referred to as 'ABF', meaning 'American breakfast') to healthier meals involving yoghurt or tropical fruit.

Midrange and chain hotels, especially in major tourist destinations, can be booked in advance and some offer discounts through their websites or online agents.

International chain hotels can be found in Bangkok, Chiang Mai, Phuket and other high-end beach resorts. The more thoughtful places have amenities such as in-room computers and free wi-fi; otherwise, it's not uncommon to have to pay a premium for the latter. Pools are almost standard, not to mention fitness and business centres, restaurants and bars. Breakfast is often buffet-style. Most top-end hotels and some midrange hotels add a 7% government

BOOK YOUR STAY ONLINE

For more accommodation reviews by Lonely Planet authors, check out http://lonelyplanet.com/hotels/. You'll find independent reviews, as well as recommendations on the best places to stay. Best of all, you can book online.

tax (VAT) and an additional 10% service charge. The additional charges are often referred to as 'plus plus'.

In provincial capitals and small towns, the only options are often ageing Thai-Chinese hotels, once the standard in all of Thailand. Most cater to Thai guests and English is usually limited. These hotels are multistorey buildings generally offering rooms ranging from bare, fan-cooled cheapies to ones with private bathrooms, air-con and TV. Although some Thai-Chinscamsese hotels are appealing for their retro charm, we've found that, unless the establishment has been recently refurbished, they are generally too old and worn to represent good value compared to guesthouses.

National Parks Accommodation

Most national parks have bungalows or campsites. Bungalows typically sleep as many as 10 people and rates range from 2000B to 3000B, depending on the park and the size of the bungalow. These are popular with extended Thai families who bring enough provisions to survive the Apocalypse.

Camping is possible at many parks for around 150B per night. Some parks rent tents and other sleeping gear, but the condition of the equipment can be poor.

Reservations for all park accommodation must be made in advance through the online system of the **National Park Office** (02 562 0760; http://nps.dnp.go.th; 61 Th Phahonyothin).

Children

Kids are welcome almost anywhere in Thailand and you'll rarely experience the sort of eye-rolling annoyance sometimes seen in the West. For more on travelling as a family in Thailand, see Travel with Children (p59).

Customs Regulations

If you have imported goods to declare, you can get the proper form from Thai customs officials at your point of entry. The **Customs Department** (nationwide 02 667 6000; www.customs.go.th) maintains a helpful website with specific information about regulations for travellers. Thailand allows

Climate

Bangkok
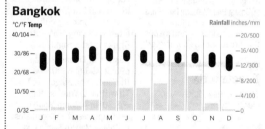

Chiang Mai
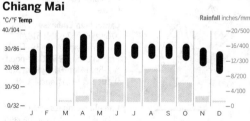

Phuket
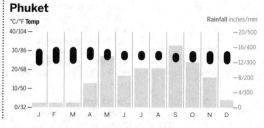

the following items to enter duty-free:

➡ reasonable amount of personal effects (clothing and toiletries)

➡ professional instruments

➡ 200 cigarettes

➡ 1L of wine or spirits

Thailand prohibits the import of the following items:

➡ firearms and ammunition (unless registered in advance with the police department)

➡ illegal drugs

➡ pornographic media

When leaving Thailand, you must obtain an export licence for any antique reproductions or newly cast Buddha images. Submit two photos of the object(s), a photocopy of your passport, the purchase receipt and the object(s) in question to the **Office of the National Museum** (Map p82; ☎02 224 1370; National Museum, 4 Th Na Phra That, Bangkok; ⊙9am-4pm Tue-Fri; 🚤Chang Pier, Maharaj Pier, Phra Chan Tai Pier). Allow four days for the application and inspection process to be completed.

Electricity

Thailand uses 220V AC electricity.

Type A
120V/60Hz

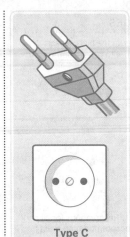

Type C
220V/50Hz

Embassies & Consulates

Foreign embassies are located in Bangkok; some nations also have consulates in Chiang Mai, Pattaya, Phuket and Songkhla.

Australian Embassy (Map p96;☎02 344 6300; www.thailand.embassy.gov.au; 181 Th Witthayu/Wireless Rd; ⊙8.30am-4.30pm Mon-Fri; ℳLumphini exit 2) Consulates in Chiang Mai, Ko Samui and Phuket.

Cambodian Embassy (Map p76;☎02 957 5851; 518/4 Soi Ramkhamhaeng 39, Th Pracha Uthit; ⊙8.30am-noon & 2-5pm Mon-Fri; ℳPhra Ram 9 exit 3 & taxi) Consulate in Sa Kaew.

Canadian Embassy (Map p96; ☎02 646 4300; www.thailand.gc.ca; 15th fl, Abdulrahim Pl, 990 Rama IV; ⊙9am-noon Mon-Fri; ℳSi Lom exit 2, 🚈Sala Daeng exit 4) Consulate in Chiang Mai (☎05 3850147; 151 Superhighway, Tambon Tahsala; ⊙9am-noon Mon-Fri).

French Embassy (Map p92; ☎02 657 5100; www.amba france-th.org; 35 Soi 36/Rue de Brest, Th Charoen Krung; ⊙8.30am-noon Mon-Fri; 🚤Oriental Pier) Consulates in Chiang Mai (Map p312; ☎053 281466; 138 Th Charoen Prathet, Chiang Mai; ⊙10am-noon Mon-Fri), Chiang Rai and Pattaya.

German Embassy (Map p96; ☎02 287 9000; www.bangkok.diplo.de; 9 Th Sathon Tai/South, Bangkok; ⊙7.30-11.30am Mon-Fri; ℳLumphini exit 2)

Irish Embassy (Map p102; ☎02 016 1360; www.dfa.ie/irish-embassy/thailand; 12th fl, 208 Th Witthayu/Wireless Rd; ⊙9.30am-12.30pm & 2.30-3.30pm Mon-Thu, 9.30-noon Fri; 🚈Phloen Chit exit 1)

Laotian Embassy (Map p76; ☎02 539 6667; 502/1-3 Soi Sahakarnpramoon, Th Pracha Uthit/Soi Ramkhamhaeng 39, Bangkok; ⊙8am-noon & 1-4pm Mon-Fri; ℳPhra Ram 9 exit 3 & taxi)

Malaysian Embassy (Map p96; ☎02 629 6800; www.kln.gov.my/web/tha_bangkok/home; 33-35 Th Sathon Tai/South; ⊙8am-4pm Mon-Fri; ℳLumphini exit 2) Consulate in Songkhla.

Myanmar Embassy (Map p98; ☎02 233 7250; www.myanmarembassybkk.com; 132 Th Sathon Neua/North, Bangkok; ⊙9am-noon & 1-3pm Mon-Fri; 🚈Surasak exit 3)

Netherlands Embassy (Map p102;☎02 309 5200; www.netherlandsworldwide.nl/countries/thailand; 15 Soi Ton Son; ⊙8.30am-noon & 1.30-4.30pm Mon-Thu, 8.30-11.30am Fri; 🚈Chit Lom exit 4)

New Zealand Embassy (Map p102;☎02 254 2530; www.nzembassy.com/thailand; 14th fl, M Thai Tower, All Seasons Pl, 87 Th Witthayu/Wireless Rd, Bangkok; ⊙8am-noon & 1-2.30pm Mon-Fri; 🚈Phloen Chit exit 5)

UK Embassy (Map p102; ☐02 305 8333; www.gov.uk/govern ment/world/organisations/ british-embassy-bangkok; 14 Th Witthayu/Wireless Rd, Bangkok; ☉8am-4.30pm Mon-Thu, to 1pm Fri; ⑤Phloen Chit exit 5)

US Embassy (Map p102; ☐02 205 4000; https://th.us embassy.gov; 95 Th Witthayu/ Wireless Rd; ☉8am-4pm Mon-Fri; ⑤Phloen Chit exit 5) Consulate in **Chiang Mai** (Map p318; ☐05 3107700; https://th.usembassy.gov; 387 Th Wichayanon; ☉8am-3.30pm Tue & Thu).

Food

For many visitors, food is one of the main reasons for choosing Thailand as a destination. Even more remarkable, however, is the locals' own love for food: Thais get just as excited as tourists when presented with a bowl of perfectly prepared noodles, or when seated at a renowned hawker stall. For more information on Thailand's food scene, see Eat & Drink Like a Local (p43).

Insurance

A comprehensive travel-insurance policy to cover theft, loss and medical problems is a good idea. Be sure that your policy covers ambulances or an emergency flight home. Some policies specifically exclude 'dangerous activities', which can include scuba diving, motorcycling and even trekking. A locally acquired motorcycle licence is not valid under some policies. You may prefer a policy that pays doctors or hospitals directly rather than you having to pay on the spot and claim later. If you have to claim later, make sure you keep all documentation.

Worldwide travel insurance is available at www.lonelyplanet.com/travel-

insurance. You can buy, extend and claim online any time – even if you're already on the road.

Internet Access

Wi-fi is almost standard in hotels, guesthouses and cafes. Signal strength deteriorates in the upper floors of a multistorey building; request a room near a router if wi-fi is essential. Cellular data networks continue to expand and increase in capability.

LGBT Travellers

Thai culture is relatively tolerant of both male and female homosexuality. There is a fairly prominent LGBT scene in Bangkok, Pattaya and Phuket. With regard to dress or mannerism, the LGBT community are generally accepted without comment. However, public displays of affection – whether heterosexual or homosexual – are frowned upon.

It's worth noting that, perhaps because Thailand is still a relatively conservative place, lesbians generally adhere to rather strict gender roles. Overtly 'butch' lesbians, called *tom* (from 'tomboy'), typically have short hair, and wear men's clothing. Femme lesbians refer to themselves as *dêe* (from 'lady'). Visiting lesbians who don't fit into one of these categories may find themselves met with confusion.

Utopia (www.utopia-asia. com) posts lots of Thailand information for LGBT travellers and publishes a gay guidebook to the kingdom.

Legal Matters

In general Thai police don't hassle foreigners, especially tourists. They usually go out of their way to avoid having to speak English with a foreigner, especially regarding minor traffic issues. Thai police do, however, rigidly enforce laws against drug possession. Do be aware that some police divisions, especially on the Thai islands, might view foreigners and their legal infractions as a money-making opportunity.

If you are arrested for any offence, the police will allow you the opportunity to make a phone call, either to your embassy or consulate in Thailand if you have one, or to a friend or relative if not. There's a whole set of legal codes governing the length of time and the manner in which you can be detained before being charged or put on trial, but a lot of discretion is left to the police. In the case of foreigners the police are more likely to bend these codes in your favour. However, as with police worldwide, if you don't show respect you will make matters worse.

Thai law does not presume an indicted detainee to be either guilty or innocent but rather a 'suspect', whose guilt or innocence will be decided in court. Trials are usually speedy.

The **tourist police** (☐24hr 1155) can be very helpful in cases of arrest. Although they typically have no jurisdiction over the kinds of cases handled by regular cops, they may be able to help with translations or with contacting your embassy. You can call the hotline to lodge complaints or to request assistance with regards to personal safety.

Money

The basic unit of Thai currency is the baht. There are 100 satang in one baht; coins include 25-satang and 50-satang pieces and baht in 1B, 2B, 5B and 10B coins. Older coins have Thai numerals only, while newer coins have Thai and Arabic numerals. The 2B coin is similar in size to the 1B coin but it is gold in colour. The two satang coins are typically only issued at supermarkets where prices aren't rounded up to the nearest baht.

Paper currency is issued in the following denominations: 20B (green), 50B (blue), 100B (red), 500B (purple) and 1000B (beige).

Most places in Thailand deal only with cash. Some foreign credit cards are accepted in high-end establishments.

ATMs & Credit/Debit Cards

Debit and ATM cards issued by a bank in your own country can be used at ATMs around Thailand to withdraw cash (in Thai baht only) directly from your account back home. ATMs are extremely ubiquitous throughout the country and can be relied on for the bulk of your spending cash. Most ATMs allow a maximum of 20,000B in withdrawals per day.

The downside is that Thai ATMs charge a 200B foreign-transaction fee on top of whatever currency conversion and out-of-network fees your home bank charges. Before leaving home, shop around for a bank account that has free international ATM usage and reimburses fees incurred at other institutions' ATMs.

Credit and debit cards can be used for purchases at some shops, hotels and restaurants. The most commonly accepted cards are Visa and MasterCard. American Express is typically only accepted at high-end hotels and restaurants.

Contact your bank and your credit-card provider before you leave home and notify them of your upcoming trip so that your accounts aren't suspended due to suspicious overseas activity.

Changing Money

Banks or private money changers offer the best foreign-exchange rates. When buying baht, US dollars is the most accepted currency, followed by British pounds and euros. Most banks charge a commission and duty for each travellers cheque cashed. Current exchange rates are posted at exchange counters.

Foreign Currency Regulations

Visitors must declare cash over US$20,000 when arriving or departing. There are also certain monetary requirements for foreigners entering Thailand; demonstration of adequate funds varies per visa type but typically does not exceed a traveller's estimated trip budget. It's rare that you'll be asked to produce such financial evidence, but be aware that these laws do exist. The **Ministry of Foreign Affairs** (☏02 203 5000; www.mfa.go.th) can provide more detailed information.

Taxes & Refunds

Thailand has a 7% value-added tax (VAT) on many goods and services. Mid-range and top-end hotels and restaurants might also add a 10% service tax. When the two are combined this becomes the 17% hit known as 'plus plus', or '++'.

You can get a refund on VAT paid on shopping, though not on food or hotels, as you leave the country. For how-to info, visit www.rd.go.th.

Tipping

Tipping is not generally expected in Thailand, though it is appreciated. The exception is loose change from a large restaurant bill – if a

---

PRACTICALITIES

Newspapers English-language newspapers include the *Bangkok Post* (www.bangkokpost.com), the business-heavy *Nation* (www.nationmultimedia.com) and *KhaoSod English* (www.khaosodenglish.com), the English-language service of a mainstream Thai newspaper. Weeklies such as the *Economist* and *Time* are sold at news stands.

Radio There are more than 400 AM and FM radio stations. Many smaller radio stations and international services are available to stream over the internet.

TV Six VHF TV networks carry Thai programming, plus TrueVision cable with international programming. Digital programming has increased programming.

Smoking Banned in restaurants and bars since 2008.

Weights & Measures The metric system is used. Gold and silver are weighed in *bàat* (15g).

meal costs 488B and you pay with a 500B note, some Thais will leave the change. It's a way of saying 'I'm not so money grubbing as to grab every last baht'. At many hotel restaurants and upmarket eateries, a 10% service charge will be added to your bill.

Opening Hours

Banks and government offices close for national holidays. Some bars and clubs close during elections and certain holidays when alcohol sales are banned. Shopping centres have banks that open late.

Banks 8.30am–4.30pm; 24hr ATMs

Bars 6pm–midnight or 1am

Clubs 8pm–2am

Government Offices 8.30am–4.30pm Monday–Friday; some close for lunch

Restaurants 8am–10pm

Shops 10am–7pm

Photography

Be considerate when taking photographs of locals. Learn how to ask politely in Thai and wait for an embarrassed nod. In some of the regularly visited hill-tribe areas, be prepared for the photographed subject to ask for money in exchange for a picture. Other hill tribes will not allow you to point a camera at them.

Post

Thailand has a very efficient postal service and local postage is inexpensive. Typical provincial post offices open from 8.30am to 4.30pm weekdays and 9am to noon on Saturdays. Larger main post offices in provincial capitals may also be open for a half-day on Sunday.

Most provincial post offices will sell DIY packing boxes. Don't send cash or other valuables through the mail.

Thailand's poste restante service is generally very reliable, though these days few tourists use it. When you receive mail, you must show your passport and fill out some paperwork.

Public Holidays

Government offices and banks close their doors on the following public holidays. For the precise dates of lunar holidays, see the Events & Festivals page of the Tourism Authority of Thailand (www.tourismthailand.org/Events-and-Festivals) website.

1 January New Year's Day

February (date varies) Makha Bucha Day; Buddhist holy day

6 April Chakri Day; commemorating the founder of the Chakri dynasty, Rama I

13–15 April Songkran Festival

1 May Labour Day

5 May Coronation Day

May/June (date varies) Visakha Bucha; Buddhist holy day

28 July King Maha Vajiralongkorn's Birthday

July/August (date varies) Asanha Bucha; Buddhist holy day

12 August Queen Sirikit's Birthday/Mother's Day

23 October Chulalongkorn Day

5 December Commemoration of Late King Bhumiphol/Father's Day

10 December Constitution Day

31 December New Year's Eve

Safe Travel

Thailand is generally a safe country to visit, but it's smart to exercise caution, especially when it comes to dealing with strangers (both Thai and foreigners) and travelling alone.

Assault

Assault of travellers is relatively rare in Thailand, but it does happen. Causing a Thai to 'lose face' (feel public embarrassment or humiliation) can sometimes elicit an inexplicably strong and violent reaction. Often alcohol is the number-one contributor.

Border Issues

Thailand now enjoys friendly relations with its neighbours, and most land borders are fully functional passages for goods and people. However, the ongoing violence in the Deep South has made the crossing at Sungai Kolok into Malaysia dangerous, and most Muslim-majority provinces (Yala, Pattani, Narathiwat and Songkhla) should be avoided by casual visitors.

Check with your government's foreign ministry for current travel warnings (p762).

Drugs

Belying Thailand's anything-goes atmosphere are strict punishments for possession and trafficking of drugs, which are not relaxed for foreigners. It is illegal to buy, sell or possess opium, heroin, amphetamines, hallucinogenic mushrooms and marijuana. Possession of drugs can result in at least one year or more of prison time. Drug smuggling – defined as attempting to cross a border with drugs in your possession – carries considerably higher sanctions, including the death penalty.

Scams

Thais can be so friendly and laid-back that some visitors are lulled into a false sense of security, making them vulnerable to scams of all kinds. Bangkok is especially good at long, involved frauds (p154) that dupe travellers into thinking they've made a friend and are getting a bargain, when in fact they are getting ripped off.

All offers of free shopping or sightseeing help from strangers should be ignored. They will invariably take a commission from your purchases.

Theft & Fraud

Exercise diligence when it comes to your personal belongings. Ensure your room is securely locked and carry your most important effects (passport, money, credit cards) on your person. Take care when leaving valuables in hotel safes.

Follow the same practice when you're travelling. A locked bag will not prevent theft on a long-haul bus.

To avoid losing all of your travel money in an instant, use a credit card that is not directly linked to your bank account so that the operator doesn't have access to immediate funds.

Touts & Commissions

Touting is a long tradition in Asia, and while Thailand doesn't have as many touts as, say, India, it has its share. In Bangkok, túk-túk drivers and other new 'friends' often take new arrivals on city tours. These almost always end up in high-pressure sales situations at silk, jewellery or handicraft shops.

Touts also steer customers to certain guesthouses that pay a commission. Travel agencies are notorious for talking newly arrived tourists into staying at inconveniently located, overpriced hotels thanks to commissions.

Some travel agencies masquerade as TAT, the government-funded tourist information office.

Shopping

Many bargains await you in Thailand, but don't go shopping in the company of touts, tour guides or friendly strangers as they will inevitably take a commission on anything you buy, thus driving prices up beyond an acceptable value and creating a nuisance for future visitors.

Antiques

Real Thai antiques are increasingly rare. Today most dealers sell antique reproductions or items from Myanmar. Bangkok and Chiang Mai are the two centres for the antique and reproduction trade.

Real antiques cannot be taken out of Thailand without a permit. No Buddha image, new or old, may be exported without the permission of the **Office of the National Museum** (Map p82; ⌖02

224 1370; National Museum, 4 Th Na Phra That, Bangkok; ⏰9am-4pm Tue-Fri; 🚢Chang Pier, Maharaj Pier, Phra Chan Tai Pier).

Ceramics

Many kinds of hand-thrown pottery, old and new, are available throughout the kingdom. Bangkok is full of modern ceramic designs, while Chiang Mai sticks to traditional styles. Ko Kret, outside of Bangkok, and Dan Kwian, in Nakhon Ratchasima Province, are two traditional pottery villages.

Clothing

Clothes tend to be inexpensive in Thailand, but ready-made items are not usually cut to fit Westerners' body types. Increasingly, larger-sized clothes are available in metropolitan shopping malls or tourist centres. Markets sell cheap everyday items while Bangkok leads the country with design-minded fashions. Finding shoes that fit larger feet is also a problem. The custom of returns is not widely accepted in Thailand, so be sure of your purchases before you leave the store.

Thailand has a long sartorial tradition, practiced mainly by Thai-Indian Sikh families. But this industry is filled with cut-rate operators and commission-paying scams. Be wary of the quickie 24-hour tailor shops; they often use inferior fabric and have poor workmanship. It's best to ask long-time foreign residents for a recommendation and then go for two or three fittings.

Fake Goods

In Bangkok, Chiang Mai and other tourist centres there's a thriving black-market street trade in fake designer goods. No one pretends they're the real thing, at least not the vendors. Technically it is illegal for these items to be produced and sold, and

Thailand has often been pressured by intellectual property enforcement agencies to close down the trade. More recently, fake goods are being imported from Chinese factories or produced by factories that no longer have an up-to-date copyright license. Police crackdowns occur when pressured from the top or when the vendors don't pay the requisite bribes. Often the vendors develop more surreptitious means of distribution. In Bangkok's Patpong market, for example, a vendor might show you a picture of a knock-off watch, you pay for it and they go around the corner to fetch it. They usually come back, but you'll wait long enough to wonder.

Furniture

Rattan and hardwood furniture items are often good purchases and can be made to order. Chiang Mai is the country's primary furniture producer with many retail outlets in Bangkok. Due to the ban on teak harvesting and the subsequent exhaustion of recycled teak, 70% of export furniture produced in Thailand is made from parawood, a processed wood from rubber trees that can no longer be used for latex production.

Gems & Jewellery

Thailand is a leading exporter of gems and ornaments, rivalled only by India and Sri Lanka. Although rough-stone sources in Thailand have decreased dramatically, stones are now imported from Myanmar, Sri Lanka and other countries to be cut, polished and traded.

Although there are a lot of gem and jewellery stores in Thailand, it has become so difficult to dodge the scammers that the country no longer represents a safe and enjoyable place to buy these goods. It is better just to window shop.

BARGAINING

Thais respect a good haggler. Always let the vendor make the first offer, then ask 'Can you lower the price?'. This usually results in a discount. Now it's your turn to make a counter-offer. Always start low, but don't bargain unless you're serious about buying. If you're buying several of an item, you have much more leverage to request and receive a lower price. It helps immeasurably to keep the negotiations relaxed and friendly.

Lacquerware

Chiang Mai is known for gold-on-black lacquerware. Lacquerware furniture and decorative items were traditionally made from bamboo and teak, but these days mango wood might be used as the base. If the item is top quality, only the frame is bamboo and horse or donkey hairs will be wound round it. With lower-quality lacquerware, the whole object is made from bamboo. The lacquer is then coated over the framework and allowed to dry. After several days it is sanded down with ash from rice husks, and another coating of lacquer is applied. A high-quality item may have seven layers of lacquer. The piece is then engraved, painted and polished to remove the paint from everywhere except in the engravings. Multicoloured lacquerware is produced by repeated applications.

It can take five or six months to produce a high-quality piece of lacquerware, which may have as many as five colours. Flexibility is one characteristic of good lacquerware: a well-made bowl can have its rim squeezed together until the sides meet without suffering damage. The quality and precision of the engraving is another thing to look for.

Textiles

The northeast is famous for *mát·mèe* cloth, a thick cotton or silk fabric woven from tie-dyed threads, similar to Indonesia's *ikat* fabrics. Surin Province is renowned for its *mát·mèe* silk, often showcasing colours and geometric patterns inherited from Khmer traditions.

In the north, silks reflect the influence of the Lanna weaving traditions, brought to Chiang Mai and the surrounding mountains by the various Tai tribes.

Fairly nice batik is available in the south in patterns that are more similar to the batik found in Malaysia than in Indonesia.

Each hill tribe has a tradition of embroidery that has been translated into the modern marketplace as bags and jewellery. Much of what you'll find in the marketplaces has been machine made, but there are many NGO cooperatives that help villagers get their handmade goods to the consumers. Chiang Mai and Chiang Rai are filled with handicraft outlets.

Telephone

The telephone country code for Thailand is ☑66 and is used when calling the country from abroad.

Domestic Calls

Inside Thailand all telephone numbers include an initial '0' plus the area code and the subscriber number. The only time you drop the initial '0' is when you're calling from outside Thailand. If the initial '0' is followed by a '6', an '8' or a '9' then you're dialling a mobile phone.

International Calls

If you want to call an international number from a telephone in Thailand, you must first dial an international access code plus the country code followed by the subscriber number.

In Thailand there are various international access codes charging different rates per minute. The standard direct-dial prefix is ☎001; it is operated by CAT and is considered to have the best sound quality. It connects to the largest number of countries, but it is also the most expensive. The next best is ☎007, a prefix operated by TOT with reliable quality and slightly cheaper rates. Economy rates are available through different carriers – do an internet search to determine promotion codes.

Mobile Phones

The easiest option is to acquire a mobile (cell) phone equipped with a local SIM card. Buying a prepaid SIM is as simple as finding a 7-Eleven. SIM cards include talk and data packages and you can add more funds with a prepaid reload card.

Time

Thailand is seven hours ahead of GMT/UTC (London). Times are often expressed according to the 24-hour clock.

Toilets

Increasingly, the Asian-style squat toilet is less of the norm in Thailand. There are still specimens in rural places, provincial bus stations, older homes and modest restaurants, but the Western-style toilet is becoming more prevalent and appears wherever foreign tourists can be found.

If you encounter a squat, here's what you should know. You should straddle the two foot pads and face the door. To flush use the plastic bowl to scoop water out of the adjacent basin and pour into the toilet bowl. Some places supply a small pack of toilet paper at the entrance (5B), otherwise bring your own stash or wipe the old-fashioned way with water.

Even in places where sit-down toilets are installed, the septic system may not be designed to take toilet paper. In such cases there will be a waste basket where you're supposed to place used toilet paper and feminine hygiene products. Some toilets also come with a small spray hose – Thailand's version of the bidet.

Tourist Information

The government-operated tourist information and promotion service, **Tourism Authority of Thailand** (TAT; ☎nationwide call centre 1672; www.tourismthailand.org), was founded in 1960 and produces excellent pamphlets on sightseeing. The TAT head office is in Bangkok and there are 35 regional offices throughout the country; check the website for contact information.

Travellers with Disabilities

Thailand presents one large, ongoing obstacle course for the mobility impaired. With its high kerbs, uneven footpaths and nonstop traffic, Thai cities can be particularly difficult. In Bangkok many streets must be crossed on pedestrian bridges flanked by steep stairways, while buses and boats don't stop long enough even for the fully mobile. Rarely are there any ramps or other access points for wheelchairs.

A number of more expensive top-end hotels make consistent design efforts to provide disabled access to their properties. Other deluxe hotels with high employee-to-guest ratios are usually good about accommodating the mobility impaired by providing staff help where building design fails. For the rest, you're pretty much left to your own resources.

Download Lonely Planet's free Accessible Travel guide from http://lptravel.to/accessibletravel. Alternatively, some organisations and publications that offer tips on international travel include the following:

Accessible Journeys (www.disabilitytravel.com)

Asia Pacific Development Centre on Disability (www.apcdfoundation.org)

Mobility International USA (www.miusa.org)

Society for Accessible Travel & Hospitality (www.sath.org)

Wheelchair Holidays @ Thailand (www.wheelchairtours.com)

Visas

For visitors from most countries, visas are generally not required for stays of up to 30 days.

The **Ministry of Foreign Affairs** (☐02 203 5000; www.mfa.go.th) oversees immigration and visa issues. There are frequent modifications of visa regulations so check the website or the nearest Thai embassy or consulate for application procedures and costs. The best online monitor is Thaivisa (www.thaivisa.com).

Tourist Visas & Exemptions

Thailand has visa-exemption and visa-on-arrival agreements with most nations (including European countries, Australia, New Zealand and the USA). Nationals from these countries can enter Thailand at no charge without pre-arranged documentation. Depending on nationality, these citizens are issued a 14- to 90-day visa exemption. Note that for some nationalities, less time (15 days rather than 30 days) is given if arriving by land rather than air. Check the **Ministry of Foreign Affairs** (☐02 203 5000; www.mfa.go.th) website for more details.

If you don'y have proof of an onward ticket and sufficient funds for your projected stay, you can be denied entry, but in practice this is a formality that is rarely checked.

If you plan to stay in Thailand for longer than 30 days, you should apply for the 60-day tourist visa from a Thai consulate or embassy before you depart for your trip. Recent changes to this visa now allow multiple entries within a six-month period. Contact the nearest Thai embassy or consulate to obtain application procedures and determine fees for tourist visas.

Non-Immigrant Visas

The non-immigrant visa is good for 90 days and is intended for foreigners entering the country for business, study, retirement and extended family visits. There are multiple-entry visas available in this visa class. If you plan to apply for a Thai work permit, you'll need to possess a non-immigrant visa first.

Visa Extensions & Renewals

If you decide you want to stay longer than the allotted time, you can extend your visa by applying at any immigration office in Thailand. The usual fee for a visa extension is 1900B. Those issued with a standard stay of 15 or 30 days can extend their stay for 30 days if the extension is handled before the visa expires. The 60-day tourist visa can be extended by up to 30 days at the discretion of Thai immigration authorities.

Another visa-renewal option is to cross a land border. A new 15- or 30-day visa exemption, depending on the nationality, will be issued upon your return. Be aware that the authorities frown upon repeated 'visa runs' and discretion is up to the visa agent. After the 2014 coup, the military government ceased issuance of land visa exemptions for a period of time. Before undertaking this option, determine the current situation.

If you overstay your visa, the usual penalty is a fine of 500B per day, which is capped at 20,000B. Fines can be paid at the airport, or in advance at an immigration office. If you've overstayed only one day, you don't have to pay. Children under 15 travelling with a parent do not have to pay the penalty.

Foreign residents in Thailand should arrange visa extensions at the immigration office closest to their in-country address.

Volunteering

There are many wonderful volunteering organisations in Thailand that provide meaningful work and cultural engagement. Volunteer Work Thailand (www.volunteerworkthailand.org) maintains a database of opportunities. For more information about volunteering in Thailand, see Responsible Travel (p752).

Women Travellers

Women travellers face relatively few problems in Thailand. It is respectful to cover up if you're going deep into rural communities, entering temples or going to and from the beach. But on the whole, local women dress in a variety of different styles (particularly in cities), so you can usually wear spaghetti strap tops and short skirts without offending Thais' modesty streak.

As in most countries, attacks and rapes do occur, especially when an attacker observes a vulnerable target. If you return home from a bar alone, be sure to have your wits about you. Avoid accepting rides from strangers late at night. Some women may prefer to avoid travelling around isolated areas alone.

Keep Thai etiquette in mind during social interactions. A Thai man could feel a loss of face if conversation, flirting or other attention is directed towards him and then diverted to another person. In extreme cases (or where alcohol is involved), this could create an unpleasant situation or even lead to violence. Women who aren't interested in romantic encounters should not presume that Thai men have merely platonic motives.

Work

Thailand is a huge destination for temporary work stints, especially those involving second-language English teaching. To work legally in the country, you will need a non-immigrant visa (p765) and a work permit – which legitimate institutions should be able to provide. An excellent online resource for background on teaching in Thailand, as well as a resource for jobs, is Ajarn. com (www.ajarn.com).

Transport

GETTING THERE & AWAY

Flights and tours can be booked online at www.lonely planet.com/bookings.

Entering the Country

Entry procedures for Thailand, by air or land, are straightforward: you'll have to show your passport and boarding pass as well as completed arrival and departure cards. You do not have to fill in a customs form on arrival unless you have imported goods to declare.

Air

Note that air fares during the high season (December to March) can be expensive and seats book up quickly.

Airports

Thai Airways is the national carrier, and Bangkok is the country's primary international and domestic gateway. Thailand's provincial airports support an extensive domestic and growing international network. Airports with international connections include the following:

Suvarnabhumi International Airport (Map p158; ☎02 132 1888; www.suvarnabhumiairport.com) The country's main air terminal is located in Samut

Prakan, 30km east of Bangkok and 110km from Pattaya. The airport's name is pronounced *sù·wán·na·poom*.

Don Mueang International Airport (Map p158; ☎02 535 2111; www.donmueangairportthai.com) Located 25km north of central Bangkok, Don Mueang was retired from service in 2006 only to reopen later as the city's de facto budget and domestic hub.

Phuket International Airport (☎076 632 7230; www.phuketairportthai.com) With several domestic and international destinations.

Chiang Mai International Airport (Map p312; ☎05 327 0222; www.chiangmaiairportthai.com) International destinations include many Asian and Southeast Asian cities.

Chiang Rai International Airport (Mae Fah Luang International Airport; ☎053 798 000; http://chiangraiairportthai.com) International destinations include Kunming, China.

Hat Yai International Airport (☎074 227131; www.hatyai-airportthai.com) International destinations are limited to Kuala Lumpur and Singapore.

Ko Samui Airport (Map p528; www.samuiairportonline.com) International destinations include Singapore.

Krabi International Airport International destinations include Doha, Kuala Lumpur, Singapore and a few cities in China.

U-Tapao Airport (UTP; ☎038 245595; www.utapao.com) International destinations include Singapore, Kuala Lumpur and a handful of cities in China and Russia.

Departure Tax

Departure tax is included in the price of a ticket.

Land

Thailand shares land borders with Cambodia, Laos, Malaysia and Myanmar. Land travel between all of these countries can be done at

---

TRAVEL AGENTS

In some cases – when travelling to neighbouring countries or to domestic destinations – it is still convenient to use a travel agent in Thailand. The amount of commission an agent will charge varies so shop around to gauge the discrepancy in prices. Agents who accept only cash should hand over the tickets straightaway and not tell you to 'come back tomorrow'.

sanctioned border crossings. With improved highways and new bridges, it is also easier to travel from Thailand to China via Laos.

Border Crossings

CAMBODIA

Cambodian tourist visas (US$30) are available at the border. Bring a passport photo and ignore the runner boys who want to issue a health certificate or other paperwork for additional fees.

Aranya Prathet to Poipet The most direct land route between Bangkok and Siem Reap (for Angkor Wat), connected by direct government bus.

Hat Lek to Krong Koh Kong The coastal crossing for travellers heading to/from Ko Chang/Sihanoukville.

Ban Pakard to Psar Pruhm A back-door route from Ko Chang (via Chanthaburi) to Battambang and Angkor Wat.

Remote crossings include O Smach to Chong Chom (periodically closed due to fighting at Khao Phra Wihan) and Choam to Chong Sa-Ngam; these aren't as convenient as you'll have to hire private transport on the Cambodian side of the border.

LAOS

It is fairly hassle-free to cross into Laos from northern and northeastern Thailand. Lao tourist visas (US$30 to US$42) can be obtained on arrival; applications require a passport photo and it's a good idea to have crisp, clean bills to pay with. Direct

buses that link major towns on both sides of the border make the border towns just a formality stop. Occasionally Lao officials will ask for an overtime fee.

Nong Khai to Vientiane The first Thai–Lao Friendship Bridge to span the Mekong River is one of the main gateways to/from Laos. Nong Khai is easily reached by train or bus from Bangkok, or air, via Udon Thani.

Chiang Khong to Huay Xai The fourth Thai–Lao Friendship Bridge has increased the popularity of this crossing that links northern Thailand with Luang Prabang via boat. Direct buses from Chiang Mai and Chiang Rai to Laos use this crossing.

Mukdahan to Savannakhet The second Thai–Lao Friendship Bridge provides a trilateral link between Thailand, Laos and Vietnam.

Nakhon Phanom to Tha Khaek The third Thai–Lao Friendship Bridge connects northeastern Thailand to southern Laos.

Chong Mek to Vangtao The border is best accessed via direct bus from Ubon Ratchathani (Thailand) and is a good option for transiting to Pakse (Laos).

In northeastern Thailand, remote crossings include Bueng Kan to Paksan (Lao visas must be arranged in advance) and Tha Li to Kaen Thao (requires chartered transport). In northern Thailand, a remote crossing links Ban Huay Kon, in Nan, and Muang Ngeun.

MALAYSIA

Malaysia, especially the west coast, is easy to reach by bus, train and even boat.

Hat Yai to Butterworth The western spur of the train line originating in Bangkok terminates at Butterworth, the mainland transfer point to Penang.

Hat Yai to Padang Besar Buses and trains originate out of the southern transit town of Hat Yai en route to a variety of Malaysian destinations. Border formalities are handled at Padang Besar.

Sungai Kolok to Rantau Panjang While this border crossing is a possibility, the continued violence in Thailand's Deep South means that we do not recommend it.

Ko Lipe to Langkawi Boats provide a convenient high-season link between these two Andaman islands. There is also boat service to/from the mainland port of Satun (Thailand) to the Malaysian island of Langkawi and the mainland town of Kuala Perlis.

There are a few other minor crossings along this border, but a private vehicle is a necessity.

MYANMAR

There are now four border crossings between Thailand and Myanmar.

Mae Sai to Tachileik This is a popular border-run crossing. It also hosts a popular border market that can be visited on a day trip from Thailand without a pre-arranged visa. For further travel, a pre-arranged visa is required. You can only travel as

---

CLIMATE CHANGE & TRAVEL

Every form of transport that relies on carbon-based fuel generates CO_2, the main cause of human-induced climate change. Modern travel is dependent on aeroplanes, which might use less fuel per kilometre per person than most cars but travel much greater distances. The altitude at which aircraft emit gases (including CO_2) and particles also contributes to their climate change impact. Many websites offer 'carbon calculators' that allow people to estimate the carbon emissions generated by their journey and, for those who wish to do so, to offset the impact of the greenhouse gases emitted with contributions to portfolios of climate-friendly initiatives throughout the world. Lonely Planet offsets the carbon footprint of all staff and author travel.

far as Kyaing Tong in Myanmar by land; onward land travel requires a permit or you can fly to Mandalay or Yangon.

Ranong to Kawthoung This is a popular visa-renewal point in the southern part of Thailand and can be used to enter/exit southern Myanmar.

Mae Sot to Myawaddy One of the most accessible land borders for points within Myanmar.

Phu Nam Ron to Htee Khee This crossing is remote and little used. You cannot enter Myanmar at this point with an e-visa but you can exit. The Thai government intends to develop this route as a link between Bangkok and Myanmar's Dawei port in the Andaman Sea.

Bus, Car & Motorcycle

Road connections exist to all of Thailand's neighbours, and these routes can be travelled by bus, shared taxi and private car. In some cases you'll take a bus to the border point, pass through immigration and then pick up another bus or shared taxi on the other side. In other cases, especially when crossing the Malaysian border, the bus will stop for immigration formalities and then continue to its destination across the border.

Taking a private vehicle across an international border requires some paperwork; it's generally not allowed to take a hired vehicle abroad.

No special permits are needed for bringing a bicycle into Thailand. It's advisable to bring a well-stocked repair kit.

Train

Thailand's and Malaysia's state railways meet at Butterworth (93km south of the Thailand–Malaysia border), which is a transfer point to Penang (by boat), or to Kuala Lumpur and Singapore (by Malaysian train).

There are several border crossings for which you can take a train to the border and

then switch to car transport on the other side. The Thai–Cambodian border crossing of Aranya Prathet to Poipet and the Thai–Lao crossing of Nong Khai to Vientiane are two examples.

Another rail line travels to the Malaysian east-coast border town of Sungai Kolok, but because of ongoing violence in Thailand's Deep South we don't recommend this route for travellers.

Sea

You can cross into and out of Thailand via public boat between the Andaman Coast and the Malaysian island of Langkawi.

GETTING AROUND

Air

Hopping around the country by air continues to be affordable. Most routes originate from Bangkok (both Don Mueang and Suvarnabhumi International Airports), but Chiang Mai, Hat Yai, Ko Samui, Phuket and Udon Thani all have a few routes to other Thai towns.

Airlines

Thai Airways (www.thaiairways.com) operates many domestic air routes from Bangkok to provincial capitals. **Bangkok Air** (www.bangkokair.com) is another established domestic carrier. **Air Asia** (www.airasia.com) and **NokAir** (www.nokair.com) are the domestic budget carriers.

It's also worth checking out the following:

Orient Thai (☑nationwide 02 229 4100; www.flyorientthai.com) From Don Mueang to Phuket.

Thai Lion Air (☑nationwide 02 529 9999; www.lionairthai.com) From Don Mueang to Chiang Mai, Chiang Rai, Hat Yai, Khon Kaen, Krabi, Nakhon Si

Thammarat, Phitsanulok, Phuket, Surat Thani, Trang and Ubon Ratchathani; Chiang Mai to Hat Yai and Surat Thani; and from Hat Yai to Udon Thani.

Thai Smile (☑nationwide 02 118 8888; www.thaismileair.com) From Suvarnabhumi to Chiang Mai, Chiang Rai, Hat Yai, Phuket, Khon Kaen, Krabi, Narathiwat, Surat Thani and Udon Thani; and from Chiang Mai to Phuket.

You may see air tickets on low-cost carriers (mostly Air Asia) that go to islands that don't have airports, such as Ko Phi Phi, Ko Lanta and Ko Ngai. These tickets fly to the nearest airport then include bus and boat transport to the island. If you don't mind being shuttled like cattle, this can be a good option since the cost is about the same as arranging the ground transport by yourself except you don't have the hassle that goes with it.

In other cases carriers may say they go to islands that have airports (like Ko Samui or Ko Pha-Ngan), but actually fly into a nearby airport and include ground and boat transportation in the cost. Make sure you check the details before booking. In these cases the ticket price is usually cheaper than flying to the island direct, although the travel time will be much longer.

Boat

The true Thai water transport is the *reu·a hǎhng yow* (longtail boat), so-called because the propeller is mounted at the end of a long driveshaft extending from the engine. The long-tail boats are a staple of transport on rivers and canals in Bangkok and neighbouring provinces, and between islands.

Between the mainland and small, less-touristed islands, the standard craft is a wooden boat, 8m to 10m long, with an inboard engine, a wheelhouse and a simple roof to shelter passengers and cargo. To more popular destinations, faster hovercraft (jetfoils) and speedboats are the norm.

Bus & Minivan

The bus network in Thailand is prolific and reliable. The Thai government subsidises the Transport Company (bò·rí·sàt kŏn sòng), usually abbreviated to Baw Khaw Saw (BKS). Every city and town in Thailand linked by bus has a BKS station, even if it's just a patch of dirt by the side of the road.

By far the most reliable bus companies in Thailand are the ones that operate out of the BKS stations. In some cases the companies are entirely state owned; in others they are private concessions.

We do not recommend using bus companies that operate directly out of tourist centres, such as Bangkok's Th Khao San, because of repeated instances of theft and commission-seeking stops. Be sure to be aware of bus scams and other common problems.

For an increasing number of destinations, minivans are superseding buses. Minivans are run by private companies and because their vehicles are smaller, they can depart from the market (instead of the out-of-town bus stations) and in some cases will deliver passengers directly to their hotel. Just don't sit in the front – that way you can avoid watching the driver's daredevil techniques!

Bus Classes

The cheapest and slowest buses are the rót tam·má·dah (ordinary fan buses) that stop in every little town and for every waving hand along the highway. Only a few of these ordinary buses still exist, mostly in rural locations or for local destinations.

Rót aa (air-con buses) come in a variety of classes, depending on the destination's distance. Short distances are usually covered by the basic 2nd-class bus, which does not have an on-board toilet. For longer routes, buses increase in comfort and amenities, ranging from 1st class to 'VIP' and 'Super VIP'. The latter two have fewer seats so that each seat reclines further; sometimes these are called rót norn (sleeper buses).

Bring a jacket for long-distance bus trips as air-con keeps the cabin at arctic temperatures. The service on these buses is usually quite good and on certain routes sometimes includes a beverage and video, courtesy of an 'air hostess'.

On overnight journeys the buses usually stop somewhere en route for a midnight meal.

Bus Reservations

You can book air-con BKS buses at any BKS terminal, or even by phone with a payment at 7-Eleven. Ordinary fan buses cannot be booked in advance. Privately run buses can be booked through most hotels or any travel agency.

Car & Motorcycle

Cars, 4WDs and vans can be hired in most major cities and airports from local companies as well as all the usual international chains. Local companies tend to have cheaper rates, but the quality of their fleets vary. Check the tyre tread and general upkeep of the vehicle before committing.

Motorcycles can be hired in major towns and tourist centres from guesthouses and small mom-and-pop businesses. Hiring a motorcycle in Thailand is relatively easy and a great way to independently tour the countryside. For daily hires most businesses will ask that you leave your passport as a deposit. Before hiring a motorcycle, check the vehicle's condition and ask for a helmet (which is required by law).

Driving Licence

In theory short-term visitors who wish to drive vehicles (including motorcycles) in Thailand need an international driving permit (IDP). In reality this is rarely enforced.

Fuel & Spare Parts

Modern petrol (gasoline) stations are plentiful. All fuel in

BICYCLE TRAVEL IN THAILAND

For exploring the more rural, less-trafficked corners of Thailand – Ayuthaya Historical Park, Pai, Sukhothai Historical Park – bicycles are a great way to get around. They can usually be hired from guesthouses for as little as 50B per day, though they aren't always high quality.

Elsewhere, lack of infrastructure and dangerous roads mean that cycling isn't generally recommended as a means of transport for the casual tourist. Exceptions are the guided bicycle tours of Bangkok and some other large cities that stick to rural routes.

Yet despite the risks, bicycle touring is an increasingly popular way to see Thailand, and most roads are sealed and have roomy shoulders. A good resource for cycling in the country is Bicycle Thailand (www.bicyclethailand.com).

Thailand is unleaded; diesel is used by trucks and some passenger cars. Thailand also uses several alternative fuels, including gasohol (a blend of petrol and ethanol that comes in either 91% or 95% octane levels) and compressed natural gas, used by taxis with bi-fuel capabilities. In more rural areas ben·sin/ nám·man rót yon (petrol containing benzene) is usually available at small roadside or village stands.

Insurance

Thailand requires a minimum of liability insurance for all registered vehicles on the road. The better hire companies include comprehensive coverage for their vehicles. Always verify that a vehicle is insured for liability before signing a rental contract; you should also ask to see the dated insurance documents. If you have an accident while driving an uninsured vehicle, you're in for some major hassles.

Road Rules & Hazards

Thais drive on the left-hand side of the road – most of the time! Other than that, just about anything goes, in spite of road signs and speed limits.

The main rule to be aware of is that right of way goes to the bigger vehicle – this is not what it says in the Thai traffic laws, but it's the reality. Maximum speed limits are 50km/h on urban roads and 80km/h to 100km/h on most highways – but on any given stretch of highway you'll see various vehicles travelling as slowly as 30km/h and as fast as 150km/h.

Indicators are often used to warn passing drivers about oncoming traffic. A flashing left indicator means it's OK to pass, while a right indicator means that someone's approaching from the

other direction. Horns are used to tell other vehicles that the driver plans to pass. When drivers flash their lights, they're telling you not to pass.

In Bangkok traffic is chaotic, roads are poorly signposted and motorcycles and random contraflows mean you can suddenly find yourself facing a wall of cars coming the other way.

Outside of the capital, the principal hazard when driving in Thailand, besides the general disregard for traffic laws, is having to contend with so many different types of vehicles on the same road – trucks, bicycles, túk-túk and motorcycles. This danger is often compounded by the lack of working lights. In village areas the vehicular traffic is lighter but you have to contend with stray chickens, dogs and water buffaloes.

Hitching

Hitching is never entirely safe in any country and we don't recommend it. Travellers who decide to hitch should understand that they are taking a small but potentially serious risk. Other than at some national parks where there isn't public transport, hitching is rarely seen these days in Thailand, so most passing motorists might not realise the intentions of the foreigner standing on the side of the road with a thumb out. Indeed, Thais don't 'thumb it'; instead, when they want a ride they wave their hand with the palm facing the ground. This is the same gesture used to flag a taxi or bus, which is why some drivers might stop and point to a bus stop if one is nearby.

ROAD SAFETY

Thailand's roads are dangerous: in 2015 the World Health Organization declared Thailand the second-deadliest country for road fatalities in the world. Several high-profile bus accidents involving foreign tourists have prompted some Western nations to issue travel advisories for highway safety due to disregard for speed limits, reckless driving and long-distance bus drivers' use of stimulants.

Fatal bus crashes make headlines, but nearly 75% of vehicle accidents in Thailand involve motorcycles. Less than half of the motorcyclists in the country wear helmets and many tourists are injured riding motorcycles because they don't know how to handle the vehicles and are unfamiliar with local driving conventions. British consular offices cited Thailand as a primary destination for UK citizens experiencing road-traffic accidents, often involving motorcyclists.

If you are a novice motorcyclist, familiarise yourself with the vehicle in an uncongested area of town and stick to the smaller 100cc automatic bikes. Drive slowly, especially when roads are slick or when there is loose gravel. Remember to distribute weight as evenly as possible across the frame of the bike to improve handling. And don't expect that other vehicles will look out for you: motorcycles are low on the traffic totem pole.

Local Transport

City Bus & Sŏrng·tǎa·ou

Bangkok has the largest city-bus system in the country, while Udon Thani and a few other provincial capitals have some city-bus services. The etiquette for riding public buses is to wait at a bus stop and hail the vehicle by waving your hand palm-side downward. You typically pay the fare once you've taken a seat or, in some cases, when you disembark.

Elsewhere, public transport is provided by sŏrng·tǎa·ou ('two rows'; a small pick-up truck outfitted with two facing benches for passengers). They sometimes operate on fixed routes, just like buses, but they may also run a shared taxi service where they pick up passengers going in the same general direction. In tourist centres, sŏrng·tǎa·ou can be chartered just like a regular taxi, but you'll need to negotiate the fare beforehand. You can usually hail a sŏrng·tǎa·ou anywhere along its route and pay the fare when you disembark.

Depending on the region, sŏrng·tǎa·ou might also run a fixed route from the centre of town to outlying areas, or even points within the provinces.

Mass Transit

Bangkok is the only city in Thailand to have an above-ground (BTS) and under-ground light-rail (MRT) public transport system.

Motorcycle Taxi

Many cities in Thailand have mor·đeu·sai ráp jâhng, motorcycle taxis that can be hired for short distances. If you're empty-handed or trav-elling with a small bag, they can't be beaten for transport in a pinch.

In most cities, you'll find motorcycle taxis clustered near street intersections. Usually they wear numbered jerseys. You'll need to estab-lish the price beforehand.

Taxi

Bangkok has the most formal system of metered taxis, although other cities have growing 'taxi meter' net-works. In some cases, fares are set in advance or require negotiation.

In bigger cities, traditional taxi alternatives and app-based taxi hailing initiatives are also available – at least, sort of.

Introduced to Thailand in 2014, Uber (www.uber. com) quickly gained popu-larity among those looking to avoid the usual Bangkok taxi headaches: communication issues, perpetual lack of change and inability to get a taxi during peak periods. Later that year, however, the service was banned because drivers and the payment sys-tem didn't meet government standards. It continues to operate, although less visibly.

Other app-based services include GrabTaxi (www. grabtaxi.com/th), All Thai Taxi (www.allthaitaxi.com) and Easy Taxi (www.easytaxi. com).

Train

Thailand's train system connects the four corners of the country and is a scenic, if slow, alternative to buses for the long journey north to Chiang Mai or south to Surat Thani. The train is also ideal for short trips to Ayuthaya and Lopburi from Bangkok, where traffic is a consideration.

The 4500km rail network is operated by the **State Railway of Thailand** (SRT; ☑nationwide 1690; www. railway.co.th) and covers four main lines: northern, south-ern, northeastern and east-ern. All long-distance trains originate from Bangkok's Hualamphong Train Station.

Most train stations have printed timetables in English, though this isn't always the case for smaller stations.

Classes

The SRT operates passenger trains in three classes – 1st, 2nd and 3rd – but each class varies considerably depend-ing on whether you're on an ordinary, rapid or express train. In 2016, SRT an-nounced the purchase of 115

SĂHM·LÓR & TÚK-TÚK

Sǎhm·lór (also spelt sǎamláw) are three-wheeled pedi-cabs that are typically found in small towns where traffic is light and old-fashioned ways persist.

The modern era's version of the human-powered sǎhm·lór is the motorised túk-túk (pronounced đúk dúk). They're small utility vehicles, powered by scream-ing engines (usually LPG-powered) with a lot of flash and sparkle.

With either form of transport the fare must be estab-lished by bargaining before departure. In tourist centres, túk-túk drivers often grossly overcharge foreigners, so have a sense of how much the fare should be before soliciting a ride. Hotel staff are helpful in providing rea-sonable fare suggestions.

Readers interested in pedicab lore and design may want to have a look at Lonely Planet's hardcover pictorial book, Chasing Rickshaws by Lonely Planet founder Tony Wheeler.

modern train carriages with seat-mounted TV screens and more comfortable bathrooms, currently in use on the northern and northeastern routes.

1st class Private, two-bunk cabins define the 1st-class carriages, which are available only on rapid, express and special-express trains.

2nd class The seating arrangements in a 2nd-class, non-sleeper carriage are similar to those on a bus, with pairs of padded seats, usually recliners, all facing towards the front of the train. On 2nd-class sleeper cars, pairs of seats face one another and convert into two fold-down berths. The lower berth has more headroom than the upper berth and this is reflected in a higher fare. Children are always assigned a lower berth. Second-class carriages are found only on rapid and express trains. There are air-con and fan 2nd-class carriages.

3rd class A typical 3rd-class carriage consists of two rows of bench seats divided into facing pairs. Each bench seat is designed to seat two or three passengers, but on a crowded rural line nobody seems to care. Express trains do not carry 3rd-class carriages at all. Commuter trains in the Bangkok area are all 3rd class.

Costs

Fares are determined on a base price with surcharges added for distance, class and train type (special express, express, rapid, ordinary). Extra charges are added if the carriage has air-con and for sleeping berths (either upper or lower).

Reservations

Advance bookings can be made from one to 60 days before your intended date of departure. You can make bookings in person from any train station. Train tickets can also be purchased at travel agencies, which usually add a service charge to the ticket price. If you're making an advance reservation from outside the country, contact a licensed travel agent; the SRT previously had an online ticket service but that has been discontinued.

It is advisable to make advanced bookings for long-distance sleeper trains between Bangkok and Chiang Mai, or from Bangkok to Surat Thani, as seats fill up quickly.

For short-distance trips you should purchase your ticket at least a day in advance for seats (rather than sleepers).

Partial refunds on tickets are available depending on the number of days prior to your departure that you arrange a cancellation. These arrangements can be handled at the train station booking office.

Station Services

You'll find that all train stations in Thailand have baggage-storage services (or 'cloak rooms'). Most stations have a ticket window that will open between 15 and 30 minutes before train arrivals. There are also newsagents, small snack vendors and some full-service restaurants.

Health

Health risks and the quality of medical facilities vary depending on where and how you travel in Thailand. The majority of cities and popular tourist areas have adequate, and even excellent, medical care. However, travel to remote rural areas can expose you to some health risks and less adequate medical care.

Travellers tend to worry about contracting exotic infectious diseases when visiting the tropics, but these are far less common than problems with pre-existing medical conditions, such as heart disease, and accidental injury (especially as a result of traffic accidents).

Other common illnesses are respiratory infections, diarrhoea and dengue fever. Fortunately most common illnesses can be prevented or are easily treated.

Our advice is a general guide and does not replace the advice of a doctor trained in travel medicine.

BEFORE YOU GO

Health Insurance

Even if you're fit and healthy, don't travel without health insurance – accidents *do* happen. You may require extra cover for adventure activities such as rock climbing or diving, as well as scooter/motorcycle riding. If your health insurance doesn't cover you for medical expenses abroad, ensure you get specific travel insurance. Most hospitals require an upfront guarantee of payment (from yourself or your insurer) prior to admission. Enquire before your trip about payment of medical charges and retain all documentation (medical reports, invoices etc) for claim purposes.

Recommended Vaccinations

The only vaccine required by international regulations is yellow fever. Proof of vaccination will only be required if you have visited a country in the yellow-fever zone within the six days prior to entering Thailand. If you are travelling to Thailand from Africa or South America you should check to see if you require proof of vaccination.

You should arrange your vaccines six to eight weeks prior to departure through a specialised travel-medicine clinic.

The Centers for Disease Control and Prevention (www.cdc.gov) has a traveller's health section that contains recommendations for vaccinations.

Medication

Pack medications in clearly labelled original containers and obtain a signed and dated letter from your physician describing your medical conditions, medications and syringes or needles. If you have a heart condition, bring a copy of your electrocardiography (ECG) taken just prior to travelling.

If you take any regular medication bring double your needs. In Thailand you can buy many medications over the counter without a doctor's prescription, but it can be difficult to find the exact medication you are taking.

Medical Checklist

Recommended items for a personal medical kit include the following, most of which are available in Thailand.

➡ alcohol-based hand gel or wipes

➡ antifungal cream, eg Clotrimazole

➡ antibacterial cream, eg Muciprocin

➡ antibiotic for skin infections, eg Amoxicillin/Clavulanate or Cephalexin

➡ antibiotics for diarrhoea include Norfloxacin, Ciprofloxacin or Azithromycin for bacterial diarrhoea; for giardiasis or amoebic dysentery take Tinidazole

➡ antihistamine – there are many options, eg Cetrizine for daytime and Promethazine for night-time

➡ antiseptic, eg Betadine

- antispasmodic for stomach cramps, eg Buscopan

- contraceptives

- decongestant

- DEET-based insect repellent

- first-aid items such as scissors, Elastoplasts, bandages, gauze, thermometer (but not one with mercury), sterile needles and syringes (with a doctor's letter), safety pins and tweezers

- ibuprofen or another anti-inflammatory

- indigestion medication, eg Quick-Eze or Mylanta

- laxative, eg Coloxyl

- migraine medicine – for migraine sufferers

- oral rehydration solution for diarrhoea (eg Gastrolyte), diarrhoea 'stopper' (eg Loperamide) and antinausea medication

- paracetamol

- permethrin to impregnate clothing and mosquito nets if at high risk

- steroid cream for allergic/itchy rashes, eg 1% to 2% hydrocortisone

- sunscreen, sunglasses and hat

- throat lozenges

- thrush (vaginal yeast infection) treatment, eg Clotrimazole pessaries or Diflucan tablet

- Ural or equivalent if prone to urinary-tract infections

IN THAILAND

Thailand has a robust healthcare infrastructure. Bangkok is a major destination for medical tourism, and is home to several internationally accredited hospitals. Hospitals and health centres can be found across the country, even in small towns and villages.

Availability & Cost of Health Care

Bangkok is considered a centre of medical excellence in Southeast Asia. Private hospitals are more expensive than other medical facilities, but offer a superior standard of care and English-speaking staff. The cost of health care is relatively cheap in Thailand compared to most Western countries.

Infectious Diseases

Cutaneous Larva Migrans

This disease, caused by dog or cat hookworm, is particularly common on the beaches of Thailand. The rash starts as a small lump, and then slowly spreads like a winding line. It is intensely itchy, especially at night. It is easily treated with medications and should not be cut out or frozen.

Dengue Fever

This mosquito-borne disease is increasingly problematic in Thailand, especially in the cities. As there is no vaccine it can only be prevented by avoiding mosquito bites. The mosquito that carries dengue is a daytime biter, so use insect-avoidance measures at all times. Symptoms include high fever, severe headache (especially behind the eyes), nausea and body aches (dengue was previously known as 'breakbone fever'). Some people develop a rash (which can be very itchy) and experience diarrhoea. Chiang Mai and the southern islands are particularly high-risk areas. There is no specific treatment, just rest and paracetamol – do not take aspirin or ibuprofen as they increase the risk of haemorrhaging. See a doctor to be diagnosed and monitored.

Dengue can progress to the more severe and life-threatening dengue haemorrhagic fever, but this is very uncommon in tourists. The risk of this increases substantially if you have previously been infected with dengue and are then infected with a different serotype.

Hepatitis A

The risk in Bangkok is decreasing, but there is still significant risk in most of the country. This food- and waterborne virus infects the liver, causing jaundice (yellow skin and eyes), nausea and lethargy. There is no specific treatment for hepatitis A. In rare instances it can be fatal for those over the age of 40. All travellers to Thailand should be vaccinated against hepatitis A.

Hepatitis B

The only sexually transmitted disease (STD) that can be prevented by vaccination, hepatitis B is spread by body fluids, including sexual contact. In some parts of Thailand up to 20% of the population are carriers of hepatitis B, and usually are

---

ONLINE RESOURCES

International Travel & Health (www.who.int/ith) Published by the World Health Organization (WHO).

Centers for Disease Control & Prevention (www.cdc.gov) Has country-specific advice.

Travelling Well (www.travellingwell.com.au) A health guidebook and website by Dr Deborah Mills.

RARE BUT BE AWARE...

Avian Influenza Most of those infected have had close contact with sick or dead birds.

Filariasis A mosquito-borne disease that is common in the local population; practice mosquito-avoidance measures.

Hepatitis E Transmitted through contaminated food and water and has similar symptoms to hepatitis A. Can be a severe problem in pregnant women. Follow safe eating and drinking guidelines.

Japanese B Encephalitis Viral disease transmitted by mosquitoes, typically occurring in rural areas. Vaccination is recommended for travellers spending more than one month outside cities, or for long-term expats.

Meliodosis Contracted by skin contact with soil. Affects up to 30% of the local population in northeastern Thailand. The symptoms are very similar to those experienced by tuberculosis (TB) sufferers. There is no vaccine, but it can be treated with medications.

Strongyloides A parasite transmitted by skin contact with soil; common in the local population. It is characterised by an unusual skin rash – a linear rash on the trunk that comes and goes. An overwhelming infection can follow. It can be treated with medications.

Tuberculosis Medical and aid workers and long-term travellers who have significant contact with the local population should take precautions. Vaccination is recommended for children spending more than three months in Thailand. The main symptoms are fever, cough, weight loss, night sweats and tiredness. Treatment is available with long-term multidrug regimens.

Typhus Murine typhus is spread by the bite of a flea; scrub typhus is spread via a mite. Symptoms include fever, muscle pains and a rash. Following general insect-avoidance measures; Doxycycline will also prevent it.

unaware of this. The long-term consequences can include liver cancer, cirrhosis and death.

HIV

HIV is now one of the most common causes of death in people under the age of 50 in Thailand. Always practice safe sex, and avoid getting tattoos or using unclean syringes.

Influenza

Present year-round in the tropics, influenza (flu) symptoms include high fever, muscle aches, runny nose, cough and sore throat. Flu is the most common vaccine-preventable disease contracted by travellers and everyone should consider vaccination. There is no specific treatment, just rest and paracetamol. Complications such as bronchitis or middle-ear infection may require antibiotic treatment.

Leptospirosis

Leptospirosis is contracted from exposure to infected surface water – most commonly after river rafting or canyoning. Early symptoms are very similar to flu and include headache and fever. It can vary from a very mild ailment to a fatal disease. Diagnosis is made through blood tests and it is easily treated with Doxycycline.

Malaria

There is an enormous amount of misinformation concerning malaria. Malaria is caused by a parasite transmitted by the bite of an infected mosquito. The most important symptom of malaria is fever, but general symptoms such as headache, diarrhoea, cough or chills may also occur – the same symptoms as many other infections. A diagnosis can only be made by taking a blood sample.

Most parts of Thailand visited by tourists, particularly city and resort areas, have minimal to no risk of malaria, and the risk of side effects from taking antimalarial tablets is likely to outweigh the risk of getting the disease itself. If you are travelling to high-risk rural areas (unlikely for most visitors), seek medical advice on the right medication and dosage for you.

Measles

This highly contagious viral infection is spread through coughing and sneezing and remains prevalent in Thailand. Measles starts with a high fever and rash and can be complicated by pneumonia and brain disease. There is no specific treatment. Ensure you are fully vaccinated.

Rabies

This disease, fatal if left untreated, is spread by the bite or lick of an infected animal – most commonly a dog or monkey. You should seek medical advice immediately after any animal bite and commence post-exposure treatment. Having a pretravel vaccination means the postbite treatment is greatly simplified.

If an animal bites you, gently wash the wound with soap and water, and apply iodine-based antiseptic. If you are not prevaccinated you will need to receive rabies immunoglobulin as soon as possible, followed by five shots of vaccine over 28 days. If prevaccinated you need just two shots of vaccine given three days apart.

STDs

Sexually transmitted diseases most common in Thailand include herpes, warts, syphilis, gonorrhoea and chlamydia. People carrying these diseases often have no signs of infection. Condoms will prevent gonorrhoea and chlamydia, but not warts or herpes. If after a sexual encounter you develop any rash, lumps, discharge or pain when passing urine, seek immediate medical attention. If you have been sexually active during your travels, have an STD check on your return home.

Typhoid

This serious bacterial infection is spread through food and water. It gives a high and slowly progressive fever, severe headache and may be accompanied by a dry cough and stomach pain. It is diagnosed by blood tests and treated with antibiotics. Vaccination is recommended for all travellers spending more than a week in Thailand, or travelling outside of the major cities. Be aware that vaccination is not 100% effective, so you must still be careful with what you eat and drink.

Environmental Hazards

Food

Eating in restaurants is the biggest risk factor for contracting traveller's diarrhoea. Ways to avoid it include eating only freshly cooked food and avoiding food that has been sitting around in buffets. Peel all fruit and cook vegetables. Eat in busy restaurants with a high turnover of customers.

Heat

For most people it takes at least two weeks to adapt to the hot climate. Prevent swelling of the feet and ankles as well as muscle cramps caused by excessive sweating by avoiding dehydration and excessive activity in the heat of the day.

Heatstroke requires immediate medical treatment. Symptoms come on suddenly and include weakness, nausea, a hot dry body with a body temperature of more than 41°C, dizziness, confusion, loss of coordination, fits and eventually collapse and loss of consciousness.

Insect Bites & Stings

Bedbugs live in the cracks of furniture and walls and then migrate to the bed at night to feed on humans. You can treat the itch with an antihistamine.

Ticks are contracted when walking in rural areas. They are commonly found behind the ears, on the belly and in armpits. If you've been bitten by a tick and a rash develops at the site of the bite or elsewhere, along with fever or muscle aches, see a doctor. Doxycycline prevents tickborne diseases.

Leeches are found in humid rainforests. They do not transmit disease, but their bites are often itchy for weeks afterwards and can easily become infected. Apply an iodine-based antiseptic to the bite to help prevent infection.

Bee and wasp stings mainly cause problems for people who are allergic to them. Anyone with a serious allergy should carry an injection of adrenalin (eg an EpiPen) for emergencies. For others, pain is the main problem – apply ice to the sting and take painkillers.

Jellyfish Stings

Box jellyfish stings are extremely painful and can even be fatal. There are two main types of box

---

MOSQUITO AVOIDANCE TIPS

Travellers are advised to prevent mosquito bites by taking these steps:

➡ use a DEET-containing insect repellent on exposed skin

➡ sleep under a mosquito net, ideally impregnated with permethrin

➡ choose accommodation with screens and fans

➡ impregnate clothing with permethrin in high-risk areas

➡ wear long sleeves and trousers in light colours

➡ use mosquito coils

➡ spray your room with insect repellent before going out

FIRST AID FOR SEVERE JELLYFISH STINGS

For severe, life-threatening envenomations, experts say the first priority is keeping the person alive. Send someone to call for medical help and start immediate CPR if they are unconscious. If the victim is conscious, douse the stung area liberally with vinegar for 30 seconds.

Vinegar can also reduce irritation from minor stings. It is best to seek medical care quickly in case any other symptoms develop over the next 40 minutes.

Australia and Thailand are now working in close collaboration to identify the species of jellyfish in Thai waters, as well as their ecology – hopefully enabling better prediction and detection of the jellyfish.

jellyfish – multi-tentacled and single-tentacled.

Multi-tentacled box jellyfish are present in Thai waters – these are the most dangerous and a severe envenomation can kill an adult within two minutes. They are generally found along sandy beaches near river mouths and mangroves during the warmer months.

There are many types of single-tentacled jellyfish, some of which can cause severe symptoms known as the Irukandji syndrome. The initial sting can seem minor; however, severe symptoms such as back pain, nausea, vomiting, sweating, difficulty breathing and a feeling of impending doom can develop between five and 40 minutes later.

There are many other jellyfish in Thailand that cause irritating stings but no serious effects. The only way to prevent these stings is to wear protective clothing.

Parasites

Numerous parasites are common in local populations in Thailand, but most of these are rare in travellers. To avoid parasitic infections, wear shoes and avoid eating raw food, especially fish, pork and vegetables.

Skin Problems

Prickly heat is a common skin rash in the tropics, caused by sweat being trapped under the skin. Treat by taking cool showers and using powders.

Two fungal rashes commonly affect travellers. The first occurs in the groin, armpits and between the toes. It starts as a red patch that slowly spreads and is usually itchy. Treatment involves keeping the skin dry, avoiding chafing and using an antifungal cream such as Clotrimazole or Lamisil. The fungus *Tinea versicolor* causes small and light-coloured patches, most commonly on the back, chest and shoulders. Consult a doctor.

Cuts and scratches become easily infected in humid climates. Immediately wash all wounds in clean water and apply antiseptic. If you develop signs of infection, see a doctor. Coral cuts can easily become infected.

Snakes

Though snake bites are rare for travellers, there are more than 85 species of venomous snakes in Thailand. Wear boots and long pants if walking in an area that may have snakes.

The Thai Red Cross produces antivenom for many of the poisonous snakes in Thailand.

Sunburn

Even on a cloudy day, sunburn can occur rapidly. Use a strong sunscreen (at least factor 30+), making sure to reapply after a swim, and always wear a wide-brimmed hat and sunglasses outdoors. If you become sunburnt stay out of the sun until you have recovered, apply cool compresses and take painkillers for the discomfort. One-percent hydrocortisone cream applied twice daily is also helpful.

Travelling with Children

Thailand is relatively safe for children. Consult a doctor who specialises in travel medicine prior to travel to ensure your child is appropriately prepared. A medical kit designed specifically for children includes liquid medicines for children who cannot swallow tables. Azithromycin is an ideal paediatric formula used to treat bacterial diarrhoea, as well as ear, chest and throat infections.

Good resources include Lonely Planet's *Travel with Children* and, for those spending longer away, Jane Wilson-Howarth's *Your Child's Health Abroad*.

TAP WATER

Although it's deemed potable by the authorities, the Thais don't drink the tap water, and neither should you. Stick to bottled or filtered water during your stay.

Traveller's Diarrhoea

Traveller's diarrhoea is by far the most common problem affecting travellers. In over 80% of cases, traveller's diarrhoea is caused by a bacteria (there are numerous potential culprits) and responds promptly to treatment with antibiotics.

Here we define traveller's diarrhoea as the passage of more than three watery bowel movements within 24 hours, plus at least one other symptom such as vomiting, fever, cramps, nausea or feeling generally unwell.

Treatment consists of staying well hydrated; rehydration solutions such as Gastrolyte are the best for this. Antibiotics such as Norfloxacin, Ciprofloxacin or Azithromycin will kill the bacteria quickly. Seek medical attention if you do not respond to an appropriate antibiotic.

Loperamide is just a 'stopper' that only treats the symptoms. It can be helpful, for example, if you have to go on a long bus ride. Don't take Loperamide if you have a fever, or blood in your stools.

Giardia lamblia is a parasite that is relatively common. Symptoms include nausea, bloating, excess gas, fatigue and intermittent diarrhoea. 'Eggy' burps are often attributed solely to giardiasis. The treatment of choice is Tinidazole, with Metronidazole being a second-line option.

Amoebic dysentery is very rare in travellers, but may be misdiagnosed by poor-quality labs. Symptoms are similar to bacterial diarrhoea. You should always seek reliable medical care if you have blood in your diarrhoea. Treatment involves two drugs: Tinidazole or Metronidazole to kill the parasite in your gut and then a second drug to kill the cysts. If left untreated complications, such as liver abscesses, can occur.

Women's Health

➡ In 2016, the Zika virus was confirmed in Thailand, and two cases of birth defects related to the virus were reported. Check the International Association for Medical Assistance for Travellers (www.iamat.org) website for updates on the situation.

➡ Sanitary products are readily available in Thailand's urban areas.

➡ Bring adequate supplies of your personal birth-control option, which may not be available.

➡ Heat, humidity and antibiotics can all contribute to thrush, which can be treated with antifungal creams and Clotrimazole. A practical alternative is one tablet of fluconazole (Diflucan).

➡ Urinary-tract infections can be precipitated by dehydration or long bus journeys without toilet stops; bring suitable antibiotics for treatment.

Language

Thailand's official language is effectively the dialect spoken and written in central Thailand, which has successfully become the lingua franca of all Thai and non-Thai ethnic groups in the kingdom.

In Thai the meaning of a single syllable may be altered by means of different tones. In standard Thai there are five: low tone, mid tone, falling tone, high tone and rising tone. The range of all five tones is relative to each speaker's vocal range, so there is no fixed 'pitch' intrinsic to the language.

➤ **low tone** – 'Flat' like the mid tone, but pronounced at the relative bottom of one's vocal range. It is low, level and has no inflection, eg bàht (baht – the Thai currency).

➤ **mid tone** – Pronounced 'flat', at the relative middle of the speaker's vocal range, eg dee (good). No tone mark is used.

➤ **falling tone** – Starting high and falling sharply, this tone is similar to the change in pitch in English when you are emphasising a word, or calling someone's name from afar, eg mâi (no/not).

➤ **high tone** – Usually the most difficult for non-Thai speakers. It's pronounced near the relative top of the vocal range, as level as possible, eg máh (horse).

➤ **rising tone** – Starting low and gradually rising, sounds like the inflection used by English speakers to imply a question – 'Yes?', eg sǎhm (three).

WANT MORE?

For in-depth language information and handy phrases, check out Lonely Planet's *Thai Phrasebook*. You'll find it at **shop. lonelyplanet.com**, or you can buy Lonely Planet's iPhone phrasebooks at the Apple App Store.

The Thai government has instituted the Royal Thai General Transcription System (RTGS) as a standard method of writing Thai using the Roman alphabet. It's used in official documents, road signs and on maps. However, local variations crop up on signs, menus etc. Generally, names in this book follow the most common practice.

In our coloured pronunciation guides, the hyphens indicate syllable breaks within words, and some syllables are further divided with a dot to help you pronounce compound vowels, eg mêu·a·rai (when).

The vowel a is pronounced as in 'about', aa as the 'a' in 'bad', ah as the 'a' in 'father', ai as in 'aisle', air as in 'flair' (without the 'r'), eu as the 'er' in 'her' (without the 'r'), ew as in 'new' (with rounded lips), oh as the 'o' in 'toe', or as in 'torn' (without the 'r') and ow as in 'now'.

Most consonants correspond to their English counterparts. The exceptions are b̶ (a hard 'p' sound, almost like a 'b', eg in 'hip-bag'); d̶ (a hard 't' sound, like a sharp 'd', eg in 'mid-tone'); ng (as in 'singing'; in Thai it can occur at the start of a word) and r (as in 'run' but flapped; in everyday speech it's often pronounced like 'l').

BASICS

The social structure of Thai society demands different registers of speech depending on who you're talking to. To make things simple we've chosen the correct form of speech appropriate to the context of each phrase.

When being polite, the speaker ends his or her sentence with kráp (for men) or kâ (for women). It is the gender of the speaker that is being expressed here; it is also the common way to answer 'yes' to a question or show agreement.

The masculine and feminine forms of phrases in this chapter are indicated where relevant with 'm/f'.

Hello.	สวัสดี	sà-wàt-dee
Goodbye.	ลาก่อน	lah gòrn
Yes./No.	ใช่/ไม่	châi/mâi
Please.	ขอ	kŏr
Thank you.	ขอบคุณ	kòrp kun
You're welcome.	ยินดี	yin dee
Excuse me.	ขออภัย	kŏr à-pai
Sorry.	ขอโทษ	kŏr tôht

How are you?
สบายดีไหม sà-bai dee măi

Fine. And you?
สบายดีครับ/ค่ะ sà-bai dee kráp/
แล้วคุณล่ะ kâ láa-ou kun lâ (m/f)

What's your name?
คุณชื่ออะไร kun chêu à-rai

My name is ...
ผม/ดิฉันชื่อ... pŏm/dì-chăn chêu ... (m/f)

Do you speak English?
คุณพูดภาษา kun pôot pah-săh
อังกฤษได้ไหม ang-grìt dâi măi

I don't understand.
ผม/ดิฉันไม่ pŏm/dì-chăn mâi
เข้าใจ kôw jai (m/f)

ACCOMMODATION

Where's a ...?	... อยู่ที่ไหน	... yòo têe năi
campsite	ค่ายพักแรม	kâi pák raam
guesthouse	บ้านพัก	bâhn pák
hotel	โรงแรม	rohng raam
youth hostel	บ้าน เยาวชน	bâhn yow-wá-chon

Do you have a ... room?	มีห้อง ... ไหม	mee hôrng ... măi
single	เดี่ยว	dèe-o
double	เตียงคู่	dee-ang kôo
twin	สองเตียง	sŏrng dee-ang

air-con	แอร์	aa
bathroom	ห้องน้ำ	hôrng nám
laundry	ห้องซักผ้า	hôrng sák pâh
mosquito net	มุ้ง	múng
window	หน้าต่าง	nâh dàhng

QUESTION WORDS

What?	อะไร	à-rai
When?	เมื่อไร	mêu·a-rai
Where?	ที่ไหน	têe năi
Who?	ใคร	krai
Why?	ทำไม	tam-mai

DIRECTIONS

Where's ...?
... อยู่ที่ไหน ... yòo têe năi

What's the address?
ที่อยู่คืออะไร têe yòo keu à-rai

Could you please write it down?
เขียนลงให้ได้ไหม kĕe-an long hâi dâi măi

Can you show me (on the map)?
ให้ดู (ในแผนที่) hâi doo (nai păn têe)
ได้ไหม dâi măi

Turn left/right.
เลี้ยวซ้าย/ขวา lée·o sái/kwăh

It's ...	อยู่ ...	yòo ...
behind	ที่หลัง	têe lăng
in front of	ตรงหน้า	drong nâh
next to	ข้างๆ	kâhng kâhng
straight ahead	ตรงไป	drong bai

EATING & DRINKING

I'd like (the menu), please.
ขอ (รายการ kŏr (rai gahn
อาหาร) หน่อย ah-hăhn) nòy

What would you recommend?
คุณแนะนำอะไรบ้าง kun náa-nam à-rai bâhng

That was delicious!
อร่อยมาก à-ròy mâhk

Cheers!
ไชโย chai-yoh

Please bring the bill.
ขอบิลหน่อย kŏr bin nòy

I don't eat ...	ผม/ดิฉัน ไม่กิน ...	pŏm/dì-chăn mâi gin ... (m/f)
eggs	ไข่	kài
fish	ปลา	blah
red meat	เนื้อแดง	néu·a daang
nuts	ถั่ว	tòo·a

NUMBERS

1	หนึ่ง	nèung
2	สอง	sŏrng
3	สาม	sǎhm
4	สี่	sèe
5	ห้า	hâh
6	หก	hòk
7	เจ็ด	jèt
8	แปด	bàat
9	เก้า	gôw
10	สิบ	sìp
11	สิบเอ็ด	sìp-èt
20	ยี่สิบ	yêe-sìp
21	ยี่สิบเอ็ด	yêe-sìp-èt
30	สามสิบ	sǎhm-sìp
40	สี่สิบ	sèe-sìp
50	ห้าสิบ	hâh-sìp
60	หกสิบ	hòk-sìp
70	เจ็ดสิบ	jèt-sìp
80	แปดสิบ	bàat-sìp
90	เก้าสิบ	gôw-sìp
100	หนึ่งร้อย	nèung róy
1000	หนึ่งพัน	nèung pan
10,000	หนึ่งหมื่น	nèung mèun
100,000	หนึ่งแสน	nèung sǎan
1,000,000	หนึ่งล้าน	nèung láhn

Key Words

bar	บาร์	bah
bottle	ขวด	kòo·at
bowl	ชาม	chahm
breakfast	อาหารเช้า	ah-hǎhn chów
cafe	ร้านกาแฟ	ráhn gah-faa
chopsticks	ไม้ตะเกียบ	mái đà-gèe·ap
cold	เย็น	yen
cup	ถ้วย	tôo·ay
dessert	ของหวาน	kŏrng wǎhn
dinner	อาหารเย็น	ah-hǎhn yen
drink list	รายการ เครื่องดื่ม	rai gahn krêu·ang dèum
fork	ส้อม	sôrm

glass	แก้ว	gâa·ou
hot	ร้อน	rórn
knife	มีด	mêet
lunch	อาหาร กลางวัน	ah-hǎhn glahng wan
market	ตลาด	đà-làht
menu	รานการ อาหาร	rai gahn ah-hǎhn
plate	จาน	jahn
restaurant	ร้านอาหาร	ráhn ah-hǎhn
spicy	เผ็ด	pèt
spoon	ช้อน	chórn
vegetarian (person)	คนกินเจ	kon gin jair
with	มี	mee
without	ไม่มี	mâi mee

Meat & Fish

beef	เนื้อ	néu·a
chicken	ไก่	gài
crab	ปู	boo
duck	เป็ด	bèt
fish	ปลา	blah
meat	เนื้อ	néu·a
pork	หมู	mŏo
seafood	อาหารทะเล	ah-hǎhn tá-lair
squid	ปลาหมึก	blah mèuk

Fruit & Vegetables

banana	กล้วย	glôo·ay
beans	ถั่ว	tòo·a
coconut	มะพร้าว	má-prów
eggplant	มะเขือ	má-kěu·a
fruit	ผลไม้	pǒn-lá-mái
guava	ฝรั่ง	fa-ràng
lime	มะนาว	má-now
mango	มะม่วง	má-môo·ang
mangosteen	มังคุด	mang-kút
mushrooms	เห็ด	hèt
nuts	ถั่ว	tòo·a
papaya	มะละกอ	má-lá-gor
potatoes	มันฝรั่ง	man fa-ràng
rambutan	เงาะ	ngó
tamarind	มะขาม	má-kǎhm

tomatoes	มะเขือเทศ	má·kěu·a têt
vegetables	ผัก	pàk
watermelon	แตงโม	đaang moh

Other

chilli	พริก	prík
egg	ไข่	kài
fish sauce	น้ำปลา	nám ƀlah
ice	น้ำแข็ง	nám kăng
noodles	เส้น	sên
oil	น้ำมัน	nám man
pepper	พริกไทย	prík tai
rice	ข้าว	kôw
salad	ผักสด	pàk sòt
salt	เกลือ	gleu·a
soup	น้ำซุป	nám súp
soy sauce	น้ำซีอิ๊ว	nám see·éw
sugar	น้ำตาล	nám đahn
tofu	เต้าหู้	đôw hôo

Drinks

beer	เบียร์	bee·a
coffee	กาแฟ	gah-faa
milk	นมจืด	nom jèut
orange juice	น้ำส้ม	nám sôm
soy milk	น้ำเต้าหู้	nám đôw hôo
sugarcane juice	น้ำอ้อย	nám ôy
tea	ชา	chah
water	น้ำดื่ม	nám dèum

EMERGENCIES

Help!	ช่วยด้วย	chôo·ay dôo·ay
Go away!	ไปให้พ้น	ƀai hâi pón

Call a doctor!
เรียกหมอหน่อย　　rêe·ak mŏr nòy

Call the police!
เรียกตำรวจหน่อย　　rêe·ak đam·ròo·at nòy

I'm ill.
ผม/ดิฉันป่วย　　pŏm/dì-chăn ƀòo·ay (m/f)

I'm lost.
ผม/ดิฉัน　　pŏm/dì-chăn
หลงทาง　　lŏng tahng (m/f)

Where are the toilets?
ห้องน้ำอยู่ที่ไหน　　hôrng nám yòo têe năi

SHOPPING & SERVICES

I'd like to buy ...
อยากจะซื้อ ...　　yàhk jà séu ...

I'm just looking.
ดูเฉย ๆ　　doo chěu·i chěu·i

Can I look at it?
ขอดูได้ไหม　　kŏr doo dâi măi

How much is it?
เท่าไร　　tôw-rai

That's too expensive.
แพงไป　　paang ƀai

Can you lower the price?
ลดราคาได้ไหม　　lót rah-kah dâi măi

There's a mistake in the bill.
บิลใบนี้ผิด　　bin bai née pit ná
นะครับ/ค่ะ　　kráp/kâ (m/f)

TIME & DATES

What time is it?
กี่โมงแล้ว　　gèe mohng láa·ou

morning	เช้า	chów
afternoon	บ่าย	bài
evening	เย็น	yen
yesterday	เมื่อวาน	mêu·a wahn
today	วันนี้	wan née

SIGNS

ทางเข้า	Entrance
ทางออก	Exit
เปิด	Open
ปิด	Closed
ที่ติดต่อสอบถาม	Information
ห้าม	Prohibited
ห้องสุขา	Toilets
ชาย	Men
หญิง	Women

tomorrow	พรุ่งนี้	prûng née
Monday	วันจันทร์	wan jan
Tuesday	วันอังคาร	wan ang-kahn
Wednesday	วันพุธ	wan pút
Thursday	วันพฤหัสฯ	wan pá-réu-hàt
Friday	วันศุกร	wan sùk
Saturday	วันเสาร์	wan sŏw
Sunday	วันอาทิตย์	wan ah-tít

TRANSPORT

Public Transport

bicycle rickshaw	สามล้อ	săhm lór
boat	เรือ	reu·a
bus	รถเมล์	rót mair
car	รถเก๋ง	rót gěng
motorcycle	มอร์เตอร์ไซค์	mor-đeu-sai
taxi	รับจ้าง	ráp jâhng
plane	เครื่องบิน	krêu·ang bin
train	รถไฟ	rót fai
túk-túk	ตุ๊ก ๆ	đúk đúk
When's	รถเมล์คัน ...	rót mair kan ...
the ... bus?	มาเมื่อไร	mah mêu·a rai
first	แรก	râak
last	สุดท้าย	sùt tái
next	ต่อไป	đòr ɓai
A ... ticket, please.	ขอตั๋ว ...	kŏr đŏo·a ...
one-way	เที่ยวเดียว	têe·o dee·o
return	ไปกลับ	ɓai glàp
I'd like	ต้องการ	đôrng gahn
a/an ... seat.	ที่นั่ง ...	têe nâng ...
aisle	ติดทางเดิน	đìt tahng deun
window	ติดหน้าต่าง	đìt nâh đàhng
platform	ชานชาลา	chan-chah-lah
ticket window	ช่องขายตั๋ว	chôrng kăi đŏo·a
timetable	ตารางเวลา	đah-rahng wair-lah

What time does it get to (Chiang Mai)?
ถึง (เชียงใหม่) tĕung (chee·ang mài)
กี่โมง gèe mohng

Does it stop at (Saraburi)?
รถจอดที่ (สระบุรี) rót jòrt têe (sà·rà·bù·ree)
ไหม măi

Please tell me when we get to (Chiang Mai).
เมื่อถึง mêu·a tĕung
(เชียงใหม่) (chee·ang mài)
กรุณาบอกด้วย gà·rú·nah bòrk dôo·ay

I'd like to get off at (Saraburi).
ขอลงที่ (สระบุรี) kŏr long têe (sà·rà·bù·ree)

Driving & Cycling

I'd like to hire a ...	อยากจะ เช่า ...	yàhk jà chôw ...
car	รถเก๋ง	rót gěng
motorbike	รถ มอร์เตอร์ไซค์	rót mor-đeu-sai
I'd like ...	ต้องการ ...	đôrng gahn ...
my bicycle repaired	ซ่อมรถ จักรยาน	sôrm rót jàk-gà-yahn
to hire a bicycle	เช่ารถ จักรยาน	chôw rót jàk-gà-yahn

Is this the road to (Ban Bung Wai)?
ทางนี้ไป tahng née ɓai
(บ้านบุ่งหวาย) ไหม (bâhn bùng wăi) măi

Where's a petrol station?
ปั๊มน้ำมันอยู่ที่ไหน ɓâm nám man yòo têe năi

Can I park here?
จอดที่นี่ได้ไหม jòrt têe née dâi măi

How long can I park here?
จอดที่นี่ได้นานเท่าไร jòrt têe née dâi nahn tôw-rai

I need a mechanic.
ต้องการช่างรถ đôrng gahn châhng rót

I have a flat tyre.
ยางแบน yahng baan

I've run out of petrol.
หมดน้ำมัน mòt nám man

Do I need a helmet?
ต้องใช้หมวก đôrng chái mòo·ak
กันน๊อก ไหม gan nórk măi

GLOSSARY

This glossary includes Thai, Pali (P) and Sanskrit (S) words and terms frequently used in this guidebook. For definitions of food and drink terms, see p781.

ajahn – *(aajaan)* respectful title for 'teacher'; from the Sanskrit term *acarya*

amphoe – *(amphur)* district, the next subdivision down from province

AUA – American University Alumni

bâhn – *(ban)* house or village

baht – *(bàat)* the Thai unit of currency

bàht – a unit of weight equal to 15g; rounded bowl used by monks for receiving alms food

BKS – Baw Khaw Saw (Thai acronym for the Transport Company)

bodhisattva (S) – in Theravada Buddhism, the term used to refer to the previous lives of the Buddha prior to his enlightenment

bòht – central sanctuary in a Thai temple used for the monastic order's official business, such as ordinations; from the Pali term *uposatha (ubohsòt)*; see also *wí·hăhn*

bòr nám rórn – hot springs

Brahman – pertaining to Brahmanism, an ancient religious tradition in India and the predecessor of Hinduism; not to be confused with 'Brahmin', the priestly class in India's caste system

BTS – Bangkok Transit System (Skytrain); Thai: *rót fai fáh*

bah·dé – batik

CAT – CAT Telecom Public Company Limited

chedi – see *stupa*

chow – folk; people

chow lair – *(chow nám)* sea gypsies

CPT – Communist Party of Thailand

doy – mountain in the Northern Thai dialect; spelt 'Doi' in proper names

đròrk – *(trok)* alley, smaller than a soi

fa·ràng –a Westerner (person of European origin); also guava

gà·teu·i – *(kàthoey)* Thailand's 'third gender', usually cross-dressing or transsexual males; also called ladyboys

gopura (S) – entrance pavilion in traditional Hindu temple architecture, often seen in Angkor-period temple complexes

hàht – beach; spelt 'Hat' in proper names

hŏr đrai – a Tripitaka (Buddhist scripture) hall

hôrng – *(hong)* room; in southern Thailand this refers to semi-submerged island caves

Isan – *(ee·săhn)* general term used for northeastern Thailand

jataka (P) – *(chah·dòk)* stories of the Buddha's previous lives

jeen – Chinese

jeen hor – literally 'galloping Chinese', referring to horse-riding Yunnanese traders

kàthoey – see *gà·teu·i*

klorng – canal; spelt 'Khlong' in proper nouns

kŏhn – masked dance–drama based on stories from the Ramakian

kŏw – hill or mountain; spelt 'Khao' in proper names

KMT – Kuomintang

KNU – Karen National Union

ku – small *stupa* that is partially hollow and open

kùtì – monk's dwelling

lăam – cape; spelt 'Laem' in proper names

làk meu·ang – city pillar

lék – little, small (in size); see also *noi*

longyi – Burmese sarong

lôok tûng – Thai country music

lôw kŏw – white whisky, often homemade rice brew

mâa chee – Thai Buddhist nun

mâa nám – river; spelt Mae Nam in proper names

mahathat – *(má·hăh tâht)* common name for temples containing Buddha relics; from the Sanskrit–Pali term *mahadhatu*

masjid – *(mát·sà·yít)* mosque

mát·mèe – technique of tie-dyeing silk or cotton threads and then weaving them into complex patterns, similar to Indonesian *ikat*; the term also refers to the patterns themselves

meu·ang – city or principality

mon·dòp – small square, spired building in a wát; from Sanskrit *mandapa*

moo·ay tai – *(muay thai)* Thai boxing

mŏr lam – an Isan musical tradition akin to *lôok tûng*

naga (P/S) – *(nâhk)* a mythical serpent-like being with magical powers

ná·kon – city; from the Sanskrit-Pali *nagara*; spelt 'Nakhon' in proper nouns

nám – water

nám đòk – waterfall; spelt 'Nam Tok' in proper nouns

neun – hill; spelt 'Noen' in proper names

nibbana (P/S) – nirvana; in Buddhist teachings, the state of enlightenment; escape from the realm of rebirth; Thai: *níp·pahn*

noi – *(nóy)* little, small (amount); see also *lék*

nôrk – outside, outer; spelt 'Nok' in proper names

ow – bay or gulf; spelt 'Ao' in proper nouns

pâh mát·mèe – *mát·mèe* fabric

pĕe – ghost, spirit

pík·sù – a Buddhist monk; from the Sanskrit *bhikshu*, Pali *bhikkhu*

PLAT – People's Liberation Army of Thailand

prá – an honorific term used for monks, nobility and Buddha images; spelt 'Phra' in proper names

prá krêu·ang – amulets of monks, Buddhas or deities worn around the neck for spiritual protection; also called *prá pim*

prá poom – earth spirits or guardians

prang – *(bprahng)* Khmer-style tower on temples

prasat – *(bprah·sàht)* small ornate building, used for religious purposes, with a cruciform ground plan and needlelike spire, located on temple grounds; any of a number of different kinds of halls or residences with religious or royal significance

rót aa – blue-and-white air-con bus

rót norn – sleeper bus

săh·lah – open-sided, covered meeting hall or resting place; from Portuguese term *sala*, literally 'room'

săhm·lór – three-wheeled pedicab

samsara (P) – in Buddhist teachings, the realm of rebirth and delusion

sangha – (P) the Buddhist community

satang – *(sà·dahng)* a Thai unit of currency; 100 satang equals 1 baht

serow – Asian mountain goat

sêua môr hôrm – blue cotton farmer's shirt

soi – lane or small street

Songkran – Thai New Year, held in mid-April

sŏrng·tăa·ou – (literally 'two rows') common name for small pick-up trucks with two benches in the back, used as buses/taxis; also spelt '*săwngthăew*'

SRT – State Railway of Thailand

stupa – conical-shaped Buddhist monument used to inter sacred Buddhist objects

tâh – pier, boat landing; spelt 'Tha' in proper nouns

tâht – four-sided, curvilinear Buddha reliquary, common in Northeastern Thailand; spelt 'That' in proper nouns

tâm – cave; spelt 'Tham' in proper nouns

tam bun – to make merit

tambon – see *đam·bon*

TAT – Tourism Authority of Thailand

Thammayut – one of the two sects of Theravada Buddhism in Thailand; founded by King Rama IV while he was still a monk

thanŏn – *(tà·nŏn)* street; spelt 'Thanon' in proper noun and shortened to 'Th'

T-pop – popular teen-music

tràwk – see *đròrk*

trimurti (S) – collocation of the three principal Hindu deities, Brahma, Shiva and Vishnu

Tripitaka (S) – Theravada Buddhist scriptures; (Pali: *Tipitaka*)

túk–túk – *(đúk–đúk)* motorised săhm·lór

vipassana (P) – *(wí·bàt·sà·nah)* Buddhist insight meditation

wâi – palms–together Thai greeting

wan prá – Buddhist holy days, falling on the days of the main phases of the moon (full, new and half) each month

wang – palace

wát – temple–monastery; from the Pali term *avasa* meaning 'monk's dwelling'; spelt 'Wat' in proper nouns

wí·hăhn – *(wihan, viharn)* any large hall in a Thai temple, usually open to laity; from Sanskrit term *vihara*, meaning 'dwelling'

Yawi – traditional language of Malay parts of Java, Sumatra and the Malay Peninsula, widely spoken in the most southern provinces of Thailand; the written form uses the classic Arabic script plus five additional letters

yài – big

Behind the Scenes

SEND US YOUR FEEDBACK

We love to hear from travellers – your comments keep us on our toes and help make our books better. Our well-travelled team reads every word on what you loved or loathed about this book. Although we cannot reply individually to your submissions, we always guarantee that your feedback goes straight to the appropriate authors, in time for the next edition. Each person who sends us information is thanked in the next edition – the most useful submissions are rewarded with a selection of digital PDF chapters.

Visit **lonelyplanet.com/contact** to submit your updates and suggestions or to ask for help. Our award-winning website also features inspirational travel stories, news and discussions.

Note: We may edit, reproduce and incorporate your comments in Lonely Planet products such as guidebooks, websites and digital products, so let us know if you don't want your comments reproduced or your name acknowledged. For a copy of our privacy policy visit lonelyplanet.com/privacy.

OUR READERS

Many thanks to the travellers who used the last edition and wrote to us with helpful hints, useful advice and interesting anecdotes: Isla Abel, Sahar Aminipour, Victoria Bailey, Werner Bruyninx, Phil Cawley, Bob De Raeve, Di Devi, Sarah Heffernan, Josh Jones, David Kabath, Magda Kwiatkowska, Jerker Lundberg, Frank McKee, Drew McMillan, Tim Mills, Eline Schoumans, Merette Schuurman, Jeremie Szeftel, Barbara Terzopoulos, Nele Van Muylder, Bryan Walker.

WRITER THANKS

Anita Isalska

Big thanks to everyone who helped me on my travels in Thailand. Gratitude to Sai and Anna for the warm welcome and insights into the wild west, to the Tourism Authority Thailand team in Kanchanaburi, and to Tim Brewer for helpful suggestions. I'd also like to thank the kids in Lopburi who helped this perplexed travel writer wriggle free from a prematurely locked temple ground. Thanks always to Normal Matt for crackly Skype calls and support.

Tim Bewer

A hearty *kòrp jai lăi lăi dôu* to the perpetually friendly people of Isan who rarely failed to live up to their reputation for friendliness and hospitality when faced with my incessant questions, in particular Prapaporn Sompakdee (especially for her crispy pork expertise)

and Julian Wright. Special thanks to my wife Suttawan for everything.

Celeste Brash

Thanks to Chiang Mai University and my beloved professors; to Samui Steve, Iain Leonard, Frans Betgem, Lee at Akha Ama and Catherine Bodry. A huge hug to Janine Brown of the Smithsonian Conservation Biology Institute for passion and insight on a tricky subject; and my family – Josh, Jasmine and Tevai – who I wish could come with me on every trip.

Austin Bush

A big thanks to Destination Editors Dora Ball and Clifton Wilkinson, as well as to all the people on the ground in Bangkok and Northern Thailand.

David Eimer

Thanks to my fellow island writers and all the Lonely Planet crew in London. Thanks also to Alex and co for the nights out on Phuket. As ever, much gratitude to everyone I met on the road who passed on tips, whether knowingly or unwittingly.

Damian Harper

Huge thanks to the late Neil Bambridge, much gratitude for everything, may you rest in peace. Also thanks to Neil's wife Ratchi, to Maurice Senseit, the jolly staff at Nira's in Thong Sala, Piotr, Gemma, James Horton, George W, Celeste Brash and everyone else who helped along the way, in whatever fashion.

Andy Symington

A great number of people, from taxi drivers to information officers, gave me excellent advice and help along the way; I'm very grateful to all of them. Specific thanks go to Siriporn Chiangpoon, Ian on Ko Chang, Maitri in Si Racha, Chayanan in Chanthaburi and the friendly Ang Sila volunteers.

ACKNOWLEDGEMENTS

Climate map data adapted from Peel MC, Finlayson BL & McMahon TA (2007) 'Updated World Map of the Köppen-Geiger Climate Classification', Hydrology and Earth System Sciences, 11, 163344.

Illustrations pp70–1 and pp72–3 by Michael Weldon.

Cover photograph: Masked Thai dancer, sutipond somnam/500px ©.

THIS BOOK

This 17th edition of Lonely Planet's *Thailand* guidebook was researched and written by Anita Isalska, Tim Bewer, Celeste Brash, Austin Bush, David Eimer, Damian Harper and Andy Symington. The last edition was written by Mark Beales, Tim Bewer, Joe Bindloss, Austin Bush, David Eimer, Bruce Evans, Damian Harper and Isabella Noble. This guidebook was produced by the following:

Destination Editors Tanya Parker, Dora Ball, Clifton Wilkinson

Product Editors Ross Taylor, Vicky Smith, Kate Chapman

Senior Cartographer Diana Von Holdt

Book Designer Wibowo Rusli

Assisting Editors Judith Bamber, Imogen Bannister, Melanie Dankel, Andrea Dobbin, Grace Dobell, Bruce Evans, Jennifer Hattam, Gabby Innes, Lou McGregor, Rosie Nicholson, Rachel Rawling, Tamara Sheward, Gabrielle Stefanos, Sam Wheeler, Amanda Williamson

Assisting Cartographer Anita Banh

Assisting Book Designer Virgina Moreno

Cover Researcher Naomi Parker

Thanks to Hannah Cartmel, Kate Kiely, Charlotte Orr, Alison Ridgway

Index

Map Legend

Sights

- Beach
- Bird Sanctuary
- Buddhist
- Castle/Palace
- Christian
- Confucian
- Hindu
- Islamic
- Jain
- Jewish
- Monument
- Museum/Gallery/Historic Building
- Ruin
- Shinto
- Sikh
- Taoist
- Winery/Vineyard
- Zoo/Wildlife Sanctuary
- Other Sight

Activities, Courses & Tours

- Bodysurfing
- Diving
- Canoeing/Kayaking
- Course/Tour
- Sento Hot Baths/Onsen
- Skiing
- Snorkelling
- Surfing
- Swimming/Pool
- Walking
- Windsurfing
- Other Activity

Sleeping

- Sleeping
- Camping
- Hut/Shelter

Eating

- Eating

Drinking & Nightlife

- Drinking & Nightlife
- Cafe

Entertainment

- Entertainment

Shopping

- Shopping

Information

- Bank
- Embassy/Consulate
- Hospital/Medical
- Internet
- Police
- Post Office
- Telephone
- Toilet
- Tourist Information
- Other Information

Geographic

- Beach
- Gate
- Hut/Shelter
- Lighthouse
- Lookout
- Mountain/Volcano
- Oasis
- Park
- Pass
- Picnic Area
- Waterfall

Population

- Capital (National)
- Capital (State/Province)
- City/Large Town
- Town/Village

Transport

- Airport
- Border crossing
- Bus
- Cable car/Funicular
- Cycling
- Ferry
- Metro/MRT/MTR station
- Monorail
- Parking
- Petrol station
- Skytrain/Subway station
- Taxi
- Train station/Railway
- Tram
- Underground station
- Other Transport

Routes

- Tollway
- Freeway
- Primary
- Secondary
- Tertiary
- Lane
- Unsealed road
- Road under construction
- Plaza/Mall
- Steps
- Tunnel
- Pedestrian overpass
- Walking Tour
- Walking Tour detour
- Path/Walking Trail

Boundaries

- International
- State/Province
- Disputed
- Regional/Suburb
- Marine Park
- Cliff
- Wall

Hydrography

- River, Creek
- Intermittent River
- Canal
- Water
- Dry/Salt/Intermittent Lake
- Reef

Areas

- Airport/Runway
- Beach/Desert
- Cemetery (Christian)
- Cemetery (Other)
- Glacier
- Mudflat
- Park/Forest
- Sight (Building)
- Sportsground
- Swamp/Mangrove

Note: Not all symbols displayed above appear on the maps in this book

David Eimer

Phuket & the Andaman Coast David has been a journalist and writer ever since abandoning the idea of a law career in 1990. After spells working in his native London and in Los Angeles, he moved to Beijing in 2005, where he contributed to a variety of newspapers and magazines in the UK. Since then he has travelled and lived across China and in numerous cities in Southeast Asia, including Bangkok, Phnom Penh and Yangon. He has been covering China, Myanmar and Thailand for Lonely Planet since 2006.

Damian Harper

Ko Samui & the Lower Gulf With two degrees (one in modern and classical Chinese from SOAS University of London), Damian has been writing for Lonely Planet for more than two decades, contributing to titles on places as diverse as China, Vietnam, Thailand, Ireland, London, Mallorca, Malaysia, Singapore, Brunei, Hong Kong and the UK. A seasoned guidebook writer, Damian has penned articles for numerous newspapers and magazines, including *The Guardian* and *The Daily Telegraph*, and currently makes Surrey, England, his home. Follow Damian on Instagram (damian.harper).

Andy Symington

Ko Chang & the Eastern Seaboard Andy has written or worked on more than a hundred books and other updates for Lonely Planet (especially in Europe and Latin America) and other publishing companies, and has published articles on numerous subjects for a variety of newspapers, magazines and websites. He part-owns and operates a rock bar, has written a novel and is currently working on several fiction and non-fiction writing projects. Originally from Australia, Andy moved to northern Spain many years ago. When he's not off with a backpack in some far-flung corner of the world, he can probably be found watching the tragically poor local football side or tasting local wines after a long walk in the nearby mountains.

OUR STORY

A beat-up old car, a few dollars in the pocket and a sense of adventure. In 1972 that's all Tony and Maureen Wheeler needed for the trip of a lifetime – across Europe and Asia overland to Australia. It took several months, and at the end – broke but inspired – they sat at their kitchen table writing and stapling together their first travel guide, *Across Asia on the Cheap*. Within a week they'd sold 1500 copies. Lonely Planet was born.

Today, Lonely Planet has offices in Franklin, London, Melbourne, Oakland, Dublin, Beijing and Delhi, with more than 600 staff and writers. We share Tony's belief that 'a great guidebook should do three things: inform, educate and amuse'.

OUR WRITERS

Anita Isalska

Curator; Central Thailand Anita is a travel journalist, editor and copywriter whose work for Lonely Planet has taken her from Greek beach towns to Malaysian jungles, and plenty of places in between. After several merry years as an in-house editor and writer – with a few of them in Lonely Planet's London office – Anita now works freelance between the UK, Australia and any Balkan guesthouse with a good wi-fi connection. Anita writes about travel, food and culture for a host of websites and magazines. Read her writing on www.anitaisalska.com.

Austin Bush

Bangkok; Northern Thailand Austin originally came to Thailand in 1999 as part of a language study program hosted by Chiang Mai University. The lure of city life, employment and spicy food eventually led him to Bangkok. City life, employment and spicy food have managed to keep him there ever since.

Austin also contributed to the Plan, Understand and Survive sections of this book.

Tim Bewer

Northeastern Thailand; Hua Hin & the Upper Gulf After briefly holding fort behind a desk as a legislative assistant, Tim decided he didn't have the ego to succeed in the political world (or the stomach to work around those who did). He quit his job at the capitol to backpack around West Africa, during which time he pondered what to do next. His answer was to write a travel guide to parks, forests, and wildlife areas of the gorgeous state of Wisconsin. He's been a freelance travel writer and photographer ever since.

Celeste Brash

Chiang Mai Province Like many California natives, Celeste now lives in Portland, Oregon. She arrived, however, after 15 years in French Polynesia, 18 months in Southeast Asia and a stint teaching English as a second language (in an American accent) in Brighton, England – among other things. She's been writing guidebooks for Lonely Planet since 2005 and her travel articles have appeared in publications from *BBC Travel* to *National Geographic*.

OVER PAGE MORE WRITERS

Published by Lonely Planet Global Limited
CRN 554153
17th edition – July 2018
ISBN 978 1 78657 058 1
© Lonely Planet 2018   Photographs © as indicated 2018
10 9 8 7 6 5 4 3 2 1
Printed in China